Contents

3 by Blackwell Publishing Ltd

t, Malden, MA 02148-5018, USA
Road, Oxford OX4 1JF, UK
550 Swansto   n South, Melbourne, Victoria 3053, Australia
mm 57, 10707 Berlin, Germany

rst published 2001
First pub   rback 2003 by Blackwell Publishing Ltd

L   ss Cataloging-in-Publication Data

A companion t   onometrics / edited by Badi H. Baltagi.
    p. cm. —   mpanions to contemporary economics)
A collection History of E in international group of scholars.
Includes bibli hn B. Da ferences and index.
    ISBN 0–631–   alk. paper) — ISBN ~~1–4051–~~ 0676–X (pb. : alk.
paper)
    1. Economet   Theoretical econometrics.   II. Baltagi, Badi H.
(Badi Hani)

HB139.C643
330′.01′5195—   00–025862

    A catalogu   title is available from the British Library.

                    0 on 12pt Book Antique
                    hicaft Ltd., Hong Kong
                    ound in the United Kingdom
    b   ational Ltd., Padstow, Cornwall

                    further information on
    b   Publishing, visit our website:
    h   w.blackwellpublishing.com

This book is to be returned on
or before the date stamped below

UNIVERSITY OF PLYMOUTH

PLYMOUTH LIBRARY

"I received the book yesterday and started to read it on the way home... and I couldn't stop. I took it to the gym and I expect people saw me smiling a lot while I was exercising and reading. This is tres 'cool'. It is fun but they cover a lot of ground and they are right to the point. I'm really impressed."

> **—Erich Gamma, IBM Distinguished Engineer,**
> **and co-author of Design Patterns**

"'Head First Design Patterns' manages to mix fun, belly-laughs, insight, technical depth and great practical advice in one entertaining and thought provoking read. Whether you are new to design patterns, or have been using them for years, you are sure to get something from visiting Objectville."

> **—Richard Helm, coauthor of "Design Patterns" with rest of the**
> **Gang of Four—Erich Gamma, Ralph Johnson, and John Vlissides**

"I feel like a thousand pounds of books have just been lifted off of my head."

> **—Ward Cunningham, inventor of the Wiki**
> **and founder of the Hillside Group**

"This book is close to perfect, because of the way it combines expertise and readability. It speaks with authority and it reads beautifully. It's one of the very few software books I've ever read that strikes me as indispensable. (I'd put maybe 10 books in this category, at the outside.)"

> **—David Gelernter, Professor of Computer Science,**
> **Yale University and author of "Mirror Worlds" and "Machine Beauty"**

"A Nose Dive into the realm of patterns, a land where complex things become simple, but where simple things can also become complex. I can think of no better tour guides than the Freemans."

> **—Miko Matsumura, Industry Analyst, The Middleware Company**
> **Former Chief Java Evangelist, Sun Microsystems**

"I laughed, I cried, it moved me."

> **—Daniel Steinberg, Editor-in-Chief, java.net**

"My first reaction was to roll on the floor laughing. After I picked myself up, I realized that not only is the book technically accurate, it is the easiest to understand introduction to design patterns that I have seen."

> **—Dr. Timothy A. Budd, Associate Professor of Computer Science at**
> **Oregon State University and author of more than a dozen books,**
> **including *C++ for Java Programmers***

"Jerry Rice runs patterns better than any receiver in the NFL, but the Freemans have out run him. Seriously...this is one of the funniest and smartest books on software design I've ever read."

> **—Aaron LaBerge, VP Technology, ESPN.com**

Other related books from O'Reilly

Making Things Happen

Applied Software Project Management

Beautiful Code

Prefactoring

The Art of Agile Development

UML 2.0 In a Nutshell

Learning UML 2.0

Other books in O'Reilly's *Head First* series

Head First Java

Head First Object-Oriented Analysis and Design (OOA&D)

Head Rush Ajax

Head First HTML with CSS and XHTML

Head First Design Patterns

Head First Servlets and JSP

Head First EJB

Head First PMP

Head First SQL

Head First JavaScript

Head First Software
Development

Wouldn't it be dreamy if there was a software development book that made me a better developer, instead of feeling like a visit to the proctologist? Maybe it's just a fantasy...

Dan Pilone
Russ Miles

Beijing • Cambridge • Köln • Paris • Sebastopol • Taipei • Tokyo

Head First Software Development

by Dan Pilone and Russ Miles

Published by O'Reilly Media, Inc., 1005 Gravenstein Highway North, Sebastopol, CA 95472.

O'Reilly Media books may be purchased for educational, business, or sales promotional use. Online editions are also available for most titles (*safari.oreilly.com*). For more information, contact our corporate/institutional sales department: (800) 998-9938 or *corporate@oreilly.com*.

Series Creators:	Kathy Sierra, Bert Bates
Series Editor:	Brett D. McLaughlin
Design Editor:	Louise Barr
Cover Designers:	Louise Barr, Steve Fehler
Production Editor:	Sanders Kleinfeld
Indexer:	Julie Hawks
Page Viewers:	Vinny, Nick, Tracey, and Corinne

Printing History:

December 2007: First Edition.

Vinny, Tracey, Nick and Dan

Russ and Corinne

No sleepovers were conducted in the writing of this book, although one author did purportedly get engaged using his prototype of the iSwoon application. And one pig apparently lost its nose, but we're confident that had nothing to do with the software development techniques espoused by this text.

RepKover. This book uses RepKover,™ a durable and flexible lay-flat binding.

ISBN-10: 0-596-52735-7

ISBN-13: 978-0-596-52735-8

[M]

To everyone who's worked on a project with us and told us where
we've gone wrong, where we've gone right, and what books to
read…here's our contribution back.

Author(s) of Head First Software Development

Russ Miles

Dan Pilone

Dan is eternally grateful to his wife Tracey for letting him finish this book. Dan is a software architect for Vangent, Inc., and has led teams for the Naval Research Laboratory and NASA, building enterprise software. He's taught graduate and undergraduate Software Engineering at Catholic University in Washington, D.C. Some of his classes were interesting.

Dan started writing for O'Reilly by submitting a proposal for this book a little over five years ago. Three UML books, some quality time in Boulder, Colorado, with the O'Reilly Head First team, and a co-author later, he finally got a chance to put this book together.

While leading a team of software developers can be challenging, Dan is waiting patiently for someone to write **Head First Parenting** to help sort out seriously complex management problems.

Russ is totally indebted to his fiancée, Corinne, for her complete love and support while writing this book. Oh, and he still can't believe she said yes to getting married next year, but I guess some guys have all the luck!

Russ has been writing for a long time and gets a huge kick out of demystifying technologies, tools, and techniques that shouldn't have been so mystified in the first place. After being a developer at various ranks for many years, Russ now keeps his days (and sometimes nights) busy by heading up a team of software developers working on super secret services for the music industry. He's also just finished up his Oxford Masters degree that only took him five years. He's looking forward to a bit of rest...but not for too long.

Russ is an avid guitar player and is relishing the spare time to get back to his guitars. The only thing he's missing is **Head First Guitar**...c'mon Brett, you know you want that one!

Table of Contents (Summary)

Table of Contents (the real thing)

Intro

Your brain on Software Development.
You're sitting around trying to *learn* something, but your *brain* keeps telling you all that learning *isn't important.* Your brain's saying, "Better leave room for more important things, like which wild animals to avoid and whether naked rock-climbing is a bad idea." So how *do* you trick your brain into thinking that your life really depends on learning how to develop great software?

1

great software development
Pleasing your customer

If the customer's unhappy, *everyone's* unhappy!

Every great piece of software starts with a customer's big idea. It's your job as a professional software developer to **bring those ideas to life**. But taking a vague idea and turning it into working code—code that **satisfies your customer**—isn't so easy. In this chapter you'll learn how to avoid being a software development casualty by delivering software that is **needed**, **on-time**, and **on-budget**. Grab your laptop and let's set out on the road to shipping great software.

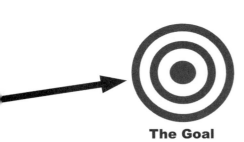

The Goal

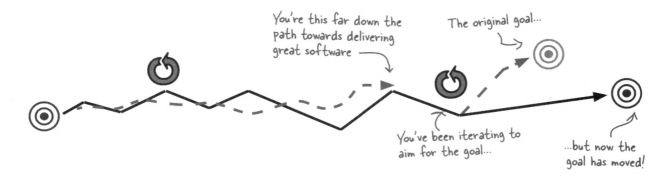

You're this far down the path towards delivering great software

The original goal...

You've been iterating to aim for the goal...

...but now the goal has moved!

gathering requirements

Knowing what the customer wants

2

You can't always get what you want...but the customer better!

Great software development delivers **what the customer wants**. This chapter is all about **talking to the customer** to figure out what their **requirements** are for your software. You'll learn how **user stories**, **brainstorming**, and the **estimation game** help you get inside your customer's head. That way, by the time you finish your project, you'll be confident you've built what your customer wants... and not just a poor imitation.

project planning

Planning for success

3

Every great piece of software starts with a great plan.

In this chapter you're going to learn how to create that plan. You're going to learn how to work with the customer to **prioritize their requirements**. You'll **define iterations** that you and your team can then work towards. Finally you'll create an achievable **development plan** that you and your team can confidently **execute** and **monitor.** By the time you're done, you'll know exactly how to get from requirements to milestone 1.0.

Here's what a programmer **SAYS**...

Sure, no problem, I can crank through that in 2 days.

...but here's what he's really **THINKING**

I'll grab a Monster on the way home, program 'til 3 AM, take a Halo break, then work through the morning. Sleep a few hours, get the guys over to hack with me, and finish at midnight. As long as nothing goes wrong... and Mom doesn't need me to pick up dinner.

user stories and tasks

Getting to the real work

4

It's time to go to work. User stories captured what you need to develop, but now it's time to knuckle down and **dish out the work that needs to be done** so that you can bring those user stories to life. In this chapter you'll learn how to **break your user stories into tasks,** and how your **task estimates** help you track your project from inception to completion. You'll learn how to update your board, moving tasks from in-progress, to complete, to finally **completing an entire user story**. Along the way, you'll handle and prioritize the inevitable **unexpected work** your customer will add to your plate.

Your first standup meeting...

Bob the junior developer.

Mark, database expert and SQL blackbelt.

Laura the UI Guru.

5

good-enough design

Getting it done with great design

Good design helps you deliver. In the last chapter things were looking pretty dire. A **bad design** was making life **hard for everyone** and, to make matters worse, an unplanned task cropped up. In this chapter you'll see how to **refactor** your design so that you and your team can be **more productive**. You'll apply **principles of good design**, while at the same time being wary of striving for the promise of the *'perfect design'*. Finally you'll **handle unplanned tasks** in exactly the same way you handle all the other work on your project using the big project board on your wall.

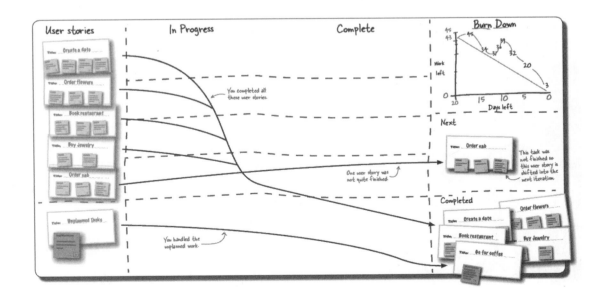

version control

Defensive development

When it comes to writing great software, *Safety First!*

Writing great software isn't easy... especially when you've got to make sure your code works, and **make sure it keeps working**. All it takes is one typo, one bad decision from a co-worker, one crashed hard drive, and suddenly all your work goes down the drain. But with **version control**, you can make sure your **code is always safe** in a code repository, you can **undo mistakes**, and you can make **bug fixes**—to new and old versions of your software.

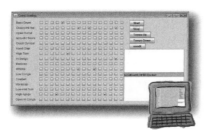

BeatBox Pro 1.0

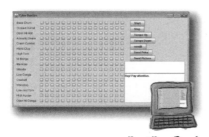

BeatBox Pro 1.x

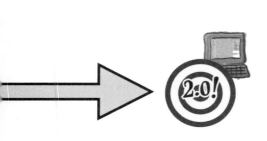

building your code

Insert tab a into slot b...

It pays to follow the instructions...

...especially when you write them yourself.

6½

It's not enough to use configuration management to ensure your code stays safe. You've also got to worry about **compiling your code** and packaging it into a deployable unit. On top of all that, which class should be the main class of your application? How should that class be run? In this chapter, you'll learn how a **build tool** allows you to **write your own instructions** for dealing with your source code.

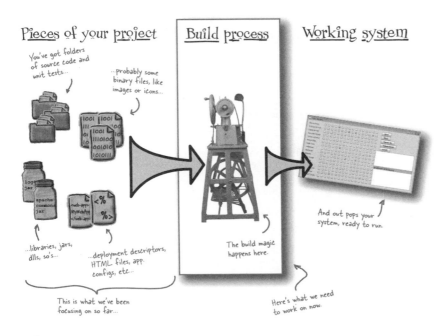

Pieces of your project

You've got folders of source code and unit tests...

...probably some binary files, like images or icons...

...libraries, jars, dlls, so's...

...deployment descriptors, HTML files, app. configs, etc...

This is what we've been focusing on so far...

Build process

The build magic happens here.

Here's what we need to work on now.

Working system

And out pops your system, ready to run.

7

testing and continuous integration

Things fall apart

Sometimes even the best developer breaks the build.

Everyone's done it at least once. You're sure **your code compiles**, you've tested it over and over again on your machine and committed it into the repository. But somewhere between your machine and that black box they call a server *someone* must have changed your code. The unlucky soul who does the next checkout is about to have a bad morning sorting out **what used to be working code**. In this chapter we'll talk about how to put together a **safety net** to keep the build in working order and you **productive**.

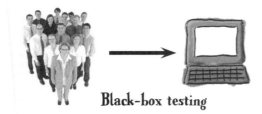

Black-box testing

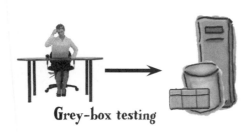

Grey-box testing

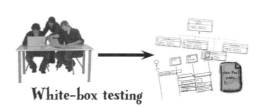

White-box testing

test-driven development

Holding your code accountable

8

Sometimes it's all about setting expectations. Good code needs to work, everyone knows that. But how do **you know your code works**? Even with unit testing, there are still parts of most code that goes untested. But what if testing was a **fundamental part of software development**? What if you did *everything* with testing in mind? In this chapter, you'll take what you know about version control, CI, and automated testing and tie it all together into an environment where you can feel **confident** about **fixing bugs**, **refactoring**, and even **reimplementing** parts of your system.

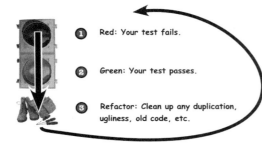

1. Red: Your test fails.

2. Green: Your test passes.

3. Refactor: Clean up any duplication, ugliness, old code, etc.

ending an iteration

It's all coming together...

You're almost finished! The team's been working hard and things are wrapping up. Your tasks and user stories are **complete**, but what's the best way to spend that extra day you ended up with? Where does **user testing** fit in? Can you squeeze in one more round of **refactoring** and **redesign**? And there sure are a lot of lingering **bugs**... when do those get fixed? It's all part of **the end of an iteration**... so let's get started on getting finished.

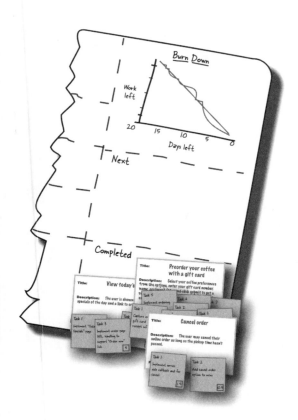

the next iteration

If it ain't broke...you still better fix it

Think things are going well?
Hold on, that just might change...

Your iteration went great, and you're delivering working software on-time. Time for the next iteration? No problem, right? Unfortunately, not right at all. Software development is all about **change,** and **moving to your next iteration** is no exception. In this chapter you'll learn how to prepare for the *next* iteration. You've got to **rebuild your board** and **adjust your stories** and expecations based on what the customer wants *NOW*, not a month ago.

10

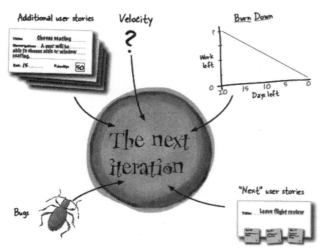

bugs

Squashing bugs like a pro

Your code, your responsibility...your bug, your reputation!

When things get tough, it's **up to you** to bring them back from the brink. **Bugs**, whether they're in your code or just in code that your software uses, are a **fact of life** in software development. And, like everything else, the way you handle bugs should fit into the rest of your process. You'll need to **prepare your board**, **keep your customer in the loop**, **confidently estimate** the work it will take to fix your bugs, and apply **refactoring** and **prefactoring** to fix and avoid bugs in the future.

the real world

Having a process in life

You've learned a lot about Software Development. But before you go pinning burn down graphs in everyone's office, there's just a little more you need to know about dealing with each project... on its own terms. There are a lot of **similarities** and **best practices** you should carry from project to project, but there are **unique** things everywhere you go, and you need to be ready for them. It's time to look at how to apply what you've learned to **your particular project**, and where to go next for **more learning**.

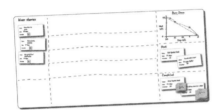

Story and Burn Down board

User Stories

Configuration Management (CM)

Continuous Integration (CI)

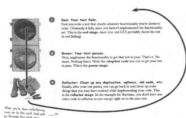

Test Driven Development (TDD)

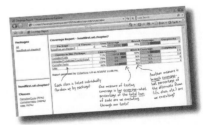

Test Coverage

appendix 1: leftovers

The top 5 things (we didn't cover)

Ever feel like something's missing? We know what you mean...

Just when you thought you were done... there's more. We couldn't leave you without a few extra things, things we just couldn't fit into the rest of the book. At least, not if you want to be able to carry this book around without a metallic case and castor wheels on the bottom. So take a peek and see what you (still) might be missing out on.

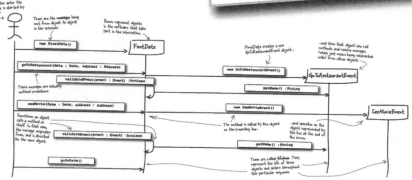

appendix 2: techniques and principles

Tools for the experienced software developer

Ever wished all those great tools and techniques were in one place? This is a roundup of all the software development **techniques** and **principles** we've covered. Take a look over them all, and see if you can **remember what each one means**. You might even want to **cut these pages out** and tape them to the bottom of your **big board**, for everyone to see in your daily standup meetings.

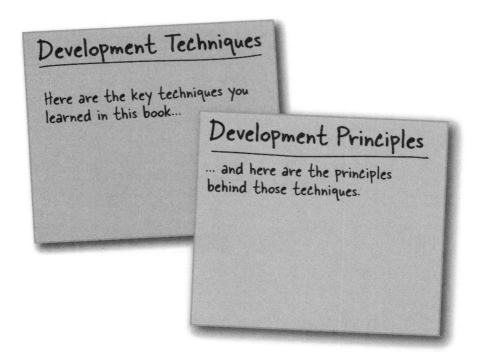

Development Techniques

Here are the key techniques you learned in this book...

Development Principles

... and here are the principles behind those techniques.

Intro

In this section we answer the burning question:
"So why DID they put that in a software
development book?"

Who is this book for?

If you can answer "yes" to all of these:

1. Do you have access to a computer and **some background in programming**?

2. Do you want to **learn techniques for building and delivering great software?** Do you want to **understand** the principles behind iterations and test-driven development?

3. Do you prefer **stimulating dinner party conversation** to **dry**, **dull**, **academic lectures**?

We use Java in the book, but you can squint and pretend it's C#. No amount of squinting will make you think it's Perl, though.

this book is for you.

Who should probably back away from this book?

If you can answer "yes" to any of these:

1. Are you <u>completely</u> new to Java?

   (You don't need to be advanced, and if you know C++ or C# you'll understand the code examples just fine.)

2. Are you a kick-butt development manager looking for a *reference* book?

3. Are you **afraid to try something different**? Would you rather have a root canal than mix stripes with plaid? Do you believe that a technical book can't be serious if iterations are anthropomorphized?

this book is not for you.

[Note from marketing: this book is for anyone with a credit card.]

We know what you're thinking

"How can *this* be a serious software development book?"

"What's with all the graphics?"

"Can I actually *learn* it this way?"

We know what your *brain* is thinking

Your brain craves novelty. It's always searching, scanning, *waiting* for something unusual. It was built that way, and it helps you stay alive.

So what does your brain do with all the routine, ordinary, normal things you encounter? Everything it *can* to stop them from interfering with the brain's *real* job—recording things that *matter*. It doesn't bother saving the boring things; they never make it past the "this is obviously not important" filter.

How does your brain *know* what's important? Suppose you're out for a day hike and a tiger jumps in front of you, what happens inside your head and body?

Neurons fire. Emotions crank up. *Chemicals surge.*

And that's how your brain knows...

This must be important! Don't forget it!

But imagine you're at home, or in a library. It's a safe, warm, tiger-free zone. You're studying. Getting ready for an exam. Or trying to learn some tough technical topic your boss thinks will take a week, ten days at the most.

Just one problem. Your brain's trying to do you a big favor. It's trying to make sure that this *obviously* non-important content doesn't clutter up scarce resources. Resources that are better spent storing the really *big* things. Like tigers. Like the danger of fire. Like the guy with the handle "BigDaddy" on MySpace probably isn't someone to meet with after 6 PM.

And there's no simple way to tell your brain, "Hey brain, thank you very much, but no matter how dull this book is, and how little I'm registering on the emotional Richter scale right now, I really *do* want you to keep this stuff around."

Your brain thinks THIS is important.

Great. Only 450 more dull, dry, boring pages.

Your brain thinks THIS isn't worth saving.

We think of a "Head First" reader as a <u>learner</u>.

So what does it take to *learn* something? First, you have to *get* it, then make sure you don't *forget* it. It's not about pushing facts into your head. Based on the latest research in cognitive science, neurobiology, and educational psychology, *learning* takes a lot more than text on a page. We know what turns your brain on.

Some of the Head First learning principles:

Make it visual. Images are far more memorable than words alone, and make learning much more effective (up to 89% improvement in recall and transfer studies). It also makes things more understandable. **Put the words within or near the graphics** they relate to, rather than on the bottom or on another page, and learners will be up to *twice* as likely to solve problems related to the content.

Use a conversational and personalized style. In recent studies, students performed up to 40% better on post-learning tests if the content spoke directly to the reader, using a first-person, conversational style rather than taking a formal tone. Tell stories instead of lecturing. Use casual language. Don't take yourself too seriously. Which would *you* pay more attention to: a stimulating dinner party companion, or a lecture?

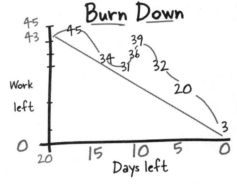

Get the learner to think more deeply. In other words, unless you actively flex your neurons, nothing much happens in your head. A reader has to be motivated, engaged, curious, and inspired to solve problems, draw conclusions, and generate new knowledge. And for that, you need challenges, exercises, and thought-provoking questions, and activities that involve both sides of the brain and multiple senses.

Get—and keep—the reader's attention. We've all had the "I really want to learn this but I can't stay awake past page one" experience. Your brain pays attention to things that are out of the ordinary, interesting, strange, eye-catching, unexpected. Learning a new, tough, technical topic doesn't have to be boring. Your brain will learn much more quickly if it's not.

Touch their emotions. We now know that your ability to remember something is largely dependent on its emotional content. You remember what you care about. You remember when you *feel* something. No, we're not talking heart-wrenching stories about a boy and his dog. We're talking emotions like surprise, curiosity, fun, "what the...?" , and the feeling of "I Rule!" that comes when you solve a puzzle, learn something everybody else thinks is hard, or realize you know something that "I'm more technical than thou" Bob from engineering *doesn't*.

Metacognition: thinking about thinking

If you really want to learn, and you want to learn more quickly and more deeply, pay attention to how you pay attention. Think about how you think. Learn how you learn.

Most of us did not take courses on metacognition or learning theory when we were growing up. We were *expected* to learn, but rarely *taught* to learn.

I wonder how I can trick my brain into remembering this stuff...

But we assume that if you're holding this book, you really want to learn how to really develop great software. And you probably don't want to spend a lot of time. If you want to use what you read in this book, you need to *remember* what you read. And for that, you've got to *understand* it. To get the most from this book, or *any* book or learning experience, take responsibility for your brain. Your brain on *this* content.

The trick is to get your brain to see the new material you're learning as Really Important. Crucial to your well-being. As important as a tiger. Otherwise, you're in for a constant battle, with your brain doing its best to keep the new content from sticking.

So just how *DO* you get your brain to treat software development like it was a hungry tiger?

There's the slow, tedious way, or the faster, more effective way. The slow way is about sheer repetition. You obviously know that you *are* able to learn and remember even the dullest of topics if you keep pounding the same thing into your brain. With enough repetition, your brain says, "This doesn't *feel* important to him, but he keeps looking at the same thing *over* and *over* and *over*, so I suppose it must be."

The faster way is to do **anything that increases brain activity,** especially different *types* of brain activity. The things on the previous page are a big part of the solution, and they're all things that have been proven to help your brain work in your favor. For example, studies show that putting words *within* the pictures they describe (as opposed to somewhere else in the page, like a caption or in the body text) causes your brain to try to makes sense of how the words and picture relate, and this causes more neurons to fire. More neurons firing = more chances for your brain to *get* that this is something worth paying attention to, and possibly recording.

A conversational style helps because people tend to pay more attention when they perceive that they're in a conversation, since they're expected to follow along and hold up their end. The amazing thing is, your brain doesn't necessarily *care* that the "conversation" is between you and a book! On the other hand, if the writing style is formal and dry, your brain perceives it the same way you experience being lectured to while sitting in a roomful of passive attendees. No need to stay awake.

But pictures and conversational style are just the beginning…

Here's what WE did:

We used **pictures**, because your brain is tuned for visuals, not text. As far as your brain's concerned, a picture really *is* worth a thousand words. And when text and pictures work together, we embedded the text *in* the pictures because your brain works more effectively when the text is *within* the thing the text refers to, as opposed to in a caption or buried in the text somewhere.

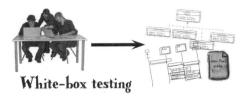

White-box testing

We used **redundancy**, saying the same thing in *different* ways and with different media types, and *multiple senses*, to increase the chance that the content gets coded into more than one area of your brain.

The software doesn't work, the code's a mess, and the CFO is going be mad as hell. I have no idea how to get things back on track...

We used concepts and pictures in **unexpected** ways because your brain is tuned for novelty, and we used pictures and ideas with at least *some* **emotional** *content*, because your brain is tuned to pay attention to the biochemistry of emotions. That which causes you to *feel* something is more likely to be remembered, even if that feeling is nothing more than a little **humor**, **surprise**, or **interest.**

We used a personalized, **conversational style**, because your brain is tuned to pay more attention when it believes you're in a conversation than if it thinks you're passively listening to a presentation. Your brain does this even when you're *reading*.

We included more than 80 **activities**, because your brain is tuned to learn and remember more when you **do** things than when you *read* about things. And we made the exercises challenging-yet-do-able, because that's what most people prefer.

PREVIOUSLY ON

We used **multiple learning styles**, because *you* might prefer step-by-step procedures, while someone else wants to understand the big picture first, and someone else just wants to see an example. But regardless of your own learning preference, *everyone* benefits from seeing the same content represented in multiple ways.

Tools for your Software Development Toolbox

We include content for **both sides of your brain**, because the more of your brain you engage, the more likely you are to learn and remember, and the longer you can stay focused. Since working one side of the brain often means giving the other side a chance to rest, you can be more productive at learning for a longer period of time.

And we included **stories** and exercises that present **more than one point of view,** because your brain is tuned to learn more deeply when it's forced to make evaluations and judgments.

We included **challenges**, with exercises, and by asking **questions** that don't always have a straight answer, because your brain is tuned to learn and remember when it has to *work* at something. Think about it—you can't get your *body* in shape just by *watching* people at the gym. But we did our best to make sure that when you're working hard, it's on the *right* things. That **you're not spending one extra dendrite** processing a hard-to-understand example, or parsing difficult, jargon-laden, or overly terse text.

We used **people**. In stories, examples, pictures, etc., because, well, because *you're* a person. And your brain pays more attention to *people* than it does to *things*.

Here's what YOU can do to bend your brain into submission

So, we did our part. The rest is up to you. These tips are a starting point; listen to your brain and figure out what works for you and what doesn't. Try new things.

Cut this out and stick it on your refrigerator.

---

(1) **Slow down. The more you understand, the less you have to memorize.**

Don't just *read*. Stop and think. When the book asks you a question, don't just skip to the answer. Imagine that someone really *is* asking the question. The more deeply you force your brain to think, the better chance you have of learning and remembering.

(2) **Do the exercises. Write your own notes.**

We put them in, but if we did them for you, that would be like having someone else do your workouts for you. And don't just *look* at the exercises. **Use a pencil.** There's plenty of evidence that physical activity *while* learning can increase the learning.

(3) **Read the "There are No Dumb Questions"**

That means all of them. They're not optional sidebars—*they're part of the core content!* Don't skip them.

(4) **Make this the last thing you read before bed. Or at least the last challenging thing.**

Part of the learning (especially the transfer to long-term memory) happens *after* you put the book down. Your brain needs time on its own, to do more processing. If you put in something new during that processing time, some of what you just learned will be lost.

(5) **Drink water. Lots of it.**

Your brain works best in a nice bath of fluid. Dehydration (which can happen before you ever feel thirsty) decreases cognitive function.

(6) **Talk about it. Out loud.**

Speaking activates a different part of the brain. If you're trying to understand something, or increase your chance of remembering it later, say it out loud. Better still, try to explain it out loud to someone else. You'll learn more quickly, and you might uncover ideas you hadn't known were there when you were reading about it.

(7) **Listen to your brain.**

Pay attention to whether your brain is getting overloaded. If you find yourself starting to skim the surface or forget what you just read, it's time for a break. Once you go past a certain point, you won't learn faster by trying to shove more in, and you might even hurt the process.

(8) **Feel something.**

Your brain needs to know that this *matters*. Get involved with the stories. Make up your own captions for the photos. Groaning over a bad joke is *still* better than feeling nothing at all.

(9) **Write a lot of software!**

There's only one way to learn to develop software: you have to **actually develop software**. And that's what you're going to do throughout this book. We're going to give you lots of requirements to capture, techniques to evaluate, and code to test and improve: every chapter has exercises that pose a problem for you to solve. Don't just skip over them—a lot of the learning happens when you solve the exercises. We included a solution to each exercise—don't be afraid to **peek at the solution** if you get stuck! (It's easy to get snagged on something small.) But try to solve the problem before you look at the solution.

Read Me

This is a learning experience, not a reference book. We deliberately stripped out everything that might get in the way of learning whatever it is we're working on at that point in the book. And the first time through, you need to begin at the beginning, because the book makes assumptions about what you've already seen and learned.

We assume you are familiar with object-oriented programming.

It would take an entire book to teach you object-oriented programming (like, say, **Head First OOA&D**). We chose to focus this book on software development principles rather than design or language basics. We picked Java for our examples because it's fairly common, and pretty self-documenting; but everything we talk about should apply whether you're using Java, C#, C++, or Visual Basic (or Ruby, or...) However, if you've never programmed using an object-oriented language, you may have some trouble following some of the code. In that case we'd strongly recommend you get familiar with one of those languages before attacking some of the later chapters in the book.

We don't cover every software development process out there.

There are tomes of information about different ways to write software. We don't try to cover every possible approach to developing code. Instead, we focus on techniques that we know work and fit well together to produce great software. Chapter 12 specifically talks about ways to tweak your process to account for unique things on your project.

The activities are NOT optional.

The exercises and activities are not add-ons; they're part of the core content of the book. Some of them are to help with memory, some are for understanding, and some will help you apply what you've learned. Some exercises are there just to make you think about **how** you would solve the problem. ***Don't skip the exercises.*** The crossword puzzles are the only thing you don't *have* to do, but they're good for giving your brain a chance to think about the words and terms you've been learning in a different context.

The redundancy is intentional and important.

One distinct difference in a Head First book is that we want you to *really* get it. And we want you to finish the book remembering what you've learned. Most reference books don't have retention and recall as a goal, but this book is about *learning*, so you'll see some of the same concepts come up more than once.

The examples are as lean as possible.

Our readers tell us that it's frustrating to wade through 200 lines of an example looking for the two lines they need to understand. Most examples in this book are shown within the smallest possible context, so that the part you're trying to learn is clear and simple. Don't expect all of the examples to be robust, or even complete—they are written specifically for learning, and aren't always fully functional.

We've placed the full code for the projects on the Web so you can copy and paste them into your text editor. You'll find them at:
   http://www.headfirstlabs.com/books/hfsd/

The Brain Power exercises don't have answers.

For some of them, there is no right answer, and for others, part of the learning experience of the Brain Power activities is for you to decide if and when your answers are right. In some of the Brain Power exercises, you will find hints to point you in the right direction.

The technical review team

Dan Francis   McClellan Francis   Faisal Jawad   Burk Hufnagel

Lisa Kellner   Kristin Stromberg   Adam Szymanski

Technical Reviewers:

This book wouldn't be anything like it is without our technical reviewers. They called us out when they disagreed with something, gave us "hurrah"s when something went right, and sent back lots of great commentary on things that worked and didn't work for them in the real world. Each of them brought a different perspective to the book, and we really appreciate that. For instance, **Dan Francis** and **McClellan Francis** made sure this book didn't turn into *Software Development for Java*.

We'd particularly like to call out **Faisal Jawad** for his thorough and supportive feedback (he started the "hurrahs"). **Burk Hufnagel** provided great suggestions on other approaches he'd used on projects and made one author's late night of updates a lot more fun with his suggestion to include, "Bad dev team. No biscuit."

Finally, we'd like to thank **Lisa Kellner** and **Kristin Stromberg** for their great work on readability and pacing. This book wouldn't be what it is without all of your input.

Acknowledgments

Our editor:

Don't let the picture fool you. **Brett** is one of the sharpest and most professional people we've ever worked with, and his contributions are on every page. Brett supported this book through every positive and negative review and spent quality time with us in Washington, D.C. to make this a success. More than once, he baited us into a good argument and then took notes while we went at it. This book is a result of his hard work and support and we really appreciate it.

Brett McLaughlin

The O'Reilly team:

↖ Lou Barr

Lou Barr is the reason these pages look so "awesome." She's responsible for turning our vaguely worded "something that conveys this idea and looks cool" comments into pages that teach the material like no other book around.

Lou's favorite American-ism...

We'd also like to thank **Laurie Petrycki** for giving us the opportunity and making the tough decisions to get this book to where it is. We'd also like to thank **Catherine Nolan** and **Mary Treseler** for getting this book kicked off. Finally we'd like to thank **Caitrin McCullough**, **Sanders Kleinfeld**, **Keith McNamara**, and the rest of the O'Reilly production team for taking this book from the rough pages we sent in to a printed, high-class book with flawless grammar.

Scrum and XP from the Trenches:

We want to extend a special thanks to Henrik Kniberg for his book **Scrum and XP from the Trenches**. This book had significant influence on how we develop software and is the basis for some of the techniques we describe in this book. We're very grateful for the excellent work he's done.

Good book... highly recommended!

Our families:

No acknowledgments page would be complete without recognizing the contributions and sacrifices our families made for this book. Vinny, Nick, and Tracey have picked up the slack in the Pilone house for almost two years while this book came together. I can't convey how much I appreciate that and how your support and encouragement while "Daddy worked on his book" made this possible. Thank you.

A massive thank you also goes out to the Miles household, that's Corinne (the boss) and Frizbee, Fudge, Snuff, Scrappy, and Stripe (those are the pigs). At every step you guys have kept me going and I really can't tell you how much that means to me. Thanks!

Safari® Books Online

 When you see a Safari® icon on the cover of your favorite technology book that means the book is available online through the O'Reilly Network Safari Bookshelf.

Safari offers a solution that's better than e-books. It's a virtual library that lets you easily search thousands of top tech books, cut and paste code samples, download chapters, and find quick answers when you need the most accurate, current information. Try it for free at `http://safari.oreilly.com`.

1 great software development

Pleasing your customer

I used to think **all** programmers got paid in bananas for their projects... but now that I'm developing great software, I get cold, hard cash.

If your customer's unhappy, *everyone's* unhappy!

Every great piece of software starts with a customer's big idea. It's your job as a professional software developer to **bring that idea to life**. But taking a vague idea and turning it into working code—code that **satisfies your customer**—isn't so easy. In this chapter you'll learn how to avoid being a software development casualty by delivering software that is **needed**, **on time**, and **on budget**. Grab your laptop, and let's set out on the road to shipping great software.

Tom's Trails is going online

Trekkin' Tom has been providing world-famous trail guides and equipment from his shack in the Rockies for years. Now, he wants to ramp up his sales using a bit of the latest technology.

No one does trail guides like mine...But the big TrailMix Conference is coming, and I want to show everybody what the next evolution in hiking looks like, Web-style.

Tom wants to take his business to the Internet.

find tools to make your adventures easier and more fun

find a trail

frequently asked questions

Your Source for Outdoor Adventure on the Web

check out our selection of hiking boots

Tom's Trails

Search Tom's Trails

the best climbing rope around

Tom's vision of Tom's Trails Online

Most projects have <u>two</u> major concerns

Talk to most customers and, besides their big idea, they've probably got two basic concerns:

How much will it cost?

No surprise here. Most customers want to figure out how much cash they'll have to spend. In this case, though, Tom has a pile of money, so that's not much of a concern for him.

Usually, cash is a limitation. In this case, Tom's got money to spare, and figures what he spends will turn into an even bigger pile.

How long will it take?

The other big constraint is time. Almost no customer ever says, "Take as long as you want!" And lots of the time, you have a specific event or date the customer wants their software ready for.

In Tom's case, he wants his website available in three months' time, ready for the big TrailMix Conference coming up.

The TrailMix Conference

This is your payday, too...if you get finished on time.

The Big Bang approach to development

With only a month to get finished, there's no time to waste.
The lead developer Tom hired gets right to work.

Flash forward: two weeks later

Tom's lead developer has pulled out all the stops to build Tom's Trails Online, putting all her finest coding skills into play and producing what she thinks Tom wants her to build.

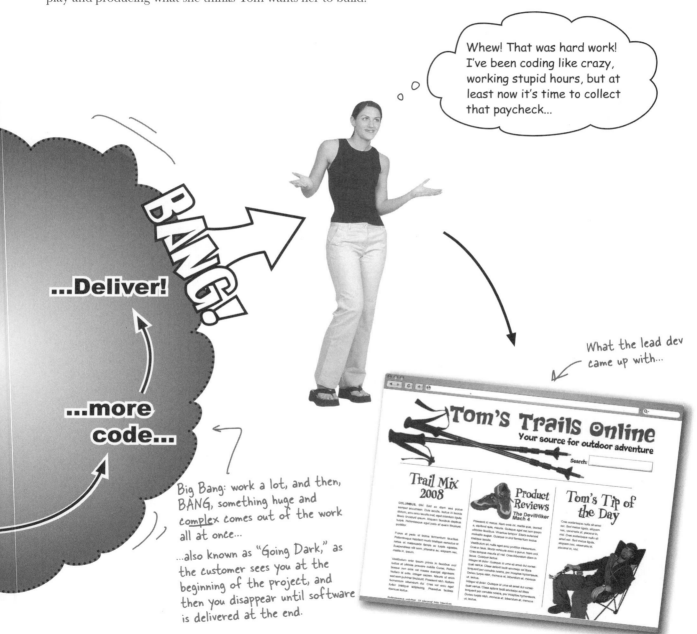

Whew! That was hard work! I've been coding like crazy, working stupid hours, but at least now it's time to collect that paycheck...

...Deliver!

BANG!

...more code...

What the lead dev came up with...

Big Bang: work a lot, and then, BANG, something huge and complex comes out of the work all at once...

...also known as "Going Dark," as the customer sees you at the beginning of the project, and then you disappear until software is delivered at the end.

Big bang development usually ends up in a BIG MESS

Even though a lot of work went into the project, Tom hasn't seen any of the (hopefully) completed work yet. Let's see what he thinks about the completed website.

> What the heck is this? The site isn't anything like I thought it would be. You couldn't have taken a little more time and gotten it right? It's like you didn't even know what I wanted...

If your customer isn't happy, you built the wrong software.

Big bang software usually means working a whole lot, but it also means not showing the customer much until your work is done. The risk with that approach is you **think** you're building what the customer wants with no real feedback until you **think** you're finished.

The emphasis here is that you think you're finished... but you may not be.

And, no matter how great YOU think your software is, it's the customer you have to make happy. So if the customer doesn't like what you've built, don't waste time trying to tell them they're wrong. Just get ready to do some rework.

But how do you figure out what the customer really wants? It's not always easy...

Sharpen your pencil

Can you figure out where things went wrong? Below are three things Tom said he wanted his site to allow for. Your job is to choose the option underneath each item that most closely matches what Tom means. And for the third one, you've got to figure out what he means on your own. Good luck!

1   **Tom says, "The customer should be able to search for trails."**

☑ The customer should see a map of the world and then enter an address to search for trails near a particular location.

☐ The customer should be able to scroll through a list of tourist spots and find trails that lead to and from those spots.

☐ The customer should be able to enter a zip code and a level of difficulty and find all trails that match that difficulty and are near that zip code.

2   **Tom says, "The customer should be able to order equipment."**

☑ The customer should be able to view what equipment Tom has and then create an order for items that are in stock.

☐ The customer should be able to order any equipment they need, but depending on stock levels the order may take longer if some of the items are back-ordered.

3   **Tom says, "The customer should be able to book a trip."**

Write what YOU think the software should do here.

> The customer should be able to enter the desired origin and destination and based on the search result, the customer should be able to book a trip.

Confused about what Tom really meant? It's okay... just do your best.

If you're having a hard time figuring out which option to choose, that's perfectly normal. Do your best, and we'll spend a lot more time in this chapter talking about how to figure out what the customer means.

Sharpen your pencil
Solution

Can you figure out where things went wrong? Your job was to choose the option underneath each item that most closely matches what Tom means. And for the third one, you had to figure out what he means on your own.

A big question mark? That's your answer? How am I supposed to develop great software when I don't even know for sure what the customer wants?

If you're not sure what the customer wants, or even if you *think* you're sure, always go back and ask

When it comes to what is needed, the customer is king. But it's really rare for the customer to know *exactly* what he wants at the beginning of the project.

When you're trying to understand what your customer wants, sometimes there's not even a right answer in the customer's head, let alone in yours! If you disappear in a hurry and start coding, you may only have half the story... or even less.

But software shouldn't be guesswork. You need to ensure that you develop great software even when what's needed is not clear up front. So go *ask* the customer what they mean. *Ask* them for more detail. *Ask* them for options about how you might implement about their big ideas.

Software development is **NOT** guesswork. You need to keep the customer in the loop to make sure you're on the right path.

Great software development is...

We've talked about several things that you'll need for successful software. You've got the customer's big ideas to deal with, their money you're spending, and a schedule you've got to worry about. You've got to get all of those things right if you're going to build consistently great software.

Great software development delivers...

> What the customer needs, otherwise called the software requirements. We'll talk more about requirements in the next chapter...

What is needed,

> When we agreed with the customer that the software would be finished.

{ On Time,

and

On Budget

> Not billing the customer for more money than was agreed upon.

 **BRAIN POWER**

Can you think of three examples of software you've been involved with where at least one of these rules was broken?

Getting to the goal with <u>ITERATION</u>

The secret to great software development is **iteration**. You've already seen that you can't simply ignore the customer during development. But iteration provides you a way to actually ask the question, at each step of development, "How am I doing?" Here are two projects: one without iteration, and one with.

Without iteration...

Suppose you take the Big Bang approach to development—or any other approach where you're not constantly checking in with the customer. The likely outcome? Missing what the customer wanted, and by a lot, not just a little.

So far, whether by luck or skill, development has stayed with the optimal path pretty closely.

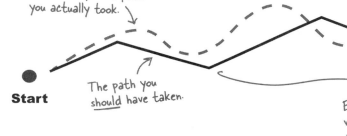

The development path you actually took.

Start

The path you <u>should</u> have taken.

Every project changes over time, with requirements subtly getting altered, or decisions about what to work on being made all the time.

With iteration...

This time, you decide that every time you make significant progress you'll check with the customer and refine what you're working on. You also don't make any major decisions without incorporating customer feedback.

Time for an early demo to see what the customer thinks.

The customer changed their mind about a feature here, but since you've been checking in, you made a small adjustment and kept going.

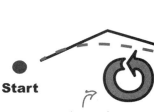

Start

Just a few days in, you clarify what the customer meant with regard to a certain feature.

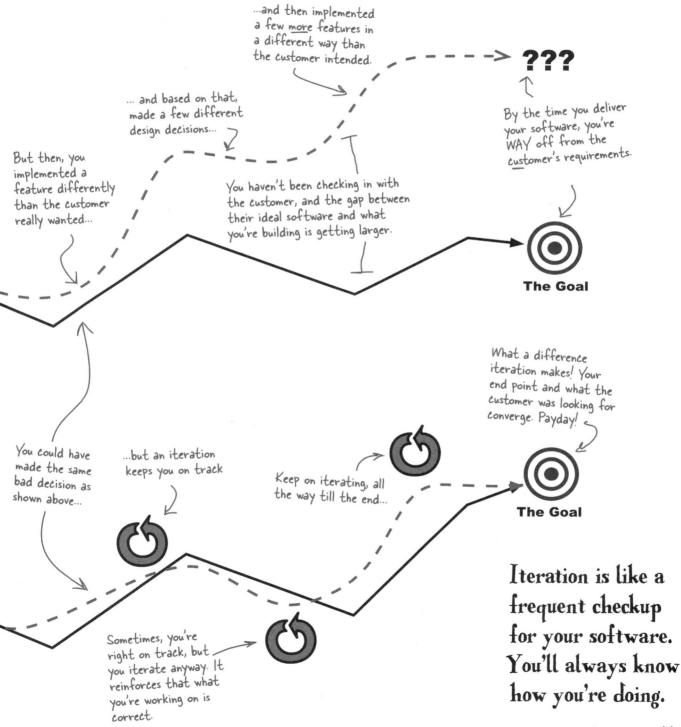

...and then implemented a few <u>more</u> features in a different way than the customer intended.

???

By the time you deliver your software, you're WAY off from the customer's requirements.

... and based on that, made a few different design decisions...

But then, you implemented a feature differently than the customer really wanted...

You haven't been checking in with the customer, and the gap between their ideal software and what you're building is getting larger.

The Goal

What a difference iteration makes! Your end point and what the customer was looking for converge. Payday!

You could have made the same bad decision as shown above...

...but an iteration keeps you on track

Keep on iterating, all the way till the end...

The Goal

Sometimes, you're right on track, but you iterate anyway. It reinforces that what you're working on is correct.

Iteration is like a frequent checkup for your software. You'll always know how you're doing.

there are no Dumb Questions

Q: What if I'm sure that I know what the customer wants at the beginning of a project? Do I still need to iterate?

A: Absolutely. Iteration and getting feedback from your customer is important *especially* when you think you know it all up front. Sometimes it can seem like a complete no-brainer on a simple piece of software, but checking back with the customer is ALWAYS worth it. Even if the customer just tells you you're doing great, and even if you actually do start out with all the right requirements, iteration is still a way to make sure you're on the right track. And, don't forget, the customer can always change their mind.

Q: My entire project is only two months long. Is it worth iterating for such a short project?

A: Yep, iteration is still really useful even on a very short project. Two months is a whopping 60 days of chances to deviate from the customer's ideal software, or misunderstand a customer's requirement. Iteration lets you catch any potential problems like this before they creep into your project. And, better yet, before you look foolish in front of your customer.

No matter how big the team, or how long the project, iteration is ALWAYS one of the keys to building great software.

Q: Wouldn't it just be better to spend more time getting to know what the customer really wants, really getting the requirements down tight, than always letting the customer change their mind midstream?

A: You'd think so, but actually this is a recipe for disaster. In the bad old days, developers used to spend ages at the beginning of a project trying to make sure they got all the customer's requirements down completely before a single line of code or design decision was made.

Unfortunately, this approach still failed. Even if you think that you completely understand what the customer needs at the beginning, the *customer* often doesn't understand. So they're figuring out what they want as much as you are.

You need a way of helping your team and your customer grow their understanding of their software as you build it, and you can't do that with a Big Bang, up-front requirements approach that expects everything to be cast in stone from day one.

Q: Who should be involved in an iteration?

A: Everyone who has a say in whether your software meets its requirements, and everyone who is involved in meeting those requirements. At a minimum, that's usually your customer, you, and any other developers working on the project.

Q: But I'm only a team of one, do I still need to iterate?

A: Good question, and the answer is yes (starting to detect a theme here?). You might only be a development team of one, but when it comes to your project there are always, at a minimum, two people who have a stake in your software being a success: your customer and you. You still have two perspectives to take into account when making sure your software is on the right path, so iteration is still really helpful even in the smallest of teams.

Q: How early in a project should I start iterating?

A: As early as you have a piece of software running that you can discuss with your customer. We normally recommend around 20 work days—1 calendar month, per iteration as a rule of thumb—but you could certainly iterate earlier. One- or two-week iterations are not unheard of. If you aren't sure about what a customer means on Day 2, call them. No sense waiting around, guessing about what you should be doing, right?

Q: What happens when my customer comes back with bad news, saying I'm way off on what I'm building. What do I do then?

A: Great question! When the worst happens and you find that you've deviated badly during an iteration, then you need to bring things back into line over the course of the next couple of iterations of development. How to do this is covered later on, but if you want to take a peek now, fast-forward to Chapter 4.

OK, I get it, iteration is important. But you said I should iterate every time I have working software, around every 30 calendar days, or 20 work days. What if I don't have anything that can run after a month? What can I show the customer?

20 working days is only a guideline. You might choose to have longer or shorter iterations for your project.

An iteration produces <u>working</u> software

With the old Big Bang approach to developing software, you probably wouldn't have any software ready until the end of the project, which is the worst time to realize that you've gone wrong!

Continuous building and testing is covered in Chapters 6 and 7.

With iteration, you check every step of the way that you're going in the right direction. That means making sure your software builds from almost day one (and more like hour one if you can manage it). You shouldn't have long periods where code doesn't work or compile, even if it's just small bits of functionality.

Then you show your customer those little pieces of functionality. It's not much, sometimes, but you can still get an OK from the customer.

A working build also makes a big difference to your team's productivity because you don't have to spend time fixing someone else's code before you can get on with your own tasks

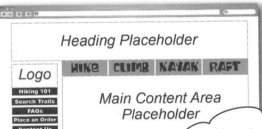

Tom got to see working software, and made some important comments you could address right away.

Hey, that's looking good. But can we go with rounded tabs? Oh, and I'd rather call it "Get in touch" than "Contact Us." Last thing... can we add an option for "Order Status?"

Here's a <u>very</u> simple portion of the Tom's Trails website. It only has the navigation, but it's still worth seeing what Tom thinks.

Instead of building the entire site at once, we broke the problem up into smaller chunks of functionality. Each chunk can then be demonstrated to the customer separately.

Each iteration is a mini-project

With iteration, you take the steps you'd follow to build the entire project, and put those steps into **each iteration**. In fact, each iteration is a mini-project, with its own requirements, design, coding, testing, etc., built right in. So you're not showing your customer junk... you're showing them well-developed bits of the final software.

Think about how most software is developed: You gather requirements (what your customer wants), build a design for the entire project, code for a long time, and then test everything. It looks a bit like this:

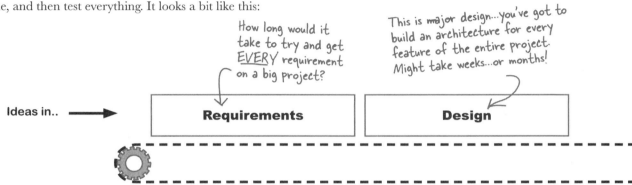

How long would it take to try and get EVERY requirement on a big project?

This is major design...you've got to build an architecture for every feature of the entire project. Might take weeks...or months!

Each iteration is <u>QUALITY</u> software

But suppose you didn't look at iteration as just a way to write big software. Think of iteration as little cycles, where you're gathering requirements, designing, writing code, and testing. Each cycle produces working, quality software:

Complete running software at the end of each iteration means we can ask the customer "Are we doing OK?" often.

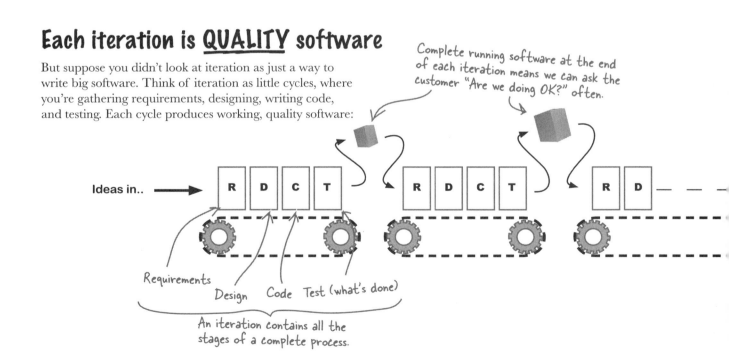

Requirements

Design   *Code*   *Test (what's done)*

An iteration contains all the stages of a complete process.

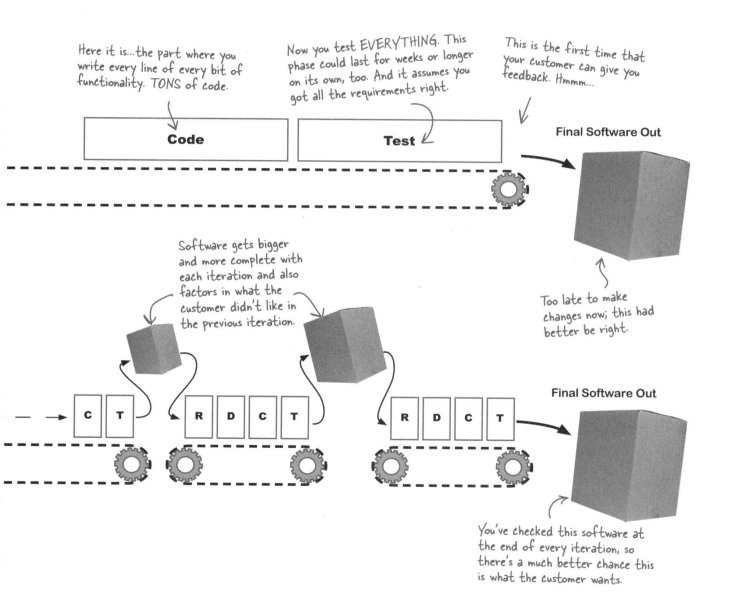

Here it is...the part where you write every line of every bit of functionality. TONS of code.

Now you test EVERYTHING. This phase could last for weeks or longer on its own, too. And it assumes you got all the requirements right.

This is the first time that your customer can give you feedback. Hmmm...

Code

Test

Final Software Out

Too late to make changes now; this had better be right.

Software gets bigger and more complete with each iteration and also factors in what the customer didn't like in the previous iteration.

C T

R D C T

R D C T

Final Software Out

You've checked this software at the end of every iteration, so there's a much better chance this is what the customer wants.

It's time to bring iterations into play on Tom's Trails. Each of the features that Tom wants for Trails Online has had estimates added to specify how long it will take to actually develop. Then we figured out how important each is to Tom and then assigned a priority to each of them (10 being the highest priority, 50 being the lowest). Take each feature and position them along the project's timeline, adding an iteration when you think it might be useful.

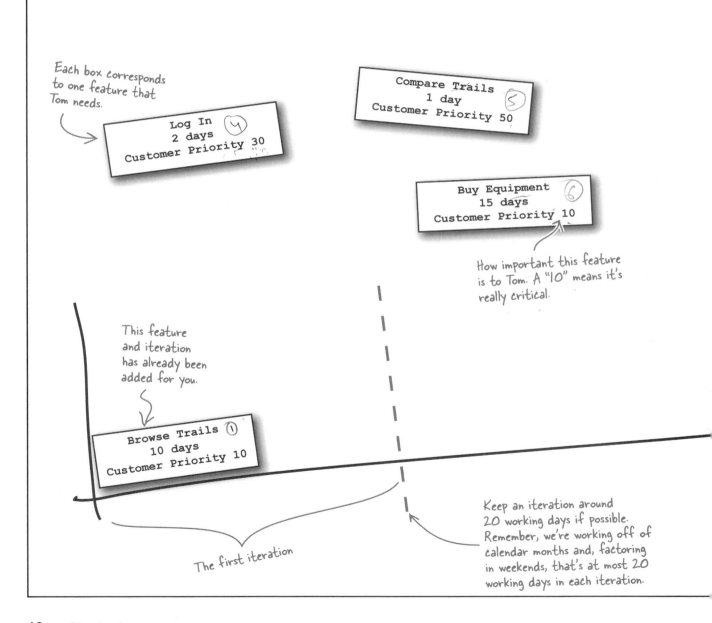

Each box corresponds to one feature that Tom needs.

Log In
2 days
Customer Priority 30

Compare Trails
1 day
Customer Priority 50

Buy Equipment
15 days
Customer Priority 10

How important this feature is to Tom. A "10" means it's really critical.

This feature and iteration has already been added for you.

Browse Trails ①
10 days
Customer Priority 10

The first iteration

Keep an iteration around 20 working days if possible. Remember, we're working off of calendar months and, factoring in weekends, that's at most 20 working days in each iteration.

Oh, one other thing. Tom doesn't want customers to be able to buy equipment unless they've logged in to the web site. Be sure and take that into account in your plan.

Each feature has an estimate to show how long it should take to develop that feature (in actual working days).

List Equipment
7 days   ③
Customer Priority 10

Add a Review   ⑧
2 days
Customer Priority 20

View Reviews
3 days   ⑦
Customer Priority 20

Search Trails ②
3 days
Customer Priority 20

10 is high priority, 50 is low. We'll look at why these priorities are in increments of 10 in Chapter 3.

Don't forget to add as many iterations as you think will be useful.

Exercise Solution

Your job was to build an iteration plan for Tom's Trails. You should have come up with something like we did, below:

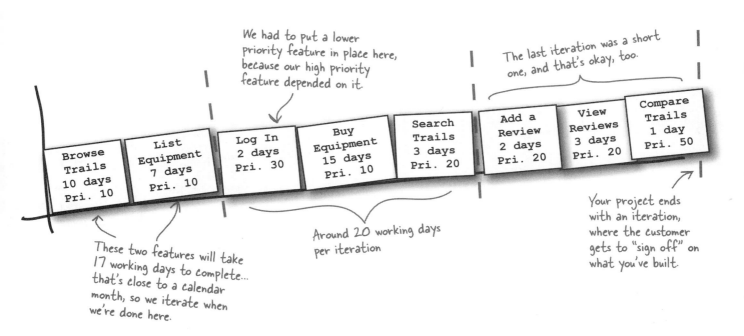

We had to put a lower priority feature in place here, because our high priority feature depended on it.

The last iteration was a short one, and that's okay, too.

| Browse Trails 10 days Pri. 10 | List Equipment 7 days Pri. 10 | Log In 2 days Pri. 30 | Buy Equipment 15 days Pri. 10 | Search Trails 3 days Pri. 20 | Add a Review 2 days Pri. 20 | View Reviews 3 days Pri. 20 | Compare Trails 1 day Pri. 50 |

These two features will take 17 working days to complete... that's close to a calendar month, so we iterate when we're done here.

Around 20 working days per iteration

Your project ends with an iteration, where the customer gets to "sign off" on what you've built.

This is probably the only plan that serves the customer's priorities, keeps iterations at a manageable length, and gets the job done. If you came up with something different, take a hard look at why you made different choices than we did.

I decided to have the customer check on the project after each feature. That's even **better** than iterating every calendar month, right?

Your iteration length should be at the right tempo for <u>YOUR</u> project

An iteration helps you stay on track, and so you might decide to have iterations that are shorter or longer than 30 days. Thirty days might seem like a long time, but factor in weekends, and that means you're probably going to get 20 days of actual productive work per iteration. If you're not sure, try 30 calendar days per iteration as a good starting point, and then you can tweak for your project as needed.

The key here is to iterate often enough to catch youself when you're deviating from the goal, but not so often that you're spending all your time preparing for the end of an iteration. It takes time to show the customer what you've done and then make course corrections, so make sure to factor this work in when you are deciding how long your iterations should be.

there are no
Dumb Questions

Q: The last feature scheduled for my iteration will push the time needed to way over a month. What should I do?

A: Consider shifting that feature into the next iteration. Your features can be shuffled around within the boundaries of a 20-day iteration until you are confident that you can successfully build an iteration within the time allocated. Going longer runs the risk of getting off course.

Q: Ordering things by customer priority is all fine and good, but what happens when I have features that need to be completed before other features?

A: When a feature is dependent on another feature, try to group those features together, and make sure they are placed within the same iteration. You can do this even if it means doing a lower-priority feature before a high-priority one, if it makes the high-priority feature possible.

This occurred in the previous exercise where the "Log In" feature was actually a low customer priority, but needed to be in place before the "Buy Equipment" feature could be implemented.

Q: If I add more people to the project, couldn't I do more in each of my iterations?

A: Yes, but be very careful. Adding another person to a project doesn't halve the time it takes to complete a feature. We'll talk more about how to factor in the overhead of multiple people in Chapter 2, when we talk about velocity.

Q: What happens when a change occurs and my plan needs to change?

A: Change is unfortunately a constant in software development, and any process needs to handle it. Luckily, an iterative process has change baked right in...turn the page and see what we mean.

The customer **WILL** change things up

Tom signed off on your plan, and Iteraton 1 has been completed. You're now well into your second iteration of development and things are going great. Then Tom calls...

> Things are really starting to look great, but I had some thoughts after that last iteration. I think it's really important that Tom's Trails Online has a mailing list, so my customers can communicate with each other.

Remember, if your software doesn't do what the customer wants, you're not going to go very far in software development.

It's up to you to make adjustments

Tom's new idea means three new features, all high-priority. And we don't even know how long they'll take, either. But you've got to figure out a way to work these into your projects.

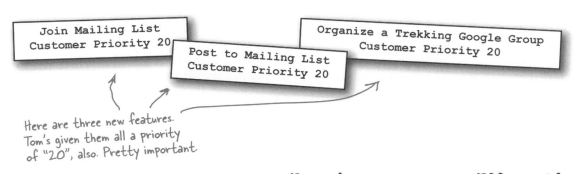

```
Join Mailing List
Customer Priority 20
```

```
Post to Mailing List
Customer Priority 20
```

```
Organize a Trekking Google Group
Customer Priority 20
```

Here are three new features. Tom's given them all a priority of "20", also. Pretty important.

But there are some **BIG** problems...

You're already <u>a long way</u> into development...

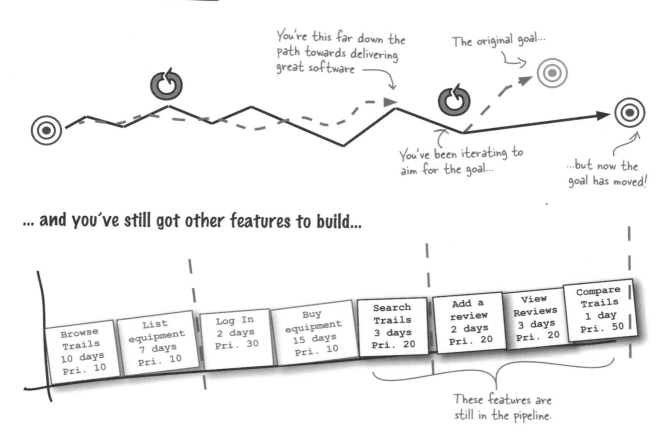

You're this far down the path towards delivering great software

The original goal...

You've been iterating to aim for the goal...

...but now the goal has moved!

... and you've still got other features to build...

| Browse Trails 10 days Pri. 10 | List equipment 7 days Pri. 10 | Log In 2 days Pri. 30 | Buy equipment 15 days Pri. 10 | Search Trails 3 days Pri. 20 | Add a review 2 days Pri. 20 | View Reviews 3 days Pri. 20 | Compare Trails 1 day Pri. 50 |

These features are still in the pipeline.

... and the deadline hasn't changed.

You are now here...

Remember the deadline from page 3? It hasn't changed, even though Tom's mind has.

A little over one month until the TrailMix conference!

Iteration handles change automatically (well, sort of)

Your iteration plan is already structured around short cycles, and is built to handle lots of individual features. Here's what you need to do:

❶ Estimate the new features

First, you need to estimate how long each of the new features is going to take. We'll talk a lot more about estimation in a few chapters, but for now, let's say we came up with these estimates for the three new features:

> Post to Mailing List
> 2 days

> Join Mailing List
> 7 days

> Organize a Trekking Group
> 10 days

You add estimates for how much work each new feature will take to add.

❷ Have your customer prioritize the new features

Tom already gave everything a priority of "20," right? But you really need him to look at the other features left to implement as well, and prioritize in relation to those.

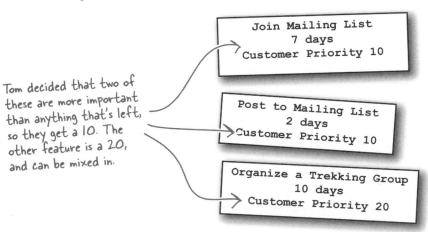

> Join Mailing List
> 7 days
> Customer Priority 10

> Post to Mailing List
> 2 days
> Customer Priority 10

> Organize a Trekking Group
> 10 days
> Customer Priority 20

Tom decided that two of these are more important than anything that's left, so they get a 10. The other feature is a 20, and can be mixed in.

A priority of 20, relative to these remaining features means we can sprinkle one more feature in anywhere before comparing trails.

> Search Trails
> 3 days
> Pri. 20

> Add a Review
> 2 days
> Pri. 20

> View Reviews
> 3 days
> Pri. 20

> Compare Trails
> 1 day
> Pri. 50

3 **Rework your iteration plan**

The ordering is set based on prioritization, and there aren't any dependencies. So now you change your plan, keeping your iteration length and the overall schedule in mind.

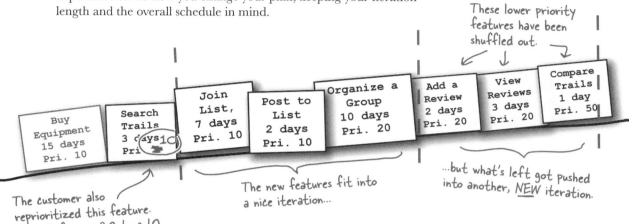

These lower priority features have been shuffled out.

Buy Equipment 15 days Pri. 10

Search Trails 3 days Pri. 10

Join List, 7 days Pri. 10

Post to List 2 days Pri. 10

Organize a Group 10 days Pri. 20

Add a Review 2 days Pri. 20

View Reviews 3 days Pri. 20

Compare Trails 1 day Pri. 50

The customer also reprioritized this feature. It went from a 20 to a 10, relative to what's left to do.

The new features fit into a nice iteration...

...but what's left got pushed into another, NEW iteration.

4 **Check your project deadline**

Remember the TrailMix Conference? You need to see if the work you've got left, including the new features, still can get done in time. Otherwise, Tom's got to make some hard choices.

Join Mailing List 7 days

Post to Mailing List 2 days

Organize a Trekking Group 10 days

Add a Review 2 days

View Reviews 3 days

Search Trails 3 days

Work left to do

(Days of work left)

–

(Days left before deadline)

Days before TrailMix Con

= **Can you do it?**

If this number is negative, you're in good shape.

> You're about to hit me with a big fancy development process, aren't you? Like if I use RUP or Quick or DRUM or whatever, I'm magically going to start producing great software, right?

A process is really just a sequence of steps

Process, particularly in software development, has gotten a bit of a bad name. A process is just a sequence of steps that you follow in order to do something—in our case, develop software. So when we've been talking about iteration, prioritization, and estimation, we've really been talking about a software development process.

Rather than being any formal set of rules about what diagrams, documentation, or even testing you should be doing (although testing is something we'd definitely recommend!), a process is really just what to do, and when to do it. And it doesn't need an acronym...it just has to work.

We don't really care what process you use, as long as it has the components that ensure you get great, quality software at the end of your development cycle.

The right software development process for YOU is one that helps YOU develop and deliver great software, on time and on budget.

> It seems like iteration could be applied to **any** process, right?

Iteration is <u>more</u> than a process

Regardless of the actual steps involved in the process you choose, iteration is a best practice. It's an approach that can be applied to **any** process, and it gives you a better chance of delivering what is needed, on time and on budget. Whatever process you end up using, iteration should be a major part.

Your software isn't complete until it's been <u>RELEASED</u>

You added the new features, and now you and your team have finished the project on time and on schedule. At every step of the way, you've been getting feedback from the customer at the end of each iteration, incorporating that feedback, and new features, into the next iteration. Now you can deliver your software, and ***then*** you get paid.

Tom isn't talking about your software running on your machine... he cares about the software running in the <u>real</u> world.

> Excellent. I'm already getting calls, and people love the new site. And our orders are up this week, mostly off of new customers that saw our online demo at TrailMix. Nice work.

The Goal

Iteration helped you reach an achievable goal that captured what your customer needed.

there are no Dumb Questions

Q: What happens when the customer comes up with new requirements and you can't fit all the extra work into your current iteration?

A: This is when customer priority comes into play. Your customer needs to make a call as to what really needs to be done for this iteration of development. The work that cannot be done then needs to be postponed until the next iteration. We'll talk a lot more about iteration in the next several chapters.

Q: What if you don't *have* a next iteration? What if you're already on the last iteration, and then a top priority feature comes in from the customer?

A: If a crucial feature comes in late to your project and you can't fit it into the last iteration, then the first thing to do is explain to the customer why the feature won't fit. Be honest and show them your iteration plan and explain why, with the resources you have, the work threatens your ability to deliver what they need by the due date.

The best option, if your customer agrees to it, is to factor the new requirement into another iteration on the end of your project, extending the due date. You could also add more developers, or make everyone work longer hours, but be wary of trying to shoehorn the work in like this. Adding more developers or getting everyone to work longer hours will often blow your budget and rarely if ever results in the performance gains you might expect (see Chapter 3).

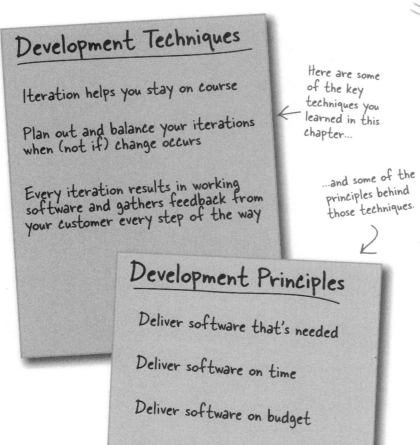

Tools for your Software Development Toolbox

Software Development is all about developing and delivering great software. In this chapter, you learned about several techniques to keep you on track. For a complete list of tools in the book, see Appendix ii.

Development Techniques

Iteration helps you stay on course

Plan out and balance your iterations when (not if) change occurs

Every iteration results in working software and gathers feedback from your customer every step of the way

Here are some of the key techniques you learned in this chapter...

...and some of the principles behind those techniques.

Development Principles

Deliver software that's needed

Deliver software on time

Deliver software on budget

BULLET POINTS

- The **feedback** that comes out of each **iteration** is the best tool for ensuring that your software meets the needs of your customers.

- An iteration is a complete project in **miniature**.

- Successful software is not developed in a vacuum. It needs **constant feedback** from your customer using iterations.

- Good software development delivers great software, **on time** and **on budget**.

- It's always better to deliver **some** of the features **working perfectly** than all of the features that don't work properly.

- Good developers develop software; **great developers** ship software!

Software Development Cross

Let's put what you've learned to use and stretch out your left brain a bit. All of the words below are somewhere in this chapter. Good luck!

Across

2. I'm the person or company who ultimately decides if your software is worth paying for.
4. Good Developers develop, great developers ....
6. An iteration produces software that is ....
7. Aim for .... working days per iteration.
9. The number of development stages that are executed within an iteration.
12. I am one thing that your software needs to do.
13. The date that you need to deliver your final software on.
15. Iteration is .... than a process.
16. The single most important output from your development process.
17. Software isn't complete until it has been ....

Down

1. A .... is really just a sequence of steps.
3. When a project fails because it costs too much, it is ....
5. I contain every step of the software development process in micro and I result in runnable software.
8. The minimum number of iterations in a 3 month project.
10. Software that arrives when the customer needs it is ....
11. An iteration is a complete mini-.........
14. The types of software development projects where you should use iteration.

Software Development Cross Solution

		¹P					²C	U	S	T	³O	M	E	R		
		R									V					
		O			⁴S	H	⁵I	P			E					
		C					T		⁶W	O	R	K	I	N	G	
⁷T	W	E	N	⁸T	Y		E				B					
		S		H			R		⁹F	O	U	R				
		S		R			A				D		¹⁰O		¹¹P	
				E			T				G		N		R	
		¹²R	E	Q	U	I	R	E	M	E	N	T	I		O	
				E			O				T		I		J	
¹³D	E	¹⁴A	D	L	I	N	E				¹⁵M	O	R	E	E	
		L						¹⁶C	O	D	E			C	
¹⁷R	E	L	E	A	S	E	D							T	

2 gathering requirements

Knowing what the customer wants

I know I said I wanted a Mustang, but I was really looking for the five-liter, turbocharged model...

You can't always get what you want...but the customer should!

Great software development delivers **what the customer wants**. This chapter is all about **talking to the customer** to figure out what their **requirements** are for your software. You'll learn how **user stories**, **brainstorming**, and the **estimation game** help you get inside your customer's head. That way, by the time you finish your project, you'll be confident you've built what your customer wants...and not just a poor imitation.

Orion's Orbits is modernizing

Orion's Orbits provides quality space shuttle services to discerning clients, but their reservation system is a little behind the times, and they're ready to take the leap into the 21st century. With the next solar eclipse just four weeks away, they've laid out some serious cash to make sure their big project is done right, and finished on time.

Orion's doesn't have an experienced team of programmers on staff, though, so they've hired you and your team of software experts to handle developing their reservation system. It's up to you to get it right and deliver on time.

We need a web site showing our current deals, and we want our users to be able to book shuttles and special packages, as well as pay for their bookings online. We also want to offer a luxury service that includes travel to and from the spaceport and accommodation in a local hotel...

BRAIN POWER

How close do you think your final software will be to what the CEO of Orion Orbits wants?

 **Sharpen your pencil**

Your job is to analyze the Orion's CEO's statement, and build some initial requirements. A requirement is a single thing that the software has to do. Write down the things you think you need to build for Orion's Orbits on the cards below.

Here's one to get you started.

Title: Show current deals

Description: The web site will show current deals to Orion's Orbits users.

Title: ....

Description: ....

Title: ....

Description: ....

Title: ....

Description: ....

Title: ....

Description: ....

Title: ....

Description: ....

Remember, each requirement should be a <u>single</u> thing the system has to do.

If you've got index cards, they're perfect for writing requirements down.

Sharpen your pencil
Solution

Let's start by breaking out the requirements from what the Orion's Orbits CEO is asking for. Take his loose ideas and turn them into snippets, with each snippet capturing one thing that you think the software will need to do...

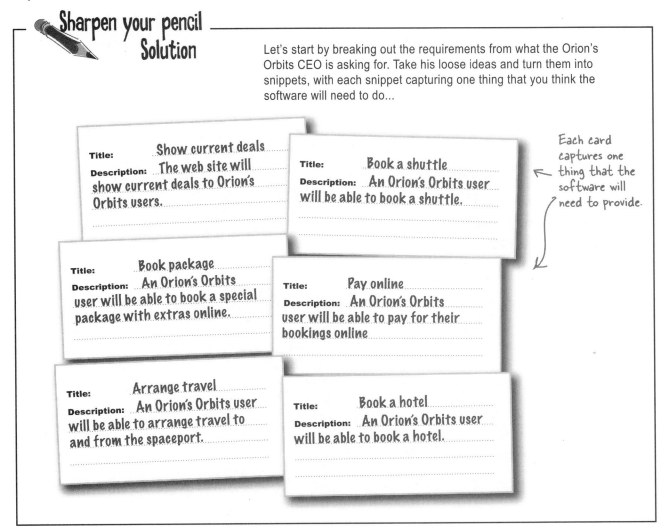

Title: Show current deals
Description: The web site will show current deals to Orion's Orbits users.

Title: Book a shuttle
Description: An Orion's Orbits user will be able to book a shuttle.

Each card captures one thing that the software will need to provide.

Title: Book package
Description: An Orion's Orbits user will be able to book a special package with extras online.

Title: Pay online
Description: An Orion's Orbits user will be able to pay for their bookings online

Title: Arrange travel
Description: An Orion's Orbits user will be able to arrange travel to and from the spaceport.

Title: Book a hotel
Description: An Orion's Orbits user will be able to book a hotel.

there are no
Dumb Questions

Q: Should we be using a specific format for writing these down?

A: No. Right now you're just grabbing and sorting out the ideas that your customer has and trying to get those ideas into some sort of manageable order.

Q: Aren't these requirements just user stories?

A: You're not far off, but at the moment they are just ideas. In just a few more pages we'll be developing them further into full-fledged user stories. At the moment it's just useful to write these ideas down somewhere.

Q: These descriptions all seem really blurry right now. Don't we need a bit more information before we can call them requirements?

A: Absolutely. There are lots of gaps in understanding in these descriptions. To fill in those gaps, we need to go back and talk to the customer some more...

Talk to your customer to get MORE information

There are always gaps in your understanding of what your software is supposed to do, especially early in your project. Each time you have more questions, or start to make assumptions, you need to go back and **talk with the customer** to get answers to your questions.

Here are a few questions you might have after your first meeting with the CEO:

1 How many different types of shuttles does the software have to support?

2 Should the software print out receipts or monthly reports (and what should be on the reports)?

3 Should the software allow reservations to be canceled or changed?

4 Does the software have an administrator interface for adding new types of shuttles, and/or new packages and deals?

5 Are there any other systems that your software is going to have to talk to, like credit card authorization systems or Air/Space Traffic Control?

6 ....
....

Can you come up with another question you might want to ask the CEO?

> OK, thanks for coming back to me. I'll get to those questions in just a bit, but I thought of something else I forgot to mention earlier...

Try to gather additional requirements.

Talking to the customer doesn't just give you a chance to get more details about *existing* requirements. You also want to find out about **additional requirements** the customer didn't think to tell you about earlier. There's nothing worse than finishing a project and the customer saying they forgot some important detail.

So how do you get the customer to think of everything you need to know, **before** you start building their software?

Bluesky with your customer

When you iterate with the customer on their requirements, **THINK BIG**. Brainstorm with other people; two heads are better than one, and ten heads are better than two, as long as everyone feels they can contribute without criticism. Don't rule out any ideas in the beginning— just capture *everything*. It's OK if you come up with some wild ideas, as long as you're all still focusing on the core needs that the software is trying to meet. This is called ***blueskying*** for requirements.

We call this blue skying because the sky's the limit.

Pay with a credit card and PayPal.

Uses Ajax for a slick user interface.

Write a review of a flight.

Order a DVD of my shuttle flight.

The developer

Your development team

The customer's team

You can include the users themselves.

Order in-flight drinks or meals.

Choose aisle or window seating.

Avoid office politics.

Nothing will stifle creative bluesky thinking like a boss that won't let people speak up. Try as much as possible to leave job descriptions and other baggage at the door when blueskying requirements. Everyone should get an equal say to ensure you get the most out of each brainstorming session.

Watch it!

Never forget to include the customer in these sessions.

Sharpen your pencil

Take four of the ideas from the bluesky brainstorm and create a new card for each potential requirement. Also, see if you can come up with two additional requirements of your own.

We can refer to each requirement easily by using its title.

Title: Pay with Visa/MC/PayPal

Description: Users will be able to pay for their bookings by credit card.

Title: ....

Description: ....

Title: ....

Description: ....

Title: ....

Description: ....

Make these two your own.

Title: ....

Description: ....

Title: ....

Description: ....

Answers on page 38.

Sometimes your bluesky session looks like this...

Sometimes, no matter how hard you try, your bluesky sessions can be as muffled as a foggy day in winter. Often the people that know what the software should really do are just not used to coming out of their shell in a brainstorming environment, and you end up with a long, silent afternoon.

Some people will give you lots of information...

Order in-flight drinks or meals.

...and others will clam up and give you the silent treatment.

< Nothing >

The zen of good requirements

The key to capturing good requirements is to get as many of the stakeholders involved as possible. If getting everyone in the same room is just not working, have people brainstorm individually and then come together and put all their ideas on the board and brainstorm a bit more. Go away and think about what happened and come back together for a second meeting.

There are **LOTS** of ways to gather good requirements. If one approach doesn't work, simply **TRY ANOTHER.**

Find out what people <u>REALLY</u> do

Everything (that's ethical and legal) is pretty much fair game when you're trying to get into your customer's head to understand their requirements. Two particularly useful techniques that help you understand the customer are **role playing** and **observation**.

Role playing

If your customer is finding it hard to visualize how they need their software to work, act it out. You pretend to be the software and your customer attempts to instruct you in what they would like you to do. Then write down each thing the software needs to do on one of your requirement cards.

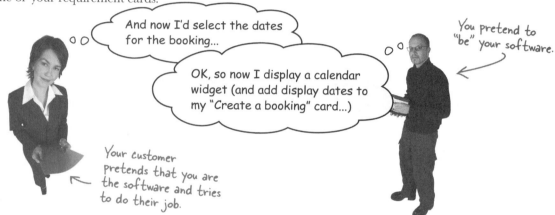

And now I'd select the dates for the booking...

OK, so now I display a calendar widget (and add display dates to my "Create a booking" card...)

You pretend to "be" your software.

Your customer pretends that you are the software and tries to do their job.

Observation

Sometimes the best way to understand how people will work with your software is to watch them, and figure out where your software will fit in. Nothing beats firsthand evidence, and observation can really help to bring out constraints and details that might have been missed in bluesky brainstorming or even in role playing. Also, try to observe the same interactions more than once with multiple observers so you don't just gain one person's impression of an event.

If you can, try three people observing on around three occasions.

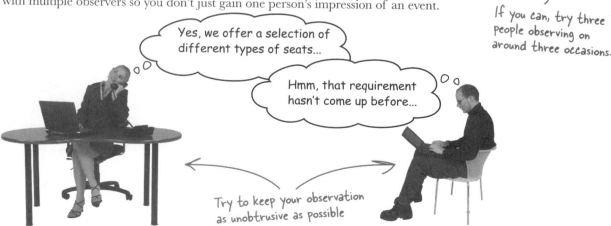

Yes, we offer a selection of different types of seats...

Hmm, that requirement hasn't come up before...

Try to keep your observation as unobtrusive as possible

Our
↗ **Sharpen your pencil**
Solution

Your job was to take each of the ideas from the bluesky session on page 35 and create a new card for each potential requirement.

You should also role play and observe. ↗

A nonfunctional constraint, but it is still captured as a user story →

Title: Support 3000 concurrent users
Description: The traffic for Orion's Orbits is expected to reach 3,000 users, all using the site at the same time.

Title: Pay with Visa/MC/PayPal
Description: Users will be able to pay for their bookings by credit card or PayPal.

Title: Review flight
Description: A user will be able to leave a review for a shuttle flight they have been on.

We've added to our cards from page 32 after the brainstorming with the customer. ↓

Title: Order Flight DVD
Description: A user will be able to order a DVD of a flight they have been on.

Title: Order in-flight meals
Description: A user will be able to specify the meals and drinks they want during a flight.

Title: Book a shuttle
Description: A user will be able to book a shuttle specifying the date and time of the flight.

These were the requirements we came up with; yours could have been different. ↘

Title: Choose seating
Description: A user will be able to choose aisle or window seating.

And we've added more detail where it was uncovered through brainstorming, role playing, or observation. ↑

Title: Use Ajax for the UI
Description: The user interface will use Ajax technologies to provide a cool and slick online experience.

The boss isn't sure he understands what this requirement is all about.

> These are really looking good, but what's Ajax? Isn't that a kitchen cleaner or something?

Your requirements must be CUSTOMER-oriented

A great requirement is actually written **from your customer's perspective** describing what the software is going to do **for the customer**. Any requirements that your customer doesn't understand are an immediate red flag, since they're not things that the customer could have possibly asked for.

A requirement should be written in the customer's language and read like a **user story**: a story about how their users interact with the software you're building. When deciding if you have good requirements or not, judge each one against the following criteria:

User stories SHOULD...

You should be able to check e<u>ach</u> box for e<u>ach</u> of your user stories.

☐ ... describe **one thing** that the software needs to do for the customer. ← Think "by the customer, for the customer"

☐ ... be written using language that **the customer understands**. ←

☐ ... be **written by the customer**. ← This means the customer drives each one, no matter who scribbles on a notecard.

☐ ... be **short**. Aim for no more than three sentences.

User stories SHOULD NOT...

☐ ... be a long essay. ← If a user story is long, you should try and break it up into multiple smaller user stories (see page 54 for tips).

☐ ... use technical terms that are unfamiliar to the customer.

☐ ... mention specific technologies.

Title: Use Ajax for the UI
Description: The user interface will use Ajax technologies to provide a cool and slick online experience.

This card is not a user story at all; it's really a design decision. Save it for later, when you start implementing the software.

DESIGN IDEAS

A user story is written from the <u>CUSTOMER'S PERSPECTIVE.</u> Both you <u>AND</u> your customer should understand what a user story means.

Great, so now you've created more user stories, and gotten a bunch more questions. What do you do with all these things you're still unclear about?

Ask the customer (yes, again).

The great thing about user stories is that it's easy for both you and the customer to read them and figure out what might be missing.

When you're writing the stories with the customer, you'll often find that they say things like "Oh, we also do this...", or "Actually, we do that a bit differently..." Those are great opportunities to refine your requirements, and make them more accurate.

If you find that you are unclear about **anything**, then it's time to have another discussion with your customer. Go back and ask them another set of questions. You're only ready to move on to the next stage when you have *no more questions* and your customer is also happy that all the user stories capture **everything** they need the software to do—for now.

there are no Dumb Questions

Q: What's the "Title" field on my user stories for? Doesn't my description field have all the information I need?

A: The title field is just a handy way to refer to a user story. It also gives everyone on the team the *same* handy way to refer to a story, so you don't have one developer talking about "Pay by PayPal," another saying, "Pay with credit card," and find out they mean the same thing later on (after they've both done needless work).

Q: Won't adding technical terms and some of my ideas on possible technologies to my user stories make them more useful to me and my team?

A: No, avoid tech terms or technologies at this point. Keep things in the language of the customer, and just describe what the software needs to do. Remember, the user stories are written from the customer's perspective. The customer has to tell you whether you've gotten the story right, so a bunch of tech terms will just confuse them (and possibly obscure whether your requirements are accurate or not).

If you do find that there are some possible technical decisions that you can start to add when writing your user stories, note those ideas down on another set of cards (cross referencing by title). When you get to coding, you can bring those ideas back up to help you at that point, when it's more appropriate.

Q: And I'm supposed to do all this refining of the requirements as user stories with the customer?

A: Yes, absolutely. After all, you're only ready for the next step when both you **and** the customer finally decide that you completely understand the software requirements. You can't make that decision on your own, so keeping your customer in the loop is essential.

Q: This seems like a lot of requirements work up front at the beginning of the project. What about when things change?

A: The work you've done so far is just your first attempt at gathering requirements at the beginning of your prject. You'll continue to refine and capture new requirements throughout your project, feeding those requirements where necessary into your project's iterations.

Develop your requirements with customer feedback

The steps we've followed so far have been all about coming to grips with the customer's ideas and refining those ideas into user stories. You execute these steps, in one form or another, at the beginning of each iteration to make sure that you always have the right set of features going into the next iteration. Let's see how that process currently looks...

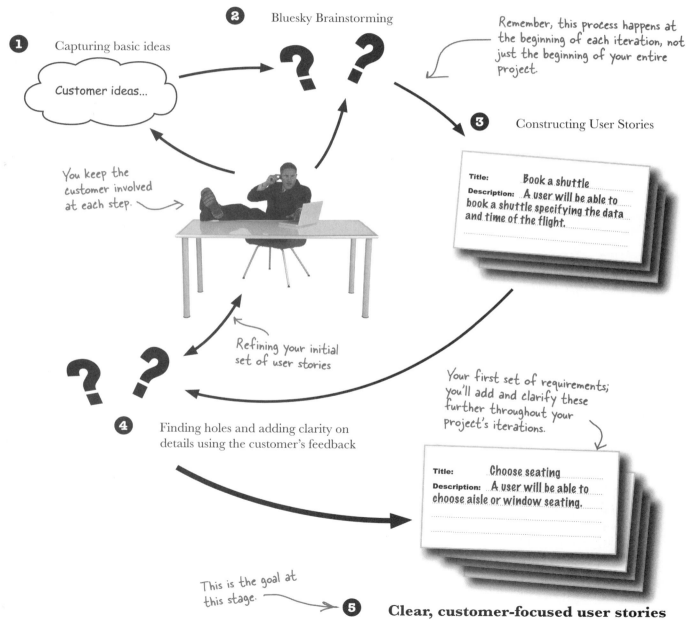

① Capturing basic ideas

Customer ideas...

② Bluesky Brainstorming

Remember, this process happens at the beginning of each iteration, not just the beginning of your entire project.

You keep the customer involved at each step.

③ Constructing User Stories

Title: Book a shuttle
Description: A user will be able to book a shuttle specifying the data and time of the flight.

Refining your initial set of user stories

Your first set of requirements; you'll add and clarify these further throughout your project's iterations.

④ Finding holes and adding clarity on details using the customer's feedback

Title: Choose seating
Description: A user will be able to choose aisle or window seating.

This is the goal at this stage.

⑤ **Clear, customer-focused user stories**

User Story Exposed

This week's interview:
The many faces of a User Story

Head First: Hello there, User Story.

User Story: Hi! Sorry it's taken so long to get an interview, I'm a bit busy at the moment...

Head First: I can imagine, what with you and your friends capturing and updating the requirements for the software at the beginning of each iteration, you must have your hands pretty full.

User Story: Actually, I'm a lot busier than that. I not only describe the requirements, but I'm also the main technique for bridging the gap between what a customer wants in his head and what he receives in delivered software. I pretty much drive everything from here on in.

Head First: But don't you just record what the customer wants?

User Story: Man, I really wish that were the case. As it turns out, I'm pretty much at the heart of an entire project. Every bit of software a team develops has to implement a user story.

Head First: So that means you're the benchmark against which every piece of software that is developed is tested?

User Story: That means if it's not in a user story somewhere, it ain't in the software, period. As you can imagine, that means I'm kept busy all the way through the development cycle.

Head First: Okay, sure, but your job is essentially done after the requirements are set, right?

User Story: I wish. If there's anything I've learned, requirements never stay the same in the real world. I might change right up to the end of a project.

Head First: So how do you handle all this pressure and still keep it together?

User Story: Well, I focus on one single thing: describing what the software needs to do from the customer's perspective. I don't get distracted by the rest of the noise buzzing around the project, I just keep that one mantra in my head. Then everything else tends to fall into place.

Head First: Sounds like a big job, still.

User Story: Ah, it's not too bad. I'm not very sophisticated, you know? Just three lines or so of description and I'm done. The customers like me because I'm simple and in their language, and the developers like me because I'm just a neat description of what their software has to do. Everyone wins.

Head First: What about when things get a bit more formal, like with use cases, main and alternate flows, that sort of thing? You're not really used then, are you?

User Story: Heck, I can smarten myself up with some more details to be a use case if that's what you need, and lots of people do dress me up that way for their bosses. The important thing is that we all describe what a piece of software needs to do, no matter how we look. Use cases are more or less user stories in a tuxedo.

Head First: Well, you heard it here first folks. Next week we'll be catching up with Test to see how he guarantees that software does what a user story requires. Until then, take care and remember, always do only what your user story says, and not an ounce more!

User stories define the WHAT of your project... estimates define the WHEN

After your initial requirement-capture stage you will have a set of clear, customer-focused user stories that you and the customer believe capture **WHAT** it is you're trying to build, at least for the first iteration or so. But don't get too comfortable, because the customer will want to know **WHEN** all those stories will be built.

This is the part where the customer asks the big question: **How long will it all take?**

> Hmm, great. Now what do I do? How do I figure out how long everything is going to take when all I have so far is a pack of user stories?

Your project estimate is the sum of the estimates for your user stories

To figure out how long it will take to complete all of the requirements captured in your user stories, you need to use a two-step process.

You need to:

If you can get this figured out...

☐ Add an estimate to each user story for how long you think it will take to develop (that is, design, code, test, and deliver) that functionality.

☐ Add up all the estimates to get a total estimate for how long your project will take to deliver the required software.

...then this will be a piece of cake.

Exercise

Welcome to the Orion's Orbits Development Diner. Below is the menu...your job is to choose your options for each dish, and come up with an estimate for that dish—ahem—user story. You'll also want to note down any assumptions you made in your calculations.

EnTRées

Pay Credit Card or Paypal

Visa ....**2 days**

Mastercard.............................**2 days**

PayPal ....**2 days**

American Express ....**5 days**

Discover ....**4 days**

Order Flight DVD

Stock titles with standard definition video ....**2 days**

Provide custom titles ....**5 days**

High Definition video...........**5 days**

Choose Seating

Choose aisle or window seat ....**2 days**

Choose actual seat on shuttle .... **10 days**

Order In-Flight Meals

Select from list of three meals & three drinks ....**5 days**

Allow special dietary needs (Vegetarian, Vegan)...............**2 days**

DesseRTs

Create Flight Review

Create a review online ....**3 days**

Submit a review by email .....**5 days**

**Estimate for each
user story in days**

Assumptions?

Title: Pay with Visa/MC/PayPal

Description: Users will be able to pay for their bookings by credit card or PayPal.

Write your estimate for the user story here.

Title: Order Flight DVD

Description: A user will be able to order a DVD of a flight they have been on.

Jot down any assumptions you think you're making in your estimate.

Title: Choose seating

Description: A user will be able to choose aisle or window seating.

Title: Order in-flight meals

Description: A user will be able to specify the meals and drinks they want during a flight.

Title: Review flight

Description: A user will be able to leave a review for a shuttle flight they have been on.

EXERCISE
SOLUTION

What did you come up with? Rewrite your estimates here. Bob and Laura also did estimates...how did yours compare to theirs?

	Your estimates	Bob's estimates	Laura's estimates

Put your estimates here.

Title: Pay with Visa/MC/PayPal	[ ]	15	10
Title:: Order Flight DVD	[ ]	20	2
Title:: Choose seating	[ ]	12	2
Title:: Order in-flight meals	[ ]	2	7
Title:: Review flight	[ ]	3	3

Well, at least we seem to agree here...

BRAIN POWER

It looks like everyone has a different idea for how long each user story is going to take. Which estimates do you think are **RIGHT**?

Cubicle conversation

So Laura, we can't both be totally wrong. But how did we get such completely different estimates?

Laura: Well, let's start with the first user story. How did you come up with 10 days?

Bob: That's easy, I just picked the most popular credit cards I could think of, and added time to support PayPal...

Laura: But lots of high-end executives only use American Express, so my assumption was that we'd have to cope with that card, too, not just Visa and MasterCard.

Bob: Okay, but I'm still not feeling entirely happy with that. Just that one assumption is making a really big difference on how long it will take to develop that user story...

Laura: I know, but what can you do, we don't know what the customer expects...

Bob: But look at this...you came up with 20 days for "Ordering a Flight DVD," but even with all the options, that should be 14 days, max!

Laura: I was actually being on the conservative side. The problem is that creating a DVD is a completely new feature, something I haven't done before. I was factoring in overhead for researching how to create DVDs, installing software, and getting everything tested. Everything I thought I'd need to do to get that software written. So it came out a lot higher.

Bob: Wow, I hadn't even thought of those things. I just assumed that they'd been thought of and included. I wonder if the rest of the estimates included tasks like research and software installation?

Laura: In my experience, probably not. That's why I cover my back.

Bob: But then ***all*** of our estimates could be off...

Laura: Well, at least we agree on the "Create a Flight Review" story. That's something.

Bob: Yeah, but I even had assumptions I made there, and that still doesn't take into account some of that overhead you were talking about.

Laura: So all we have are a bunch of estimates we don't feel that confident about. How are we going to come up with a number for the project that we believe when we don't even know what everyone's assumptions are?

Getting rid of assumptions is the most important activity for coming up with estimates you believe in.

Playing planning poker

To come up with accurate estimates, you need to get rid of all those assumptions that put your estimates at risk of being wrong. You want a set of estimates that **everyone believes in** and are confident that they can deliver, or at the very least you want a set of estimates that let you know what assumptions everyone is making before you sign on the dotted line. It's time to grab everyone that's going to be involved in estimating your user stories, sit them around a table, and get ready to play "planning poker."

1 **Place a user story in the middle of the table**
This focuses everyone on a specific user story so they can get their heads around what their estimates and assumptions might be.

> **Title:** Pay with Visa/MC/PayPal
> **Description:** Users will be able to pay for their bookings by credit card or PayPal.

We want a solid estimate for how long it will take to develop this story. Don't forget that development should include designing, coding, testing, and delivering the user story.

2 **Everyone is given a deck of 13 cards. Each card has an estimate written on one side.**
You only need a small deck, just enough to give people several options:

All of these estimates are developer-days (for instance, two man-days split between two workers is still two days).

This card means "It's already done." →

Ø days — 1/2 day — 1 day — 2 days — 3 days — 5 days

8 days — 13 days — 20 days — 40 days — 100 days — ? —

Everyone has each of these cards.

Hmmm...any thoughts on what it means if someone plays one of these cards for their estimate?

Don't have enough info to estimate? You might consider using this card.

If any player uses this card, you need to take a break from estimating for a bit.

3 **Everyone picks an estimate for the user story and places the corresponding card face down on the table.**

You pick the card that you think is a reasonable estimate for the user story. Don't discuss that estimate with anyone else, though.

Make sure your estimate is for the whole user story, not just a part of it.

Place your choice face-down so you keep your estimate from everyone else

The user story is still in the middle... still the focus.

4 **Everyone then turns over their cards at exactly the same time.**

Each player at the table shows their hand, which gives their honest estimate for the user story.

These almost never all match up... that's okay.

5 **The dealer marks down the spread across each of the estimates.**

Whoever is running the game notes the spread across each of the estimates that are on the cards. Then you do a little analysis:

Ask the developer who played this card what they were thinking about; don't ignore them, try to pull out the assumptions they made.

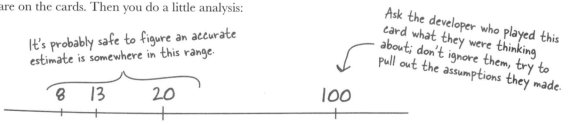

It's probably safe to figure an accurate estimate is somewhere in this range.

8   13   20   100

The larger the <u>difference</u> between the estimates, the <u>less</u> <u>confident</u> you are in the estimate, and the more assumptions you need to root out.

How does this help with assumptions? And what about that guy who chose 100? We can't just ignore him, can we?

Large spreads can be a misunderstanding

When you see large gaps between the estimates on a particular user story's spread, something is probably missing. It could be that some of your team misunderstood the user story, in which case it's time to revisit that story. Or it could be that some members of your team are just unsure of something that another part of your team is completely happy with.

In either case, it's time to look at the assumptions that your team is making and decide if you need to go back and speak to the customer to get some more feedback and clarification on your user stories—and the assumptions you're making about them.

In fact, even if everyone's estimate is within the same narrow range, it's worth asking for everyone's assumptions to make sure that EVERYONE is not making the same wrong assumption. It's unlikely that they are, but just in case, always discuss and document your assumptions after every round of planning poker.

Try writing your assumptions on the back of your user story cards.

Put assumptions on trial for their lives

When it comes to requirements, ***no assumption is a good assumption***. So whenever planing poker turns up your team's assumptions, don't let that assumption into your project without first doing everything you can to ***beat it out*** of your project...

> **Put every assumption on trial**
> You're aiming for as few assumptions as possible when making your estimates. When an assumption rears its head in planning poker, even if your entire team shares the assumption, expect that assumption to be wrong **until it is clarified by the customer**.

As opposed to not knowing what you don't know...

At least you know what you don't know

No matter how hard you try, some assumptions really will survive clarification with the customer. That's OK. Sometimes the customer doesn't have a great answer to a particular assumption at the beginning of a project, and in those cases you need to live with the assumption. The important thing is that you know that there is an assumption being made, and you can write it down as a risk for that user story (like on the back of your user story card). This helps you keep an eye on and track your risks, knocking them out at a later stage in your project.

Depending on customer priority, you might even decide to delay the development of a user story that has a number of surviving assumptions until they can be clarified.

While you can't always get rid of all assumptions, the goal during estimation is to <u>eliminate</u> as many assumptions as possible by <u>clarifying</u> those assumptions with the customer. Any surviving assumptions then become <u>risks.</u>

> With all this talk of customer clarification, it seems to me that you could be bothering the customer too much. You might want to think about how you use the customer's time effectively...

Value your customer's time.

Putting all your asssumptions on trial for their life and seeking clarification from the customer can become a lot of work. You can easily spend a lot, if not all, of your time with your customer. That might be OK with some customers, but what about the ones that are too busy to talk with you every 15 minutes?

In those cases you need to use your customer's time carefully. Even though you're trying to make sure you've gotten things right on their project, you don't want to come across as being not up to the job. So when you do spend time with your customer, make sure that time is organized, efficient, and well-spent.

Try gathering a collection of assumptions together and then clarifying those all at once with the customer. Rather than bothering the customer at the end of every round of planing poker, schedule an **assumption-busting session** where you take in the collected assumptions and try to blast as many of them away as possible.

Once you have your answers, head back for a final round of planning poker.

Once you've gotten a significant number of your assumptions beaten out in your assumption-busting session with the customer, it's time to head back and play a final round of planning poker so that you and your team can come up with estimates that factor in the new clarifications.

there are no
Dumb Questions

Q: **Why is there a gap between 40 and 100 days on the planning poker cards?**

A: Well, the fact is that 40 is a pretty large estimate, so whether you feel that the estimate should be 41 or even 30 days is not really important at this point. 40 just says that you think there's a lot to do in this user story, and you're just on the boundary of not being able to estimate this user story at all...

Q: **100 days seems *really* long; that's around half a year in work time! Why have 100 days on the cards at all?**

A: Absolutely, 100 days is a **very** long time. If someone turns up a 100-days card then there's something seriously misunderstood or wrong with the user story. If you find that it's the user story that's simply too long, then it's time to break that user story up into smaller, more easily estimatable stories.

Q: **What about the question-mark card? What does that mean?**

A: That you simply don't feel that you have enough information to estimate this user story. Either you've misunderstood something, or your assumptions are so big that you don't have any confidence that *any* estimate you place down on the table could be right.

Q: **Some people are just bound to pick nutty numbers. What do I do about them?**

A: Good question. First, look at the trends in that individual's estimates to see if they really are being "nutty," or whether they in fact tend to be right! However, some people really are inclined to just pick extremely high or very low numbers most of the time and

get caught up in the game. However, every estimate, particularly ones that are out of whack with the rest of the player's estimates, should come under scrutiny after every round to highlight the assumptions that are driving those estimates.

After a few rounds where you start to realize that those wacky estimates are not really backed up by good assumptions, you can either think about removing those people from the table, or just having a quiet word with them about why they always insist on being off in left field.

Q: **Should we be thinking about who implements a user story when coming up with our estimates?**

A: No, every player estimates how long they think it will take for them to develop and deliver the software that implements the user story. At estimation time you can't be sure who is going to actually implement a particular user story, so you're trying to get a feel for the capability of anyone on your team to deliver that user story.

Of course, if one particular user story is perfect for one particular person's skills, then they are likely to estimate it quite low. But this low estimate is balanced by the rest of your team, who should each assume that they are individually going to implement that user story.

In the end, the goal is to come up with an estimate that states "We as a team are all confident that this is how long it will take any one of us to develop this user story."

Q: **Each estimate is considering more than just implementation time though, right?**

A: Yes. Each player should factor in how much time it will take them to develop and

deliver the software including any other deliverables that they think might be needed. This could include documentation, testing, packaging, deployment—basically everything that needs to be done to develop and deliver the software that meets the user story.

If you're not sure what other deliverables might be needed, then that's an assumption, and might be a question for the customer.

Q: **What if my team all agree on exactly the same estimate when the cards are turned over. Do I need to worry about assumptions?**

A: Yes, for sure. Even if everyone agrees, it's possible that everyone is making the same wrong assumptions. A large spread of different estimates indicates that there is more work to be done and that your team is making different and possibly large assumptions in their estimates. A tiny spread says that your team might be making the same assumptions in error, so examining assumptions is critical regardless of the output from planning poker.

It's important to get any and all assumptions out in the open *regardless* of what the spread says, so that you can clarify those assumptions right up front and keep your confidence in your estimates as high as possible.

Don't make assumptions about your assumptions... talk about EVERYTHING.

A <u>BIG</u> user story estimate is a <u>BAD</u> user story estimate

> We all agree, we don't need any more information. This user story will take 40 days to develop...

Your user story is too big.

Remember this from Chapter 1?

40 days is a long time, and lots can change. Remember, 40 days is *2 months* of work time.

An *entire iteration* should ideally be around **1 calendar month** in duration. Take out weekends and holidays, and that's about 20 working days. If your estimate is 40 days for just *one* user story, then it won't even fit in one iteration of development unless you have two people working on it!

If you have to have long estimates like this, then you need to be talking as a team as often as possible. We'll get to that in a few pages.

As a rule of thumb, estimates that are longer than 15 days are *much less likely* to be accurate than estimates below 15 days.

In fact, some people believe that estimates longer than seven days should be double-checked.

When a user story's estimate breaks the 15-day rule you can either:

1 **Break your stories into smaller, more easily estimated stories**
Apply the AND rule. Any user story that has an "and" in its title or description can probably be split into two or more smaller user stories.

2 **Talk to your customer...again.**
Starting to sense a pattern?
Maybe there are some assumptions that are pushing your estimate out. If the customer could clarify things, those assumptions might go away, and cut down your estimates significantly.

Estimates greater than 15 days per user story allow too much room for error.

When an estimate is too long, apply the AND rule to break the user story into smaller pieces.

Exercise

The two user stories below resulted in estimates that broke the 15-day rule. Take the two user stories and apply the AND rule to them to break them into smaller, more accurately estimatable stories.

Title: Choose seating

Description: A user will choose aisle or window seating, be able to select the seat they want, and change that seat up to 24 hours before the flight.

Title: Order in-flight meals

Description: A user will choose which meal option they want, from a choice of three, and be able to indicate if they are vegetarian or vegan.

Title:

Description:

Title:

Description:

Title:

Description:

Title:

Description:

Title:

Description:

Title:

Description:

Exercise Solution

Your job was to take the longer user stories at the top of each column and turn them into smaller, easily estimatable user stories.

Title: Choose seating

Description: A user will choose aisle or window seating, be able to select the seat they want, and change that seat up to 24 hours before the flight.

Title: Order in-flight meals

Description: A user will choose which meal option they want, from a choice of three, and be able to indicate if they are vegetarian or vegan.

Title: Choose aisle/window seat

Description: A user can choose either aisle or window seating.

Title: Select from meal options

Description: A user can choose the meal they want from a set of three meal options.

Title: Choose specific seat

Description: A user can choose the actual seat that they want for a shuttle flight.

Title: Specify vegetarian meal

Description: A user will be able to indicate that they are vegetarian when selecting their meal options.

Title: Change seating

Description: A user can change their seat up to 24 hours before launch, provided other seat options are available.

Title: Specify vegan meal

Description: A user will be able to indicate that they are vegan when selecting their meal options.

The goal is <u>convergence</u>

After a solid round of planning poker, you should not only have estimates for each user story but be *confident* in those estimates. The goal now is to get rid of as many assumptions as possible, and to **converge** all of the points on each user story's spread of estimates.

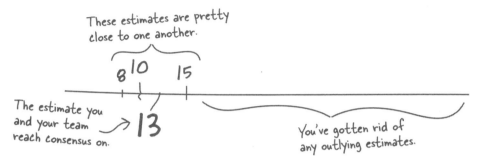

These estimates are pretty close to one another.

8 10   15

The estimate you and your team reach consensus on. → 13

You've gotten rid of any outlying estimates.

Run through this cycle of steps till you reach a consensus:

① Talk to the customer
First and foremost, get as much information and remove as many assumptions and misunderstandings as possible by talking to your customer.

② Play planning poker
Play planning poker with each of your user stories to uproot any hidden assumptions. You'll quickly learn how confident you are that you can estimate the work that needs to be done.

Head back to Step 1 if you find assumptions that only the customer can answer.

③ Clarify your assumptions
Using the results of planning poker, you'll be able to see where your team may have misunderstood the user stories, and where additional clarification is needed.

④ Come to a consensus
Once everyone's estimates are close, agree on a figure for the user story's estimate.

It can also be useful to note the low, converged, and high estimates to give you an idea of the best and worst case scenarios.

How close is "close enough"?

Deciding when your estimates are close enough for consensus is really up to you. When you feel **confident in an estimate**, and you're **comfortable with the assumptions** that have been made, then it's time to write that estimate down on your user story card and move on.

there are no
Dumb Questions

Q: How can I tell when my estimates are close enough, and have really converged?

A: Estimates are all about confidence. You have a good estimate if you and your team are truly confident that you can deliver the user story's functionality within the estimate.

Q: I have a number of assumptions, but I still feel confident in my estimate. Is that okay?

A: Really, you should have no assumptions in your user stories or in you and your team's understanding of the customer's requirements.

Every assumption is an opportunity to hit unexpected problems as you develop your software. Worse than that, every assumption increases the chances that your software development work will be delayed and might not even deliver what was required.

Even if you're feeling relatively confident, knock out as many of those assumptions as you possibly can by speaking to your team and, most importantly, speaking to your customer.

With a *zero-tolerance attitude to assumptions*, you'll be on a much more secure path to delivering your customer the software that's needed, on time and on budget. However, you will probably always have some assumptions that survive the estimation process. This is OK, as assumptions are then turned into risks that are noted and tracked, and at least you are aware of those risks.

Q: I'm finding it hard to come up with an estimate for my user story, is there a way I can better understand a user story to come up with better initial estimates?

A: First, if your user story is complicated, then it may be too big to estimate confidently. Break up complex stories into simpler ones using the AND rule or common sense.

Sometimes a user story is just a bit blurry and complicated. When that happens, try breaking the user story into tasks in your head—or even on a bit of paper—you've got next to you at your planning poker sessions.

Think about the jobs that will be needed to be done to build that piece of software. Imagine you are doing those jobs, figure out how long you would take to do each one, and then add them all up to give you an estimate for that user story.

Q: How much of this process should my customer actually see?

A: Your customer should only see and hear your questions, and then of course your user stories as they develop. In particular, your customer is *not* involved in the planning poker game. Customers will want lower-than-reasonable estimates, and can pressure you and your team to get overly aggressive.

When there is a question about what a piece of the software is supposed to do in a given situation, or when an assumption is found, then involving the customer is absolutely critical. When you find a technical assumption being made by your team that you can clarify without the customer, then you don't have to go back and bother them with details they probably won't understand anyway.

But when you're playing planning poker, you are coming up with estimates of how long *you* believe that *your team* will take to develop and deliver the software. So it's *your* neck on the line, and *your* promise. So the customer shouldn't be coming up with those for you.

Your estimates are your PROMISE to your customer about how long it will take you and your team to DELIVER.

A bunch of techniques for working with requirements, in full costume, are playing a party game, "Who am I?" They'll give you a clue and then you try to guess who they are based on what they say. Assume they always tell the truth about themselves. Fill in the blanks next to each statement with the name (or names) of each attendee that the statement is true for. Attendees may be used in more than one answer

Tonight's attendees:

Blueskying – Role playing – Observation
User story – Estimate – Planning poker

You can dress me up as a use case for a formal occasion.   *User Story*

The more of me there are, the clearer things become.   *Planning poker*

I help you capture EVERYTHING.   *Observation*

I help you get more from the customer.   *Role playing*

In court, I'd be admissible as firsthand evidence.   *User story* ✗

Some people say I'm arrogant, but really I'm just about confidence.   *estimates*

Everyone's involved when it comes to me.   *Bluesking*

⟶ Answers on page 62.

The requirement to estimate iteration cycle

We've now added some new steps in our iterative approach to requirements development. Let's look at how estimation fits into our process...

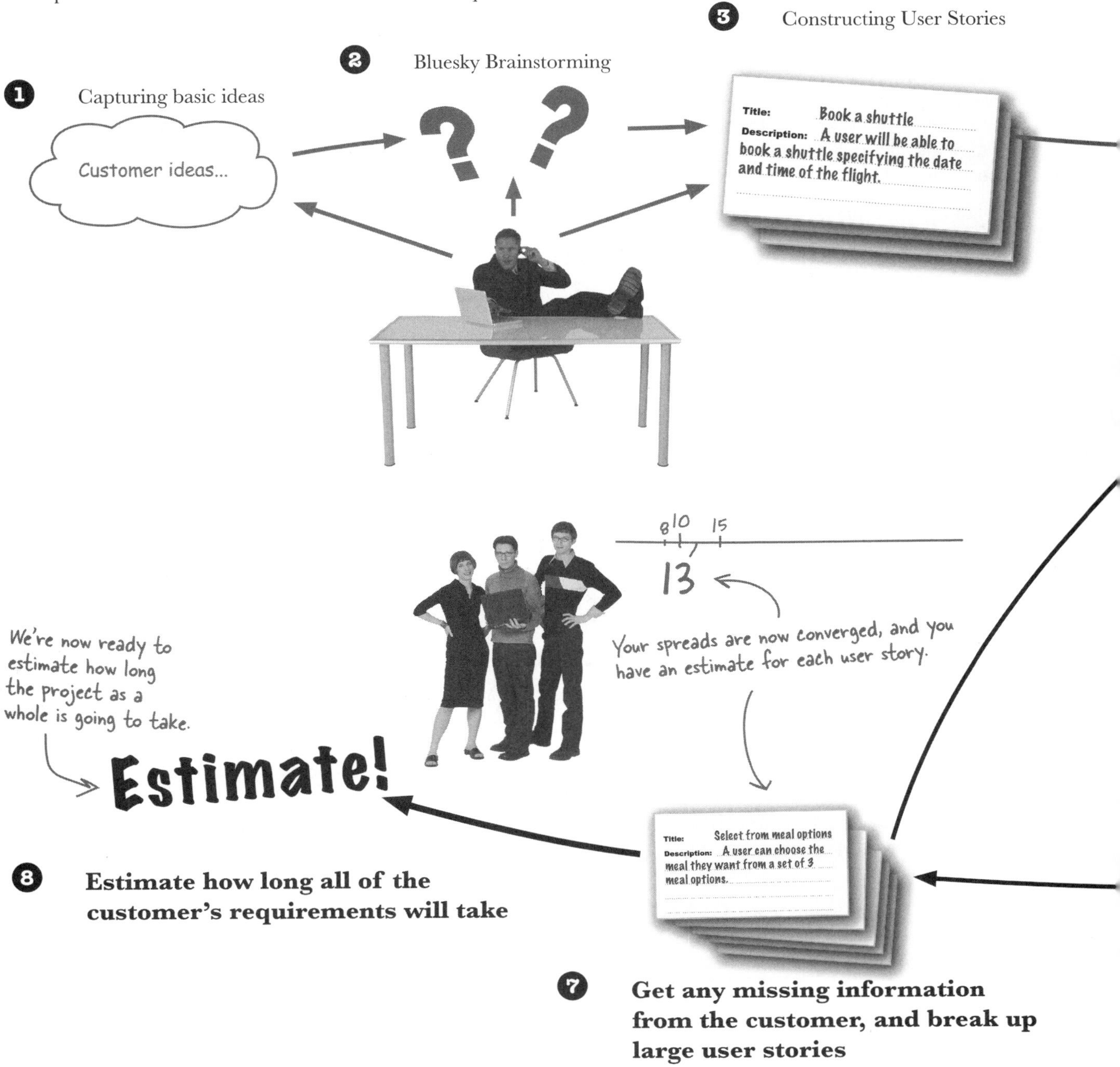

3 Constructing User Stories

1 Capturing basic ideas

Customer ideas...

2 Bluesky Brainstorming

? **?**

> **Title:** Book a shuttle
> **Description:** A user will be able to book a shuttle specifying the date and time of the flight.

8 ^{10} 15
13 ←

Your spreads are now converged, and you have an estimate for each user story.

We're now ready to estimate how long the project as a whole is going to take.

→ **Estimate!**

> **Title:** Select from meal options
> **Description:** A user can choose the meal they want from a set of 3 meal options.

8 **Estimate how long all of the customer's requirements will take**

7 **Get any missing information from the customer, and break up large user stories**

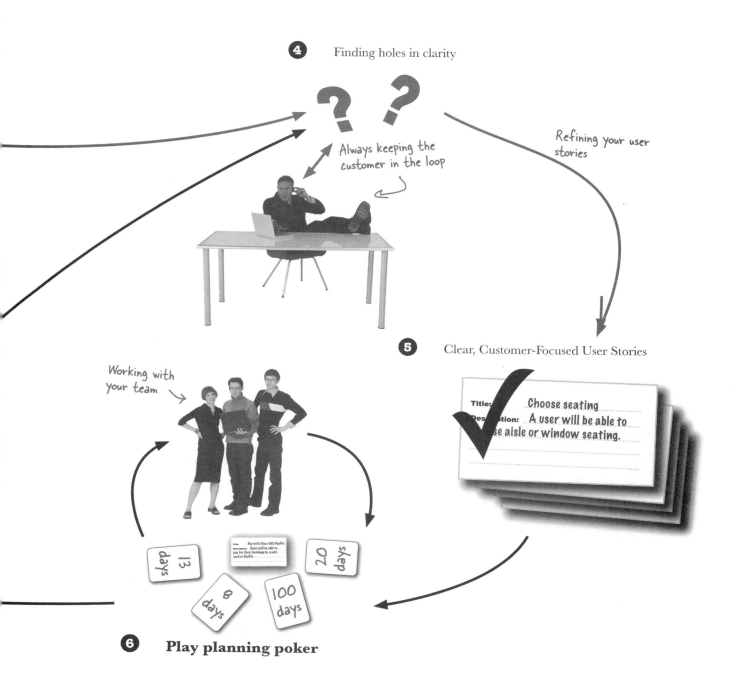

4 Finding holes in clarity

Refining your user stories

Always keeping the customer in the loop

5 Clear, Customer-Focused User Stories

Title: Choose seating
Description: A user will be able to ...se aisle or window seating.

Working with your team

13 days

Pay with Visa/MC/PayPal
Description: Users will be able to pay for their bookings by credit card or PayPal.

20 days

8 days

100 days

6 **Play planning poker**

A bunch of techniques for working with requirements, in full costume, are playing a party game, "Who am I?" They'll give you a clue and then you try to guess who they are based on what they say. Assume they always tell the truth about themselves. Fill in the blanks next to each statement with the name (or names) of each attendee that the statement is true for. Attendees may be used in more than one answer

Who am I? Solutions

Tonight's attendees:

**Blueskying – Role playing – Observation
User story – Estimate – Planning poker**

You can dress me up as a use case for a formal occasion.	*User Story*
The more of me there are, the clearer things become.	*User Story*
I help you capture EVERYTHING.	*Blueskying, Observation*
I help you get more from the customer.	*Role playing, Observation*
In court, I'd be admissible as firsthand evidence.	*Observation*
Some people say I'm arrogant, but really I'm just about confidence.	*Estimate*
Everyone's involved when it comes to me.	*Blueskying*

Did you say planning poker? Customers aren't involved in that activity.

Finally, you're ready to estimate the whole project...

You've got short, focused user stories, and you've played planning poker on each story. You've dealt with all the assumptions that you and your team were making in your estimates, and now you have a set of estimates that you all believe in. It's time to get back to the customer with your total project estimate...

You've got an estimate for each story now.

☒ Add an estimate to each user story for how long you think it will take to develop that functionality.

☐ Add up all the estimates to get a **total estimate** for how long your project will take to deliver the required software.

Now you can get a total estimate.

And the total project estimate is...

Add up the each of the converged estimates for your user stories, and you will find the total duration for your project, if you were to develop everything the customer wants.

15	16
20	19
12	15

Sum of user story estimates

= 489 days!

**489 days for the project?
That's almost two years!!!**

No kidding! That's way too long,
By the time you've developed the
software, my competition will
have beaten us into the ground!

What do you do when your estimates are <u>WAY</u> too long?

You've finally got an estimate you believe in, and that takes into account all the requirements that the customer wants. But you've ended up with a monster project that is just going to take too long.

Is it time to go back to the drawing board? Do you admit defeat and hand the work over to someone else? Or do you just ask the customer how long he thinks would work, forgetting about all your hard work to come up with you estimates in the first place?

You'll have to solve a crossword puzzle and work your way to Chapter 3 to find out how to get Orion's Orbits back on track.

Requirements and Estimation Cross

Let's put what you've learned to use and stretch out your left brain a bit.
All of the words below are somewhere in this chapter: Good luck!

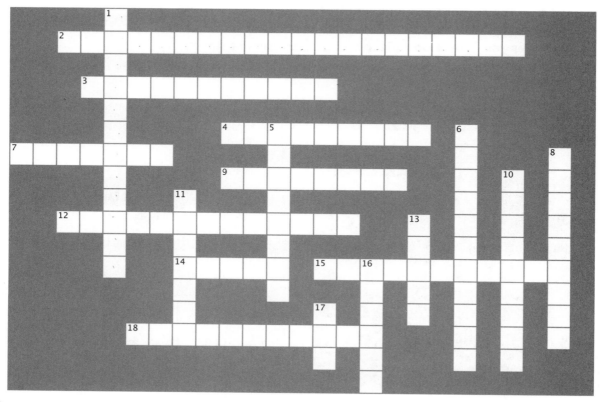

Across

2. When you and the customer are really letting your ideas run wild you are ....
3. When coming up with estimates, you are trying to get rid of as many .... as possible.
4. None of this language is allowed in a user story.
7. If a requirement is the what, an estimate is the ....
9. Requirements are oriented towards the ....
12. The best way to get honest estimates and highlight assumptions.
14. A User Story is made up of a .... and a description.
15. .... is a great way of getting first hand evidence of exactly how your customer works at the moment.
18. The goal of estimation is ....

Down

1. When you just have no idea how to estimate a user story, use a card with this on it.
5. User stories are written from the perspective of the ....
6. When you and the customer act out a particular user story, you are ....
8. When everyone agrees on an estimate, it is called a ....
10. An estimate is good when eveyone on your team is feeling ....
11. The maximum number of days that a good estimate should be for one user story.
13. A great user story is about .... lines long.
16. After a round of planning poker, you plot all of the estimates on a ....
17. You can use the .... rule for breaking up large user stories.

CHAPTER 2

Tools for your Software Development Toolbox

Software Development is all about developing and delivering the software that the customer actually wants. In this chapter, you learned about several techniques to help you get inside the customer's head and capture the requirements that represent what they really want... For a complete list of tools in the book, see Appendix ii.

Development Techniques

Bluesky, Observation and Roleplay

User Stories

Planning poker for estimation

Development Principles

The customer knows what they want, but sometimes you need to help them nail it down

Keep requirements customer-oriented

Develop and refine your requirements iteratively with the customer

BULLET POINTS

- **Blueskying** gets your customer to **think big** when coming up with their requirements.

- A **user story** captures one interaction with the software from the customer's perspective.

- User stories should be **short**, around three sentences in length.

- A short user story is an **estimatable user story**.

- A user story should not take one developer more than 15 days to deliver.

- **Iteratively develop** your requirements with your customer to keep them in the loop at every step of the process.

Requirements and Estimation Cross Solution

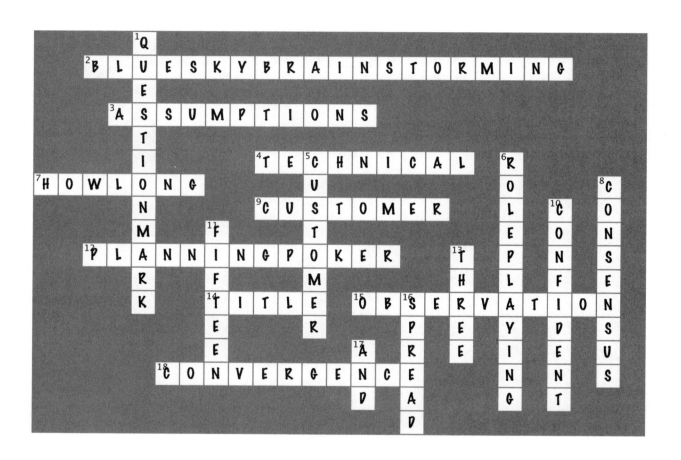

3 project planning

Planning for success

Really darling, my software development is so well planned I'll be home on time every day for us to watch NASCAR together!

Every great piece of software starts with a great plan.

In this chapter you're going to learn how to create that plan. You're going to learn how to work with the customer to **prioritize their requirements**. You'll **define iterations** that you and your team can then work toward. Finally you'll create an achievable **development plan** that you and your team can confidently **execute** and **monitor.** By the time you're done, you'll know exactly how to get from requirements to your first deliverable.

Customers want their software <u>NOW!</u>

Customers want their software **when they need it**, and not a moment later. You've come to grips with the customer's ideas using brainstorming, you've got a set of user stories that describe everything the customer might need the software to do, and you've even added an estimate to each user story that helped you figure out how long it will take to deliver everything the customer wants. The problem is, developing **everything** the customer said they needed will take **too long**...

Our Estimate

489 days

The total after summing up all the estimates for your user stories

What the customer wants

90 days!

> Well you obviously can't do everything that the customer wants in 90 days. Why not just cut back and prioritize?

Exercise

Orion's Orbits still wants to modernize their booking system; they just can't wait almost two years for the software to get finished. Take the following snippets from the Orion's Orbits user stories, along with their estimates, and circle the ones you think you should develop to come up with a chunk of work that will take **no longer than 90 days**.

Title: Book a shuttle	**Title:** Pay with Visa/MC/PayPal
Estimate: 15 days	**Estimate:** 15 days

Title: Review flight
Estimate: 13 days

Title: Order in-flight meals
Estimate: 13 days

Title: Order Flight DVD
Estimate: 12 days

Title: Book Segway in spaceport transport
Estimate: 15 days

Title: View Space Miles Account
Estimate: 14 days

Title: Choose seating
Estimate: 12 days

Title: Apply for "frequent astronaut" card
Estimate: 14 days

Title: Take pet reservation
Estimate: 12 days

Title: Manage special offers
Estimate: 13 days

Total Estimate: ⌐ ¬
                    ⌊ ⌋

← Total estimate for all of the user stories you've circled

Problems? ....

....

....

....

See any problems with this approach? Write them down here. ↙

Assumptions? ....

....

....

....

Note down any assumptions you think you are making here.

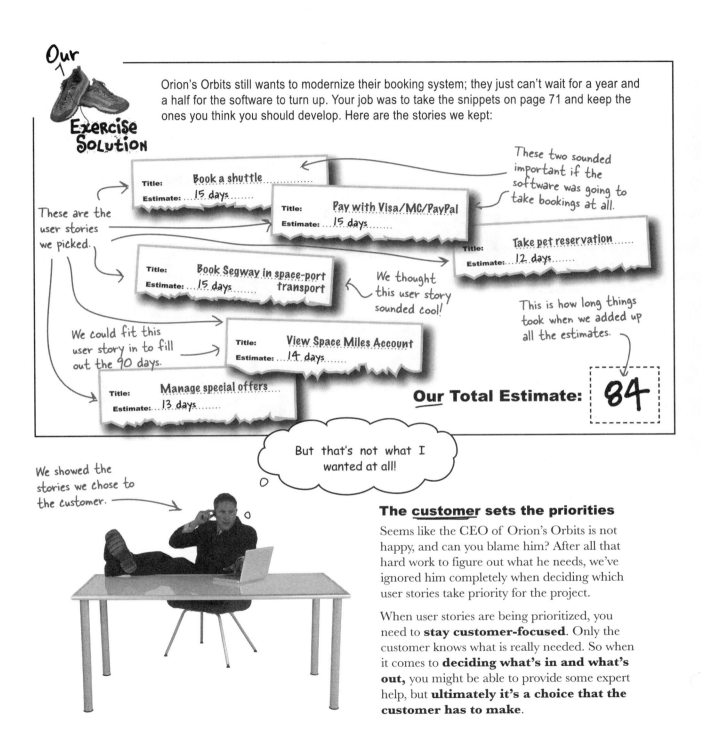

Our

Exercise Solution

Orion's Orbits still wants to modernize their booking system; they just can't wait for a year and a half for the software to turn up. Your job was to take the snippets on page 71 and keep the ones you think you should develop. Here are the stories we kept:

These two sounded important if the software was going to take bookings at all.

These are the user stories we picked.

Title: Book a shuttle
Estimate: 15 days

Title: Pay with Visa/MC/PayPal
Estimate: 15 days

Title: Take pet reservation
Estimate: 12 days

Title: Book Segway in space-port transport
Estimate: 15 days

We thought this user story sounded cool!

This is how long things took when we added up all the estimates.

We could fit this user story in to fill out the 90 days.

Title: View Space Miles Account
Estimate: 14 days

Title: Manage special offers
Estimate: 13 days

Our Total Estimate: 84

But that's not what I wanted at all!

We showed the stories we chose to the customer.

The customer sets the priorities

Seems like the CEO of Orion's Orbits is not happy, and can you blame him? After all that hard work to figure out what he needs, we've ignored him completely when deciding which user stories take priority for the project.

When user stories are being prioritized, you need to **stay customer-focused**. Only the customer knows what is really needed. So when it comes to **deciding what's in and what's out,** you might be able to provide some expert help, but **ultimately it's a choice that the customer has to make**.

Prioritize <u>with</u> the customer

It's your **customer's call** as to what user stories take priority. To help the
customer make that decision, shuffle and lay out all your user story cards on
the table. Ask your customer to order the user stories by priority (the story
most important to them first) and then to select the set of features that need
to be delivered in Milestone 1.0 of their software.

Order Flight DVD
ion: A user will be able to
DVD of a flight they have
n.
12 days

Title: Review Flight
Description: A user will be able to
leave a review for a shuttle flight
they have been on.
Est: 13 days

Title: Choose seating
Description: A user will be
choose aisle or window seat
Est: 12 days

Pay with Visa/MC/PayPal
ion: Users will be able to
their bookings by credit
PayPal.
days

Title: Order in-flight meals
Description: A user will be able to
specify the meals and drinks they
want during a flight.
Est: 13 days

Title: Book a shuttle
Description: A user will be
to book a shuttle specifying
data and time of the flight
Est: 15 days

*Lay out all your user stories
and ask the customer to
order them by priority.*

What is "Milestone 1.0"?

Milestone 1.0 is your **first major release** of the software to the customer. Unlike
smaller iterations where you'll show the customer your software for feedback, this
will be the first time you actually **deliver your software** (and expect to get paid for
the delivery). Some Do's and Don'ts when planning Milestone 1.0:

Do... balance functionality with customer impatience

Help the customer to understand **what can be done in the time
available**. Any user stories that don't make it into Milestone 1.0 are not
ignored, just postponed until Milestone 2, or 3...

Don't... get caught planning nice-to-haves

Milestone 1.0 is about **delivering what's needed**, and that means a set
of functionality that meets the most important needs of the customer.

Don't... worry about length (yet)

At this point you're just asking your customer which are the most important
user stories. **Don't get caught up on how long** those user stories will
take to develop. You're just trying to understand the customer's priorities.

*Don't worry,
we're not
ignoring
estimation.
We'll come
right back
to this.*

We know what's in Milestone 1.0 (well, maybe)

From all of the user stories developed from the customer's ideas, organized into prority order, the customer then selects the user stories that they would like to be a part of Milestone 1.0 of the software...

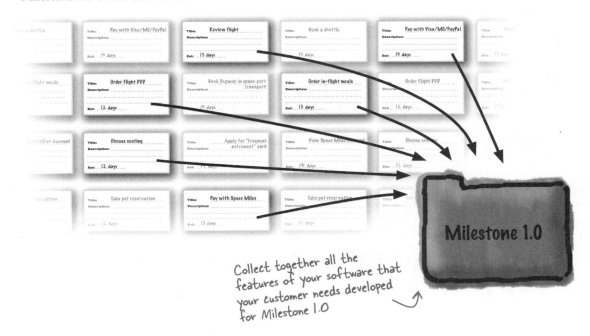

Collect together all the features of your software that your customer needs developed for Milestone 1.0

Sanity-check your Milestone 1.0 estimate

Now that you know what features the customer wants in Milestone 1.0, it's time to find out if you now have a reasonable length of project if you develop and deliver all of those most important features...

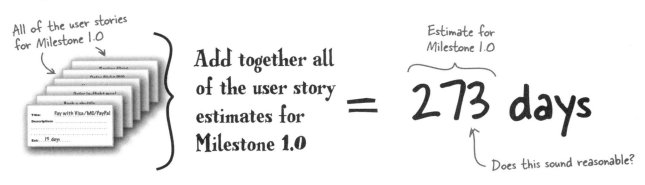

All of the user stories for Milestone 1.0

Add together all of the user story estimates for Milestone 1.0

Estimate for Milestone 1.0

= **273 days**

Does this sound reasonable?

If the features don't fit, <u>reprioritize</u>

You've got 273 days of work for Milestone 1.0, and Orion's Orbits want delivery in **90 days**. Don't worry, this is pretty common. Customers usually want more than you can deliver, and it's your job to go back to them and reprioritize until you come up with a workable feature set.

To reprioritize your user stories for Milestone 1.0 with the customer...

❶ **Cut out more FUNCTIONALITY**

The very first thing you can look at doing to shorten the time to delivering Milestone 1.0 is to cut out some functionality by removing user stories that are not ***absolutely*** ***crucial*** to the software working.

⤺ Once you explain the schedule, most customers will admit they don't really need everything they originally said they did.

❷ **Ship a milestone build as early as possible**

Aim to deliver a significant milestone build of your software as early as possible. This keeps your development momentum up by allowing you and your team to focus on a deadline that's <u>not</u> <u>too</u> <u>far</u> off.

⤺ Don't let customers talk you into longer development cycles than you're comfortable with. The sooner your deadline, the more focused you and your team can be on it.

❸ **Focus on the BASELINE functionality**

Milestone 1.0 is all about delivering ***just*** the functionality that is needed for a working version of the software. Any features beyond that can be scheduled for later milestones.

there are no Dumb Questions

Q: **What's the difference between a milestone and a version?**

A: Not much. In fact you could call your first milestone "Version 1" if you like. The big difference between a milestone and a version is that a milestone marks a point at which you deliver signficant software and get paid by your customer, whereas a version is more of a simple descriptive term that is used to identify a particular release of your software.

The difference is really quite subtle, but the simple way to understand it is that "Version" is a label and doesn't mean anything more, whereas "Milestone" means you deliver signficant functionality and you get paid. It could be that Version 1.0 coincides with Milestone 1.0, but equally Milestone 1.0 could be Version 0.1, 0.2 or any other label you pick.

Q: **So what exactly is my software's baseline functionality?**

A: The **baseline functionality** of your software is the smallest set of features that it needs to have in order for it to be at all useful to your customer and their users.

Think about a word processing application. Its core functionality is to let you load, edit, and save text to a file. Anything else is beyond core functionality, no matter how useful those features are. Without the ability to load, edit, and save a document with text in it, a word processor simply *is not useful*.

That's the rule of thumb: If you can get by without a feature, then it isn't really baseline functionality, and it's probably a good candidate for pushing out to a later milestone than Milestone 1.0 if you don't have time to get everything done.

Q: **I've done the math and no matter how I cut the user stories up, I just can't deliver what my customer wants when they want me to. What can I do?**

A: It's time to confess, unfortunately. If you really can't build the software that is required in the time that it's needed by, and your customer simply won't budge when it comes to removing some user stories from the mix, then you might need to walk away from the project and know that at least you were honest with the customer.

Another option is to try to beef up your team with new people to try and get more work done quicker. However, adding new people to the team will up the costs considerably, and won't necessarily get you all the advantages that you'd think it might.

Hello?! Can't we just add some more people to cut down our estimates? Add two developers, and we'll get done in 1/3 the time, right?

If it takes you 273 days, with 2 more people like you, that would reduce the overall development time by a factor of 3, right?

It's about more than just development time

While adding more people can look really attractive at first, it's really not as simple as "double the people, halve the estimate."

Every new team member needs to **get up to speed on the project**; they need to **understand the software**, the **technical decisions**, and **how everything fits together**, and while they're doing that *they can't be 100% productive*.

Then you need to get that new person set up with the right tools and equipment to work with the team. This could mean buying new licenses and purchasing new equipment, but even if it just means downloading some free or open source software, *it all takes time* and that time needs to be factored in as you reassess your estimates.

Finally, every person you add to your team makes the job of keeping everyone focused and knowing what they are doing harder. Keeping everyone moving in the same direction and on the same page can become a full-time job, and as your team gets larger you will find that this complex communication can start to hit your team's overall ability to be productive and develop great software.

In fact, there is a maximum number of people that your team can contain and still be productive, but it will depend very much on your project, your team, and who you're adding. The best approach is to monitor your team, and if you start to see your team actually get *less productive*, even though you have *more people*, then it's time to re-evaluate the amount of work you have to do or the amount of time in which you have to do it.

Later on in this chapter you'll be introduced to the burn-down rate graph. This is a great tool for monitoring the performance of your team.

More people sometimes means diminishing returns

Adding more people to your team doesn't always work as you'd expect. If 1 person takes 273 days to complete Milestone 1.0, then 3 people **won't** necessarily take 91. In fact they could actually take much longer! Take a look...performance doesn't always increase with the size of your team:

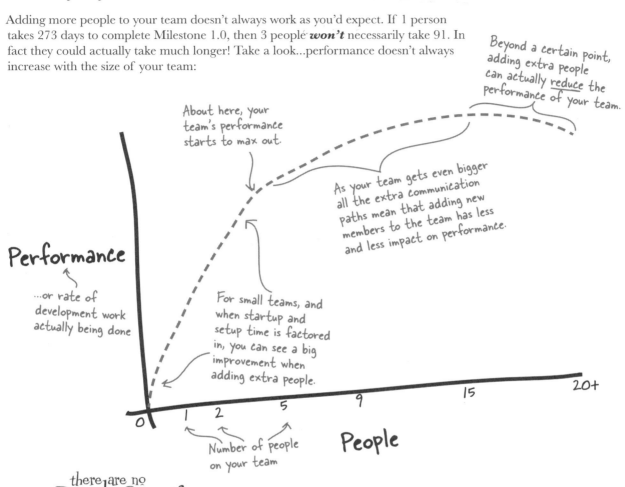

Beyond a certain point, adding extra people can actually <u>reduce</u> the performance of your team.

About here, your team's performance starts to max out.

As your team gets even bigger all the extra communication paths mean that adding new members to the team has less and less impact on performance.

Performance

...or rate of development work actually being done

For small teams, and when startup and setup time is factored in, you can see a big improvement when adding extra people.

0   1   2   5   9   15   20+

People

Number of people on your team

there are no Dumb Questions

Q: Is there a maximum team size that I should never go over?

A: Not really. Depending on your experience you may find that you can happily handle a 20-person team, but that things become impossible when you hit 21. Alternatively you might find that any more than three developers, and you start to see a dip in productivity. The best approach is to monitor performance closely and make amendments based on your observations.

BRAIN POWER

Do you think the size of your project affects this graph? What about if you broke your project up into smaller sub-projects?

Work your way to a <u>reasonable</u> Milestone 1.0

With Orion's Orbits, going from one person to three—by adding two more developers—can have a positive impact. So let's see how that works out:

First you add two new people to your team...

Adding two developers to your team (that's three including you) helps, but it's not a magical solution. Two developers can add a lot of work time to your project, but there's still work left:

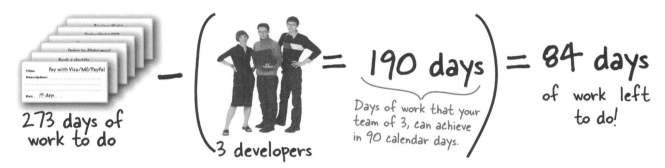

273 days of work to do

− (3 developers = 190 days

Days of work that your team of 3, can achieve in 90 calendar days.

) = 84 days of work left to do!

...then you reprioritize with the customer

Now you've got a nice way to figure out what has to be removed. We've got 189 days of work time, and 273 days of work. So we need to talk to the customer and remove around 84 days of work by shifting out some user stories from Milestone 1.0.

273 days of work to do

− Customer removed features = 184 days

Looking better, with a few days left over to give you a bit of breathing space in your milestone.

there are no Dumb Questions

Q: But 190 days of work is less than the 190 days that our three-developer team can produce, shouldn't we add some more features with the customer?

A: The overall estimate doesn't actually have to be exactly 189 days. Given that we're dealing with estimates anyway, which are rarely 100% accurate, and that we tend to be slightly optimistic in our estimates then 165 days is close enough to the 189-day mark to be reasonably confident of delivering in that time.

Q: How did you come up with 190 days when you added two new developers?

A: At this point this number is a guesstimate. We've guessed that adding two people to build a team of three will mean we can do around 190 days of work in 90 calendar days. There are ways to back up this guess with some evidence using something called "team velocity," but we'll get back to that later on in this chapter.

BE the Customer

Think about baseline functionality. If a feature isn't essential, it's probably not a 10.

Now it's your chance to be the customer. You need to build a plan for when you are going to develop each of the user stories for Milestone 1.0, and to do that you need to ask the customer what features are most important so that you can develop those first. Your job is to play the customer by assigning a priority to the Milestone 1.0 user stories. For each user story, assign it a ranking in the square provided, depending on how important you think that feature is using the key at the bottom of the page.

Title: Login to "Frequent Astronaut" account
Est: 15 days
Priority: ☐

Title: Order In-flight meals
Est: 13 days
Priority: 10

Title: Pay using "Space Miles"
Est: 15 days
Priority: ☐

Title: Book a shuttle
Est: 15 days
Priority: 10

Title: Review flight
Est: 13 days
Priority: 10

Title: Manage special offers
Est: 13 days
Priority: 10

Title: Pay with Visa/MC/PayPal
Est: 15 days
Priority: 10

Title: View "Space Miles" account
Est: 14 days
Priority: ☐

Title: View flight reviews
Est: 12 days
Priority: ☐

Priorities Key

10	- Most Important
20	
30	↓
40	
50	- Least Important

Title: Choose seating
Est: 12 days
Priority: 10

Title: Apply for "frequent astronaut" card
Est: 14 days
Priority: ☐

For each user story, specify what priority it is in the box provided.

Title: View shuttle deals
Est: 12 days
Priority: 10

Our ᐱ BE the Customer Solution

Your job was to play the customer and prioritize the Milestone 1.0 user stories. Here are the priorities that we assigned to each of the user stories. We also laid out the user stories in order of

Order of priority, most to least important to the customer

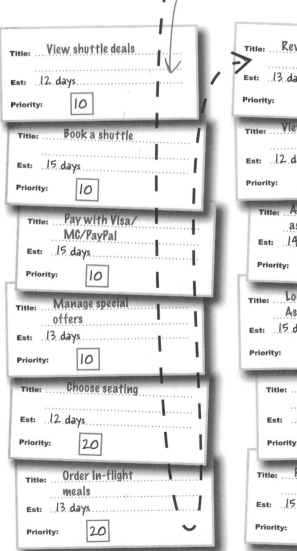

Title:	View shuttle deals
Est:	12 days
Priority:	10

Title:	Book a shuttle
Est:	15 days
Priority:	10

Title:	Pay with Visa/ MC/PayPal
Est:	15 days
Priority:	10

Title:	Manage special offers
Est:	13 days
Priority:	10

Title:	Choose seating
Est:	12 days
Priority:	20

Title:	Order In-flight meals
Est:	13 days
Priority:	20

Title:	Review flight
Est:	13 days
Priority:	30

Title:	View flight reviews
Est:	12 days
Priority:	30

Title:	Apply for "frequent astronaut" card
Est:	14 days
Priority:	40

Title:	Login to "Frequent Astronaut" account
Est:	15 days
Priority:	50

Title:	View "Space Miles" account
Est:	14 days
Priority:	50

Title:	Pay using "Space Miles"
Est:	15 days
Priority:	50

there are no Dumb Questions

Q: Why are the priorities 10, 20, 30, 40, and 50?

A: Powers of ten get the brain thinking about groupings of features, instead of ordering each and every feature separately with numbers like 8 or 26 or 42. You're trying to get the customer to decide what is most important, but not get too hung up on the exact numbers themselves. Also, powers of ten allow you to occasionally specify, say, a 25 for a particular feature when you add something in later, and need to squeeze it between existing features.

Q: If it's a 50, then maybe we can leave it out, right?

A: No, 50 doesn't mean that a user story is a candidate for leaving out. At this point, we're working on the user stories for Milestone 1.0, and so these user stories have *already* been filtered down to the customer's most important features. The goal here is to prioritize, not figure out if any of these features aren't important. So a 50 just says it can come later, not that it's not important to the customer

Q: What if I have some non–Milestone 1.0 user story cards?

A: Assign a priority of 60 to those cards for now, so they don't get mixed in with your Milestone 1.0 features.

Q: And the customer does all this work?

A: You can help out and advise, maybe mentioning dependencies between some of the user stories. But the final decision on priorities is *always* the customer's to make.

Now that you have your user stories for Milestone 1.0 in priority order, it's time to build some iterations. Lay out the user stories so they make iterations that make sense to you. Be sure and write down the total days of work, and how long that will take for your team of three developers.

Exercise

First one added for you

Iteration 1

Title: **View shuttle deals**

Est: 12 days

Priority: 10

Book → shuttle.   Pay with Any/Visa

15 days.   15 days.

Total Days: 42   Divide by 3 developers: 14

Iteration 2

13 + 12 + 12 + 13

Total Days: 51   Divide by 3 developers: 17

Iteration 3

12 + 14 + 15 + 14

Total Days: [ ]   Divide by 3 developers: [ ]

Bonus question

What do you think you should do at the end of an iteration?

Take feedback from client

Answers on page 84.

Fireside Chats

Tonight's talk: **A sit-down discussion between an iteration and a milestone.**

Milestone:

Hello there, iteration, seems like it's only been a month since I saw you last.

So how are things going on the project? It seems like you're always showing up, and I just arrive for the big finish. Actually, what's your purpose?

Naive? Look, just because I've had a few customer run-ins before doesn't mean I'm not important. I mean, without me, you wouldn't have software at all ,let alone get paid! Besides, just because I've shown up and surprised the occasional customer from time to time...

I used to try that, too. I'd try and soften the blow by explaining to the customer that all of their problems would be fixed in the next version of the software, but that wasn't what they wanted to hear. Lots of yelling, and I'd slink off, ready to go back to work for a year or so, and see if the customer liked me better next time.

Iteration:

Almost exactly a month. And you'll see me again next month, I can guarantee it. About three times, and we're ready for you, Milestone 1.0.

To make sure things go great, of course. That's my job really, to make sure that every step of the way from day 1 to day 90, the project stays on track. What, you thought you could just show up three months into the project and everything would be just like the customer wants it? A bit naive, aren't you?

Oh, I really sympathize with you there. I hate it when the customer isn't happy with me. But then again, there's a lot more time to fix things. I mean, we get together, you know, me and the customer, at least once a month. And, if things are bad, I just let the customer know it'll be better next time.

But you're shorter than a year now, right?

Milestone:

Well, I try to be, but sometimes that's just how long it takes, although I just love seeing the customer more often. At least once a quarter seems to line up with their billing cycles. And not so long that I get forgotten about; there's nothing worse than that.

Are you kidding? You're not even an alpha or a beta....just some code glued together, probably an excuse for everyone to wear jeans to work and drink beer on Friday afternoon.

Ha! Where would I be? Same place I am right now, getting ready to show the customer some real...

...software. Hey, wait. Hopefully? I've got a few hopes for you, you little...

Ungrateful little punk...release this!

Iteration:

Yeah, nobody forgets about me. Around every month, there I am, showing up, putting on a song and dance, pleasing the customer. Really, I can't imagine how you ever got by without me.

Oh, it's a little more than that, don't you think? Where would you be without me paving the way, making sure we're on track, handling changes and new features, and even removing existing features that aren't needed any more.

...*hopefully* working?

Well, you got the little part right. Why don't you just shuffle off for another 30 days or so, we'll call you when all the work's done. Then we'll see who Friday beers are on, OK?

Sure thing, and since I do my job, I'm sure you'll work just fine. I'm outta here, plenty of work left to be done...

EXERCiSE SOLUTION

Your job was to lay out the user stories so they make iterations that make sense. Here's what we came up with... note that all our iterations are within one calendar month, about 20 working days (or less).

Your answers could be different, but make sure you went in order of priority...

Title: Manage special offers
Est: 13 days
Priority: 10

Title: Book a shuttle
Est: 15 days
Priority: 10

Title: Pay with Visa/ MC/PayPal
Est: 15 days
Priority: 10

Title: View Shuttle deals
Est: 12 days
Priority: 10

Iteration 1

...and make sure you kept your iterations short.

Total Days: 57 Divide by 3 developers: 19

Title: Choose seating
Est: 12 days
Priority: 20

Title: Order In-flight meals
Est: 13 days
Priority: 20

Title: Review flight
Est: 13 days
Priority: 30

Title: View flight reviews
Est: 12 days
Priority: 30

Iteration 2

Total Days: 50 Divide by 3 developers: 17

Title: Apply for "frequent astronaut" card
Est: 14 days
Priority: 40

Title: Login to "Frequent Astronaut" account
Est: 15 days
Priority: 50

Title: View "Space Miles" account
Est: 14 days
Priority: 50

Title: Pay using "Space Miles"
Est: 15 days
Priority: 50

Iteration 3

Total Days: 58 Divide by 3 developers: 20

What do you think you should do at the end of an iteration? Show the customer and get their feedback

there are no Dumb Questions

Q: What if I get to the end of an iteration, and I don't have anything to show my customer?

A: The only way you should end up at the end of an iteration and not have something to show the customer is if no user stories were completed during the iteration. If you've managed to do this, then your project is out of control and you need to get things back on track as quickly as possible.

Keep your software **continuously building** and your software **always runnable** so you can always get feedback from the customer at the end of an iteration.

Iterations should be short and sweet

So far Orion's Orbits has focussed on ***30-day iterations***, with 3
iterations in a 90-day project. You can use different size iterations,
but make sure you keep these basic principles in mind:

 ## Keep iterations short

The shorter your iterations are, the more chances you get to
find and deal with change and unexpected details ***as they
arise***. A short iteration will get you feedback earlier and bring
changes and extra details to the surface sooner, so you can
adjust your plans, and even change what you're doing in the
next iteration, before you release a faulty Milestone 1.0.

 ## Keep iterations balanced

Each iteration should be a balance between dealing with change,
adding new features, beating out bugs, and accounting for real
people working. If you have iterations every month, that's not
really 30 days of work time. People take weekends off (at least
once in a while), and you have to account for vacation, bugs,
and things that come up along the way. A 20-work-day iteration
is a safe bet of work time you can handle in an actual 30-day,
calendar-month iteration.

*← 30-day iterations
are basically 30
CALENDAR days...*

*...which you can assume turn
into about 20 WORKING
days of productive
development.*

<u>SHORT</u> iterations help you deal with <u>ch</u>ange and keep you and your team motivated and focused.

WHO DOES WHAT?

Below is a particular aspect of a user story, iteration, milestone...or perhaps two, or even all three! Your job is to check off the boxes for the different things that each aspect applies to.

	User story	Iteration	Milestone
I result in a buildable and runnable bit of software.	☐	☑	☐
I'm the smallest buildable piece of software.	☑	☑	☐
In a full year, you should deliver me a maximum of four times.	☐	☐	☑
I contain an estimate set by your team.	☑	☐	☐
I contain a priority set by the customer.	☑	☑	☐
When I'm done, you deliver software to the customer and get paid.	☐	☐	☑
I should be done and dusted in 30 days.	☐	☑	☐

Answers on page 88.

Comparing your plan to reality

It looks like we'll be doing fine on the plan as long as we can all fit in a full five-day week.

Bob: Oh, just so you know, Nick is coming in at 11 today, he's got a doctor's appointment...

Laura: What?

Bob: And while we're talking, the IT guys are installing Oracle 9 on my machine this afternoon, so you might want to keep that in mind, too.

Laura: Oh great, any other nasty surprises in there that I should be aware of?

Bob: Well, I have got a week of vacation this month, and then there's Labor Day to take into account...

Laura: Perfect, how can we come up with a plan that factors all these overheads in so that when we go get signoff from the CEO of Orion's Orbits we know we have a plan we can deliver?

Do you think our current 20-work-day iterations take these sorts of issues into account?

Sharpen your pencil

See if you can help Bob out. Check all the things that you need to account for when planning your iterations.

☑ Paperwork	☐ Equipment failure	☑ Holidays
☑ Sickness	☑ Software upgrades	☐ Frank winning the lottery

Exercise Solution

Below is a particular aspect of a user story, iteration, milestone...or perhaps two, or even all three! Your job is to check off the boxes for the different things that each aspect applies to.

	User Story	Iteration	Milestone
I result in a buildable and runnable bit of software.		☒	☒
I'm the smallest buildable piece of software.		☒	
In a full year, you should deliver me a maximum of four times.			☒
I contain an estimate set by your team.	☒	☒	☒
I contain a priority set by the customer.	☒		
When I'm done, you deliver software to the customer and get paid.			☒
I should be done and dusted in 30 days.		☒	

Sharpen your pencil

See if you can help Bob out. Check all the things that you need to account for when planning your iterations.

Things like this <u>always</u> occur... so we have to plan for them.

☒ Paperwork   ☐ Equipment failure   ☒ Holidays

☒ Sickness   ☒ Software upgrades   ☐ Frank winning the lottery

You really can't factor in complete surprises

Velocity accounts for overhead in your estimates

It's time to add a little reality to your plan. You need to factor in all those annoying bits of overhead by looking at how fast you and your team actually develop software. And that's where **velocity** comes in. Velocity is a percentage: given X number of days, how much of that time is productive work?

> But how can I know how fast my team performs? We've only just gotten started!

Start with a velocity of 0.7.

On the first iteration with a new team it's fair to assume that your team's working time will be about 70% of their available time. This means your team has a velocity value of 0.7. In other words, for every 10 days of work time, about 3 of those days will be taken up by holidays, software installation, paperwork, phone calls, and other nondevelopment tasks.

That's a conservative estimate, and you may find that over time, your team's actual velocity is higher. If that's the case, then, at the end of your current iteration, you'll adjust your velocity and use that new figure to determine how many days of work can go into the next iteration.

Yet another reason to have short iterations: you can adjust velocity frequently.

Best of all, though, you can apply velocity to your amount of work, and get a **realistic estimate** of how long that work will actually take.

Take the days of work it will take you to develop a user story, or an iteration, or even an entire milestone...

The result should always be BIGGER than the original days of work, to account for days of administration, holidays, etc.

$$\frac{\text{days of work}}{\text{velocity}} = \text{days required to get work done}$$

...and DIVIDE that number by your velocity, which should be between 0 and 1.0. Start with 0.7 on a new project as a good conservative estimate.

Seeing a trend? 30 days of a calendar month was really 20 days of work, and 20 days of work is really only about 15 days of productive time.

Programmers think in <u>UTOPIAN</u> days...

Ask a programmer how long it takes to get something done, like writing a PHP interface to a MySQL database, or maybe screen-scraping World Series scores from *espn.com*. They're going to give you a ***better-than-best-case estimate***.

Here's what a programmer <u>SAYS</u>...

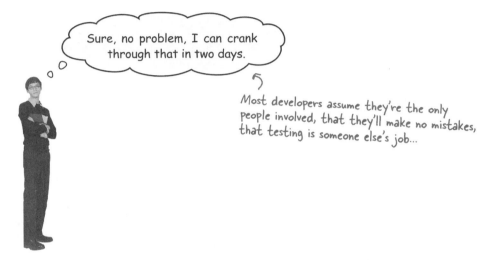

Sure, no problem, I can crank through that in two days.

Most developers assume they're the only people involved, that they'll make no mistakes, that testing is someone else's job...

...but here's what he's really <u>THINKING</u>

I'll grab a Monster on the way home, program till 3 A.M., take a Halo break, then work through the morning. Sleep a few hours, get the guys over to hack with me, and finish at midnight. As long as nothing goes wrong... and Mom doesn't need me to pick up dinner.

But there are about 10 assumptions in here...and these are just the ones the developer knows about!

Developers think in <u>REAL-WORLD</u> days...

To be a software developer, though, you have to deal with reality. You've probably got a team of programmers, and you've got a customer who won't pay you if you're late. On top of that, you may even have other people depending on you—so your estimates are more conservative, and take into account real life:

You start with a month, but take away weekends and holidays.

1 calendar month

20 workable days

Then, apply velocity to account for time in the office that isn't focused on actual development.

velocity

14 days of <u>REAL</u> work

This is a lot lower number of days, but you can be more <u>CONFIDENT</u> in this number.

Sharpen your pencil

Take your original estimates for each iteration from the solution on page 84 and apply a 70% velocity so that you can come up with a more confident estimate for all the work in Milestone 1.0.

Iteration 1
57 days of work / 0.7 = ...

Iteration 2
50 days of work / 0.7 = ...

Iteration 3
58 days of work / 0.7 = ...

Milestone 1.0 = ...

When is your iteration too long?

Suppose you have three developers on your team who are working at a velocity of 0.7. This means that to calculate **how long an iteration will really take *your team***, you need to apply your velocity to the iteration's estimate:

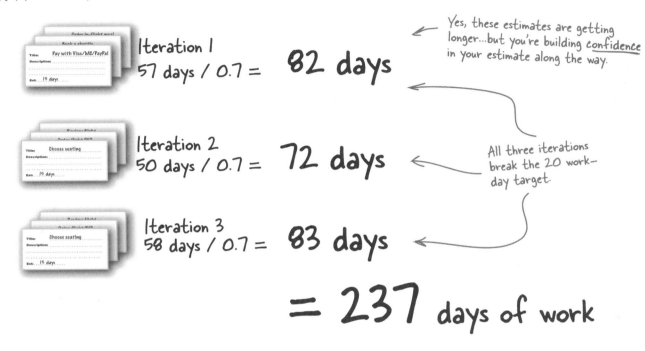

Iteration 1
57 days / 0.7 = **82 days**

Yes, these estimates are getting longer...but you're building <u>confidence</u> in your estimate along the way.

Iteration 2
50 days / 0.7 = **72 days**

All three iterations break the 20 work-day target.

Iteration 3
58 days / 0.7 = **83 days**

= **237** days of work

So if you have **3** developers, each of them has to work **79** days in **3** months... but there are only **60** working days.

Even with three people, we still can't deliver Milestone 1.0 in time!

BRAIN POWER

How would you bring your estimates back to 20 work-day cycles so you can deliver Milestone 1.0 on time, without working weekends?

Deal with velocity <u>BEFORE</u> you break into iterations

A lot of this pain could actually have been avoided if you'd applied velocity at the *beginning* of your project. By applying velocity up front, you can calculate how many days of work you and your team can produce in each iteration. Then you'll know exactly what you can *really* deliver in Milestone 1.0.

First, apply your team velocity to each iteration

By taking the number of people in your team, multiplied by the number of actual working days in your iteration, multiplied finally by your team's velocity, you can calculate how many **days of actual work** your team can produce in one iteration:

$$3 \times 20 \times 0.7 = 42$$

The number of people on your team.

20 working days in your iteration

Your team's first pass velocity.

The amount of work, in person-days, that your team can handle in one iteration.

Add your iterations up to get a total milestone estimate

Now you should estimate the number of iterations you need for your milestone. Just multiply your days of work per iteration by the number of iterations, and you've got the number of working days you can devote to user stories for your milestone:

$$42 \times 3 = 126$$

Number of iterations in Milestone 1.0.

Amount of work in days that you and your team can do before Milestone 1.0 needs to be shipped.

---

there are no Dumb Questions

Q: That sucks! So I only have 14 days of actual productive work per iteration if my velocity is 0.7?

A: 0.7 is a conservative estimate for when you have new members of your team coming up to speed and other overheads. As you and your team complete your iterations, you'll keep coming back to that velocity value and updating it to reflect how productive you really are.

Q: With velocity, my Milestone 1.0 is now going to take 79 working days, which means 114 calendar days. That's much more than the 90-day/3-month deadline that Orion's Orbits set, isn't that too long?

A: Yes! Orion's Orbits need Milestone 1.0 in 90 calendar days, so by applying velocity, you've now got too much work to do to meet that deadline. You need to reassess your plan to see what you really can do with the time and team that you have.

Long Exercise

When your iterations contain too much work for your team, there's nothing else to do but reshuffle work until your iterations are manageable. Take the Orion's Orbits Milestone 1.0 user stories and organize them into iterations that each contain no more than 42 days of work.

The maximum amount of work your team can do in a 20-day iteration, factoring in your velocity this time.

Title:	View shuttle deals
Est:	12 days
Priority:	10

Title:	Book a shuttle
Est:	15 days
Priority:	10

Title:	Pay with Visa/ MC/PayPal
Est:	15 days
Priority:	10

Title:	Manage special offers
Est:	13 days
Priority:	10

Remember to respect the customer's original order of priority in your iterations.

Title:	Choose seating
Est:	12 days
Priority:	20

Title:	Order In-flight meals
Est:	13 days
Priority:	20

Title:	Review flight
Est:	13 days
Priority:	30

Title:	View flight reviews
Est:	12 days
Priority:	30

Title:	Apply for "frequent astronaut" card
Est:	14 days
Priority:	40

Title:	Login to "Frequent Astronaut" account
Est:	15 days
Priority:	50

Title:	View "Space Miles" account
Est:	14 days
Priority:	50

Title:	Pay using "Space Miles"
Est:	15 days
Priority:	50

Plan out each iteration by adding user stories that come out to around 42 days of work.

Iteration 1

Total Days of work: ☐

Iteration 2

Total Days of work: ☐

Iteration 3

Total Days of work: ☐

Put any user stories that won't fit in the three iterations for Milestone 1.0 here

User stories that won't fit

LONG EXERCISE SOLUTION

Your job was to to take the Orion's Orbits user stories and aim for iterations that contain no more than 42 days of work each.

Title: View shuttle deals
Est: 12 days
Priority: 10

Title: Book a shuttle
Est: 15 days
Priority: 10

Title: Pay with Visa/ MC/PayPal
Est: 15 days
Priority: 10

Iteration 1

Total Days of work: 42

Title: Manage special offers
Est: 13 days
Priority: 10

Title: Choose seating
Est: 12 days
Priority: 20

Title: Order In-flight meals
Est: 13 days
Priority: 20

Iteration 2

Total Days of work: 38

Title: Review flight
Est: 13 days
Priority: 30

Title: View flight reviews
Est: 12 days
Priority: 30

Title: Apply for Space Miles Loyalty Card
Est: 14 days
Priority: 40

Iteration 3

Total Days of work: 39

These user stories dropped off of the plan...

Title: Login to "Frequent Astronaut" account
Est: 15 days
Priority: 50

Title: View "Space Miles" account
Est: 14 days
Priority: 50

Title: Pay using "Space Miles"
Est: 15 days
Priority: 50

User stories that won't fit

Time to make an evaluation

So what's left? You've probably got a lot of user stories that still fit into Milestone 1.0...and maybe a few that don't. That's because we didn't figure out our velocity before our iteration planning.

Estimates without velocity can get you into real trouble with your customer.

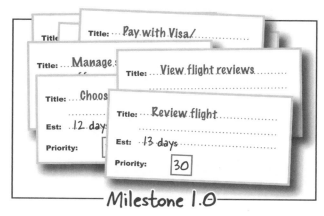

Title: ...Pay with Visa/

Title: ...Manage...

Title: ...Choos...

Title: ...View flight reviews...........

Title: ...Review flight........

Est: ..12 days

Est: ..13 days......

Priority: 30

Milestone 1.0

All the work that can be done for Milestone 1.0

Title: ...Pay using "Space Miles"...

Est: ..15 days......

Priority: 50

Milestone .Next

The user stories that fell out of Milestone 1.0

Deliver the bad news to the customer

It's the time that every software developer dreads. You've planned out your iterations, factored in the velocity of your team, but you still can't get everything your customer wants done in time for their deadline. There's nothing else to do but come clean...

That sucks! So you can do everything except the online "Space Miles" features. Hmm...Let me think about it...

There's no magic trick here...you have to tell the customer and see what they want to do.

[Note from human resources: we prefer the term <u>unsympathetic</u> customers.]

Managing ~~pissed off~~ customers

Customers usually aren't happy when you tell them you can't get everything done in the time they want. Be honest, though; you want to come up with a plan for Milestone 1.0 that you can achieve, not a plan that just says what the customer wants it to say.

...and has you on a fast track to failure!

So what do you do when this happens?

It's almost inevitable that you're not going to be able to do everything, so it helps to be prepared with some options when you have to tell the customer the bad news...

1 **Add an iteration to Milestone 1.0**
Explain that the extra work can be done if an additional iteration is added to the plan. That means a longer development schedule, but the customer will get what they want in Milestone 1.0.

$$42 \times \cancel{3}4 = \cancel{126} 168$$

Another iteration gives your team plenty of time to develop all the customer's stories—but that pushes out the release date of Milestone 1.0, too.

2 **Explain that the overflow work is not lost, just postponed**
Sometimes it helps to point out that the user stories that can't make it into Milestone 1.0 are not lost; they are just put on the back burner until the next milestone.

Milestone 1.0

Milestone .Next

These extra stories aren't trashed—they just fall into Milestone 2.0. Are space miles so important that they're worth starting over with a new development team?

3 **Be transparent about how you came up with your figures**
It sounds strange, but your customer only has your word that you can't deliver everything they want within the deadline they've given you, so it sometimes helps to explain where you're coming from. If you can, show them the calculations that back up your velocity and how this equates to their needs. And tell your customer you ***want*** to deliver them successful software, and that's why you've had to sacrifice some features to give yourself a plan that you are confident that you can deliver on.

there are no Dumb Questions

Q: If I'm close on my estimates, can I fudge a little and squeeze something in?

A: We REALLY wouldn't recommend this. Remember, your estimates are only educated guesses at this point, and they are actually more likely to take slightly longer than originally thought than shorter.

It's a much better idea to leave some breathing room around your estimates to really be confident that you've planned a successful set of iterations.

Q: I have a few days left over in my Milestone 1.0. Can't I add in a user story that breaks my day limit just a little bit?

A: Again, probably not a good idea. If your stories add up to leave you one or two days at the end of the iteration, that's OK. (In Chapter 9 we'll talk about what you can do to round those out.)

Q: OK, without squeezing my last user story in I end up coming under my work-day limit by a LONG way. I have 15 days free at the end of Milestone 1.0! Is there anything I can do about that?

A: To fit a story into that space, try and come up with two simpler stories and fit one of those into Milestone 1.0 instead.

Q: 0.7 seems to add up to a LOT of lost time. What sorts of activities could take up that sort of time?

A: 0.7 is a safe first guess at a team's velocity. One example is where you are installing a new piece of software, like an IDE or a database (naming no specific manufacturers here, of course). In cases like these two hours of interrupted work can actually mean FOUR hours of lost time when you factor in how long it can take a developer to get back in "the zone" and developing productively.

It's also worth bearing in mind that velocity is recalculated at the end of every iteration. So even if 0.7 seems low for your team right now, you'll be able to correct as soon as you have some hard data. In Chapter 9 we'll be refining your velocity based on your team's performance during Iteration 1.

Alright, it's worth it to me to lose space miles in Milestone 1.0 to keep things moving. Let's do it.

Stay confident that you can achieve the work you sign up for. You should pr<u>omise</u> and <u>deliver</u> rather than <u>overpromise</u> and <u>fail.</u>

The <u>Big Board</u> on your wall

Once you know exactly what you're building, it's time to set up your **software development dashboard** for Iteration 1 of development. Your dashboard is actually just a **big board** on the wall of your office that you can use to keep tabs on **what work is in the pipeline**, **what's in progress,** and **what's done**.

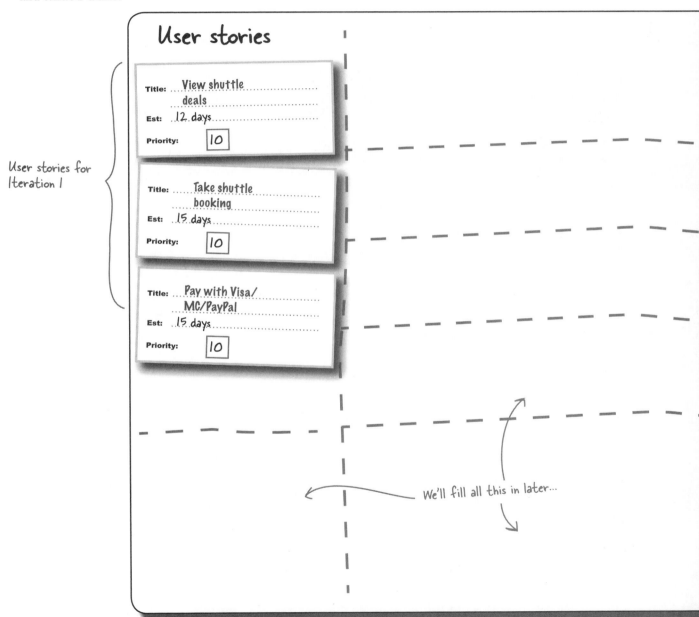

User stories

Title: View shuttle deals
Est: 12 days
Priority: 10

Title: Take shuttle booking
Est: 15 days
Priority: 10

Title: Pay with Visa/ MC/PayPal
Est: 15 days
Priority: 10

User stories for Iteration 1

We'll fill all this in later...

Usually your project board is a whiteboard, so you can use it again and again between iterations and projects.

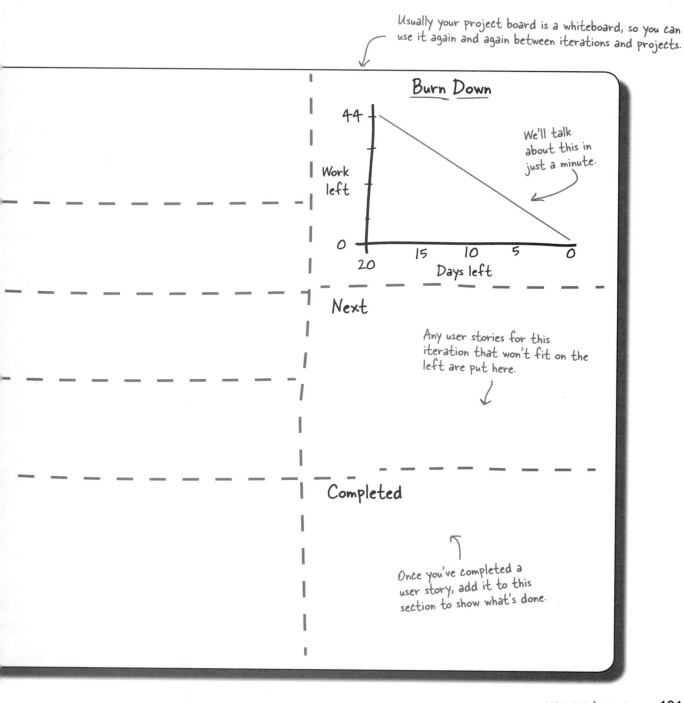

Burn Down

44

Work left

0

20   15   10   5   0

Days left

We'll talk about this in just a minute.

Next

Any user stories for this iteration that won't fit on the left are put here.

Completed

Once you've completed a user story, add it to this section to show what's done.

Exercise

You may have noticed a graph at the top right of your development dashboard, but what is it for? Take a few minutes to glance over the burn-down graph below and write on it what you think the different parts of the graph are for and how it is one of the key tools for monitoring your software development progress and ensuring that you deliver on time.

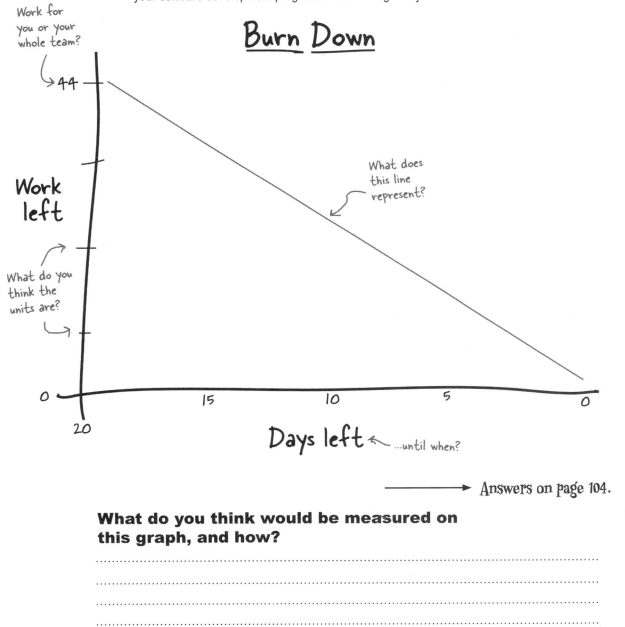

Work for you or your whole team?

44

Burn Down

What does this line represent?

Work left

What do you think the units are?

0

20

15   10   5   0

Days left ←....until when?

⟶ Answers on page 104.

What do you think would be measured on this graph, and how?

....
....
....
....

How to ruin your team's lives

It's easy to look at those long schedules, growing estimates, and diminishing iteration cycles, and start to think, "**My team can work longer weeks!**" If you got your team to agree to that, then you're probably setting yourself up for some trouble down the line.

Personal lives matter

Long hours are eventually going to affect your personal life and the personal lives of the developers on your team. That might seem trite, but a happier team is a more productive team.

Fatigue affects productivity

Tired developers aren't productive. Lots of studies suggest that developers are really only incredibly productive for about three hours a day. The rest of the day isn't a loss, but the more tired your developers are, the less likely they'll even get to that three hours of really productive time.

> Be confident in your plans by applying velocity and not overworking yourself and your team.

BULLET POINTS

- The first step to planning what you are going to develop is to ask the customer to **prioritize their requirements**.

- **Milestone 1.0** should be delivered as **early** as you can.

- During Milestone 1.0 try to **iterate around once a month** to keep your development work on track.

- When you don't have enough time to build everything, ask the **customer** to **reprioritize**.

- Plan your iterations by factoring in your team's **velocity** from the **start**.

- If you really can't do what's needed in the time allowed, **be honest** and **explain why** to the customer.

- Once you have an agreed-upon and achievable set of user stories for Milestone 1.0, it's time to set up your **development dashboard** and get developing!

Exercise Solution

You were asked to take a few minutes to glance over the burn-down graph below and describe what you think the different parts of the graph are for and how it is one of the key tools for monitoring your software development progress and ensuring that you deliver on time.

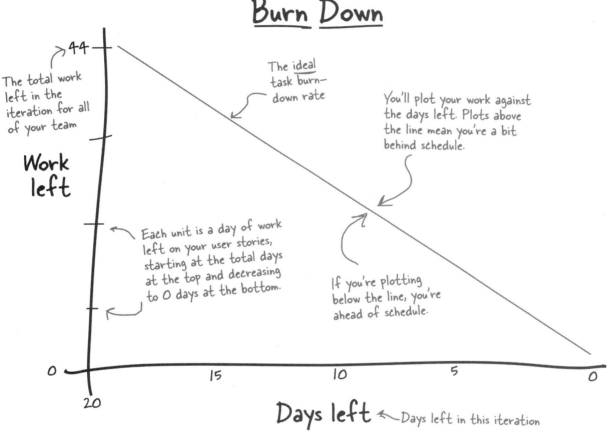

Burn Down

44 — The total work left in the iteration for all of your team

Work left

Each unit is a day of work left on your user stories, starting at the total days at the top and decreasing to 0 days at the bottom.

The ideal task burn-down rate

You'll plot your work against the days left. Plots above the line mean you're a bit behind schedule.

If you're plotting below the line, you're ahead of schedule.

0

20

15   **10**   **5**   **0**

Days left ← Days left in this iteration

What do you think would be measured on this graph, and how?

This graph monitors how quickly you and your team are completing your work, measured in days on the vertical axis. This chart then plots how quickly you tick off your work remaining against the number of days left in your iteration.

Relax

We'll talk a lot more about burn-down in the next few chapters.

Don't worry if you're still a little fuzzy on how burn-down rates work, and how to track it. You'll start creating a chart of your own in the next chapter, tracking your project's progress.

Software Development Planning Cross

Let's put what you've learned to use and stretch out your left brain a bit!
All of the words below are somewhere in this chapter: Good luck!

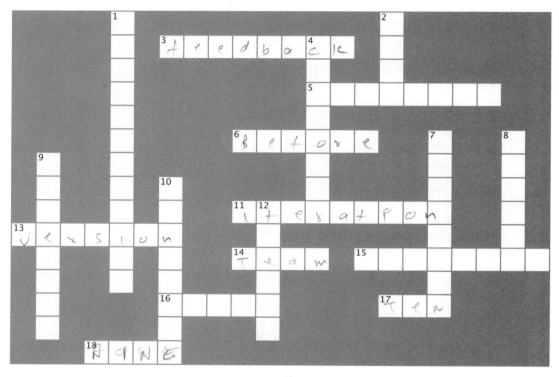

Across

3. At the end of an iteration you should get .... from the customer.
5. Velocity does not account for .... events.
6. Ideally you apply velocity .... you break your Version 1.0 into iterations.
11. You should have one .... per calendar month.
13. Every 3 iterations you should have a complete and running and releasable .... of your software.
14. Velocity is a measuer of your ....'s work rate.
15. 0.7 is your first pass .... for a new team.
16. At the end of an iteration your software should be ....
17. When priotitizing, the highest priority (the most important to the customer) is set to a value of ....
18. Any more than .... people in a team and you run the risk of slowing your team down.

Down

1. Your customer can remove some less important user stories when .... them.
2. Every 90 days you should .... a complete version of your software.
4. The .... sets the priority of each user stor.
7. The rate that you complete user stories across your entire project.
8. You should always try be .... with the customer.
9. The set of features that must be present to have any working software at all is called the .... functionality.
10. At the end of an iteration your software should be ....
12. You should assume .... working days in a calendar month.

CHAPTER 3

Tools for your Software Development Toolbox

Software Development is all about developing and delivering great software. In this chapter, you added several new techniques to your toolbox... For a complete list of tools in the book, see Appendix ii.

Development Techniques

Iterations should ideally be no longer than a month. That means you have 20 working calendar days per iteration

Applying velocity to your plan lets you feel more confident in your ability to keep your development promises to your customer

Use (literally) a big board on your wall to plan and monitor your current iteration's work

Get your customer's buy-in when choosing what user stories can be completed for Milestone 1.0, and when choosing what iteration a user story will be built in.

Development Principles

Keep iterations short and manageable

Ultimately, the customer decides what is in and what is out for Milestone 1.0

Promise, and deliver

ALWAYS be honest with the customer

BULLET POINTS

- Your **customer prioritizes** what is in and what is out for Milestone 1.0.

- Build **short iterations** of about 1 calendar month, **20 calendar days** of work.

- Throughout an iteration your software should be **buildable** and **runnable**.

- Apply your team's **velocity** to your estimates to figure out exactly how much work you can **realistically manage** in your first iteration.

- Keep your customers happy by coming up with a Milestone 1.0 that **you can achieve** so that you can be confident of delivering and getting paid. Then if you deliver more, they'll be even happier.

Software Development Planning Cross Solution

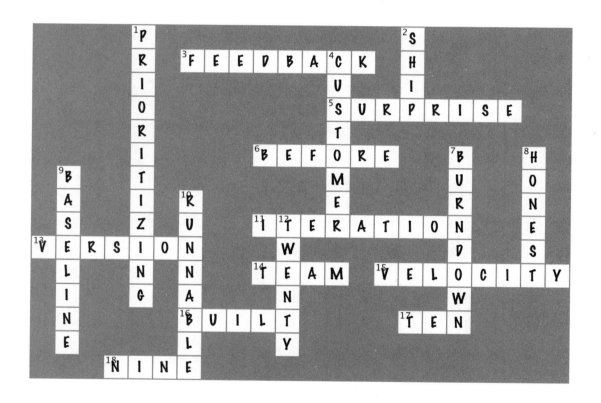

4 user stories and tasks

Getting to the real work

I'm sure that eighth layer of wax is important, but couldn't we get going? We should already be there...

It's time to go to work. User stories capture what you need to develop, but now it's time to knuckle down and **dish out the work that needs to be done** so that you can bring those user stories to life. In this chapter you'll learn how to **break your user stories into tasks,** and how **task estimates** help you track your project from inception to completion. You'll learn how to update your board, moving tasks from in progress to complete, to finally **completing an entire user story**. Along the way, you'll handle and prioritize the inevitable **unexpected work** your customer will add to your plate.

Introducing iSwoon

Welcome to iSwoon, soon to be the world's finest desktop date planner! Here's the big board, already loaded with user stories broken down into 20-work-day iterations:

Date Rights Management (DRM) included

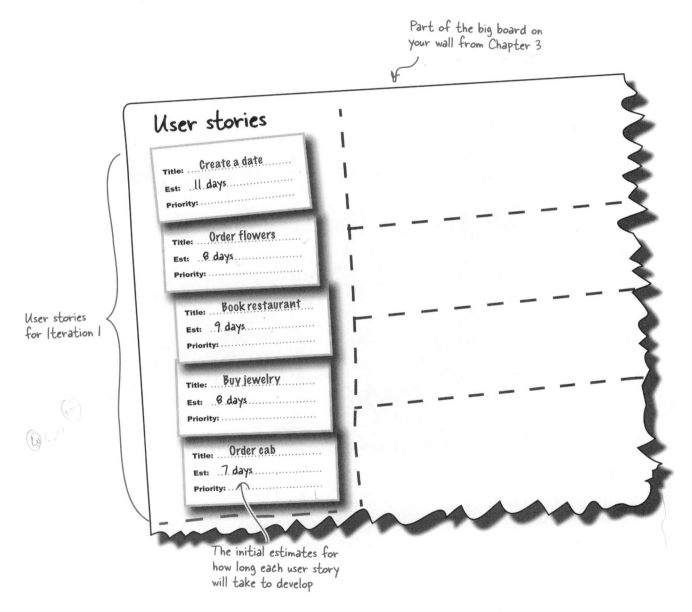

Part of the big board on your wall from Chapter 3

User stories

Title: Create a date
Est: 11 days
Priority:

Title: Order flowers
Est: 8 days
Priority:

Title: Book restaurant
Est: 9 days
Priority:

Title: Buy jewelry
Est: 8 days
Priority:

Title: Order cab
Est: 7 days
Priority:

User stories for Iteration 1

The initial estimates for how long each user story will take to develop

Exercise

It's time to get you and your team of developers working. Take each of the iSwoon user stories for Iteration 1 and assign each to a developer by drawing a line from the user story to the developer of your choice...

Title: Order flowers
Est: 8 days
Priority:

Title: Book restaurant
Est: 9 days
Priority:

Title: Create a date
Est: 11 days
Priority:

Title: Buy Jewelry
Est: 8 days
Priority:

Title: Order cab
Est: 7 days
Priority:

Mark, database expert and SQL black belt

Laura, the UI guru

Bob, the junior developer

> Wait a second, we can't just assign user stories to developers; things aren't that simple! Some of those user stories have to happen before others, and what if I want more than one developer on a single story?

Your work is more granular than your user stories.

Your user stories were ***for your user***; they helped describe exactly what you software needed to do, from the customer's perspective. But now that it's time to start coding, you'll probably need to look at these stories differently. Each story is really a collection of specific **tasks**, small bits of functionality that can combine to make up one single user story.

A **task** specifies a piece of development work that needs to be carried out by ***one developer*** in order to construct part of a user story. Each task has a ***title*** so you can easily refer to it, a ***rough description*** that contains details about how the development of that task should be done, and an ***estimate***. Each task has its own estimate and—guess what—the best way to come up with those estimates is by playing planning poker again with your team.

We already used this to get estimates for user stories in Chapter 2, and it works for tasks, too.

Sharpen your pencil

Now it's your turn. Take the user story of creating a date and break it into tasks you think you and your team need to execute. Write one task down on each of the sticky notes, and don't forget to add an estimate to each task.

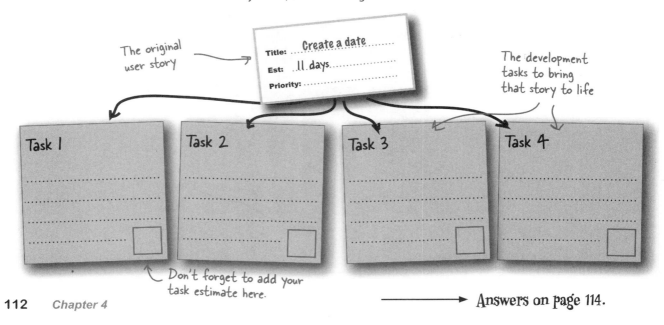

The original user story

Title: Create a date
Est: 11 days
Priority:

The development tasks to bring that story to life

Task 1

Task 2

Task 3

Task 4

Don't forget to add your task estimate here.

Answers on page 114.

Do your tasks add up?

Did you notice a possible problem with your estimates? We've got a user story with an estimate, but now we're adding *new* estimates to our tasks. What happens when the two sets of estimates don't agree?

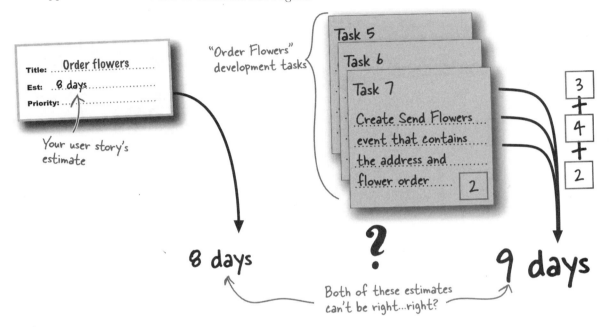

"Order Flowers" development tasks

Task 5
Task 6
Task 7
Create Send Flowers
event that contains
the address and
flower order
2

Title: Order flowers
Est: 8 days
Priority:

Your user story's estimate

8 days

? Both of these estimates can't be right...right?

9 days

3
+
4
+
2

Task estimates add confidence to user story estimates

Your user story estimates kept you in the right ballpark when you were planning your iterations, but tasks really add another level of detail specific to the actual coding you'll do for a user story.

In fact, it's often best to break out tasks from your user stories right **at the beginning** of the estimation process, if you have time. This way you'll add even more confidence to the plan that you give your customer. **It's always best to rely on the task estimates.** Tasks describe the actual software development work that needs to be done and are far less of a guesstimate than a coarse-grained user story estimate.

Break user stories into tasks to add CONFIDENCE to your estimates and your plan.

And the earlier you can do this, the better.

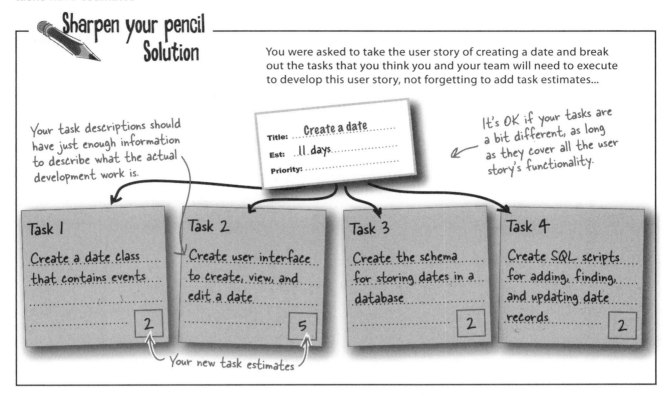

Sharpen your pencil Solution

You were asked to take the user story of creating a date and break out the tasks that you think you and your team will need to execute to develop this user story, not forgetting to add task estimates...

Your task descriptions should have just enough information to describe what the actual development work is.

Title: Create a date
Est: 11 days
Priority:

It's OK if your tasks are a bit different, as long as they cover all the user story's functionality.

Task 1
Create a date class that contains events
2

Task 2
Create user interface to create, view, and edit a date
5

Task 3
Create the schema for storing dates in a database
2

Task 4
Create SQL scripts for adding, finding, and updating date records
2

Your new task estimates

there are no Dumb Questions

Q: My tasks add up to a new estimate for my user story, so were my original user story estimates wrong?

A: Well, yes and no. Your user story estimate was accurate enough in the beginning to let you organize your iterations. Now, with task estimates, you have a set of **more accurate data** that either backs up your user story estimates or conflicts with them.

You always want to rely on data that you trust, the estimates that you feel are most accurate. In this case, those are your task estimates.

Q: How big should a task estimate be?

A: Your task estimates should ideally be between 1/2 and 5 days in length. A shorter task, measured in hours, is too small a task. A task that is longer than five days spreads across more than one working week, and that gives the developer working on the task too much time to lose focus.

Q: What happens when I discover a big missing task?

A: Sometimes—hopefully not too often—you'll come across a task that just breaks your user story estimate completely. You might have forgotten something important when first coming up with the user story estimates, and suddenly the devil in the details rears its ugly head, and you have a more accurate, task-based estimate that completely blows your user story estimate out of the water.

When this happens you can really only do one thing, and that's adjust your iteration. To keep your iteration within 20 working days, you can postpone that large task (and user story) until the next iteration, reshuffling the rest of your iterations accordingly.

To avoid these problem, you could break your user stories into tasks earlier. For instance, you might break up your user stories into tasks when you initially plan your iterations, always relying on your task estimates over your original user story estimates as you balance out your iterations to 20 working days each.

Plot just the work you have left

Remember that burn-down rate chart from Chapter 3? Here's where it starts to help us track what's going on in our project. Every time we do any work or review an estimate, we update our new estimates, and the time we have left, on our burn-down chart:

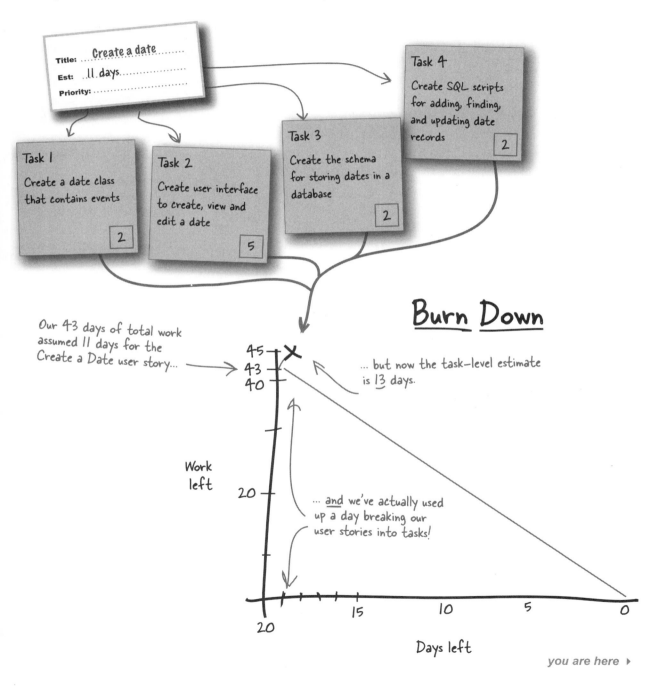

Title: Create a date

Est: 11 days

Priority:

Task 4

Create SQL scripts for adding, finding, and updating date records

2

Task 1

Create a date class that contains events

2

Task 2

Create user interface to create, view and edit a date

5

Task 3

Create the schema for storing dates in a database

2

Our 43 days of total work assumed 11 days for the Create a Date user story...

Burn Down

... but now the task-level estimate is 13 days.

... and we've actually used up a day breaking our user stories into tasks!

Work left

45
43
40

20

20

15   10   5   0

Days left

Add your tasks to your board

You and your team are now almost ready to start working on your tasks, but first you need to update the big board on your wall. Add your task sticky notes to your user stories. and also add an In Progress and Complete section for tracking tasks and user stories:

User stories ← ... for this iteration

In Progress

Sticky notes are perfect for tasks; they can hang on the bottom of the user story they belong to.

Title: **Create a date**

Task 1 — Create a date class that contains events

Task 2 — Create user interface to create, view and edit a date

Task 3 — Create the schema for storing dates in a database

Task 4 — Create GUI events for adding, finding and updating date records

Title: **Order flowers**

Task 7 — Create send flowers event that contains the address and flower order

Task 5 — Develop email client to send order to florist

Task 6 — Develop UI for tracking flower order and routing to florist

Title: **Book restaurant**

Task 8 — Create user interface to find and add restaurant's details for a date

Task 10 — Create a Book Restaurant event class

Task 9 — Develop email code to send booking request to restaurant

Title: **Buy jewelry**

Task 11 — Syndicate deal feeds from various jewelry stores

Task 12 — Add parsing code to HTTP request when an item is selected

Title: **Order cab**

Task 13 — Add cab order event to database

Task 15 — Add order cab event

Task 14 — Develop code that instantiates the notifying a cab for pickup if one hasn't arrived

This is where you put tasks that are in progress—and none are yet.

Soon, we'll start working on tasks, and move the matching sticky into the In Progress area.

The original user story estimates are now gone...

...and now you're relying on the combined estimates of all of the tasks for all the user stories for the iteration.

A user story's tasks first move to the In Progress swimlane for that user story...

This isn't a virtual board—it should be a <u>real</u> bulletin or whiteboard hanging somewhere, like a common area or maybe the office where you and your team meet each morning.

Yes, you should meet each morning! More on that in just a minute...

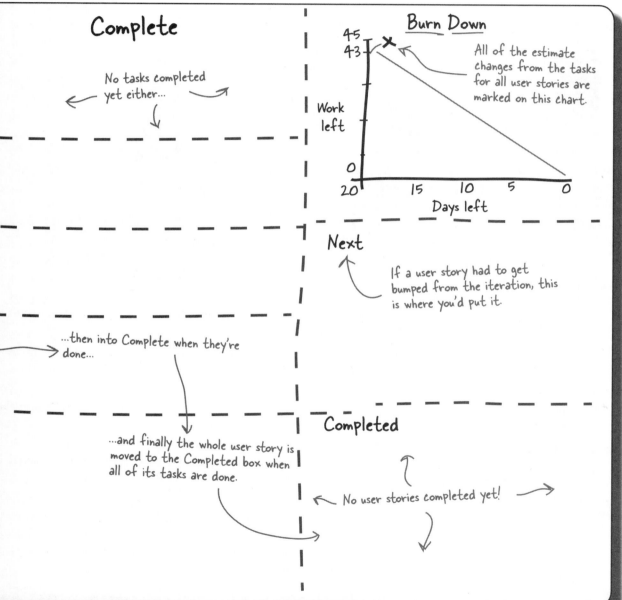

Complete

No tasks completed yet either...

Burn Down

45
43
x

All of the estimate changes from the tasks for all user stories are marked on this chart.

Work left

0

20   15   10   5   0

Days left

Next

If a user story had to get bumped from the iteration, this is where you'd put it.

...then into Complete when they're done...

...and finally the whole user story is moved to the Completed box when all of its tasks are done.

Completed

No user stories completed yet!

Start working on your tasks

It's time to bring that burn-down rate back under control by getting started developing on your first user story. And, with small tasks, you can assign your team work in a sensible, trackable way:

Title: Create a date

Est: 11 days

Priority:

Write down the initials of the developer working on each task on its sticky.

Task 1   BJD

Create a date class that contains events

2

Task 2   LUG

Create user interface to create, view, and edit a date

5

Task 3   MDE

Create the schema for storing dates in a database

2

Task 4   MDE

Create SQL queries for adding, finding, and updating date records

2

All the tasks from the first user story

This story is best done first, because most of the other stories depend on the "Create a Date" user story.

there are no Dumb Questions

Q: How do I figure out who to assign a task to?

A: There are no hard-and-fast rules about who to give a task to, but it's best to just apply some common sense. Figure out who would be most productive or—if you have the time, will learn most from a particular task by looking at their own expertise—and then allocate the task to the best-suited developer, or the one who will gain the most, that's not already busy.

Q: Why allocate tasks just from the first user story. Why not take one task from each user story?

A: One good reason is so that so that you don't wind up with five stories in a half-done state, and instead can wrap up a user story and move on to the next. If you've got one story your other stories depend on, you may want to get all that first story's tasks done at once. However, if your stories are independent of each other, you may work on tasks from multiple stories all at the same time.

Q: I'm still worried about that burn-down rate being way up, is there anything I can do right now to fix that?

A: A burn-down rate that's going up is always a cause for concern, but since you're early on, let's wait a bit and see if we catch up.

A task is only in progress when it's <u>IN PROGRESS</u>

Now that everyone's got some work to do, it's time to move those task stickies off of user story cards, and onto the In Progress area of your big board. But you only put tasks that are **actually being worked on** in the In Progress column—even if you already know who'll be working on tasks yet to be tackled.

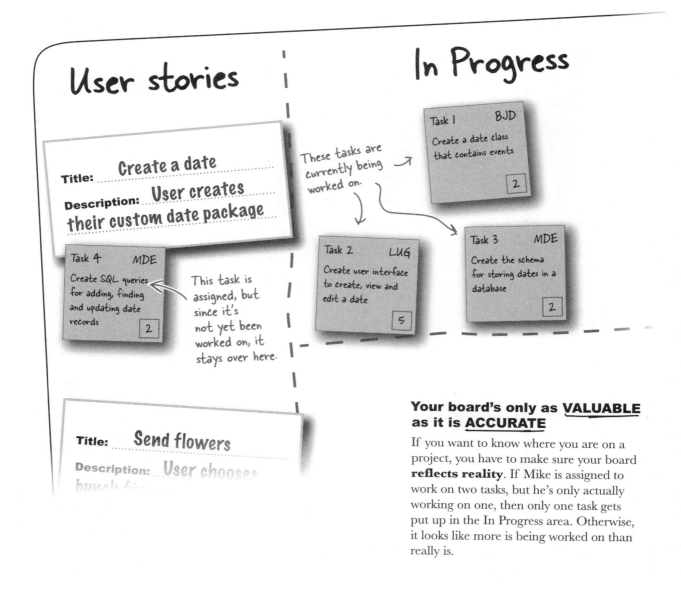

User stories

In Progress

Title: Create a date
Description: User creates their custom date package

Task 4   MDE
Create SQL queries for adding, finding and updating date records   2

This task is assigned, but since it's not yet been worked on, it stays over here.

These tasks are currently being worked on.

Task 1   BJD
Create a date class that contains events   2

Task 2   LUG
Create user interface to create, view and edit a date   5

Task 3   MDE
Create the schema for storing dates in a database   2

Title: Send flowers
Description: User chooses bunch f...

Your board's only as <u>VALUABLE</u> as it is <u>ACCURATE</u>

If you want to know where you are on a project, you have to make sure your board **reflects reality**. If Mike is assigned to work on two tasks, but he's only actually working on one, then only one task gets put up in the In Progress area. Otherwise, it looks like more is being worked on than really is.

What if I'm working on two things at once?

Not all tasks are best executed in isolation. Sometimes two tasks are related, and, because there is so much overlap, it's actually more work to tackle one, and then the other separately. In these cases the most productive thing to do is work on those tasks **at the same time**...

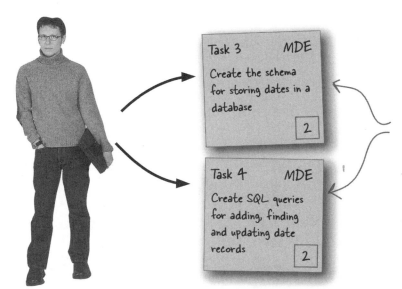

Task 3   MDE

Create the schema for storing dates in a database

2

Task 4   MDE

Create SQL queries for adding, finding and updating date records

2

Both these tasks involve writing database scripts, so in this case it might make more sense for Mark to be allocated both of these tasks at the same time.

Sometimes working on both tasks at the same time **IS** the best option

When you have two tasks that are closely related. then it's not really a problem to work on them both at the same time.

This is especially the case where the work completed in one task could ***inform decisions*** made in the work for another task. Rather than completing one task and starting the next, and then realizing that you need to do some work on the first task again, it is far more efficient to work both tasks at the same time.

Rules of Thumb

- Try to double-up tasks that are related to each other, or at least focus on roughly the same area of your software. The less thought involved in moving from one task to another, the faster that switch will be.

- Try not to double-up on tasks that have large estimates. It's not only difficult to stay focused on a long task, but you will be more confident estimating the work involved the shorter the task is.

Exercise

Someone's been tampering with the board and things are a real mess. Take a look at the project below and annotate all of the problems you can spot.

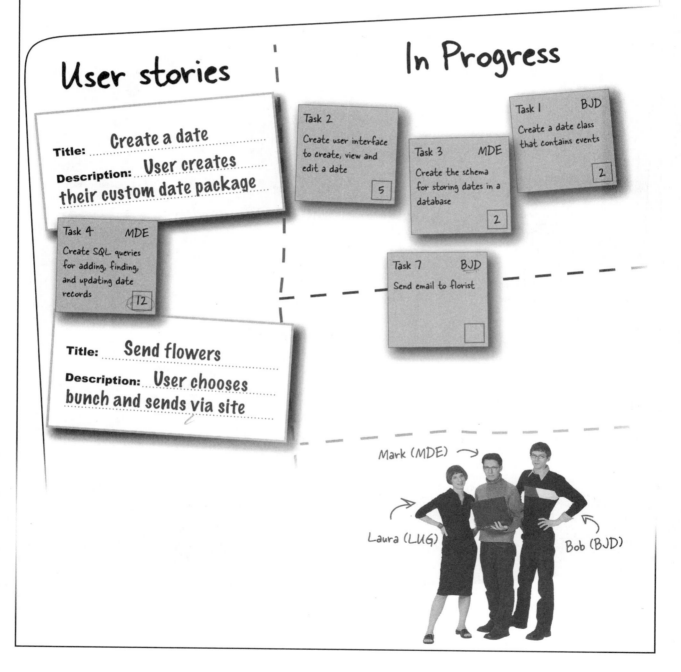

User stories

Title: .... Create a date ....

Description: .... User creates .... their custom date package

Task 4   MDE

Create SQL queries for adding, finding, and updating date records

12

Title: .... Send flowers ....

Description: .... User chooses .... bunch and sends via site

In Progress

Task 2

Create user interface to create, view and edit a date

5

Task 3   MDE

Create the schema for storing dates in a database

2

Task 1   BJD

Create a date class that contains events

2

Task 7   BJD

Send email to florist

Mark (MDE) →

Laura (LUG) →

Bob (BJD) ↖

Exercise
Solution

Your job was to to take a look at the project below and annotate
all of the problems you could spot...

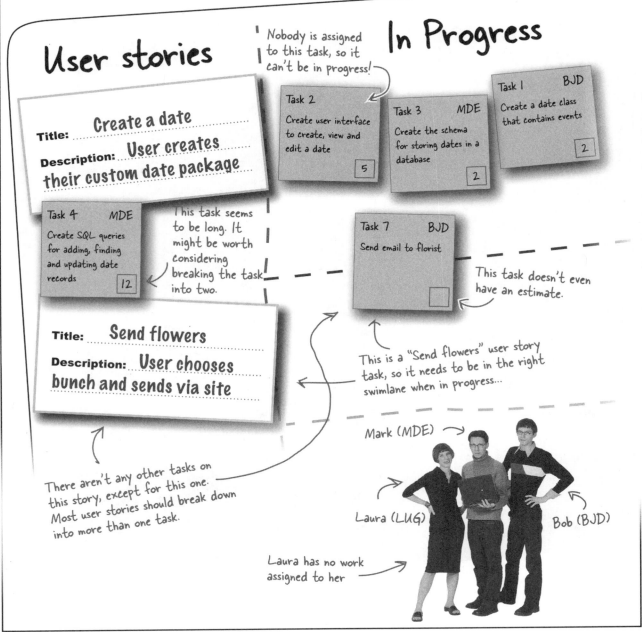

User stories

Nobody is assigned to this task, so it can't be in progress!

In Progress

Title: Create a date

Description: User creates their custom date package

Task 2
Create user interface to create, view and edit a date
5

Task 3   MDE
Create the schema for storing dates in a database
2

Task 1   BJD
Create a date class that contains events
2

Task 4   MDE
Create SQL queries for adding, finding and updating date records
12

This task seems to be long. It might be worth considering breaking the task into two.

Task 7   BJD
Send email to florist

This task doesn't even have an estimate.

Title: Send flowers

Description: User chooses bunch and sends via site

This is a "Send flowers" user story task, so it needs to be in the right swimlane when in progress...

There aren't any other tasks on this story, except for this one. Most user stories should break down into more than one task.

Mark (MDE) →

Laura (LUG)

Bob (BJD)

Laura has no work assigned to her →

Your first <u>standup</u> meeting...

A meeting so quick you don't even have time to sit down.

You've now got some tasks in progress, and so to keep everyone in the loop, while not taking up too much of their time, you conduct a quick standup meeting every day.

G'morning everyone, it's day 1 and I thought I'd call a quick meeting so we can update the board and get everything set for today's development...

Mark: So, we've all had our tasks for one day now. How are we doing?

Bob: Well, I haven't hit any big problems yet, so nothing new really to report.

Mark: That's great. I've had a bit of success and finished up on the scripts to create tables in the database...

Laura: Things are still in progress on my user interface task.

Mark: OK, that all sounds good, I'll update the board and move my task into Completed. We can update the burn rate, too; maybe we're making up for some of that time we lost earlier. Any other successes or issues to report?

Bob: Well, I guess I should probably mention that I'm finding creating the right Date class a little tricky...

Mark: That's fine. I'm really glad you brought it up, though. That's a two-day task and we need it done tomorrow, so I'll get you some help on that as soon as possible. OK, it's been about seven minutes, I think we're done here...

Your daily standup meetings should:

- **Track your progress.** Get everyone's input about how things are going.

- **Update your burn-down rate.** It's a new day so you need to update your burndown rate to see how things are going.

- **Update tasks.** If a task is completed then it's time to move it over into the Completed area and check those days off of your burn-down rate.

- **Talk about what happened yesterday and what's going to happen today.**

Bring up any successes that happened since yesterday's standup meeting and make sure everyone knows what they're doing today.

- **Bring up any issues.** The standup meeting is not a place to be shy, so encourage everyone to bring up any problems they've encountered so that you all as a team can start to fix those problems.

- **Last between 5 and 15 minutes.** Keep things brief and focused on the short-term tasks at hand.

> **A daily standup meeting should keep everyone motivated, keep your board up-to-date, and highlight any problems <u>early</u>.**

Task 1: Create the Date class

Bob's been busy creating the classes that bring the "Create a Date" user story to life, but he needs a hand. Here's a UML class diagram that describes the design he's come up with so far.

A UML class diagram shows the classes in your software and how they relate to each other.

The Date class is split into three classes, one class for each type of date...

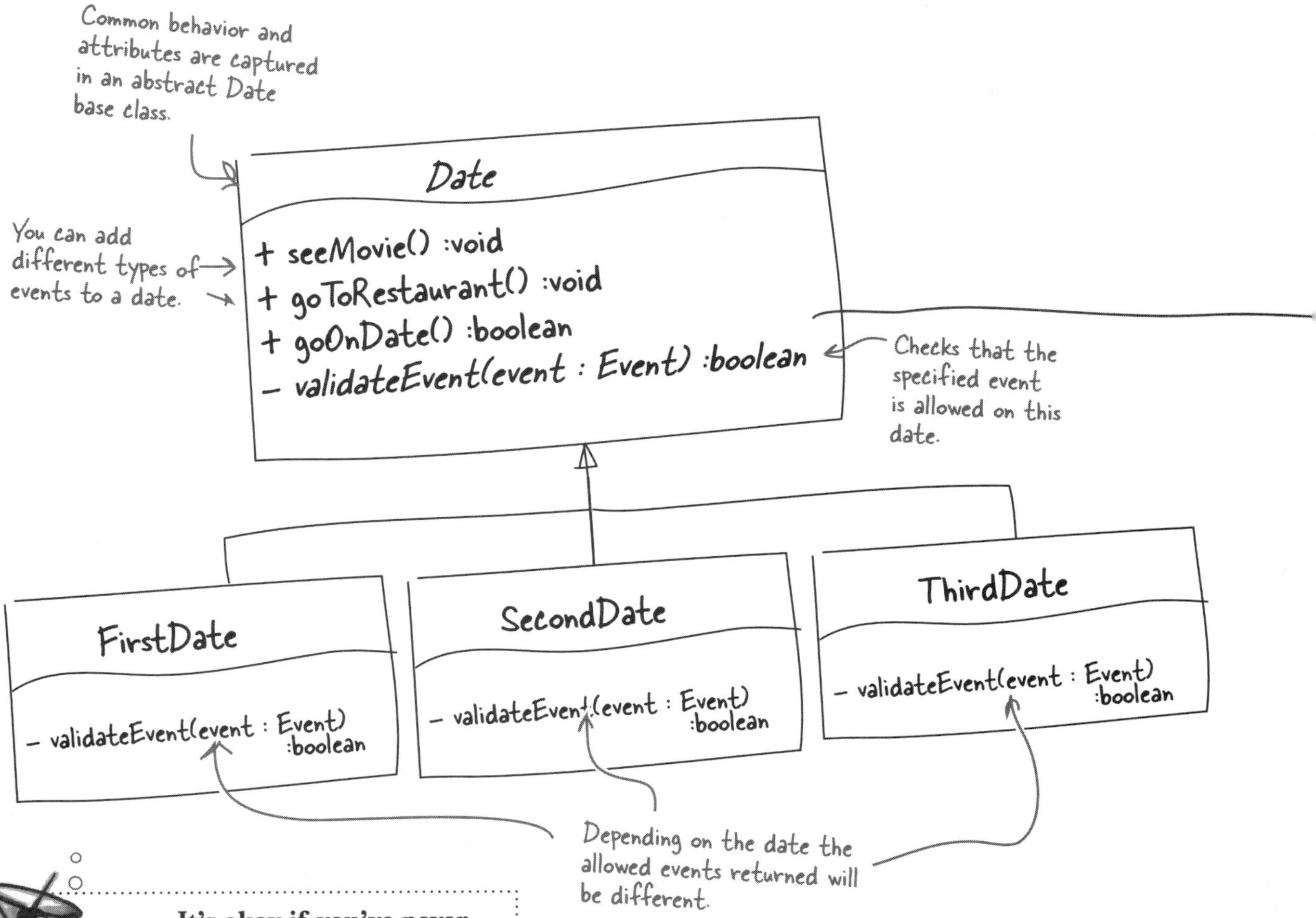

Common behavior and attributes are captured in an abstract Date base class.

You can add different types of events to a date.

Date

+ seeMovie() :void
+ goToRestaurant() :void
+ goOnDate() :boolean
− validateEvent(event : Event) :boolean

Checks that the specified event is allowed on this date.

FirstDate

− validateEvent(event : Event) :boolean

SecondDate

− validateEvent(event : Event) :boolean

ThirdDate

− validateEvent(event : Event) :boolean

Depending on the date the allowed events returned will be different.

Relax

It's okay if you've never seen UML before!

Don't worry if you don't know your UML class diagrams from your sequences; there's a short overview in Appendix i to help you get comfortable with UML notation as quickly as possible.

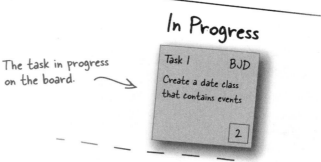

The task in progress on the board.

In Progress

Task 1   BJD

Create a date class that contains events

2

Each Date can then have a number of Events added to it...

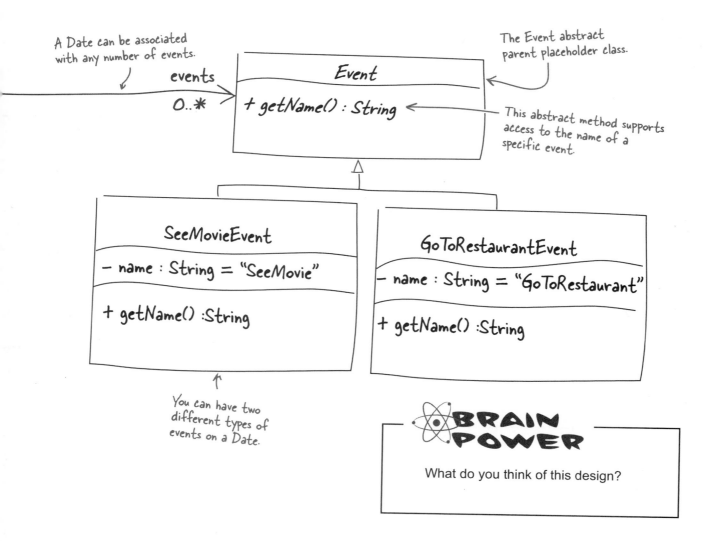

A Date can be associated with any number of events.

events

0..*

The Event abstract parent placeholder class.

Event

+ getName() : String

This abstract method supports access to the name of a specific event.

SeeMovieEvent

– name : String = "SeeMovie"

+ getName() :String

GoToRestaurantEvent

– name : String = "GoToRestaurant"

+ getName() :String

You can have two different types of events on a Date.

BRAIN POWER

What do you think of this design?

Task 1: Creating dates

Let's test out the Date and Event classes by bringing them to life on a sequence diagram. Finish the sequence diagram by adding the right method names to each interaction between objects so that you are creating and validating that a first date that has two events, going to a restaurant and seeing a movie.

A diagram that brings objects to life, showing how they work together to make an interaction happen

Exercise

The user begins the process by creating a new first date.

The first method calls are done for you.

Each arrow is a method call on the different objects involved in the interaction

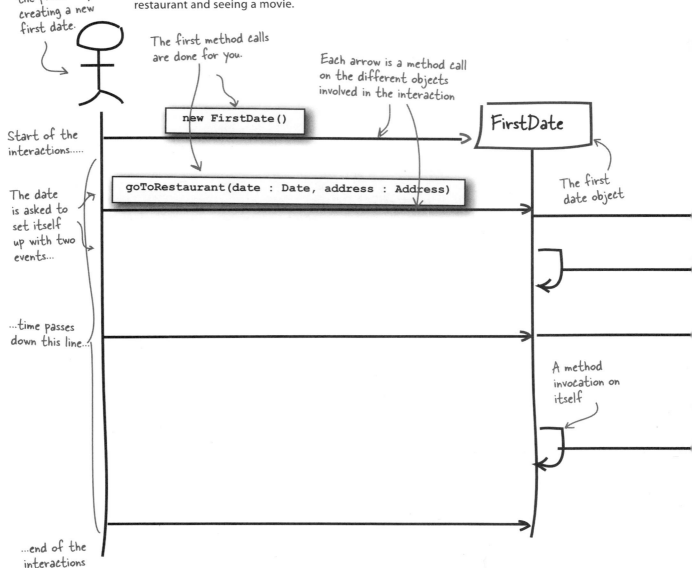

```
new FirstDate()
```

```
goToRestaurant(date : Date, address : Address)
```

FirstDate

Start of the interactions.....

The date is asked to set itself up with two events...

The first date object

...time passes down this line...

A method invocation on itself

...end of the interactions

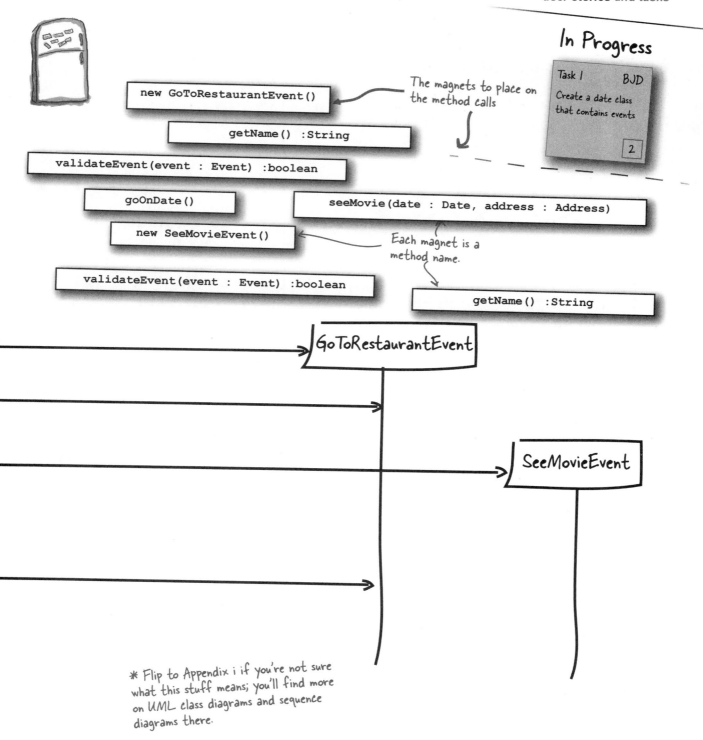

In Progress

Task I   BJD
Create a date class that contains events

2

new GoToRestaurantEvent()

The magnets to place on the method calls

getName() :String

validateEvent(event : Event) :boolean

goOnDate()

seeMovie(date : Date, address : Address)

new SeeMovieEvent()

Each magnet is a method name.

validateEvent(event : Event) :boolean

getName() :String

GoToRestaurantEvent

SeeMovieEvent

* Flip to Appendix i if you're not sure what this stuff means; you'll find more on UML class diagrams and sequence diagrams there.

Exercise
Solution

Your job was to test out the Date and Event classes by bringing them to life on a sequence diagram. You should have finished the sequence diagram so that you plan and go on a first date with two events, going to a restaurant and seeing a movie.

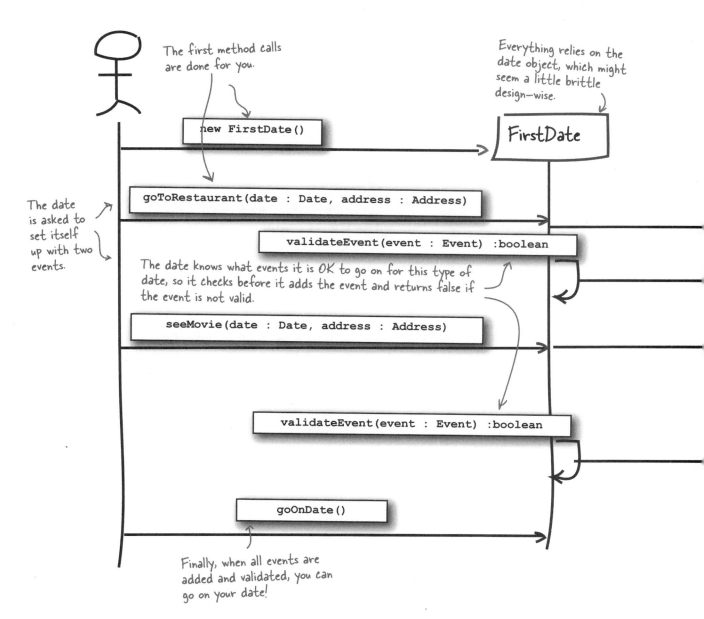

The first method calls are done for you.

Everything relies on the date object, which might seem a little brittle design-wise.

new FirstDate()

FirstDate

The date is asked to set itself up with two events.

goToRestaurant(date : Date, address : Address)

validateEvent(event : Event) :boolean

The date knows what events it is OK to go on for this type of date, so it checks before it adds the event and returns false if the event is not valid.

seeMovie(date : Date, address : Address)

validateEvent(event : Event) :boolean

goOnDate()

Finally, when all events are added and validated, you can go on your date!

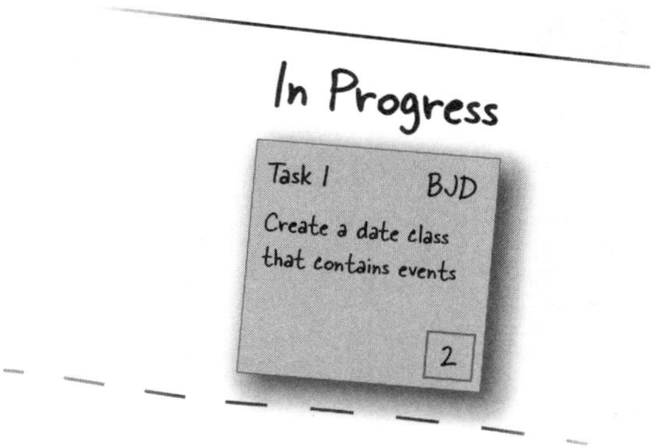

In Progress

Task 1   BJD

Create a date class
that contains events

2

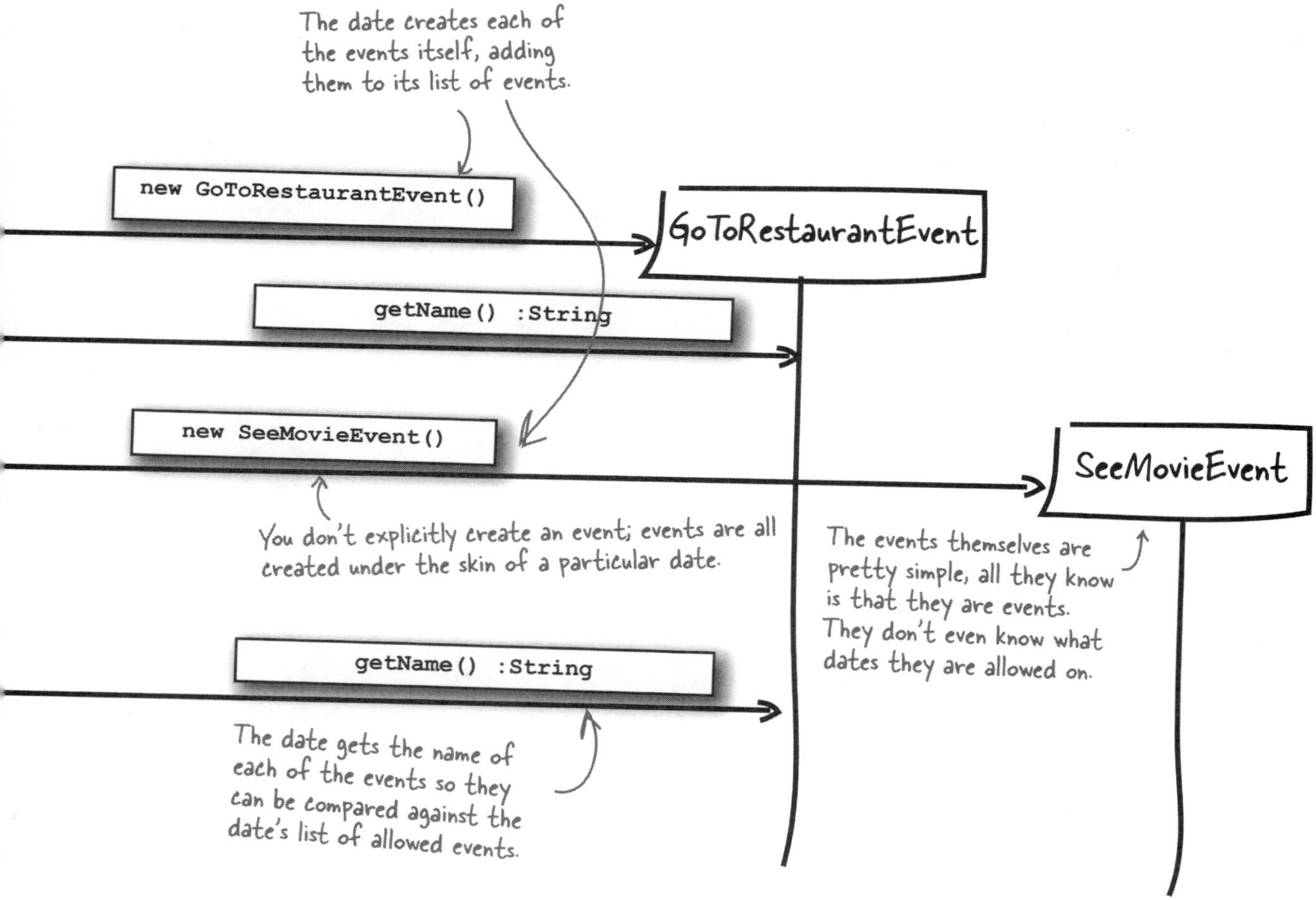

The date creates each of
the events itself, adding
them to its list of events.

`new GoToRestaurantEvent()`

GoToRestaurantEvent

`getName() :String`

`new SeeMovieEvent()`

SeeMovieEvent

You don't explicitly create an event; events are all
created under the skin of a particular date.

The events themselves are
pretty simple, all they know
is that they are events.
They don't even know what
dates they are allowed on.

`getName() :String`

The date gets the name of
each of the events so they
can be compared against the
date's list of allowed events.

Standup meeting: Day 5, end of Week 1...

So, one day left in the first week, how are we doing according to the big board?

Bob: Well, I finally got the date class finished with a little help, ran late by a day though...

Laura: That's OK, this time around. We can hopefully make some of that time up later.

Mark: All work on the database is now done; I'm all set for the next set of tasks.

Laura: Great, and I got my work done on the user interface pieces, so we've actually got something running.

Bob: Always a good week when you head out of the office with something working...

Laura: Absolutely. OK, it's time to update the board and our burn-down rate to get things set up for next week.

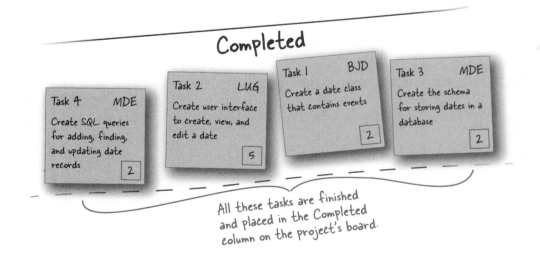

Completed

Task 4   MDE
Create SQL queries for adding, finding, and updating date records   2

Task 2   LUG
Create user interface to create, view, and edit a date   5

Task 1   BJD
Create a date class that contains events   2

Task 3   MDE
Create the schema for storing dates in a database   2

All these tasks are finished and placed in the Completed column on the project's board.

there are no
Dumb Questions

Q: Do I REALLY have to get everyone to stand up during a standup meeting?

A: No, not really. A standup meeting is called "standup" because it is meant to be a fast meeting that lasts a **maximum** of 15 minutes; you should ideally be aiming for 5 minutes.

We've all been stuck in endless meetings where nothing gets done, so the idea with a standup meeting is to keep things so short you don't even have time to find chairs. This keeps the focus and the momentum on only two agenda items:

• Are there any issues?

• Have we finished anything?

With these issues addressed, you can update your project board and get on with the actual development work.

Q: An issue has come up in my standup meeting that is going to take some discussion to resolve. Is it OK to lengthen the standup meeting to an hour to solve these bigger problems?

A: Always try to keep a standup meeting to less than 15 minutes. If an issue turns out to be something that requires further discussion, then schedule another meeting *specifically for that issue*. The standup meeting has highlighted the issue, and so it's done its job.

Q: Do standup meetings have to be daily?

A: It certainly helps to make your standup meetings daily. With the pace of modern software development, issues arise on almost a daily basis, so a quick 15 minutes with your team is essential to keeping your finger on the pulse of the project.

Q: Is it best to do a standup meeting in the morning or the afternoon?

A: Ideally, standup meetings should be first thing in the morning. The meeting sets everyone up for the day's tasks and gives you time to hit issues straight away.

Still, there may be situations when you can't all meet in the morning, especially if you have remote employees. In those cases, standup meetings should be conducted when the majority of your team begin their working day. This isn't ideal for everyone, but at least most people get the full benefit of early feedback from the meeting.

On rare occasions, you can split the standup meeting in two. You might do this if part of your team works in a completely different time zone. If you go with this approach, keeping your board updated is even more critical, as this is the place where everyone's status from the standup meeting is captured for all to see.

Standup meetings keep your peers, employees, and managers up to date, and keep your finger on the pulse of how your development work is going.

BULLET POINTS

■ Organize **daily standup meetings** to make sure you catch issues early.

■ Keep standup meetings **less than 15 minutes**.

■ A standup meeting is all about **progress, problematic issues**, and **updating your board**.

■ Try to schedule your standup meetings for the **morning** so that everyone knows where they are at the **beginning of the working day**.

LONG EXERCISE

It's the end of Week 1, and you and the team have just finished your standup meeting. It's time to update the project board. Take a look at the board below and write down what you think needs to be changed and updated on the board to get it ready for Week 2.

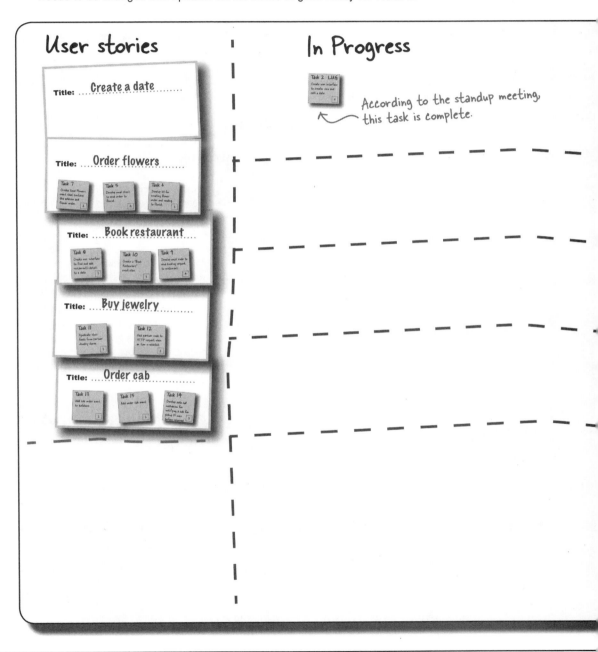

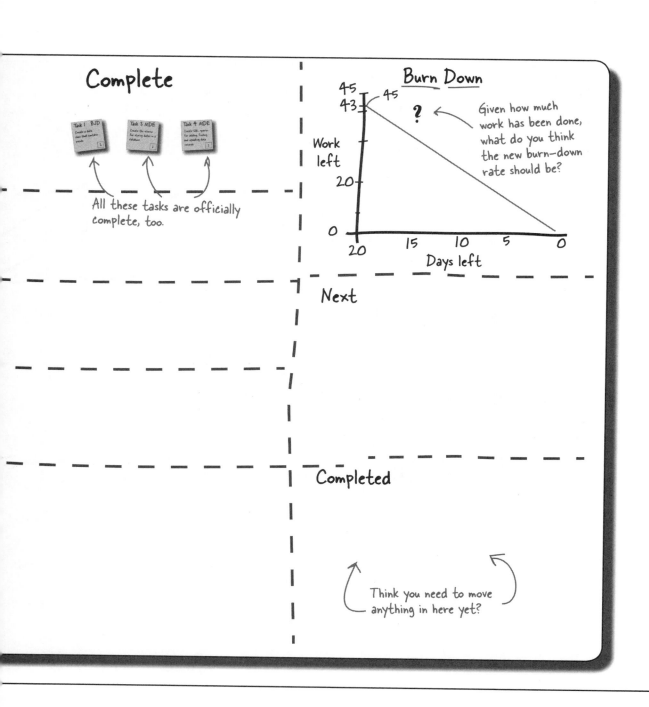

Complete

All these tasks are officially complete, too.

Burn Down

45
43
45

Work left

20

0

20   15   10   5   0

Days left

? ← Given how much work has been done, what do you think the new burn-down rate should be?

Next

Completed

Think you need to move anything in here yet?

Long Exercise Solution

You were asked to update the board and write down what you think needs to be changed to get it ready for Week 2.

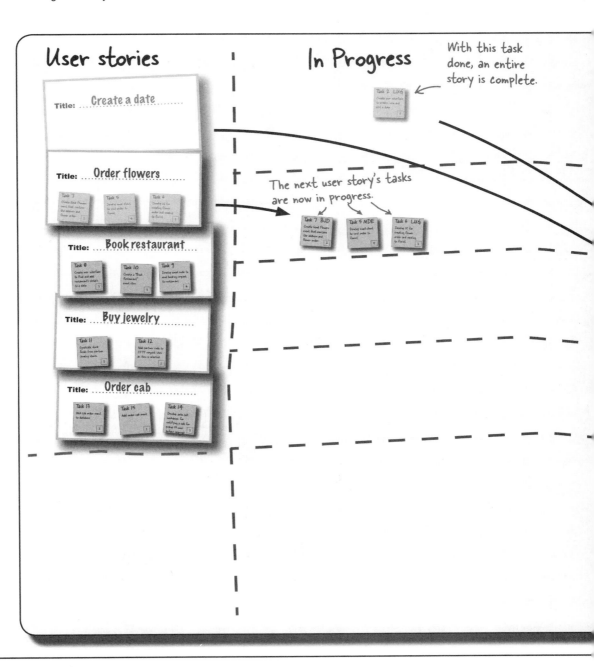

User stories

Title: .....Create a date.....

Title: .....Order flowers.....

Task 7   Task 5   Task 6

Title: .....Book restaurant.....

Task 8   Task 10   Task 9

Title: .....Buy jewelry.....

Task 11   Task 12

Title: .....Order cab.....

Task 13   Task 15   Task 14

In Progress

With this task done, an entire story is complete.

Task 2 LUG

The next user story's tasks are now in progress.

Task 7 BJD   Task 5 MDE   Task 6 LUG

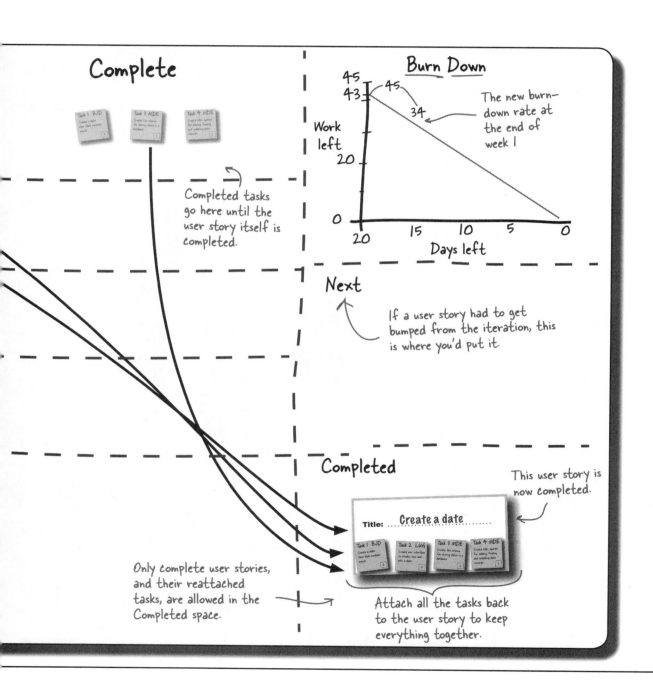

Complete

Completed tasks go here until the user story itself is completed.

Burn Down

45
43
45
34

The new burn-down rate at the end of week 1

Work left

20

0

20   15   10   5   0

Days left

Next

If a user story had to get bumped from the iteration, this is where you'd put it.

Completed

This user story is now completed.

Title: ....Create a date........

Only complete user stories, and their reattached tasks, are allowed in the Completed space.

Attach all the tasks back to the user story to keep everything together.

Standup meeting: Day 2, Week 2...

One of the In Progres tasks from the board.

In-Progress

Task 7   BJD

Create send flowers event that contains the address and flower order

3

> Hey guys, I've been busy working on my task and I noticed a way of saving us some time and effort by extending our design a little...

Laura's acting as the team lead, at least on this iteration.

Laura: How are you going to do that?

Bob: Well, if you treat someone ordering flowers as just another type of event, then we can add it straight into our current class tree, and that should save us some time in the long run.

Laura: That's sounds good. What do you think, Mark?

Mark: I don't see any problems right now...

Bob: Apart from it might take an extra day right now to make the changes, but in the long run this should save us some time.

Laura: Mmm. We're still a little behind, but we can probably lose a day on the burn-down rate now if it saves us time later on in the iteration. OK, I'm sold, let's go for it...

The change that Bob's suggesting

Event

+ *validate(Date) :boolean*

SeeMovie

+ validate(Date) :boolean

GoToRestaurant

+ validate(Date) :boolean

OrderFlowers

+ validate(Date) :boolean

It's okay to think about the big picture, even when you're working on granular tasks.

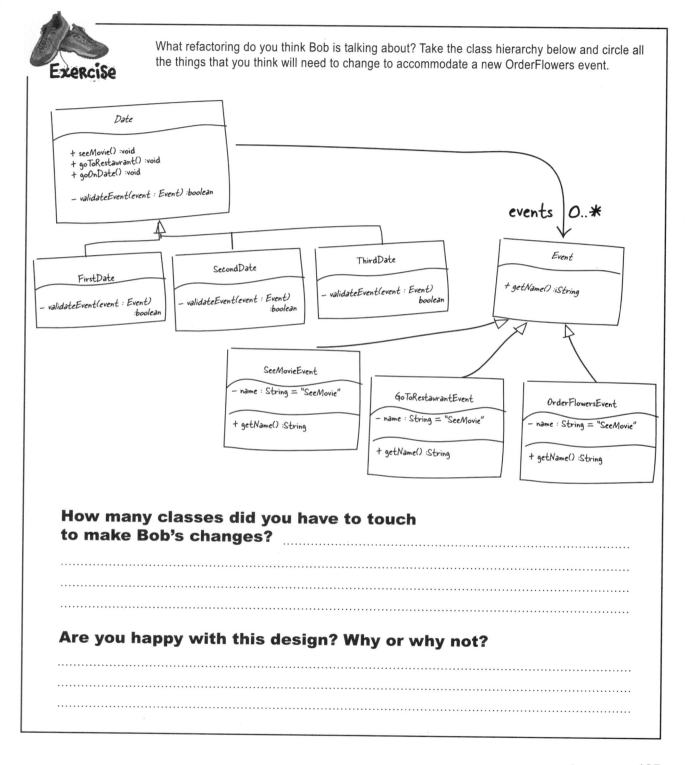

What refactoring do you think Bob is talking about? Take the class hierarchy below and circle all the things that you think will need to change to accommodate a new OrderFlowers event.

How many classes did you have to touch to make Bob's changes?

....

....

....

....

Are you happy with this design? Why or why not?

....

....

....

Exercise Solution

You were asked to take the class hierarchy below and circle all the places that you think will need to change to accommodate a new OrderFlowersEvent...

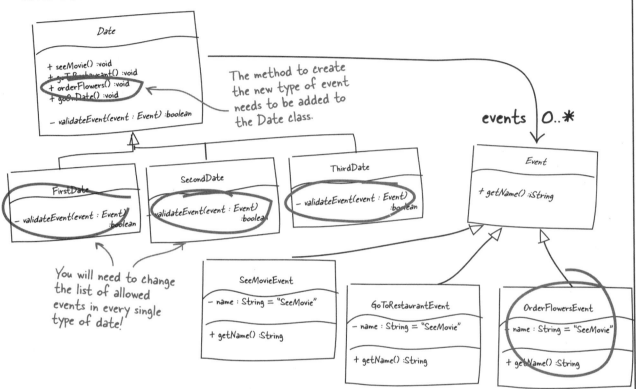

Date

+ seeMovie() :void
+ goToRestaurant() :void
+ orderFlowers() :void
+ goOnDate() :void

– validateEvent(event : Event) :boolean

The method to create the new type of event needs to be added to the Date class.

events 0..*

Event

+ getName() :String

FirstDate

– validateEvent(event : Event) :boolean

SecondDate

– validateEvent(event : Event) :boolean

ThirdDate

– validateEvent(event : Event) :boolean

You will need to change the list of allowed events in every single type of date!

SeeMovieEvent

– name : String = "SeeMovie"

+ getName() :String

GoToRestaurantEvent

– name : String = "SeeMovie"

+ getName() :String

OrderFlowersEvent

– name : String = "SeeMovie"

+ getName() :String

How many classes did you have to touch to make Bob's changes?

Five classes were changed or added to add just this one new type of event. First the "OrderFlowersEvent" class needed to be added, and then the method to order flowers on a date needed to be added to the Date class. Finally I had to update each of the different types of date to allow, or reject, the new type of event depending on whether it's allowed on that date or not

Are you happy with this design? Why or why not?

Five classes being changed seems like a LOT when all I'm adding is ONE new event. What happens when I have to add, say, a dozen new types of event; is it always going to involve this much work?

All done. It took a bit of work but we now have a Send Flowers event that you can add to a date.

Laura: Hey, isn't "Buy jewelry" coming down the line? That works as just another event, too, right?

Bob: Yeah, but we'll need to add some time to make those changes to all the classes again.

Mark: Can't we come up with a more flexible design, so we can avoid this pain and effort each time we add a new event?

Bob: That's exactly what I was thinking.

Laura: But that will take even more time, right? I guess we're invested, though, huh? This will save us time later, I hope...

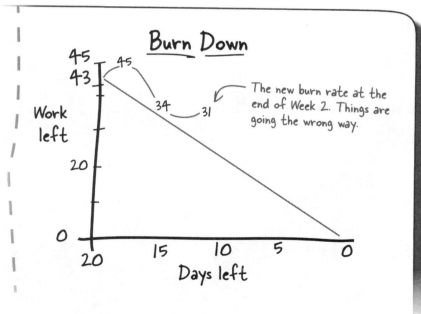

Burn Down

45
43
45
34
31

The new burn rate at the end of Week 2. Things are going the wrong way.

Work left

20

0

20   15   10   5   0

Days left

We interrupt this chapter...

You're already getting behind on your burn-down rate and then the inevitable happens: the customer calls with a last-minute request...

Hey! The CEO of Starbuzz just called, and he wants to see a demo of ordering coffee as part of a date. Can you show me that tomorrow?

Your customer, iSwoon's CEO

You <u>have</u> to track unplanned tasks

So far, your board has kept track of everything going on in your project. But what happens when somthing unplanned comes up? You have to track it, just like anything else. It affects your burn-down rate, the work you're doing on user stories, and more...

Let's take a look at a part of the board we haven't used yet:

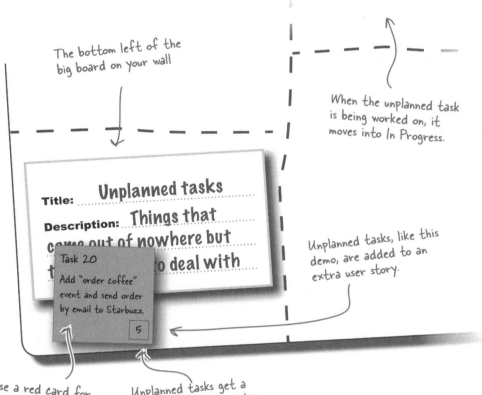

The bottom left of the big board on your wall

When the unplanned task is being worked on, it moves into In Progress.

Title: Unplanned tasks

Description: Things that come out of nowhere but that you have to deal with

Task 20
Add "order coffee" event and send order by email to Starbuzz

5

Unplanned tasks, like this demo, are added to an extra user story.

Use a red card for unplanned tasks, so you can tell them apart from regular planned tasks.

Unplanned tasks get a number and a description just like any other task.

An unplanned task is STILL a task. It has to be tracked, put in progress, completed, and included in the burn-down rate just like <u>EVERY OTHER TASK</u> you have.

> Wait a sec! You're saying we have to do the demo? What if it blows our deadlines?

Yes, you've heard it before, but talking to the customer is the answer to most scheduling- and deadline-related problems.

Talk to the customer

You've been hit by the unexpected, but that's part of software development. You can't do everything, but you also can't make the choice about what takes priority. Remember, **the customer sets priorities**, not you.

You need to deal with new tasks like customer demos, and the best way to do this is to ask the customer what takes priority. Give the customer a chance to make a considered decision by estimating the amount of work that the new task requires and explaining how that will affect the current schedule. Ultimately, the customer rules, so as long as they have all the information needed to make a choice, then you need to be prepared to go with their decision by reshuffling your existing tasks and user stories to make room for the surprise work.

Ultimately you need to keep your customer in the picture as to what is in and what is out. Adding new unplanned work is not the end of the world, but your customer needs to understand that the work has an impact, and then they can choose what that impact is.

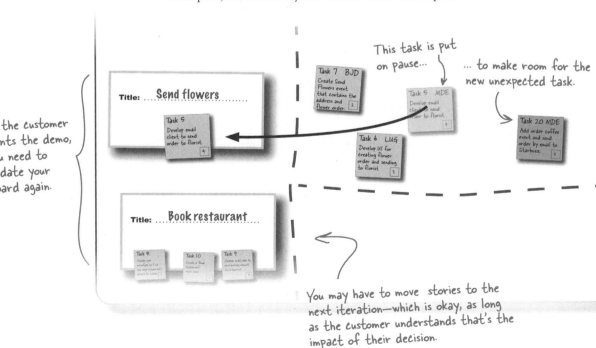

If the customer wants the demo, you need to update your board again.

This task is put on pause...

... to make room for the new unexpected task.

You may have to move stories to the next iteration—which is okay, as long as the customer understands that's the impact of their decision.

Unexpected tasks raise your burn-down rate

Unexpected task mean extra work. If the unexpected tasks can't be pushed into another iteration, then they need to be factored into your board. All of this means that your burn-down rate is affected, and not in a good way...

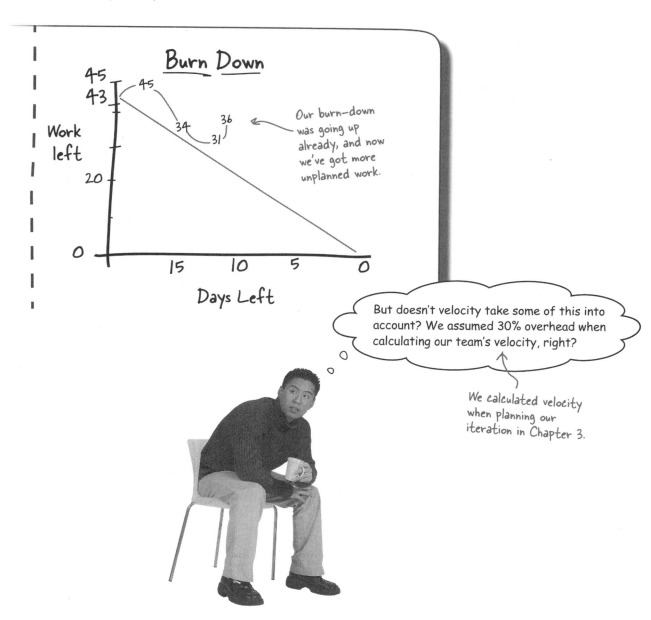

Burn Down

45
43

Work left

20

0

45

34
36
31

← Our burn-down was going up already, and now we've got more unplanned work.

15   10   5   0

Days Left

But doesn't velocity take some of this into account? We assumed 30% overhead when calculating our team's velocity, right?

↑ We calculated velocity when planning our iteration in Chapter 3.

Velocity helps, but...

You've got more work thanks to some unexpected requirements from your customer, but didn't you factor this in when you calculated your team's velocity? Unfortunately, velocity is there to help you gauge how fast your team performs, but it's not there to handle unplanned tasks.

We originally calculated velocity as...

$$3 \times 20 \times 0.7 = 42$$

Remember this equation from Chapter 3?

The number of people in your team

Your team's first pass velocity, which is actually a guess at this point

The amount of work in days that your team can handle in one iteration

So we have this much "float"...

$$3 \times 20 - 42 = 18$$

These are the possible days we could have, if everyone worked at 100% velocity...

... but it may not be enough!

Float—the "extra" days in your schedule—disappear quickly.

An employee's car breaks down, someone has to go to the dentist, your daily standup meetings...those "extra" days disappear quickly. And remember, *float is in work time, not actual time*. So if your company gives an extra Friday off for great work, that's *three* days of float lost because you are losing *three* developers for the whole day.

So when unplanned tasks come up, you may be able to absorb some of the extra time, but velocity won't take care of all of it.

> So what do we do? This is major panic time, right? We're going to miss our deadlines...

there are no
Dumb Questions

Q: You said to add unplanned tasks as red sticky notes. Do I have to use colored sticky notes? And why red?

A: We picked red because regular tasks are usually on regular yellow sticky notes, and because red stands out as a warning color. The idea is to quickly see what's part of your planned stories (the normal stickies), and what's unplanned (red). And red is a good "alert" color, since most unplanned tasks are high-priority (like that customer demo that came out of nowhere).

It's also important to know at the end of an iteration what you worked on. The red tasks make it easy to see what you dealt with that wasn't planned, so when you're recalculating velocity and seeing how good your estimates were, you know what was planned and what wasn't.

Q: So later on we're going to recalculate velocity?

A: Absolutely. Your team's velocity will be recalculated at the beginning of every single iteration. That way, you can get a realistic estimate of *your* team's productivity. 0.7 is just a good conservative place to start when you don't have any previous iterations to work from.

Q: So velocity is all about how me and my team performed in the last iteration?

A: Bingo. Velocity is a measure of how fast **you** and **your team** are working. The only way you can *reliably* come up with a figure for that is by looking at how well you performed in previous iterations.

Q: I really don't think 0.7 captures my team's velocity. Would it be OK to pick a faster or slower figure to start out with? Say 0.65, or 0.8?

A: You can pick a different starting velocity, but you have to stand by what you pick. If you know your team already at the beginning of a project, then it's perfectly alright to pick a velocity that matches your team's performance on other projects, although you should still factor in a slightly slower velocity at the beginning of any project. It always takes a little extra time to get your heads around what needs to be developed on a new project.

Remember, velocity is about how fast you and your team can comfortably work, for real. So you're aiming for a velocity that you believe in, and it's better to be slightly on the conservative side at the beginning of a new project, and then to refine that figure with hard data before each subsequent iteration.

Velocity is NOT a substitute for good estimation; it's a way of factoring in the <u>real-world</u> performance of you and your team.

We have a lot to do...

You're in a tough spot. Doing some refactoring work is going to cost you time now, but the hope is that it will save you time in the long run. In addition you have the new demo that you need to prepare for the iSwoon CEO....

The "surprise" work that's needed for the demo that the CEO of iSwoon is giving to the CEO of Starbuzz. Talk about pressure!

You've got more work to do...

> Task 19
>
> Refactor design to make it easier to add new types of event
>
> 3

The task that came out of Bob's refactoring suggestion

> Task 20
>
> Add "Order Coffee" event and order by email to Starbuzz
>
> 5

...and your burn-down rate is going in the wrong direction.

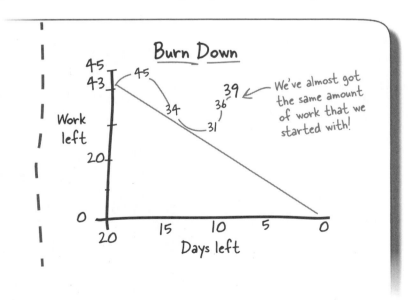

Burn Down

45
43
45
34
31
36
39

We've almost got the same amount of work that we started with!

Work left

20
0

20   15   10   5   0

Days left

...but we know <u>EXACTLY</u> where we stand

 The <u>customer</u> knows where you are

At every step you've kept the customer involved so they know exactly what work they've added, and you can show them exactly what the changes will impact.

 <u>YOU</u> know where you are

You and your development team are also on exactly the same page thanks to your board and the burn-down rate. This means that although things look a bit bleak, at least no one is burying their heads in the sand. The challenges are right there on your wall.

You know there are challenges, <u>NOW</u>.

Because you're monitoring your project using your board you know right now that there are challenges ahead if you're going to keep things on track. Compare this with the Big Bang "See you later, I'll deliver something in 3 months" approach from Chapter 1.

With the Big Bang approach, you didn't know you were in trouble until day 30, or even day 90! With your board and your burn-down rate you know immediately what you're facing, and that gives you the edge to make the calls to keep your development heading towards success.

Sometimes you'll hear this referred to as the <u>waterfall</u> approach

Successful software development is about <u>knowing</u> <u>where</u> <u>you</u> <u>are</u>.

With an understanding of your progress and challenges, you can keep your customer in the loop, and deliver software when it's needed.

All is far from lost! We'll tackle all these problems in Chapter 5, when we dig deeper into good class and application design, and handle the customer demo.

Velocity Exposed

This week's interview:
Keeping pace with Velocity

Head First: Welcome, Velocity, glad you could make time in your busy day to come talk with us.

Velocity: My pleasure, it's nice to be here.

Head First: So some would say that you have the potential to save a project that's in crisis, due perhaps to surprise changes or any of the other pieces of extra work that can hit a plan. What would you say to those people?

Velocity: Well, I'm really no superhero to be honest. I'm more of a safety net and confidence kinda guy.

Head First: What do you mean by "confidence"?

Velocity: I'm most useful when you're trying to come up with realistic plans, but not for dealing with the unexpected.

Head First: So you're really only useful at the beginning of a project?

Velocity: Well, I'm useful then, but at that point I'm usually just set to my default value of 0.7. My role gets much more interesting as you move from Iteration 1 to Iteration 2 and onwards.

Head First: And what do you offer for each iteration, confidence?

Velocity: Absolutely. As you move from one iteration to the next you can recalculate me to make sure that you can successfully complete the work you need to.

Head First: So you're more like a retrospective player?

Velocity: Exactly! I tell you how fast you were performing in the last iteration. You can then take that value and come up with a chunk of work in the next iteration that you can be much more confident that you can accomplish.

Head First: But when the unexpected comes along...

Velocity: Well, I can't really help too much with that, except that if you can increase your team's velocity, you might be able to fit in some more work. But that's a risky approach...

Head First: Risky because you really represent how fast your team works?

Velocity: That's exactly my point! I represent how fast your team works. If I say that you and your team, that's 3 developers total, can get 40 days of work done in an iteration, that's 20 work days long, that doesn't mean that there's 20 days there that you could possibly use if you just worked harder. Your team is always working as hard as they can, and I'm a measure of that. The danger is when people start using me as a pool of possible extra days of work...

Head First: So, if you could sum yourself up in one sentence, what would it be?

Velocity: I'm the guy that tells you how fast your team worked in the last iteration. I'm a measure of how you perform in reality, based on how you performed in the past, and I'm here to help you plan your iterations realistically.

Head First: Well, that's actually two sentences, but we'll let you get away with that. Thanks for making the time to come here today, Velocity.

Velocity: It's been a pleasure, nice to get some of these things off of my chest.

5 good-enough design

Getting it done with great design

Well, he's not really perfect, but he's here, and sometimes that's good enough...

Good design helps you deliver. In the last chapter things were looking pretty dire. A bad design was making life **hard for everyone**, and, to make matters worse, an unplanned task cropped up. In this chapter you'll see how to **refactor** your design so that you and your team can be **more productive**. You'll apply **principles of good design**, while at the same time be wary of striving for the promise of the **"*perfect design*."** Finally you'll **handle unplanned tasks** in exactly the same way you handle all the other work on your project using the big project board on your wall.

iSwoon is in serious trouble...

In the last chapter things were in pretty bad shape at iSwoon. You had some refactoring work to do to improve your design that was going to impact your deadlines, and the customer had piped in with a surprise task to develop a demonstration for the CEO of Starbuzz. All is not lost, however. First let's get the refactoring work done so that you can turn what looks like a slip into a way of speeding up your development work. The current design called for lots of changes just to add a new event:

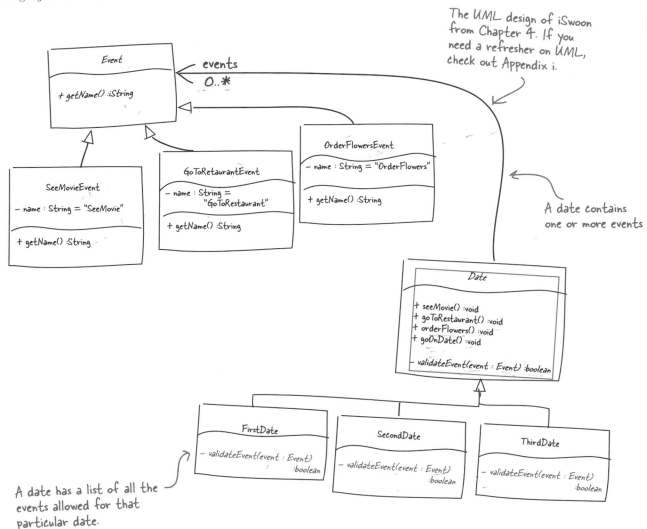

The UML design of iSwoon from Chapter 4. If you need a refresher on UML, check out Appendix i.

A date contains one or more events

A date has a list of all the events allowed for that particular date.

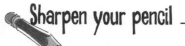

Sharpen your pencil

Write down the changes you think would be needed if...

What would you have to do to the software to implement these changes?

...you needed to add three new event types?

....
....
....
....
....
....

...you needed to add a new event type called "Sleeping over," but that event was only allowed on the third date?

....
....
....
....
....
....

The validateEvent( ) method will certainly come in handy here.

...you changed the value of the name attribute in the OrderFlowersEvent class to "SendFlowers"?

....
....
....
....
....
....

Sharpen your pencil
Solution

You were asked to write down the changes you think would be needed if...

...you needed to add three new event types?

We'd need a new event class for each of the new types. Three new methods, one for each type of event, would need to be added to the abstract parent Date class. Then, each of the date classes, however many there are, will need to be updated to allow (or disallow) the three new types of event, depending on if the event is allowed for that date.

...you needed to add a new event type called "Sleeping over," but that event was only allowed on the third date?

A new event class would be added, called something like "SleepingOverEvent." Then a new method called "sleepOver" needs to be added to the Date class so the new event can be added to a date. Finally, all three of the existing date classes would need to be updated in order to specify that only the third date allows a SleepingOverEvent to be specified.

...you changed the value of the name attribute in the OrderFlowersEvent class to "SendFlowers"?

All three of the different concrete classes of Date would need to be updated so that the logic that decides if a particular event is allowed now uses the new name in regards to the OrderFlowersEvent class's name attribute value change. Also, the value of OrderFlowerEvent's name will need to change from "OrderFlowers" to "SendFlowers," then finally the class name will need to be changed to SendFlowersEvent so it follows the naming convention we're currently using for date events.

> Wow, that's not good...a single change means we have to mess with a bunch of classes. Can't we do something about that in our design?

Well-designed classes are <u>singularly</u> <u>focused</u>.

The problem here is that for any particular behavior—like sending flowers—the logic for that behavior is spread out over a lot of different classes. So what seems like a simple change, like the name in `OrderFlowersEvent` being changed to "SendFlowers," turns into a multi-class mess of modifications.

This design breaks the <u>single responsibility principle</u>

iSwoon is such a headache to update because it breaks one of the fundamental principles of good object oriented design, the **single responsibility principle** (or **SRP** for short).

> ### Single responsibility principle
> *Every object in your system should have a **single responsibility**, and all the object's services should be focused on carrying out that single responsibility.*

Both the Date and Event class break the single responsibility principle

When a new type of event is added, the single responsibility principle states that all you should really need to do is add the new event class, and then you're done. However, with the current design, adding a new event also requires changes in the Date class *and* all of its subclasses.

You've implemented the single responsibility principle correctly when each of your objects has <u>only one reason</u> <u>to change.</u>

If you add a new event type, you have to add a method here...

```
           Date
─────────────────────────
 - allowedEvents : String[]
─────────────────────────
 + seeMovie() :void
 + goToRestaurant() :void
 + goOnDate() :boolean

 - validateEvent(event : Event)
                     :boolean
```

```
        FirstDate
─────────────────────────
 - validateEvent(event : Event)
                     :boolean
```

```
       SecondDate
─────────────────────────
 - validateEvent(event : Event)
                     :boolean
```

```
        ThirdDate
─────────────────────────
 - validateEvent(event : Event)
                     :boolean
```

...and then update each of these subclasses of Date to allow or disallow the new event type.

All these classes can change because their behavior changes, but also if other classes in the system change behavior.

⚙️ LONG EXERCISE

Your design at the moment makes it hard work to add events, change event names, and even deal with additional dates. Take a look at the current design and mark up what changes you'd make to apply the single responsibility principle to the iSwoon design (and in the process, make it easier to add new events and dates).

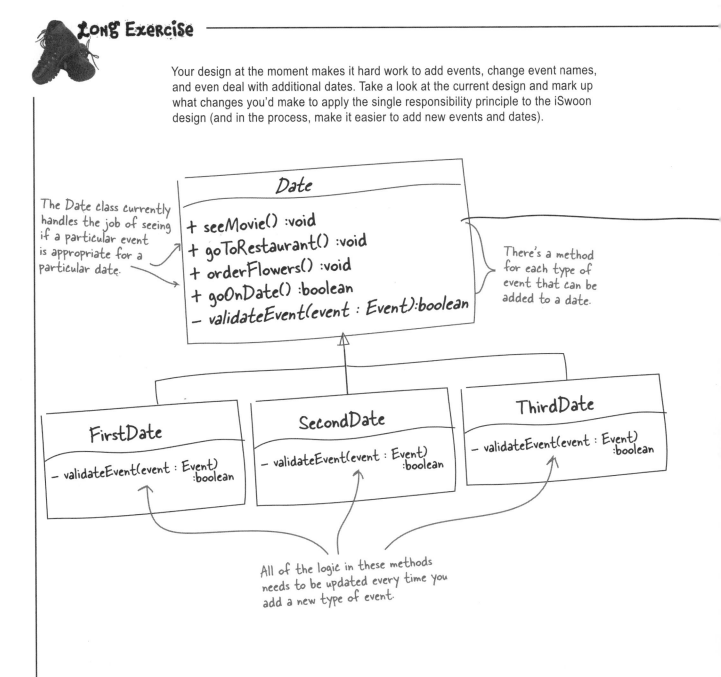

The Date class currently handles the job of seeing if a particular event is appropriate for a particular date.

Date

+ seeMovie() :void
+ goToRestaurant() :void
+ orderFlowers() :void
+ goOnDate() :boolean
− validateEvent(event : Event):boolean

There's a method for each type of event that can be added to a date.

FirstDate

− validateEvent(event : Event) :boolean

SecondDate

− validateEvent(event : Event) :boolean

ThirdDate

− validateEvent(event : Event) :boolean

All of the logic in these methods needs to be updated every time you add a new type of event.

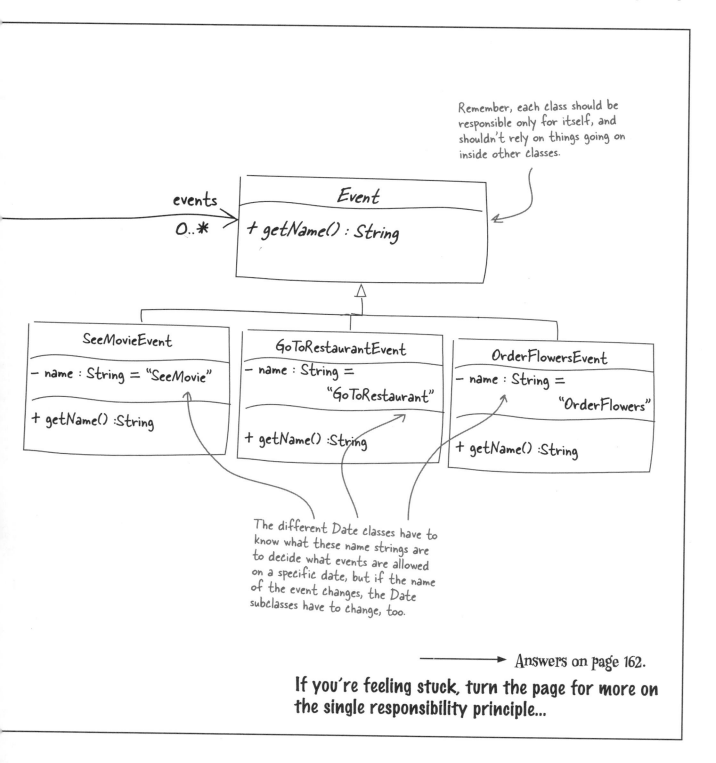

Remember, each class should be responsible only for itself, and shouldn't rely on things going on inside other classes.

events
0..*

Event

+ getName() : String

SeeMovieEvent

− name : String = "SeeMovie"

+ getName() :String

GoToRestaurantEvent

− name : String = "GoToRestaurant"

+ getName() :String

OrderFlowersEvent

− name : String = "OrderFlowers"

+ getName() :String

The different Date classes have to know what these name strings are to decide what events are allowed on a specific date, but if the name of the event changes, the Date subclasses have to change, too.

Answers on page 162.

If you're feeling stuck, turn the page for more on the single responsibility principle...

Spotting multiple responsibilies in your design

Most of the time, you can spot classes that aren't using the SRP
with a simple test:

1 On a sheet of paper, write down a bunch of lines like this: The [blank]
[blanks] itself. You should have a line like this for every method in the class
you're testing for the SRP.

2 In the first blank of each line, write down the class name. In the second
blank, write down one of the methods in the class. Do this for each
method in the class.

3 Read each line out loud (you may have to add a letter or word to get it to
read normally). Does what you just said make any sense? Does your class
really have the responsibility that the method indicates it does?

> **If what you've just said doesn't make sense,
> then you're probably violating the SRP with that
> method. The method might belong in a different
> class—think about moving the method.**

*Here's what your
SRP analysis sheet
should look like.*

SRP Analysis for _____

*Write the class name
in this blank, all the
way down the sheet.*

*Write each method
from the class in this
blank, one per line.*

The _____ _____ itself.

The _____ _____ itself.

The _____ _____ itself.

*Repeat this line for each
method in your class.*

Sharpen your pencil

Apply the SRP to the Automobile class.

Do an SRP analysis on the Automobile class shown below. Fill out the sheet with the class name methods in Automobile, like we've described on the last page. Then, decide if you think it makes sense for the Automobile class to have each method, and check the right box.

```
                    Automobile
─────────────────────────────────────────
+ start() :void
+ stop() :void
+ changeTires(tires : Tire[]) :void
+ drive() :void
+ wash() :void
+ checkOil() :void
+ getOil() :int
```

SRP Analysis for ___Automobile___

	Follows SRP	**Violates SRP**
The _____ _____ itself.	☐	☐
The _____ _____ itself.	☐	☐
The _____ _____ itself.	☐	☐
The _____ _____ itself.	☐	☐
The _____ _____ itself.	☐	☐
The _____ _____ itself.	☐	☐
The _____ _____ itself.	☐	☐

← If what you read doesn't make sense, then the method on that line is probably violating the SRP.

Sharpen your pencil
Solution

Apply the SRP to the Automobile class.

Your job was to do an SRP analysis on the Automobile class shown below. You should have filled out the sheet with the class name methods in Automobile, and decided if you think it makes sense for the Automobile class to have each method.

It makes sense that the automobile is responsible for starting and stopping. That's a function of the automobile.

An automobile is *NOT* responsible for changing its own tires, washing itself, or checking its own oil.

SRP Analysis for _Automobile_

You may have to add an "s" or a word or two to make the sentence readable.

The	_Automobile_	start[s]	itself.	Follows SRP ☑	Violates SRP ☐
The	_Automobile_	stop[s]	itself.	☑	☐
The	_Automobile_	changesTires	itself.	☐	☑
The	_Automobile_	drive[s]	itself.	☐	☑
The	_Automobile_	wash[es]	itself.	☐	☑
The	_Automobile_	check[s] oil	itself.	☐	☑
The	_Automobile_	get[s] oil	itself.	☑	☐

You should have thought carefully about this one, and what "get" means. This is a method that just returns the amount of oil in the automobile—and that is_something that the automobile should do.

This one was a little tricky—we thought that while an automobile might start and stop itself, it's really the responsibilty of a <u>driver</u> to drive the car.

Cases like this are why SRP analysis is just a <u>guideline</u>. You still are going to have to make some judgment calls using common sense and your own experience.

Going from multiple responsibilies to a single responsibility

Once you've done an analysis, you can take all the methods that don't make sense on a class, and move those methods to classes that do make sense for that particular responsibility.

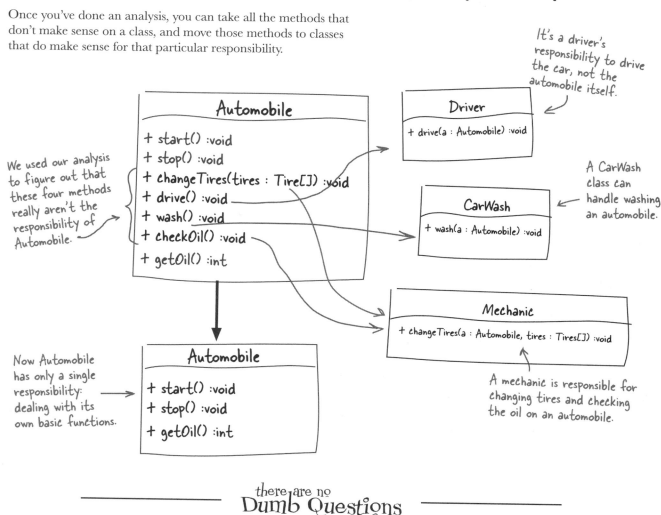

It's a driver's responsibility to drive the car, not the automobile itself.

We used our analysis to figure out that these four methods really aren't the responsibility of Automobile.

A CarWash class can handle washing an automobile.

Now Automobile has only a single responsibility: dealing with its own basic functions.

A mechanic is responsible for changing tires and checking the oil on an automobile.

there are no Dumb Questions

Q: How does SRP analysis work when a method takes parameters, like wash(Automobile) on the CarWash class?

A: Good question! For your SRP analysis to make any sense, you need to include the parameter of the method in the method blank. So you would write "The <u>CarWash</u> washes [an] automobile itself." That method makes sense (with the **Automobile** parameter), so it would stay on the **CarWash** class.

Q: But what if CarWash took in an Automobile parameter as part of its constructor, and the method was just wash()? Wouldn't SRP analysis give you a wrong result?

A: It would. If a parameter that might cause a method to make sense, like an **Automobile** for the **wash()** method on **CarWash**, is passed into a class's constructor, your SRP analysis might be misleading. But that's why you always need to apply a good amount of your own common sense and knowledge of the system in addition to what you learn from the SRP analysis.

Your design should obey the SRP, but also be <u>DRY</u>...

The SRP is all about responsibility, and which objects in your system do what. You want each object that you design to have **just one responsibility** to focus on—and when something about that responsibility changes, you'll know exactly where to look to make those changes in your code. Most importantly you'll avoid what's called the **ripple effect**, where one small change to your software can cause a ripple of changes throughout your code.

But there's a principle that goes hand in hand with SRP, and that's DRY:

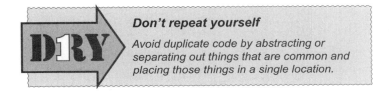

Don't repeat yourself

Avoid duplicate code by abstracting or separating out things that are common and placing those things in a single location.

The different Date classes are not DRY

Each of the different `Date` classes (`FirstDate`, `SecondDate`, `ThirdDate`) have almost identical behavior in their `validateEvent()` methods. This not only breaks the SRP, but means that one change in logic—like specifying that you can actually Sleep Over on the second date—would result in changes to the logic in all three classes.

This quickly turns into a maintenance nightmare.

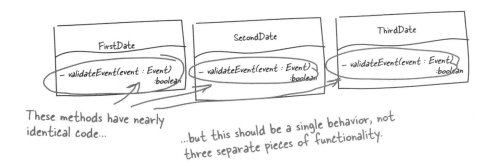

These methods have nearly identical code...

...but this should be a single behavior, not three separate pieces of functionality.

DRY is about having each piece of information and behavior in your system in a <u>single</u>, <u>sensible</u> place.

there are no
Dumb Questions

Q: SRP sounded a lot like DRY to me. Aren't both about a single class doing the one thing it's supposed to do?

A: They are related, and often appear together. DRY is about putting a piece of functionality in a single place, such as a class; SRP is about making sure that a class does only one thing, and that it does that one thing well. In well-designed applications, one class does one thing, and does it well, and no other classes share that behavior.

Q: Isn't having each class do only one thing kind of limiting?

A: It's not, when you realize that the one thing a class does can be a pretty *big* thing. For example, the `Event` class in iSwoon and its subclasses only store and manage one thing, the details of the specific event. Currently those details are only the name of the event, but those classes could store any of a host of details about an event, such as times, dates, notifications and alarms, even addresses. However all this extra information is still only about *one thing*, describing an event. The different `Event` classes do that one thing, and that's all they do, so they are great examples of the SRP.

Q: And using SRP will help my classes stay smaller, since they're only doing one thing, right?

A: Actually, the SRP will often make your classes bigger. Since you're not spreading out functionality over a lot of classes—which is what many programmers not familiar with the SRP will do—you're often putting more things into a class.

But using the SRP will usually result in fewer classes, and that generally makes your overall application a lot simpler to manage and maintain.

Q: I've heard of something called cohesion that sounds a lot like this. Are cohesion and the SRP the same thing?

A: Cohesion is actually just another name for the SRP. If you're writing **highly cohesive software**, then you're correctly applying the SRP. In the current iSwoon design, a `Date` does two things: it creates events *and* it stores the events that are happening on that specific date. When a class is cohesive, it has **one** main job. So in the case of the `Date` class, it makes more sense for the class to focus on storing events, and give up the responsibility for actually creating the events.

Want to know more about design principles? Check out Head First Object-Oriented Analysis and Design.

You've been loaded up with hints on how to make the iSwoon design, now make sure you've worked through and solved the exercise on pages 154 and 155 before turning the page...

For extra points, try to apply DRY as well as SRP to come up with a really great design.

Long Exercise Solution

You were asked to take a look at the current design and mark up what changes you'd make to apply the single responsibility principle to the iSwoon design to make it a breeze to update your software.

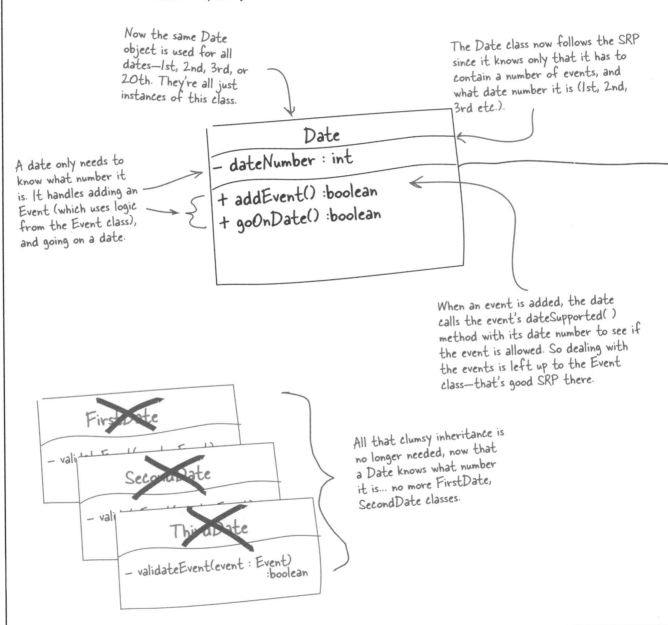

Now the same Date object is used for all dates—1st, 2nd, 3rd, or 20th. They're all just instances of this class.

The Date class now follows the SRP since it knows only that it has to contain a number of events, and what date number it is (1st, 2nd, 3rd etc.).

A date only needs to know what number it is. It handles adding an Event (which uses logic from the Event class), and going on a date.

Date

- dateNumber : int

+ addEvent() : boolean
+ goOnDate() : boolean

When an event is added, the date calls the event's dateSupported() method with its date number to see if the event is allowed. So dealing with the events is left up to the Event class—that's good SRP there.

~~FirstDate~~
~~- validateEvent(...)~~

~~SecondDate~~
~~- vali...~~

~~ThirdDate~~
~~- validateEvent(event : Event) : boolean~~

All that clumsy inheritance is no longer needed, now that a Date knows what number it is... no more FirstDate, SecondDate classes.

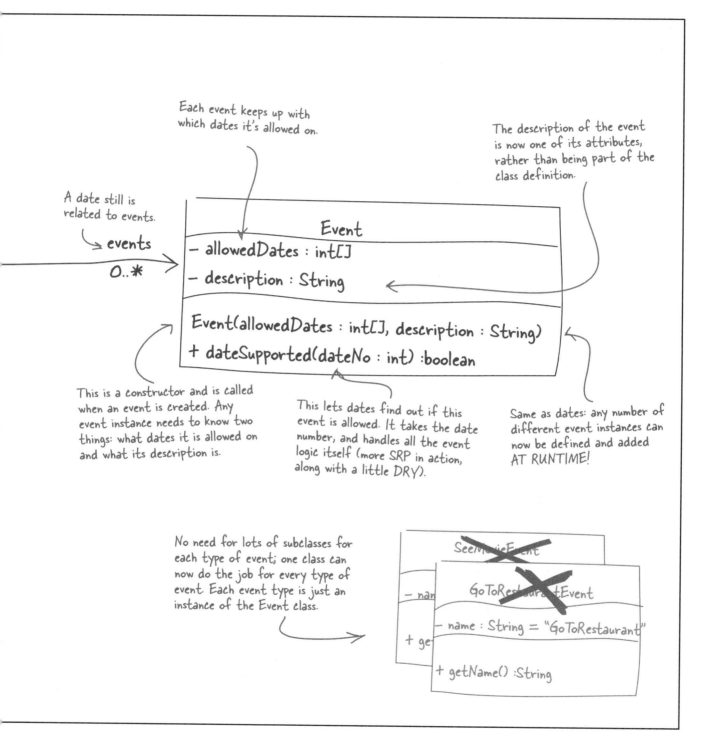

Each event keeps up with which dates it's allowed on.

The description of the event is now one of its attributes, rather than being part of the class definition.

A date still is related to events.

events
0..*

Event

− allowedDates : int[]

− description : String

Event(allowedDates : int[], description : String)

+ dateSupported(dateNo : int) :boolean

This is a constructor and is called when an event is created. Any event instance needs to know two things: what dates it is allowed on and what its description is.

This lets dates find out if this event is allowed. It takes the date number, and handles all the event logic itself (more SRP in action, along with a little DRY).

Same as dates: any number of different event instances can now be defined and added AT RUNTIME!

No need for lots of subclasses for each type of event; one class can now do the job for every type of event. Each event type is just an instance of the Event class.

SeeMovieEvent

GoToRestaurantEvent

− nam

+ ge

− name : String = "GoToRestaurant"

+ getName() :String

The post-refactoring standup meeting...

So, it's halfway through Week 3, how are we doing?

Bob: Got it all done, we now have a really flexible piece of software that can support any number of different types of dates and events.

Laura: That's great! Sounds like the extra work might pay off for us; we've got a ton of new events to add...

Bob: Oh, it will. Now we can just write one or two lines of code, and, boom, the new event is in the system. We allowed between two and five days for each event, and now it only takes a day, at most.

Mark: You're not kidding. I've already added all the new events. And I'm sure we could make some more improvements as well...

Laura: Wait, just hang on a sec. For now the software is *more* than good enough, actually. Let's not starting making more changes just because we can.

Mark: So what's next?

Bob: Well, now that I've got the refactoring done, it looks like we have some time to focus on the demo that the Starbuzz CEO wanted...

there are no
Dumb Questions

Q: When Laura says that the code is good enough, what does she mean?

A: Good question! We'll talk a lot more about testing in Chapters 7 and 8 and how you can be confident, and prove that your code does what it should.

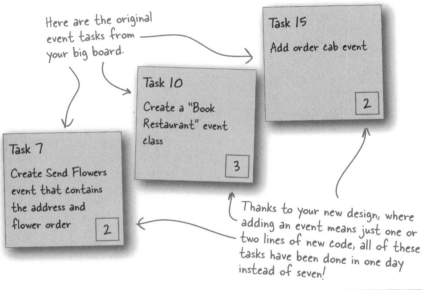

Here are the original event tasks from your big board.

Task 15

Add order cab event

2

Task 10

Create a "Book Restaurant" event class

3

Task 7

Create Send Flowers event that contains the address and flower order

2

Thanks to your new design, where adding an event means just one or two lines of new code, all of these tasks have been done in one day instead of seven!

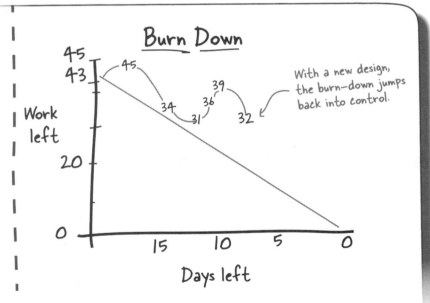

Burn Down

Work left

45
43
45
34
31
36
39
32

20

0

With a new design, the burn-down jumps back into control.

15   10   5   0

Days left

A great design helps you be more PRODUCTIVE as well as making your software more FLEXIBLE.

Unplanned tasks are still just tasks

The Starbuzz CEO's demo is an unplanned task, but you deal with it just like all the other tasks on your board. You estimate it, move it to the In Progress section of your board, and then go to work.

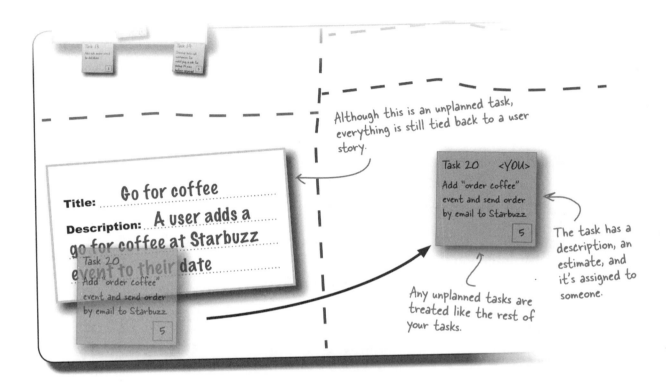

Although this is an unplanned task, everything is still tied back to a user story.

Task 20   <YOU>
Add "order coffee" event and send order by email to Starbuzz
5

The task has a description, an estimate, and it's assigned to someone.

Title: Go for coffee

Description: A user adds a go for coffee at Starbuzz event to their date

Task 20
Add "order coffee" event and send order by email to Starbuzz
5

Any unplanned tasks are treated like the rest of your tasks.

Unplanned tasks *on the board* become <u>planned</u>.

An unplanned task may start out differently, but once it goes on your board, it's treated just like all your planned tasks. In fact, as soon as you assign the task and give it an estimate, it really isn't unplanned anymore. It's just another task that has to be handled, along with everything else in your project.

And that's how you handle a task that starts out unplanned from its inception to completion: just like any other task. You estimate it, move it to the In Progress section of your board, and work it until it's done. Then you move it into the Completed section and move on.

> It doesn't matter how a task starts out. Once it's on your board, it's got to be <u>assigned</u>, <u>estimated</u>, and <u>worked</u> on until it's complete.

Part of your task is the demo itself

In addition to the time you'd spend working on the demo, you've got to think about time spent actually **doing** the demo. If you and your lead web programmer both spend a day traveling to Starbuzz and showing off iSwoon, that's got to be part of your task estimate.

 ## Your estimates should be <u>complete</u>

When you're estimating your tasks, you should come up with the time it takes to complete the task—and sometimes that involves more than just code. If you've got to demo the code or meet with a stakeholder, include time for those activities, too.

Task 20   <YOU>

Add "order coffee" event and send order by email to Starbuzz

5

Four days to do the development, and another day for the actual demo and to field follow-up questions

Nice...can you email me the minimum system requirements? And does it work on Safari and Firefox, too? I want to start spreading the word to our customers right away.

Look! More unplanned tasks.

The Starbuzz CEO, now a happy iSwoon partner

Fireside Chats

Tonight's talk: **A sit-down discussion between Perfect Design and "Good Enough" Design.**

"Good Enough" Design

Hi! So you're a Perfect Design? Man, I've always dreamed about meeting you!

Why's that?

Yeah, I suppose so. As long as I help everyone be productive and meet their deadlines, and the customer is getting the software they need, then I'm doing my job.

Huh, I never thought of it like that. I thought when you came along everyone would be all hugs and kisses...

What do you mean? After all that hard work your team might still be able to make you even more, err...perfect?

Perfect Design:

Thanks. Designs like me are pretty rare. In fact I may be the only one you'll ever meet.

Well, the problem is that it's really hard to come up with a design that everyone thinks is perfect. There's always somebody out to get me with their criticisms. And with refactoring, I keep getting changed. But you're pretty valuable yourself, you know...

You see, that's the thing. People spend so much time on me that they never meet their deadlines, they never deliver software, and they never get paid. That can make me pretty unpopular. It kind of sucks, really.

Not at all. Usually by the time I show up, the team is running late and I can't help out anywhere near as much as as they thought. And then there's always the danger that I'm not completely perfect...

Unfortunately, yes. You see, perfection is a bit of a moving target. Sometimes, I just wish I could be like you and actually deliver. Maybe not great, but—

"Good Enough" Design:

Hey, wait a second. That sounded pretty condescending.

Yeah, I suppose everyone is pretty stoked when I help them get great software out of the door. But I always figured that I was second class somehow and that they loved you...

So really what you're saying is that you'd like to be a design for software that actually got delivered?

So, I guess I'm good enough to get the job done, to meet the customer's needs, and to be easy enough to work with that my developers can develop code on time. That's what really matters.

Perfect Design:

Well, sure. Everyone ships you out because you draw a line in the sand and say you're finished when the customer gets what they want. So even though you're not perfect you deliver. And a developer who delivers great software, whether it's designed perfectly or not, is a happy developer.

If by love, you mean "never have time for," then you're right.

Exactly! I aspire to be you, in many respects. People *want* to meet their deadlines and to ship software that the customer will sign off on. That's not settling; that's just being good developers and getting paid. You know developers, right, those guys that get paid for delivering? Well, I'm not in their good graces when they've come up with me and no software to actually ship...

Yep, don't ever put yourself down. In this world it's nice to be perfect, but it's better to be ready and shipping.

When everything's complete, the iteration's done

Once you finish all your tasks, including any unplanned demos for forward-looking coffee addicts, you should end up with all your user stories, and the tasks that make them up, in your completed area of the board. And when you've got that, you're finished! There's nothing magical about it: when the work is done, so is your iteration.

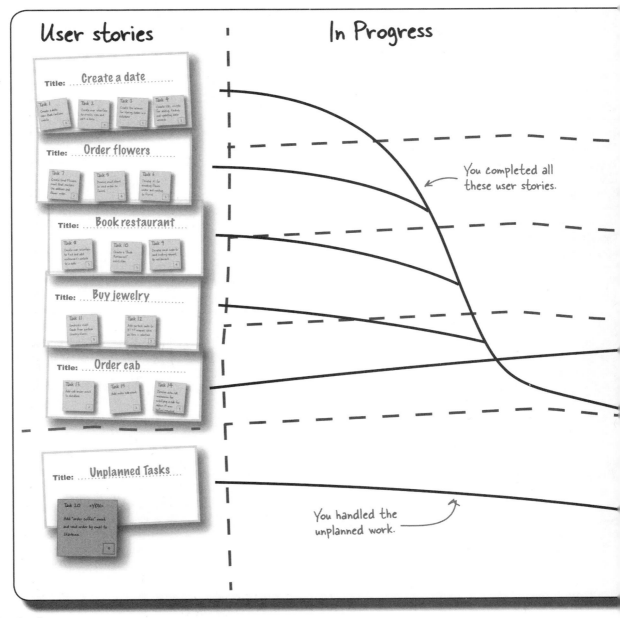

You completed all these user stories.

You handled the unplanned work.

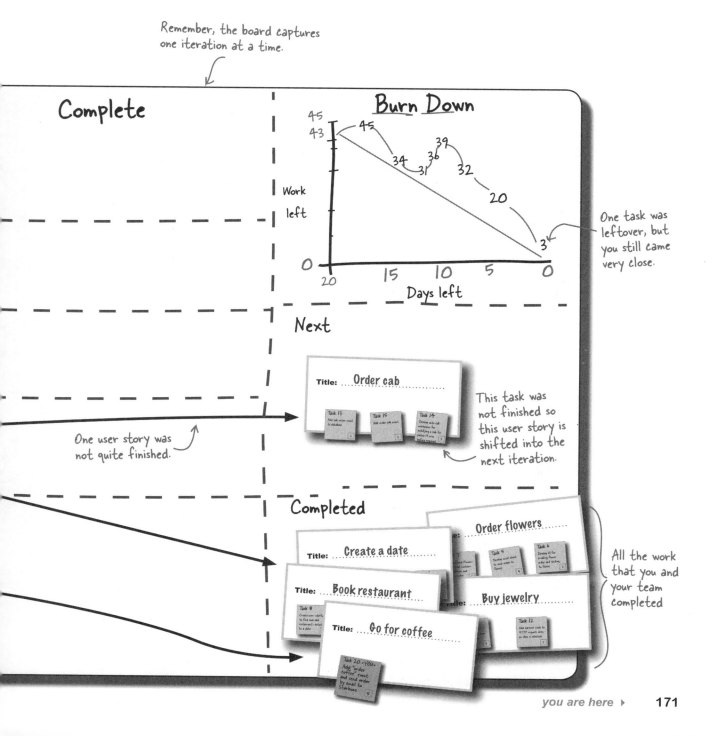

Remember, the board captures one iteration at a time.

Complete

Burn Down

Work left

One task was leftover, but you still came very close.

Days left

Next

Title: Order cab

Task 13 — Add cab order event to database

Task 15 — Add order cab event

Task 14 — Develop into call notification for notifying a cab for pickup 15 min before restaurant

This task was not finished so this user story is shifted into the next iteration.

One user story was not quite finished.

Completed

Title: Create a date

Title: Order flowers

Title: Book restaurant

Title: Buy jewelry

Title: Go for coffee

All the work that you and your team completed

WHAT'S MY PURPOSE?

Take each of the following techniques and artifacts from this chapter
and match it to what it does.

Unplanned tasks and user stories ⟨7⟩

    I help you make sure that everything
has its place, and that place is only
one place.

Perfect design ⟨6⟩

    With me, the design gets better with
small improvements throughout your
code.

SRP ⟨5⟩

    I make sure that the unexpected
becomes the expected and managed.

Refactoring ⟨2⟩

    My mantra is, "Perfect is great, but I
deliver."

DRY ⟨1⟩

    I make sure that all the parts of your
software have one well-defined job.

Good-enough design ⟨4⟩

    I'm what you strive for, but ultimately
you might not deliver.

Software Development Design Cross

Let's put what you've learned to use and stretch out your left brain a bit!
All of the words below are somewhere in this chapter. Good luck!

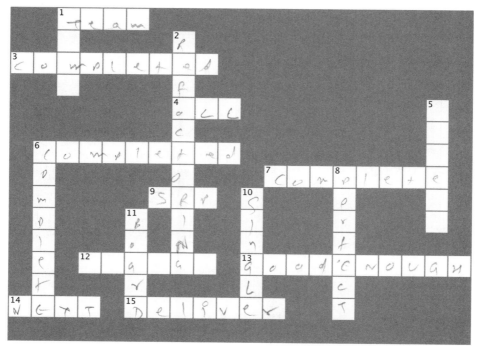

Across

1. Great developers ....
3. When an unplanned task is finished it is moved into the .... column.
4. Your burn down rate should show .... the work on your board, including any new unplanned tasks.
6. When a task is finished it goes in the .... column.
7. An unplanned user story and its tasks are moved into the .... bin on your project board when they are all finished.
9. If you find you are cutting and pasting large blocks of your design and code then there's a good chance that you're breaking the .... principle.
12. .... is the only constant in software development.
13. When a design helps you meet your deadlines, it is said to be a .... design.
14. If a user story is not quite finished at the end of an iteration, it is moved to the .... bin on your project board.
15. A good enough design helps you ....

Down

1. Unplanned tasks are treated the .... as unplanned tasks once they are on your board.
2. When you improve a design to make it more flexible and easier to maintain you are .... the design.
5. You should always be .... with your customer.
6. When all the tasks in a user story are finished, the user story is transferred to the .... bin
8. Striving for a .... design can mean that you never actually cut any code.
10. When a class does one job and it's the only class that does that job it is said to obey the .... responsibility principle.
11. An unplanned task is going to happen in your current iteration once you have added it to your ....

SOLUTION

Take each of the following techniques and artifacts from this chapter
and match it to what it does.

Unplanned tasks and user stories

Perfect design

SRP

Refactoring

DRY

Good-enough design

I help you make sure that everything has its place, and that place is only **one** place.

With me, the design gets better with small improvements throughout your code.

I make sure that the unexpected becomes the expected and managed.

My mantra is, "Perfect is great, but I deliver."

I make sure that all the parts of your software have one well-defined job.

I'm what you strive for, but ultimately you might not deliver.

Software Development Design Cross Solution

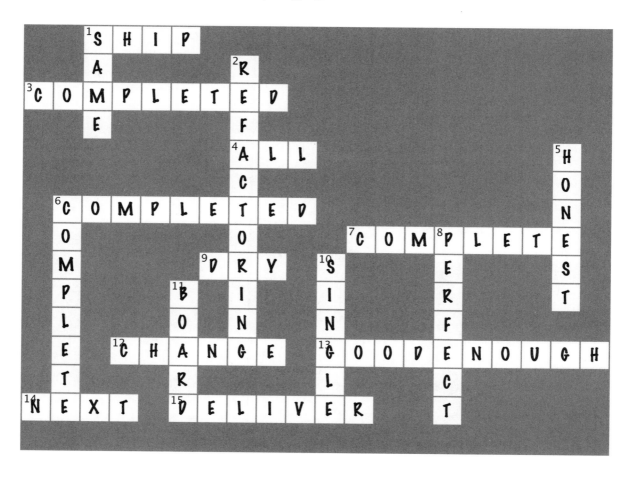

6 version control

Defensive development

Alright guys, listen up. Bob's writing new code. You've got to keep him safe, no matter what happens, understand?

When it comes to writing great software, *Safety First!*

Writing great software isn't easy...especially when you've got to make sure your code works, and **make sure it keeps working**. All it takes is one typo, one bad decision from a co-worker, one crashed hard drive, and suddenly all your work goes down the drain. But with **version control**, you can make sure your **code is always safe** in a code repository, you can **undo mistakes**, and you can make **bug fixes**—to new and old versions of your software.

You've got a new contract—BeatBox Pro

Congratulations—you've been getting rave reviews from iSwoon, and you've landed a new contract. You've been hired to add two new features to the legendary *Head First Java* BeatBox project. BeatBox is a multi-player drum machine that lets you send messages and drum loops to other users over the network.

Like every other software development project out there, the customer wants things done as soon as possible. They even let you bring along Bob, one of your junior developers, to help out. Since the stories aren't big enough to have more than one person work on them at a time, you'll work on one and Bob will work on the other. Here are the user stories for the new features you've got to add:

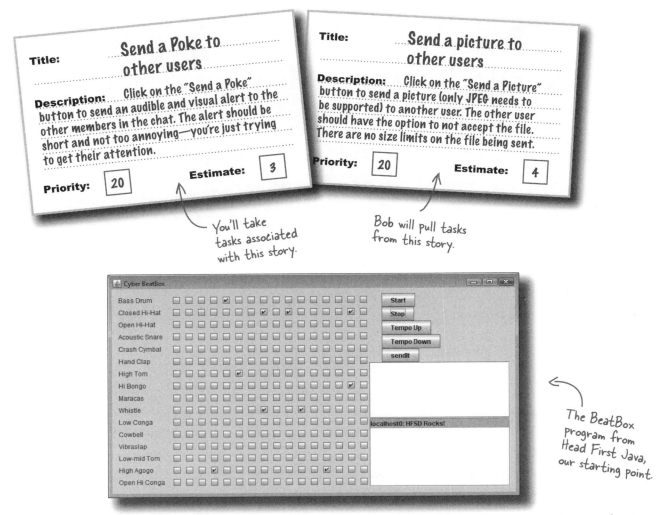

Title: Send a Poke to other users

Description: Click on the "Send a Poke" button to send an audible and visual alert to the other members in the chat. The alert should be short and not too annoying—you're just trying to get their attention.

Priority: 20   **Estimate:** 3

You'll take tasks associated with this story.

Title: Send a picture to other users

Description: Click on the "Send a Picture" button to send a picture (only JPEG needs to be supported) to another user. The other user should have the option to not accept the file. There are no size limits on the file being sent.

Priority: 20   **Estimate:** 4

Bob will pull tasks from this story.

The BeatBox program from *Head First Java*, our starting point.

*You can download the code that we're starting with from http://www.headfirstlabs.com/books/hfsd/

Task Stickies ~~Magnets~~

Let's get right to the new features. Here's a snippet from the
BeatBox client code. Your job is to map the task stickies to the
code that implements each part of the "Send a Poke..." story. We'll
get to the GUI work in a minute.

```java
// ... more BeatBox.java code above this

public class RemoteReader implements Runnable {
  boolean[] checkboxState = null;
  String nameToShow = null;
  Object obj = null;

  public void run() {
    try {
      while((obj=in.readObject()) != null) {
        System.out.println("got an object from server");
        System.out.println(obj.getClass());
        String nameToShow = (String) obj;
        checkboxState = (boolean[]) in.readObject();

        if (nameToShow.equals(POKE_START_SEQUENCE)) {
          playPoke();
          nameToShow = "Hey! Pay attention.";
        }

        otherSeqsMap.put(nameToShow, checkboxState);
        listVector.add(nameToShow);
        incomingList.setListData(listVector);
      } // close while
    } catch (Exception ex) { ex.printStackTrace(); }
  } // close run

  private void playPoke() {
    Toolkit.getDefaultToolkit().beep();
  }
} // close inner class
```

Task 1   MDE

Sound an audible alert
when receiving a poke
message (can't be
annoying!)   .5

Task 2   LUG

Add support for
checking for the Poke
command and creating
a message.   .5

Task 4   BJD

Merge Poke visual
alert into message
display system.
                         .5

Task 3   MDE

Implement receiver
code to read the
data off of the
network.   1

Stickies
Task ~~Magnets~~ Solution

We're not in *Head First Java* anymore; let's get right to the new features. Here's a snippet from the BeatBox client code. Your job was to map the task magnets to the code that implements each part of the "Send a Poke..." story.

All of this code goes into BeatBox.java.

Here's the code that will run in the new thread context for BeatBox.

This is the inner class that receives data from the server.

This is original code—it reads messages sent from the server.

```java
// ... more BeatBox.java code above this

public class RemoteReader implements Runnable {
    boolean[] checkboxState = null;
    String nameToShow = null;
    Object obj = null;

    public void run() {
        try {
            while((obj=in.readObject()) != null) {
                System.out.println("got an object from server");
                System.out.println(obj.getClass());
                String nameToShow = (String) obj;
                checkboxState = (boolean[]) in.readObject();

                if (nameToShow.equals(POKE_START_SEQUENCE)) {
                    playPoke();
                    nameToShow = "Hey! Pay attention.";

                }

                otherSeqsMap.put(nameToShow, checkboxState);
                listVector.add(nameToShow);
                incomingList.setListData(listVector);
            } // close while
        } catch (Exception ex) { ex.printStackTrace(); }
    } // close run

    private void playPoke() {
        Toolkit.getDefaultToolkit().beep();
    }
} // close inner class
```

Task 3   MDE

Implement receiver code to read the data off of the network.

`1`

If we get the POKE_START_SEQUENCE, we play the poke sound and replace the message with our alert text.

Here's our new playPoke() method that just beeps for now. If you want a real challenge, add MP3 poke-sound support.

Task 2   LUG

Add support for checking for the Poke command and creating a message.

`.5`

Task 4   BJD

Merge Poke visual alert into message display system.

`.5`

Task 1   MDE

Sound an audible alert when receiving a poke message (can't be annoying!)

`.5`

there are no Dumb Questions

Q: This isn't a Java programming book. Why are we wasting time looking through all this code?

A: Software development techniques cover everything related to a project, from organization and estimation down through code. Earlier, we talked about the planning and execution parts of a project, and then we got a little closer to code and talked about design. Now, we need to dive all the way down and talk about some tools and techniques you can use *on your code itself*. Software development isn't just about prioritization and estimation; you've still got to write good, working, reliable code.

Q: I don't develop in Java. I'm not sure what some of the code in there does. What do I do?

A: That's OK. Do your best to understand what the code is doing, and don't worry about all the Java-specific details. The main thing is to get an idea of how to handle and think about code in a solid software development process. The tools and techniques we'll talk about should make sense whether you know what a Java thread is or not.

Q: I think I must have...misplaced... my copy of *Head First Java*. What's this whole BeatBox thing about?

A: BeatBox is a program first discussed in Head First Java. It has a backend `MusicServer` and a Java Swing–based client piece (that's Java's graphical toolkit API). The client piece uses the Java Sound API to generate sound sequences that you can control with the checkboxes on the form's main page. When you enter a message and click "sendit," your message and your BeatBox settings are sent to any other copies of BeatBox connected to your `MusicServer`. If you click on the received message, then you can hear the new sequence that was just sent.

Q: So what's the deal with that POKE_START_SEQUENCE thing?

A: Our story requires us to send a poke message to the other BeatBoxes connected to the `MusicServer`. Normally when a message gets sent it's just a string that is displayed to the user. We added the Poke functionality on top of the original BeatBox by coming up with a unique string of characters that no one should ever type

on purpose. We can use that to notify the other BeatBoxes that a "poke" was sent. This sequence is stored in the `POKE_START_SEQUENCE` constant (the actual string value is in the `BeatBox.java` file in the code you can download from *http://www.headfirstlabs.com/books/hfsd/*).

When other BeatBox instances see the `POKE_START_SEQUENCE` come through, they replace it with our visual alert message, and the receiving user never actually sees that code sequence.

Q: What's all this threading and Runnable stuff about?

A: BeatBox is always trying to grab data from the network so it can display incoming messages. However, if there's nothing available on the network, it could get stuck waiting for data. This means the screen wouldn't redraw and users couldn't type in a new message to send. In order to split those two things apart, BeatBox uses threads. It creates a thread to handle the network access, and then uses the main thread to handle the GUI work. The `Runnable` interface is Java's way of wrapping up some code that should be run in another thread. The code you just looked at, in the last exercise, is the network code.

BRAIN POWER

Bob's making good progress on his end, too. Can you think of anything else you should be worrying about at this point?

And now the GUI work...

We need one more piece of code to get this story together. We need to add a button to the GUI that lets the user actually send the Poke. Here's the code to take care of that task:

```java
// The code below goes in BeatBox.java,
//   in the buildGUI() method
   JButton sendIt = new JButton("sendIt");
   sendIt.addActionListener(new MySendListener());
   buttonBox.add(sendIt);

   JButton sendPoke = new JButton("Send Poke");
   sendPoke.addActionListener(new MyPokeListener());
   buttonBox.add(sendPoke);

   userMessage = new JTextField();
   buttonBox.add(userMessage);
```

First we need to create a new button for our Poke feature.

Then we set up a listener so we can react when it's clicked.

Finally, add the button to the box holding the other buttons.

```java
// Below is new code we need to add, also to BeatBox.java
public class MyPokeListener implements ActionListener {

   public void actionPerformed(ActionEvent a) {
     // We'll create an empty state array here
     boolean[] checkboxState = new boolean[255];

     try {
       out.writeObject(POKE_START_SEQUENCE);
       out.writeObject(checkboxState);
     } catch (Exception ex) {
       System.out.println("Failed to poke!");
     }
   }
}
```

Here we create an array of booleans for our state. We can leave them all false because the receiving side ignores them when it gets the POKE command.

Here's the magic: to send a poke we send the magic POKE_START_SEQUENCE and our array of booleans to the server. The server will relay our magic sequence to the other clients, and they'll beep at the user because of the earlier code we wrote (back on page 180).

And a quick test...

Now that both the client and server are implemented it's time to make sure things work. No software can go out without testing so...

1 First compile and start up the MusicServer.

The MusicServer will listen for connections and print out a line each time it gets one.

```
File  Edit  Window  Help  Buildin'
hfsd> mkdir bin
hfsd> javac -d bin src\headfirst\sd\chapter6\*.java
hfsd> java -cp bin headfirst.sd.chapter6.MusicServer
```

The "-d" tells the java compiler to put the classes in the bin directory.

2 Then start the new BeatBox—we'll need two instances running so we can test the Poke.

We use different names here so we know which is which.

```
File  Edit  Window  Help  Ouch
hfsd> java -cp bin headfirst.sd.chapter6.BeatBox PokeReceiver
```
```
File  Edit  Window  Help  Hah
hfsd> java -cp bin headfirst.sd.chapter6.BeatBox PokeSender
```

3 Now send off a Poke by clicking the "Send Poke" button on the instance we named PokeSender.

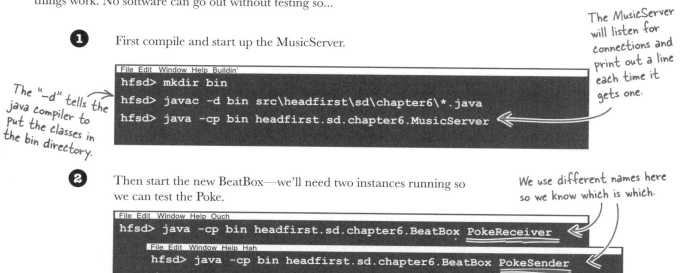

Here's our new Poke button.

Here's our PokeReceiver instance.

Here's our alert message.

DING! (Seriously, it sounds like that.)

Excellent! Your changes work as advertised. We'll copy the code up to the demo server, and all that's left is for Bob to merge his stuff in. Time to call it a night.

And Bob does the same...

Bob finished up the tasks related to his story and ran a quick test on his end. His task is working, so he copies his code up to the server. In order to do the final build he merges his code in with ours, gets everything to compile, and retests sending a picture. Everything looks good. Tomorrow's demo is going to rock...

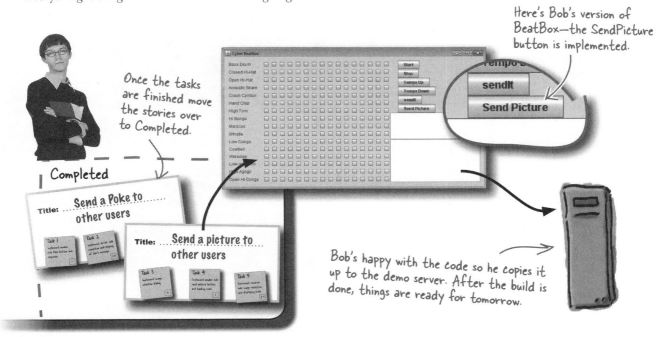

Once the tasks are finished move the stories over to Completed.

Completed

Here's Bob's version of BeatBox—the SendPicture button is implemented.

Bob's happy with the code so he copies it up to the demo server. After the build is done, things are ready for tomorrow.

there are no
Dumb Questions

Q: **I'm not familiar with networking code. What's happening in that code we just added?**

A: On the sending side we represent the sequence settings as an array of checkboxes. We don't really care what they're set to, since we won't use them on the receiving side. We still need to send something, though, so the existing code works. We use Java's object serialization to stream the array of checkboxes and our secret message that triggers the alert on the other side.

On the receiving side we pull off the secret sequence and the array of checkboxes. All of the serialization and deserialization is handled by Java.

Q: **Why did we make the bin directory before we compiled the code?**

A: We'll talk more about this in the next chapter, but in general it's a good idea to keep your compiled code separate from the source. It makes it a lot simpler to clean up and rebuild when you make changes. There's nothing special about the name "bin"; it's just convention and is short for "binaries"—i.e., compiled code.

Q: **Wait, did Bob just merge code on the demo server?**

A: Yup...

Demo the new BeatBox for the customer

We're all set to go. Your code is written, tested, and copied up to the demo server. Bob did the final build, so we call the customer and prepare to amaze the crowds.

Here's our button—and the "Send Picture" button is from Bob's code.

Uh oh, this doesn't look good. What's going on?

Unhappy customer. Not good.

I'm not hearing any alert. And what's SECRET_POKE_SEQUENCE? I'm not impressed.

So what went wrong?

Our code worked just a few pages ago. So what went wrong? More importantly, what would you do differently in the future to make sure nothing like this ever happens again?

Think beyond, "Do more testing." How can you prevent this problem from occurring in the first place?

Exercise

Something's clearly gone wrong. Below is some code we compiled on our machine and the same section of code from the demo machine. See if you can figure out what happened.

```
public class RemoteReader implements Runnable {
    boolean[] checkboxState = null;
    String nameToShow = null;
    Object obj = null;

    public void run() {
        try {
            while((obj=in.readObject()) != null) {
                System.out.println("got an object from server");
                System.out.println(obj.getClass());
                String nameToShow = (String) obj;
                checkboxState = (boolean[]) in.readObject();
                if (nameToShow.equals(POKE_START_SEQUENCE)) {
                    playPoke();
                    nameToShow = "Hey! Pay attention.";
                }
                otherSeqsMap.put(nameToShow, c
                listVector.add(nameToShow);
                incomingList.setListData(list
            } // close while
        } catch (Exception ex) { ex.print
    } // close run
```

Here's the code from our machine—it worked fine when we ran it.

And here's the code on the demo server—the code that tanked.

```
public class RemoteReader implements Runnable {
    boolean[] checkboxState = null;
    String nameToShow = null;
    Object obj = null;

    public void run() {
    try {
        while ((obj = in.readObject()) != null) {
            System.out.println("got an object from server");
            System.out.println(obj.getClass());
            String nameToShow = (String) obj;
            checkboxState = (boolean[]) in.readObject();
            if (nameToShow.equals(PICTURE_START_SEQUENCE)) {
                receiveJPEG();
            }
            else {
                otherSeqsMap.put(nameToShow, checkboxState);
                listVector.add(nameToShow);
                incomingList.setListData(listVector);
            }
        } // close while
    } catch (Exception ex) {
        ex.printStackTrace();
    }
    } // close run
} // close run
```

What went wrong?.....................................
....
....

How did this happen?..............................
....
....

What would you do?.................................
....
....

Standup meeting

Your team, after the big flop at the customer demo

Mark: Wow. Bob really blew it with that demo.

Bob: What are you talking about? My code worked!

Laura: But you broke the other story we were trying to demo! It worked fine before you got to it.

Bob: Wait a minute—why am I getting blamed for this? You asked me to copy my code up to the demo server so we could build it. When I did that, I saw you guys had changed a lot of the same stuff. It was a mess.

Mark: So you just overwrote it??

Bob: No way—I spent a bunch of time comparing the files trying to figure out what you had changed and what I had changed. To make things worse, you guys had some variables renamed in your code so I had to sort that out, too. I got the button stuff right, but I guess I missed something in the receiver code.

Laura: So do we still have the working Poke code on there?

Bob: I doubt it. I copied my stuff up with a new name and merged them into the files you had up there. I didn't think to snag a copy of your stuff.

Mark: Not good. I probably have a copy on my machine, but I don't know if it's the latest. Laura, do you have it?

Laura: I might, but I've started working on new stuff, so I'll have to try and back all my changes out. We really need to find a better way to handle this stuff. This is costing us a ton of time to sort out and we're probably adding bugs left and right...

Not to mention we're going the <u>wrong</u> w<u>a</u>y on our burn-down rate again.

Let's start with VERSION CONTROL

You'll also see this referred to as configuration management, which is a little more formal term for the same thing.

Keeping track of source code (or any kind of files for that matter) across a project is tricky. You have lots of people working on files—sometimes the same ones, sometimes different. Any serious software project needs **version control**, which is also often called **configuration management**, or **CM** for short.

Version control is a tool (usually a piece of software) that will keep track of changes to your files and help you coordinate different developers working on different parts of your system at the same time. Here's the rundown on how version control works:

❷ Bob **makes some changes** to the code and tests them.

Bob's Machine

❶ Bob **checks out** BeatBox.java from the server.

"Check out" means you get a copy of BeatBox.java that you can work on.

I need the BeatBox.java file.

The version control server looks up files and returns the latest version to the developers.

Found it, here ya go...

I need the BeatBox.java file, too.

1.5 The rest of your team can **check out** Version 1 of BeatBox.java while Bob works on his version.

Found it, here ya go...

Other people can get a copy of the original file while Bob works on his changes on his local machine.

The server running version control software

3 Bob **checks in** his changes.

All done!

Checking the code back in means your changes are sent to the server so others can get them.

3.5 After Bob checks in his changes, the team can **get an update** from the server with the new code.

I need the latest BeatBox.java file.

Found it, here ya go...

Some systems prevent other people from modifying the file that's being edited by someone, while other systems handle merging the changes.

there are no Dumb Questions

Q: So if version control is a piece of software, which version control product should I use?

A: There are lots of choices out there for version control tools, both commercial and open source. One of the most popular open source ones is called Subversion, and that's the one we'll use in this chapter. Microsoft tools such as Visual Studio like to work with Microsoft's version control tool, called Visual SourceSafe, or Microsoft's new Team Foundation product.

Version control tools all do pretty much the same thing, but some offer different ways to do it. For example, some commercial systems have strict access control on where you can commit code so that your organization can control what goes into what build. Other tools show you the different versions of files as virtual directories.

Q: You're only showing one file and two developers. I'm guessing it can do more than that, right?

A: You bet. In fact, a good version control tool is really the only way you can **scale a team**. We'll need some of those more sophisticated features (like merging changes, tagging versions, etc.) in just a minute...

First set up your project...

We're assuming you've got your version control software installed. If not, you can download it from the Subversion web site.

The first step in using a version control tool is to put your code in the **repository**; that's where your code is stored. There's nothing tricky about putting your code in the repository, just get the original files organized on your machine and create the project in the repository:

1 First create the repository—you only need to do this once for each version control install. After that you just add projects to the same repository.

```
File Edit  Window  Help  TakeBacks
hfsd> svnadmin create c:\Users\Developer\Desktop\SVNRepo
hfsd>
```

This tells Subversion to create a new repository...

...in this directory.

After that runs, we have our repository.

2 Next you need to import your code into the repository. Just go to the directory above your code and tell your version control server to import it. So, for your BeatBox project, you'd go to the directory that contains your beat box code. If you're using the downloaded files, that directory is called Chapter6:

Now you want all your code in that repository, in a project called BeatBox.

Here you tell Subversion to import your code.

This is the repository you created in step 1. On Windows you'll need to use forward slash notation.

This is just a comment describing what we're doing; we'll talk more about this later, too.

```
File Edit  Window  Help  Tariffs
hfsd> svn import Chapter6 file:///c:/Users/Developer/Desktop/
SVNRepo/BeatBox/trunk -m "Initial Import"
Adding          Chapter6\src
Adding          Chapter6\src\headfirst
Adding          Chapter6\src\headfirst\sd
Adding          Chapter6\src\headfirst\sd\chapter6
Adding          Chapter6\src\headfirst\sd\chapter6\BeatBox.java
Adding          Chapter6\src\headfirst\sd\chapter6\MusicServer.java

Committed revision 1.

hfsd>
```

Here's what we want our project to be called—ignore the "trunk" thing for right now.

Subversion adds each file it finds into your repository for the BeatBox project.

* You can get the full Subversion documentation here: http://svnbook.red-bean.com/

...then you can check code in and out.

Now that your code is in the repository, you can check it out, make your changes, and check your updated code back in. A version control system will keep track of your original code, all of the changes you make, and also handle sharing your changes with the rest of your team. First, check out your code (normally your repository wouldn't be on your local machine):

1 To check out your code, you just tell your version control software what project you want to check out, and where to put the files you requested.

This tells Subversion to check out a copy of the code.

This pulls code from the BeatBox project in the repository and puts it in a local directory called BeatBox.

```
File Edit Window Help Girvue
hfsd> svn checkout file:///c:/Users/Developer/Desktop/SVNRepo/
BeatBox/trunk BeatBox

A        BeatBox\src
A        BeatBox\src\headfirst
A        BeatBox\src\headfirst\sd
A        BeatBox\src\headfirst\sd\chapter6
A        BeatBox\src\headfirst\sd\chapter6\BeatBox.java
A        BeatBox\src\headfirst\sd\chapter6\MusicServer.java

Checked out revision 1.

hfsd>
```

Subversion pulls your files back out of the repository and copies them into a new BeatBox directory (or an existing one if you've already got a BeatBox directory).

2 Now you can make changes to the code just like you normally would. You just work directly on the files you checked out from your version control system, compile, and save.

You can re-implement the Poke story, since Bob broke that feature when he wrote code for the Send Picture story.

This is a normal .java file. Subversion doesn't change it in any way...it's still just code.

3 Then you commit your changes back into the repository with a message describing what changes you've made.

This tells Subversion to commit your changes; it will figure out what files you've changed.

This is a log message, indicating what you did.

```
File Look What IDid
hfsd> svn commit -m "Added POKE support."

Sending          src\headfirst\sd\chapter6\BeatBox.java
Transmitting file data .
Committed revision 2.

hfsd>
```

Since you only changed one file, that's all that subversion sent to the repository—and notice that now you have a new revision number.

Most version control tools will try and solve problems for you

Suppose you had a version control system in place before the great BeatBox debacle of '08. You'd check in your code (with `commit`) to implement Send Poke, and then Bob would change his code, and try to commit his work on Send Picture:

Bob tries to check in his code...

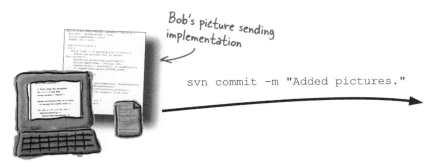

Bob's picture sending implementation

```
svn commit -m "Added pictures."
```

Here's your code—safe and sound in the repository.

...but quickly runs into a problem.

You and Bob both made changes to the same file; you just got yours into the repository first.

The code on the server, with your changes

Bob's code

```java
public class RemoteReader implements Runnable {
  boolean[] checkboxState = null;
  String nameToShow = null;
  Object obj = null;

  public void run() {
  try {
    while ((obj = in.readObject()) != null) {
      System.out.println("got an object from server")
      System.out.println(obj.getClass());
      String nameToShow = (String) obj;
      checkboxState = (boolean[]) in.readObject();
      if (nameToShow.equals(PICTURE_START_SEQUENCE)) {
        receiveJPEG();
      }
      else {
        otherSeqsMap.put(nameToShow, checkboxState);
        listVector.add(nameToShow);
        incomingList.setListData(listVector);
        // now reset the sequence to be this
      }
    } // close while
  } catch (Exception ex) {
    ex.printStackTrace();
  }
} // close run
} // close inner class
```

Bob's BeatBox.java

```java
public class RemoteReader implements Runnable {
  boolean[] checkboxState = null;
  String nameToShow = null;
  Object obj = null;

  public void run() {
  try {
    while((obj=in.readObject()) != null) {
      System.out.println("got an object from server");
      System.out.println(obj.getClass());
      String nameToShow = (String) obj;
      checkboxState = (boolean[]) in.readObject();
      if (nameToShow.equals(POKE_START_SEQUENCE)) {
        playPoke();
        nameToShow = "Hey! Pay attention.";
      }
      otherSeqsMap.put(nameToShow, checkboxState);
      listVector.add(nameToShow);
      incomingList.setListData(listVector);
    } // close while
  } catch(Exception ex) {ex.printStackTrace();}
  } // close run

  private void playPoke() {
    Toolkit.getDefaultToolkit().beep();
  }
} // close inner class
```

BeatBox.java

The server tries to <u>MERGE</u> your changes

If two people make changes to the same file but in different places, most version control systems try to merge the changes together. This isn't *always* what you want, but most of the time it works great.

Nonconflicting code and methods are easy

In `BeatBox.java`, you added a `playPoke()` method, so the code on the version control server has that method. But Bob's code has no `playPoke()` method, so there's a potential problem.

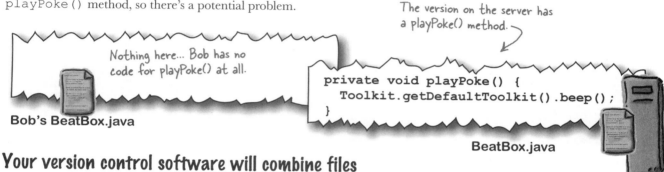

The version on the server has a playPoke() method.

Nothing here... Bob has no code for playPoke() at all.

Bob's BeatBox.java

```
private void playPoke() {
    Toolkit.getDefaultToolkit().beep();
}
```

BeatBox.java

Your version control software will combine files

In a case like this, your version control server can simply combine the two files. In other words, the `playPoke()` method gets combined with nothing in Bob's file, and you end up with a `BeatBox.java` on the server that still retains the `playPoke()` method. So no problems yet...

But conflicting code <u>IS</u> a problem

But what if you have code in the same method that is different? That's exactly the case with Bob's version of `BeatBox.java`, and the version on the server, in the `run()` method:

These two bits of code are in the same place, but it's not clear how to merge them.

```
if (nameToShow.equals(PICTURE_START_SEQUENCE)) {
    receiveJPEG();
} else {
    otherSeqsMap.put(nameToShow, checkboxSt
    listVector.add(nameToShow);
    incomingList.setListData(listVector);
}
```

Bob's BeatBox.java

```
if (nameToShow.equals(POKE_START_SEQUENCE)) {
    playPoke();
    nameToShow = "Hey! Pay attention.";
}
otherSeqsMap.put(nameToShow, checkboxState)
listVector.add(nameToShow);
incomingList.setListData(listVector);
```

BeatBox.java

If your software can't merge the changes, it issues a conflict

If two people made changes to the same set of lines, there's no way for a version control system to know what to put in the final server copy. When this happens, most systems just punt. They'll kick the file back to the person trying to commit the code and ask them to sort out the problems.

Subversion rejects your commit. You can use the update command to pull the changes into your code, and Subversion will mark the lines where there are conflicts in your files... after you sort out the conflicts, you can recommit.

```java
public class RemoteReader implements Runnable {
  boolean[] checkboxState = null;
  String nameToShow = null;
  Object obj = null;

  public void run() {
  try {
    while ((obj = in.readObject()) != null) {
      System.out.println("got an object from server");
      System.out.println(obj.getClass());
      String nameToShow = (String) obj;
      checkboxState = (boolean[]) in.readObject();
      if (nameToShow.equals(PICTURE_START_SEQUENCE)) {
        receiveJPEG();
      }
      else {
        otherSeqsMap.put(nameToShow, checkboxState);
        listVector.add(nameToShow);
        incomingList.setListData(listVector);
        // now reset the sequence to be this
      }
    } // close while
  } catch (Exception ex) {
    ex.printStackTrace();
  }
} // close run
}  se inner class
```

Bob's BeatBox.java

Your version control software doesn't know what to do with this conflicting code, so to protect everyone, it refuses to commit the new code, and marks up where problems might be.

```java
public class RemoteReader implements Runnable {
  boolean[] checkboxState = null;
  String nameToShow = null;
  Object obj = null;

  public void run() {
   try {
     while((obj=in.readObject()) != null) {
       System.out.println("got an object from server");
       System.out.println(obj.getClass());
       String nameToShow = (String) obj;
       checkboxState = (boolean[]) in.readObject();
       if (nameToShow.equals(POKE_START_SEQUENCE)) {
         playPoke();
         nameToShow = "Hey! Pay attention.";
       }
       otherSeqsMap.put(nameToShow, checkboxState);
       listVector.add(nameToShow);
       incomingList.setListData(listVector);
     } // close while
   } catch(Exception ex) {ex.printStackTrace();}
   } // close run

  private void playPoke() {
    Toolkit.getDefaultToolkit().beep();
  }
} // close inner class
```

BeatBox.java

Exercise

Conflict Resolution: Here's the file the version control software kicked back to Bob, with all the conflicts marked. What should the final code look like that Bob commits back in?

```
public class RemoteReader implements Runnable {
  // variable declarations
  public void run() {
  try {
    // code without problems

<<<<<<< .mine
      if (nameToShow.equals(
                    PICTURE_START_SEQUENCE)) {
        receiveJPEG();
      } else {
        otherSeqsMap.put(
                nameToShow, checkboxState);
        listVector.add(nameToShow);
        incomingList.setListData(listVector);
        // now reset the sequence to be this
      }
=======
      if (nameToShow.equals(
                    POKE_START_SEQUENCE)) {
        playPoke();
        nameToShow = "Hey! Pay attention.";
      }
      otherSeqsMap.put(
                nameToShow, checkboxState);
      listVector.add(nameToShow);
      incomingList.setListData(listVector);
>>>>>>> .r2
    } // close while
  // more code without problems
} // close run
} // close inner class
```

Files with conflicts get both the local changes (Bob's changes) and the changes from the server. The ones between "<<<<<<< .mine" and the ===='s are Bob's—the ones after that up to the ">>>>>>> .r2" are the ones from the server.

```
public class RemoteReader implements
Runnable {
  // variable declarations
  public void run() {
  try {
    // code without problems

.................................................
.................................................
.................................................
.................................................
.................................................
.................................................
.................................................
.................................................
.................................................
.................................................
.................................................
.................................................
.................................................
.................................................
.................................................
.................................................
.................................................
.................................................
    } // close while
  // more code without problems
} // close run
} // close inner class
```

Exercise
Solution

Conflict Resolution: Here's the file version control kicked back to Bob with both changes in it. What should the final section look like that Bob commits back in?

```
public class Remote
  // variable decla
  public void run()
  try {
    // code without
<<<<<<< .mine
     if (nameTosho

       receiveJPEG
     } else {
       otherSeqsMa
              na
       listVector.
       incomingLis
       // now rese
     }
=======
     if (nameTosh

       playPoke()
       nameToshow
     }
       otherSeqsMap
              nam
       listVector.a
       incomingList
>>>>>>> .r2
     } // close whil
     // more code with
  } // close run
  } // close inner cl
```

```
public class RemoteReader implements Runnable {
  // variable declarations
  public void run() {
  try {
    while ((obj = in.readObject()) != null) {
      System.out.println("got an object from server");
      System.out.println(obj.getClass());
      String nameToShow = (String) obj;
      checkboxState = (boolean[]) in.readObject();
      if (nameToShow.equals(PICTURE_START_SEQUENCE)) {
        receiveJPEG();
      }
      else {
       if (nameToShow.equals(POKE_START_SEQUENCE)) {
         playPoke();
         nameToShow = "Hey! Pay attention.";
       }

         otherSeqsMap.put(nameToShow, checkboxState);
         listVector.add(nameToShow);
         incomingList.setListData(listVector);
         // now reset the sequence to be this
       }
    } // close while
  } catch (Exception ex) {
      ex.printStackTrace();
  }
} // close run
} // close inner class
```

We need to support both the picture sequence and the poke sequence so we need to merge the conditionals.

Make sure you delete the conflict characters (<<<<<<<, =======, and >>>>>>>).

Make these changes to your own copy of `BeatBox.java`, and commit them to your code repository:

First, tell Subversion you resolved the conflict in the file using the "resolved" command and the path to the file.

You can skip this step if you didn't really get a conflict from Subversion.

Now, commit the file to your server, adding a comment indicating what you did.

```
File Edit Window Help Tranquility
hfsd> svn resolved src/headfirst/sd/chapter6/BeatBox.java
Resolved conflicted state of `BeatBox.java'

hfsd> svn commit -m "Merged picture support with Poke stuff."
Sending          src\headfirst\sd\chapter6\BeatBox.java
Transmitting file data .
Committed revision 3.

hfsd>
```

Now show the customer...

Send Poke **and** Send Picture work.

---

there are no Dumb Questions

Q: I see how checking out and committing works, but how do other people on the team get my changes?

A: Once you've got your project checked out, you can run `svn update`. That tells the version control server to give you the latest versions of all files in the project. Lots of teams run an update every morning, to make sure they're current with everyone else's work.

Q: This whole conflict thing seems pretty hairy. Can't my version control software do anything besides erroring out?

A: Some can. Certain version control tools work in a *file locking mode*, which means when you check out files, the system locks those files so no one else can check them out. Once you make your changes and check the files back in, the system unlocks the files. This prevents conflicts, since only one person can edit a file at a time. But, it also means you might not be able to make changes to a file when you want to; you might need to wait for someone else to finish up first. To get around that, some locking version control systems allow you to check out a file in read-only mode while it's locked. But that's a bit heavy-handed, so other tools like Subversion allow multiple people to work on the same file at once. Good design, good division of labor, frequent commits, and good communication help reduce the number of manual merges you actually have to do.

Q: What is all this trunk business you keep saying to ignore?

A: The Subversion authors recommend putting your code into a directory called `trunk`. Then, other versions would go into a directory called `branches`. Once you've imported your code, the trunk thing doesn't really show up again, except during an initial checkout. We'll talk more about branches later in the chapter, but for now, stick with the `trunk`.

Q: Where are all of my messages going when I do a commit?

A: Subversion keeps track of each time you commit changes into the repository and associates your message with those changes. This lets you look at why people made a certain change—for instance, if you need to go back and figure out why something was done. That's why you should always use a sensible, explanatory message when you do a commit. The first time you go back through old commits and find "I changed stuff" as the log message, you'll be pretty cranky.

Q: Do I have to commit all of my changes at the same time?

A: Nope! Just put the path to the filename on the `commit` command like you did for the `resolved` command. Subversion will commit just the file(s) you specify.

More iterations, more stories...

Things are going well. The customer was happy with our Poke and
Picture support, and after one more iteration, felt we had enough
for Version 1.0. A few iterations later and everyone's looking
forward to Version 2.0. Just a few more stories to implement...

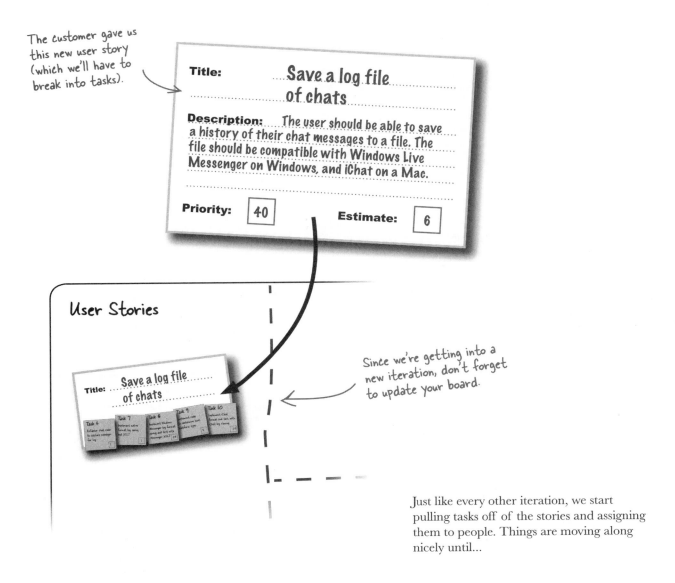

The customer gave us
this new user story
(which we'll have to
break into tasks).

Title: Save a log file
of chats

Description: The user should be able to save
a history of their chat messages to a file. The
file should be compatible with Windows Live
Messenger on Windows, and iChat on a Mac.

Priority: 40   **Estimate:** 6

User Stories

Title: Save a log file
of chats

Since we're getting into a
new iteration, don't forget
to update your board.

Just like every other iteration, we start
pulling tasks off of the stories and assigning
them to people. Things are moving along
nicely until...

Standup meeting

Bob: Hey guys. Good news: I'm just about done with the Windows Messenger version, and it's working well. But there's bad news, too. I just found a bug in the way images are handled in our Send Picture feature from way back in the first iteration.

Laura: That's not good. Can we wait on fixing it?

Bob: I don't think so—it's a potential security hole if people figure out how to send a malicious picture. The users will be pretty annoyed over this.

Mark: Which means the customer is going to be *really* annoyed over this. Can you fix it?

Bob: I can fix it—but I've got a ton of code changes in there for the new story, the log files, that aren't ready to go out yet.

Laura: So we're going to have to roll your changes back and send out a patched 1.0 version.

Mark: What do we roll it back to? We have lots of little changes to lots of files. How do we know where version 1.0 was?

Bob: Forget version 1.0, what about all of my work?? If you roll back, you're going to drop everything I did.

The team's in a tough spot—there's a pretty serious bug in the released version, but there's a lot effort invested in the new version. The new version isn't ready to go out the way it is. What would you do?

We have more than one version of our software...

The real problem here is that we have more than one version of our software—or more accurately, more than one version of our source code—that we need to make changes to. We have version 1.0 of the code built and out there, but Bob found a pretty serious bug. On top of that, we've got version 2.0 in the works, but it's full of untested, unworking features.

We need to separate them somehow...

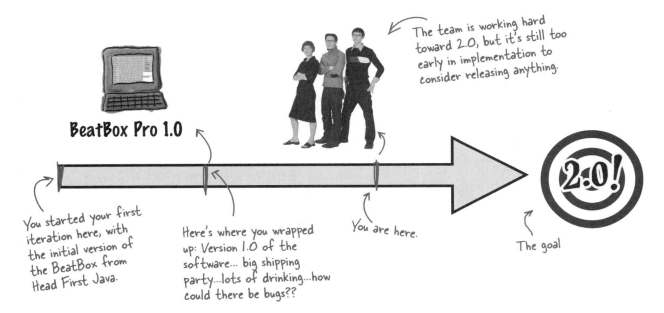

The team is working hard toward 2.0, but it's still too early in implementation to consider releasing anything.

BeatBox Pro 1.0

You started your first iteration here, with the initial version of the BeatBox from Head First Java.

Here's where you wrapped up: Version 1.0 of the software... big shipping party...lots of drinking...how could there be bugs??

You are here.

The goal

BULLET POINTS

- Bugs to released versions are usually a higher priority to the customer than implementing new features.

- Your bug fixes should affect released software and still be implemented in in-progress versions of your software.

- Effective bug fixing depends on being able to locate specific versions of your software and make changes to those versions without affecting current development.

You'll always have tension between bugs cropping up in released versions, and new features in upcoming versions. It's up to you to work with the customer to BALANCE those tensions.

> You keep saying "Version 1.0," but what does that mean? We've committed tons of changes since then into the repository....

By default, your version control software gives you code from the <u>trunk</u>. ←

Some systems call this the HEAD or the main line.

You're right. When you check out the code from your version control system, you're checking it out from the **trunk**. That's the latest code by default and (assuming people are committing their changes on a regular basis) has all of the latest ~~bugs~~ features.

Remember the trunk thing that keeps coming up? That's the place where all the latest and greatest code is stored.

```
File Edit  Window Help
hfsd> svn checkout file:///c:/Users/Developer/Desktop/SVNRepo/
BeatBox/trunk BeatBox
A        BeatBox\src
A        BeatBox\src\headfirst
A        BeatBox\src\headfirst\sd
A        BeatBox\src\headfirst\sd\chapter6
A        BeatBox\src\headfirst\sd\chapter6\BeatBox.java
A        BeatBox\src\headfirst\sd\chapter6\MusicServer.java

Checked out revision 1.

hfsd>
```

> But we **do** have the 1.0 code **somewhere**, even if it's not labeled, right? We just have to find it on our server somehow...

Version control software stores <u>ALL</u> your code.

Every time you commit code into your version control system, a revision number was attached to the software at that point. So, if you can figure out which revision of your software was released as Version 1.0, you're good to go.

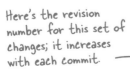

Here's the revision number for this set of changes; it increases with each commit.

```
File Edit  Window Help
hfsd> svn commit -m "Added POKE support."

Sending          src\headfirst\sd\chapter6\BeatBox.java
Transmitting file data .
Committed revision 18.

hfsd>
```

Good commit messages make finding older software easier

You've been putting nice descriptive messages each time you committed code into your version control system, right? Here's where they matter. Just as each commit gets a revision number, your version control software also keeps your commit messages associated with that revision number, and you can view them in the log:

...and specify which file to get the log for.

To get the log we use the "log" command...

Subversion responds by giving us all of the log entries for that file.

Here's the revision number...

And here's the log message to go with it.

Subversion keeps track of who made the changes and when.

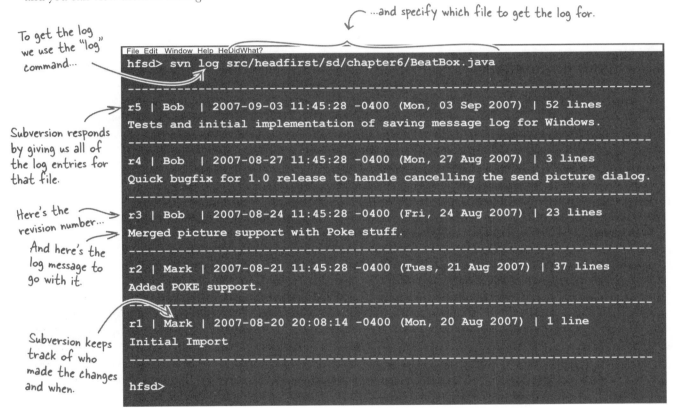

```
File Edit Window Help HeDidWhat?
hfsd> svn log src/headfirst/sd/chapter6/BeatBox.java
------------------------------------------------------------------------
r5 | Bob | 2007-09-03 11:45:28 -0400 (Mon, 03 Sep 2007) | 52 lines
Tests and initial implementation of saving message log for Windows.
------------------------------------------------------------------------
r4 | Bob | 2007-08-27 11:45:28 -0400 (Mon, 27 Aug 2007) | 3 lines
Quick bugfix for 1.0 release to handle cancelling the send picture dialog.
------------------------------------------------------------------------
r3 | Bob | 2007-08-24 11:45:28 -0400 (Fri, 24 Aug 2007) | 23 lines
Merged picture support with Poke stuff.
------------------------------------------------------------------------
r2 | Mark | 2007-08-21 11:45:28 -0400 (Tues, 21 Aug 2007) | 37 lines
Added POKE support.
------------------------------------------------------------------------
r1 | Mark | 2007-08-20 20:08:14 -0400 (Mon, 20 Aug 2007) | 1 line
Initial Import
------------------------------------------------------------------------
hfsd>
```

Play "Find the features" with the log messages

You've got to figure out which features were in the software—in this case, for Version 1.0. Then, figure out which revision that matches up with.

Using the log messages above, which revision do you think matches up with Version 1.0 of BeatBox Pro?

....

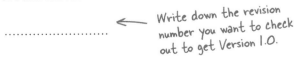

Write down the revision number you want to check out to get Version 1.0.

<u>Now</u> you can check out Version 1.0

In Subversion, -r indicates you want a specific revision of code. We're grabbing revision 4.

1 Once you know which revision to check out, your version control server can give you the code you need:

This puts the code in a new directory, for Version 1.0.

```
File Edit Window Help ThatOne
hfsd> svn checkout -r 4 file:///c:/Users/Developer/Desktop/
SVNRepo/BeatBox/trunk BeatBoxV1.0
A       BeatBoxV1.0\src
A       BeatBoxV1.0\src\headfirst
A       BeatBoxV1.0\src\headfirst\sd
A       BeatBoxV1.0\src\headfirst\sd\chapter6
A       BeatBoxV1.0\src\headfirst\sd\chapter6\BeatBox.java
A       BeatBoxV1.0\src\headfirst\sd\chapter6\MusicServer.java

Checked out revision 4.

hfsd>
```

2 Now you can fix the bug Bob found...

BeatBox.java

Once again, the version control server gives you normal Java code you can work on.

3 With the changes in place, commit the code back to your server...

Uh oh, looks like the server isn't happy with your updated code.

```
File Edit Window Help Trouble
hfsd> svn commit src/headfirst/sd/chapter6/BeatBox.java -m
"Fixed the critical security bug in 1.0 release."

Sending         src\headfirst\sd\chapter6\BeatBox.java
svn: Commit failed (details follow):

svn: Out of date: '/BeatBox/trunk/src/headfirst/sd/chapter6/
BeatBox.java' in transaction '6-1'

hfsd>
```

Sharpen your pencil

What happened? ....

....

Why? ....

....

So now what do we do? ....

....

(Emergency) standup meeting

← If you're having a problem, don't wait for the next day. Just grab everyone and have an impromptu standup meeting.

Laura: We could check out the version 1.0 code just fine, but now the version control server won't let us commit our changes back in. It says our file is out of date.

Mark: Oh—ya know, that's probably a good thing. If we could commit it, wouldn't that become revision 6, meaning the latest version of the code wouldn't have Bob's changes?

Bob: Hey that's right—you'd leapfrog my code with old version 1.0 code. I don't want to lose all of my work!

Laura: You still have your work saved locally, right? Just merge it in with the new changes and recommit it. You'll be fine.

Bob: Uggh, all that merging stuff sucks; it's a pain. And what about the next time we find a bug we need to patch in Version 1.0?

Mark: We'll have to remember what the new 1.0 revision is. Once we figure out how to commit this code, we'll write down the revision number and use that as our base for any other 1.0 changes.

Laura: New 1.0 changes? Wouldn't we be at Version 1.1 now?

Bob: Yeah, that's right. But this is still a mess...

Sharpen your pencil

Write down three problems with the approach outlined above for handling future changes to Version 1.0 (or is it 1.1?).

1. ....

2. ....

3. ....

Answers on page 217.

Tag your versions

The revision system worked great to let us get back to the version of the code we were looking for, and we got lucky that the log messages were enough for us to figure out what revision we needed. Most version control tools provide a better way of tracking which version corresponds to a meaningful event like a release or the end of an iteration. They're called **tags**.

Let's tag the code for BeatBox Pro we just located as Version 1.0:

1 First you need to create a directory in the repository for the tags. You only need to do this once for the project (and this is specific to Subversion; most version control tools support tags without this kind of directory).

Instead of trunk, specify the tags directory here.

You can use the mkdir command to create the tags directory.

```
File Edit Window Help Storage
hfsd> svn mkdir file:///c:/Users/Developer/Desktop/SVNRepo/BeatBox/tags

-m "Created tags directory"

Committed revision 6.

hfsd>
```

Here's the log message — and notice it creates a revision. This is a change to the project, so Subversion tracks it.

2 Now tag the initial 1.0 release, which is revision 4 from the repository.

We want revision 4 of the trunk...

With Subversion, you create a tag by copying the revision you want into the tags directory. Subversion actually just relates that version tag to the release.

```
File Edit Window Help YourIt
hfsd> svn copy -r 4 file:///c:/Users/Developer/Desktop/SVNRepo/BeatBox/
trunk file:///c:/Users/Developer/Desktop/SVNRepo/BeatBox/tags/version-1.0

-m "Tagging the 1.0 release of BeatBox Pro."

Committed revision 6.

hfsd>
```

And we want to put that code into a tag called version-1.0

So what?

So what did that get us? Well, instead of needing to know the revision number for version 1.0 and saying `svn checkout -r 4 ...`, you can check out Version 1.0 of the code like this:

```
svn checkout file:///c:/Users/Developer/Desktop/SVNRepo/BeatBox/tags/version-1.0
```

And let Subversion remember which revision of the repository that tag relates to.

So now I know where Version 1.0 is, great. But we still only have the 1.0 code, and need to commit those changes. Do we just commit our updated code into the Version 1.0 tag?

No! The tag is just that; it's a snapshot of the code at the point you made the tag. You don't want to commit any changes into that tag, or else the whole "version-1.0" thing becomes meaningless. Some version control tools treat tags so differently that it's impossible to commit changes into tags at all (Subversion doesn't. It's possible to commit into a tag, but it's a very, very bad idea).

BUT we can use the same idea and make a copy of revision 4 that we will commit changes into; this is called a branch. So a **tag** is a snapshot of your code at a certain time, and a **branch** is a place where you're working on code that isn't in the main development tree of the code.

1 Just like with tags, we need to create a directory for branches in our project.

Instead of trunk, we specify the branches directory here.

Use the mkdir command again to create the branches directory.

```
File Edit  Window Help  Expanding
hfsd> svn mkdir file:///c:/Users/Developer/Desktop/SVNRepo/BeatBox/branches

-m "Created branches directory"

Committed revision 8.

hfsd>
```

2 Now create a `version-1` branch from revision 4 in our repository.

We want revision 4 of the trunk...

```
File Edit  Window Help  Duplicating
hfsd> svn copy -r 4 file:///c:/Users/Developer/Desktop/SVNRepo/BeatBox/trunk
file:///c:/Users/Developer/Desktop/SVNRepo/BeatBox/branches/version-1

-m "Branched the 1.0 release of BeatBox Pro."

Committed revision 9.

hfsd>
```

With Subversion you create a branch just like a tag; you copy the revision you want into the branches directory. It won't actually copy anything; it just stores the revision number you supplied.

And we want to put it into a branch called version-1 (not Version 1.0, because we'll use this for Version 1.1, 1.2, etc.).

Tags, branches, and trunks, oh my!

Your version control system has got a lot going on now, but most of the complexity is managed by the server and isn't something you have to worry about. We've tagged the 1.0 code, made fixes in a new branch, and still have current development happening in the trunk. Here's what the repository looks like now:

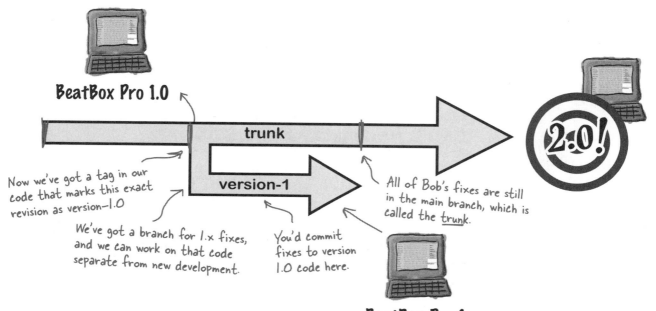

BeatBox Pro 1.0

trunk

version-1

Now we've got a tag in our code that marks this exact revision as version-1.0

We've got a branch for 1.x fixes, and we can work on that code separate from new development.

You'd commit fixes to version 1.0 code here.

All of Bob's fixes are still in the main branch, which is called the <u>trunk</u>.

2.0!

BeatBox Pro 1.x

Tags are snapshots of your code. You should always commit to a <u>branch</u>, and never to a <u>tag</u>.

BULLET POINTS

- The **trunk** is where your active development should go; it should always represent the latest version of your software.

- A **tag** is a name attached to a specific revision of the items in your repository so that you can easily retrieve that revision later.

- Sometimes you might need to **commit the same changes to a branch and the trunk** if the change applies to both.

- **Branches** are copies of your code that you can make changes to without affecting code in the trunk. Branches often start from a tagged version of the code.

- **Tags are static**—you don't commit changes into them. **Branches** are for **changes that you don't want in the trunk** (or to keep code away from changes being made in the trunk).

Fixing Version 1.0...for real this time.

When we had everything in the trunk, we got an error trying to commit old
patched code on top of our new code. Now, though, we've got a tag for version
1.0 and a branch to work in. Let's fix Version 1.0 in that branch:

1 First, check out the `version-1` branch of the BeatBox code:

*Notice we didn't need to specify a revision here.
The branch is a copy of the version 1.0 code.*

We'll put this in the BeatBoxV1 directory this time.

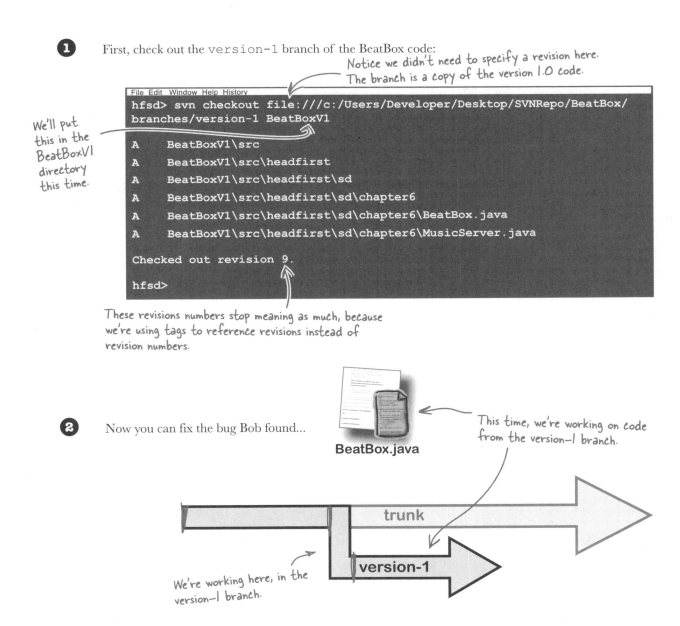

```
File Edit  Window  Help History
hfsd> svn checkout file:///c:/Users/Developer/Desktop/SVNRepo/BeatBox/
branches/version-1 BeatBoxV1

A       BeatBoxV1\src

A       BeatBoxV1\src\headfirst

A       BeatBoxV1\src\headfirst\sd

A       BeatBoxV1\src\headfirst\sd\chapter6

A       BeatBoxV1\src\headfirst\sd\chapter6\BeatBox.java

A       BeatBoxV1\src\headfirst\sd\chapter6\MusicServer.java

Checked out revision 9.

hfsd>
```

*These revisions numbers stop meaning as much, because
we're using tags to reference revisions instead of
revision numbers.*

2 Now you can fix the bug Bob found...

BeatBox.java

*This time, we're working on code
from the version-1 branch.*

trunk

version-1

*We're working here, in the
version-1 branch.*

3 ...and commit our changes back in. This time, though, no conflicts:

```
File Edit Window Help Sweet
hfsd> svn commit src/headfirst/sd/chapter6/BeatBox.java -m "Fixed the
critical security bug in 1.0 release."

Sending            src\headfirst\sd\chapter6\BeatBox.java

Committed revision 10.

hfsd>
```

The fix is in the branch.

We have **TWO** code bases now

With all these changes, we've actually got two different sets of code: the 1.x branch, where fixes are made to Version 1.0, and the trunk, which has all the new development.

☑ Our `trunk` directory in the repository has the latest and greatest code that's still in development (and Bob applied the security fix there, too).

☑ We have a `version-1.0` tag in our `tags` directory so we can pull out Version 1.0 whenever we want.

☑ We have a `version-1` branch in our `branches` directory that has all of our critical patches that have to go out as a 1.x version without any of the new development work.

Don't forget: when you actually do release v1.1 with these patches, create a version-1.1 tag in the tags directory so you can get back to that version later if you have to.

there are no
Dumb Questions

Q: I've heard branches are a bad idea and should be avoided. Why are we talking about them?

A: Branches aren't always a bad thing; they have an important place in software development. But, they do come with a price. We'll talk about that over the next few pages.

Q: What else can tags be used for?

A: Tags are great for tracking released versions of software, but you can also use them for keeping track of versions as software goes through testing or QA—think `alpha1`, `alpha2`, `beta1`, `ReleaseCandidate1`, `ReleaseCandidate2`, `ExternalTesting`, etc. It's also a good practice to tag the project at the end of each iteration.

Q: Earlier, you said not to commit changes to a tag. What's that supposed to mean? And how can you prevent people from doing it?

A: The issue with commiting changes to a tag is really a Subversion peculiarity; other tools explicitly prohibit commiting to a tag. Since Subversion uses the copy command to create a tag, exactly like it does a branch, you technically can commit into a tag just like any other place in the repository. However, this is almost always a bad idea. The reason you tagged something was to be able to get back to the code *just as it was when you tagged it*. If you commit changes into the tag, it's not the same code you originally tagged.

Subversion does have ways of putting permission controls on the tags directory so that you can prevent people from committing into it. However, once people get used to Subversion, it's usually not a major problem, and you can always revert changes to a tag in the odd case where it happens.

Q: We've been using file:///c:/... for our repository. How is that supposed to work with multiple developers?

A: Great question—there are a couple things you can do here. First, Subversion has full support for integration with a web server, which lets you specify your repository location as http:// or https://. That's when things get really interesting. For example, with https you get encrypted connections to your repository. With either web approach, you can share your repository over a much larger network without worrying about mapping shared drives. It's a little more work to configure, but it's great from the developer perspective. If you can't use http access for your repository, Subversion also supports tunneling repository access through SSH. Check out the Subversion documentation (*http://svnbook.red-bean.com/*) for more information on how to set these up.

Q: When I run the log command, I see the same revision number all over the place. What's that about?

A: Different tools do versioning (or revisioning) differently. What you're seeing is how Subversion does its revision tracking. Whenever you commit a file, Subversion applies a revision number *across the whole project*. Basically, that revision says that "The entire project looked like this at revision 9." This means that if you want to grab the project at a certain point you only need to know *one* revision number. Other tools version each file separately (most notably the version control tool called CVS which was a predecessor to Subversion). That means that to get a copy of a project at a certain state, you need to know the version numbers *of each file*. This really isn't practical, so tags become even more critical.

Q: Why did we branch the Version 1.0 code instead of leaving Version 1.0 in the trunk, and branch the new work?

A: That would work, but the problem with that approach is you end up buried in branches as development goes on. The trunk ends up being ancient code, and all the new work happens several branches deep. So you'd have a branch for the next version, and another branch for the next...

With branches for older software, you'll eventually stop working with some of those branches. (Do you think Microsoft is still making fixes to Word 95?)

Q: To create tags and branches with Subversion, we used the copy command. Is that normal?

A: Well, it's normal for Subversion. That's because Subversion was designed for very "cheap" copies, which just means a copy doesn't create lots of overhead. When you create a copy, Subversion actually just marks the revision you copied from, and then stores changes relative to that. Other version control tools do things differently. For example, CVS has an explicit tag command, and branches result in "real" copies of files, meaning they take a lot of time and resources.

Sharpen your pencil

WIth the security fix to Version 1.0 taken care of, we're back to our original user story. Bob needs to implement two different saving mechanisms for the BeatBox application: one for when the user is on a Mac, and one for when a user is on a Windows PC. Since these are two completely different platforms, what should Bob do here?

What should Bob do? ....

....

....

....

Why? ....

....

....

....

When <u>NOT</u> to branch...

Did you say that Bob should branch his code to support the two different features? Modern version control tools do make branching cheap from a **technical perspective.** The problem is there's a lot of hidden cost from the **people perspective**. Each branch is a separate code base that needs to be maintained, tested, documented, etc.

For example, remember that critical security fix we made to Version 1.0 of BeatBox? Did that fix get applied to the trunk so that it stays fixed in Version 2.0 of the software? Has the trunk code changed enough that the fix isn't a straightforward copy, and we need to so something differently to fix it?

The same would apply with branching to support two different platforms. New features would have to be implemented to **both** branches. And then, when you get to a new version, what do you do? Tag both branches? Branch both branches? It gets confusing, fast. Here are some rules of thumb for helping you know when *not* to branch:

Branch when...

☐   You have released a **version of the software** that you need to maintain **outside of the main development cycle**.

☐   You want to try some **radical changes to code** that you might need to throw away, and you **don't want to impact the rest of the team** while you work on it.

Do not branch when...

☐   You can accomplish your goal by **splitting code into different files** or libraries that can be built as appropriate on different platforms.

☐   You have a bunch of developers that can't keep their code compiling in the trunk so you try to **give them their own sandbox** to work in.

There are other ways to keep people from breaking other people's builds. We'll talk about those in a later chapter.

The Zen of good branching

Branch only when you absolutely have to. Each branch is a potentially large piece of software you have to maintain, test, release, and keep up with. If you view branching as a major decision that doesn't happen often, you're ahead of the game.

We fixed Version 1...

Good catch on the security bug! You guys even got a patch out before we hit the news!

Version 1.1 is released, and the security bug is no more.

... and Bob finished Version 2.0 (so he says)

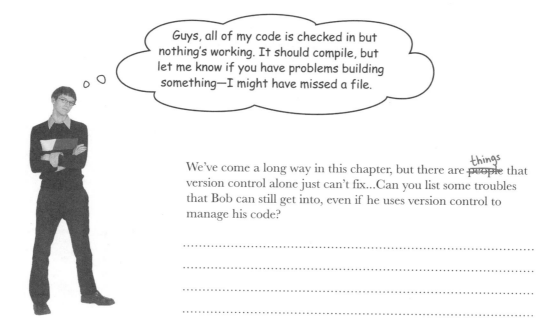

Guys, all of my code is checked in but nothing's working. It should compile, but let me know if you have problems building something—I might have missed a file.

We've come a long way in this chapter, but there are ~~people~~ things that version control alone just can't fix...Can you list some troubles that Bob can still get into, even if he uses version control to manage his code?

....

....

....

....

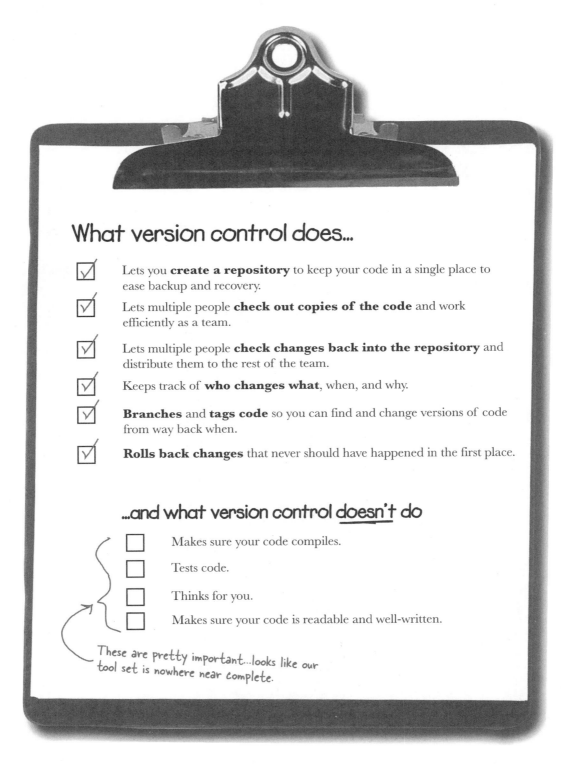

What version control does...

☑ Lets you **create a repository** to keep your code in a single place to ease backup and recovery.

☑ Lets multiple people **check out copies of the code** and work efficiently as a team.

☑ Lets multiple people **check changes back into the repository** and distribute them to the rest of the team.

☑ Keeps track of **who changes what**, when, and why.

☑ **Branches** and **tags code** so you can find and change versions of code from way back when.

☑ **Rolls back changes** that never should have happened in the first place.

...and what version control **doesn't** do

☐ Makes sure your code compiles.

☐ Tests code.

☐ Thinks for you.

☐ Makes sure your code is readable and well-written.

These are pretty important...looks like our tool set is nowhere near complete.

Version control can't make sure your code actually <u>works</u>...

Wouldn't it be dreamy if there was a tool that made sure my code actually compiled and worked before it showed up in a broken customer demo? But I guess it's just a fantasy...

Tools for your Software Development Toolbox

Software Development is all about developing
and delivering great software. In this chapter,
you learned about several techniques to keep
you on track. For a complete list of tools in the
book, see Appendix ii.

BULLET POINTS

- **Back up** your version control repository! It should have all of your code and a history of changes in it.

- Always use a **good commit message** when you commit your code—you and your team will appreciate it later.

- **Use tags liberally**. If there's any question about needing to know what the code looked like before a change, tag that version of your code.

- **Commit frequently** into the repository, but be careful about breaking other people's code. The longer you go between commits, the harder merges will be.

- There are lots of **GUI tools** for version control systems. They help a lot with merges and dealing with conflicts.

Development Techniques

Use a version control tool to track and distribute changes in your software to your team

Use tags to keep track of major milestones in your project (ends of iterations, releases, bug fixes, etc.)

Use branches to maintain a separate copy of your code, but only branch if absolutely necessary

Here are some of the key techniques you learned in this chapter...

... and some of the principles behind those techniques.

Development Principles

Always know where changes should (and shouldn't) go

Know what code went into a given release – and be able to get to it again

Control code change and distribution

Sharpen your pencil
Solution

Write down three problems with the approach outlined above for handling future changes to version 1.0 (or is it 1.1?).

1. You need to keep track of what revisions go with what version of the software.

2. It's going to be very difficult to keep 2.0 code changes from slipping into v1.x patches.

3. Changes for Version 2.0 could mean you need to delete a file or change a class so much that it would be very difficult to keep a v1.x patch without conflicting.

6 ½ building your code

Insert tab a into slot b...

I tried building this thing without instructions, and what a mess... Who knew you could build a gondola out of the parts you'd use to make a treehouse?

It pays to follow the instructions...
...especially when you write them yourself.

It's not enough to use version control to ensure your code stays safe. You've also got to worry about **compiling your code** and packaging it into a deployable unit. On top of all that, which class should be the main class of your application? How should that class be run? In this chapter, you'll learn how a **build tool** allows you to **write your own instructions** for dealing with your source code.

Developers aren't mind readers

Suppose you've got a new developer on your team. He can check out code from your version control server, and you're protected from his overwriting your code, too. But how does your new team member know which dependencies he's got to worry about? Or which class he should run to test things out?

I had no problems checking out the code, but there are 4 classes with main methods. I have no idea how to compile or run any of this.

Our version control server from Chapter 6.

svn checkout ...

How can you make sure your new developer knows what to do with your code?

There are lots of things you could do with source code: compile it all at once, run a particular class (or a set of classes); package classes up into a single JAR or DLL file, or multiple library files; include a bunch of dependencies... and these details change for every project you'll work on.

Software must be usable

It doesn't do you much good to put in a version control server if you can't also be sure your code is used properly once it's checked out. And that's where build scripts come in.

Good code is easy to USE, as well as easy to GET.

Building your project in one step

When someone wants to run your project, they need to do more than just compile source code—they need to **build** the project. Compiling source code into binary files is important, but building a project usually involves *finding dependencies*, *packaging up your project* into a usable form, and more.

And since tasks like these are the same each time they're run, building a project is a perfect candidate for **automation**: using a tool to handle the repetitive work for you. If you're using an IDE to write your code, a lot of this is handled for you when you click "Build." But there's a lot of work going on when you press that "Build" button:

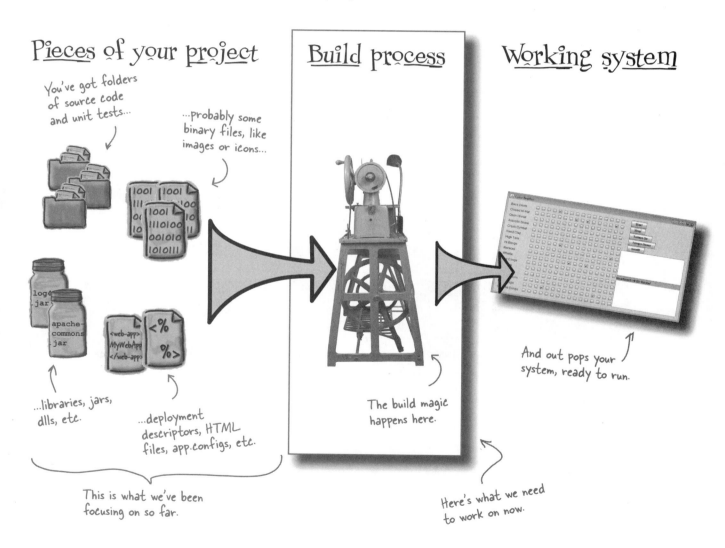

Pieces of your project

You've got folders of source code and unit tests...

...probably some binary files, like images or icons...

...libraries, jars, dlls, etc.

...deployment descriptors, HTML files, app.configs, etc.

This is what we've been focusing on so far.

Build process

The build magic happens here.

Working system

And out pops your system, ready to run.

Here's what we need to work on now.

Ant: a build tool for Java projects

Ant is a build tool for Java that can compile code, create and delete directories, and even package up files for you. It all centers around a **build script**. That's a file you write, in XML for Ant, that tells the tool what to do when you need to build your program.

You can download Ant from http://ant.apache.org/

The steps to build your project are stored in an XML file, usually named build.xml.

This whole file is called a build script.

Each build file represents a single project.

```xml
<project name="HFSDCoverage" default="dist" basedir=".">

    <property name="src" location="src"/>
    <property name="bin" location="bin"/>
    <property name="bin-instrumented" location="bin-
instrumented"/>
    <property name="reportdir" location="reportdir"/>

    <target name="clean">
        <delete dir="${bin}"/>
        <delete dir="${reportdir}"/>
        <delete dir="${bin-instrumented}"/>
        <delete file="cobertura.ser"/>
    </target>

    <target name="init">
        <mkdir dir="${bin}"/>
        <mkdir dir="${reportdir}"/>
        <mkdir dir="${bin-instrumented}"/>
    </target>
```

What's needed to build your project is broken up into steps called targets. Each target can have more than one task.

You just kick off a build with a single command. Ant runs the default target in build.xml, and follows your instructions.

```
File Edit Window Help DoIt
hfsd> ant
Buildfile: build.xml

init:
    [mkdir] Created dir: C:\Users\Developer\workspaces\HFSD\BeatBox\bin
    [mkdir] Created dir: C:\Users\Developer\workspaces\HFSD\BeatBox\dist

compile:
    [javac] Compiling 4 source files to C:\Users\Developer\workspaces\HFSD\BeatBox\bin

dist:
    [jar] Building jar: C:\Users\Developer\workspaces\HFSD\BeatBox\dist\BeatBox.jar

BUILD SUCCESSFUL
Total time: 16 seconds

hfsd>
```

In this case, Ant creates a directory structure...

...compiles code into that structure...

...and builds a JAR file.

Projects, properties, targets, tasks

An Ant build file is broken into four basic chunks:

1 **Projects**

Everything in your build file is part of a single project:

Everything in Ant is represented by an XML element tag.

In this case, Ant will run the dist target when the script is run.

```
<project name="BeatBox" default="dist">
```

Your project should have a name and a default target to run when the script is run.

Everything else in the build file is nested inside the project tag.

2 **Properties**

Ant properties are a lot like constants. They let you refer to values in the script, but you can change those values in a single place:

A property has a name and a value.

You can use properties with ${property-name}, like this.

```
<property name="version" value="1.1" />
<property name="src" location="src" />
<property name="xerces-src" location="${src}/xerces" />
```

You can use location instead of value if you're dealing with paths.

3 **Targets**

You can group different actions into a target, which is just a set of work. For example, you might have a `compile` target for compilation, and an `init` target for setting up your project's directory structure.

A target has a bunch of tasks nested within it.

```
<target name="compile" depends="init">
```

A target has a name, and optionally a list of targets that must be run before it.

4 **Tasks**

Tasks are the work horses of your build script. A task in Ant usually maps to a specific command, like `javac`, `mkdir`, or even `javadoc`:

This makes a new directory, using the value of the src property.

```
<mkdir dir="${src}">
<javac srcdir="${src}" destdir="${bin}" />
```

Each Ant task has different parameters, depending on what the task does and is used for.

Relax

The syntax here is particular to Ant, but the principles work with all build tools, in any language.

Ant is great for Java, but not everyone uses Java. For now, though, focus on what a good build tool gives you: a way to manage projects, constants, and specific tasks. In a few pages, we'll talk about build tools that work with other languages, like PHP, Ruby, and C#.

Are you kidding? I'm supposed to learn a whole new language just so I can compile my project?

No... you're supposed to learn a new tool so *someone (or something) ELSE* can *build* your project.

It's easy to see a build tool as just one more thing to learn and keep up with. But most build tools, like Ant, are really easy to learn. In fact, you're just about to put together your first build script, and you already know more than you think!

On top of that, your build tool is just that: *a tool*. It helps you get things done faster, especially over a lot of projects. You'll learn a little bit of syntax for your build tool, and hardly need to learn anything else about it.

Oh, and remember: ***the build tool is for your team, not just you***. While you may know how to compile your project, and keep up with its dependencies, everyone else might not. A build tool and build script lets everyone on your team use the same process to turn source code into a running application. With a good build script all it takes is one command to build the software; it's impossible for a developer to accidentally leave a step out—even after working on two other projects for six months.

Ant Build Magnets

Ant files are easier to use—and write—than you think. Below is part of a build script, but lots of pieces are missing. It's up to you to use the build magnets at the bottom of the page to complete the build script.

Put the magnets between the target elements to complete the build.xml file.

```
<project name="BeatBox" default="dist">
  <target name="init"
          description="Creates the needed directories.">
  _____
  _____
  </target>

  <target name="clean"
          description="Cleans up the build and dist directories.">
  _____
  _____
  </target>

  <target name="compile" depends="init"
          description="_____">
  _____
  _____
  </target>

  <target name="dist" depends="_____"
          description="Packages up BeatBox into BeatBox.jar">

  _____
  _____

</project>
```

Seems like there are a couple of extra magnets, so be careful.

destfile="dist/BeatBox.jar"

Compiles the source files to the bin directory.

debug="true"

Compiles the binary files to the src directory.

<jarc

<mkdir dir="bin"/>

/>

>

compile

init

dist

<jar

<javac

srcdir="src"

<delete dir="bin"/>

clean

init   compile

clean

<java

destdir="bin"

<delete dir="dist"/>

dist

basedir="bin"

</target>

<mkdir dir="dist"/>

</target>

/>

>

Ant Build Magnet Solutions

Your task was to reassemble a working build file for building
the BeatBox application.

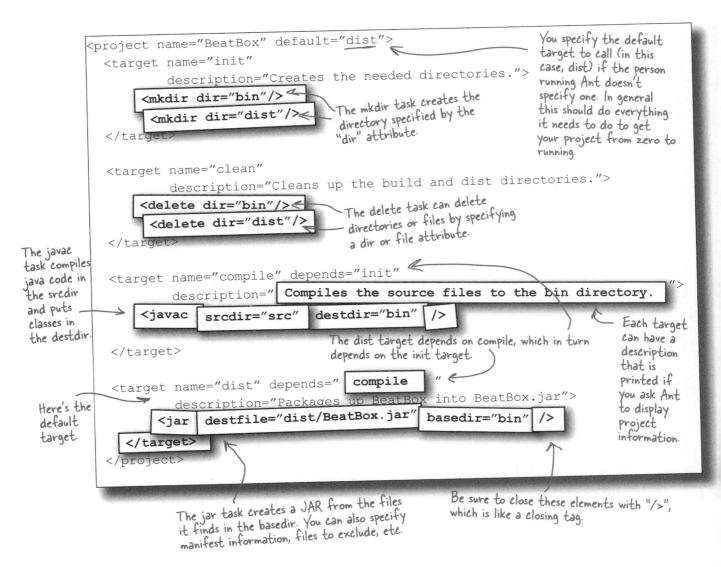

You specify the default target to call (in this case, dist) if the person running Ant doesn't specify one. In general this should do everything it needs to do to get your project from zero to running.

```
<project name="BeatBox" default="dist">
  <target name="init"
          description="Creates the needed directories.">
    <mkdir dir="bin"/>
    <mkdir dir="dist"/>
  </target>

  <target name="clean"
          description="Cleans up the build and dist directories.">
    <delete dir="bin"/>
    <delete dir="dist"/>
  </target>

  <target name="compile" depends="init"
          description="Compiles the source files to the bin directory.">
    <javac srcdir="src" destdir="bin" />
  </target>

  <target name="dist" depends="compile"
          description="Packages up BeatBox into BeatBox.jar">
    <jar destfile="dist/BeatBox.jar" basedir="bin" />
  </target>
</project>
```

The mkdir task creates the directory specified by the "dir" attribute.

The delete task can delete directories or files by specifying a dir or file attribute.

The javac task compiles java code in the srcdir and puts classes in the destdir.

The dist target depends on compile, which in turn depends on the init target.

Each target can have a description that is printed if you ask Ant to display project information.

Here's the default target.

The jar task creates a JAR from the files it finds in the basedir. You can also specify manifest information, files to exclude, etc.

Be sure to close these elements with "/>", which is like a closing tag.

there are no
Dumb Questions

Q: My project isn't in Java—do I still need a build tool?

A: Probably, and depending on what environment you're working in, you might already be using one. If you're developing in Microsoft Visual Studio, you're almost certainly *already* using their build system, called MSBuild (open your csproj file in Notepad...seriously). It uses an XML description of the build process similar to the way Ant does. Visual Studio started that file for you, but there's a whole lot more MSBuild can do for you that the IDE doesn't expose. If you're not in Visual Studio but are doing .NET development, you might want to check out NAnt. It's basically a port of Ant for the .NET world. Ruby uses a tool called rake to kick off tests, package up the application, clean up after itself, etc.

But there are some technologies, like Perl or PHP, where build scripts aren't quite as valuable, because those languages don't compile or package code. However, you can still use a build tool to package, test, and deploy your applications, even if you don't need everything a build tool brings to the table.

Q: I'm using an IDE that builds everything for me. Isn't that enough?

A: It might be enough for *you*, but what about everyone else on your team? Does everyone on your team have to use that IDE? This can be a problem on larger projects where there's an entirely separate group responsible for building and packaging your project for other teams like testers or QA.

Then there are tasks that your IDE *doesn't* do... (If you can't think of anything like that, we'll talk about some great ones in the next few chapters). In general, if your project is more than a one-person show (or you want to use

any of the best practices we're going to talk about in the next few chapters) you need to think about a build tool.

Q: Where did you come up with those bin, dist, and src directory names?

A: Those directories are an unofficial standard for Java projects. A few others you're likely to see are `docs` for generated documenation, `generated` for things like web-service-generated clients and stubs, and `lib` for library dependencies you might need.

There's nothing about these directory names that's set in stone, and you can adjust your build file to deal with whatever you use on your project. However, if you stick with common conventions, it makes it easier for new team members to get their heads around your project.

Q: Why are you even talking about Ant? Don't you know about Maven?

A: Maven is a Java-oriented "software project management and comprehension tool." Basically, it goes beyond the smaller-scale Ant tasks we've been talking about and adds support for automatically fetching library dependencies, publishing libraries you build to well-known places, test automation, etc. It's a great tool, but it masks a lot of what's going on behind the scenes. To get the most out of Maven you need to structure your project in a particular way.

For most small- to medium-sized projects, Ant can do everything you'll need. That's not to discourage you from checking out Maven, but it's important to understand the underlying concepts that Maven does such a great job of hiding. You can find out more about Maven at *http://maven.apache.org/*.

Q: What should my default target be? Should it compile my code, package it, generate documentation, all of the above?

A: That really depends on your project. If someone new was to check out your code, what are they most likely looking to do with it? Would they want to be able to check out your project and expect to be able to run it in one step? If so, you probably want your default target to do everything. But if "everything" means signing things with encryption keys and generating an installer with InstallShield and so on, you probably don't want that by default. A lot of projects actually set up the default target to output the project help information so that new people can see what their options are and pick appropriately.

Q: The build.xml file has directory names repeated all over the place. Is that a good idea?

A: Great catch! For a build script the size of the one we're using here, it's OK. But if you're writing a more complex build file, it's generally a good idea to use properties to let you define the directories once, and refer to them by aliases throughout the rest of the file. In Ant, you'd use the `property` tag for this, like on page 223.

Q: Couldn't I just do all of this with a batch file or shell script?

A: Technically, yes. But a build system comes with lots of software-development-oriented tasks that you'd either have to write yourself or lean on external tools to handle. Build tools also integrate into continuous integration systems, which we'll talk about in the next chapter.

Good build scripts...

A build script captures the details that developers probably don't need to know right from the start about how to compile and package an application, like BeatBox. The information isn't trapped in one person's head; it's captured in a version-controlled, repeatable process. But what exactly should a standard build script do?

You'll probably add tasks to your own build scripts, but all build scripts should do a few common things...

...generate documentation

Remember those description tags in the build file? Just type `ant -projecthelp` and you'll get a nice printout of what targets are available, a description of each, and what the default target is (which is usually what you want to use).

Your build tool probably has a way to generate documentation about itself and your project, even if you're not using Ant and Java.

```
File Edit  Window Help Huh?
hfsd> ant -projecthelp
Buildfile: build.xml

Main targets:

  clean    Cleans up the build and dist directories.
  compile  Compiles the source files to the bin directory.
  dist     Packages up BeatBox into BeatBox.jar
  init     Creates the needed directories.
Default target: dist

hfsd>
```

...compile your project

Most importantly, your build scripts compile the code in your project. And in most scripts, you want a single command that you can run to handle everything, from setup to compilation to packaging.

Here you can see the target dependencies in action: our build script tells Ant to run the dist target by default, but in order to do that, it has to run compile, and in order to do that, it has to run init.

```
File Edit  Window Help Build
hfsd> ant
Buildfile: build.xml

init:
    [mkdir] Created dir: C:\Users\Developer\workspaces\HFSD\BeatBox\bin
    [mkdir] Created dir: C:\Users\Developer\workspaces\HFSD\BeatBox\dist

compile:
    [javac] Compiling 4 source files to C:\Users\Developer\workspaces\HFSD\BeatBox\bin

dist:
    [jar] Building jar: C:\Users\Developer\workspaces\HFSD\BeatBox\dist\BeatBox.jar

BUILD SUCCESSFUL
Total time: 16 seconds

hfsd>
```

This is cool. But I saw there's a clean target in the build file we haven't talked about yet...

Good catch—a clean target is there to clean up the scraps of things that compiling leaves laying around. It's important to have a target that will get the project back to what it would look like if you checked the project out from the repository. That way, you can test things from a new developer's perspective.

Your tool may call this something else, but the idea is the same—clean up the mess made by building your project.

...clean up the mess they make

The final target we'll discuss in the BeatBox build script deletes the directories created during the build process: the `bin` directory for compiled classes and the `dist` directory for the final JAR file.

Since dist is the default target, you have to explicitly tell Ant to run the clean target.

```
File Edit Window Help Scrub
hfsd> ant clean
Buildfile: build.xml

clean:
   [delete] Deleting directory C:\Users\Developer\workspaces\HFSD\BeatBox\bin
   [delete] Deleting directory C:\Users\Developer\workspaces\HFSD\BeatBox\dist

BUILD SUCCESSFUL
Total time: 3 seconds

hfsd>
```

Ant runs the delete tasks to clean up the bin and dist directories and remove all of their contents.

Good build scripts go **BEYOND** the basics

Even though there are some standard things your scripts should do, you'll find plenty of places a good build tool will let your script go beyond the basics:

 Reference libraries your project needs

You can add libraries to your build path in Ant by using the `classpath` element in the `javac` task:

Each pathelement points to a single JAR to add to the classpath. You can also point to a directory if you need to.

```
<javac srcdir="src" destdir="bin">
  <classpath>
    <pathelement location="libs/junit.jar"/>
    <pathelement location="libs/log4j.jar"/>
  </classpath>
</javac>
```

If your project depends on libraries you don't want to include in your `libs` directory, you can also have Ant download libraries using FTP, HTTP, SCP, etc., using additional Ant tasks (check out the Ant task documentation for details).

2 **Run your application**

Sometimes it's not just compiling your application that requires some background knowledge; running it can be tricky, too. Suppose your app requires the setting of a complex library path or a long string of command-line options. You can wrap all of that up in your build script using the `exec` task:

```
<exec executable="cmd">
  <arg value="/c"/>
  <arg value="iexplorer.exe"/>
  <arg value="http://www.headfirstlabs.com/"/>
</exec>
```

Executing something on the system directly is obviously going to be platform-dependent. Don't try to run iexplorer.exe on Linux.

(but do go to Head First Labs)

or the `java` task:

```
<java classname="headfirst.sd.chapter6.BeatBox">
  <arg value="HFBuildWizard"/>
  <classpath>
    <pathelement location="dist/BeatBox.jar"/>
  </classpath>
</java>
```

If you wrap this in a target then you won't ever have to type "java –cp blahblah..." again to launch BeatBox.

③ Generate documentation

You've already seen how Ant can display documentation for the build file, but it can also generate JavaDoc from your source code:

```
<javadoc packagenames="headfirst.sd.*"
    sourcepath="src"
    destdir="docs"
    windowtitle="BeatBox Documentation"/>
```

> *Note that Ant can generate your HTML files for you—but it can't <u>write</u> the documentation you've been putting off.*

> *There are other elements you can include in the JavaDoc task to generate headers and footers for each page if you need to.*

④ Check out code, run tests, copy builds to archival directories, encrypt files, email you when the build finishes, execute SQL...

There are lots more tasks you can use depending on what you need your build file to do. Now that you know the basics, all of the other tasks look pretty much the same. To get a look at the tasks Ant offers go to: http://ant.apache.org/manual/index.html.

Automation lets you focus on code, not repetitive tasks.

With a good build script, you can automate a pretty sophisticated build process. It's not uncommon to see multiple build files on a single project, one for each library or component. In cases like that, you might want to think about a master build file (sometimes called a **bootstrap** script) that ties everything together.

Your build script is code, too

You've put a lot of work into your build script. In fact, ***it's really code***, just like your source files and deployment descriptors. When you look at your build script as code, you'll realize there are lots of clever things you can do with it, like deal with platform differences between Windows and Unix, use timestamps to track builds or figure out what needs to be recompiled—all completely hidden from the person trying to do the build. But, like all other code, it belongs in a repository...

You should always check your build script into your code repository:

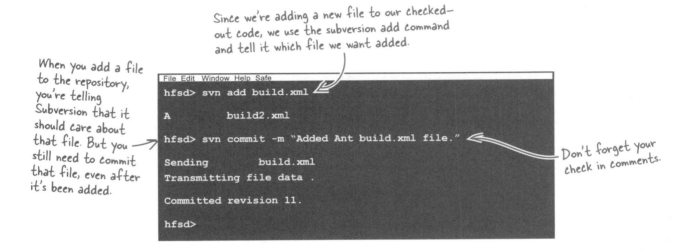

Since we're adding a new file to our checked-out code, we use the subversion add command and tell it which file we want added.

When you add a file to the repository, you're telling Subversion that it should care about that file. But you still need to commit that file, even after it's been added.

Don't forget your check in comments.

With your build script in the repository, it's available to everyone else when they do an update. Your version control software will track any changes to the script, and the script gets tagged with everything else whenever you do a release. This means that you won't have to remember all the magic commands you needed to build the nostalgic Version 1.0 in a few years at your IPO party!

Your build script is code...ACT LIKE IT! Code belongs in a version control system, where it's versioned, tagged, and saved for later use.

New developer, take two

We haven't written any new classes, talked to the customer, broken tasks up into stories, or demoed software for the customer...but things are still looking a lot better. With a build tool in place, let's see what bringing on the new developer looks like:

Nice...I checked out the project, ran the build script, and now I can get right to work.

Our version control server from Chapter 6.

svn checkout ...

Your new developer's productive within minutes, instead of hours (or worse, days) and won't spend that time bugging you for help on how to build the system.

BULLET POINTS

- A build tool is simply a **tool**. It should make building your project **easier**, not harder.

- Most build tools use a **build script**, where you can specify what to build, several different instruction sets, and locations of external files and resources.

- Be sure you create a way to **clean up** any files your script creates.

- Your build script is **code** and should be versioned and checked into your code repository.

- **Build tools are for your team**, not just you. Choose a build tool that works for everyone on your team.

Tools for your Software Development Toolbox

Software Development is all about developing and delivering great software. In this chapter, you learned about several techniques to keep you on track. For a complete list of tools in the book, see Appendix ii.

Development Techniques

Use a build tool to script building, packaging, testing, and deploying your system

Most IDEs are already using a build tool underneath. Get familiar with that tool, and you can build on what the IDE already does

Treat your build script like code and check it into version control

Here are some of the key techniques you learned in this chapter...

... and some of the principles behind those techniques.

Development Principles

Building a project should be repeatable and automated

Build scripts set the stage for other automation tools

Build scripts go beyond just step-by-step automation and can capture compilation and deployment logic decisions

BULLET POINTS

- All but the smallest projects have a **nontrivial build process**.

- You want to **capture** and **automate** the knowledge of **how to build your system**—ideally in a single command.

- **Ant** is a build tool for **Java projects** and captures build information in an XML file named build.xml.

- The more you take advantage of **common conventions**, the more **familiar** your project will look to someone else, and the easier the project will be to integrate with external tools.

- Your **build script** is just as much a part of your project as **any other piece of code**. It should be checked into version control with everything else.

7 testing and continuous integration

Things fall apart

I swear, Mac, I'll get it working again...just give me 48 hours. I'll make good on my marker, okay?

Sometimes even the best developer breaks the build.

Everyone's done it at least once. You're sure **your code compiles**; you've tested it over and over again on your machine and committed it into the repository. But somewhere between your machine and that black box they call a server, *someone* must have changed your code. The unlucky soul who does the next checkout is about to have a bad morning sorting out **what used to be working code**. In this chapter we'll talk about how to put together a **safety net** to keep the build in working order and you **productive**.

Things will ALWAYS go wrong...

Everyone who's ever done development knows what it's like. It's late, you're on you're eleventh can of Rock Star energy drink, and you still leave out that one ++ operator somewhere. Suddenly, your elegant code goes to pieces...bad news is, you don't *realize* you've got a problem.

At least, not until you're demoing the software for your boss. Remember the issues we had with Bob's code in Chapter 6?

Bob's code seemed to work in some places...

...but not in others.

I'm not hearing any alert. And what's SECRET_POKE_ SEQUENCE? I'm not impressed.

The real problem was that we were as surprised as the customer was when things went wrong.

⚛ **BRAIN POWER**

What other kinds of things can go wrong on a development project? What about with a small team? Do you have the same problems with a bigger team? Different problems?

Standup meeting

If Bob had just made sure his code compiled, none of this would even be an issue.

Bob: I did get it compiling! It took me forever to integrate the changes and get everything building again. It's not my fault.

Mark: Yeah, the code compiled; it just didn't work. So he didn't screw up as badly as it looks, really.

Laura: Didn't you test things?

Bob: Well, the code worked fine on my machine. I ran it and everything seemed fine...

Mark: OK, but running your code and doing a quick checkover is not really putting your code to the test.

Laura: Exactly. The functionality of your software is part of your responsibility, not just that the code "seems to work"; that's never going to wash with the customer...

Bob: Well, now that we have a version control server and build tool in place, this shouldn't be a problem anymore. So enough beating up on me, alright?

Mark: Hardly! Our build tool makes sure the code compiles, and we can back out changes with version control, but that doesn't help making sure things work right. Your code compiled; that was never the problem. It's the functionality of the system that got screwed up, and our build tool does nothing for that.

Laura: Yeah, you didn't even realize anything had gone wrong...

There are three ways to look at your system...

Good testing is essential on any software project. If your software doesn't work, it won't get used—and there's a good chance you won't get paid. So before getting into the nitty-gritty of software testing, it's important to step back and remember that different people look at your system from totally different perspectives, or views.

For more on these different types of testing, see Appendix i.

Your users see the system from the <u>outside</u>

Your users don't see your code, they don't look at the database tables, they don't evaluate your algorithms...and generally *they don't want to*. Your system is a **black box** to them; it either does what they asked it to do, or it doesn't. Your users are all about **functionality**.

Testers peek <u>under</u> <u>the</u> <u>covers</u> a little

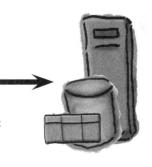

Testers are a different breed. They're looking for functionality, but they're usually poking underneath to make sure things are really happening the way you said they would. Your system is more of a **grey box** to them. Testers are probably looking at the data in your database to make sure things are being cleaned up correctly; they might be checking that ports are closed, network connections dropped, and that memory usage is staying steady.

Developers let it <u>all</u> <u>hang</u> <u>out</u>

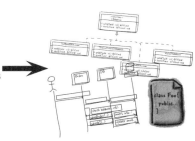

Developers are in the weeds. They see good (and sometimes bad) class design, patterns, duplicated code, inconsistencies in how things are represented. The system is wide open to them. If users see a system as a closed black box, developers see it as an open **white box**. But sometimes because developers see so much detail, it's possible for them to miss broken functionality or make an assumption that a tester or end user might not.

...and you need to consider each of these views

Each view of your system is valid, and you have to test from each of those three perspectives.

Black-box testing focuses on <u>INPUT</u> and <u>OUTPUT</u>

Your users are outside your system. They only see what they put into the system and what comes back out. When you do black-box testing you should look for:

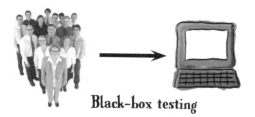

Black-box testing

☐   **Functionality**. Hands down, this is the most important black box testing. Does the system do what the user story says it is supposed to do? With black box testing, you don't care if your data is being stored in a text file or a massively parallel clustered database. You just care that the data gets in there like the story says and you get back the results the story says you should.

This isn't "the OrderProcessor class can handle GiftCard objects" functionality; it's about if a customer can buy a drink with their gift card.

☐   **User input validation**. Feed your system 3.995 for a dollar amount or -1 for your birthday. If you're writing a web application, put some HTML in your name field or try some SQL. The system better reject those values, and do it in a way that a typical end user can understand.

☐   **Output results**. Hand-check numerical values that your system returns. Make sure all of the functional paths have been tested ("if the user enters an invalid ending location, and then clicks "Get Directions"...") It's often helpful to put together a table showing the various inputs you could give the system, and what you'd expect the results to be for each input.

Error conditions are usually the last thing most developers think about, but it's the first thing most customers notice.

☐   **State transitions**. Some systems need to move from one state to another according to very specific rules. This is similar to output results, but it's about making sure your system handles moving from state to state like it's supposed to. This is particularly critical if you're implementing some kind of protocol like SMTP, a satellite communications link, or GPS receiver. Again, having a map of the states and what it takes to move the system from one to the other is very useful here.

☐   **Boundary cases and off-by-one errors**. You should test your system with a value that's just a little too small or just outside the maximum allowable value. For example, checking month 12 (if your months go from 0–11) or month 13 will let you know if you've got things just right, or if someone slipped up and forgot about zero-based arrays.

Customers don't usually make huge mistakes—they make <u>little</u> typos, and those are the things you're testing for here.

Grey-box testing gets you <u>CLOSER</u> to the code

Black-box testing works great for a lot of applications, but there are situations where you need more. Sometimes you just can't get the results out of a system easily without looking inside, at least a little. This is particularly true with a lot of web applications, where the web interface just moves data around in a database. You've got to deal with the database code *as well as* the web interface itself.

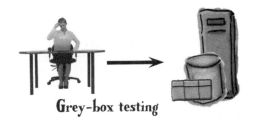

Grey-box testing

Grey-box testing is like black-box testing...but you can peek

When doing grey box testing, you're generally looking for the same things as black box testing, but you can dig around a little to make sure the system works as it's supposed to below the surface. Use grey box testing for things like:

☐ **Verifying auditing and logging**. When important data (or money) is on the line, there's usually a lot of auditing and logging going on inside a system. This information isn't usually available through the normal user interface, either. You might need to use a log viewing tool or auditing report, or maybe just query some database tables directly.

But be careful of logging confidential information to unsecured places, you won't make the right sorts of friends that way...

☐ **Data destined for other systems**. If you're building a system that sends information to another system at a later time (say an order for 50 copies of *Head First Software Development*), you should check the output format and data you're sending to the other systems...and that means looking underneath what's exposed by the system.

☐ **System-added information**. It's common for applications to create checksums or hashes of data to make sure things are stored correctly (or securely). You should hand-check these. Make sure system-generated timestamps are being created in the right time zone and stored with the right data.

☐ **Scraps left laying around**. It's so easy as a developer to miss doing cleanup after a system is done with data. This can be a security risk as well as a resource leak. Make sure data is really deleted if it's supposed to be, and make sure it isn't deleted if it's not. Check that the system isn't leaking memory while it's running. Look for things that might leave scraps of files or registry entries after they should have been cleaned up. Verify that uninstalling your application leaves the system clean.

Exercise

Below is a user story from BeatBox Pro. Your job is to write up three ideas for black or grey box tests, and descriptions of what you'd do to implement those tests.

Title: Send a picture to other users

Description: Click on the "Send a Picture" button to send a picture (only JPEG needs to be supported) to the other users. They should have the option to not accept the file. There are no size limits on the file right now.

Priority: 20   **Estimate:** 4

1. Test for... sending a small JPEG to another user

Here's one to get you started.

How would you test this? Describe the test case in plain English.

2. Test for...

Think about the different ways the fuctionality in the user story could be tested, like testing when it handles things going wrong...

3. Test for...

Exercise Solution

Below is a user story from BeatBox Pro. Your job was to write up three ideas for black or grey box tests, and descriptions of what you'd do to implement those tests.

Title: Send a picture to other users

Description: Click on the "Send a Picture" button to send a picture (only JPEG needs to be supported) to the other users. They should have the option to not accept the file. There are no size limits on the file right now.

Priority: 20   **Estimate:** 4

* Here are the three tests we came up with. It's okay if you have three different ones... you'll just have more ideas for actual tests.

1. Test for... sending a small JPEG to another user.

Get two instances of BeatBox Pro running. On the first instance, click the Send Picture button. When the image selection dialog pops up, select SmallImage.jpg and click OK.

Then check and make sure that the second BeatBox displays a Receive Image dialog box. Click OK to accept the image. Check that the image displays correctly.

This is a black-box test. Also notice that we needed some JPEG resources to support the test. That's OK; using sample input is fine. You should version-control those resources, though, for later reuse.

2. Test for... sending an invalid JPEG to another user.

Get two instances of BeatBox Pro running. On the first instance, click the Send Picture button. When the image selection dialog pops up, select InvalidImage.jpg and click OK.

Check that BeatBox shows a dialog telling you that the image is invalid and can't be sent. Confirm that the second BeatBox did not display a Receive Image dialog. Also make sure no exceptions were thrown from either instance.

These tests are a little more on the grey side. You need to know how BeatBox Pro should handle these conditions, and where exceptions would be sent if an error occurred.

3. Test for... losing connectivity while transferring an image.

Start two instances of BeatBox Pro. On the first instance, click the Send Picture button. When the image selection dialog pops up, select GiantImage.jpg and click OK.

Check that the second BeatBox shows a Receive Image dialog box and click OK. While this image is transferring (make the image several MB so it will take a while), kill the second BeatBox instance. Check that the first BeatBox displays a dialog saying the transfer failed and that no exceptions were thrown.

White-box testing uses inside knowledge

At the deepest levels of testing, you'll find white box tests. This is where you know exactly what's going on inside the code, and you do your best to make that code break. If you put aside the fact that you have to fix the code when it does break, white-box testing can actually be fun: it becomes a challenge to dig into code and generate problem situations that will cause errors and crashes.

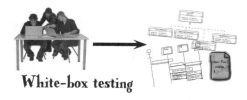

White-box testing

When doing white-box testing you should be familiar with the code you're about to test. You still care about functionality, but you should also be thinking about the fact that method X is going to divide by one of the numbers you're sending in... is that number being checked properly? With white-box testing you're generally looking for:

☐ **Testing all the different branches of code**. With white-box testing you should be looking at *all* of your code. You can see all of the `if/ elses` and all the case and switch statements. What data do you need to send in to get the class you're looking at to run each of those branches?

Most code works great when things are going as expected—the so-called "happy path"—but what about when things go off-track?

☐ **Proper error handling**. If you do feed invalid data into a method, are you getting the right error back? Is your code cleaning up after itself nicely by releasing resources like file handles, mutexes, or allocated memory?

☐ **Working as documented**. If the method claims it's thread-safe, test the method from multiple threads If the documentation says you can pass null in as an argument to a method and you'll then get back a certain set of values, is that what's really going on? If a method claims you need a certain security role to call it, try the method with and without that role.

Black-box testing looked at error messages, but what about what the code left around when things go wrong? That's for white-box testing to examine.

☐ **Proper handling of resource constraints**. If a method tries to grab resources—like memory, disk space, or a network connection—what does the code do if it can't get the resource it needs? Are these problems handled gracefully? Can you write a test to force the code into one of those problematic conditions?

White-box tests tend to be <u>code-on-code</u>

Since white-box tests tend to get up close and personal with the code they're trying to test, it's common to see them written in code and run on a machine rather than exercised by a human. Let's write some code-on-code tests now...

Exercise

Below is the block of code that Bob built for the BeatBox Pro demo (the one that failed spectacularly), and the two user stories that version of the software was focused on. On the next page are three tests that need to pass. How would you test these in code?

Title: ...Send a poke to... ...other users...

Description: Click on the "Send a Poke" button to send an audible and visual alert to the other members in the chat. The alert should be short and not too annoying—you're just trying to get their attention.

Priority: 20   Estimate: 3

Title: ...Send a picture... ...to other users...

Description: Click on the "Send a Picture" button to send a picture (only JPEG needs to be supported) to the other users. They should have the option to not accept the file. There are no size limits on the file right now.

Priority: 20   Estimate: 4

These stories have to work in the demo—you have to test for this functionality.

```
public class RemoteReader implements Runnable {
  boolean[] checkboxState = null;
  String nameToShow = null;
  Object obj = null;

  public void run() {
  try {
    while ((obj = in.readObject()) != null) {
      System.out.println("got an object from server");
      System.out.println(obj.getClass());
      String nameToShow = (String) obj;
      checkboxState = (boolean[]) in.readObject();
      if (nameToShow.equals(PICTURE_START_SEQUENCE)) {
        receiveJPEG();
      }
      else {
        otherSeqsMap.put(nameToShow, checkboxState);
        listVector.add(nameToShow);
        incomingList.setListData(listVector);
        // now reset the sequence to be this
      }
    } // close while
  } catch (Exception ex) {
    ex.printStackTrace();
  }
  } // close run
}
```

Remember that Bob overwrote the code to handle the POKE_START_SEQUENCE command.

How could you test this code to make sure it works, even if another problem comes up?

Definitely pseudocode...if you need a resource, assume you can get it. This is just the basic code-level steps you'd need.

1. Test for... a picture start sequence to test picture functionality.

establish a new network connection
send the PICTURE_START_SEQUENCE
send over an empty array of check boxes (no audio)
send the picture data
verify picture data received and displayed properly

Here's what you need to test.

This one is done for you to give you an idea of the pseudocode to use to describe a test.

2. Test for... a poke start sequence to test for poke functionality.

establish a new network connection

What would this test do? This should be pseudocode. What code are you going to have to write to implement this test?

3. Test for... a normal text message that's sent to all clients.

establish a new network connection

Exercise Solution

Below is the block of code that Bob built for the demo (the one that failed spectacularly), and the two user stories this version of the software was focused on. Your job was to figure out how to white-box-test for at least three problem situations.

test for   a picture start sequence to test picture functionality. ⟵ ·········

This is to test the basic picture functionality, since it was one of our new stories, but digs into the code involved.

establish a new network connection
send the PICTURE_START_SEQUENCE
send over an empty array of checkboxes (no audio)
send the picture data
verify picture data received and displayed properly. ⟵

This is more in-depth than just using the GUI: you're really testing specific methods, with specific inputs, to make sure the result is what's expected.

test for   a poke start sequence to test for poke functionality.

establish a new network connection
send the POKE_START_SEQUENCE
send over an empty array of check boxes (no audio)
verify alert sound is heard and the alert message is shown. ⟵

You'll probably need to verify this works by watching a running chat client—that's okay, use whatever you need to test properly.

With a test to check the POKE_START_SEQUENCE, you can see if it fails before showing it the customer, and avoid any surprises.

This one is based on the other story, and is a lot like the picture test.

test for   a normal text message is sent to all clients. ⟵

establish a new network connection
send the message, "Test message"
send an array of valid checkbox options
verify the test message was received by all clients and the
checkboxes are updated to match the array values. ⟵

Don't forget to test stuff that should still be working! This is just as important as testing new functionality.

There are lots more tests you could have come up with—things like testing that clicking on one of the messages retrieves the checkboxes correctly, and testing for failure conditions. What happens if too many checkbox values are sent in an array? Or too few? See how many ways you can break BeatBox Pro.

But aren't there testing frameworks out there to do this for us? Why are we writing all this code ourselves?

Coming up with tests is <u>YOUR</u> job.

There are lots of good frameworks out there, but they ***run*** your tests; they don't write them for you.✱ A testing frameworks is really just a collection of tools that help you express your tests. Even though that makes them really useful, there are a few things you still need to keep in mind:

First, **you still need to figure out what you have to test**. Figuring out what to test and how you express that test are usually two different things. Regardless of your framework, you need to think about functional testing, performance testing, boundary or edge cases, race conditions, security risks, valid data, invalid data, etc.

Next, **your choice of testing frameworks is almost certainly going to impact how you test**. That's not always a bad thing, but don't forget about it. This might mean you need more than one way to test your software. For example, if you decide to use a code-level testing framework for your desktop application, you're still leaving yourself open for bugs in your GUI, so you'll probably want something to test that, too. Another great example: say you're writing a 3-D game. Testing the backend code isn't too hard, but making sure that the game renders correctly and people can't walk through walls or fall through small cracks in your world...well, that's a mess, and no framework can generate those tests for you.

✱ Actually, some frameworks can generate tests for you, but they have very specific goals in mind. Security frameworks are a common example: the framework can throw tons of common security errors at your software and see what happens. But this doesn't replace real application testing to make sure the system does what you think it does (and what the customer actually wants it to do).

Hanging your tests on a framework

We're talking about frameworks, but what does that really mean? The obvious way to test is to have someone **use your application**. But, if we can automate our tests we can ~~get paid while the computer tests our stuff~~ be more effective and know that our tests are run exactly the same way each time. That's important, because consistency in how a test is run isn't something humans are very good at.

Testing EVERYTHING with one step ⌐ Well, one command actually

There are lots more advantages to automating your tests. As well as not requiring you to sit there and manually run the tests yourself, you also build up a **library of tests** that are all run at the same time to test your software completely every time you run the **test suite**:

1 **Build up a suite of tests**

As your software grows so will the tests that need to be applied to it. At first, this might seem a little scary, especially if you're running tests by hand. Large software systems can have literally thousands of tests that take days of developer time to run. If you automate your tests you can collect all the tests for your software into one library and then run those tests at will, without having to rely on having somebody, probably a poor test engineer who looked at you wrong, running those tests manually for a day or so.

2 **Run all your tests with one command**

Once you have a suite of tests that can be run automatically in a framework, the next step is to build that set of tests such that they can all be run with just one command. The easier a test suite is to run, the more often it will actually be used and that can only mean that your software quality will improve. Any new tests are simply added to the test suite, and bang, everyone gets the benefit of the test you have written.

3 **Get regression testing for free**

The big advantage of creating a one-command suite of tests that you continually add to as you add more code to your software is that you get **regression testing** for free. Detecting when a new change that you've made to your software has actually introduced bugs in the older code, called **software regression**, is a danger for any developer working with old or inherited code. The best way to deal with the threat of regression problems is to not only run your own tests for your newly added code, but to run all the older tests as well.

Now, because you'll be adding your new tests into your test suite, you'll get this for free. All you have to do is add your new tests to the existing test suite and kick things off with one command—you'll have regression tested your changes.

Of course, this relies on the existing code base having a suite of tests available for you to extend. Check out Chapter 10 for what to do when that isn't the case.

Hmm, won't testing everything every time make testing take a long time? Isn't there a way of tuning things so that developers can regression-test everything when they need to, and just fit testing in manually

Tailor your test suites to suit the occasion

It's unfortunately true that large unit test suites become ungainly and, therefore, tend to get used less. One technique is to break out fast and slow tests so that a developer can run all the fast tests often while they are changing and adding code, but only run the full suite when they think they need to.

What tests fall into the fast or slow categories is really up to your particular project, and which category specific tests fall into can change depending on the development work that you are doing. For example, if you have barely-ever-changes code that takes a long time to test, then that would be a good candidate for the slow test suite. However if you were working on code that might well impact the barely-ever-changes code, then you might consider moving its tests into the fast test suite while you are working those changes.

Let's try it out with a popular free testing framework for Java, called JUnit.

To download the JUnit framework, go to http://www.junit.org

You can also speed up slow tests using mocks; see Chapter 8 for more on those.

there are no
Dumb Questions

Q: So how often should we run our entire test suite?

A: This is really up to you and your team. If you're happy with running your full test suite once a day, and know that any regression bugs will only be caught once a day, then that's fine. However, we'd still recommend you have a set of tests that can be run much more frequently.

Keep the time it takes to run your tests as short as possible. The longer a test suite takes to run, the less often it is likely to be run!

Automate your tests with a testing framework

Let's take a simple test case and automate it using JUnit. JUnit provides common resources and behaviors you need for your tests, and then invokes each of your tests, one at a time. JUnit gives you a nice GUI to see your tests run, as well, but that's really a small thing compared to the power of automating your tests.

JUnit also has a text-based test runner and plug-ins for most popular IDEs.

You've got to import the JUnit classes.

Here's a static final of empty checkboxes that can be used in several different tests.

JUnit calls setUp() before each test is run, so here's where to initialize variables used in the test methods.

tearDown() is for cleaning up. JUnit calls this method when each test is finished.

Here's an actual test. You annotate it with @Test so JUnit knows it's a test and can run it. The method just sends a test message and a checkboxState.

These are objects used in several of the test cases.

Since these are annotated with @Before and @After, they'll get called by JUnit before and after each test.

```java
package headfirst.sd.chapter7;
import java.io.*;
import java.net.Socket;
import org.junit.*;

public class TestRemoteReader {
    private Socket mTestSocket;
    private ObjectOutputStream mOutStream;
    private ObjectInputStream mInStream;

    public static final boolean[] EMPTY_CHECKBOXES = new boolean[256];

    @Before
    public void setUp() throws IOException {
        mTestSocket = new Socket("127.0.0.1", 4242);
        mOutStream =
            new ObjectOutputStream(mTestSocket.getOutputStream());
        mInStream =
            new ObjectInputStream(mTestSocket.getInputStream());
    }

    @After
    public void tearDown() throws IOException {
        mTestSocket.close();
        mOutStream = null;
        mInStream = null;
        mTestSocket = null;
    }

    @Test
    public void testNormalMessage() throws IOException {
        boolean[] checkboxState = new boolean[256];
        checkboxState[0] = true;
        checkboxState[5] = true;
        checkboxState[19] = true;
        mOutStream.writeObject("This is a test message!");
        mOutStream.writeObject(checkboxState);
    }
}
```

You can use mOutStream because it was set up in the setup() method that JUnit will already have called.

Use your framework to run your tests

Invoke the JUnit test runner, `org.junit.runner.JUnitCore`. The only information you need to give the runner is which test class to run: `headfirst.sd.chapter7.TestRemoteReader`. The framework handles running each test in that class::

Don't forget to start the MusicServer and a copy of the BeatBox Pro. JUnit won't take care of that for you, unless you add code for that into setUp().

Don't forget to put junit.jar in your classpath.

JUnit will print a dot for each test it ran. Since this class has only one test, you get a single dot.

"OK" is JUnit's understated way of saying all the tests ran.

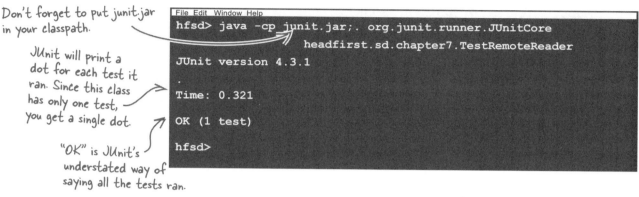

```
File  Edit  Window  Help
hfsd> java -cp junit.jar;. org.junit.runner.JUnitCore
                    headfirst.sd.chapter7.TestRemoteReader
JUnit version 4.3.1
.
Time: 0.321

OK (1 test)

hfsd>
```

And here's what BeatBox Pro looks like after the test has run. Checkmarks are where they're supposed to be and the test message is in the log.

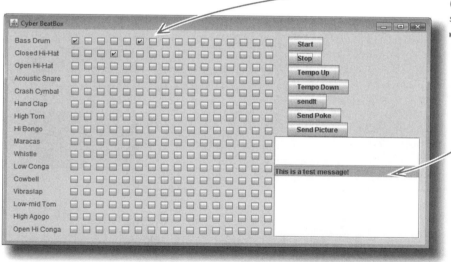

With a framework in place, you can easily add the other tests from page 246. Just add more test methods and annotate them with `@Test`. You can then run your test classes and watch the results.

> Wouldn't it be dreamy if there was a tool that ran all my tests for me, every time I checked in code, so I wouldn't be embarrassed in front of my team?

Continuous integration tools run your tests when you check in your code

We've already got a version control tool that keeps track of our code, and now we've got a set of automated tests. We just need a way to tie these two systems together. There are version control tools (or applications that integrate with version control tools) that will compile your code, run your automated tests, and even display and mail out reports—as soon as you (or Bob) commit code into your repository.

This is all part of **continuous integration** (CI), and it looks like this:

Sometimes the CI tool watches your repository for changes, but the end result is the same—the whole thing is automatic.

(2) **The version control tool notifies your CI tool that there's new code available.**

For you and your team, nothing changes from the version control process you already have. You start out by updating some code, and then checking it in.

New code's available!

(1) **Bob checks in some code.**

Here's some code.

The version control server does its normal check-in procedures, like updating the revision number, but now it has a continuous integration tool it works with, too.

Under the Hood

The great thing about version control and CI is that they happen without you having to do anything— it's all going on "under the hood."

Continuous integration and build tools are two more processes that improves communication amongst your team.

(3) **The CI tool checks out the new code, compiles it, and runs all your tests. Most build tools create web pages and emails to let everyone know how the builds are going.**

This particular build tool is called CruiseControl, but there are lots of similar products out there.

there are no Dumb Questions

Q: Does CI have to build and test my code every time I check it in? My project is so large that could really slow things down.

A: No, defnitely not. Although building and running your tests every time you commit changes to version control is a good practice, sometimes it's not entirely practical. If you have a really large set of tests that use significant computing resources, you might want to schedule things a bit differently.

> **Continuous integration wraps version control, compilation, and testing into a <u>single</u> repeatable process.**

At the wheel of CI with CruiseControl

The three main jobs of a CI tool are to get a version of the code from your repository, build that code, and then run a suite of tests against it. To give you a flavor of how CI is set up, let's take a look at how that works in CruiseControl:

1 **Add your JUnit test suite to your Ant build**

Before you build your CruiseControl project, you need to add your JUnit tests into your Ant build file.

You last saw Ant in Chapter 6.5.

```
<target name="test" depends="compile">

  <junit>

    <classpath refid="classpath.test" />

    <formatter type="brief" usefile="false" />

    <batchtest>

      <fileset dir="${tst-dir}" includes="**/Test*.class" />

    </batchtest>

  </junit>

</target>

<target name="all" depends="test" />
```

A new target called "test" that depends on the "compile" target having finished successfully

Here's where the magic happens. All of the classes in your project that begin with the word "Test" are automatically executed as JUnit tests. No need for you to specify each one individually.

The "all" target is just a nicer way of saying "compile, build, and test everything."

2 **Create your CruiseControl project**

The next step is to create a CruiseControl project and begin to define your build and test process.

```
<cruisecontrol>

  <project name="BeatBox" buildafterfailed="true">

    <!-- This is where the rest of your project configuration will go -->

  </project>

</cruisecontrol>
```

The project tag bounds all of your project's configuration.

In CruiseControl, your project is described using an XML document, much the same as in Ant, except this script describes what is going be done, and when.

③ **Check to see if there have been any changes in the repository**

Inside your CruiseControl project you can describe where to get your code from and then what to do with it. In this case, code changes are grabbed from your subversion repository. If the code has changed, then a full build is run; otherwise the scheduled build is skipped.

The "modificationset" tells the repository to check against the local copy to see if it actually needs to build changes in or not

```
<modificationset quietperiod="10">

  <svn LocalWorkingCopy="hfsd/chapter7/cc"
    RepositoryLocation="file:///c:/Users/Developer/Desktop/SVNRepo/BeatBox/trunk"/>

</modificationset>
```

Here you declare what local copy and remote repository to check against for changes

④ **Schedule the build**

Finally, you describe how often you want your continuous integration build to take place. In CruiseControl this is done with the schedule tag, inside of which you describe the type of build that you want to perform.

Schedules the build to occur every 60 minutes.

```
<schedule interval="60">
  <ant antworkingdir="hfsd/chapter7/cc"

      buildfile="build.xml"

      uselogger="true"

      usedebug="true"

      target="all"/>
</schedule>
```

Here, you plug in your Ant build script.

Building the "all" target

Testing guarantees things will work... right?

Version control, CI, test frameworks, build tools...you've come a long way since it was you and your college buddies hacking away on laptops in your garage. With all your testing, you should be confident showing the customer what you've built:

The customer clicked on a Poke message in the log, and suddenly a nasty stack trace spit out onto the console window.

This is really starting to get old... can't you get **anything** right?

ExeRciSe

Here's the code we changed in Chapter 6. The bug has to be related to this stuff somewhere. Find the bug that bit us this time.

```
public void buildGUI() {
  // code from buildGUI
  JButton sendIt = new JButton("sendIt");
  sendIt.addActionListener(new MySendListener());
  buttonBox.add(sendIt);
  JButton sendPoke = new JButton("Send Poke");
  sendPoke.addActionListener(new MyPokeListener());
  buttonBox.add(sendPoke);
  userMessage = new JTextField();
  buttonBox.add(userMessage);
  // more code in buildGUI()
}

public class MyPokeListener implements ActionListener {
  public void actionPerformed(ActionEvent a) {
    // We'll create an empty state array here
    boolean[] checkboxState = new boolean[255];
    try {
      out.writeObject(POKE_START_SEQUENCE);
      out.writeObject(checkboxState);
    } catch (Exception ex) {
        System.out.println("Failed to poke!"); }
    }
  }
  // other code in BeatBoxFinal.java
}
```

Here's the code we modified from BeatBox.java's buildGUI() method.

This inner class is from BeatBox.java, too.

What went wrong in this code? ....
....

Why didn't our tests catch this? ....
....

What would you do differently? ....
....

Exercise Solution

Here's the code we changed in Chapter 6. The bug has to be related to this stuff somewhere. Find the bug that bit us this time.

```java
public void buildGUI() {
  // code from buildGUI
  JButton sendIt = new JButton("sendIt");
  sendIt.addActionListener(new MySendListener());
  buttonBox.add(sendIt);
  JButton sendPoke = new JButton("Send Poke");
  sendPoke.addActionListener(new MyPokeListener());
  buttonBox.add(sendPoke);
  userMessage = new JTextField();
  buttonBox.add(userMessage);
  // more code in buildGUI()
}

public class MyPokeListener implements ActionListener {
  public void actionPerformed(ActionEvent a) {
    // We'll create an empty state array here
    boolean[] checkboxState = new boolean[255];
    try {
      out.writeObject(POKE_START_SEQUENCE);
      out.writeObject(checkboxState);
    } catch (Exception ex) {
        System.out.println("Failed to poke!"); }
    }
  }
}
// other code in BeatBoxFinal.java
```

Here's the bug.
We create an
array of 255
booleans instead
of 256.

What went wrong in this code? When we send the dummy array of checkboxes, we're off by one—we only send 255 checkboxes, and it should be 256 (16x16).

Why didn't our tests catch this? Our tests sent valid arrays to our receiver code, but we didn't really test the GUI side of the application.

What would you do differently? We need a way to test more of our code. We should add a test that will catch this. (But what else are we missing?)

Wait. This is code from a while back. We could write tests forever and never come up with everything. And when do we get to go back to work on developing new code? That burn-down rate is gonna kill us...

Code that doesn't work isn't complete!

Complete code is *working* code. Not many people will pay you to write code that doesn't do what it's supposed to. Writing tests is very much a part of getting your work done. In fact, tests let you know when you've written the code you meant to write, and when it does what it's supposed to do.

But how many tests do you need? Well, it becomes a trade-off between how much of the code you test versus how likely are you to find a bug in the part you *haven't* tested. A hundred tests that all test the same 50-line method in a 100,000-line system isn't going to give you much confidence—that leaves a whopping 99,950 lines of untested code, no matter how many tests you've written.

Instead of talking about number of tests, it's better to think about **code coverage**: what percentage of your code are your tests actually testing?

Your code's not finished until it passes its tests.

You should be writing your tests to make sure your code does what it's supposed to. If you don't have a test for a certain piece of functionality, how do you know your code really implements that functionality? And if you do have a test and it's not passing, your code doesn't work.

Hmm...lemme guess, there's a tool that we can tie into our process that checks this for us, right?

Tools are your friends.

Tools and frameworks can't do your work for you, but they can make it easier for you to get to your work—and figure out what you should be working on. Code coverage is no different.

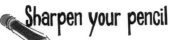

Sharpen your pencil

Below is some code from the BeatBox Pro application. Your job is to come up with tests to get 100% coverage on this code... or as close to it as you can get.

This is the code that handles the picture and poke sequences, as well as normal messages.

```java
public class RemoteReader implements Runnable {
    boolean[] checkboxState = null;
    String nameToShow = null;
    Object obj = null;

    public void run() {
        try {
            while ((obj = in.readObject()) != null) {
                System.out.println("got an object from server");
                System.out.println(obj.getClass());
                String nameToShow = (String) obj;
                checkboxState = (boolean[]) in.readObject();

                if (nameToShow.equals(PICTURE_START_SEQUENCE)) {
                    receiveJPEG();
                } else {
                    if (nameToShow.equals(POKE_START_SEQUENCE)) {
                        playPoke();
                        nameToShow = "Hey! Pay attention.";
                    }

                    otherSeqsMap.put(nameToShow, checkboxState);
                    listVector.add(nameToShow);
                    incomingList.setListData(listVector);
                    // now reset the sequence to be this
                }
            } // close while
        } catch (Exception ex) {
            ex.printStackTrace();
        }
    } // close run
} // close inner class
```

Circle any code that your tests don't cover.

1   Write a test to exercise this section of the code (pseudocode is fine).

....

....

....

....

....

Some of these tests may test more than just the section of code bracketed—write notes indicating what else your tests exercise.

2   Write a test to exercise this section of the code.

....

....

....

....

....

3   Write a test to exercise this section of the code.

....

....

....

....

....

4   Did we get 100% coverage? What else would you test? How?

....

....

....

....

Sharpen your pencil Solution

Below is some code from the BeatBox Pro application. Your job was to come up with tests to get 100% coverage on this code...or as close to it as you can get.

```
public class RemoteReader impleme
  boolean[] checkboxState = null
  String nameToShow = null;
  Object obj = null;

  public void run() {
    try {
      while ((obj = in.readObject()
        System.out.println("got an object from server");
        System.out.println(obj.getClass());
        String nameToShow = (String)
        checkboxState = (boolean[]) i

        if (nameToShow.equals(PICTURE
          receiveJPEG();
        } else {
          if (nameToShow.equals(POKE_START_SEQUENCE)) {
            playPoke();
            nameToShow = "Hey! Pay attent

          }

          otherSeqsMap.put(nameToShow, c
          listVector.add(nameToShow);
          incomingList.setListData(listVector);
          // now reset the sequence to be this

        }
      } // close while
    } catch (Exception ex) {
      ex.printStackTrace();
    }
  } // close run
} // close inner class
```

All three of these tests cover the code before the if statement.

1 @Test
```
public void testNormalMessage() throws IOException {
  boolean[] checkboxState = new boolean[256];
  checkboxState[0] = true;
  checkboxState[5] = true;
  checkboxState[19] = true;
  mOutStream.writeObject("This is a test message!");
  mOutStream.writeObject(checkboxState);
}
```

2 @Test
```
public void testPictureMessage() throws IOException {
  mOutStream.writeObject(PICTURE_START_SEQUENCE);
  mOutStream.writeObject(EMPTY_CHECKBOXES);
  sendJPEG(TEST_JPEG_FILENAME);
}
```

3 @Test
```
public void testPoke() throws IOException {
  mOutStream.writeObject(POKE_START_SEQUENCE);
  mOutStream.writeObject(EMPTY_CHECKBOXES);
}
```

This test exercises multiple chunks of code. In fact, most tests aren't isolated to just a few lines, even though it might be the only test that covers those few lines.

4 Did we get 100% coverage? What else would you test? How?

We didn't test the exception-handling code, so we'd need to create exceptional situations. We also didn't test the GUI at all—that would take someone playing with the interface.

Standup meeting

Ok, so if we test every single method, we'll have 100% coverage, right?

Mark: No, I don't think so; running every method doesn't mean every *line* of each method will run. We need to have different kinds of tests to get to all the different error conditions and branches.

Laura: Wow...so I guess every variation of every method should have a separate test?

Bob: But how are we going to do all that? We'll have to make up all kinds of bogus data to get every weird error condition. That could take forever...

Mark: And that's not all. We've got to try things like pulling the network plug at some point to test what happens if the network goes down and I/O problems crop up.

Bob: You don't think that's going a little too far?

Mark: Well, if we want to catch all of the corner cases and every bit of exception handling...

Laura: But a lot of that stuff never really happens...

Bob: Then why did I bother to write all that exception-handling code? I've got all kinds of logging and reconnection code in my methods. Now you're saying I didn't need to write that?

Mark: You did, but—

Laura: This is impossible!

Testing all your code means testing EVERY BRANCH

Some of the easiest areas to miss are methods or code that have lots of branches. Suppose you've got login code like this:

```java
public class ComplexCode {
  public class UserCredentials {
    private String mToken;

    UserCredentials(String token) {
      mToken = token;
    }
    public String getUserToken() { return mToken; }
  }

  public UserCredentials login(String userId, String password) {
    if (userId == null) {
      throw new IllegalArgumentException("userId cannot be null");
    }
    if (password == null) {
      throw new IllegalArgumentException("password cannot be null");
    }
    User user = findUserByIdAndPassword(userId, password);
    if (user != null) {
      return new UserCredentials(generateToken(userId, password,
              Calendar.getInstance().getTimeInMillis()));
    }
    throw new RuntimeException("Can't find user: " + userId);
  }

  private User findUserByIdAndPassword(String userId, String password) {
    // code here only used by class internals
  }

  private String generateToken(String userId, String password,
                    long nonce) {
    // utility method used only by this class
  }
}
```

You'd probably only need one test case for all of the UserCredential code, since there's no behavior, just data to access and set.

You'll need lots of tests for this method. One with a valid username and password...

...one where the userId is null...

...another where the password is null...

...and one where the username is valid but the password is wrong.

...one where the userId isn't null but isn't a valid ID...

And then there are these private methods...We can't get to these directly.

Use a coverage report to see what's covered

Most coverage tools—especially ones like CruiseControl that integrate with other CI and version control tools—can generate a report telling you how much of your code is covered.

Here's a report for testing the `ComplexCode` class on the last page, and providing a valid username and password:

> Code complexity basically tells us how many different paths there are through a given class's code. If there are lots of conditionals (more complicated code), this number will be high.

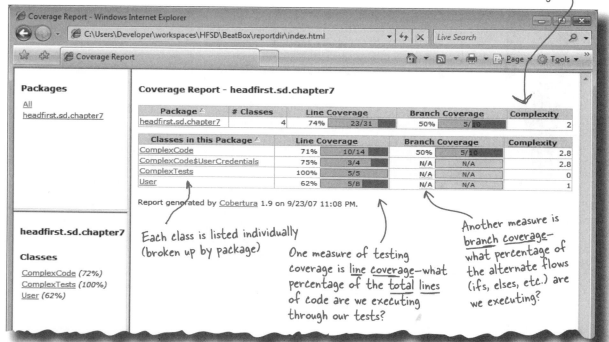

Each class is listed individually (broken up by package)

One measure of testing coverage is <u>line coverage</u>—what percentage of the total lines of code are we executing through our tests?

Another measure is branch <u>coverage</u>— what percentage of the alternate flows (ifs, elses, etc.) are we executing?

So the above test manages to test 62% of the `User` class, 71% of the `ComplexCode` class, and 75% of `UserCredentials`. Things get a lot better if you add in all the failure cases described on page 264.

> Add in the failure cases and we're in much better shape with the ComplexCode class. Still need work on the User class though...

> Are you kidding me? All that testing, and we're still not at 100%? How could you ever do this on a real project?

Good testing takes lots of time.

In general, it's not practical to always hit 100% coverage. You'll get diminishing returns on your testing after a certain point. For most projects, aim for about 85%–90% coverage. More often than not, it's just not possible to tease out that last 10%–15% of coverage. In other cases, it's possible but just far too much work to be worth the trouble.

You should decide on a coverage goal on a per-project, and sometimes even a per-class, basis. Shoot for a certain percentage when you first start, say 80%, and then keep track of the number of bugs found, first using your tests, and then after you release your code. If you get more bugs back after you release your code than you're comfortable with, then increase your coverage requirement by 5% or so.

Keep track of your numbers again. What's the ratio between bugs found by your testing versus bugs found after release? At some point you'll see that increasing your coverage percentage is taking a long time, but not really increasing the number of bugs you find internally. When you hit that point, then back off a little and know you've found a good balance.

---

there are no
Dumb Questions

Q: How do coverage tools work?

A: There are basically three approaches coverage tools can take:

1. They can inspect the code during compilation time

2. They can inspect it after compilation, or

3. They can run in a customized environment (JVM)

Q: We want to try doing coverage analysis on our project, but right now our tests cover hardly anything. How do we get started?

A: Start small. Set your target at 10%. Then when you hit it, celebrate, then bump it to 15%. If you've never done automated testing on your project before, you might find that some parts of your system are really hard to automate. We'll talk more about that in Chapter 8. Get as far as you can, though—some testing is way better than no testing.

Q: Don't you end up with a lot of test code?

A: Absolutely. You'll have a 2-to-1 or 3-to-1 test-to-production code ratio if you're really doing good testing. But finding bugs early is so much easier than having your customer find them. It's more code to maintain, but if your environment is in place, the extra code and effort is generally worth the trade-off. More satisfied customers, more business, and more money!

Getting good coverage isn't always easy...

Now that we've gotten our heads around coverage, let's look
back at BeatBox Pro. Now that we know what to look for,
there are all kinds of things not being tested:

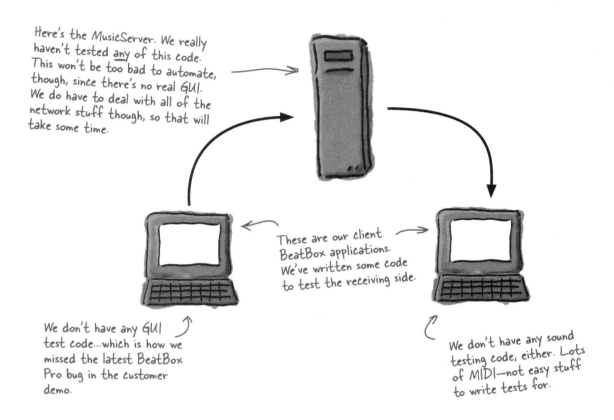

Here's the MusicServer. We really
haven't tested any of this code.
This won't be too bad to automate,
though, since there's no real GUI.
We do have to deal with all of the
network stuff though, so that will
take some time.

These are our client
BeatBox applications.
We've written some code
to test the receiving side.

We don't have any GUI
test code...which is how we
missed the latest BeatBox
Pro bug in the customer
demo.

We don't have any sound
testing code, either. Lots
of MIDI—not easy stuff
to write tests for.

There are some things that are just inherently hard to test. GUIs actually
aren't impossible; there are tools available that can simulate button clicks and
keyboard input. Things like audio or 3-D graphics, though, those are tough. The
answer? **Get a real person to try things out.** Software tests can't cover all the
different variations of an animated game or audio in a music program.

So what about code you just can't seem to reach? Private methods, third-party
libraries, or maybe your own code that's abstracted away from the inputs and
outputs of your main interface modules? Well, we'll get to that in just a few more
pages, in Chapter 8.

And then...enter **test-driven development**.

Sharpen your pencil

Check off all of the things you should do to get good coverage when testing.

☐ Test the success cases ("happy paths").

☐ Test failure cases.

☐ Stage known input data if your system uses a database so you can test various backend problems.

☐ Read through the code you're testing.

☐ Review your requirements and user stories to see what the system is supposed to do.

☐ Test external failure conditions, like network outages or people shutting down their web browsers.

☐ Test for security problems like SQL injection or cross-site scripting (XSS).

☐ Simulate a disk-full condition.

☐ Simulate high-load scenarios.

☐ Use different operating systems, platforms, and browsers.

⟶ Answers on page 272.

Standup meeting

Laura: I really wish we knew all this going in...before we started doing demos with the customer.

Bob: Yeah, I could have run tests on my code, and known I'd screwed up the other user story when I got mine to work. Anything to get us to full coverage...

Mark: Whoa, I'm not sure full coverage is reasonable. You ever heard of the 80/20 rule? Why spend all our time on a tiny bit of the code that probably **won't** ever get run?

Bob: Well, I'm going for 100%. I figure with another few days of writing tests, I can get there.

Mark: A few **days**? We don't have time for that; don't you have a lot of GUI code to work on?

Laura: I agree. But I'm not sure we can even get to 80% coverage: there's a lot of complex code buried pretty deep in the GUI, and I'm not sure how to write tests to get to all of that stuff.

Mark: Hmmm...what about 50%? We could start there, and then add tests for things we think are missing. The coverage report will tell us what we're missing, right?

Bob: Yeah, we can look at which methods we're not calling. If we could hit every method, and then test the edge cases on code that's used a lot, that's pretty good...

Laura: Sounds like a plan...You just committed some stuff, right? I'll check the coverage report as soon as CruiseControl finishes its build.

What ~~version control~~ does...
your environment ^

☑ Lets you **create a repository** to keep your code in a secure place.

☑ Lets multiple people **check out copies of the code** and work efficiently as a team.

☑ Lets multiple people **check changes back into the repository** and distribute them to the rest of the team.

☑ Keeps track of **who changes what**, when, and why.

☑ **Branches** and **tags code** so you can find and change versions of code from way back when.

☑ **Rolls back changes** that never should have happened in the first place.

☑ Makes sure **your code compiles**.

☑ **Tests** your code.

☑ Tells us **how well we're testing.**

You've gotten a couple of these things into your environment now with a continuous integration tool.

... and what version control <u>doesn't</u> do

☐ ~~Makes sure your code compiles~~

☐ ~~Tests code.~~

☐ Thinks for you.

☐ Makes sure your code is readable and well-written.

Testcross

Take some time to sit back and test the right side of your brain (get it?).

Across

5. The practice of automatically building and testing your code on each commit.
7. This should fail if a test doesn't pass.
8. Instead of running your tests by hand, use ....
10. Coverage tells you how much .... you're actually testing.
11. When white box testing you want to exercise each of these.
12. Ability to be climbed - or support a lot of users.
13. 3 lines of this to 1 line of production isn't crazy.

Down

1. Just slightly outside the valid range, this case can be bad news.
2. All of your functional testing ties back to these.
3. Peeking under the covers a little, you might check out some DB tables when you use this kind of testing.
4. 85% of this and you're doing ok.
6. Continuous integration watches this to know when things change.
7. Test the system like a user and forget how it works inside.
9. You're done when all your ....

Sharpen your pencil
Solution

Check off all of the things you should do to get good coverage when testing.

- ☑ Test the success cases ("happy paths").

- ☑ Test failure cases.

- ☑ Stage known input data if your system uses a database so you can test various backend problems.

- ☑ Read through the code you're testing.

- ☑ Review your requirements and user stories to see what the system is supposed to do.

- ☑ Test external failure conditions, like network outages or people shutting down their web browsers.

- ☑ Test for security problems like SQL injection or cross-site scripting (XSS).

- ☑ Simulate a disk-full condition.

- ☑ Simulate high-load scenarios.

- ☑ Use different operating systems, platforms, and browsers.

* Depending on your app, all _of these_ are critical to getting good tests. But, if you're using a coverage tool, you can figure out where you might be missing tests on part of your system.

 Testcross Solution

Across

5. CONTINUOUSINTEGRATION
7. BUILD
8. AUTOMATION
10. CODE
11. BRANCHES
12. SCALABILITY
13. TESTCODE

Down

1. BUNDCASE / B U N D C A S E
2. USERSTORIES
3. GREYBOX
4. COVERAGE
6. REPOSITORY
7. BLACKBOX
9. TESTSTPSPASS

Tools for your Software Development Toolbox

Software Development is all about developing and delivering great software. In this chapter, you learned about several techniques to keep you on track. For a complete list of tools in the book, see Appendix ii.

CHAPTER 7

Development Techniques

There are different views of your system, and you need to test them all

Testing has to account for success cases as well as failure cases

Automate testing whenever possible

Use a continuous integration tool to automate building and testing your code on each commit

Here are some of the key techniques you learned in this chapter...

... and some of the principles behind those techniques.

Development Principles

Testing is a tool to let you know where your project is at all times

Continuous integration gives you confidence that the code in your repository is correct and builds properly

Code coverage is a much better metric of testing effectiveness than test count

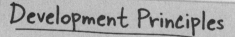

BULLET POINTS

- Using **Continuous Integration** tools means something is always watching over the quality of the code in the repository.

- **Automated testing** can be addictive. You still get to write code, so it's fun. And sometimes you break things. Also fun.

- Make the results of your continuous integration builds and coverage reports **public to the team**—the team owns the project and should feel responsible.

- Have your continuous integration tool **fail a build** if an automated test fails. Then have it **email the committer** until they fix it.

- Testing for **overall functionality** is critical to declaring a project as working.

8 test-driven development

Holding your code accountable

Alright John—here's what I'm expecting out of you: If someone doesn't know their password, they don't get in. Never heard of the guy? They don't get in...

Sometimes it's all about setting expectations. Good code needs to work, everyone knows that. But how do **you know your code works**? Even with unit testing, there are still parts of most code that go untested. But what if testing was a **fundamental part of software development**? What if you did *everything* with testing in mind? In this chapter, you'll take what you know about version control, CI, and automated testing and tie it all together into an environment where you can feel **confident** about **fixing bugs**, **refactoring**, and even **reimplementing** parts of your system.

Test **FIRST**, not last

Instead of trying to retrofit testing onto an existing project, let's look
at a project from the ground up using a new technique, **test-driven
development**, and write your code with testing in mind right from the start.

Starbuzz Coffee has been selling gift cards for several months, but now they
need a way to accept those gift cards as payment for their drinks. Starbuzz
already knows how their page should look, so your job is to focus on the design
and implementation of the gift card ordering system itself.

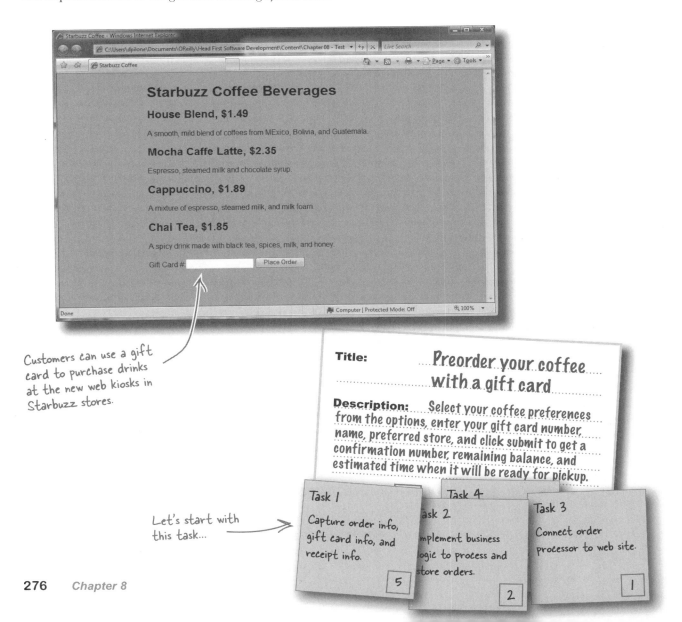

Customers can use a gift
card to purchase drinks
at the new web kiosks in
Starbuzz stores.

Title: Preorder your coffee with a gift card

Description: Select your coffee preferences
from the options, enter your gift card number,
name, preferred store, and click submit to get a
confirmation number, remaining balance, and
estimated time when it will be ready for pickup.

Let's start with
this task...

Task 1
Capture order info,
gift card info, and
receipt info.

5

Task 2
Implement business
logic to process and
store orders.

2

Task 4

Task 3
Connect order
processor to web site.

1

So we're going to test <u>FIRST</u>...

Task 1

Capture order info, gift card info, and receipt info.

5

The Starbuzz Gift Cards story is broken down into tasks, so if we're going to test first, we need to begin by looking at our first task, which is capturing information about orders, gift cards, and receipts. Remember, if we jump right into code, we'll end up right back where we did in the last few chapters...

Lingo alert: "customer" in these cases refers to shoppers at Starbuzz—in fact, your customer's customer. That's typical language for user stories.

Analyze the task

First break down the task. For this task you'll need to...

☐ **Represent the order information.** You need to capture the customer's name, the drink description, the store number the <u>customer</u> wants to pick up the drink from, and a gift card number.

Usually, tasks are just one thing, but the three items in this task are so small, they're easier to treat as a single unit of work.

☐ **Represent gift card information.** You need to capture the activation date, the expiration date, and the remaining balance.

☐ **Represent receipt information.** You need to capture the confirmation number and the pickup time, as well as the remaining balance on a gift card.

Write the test BEFORE any other code

We're testing first, remember? That means you have to actually write a test... ***first***. Start with the order information part of the task. Now, using your <u>test framework</u>, you need to write a test for that functionality.

Just like in Chapter 7, you can use any testing framework you want—although an automated framework is easiest to integrate into your version control and CI processes.

Welcome to <u>test-driven</u> <u>development</u>

When you're writing tests before any code, and then letting those tests drive your code, you're using **test-driven development**, or **TDD**. That's just a formal term to describe the process of testing from the outset of development—and writing every line of code specifically as a response to your tests. Turn the page for a lot more on TDD.

Your first test...

The first step in writing a test is to figure out what **exactly** it is you should be testing. Since this is testing at a really fine-grained level—**unit testing**—you should start small. What's the **smallest test you could write** that uses the order information you've got to store as part of the first task? Well, that's just creating the object itself, right? Here's how to test creating a new `OrderInformation` object:

This is a JUnit test... a single method that tests object creation.

```java
package headfirst.sd.chapter8;

import org.junit.*;

public class TestOrderInformation {
  @Test
  public void testCreateOrderInformation() {
    OrderInformation orderInfo = new OrderInformation();
  }
}
```

Keep it as simple as possible: just create a new OrderInformation object.

> Wait—what are you doing? There's no way this test is going to work; it's not even going to compile. You're just making up class names that don't exist. Where did you get OrderInformation from?

You're exactly right! We're writing

tests **first**, remember? We have **no code**. There's no way this test could (or should) pass the first time through. In fact, this test won't even compile, and that's OK, too. We'll fix it in a minute. The point here is that at first, your test...

...fails miserably.

Unlike pretty much everything else in life, in TDD **you want your tests to fail when you first write them.** The point of a test is to establish a measurable success—and in this case, that measure is a compiling `OrderInformation` object that you can instantiate. And, because you've got a failing test, now it's clear what you have to do to make sure that test passes.

The first rule of effective test-driven development

 Rule #1: Your test should always FAIL, before you implement any code.

NOW write code to get the test to pass.

You've got a failing test...but that's OK. Before going any further, either writing more tests or working on the task, *write the simplest code possible to get just this test to pass*. And right now, the test won't even compile!

Running our first test isn't even possible yet; it fails when you try to compile.

```
File  Edit  Window  Help
hfsd> javac -cp junit.jar
             headfirst.sd.chapter8.TestOrderInformation.java
TestOrderInformation.java:8: cannot find symbol
symbol  : class OrderInformation
location: class headfirst.sd.chapter8.TestOrderInformation
    OrderInformation orderInfo = new OrderInformation();
    ^
TestOrderInformation.java:8: cannot find symbol
symbol  : class OrderInformation
location: class headfirst.sd.chapter8.TestOrderInformation
    OrderInformation orderInfo = new OrderInformation();
                                     ^
2 errors

hfsd>
```

Sharpen your pencil

We have a failing test that we need to get to pass. What's the simplest thing you can do to get this test passing?

....

....

....

Get your tests to GREEN

The only goal you should have at this point is to get your test to pass. So write *just the code you have to* in order for your test to pass; that's called **getting your tests to green**.

Green refers to the green bar that JUnit's GUI displays when all tests pass. If any test failed, it displays a red bar.

```
public class OrderInformation {


}
```

Here's the UML for the new class. No attributes, no methods—just an empty class.

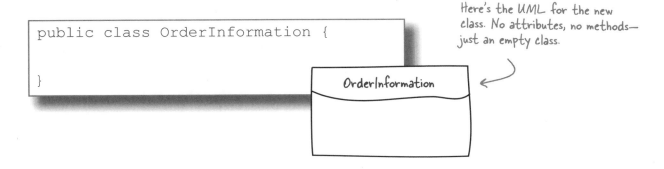

OrderInformation

Yes, that's it. An empty class. Now try running your test again:

```
File Edit  Window Help  Classy
hfsd> javac -d bin -cp junit.jar *.java

hfsd> java -cp junit.jar;.\bin org.junit.runner.
JUnitCore headfirst.sd.chapter8.TestOrderInformation

JUnit version 4.4

.

Time: 0.018        SUCCESS!

OK (1 test)

hfsd>
```

The test compiles now, as does the OrderInformation class.

With this test passing, you're ready to write the next test, still focusing on your first task. That's it—you've just made it through your first round of test-driven development. Remember, the goal was to write just the code you needed to get that test to pass.

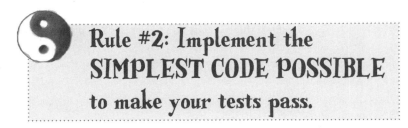

Rule #2: Implement the
SIMPLEST CODE POSSIBLE
to make your tests pass.

Seriously? You made an empty class to get a test to pass and you call that SUCCESS?

Test-driven development is about doing the <u>simplest</u> <u>thing</u> you can to get your test to pass.

Resist the urge to add anything you *might need in the future*. If you need that something later, you'll write a test then and the code to pass that test. In the meantime, leave it alone. Obviously you can't stop here—you need to move on to the next test—but **focusing on small bits of code** is the heart and soul of test-driven development.

This is the YAGNI principle... You Ain't Gonna Need It.

Red, green, refactor...

Test-driven development works on a very simple cycle:

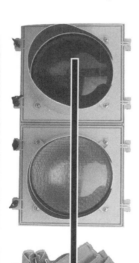

① Red: Your test fails.
First you write a test that checks whatever functionality you're about to write. Obviously it fails, since you haven't implemented the functionality yet. This is the **red stage**, since your test GUI probably shows the test in red (failing).

② Green: Your test passes.
Next, implement the functionality to get that test to pass. That's it. No more. Nothing fancy. Write the ***simplest code*** you can to get your test to pass. This is the **green stage**.

③ Refactor: Clean up any duplication, ugliness, old code, etc.
Finally, after your test passes, you can go back in and clean up some things that you may have noticed while implementing your code. This is the **refactor stage**. In the example for Starbuzz, you don't have any other code to refactor, so you can go right on to the next test.

When you're done refactoring, move on to the next test and go through the cycle again.

Exercise

Below is the task we're working on and the user story it came from. Your job is to add the next test to the `TestOrderInformation` class to make progress on this task.

Title: Preorder your coffee with a gift card

You should always look to the story to figure out what you should be testing at a higher, functional level.

Description: Select your coffee preferences from the options, enter your gift card number, name, preferred store, and click submit to get a confirmation number, remaining balance, and estimated time when it will be ready for pickup.

Priority: 20

Task 1

Capture order info, gift card info, and receipt info.

5

For this test you should be focusing on the OrderInformation class. We'll get to the gift card and receipt later.

```java
import org.junit.*;

public class TestOrderInformation {
  @Test
  public void testCreateOrderInformationInstance() {
    OrderInformation orderInfo = new OrderInformation();
  }

  @Test
  public void testOrderInformation() {
    ..........................................................................................................
    ..........................................................................................................
    ..........................................................................................................
    ..........................................................................................................
    ..........................................................................................................
  }
}
```

* If you're not a Java programmer, try and write out the test in the framework you're using, or type it into your IDE.

Now implement the code to make your test pass. Remember, you just
want the simplest code possible to get the test passing.

Here's the OrderInformation class created
to pass the first test. You need to fill it
out to pass the test you just wrote.

```
public class OrderInformation {

    ...............................................................
    ...............................................................
    ...............................................................
    ...............................................................
    ...............................................................
    ...............................................................
    ...............................................................
    ...............................................................
    ...............................................................
    ...............................................................
    ...............................................................
    ...............................................................
    ...............................................................
    ...............................................................

}
```

OrderInformation

Update the OrderInformation
class diagram, too.

Exercise Solution

Below is the task we're working on and the user story it came from. Your job is to add the next test to the `TestOrderInformation` class to make progress on this task.

Title: Preorder your coffee with a gift card

Description: Select your coffee preferences from the options, enter your gift card number, name, preferred store, and click submit to get a confirmation number, remaining balance, and estimated time when it will be ready for pickup.

To get the rest of the OrderInformation class together, you need to add coffee preference, gift card number, customer name, and preferred store to the order information.

Priority: 20

Task 1

Capture order info, gift card info, and receipt info.

5

```java
import org.junit.*;

public class TestOrderInformation {
  @Test
  public void testCreateOrderInformationInstance() { // existing test }

  @Test
  public void testOrderInformation() {
    OrderInformation orderInfo = new OrderInfomation();
    orderInfo.setCustomerName("Dan");
    orderInfo.setDrinkDescription("Mocha cappa-latte-with-half-whip-skim-fracino");
    orderInfo.setGiftCardNumber(123456);
    orderInfo.setPreferredStoreNumber(8675309);
    assertEqual(orderInfo.getCustomerName(), "Dan");
    assertEqual(orderInfo.getDrinkDescription(),
      "Mocha cappa-latte-with-half-whip-skim-fracino");
    assertEqual(orderInfo.getGiftCardNumber(), 123456);
    assertEqual(orderInfo.getPreferredStoreNumber(), 8675309);
  }
}
```

Our test simply creates the OrderInformation, sets each value we need to track, and then checks to make sure we get the same values out.

You might want to use constants in your own code, so you don't have any typos beween setting values and checking against the returned values (especially in those long coffee-drink names).

Now implement the code to make your test pass. Remember, you just want the simplest code possible to get the test passing.

```java
public class OrderInformation {

    private String customerName;
    private String drinkDescription;
    private int giftCardNumber;
    private int preferredStoreNumber;

    public void setCustomerName(String name) {
        customerName = name;
    }
    public void setDrinkDescription(String desc) {
        drinkDescription = desc;
    }
    public void setGiftCardNumber(int gcNum) {
        giftCardNumber = gcNum;
    }
    public void setPreferredStoreNumber(int num) {
        preferredStoreNumber = num;
    }
    public String getCustomerName() {
        return customerName;
    }
    public String getDrinkDescription() {
        return drinkDescription;
    }
    public int getGiftCardNumber() {
        return giftCardNumber;
    }
    public int getPreferredStoreNumber() {
        return preferredStoreNumber;
    }
}
```

This class is really just a few member variables, and then methods to get and set those variables.

Is there anything <u>less</u> you could do here and still pass the test case?

OrderInformation

- customerName : String
- drinkDescription : String
- giftCardNumber : int
- preferredStoreNumber : int

+ setCustomerName(name : String)
+ setDrinkDescription(desc : String)
+ setGiftCardNumber(gcNum : int)
+ setPreferredStoreNumber(num : int)
+ getCustomerName() : String
+ getDrinkDescription() : String
+ getGiftCardNumber() : int
+ getPreferredStoreNumber() : int

In TDD, tests <u>DRIVE</u> your implementation

Now you've got a working and tested `OrderInformation` class. And, because of the latest test, you've got getters and setters that all work, too. In fact, the things you put in the class were completely driven by your tests.

Test-driven development is different from just *test-first development* in that it drives your implementation ***all the way through development***. By writing your tests before your code, you have to focus on the functionality right away. What exactly is the code you're about to write actually supposed to do?

To help keep your tests manageable and effective, there are some good habits to get into:

1 **Each test should verify ONLY ONE THING**
To keep your tests straightforward and focused on what you need to implement, try to make each test only test one thing. In the Starbuzz system, each test is a method on our test class. So `testCreateOrderInformation()` is an example of a test that only checks one thing: all it does is test creating a new order object. The next test, which tests multiple methods, still tests only one piece of functionality: that the order stores the right information within it.

2 **AVOID DUPLICATE test code**
You should try to avoid duplicated test code just like you'd try to avoid duplicated production code. Some testing frameworks have setup and teardown methods that let you consolidate code common to all your tests, and you should use those liberally. You also may need to mock up test objects—we'll talk more about how to do that later in this chapter.

Suppose you need a database connection: you could set that up in your setup() method, and release the connection in your teardown() method of your test framework.

3 **Keep your tests in a MIRROR DIRECTORY of your source code**
Once you start using TDD on your project, you'll write tons of tests. To help keep things organized, keep the tests in a separate directory (usually called `test/`) at the same level as your source directory, and with the same directory structure. This helps avoid problems with languages that assume that directories map to package names (like Java) while keeping your tests cases out of the way of your production code. This also makes things easier on your build files, too; all tests are in one place.

there are no Dumb Questions

Q: If TDD drives my implementation, when do we do design?

A: TDD is usually used with what's called **evolutionary design**. Note that this **doesn't** mean code all you want, and magically you'll end up with a nicely designed system. The critical part of getting to a good design is the refactoring step in TDD. Basically TDD works hard to prevent overdesigning something. As you add functionality to your system, you'll be increasing the code base. After a while you'll see things getting naturally disorganized, so after you get your test to pass, refactor it. Redesign it, apply the appropriate design patterns, whatever it takes. And all along your tests should keep passing and let you know that you haven't broken anything.

Q: What if I need more than one class to implement a piece of functionality?

A: That's fine functionally, but you should really consider adding tests for each class you need to realize the functionality. If you add tests for each class, you'll add a test, implement the code, add a test, etc., and build up your functionality with the red, green, refactor cycle.

Q: The test example we just did had us writing tests for getter and setter methods. I thought we weren't supposed to test those.

A: There's nothing wrong with testing setters and getters; you just don't get much bang for the buck. The setter and getter example was just the beginning. The next few pages really dig into a challenging TDD problem.

Q: So when I implement code to make a particular test pass, I know what the next test I have to write is. Can't I just add the code I'm going to need for that test too?

A: No. There's a couple problems with that approach. First, it's a really slippery slope once you start adding things that are outside of the scope of the test you're trying to get to pass. You might think you need it, but until a test says you do, don't tempt yourself.

The second, and possibly more severe problem is that if you add code now for the next test you're going to write, that second test probably won't fail. Which means you don't know that it's actually testing what you think it is. You can't be sure that it will let you know if the underlying code breaks. Write the test—then implement code for that test.

> Test-driven development is all about creating tests for specific functionality, and then writing code to satisfy that functionality.
>
> Anything beyond that functionality is **NOT IMPORTANT** to your software (right now).

Exercise

Finish up the remaining work on the current Starbuzz task by writing tests and then the implementation for the gift card and receipt objects.

We've left the answers out on this one...it's up to you to write these tests on your own.

Completing a task means you've got all the tests you need, and they all pass

To finish up the first task, you'll need to be able to test that order, gift card, and receipt information can be captured and accessed. You should have created objects for all three of these items. Here's how we implemented each object...

Task 1

Capture order info, gift card info, and receipt info.

5

Here are the classes that came out of our first task. All of the fields came from data the story said was captured.

Receipt

- confirmationNumber : int
- pickupTime : Date
- gcBalance : BigDecimal

+ setConfirmationNumber(no : int)
+ setPickupTime(date : Date)
+ setGCBalance(bal : BigDecimal)
+ getConfirmationNumber() : int
+ getPickupTime() : Date
+ getGCBalance() : BigDecimal

OrderInformation

- customerName : String
- drinkDescription : String
- giftCardNumber : int
- preferredStoreNumber : int

+ setCustomerName(name : String)
+ setDrinkDescription(desc : String)
+ setGiftCardNumber(gcNum : int)
+ setPreferredStoreNumber(num : int)
+ getCustomerName() : String
+ getDrinkDescription() : String
+ getGiftCardNumber() : int
+ getPreferredStoreNumber() : int

GiftCard

- activationDate : Date
- expirationDate : Date
- balance : BigDecimal

+ getActivationDate() : Date
+ getExpirationDate() : Date
+ getBalance() : BigDecimal
+ setBalance(BigDecimal) : void
+ equals(object : Object) : boolean

When your tests pass, move on!

The first task is complete and we have `Receipt`, `GiftCard`, and `OrderInformation` classes written and tested. Now it's time to try our TDD approach on a tougher task: implementing the business logic to process and store orders.

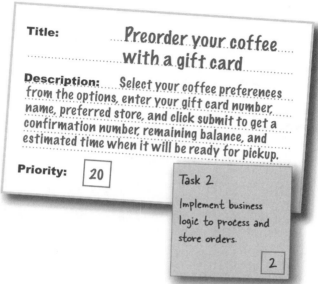

Title: ....Preorder your coffee.... ....with a gift card....

Description: ...Select your coffee preferences... from the options, enter your gift card number, name, preferred store, and click submit to get a confirmation number, remaining balance, and estimated time when it will be ready for pickup.

Priority: 20

Task 2

Implement business logic to process and store orders.

2

Different task, same process

This task is no different than the last one. We'll just follow the same approach. Write a test that fails, implement the code to get the test passing, perform any cleanup, and then repeat.

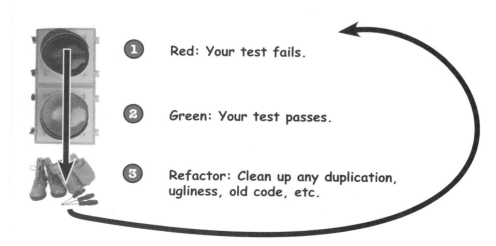

1. **Red:** Your test fails.

2. **Green:** Your test passes.

3. **Refactor:** Clean up any duplication, ugliness, old code, etc.

Red: write (failing) tests

The first step is to write a test. The user story says we need to process and store order information, so let's assume we'll need a new class for that, called OrderProcessor:

```
import org.junit.*;

public class TestOrderProcessor {
  @Test
  public void testCreateOrderProcessor() {
    OrderProcessor orderProcessor = new OrderProcessor();
  }
}
```

There's nothing special about the name OrderProcessor. It's just a place to put business logic, since the only other classes in the app are for storing data.

```
File Edit Window Help Failure
hfsd> javac -cp junit.jar
         headfirst.sd.chapter8.TestOrderProcessor.java

TestOrderProcessor.java:8: cannot find symbol
symbol   : class OrderProcessor
location: class headfirst.sd.chapter8.TestOrderProcessor
    OrderProcessor orderProcessor = new OrderProcessor();
    ^
TestOrderProcessor.java:8: cannot find symbol
symbol   : class OrderProcessor
location: class headfirst.sd.chapter8.TestOrderProcessor
    OrderProcessor orderProcessor = new OrderProcessor();
                                        ^
2 errors

hfsd>
```

As you would expect, this test will fail— you don't have an OrderProcessor yet. So now you can fix that pretty easily.

This test doesn't even compile, let alone pass.

Green: write code to pass tests

To get your first test to pass, just add an empty OrderProcessor class:

```
public class OrderProcessor {
}
```

Green: test compiles and passes.

```
File Edit Window Help Success
hfsd> javac -d bin -cp junit.jar *.java

hfsd> java -cp junit.jar;.\bin org.junit.runner.
JUnitCore headfirst.sd.chapter8.TestOrderProcessor
JUnit version 4.4

Time: 0.018
OK (1 test)

hfsd>
```

That's it. Recompile, retest, and you're back to green. The user story says you need to process and store order information. You've already got classes that represent order information (and a receipt), so use those now along with the OrderProcessor class that you just created.

Exercise

Red

Below is a new test method. Implement a test that will verify your software can process a simple order.

You'll need to put the pieces together to describe the order...

...and then pass it on to the order processor and make sure it worked.

```
// other tests

@Test
public void testSimpleOrder() {
  OrderProcessor orderProcessor = new OrderProcessor();
  ..................................................................
  ..................................................................
  ..................................................................
  ..................................................................
  ..................................................................
  ..................................................................
  ..................................................................
  ..................................................................
  ..................................................................
  ..................................................................
  ..................................................................
  ..................................................................
  ..................................................................
  ..................................................................
  ..................................................................
  ..................................................................
  ..................................................................
  ..................................................................
}
```

Don't forget about your classes from the last task.

OrderInformation

- customerName : String
- drinkDescription : String
- giftCardNumber : int
- preferredStoreNumber : int

+ setCustomerName(name : String)
+ setDrinkDescription(desc : String)
+ setGiftCardNumber(gcNum : int)
+ setPreferredStoreNumber(num : int)
+ getCustomerName() : String
+ getDrinkDescription() : String
+ getGiftCardNumber() : int
+ getPreferredStoreNumber() : int

Receipt

- confirmationNumber : int
- pickupTime : Date
- gcBalance : BigDecimal

+ setConfirmationNumber(no : int)
+ setPickupTime(date : Date)
+ setGCBalance(bal : BigDecimal)
+ getConfirmationNumber() : int
+ getPickupTime() : Date
+ getGCBalance() : BigDecimal

GiftCard

- activationDate : Date
- expirationDate : Date
- balance : BigDecimal

+ getActivationDate() : Date
+ getExpirationDate() : Date
+ getBalance() : BigDecimal
+ setBalance(BigDecimal) : void
+ equals(object : Object) : boolean

Exercise Solution

Red

Your job was to implement a test that will verify your software can process a simple order.

You can just make up a gift card number here...

The simplest thing here is to not worry about the balance on the card... this is just testing the simplest version of order processing.

```
// existing tests

@Test
public void testSimpleOrder() {

    // First create the order processor
    OrderProcessor orderProcessor = new OrderProcessor();

    // Then you need to describe the order that should be placed
    OrderInformation orderInfo = new OrderInformation();
    orderInfo.setCustomerName("Dan");
    orderInfo.setDrinkDescription("Bold with room");
    orderInfo.setGiftCardNumber(12345);
    orderInfo.setPreferredStoreNumber(123);

    // Hand the order off to the order processor and check the receipt
    Receipt receipt = orderProcessor.processOrder(orderInfo);
    assertNotNull(receipt.getPickupTime());
    assertTrue(receipt.getConfirmationNumber() > 0);
    assertTrue(receipt.getGCBalance().equals(0));

}
```

there are no Dumb Questions

Q: How can you just assume that the gift card has the right amount on it? Isn't that an assumption? Aren't those bad?

A: We're writing our first test, and then we need to make it pass. So, we're sort of assuming that the gift card has enough on it, but since we're about to implement the backend code, we can make sure it does then. What we are setting ourselves up for is some refactoring. Once we get this test passing we'll obviously need to add a test for a gift card that doesn't have enough money on it. When we do that, we'll certainly have to revisit the code we wrote to get this test going and rework it to support different gift cards and different values. But, this is going to take some thought. Read on...

Q: There are a bunch of values in that test that aren't constants—should I care?

A: Yes, you should. To keep the code sample short we didn't pull those values into constants, but you should treat your test code just like production code you write and apply the same style and discipline. Remember, this isn't throwaway code; it lives in the repository with the rest of your system, and you rely on it to let you know if things aren't working right. Treat it with respect.

Simplicity means avoiding dependencies

Let's add a `processOrder()` method to `OrderProcessor`, since that's what our latest test needs to pass. The method should return a `Receipt` object, like this:

OrderProcessor
+ processOrder(orderInfo : OrderInformation) : Receipt

But here's where things get tricky: `processOrder()` needs to connect to the Starbuzz database. Here's the task that involves that piece of the system's functionality:

Task 4

Implement DB backend for gift cards, drink info, customer info, and receipt

`1`

Title: ...Preorder your coffee... ...with a gift card...

Description: Select your coffee preferences from the options, enter your gift card number, name, preferred store and click submit to get a confirmation number, remaining balance, and estimated time when it will be ready for pickup.

Priority: `40`   **Estimate:** `5`

> Wait a second...what happened to the simplest code possible? Can't we just simulate a database, and save writing the actual database code for when we get to the later task?

Dependencies make your code more complex, but the point of TDD is to keep things as simple as possible.

You've got to have `processOrder()` talk to a database, but the database access code is part of another task you haven't dealt with yet.

On top of that, is the simplest code possible to get this test to pass really to write database-access code?

What would you do in this situation?

Always write testable code

When you first start practicing TDD, you will often find yourself in situations where the code you want to test seems to depend on everything else in your project. This can often be a maintenance problem later on, but it's a huge problem **right now** when it comes to TDD. Remember our rules? We really don't want that "simplest thing" to be "an order processor with a database connection, four tables, and a full-time DBA."

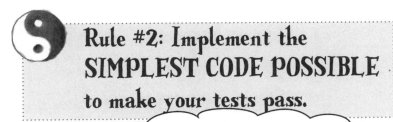

Rule #2: Implement the **SIMPLEST CODE POSSIBLE** to make your tests pass.

And our problem is that the code for this task is all tied up with other tasks, and with database code, right?

All real-world code has dependencies

When you only have basic classes in your system, it's not too hard to split things up so you can test pieces one thing at a time. But eventually, you're going to have code that depends on something external to your system, like a database.

This can show up lots of other ways too, though: your system might depend on a network connection to send or receive data, or you might need to read data from files that are created by another application, or you might need to use a sound API to generate annoying thumps and beeps. In all of these cases, the dependencies make it hard to test one thing at a time.

Hmmm...like a Java-based chat client with BeatBox capabilities?

But that doesn't mean you don't have to test. It just means you have to figure out a way to test things **independent** of all those dependencies.

When things get hard to test, examine your design

One of the first things you can do to remove dependencies is to see if you can remove the dependencies. Take a look at your design, and see if you really need everything to be as **tightly coupled**—or interdependent—as your current design calls for. In the case of Starbuzz, here's what we've assumed so far:

What we have...

The order processor has to fetch gift cards from the database, check the order, save it, and update the gift card (again in the database). So processOrder() is hardwired to connect to the database...and that's what makes testing the method tricky.

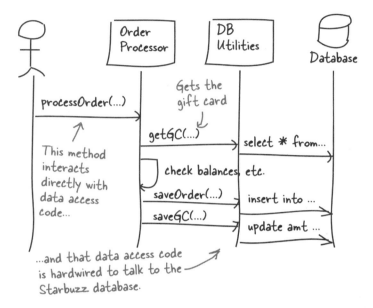

What we need...

How can we have processOrder() make the same calls, but avoid database access code? We need a way to get data **without** requiring a database—it's almost like we need a fake data access layer.

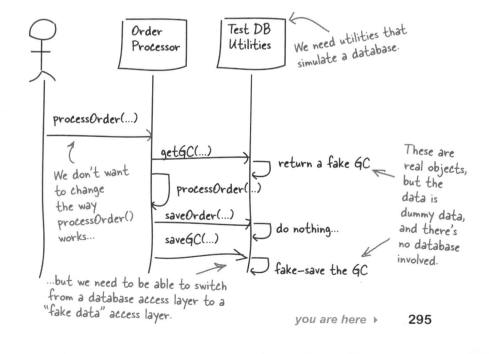

The strategy pattern provides for multiple implementations of a single interface

We want to hide how the system gets gift cards, and vary it depending on whether we're testing the code or we're running the system in production. Flip to Chapter 1 of *Head First Design Patterns* and you'll find there's a ready made pattern to help us deal with just this problem: the **strategy pattern**.

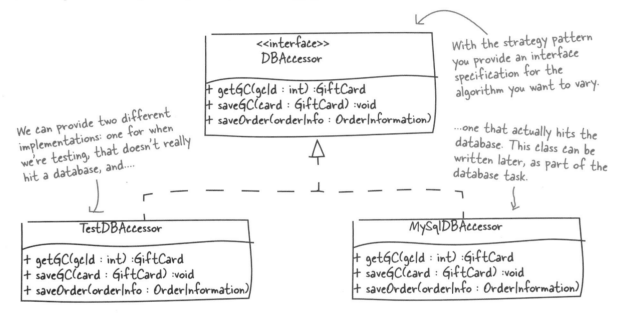

With the strategy pattern you provide an interface specification for the algorithm you want to vary.

We can provide two different implementations: one for when we're testing, that doesn't really hit a database, and....

...one that actually hits the database. This class can be written later, as part of the database task.

Now we've got two *different* ways of hitting the database, and `OrderProcessor` doesn't need to know which one it's using. Instead, it just talks to the `DBAccessor` interface, which hides the details about which implementation is actually used.

All we need to do now is add a way to give the OrderProcessor the correct DBAccessor implementation, based on whether the test code or the system is providing it.

* If your customer was unsure about what database they might use in production, this same approach would make it easy to swap out database vendors and implementations.

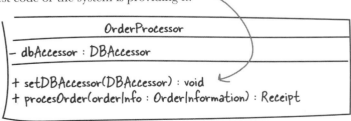

The strategy pattern encapsulates a family of algorithms and makes them interchangeable.

Exercise

Getting to Green... again

Now you've got a way to isolate the OrderProcessor class from the database. Implement the processOrder() method using the right database strategy.

You'll need to pull the gift card from the database

...save the order...

...then save the updated gift card back out.

This allows the right database accessor to be set for order processing.

```
// existing code

private DBAccessor mDBAccessor;
public void setDBAccessor(DBAccessor accessor) {
  dbAccessor = accessor;
}
public Receipt processOrder(OrderInformation orderInfo) {
  ................................................................
  ................................................................
  ................................................................
  ................................................................
  ................................................................
  ................................................................
  ................................................................
  ................................................................
  ................................................................
  ................................................................
  ................................................................
  ................................................................
  ................................................................
  ................................................................
  ................................................................
  ................................................................

  }
}
```

OrderInformation

- customerName: : String
- drinkDescription : String
- giftCardNumber : int
- preferredStoreNumber : int

+ setCustomerName(name : String)
+ setDrinkDescription(desc : String)
+ setGiftCardNumber(gcNum : int)
+ setPreferredStoreNumber(num : int)
+ getCustomerName() : String
+ getDrinkDescription() : String
+ getGiftCardNumber() : int
+ getPreferredStoreNumber() : int

Receipt

- confirmationNumber : int
- pickupTime : Date
- gcBalance : BigDecimal

+ setConfirmationNumber(no : int)
+ setPickupTime(date : Date)
+ setGCBalance(bal : BigDecimal)
+ getConfirmationNumber() : int
+ getPickupTime() : Date
+ getGCBalance() : BigDecimal

GiftCard

- activationDate : Date
- expirationDate : Date
- balance : BigDecimal

+ getActivationDate() : Date
+ getExpirationDate() : Date
+ getBalance() : BigDecimal
+ setBalance(BigDecimal) : void
+ equals(object : Object) :boolean

EXERCISE SOLUTION

Getting to Green…again.

Now you've got a way to isolate the OrderProcessor class from the database. Implement the processOrder() method using the right database strategy.

Remember, as long as you're using the test DBAccessor this is just a placeholder.

The test wants a zero-balance gift card at the end. So we simulate that.

Hmm, this isn't good; this is what the test wants but we're obviously going to have to revisit this. We'll need another test.

Remember, this is just the code needed to get our test passing; it's OK that we're going to have to revisit this code for the next test.

```
// existing code

private DBAccessor dbAccessor;
public void setDBAccessor(DBAccessor accessor) {
  mDBAccessor = accessor;
}
public Receipt processOrder(OrderInformation orderInfo) {

  GiftCard gc = dbAccessor.getGC(orderInfo.getGiftCardNumber());
  dbAccessor.saveOrder(orderInfo);

  // This is what our test is expecting
  gc.setBalance(new BigDecimal(0));

  dbAccessor.saveGC(gc);

  Receipt receipt = new Receipt();
  receipt.setConfirmationNumber(12345);
  receipt.setPickupTime(new Date());
  receipt.setGCBalance(gc.getBalance());

  return receipt;

}
}
```

there are no Dumb Questions

Q: I just don't buy it. We just wrote a bunch of code that we know is wrong. How is this helping me?

A: The test we wrote is valid—we need that test to work. The code we wrote makes that test work so we can move on to the next one. That's the principle behind TDD—just like we broke stories into tasks to get small pieces, we're breaking our functionality into small code pieces. It didn't take long to write the code to get the first test to pass and it won't take long to refactor it to get the second one to pass, or the third. When you're finished you'll have a set of tests that makes sure the system does what it needs to, and you won't have any more code than necessary to do it.

Keep your test code <u>with</u> <u>your</u> <u>tests</u>

All that's left is to write up an implementation of DBAccessor for the
processOrder() method to use, and finish the testSimpleOrder()
test method. But the test implementation of DBAccessor is really only used
for tests, so it belongs with your testing classes, ***not*** in your production code:

All this code is in our test class,
which is in a separate directory from
production code.

```java
public class TestOrderProcessing {
  // other tests

  public class TestAccessor implements DBAccessor {
    public GiftCard getGC(int gcId) {
      GiftCard gc = new GiftCard();
      gc.setActivationDate(new Date());
      gc.setExpirationDate(new Date());
      gc.setBalance(new BigDecimal(100));
    }
    // ... the other DBAccessor methods go here...
  }
```

Here's a simple DBAccessor
implementation that
returns the values we want.

Since this is only used for
testing, it's defined <u>inside</u>
our test class.

```java
  @Test
  public void testSimpleOrder() {
    // First create the order processor
    OrderProcessor orderProcessor = new OrderProcessor();
    orderProcessor.setDBAccessor(new TestAccessor());

    // Then we need to describe the order we're about to place
    OrderInformation orderInfo = new OrderInformation();
    orderInfo.setCustomerName("Dan");
    orderInfo.setDrinkDescription("Bold with room");
    orderInfo.setGiftCardNumber(12345);
    orderInfo.setPreferredStoreNumber(123);


    // Hand it off to the order processor and check the receipt
    Receipt receipt = orderProcessor.processOrder(orderInfo);
    assertNotNull(receipt.getPickupTime());
    assertTrue(receipt.getConfirmationNumber() > 0);
    assertTrue(receipt.getGCBalance().equals(0));
  }
}
```

Set the OrderProcessor
object to use the test
implementation for
database access—which
means no real database
access at all.

With the testing
database accessor,
we can test this
method, even
without hitting a
live database.

Remember, this was all about the
simplest code possible to return the
expected values here.

Testing produces <u>better</u> code

We've been working on testing, but writing tests first has done more than just test our system. It's caused us to organize code better, keeping production code in one place, and everything else in another. We've also written simpler code—and although not everything in the system works yet, the parts that do are streamlined, without anything that's not absolutely required.

And, because of the tight coupling between our system's business logic and database code, we implemented a design pattern, the strategy pattern. Not only does this make testing easier, it decouples our code, and even makes it easy to work with different types of databases.

So testing first has gotten us a lot of things:

☑ **Well-organized code.** Production code is in one place; testing code is in another. Even implementations of our database access code used for testing are separate from production code.

☑ **Code that always does the same thing.** Lots of approaches to testing result in code that does one thing in testing, but another in production (ever seen an `if (debug)` statement?). TDD means writing production code, all the time.

Our test uses a testing-specific implementation of DBAccessor, but the order processor runs the same code, because of our strategy pattern, in testing or in production.

☑ **Loosely coupled code.** Tightly coupled systems are brittle and difficult to maintain, not to mention really, really hard to test. Because we wanted to test our code, we ended up breaking our design into a loosely coupled, more flexible system.

Ever heard your computer science professor or lead architect talking about low coupling and high cohesion? This is what they were talking about. We have low coupling because of our use of interfaces and the strategy pattern, and we've got high cohesion by having our database and business logic code concentrated into separate but well defined classes.

Remember the single responsibility principle?

Because of the interface approach of the strategy pattern, you've reduced the coupling between the OrderProcessor and your DB code.

```
          <<interface>>
           DBAccessor
+ getGC(gcId : int) :GiftCard
+ saveGC(card : GiftCard) :void
+ saveOrder(orderInfo : OrderInformation)
```

```
            OrderProcessor
- mDBAccessor : DBAccessor

+ setDBAccessor(DBAccessor) : void
+ processOrder(orderInfo : OrderInformation) : Receipt
```

OrderProcessor has the business logic to handle an order, and doesn't worry about databases. So it's got high cohesion.

```
            TestDBAccessor

+ getGC(gcId : int) :GiftCard
+ saveGC(card : GiftCard) :void
+ saveOrder(orderInfo : OrderInformation)
```

```
            MySqlDBAccessor

+ getGC(gcId : int) :GiftCard
+ saveGC(card : GiftCard) :void
+ saveOrder(orderInfo : OrderInformation)
```

These accessors worry about database access, and only database access. That's high cohesion.

Are you kidding me? Did you look at that code we just wrote? We never once look at the expiration date on a gift card, and we always set the balance to 0. How can you call this **better code**?

Your code may be incomplete, but it's still in better shape.

Remember the second rule of test-driven development?

Rule #2: Implement the **SIMPLEST CODE POSSIBLE** to make your tests pass.

Even though not everything works, the code that we do have works, is testable, and is slim and uncluttered. However, it's pretty clear that we still have lots of work left. The goal is getting everything else working and keeping any additional code just as high-quality as what you've got so far.

So once you get your basic tests, start thinking about what else you need to test...which will motivate the next piece of functionality to write code for. Sometimes it's obvious what to test next, like adding a test to deal with gift card balances. Other times, the user story might detail additional functionality to work on. And once all that's done, think about things like testing for boundary conditions, passing in invalid values, scalability tests, etc.

All of this...testing for functionality, edge cases, and hokey implementations, adds up to a complete testing approach.

BRAIN POWER

We've implemented the basic success-case test for processing an order, but there are clearly problems with our implementation. Write another test that finds one of those problems, and then write code to get the test to pass.

More tests always means ^lots more code

The gift card class for Starbuzz has four attributes, so we're going to need several tests to exercise those attributes. We could test for:

- ☐ A gift card with more than enough to cover the cost of the order
- ☐ A gift card without enough to cover the cost of the order
- ☐ An invalid gift card number
- ☐ A gift card with exactly the right amount
- ☐ A gift card that hasn't been activated
- ☐ A gift card that's expired

In each case, we need a gift card object with a slightly different set of values, so we can test each variation in our order processing class.

And that's just for the gift cards. You'll need tests for variations on the `OrderInformation` class, too...and we still haven't tested for the bigger failure cases, like what happens if the database fails to save an order.

> These are really important things to test, but not only are we going to have to write tests for these cases, we're going to have to write up a bunch of strategies too...

Automated test-driven development means a **LOT** of test code.

The more functionality you have, the more tests you'll need. And more tests means more code... lots and lots of code. But all that code also means a lot more stability. You'll know your system is working, at every step of the way.

And sometimes, you may not need quite as much code as you first thought...

Strategy patterns, loose couplings, object stand ins...

Suppose we used the strategy pattern again for all the different variations on the types of gift card a database could return, like this:

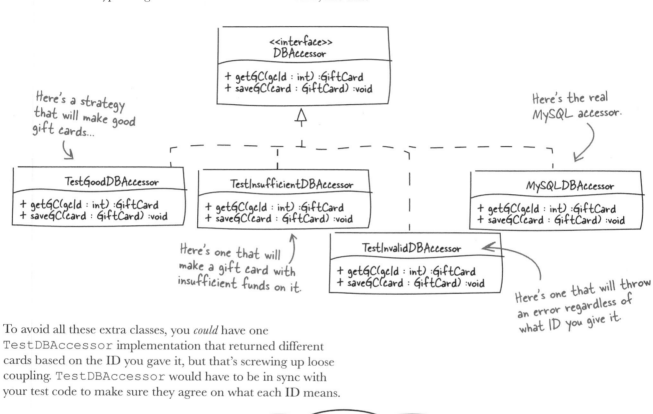

Here's a strategy that will make good gift cards...

Here's the real MySQL accessor.

<<interface>>
DBAccessor

+ getGC(gcId : int) :GiftCard
+ saveGC(card : GiftCard) :void

TestGoodDBAccessor

+ getGC(gcId : int) :GiftCard
+ saveGC(card : GiftCard) :void

TestInsufficientDBAccessor

+ getGC(gcId : int) :GiftCard
+ saveGC(card : GiftCard) :void

MySQLDBAccessor

+ getGC(gcId : int) :GiftCard
+ saveGC(card : GiftCard) :void

TestInvalidDBAccessor

+ getGC(gcId : int) :GiftCard
+ saveGC(card : GiftCard) :void

Here's one that will make a gift card with insufficient funds on it.

Here's one that will throw an error regardless of what ID you give it.

To avoid all these extra classes, you *could* have one `TestDBAccessor` implementation that returned different cards based on the ID you gave it, but that's screwing up loose coupling. `TestDBAccessor` would have to be in sync with your test code to make sure they agree on what each ID means.

> But each test gift card accessor shares a lot of code, and that's bad, too...so what do we do?

We need lots of different, but similar, objects

The problem right now is that we have a sequence like this:

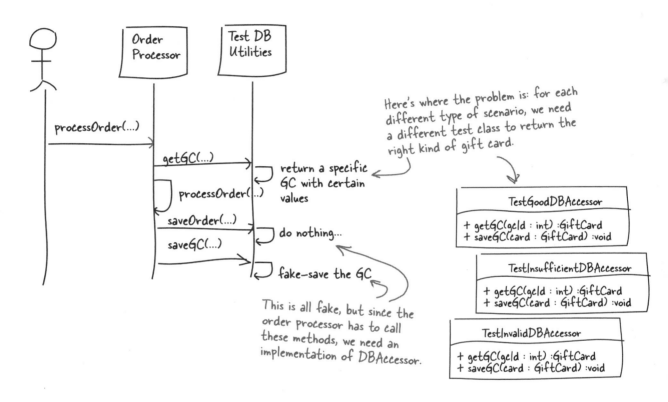

Here's where the problem is: for each different type of scenario, we need a different test class to return the right kind of gift card.

TestGoodDBAccessor
+ getGC(gcId : int) :GiftCard
+ saveGC(card : GiftCard) :void

TestInsufficientDBAccessor
+ getGC(gcId : int) :GiftCard
+ saveGC(card : GiftCard) :void

TestInvalidDBAccessor
+ getGC(gcId : int) :GiftCard
+ saveGC(card : GiftCard) :void

return a specific GC with certain values

do nothing...

fake-save the GC

This is all fake, but since the order processor has to call these methods, we need an implementation of DBAccessor.

What if we **generated** objects?

Instead of writing all these DBAccessor implementations, what if we had a tool—or a framework—that we could tell to create a new object, conforming to a certain interface (like DBAccessor), and that would behave in a certain way, like returning a gift card with a zero balance provided a certain input was passed in?

Your testing code tells the framework what it needs.

I want a DBAccessor implementation that returns a GiftCard with a zero balance, please.

Your test code can use this object like any other... it implements DBAccessor and looks just like a real class that you'd write yourself.

Here's an object... if you call getGC() with a value of "12345," it will do just what you want.

Mock Object

Mock Object Framework

Most languages have a framework just like this—just Google "mock objects."

A mock object <u>stands</u> <u>in</u> for real objects

There's really no need for three different accessors, all of which create a new `GiftCard` object and populate it with different data. That's a lot of extra code to instantiate a `GiftCard` and call some setter methods.

Since we have an interface that describes what each of these implementations should look like, we can take advantage of a **mock object framework** to do the heavy lifting. Instead of implementing all of the classes ourselves, we can give the framework the interface we want implemented and then tell it what we expect to happen.

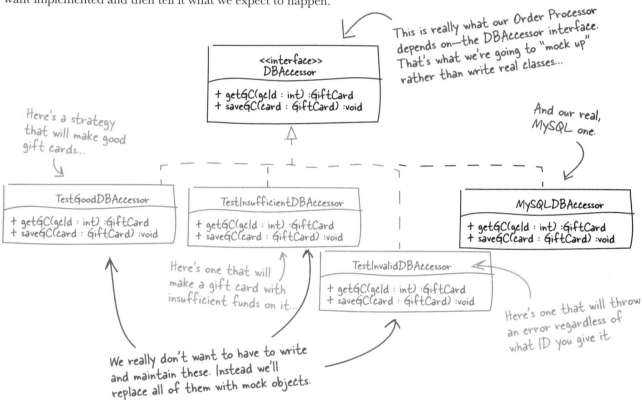

This is really what our Order Processor depends on—the DBAccessor interface. That's what we're going to "mock up" rather than write real classes...

And our real, MySQL one.

Here's a strategy that will make good gift cards...

Here's one that will make a gift card with insufficient funds on it...

Here's one that will throw an error regardless of what ID you give it.

We really don't want to have to write and maintain these. Instead we'll replace all of them with mock objects.

The mock framework will handle creating implementations of the interface and keeping track of what methods we say should be called, what they should return when they are called, what shouldn't be called, etc. The mock framework's implementation of our interface will track all of this and throw an error if something doesn't go according to the plan we gave it.

* We're going to use the EasyMock framework here but a mock object framework exists for most languages and they all work similarly.

Mock objects are working object stand-ins

Let's look at a mock object framework in action. Below is a test that uses the EasyMock framework, a mock object framework for Java. A good mock object framework allows you to **simulate an object's behavior**, without writing code for that object.

```java
import org.easymock.*;
// This test will test placing an order with a valid gift card
// with exactly the right amount of money on it.
@Test
public void testSimpleOrder() {
  // Set everything up and get ready
  OrderInformation orderInfo = new OrderInformation();
  orderInfo.setCustomerName("Dan");
  orderInfo.setDrinkDescription("Bold with room");
  orderInfo.setGiftCardNumber(12345);
  orderInfo.setPreferredStoreNumber(123);
  Date activationDate = new Date(); // Valid starting today
  Date expirationDate = new Date(activationDate.getTime() + 3600);
  BigDecimal gcValue = new BigDecimal("2.75"); // Exactly enough
  GiftCard startGC =
    new GiftCard(activationDate, expirationDate, gcValue);
  BigDecimal gcEndValue = new BigDecimal("0"); // Nothing left
  GiftCard endGC =
    new GiftCard(activationDate, expirationDate, gcEndValue);

  // Here's where the mock object creation happens
  DBAccessor mockAccessor = EasyMock.createMock(DBAccessor.class);
```

Whatever framework you use, you'll need to import the right classes.

This is all part of the test orderInfo object we want to use.

This sets up test values that we'll use in the GiftCard we're testing.

This is all "normal" test code... no mock objects involved yet.

We need a gift card representing the starting values we're testing...

...and then an "ending" gift card. This has what <u>should</u> be returned from testing order processing.

We want an object that implements this interface...

...so we tell our framework to create a mock object that implements the right interface.

At this point, the mock object framework doesn't know much—just that it has to create a stand-in for the DBAccessor class. So it knows the methods it "mocks", but nothing more than that—no behavior yet at all.

Once you create a mock object, it's in "record mode." That means you tell it what to expect and what to do...so when you put it in replay mode, and your tests use it, you've set up exactly *what* the mock object should do.

Remember, you haven't had to write your own class... that's the big win here.

```
// Tell our test framework what to call, and what to expect
EasyMock.expect(mockAccessor.getGC(12345)).andReturn(startGC);
```

First, expect a call to getGC() with the value 12345... that matches up with the orderInfo object we created over here.

When getGC() is called with that value, return the startGC object... this simulates getting a card from the database, and we've supplied the *exact* values we want for this test scenario.

```
// Simulate processing an order
mockAccessor.saveOrder(orderInfo);
```

This doesn't do anything...but it tells the mock object that you should have saveOrder() called, with orderInfo as the parameter. Otherwise, something's gone wrong, and it should throw an exception.

```
// Then the processor should call saveGC(...) with an empty GC
mockAccessor.saveGC(endGC);
```

Then, the mock object should have saveGC() called on it, with the endGC gift card simulating the right amount of money being spent. If this isn't called, with these values, then the test should fail.

```
// And nothing else should get called on our mock.
EasyMock.replay(mockAccessor);
```

Calling replay() tells the mock object framework "OK, something is going to replay these activities, so get ready."

This is like activating the object; it's ready to be used now.

```
// Create an OrderProcessor...
OrderProcessor processor = new OrderProcessor();
processor.setDBAccessor(mockAccessor);
Receipt rpt = processor.processOrder(orderInfo);


// Validate receipt...
}
```

And here's where we use the mock object as a stand-in for a DBAccessor implementation: we test order processing, never having to write a custom implementation for this particular test case (or for any of the other specific test cases we need to check out).

This might seem like a good bit of work here, but we've saved one class. Add in all the other variations of testing for specific gift card things, and you'll save <u>lots</u> of classes...and that's a big deal.

there are no
Dumb Questions

Q: These mock objects don't seem to be doing anything I couldn't do myself. What are they buying me again?

A: Mock objects give you a way to create custom implementations of interfaces without needing to actually write the code. Just look at page 303. We needed three different variations of gift cards (if you count the testInvalidGiftCard one). Two of them had different behavior, not just different values. Without the mock objects we'd have to implement that code ourselves. You could do it, but why?

Q: Why didn't we use mock objects for the gift cards themselves?

A: Well, two reasons. First, we'd have to introduce an interface for the gift cards. Since we don't have any behavioral variations it really doesn't make a lot of sense to put an interface here. Second, all we're really changing are the values it returns since it's pretty much a simple data object anyway. We can get that same result by just instantiating a couple different gift cards at the beginning of our test and set them to have the values we want. Mock objects (and the required interface) would be overkill here.

Q: Speaking of interfaces, doesn't this mean I'll need an interface at any point I'd want a mock object in my tests?

A: Yes—and truthfully sometimes you end up putting interfaces in places that you really don't ever intend on having more than one implementation. It's not ideal, but as long as you're aware that you're adding the interface strictly for testing it's not usually a big deal. Generally the value you get from being able to unit-test effectively with less test code makes it worth the trade-off.

Q: What's that replay(...) method all about?

A: That's how you tell the mock object that you're done telling it what's about to happen. Once you call replay on the mock object it will verify any method calls it gets after that. If it gets calls it wasn't expecting, in a different order, or with different arguments, it will throw an exception (and thereby fail your test).

Q: What about arguments...you say they're compared with Java's equals( ) method?

A: Right—EasyMock tests the arguments the mock object gets during execution against the ones you said it should get by using the `equals()` method. This means you need to provide an `equals()` method on classes you use for arguments to methods. There are other comparison operators to help you deal with things like arrays where the reference value is actually compared. Check out the EasyMock docs (*www.easymock.org/Documentation*) for more details.

Q: So we changed our design a pretty good bit to get all this testing stuff going. The design feels.. upside-down. We're telling the OrderProcessor how to talk to the database now...

A: Yes, we are. This pattern is called **dependency injection**, and it shows up in a lot of frameworks. Specifically the Spring Framework is built on the concepts of dependency injection and inversion of control. In general, dependency injection really supports testing—particularly in cases where you need to hide something ugly like a database or the network. It's all about dependency management and limiting how much of the system you need to be concerned about for any given test.

Q: So do you need dependency injection to do good testing or mock objects?

A: No. You could do a lot of what we did with the DBAccessor by using a factory pattern that can create different kinds of DBAccessors. However, some people feel that dependency injection just feels cleaner. It does have an impact on your design, and it does often mean adding an interface where you might not have put one before, but those typically aren't the parts of your design that cause problems; it's usually that part of the code that no one bothered to look at because time was getting tight and the project had to ship.

Good software is testable...

There are lots of things to think about when designing software: reusability, clean APIs, design patterns, etc. Equally important is to think about your code's testability. We've talked about a few measures of testability like well-factored code and code coverage. However, don't forget that just because you have JUnit running on every commit that your code isn't guaranteed to be good.

There are a few testing bad habits you need to watch out for:

A whole-lotta-nuthin'

If you're new to test driven development it's very easy to write a whole lot of test code but not really test anything. For example, you could write a test that places a Starbuzz order but never checks the gift card value or receipt after the order is placed "Didn't throw an exception? Good to go." That's a lot like saying "it compiles—ship it."

It's still me...

In an overeager attempt to validate data it's easy to go crazy testing fake data you fed into the system initially and miss the actual code you need to test. For example, suppose you write a test that checks that the gift card value and expiration date are correct when you call `getGC()` ... on our `TestDBAccessor`. This is a simplistic example but if you're traversing a few layers of code with your test, it's not too hard to forget that you put the value you're about to test in there in the first place.

Ghosts from the past

You need to be extremely careful that your system is in a known state every time your automated tests kick off. If you don't have an established pattern for how to write your tests (like rolling back database transactions at the end of each test) it's very easy to leave scraps of test results laying around in the system. Even worse is writing other tests that **rely** on these scraps being there. For example, imagine if our end-to-end testing placed an order, and then a subsequent test used the same gift card to test the "insufficient funds" test. What happens the second time this pair of tests execute? What if someone just reruns the second test? Each test should execute from a known, restorable state.

There are a lot of ways to write bad tests—these are just a few of them. Pick your search engine of choice and do a search for "TDD antipatterns" to find a whole lot more. Don't let the possibility of bad tests scare you off, though—just like everything else, the more tests you write the better you'll get at it!

It's not easy bein' green...

You did it—through the help of the strategy pattern, dependency injection (see the previous No Dumb Questions), and mock objects, you have a really powerful, but not too bulky, suite of unit tests. You now have piles of tests that make sure your system does what it's supposed to be doing at all times. So to keep your system in line:

1 Always write a test before you write the real production code.

2 Make sure your test fails, and then implement the simplest thing that will make that test pass.

3 Each test should really only test one thing; that might mean more than one assertion, but one real concept.

4 Once your're back to green (your test passes) you can refactor some surrounding code if you saw something you didn't like. No new functionality—just cleanup and reorganization.

5 Start over with the next test. When you're out of tests to write, you're done!

When all of your tests pass, you're done

Before we never really had a way of knowing when we were finished. You wrote a bunch of code, probably ran it a few times to make sure it seemed to be working, and then moved on. Unless someone said something bad happened, most developers won't look back. With test-driven development we know exactly when we're done—and exactly what works.

Which do you think is better?

I'm pretty sure I'm done. Things seem to be working OK.

Bob again...

vs

```
File Edit Window Help Bliss
hfsd> java -cp junit.jar;. org.junit.runner.JUnitCore
                    headfirst.sd.chapter8.TestOrderProcessor

JUnit version 4.4

. . . . . . . . . . . . . . . . . . . . . . . . . . . . . . .
. . . . .

Time: 0.321

OK (86 test)

hfsd>
```

↖ Our test suite in action

* If you said Bob, please donate this book to your library.

TDDcross

The crossword tests are below; fill in
the answers to make each one pass.

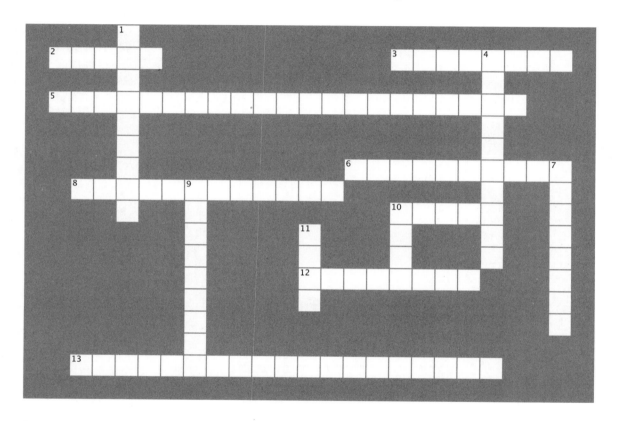

Across

2. You ain't gonna need it.
3. Red, Green, ...
5. TDD.
6. Mock objects realize ....
8. Bad approaches to TDD are called ....
10. TDD means writing tests ....
12. To do effective TDD you need to have low ....
13. To help reduce dependencies to real classes you can
use ....

Down

1. Fine grained tests.
4. When you should test.
7. Write the .... code that will get the test to pass.
9. .... testing is essential to TDD.
10. Your tests should .... at first.
11. To help reduce test code you can use .... objects.

————————➤ Answers on page 315.

A day in the life of a test-driven developer...

Once you have your tests passing, you know you built what you set out to. You're done. Check the code in, knowing that your version control tool will ping your CI tool, which will diligently check out your new code, build it, and run your tests. All night. All the next day. Even when Bob checks in some code that breaks yours...✱

Then the automated mail starts....

(1) **Start with the task you're going to work on.**

(5) **Write code to get your test to pass, refactor, add another test, and get it to pass. Repeat until you run out of tests to add.**

Once your code is passing, it's time to check it into your repository and move onto the next task.

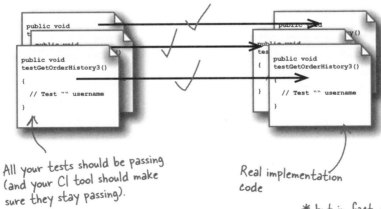

All your tests should be passing (and your CI tool should make sure they stay passing).

Real implementation code

✱ but in fact, with TDD, Bob will know instantly because the tests will fail and he will know exactly what code he broke.

② Work up the first test for the very
first piece of functionality you need
to implement. You're now Red.

```
public void
testGetOrderHistory3()
{
    // Test "" username
}
```

This test is going to fail.
Everyone knows it. It's OK.

③ Write the simplest implementation
code you can to get the test to pass.
You're now Green.

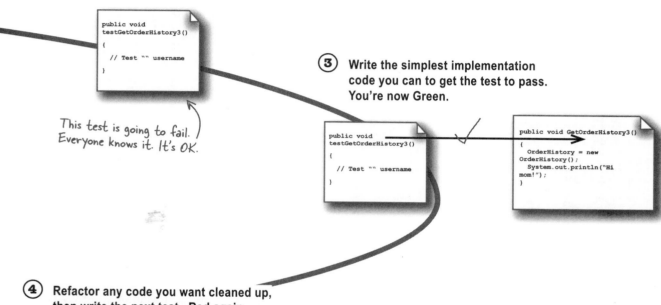

```
public void
testGetOrderHistory3()
{
    // Test "" username
}
```

```
public void GetOrderHistory3()
{
    OrderHistory = new
OrderHistory();
    System.out.println("Hi
mom!");
}
```

④ Refactor any code you want cleaned up,
then write the next test...Red again.

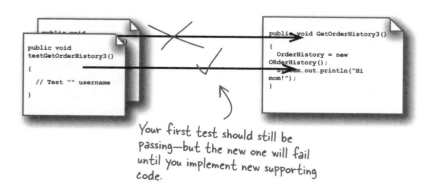

```
public void
testGetOrderHistory3()
{
    // Test "" username
}
```

```
public void GetOrderHistory3()
{
    OrderHistory = new
ORderHistory();
    System.out.println("Hi
mom!");
}
```

Your first test should still be
passing—but the new one will fail
until you implement new supporting
code.

Tools for your Software Development Toolbox

Software Development is all about developing and delivering great software. In this chapter, you learned about several techniques to keep you on track. For a complete list of tools in the book, see Appendix ii.

Development Techniques

Write tests first, then code to make those tests pass

Your tests should fail initially; then after they pass you can refactor

Use mock objects to provide variations on objects that you need for testing

Here are some of the key techniques you learned in this chapter...

... and some of the principles behind those techniques.

Development Principles

TDD forces you to focus on functionality

Automated tests make refactoring safer; you'll know immediately if you've broken something

Good code coverage is much more achievable in a TDD approach

BULLET POINTS

- TDD means you'll be **refactoring code** a lot. Break something pretty bad? Just use your version control tool to roll back to where you were earlier and try again.

- Sometimes testing will **influence your design**—be aware of the trade-offs and deliberately make the choice as to whether it's worth the **increased testability**.

- Use the **strategy pattern** with **dependency injection** to help **decouple classes**.

- Keep your tests in a **parallel structure** to your source code, such as in a `tests/` directory. Most build and automated testing tools play nicely with that setup.

- **Try to keep your build and test execution time down** so running the full suite of tests doesn't hold back your development speed.

TDDcross Solution

The crossword tests are below—fill in
the answers to make each one pass.

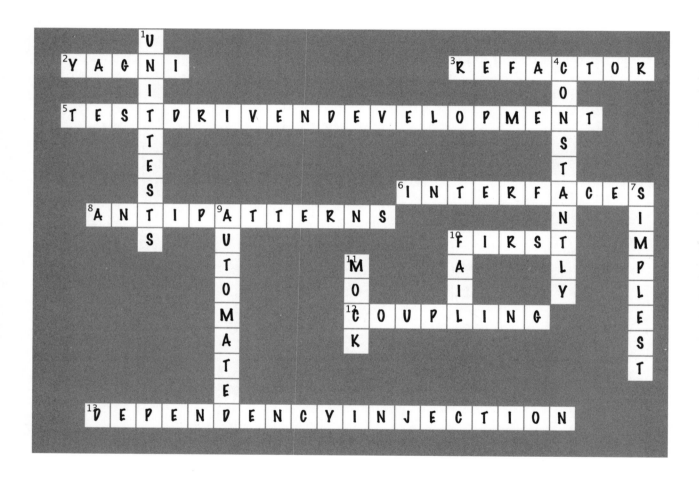

9 ending an iteration

It's all coming together...

> Wait until you try this.
> I've been working on it all month,
> and it's exactly how you like it.

You're almost finished! The team's been working hard, and things are wrapping up. Your tasks and user stories are **complete**, but what's the best way to spend that extra day you ended up with? Where does **user testing** fit in? Can you squeeze in one more round of **refactoring** and **redesign**? And there sure are a lot of lingering **bugs**...when do those get fixed? It's all part of **the end of an iteration**... so let's get started on getting finished.

Your iteration is just about complete...

You've made it! You've successfully put your process in place: the stories have piled up in the Completed section of your board, and everyone's ready for a little breather. Before people head out for the weekend, though, let's do a quick status check:

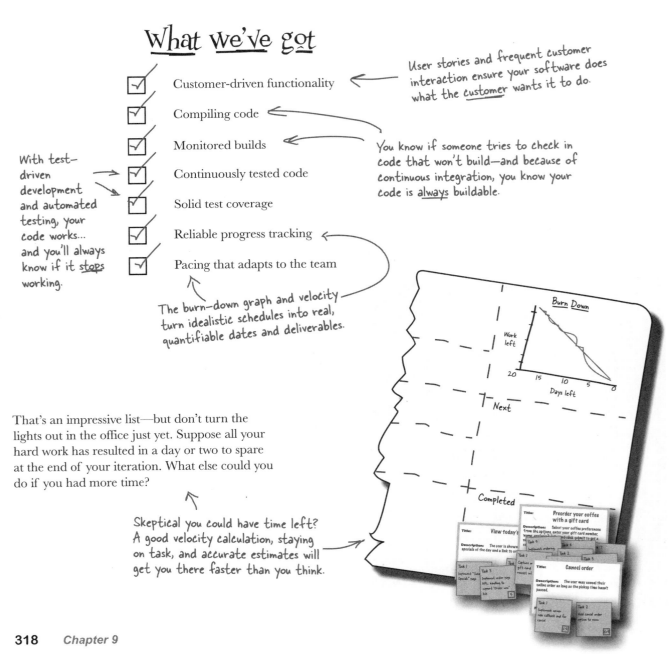

What we've got

☑ Customer-driven functionality

User stories and frequent customer interaction ensure your software does what the customer wants it to do.

☑ Compiling code

☑ Monitored builds

You know if someone tries to check in code that won't build—and because of continuous integration, you know your code is always buildable.

☑ Continuously tested code

With test-driven development and automated testing, your code works... and you'll always know if it stops working.

☑ Solid test coverage

☑ Reliable progress tracking

☑ Pacing that adapts to the team

The burn-down graph and velocity turn idealistic schedules into real, quantifiable dates and deliverables.

Burn Down

Work left

20   15   10   5   0

Days left

Next

Completed

That's an impressive list—but don't turn the lights out in the office just yet. Suppose all your hard work has resulted in a day or two to spare at the end of your iteration. What else could you do if you had more time?

Skeptical you could have time left? A good velocity calculation, staying on task, and accurate estimates will get you there faster than you think.

...but there's lots left you <u>could</u> do

There are always more things you can do on a project. One benefit of iterative development is that you get a chance to step back and think about what you've just built every month or so. But lots of the time, you'll end up wishing you'd done a few things differently. Or, maybe you'll think of a few things you wish you could **still** do...

You've worked hard putting this process together, but the whole point of iterative development is to learn from each iteration... how can you improve your processes on the next iteration?

What we <u>don't</u> have

You've got unit tests, but users haven't tried the system out yet. And users always find things the best testers miss...

☐ Process improvements

Everyone documented their code, right? No typos, misspelliins, or incomplete ?

☐ System testing

☐ Refactoring of code using lessons you've learned

☐ Code cleanup and documentation updates

No matter how slick your design seemed early on, you'll always come up with just a little something that will make it so much sweeter. Do you do that now?

Sometimes a design pattern doesn't really show itself until you've implemented something more than once. Maybe you didn't need a factory in the first iteration... or the second. But by the time you add more code in the third iteration, things are screaming for a helpful pattern.

☐ More design patterns?

☐ Development environment updates

☐ R&D on a new technology you're considering

☐ Personal development time to let people explore new tools or read

There's always some new tool out there that will "revolutionize" your build environment—or maybe you just need to reorganize dependencies. Either way, when do you update your environment?

You may be cutting-edge now, but when do you have time to learn about even newer technologies and work them into your projects?

 **BRAIN POWER**

Which of these things would you feel like you **have** to do? Which ones do you think you **should** do? Are there things that can be put off indefinitely? Are there other things you'd like to do that are not on this list?

Standup Meeting

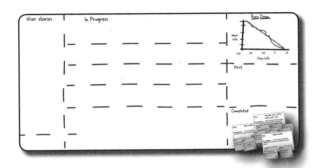

Laura: OK, my code's all checked in. But I need another couple days to refactor it. A way better design came to me last night at the gym!

Mark: No way. Have you seen some of the documentation Bob put in there? I mean, it's English, I guess, but it needs some work. So no time for more code changes; we've got to work on the documentation.

Bob: Hey—back off. It says what the code does, right? Besides, we really need to test more. Everybody's tests pass, but I'm just not convinced the user isn't going to get confused navigating through some of the site's pages. And I'd like to run the app for at least a day straight, make sure we're not chewing up resources somewhere.

Laura: But we're going to have to add more complex ordering in the next iteration; the current framework just isn't going to hold up. I need to get in there and sort this out before we build more on top of it.

Mark: Are you listening? The documentation's *awful*; that's got to be the priority with the time we've got left.

Bob: We need to focus on the project—how did our burn-down rate look this iteration? Where did we spend our time?

Standup Meeting Tips for Pros

- Keep them to 10 people or less.

- Literally stand up to help keep them short—ideally 15 minutes or less, 30 if you absolutely have to, but then kick everyone out.

- Meet at the same time, same place, every day, ideally in the morning, and make them mandatory.

- Only people with direct, immediate impact on the progress of the iteration should participate; this is typically the development team and possibly a tester, marketing, etc.

- Everyone must feel comfortable talking honestly: standups are about communication and bringing the whole team to bear on immediate problems.

- Always report on *what you did yesterday, what you're going to do today*, and *what is holding you up*. Focus on the outstanding tasks!

- Take things offline to solve bigger issues—remember, 15 minutes.

- Standups should build the sense of team: be supportive, solve hard issues offline, and communicate!

Exercise

Do you think the tasks you'd do at the end of an iteration should be changed based on how the iteration progressed? Below are three different burn-down graphs. Can you figure out how the iteration went in each case? Describe what you think happened in the provided blanks.

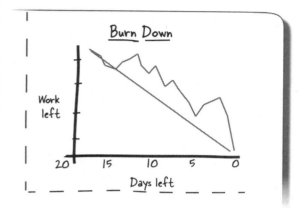

....
....
....
....
....
....
....
....
....
....

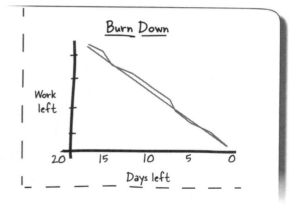

....
....
....
....
....
....
....
....
....
....
....
....

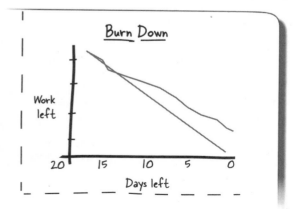

....
....
....
....
....
....
....
....
....
....

Exercise Solution

Before we go on let's take a look at some burn rates. Your job was to take a look at each graph and figure out what probably went on during that iteration.

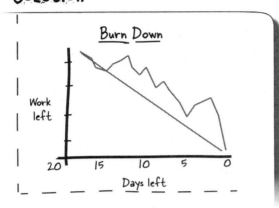

In this graph, the work remaining kept increasing as the iteration progressed. The team probably missed some things in their user stories: maybe lots of unplanned tasks—remember, red stickies are great for those—or bad estimates that got uncovered when user stories were broken down into tasks. Note the steep drop at the end—odds are that the team had to cut out things, or drop stories altogether, as deadlines started creeping up.

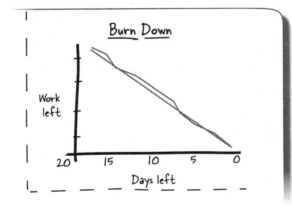

This is a perfect graph—what every team wants. The team probably had a good idea what they were getting into, their estimates were pretty close at both the user story and task level, and they moved through tasks and stories at a nice predictable pace. Remember, a good iteration doesn't have lots of time at the end—it ends right when it's scheduled to.

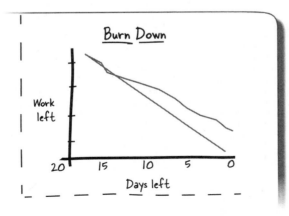

In this graph, the work left just keeps drifting to the right of the ideal burn-down rate. Chances are this is an estimate problem. There aren't any real spikes in the work left, so it's not likely that there were too many things the team didn't account for, but they just severely underestimated how long things would take. Notice they didn't make it to zero here... The team probably should have dropped a few stories to end the iteration on time.

there are no Dumb Questions

Q: How do you know the first graph is things the team missed? Couldn't it be things they didn't expect, like extra demos or presentations?

A: Absolutely. The burn-down graph isn't enough to go on to determine where all those extra work items came from. You need to look at the completed tasks and figure out whether the extra work came from outside forces that you couldn't control or if they were a result of not really understanding what the team was getting into. Either way, it's important to make progress in addressing the extra work before the next iteration. If the work came from outside sources, can you do something to limit that from happening again, or at least incorporate it into your work for the estimate? For example, if the marketing team keeps asking you for demos, can you pick one day a week where they could get a demo if needed? You can block that time off and count it toward the total work left. You can use the same approach if things like recruiting or interviewing candidate team members is taking time away from development. Remember—your job is to do **what the customer wants**. However, it's also your responsibility to know where your time is going and prioritize appropriately.

If the extra work came from not understanding what you were getting into, do you have a better sense now, after working on the project for another iteration? Would spending more time during task breakdowns help the team get a better sense of what has to be done? Maybe some more up-front design, or possibly quick-and-dirty code (called spike implementations) to help shake out the details?

Q: So spending more time doing up-front design usually helps create better burn-down rates, right?

A: Maybe...but not necessarily. First, remember that by the time you start doing design, you're *already* into your iteration. Ideally you'd find those issues earlier.

It's also important to think about **when** is the right time to do the design for an iteration. Some teams do most of the detailed design work at the beginning of the iteration to get a good grasp of everything that needs to be done. That's not necessarily a bad approach, but keep an eye on how efficient you are with your designs. If you had driven a couple stories to completion before you worked up designs for some of the remaining ones, would you have known more about the rest of the iteration? Would the design work have gone faster, or would you realize things you'd need to go back and fix in the first few stories? It's a trade off between how much up-front design you do before you start coding.

Having said all of that, sometimes doing some rough whiteboard design sketches and spending a little extra time estimating poorly understood stories can help a lot with identifying any problem issues.

Q: For that third graph, couldn't the velocity be a big part of the problem?

A: That's a possibility, for sure. It could either be that the team's estimates were wrong and things just took a lot longer than they thought the would, or their estimates were reasonable but they just couldn't implement as fast as they thought. At the end of the day it doesn't make too much difference. As long as a team is consistent with their estimates, then velocity can be tweaked to compensate for over- or underestimating. What you **don't** want to do is keep shifting your estimates around. Keep trying to estimate for that **ideal workday for your average developer**—if that person was locked in a room with a computer and a case of Jolt, how long would it take? Then, use velocity to adjust for the reality of your work environment and mixed skill level on your team.

Q: So should the team with the third graph just add time to the end of their iteration to get the extra work done?

A: In general that's not a great idea. Typically, when the burn-down graph looks like that, people are already working hard and feeling stressed. Remember one of the benefits of that graph on the board is communication—everyone sees it at each standup, and they know things are running behind. Adding a day or two is usually OK in a crisis, but not something you want to do on a regular basis. Adding a week or two... well, unless it's your last iteration, that's probably not a good idea. It's generally better to punt on a user story or two and move them to the next iteration. Clean up the stories you finished, get the tests passing, and let everyone take a breather. You can adjust your velocity and get a handle on what went wrong before you start the next iteration, and go into it with a refreshed team and a more realistic pace.

Q: We have one guy who just constantly underestimates how long something is going to take and wrecks our burn-down. How do we handle that?

A: First, try to handle the bad estimates during estimation, and remember, you should be estimating as a team. Try reminding the person that they aren't estimating for themselves, but for the average person on your team. If that still doesn't work, try keeping track of the date a task gets moved to In Progress, and then the date it gets moved to Done. At the end of your iteration, use that information to calibrate your estimations. Remember, this isn't about making anyone feel bad because they took longer than originally expected; it's to calibrate your estimates from the beginning.

System testing **MUST** be done...

Your system has to work, and that means **using the system**. So you've got to either have a dedicated end-to-end system testing period, or you actually let the real users work on the system (even if it's on a beta release). No matter which route you go, you've got to test the system in a situation that's as close to real-world as you can manage. That's called **system testing**, and it's all about reality, and the system as a whole, rather than all its individual parts.

> We've written a ton of tests to cover all kinds of conditions. Aren't we already doing system testing?

So far, we've been **unit testing**. Our tests focus on small pieces of code, one at a time, and deliberately try to isolate components from each other to minimize dependencies. This works great for automated test suites, but can potentially miss bugs that only show up when components interact, or when real, live users start banging on your system.

And that's where **system testing** comes in: hooking everything together and treating the system like a black box. You're not thinking about how to avoid garbage collection, or creating a new instance of your `RouteFinder` object. Instead, you're focusing on the functionality the customer asked for... and making sure your system handles that functionality.

> System testing exercises the **FUNCTIONALITY** of the system from front to back in real-world, black-box scenarios.

...but <u>WHO</u> does system testing?

You should try your best to have a **different set of people** doing your system testing. It's not that developers aren't really bright people; it's just that dedicated testers bring a testing mentality to your project.

<u>Developer</u> testing

Sweet! My tests pass, and this new interface is just as powerful as I planned.

Developers come preloaded with lots of knowledge about the system and how things work underneath. No matter how hard they try, it's really tough for developers to *put themselves in the shoes of end users* when they use the system. Once you've seen the guts, you just can't go back.

<u>Tester</u> testing

Hmm, no one is ever going to figure this out. And what are all these extra options? They're confusing.

Testers can often bring a fresh perspective to the project. They approach the system with a fundamentally different view. They're *trying* to find bugs. They don't care how slick your multithreaded, templated, massively parallel configuration file parser is. ***They just want the system to work.***

---

there are no Dumb Questions

Q: So developers can't be testers? We can't afford a separate test team!

A: Ideally, you'd have developers doing your unit testing with an automated approach, and a different group of people doing the full, black-box system testing. But, if that's not doable, then *at a*

minimum, don't let a developer black-box-test their own code. They just know too much about the code, and it's way too easy to steer clear of that sketchy part of the code that just might fail.

Never system-test your own code! You know it <u>too</u> <u>well</u> to be unbiased.

System testing depends on a complete system to test

If you're velocity is pretty accurate and your estimates are on, you should have a reasonably full iteration. It also means you don't have a stack of empty days for system testing...and on top of that, you won't have a system to test until the end of your iteration.

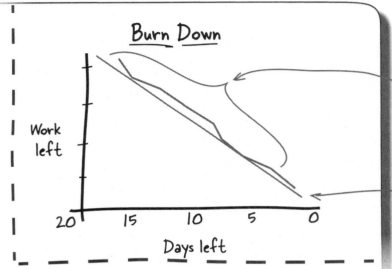

You should be testing all along, but that's unit testing—focusing on lots of smaller components. You don't have a working system to test at a big-picture, functional level.

You don't have a system that's really testable until the end of your iteration. It will build at every step, but that doesn't mean you've got enough functionality to really exercise.

At a minimum, the system needs to get out for system testing at the end of each iteration. The system won't have all of its functionality in the early iterations, but there should always be some completed stories that can be tested for functionality.

there are no Dumb Questions

Q: Can't we start system testing earlier?

A: Technically, you can start system testing earlier in an iteration, but you really have to think about whether that makes much sense. Within an iteration, developers often need to refactor, break, fix, clean up, and implement code. Having to deliver a build to another group in the middle of an iteration is extremely distracting and likely to including half-baked features. You also want to try to avoid doing bug fix builds in the middle of an iteration—an iteration is a fixed amount of time the team has to make changes to the system.

They need to have the freedom to get work done without worrying about what code goes in which build during the iteration. Builds get distributed at the end of an iteration—protect your team in between!

Q: So what about the people doing testing? Where do they fit in?

A: It's definitely best to have a separate group doing system testing, but as for what they should do while your main team is writing code, that's a good question. And even if you have other developers do system testing, the question still applies...

Good system testing requires <u>TWO</u> iteration cycles

Iterations help your team stay focused, deal with just a manageable amount of user stories, and keep you from getting too far ahead without built-in checkpoints with your customer.

But you need all the same things for good system testing. So what if you had **two** cycles of iterations going on?

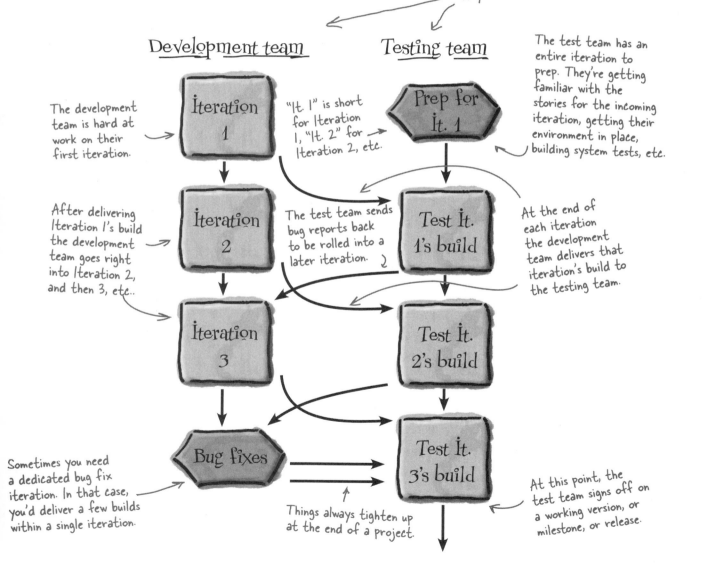

This assumes you've got two separate teams: one working on code, the other handling system testing. But the same principles apply if your second team is other developers.

Development team

Testing team

The test team has an entire iteration to prep. They're getting familiar with the stories for the incoming iteration, getting their environment in place, building system tests, etc.

The development team is hard at work on their first iteration.

Iteration 1

"It. 1" is short for Iteration 1, "It. 2" for Iteration 2, etc.

Prep for It. 1

After delivering Iteration 1's build the development team goes right into Iteration 2, and then 3, etc..

Iteration 2

The test team sends bug reports back to be rolled into a later iteration.

Test It. 1's build

At the end of each iteration the development team delivers that iteration's build to the testing team.

Iteration 3

Test It. 2's build

Bug fixes

Sometimes you need a dedicated bug fix iteration. In that case, you'd deliver a few builds within a single iteration.

Test It. 3's build

Things always tighten up at the end of a project.

At this point, the test team signs off on a working version, or milestone, or release.

More iterations means more problems

System testing works best with two separate teams, working two separate iteration cycles. But with more iterations comes more trouble—problems that aren't easy to solve.

Running two cycles of iterations means you've got to deal with:

LOTS more communication

Now, not only do you have inter-team communication issues, but you've got two teams trying to work together. The testing team will have questions on an iteration, especially about error conditions, and the development team wants to get on to the next story, not field queries. One way to help this is to bring a representative from the test team into your standup meetings as an observer. He'll get a chance to hear what's going on each day and get to see the any notes or red stickies on the board as the iteration progresses. Remember that your standup meeting is *your* meeting, though—it's not a time to prioritize bugs or ask questions about how to run things.

The test team (reasonably) needs to know some details that the development team probably doesn't have yet. Error codes, invalid values, API information, how to set things up, etc.

The testing team is looking ahead to what's coming at the end of Iteration 1, even while your developers are still coding.

Testing in a FIXED iteration length

If you're keeping your two iteration cycles in sync—and that's the best way to keep the testing team caught up—you're forcing testing to fit into a length that might not be ideal. To help give the test team a voice in iterations, you can have them provide you a testing estimate for stories you're planning on including in your iteration. Even if you don't use that to adjust what's in your iteration (remember, you're priority-driven) it might give you some insight into where the testing team might get hung up or need some help to get through a tough iteration.

A fixed iteration length forces testing into the same time box as development. But if you've got different teams and different schedules, this may be tricky, if even possible at all.

Fixing bugs while you keep working

The development team will start getting bug reports on their first iteration about the time they're getting into the **third** iteration! And then you have to figure out if the bug's important enough to fix right away, roll into the current iteration, or put off for later. We'll talk more about this in a minute, but the straightforward approach is to treat a bug like any other story. Prioritize it against everything else and bump lower-priority stories if you need to in order to get it done sooner.

Another approach is to carve off a portion of time every week that you'll dedicate to bug fixes. Take this off of the available hours when you do your iteration planning, so you don't need to worry about it affecting your velocity. For example, you could have everyone spend one day a week on bug fixes—about 20% of their time.

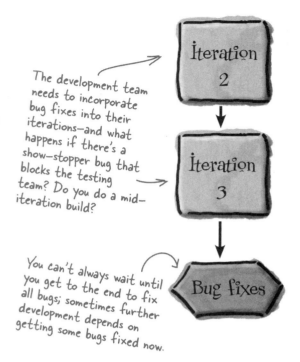

The development team needs to incorporate bug fixes into their iterations—and what happens if there's a show-stopper bug that blocks the testing team? Do you do a mid-iteration build?

You can't always wait until you get to the end to fix all bugs; sometimes further development depends on getting some bugs fixed now.

Writing tests for a moving target

Functionality in user stories—even if it's agreed upon by the customer—can change. So lots of times, tests and effort are being put into something that changes 30 days later. That's a source of a lot of irritation and frustration for people working on tests. There's not much you can do here except **communicate**. Communicate as soon as you think something might change. Make sure testing is aware of ongoing discussions or areas most likely to be revisited. Have formal turnover meetings that describe new features and bug fixes as well as known issues. One subtle trick that people often miss is to *communicate how the process works*. Make sure the testing team understands to expect change. It's a lot easier to deal with change if it's just part of your job rather than something that's keeping you from completing your job.

Development has moved on... and user stories may have changed already.

Iteration 3

Test I2's build

The test team is writing tests for code that isn't stabilized yet. And remember, features can change each iteration since the customer can reprioritize or change things.

> But this is the same sort of stuff we were dealing with anyway, right? There's nothing really new here...

More iterations really just means more communication.

During an iteration there are some messy things to deal with: multiple team members, your customer changing requirements and user stories, priorities of different pieces of functionality, and sometimes having to guess at what you're going to build before your requirements are complete.

Adding another cycle of iterations might mean more of the same issues, but you won't have any new ones. That means you can rely on the same things you've already been doing: standup meetings, tracking everything you do on your big board, using velocity to account for real life, and lots and lots of communication—with your team, with the testing team, and, of course, with your customer.

The key to most problems you'll run into in software development is COMMUNICATION.

When in doubt, TALK to your team, other teams, and your customer.

Sharpen your pencil

Below are some different approaches to testing, all of which involve just one cycle of iterations. What are some **good things** about these approaches? What are some **bad things**?

This approach has one big testing iteration at the end.

| Iteration 1 | → | Iteration 2 | → | Iteration 3 | → | Test Iteration | → | Bug fixes |

....
....
....
....
....
....

This approach adds a testing iteration after every coding iteration.

| Iteration 1 | → | Test I1 | → | Iteration 2 | → | Test I2 | → | Iteration 3... |

....
....
....
....
....
....

Sharpen your pencil
Solution

Below are some different approaches to testing, all of which involve just one cycle of iterations. What are some **good things** about these approaches? What are some **bad things**?

If you only have one team to work with, this approach isn't too bad. One big drawback is that serious system testing starts very late in the process. If you take this approach, it's critical that the results of each iteration get out to <u>at</u> <u>least</u> a set of beta users and the customer. You can't wait until the end of the third iteration to start any testing and collecting feedback.

This approach also works pretty well if you need to do formal testing with the customer before they sign off on your work. Since you've been doing automated testing during each iteration and releasing your software to users at the end of each iteration you have a pretty good sense that you're building the right software and it's more or less working as expected. The test iteration at the end is where the formal "check-off" happens before you start looking at Version 2.0.

This is usually called <u>acceptance</u> <u>testing</u>.

This approach requires a <u>lot</u> of iterations, and <u>50%</u> of your time is spent in testing. It really would only work in situations where your customer is willing to expend a lot of time on testing and debugging. Let's say that your customer is thrilled with the idea of monthly releases to the public; it keeps the site fresh and dynamic in their users' eyes. However, the customer insists on a formal validation process before the code goes anywhere. If you don't have a separate acceptance- and system-testing team, you're going to be looking at a situation a lot like this.

Top 10 Traits of Effective System Testing

10 **Good, frequent communication** between the customer, development team, and testing team.

9 **Know the starting and ending state of the system.** Make sure you start with a known set of test data, and that the data ends up exactly like you'd expect it at the end of your tests.

8 **Document your tests.** Don't rely on that one awesome tester who knows the system inside and out to always be around to answer questions. Capture what each tester is doing, and do those same things at each round of system testing (along with adding new tests).

7 **Establish clear success criteria.** When is the system good enough to go live? Testers can test forever—know before you start what it means to be finished. A **zero-bug-bounce** (when you get to zero outstanding bugs, even if you bounce back up after that) is a good sign you're getting close.

6 **Good, frequent communication** between the customer, development team, and testing team.

5 **Automate your testing wherever possible.** People just aren't great at performing repetitive tasks carefully, but computers are. Let the testers exercise their brains on new tests, not on repeating the same five over and over and over again.

4 **A cooperative dynamic between the development team and testing team.** Everyone should want solid, working software that they can be proud of. Remember, testers help developers look good.

3 **A good view of the big picture by the testing team.** Make sure that all your testers understand the overall system and how the pieces fit together.

2 **Accurate system documentation** (stories, use cases, requirements documents, manuals, whatever). In addition to testing docs, you should capture all of the subtle changes that happen during an iteration, and especially *between* iterations.

1 **Good, frequent communication** between the customer, development team, and testing team.

The life (and death) of a bug

Eventually, your testers are going to find a bug. In fact, they'll probably find a lot of them. So what happens then? Do you just fix the bug, and not worry about it? Do you write it down? What really happens to bugs?

Just like with version control and building, there are great tools for tracking and storing bugs.

> Hmm, no one is ever going to figure this out. And what are all these extra options? They're confusing.

At the system-testing level, bugs aren't always code; sometimes they're confusing or malfunctioning user interfaces.

② **The tester FILES A BUG REPORT**
This is one of the most critical steps: *you have to track bugs!* It doesn't matter who reports a bug, but level of detail is crucial. Always record what you were trying to do, and if possible, the steps to re-create the bug, any error messages, what you did immediately before the bug occurred, and what you would have expected to happen.

① **A tester FINDS A BUG**
A bug doesn't have to be something that's clearly failing. It could be ambiguity in the documentation, a missing feature, or a break from the style guide for a web site.

⑥ **UPDATE the bug report**
Once the tester (and original reporter) are happy with the fix, close the bug report. The updated report can be used as a script to retest. Don't delete it...you never know when you might want to refer back to it.

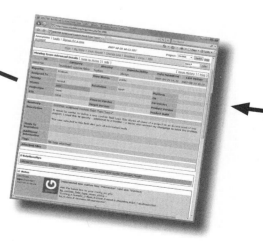

Some teams work with their customer to prioritize which bugs get fixed using the bug tracker, and don't create stories or tasks for ones that aren't going to get fixed in the current iteration. Other teams create the stories and tasks right away and let the customer prioritize the bugs like any other story. Either way works great as long as things are being prioritized by the customer.

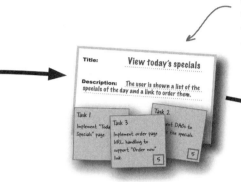

Title: View today's specials

Description: The user is shown a list of the specials of the day and a link to order them.

Task 1
Implement "Today Specials" page

Task 3
Implement order page URL handling to support "Order now" link

Task 2
...ent DAOs to ...the specials

A bug is just like an unplanned task. Once it's on the board, it's handled like any other story and task.

③ **CREATE A STORY (or task) to fix the bug**
Bugs are just work that has to be done in your system—sometimes in the current iteration, sometimes in a later one. You'll need to capture them and prioritize each bug with the customer. These are tricky to estimate, though, because it's not always clear what's wrong. Some teams have a "Bug Fix" story that they just keep around, and they add tasks to it as needed.

A build usually has more than just one bug fix in it, but it can depend on how critical the bug was.

④ **FIX THE BUG**
The development team works on the bug as part of an iteration. Start by writing a test that exposes the bug (the test should fail before you change any code). Once the team's fixed the bug (and the test lets you know when that is), they should mark it as "Fixed" in the bug tracker. But don't mark it as tested, closed, or verified—that's for the original reporter to take care of. This also helps you get a list of what's ready for turnover to the test team.

⑤ **CHECK THE FIX and verify it works**
The tester (or original reporter) verifies the new build and makes sure they're happy with the resolution. *Now* the bug can be marked as closed (or verified).

So you found a bug....

No matter how hard you work at coding carefully, some bugs are going to slip through. Sometimes they're programming errors; sometimes they're just functional issues that no one picked up on when writing the user stories. Either way, a bug is an issue that you ***have*** to address.

Bugs belong in a bug tracker

The most important thing about dealing with bugs on a software project is making sure they get recorded and tracked. For the most part it doesn't matter which bug tracking software you use; there are free ones like Bugzilla and Mantis or commercial ones like TestTrackPro and ClearQuest. The main thing is to make sure the whole team knows how to use whatever piece of software you choose.

You should also use your tracker for more than just writing down the bug, too. Make sure you:

1 **Record and communicate priorities**
Bug trackers can record priority and severity information for bugs. One way to work this in with your board is to pick a priority level—say priority 1, for example—and all bugs of that priority level get turned into stories and prioritized with everything else for the next iteration. Any bugs below priority 1 stay where they are until you're out of priority 1 bugs.

Bug trackers usually work off priorities like 1, 2, and 3, even though your user stories have priorities more like 10, 20, and 30.

2 **Keep track of **
Bug trackers can record a history of discussion, tests, code changes, verification, and decisions about a bug. By tracking everything, your entire team knows what's going on with a bug, how to test it, or what the original developer thought they did to fix it.

3 **Generate metrics**
Bug trackers can give you a great insight into what's really going on with your project. What's your new-bug submission rate? And is it going up or down? Do a significant number of bugs seem to come from the same area in the code? How many bugs are left to be fixed? What's their priority? Some teams look for a **zero-bug-bounce** before even discussing a production release; that means all of the outstanding bugs are fixed (bug count at zero) before a release.

We'll talk more about delivering software in Chapter 12.

Anatomy of a bug report

Different bug tracking systems give you different templates for submitting a bug, but the basic elements are the same. As a general rule of thumb, the more information you can provide in a bug report, the better. Even if you work on a bug and don't fix it, you should record what you've done, and any ideas about what else might need to be done. You—or another developer—might save hours by referring to that information when you come back to that bug later.

A good bug report should have:

☐ **Summary:** Describe your bug in a sentence or so. This should be a detailed action phrase like "Clicking on received message throws ArrayOutOfBoundsException," not something like "Exception thrown." You should be able to read the summary and have a clear understanding of what the problem is.

☐ **Steps to reproduce:** Describe how you got this bug to happen. You might not always know the exact steps to reproduce it, but list everything you think might have contributed. If you can reproduce the bug, then explain the steps in detail:
   1. Type "test message" into message box.
   2. Click "sendIt."
   3. Click on the received message in the second application.

☐ **What you expected to happen and what really did happen:** Explain what you thought was going to happen, and then what actually *did* happen. This is particularly helpful in finding story or requirement problems where a user expected something that the developers didn't know about.

☐ **Version, platform, and location information:** What version of the software were you using? If your application is web-based, what URL were you hitting? If the app's installed on your machine, what kind of installation was it? A test build? A build you compiled yourself from the source code?

☐ **Severity and priority:** How bad is the impact of this bug? Does it crash the system? Is there data corruption? Or is it just annoying? How important is it that the bug gets fixed? Severity and priority are often two different things. It's possible that something is severe (kills a user's session or crashes the application) but happens in such a contrived situation (like the user has to have a particular antivirus program installed, be running as a non-Administrator user, and have their network die while downloading a file) that it's a low-priority fix.

BRAIN POWER

What else would you want to see in a bug report? What kind of information would you want to see from the user? How about any kind of output from the system?

But there's still plenty left you COULD do...

So you've handled system testing and dealt with the major bugs you wanted to tackle this iteration. Now what?

What we don't have

☐ Process improvements

☑ System testing ←

System testing is taken care of, and you've knocked out your bug reports (or you're waiting on some to get filed).

☐ Review the iteration for what worked and what didn't

☐ Refactor code using lessons you've learned

☐ Code cleanup and documentation updates

☐ More design patterns?

☐ Development environment updates

☐ R&D on a new technology you're considering

☐ Personal development time to let people explore new tools or read

The right thing to do at any time on your project is the right thing to do AT THAT TIME on YOUR project.

There are no hard-and-fast rules—you've got to make this decision yourself.

A good software process is all about **prioritization**. You want to make sure you're doing the right thing on the project at all times.

Producing working software is critical, but what about quality code? Could you be writing even better code if your process was improved? Or if you dropped a couple thousand lines by incorporating that new persistence framework?

Exercise

Below are three burn-down graphs. It's up to you to decide what to do next.

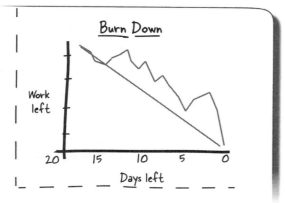

What would you do next?

....
....
....
....
....
....
....
....
....
....
....

What would you do next?

....
....
....
....
....
....
....
....
....
....

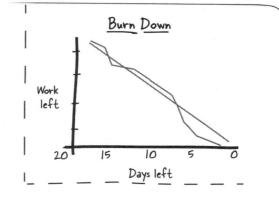

What would you do next?

....
....
....
....
....
....
....
....
....
....

Below are three burn-down graphs. It's up to you to decide what to do next.

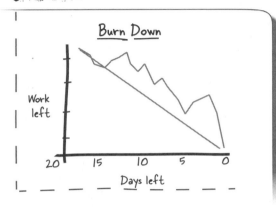

What would you do next?

Here, the team just got finished at the end of the iteration, so there's likely nothing you can squeeze in. However, that steep drop at the end probably means something was skipped. Testing is going to be vital after this iteration, and you should probably expect to schedule some time next iteration for refactoring and cleanup, to recover from the rush. You could probably revisit your task breakdown approach, too, as well as take a look at adjusting velocity.

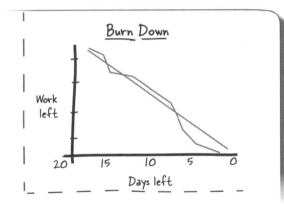

What would you do next?

In this iteration, things wrapped up early; the team may have a couple of days at the end of the iteration. If the project has been ticking along for a little bit, you may have a backlog of bugs you can start to tick off. Or, depending on how big your stories are, you might be able to grab the highest priority story waiting for the next iteration and get started on that.

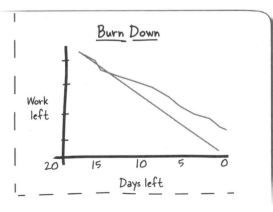

What would you do next?

Nothing! This team is late already. Before the next iteration, you should look at what caused the slowdown and whether it's a velocity problem, an estimation problem, or something else. Chances are there's unfinished code, too, which means there are going to be bugs coming your way. Make sure you leave room in the next iteration to cover any problems that come up.

How can you decide what to do next when you haven't even seen the code the team is working on?

Each project *is* different...sort of.

Remember, software development isn't about just code. It's about good habits and approaches to deliver working software, on time and on budget. Besides, we already have:

- ☑ Compiling code

- ☑ Automated unit testing

- ☑ User stories and tasks that capture what needs to happen

- ☑ A process for prioritizing what gets done next

- ☑ A working build of the software we can deliver to the customer

So this is about how to prioritize additional, nice-to-have tasks, if you've got extra time. And that's all about **where you are in your project.** Early on you'll likely need more refactoring to refine your design. Later, when the project is a little more stable, you'll probably spend more time on documentation or looking at alternatives to that aging technology the team started with six months ago.

Time for the <u>iteration</u> review

It's here: the end of your iteration. You're remaining work is at zero, you've hit the last day of the iteration, and it's time to start getting ready for the next iteration.

But, before you prioritize your next stories, remember: it's not just software we're developing iteratively. You should develop and define your process iteratively, too. At the end of each iteration, take some time to do an iteration review with your team. Everyone has to live with this process so make sure you incorporate their opinions.

<u>Elements of an iteration review</u>

(1) **Prepare ahead of time**
An iteration review is a chance for the team to give you their input on how the iteration went, not a time for you to lecture. However, it's important to keep the review focused, too. Bring a list of things you want to make sure get discussed and introduce them when things start wandering off.

(2) **Be forward-looking**
It's OK if the last iteration was tragic or if one if the developers consistently introduced bugs, as long as the team has a way to address it in the next iteration. People need to vent sometimes, but don't let iteration reviews turn into whining sessions; it demoralizes everyone in the end.

(3) **Calculate your metrics**
Know what your velocity and coverage were for the iteration that just completed. In general, it's best to add up all of the task estimates and divide by the theoretical person-days in your iteration to get your velocity. Whether or not you reveal the actual number during the review is up to you (sometimes it helps to not give the actual number just yet so as not to bias any upcoming estimates), but you should convey whether the team's velocity went up or down.

> The actual time spent on a task versus the estimated time isn't too important since your velocity calculation should account for any mismatch. We'll talk about velocity again in the next chapter.

(4) **Have a standard set of questions to review**
Have a set of questions you go through at the end of each iteration. The set of questions can change if someone would like to add something or a question really doesn't make sense for your team. Having recurring discussion topics means people will expect the questions and prepare (even unconsciously during an iteration) for the review.

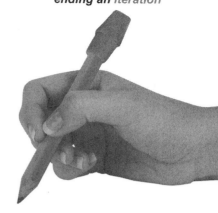

Some iteration review questions

Here is a set of review questions you can use to put together your first iteration review. Add or remove questions as appropriate for your team, but try to touch on each of the general areas.

Iteration Review Questions

☐ Is everyone happy with the quality of work? Documentation? Testing?

☐ How did everyone feel about the pace of the iteration? Was it frantic? Reasonable? Boring?

☐ Is everyone comfortable with the area of the system they were working in?

☐ Are there any tools particularly helping or hurting productivity? Are there any new tools the team should consider incorporating?

☐ Was the process effective? Were any reviews conducted? Were they effective? Are there any process changes to consider? ← *See Chapter 12 for more on this.*

☐ Was there any code identified that should be revisited, refactored, or rewritten?

☐ Were any performance problems identified?

☐ Were any bugs identified that must be discussed before prioritization?

☐ Was testing effective? Is our test coverage high enough for everyone to have confidence in the system?

☐ Is deployment of the system under control? Is it repeatable?

Any of these questions could turn into things you'd like to get done next iteration. Remember, you should be story-driven, so make sure any changes you want to introduce support some customer need (either directly or indirectly) and get prioritized along with everything else. It might mean you need to make a case for a technology or process change to the customer, but it's important to remember why you're writing the software in the first place.

A <u>GENERAL</u> priority list for getting <u>EXTRA</u> things done...

You've got to figure out what's best for your project, but here are some general things you can look at if you've got extra time in your iteration.

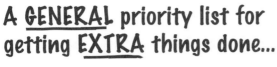

Fix bugs

Obviously this depends on what your bug backlog looks like. Remember to prioritize bugs with the customer, too. There might be some bugs that are vital to the customer, and others they just don't care that much about.

Pull in stories that are on deck for next iteration

Since the customer has prioritized more stories than typically fit in an iteration, you can try pulling in a story from the next iteration and get working on it now. Be careful doing this, though, as the customer's priorities or ideas for the story may have changed during your iteration. It's also good to make sure you know whether or not the test team has time to test any extra stories you pull in.

Prototype solutions for the next iteration

If you have an idea about what's likely coming in the next iteration, you might want to take advantage of an extra day or two to start looking ahead. You could try writing some prototype code or testing technologies or libraries you might want to include. You probably won't commit this code into the repository, but you can get some early experience with things you plan on rolling into the next iteration. It will almost certainly help your estimates when you get back to planning poker.

Training or learning time

This could be for your team or for your users. Maybe the team goes to a local users group's session during work hours. Get a speaker or technology demo setup. Run a team-building exercise like sailing or paintball. **Care and feeding of your team** is an important part of a successful project.

there are no Dumb Questions

Q: Seriously, do people ever really have time at the end of the iteration?

A: Yes, absolutely! It usually goes something like this: The first iteration or two are bad news. People always underestimate how long something is going to take early on. At the end of each iteration, you adjust your velocity, so you end up fitting less into subsequent iterations. As the team gets more experienced, their estimates get better, and they get more familiar with the project. That means that the velocity from previous iterations is actually *too low*. This ends up leaving room at the end of an iteration—at least until you recalculate the team's velocity. And believe it or not, sometimes, well, things just go right and you have extra time.

Q: Wait, you said the first two iterations will be bad?

A: You don't want them to be, but realize that people almost always underestimate how long things will take—or how much time they're spending on little things that no one is thinking about, like setting up a co-worker's environment or answering questions on the user's mailing list.

Those are all important things, but need to be accounted for in your work estimates. That's part of why a velocity of 0.7 for your first iteration is a good idea. It gives you some breathing room until you really know how things are going. You'll be surprised how fast you can fill an iteration with user stories, too. Strike a balance between getting a lot squeezed in and being realistic about what you can hope to get done.

Q: We seem to always have extra time at the end of our iterations—and lots of it. What's going on?

A: One idea is that your velocity might be way off. Are you updating it at the end of each iteration? (We'll talk more about that in the next chapter) Another idea is that your estimates are off—on the high side. If you've recently had an iteration where things got really tight at the end, people will naturally be more conservative in their estimates in the next iteration. That's OK, though. If you have lots of time, pull in another story or two at the end of the iteration, and when you update your velocity it will all balance back out.

Q: We tried pulling a story into our iteration, but now it's not finished and we're just about out of time.

A: Punt on the story. Remember, you're working ahead of the curve anyway. It's better to punt on the story and put it back into the next iteration than it is to commit half-written, untested code and just "wrap that up" next iteration. Remember, you're going to send your iteration's build out into the wild. You want it as stable and clean as possible.

If there is extra time at the end of an iteration some teams will tag their code before they pull anything else into the repository. That way, if things go south, they have no problems releasing a stable build by using the tag.

Q: You keep saying to prioritize bugs... but we're in the middle of an iteration. So how do bugs fit in?

A: Some projects have regularly scheduled bug reviews with the customer once a week or so to prioritize outstanding bugs. In those cases, there's always a pool of work to pull from if there's time available. If you don't meet with your customer to talk about bugs regularly, you might want to think about that...although be sure to factor in the time you'll spend on your burn rate and big board. Remember, if the bug is sufficiently important to fix, it should get scheduled into an iteration like anything else.

It's important to note we're talking about bugs found outside of developing a story. If you find a bug in a story you're working on, you should almost always fix it (after adding a test!). Nothing is "done" until it works according to the story—and the tests are proving it.

You shouldn't have LOTS of time left over. So choose SMALL TASKS to take on with any extra time you have... and get ready for the NEXT iteration.

Tools for your Software Development Toolbox

Software Development is all about developing and delivering great software. In this chapter, you learned how to end an iteration effectively. For a complete list of tools in the book, see Appendix ii.

Development Techniques

Pay attention to your burn-down rate—especially after the iteration ends

Iteration pacing is important—drop stories if you need to keep it going

Don't punish people for getting done early—if their stuff works, let them use the extra time to get ahead or learn something new

> Here are some of the key techniques you learned in this chapter...

> ... and some of the principles behind those techniques.

Development Principles

Iterations are a way to impose intermediate deadlines—stick to them

Always estimate for the ideal day for the average team member

Keep the big picture in mind when planning iterations—and that might include external testing of the system

Improve your process iteratively through iteration reviews

BULLET POINTS

- If you have some room at the end of an iteration, that's a good time to **brainstorm for new stories** that might have come up. They'll need to be prioritized with everything else, but it's great to capture them.

- **Resist the temptation** to forget about all of your good habits in the last day or two of an iteration. Don't just "sneak in" that one quick feature that has a low priority because you have a day or make that little refactoring that you're "sure won't break anything." You worked really hard to get done a day or so early, **don't blow it**.

- Work hard to keep a **healthy relationship** with your **testing team**. The two teams can make each other miserable if communication goes bad.

- Recording actual time spent on a task versus estimated time on a task isn't necessary since your velocity will account for estimation errors. But, if you know something went really wrong, **it's worth discussing in the iteration review**.

Iterationcross

You've reached the end of your iteration. Take a breather and enjoy a nice crossword puzzle.

Across

4. Estimate for the .... day and the .... team member.
5. Pay attention to your .... rate to help understand how your team is doing.
6. Make sure your testing team understands the ....
9. Standup meetings are about ....
11. Try really hard to end an iteration ....
12. A quick and dirty test implementation is a .... solution.
13. System testing is usually .... testing, but sometimes .... testing.

Down

1. Since testing can usually go on forever, make sure you have this defined and agreed to by everyone.
2. When your bug fixing rate exceeds your bug finding rate for a while.
3. You should estimate consistently because random disruptions are included in your ....
7. A good way to work through a bug backlog is to treat them as ....
8. .... system testing whenever possible.
10. System testing should really be done by a .... team.

 # Iterationcross Solution

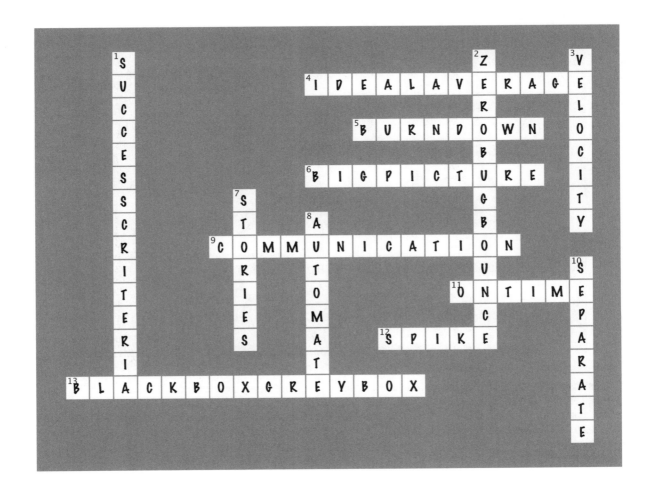

10 the next iteration

If it ain't broke...
you still better fix it

So then he said, "I don't *want* to wear a white shirt this time; I want to wear a blue shirt." How am I supposed to react to that?

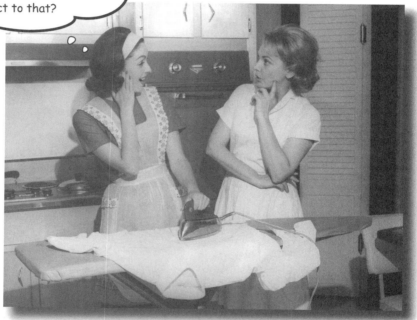

Think things are going well?
Hold on, that just might change...

Your iteration went great, and you're delivering working software on time. Time for the next iteration? No problem, right? Unfortunately, not right at all. Software development is all about **change,** and **moving to your next iteration** is no exception. In this chapter you'll learn how to prepare for the *next* iteration. You've got to **rebuild your board** and **adjust your stories** and expecations based on what the customer wants *NOW*, not a month ago.

What is working software?

When you come to the end of an iteration, you should have a
buildable piece of software. But complete software is more than just
code. It's also...

...completing your iteration's work

You're getting paid to get a certain amount of work done. No matter
how clever your code, you've got to complete tasks to be successful.

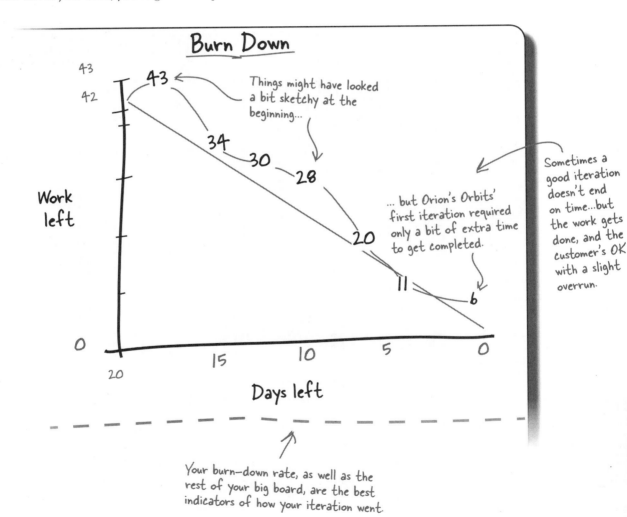

...passing all your tests

Unit tests, system tests, black- and white-box tests...if your
system doesn't pass your tests, it's not working.

```
File Edit  Window  PleaseWork
hfsd> java -cp junit.jar;. org.junit.runner.JUnitCore
                    headfirst.sd.chapter7.TestRemoteReader
JUni  version 4.3.1

Ti  : 97.825

      (112 tests)

hfsd>
```

...satisfying your customer

Software that does what it's supposed to do, in the time you
promised it, usually makes customers pretty excited. And in lots
of cases, it means you've got another iteration's worth of work.

Great. So you'll start on the
next iteration tomorrow, right?

✹BRAIN POWER

What would you do to get
going on the next iteration?

You need to pl<u>an</u> for the next iteration

Before diving into the next iteration, there are several things that all play a crucial part in getting ready. Here are the key things to pay attention to:

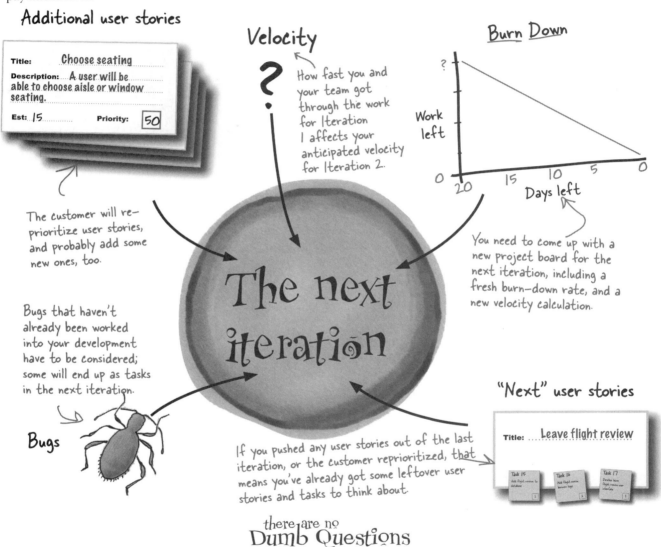

Additional user stories

Title: Choose seating
Description: A user will be able to choose aisle or window seating.
Est: 15   **Priority:** 50

Velocity

?

How fast you and your team got through the work for Iteration 1 affects your anticipated velocity for Iteration 2.

Burn Down

?

Work left

0 20 15 10 5 0

Days left

You need to come up with a new project board for the next iteration, including a fresh burn-down rate, and a new velocity calculation.

The customer will re-prioritize user stories, and probably add some new ones, too.

The next iteration

Bugs that haven't already been worked into your development have to be considered; some will end up as tasks in the next iteration.

Bugs

If you pushed any user stories out of the last iteration, or the customer reprioritized, that means you've already got some leftover user stories and tasks to think about.

"Next" user stories

Title: Leave flight review

Task 15 — Add flight review to database

Task 16 — Add flight review button logic

Task 17 — Develop leave flight review user interface

there are no Dumb Questions

Q: So what happend to the board from Iteration 1?

A: Once the iteration is finished, you can archive everything on the old Iteration 1 board. You might want to take a photo of it for archival purposes, but the important thing is to capture how much work you managed to get through in the iteration, how much work was planned, and, of course, to also take any user stories that ended up in the "Next" section back into the pack of candidate user stories for Iteration 2.

> We can fit more user stories in this next iteration, right? We should have gotten over a lot of setup stuff, and understand the overall app better now, right?

You need to revise your story and task estimates and your team's velocity.

When originally planning Orion's Orbits, you and your team came up with estimates for each of the user stories for Version 1.0, and then the tasks associated with each of those user stories. Now that it's time to kick off another iteration, you have a lot more knowledge about how things will work. So it's time to revisit those estimates for the remaining user stories and tasks.

Also, when you originally calculated how much work you could complete in the first iteration, you didn't know how fast your team could develop software and complete their tasks. You probably used an <u>initial</u> value of something like 0.7 for your team's velocity. But that was just a rough guess...now, you and your team have completed an iteration. That means you've got hard data you can use for recalculating velocity, and getting a more accurate figure.

Remember, your estimates and your velocity are about providing confident statements to your customer about what can be done, and when it will be done. You should revise both your estimates and your velocity at every iteration.

Velocity accounts for overhead in your estimates. A value of 0.7 says that you expect 30% of your team's time to be spent on other things than the actual development work. Flip back to Chapter 3 for more on velocity.

Recalculate your estimates and velocity at each iteration, applying the things you learned from the previous iteration.

Long Exercise

It's time to plan out the work for another iteration at Orion's. First, calculate your team's new velocity according to how well everyone performed in the last iteration. Then, calculate the maximum amount of days of work you can fit into this next iteration. Finally, fill out your project board with user stories and other tasks that will fit into this next iteration using your new velocity, the time that gives you, and your customer's estimates.

1 **Calculate your new velocity**

Take your team's performance from the previous iteration and calculate a new value for this iteration's velocity.

Enter your team's new velocity.

$$38 \; / \; (20 \times 3) = \boxed{}$$

This is the total days of work you accomplished, based on what you actually completed.

Number of actual working days in the last iteration.

Remember, we used calendar days here.

The number of developers on your team during the last iteration.

This number helps you figure out how many days of work you can handle for stories and tasks.

2 **Calculate the work days you have available**

Now that you have your team's velocity. you can calculate the maximum number of work days that you can fit into this iteration.

$$3 \times 20 \times \boxed{} = \boxed{}$$

The number of people on your team

The next iteration is a month long again, so that's 20 calendar days

The new velocity you just calculated

The amount of work, in days, that your team can handle in this next iteration

③ **Fill up the board with new work**

You know how many work days you've got, so all that's left is to take the candidate user stories and bugs, as well as stories left over the last iteration, and add them to your board—make sure you have a manageable workload.

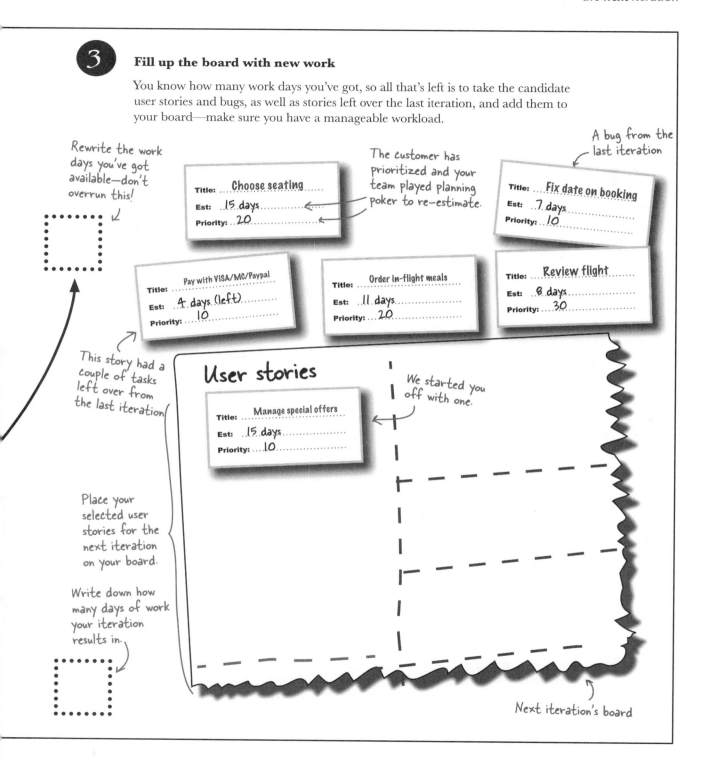

Rewrite the work days you've got available—don't overrun this!

A bug from the last iteration

The customer has prioritized and your team played planning poker to re-estimate.

Title: Choose seating
Est: 15 days
Priority: 20

Title: Fix date on booking
Est: 7 days
Priority: 10

Title: Pay with VISA/MC/Paypal
Est: 4 days (left)
Priority: 10

Title: Order in-flight meals
Est: 11 days
Priority: 20

Title: Review flight
Est: 8 days
Priority: 30

This story had a couple of tasks left over from the last iteration

User stories

Title: Manage special offers
Est: 15 days
Priority: 10

We started you off with one.

Place your selected user stories for the next iteration on your board.

Write down how many days of work your iteration results in.

Next iteration's board

Long Exercise Solution

Your job was to calculate your team's new velocity, the maximum amount of days of work you can fit into the next iteration, and then to fill out your project board with user stories and other tasks that will fit into this next iteration.

1 **Calculate your new velocity**

Take your team's performance from the previous iteration and calculate a new value for this iteration's velocity.

$$38 \ / \ (20 \times 3) = 0.6$$

Your team's velocity has actually dropped...

You got 38 days of work done, including unplanned tasks that hit the board.

Remember, velocity is a measure of how fast you and your team can get through work on your board. Regardless of whether that work is unplanned or not, it all counts.

2 **Calculate the work days you have available**

Now that you have your team's velocity, you can calculate the maximum number of work days that you can fit into this iteration.

$$3 \times 20 \times 0.6 = 36$$

... as has the total amount of work that your team can execute in the next iteration.

Fill up the board with new work

You know how many work days you've got, so all that's left is to take the candidate user stories and bugs, as well as stories left over the last iteration, and add them to your board—make sure you have a manageable work load.

Rewrite the work days you've got available—don't overrun this!

36

Title: Choose seating
Est: 15 days
Priority: 20

These stories dropped off either because they were a lower priority or wouldn't fit within the work days left in the iteration.

Title: Order in-flight meals
Est: 11 days
Priority: 20

User stories

Title: Manage special offers
Est: 15 days
Priority: 10

These stories had the highest priority.

Title: Fix date on booking
Est: 7 days
Priority: 10

The work required for the next iteration didn't exceed the available 36 days

Title: Pay with VISA/MC/PayPal
Est: 4 days (left)
Priority: 10

This bug was high-priority to the customer, so it was scheduled ahead of additional functionality.

34

Title: Review flight
Est: 8 days
Priority: 30

This story fit within the remaining 10 work days of the iteration.

there are no
Dumb Questions

Q: A team velocity of 0.6!? That's even slower than before. What happened?

A: Based on the work done in the last iteration, it turned out that your team was actually working a little *slower* than 0.7.

Q: Shouldn't my velocity get quicker as my iterations progress?

A: Not always. Remember, velocity is a measure of how fast *your* team can burn through their tasks, and 0.7 was just an original rough guess when you had nothing else to go by.

It's not uncommon for you and your team to have a tough first iteration, which will result in a lower velocity for the next iteration. But you'll probably see your velocity get better over the *next* several iterations, so you've got something to look forward to.

Q: Hmm, I noticed that some of the estimates for the Orion's Orbits user stories have changed from when we last saw them in Chapter 3. What gives?

A: Good catch! Based on the knowledge that you and your team have built up in the last iteration, you should **re-estimate** all your stories and tasks. Now you know much more about the work that will be involved so new estimates should be even more accurate, and keep you from missing something important, and taking longer than you expect.

Q: So the estimates for our user stories and their tasks will get smaller?

A: Not necessarily. They could get smaller, or bigger, but the important thing is that they will likely get more and more **accurate** as you progress through your iterations.

Q: I see that bug fixing is also represented as a user story. Doesn't that break the definition of a user story a bit?

A: A little, but a user story really ends up being—when it is broken into tasks—nothing more than work that you have to do. And a bug fix is certainly work for you to take on. The user story in this case is a description of the bug, and the tasks will be the work necessary to fix that bug (as far as you and your team can gauge from the description).

Q: I'm really struggling coming up with estimates for my bugs. Am I just supposed to take my best guess?

A: Unfortunately, you will be taking a best guess. And when it comes to bugs, it pays to guess conservatively. Always give yourself an amount of time that feels really comfortable to you. And remember, you've got to figure out what caused the bug as well as fix it; both steps take time.

One technique you can use is to look for similar bugs in the past and see how long they took to find and fix. That information will at least give you some guide when estimating a particular bug's work.

Q: If I have a collection of bugs, how do I decide what ones should make it into the board and be fixed in the next iteration?

A: " You don't! **Priority is always set by the customer.** So the customer sets a priority for each of the bugs, and that's what tells you what to deal with in each iteration

Besides, this approach lets the customer see that for each bug that is added to the iteration, other work—like new functionality—has to be sacrificed.

The decision is functionality versus bug fixes, and it's the customer who has to make that call... because it's the customer who decides ultimately what they want delivered at the end of the *next* iteration.

Q: I understand why the high-priority stories made it onto the next iteration's board, but wouldn't it be a better idea to add in another high-priority user story that slightly breaks the maximum work limit, rather than schedule in a lower priority task that fits?

A: **Never** break the maximum working days that your team can execute in an iteration. That value of 36 days for the maximum amount of work your team can handle for an iteration of 20 days is exactly that: the **maximum**.

The only way that you could add more work into the iteration is to extend the iteration. You could fit in more work if your iteration were extended to, say, 22 days, but be very careful when doing this. As you saw in Chapter 1, iterations are kept small so that you can check your software with the customer often. Longer iterations mean less checks and more chance that you'll deviate further from what your customer needs.

Velocity accounts for...
the <u>REAL</u> <u>WORLD</u>

Velocity is a key part of planning out your next iteration. You're looking for a value that corresponds to how fast your team **actually works**, in reality, based on how they've worked in the past.

This is why you only factor in the work that has been completed in your last iteration. Any work that got put off doesn't matter; you want to know what was done, and how long it took to get done. That's the key information that tells you what to expect in the next iteration.

Velocity tells you what your team can expect to get done in the <u>NEXT</u> iteration

Be confident in your estimates

Velocity gives you an accurate way to forecast your productivity. Use it to make sure you have the right amount of work in your next iteration, and that you can successfully deliver on your promises to the customer.

It's not that I *think* we can deliver on time anymore...I **know** we can deliver.

By calculating velocity, you take into account the <u>REALITY</u> of how you and your team develop, so that you can plan your next iteration for <u>SUCCESS.</u>

And it's __STILL__ about the customer

Let's say you've calculated your new velocity. You collected bugs and put them all in a bug tracker. You waded through all the piles of unfinished and delayed tasks and stories, and had the customer reprioritize those along with stories planned for the next iteration. You've got your board ready to go.

You still have to go back and get your customer's approval on your overall plan. And that's when things can go really wrong...

This looks great, but I've got big news...We've just bought Mercury Meals, the galaxy's premiere in-space catering company, and we need to integrate their ordering system into our code ASAP! Throw out everything else; this is top priority now.

All your estimates from planning poker, your stories, your nice organized big board...they all have to get trashed (well, not the board itself) if the customer makes a big change.

You've suddenly got a ton of new code that you know nothing about, and it replaces a lot of what you had planned for the next iteration.

Now hang on a second! That's a LOT of work to just toss out. Couldn't we have checked with the customer earlier? Or done something else to avoid all this wasted time?

Software is still about CHANGE

Sometimes the customer is going to come up with a big change at the last minute. Or your best plans break down when your star programmer takes a new job. Or the company you're working for lays off an entire department...

But even though what you're working on has changed, the mechanics of planning haven't. You have a new velocity, and you know how many days of work your team has available. So you simply need to build new user stories, reprioritize, and replan.

You already know how to...

☐ Calculate your team's velocity

☐ Estimate your team's user stories and tasks

☐ Calculate your iteration size in days of work that your team can handle

BRAIN POWER

You've got a ton of new code that you've never seen or used before. What would be the first thing you do to try and estimate the time it will take to integrate that code into the Orion's system?

Someone else's software is <u>STILL</u> just software

Even though the Mercury Meals library is not code you have written, you still treat the work necessary to integrate the code into Orion's Orbits as you would any other software development activities. You'll need to tackle all the same basic activities:

User stories

Every change to the software is motivated by and written down as a user story. In this case, your story card will be a description of how the Mercury Meals code is used by the Orion's Orbit system to achieve some particular piece of functionality.

Estimates

Every user story needs an estimate. So each of the user stories that the Mercury Meals code library plays a part in has to be estimated. How much time will it take to build that functionality, including time spent integrating the Mercury Meals code?

Priorities

The final piece of the puzzle is, of course, priorities. Each of the user stories associated with the Mercury Meals code needs to have an associated priority from your customer so that you can plan out the work for the next iteration, in the order that your customer wants it done.

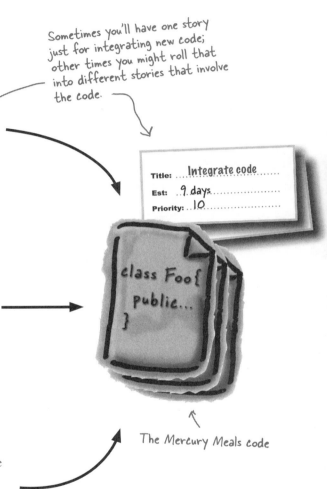

Sometimes you'll have one story just for integrating new code; other times you might roll that into different stories that involve the code.

Title: .....Integrate code.....
Est: ..9 days...............
Priority: ..10.................

class Foo{
public...
}

The Mercury Meals code

Exercise

You've got new stories related to Mercury Meals, as well as the stories you thought you'd be doing in this next iteration. Your job is to re-create the board using your velocity and the customer's priorities. (We've left out the stories that didn't make the first-pass plan.)

Title: Order Regular Meal
Est: 12 days
Priority: 10

The new Mercury Meals user stories

Title: Order vegetarian or vegan meal
Est: 6 days
Priority: 20

Title: View all the orders for a flight
Est: 4 days
Priority: 10

Title: Edit Special Deals
Est: 15 days
Priority: 10

Title: Fix date on booking
Est: 7 days
Priority: 10

Title: Leave flight review
Est: 8 days
Priority: 30

Title: Pay with Visa/MC/PayPal
Est: 4 days (left)
Priority: 10

These were the user stories that made it onto your board the first planning pass.

36

The number of people in your team and their velocity hasn't changed since your first attempt at a project board for this iteration, so neither has the number of work days you've got.

Add up your new total work for the next iteration.

User stories

EXERCISE SOLUTION

Your job was to re-create the board using your velocity and the customer's priorities.

Title: Order vegetarian or vegan meal
Est: 6 days
Priority: 20

This Mercury Meals user story was a lower priority and so will have to wait until the following iteration.

Title: Leave flight review
Est: 8 days
Priority: 30

Title: Fix date on booking
Est: 7 days
Priority: 10

Even though it's a high priority, we couldn't fit in this bug fix so it'll be first up for the <u>following</u> iteration, assuming that's what the customer still wants then.

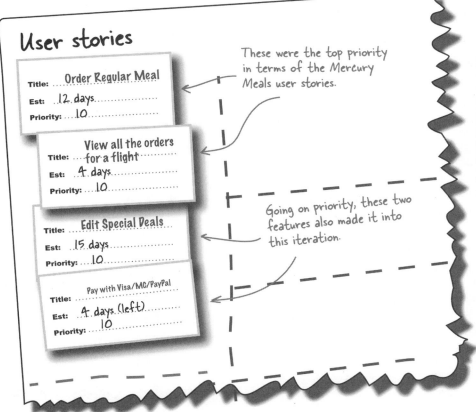

36

Your budget was 36 days of work for your team, factoring in velocity...

User stories

Title: Order Regular Meal
Est: 12 days
Priority: 10

These were the top priority in terms of the Mercury Meals user stories.

Title: View all the orders for a flight
Est: 4 days
Priority: 10

Title: Edit Special Deals
Est: 15 days
Priority: 10

Going on priority, these two features also made it into this iteration.

Title: Pay with Visa/MC/PayPal
Est: 4 days (left)
Priority: 10

... and you've planned out 35.

35

Customer approval? Check!

Once again, you've got to get customer approval
once everything's planned out. And this time, there
aren't any surprises...

> This looks great! It's a shame we can't do everything, but
> I'm really excited to see us using the new Mercury Meals
> code. I can't wait to tell the CFO! I'll let her know right
> now, and I'll even mention your name.

*Yes, it's really possible to get reactions like
this from a customer. Good planning and
giving your customer a chance for frequent
feedback is a sure way to get your customer
on board and excited.*

---
there are no
Dumb Questions

**Q: Can you tell me again why we've got user stories for
working with third-party code? And why did you estimate 12
days for ordering a meal? Isn't the whole point of getting third-
party code that it saves us time?**

A: A user story isn't as much about writing code as it is about what
a user needs your system to do. So no matter who wrote the code, if
you're responsible for functionality, capture it as a user story.
As for why the estimates are pretty large, reuse is great, but you're
still going to have to write some code that interacts with the third-
party software. But just think how long it would take if you had to
write all the Mercury Meals code yourself.

**Q: Are there any times when I shouldn't consider reusing
someone else's code library or API?**

A: Reuse can really give your development work a shot in the
arm, but third-party code has to be used with care. When you use
someone else's software, you're **relying** on that software, placing
your success in the hands of the people that developed the code that
your code now uses.

So if you're using someone else's work, you better be sure you can
trust that work.

Exercise

It's time to write the code for the two Mercury Meals user stories, "Order Regular Meals" and "View all the orders for a flight." On the left you have the Mercury Meals code's interface, which is a collection of methods that you can call from your own code. On the right, you need to wire up your code so that it uses the Mercury Meals API to bring both of the user stories below to life.

Title: ....Order Regular Meal....

Est: ...12. days...................

Priority: ....10......................

Title: .....View all the orders....
.....for a flight.............

Est: ...4. days....................

Priority: ...10.....................

The two stories you have to implement

Reality <u>check</u>: assume your team spent several days getting class diagrams together for the Mercury Meals API.

The main interface to the Mercury Meals code

How you get access to the MercuryMeals object

MercuryMeals

+ getInstance() :MercuryMeals   Creates a blank order

+ createOrder() :Order

+ submitOrder(order : Order) :boolean   Submits a completed order to Mercury Meals

+ getMealOption(name : String) :MealOption   Returns a meal option, like "Roast Beef"

+ getOrdersThatMatchKeywords(keywords : String[]) :Order[]

Methods on the interface that can be called from your code

Returns a list of orders that match a specific set of keywords

Interface that represents an order for a meal

Order

+ addMealOption(mealOption : MealOption) :void

+ addKeyword(keyword : String) :void

You can add options to an order...

...and add keywords that you can then search on later to retrieve a set of orders.

You can download the Mercury Meals code from
http://www.headfirstlabs.com/books/hfsd

```
return mercuryMeals.getOrdersThatMatchKeyword({flightNo});
```

```
//...
// Adds a meal order to a flight
public void orderMeal(String[] options, String flightNo)
                                    throws MealOptionNotFoundException,
                                           OrderNotAcceptedException {
```

The first line of code has already
been added for you.

```
MercuryMeals mercuryMeals = MercuryMeals.getInstance();
```

```
for (int x = 0; x < options.length;x++) {
```

```
Order order = mercuryMeals.createOrder();
```

```
order.addKeyword(flightNo);
```

Add these code magnets
into the main program.

```
MercuryMeals mercuryMeals = MercuryMeals.getInstance();
```

```
if (!mercuryMeals.submitOrder(order)) {
    throw new OrderNotAcceptedException(order);
}
```

```
MealOption mealOption = mercuryMeals.getMealOption(options[x]);
```

```
    }
```

```
    }
```

```
// Finds all the orders for a specific flight
public String[] getAllOrdersForFlight(String flightNo) {
```

```
if (mealOption != null) {
    order.addMealOption(mealOption);
} else {
    throw new MealOptionNotFoundException(mealOption);
}
```

```
    }
```

```
// ...
```

Exercise Solution

Your job was to complete the code so that it uses the Mercury Meals API to bring both of the user stories to life.

```
//...
// Adds a meal order to a flight

public void orderMeal(String[] options, String flightNo)
                                    throws MealOptionNotFoundException,
                                    OrderNotAcceptedException {

    MercuryMeals mercuryMeals = MercuryMeals.getInstance();

    Order order = mercuryMeals.createOrder();

    for (int x = 0; x < options.length;x++) {

        MealOption mealOption = mercuryMeals.getMealOption(options[x]);

        if (mealOption != null) {

            order.addMealOption(mealOption);

        } else {

            throw new MealOptionNotFoundException(mealOption);

        }

    }

    order.addKeyword(flightNo);

    if (!mercuryMeals.submitOrder(order)) {

        throw new OrderNotAcceptedException(order);

    }

}


// Finds all the orders for a specific flight

public Order[] getAllOrdersForFlight(String flightNo) {

    MercuryMeals mercuryMeals = MercuryMeals.getInstance();

    return mercuryMeals.getOrdersThatMatchKeyword({flightNo});

}

// ...
```

This gets a Mercury Meals object for this code to use.

Creates a new blank order

For each of the options selected, a new option is added to the order.

If an option isn't found, then an exception is raised.

The flight number is added to the order as a keyword so that the orders for a particular flight can be retrieved.

Attempt to submit the new complete order to Mercury Meals.

Searches for and returns all orders that have the specified flight number as a keyword

there are no
Dumb Questions

Q: That was easy. Why did we estimate 16 days for integrating the Mercury Meals code?

A: There's more going on here than just integrating code. First you and your team will have to come to grips with the Mercury Meals documentation. There'll be sequence diagrams to understand and class diagrams to pick through, all of which takes time. Factor in your own updates to your design and thinking about how best to integrate the code in the first place, and you've got a meaty task on your hands. In fact, it's often the thinking time up front that takes longer than the actual implementation.

Q: Does it matter if the third-party code is compiled or not?

A: If the library works then it doesn't matter if it's in source code or compiled form. You have to add in extra time to compile the code if it comes as source, but often that's an easy comand-line job and you'll have a compiled library anyway.

However, if the library doesn't work for any reason, then it really does matter if you can get at the source or not. If you are reusing a compiled library of code then you are limited to simply using that code, according to its accompanying documentation. You might be able to decompile the code, but if you're not careful, that can mean you are breaking the license of the third-party software. With compiled libraries you usually can't actually delve into the code in the library itself to fix any problems. If there's an issue, you have to try and get back in touch with the person who originally wrote the code.

However, if you are actually given the source code to the library—if it's open source or something that you've purchased—then you can get into the library itself to fix any problems. This sounds great, but bear in mind that in both cases you're trusting the third-party library to work. Otherwise you're either signing up for a barrage of questions being sent to the original developers, or for extra work to develop fixes in the code itself.

Q: What if the third-party code doesn't work?

A: Then your trust in that library quickly disappears, and you have two choices: You can continue to persevere with the library, particularly if you have the source code and can perform some serious debugging to see what is going wrong. Or you can discard the library for another, if one's available, or try to write the code yourself, if you know how.

With any of these options you are taking on extra work. That's why when you consider using third-party code, you have to think very carefully. Sometimes that code is forced upon you, like with Mercury Meals, but often you have a choice. You need to be aware of just how much trust you are putting in that library working.

> **Be careful when deciding to reuse something. When you reuse code, you are assuming that code WORKS.**

Exercise

This is a good time to go grab the code!
The code for Mercury Meals is available from the Head First Labs site. Just go to *http://www.headfirstlabs.com/books/hfsd/*, and follow the links to download the code for Chapter 10.

Testing your code

Make sure you've downloaded the Mercury Meals and Orion's Orbits code from Head First Labs. Make the additions shown on page 368, <u>compile everything</u>, and give things a whirl...

You should have a build tool that makes this a piece of cake.

```
> java OrionsOrbits
Adding order...
```

This doesn't look good...the application hangs. No output, no errors, nothing...

You're kidding, right? The customer's CFO got so excited about the new improvements, she booked herself on the inaugural flight of Orion's Orbits. You're telling me she won't even be able to pick her meal?

Houston, we really do have a problem...

All that hard work has resulted in a big fat nothing. Your code...or the
Mercury Meals code...***some*** code isn't working. Somewhere. And
your customer, and your customer's *boss*, is about to really be upset...

Sharpen your pencil

You've just integrated a huge amount of third-party code, and
something's not working. Time's short, and the pressure's on.

What would you do? ....

....

....

....

....

....

....

Standup meeting

OK, what the heck happened guys, we coded things up and nothing worked...

Laura: We assumed that the Mercury Meals code would work, and it clearly doesn't, or at least doesn't in the way we expect. What a mess.

Bob: Well, that sounds like a reasonable assumption to me. *We* would never release code that doesn't work...

Mark: Yeah, but that's us. Who knows what the developers at Mercury Meals were doing?

Laura: We just took the code and assumed it would work, maybe we should have tested it out first...

Bob: So you think the developers at Mercury Meals just kicked out a dud piece of code?

Laura: It certainly looks like it. Who knows if it was ever even run, it could have been only half a project.

Mark: But it's our code and our problem now...

Bob: And it's way too late to start from scratch...

Mark: ...and we don't know how the Mercury Meals system works anyhow...

Laura: And worse than all of that, what are we going to tell the CFO? Our butts are seriously on the line here...

Trust <u>NO</u> <u>ONE</u>

When it comes to code that someone else has written, it's all about trust, and the real lesson here is to ***trust no one*** when it comes to code. Unless you've *seen* a piece of code running, or run your own tests against it, someone else's code could be a ticking time bomb that's just waiting to explode—right when you need it the most.

When you take on code from a third party, you are relying on that code to work. It's no good complaining that it doesn't work if you never tried to use it, and until you have seen it running, it's best to assume that third-party code doesn't really work at all.

Your software...your responsibility

You're responsible for how your software works. It doesn't matter if the buggy code in the software wasn't code you wrote. A bug is a bug, and as a pro software developer, you're responsible for *all* the software you deliver.

A third party is not you. That might sound a little obvious, but it's really important when you're tempted to assume that just because you use a great testing and development process, everyone else does, too.

Never assume that other people are following your process

Treat every line of code developed elsewhere with suspicion until you've tested it, because not everyone is as professional in their approach to software development as you are.

> It doesn't matter who wrote the code. If it's in <u>YOUR</u> software, it's <u>YOUR</u> responsibility.

Exercise

The Mercury Meals classes are now **your** code...but they're a mess. Circle and annotate all the problems you can see in the code below. You're looking for everything from readability of the code right through to problems with functionality.

```java
// Follows the Singleton design pattern
public class MercuryMeals
{
    public MercuryMeals meallythang;
    private Order cO;
    private String qk = "select * from order-table where keywords like %1;";


public MercuryMeals() {

}


public MercuryMeals getInstance()
{
    this.meallythang = new MercuryMeals();
    return this.instance;
}
    // TODO Really should document this at some point... TBD
    public Order createOrder {
        return new Order();}


public MealOption getMealOption(String option)
throws MercuryMealsConnectionException {
    if (MM.establish().isAnyOptionsForKey(option))
    { return MM.establish.getMealOption(option).[0] };
    return null;
}
```

```
// Mercury Meals class continued...




    public boolean submitOrder(Order cO)
{

    try {
      MM mm = MM.establish();
      mm.su(this.cO);
    catch (Exception e)
    { // write out an error message } return false; }




    public Order[] getOrdersThatMatchKeyword(String qk)
                            throws MercuryMealsConnectionException {
      Order o = new Order[];
      try {
          o = MM.establish().find(qk, qk);
        } catch (Exception e) {
          return null;
        }
      return o;
    }}
```

Exercise Solution

Your job was to to circle and annotate all the problems you can see in this Mercury Meals code.

```
// Follows the Singleton design pattern

public class MercuryMeals

{
    public MercuryMeals meallythang;

    private Order cO;

    private String qk = "select * from order-table where keywords like %1;";

    private MercuryMeals instance;

    public MercuryMeals() {

    }


    public MercuryMeals getInstance()

    {

        this.instance = new MercuryMeals();

        return this.instance;

    }

    // TODO Really should document this at some point... TBD

    public Order createOrder {

        return new Order();}


    public MealOption getMealOption(String option)

        throws MercuryMealsConnectionException {

        if (MM.establish().isAnyOptionsForKey(option))

            { return MM.establish().getMealOption(option).[0] };

        return null;

    }
```

No real documentation on the class, other than the fact that it tries to implement the Singleton pattern...

Not the most descriptive of attribute names.

This attribute is public! That's a major object-oriented no-no.

Why is there an Order attribute? Even a few comments would help...

Surely this should be a constant? And does qk make any sense as an attribute name?

Why have an explicit constructor declared that does nothing?

Hang on! This class is supposed to be implementing the singleton pattern but this looks like it creates a new instance of MercuryMeals every time this method is called...

Looks like the original developer just didn't ever finish this bit off.

This method seems to not do anything of any real value at the moment. You could just as easily create an order without the Mercury Meals class—and as for the indentation, it's all over the place.

Why not establish the connection just once?

Returning null is a bad practice. It's a better idea to raise an exception that gives the caller more info to work with.

```
// Mercury Meals class continued...
```

No documentation on any of this class's methods.
Something that described what the methods are
supposed to do would make life a LOT easier.

```
public boolean submitOrder(Order cO)
{
    try {
        MM mm = MM.establish();
        mm.su(this.cO);
    catch (Exception e)
    { // write out an error message } } return false; }
```

No wonder the software gave no indication whether
it was working or not (except by just hanging...) This
method swallows all exceptions that are raised. This is
a classic exception anti-pattern. If an exception gets
raised, and you can't deal with it locally, then pass
the exception up to the caller so they can at least
know what went wrong.

The code indentation is still all
over the place. This makes things
very hard to read.

```
public Order[] getOrdersThatMatchKeyword(String qk)

                        throws MercuryMealsConnectionException {

    Order o = new Order[];
    try {

        o = MM.establish().find(qk, qk);
    } catch (Exception e) {

        return null;

    }
    return o;
}}
```

Which qk is being used here? This
doesn't make sense, and might be a bug.

Hiding exceptions again! The caller of
this method will never have to handle a
MercuryMealsConnectionException or any other
exception because this method is hiding anything
that goes wrong and just returning null.

Believe it or not, this bracket here
closes the class, but from the poor use of
indentation, you'd be hard-pressed to be
sure of that from looking.

You <u>without</u> your process

Right now things are looking pretty bleak, and without
your process you would really be in trouble...

You **with** your process

It's not a perfect world. When your code—or someone else's code you depend on—isn't working, and your customer is breathing down your neck, it's easy to panic or catch the next flight to a non-extradition country. But that's when a good process can be your best friend.

> We need to get a good estimate of how long it will take to fix this code.

> Once we get the third-party stuff working, we're done and we can do that demo...

> So let's update the burn rate and get back to it!

BULLET POINTS

- When you're gearing up for the next iteration, always **check back with the customer** to make sure that the work you are planning is the work that they want done.

- You and your team's **velocity is recalculated** at the end of every iteration.

- Let your customer **reprioritize your user stories** for a new iteration, based on the working days you've got available for that iteration.

- Whether you're writing new code or reusing someone else's **it's all still just software** and your **process remains the same**.

- Every piece of code in your software, whether it be your own code or a third party's like Mercury Meals, should be represented by at least one user story.

- **Never assume anything** about code you are reusing.

- A great interface to a library of code is no guarantee that the code works. **Trust nothing** until you've seen it work for yourself.

- **Code is written once but read (by others) many times.** Treat your code as you would any other piece of work that you present to other people. It should be readable, reliable, and easy to understand.

there are no Dumb Questions

Q: Things seem to be in a really bad shape right now. What good is our process if we still end up in crappy situations like this?

A: The problem here is that when you reused Mercury Meals' software, you and your team brought in code that was developed under a different process than yours, with an entirely different result—broken code.

Not everyone developing software is going to test first, use version control and continuous integration, and track bugs. Sometimes, it's up to you to take software you didn't develop and deal with it.

Q: So how common is this situation? Couldn't I just always use my own code?

A: Most software developed today is created on really tight timelines. You have to be productive and deliver great software quicker and quicker, and often with success, so the tempo rises as your customers demand even more.

One of the best ways to save time in those situations is to reuse code—often code that your team didn't write. So the better you get at development, the more reuse will be part of your normal routine.

And when you start to reuse code, there's always that crucial time when you encounter code that simply does not work, and it's easier to fix that code than to start over. But hold on...Chapter 11 is all about just how to do that, without abandoning your process.

Dealing with code that doesn't work is part of software development!

In Chapter 11, you'll see how your process can handle the heat.

Software Development Cross

Let's put what you've learned to use and stretch out your left brain a bit! Good luck!

Across

2. If your software doesn't work, it's your .... to get it fixed.

6. If you .... that a piece of code works you are heading for a world of pain.

8. The .... decides what is in or out for iteration 2.

11. Your velocity helps you calculate how many .... days you can handle in iteration 2.

12. .... deals with the real world when you're planning your next iteration.

13. Mercury Meals, other frameworks, code libraries and even code samples are all cases where you will want to consider .... code.

14. .... are also included in the candidate work for the next iteration.

Down

1. Code .... is one very useful technique to get you developing quickly and productively.

3. Any work for the next iteration should appear on the .... for the iteration.

4. Trust .... when it comes to reusing software.

5. Never .... any code you haven't written or run in some way.

7. You should let your customer .... your user stories, bug reports and other pieces of work before you begin planning iteration 2.

9. You treat third party code the .... as your own code.

10. You may be following a great ...., but don't assume that anyone else is.

Software Development Cross Solution

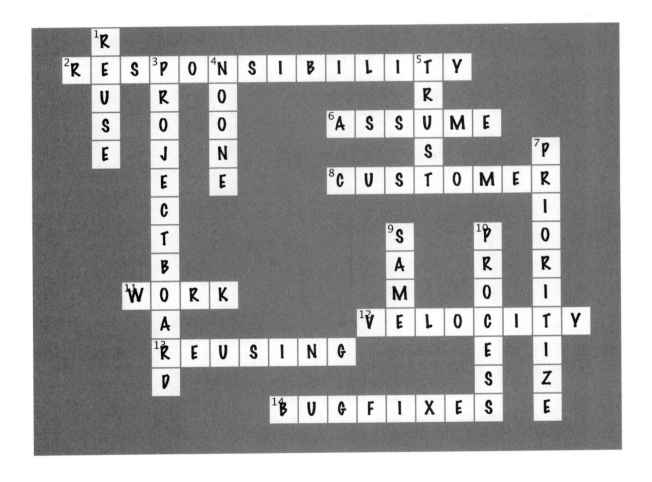

11 bugs

Squashing bugs like a pro

> Some call me vain, but I'm just proud of what I've accomplished. It takes a lot of work to be flawless.

Your code, your responsibility...your bug, your reputation!

When things get tough, it's **up to you** to bring them back from the brink. **Bugs**, whether they're in your code or just in code that your software uses, are a **fact of life** in software development. And, like everything else, the way you handle bugs should fit into the rest of your process. You'll need to **prepare your board**, **keep your customer in the loop**, **confidently estimate** the work it will take to fix your bugs, and apply **refactoring** and **prefactoring** to fix and avoid bugs in the future.

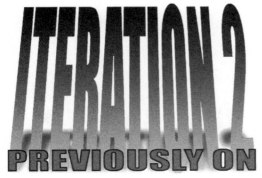

You with **your** process

It's not a perfect world and when your code is not working and your customer is breathing down your neck it can feel like a perfect hell. Luckily your process has the unexpected, and the desperate, situation also baked right in. With your process, you have a plan...

Once we get the third party stuff working, we're done and we can do that demo...

We need to get a good estimate of how long it will take to fix this code.

So let's update the burn rate and get back to it!

At the end of the last chapter, things were in a pretty bad way. You'd added Mercury Meals' code into Orion's Orbits and were all set to demo things to the CFO when you hit a problem. Well, actually **three** problems—and that adds up to **one big mess**...

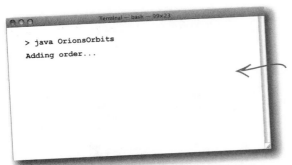

> java OrionsOrbits
> Adding order...

Your system freezes when you try and run it...it just stops doing anything.

Orion's Orbits is NOT working.

Your customer added three new user stories that relied on some new code from Mercury Meals. Everything looked good, the board was balanced and you completed the integration work when, BOOM!, you ran your code and absolutely nothing happened. The application just froze...

You have a LOT of ugly new code.

When you dug into the Mercury Meals code, you found a ton of problems. What's causing the problems in Orion's Orbits, and where should you start looking?

Title: Order Regular Meal
Est: 12
Priority: 10

Title: Order vegetarian or vegan meal
Est: 6
Priority: 20

Title: View all the orders for a flight
Est: 4
Priority: 10

You have THREE user stories that rely on your code working.

All of this would be bad enough, but there are three user stories that rely on the Mercury Meals code working, not just one.

To make matters even worse, the CEO of Orion's Orbits has talked you up to the CFO, and both are looking forward to seeing everything working, and soon...

Sharpen your pencil

Your software isn't working, you've got code to fix, and the CEO of Orion's Orbits is breathing down your neck, because the CFO is soon to be breathing down his. But how does any of this fit into your process?

What would you do next?

....

....

....

....

....

....

....

Wait! Think through what you would do next and fill in the blanks above before turning the page...

You, too, impatient developer... come up with a good answer, and <u>then</u> go on to the next section.

First, you've got to talk to the customer

Whenever something changes, talk it over with your team. If the impact is significant, in terms of functionality or schedule, then you've got to go back to the customer. And this is a big issue, so that means making a tough phone call...

Great. Yeah, I'm gonna get screamed at, but I'll tell the CFO we're pushing things back. But I need a date...when will this be done? And don't tell me you don't know, I pay you way too much to not know.

The customer's right. You need to get things to a point where you can make a confident estimate as to how long this mess will take to fix...and get that estimate FAST.

Standup meeting

Y'know, I wish I could just get my hands on one of those Mercury Meals developers; their code really sucks...

Laura: Well, that's why they were fired after the merger. It doesn't really matter that they screwed up, though, it's our code now...

Bob: I know, I know. But poorly written code just burns me up. It makes us look like idiots.

Mark: Look, can we move on? What do we do next?

Laura: Well, we're stuck with this code. So better start treating it like it's ours.

Mark: I think you might be on to something there...

Laura: We already know how to deal with our own new code. if we treat Mercury Meals the same way, that should at least give us a good starting point.

Bob: Ugh...you mean we have to manage its configuration, build it, and test it, don't you? Build scripts and CI all around?

Mark: Yep, we're going to have to maintain this stuff so the best first step would be to get all the Mercury Meals code into our code repository and building correctly before we can even start to fix the problem.

It's <u>your</u> <u>code</u>, so the first step is to get it building...

Broken Code Magnets

Here are a bunch of things you could do to work your way through the Mercury Meals code. Put them in the order you think you should do them. Be careful, though, there might be some you don't think will be worth doing at all.

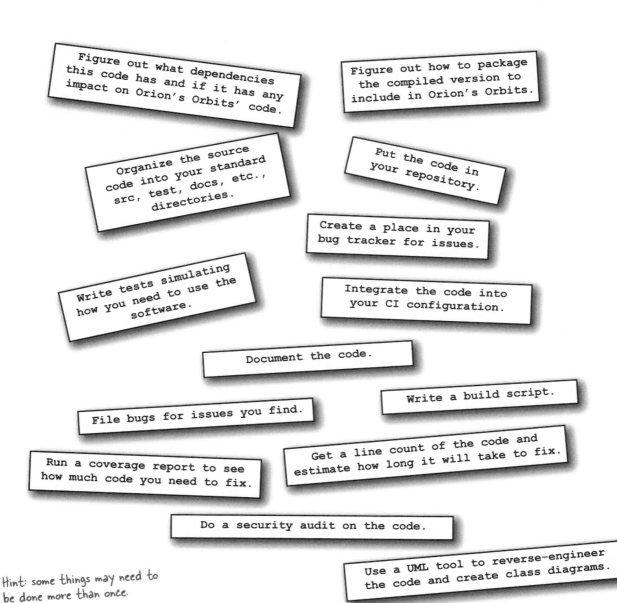

Figure out what dependencies this code has and if it has any impact on Orion's Orbits' code.

Figure out how to package the compiled version to include in Orion's Orbits.

Organize the source code into your standard src, test, docs, etc., directories.

Put the code in your repository.

Create a place in your bug tracker for issues.

Write tests simulating how you need to use the software.

Integrate the code into your CI configuration.

Document the code.

Write a build script.

File bugs for issues you find.

Get a line count of the code and estimate how long it will take to fix.

Run a coverage report to see how much code you need to fix.

Do a security audit on the code.

Use a UML tool to reverse-engineer the code and create class diagrams.

Hint: some things may need to be done more than once.

Put your magnets on here in
the order you would do them.

To-Do List

Broken Code Magnets

Here are a bunch of things you could do to work your way through the
Mercury Meals code. Put them in the order you think you should do them.
Be careful, though, there might be some you don't think will be worth doing
at all.

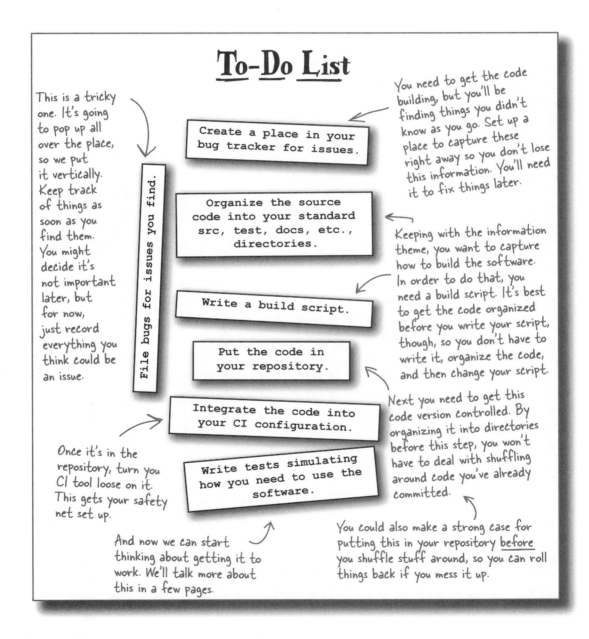

To-Do List

This is a tricky
one. It's going
to pop up all
over the place,
so we put
it vertically.
Keep track
of things as
soon as you
find them.
You might
decide it's
not important
later, but
for now,
just record
everything you
think could be
an issue.

File bugs for issues you find.

Create a place in your
bug tracker for issues.

You need to get the code
building, but you'll be
finding things you didn't
know as you go. Set up a
place to capture these
right away so you don't lose
this information. You'll need
it to fix things later.

Organize the source
code into your standard
src, test, docs, etc.,
directories.

Keeping with the information
theme, you want to capture
how to build the software.
In order to do that, you
need a build script. It's best
to get the code organized
before you write your script,
though, so you don't have to
write it, organize the code,
and then change your script.

Write a build script.

Put the code in
your repository.

Integrate the code into
your CI configuration.

Next you need to get this
code version controlled. By
organizing it into directories
before this step, you won't
have to deal with shuffling
around code you've already
committed.

Once it's in the
repository, turn you
CI tool loose on it.
This gets your safety
net set up.

Write tests simulating
how you need to use the
software.

And now we can start
thinking about getting it to
work. We'll talk more about
this in a few pages.

You could also make a strong case for
putting this in your repository <u>before</u>
you shuffle stuff around, so you can roll
things back if you mess it up.

**So what about all the magnets we didn't use?
They're not necessarily bad ideas, but here's
why we didn't put them on our short list.**

Figure out what dependencies
this code has and if it has any
impact on Orion's Orbits' code.

This is important, but we don't know what changes we're going to have to make to the code yet. We're just not ready to focus on library versions.

Figure out how to package
the compiled version to
include in Orion's Orbits.

This is going to be important once this code is stable, but until we get things tested and working, it's not much use worrying about how to package anything up beyond the library we already have.

Document the code.

Another important one, and it almost got a vertical spot next to "File bugs...". But since we're not making changes to the code yet, and don't even know what parts we'll need, we decided to leave this one off of our short list...although we might come back to it later.

Run a coverage report to see
how much code you need to fix.

This one just can't happen yet. We don't have tests, we don't know what code we actually need, and we know some of the code isn't working. Test coverage at this point won't tell us much of value.

Get a line count of the code and
estimate how long it will take to fix.

This is oh-so-tempting. It provides a solid metric to latch onto, which seems like a good thing. The problem with this is that we don't know how much of the code we'll need, and we have absolutely no idea how much is missing. What if there is a stubbed-out class where a whole section of the library is supposed to be? Concerns like this make a metric here useless.

Do a security audit on the code.

At some point this will be a great idea, but like some of the other tasks, we don't know what code we need yet, and we're about to go changing things anyway, so let's hold off on this for now.

Use a UML tool to reverse-engineer
the code and create class diagrams.

Of all the tasks we didn't choose to do, this is the most likely candidate to get added back in. But right now, we don't know how much of the library we need. Let's get a handle on what we have to use; then we'll try and figure out how it's supposed to work.

Priority one: get things buildable

The code is in version control, you've written build scripts, and you've
added continuous integration with CruiseControl. Mercury Meals is still a
junky piece of nonworking code, but at least you should have a little bit of
control over the code...and that's your first priority.

*An email generated by your
continuous integration tool
when the Mercury Meals
build is run.*

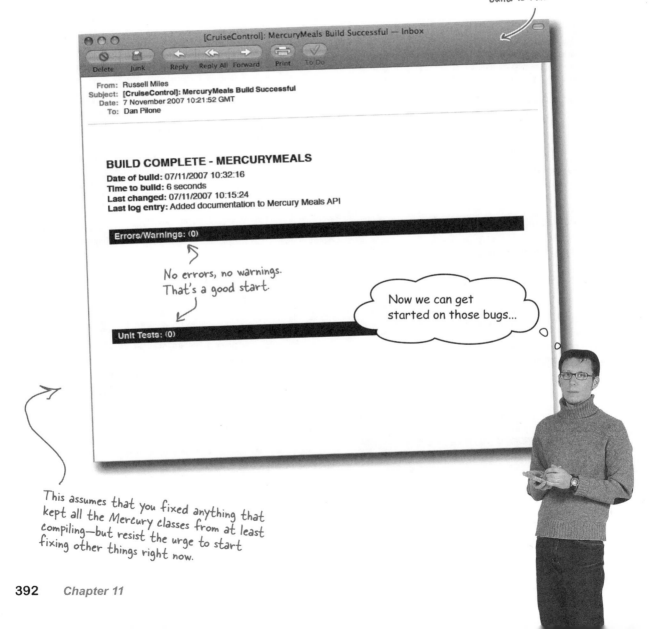

*No errors, no warnings.
That's a good start.*

*Now we can get
started on those bugs...*

*This assumes that you fixed anything that
kept all the Mercury classes from at least
compiling—but resist the urge to start
fixing other things right now.*

> Great,
> you're a real wunderkind; all
> that time and nothing works, still. Give
> that guy a promotion, huh?

A <u>little</u> time now can save a <u>LOT</u> of time later.

None of the original bugs are fixed just yet, but that's OK. You've got a development environment set up, your code's under version control, and you can easily write tests and run them automatically. In other words, you've just prevented all the problems you've seen over the last several hundred pages from sneaking up and biting you in the ass.

You know that the code doesn't work, but now that everything is dialed into your process, you're ready to attack bugs in a sensible way. You've taken ownership of the Mercury Meals code, and anything you fix from here on out will stay fixed... saving you wasted time on the back end.

Get the code under source control and building successfully <u>before</u> you change anything... including fixing bugs.

We could fix code...

Now it's time to figure out what needs to be fixed. At the end of
Chapter 10 you took a look at the Mercury Meals code, and the
prognosis was not good...

All of these problems were
found, and this was only when
you peeked into the first layer
of the Mercury Meals code.

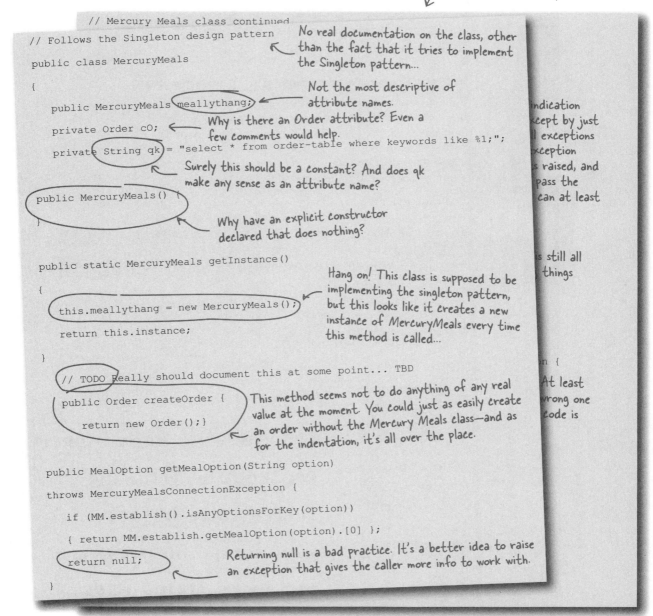

```
// Mercury Meals class continued
// Follows the Singleton design pattern

public class MercuryMeals

{
    public MercuryMeals meallythang;

    private Order cO;

    private String qk = "select * from order-table where keywords like %1;";

    public MercuryMeals() {

    }

    public static MercuryMeals getInstance()

    {
        this.meallythang = new MercuryMeals();

        return this.instance;

    }

    // TODO Really should document this at some point... TBD

    public Order createOrder {

        return new Order();}


    public MealOption getMealOption(String option)

    throws MercuryMealsConnectionException {

        if (MM.establish().isAnyOptionsForKey(option))

        { return MM.establish.getMealOption(option).[0] };

        return null;

    }
```

No real documentation on the class, other
than the fact that it tries to implement
the Singleton pattern...

Not the most descriptive of
attribute names.

Why is there an Order attribute? Even a
few comments would help.

Surely this should be a constant? And does qk
make any sense as an attribute name?

Why have an explicit constructor
declared that does nothing?

Hang on! This class is supposed to be
implementing the singleton pattern,
but this looks like it creates a new
instance of MercuryMeals every time
this method is called...

This method seems not to do anything of any real
value at the moment. You could just as easily create
an order without the Mercury Meals class—and as
for the indentation, it's all over the place.

Returning null is a bad practice. It's a better idea to raise
an exception that gives the caller more info to work with.

...but we need to fix functionality

But things might not be quite as bad as they look. You don't have to fix **all** the bugs in Mercury Meals; **you just have to fix the bugs that affect the functionality that you need**. Don't worry about the rest of the code—focus just on the functionality in your user stories.

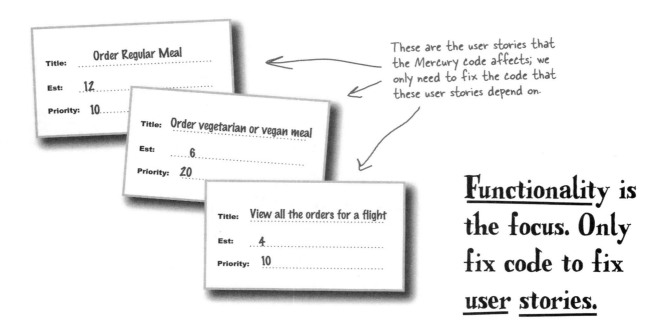

These are the user stories that the Mercury code affects; we only need to fix the code that these user stories depend on.

Functionality is the focus. Only fix code to fix <u>user</u> stories.

BULLET POINTS

- Everything revolves around **customer-oriented functionality**.

- You write and fix code to **satisfy user stories**.

- You **only fix what is broken**, and you know what is broken because you have **tests that fail**.

- **Tests are your safety net**. You use tests to make sure you didn't break anything and to know when you've fixed something.

- If there's **no test** for a piece of functionality, then it's the same as saying that functionality is broken.

- While beautiful code is great, **functional code trumps beautiful code every single time**. This doesn't mean to let things stay sloppy, but always keep in mind why you're working on this code in the first place: **for the customer**.

Figure out what <u>functionality</u> works

You know that Orion's Orbits was working fine until you integrated the Mercury Meals library, so let's focus on that code. The first step is to find out what's actually working, and that means tests. Remember, if it's not testable, assume it's broken.

Here's the main interface to the Mercury Meals code.

MercuryMeals uses the singleton pattern; you call the static getInstance() method to get an instance, instead of instantiating the class with the "new" keyword.

Design note: Naming a class with your company's name is a lousy idea—Mercur really was an awful development shop!

MercuryMeals

+ getInstance(): MercuryMeals

+ createOrder(): Order

+ submitOrder(order: Order): boolean

+ getMealOption(name: String): MealOption

+ getOrdersThatMatchKeywords(keywords: String[]): Order[]

You've got two basic interfaces to work with, along with any helper code that might be hiding in these classes.

Order

+ addMealOption(mealOption: MealOption): void

+ addKeyword(keyword: String): void

Remember, we want to use the flight number as the keyword for a meal.

Exercise

Your job is to create a unit test that exercises all of the functionality your user stories need. The "Order Regular Meal" test creates an order, adds a regular meal option to it (in this case, "Fish and chips"), and then submits the order to Mercury Meals. Using the class diagrams on the lefthand page, write the code for this test of the "Order Regular Meal" user story in the spaces provided below.

```
package test.com.orionsorbits.mercurymeals;
import com.orionsorbits.mercurymeals.*;
import org.junit.*;

public class TestMercuryMeals {
    String[] options;
    String flightNo;

    @Before
    public void setUp() {
        options = {"Fish and chips");
        flightNo = "VS01";
    }

    @After
    public void tearDown() {
        options = null;
        flightNo = null;
    }

    @Test
    public void testOrderRegularMeal()
        throws MealOptionNotFoundException, OrderNotAcceptedException {

        MercuryMeals mercuryMeals = MercuryMeals.getInstance();
```

> Title: ....Order Regular Meal.
> Est: .12 days.................
> Priority: ....10.....................

The user story this test focuses on.

This should be a valid meal option.

The code for setUp() and tearDown() are already in place.

Throw a MealOptionNotFoundException if the meal isn't found, and an OrderNotAcceptedException if the order can't be submitted.

You may need more—or fewer—lines to implement your solution... this is what it took to get our test written.

```
        .................................................................................
        .................................................................................
        .................................................................................
        .................................................................................
        .................................................................................
        .................................................................................
        .................................................................................
        .................................................................................
        .................................................................................
        .................................................................................
        .................................................................................

    }
}
```

Exercise Solution

Your job was to create a unit test that exercises all of the functionality your user stories need. The "Order Regular Meal" test creates an order, adds a regular meal option to it (in this case, "Fish and chips"), and then submits the order to Mercury Meals.

```java
package test.com.orionsorbits.mercurymeals;
import com.orionsorbits.mercurymeals.*;
import org.junit.*;

public class TestMercuryMeals {
   String[] options;
   String flightNo;

   @Before
   public void setUp() {
     options = {"Fish and chips"};
     flightNo = "VS01";
   }

   @After
   public void tearDown() {
     options = null;
     flightNo = null;
   }

   @Test
   public void testOrderRegularMeal()
      throws MealOptionNotFoundException, OrderNotAcceptedException {

      MercuryMeals mercuryMeals = MercuryMeals.getInstance();
      Order order = mercuryMeals.createOrder();
      MealOption mealOption = mercuryMeals.getMealOption(options[0]);
      if (mealOption != null) {
        order.addMealOption(mealOption);
      } else {
        throw new MealOptionNotFoundException(mealOption);
      }

      order.addKeyword(flightNo);
      if (!mercuryMeals.submitOrder(order)) {
        throw new OrderNotAcceptedException(order);
      }
   }
}
```

Title: ....**Order Regular Meal**.
Est: ..**12 days**................
Priority: ....**10**....................

Here's the user story you're testing Mercury Meals functionality for.

Even though you don't know exactly how this code works, it should be clear what it should do.

Create an order and get the single meal option that was set up prior to the test being run.

Add the "Fish and chips" meal option to the order, tie the order to the flight number, and then submit the order to Mercury Meals.

These exceptions are just ways to cause the test to fail, and say something in the Mercury Meals API didn't work.

NOW you know what's ^not working

Here's the build and test report email from your automated testing tool.

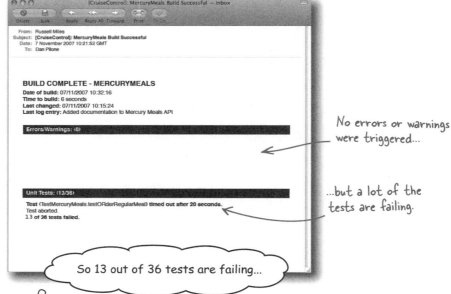

No errors or warnings were triggered...

...but a lot of the tests are failing.

So 13 out of 36 tests are failing...

Laura: Right, about 30% of the code we need to use is failing our tests.

Mark: But that doesn't tell us anything about how much work it will take to fix thing. And it's 30% of the code that's written...how much of that do we need?

Bob: And there could be whole chunks of code completely missing, too. I don't know how much new code we're going to have to write.

Mark: How do we estimate this?

Bob: There has to be a better way to come up with an estimate besides just guessing, right?

What would you do?

<u>Spike</u> <u>test</u> to estimate

30% of the tests you wrote are failing, but you really have no idea if a single line of code would fix most of that, or if even passing one more test could take new classes and hundreds of lines of code. There's no way to know how big a problem those 13 test failures really represent. So what if we take a little time to work on the code, see what we can get done, and then extrapolate out from that?

This is called **spike testing**: you're doing one burst of activity, seeing what you get done, and using that to estimate how much time it will take to get everything else done.

 Take a week to conduct your spike test

Get the customer to give you five working days to work on your problem. That's not a ton of time, and at the end, you should be able to supply a reasonable estimate.

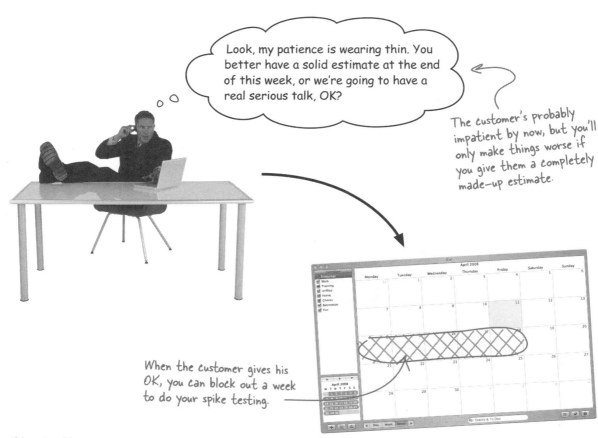

Look, my patience is wearing thin. You better have a solid estimate at the end of this week, or we're going to have a real serious talk, OK?

The customer's probably impatient by now, but you'll only make things worse if you give them a completely made-up estimate.

When the customer gives his OK, you can block out a week to do your spike testing.

② Pick a random sampling from the tests that are failing

Take a random sample of the tests that are failing, and try to fix just those tests. But be sure it's random—don't pick just the easy tests to fix, or the really hard ones. You want to get a real idea of the work to get things going again.

OK, we'll work on a bug each. Let's just draw bugs out of a hat, and see if we can knock one out as quickly as possible. Then, on to the next bug...

Write code the right way... don't rush. You're getting an estimate, not running a race, so make sure you're following your process, even in spike testing.

Use your bug tracker. Note what you're working on, what happened, and how you made the fix. Remember, spike testing should fit into your normal development process.

③ At the end of the week, calculate your bug fix rate

Look at how fast you and your team are knocking off bugs, and come up with a more confident estimate for how long you think it will take to fix all the bugs, based on your current fix rate.

$$\text{Bugs fixed} / 5 = \text{Your daily bug fix rate}$$

Total bugs your entire team fixed

Number of days in the spike test

Bugs likely to be fixed per day, assuming this rate stays steady

What do the spike test results tell you?

Your tests gave you an idea as to how much of your code was failing. With the results of your spike test, you should have an idea about how long it will take to fix the remaining bugs.

The number of bugs fixed during the week-long spike test

$$4 \; / \; 5 \; = \; 0.8 \text{ bugs per day}$$

The number of work days in the spike test

Your team's bug fix rate for the spike test

You can then figure out how long it will take for your team to fix all the bugs

The bugs left, after you fixed some on the spike test.

$$0.8 \; \times \; (13 - 4) \; = \; 7 \text{ days}$$

Your bug fix rate.

How long it would take your whole team to fix all the remaining bugs

So we fixed some bugs AND we now know how long it will take for the entire team to fix all the problems. But I'm still not feeling very confident...

Hmm, are you sure a team will always squash bugs like they did in the spike test? How can you have any confidence that you'll fix all the bugs in seven

When it comes to bug fixing, *we really can't be sure*

When it comes down to it, a spike test really only gives you a more accurate estimate than a pure guess. It's not 100% accurate, and may not even be close.

But the spike test does give you **quantitative data** upon which you can base your estimates. You know how many bugs you fixed, and it was a random sample, so you can say with a certain degree of confidence that you should be able to fix the same number of further bugs in roughly the same amount of time.

However, a spike test does not give you any **qualitative data**. This means that we really only know how fast you can fix the bugs that we just worked on. We *don't* really know how bad things might be in stuff waiting to be fixed. There's still the potential for a bug to be in Mercury Meals that will blow your estimate out of the water, and unfortunately, that's a fact of life when it comes to bug fixing, especially on third-party software.

Your team's gut feeling matters

One quick way that you can add some qualitative feedback into your bug fix estimate is by factoring in the confidence of your team. During the spike test week, you've all have seen the Mercury Meals code, probably in some depth, so now's the time to run your fix rate past your team to factor in their confidence in that number.

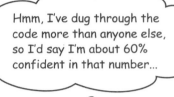

> Hmm, I've dug through the code more than anyone else, so I'd say I'm about 60% confident in that number...

> I'd split the different, about 70% confident in the seven-day estimate.

> Looks pretty reasonable to me. I'd say I'm 80% confident that it will take seven days to fix the rest of the bugs.

Feed confidence into your estimate

$$\frac{(80\% + 60\% + 70\%)}{3}$$

Take the average of your team's confidence, in this case 70%, and factor that into your estimate to give you some wiggle room:

$$\left(0.8 \times (13 - 4) \right) \times \frac{1}{70\%}$$

The estimate for your customer

$$= 10 \text{ days}$$

to fix the remaining bugs

there are no
Dumb Questions

Q: How many people should be involved in a spike test?

A: Ideally you'd get everyone that you think will be involved in the actual bug fixing involved in the spike test. This means that you not only get a more accurate estimate, because the actual people who will finish off the bug fixing will be involved in the future estimated fixing task, but those individuals also have a week to get familiar with the code.

This especially helps when you ask those members of your team to assess their confidence in the estimate that comes out of your spike test. They'll have seen the code base and have a feel for how big all the problems might have been, so their gut feeling is worth that much more.

Q: How do I pick the right tests to be part of the spike testing when I have *thousands* of tests failing?!

A: Try to pick a random sampling, but with an eye towards getting a selection of bugs that vary in difficulty. So what you're looking for first is a random sample, but then you want to make sure that you have a cross-section of bugs that, at a glance, at least appear to be challenging and not just the easiest things to fix.

Q: I thought in test-driven development, we fixed each test as we came across it. Are we not using TDD anymore?

A: This is still TDD, for sure. But this is about existing code, not writing tests for new code. You don't want to stop and try to fix each test just yet. We need a big picture view of the code right now.

However, this does cause a problem if you're using CI, and your build fails when a test fails. In that case, after you get a count of failing tests it might make sense to cheat a little and comment out the failing tests. Then add them back in one at a time. This is risky, and might get you on the TDD Most Wanted list in no time flat, but practically speaking you might want to consider it. The most important thing is you get all of those tests passing, and nothing's left commented out.

Q: Why did we add in that confidence factor again?

A: Factoring in confidence gives you that qualitative input into your estimates where your team gets a chance to say how difficult they feel the rest of the bugs may be to fix. You can take this pretty far, by playing planning poker with your bugs, but remember that the longer you spend assessing confidence, the less time you have to actually fix the bugs.

It's always a compromise between getting an absolute estimate for how long it will take to fix the bugs (and this can really only be obtained by actually fixing them all) and getting a good enough feel for how fast you can squash bugs and getting that estimate to your customer.

Q: Why five days for a spike test?

A: Good question. Five days is a good length because it focuses your team on just the spike test for a week (rather than attempting to multitask during that week), and it gives everyone enough time to do some serious bug fixing.

Q: Can I use a shorter length?

A: You can, but this will affect how many bugs your team can work through, and that affects your confidence in your final estimate. In the worst case scenario, no bugs at all are fixed in your spike test, and you're left confused and without a real end in sight.

Five days is enough time for some serious bugs to be fixed and for you to be able to come out of the spike test with some confidence in your estimate for fixing the remainder of the bugs. And in the best case scenario, you come out of the spike test week with no bugs at all!

Q: So should I do this on code we've developed, too?

A: You really shouldn't need to. First of all, you shouldn't have a massive stack of failing tests. If a test is failing, the build should be failing, and you should fix things immediately. And with bugs, they should be prioritized in with your other work, so it's unlikely you'll suddenly get a giant stack of bugs you need to sort through. And finally, you and your team should know your code base pretty well. Your coverage reports provide value, and you know there can't be too much code involved in any given bug.

Q: How can I be absolutely sure that, even when I've factored in my team's confidence, that 10 days is definitely enough to fix all these bugs?

A: You can't. Ten days is still just an estimate, and so it's how long you think it will take, based on your spike test and your team's gut feelings. You've done everything you can to be confident in your estimate, but it is still *just an estimate*. When it comes to bugs, you need to be aware that there is a risk that your estimates will be wrong, and that's a message that you need to convey to your customer too...

Give your customer the bug fix estimate

You've got an estimate you can be reasonably confident in, so head back to the customer. Tell him how long it will take to fix the bugs in the Mercury Meals code, and see if you can get fixing.

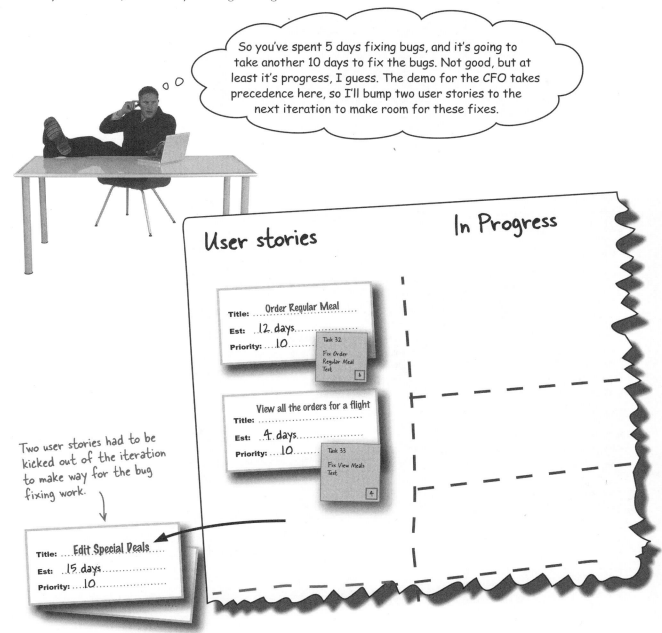

So you've spent 5 days fixing bugs, and it's going to take another 10 days to fix the bugs. Not good, but at least it's progress, I guess. The demo for the CFO takes precedence here, so I'll bump two user stories to the next iteration to make room for these fixes.

Two user stories had to be kicked out of the iteration to make way for the bug fixing work.

Exercise

Back to the magnets we didn't use on page 391. Would you do any of these activities now? Why? Any others you might add that aren't on this list?

Figure out what dependencies this code has and if it has any impact on Orion's Orbits' code.

Would you do this now? Why? ....
....
....
....

Figure out how to package the compiled version to include in Orion's Orbits.

Would you do this now? Why? ....
....
....
....

Document the code.

Would you do this now? Why? ....
....
....
....

Run a coverage report to see how much code you need to fix.

Would you do this now? Why? ....
....
....
....

Get a line count of the code and estimate how long it will take to fix.

Would you do this now? Why? ....
....
....
....

Do a security audit on the code.

Would you do this now? Why? ....
....
....
....

Use a UML tool to reverse-engineer the code and create class diagrams.

Would you do this now? Why? ....
....
....
....

ExercisE SoLUTioN

Back to the magnets we didn't use on page 391. Would you do any of these activities now? Why? Any others you might add that aren't on this list?

Figure out what dependencies this code has and if it has any impact on Orion's Orbits' code.

Would you do this now? Why? Maybe. It's possible that some kind of library conflict is behind one of our bugs. You're going to need to figure this out to get everything working by the end of the iteration anyway.

Figure out how to package the compiled version to include in Orion's Orbits.

Would you do this now? Why? Only if the current packaging approach isn't going to cut it. This is basically refactoring at the packaging level. If things are working and it's maintainable, you should probably skip this.

Document the code.

Would you do this now? Why? Absolutely! Every file you touch should come out of your cleanup with clear documentation. At a minimum, explain the code you've touched while fixing a bug.

Run a coverage report to see how much code you need to fix.

Would you do this now? Why? Probably. You now have a set of tests that scope how much of the system you need. This will give you an idea of how much of the overall code base you actually use, which is a useful metric.

Get a line count of the code and estimate how long it will take to fix.

Would you do this now? Why? Nope. Still not a terribly useful measure. Who cares how big a code base is, except as to how it relates to the functionality you need to get working?

Do a security audit on the code.

Would you do this now? Why? Yes. Any code that gets touched with your tests should be checked for security issues. If you can fix any problems as part of getting your test to pass, go for it. If not, capture it and prioritize it in a later iteration.

Use a UML tool to reverse-engineer the code and create class diagrams.

Would you do this now? Why? Maybe—it depends on how complicated the code is. If you're having trouble figuring out what a block of code is trying to do, this might help you get your head around it.

there are no
Dumb Questions

Q: I noticed that the bug fixing tasks on page 406 both had estimates. Where did those estimates come from?

A: Good catch! Bug fixing tasks are just like any other type of task; they need an estimate, and there are a number of ways that you can come up with that.

You can derive the estimate, dividing the total amount of days you've calculated evenly by the number of bugs to fix, or you can play planning poker with your team. Whichever approach you take, your total planned tasks for bug fixes must never be greater than the number of days calculated from your spike test.

Q: When fixing bugs, how much time should I spend on cleaning up other problems I notice, or just generally cleaning up the code?

A: This is a tough call. It would be great to fix every bug or problem you see, but then you'll likely finish all your tasks late or, worse, end up refactoring your code indefinitely.

The best guideline is to get the code into a working, pretty decent state, within the time allotted for your bug fixing task, and then move on to the next task. First priority is to get the code working; second is to make it as easily readable and understandable as possible so that bugs are not accidentally introduced in the future. If there are problems you found but couldn't get to, file them as new bugs and prioritize them into a later iteration.

Q: What did that five-day spike test period do to our iteration length?

A: Right now, we're getting ready for the next iteration so we're between iterations. If there's a master schedule, the five days needs to be accounted for there, but in terms of iteration time, it's basically off the clock. After you get your board sorted out and everything approved by the customer, though, you should kick off a normal iteration. If you're forced to do a spike test in the middle of an iteration, that's a case where it's probably OK to slip the iteration end date by a week, assuming nearly everyone is participating.

If only a small number of developers are participating in the spike test and everyone else is continuing the iteration, you probably want to drop that five days' worth of other work from the iteration, but still end on time.

Remember, this is five days per person, not five days total.

Q: You said try and get code into a "pretty decent" state. What does that really mean?

A: This is really a judgment call, and in fact this is where you get into the aesthetics of code, which is a whole book on its own. However there are some rules of thumb that can help you decide when your code is good enough and you can move on.

First, **the code must work according to your tests**. Those tests must exercise your code thoroughly, and you should feel very confident that the code works as it should.

Secondly, **your code should be readable**. Do you have cryptic variable names? Do the lines of code read like Sanskrit? Are you using too much complicated syntax just because you can? These are all huge warning signs that your code needs to be improved in readability.

And finally, **you should be proud of your code**. When your code is correct and easily readable by another developer, then you've really done your job. It doesn't have to be perfect, but "pretty decent" starts with your code doing what it should and ends with it being readable.

Q: This sounds like the same approach as the perfect-versus-good-enough design stuff we talked about earlier, right?

A: Yes, it's based on exactly the same principle. Just as you can spend hours improving a design, trying to reach perfection, you can waste exactly the same time in your coding. Don't fall into the trap of perfection. If you achieve it, then that's great, but what you're aiming for is code that does what it should, and that can be read and understood by others. Do that, and you're coding like a pro.

Beautiful code is nice, but <u>tested</u> and <u>readable</u> code is <u>delivered</u> on time.

Things are looking good...

So you've picked off all the bugs from Orion's Orbits, and all functionality is working according to the results of your continuous integration build process...

Your CI tool is happy again; everything builds and passes its tests.

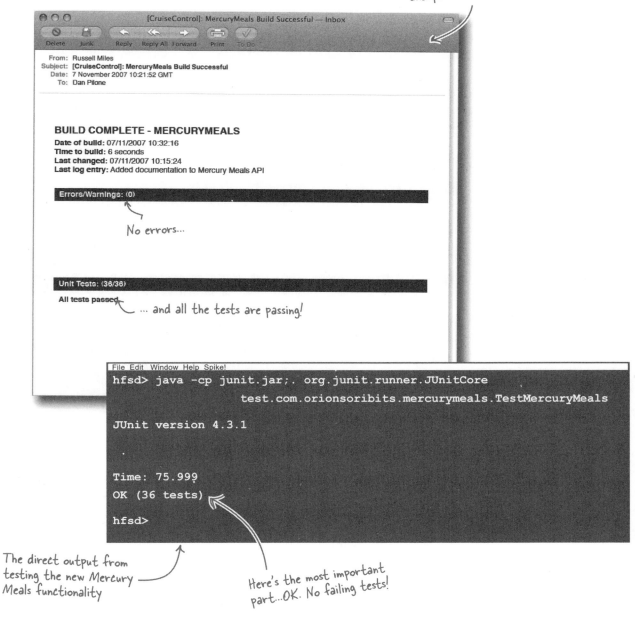

From: **Russell Miles**
Subject: **[CruiseControl]: MercuryMeals Build Successful**
Date: 7 November 2007 10:21:52 GMT
To: Dan Pilone

BUILD COMPLETE - MERCURYMEALS
Date of build: 07/11/2007 10:32:16
Time to build: 6 seconds
Last changed: 07/11/2007 10:15:24
Last log entry: Added documentation to Mercury Meals API

Errors/Warnings: (0)

No errors...

Unit Tests: (36/36)

All tests passed *... and all the tests are passing!*

```
File  Edit  Window  Help  Spike!
hfsd> java -cp junit.jar;. org.junit.runner.JUnitCore
                    test.com.orionsoribits.mercurymeals.TestMercuryMeals

JUnit version 4.3.1

    .

Time: 75.999
OK (36 tests)

hfsd>
```

The direct output from testing the new Mercury Meals functionality

Here's the most important part...OK. No failing tests!

...and you finish the iteration <u>successfully!</u>

You've reached the end of this iteration and, by managing the work and keeping the customer involved, you've successfully overcome the Mercury Meals bug nightmare. Most importantly, you've developed what your customer needed.

Remember, success changes as your iteration goes on. In this case, success turned out to mean dropping two stories, but getting the CFO demo done.

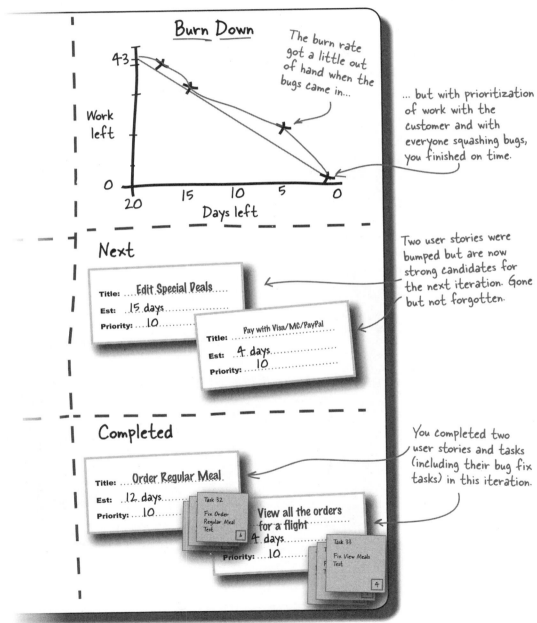

Burn Down

The burn rate got a little out of hand when the bugs came in...

... but with prioritization of work with the customer and with everyone squashing bugs, you finished on time.

Next

Title: ....Edit Special Deals....
Est: ..15 days............
Priority: ....10.........

Title: .....Pay with Visa/MC/PayPal......
Est: ..4 days.........
Priority: 10

Two user stories were bumped but are now strong candidates for the next iteration. Gone but not forgotten.

Completed

Title: ....Order Regular Meal.
Est: ..12 days........
Priority: ....10........

Task 32
Fix Order Regular Meal Test

View all the orders for a flight
4 days..........
Priority: ....10........

Task 33
Fix View Meals Test

You completed two user stories and tasks (including their bug fix tasks) in this iteration.

AND the customer is happy

most importantly

You and your team of developers, by applying your best practices and professional process, have overcome the perils of integrating third-party code, fixed the bugs that arose from that integration, and have delivered the demo on time. The CFO, who just cares that things work, is pretty stoked.

You got the Mercury Meals integration working!? That's fantastic, guys; you really deliver! You'll all be featured in my review to the board—better start ordering those PlayStation 3's now!

The all-new Orion's Orbits, with the Mercury Meals features

The Orion's Orbits CFO...you know, the woman who signs your paychecks (and approves raises)

But wait a sec, isn't there a lot of code in Mercury's Meals that we haven't tested? We've only proven the parts of the Mercury Meals code that are used by our user stories, but doesn't that mean you're shipping software that could contain a stack of buggy code? That can't be right, can it?

You've uncovered an unfortunate truth.

Yes, there may be bugs in the code, particularly in the Mercury Meals code that you inherited. ***But you delivered code that worked.***

Yes, there are potentially large pieces of that library that haven't yet been covered by tests. ***But you have tested all the code that you actually use to complete your user stories.***

The bottom line is that pretty much *all software has some bugs*. However, by applying your process you can avoid those bugs rearing their ugly head in your software's functionality.

Remember, your code doesn't have to be perfect, and often good enough is exactly that: good enough. But as long as any problems in the code don't result in bugs (or software bloat), and you deliver the functionality that your customer needs, then you'll be a success, and get paid, every time.

Security issues are the one exception. You need to be careful that code that isn't tested isn't available for people to use—either accidentally or deliberately. Your coverage report can help identify which code you're actually using.

Real success is about DELIVERING FUNCTIONALITY, period.

Tools for your Software Development Toolbox

Software Development is all about developing and delivering great software. In this chapter, you learned how to debug like a pro. For a complete list of tools in the book, see Appendix ii.

Development Techniques

Before you change a single line of code, make sure it is controlled and buildable

When bugs hit code you don't know, use a spike test to estimate how long it will take to fix them

Factor in your team's confidence when estimating the work remaining to fix bugs

Use tests to tell you when a bug is fixed

Here are some of the key techniques you learned in this chapter...

...and some of the principles behind those techniques.

Development Principles

Be honest with your customer, especially when the news is bad

Working software is your top priority

Readable and understandable code comes a close second

If you haven't tested a piece of code, assume that it doesn't work

Fix functionality

Be proud of your code

All the code in your software, even the bits you didn't write, is your responsibility

BULLET POINTS

- Before you change a single line of code, **take ownership** of it by adding it into your build process and putting it under source code management.

- **Take responsibility** for all the code in your software. If you see a problem, then don't cry "it's someone else's code"; write a test, then **fix it**.

- **Don't assume** a single line of **code works** until there is a **test** that proves it.

- **Working software** comes first; **beautiful code** is second.

- Use the **pride test**. If you'd be happy for someone else to read your code and rely on your software, then it's probably in good shape.

BugSquashingCross

Flex your brain with this crossword puzzle. All of the words below are somewhere in this chapter.

Across

2. At the end of a spike test you have a good idea what your team's .... is

4. When you apply your refactoring experience to avoid problems up front, that is called ....

9. When new bug fix tasks appear on your board, your customer might need to re-.... the work left in the current iteration.

10. When fixing bugs you are fixing ....

11. Fixing bugs becomes .... or sometimes full stories on your board.

12. A spike test should be around a .... in duration.

14. Close second priority is for your code to be .... and understandable by other developers

15. You should always be .... with your customer

16. The first step when dealing with a new chunk of unfamiliar code is to get it under source code ....

17. Before you change anything, get all your code ....

Down

1. Take .... for all the code in your software, not just the bits that you wrote

3. The best spike tests include attempting to fix a .... of the bugs.

5. You should be .... of your software.

6. When you change code to make it work or just to tidy it up, this is called ....

7. You can account for your team's gut feeling about a collection of bugs by factoring in their .... in your big fixing estimate.

8. To help you estimate how long it will take to fix a collection of bugs in software you are unfamiliar with, use a ....

13. Top priority is for your code to ....

 BugSquashingCross Solution

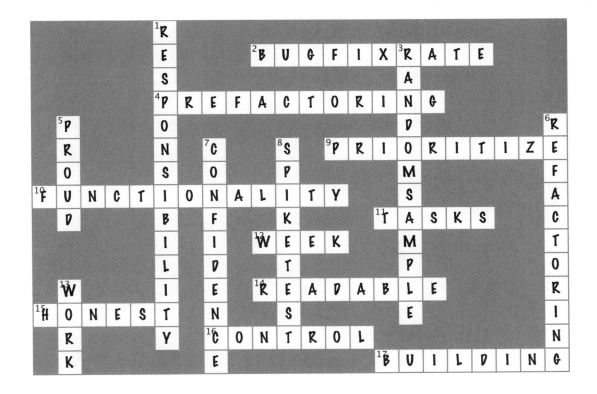

12 the real world

Having a process in life

Now I know that everything **isn't** a nail! It's about using the right tool for the job.

You've learned a lot about software development. But before you go pinning burn-down graphs in everyone's office, there's just a little more you need to know about dealing with each project—on its own terms. There are a lot of **similarities** and **best practices** you should carry from project to project, but there are **unique** things everywhere you go, and you need to be ready for them. It's time to look at how to apply what you've learned to **your particular project**, and where to go next for **more learning**.

Pinning down a software development process

You've read a lot of pages about software development process, but we haven't pinned down exactly what that term really means.

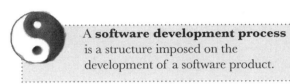

A **software development process** is a structure imposed on the development of a software product.

Wikipedia's definition of a software development process.

Notice that definition doesn't say "a software development process is four-week iterations with requirements written on index cards from a user-focused point of view…" ***A software development process is a framework that should enable you to make quality software.***

There is no silver-bullet process

There's no single process that magically makes software development succeed. A good software process is one that lets ***your*** development team be successful. However, there are some common traits among processes that work:

☐ **Develop iteratively**. Project after project and process after process have shown that big-bang deliveries and waterfall processes are extremely risky and prone to failure. Whatever process you settle on, make sure it involves developing in iterations.

☐ **Always evaluate and assess**. No process is going to be perfect from day one. Even if your process is really, really good, your project will change as you work on it. People will be promoted or quit, new developers will join the team, requirements will change. Be sure to incorporate some way of evaluating how well your process is working, and be willing to change parts of the process where it makes sense.

☐ **Incorporate best practices**. Don't do something just because it's trendy, but don't avoid something because it's trendy either. Most of the things that people takes for granted as good software development started out as a goofy idea at some point. Be critical—but fair—about other processes' approaches to problems, and incorporate those approaches when they might help your project. Some people call this ***process***

A great software process is a process that lets <u>YOUR</u> development team be successful.

A good process delivers good software

Let's say your team loves its process. But suppose your team has yet to deliver a project on time, or deliver software that's working correctly. If that's the case, you may have a **process problem**. The ultimate measure of a process is how good the software is that the process produces. So you and your team might need to change a few things around.

Before you go changing things, you need to be careful—there are lots of wrong ways to change things. Here are a few rules to think about if you're considering changing part (or even all) of your process:

1 **Unless someone is on fire, don't change things mid-iteration.**
Changes are usually disruptive to a project, no matter how well-planned they are. It's up to you to minimize disruptions to other developers. Iterations give you a very natural breaking point. And good iterations are short, so if you need to change your process, *wait until the end of your current iteration*.

2 **Develop metrics to determine if your changes are helping.**
If you're going to change something, you'd better have a good reason. And you should also have a way to measure whether or not your change worked. This means every change is examined at least twice: first, to decide to make the change, and then again—at least an iteration later—to measure if the change was a good idea or not. Try to avoid touchy-feely measures of success, too. Look at things like test coverage, bug counts, velocity, standup meeting durations. If you're getting better numbers and better results, you've made a good change. If not, wait for the next iteration, and be willing to change again.

3 **Value the other members of your team.**
The single biggest determinant of success or failure on a project are the people on your team. No process can overcome bad people, but good people can sometimes overcome a bad process. Respect your fellow team members—and their opinions—when evaluating your process and any changes you might want to make. This doesn't necessarily mean you have to run everything by committee, but it does mean you should try and build consensus whenever possible.

BRAIN POWER

If you could change one thing about your current software process, what would it be? Why? How would you measure whether or not your change was effective?

Exercise

Below are some of the best practices you've learned about in earlier chapters. For each technique, write down what you think it offers to a software process, and then how you could measure whether or not that technique helped *your* project.

What does this technique offer? ....

....

....

How do you know if it worked? ....

....

....

The big board

What does this technique offer? ....

....

....

How do you know if it worked? ....

....

....

User stories

What does this technique offer? ....

....

....

How do you know if it worked? ....

....

....

Version control

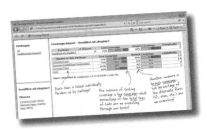

Continuous integration (CI)

What does this technique offer? . . . .

. . . .

. . . .

How do you know if it worked? . . . .

. . . .

. . . .

Test-driven development (TDD)

What does this technique offer? . . . .

. . . .

. . . .

How do you know if it worked? . . . .

. . . .

. . . .

Test coverage

What does this technique offer? . . . .

. . . .

. . . .

How do you know if it worked? . . . .

. . . .

Exercise Solution

Below are some of the best practices you've learned about in earlier chapters. For each technique, you were asked to write down what you think each technique offers, and then how you could measure whether or not that technique helped *your* project.

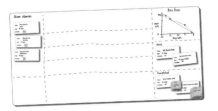

The big board

What does this technique offer? _Everyone on the team knows where they are, what else needs to be done, and what has to happen in this iteration. You can also see if you're on schedule._

How do you know if it worked? _There should be fewer bugs resulting from missed features, better handling of unplanned items, and an idea of exactly what's done during this iteration._

User stories

What does this technique offer? _A way to split up software requirements, track those requirements, and make sure the functionality the customer wants is captured correctly._

How do you know if it worked? _There should be fewer misunderstandings about functionality. Velocity on a project should also go up, since developers know what to build better._

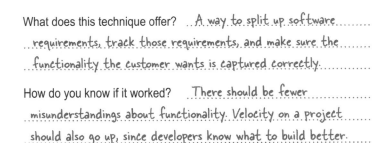

Version control

What does this technique offer? _Changes can be distributed across a team without risking file loss and overwrites. You can also tag and branch and keep up with multiple versions._

How do you know if it worked? _No code overwrites, no code lost from bad merges, and changes to one part of software shouldn't affect other pieces and cause them to break._

Continuous integration (CI)

What does this technique offer?   *The repository always builds because compilation and testing are part of check-in, and the code in the repository always works.*

How do you know if it worked?   *Nobody checks out code and finds out it doesn't work, or doesn't compile. Bug reports should go down, since code must pass tests to be checked in.*

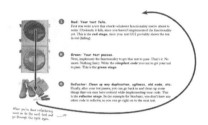

Test-driven development (TDD)

What does this technique offer?   *A way to ensure your code is testable from the very beginning of development. Also introduces test-friendly patterns into your code.*

How do you know if it worked?   *Fewer bugs because testing starts earlier. Better coverage, and every line of code matters. Possibly better design, and less legacy code.*

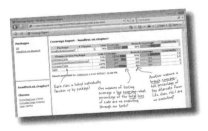

Test coverage

What does this technique offer?   *Better metrics on how much code is being tested and used. A way to find bugs because they usually exist in untested and uncovered code.*

How do you know if it worked?   *Bugs becomes focused on edge cases because the main parts of code are well-tested. Less unused or "cruft" code that's uncovered and not useful.*

Formal attire required...

There are projects where you may need more formality than index cards and sticky notes. Some customers and companies want documents that are a little more formal. It's OK, though; everything you've learned still applies, and you don't need to scrap a process that's working just to dress up your development a bit.

First, remember that unless you absolutely have to, wait until the end of your current iteration to make any changes to your process. Next, know why you're making a change and how you're going to measure its effectiveness. "The customer won't pay me unless we have design documentation" is a perfectly reasonable starting point for dressing up your process. However, it's still important to know how you're going to measure effectiveness. Most customers are (rightfully) concerned about their business and aren't just looking to give you extra work.

If you're going to put together more documentation, project plans, use cases, or anything else, make sure it helps your customer—and hopefully your team—be better at communication. That's a result that is good for your project.

Do what you're doing...just prettier

Most of the work you're doing can be captured and reported in a more formal fashion. With software and a little extra polish, everything from your big board to your user stories can be converted into something that meets your customer's needs.

Your class diagrams might need to be translated into a tool like Rational Rose, or captured in design documents.

You may need to turn your user stories into use cases. Flip to Appendix i for some examples of use cases.

You can usually capture most of what's on your board in software like Microsoft Project if you need more formal project planning.

there are no
Dumb Questions

Q: Isn't less formality better? Can't I convince my customer that index cards are all I need?

A: It's not about more formal versus less formal. It's about what works to get the right software written. The board with stories and tasks works well for lots of teams because it's simple, visual, and effective at communicating what needs to be done. It's not effective at lining up external teams that might be relying on your software or for when marketing should schedule the major release events and start shipping leaflets. Don't add formality for the sake of being formal, but there are times when you will need more than index cards.

Q: If we have to use a project planning tool, should I keep the board too?

A: Yes. There'll be some duplication of effort, but the board works so well with small teams that it's very hard to get anything more effective. The tangible tasks hanging on the board that team members physically move around just keeps the team in sync better than a screenshot or printout does.

Q: My customer wants design documentation and just doesn't get that my design just "evolves"...

A: Be careful with this one. Refactoring and evolutionary design work well with experienced teams who know their product, but it's very easy to get something wrong. On top of that, not giving your customer the design documentation they want is asking them to take a huge leap of faith in what you're doing—and that leap might not be justified yet. Most successful teams do at least some up-front design each iteration. You need to make sure the design documentation they're asking for is providing value, but design material is usually pretty useful for both you and the customer. Just make sure you account for the work in your estimates. Don't let TDD or "evolutionary design" be an excuse for "random code that I typed in late last night."

Q: My customer wants a requirements document, but user stories are working really well for my team. Now what?

A: If your customer has a history with more formal requirements documents, it may be very difficult to make the shift to user stories. In general, you don't want more than one requirement document directing how things should be implemented. It's very difficult to keep a document and user stories in sync, and someone always gets stuck resolving the conflicts.

Instead, try starting with a user story and at the end of the iteration break up the user story into "the user shall" statements that can fit into a formal requirements document. Or, if the customer wants nothing to do with user stories, you can try going the other direction: pull several "The user shall" type statements into a user story and work from the stories. But watch out—those "the user shall" type requirements often don't give you a lot of context about the application as a whole, and what it's doing.

Neither approach is ideal, but one may be a compromise that's workable. You need to be absolutely diligent about changes in both directions, though.

Choose a process that works for <u>YOUR</u> team and <u>YOUR</u> project...

...and then tailor the artifacts it produces to match what <u>YOUR</u> customer wants and needs.

Some additional resources...

Even with all of the new tools available to you, there's always more to learn. Here are some places to go for some more great information on software development, and the techniques and approaches you've been learning about.

Head First PMP

If you've managing your team, there's more to good software—and project management—than just the big board. PMP takes you beyond the basics into a tried-and-true project management process—and help you get certified along the way.

Even if you've never considered yourself a project manager, if you're leading or in charge of a team, this book could help.

Test-driven development Yahoo! group

One of the all-time great resources for information on test-driven development is on the "Test-driven Development" group at Yahoo!. The group is pretty active, with current discussions and debates as well as some great historical information. You can find the group online at `http://tech.groups.yahoo.com/group/testdrivendevelopment/`.

Head First Object-Oriented Analysis and Design

Want to get deeper into code? To learn more about object-oriented principles of design and implementation? If you loved drawing class diagrams and implementing the strategy pattern, check out this book for a lot more on getting down deep with code.

Rational Unified Process web site

One of the founding iterative processes is the Rational Unified Process (RUP). It's a pretty heavy process out-of-the-box, but it's designed to be tailored to your needs. It's also a common approach to large-scale enterprise development. Be sure and read this and some Agile- or XP-leaning sites, so you get a balanced picture. Check it out online at `http://www-306.ibm.com/software/awdtools/rup/`.

The Agile Alliance

The Agile Alliance is a great kickoff point for information on Agile processes like extreme programming, Scrum, or Crystal. Agile processes are very lightweight, and you'll see many of the things you learned about, albeit from a different perspective at times. Check it out at `http://www.agilealliance.org/`.

More knowledge == better process

There are tons more resources than just these. Part of good software development is keeping on top of what's going on. And that means reading, Googling, asking your buddies on other projects—anything you can do to find out what other people are doing, and what works for them.

And never be afraid to try something new, even for just an iteration. You never know what might work, or what you might pick up that's just perfect for **your** project.

Tools for your Software Development Toolbox

Software Development is all about developing and delivering great software. In this chapter, you got some additional resources to help you take your knowledge out into the real world. For a complete list of tools in the book, see Appendix ii.

Development Techniques

Critically evaluate any changes to your process with real metrics.

Formalize your deliverables if you need to, but always know how it's providing value.

Try hard to only change your process between iterations.

Here are some of the key techniques you learned in this chapter...

...and some of the principles behind those techniques.

Development Principles

Good developers develop—great developers ship.

Good developers can usually overcome a bad process.

A good process is one that lets your team be successful.

BULLET POINTS

- **Take your team's opinion into account** whenever you're going to make changes to the process; they have to live with your changes, too.

- Any process change should show up **twice**: once to **decide to do it** and once to **evaluate whether or not it worked**.

- Steer clear of **more than one place to store requirements**. It's always a maintenance nightmare.

- Be **skeptical** of magic, **out-of-the-box processes**. Each project has something **unique** to it, and your process should be flexible.

SoftwareDevelopmentcross

This is it, the last crossword. This time the solutions are from anywhere in the book.

Across

3. Project planning tools can help with projections and presentation of schedule, but do them in parallel with your.........

4. No more than 15 minutes, these keep the team functioning as a team toward a common goal.

7. Every iteration involves ....

8. This is an approach where you write your tests first and refactor like mad.

10. This is a process that checks out your code, builds it, and probably runs tests.

11. High stakes game of estimation.

13. Good Developers develop, Great developers ....

14. The team member you should estimate for.

15. No matter what process you pick, develop ....

17. Every iteration involves ....

Down

1. This means to evaluate processes critically and demand results from each of the practices they promote.

2. Shows how you're progressing through an iteration.

5. What you should be estimating in.

6. Every iteration involves ....

9. How you rack and stack your user stories.

12. The greatest indicator of success or failure on a project.

16. This is a process that tracks changes to your code and distributes them among developers.

SoftwareDevelopmentcross

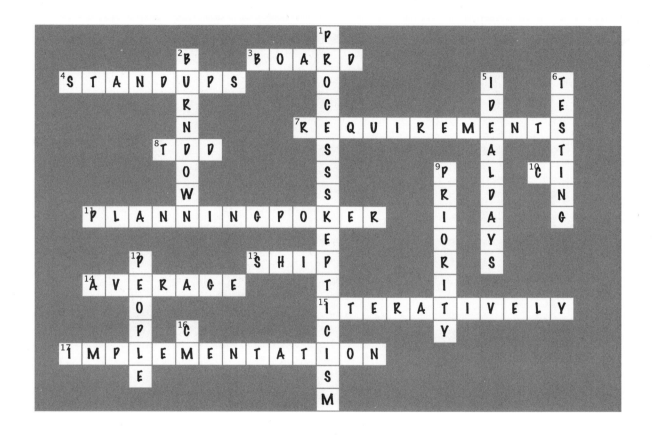

It's time to leave a mark on the ~~board~~ world!

There are exciting times ahead! Armed with all of your software development knowledge, it's time to put what you know to work...so get out there and change the world. Don't forget that the realm of software never stops changing, either. Keep reading, learning, and please, if you can schedule it in your iteration, swing by Head First Labs (*www.headfirstlabs.com*) and drop us a note on how these tools have helped you out.

And be sure and move your "Visit Head First Labs" task to Completed when you're through.

i leftovers

The top 5 topics
(we didn't cover)

Ever feel like something's missing? We know what you mean...

Just when you thought you were done... there's more. We couldn't leave you without a few extra things, things we just couldn't fit into the rest of the book. At least, not if you want to be able to carry this book around without a metallic case and castor wheels on the bottom. So take a peek and see what you (still) might be missing out on.

#1. UML class diagrams

When you were developing the iSwoon application in Chapters 4 and 5, we described the design using UML, the ***Unified Modeling Language***, which is a language used to communicate just the **important details** about your **code** and **application's structure** that other developers and customers need, without getting into things that *aren't* necessary.

UML is a great way of working through your design for iSwoon without getting too bogged down in code. After all, it's pretty hard to look at 200 lines of code and focus on the big picture.

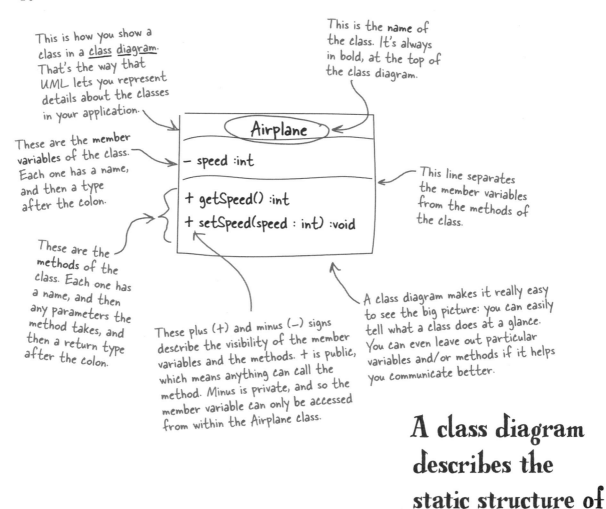

This is how you show a class in a <u>class diagram</u>. That's the way that UML lets you represent details about the classes in your application.

This is the name of the class. It's always in bold, at the top of the class diagram.

These are the member variables of the class. Each one has a name, and then a type after the colon.

This line separates the member variables from the methods of the class.

These are the methods of the class. Each one has a name, and then any parameters the method takes, and then a return type after the colon.

These plus (+) and minus (−) signs describe the visibility of the member variables and the methods. + is public, which means anything can call the method. Minus is private, and so the member variable can only be accessed from within the Airplane class.

A class diagram makes it really easy to see the big picture: you can easily tell what a class does at a glance. You can even leave out particular variables and/or methods if it helps you communicate better.

A class diagram describes the <u>static structure</u> of your classes.

Class diagrams show relationships

Classes in your software don't exist in a vacuum, they interact with each other at runtime and have relationships to each other. In this book you've seen two relationships, called association and inheritance.

Association

Association is where one class is made up of objects of another class. For example, you might say "A Date is associated with a collection of Events."

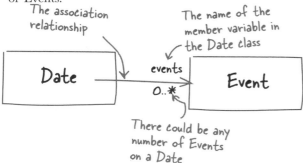

The association relationship

The name of the member variable in the Date class

There could be any number of Events on a Date

Inheritance

Inheritance is useful when a class inherits from another class. For example, you might "A Sword inherits from Weapon."

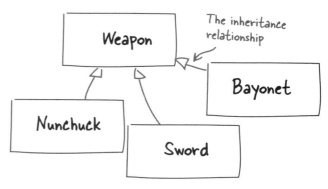

The inheritance relationship

there are no
Dumb Questions

Q: Don't I need a big expensive set of tools to create UML diagrams?

A: No, not al all. The UML language was originally designed such that you could jot down a reasonably complex design with just a pencil and some paper. So if you've got access to a heavyweight UML modeling tool then that's great, but you don't actually need it to use UML.

Q: So the class diagram isn't a very complete representation of a class, is it?

A: No, but it's not meant to be. Class diagrams are just a way to communicate the basic details of a class's variables and methods. It also makes it easy to talk about code without forcing you to wade through hundreds of lines of Java, or C, or Perl.

Q: I've got my own way of drawing classes; what's wrong with that?

A: There's nothing wrong with your own notation, but it can make things harder for other people to understand. By using a standard like UML, we can all speak the same language and be sure we're talking about the same thing in our diagrams

Q: So who came up with this UML deal, anyway?

A: The UML specification was developed by Rational Software, under the leadership of Grady Booch, Ivar Jacobson, and Jim Rumbaugh (three really smart guys). These days it's managed by the OMG, the Object Management Group.

Q: Sounds like a lot of fuss over that simple little class diagram thing.

A: UML is actually a lot more than that class diagram. UML has diagrams for the state of your objects, the sequence of events in your application, and it even has a way to represent customer requirements and interactions with your system. And there's a lot more to learn about class diagrams, too.

#2. Sequence diagrams

A static class diagram only goes so far. It shows you the classes that make up your software, but it doesn't show how those classes work together. For that, you need a UML **sequence diagram**. A sequence diagram is just what it sounds like: a visual way to show the order of events that happen, such as invoking methods on classes, between the different parts of your software.

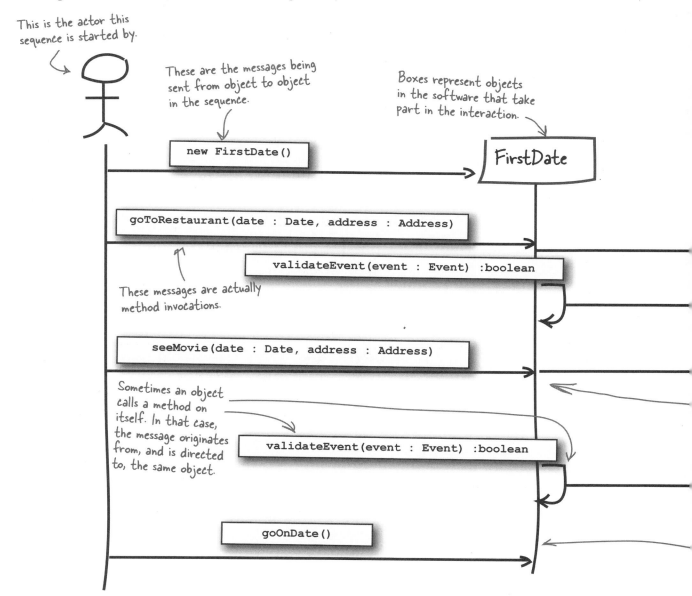

This is the actor this sequence is started by.

These are the messages being sent from object to object in the sequence.

Boxes represent objects in the software that take part in the interaction.

new FirstDate()

FirstDate

goToRestaurant(date : Date, address : Address)

validateEvent(event : Event) :boolean

These messages are actually method invocations.

seeMovie(date : Date, address : Address)

Sometimes an object calls a method on itself. In that case, the message originates from, and is directed to, the same object.

validateEvent(event : Event) :boolean

goOnDate()

Sequence diagrams show how your objects <u>interact</u> <u>at</u> <u>runtime</u> to bring your software's functionality to life.

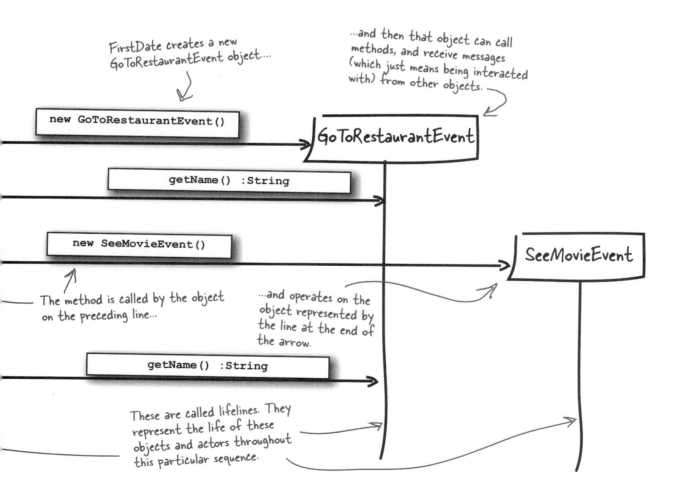

FirstDate creates a new GoToRestaurantEvent object....

...and then that object can call methods, and receive messages (which just means being interacted with) from other objects.

new GoToRestaurantEvent()

GoToRestaurantEvent

getName() :String

new SeeMovieEvent()

SeeMovieEvent

The method is called by the object on the preceding line...

...and operates on the object represented by the line at the end of the arrow.

getName() :String

These are called lifelines. They represent the life of these objects and actors throughout this particular sequence.

#3. User stories and use cases

You used user stories throughout this book to capture your requirements. User stories are really great at getting a neat description of exactly what the customer needs your software to do. But a lot of more formal processes recommend something called a **use case**.

Luckily, there's easily enough overlap between user stories and use cases for you to use either technique to capture your customer's requirements:

A user story that describes sending a picture using the Beatbox software from chapter 6.

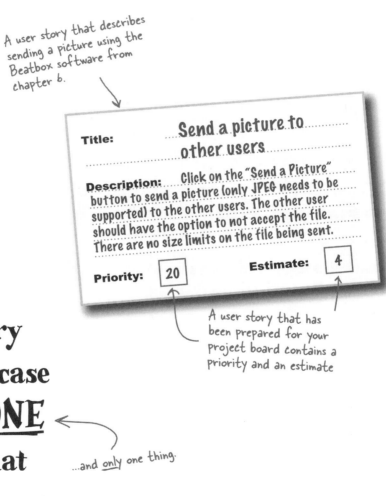

Title: Send a picture to other users

Description: Click on the "Send a Picture" button to send a picture (only JPEG needs to be supported) to the other users. The other user should have the option to not accept the file. There are no size limits on the file being sent.

Priority: 20   **Estimate:** 4

A user story that has been prepared for your project board contains a priority and an estimate

A user story and a use case describe <u>ONE</u> THING that your software needs to do.

...and <u>only</u> one thing.

An equivalent Use Case that describes the same "Send a picture to other users" requirement

You can add more detail to your user story, or modify your use case to have a little less detail... it's really up to you and your customer.

Send a picture to other users

1. Click on the "Send a Picture button"
2. Display users the picture can be sent to in the address book list box.
   2a. Enter the destination user's name in the search box
   2b. Click on search to find the user
3. Select the user to send the picture to
4. Click on send
5. The receiver is asked if they want to accept the photo
   5a.1. The receiver accepts the photo
   5a.2. The receiver views the photo
   5b.1. The recevier rejects the photo
   5b.2. The photo is trashed.

Observation is a key component in getting good use cases written.

A use case's sequence normally contains more steps and detail than a user story. This makes it easier to work to for developers, but means extra work with the customer to nail these details down.

There are a number of different ways that you can write down a use case. This one describes the interactions that a user has with the software, step by step.

So what's the big difference?

Well, actually not a lot, really. User stories are usually around three lines long, and are accompanied by an estimate and a priority, so the information is all in one bite-sized place. Use cases are usually reasonably more detailed descriptions of a user's interaction with the software. Use cases also aren't usually written along with a priority or an estimate—those details are often captured elsewhere, in more detailed design documentation.

User stories are ideally written by the customer, whereas traditionally use cases are not. Ultimately either approach does the same job, capturing what your customer needs your software to do. And one use case, with alternate paths (different ways to use the software in a specific situation) may capture more than one user story.

#4. System tests vs. unit tests

In chapters 7 and 8, you learned how to build testing and continuous integration into your development process. Testing is one of the key tools you have to prove that **your code works** and **meets the requirements** set by your customer. These two different goals are supported by two different types of tests.

Unit tests test your CODE

Unit tests are used to test that your code *does what it should*. These are the tests that you build right into your continuous build and integration cycle, to make sure that any changes that you make to code don't break these tests, on your code and the rest of the code base.

Ideally, every class in your software should have an associated unit test. In fact, with test-driven development, your tests are developed before any code is even written, so there is no code without a test. Unit tests have their limits, though. For example, maybe you make sure that calling `drive()` on the `Automobile` class works... but what happens when other instances of `Automobile` are also driving, and using the same `RaceTrack` object, too?

Unit testing is at a very low level... source files and XML descriptors.

System tests test your SOFTWARE

System tests pick up where unit tests leave off. A system test tests your code when it is integrated into a **fully functional system**. System tests are sometimes automated, but often involve someone actually exercising your entire system in very much the same way as the end user will.

For example, you might fire up the GUI for monitoring a race, press the "Start Race" button, watch animated versions of cars spin around the track, and then initiate a wreck. Does everything work the way the customer expects? That's a system test.

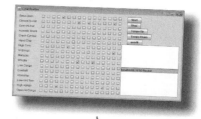

System testing looks at your application as a whole.

there are no Dumb Questions

Q: In addition to unit and system tests, aren't there lots of other types of tests as well?

A: Yes. Testing is a BIG field of work. There are various names for testing, conducted at anything from the source code level to enterprise software integration level. For example, you may hear of **acceptance tests**. Acceptance tests are often conducted with the customer, where the customer either accepts or rejects your software as doing what they need..

Unit tests prove that your code WORKS. System tests prove that your software meets its REQUIREMENTS.

#5. Refactoring

Refactoring is the process of modifying the structure of your code, *without* modifying its behavior. Refactoring is done to increase the cleanness, flexibility, and extensibility of your code, and usually is related to a **specific improvement in your design**.

Most refactorings are fairly simple, and focus on one specific design aspect of your code. For example:

```
public double getDisabilityAmount() {
  // Check for eligibility
  if (seniority < 2)
    return 0;
  if (monthsDisabled > 12)
    return 0;
  if (isPartTime)
    return 0;
  // Calculate disability amount and return it
}
```

While there's nothing particularly wrong with this code, it's not as maintainable as it could be. The `getDisabilityAmount()` method is really doing two things: checking the eligibility for disability, and then calculating the amount.

By now, you should know that violates the Single Responsibility Principle. We really should separate the code that handles eligibility requirements from the code that does disability calculations. So we can *refactor* this code to look more like this:

```
public double getDisabilityAmount() {
  // Check for eligibility
  if (isEligibleForDisability()) {
    // Calculate disability amount and return it
  } else {
    return 0;
  }
}
```

We've taken two responsibilities, and placed them in two separate methods, adhering to the SRP.

Now, if the eligibility requirements for disability change, only the `isEligibleForDisability()` methods needs to change—and the method responsible for calculating the disability amount doesn't.

Think of refactoring as a checkup for your code. It should be an ongoing process, as code that is left alone tends to become harder and harder to reuse. Go back to old code, and refactor it to take advantage of new design techniques you've learned. The programmers who have to maintain and reuse your code will thank you for it.

> **Refactoring changes the internal structure of your code <u>WITHOUT</u> affecting your code's behavior.**

Tools for the experienced software developer

Development Techniques

Iteration helps you stay

Plan out and balance y
when (not if) change o

Every iteration result:
software to get feed
customer every step o

Development Principles

Be honest with your customer, especially when the news is bad.

Working software is your top priority.

Readable and understandable code comes a close second.

If you haven't tested a piece of code, assume that it doesn't work.

Fix functionality.

Be proud of your code.

All the code in your software, even the bits you didn't write, is your responsibility.

Ever wished all those great tools and techniques were in one place? This is a roundup of all the software development **techniques** and **principles** we've covered. Take a look over them all, and see if you can **remember what each one means**. You might even want to **cut these pages out** and tape them to the bottom of your **big board**, for everyone to see in your daily standup meetings.

Development Techniques

CHAPTER 1

Iteration helps you stay on course

Plan out and balance your iterations when (not if) change occurs

Every iteration results in working software and gathers feedback from your customer every step of the way

CHAPTER 4

You didn't think the exercises were over, did you? Write your own techniques for Chapters 4 and 5.

CHAPTER 2

Bluesky, Observation, and Roleplay to figure out how your system should behave

Use user stories to keep the focus on functionality

Play planning poker for estimation

CHAPTER 5

CHAPTER 3

Iterations should ideally be no longer than a month. That means you have 20 working calendar days per iteration

Applying velocity to your plan lets you feel more confident in your ability to keep your development promises to your customer

Use (literally) a big board on your wall to plan and monitor your current iteration's work

Get your customer's buy-in when choosing what user stories can be completed for Milestone 1.0, and when choosing what iteration a user story will be built in

CHAPTER 6

Use a version control tool to track and distribute changes in your software to your team

Use tags to keep track of major milestones in your project (ends of iterations, releases, bug fixes, etc.)

Use branches to maintain a separate copy of your code, but only branch if absolutely necessary

CHAPTER 6.5

Use a build tool to script building, packaging, testing, and deploying your system

Most IDEs are already using a build tool underneath. Get familiar with that tool, and you can build on what the IDE already does

Treat your build script like code and check it into version control

CHAPTER 10

↑

What did you learn in Chapter 10? Write it down here.

CHAPTER 7

There are different views of your system, and you need to test them all

Testing has to account for success cases as well as failure cases

Automate testing whenever possible

Use a continuous integration tool to automate building and testing your code on each commit

CHAPTER 11

Before you change a single line of code, make sure it is controlled and buildable

When bugs hit code you don't know, use a spike test to estimate how long it will take to fix them

Factor in your team's confidence when estimating the work remaining to fix bugs

Use tests to tell you when a bug is fixed

CHAPTER 8

Write tests first, then code to make those tests pass

Your tests should fail initially; then after they pass you can refactor

Use mock objects to provide variations on objects that you need for testing

CHAPTER 12

Critically evaluate any changes to your process with real metrics

Formalize your deliverables if you need to, but always know how it's providing value

Try hard to only change your process between iterations

CHAPTER 9

Pay attention to your burn-down rate—especially after the iteration ends

Iteration pacing is important—drop stories if you need to keep it going

Don't punish people for getting done early—if their stuff works, let them use the extra time to get ahead or learn something new

Development Principles

CHAPTER 1

Deliver software that's needed

Deliver software on time

Deliver software on budget

CHAPTER 2

The customer knows what they want, but sometimes you need to help them nail it down

Keep requirements customer-oriented

Develop and refine your requirements iteratively with the customer

CHAPTER 3

Keep iterations short and manageable

Ultimately, the customer decides what is in and what is out for Milestone 1.0

Promise, and deliver

ALWAYS be honest with the customer

CHAPTER 4

↖ We didn't add any techniques and principles to Chapter 4... can you come up with a few and write them here?

CHAPTER 5

↙ Be the author... write your own principles based on what you learned in Chapter 5.

CHAPTER 6

Always know where changes should (and shouldn't) go

Know what code went into a given release—and be able to get to it again

Control code change and distribution

CHAPTER 6.5

Building a project should be repeatable and automated

Build scripts set the stage for other automation tools

Build scripts go beyond just step-by-step automation and can capture compilation and deployment logic decisions

CHAPTER 7

Testing is a tool to let you know where your project is at all times

Continuous integration gives you confidence that the code in your repository is correct and builds properly

Code coverage is a much better metric of testing effectiveness than test count

CHAPTER 8

TDD forces you to focus on functionality

Automated tests make refactoring safer; you'll know immediately if you've broken something

Good code coverage is much more achievable in a TDD approach

CHAPTER 9

Iterations are a way to impose intermediate deadlines—stick to them

Always estimate for the ideal day for the average team member

Keep the big picture in mind when planning iterations—and that might include external testing of the system

Improve your process iteratively through iteration reviews

CHAPTER 10

Chapter 10 was all about third-party code. What principles did you pick up?

CHAPTER 11

Be honest with your customer, especially when the news is bad

Working software is your top priority

Readable and understandable code comes a close second

If you haven't tested a piece of code, assume that it doesn't work

Fix functionality

Be proud of your code

All the code in your software, even the bits you didn't write, is your responsibility

CHAPTER 12

Good developers develop—great developers ship

Good developers can usually overcome a bad process

A good process is one that lets YOUR team be successful

Index

H

Head First Java BeatBox project 178–183
  demo failure 185
  GUI 182
  networking code 184
  testing 183
honesty 75, 96, 98, 103, 106

I

inheritance 435

input and output 239

interdependencies 295

interfaces, multiple implementations of a single interface 296

iteration 10–15, 19, 84
  adding more people to project 19
  adding time to end of 323
  bad 345
  balanced 85
  changing features 22–23
  communication and 329–330
  estimates 60–61
  Fireside Chats 82–83
  fixed iteration length 328
  handling each as mini-project 14–15
  length of iteration and spike testing 409
  monitoring 100–102, 104, 106
  necessity of 12
  not enough time for story 345
  pacing 346
  prototyping solutions 344
  pulling stories for next 344
  reviewing 342–343
    elements of review 342
    review questions 343
  reworking plans 23
  short 85
  short projects 12
  software development process 418

system testing 327–329
  fixing bugs while continuing working 329
time at end 345
versus process 24
when everything is complete 170–171
when new requirements come in during last 25
when new requirements won't fit current 25
when to begin 12
when too long 92
(see also iteration, next)
iteration, next 352–382
  bugs 358
  customer approval 360
  planning for 352
  recalculating estimates and velocity 353
  velocity 359

J

Java's equals method 308

Java programming 181

Java projects 227

JUnit 247, 250–251
  adding to Ant build 254
  invoking test runner 251

L

learning time 344

logging 240

loosely coupled code 300, 303

M

Mantis 336

maximum team size 77

Mercury Meals project 360–382
  building project 392
  estimates 362
  figuring out what functionality works 396, 399
  fixing functionality 394–395

Praise for *Head First Object-Oriented Analysis and Design*

"*Head First Object-Oriented Analysis and Design* is a refreshing look at the subject of OOA&D. What sets this book apart is its focus on learning. There are too many books on the market that spend a lot of time telling you why, but do not actually enable the practitioner to start work on a project. Those books are very interesting, but not very practical. I strongly believe that the future of software development practice will focus on the practitioner. The authors have made the content of OOA&D accessible and usable for the practitioner "

> **— Ivar Jacobson, Ivar Jacobson Consulting**

"I just finished reading *HF OOA&D*, and I loved it! The book manages to get across the essentials of object-oriented analysis and design with UML and use cases, and even several lectures on good software design, all in a fast-paced, easy to understand way. The thing I liked most about this book was its focus on why we do OOA&D—to write great software! By defining what great software is and showing how each step in the OOA&D process leads you towards that goal, it can teach even the most jaded Java programmer why OOA&D matters. This is a great 'first book' on design for anyone who is new to Java, or even for those who have been Java programmers for a while but have been scared off by the massive tomes on OO Analysis and Design."

> **— Kyle Brown, Distinguished Engineer, IBM**

"Finally a book on OOA&D that recognizes that the UML is just a notation and that what matters when developing software is taking the time to think the issues through."

> **— Pete McBreen, Author,** *Software Craftsmanship*

"The book does a good job of capturing that entertaining, visually oriented, 'Head First' writing style. But hidden behind the funny pictures and crazy fonts is a serious, intelligent, extremely well-crafted presentation of OO Analysis and Design. This book has a strong opinion of how to design programs, and communicates it effectively. I love the way it uses running examples to lead the reader through the various stages of the design process. As I read the book, I felt like I was looking over the shoulder of an expert designer who was explaining to me what issues were important at each step, and why."

> **— Edward Sciore, Associate Professor, Computer Science Department**
> **Boston College**

"This is a well-designed book that delivers what it promises to its readers: how to analyze, design, and write serious object-oriented software. Its contents flow effortlessly from using use cases for capturing requirements to analysis, design, implementation, testing, and iteration. Every step in the development of object-oriented software is presented in light of sound software engineering principles. The examples are clear and illustrative. This is a solid and refreshing book on object-oriented software development."

> **— Dung Zung Nguyen, Lecturer**
> **Rice University**

Adv `D1330421` **Software Development**

"*Head First Software Development* is a whi
diagrams and clever illustrations mear
brain. It's a whole new kind of book."

> — **Scott Hanselman**
> **Software Developer, Speaker, Author**
> *Scott Hanselman's*

"This is one of those books experie
I'm one of them."

> — **Burk Hufnagel,**

"I could have avoided a whole wo

> — **This developer**
> **wouldn't be ups**

"*Head First Software Development* te
software on time and on budget.
project on track from start to fini
Software Development will give you

> — **Adam Z. Szyma**

"The ideas in this book can be u
overall software development pr

> — **Dan Francis, S**

"A fresh new perspective on the
development team from require

> — **McClellan Fra**

information
directly into YOUR

Figures

Tables

Contributors

Lee C. Adkins, Oklahoma State University
Luc Anselin, University of Illinois
Paul Bekker, University of Groningen
Anil K. Bera, University of Illinois
Herman J. Bierens, Pennsylvania State University
A. Colin Cameron, University of California – Davis
Russell Davidson, Queen's University, Ontario, and GREQAM, Marseilles
Juan Dolado, Universidad Carlos III de Madrid
Jean-Marie Dufour, University of Montreal
Denzil G. Fiebig, University of Sydney
A. Flores-Lagunes, University of Arizona
John Geweke, University of Minnesota and University of Iowa
Eric Ghysels, Pennsylvania State University
Jesús Gonzalo, Universidad Carlos III de Madrid
Christian Gouriéroux, CREST and CEPREMAP, Paris
Clive W.J. Granger, University of California – San Diego
William E. Griffiths, University of Melbourne
Alastair R. Hall, North Carolina State University
R. Carter Hill, Louisiana State University
Daniel Houser, University of Arizona
Cheng Hsiao, University of Southern California
Joann Jasiak, York University
Michael Keane, University of Minnesota and New York University
Lynda Khalaf, University of Laval
Maxwell L. King, Monash University
Gary Koop, University of Glasgow
Lung-fei Lee, Hong Kong University of Science & Technology
Helmut Lütkepohl, Humboldt University
Esfandiar Maasoumi, Southern Methodist University, Dallas
James MacKinnon, Queen's University, Ontario

G.S. Maddala, Ohio State University
Roberto S. Mariano, University of Pennsylvania
Francesc Marmol, Universidad Carlos III de Madrid
Erik Meijer, University of Groningen
Denise R. Osborn, University of Manchester
M. Hashem Pesaran, Cambridge University
Benedikt M. Pötscher, University of Vienna
Gamini Premaratne, University of Illinois
Ingmar R. Prucha, University of Maryland
Paulo M.M. Rodrigues, University of Algarve
Aris Spanos, Virginia Polytechnic Institute and State University
Mark F.J. Steel, University of Kent
James H. Stock, Harvard University
P.A.V.B. Swamy, Department of the Treasury, Washington
George S. Tavlas, Bank of Greece
Pravin K. Trivedi, Indiana University
Aman Ullah, University of California – Riverside
Tom Wansbeek, University of Groningen
Melvyn Weeks, Cambridge University
Jeffrey M. Wooldridge, Michigan State University

Preface

This companion in theoretical econometrics is the first in a series of companions in economics published by Blackwell. The emphasis is on graduate students of econometrics and professional researchers who need a guide, a friend, a companion to lead them through this exciting yet ever growing and expanding field. This is not a handbook of long chapters or exhaustive surveys on the subject. These are simple chapters, written by international experts who were asked to give a basic introduction to their subject. These chapters summarize some of the well known results as well as new developments in the field and direct the reader to supplementary reading. Clearly, one single volume cannot do justice to the wide variety of topics in theoretical econometrics. There are five handbooks of econometrics published by North-Holland and two handbooks of applied econometrics published by Blackwell, to mention a few. The 32 chapters in this companion give only a sample of the important topics in theoretical econometrics. We hope that students, teachers, and professionals find this companion useful. I would like to thank Al Bruckner who approached me with this idea and who entrusted me with the editorial job, the 50 authors who met deadlines and page limitations.

I would also like to thank the numerous reviewers who read these chapters and commented on them. These include Seung Ahn, Paul Bekker, Anil Bera, Herman Bierens, Erik Biorn, Siddahrtha Chib, James Davidson, Francis Diebold, Juan Dolado, Jean-Marie Dufour, Neil Ericsson, Denzil Fiebig, Philip Hans Franses, John Geweke, Eric Ghysels, David Giles, Jesús Gonzalo, Clive Granger, William Greene, William Griffith, Alastair Hall, Bruce Hansen, R. Carter Hill, Cheng Hsiao, Hae-Shin Hwang, Svend Hylleberg, Michael Keane, Lynda Khalaf, Gary Koop, Lung-fei Lee, Qi Li, Oliver Linton, Helmut Lütkepohl, Essie Maasoumi, James MacKinnon, G.S. Maddala, Masao Ogaki, Denise Osborn, Pierre Perron, Peter Phillips, Ingmar Prucha, Peter Schmidt, Mark Steel, James Stock, Pravin Trivedi, Aman Ullah, Marno Verbeek, Tom Wansbeek, Rainer Winkelmann, and Jeffrey Wooldridge.

On a sad note, G.S. Maddala, a contributing author to this volume, died before this book was published. He was a leading figure in econometrics and a prolific researcher whose writings touched students all over the world. He will be sorely missed.

Finally, I would like to acknowledge the support and help of Blackwell Publishers and the secretarial assistance of Teri Bush at various stages of the preparation of this companion.

BADI H. BALTAGI
Texas A&M University
College Station, Texas

Abbreviations

2SLS	two-stage least squares
3SLS	three-stage least squares
a.s.	almost sure
ACD	Autoregressive Conditional Duration
ADF	Augmented Dickey–Fuller
AE	asymptotically equivalent
AIC	Aikake's information criteria
AIMA	asymptotically ideal model
AIMSE	average integrated mean square error
AR	autoregressive
AR(1)	first-order autoregressive
ARCH	autoregressive conditional heteroskedasticity
ARFIMA	autoregressive fractionally integrated moving average
ARIMA	autoregressive integrated moving average
ARMA	autoregressive moving average
BDS	Brock, Dechert, and Scheinkman
BIC	Bayesian information criteria
BKW	Belsley, Kuh, and Welsch
BLUE	best, linear unbiased estimator
BMC	bound Monte Carlo
CAPM	capital asset pricing model
CAPS	consistent adjusted least squares
CDF (or cdf)	cumulative distribution function
CES	constant elasticity of substitution
CFI	comparative fit index
CG matrix	matrix of contributions to the gradient
CI	confidence interval
CLT	central limit theorem
CM	conditional moment
CME	conditional mean encompassing

CMT	conditional moment test
CPI	consumer price index
CPS	current population survey
CUAN	consistent and uniformly asymptotic normal
DEA	data envelopment analysis
DF	Dickey–Fuller
DGLS	dynamic generalized least squares
DGM	data generating mechanism
DGP	data generating process
DHF	Dickey, Hasza, and Fuller
DLR	double-length artificial regression
DOLS	dynamic ordinary least squares
DW	Durbin–Watson
DWH	Durbin–Wu–Hausman
EBA	elimination-by-aspects
ECM	expectation conditional maximization
EM	expectation maximization
EPE	estimated prediction error
ESS	explained sums of squares
ESS_R	restricted sum of squares
ESS_U	unrestricted error sum of squares
EWMA	exponentially weighted moving average
FCLT	functional central limit theorem
FGLS	feasible generalized least squares
FIML	full information maximum likelihood
FIVE	full information instrumental variables efficient
FM-OLS	fully modified ordinary least squares estimator
FSD	first-order stochastic dominate
FWL	Frisch–Waugh–Lovell
GARCH	generalized autoregressive conditional heteroskedastic
GEV	generalized extreme value
GHK	Geweke, Hajivassiliou, and Keane
GHM	Gouriéoux, Holly, and Montfort
GIS	geographic information systems
GL	generalized Lorenz
GLM	generalized linear model
GLN	Ghysels, Lee, and Noh
GLS	generalized least squares
GML	generalized maximum likelihood
GMM	generalized method of moments
GNR	Gauss–Newton regression
GSUR	generalized seemingly unrelated regression
HAC	heteroskedasticity and autocorrelation consistent
HEBA	hierarchical elimination-by-aspects
HEGY	Hylleberg, Engle, Granger, and Yoo
H–K	Honoré and Kyriazidou

HRGNR	heteroskedasticity-robust Gauss–Newton regression
i.p.	in probability
IC	information criteria
ID	independently distributed
IIA	independence of irrelevant alternatives
IID	independently identically distributed
IIV	iterated instrumental variable
ILS	indirect least squares
IM	information matrix
IMSE	integrated mean square error
INAR	integer autoregressive
IP	industrial production
IV	instrumental variable
JB	Jarque–Bera
KLIC	Kullback–Leibler information criterion
KPSS	Kwiatkowski, Phillips, Schmidt, and Shin
KS	Kolmogorov–Smirnov
KT	Kuhn–Tucker
LBI	locally best invariant
LCLS	local constant least squares
LEF	linear exponential family
LI	limited information
LIML	limited information maximum likelihood
LIVE	limited information instrumental variables efficient
LL	local linear
LLLS	local linear least squares
LLN	law of large numbers
LLS	local least squares
LM	Lagrange multiplier
LMC	local Monte Carlo
LMP	locally most powerful
LMPU	locally most powerful unbiased
LPLS	local polynomial least squares
LR	likelihood ratio
LS	least squares
LSE	least squares estimation
LSTAR	logistic smooth transition autoregression
M2SLS	modified two-stage least squares
MA	moving average
MA(1)	first-order moving average
MC	Monte Carlo
MCMC	Markov Chain Monte Carlo
MD	martingale difference
MDML	multivariate dynamic linear regression
MIMIC	multiple indicators-multiple causes
ML	maximum likelihood

MLE	maximum likelihood estimation
MLR	multivariate linear regression
MM	method of moments
MMC	maximized Monte Carlo
MML	maximum marginal likelihood
MNL	multinomial logit
MNP	multinomial probit
MP	most powerful
MS	maximum score
MSE	mean square error
MSFE	mean squared forecast error
MSL	method of simulated likelihood
MSM	method of simulated moments
MSS	method of simulated scores
NB	negative binomial
NFI	normed fit index
NLS	nonlinear least squares
NMNL	nested multinomial logit
NN	neural network
N–P	Neyman–Pearson
NPRSS	nonparametric residual sum of squares
N–W	Nadaraya–Watson
NYSE	New York Stock Exchange
OLS	ordinary least squares
OPG	outer-product-of-the-gradient
PDF	probability distribution function
PLS	predictive least squares
PML	pseudo-ML
PP	Phillips–Perron
PR	probabilistic reduction
PRSS	parametric residual sum of squares
psd	positive semi-definite
PSP	partial sum process
QML	quasi-ML
QP	quadratic programming
QRM	qualitative response model
RCM	random coefficient models
RESET	regression error specification test
RIS	recursive importance sampling
RLS	restricted least squares
RMSE	root mean squared error
RMSFE	root mean squared forecast error
RNI	relative noncentrality index
RRR	reduced rank regression
RS	Rao's score
RSS	residual sum of squares

s/n	signal-to-noise
SA	simulated annealing
SAR	spatial autoregressive
SD	stochastic dominance
SEM	simultaneous equations model
SET	score encompassing test
SMA	spatial moving average
SML	simulated maximum likelihood
SNP	semi-nonparametric
SP	semiparametric
SSD	second-order stochastic dominate
SSE	sum of square error
SSR	sum of squared residuals
STAR	smooth transition autoregression
SUR(E)	seemingly unrelated regression
SVD	Stochastic Volatility Duration
TAR	transition autoregression
TSD	third-order stochastic
UI	union intersection
UL	uniform linear
ULLN	uniform law of large numbers
UMP	uniformly most powerful
UMPI	uniformly most powerful invariant
UMPU	uniformly most powerful unbiased
VAR	vector autoregression
VECM	vector error correction model
VIF	variance-inflation factor
VNM	von Neumann–Morgenstern
W	Wald
WET	Wald encompassing test
wrt	with respect to

Introduction

Badi H. Baltagi

This is the first companion in econometrics. It covers 32 chapters written by international experts in the field. The emphasis of this companion is on "keeping things simple" so as to give students of econometrics a guide through the maze of important topics in econometrics. These chapters are helpful for readers and users of econometrics who are not looking for exhaustive surveys on the subject. Instead, these chapters give the reader some of the basics and point to further readings on the subject. The topics covered vary from basic chapters on serial correlation and heteroskedasticity, which are found in standard econometrics texts, to specialized topics that are covered by econometric society monographs and advanced books on the subject like count data, panel data, and spatial correlation. The authors have done their best to keep things simple. Space and time limitations prevented the inclusion of other important topics, problems and exercises, empirical applications, and exhaustive references. However, we believe that this is a good start and that the 32 chapters contain an important selection of topics in this young but fast growing field.

Chapter 1 by Davidson and MacKinnon introduces the concept of an artificial regression and gives three conditions that an artificial regression must satisfy. The widely used Gauss–Newton regression (GNR) is used to show how artificial regressions can be used for minimizing criterion functions, computing one-step estimators, calculating covariance matrix estimates, and more importantly computing test statistics. This is illustrated for testing the null hypothesis that a subset of the parameters of a nonlinear regression model are zero. It is shown that the test statistic can be computed as an explained sum of squares of the GNR divided by a consistent estimate of the residual variance. Two ways of computing this statistic are: (i) the sample size times the uncentered R^2 of the GNR, or (ii) an ordinary F-statistic testing the subset of the parameters are zero from the GNR. The two statistics are asymptotically equivalent under the null hypothesis. The GNR can be used for other types of specification tests, including serial correlation, nonnested hypothesis and obtaining Durbin–Wu–Hausman type tests. This chapter also shows how to make the GNR robust to heteroskedasticity of unknown form. It also develops an artificial regression for the generalized method of moments (GMM) estimation. The outer-product-of-the-gradient (OPG) regression is also discussed. This is a simple artificial regression which can be used with most models estimated by maximum likelihood. It is shown that the OPG satisfies the three conditions of an artificial regression and has the usual uses of an artificial regression. It is appealing because it requires only first derivatives. However, it is demonstrated that the OPG regression yields relatively poor estimates of the covariance matrices and unreliable test statistics in small samples. In fact, test statistics based on the OPG regression tend to overreject, often very severely. Davidson and MacKinnon also discuss double-length or triple-length artificial regressions where each observation makes two or three contributions to the criterion function. In this case, the artificial regression has twice or three times the sample size. This artificial regression can be used for many purposes, including tests of models with different functional forms. Finally, this chapter extends the GNR to binary response models such as the logit and probit models. For further readings on this subject, see Davidson and MacKinnon (1993).

Chapter 2 by Bera and Premaratne gives a brief history of hypothesis testing in statistics. This journey takes the reader through the basic testing principles leading naturally to several tests used by econometricians. These tests are then linked back to the basic principles using several examples. This chapter goes through the Neyman–Pearson lemma and the likelihood ratio test. It explains what is meant by locally most powerful tests and it gives the origins of the Rao-score test. Next, locally most powerful unbiased tests and Neyman's smooth test are reviewed. The interrelationship among the holy trinity of test statistics, i.e., the Wald, likelihood ratio, and Rao-score tests is brought home to the reader by an amusing story. Neyman's $C(\alpha)$ test is derived and motivated. This approach provides an attractive way of dealing with nuisance parameters. Next, this chapter goes through some of the application of testing principles in econometrics. Again a brief history of hypothesis testing in econometrics is given beginning with the work of Ragnar Frisch and Jan Tinbergen, going into details through the Durbin–Watson statistic linking its origins to the Neyman–Pearson lemma. The use of the popular Rao-score test in econometrics is reviewed next, emphasizing that several tests in econometrics old and new have been given a score test interpretation. In fact, Bera and Premaratne consider the conditional moment test developed by Newey (1985) and Tauchen (1985) and derive its score test interpretation. Applications of Neyman's $C(\alpha)$ test in econometrics are cited and some of the tests in econometrics are given a smooth test interpretation. The chapter finishes with a double warning about testing: be careful how you interpret the test results. Be careful what action you take when the null is rejected.

Chapter 3 by King surveys the problem of serial correlation in econometrics. Ignoring serial correlation in the disturbances can lead to inefficient parameter estimates and a misleading inference. This chapter surveys the various ways of modeling serial correlation including Box–Jenkins time series models. Autoregressive and moving average (ARMA) models are discussed, highlighting the contributions of Cochrane and Orcutt (1949) for the AR(1) model; Thomas and Wallis (1971) for the restricted AR(4) process and Nichols, Pagan, and Terrell

(1975) for the MA(1) process. King argues that modeling serial correlation involves taking care of the dynamic part of model specification. The simple version of a dynamic model includes the lagged value of the dependent variable among the regressors. The relationship between this simple dynamic model and the AR(1) model is explored. Estimation of the linear regression model with ARMA disturbances is considered next. Maximum likelihood estimation (MLE) under normality is derived and a number of practical computation issues are discussed. Marginal likelihood estimation methods are also discussed which work well for estimating the ARMA process parameters in the presence of nuisance parameters. In this case, the nuisance parameters include the regression parameters and the residual variance. Maximizing marginal likelihoods were shown to reduce the estimation bias of maximum likelihood methods. Given the nonexperimental nature of economic data and the high potential for serial correlation, King argues that it is important to test for serial correlation. The von Neuman as well as Durbin–Watson (DW) tests are reviewed and their statistical properties are discussed. For example, the power of the DW test tends to decline to zero when the AR(1) parameter ρ tends to one. In this case, King suggests a class of point optimal tests that provide a solution to this problem. LM, Wald and LR tests for serial correlation are mentioned, but King suggests constructing these tests using the marginal likelihood rather than the full likelihood function. Testing for AR(1) disturbances in the dynamic linear regression model is also studied, and the difficulty of finding a satisfactory test for this model is explained by showing that the model may suffer from a local identification problem. The last section of this chapter takes up the problem of deciding what lags should be used in the ARIMA model. Model selection criteria are recommended rather than a test of hypotheses and the Bayesian information criteria is favored because it is consistent. This means that as the sample size goes to infinity, this criteria selects the correct model from a finite number of models with probability one.

Chapter 4 by Griffiths gives a lucid treatment of the heteroskedasticity problem. The case of a known variance covariance term is treated first and generalized least squares is derived. Finite sample inference under normality as well as large sample inference without the normality assumption are summarized in the context of testing linear restrictions on the regression coefficients. In addition, inference for nonlinear restrictions on the regression coefficients is given and the consequences of heteroskedasticity on the least squares estimator are explained. Next, the case of the unknown variance covariance matrix is treated. In this case, several specifications of the form of heteroskedasticity are entertained and maximum likelihood estimation under normality is derived. Tests of linear restrictions on the regression coefficients are then formulated in terms of the ML estimates. Likelihood ratio, Wald and LM type tests of heteroskedasticity are given under normality of the disturbances. Other tests of heteroskedasticity as well as Monte Carlo experiments comparing these tests are cited. Adaptive estimators that assume no form of heteroskedasticity are briefly surveyed as well as several other miscellaneous extensions. Next, this chapter discusses Bayesian inference under heteroskedasticity. The joint posterior probability density function is specified assuming normality for the regression and uninformative priors on heteroskedasticity. An algorithm for obtaining the marginal posterior probability density function is given.

Chapter 5 by Fiebig, surveys the most recent developments on seemingly unrelated regressions (SUR) including both applied and theoretical work on the specification, estimation and testing of SUR models. This chapter updates the survey by Srivastava and Dwivedi (1979) and the book by Srivastava and Giles (1987). A basic introduction of the SUR model introduced by Zellner (1962), is given along with extensions of the model to allow for more general stochastic specifications. These extensions are driven in part by diagnostic procedures as well as theoretical economic arguments presented for behavioral models of consumers and producers. Here the problem of testing linear restrictions which is important for testing demand systems or estimating say a cost function with share equations is studied. In addition, tests for the presence of contemporaneous correlation in SUR models as well as spatial autocorrelation are discussed. Next, SUR with missing observations and computational matters are reviewed. This leads naturally to a discussion of Bayesian methods for the SUR model and improved estimation methods for SUR which include several variants of the Stein-rule family and the hierarchical Bayes estimator. Finally, a brief discussion of misspecification, robust estimation issues, as well as extensions of the SUR model to time series modeling and count data Poisson regressions are given.

Chapter 6 by Mariano, considers the problem of estimation in the simultaneous equation model. Both limited as well as full information estimators are discussed. The inconsistency of ordinary least squares (OLS) is demonstrated. Limited information instrumental variable estimators are reviewed including two-stage least squares (2SLS), limited information instrumental variable efficient (LIVE), Theil's k-class, and limited information maximum likelihood (LIML). Full information methods including three-stage least squares (3SLS), full information instrumental variables efficient (FIVE) and full information maximum likelihood (FIML) are studied next. Large sample properties of these limited and full information estimators are summarized and conditions for their consistency and asymptotic efficiency are stated without proof. In addition, the finite sample properties of these estimators are reviewed and illustrated using the case of two included endogenous variables. Last, but not least, practical implications of these finite sample results are given. These are tied up to the recent literature on weak instruments.

Chapter 7 by Bekker and Wansbeek discusses the problem of identification in parametric models. Roughly speaking, a model is identified when meaningful estimates of its parameters can be obtained. Otherwise, the model is under-identified. In the latter case, different sets of parameter values agree well with the statistical evidence rendering scientific conclusions based on any estimates of this model void and dangerous. Bekker and Wansbeek define the basic concepts of observational equivalence of two parameter points and what is meant by local and global identification. They tie up the notion of identification to that of the existence of a consistent estimator, and provide a link between identification and the rank of the information matrix. The latter is made practically useful by presenting it in terms of the rank of a Jacobian matrix. Although the chapter

is limited to the problem of parametric identification based on sample information and exact restrictions on the parameters, extensions are discussed and the
reader is referred to the book by Bekker, Merckens, and Wansbeek (1994) for
further analysis.

Chapter 8 by Wansbeek and Meijer discusses the measurement error problem
in econometrics. Many economic variables like permanent income, productivity
of a worker, consumer satisfaction, financial health of a firm, etc. are latent variables that are only observed with error. This chapter studies the consequences of
measurement error and latent variables in econometric models and possible solutions to these problems. First, the linear regression model with errors in variables
is considered, the bias and inconsistency of OLS is demonstrated and the attenuation phenomenon is explained. Next, bounds on the parameters of the model
are obtained by considering the reverse regression. Solutions to the errors in
variables include restrictions on the parameters to identify the model and hence
yield consistent estimators of the parameters. Alternatively, instrumental variables estimation procedures can be employed, or nonnormality of the errors may
be exploited to obtain consistent estimates of these parameters. Repeated measurements like panel data on households, firms, regions, etc. can also allow the
consistent estimation of the parameters of the model. The second part of this
chapter gives an extensive discussion of latent variable models including factor
analysis, the multiple indicators-multiple causes (MIMIC) model and a frequently
used generalization of the MIMIC model known as the reduced rank regression
model. In addition, general linear structural equation models estimated by LISREL
are considered and maximum likelihood, generalized least squares, test statistics,
and model fit are studied.

Chapter 9 by Wooldridge provides a comprehensive account of diagnostic
testing in econometrics. First, Wooldridge explains how diagnostic testing differs
from classical testing. The latter assumes a correctly specified parametric model
and uses standard statistics to test restrictions on the parameters of this model,
while the former tests the model for various misspecifications. This chapter considers diagnostic testing in cross section applications. It starts with diagnostic
tests for the conditional mean in the linear regression model. Conditional mean
diagnostics are computed using variable addition statistics or artificial regressions (see Chapter 1 by Davidson and MacKinnon). Tests for functional form are
given as an example and it is shown that a key auxiliary assumption needed
to obtain a usable limiting distribution for the usual nR^2 (LM) test statistic is
homoskedasticity. Without this assumption, the limiting distribution of the LM
statistic is not χ^2 and the resulting test based on chi-squared critical values may
be asymptotically undersized or oversized. This LM statistic is adjusted to allow
for heteroskedasticity of unknown form under the null hypothesis. Next, testing
for heteroskedasticity is considered. A joint test of the conditional mean and conditional variance is an example of an omnibus test. However, if this test rejects
it is difficult to know where to look. A popular omnibus test is White's (1982)
information matrix test. This test is explicitly a test for homoskedasticity, conditional symmetry and homokurtosis. If we reject, it may be for any of these reasons
and it is not clear why one wants to toss out a model because of asymmetry, or

because its fourth and second moments do not satisfy the same relationship as that for a normal distribution. Extensions to nonlinear models are discussed next as well as diagnostic tests for completely specified parametric models like limited dependent variable models, probit, logit, tobit, and count data type models. The last section deals with diagnostic testing in time series models. In this case, one can no longer assume that the observations are independent of one another and the discussion of auxiliary assumptions under the null is more complicated. Wooldridge discusses different ways to make conditional mean diagnostics robust to serial correlation as well as heteroskedasticity. Testing for heteroskedasticity in time series contexts and omnibus tests on the errors in time series regressions, round up the chapter.

Chapter 10 by Pötscher and Prucha gives the basic elements of asymptotic theory. This chapter discusses the crucial concepts of convergence in probability and distribution, the convergence properties of transformed random variables, orders of magnitude of the limiting behavior of sequences of random variables, laws of large numbers both for independent and dependent processes, and central limit theorems. This is illustrated for regression analysis. Further readings are suggested including the recent book by Pötscher and Prucha (1997).

Chapter 11 by Hall provides a thorough treatment of the generalized method of moments (GMM) and its applications in econometrics. Hall explains that the main advantage of GMM for econometric theory is that it provides a general framework which encompasses many estimators of interest. For econometric applications, it provides a convenient method of estimating nonlinear dynamic models without complete knowledge of the distribution of the data. This chapter gives a basic definition of the GMM estimation principle and shows how it is predicated on the assumption that the population moment condition provides sufficient information to uniquely determine the unknown parameters of the correctly specified model. This need not be the case, and leads naturally to a discussion of the concepts of local and global identification. In case the model is overidentified, Hall shows how the estimation effects a decomposition on the population moment condition into identifying restrictions upon which the estimation is based, and overidentifying restrictions which are ignored in the estimation. This chapter describes how the estimated sample moment can be used to construct the overidentification restrictions test for the adequacy of the model specification, and derives the consistency and asymptotic distribution of the estimator. This chapter also characterizes the optimal choice of the weighting matrix and shows how the choice of the weight matrix impacts the GMM estimator via its asymptotic variance. MLE is shown to be a special case of GMM. However, MLE requires that we know the distribution of the data. GMM allows one to focus on the information used in the estimation and thereby determine the consequences of choosing the wrong distribution. Since the population moment condition is not known in practice, the researcher is faced with a large set of alternatives to choose from. Hall focuses on two extreme scenarios where the best and worst choices are made. The best choice is the population moment condition which leads to the estimator with the smallest asymptotic variance. The worst choice is when the population moment condition does not provide enough information to identify the unknown parameters of our model. This leads to a discussion of nearly uninformative population moment conditions, their consequence and how they might be circumvented.

Chapter 12 by Hill and Adkins gives a lucid discussion of the collinearity problem in econometrics. They argue that collinearity takes three distinct forms. The first is where an explanatory variable exhibits little variability and therefore makes it difficult to estimate its effect in a linear regression model. The second is where two explanatory variables exhibit a large correlation leaving little independent variation to estimate their separate effects. The third is where there may be one or more nearly exact linear relationships among the explanatory variables, hence obscuring the effects of each independent variable on the dependent variable. Hill and Adkins examine the damage that multicollinearity does to estimation and review collinearity diagnostics such as the variance decomposition of Belsley, Kuh, and Welsch (1980), the variance-inflation factor and the determinant of $X'X$, the sum of squares and cross-product of the regressor matrix X. Once collinearity is detected, this chapter discusses whether collinearity is harmful by using Belsley's (1982) test for adequate signal to noise ratio in the regression model and data. Next, remedies to harmful collinearity are reviewed. Here the reader is warned that there are only two safe paths. The first is obtaining more and better data which is usually not an option for practitioners. The second is imposing additional restrictions from economic theory or previous empirical research. Hill and Adkins emphasize that although this is a feasible option, only good nonsample information should be used and it is never truly known whether the information introduced is good enough. Methods of introducing exact and inexact nonsample information including restricted least squares, Stein-rule estimators, inequality restricted least squares, Bayesian methods, the mixed estimation procedure of Theil and Goldberger (1961) and the maximum entropy procedure of Golan, Judge, and Miller (1996) are reviewed. In addition, two estimation methods designed specifically for collinear data are discussed if only to warn the readers about their use. These are ridge regression and principal components regression. Finally, this chapter extends the collinearity analysis to nonlinear models.

Chapter 13 by Pesaran and Weeks gives an overview of the problem of non-nested hypothesis testing in econometrics. This problem arises naturally when rival economic theories are used to explain the same phenomenon. For example, competing theories of inflation may suggest two different sets of regressors neither of which is a special case of the other. Pesaran and Weeks define non-nested models as belonging to separate families of distributions in the sense that none of the individual models may be obtained from the remaining either by imposition of parameter restrictions or through a limiting process. This chapter discusses the problem of model selection and how it relates to non-nested hypothesis testing. By utilizing the linear regression model as a convenient framework, Pesaran and Weeks examine three broad approaches to non-nested hypotheses testing: (i) the modified (centered) log-likelihood ratio procedure also known as the Cox test; (ii) the comprehensive models approach, whereby the non-nested models are tested against an artificially constructed general model that includes the non-nested models as special cases; and (iii) the encompassing approach, where the ability of one model to explain particular features of an alternative model is tested directly. This chapter also focuses on the Kullback-Leibler divergence measure which has played a pivotal role in the development of a number of non-nested test statistics. In addition, the Vuong (1989) approach to model selection, viewed as a hypothesis testing problem is also discussed. Finally, practical problems involved in the implementation of the Cox procedure are considered. This involves finding an estimate of the Kullback-Leibler measure of closeness of the alternative to the null hypothesis which is not easy to compute. Two methods are discussed to circumvent this problem. The first examines the simulation approach and the second examines the parametric bootstrap approach.

Chapter 14 by Anselin provides an excellent review of spatial econometrics. These methods deal with the incorporation of spatial interaction and spatial structure into regression analysis. The field has seen a recent and rapid growth spurred both by theoretical concerns as well as the need to apply econometric models to emerging large geocoded databases. This chapter outlines the basic terminology and discusses in some detail the specification of spatial effects including the incorporation of spatial dependence in panel data models and models with qualitative variables. The estimation of spatial regression models including maximum likelihood estimation, spatial 2SLS, method of moments estimators and a number of other approaches are considered. In addition, specification tests for spatial effects as well as implementation issues are discussed.

Chapter 15 by Cameron and Trivedi gives a brief review of count data regressions. These are regressions that involve a dependent variable that is a count, such as the number of births in models of fertility, number of accidents in studies of airline safety, hospital or doctor visits in health demand studies, number of trips in models of recreational demand, number of patents in research and development studies or number of bids in auctions. In these examples, the sample is concentrated on a few discrete values like 0, 1 and 2. The data is skewed to the left and the data is intrinsically heteroskedastic with its variance increasing with the mean. Two methods of dealing with these models are considered. The first is a fully parametric approach which completely specifies the distribution of the data and restricts the dependent variable to nonnegative integer values. This includes the Poisson regression model which is studied in detail in this chapter including its extensions to truncated and censored data. Limitations of the Poisson model, notably the excess zeros problem and the overdispersion problem are explained and other parametric models, superior to the Poisson are presented. These include continuous mixture models, finite mixture models, modified count models and discrete choice models. The second method of dealing with count data is a partial parametric method which focuses on modeling the data via the conditional mean and variance. This includes quasi-maximum likelihood estimation, least squares estimation and semiparametric models. Extensions to other types of data notably time series, multivariate, and panel data are discussed and the chapter concludes with some practical recommendations. For further readings and diagnostic procedures, the reader is referred to the recent econometric society monograph on count data models by Cameron and Trivedi (1998).

Chapter 16 by Hsiao gives a selected survey of panel data models. First, the benefits from using panels are discussed. This includes more degrees of freedom, controlling for omitted variable bias, reducing the problem of multicollinearity and improving the accuracy of parameter estimates and predictions. A general encompassing linear panel data model is provided which includes as special cases the error components model, the random coefficients model and the mixed fixed and random coefficients model. These models assume that some variables are subject to stochastic constraints while others are subject to deterministic constraints. In practice, there is little knowledge about which variables are subject to stochastic constraints and which variables are subject to deterministic constraints. Hsiao recommends the Bayesian predictive density ratio method for selecting between two alternative formulations of the model. Dynamic panel data models are studied next and the importance of the initial observation with regards to the consistency and efficiency of the estimators is emphasized. Generalized method of moments estimators are proposed and the problem of too many orthogonality conditions is discussed. Hsiao suggests a transformed maximum likelihood estimator that is asymptotically more efficient than GMM. Hsiao also reports that the mean group estimator suggested by Pesaran and Smith (1995) does not perform well in finite samples. Alternatively, a hierarchical Bayesian approach performs well when T is small and the initial value is assumed to be a fixed constant. Next, the existence of individual specific effects in nonlinear models is discussed and the conditional MLE approach of Chamberlain (1980) is given. The problem becomes more complicated if lagged dependent variables are present. $T \geq 4$ is needed for the identification of a logit model and this conditional method will not work with the presence of exogenous variables. In this case, a consistent and asymptotically normal estimator proposed by Honoré and Kyriazidou (1997) is suggested. An alternative semiparametric approach to estimating nonlinear panel models is the maximum score estimator proposed by Manski (1975). This applies some data transformation to eliminate the individual effects if the nonlinear model is of the form of a single index model with the index possessing a linear structure. This estimator is consistent but not root n consistent. A third approach proposed by Lancaster (1998) finds an orthogonal reparametrization of the fixed effects such that the new fixed effects are independent of the structural parameters in the information matrix sense. Hsiao discusses the limitations of all three methods, emphasizing that none of these approaches can claim general applicability and that the consistency of nonlinear panel data estimators must be established on a case by case basis. Finally, Hsiao treats missing observations in panels. If individuals are missing randomly, most estimators in the balanced panel case can be easily generalized to the unbalanced case. With sample selection, Hsiao emphasizes the dependence of the MLE and Heckman's (1979) two-step estimators on the exact specification of the joint error distribution. If this distribution is misspecified, then these estimators are inconsistent. Alternative semiparametric methods are discussed based on the work of Ahn and Powell (1993), Kyriazidou (1997), and Honoré and Kyriazidou (1998).

Chapter 17 by Maddala and Flores-Lagunes gives an update of the econometrics of qualitative response models. First, a brief introduction to the basic material on the estimation of binary and multinomial logit and probit models is given and the reader is referred to Maddala (1983) for details. Next, this chapter reviews specification tests in qualitative response models and the reader is referred to the recent review by Maddala (1995). Panel data with qualitative variables and semiparametric estimation methods for qualitative response models are reviewed including Manski's maximum score, quasi-maximum likelihood, generalized maximum likelihood and the semi-nonparametric estimator. Maddala and Flores-Lagunes comment on the empirical usefulness and drawbacks of the different methods. Finally, simulation methods in qualitative response models are reviewed. The estimation methods discussed are the method of simulated moments, the method of simulated likelihood and the method of simulated scores. Some examples are given comparing these simulation methods.

Chapter 18 by Lee gives an extensive discussion of the problem of self-selection in econometrics. When the sample observed is distorted and is not representative of the population under study, sample selection bias occurs. This may be due to the way the sample was collected or it may be due to the self-selection decisions by the agents being studied. This sample may not represent the true population no matter how large. This chapter discusses some of the conventional sample selection models and counterfactual outcomes. A major part of this chapter concentrates on the specification, estimation, and testing of parametric models of sample selection. This includes Heckman's two-stage estimation procedure as well as maximum likelihood methods, polychotomous choice sample selection models, simulation estimation methods, and the estimation of simultaneous equation sample selection models. Another major part of this chapter focuses on semiparametric and nonparametric approaches. This includes semiparametric two-stage estimation, semiparametric efficiency bound and semiparametric maximum likelihood estimation. In addition, semiparametric instrumental variable estimation and conditional moments restrictions are reviewed, as well as sample selection models with a tobit selection rule. The chapter concludes with the identification and estimation of counterfactual outcomes.

Chapter 19 by Swamy and Tavlas describes the purpose, estimation, and use of random coefficient models. Swamy and Tavlas distinguish between first generation random coefficient models that sought to relax the constant coefficient assumption typically made by researchers in the classical tradition and second generation random coefficient models that relax the assumptions made regarding functional forms, excluded variables, and absence of measurement error. The authors argue that the latter are useful approximations to reality because they provide a reasonable approximation to the underlying "true" economic relationship. Several model validation criteria are provided. Throughout, a demand for money model is used as a backdrop to explain random coefficient models and an empirical application to United Kingdom data is given.

Chapter 20 by Ullah provides a systematic and unified treatment of estimation and test of hypotheses for nonparametric and semiparametric regression models. Parametric approaches to specifying functional form in econometrics may lead to misspecification. Nonparametric and semiparametric approaches provide alternative estimation procedures that are more robust to functional form misspecification. This chapter studies the developments in the area of kernel estimation in econometrics. Nonparametric estimates of conditional means as well as higher order moments and function derivatives are reviewed. In addition, some new goodness of fit procedures for nonparametric regressions are presented and their application to determining the window width and variable selection are discussed. Next, a combination of parametric and nonparametric regressions that takes into account the tradeoff between good fit (less bias) and smoothness (low variance) is suggested to improve (in mean-squared error sense) the drawbacks of each approach used separately. Additive nonparametric regressions and semiparametric models are given as possible solutions to the curse of dimensionality. The chapter concludes with hypothesis testing in nonparametric and semiparametric models.

Chapter 21 by Gourieroux and Jasiak gives a review of duration models. These models have been used in labor economics to study the duration of individual unemployment spells and in health economics to study the length of hospital stays to mention just two examples. Gourieroux and Jasiak discuss the main duration distribution families including the exponential, gamma, Weibull, and lognormal distributions. They explain what is meant by survivor functions, hazard functions, and duration dependence. Maximum likelihood estimation for the exponential duration model without heterogeneity as well as the gamma distributed heterogeneity model are given. The latter leads to the Pareto regression model. Next, the effect of unobservable heterogeneity and its relationship with negative duration dependence as well as the problem of partial observability of duration variables due to truncation or censoring effects are considered. Semiparametric specifications of duration models are also studied. These distinguish a parametric scoring function and an unconstrained baseline distribution. Accelerated and proportional hazard models are introduced and the estimation methods for the finite dimensional functional parameters are given. Finally, dynamic models for the analysis of time series durations are given. These are especially useful for applications to financial transactions data. Some recent developments in this field are covered including the Autoregressive Conditional Duration (ACD) model and the Stochastic Volatility Duration (SVD) model.

Chapter 22 by Geweke, Houser, and Keane provides a detailed illustration of how to implement simulation methods to dynamic discrete choice models where one has available a panel of multinomial choice histories and partially observed payoffs. The advantages of this procedure is that it does not require the econometrician to solve the agents' dynamic optimization problem, or to make strong assumptions about the way individuals form expectations. The chapter focuses exclusively on simulation based Bayesian techniques. Monte Carlo results demonstrate that this method works well in relatively large state-space models with only partially-observed payoffs, where very high dimensional integrations are required.

Chapter 23 by Dufour and Khalaf reviews Monte Carlo test methods in econometrics. Dufour and Khalaf demonstrate that this technique can provide exact randomized tests for any statistic whose finite sample distribution may be intractable but can be simulated. They illustrate this technique using several specification tests in linear regressions including tests for normality, tests for independence, heteroskedasticity, ARCH, and GARCH. Also, nonlinear hypotheses in univariate and SUR models, tests on structural parameters in instrumental variable regressions, tests on long-run multipliers in dynamic models, long-run identification constraints in VAR (vector autoregression) models and confidence intervals on ratios of coefficients in discrete choice models. Dufour and Khalaf demonstrate, using several econometric examples, that standard testing procedures that rely on asymptotic theory can produce questionable p-values and confidence intervals. They recommend Monte Carlo test methods over these standard testing procedures because the former procedures produce a valid inference in small samples.

Chapter 24 by Koop and Steel uses the stochastic frontier models to illustrate Bayesian methods in econometrics. This is contrasted with the classical econometric stochastic frontier methods and the strengths and weaknesses of both approaches are reviewed. In particular, the stochastic frontier model with cross-sectional data is introduced with a simple log-linear model (e.g., Cobb–Douglas or translog) and a simple Gibbs sampler is used to carry out Bayesian inference. This is extended to nonlinear production frontiers (e.g., constant elasticity of substitution or the asymptotically ideal model) where more complicated posterior simulation methods are necessary. Next, the stochastic frontier model with panel data is considered and the Bayesian fixed effects and random effects models are contrasted with their classical alternatives. Koop and Steel show that the Bayesian fixed effects model imposes strong and possibly unreasonable prior assumptions. In fact, only relative efficiencies and not absolute efficiencies can be computed by this model and it is shown to be quite sensitive to prior assumptions. In contrast, the Bayesian random effects model makes explicit distributional assumptions for the inefficiencies and allows robust inference on the absolute efficiencies.

Chapter 25 by Maasoumi summarizes some of the technical and conceptual advances in testing multivariate linear and nonlinear inequality hypotheses in econometrics. This is done in the context of substantive empirical settings in economics in which either the null, or the alternative, or both hypotheses define more limited domains than the two-sided alternatives typically tested in classical hypotheses testing. The desired goal is increased power. The impediments are a lack of familiarity with implementation procedures, and characterization problems of distributions under some composite hypotheses. Several empirically important cases are identified in which practical "one-sided" tests can be conducted by either the mixed χ^2 distribution, or the union intersection mechanisms based on the Gaussian variate, or the popular resampling/simulation techniques. Point optimal testing and its derivatives find a natural medium here whenever unique characterization of the null distribution for the "least favorable" cases is not possible. Applications in the parametric, semiparametric and nonparametric testing area are cited.

Chapter 26 by Granger gives a brief introduction to the problem of spurious regressions in econometrics. This problem is traced historically from its origins (see Yule 1926). A definition of spurious correlation is given and the problem is

The Gauss–Newton regression can be derived as an approximation to *Newton's Method* for the minimization of Q(β). In this case, Newton's Method consists of the following iterative procedure. One starts from some suitably chosen starting value, $\beta_{(0)}$. At step m of the procedure, $\beta_{(m)}$ is updated by the formula

$$\beta_{(m+1)} = \beta_{(m)} - H_{(m)}^{-1} g_{(m)},$$

where the $k \times 1$ vector $g_{(m)}$ and the $k \times k$ matrix $H_{(m)}$ are, respectively, the gradient and the Hessian of Q(β) with respect to β, evaluated at $\beta_{(m)}$. For general β, we have

$$g(\beta) = -X^{\top}(\beta)(y - x(\beta)),$$

where the matrix $X(\beta)$ is an $n \times k$ matrix with tith element the derivative of $x_t(\beta)$ with respect to β_i, the ith component of β. A typical element of the Hessian $H(\beta)$ is

$$H_{ij}(\beta) = -\sum_{t=1}^{n} \left((y_t - x_t(\beta))\frac{\partial X_{ti}(\beta)}{\partial \beta_j} - X_{ti}(\beta)X_{tj}(\beta) \right), \quad i, j = 1, \ldots, k. \tag{1.5}$$

The Gauss–Newton procedure is one of the set of so-called **quasi-Newton** procedures, in which the exact Hessian is replaced by an approximation. Here, only the second term in (1.5) is used, so that the H(β) of Newton's method is replaced by the matrix $X^{\top}(\beta)X(\beta)$. Thus the Gauss–Newton updating formula is

$$\beta_{(m+1)} = \beta_{(m)} + (X_{(m)}^{\top}X_{(m)})^{-1}X_{(m)}^{\top}(y - x_{(m)}), \tag{1.6}$$

where we write $X_{(m)} = X(\beta_{(m)})$ and $x_{(m)} = x(\beta_{(m)})$. The updating term on the right-hand side of (1.6) is the set of OLS parameter estimates from the *Gauss–Newton regression*, or *GNR*,

$$y - x(\beta) = X(\beta)b + \text{residuals}, \tag{1.7}$$

where the variables $r(\beta) \equiv y - x(\beta)$ and $R(\beta) \equiv X(\beta)$ are evaluated at $\beta_{(m)}$. Notice that there is no regressor in (1.7) corresponding to the parameter σ^2, because the criterion function Q(β) does not depend on σ^2. This is one of the features of the GNR that makes it a nonstandard artificial regression.

The GNR is clearly a linearization of the nonlinear regression model (1.3) around the point β. In the special case in which the original model is linear, $x(\beta) = X\beta$, where X is the matrix of independent variables. Since $X(\beta)$ is equal to X for all β in this special case, the GNR will simply be a regression of the vector $y - X\beta$ on the matrix X.

An example is provided by the nonlinear regression model

$$y_t = \beta_1 Z_{t1}^{\beta_2} Z_{t2}^{1-\beta_2} + u_t, \quad u_t \sim \text{iid}(0, \sigma^2), \tag{1.8}$$

where Z_{t1} and Z_{t2} are independent variables. The regression function here is nonlinear and has the form of a Cobb–Douglas production function. In many cases, of course, it would be reasonable to assume that the error term is multiplicative, and it would then be possible to take logarithms of both sides and use ordinary least squares. But if we wish to estimate (1.8) as it stands, we must use nonlinear least squares. The GNR that corresponds to (1.8) is

$$y_t - \beta_1 Z_{t1}^{\beta_2} Z_{t2}^{1-\beta_2} = b_1 Z_{t1}^{\beta_2} Z_{t2}^{1-\beta_2} + b_2 \beta_1 Z_{t2} \left(\frac{Z_{t1}}{Z_{t2}}\right)^{\beta_2} \log\left(\frac{Z_{t1}}{Z_{t2}}\right) + \text{residual.}$$

The regressand is y_t minus the regression function, the first regressor is the derivative of the regression function with respect to β_1, and the second regressor is the derivative of the regression function with respect to β_2.

Now consider the defining conditions of an artificial regression. We have

$$R^\top(\theta)r(\theta) = X^\top(\beta)(y - x(\beta)), \tag{1.9}$$

which is just minus the gradient of $Q(\beta)$. Thus condition (1.1′) is satisfied.

Next, consider condition (3). Let $\acute{\beta}$ denote a vector of initial estimates, which are assumed to be root-n consistent. The GNR (1.7) evaluated at these estimates is

$$y - \acute{x} = \acute{X}b + \text{residuals,}$$

where $\acute{x} \equiv x(\acute{\beta})$ and $\acute{X} \equiv X(\acute{\beta})$. The estimate of b from this regression is

$$\acute{b} = (\acute{X}^\top \acute{X})^{-1} \acute{X}^\top (y - \acute{x}). \tag{1.10}$$

The *one-step efficient estimator* is then defined to be

$$\grave{\beta} \equiv \acute{\beta} + \acute{b}. \tag{1.11}$$

By Taylor expanding the expression $n^{-1/2}\acute{X}^\top(y - \acute{x})$ around $\beta = \beta_0$, where β_0 is the true parameter vector, and using standard asymptotic arguments, it can be shown that, to leading order,

$$n^{-1/2}\acute{X}^\top(y - \acute{x}) = n^{-1/2}X_0^\top u - n^{-1}X_0^\top X_0 n^{1/2}(\acute{\beta} - \beta_0),$$

where $X_0 \equiv X(\beta_0)$. This relation can be solved to yield

$$n^{1/2}(\acute{\beta} - \beta_0) = (n^{-1}X_0^\top X_0)^{-1}(n^{-1/2}X_0^\top u - n^{-1/2}\acute{X}^\top(y - \acute{x})). \tag{1.12}$$

Now it is a standard result that, asymptotically,

$$n^{1/2}(\hat{\beta} - \beta_0) = (n^{-1}X_0^\top X_0)^{-1}(n^{-1/2}X_0^\top u); \tag{1.13}$$

see, for example, Davidson and MacKinnon (1993, section 5.4). By (1.10), the second term on the right-hand side of (1.12) is asymptotically equivalent to $-n^{1/2}\acute{b}$. Thus (1.12) implies that

$$n^{1/2}(\acute{\beta} - \beta_0) = n^{1/2}(\hat{\beta} - \beta_0) - n^{1/2}\acute{b}.$$

Rearranging this and using the definition (1.11), we see that, to leading order asymptotically,

$$n^{1/2}(\acute{\beta} - \beta) = n^{1/2}(\acute{\beta} + \acute{b} - \beta_0) = n^{1/2}(\hat{\beta} - \beta_0).$$

In other words, after both are centered and multiplied by $n^{1/2}$, the one-step estimator $\acute{\beta}$ and the NLS estimator $\hat{\beta}$ tend to the same random variable asymptotically. This is just another way of writing condition (3) for model (1.3).

Finally, consider condition (2). Since $X(\beta)$ plays the role of $R(\theta)$, we see that

$$\frac{1}{n}R^{\top}(\theta)R(\theta) = \frac{1}{n}X^{\top}(\beta)X(\beta). \tag{1.14}$$

If the right-hand side of (1.14) is evaluated at any root-n consistent estimator $\acute{\beta}$, it must tend to the same probability limit as $n^{-1}X_0^{\top}X_0$. It is a standard result, following straightforwardly from (1.13), that, if $\hat{\beta}$ denotes the NLS estimator for the model (1.3), then

$$\lim_{n\to\infty} \mathrm{var}(n^{1/2}(\hat{\beta} - \beta_0)) = \sigma_0^2 \plim_{n\to\infty} (n^{-1}X_0^{\top}X_0)^{-1}, \tag{1.15}$$

where σ_0^2 is the true variance of the error terms; see, for example, Davidson and MacKinnon (1993, ch. 5). Thus the GNR would satisfy condition (2) except that there is a factor of σ_0^2 missing. However, this factor is automatically supplied by the regression package. The estimated covariance matrix will be

$$\widehat{\mathrm{var}}(\acute{b}) = \acute{s}^2(\acute{X}^{\top}\acute{X})^{-1}, \tag{1.16}$$

where $\acute{s}^2 = \mathrm{SSR}/(n-k)$ is the estimate of σ^2 from the artificial regression. It is not hard to show that $\acute{s}^2$ estimates σ_0^2 consistently, and so it is clear from (1.15) that (1.16) provides a reasonable way to estimate the covariance matrix of $\acute{\beta}$.

It is easy to modify the GNR so that it actually satisfies condition (2). We just need to divide both the regressand and the regressors by s, the standard error from the original, nonlinear regression. When this is done, (1.14) becomes

$$\frac{1}{n}R^{\top}(\theta)R(\theta) = \frac{1}{ns^2}X^{\top}(\beta)X(\beta),$$

and condition (2) is seen to be satisfied. However, there is rarely any reason to do this in practice.

Although the GNR is the most commonly encountered artificial regression, it differs from most artificial regressions in one key respect: there is one parameter, σ^2, for which there is no regressor. This happens because the criterion function, $Q(\beta)$, depends only on β. The GNR therefore has only as many regressors as β has components. This feature of the GNR is responsible for the fact that it does not quite satisfy condition (2). The fact that $Q(\beta)$ does not depend on σ^2 also causes the asymptotic covariance matrix to be block diagonal between the $k \times k$ block that corresponds to β and the 1×1 block that corresponds to σ^2.

4   USES OF THE GNR

The GNR, like other artificial regressions, has several uses, depending on the parameter values at which the regressand and regressors are evaluated. If we evaluate them at $\hat{\beta}$, the vector of NLS parameter estimates, regression (1.7) becomes

$$y - \hat{x} = \hat{X}b + \text{residuals},\tag{1.17}$$

where $\hat{x} \equiv x(\hat{\beta})$ and $\hat{X} \equiv X(\hat{\beta})$. By condition (1), which follows from the first-order conditions for NLS estimation, the OLS estimate $\hat{b}$ from this regression is a zero vector. In consequence, the explained sum of squares, or ESS, from regression (1.17) will be 0, and the SSR will be equal to

$$\|y - \hat{x}\|^2 = (y - \hat{x})^\top (y - \hat{x}),$$

which is the SSR from the original nonlinear regression.

Although it may seem curious to run an artificial regression all the coefficients of which are known in advance to be zero, there can be two very good reasons for doing so. The first reason is to check that the vector $\hat{\beta}$ reported by a program for NLS estimation really does satisfy the first-order conditions. Computer programs for calculating NLS estimates do not yield reliable answers in every case; see McCullough (1999). The GNR provides an easy way to see whether the first-order conditions are actually satisfied. If all the t-statistics for the GNR are not less than about 10^{-4}, and the R^2 is not less than about 10^{-8}, then the value of $\hat{\beta}$ reported by the program should be regarded with suspicion.

The second reason to run the GNR (1.17) is to calculate an estimate of $\text{var}(\hat{\beta})$, the covariance matrix of the NLS estimates. The usual OLS covariance matrix from regression (1.17) is

$$\widehat{\text{var}}(\hat{b}) = s^2(\hat{X}^\top \hat{X})^{-1},\tag{1.18}$$

which is similar to (1.16) except that everything is now evaluated at $\hat{\beta}$. Thus running the GNR (1.17) provides an easy way to calculate what is arguably the best estimate of $\text{var}(\hat{\beta})$. Of course, for (1.18) to provide an asymptotically valid covariance matrix estimate, it is essential that the error terms in (1.2) be independent and identically distributed, as we have assumed so far. We will discuss ways to drop this assumption in Section 7.

Since the GNR satisfies the one-step property, it and other artificial regressions can evidently be used to obtain one-step efficient estimates. However, although one-step estimation is of considerable theoretical interest, it is generally of modest practical interest, for two reasons. First, we often do not have a root-n consistent estimator to start from and, secondly, modern computers are so fast that the savings from stopping after just one step are rarely substantial.

What is often of great practical interest is the use of the GNR as part of a numerical minimization algorithm to find the NLS estimates $\hat{\beta}$ themselves. In practice, the classical Gauss–Newton updating procedure (1.6) should generally be replaced by

$$\beta_{(m)} = \beta_{(m-1)} + \alpha_{(m)}b_{(m)},$$

where $\alpha_{(m)}$ is a scalar that is chosen in various ways by different algorithms, but always in such a way that $Q(\beta_{(m+1)}) < Q(\beta_{(m)})$. Numerical optimization methods are discussed by Press *et al.* (1992), among many others. Artificial regressions other than the GNR allow these methods to be used more widely than just in the least squares context.

5   HYPOTHESIS TESTING WITH ARTIFICIAL REGRESSIONS

Artificial regressions like the GNR are probably employed most frequently for hypothesis testing. Suppose we wish to test a set of r equality restrictions on θ. Without loss of generality, we can assume that these are zero restrictions. This allows us to partition θ into two subvectors, θ_1 of length $k - r$, and θ_2 of length r, the restrictions being that $\theta_2 = 0$. If the estimator $\hat{\theta}$ is not only root-n consistent but also asymptotically normal, an appropriate statistic for testing these restrictions is

$$\hat{\theta}_2^{\top}(\widehat{\text{var}}\,(\hat{\theta}_2))^{-1}\hat{\theta}_2, \tag{1.19}$$

which will be asymptotically distributed as $\chi^2(r)$ under the null if $\widehat{\text{var}}(\hat{\theta}_2)$ is a suitable estimate of the covariance matrix of $\hat{\theta}_2$.

Suppose that $r(\theta)$ and $R(\theta)$ define an artificial regression for the estimator $\hat{\theta}$. Let $\acute{\theta} \equiv [\acute{\theta}_1 \vdots 0]$ be a vector of root-n consistent estimates under the null. Then, if the variables of the artificial regression are evaluated at $\acute{\theta}$, the regression can be expressed as

$$r(\acute{\theta}_1, 0) = R_1(\acute{\theta}_1, 0)b_1 + R_2(\acute{\theta}_2, 0)b_2 + \text{residuals}, \tag{1.20}$$

where the partitioning of $R = [R_1 \; R_2]$ corresponds to the partitioning of θ as $[\theta_1 \vdots \theta_2]$. Regression (1.20) will usually be written simply as

$$\acute{r} = \acute{R}_1 b_1 + \acute{R}_2 b_2 + \text{residuals},$$

although this notation hides the fact that $\acute{\theta}$ satisfies the null hypothesis.

regression, a particularly simple artificial regression that can be used with most models that are estimated by maximum likelihood. Suppose we are interested in a model of which the loglikelihood function can be written as

$$\ell(\theta) = \sum_{t=1}^{n} \ell_t(\theta), \tag{1.27}$$

where $\ell_t(\cdot)$ denotes the contribution to the loglikelihood function associated with observation t. This is the log of the density of the dependent variable(s) for observation t, conditional on observations $1, \ldots, t-1$. Thus lags of the dependent variable(s) are allowed. The key feature of (1.27) is that $\ell(\theta)$ is a sum of contributions from each of the n observations.

Now let $G(\theta)$ be the matrix with typical element

$$G_{ti}(\theta) \equiv \frac{\partial \ell_t(\theta)}{\partial \theta_i}; \quad t = 1, \ldots, n, i = 1, \ldots, k.$$

The matrix $G(\theta)$ is called the *matrix of contributions to the gradient*, or the *CG matrix*, because the derivative of the sample loglikelihood (1.27) with respect to θ_i, the ith component of θ, is the sum of the elements of column i of $G(\theta)$. The OPG regression associated with (1.27) can be written as

$$\iota = G(\theta)b + \text{residuals}, \tag{1.28}$$

where ι denotes an n-vector of 1s.

It is easy to see that the OPG regression (1.28) satisfies the conditions for it to be an artificial regression. Condition (1.1′) is evidently satisfied, since $R^\top(\theta)r(\theta) = G^\top(\theta)\iota$, the components of which are the derivatives of $\ell(\theta)$ with respect to each of the θ_i. Condition (2) is also satisfied, because, under standard regularity conditions, if θ is the true parameter vector,

$$\operatorname*{plim}_{n \to \infty} (n^{-1}R^\top(\theta)R(\theta)) = \operatorname*{plim}_{n \to \infty} (n^{-1}G^\top(\theta)G(\theta)) = \mathcal{J}(\theta).$$

Here $\mathcal{J}(\theta)$ denotes the information matrix, defined as

$$\mathcal{J}(\theta) = \lim_{n \to \infty} \frac{1}{n} \sum_{t=1}^{n} E(G_t^\top(\theta)G_t(\theta)),$$

where $G_t(\cdot)$ is the tth row of $G(\cdot)$. Since, as is well known, the asymptotic covariance matrix of $n^{1/2}(\hat{\theta} - \theta_0)$ is given by the inverse of the information matrix, condition (2) is satisfied under the further weak regularity condition that $\mathcal{J}(\theta)$ should be continuous in θ. Condition (3) is also satisfied, since it can be shown that one-step estimates from the OPG regression are asymptotically equivalent to maximum likelihood estimates. The proof is quite similar to the one for the GNR given in Section 3.

It is particularly easy to compute an LM test by using the OPG regression. Let $\tilde{\theta}$ denote the constrained ML estimates obtained by imposing r restrictions when maximizing the loglikelihood. Then the ESS from the OPG regression

$$\iota = G(\tilde{\theta})b + \text{residuals}, \tag{1.29}$$

which is equal to n times the uncentered R^2, is the OPG form of the LM statistic. Like the GNR, the OPG regression can be used for many purposes. The use of what is essentially the OPG regression for obtaining maximum likelihood estimates and computing covariance matrices was advocated by Berndt, Hall, Hall, and Hausman (1974). Using it to compute Lagrange Multiplier, or LM, tests was suggested by Godfrey and Wickens (1981), and using it to compute information matrix tests was proposed by Chesher (1983) and Lancaster (1984). The OPG regression is appealing for all these uses because it applies to a very wide variety of models and requires only first derivatives. In general, however, both estimated covariance matrices and test statistics based on the OPG regression are not very reliable in finite samples. In particular, a large number of papers, including Chesher and Spady (1991), Davidson and MacKinnon (1985a, 1992), and Godfrey, McAleer, and McKenzie (1988), have shown that, in finite samples, LM tests based on the OPG regression tend to overreject, often very severely.

Despite this drawback, the OPG regression provides a particularly convenient way to obtain various theoretical results. For example, suppose that we are interested in the variance of $\hat{\theta}_2$, the last element of $\hat{\theta}$. If θ_1 denotes a vector of the remaining $k - 1$ elements, and $G(\theta)$ and b are partitioned in the same way as θ, the OPG regression becomes

$$\iota = G_1(\theta)b_1 + G_2(\theta)b_2 + \text{residuals},$$

and the FWL regression derived from this by retaining only the last regressor is

$$M_1\iota = M_1G_2b_2 + \text{residuals},$$

where $M_1 \equiv I - G_1(G_1^\top G_1)^{-1}G_1^\top$, and the dependence on θ has been suppressed for notational convenience. The covariance matrix estimate from this is just

$$(G_2^\top M_1 G_2)^{-1} = (G_2^\top G_2 - G_2^\top G_1(G_1^\top G_1)^{-1}G_1^\top G_2)^{-1}. \tag{1.30}$$

If we divide each of the components of (1.30) by n and take their probability limits, we find that

$$\lim_{n \to \infty} \text{var}(n^{1/2}(\hat{\theta}_2 - \theta_{20})) = (\mathcal{I}_{22} - \mathcal{I}_{21}\mathcal{I}_{11}^{-1}\mathcal{I}_{12})^{-1},$$

where θ_{20} is the true value of θ_2. This is a very well-known result, but, since its relation to the FWL theorem is not obvious without appeal to the OPG regression, it is not usually obtained in such a convenient or illuminating way.

7 AN ARTIFICIAL REGRESSION FOR GMM ESTIMATION

Another useful artificial regression, much less well known than the OPG regression, is available for a class of models estimated by the generalized method of moments (GMM). Many such models can be formulated in terms of functions $f_t(\theta)$ of the model parameters and the data, such that, when they are evaluated at the true θ, their expectations conditional on corresponding information sets, Ω_t, vanish. The Ω_t usually contain all information available prior to the time of observation t, and so, as with the GNR and the OPG regression, lags of dependent variables are allowed.

Let the $n \times l$ matrix W denote the instruments used to obtain the GMM estimates. The tth row of W, denoted W_t, must contain variables in Ω_t only. The dimension of θ is k, as before, and, for θ to be identified, we need $l \geq k$. The GMM estimates with $l \times l$ weighting matrix A are obtained by minimizing the criterion function

$$Q(\theta) = \tfrac{1}{2} f^\top(\theta) W A W^\top f(\theta) \tag{1.31}$$

with respect to θ. Here $f(\theta)$ is the n-vector with typical element $f_t(\theta)$. For the procedure known as efficient GMM, the weighting matrix A is chosen so as to be proportional, asymptotically at least, to the inverse of the covariance matrix of $W^\top f(\theta)$. In the simplest case, the $f_t(\theta)$ are serially uncorrelated and homoskedastic with variance 1, and so an appropriate choice is $A = (W^\top W)^{-1}$. With this choice, the criterion function (1.31) becomes

$$Q(\theta) = \tfrac{1}{2} f^\top(\theta) P_W f(\theta), \tag{1.32}$$

where P_W is the orthogonal projection on to the columns of W.

Let $J(\theta)$ be the negative of the $n \times k$ Jacobian matrix of $f(\theta)$, so that the tith element of $J(\theta)$ is $-\partial f_t / \partial \theta_i(\theta)$. The first-order conditions for minimizing (1.32) are

$$J^\top(\theta) P_W f(\theta) = 0. \tag{1.33}$$

By standard arguments, it can be seen that the vector $\hat{\theta}$ that solves (1.33) is asymptotically normal and asymptotically satisfies the equation

$$n^{1/2}(\hat{\theta} - \theta_0) = (n^{-1} J_0^\top P_W J_0)^{-1} n^{-1/2} J_0^\top P_W f_0, \tag{1.34}$$

with $J_0 = J(\theta_0)$ and $f_0 = f(\theta_0)$. See Davidson and MacKinnon (1993, ch. 17), for a full discussion of GMM estimation.

Now consider the artificial regression

$$f(\theta) = P_W J(\theta) b + \text{residuals}. \tag{1.35}$$

By the first-order conditions (1.33) for θ, this equation clearly satisfies condition (1), and in fact it also satisfies condition (1') for the criterion function $Q(\theta)$ of (1.32). Since the covariance matrix of $f(\theta_0)$ is just the identity matrix, it follows from (1.34) that condition (2) is also satisfied. Arguments just like those presented in Section 3 for the GNR can be used to show that condition (3), the one-step property, is also satisfied by (1.35).

If the $f_t(\theta_0)$ are homoskedastic but with unknown variance σ^2, regression (1.35) can be used in exactly the same way as the GNR. Either the regressand and regressors can be divided by a suitable consistent estimate of σ, or else all test statistics can be computed as ratios, in F or nR^2 form, as appropriate.

An important special case of (1.35) is provided by the class of regression models, linear or nonlinear, estimated with instrumental variables (IV). Such a model can be written in the form (1.3), but it will be estimated by minimizing, not the criterion function (1.4) related to the sum of squared residuals, but rather

$$Q(\beta) \equiv \tfrac{1}{2}(y - x(\beta))^\top P_W(y - x(\beta)),$$

where W is an $n \times l$ matrix of instrumental variables. This criterion function has exactly the same form as (1.32), with β instead of θ, and with $f(\beta) = y - x(\beta)$. In addition, $J(\beta) = X(\beta)$, where $X(\beta)$ is defined, exactly as for the GNR, to have the tith element $\partial x_t / \partial \beta_i(\beta)$. The resulting artificial regression for the IV model, which takes the form

$$y - x(\beta) = P_W X(\beta)b + \text{residuals}, \tag{1.36}$$

is often referred to as a GNR, because, except for the projection matrix P_W, it is identical to (1.7): See Davidson and MacKinnon (1993, ch. 7).

8 ARTIFICIAL REGRESSIONS AND HETEROSKEDASTICITY

Covariance matrices and test statistics calculated via the GNR (1.7), or via artificial regressions such as (1.35) and (1.36), are not asymptotically valid when the assumption that the error terms are iid is violated. Consider a modified version of the nonlinear regression model (1.3), in which $E(uu^\top) = \Omega$, where Ω is an $n \times n$ diagonal matrix with tth diagonal element ω_t^2. Let $\hat{\Omega}$ denote an $n \times n$ diagonal matrix with the squared residual $\hat{u}_t^2$ as the tth diagonal element. It has been known since the work of White (1980) that the matrix

$$(\hat{X}^\top \hat{X})^{-1} \hat{X}^\top \hat{\Omega} \hat{X}(\hat{X}^\top \hat{X})^{-1} \tag{1.37}$$

provides an estimator of $\text{var}(\hat{\beta})$, which can be used in place of the usual estimator, $s^2(\hat{X}^\top \hat{X})^{-1}$. Like the latter, this *heteroskedasticity-consistent covariance matrix estimator*, or *HCCME*, can be computed by means of an artificial regression. We will refer to this regression as the *heteroskedasticity-robust Gauss–Newton regression*, or *HRGNR*.

In order to derive the HRGNR, it is convenient to begin with a linear regression model $y = X\beta + u$, and to consider the criterion function

$$Q(\beta) = \tfrac{1}{2}(y - X\beta)^\top X(X^\top \Omega X)^{-1}X^\top(y - X\beta).$$

The negative of the gradient of this function with respect to β is

$$X^\top X(X^\top \Omega X)^{-1}X^\top(y - X\beta), \tag{1.38}$$

and its Hessian is the matrix

$$X^\top X(X^\top \Omega X)^{-1}X^\top X, \tag{1.39}$$

of which the inverse is the HCCME if we replace Ω by $\hat{\Omega}$. Equating the gradient to zero just yields the OLS estimator, since $X^\top X$ and $X^\top \Omega X$ are $k \times k$ nonsingular matrices.

Let V be an $n \times n$ diagonal matrix with tth diagonal element equal to ω_t; thus $V^2 = \Omega$. Consider the $n \times k$ regressor matrix R defined by

$$R = VX(X^\top V^2 X)^{-1}X^\top X = P_{VX}V^{-1}X, \tag{1.40}$$

where P_{VX} projects orthogonally on to the columns of VX. We have

$$R^\top R = X^\top X(X^\top \Omega X)^{-1}X^\top X, \tag{1.41}$$

which is just the Hessian (1.39). Let $U(\beta)$ be a diagonal matrix with tth diagonal element equal to $y_t - X_t\beta$. Then, if we define $R(\beta)$ as in (1.40) but with V replaced by $U(\beta)$, we find that $\hat{R}^\top \hat{R}$ is the HCCME (1.37).

In order to derive the regressand $r(\beta)$, note that, for condition (1') to be satisfied, we require

$$R^\top(\beta)r(\beta) = X^\top X(X^\top U^2(\beta)X)^{-1}X^\top(y - X\beta);$$

recall (1.38). Since the tth element of $U(\beta)$ is $y_t - X_t\beta$, this implies that

$$r(\beta) = U^{-1}(\beta)(y - X\beta) = \iota.$$

In the general nonlinear case, X becomes $X(\beta)$, and the HRGNR has the form

$$\iota = P_{U(\beta)X(\beta)}U^{-1}(\beta)X(\beta)b + \text{residuals}, \tag{1.42}$$

where now the tth diagonal element of $U(\beta)$ is $y_t - x_t(\beta)$. When $\beta = \hat{\beta}$, the vector of NLS estimates,

$$\begin{aligned}
\hat{r}^\top \hat{R} &= \iota^\top P_{\hat{U}\hat{X}}\hat{U}^{-1}\hat{X} \\
&= \iota^\top \hat{U}\hat{X}(\hat{X}^\top \hat{U}\hat{U}\hat{X})^{-1}\hat{X}^\top \hat{U}\hat{U}^{-1}\hat{X} \\
&= \hat{u}^\top \hat{X}(\hat{X}^\top \hat{\Omega}\hat{X})^{-1}\hat{X}^\top \hat{X} = 0,
\end{aligned} \tag{1.43}$$

because the NLS first-order conditions give $\hat{X}^\top\hat{u} = 0$. Thus condition (1) is satisfied for the nonlinear case. Condition (2) is satisfied by construction, as can be seen by putting hats on everything in (1.41).

For condition (3) to hold, regression (1.42) must satisfy the one-step property. We will only show that this property holds for linear models. Extending the argument to nonlinear models would be tedious but not difficult. In the linear case, evaluating (1.42) at an arbitrary $\acute{\beta}$ gives

$$\acute{b} = (X^\top\acute{U}^{-1}P_{\acute{U}X}\acute{U}^{-1}X)^{-1}X^\top\acute{U}^{-1}P_{\acute{U}X}\iota.$$

With a little algebra, it can be shown that this reduces to

$$\acute{b} = (X^\top X)^{-1}X^\top\acute{u} = (X^\top X)^{-1}X^\top(y - X\acute{\beta}) = \hat{\beta} - \acute{\beta}, \tag{1.44}$$

where $\hat{\beta}$ is the OLS estimator. It follows that the one-step estimator $\acute{\beta} + \acute{b}$ is equal to $\hat{\beta}$, as we wished to show. In the nonlinear case, of course, we obtain an asymptotic equality rather than an exact equality.

As with the ordinary GNR, the HRGNR is particularly useful for hypothesis testing. If we partition β as $[\beta_1 \mathbin{\vdots} \beta_2]$ and wish to test the r zero restrictions $\beta_2 = 0$, we need to run two versions of the regression and compute the difference between the two SSRs or ESSs. The two regressions are:

$$\iota = P_{\tilde{U}\tilde{X}}\tilde{U}^{-1}\tilde{X}_1 b_1 + \text{residuals, and} \tag{1.45}$$

$$\iota = P_{\tilde{U}\tilde{X}}\tilde{U}^{-1}\tilde{X}_1 b_1 + P_{\tilde{U}\tilde{X}}\tilde{U}^{-1}\tilde{X}_2 b_2 + \text{residuals.} \tag{1.46}$$

It is important to note that the first regression is *not* the HRGNR for the restricted model, because it uses the matrix $P_{\tilde{U}\tilde{X}}$ rather than the matrix $P_{\tilde{U}\tilde{X}_1}$. In consequence, the regressand in (1.45) will not be orthogonal to the regressors. This is why we need to run two artificial regressions. We could compute an ordinary F-statistic instead of the difference between the SSRs from (1.45) and (1.46), but there would be no advantage to doing so, since the F-form of the test merely divides by a stochastic quantity that tends to 1 asymptotically.

The HRGNR appears to be new. The trick of multiplying $X(\beta)$ by $U^{-1}(\beta)$ in order to obtain an HCCME by means of an OLS regression was used, in a different context, by Messer and White (1984). This trick does cause a problem in some cases. If any element on the diagonal of the matrix $U(\beta)$ is equal to 0, the inverse of that element cannot be computed. Therefore, it is necessary to replace any such element by a small, positive number before computing $U^{-1}(\beta)$.

A different, and considerably more limited, type of heteroskedasticity-robust GNR, which is applicable only to hypothesis testing, was first proposed by Davidson and MacKinnon (1985b). It was later rediscovered by Wooldridge (1990, 1991) and extended to handle other cases, including regression models with error terms that have autocorrelation as well as heteroskedasticity of unknown form.

It is possible to construct a variety of artificial regressions that provide different covariance matrix estimators for regression models. From (1.43) and (1.44), it follows that any artificial regression with regressand

$$r(\beta) = U^{-1}(\beta)(y - x(\beta))$$

and regressors

$$R(\beta) = P_{U(\beta)X(\beta)}U^{-1}(\beta)X(\beta)$$

satisfies properties (1) and (3) for the least-squares estimator, for any nonsingular matrix $U(\beta)$. Thus any sandwich covariance matrix estimator can be computed by choosing $U(\beta)$ appropriately; the estimator (1.37) is just one example. In fact, it is possible to develop artificial regressions that allow testing not only with a variety of different HCCMEs, but also with some sorts of heteroskedasticity and autocorrelation consistent (HAC) covariance matrix estimators. It is also a simple matter to use such estimators with modified versions of the artificial regression (1.35) used with models estimated by GMM.

9   Double-Length Regressions

Up to this point, the number of observations for all the artificial regressions we have studied has been equal to n, the number of observations in the data. In some cases, however, artificial regressions may have $2n$ or even $3n$ observations. This can happen whenever each observation makes two or more contributions to the criterion function.

The first *double-length artificial regression*, or *DLR*, was proposed by Davidson and MacKinnon (1984a). We will refer to it as *the* DLR, even though it is no longer the only artificial regression with $2n$ observations. The class of models to which the DLR applies is a subclass of the one used for GMM estimation. Such models may be written as

$$f_t(y_t, \theta) = \varepsilon_t, \quad t = 1, \ldots, n, \quad \varepsilon_t \sim \text{NID}(0, 1), \tag{1.47}$$

where, as before, each $f_t(\cdot)$ is a smooth function that depends on the data and on a k-vector of parameters θ. Here, however, the f_t are assumed to be normally distributed conditional on the information sets Ω_t, as well as being of mean zero, serially uncorrelated, and homoskedastic with variance 1. Further, f_t may depend only on a scalar dependent variable y_t, although lagged dependent variables are allowed as explanatory variables.

The class of models (1.47) is much less restrictive than it may at first appear to be. In particular, it is not essential that the error terms follow the normal distribution, although it is essential that they follow some specified, continuous distribution, which can be transformed into the standard normal distribution, so as to allow the model to be written in the form of (1.47). A great many models that involve transformations of the dependent variable can be put into the form of (1.47). For example, consider the Box–Cox regression model

$$\tau(y_t, \lambda) = \sum_{i=1}^{k} \beta_i \tau(X_{ti}, \lambda) + \sum_{j=1}^{l} \gamma_j Z_{tj} + u_t, \quad u_t \sim N(0, \sigma^2), \tag{1.48}$$

where $\tau(x, \lambda) = (x^\lambda - 1)/\lambda$ is the Box–Cox transformation (Box and Cox, 1964), y_t is the dependent variable, the X_{ti} are independent variables that are always positive, and the Z_{tj} are additional independent variables. We can rewrite (1.48) in the form of (1.47) by making the definition

$$f_t(y_t, \theta) = \frac{1}{\sigma}\left(\tau(y_t, \lambda) - \sum_{i=1}^{k} \beta_i \tau(X_{ti}, \lambda) - \sum_{j=1}^{l} \gamma_j Z_{tj}\right).$$

For the model (1.47), the contribution of the tth observation to the loglikelihood function $\ell(y, \theta)$ is

$$\ell_t(y_t, \theta) = -\tfrac{1}{2}\log(2\pi) - \tfrac{1}{2}f_t^2(y_t, \theta) + k_t(y_t, \theta),$$

where

$$k_t(y_t, \theta) \equiv \log\left|\frac{\partial f_t(y_t, \theta)}{\partial y_t}\right|$$

is a Jacobian term. Now let us make the definitions

$$F_{ti}(y_t, \theta) \equiv \frac{\partial f_t(y_t, \theta)}{\partial \theta_i} \quad \text{and} \quad K_{ti}(y_t, \theta) \equiv \frac{\partial k_t(y_t, \theta)}{\partial \theta_i}$$

and define $F(y, \theta)$ and $K(y, \theta)$ as the $n \times k$ matrices with typical elements $F_{ti}(y_t, \theta)$ and $K_{ti}(y_t, \theta)$ and typical rows $F_t(y, \theta)$ and $K_t(y, \theta)$. Similarly, let $f(y, \theta)$ be the n-vector with typical element $f_t(y_t, \theta)$.

The DLR, which has $2n$ artificial observations, may be written as

$$\begin{bmatrix} f(y, \theta) \\ \iota \end{bmatrix} = \begin{bmatrix} -F(y, \theta) \\ K(y, \theta) \end{bmatrix}b + \text{residuals.} \tag{1.49}$$

Since the gradient of $\ell(y, \theta)$ is

$$g(y, \theta) = -F^\top(y, \theta)f(y, \theta) + K^\top(y, \theta)\iota, \tag{1.50}$$

we see that regression (1.49) satisfies condition (1′). It can also be shown that it satisfies conditions (2) and (3), and thus it has all the properties of an artificial regression.

The DLR can be used for many purposes, including nonnested hypothesis tests of models with different functional forms (Davidson and MacKinnon, 1984a), tests of functional form (MacKinnon and Magee, 1990), and tests of linear and loglinear regressions against Box–Cox alternatives like (1.48) (Davidson and MacKinnon, 1985a). The latter application has recently been extended to models with AR(1) errors by Baltagi (1999). An accessible discussion of the DLR may be found in Davidson and MacKinnon (1988). When both the OPG regression and the DLR are available, the finite-sample performance of the latter always seems to be very much better than that of the former.

As we remarked earlier, the DLR is not the only artificial regression with $2n$ artificial observations. In particular, Orme (1995) showed how to construct such a regression for the widely-used tobit model, and Davidson and MacKinnon (1999) provided evidence that Orme's regression generally works very well. It makes sense that a double-length regression should be needed in this case, because the tobit loglikelihood is the sum of two summations, which are quite different in form. One summation involves all the observations for which the dependent variable is equal to zero, and the other involves all the observations for which it takes on a positive value.

10   An Artificial Regression for Binary Response Models

For binary response models such as the logit and probit models, there exists a very simple artificial regression that can be derived as an extension of the Gauss–Newton regression. It was independently suggested by Engle (1984) and Davidson and MacKinnon (1984b).

The object of a binary response model is to predict the probability that the binary dependent variable, y_t, is equal to 1 conditional on some information set Ω_t. A useful class of binary response models can be written as

$$E(y_t \mid \Omega_t) = \Pr(y_t = 1) = F(Z_t\beta). \tag{1.51}$$

Here Z_t is a row vector of explanatory variables that belong to Ω_t, β is the vector of parameters to be estimated, and $F(x)$ is the differentiable cumulative distribution function (CDF) of some scalar probability distribution. For the probit model, $F(x)$ is the standard normal CDF. For the logit model, $F(x)$ is the logistic function

$$\frac{\exp(x)}{1 + \exp(x)} = (1 + \exp(-x))^{-1}.$$

The loglikelihood function for this class of binary response models is

$$\ell(\beta) = \sum_{t=1}^{n} \left((1 - y_t) \log\left(1 - F(Z_t\beta)\right) + y_t \log\left(F(Z_t\beta)\right)\right), \tag{1.52}$$

If $f(x) = F'(x)$ is the density corresponding for the CDF $F(x)$, the first-order conditions for maximizing (1.52) are

$$\sum_{t=1}^{n} \frac{(y_t - \hat{F}_t)\hat{f}_t Z_{ti}}{\hat{F}_t(1 - \hat{F}_t)} = 0, \quad i = 1, \ldots, k, \tag{1.53}$$

where Z_{ti} is the tth component of Z_t, $\hat{f}_t \equiv f(Z_t\hat{\beta})$ and $\hat{F}_t \equiv F(Z_t\hat{\beta})$.

There is more than one way to derive the artificial regression that corresponds to the model (1.51). The easiest is to rewrite it in the form of the nonlinear regression model

$$y_t = F(Z_t\beta) + u_t. \tag{1.54}$$

The error term u_t here is evidently nonnormal and heteroskedastic. Because y_t is like a Bernoulli trial with probability p given by $F(Z_t\beta)$, and the variance of a Bernoulli trial is $p(1 - p)$, the variance of u_t is

$$v_t(\beta) \equiv F(Z_t\beta)(1 - F(Z_t\beta)). \tag{1.55}$$

The ordinary GNR for (1.54) would be

$$y_t - F(Z_t\beta) = f(Z_t\beta)Z_t b + \text{residual},$$

but the ordinary GNR is not appropriate because of the heteroskedasticity of the u_t. Multiplying both sides by the square root of the inverse of (1.55) yields the artificial regression

$$v_t^{-1/2}(\beta)(y_t - F(Z_t\beta)) = v_t^{-1/2}(\beta)f(Z_t\beta)Z_t b + \text{residual}. \tag{1.56}$$

This regression has all the usual properties of artificial regressions. It can be seen from (1.53) that it satisfies condition (1′). Because a typical element of the information matrix corresponding to (1.52) is

$$\mathcal{I}_{ij}(\beta) = \plim_{n\to\infty}\left(\frac{1}{n}\sum_{t=1}^{n} Z_{ti}Z_{tj}\frac{f(Z_t\beta)^2}{F(Z_t\beta)(1 - F(Z_t\beta))}\right),$$

it is not difficult to show that regression (1.56) satisfies condition (2). Finally, since (1.56) has the structure of a GNR, the arguments used in Section 3 show that it also satisfies condition (3), the one-step property.

As an artificial regression, (1.56) can be used for all the things that other artificial regressions can be used for. In particular, when it is evaluated at restricted estimates $\tilde{\beta}$, the explained sum of squares is an LM test statistic for testing the restrictions. The normalization of the regressand by its standard error means that other test statistics, such as nR^2 and the ordinary F-statistic for the coefficients on the regressors that correspond to the restricted parameters to be zero, are also asymptotically valid. However, they seem to have slightly poorer finite-sample properties than the ESS (Davidson and MacKinnon, 1984b). It is, of course, possible to extend regression (1.56) in various ways. For example, it has been extended to tests of the functional form of $F(x)$ by Thomas (1993) and to tests of ordered logit models by Murphy (1996).

11 CONCLUSION

In this chapter, we have introduced the concept of an artificial regression and discussed several examples. We have seen that artificial regressions can be useful for minimizing criterion functions, computing one-step estimates, calculating covariance matrix estimates, and computing test statistics. The last of these is probably the most common application. There is a close connection between the artificial regression for a given model and the asymptotic theory for that model. Therefore, as we saw in Section 6, artificial regressions can also be very useful for obtaining theoretical results.

Most of the artificial regressions we have discussed are quite well known. This is true of the Gauss–Newton regression discussed in Sections 3 and 4, the OPG regression discussed in Section 6, the double-length regression discussed in Section 9, and the regression for binary response models discussed in Section 10. However, the artificial regression for GMM estimation discussed in Section 7 does not appear to have been treated previously in published work, and we believe that the heteroskedasticity-robust GNR discussed in Section 8 is new.

References

Baltagi, B. (1999). Double length regressions for linear and log-linear regressions with AR(1) disturbances. *Statistical Papers* 4, 199–209.

Berndt, E.R., B.H. Hall, R.E. Hall, and J.A. Hausman (1974). Estimation and inference in nonlinear structural models. *Annals of Economic and Social Measurement* 3, 653–65.

Box, G.E.P., and D.R. Cox (1964). An analysis of transformations. *Journal of the Royal Statistical Society*, Series B 26, 211–52.

Chesher, A. (1983). The information matrix test: simplified calculation via a score test interpretation. *Economics Letters* 13, 45–8.

Chesher, A., and R. Spady (1991). Asymptotic expansions of the information matrix test statistic. *Econometrica* 59, 787–815.

Davidson, R., and J.G. MacKinnon (1981). Several tests for model specification in the presence of alternative hypotheses. *Econometrica* 49, 781–93.

Davidson, R., and J.G. MacKinnon (1984a). Model specification tests based on artificial linear regressions. *International Economic Review* 25, 485–502.

Davidson, R., and J.G. MacKinnon (1984b). Convenient Specification Tests for Logit and Probit Models. *Journal of Econometrics* 25, 241–62.

Davidson, R., and J.G. MacKinnon (1985a). Testing linear and loglinear regressions against Box–Cox alternatives. *Canadian Journal of Economics* 18, 499–517.

Davidson, R., and J.G. MacKinnon (1985b). Heteroskedasticity-robust tests in regression directions. *Annales de l'INSEE* 59/60, 183–218.

Davidson, R., and J.G. MacKinnon (1988). Double-length artificial regressions. *Oxford Bulletin of Economics and Statistics* 50, 203–17.

Davidson, R., and J.G. MacKinnon (1990). Specification tests based on artificial regressions. *Journal of the American Statistical Association* 85, 220–7.

Davidson, R., and J.G. MacKinnon (1992). A new form of the information matrix test. *Econometrica* 60, 145–57.

Davidson, R., and J.G. MacKinnon (1993). *Estimation and Inference in Econometrics*. New York: Oxford University Press.

Davidson, R., and J.G. MacKinnon (1999). Bootstrap testing in nonlinear models. *International Economic Review* 40, 487–508.

Delgado, M.A., and T. Stengos (1994). Semiparametric specification testing of non-nested econometric models. *Review of Economic Studies* 61, 291–303.

Engle, R.F. (1984). Wald, Likelihood Ratio and Lagrange Multiplier Tests in Econometrics. In Zvi Griliches and Michael D. Intriligator (eds.). *Handbook of Econometrics*, Vol. II, Amsterdam: North-Holland.

Godfrey, L.G. (1978). Testing against general autoregressive and moving average error models when the regressors include lagged dependent variables. *Econometrica* 46, 1293–301.

Godfrey, L.G., and M.R. Wickens (1981). Testing linear and log-linear regressions for functional form. *Review of Economic Studies* 48, 487–96.

Godfrey, L.G., M. McAleer, and C.R. McKenzie (1988). Variable addition and Lagrange Multiplier tests for linear and logarithmic regression models. *Review of Economics and Statistics* 70, 492–503.

Lancaster, T. (1984). The covariance matrix of the information matrix test. *Econometrica* 52, 1051–3.

MacKinnon, J.G., and L. Magee (1990). Transforming the dependent variable in regression models. *International Economic Review* 31, 315–39.

McCullough, B.D. (1999). Econometric software reliability: EViews, LIMDEP, SHAZAM, and TSP. *Journal of Applied Econometrics* 14, 191–202.

Messer, K., and H. White (1984). A note on computing the heteroskedasticity consistent covariance matrix using instrumental variable techniques. *Oxford Bulletin of Economics and Statistics* 46, 181–4.

Murphy, A. (1996). Simple LM tests of mis-specification for ordered logit models. *Economics Letters* 52, 137–41.

Orme, C. (1995). On the use of artificial regressions in certain microeconometric models. *Econometric Theory* 11, 290–305.

Press, W.H., S.A. Teukolsky, W.T. Vetterling, and B.P. Flannery (1992). *Numerical Recipes in C*, 2nd edn., Cambridge: Cambridge University Press.

Thomas, J. (1993). On testing the logistic assumption in binary dependent variable models. *Empirical Economics* 18, 381–92.

White, H. (1980). A heteroskedasticity-consistent covariance matrix estimator and a direct test for heteroskedasticity. *Econometrica* 48, 817–38.

Wooldridge, J.M. (1990). A unified approach to robust, regression-based specification tests. *Econometric Theory* 6, 17–43.

Wooldridge, J.M. (1991). On the application of robust, regression-based diagnostics to models of conditional means and conditional variances. *Journal of Econometrics* 47, 5–46.

CHAPTER TWO

General Hypothesis Testing

Anil K. Bera and Gamini Premaratne*

1 INTRODUCTION

The history of statistical hypothesis testing is, indeed, very long. Neyman and Pearson (1933) traced its origin to Bayes (1763). However, systematic applications of hypothesis testing began only after the publication of Karl Pearson's (1900) goodness-of-fit test, which is regarded as one of the 20 most important scientific breakthroughs in this century. In terms of the development of statistical methods, Ronald Fisher took up where Pearson left off. Fisher (1922) can be regarded as the analytical beginning of statistical methods. In his paper Fisher advocated the use of maximum likelihood estimation and provided the general theory of parametric statistical inference. In order to develop various statistical techniques, Fisher (1922) also introduced such basic concepts as consistency, efficiency, and sufficiency that are now part of our day-to-day vocabulary. Fisher, however, was not particularly interested in testing *per se*, and he occupied himself mostly in solving problems of estimation and sampling distributions. Neyman and Pearson (1928) suggested the likelihood ratio (LR) test, but that was mostly based on intuitive arguments. The foundation of the theory of hypothesis testing was laid by Neyman and Pearson (1933), and for the first time the concept of "optimal test" was introduced through the analysis of "power function." The result was the celebrated Neyman–Pearson (N–P) lemma. This lemma provides a way to find the most powerful (MP) and uniformly most powerful (UMP) tests. Neyman and Pearson (1936) generalized the basic N–P lemma to restrict optimal tests to suitable subclasses since the UMP test rarely exists. On the basis of Neyman–Pearson's foundation in testing, several general test principles were gradually developed, such as Neyman's (1937) smooth test, Wald (1943), Rao's (1948) score test and Neyman's (1959) $C(\alpha)$ test. During the last four decades no new fundamental test principle has emerged. However, econometricians have produced a large number of general test procedures such as those in Hausman (1978), Newey (1985), Tauchen (1985), and White (1982). Also, simultaneously, econometricians applied the basic test principles, most notably Rao's score test, and developed model diagnostic and evaluation techniques for the basic assumptions such as serial independence, homoskedasticity, and normality for the regression models, and these procedures are now routinely used in applied econometrics.

The aim of this chapter is very modest. Our main purpose is to explain the basic test principles with examples in a simple way and discuss how they have been used by econometricians to develop procedures to suit their needs. In the next section, we review the general test procedures suggested in the statistics literature. In Section 3, we discuss some standard tests in econometrics and demonstrate how they are linked to some basic principles. The last section offers some concluding remarks. At the outset we should state that there is nothing original about the material covered in this chapter. Students of econometrics are sometimes not aware of the origin of many of the tests they use. Here, we try to provide intuitive descriptions of some test principles with simple examples and to show that various econometric model evaluations and diagnostic procedures have their origins in some of the basic statistical test principles. Much of what we cover can be found, though in a scattered fashion, in Lehmann (1986, 1999), Godfrey (1988), Bera and Ullah (1991), Davidson and MacKinnon (1993), Gouriéroux and Monfort (1995), Bera (2000), Bera and Billias (2000) and Rao (2000).

2 SOME TEST PRINCIPLES SUGGESTED IN THE STATISTICS LITERATURE

We start by introducing some notation and concepts. Suppose we have n independent observations $y_1, y_2, \ldots, y_n$ on a random variable Y with density function $f(y; \theta)$, where θ is a $p \times 1$ parameter vector with $\theta \in \Theta \subset \Re^p$. It is assumed that $f(y; \theta)$ satisfies the regularity conditions stated in Rao (1973, p. 364) and Serfling (1980, p. 144). The likelihood function is given by

$$L(\theta, \text{y}) \equiv L(\theta) = \prod_{i=1}^{n} f(y_i; \theta), \tag{2.1}$$

where $\text{y} = (y_1, y_2, \ldots, y_n)'$ denotes the sample.

Suppose we are interested in testing a simple hypothesis $H_0 : \theta = \theta_0$ against another simple hypothesis $H_1 : \theta = \theta_1$. Let S denote the sample space. In standard test procedures, S is partitioned into two regions, ω and its compliment ω^c. We reject the null hypothesis if the sample $\text{y} \in \omega$; otherwise, we do not reject H_0. Let us define a test function $\phi(\text{y})$ as: $\phi(\text{y}) = 1$ when we reject H_0, and $\phi(\text{y}) = 0$ when we do not reject H_0. Then,

$$\phi(\text{y}) = 1 \quad \text{if} \quad \text{y} \in \omega$$
$$= 0 \quad \text{if} \quad \text{y} \in \omega^c. \tag{2.2}$$

Therefore, the probability of rejecting H_0 is given by

$$\gamma(\theta) = E_\theta[\phi(y)] = \int \phi(y)L(\theta)dy, \tag{2.3}$$

where E_θ denotes expectation when $f(y; \theta)$ is the probability density function. Type-I and type-II error probabilities are given by, respectively,

$$\Pr(\text{Reject } H_0 \mid H_0 \text{ is true}) = E_{\theta_0}[\phi(y)] = \gamma(\theta_0) \tag{2.4}$$

and

$$\Pr(\text{Accept } H_0 \mid H_1 \text{ is true}) = E_{\theta_1}[1 - \phi(y)] = 1 - \gamma(\theta_1). \tag{2.5}$$

Note that $\gamma(\theta_1)$ is the probability of making a correct decision and it is called the power of the test. An ideal situation would be if we could simultaneously minimize $\gamma(\theta_0)$ and maximize $\gamma(\theta_1)$. However, because of the inverse relationship between the type-I and type-II error probabilities and also because Neyman and Pearson (1933) wanted to avoid committing the error of first kind and did not want $\gamma(\theta_0)$ to exceed a preassigned value, they suggested maximizing the power $\gamma(\theta_1)$ after keeping $\gamma(\theta_0)$ at a low value, say α, that is, maximize $E_{\theta_1}[\phi(y)]$ subject to $E_{\theta_0}[\phi(y)] = \alpha$ [see also Neyman, 1980, pp. 4–5]. A test $\phi^*(y)$ is called a most powerful (MP) test if $E_{\theta_1}[\phi^*(y)] \geq E_{\theta_1}[\phi(y)]$ for any $\phi(y)$ satisfying $E_{\theta_0}[\phi(y)] = \alpha$. If an MP test maximizes power uniformly in $\theta \in \Theta_1 \subset \Theta$, the test is called a uniformly most powerful (UMP) test. A UMP test, however, rarely exists, and therefore, it is necessary to restrict optimal tests to a suitable subclass by requiring the test to satisfy other criteria such as local optimality, unbiasedness, and invariance, etc. For the N–P Lemma, there is only one side condition, that is, the size (α) of the test. Once the test is restricted further, in addition to the size there will be more than one side condition, and one must use the generalized N–P lemma given in Neyman and Pearson (1936).

2.1   Neyman–Pearson generalized lemma and its applications

The lemma can be stated as follows:

Let $g_1, g_2, \ldots, g_m, g_{m+1}$ be integrable functions and ϕ be a test function over S such that $0 \leq \phi \leq 1$, and

$$\int \phi g_i dy = c_i \quad i = 1, 2, \ldots, m, \tag{2.6}$$

where $c_1, c_2, \ldots, c_m$ are given constants. Further, let there exist a ϕ^* and constants $k_1, k_2, \ldots, k_m$ such that ϕ^* satisfies (2.6), and

$$\phi^* = 1 \quad \text{if} \quad g_{m+1} > \sum_{i=1}^{m} k_i g_i$$

$$= 0 \quad \text{if} \quad g_{m+1} < \sum_{i=1}^{m} k_i g_i \tag{2.7}$$

then,

$$\int \phi^* g_{m+1} dy \geq \int \phi g_{m+1} dy. \tag{2.8}$$

For a proof, see, for example, Rao (1973, pp. 446–8) and Lehmann (1986, pp. 96–101). Several results can be derived from the above lemma as discussed below.

N–P LEMMA AND THE LIKELIHOOD RATIO TEST

To obtain the basic N–P lemma, we put $m = 1$, $g_1 = L(\theta_0)$, $g_2 = L(\theta_1)$, $c_1 = \alpha$ and $k_1 = k$. Then among all test functions $\phi(y)$ having size α, that is,

$$\int \phi(y) L(\theta_0) dy = \alpha, \tag{2.9}$$

the function $\phi^*(y)$ defined as

$$\phi^*(y) = 1 \quad \text{when} \quad L(\theta_1) > kL(\theta_0)$$

$$= 0 \quad \text{when} \quad L(\theta_1) < kL(\theta_0),$$

and also satisfying (2.9), we will have

$$\int \phi^*(y) L(\theta_1) dy \geq \int \phi(y) L(\theta_1) dy, \tag{2.10}$$

that is, $\phi^*(y)$ will provide the MP test. Therefore, in terms of critical region,

$$\omega = \left\{ y \left| \frac{L(\theta_1)}{L(\theta_0)} > k \right. \right\}, \tag{2.11}$$

where k is such that $\Pr\{\omega \,|\, H_0\} = \alpha$, is the MP critical region.

The N–P lemma also provides the logical basis for the LR test. To see this, consider a general form of null hypothesis, $H_0 : h(\theta) = c$ where $h(\theta)$ is an $r \times 1$ vector function of θ with $r \leq p$ and c a known constant vector. It is assumed that $H(\theta) = \frac{\partial h(\theta)}{\partial \theta}$ has full column rank, that is, rank$[H(\theta)] = r$. We denote the maximum likelihood estimator (MLE) of θ by $\hat{\theta}$, and by $\tilde{\theta}$, the restricted MLE of θ, that is,

Therefore, we reject H_0 if $y > k$, where $k = Z_\alpha$, the upper α percent cut-off point of standard normal. The power of this test is $1 - \Phi(Z_\alpha - \mu)$, where $\Phi(\cdot)$ is the distribution function of the standard normal density. And as $\mu \to \infty$, the power of the test goes to 1. Therefore, the test $y > Z_\alpha$ is not only LMP, it is also uniformly most powerful (UMP) for all $\mu > 0$.

Now let us consider what happens to the power of this test when $\mu < 0$. The power function $\Pr(y > Z_\alpha \mid \mu < 0)$ still remains $1 - \Phi(Z_\alpha - \mu)$, but it is now less than α, the size of the test. Therefore, the test is not MP for all $\mu \neq 0$. To get an MP test for *two-sided* alternatives, we need to add unbiasedness as an extra condition in our requirements.

LOCALLY MOST POWERFUL UNBIASED (LMPU) TEST

A test $\phi(y)$ of size α is unbiased for $H_0 : \theta \in \Omega_0$ against $H_1 : \theta \in \Omega_1$ if $E_\theta[\phi(y)] \leq \alpha$ for $\theta \in \Omega_0$ and $E_\theta[\phi(y)] \geq \alpha$ for $\theta \in \Omega_1$. Suppose we want to find an LMPU test for testing $H_0 : \theta = \theta_0$ against $H_1 : \theta \neq \theta_0$. By expanding the power function $\gamma(\theta)$ in (2.3) around $\theta = \theta_0$ for local alternatives, we have

$$\gamma(\theta) = \gamma(\theta_0) + (\theta - \theta_0)\gamma'(\theta_0) + \frac{(\theta - \theta_0)^2}{2}\gamma''(\theta_0) + o(n^{-1})$$

$$= \alpha + \frac{(\theta - \theta_0)^2}{2}\gamma''(\theta_0) + o(n^{-1}). \tag{2.22}$$

Unbiasedness requires that the "power" should be minimum at $\theta = \theta_0$, and, hence, $\gamma'(\theta_0) = 0$. To maximize the local power, we, therefore, need to maximize $\gamma''(\theta_0)$ for both $\theta > \theta_0$ and $\theta < \theta_0$, and this leads to the LMPU test. Neyman and Pearson (1936, p. 9) called the corresponding critical region "type-A region," and this requires maximization of $\gamma''(\theta_0)$ subject to two side-conditions $\gamma(\theta_0) = \alpha$ and $\gamma'(\theta_0) = 0$. In the N–P generalized lemma, let us put $m = 2$, $c_1 = 0$, $c_2 = \alpha$, $g_1 = \frac{\partial L(\theta_0)}{\partial \theta}$, $g_2 = L(\theta_0)$ and $g_3 = \frac{\partial^2 L(\theta_0)}{\partial \theta^2}$, then from (2.7) and (2.8), the optimal test function $\phi^* = 1$ if

$$\frac{\partial^2 L(\theta_0)}{\partial \theta^2} > k_1 \frac{\partial L(\theta_0)}{\partial \theta} + k_2 L(\theta_0) \tag{2.23}$$

and $\phi^* = 0$, otherwise. Critical region (2.23) can be expressed in terms of the derivatives of the loglikelihood function as

$$\frac{\partial^2 l(\theta_0)}{\partial \theta^2} + \left[\frac{\partial l(\theta_0)}{\partial \theta}\right]^2 > k_1 \frac{\partial l(\theta_0)}{\partial \theta} + k_2. \tag{2.24}$$

In terms of the score function $s(\theta) = \partial l(\theta)/\partial \theta$ and its derivative $s'(\theta)$, (2.24) can be written as

$$s'(\theta_0) + [s(\theta_0)]^2 > k_1 s(\theta_0) + k_2. \tag{2.25}$$

Example 2. (*continued*) For this example, consider now testing $H_0 : \mu = 0$ against $H_1 : \mu \neq 0$. It is easy to see that $s(\theta_0) = y$, $s'(\theta_0) = -1$. Therefore, a uniformly most powerful unbiased test (UMPU) will reject H_0 if

$$y^2 + k_1' y + k_2' > 0$$

or

$$y < k_1'' \quad \text{and} \quad y > k_2'',$$

where k_1', k_2', k_1'', and k_2'' are some constants determined from satisfying the size and unbiasedness conditions. After some simplification, the LMPU principle leads to a symmetric critical region of the form $y < -Z_{\alpha/2}$ and $y > Z_{\alpha/2}$.

In many situations, $s'(\theta)$ can be expressed as a linear function of the score $s(\theta)$. For those cases, LMPU tests will be based on the score function only, just like the LMP test in (2.15). Also for certain test problems $s(\theta_0)$ vanishes, then from (2.25) we see that an LMPU test can be constructed using the second derivative of the loglikelihood function.

Example 3. (Godfrey, 1988, p. 92). Let $y_i \sim N(0, (1 + \theta^2 z_i))$, $i = 1, 2, \ldots, n$, where z_is are given positive constants. We are interested in testing $H_0 : \theta = 0$, that is, y_i has constant variance. The loglikelihood function and the score function are, respectively, given by

$$l(\theta) = \text{const} - \frac{1}{2} \sum_{i=1}^{n} \ln(1 + \theta^2 z_i) - \frac{1}{2} \sum_{i=1}^{n} y_i^2 / (1 + \theta^2 z_i), \tag{2.26}$$

and

$$s(\theta) = \frac{\partial}{\partial \theta} l(\theta) = -\theta \sum_{i=1}^{n} \left[\frac{z_i}{(1 + \theta^2 z_i)} - \frac{z_i y_i^2}{(1 + \theta^2 z_i)^2} \right]. \tag{2.27}$$

It is clear that $s(\theta) = 0$ at $H_0 : \theta = 0$. However,

$$s'(\theta) \big|_{\theta=0} = \frac{\partial s(\theta)}{\partial \theta} \bigg|_{\theta=0} = \frac{1}{2} \sum_{i=1}^{n} z_i (y_i^2 - 1) \tag{2.28}$$

and from (2.25), the LMPU test could be based on the above quantity. In fact, it can be shown that (Godfrey, 1988, p. 92)

$$\frac{\sum_{i=1}^{n} z_i (y_i^2 - 1)}{\sqrt{2 \sum_{i=1}^{n} z_i^2}} \xrightarrow{d} N(0, 1). \tag{2.29}$$

where $\xrightarrow{d}$ denotes convergence in distribution.

NEYMAN'S SMOOTH TEST

Pearson (1900) suggested his goodness-of-fit test to see whether an assumed probability model adequately described the data at hand. Suppose we divide data into j-classes and the probability of the jth class is θ_j, $j = 1, 2, \ldots, p$, and $\sum_{j=1}^{p} \theta_j = 1$. Suppose according to the assumed probability model $\theta_j = \theta_{j0}$; therefore, our null hypothesis could be stated as $H_0 : \theta_j = \theta_{j0}$, $j = 1, 2, \ldots, p$. Let n_j denote the observed frequency of the jth class, with $\sum_{j=1}^{p} n_j = n$. Pearson (1900) suggested the goodness-of-fit statistic

$$P = \sum_{j=1}^{p} \frac{(n_j - n\theta_{j0})^2}{n\theta_{j0}} = \sum_{j=1}^{p} \frac{(O_j - E_j)^2}{E_j}, \tag{2.30}$$

where O_j and E_j denote, respectively, the observed and expected frequencies for the jth class.

Neyman's (1937) criticism to Pearson's test was that (2.30) does not depend on the order of positive and negative differences $(O_j - E_j)$. Neyman (1980) gives an extreme example represented by two cases. In the first, the signs of the consecutive differences $(O_j - E_j)$ are not the same, and in the other, there is run of, say, a number of "negative" differences, followed by a sequence of "positive" differences. These two possibilities might lead to similar values of P, but Neyman (1937, 1980) argued that in the second case the goodness-of-fit should be more in doubt, even if the value of P happens to be small.

Suppose we want to test the null hypothesis (H_0) that $f(y; \theta)$ is the true density function for the random variable Y. The specification of $f(y; \theta)$ will be *different* depending on the problem on hand. Let us denote the alternative hypothesis as $H_1 : Y \sim g(y)$. Neyman (1937) transformed any hypothesis-testing problem of this type to testing only *one kind of hypothesis*. Let $z = F(y)$ denote the distribution function of Y, then the density of the random variable Z is given by

$$h(z) = g(y)\frac{dy}{dz} = \frac{g(y)}{f(y; \theta)}, \tag{2.31}$$

when $H_0 : Y \sim f(y; \theta)$, then

$$h(z) = 1 \quad 0 < z < 1. \tag{2.32}$$

Therefore, testing H_0 is equivalent to testing whether Z has uniform distribution in the interval $(0, 1)$, irrespective of the specification of $f(y; \theta)$. As for the specific alternative to the uniform distribution, Neyman (1937) suggested a *smooth* class. By smooth alternatives Neyman meant those densities that have few intersections with the null density function and that are close to the null. He specified the alternative density as

$$h(z) = C(\delta)\exp\left[\sum_{j=1}^{r} \delta_j \pi_j(z)\right], \tag{2.33}$$

where $C(\delta)$ is the constant of integration that depends on the δ_j values, and $\pi_j(z)$ are orthogonal polynomials satisfying

$$\int_0^1 \pi_j(z)\pi_k(z)dy = 1 \quad \text{for} \quad j = k$$

$$= 0 \quad \text{for} \quad j \neq k. \tag{2.34}$$

Under the hypothesis $H_0 : \delta_1 = \delta_2 = \ldots = \delta_r = 0$, $C(\delta) = 1$ and $h(z)$ in (2.33) reduces to the uniform density (2.32). Using the generalized N–P lemma, Neyman (1937) derived a locally most powerful symmetric unbiased test for H_0, and the test statistic is given by

$$\psi_r^2 = \sum_{j=1}^{r} \frac{1}{n}\left[\sum_{i=1}^{n} \pi_j(z_i)\right]^2. \tag{2.35}$$

The test is symmetric in the sense that the asymptotic power of the test depends only on the "distance" $\sum_{j=1}^{r}\delta_j^2$ between the null and alternative hypotheses.

2.2 Tests based on score function and Wald's test

We have already discussed Rao's (1948) score principle of testing as an LMP test in (2.15) for the scalar parameter $\theta(p = 1)$. For the $p \geq 2$ case, there will be scores for each individual parameter, and the problem is to combine them in an "optimal" way. Let $H_0 : \theta = \theta_0$, where now $\theta = (\theta_1, \theta_2, \ldots, \theta_p)'$ and $\theta_0 = (\theta_{10}, \theta_{20}, \ldots, \theta_{p0})'$, and the (local) alternative hypothesis be as $H_1 : \theta = \theta_\delta$, where $\theta_\delta = (\theta_{10} + \delta_1, \theta_{20} + \delta_2, \ldots, \theta_{p0} + \delta_p)'$. The proportionate change in the loglikelihood function for moving from θ_0 to θ_δ is given by $\delta's(\theta_0)$, where $\delta = (\delta_1, \delta_2, \ldots, \delta_p)'$ and $s(\theta_0)$ is the score function evaluated at $\theta = \theta_0$. Let us define the information matrix as

$$I(\theta) = -E\left[\frac{\partial^2 l(\theta)}{\partial\theta\partial\theta'}\right]. \tag{2.36}$$

Then, the asymptotic variance of $\delta's(\theta_0)$ is $\delta'I(\theta_0)\delta$; and, if δ' were known, a test could be based on

$$\frac{[\delta's(\theta_0)]^2}{\delta'I(\theta_0)\delta}, \tag{2.37}$$

which under H_0 will be asymptotically distributed as χ_1^2. To eliminate the δ's and to obtain a linear function that would yield maximum discrimination, Rao (1948) maximized (2.37) with respect to δ and obtained[2]

$$\sup_\delta \frac{[\delta's(\theta_0)]^2}{\delta'I(\theta_0)\delta} = s(\theta_0)'I(\theta_0)^{-1}s(\theta_0) \tag{2.38}$$

with optimal value $\delta = I(\theta_0)^{-1}s(\theta_0)$. In a sense, $\delta = I(\theta_0)^{-1}s(\theta_0)$ signals the *optimal* direction of the alternative hypothesis that we should consider. For example, when $p = 1$, $\delta = +1$ or -1, as we have seen in (2.16). Asymptotically, under the null, the statistic in (2.38) follows a χ_p^2 distribution in contrast to (2.37), which follows χ_1^2. When the null hypothesis is composite, like $H_0 : h(\theta) = c$ with $r \le p$ restrictions, the general form of Rao's score (RS) statistic is

$$RS = s(\tilde{\theta})' I(\tilde{\theta})^{-1}s(\tilde{\theta}), \tag{2.39}$$

where $\tilde{\theta}$ is the restricted MLE of θ. Under $H_0 : RS \xrightarrow{d} \chi_r^2$. Therefore, we observe *two* optimality principles behind the RS test; first, in terms of the LMP test as given in (2.15), and second, in deriving the "optimal" direction for the multi-parameter case.

Rao (1948) suggested the score test as an alternative to the Wald (1943) statistic, which for testing $H_0 : h(\theta) = c$ is given by

$$W = (h(\hat{\theta}) - c)'[H(\hat{\theta})' I(\hat{\theta})^{-1}H(\hat{\theta})]^{-1}(h(\hat{\theta}) - c). \tag{2.40}$$

Rao (1948, p. 53) stated that his test "besides being simpler than Wald's has some theoretical advantages," such as invariance under transformation of parameters. Rao (2000) recollects the motivation and background behind the development of the score test.

The three statistics LR, W, and RS given, respectively in (2.12), (2.40), and (2.39) are referred to as the "holy trinity." We can look at these statistics in terms of different measures of distance between the null and alternative hypotheses. When the null hypothesis is true, we would expect the restricted and unrestricted MLEs of θ, $\hat{\theta}$, and $\tilde{\theta}$ to be close, and likewise the loglikelihood functions. Therefore the LR statistic measures the distance through the loglikelihood function and is based on the the difference $l(\hat{\theta}) - l(\tilde{\theta})$. To see the intuitive basis of the score test, note that $s(\hat{\theta})$ is zero by construction, and we should expect $s(\tilde{\theta})$ to be close to zero if H_0 is true. And hence the RS test exploits the distance through the score function $s(\theta)$ and can be viewed as being based on $s(\tilde{\theta}) - s(\hat{\theta})$. Lastly, the W test considers the distance directly in terms of $h(\theta)$ and is based on $[h(\hat{\theta}) - c] - [h(\tilde{\theta}) - c]$, where by construction $h(\tilde{\theta}) = c$. This reveals a duality between the Wald and score tests. At the unrestricted MLE $\hat{\theta}$, $s(\hat{\theta}) = 0$, and the Wald test checks whether $h(\hat{\theta})$ is away from c. On the other hand, at the restricted MLE $\tilde{\theta}$, $h(\tilde{\theta}) = c$ by construction, and the score test verifies whether $s(\tilde{\theta})$ is far from a null vector.[3]

Example 4. Consider a multinomial distribution with p classes and let the probability of an observation belonging to the jth class be θ_j, so that $\sum_{j=1}^p \theta_j = 1$. Denote the frequency of jth class by n_j with $\sum_{j=1}^p n_j = n$. We are interested in testing $H_0 : \theta_j = \theta_{j0}, j = 1, 2, \ldots, p$, where θ_{j0}s are known constants. It can be shown that for this problem the score statistic is given by

$$s(\theta_0)' I(\theta_0)^{-1}s(\theta_0) = \sum_{j=1}^p \frac{(n_j - n\theta_{j0})^2}{n\theta_{j0}}, \tag{2.41}$$

where $\theta_0 = (\theta_{10}, \ldots, \theta_{p0})'$. Therefore, the RS statistic is the same as Pearson's P given in (2.30). It is quite a coincidence that Pearson (1900) suggested a score test mostly based on intuitive grounds almost 50 years before Rao (1948). For this problem, the other two test statistics LR and W are given by

$$LR = 2\sum_{i=1}^{p} n_j \ln\left(\frac{n_j}{n\theta_{j0}}\right) = \sum_{j=1}^{p} O_j \ln\left(\frac{O_j}{E_j}\right) \tag{2.42}$$

and

$$W = \sum_{j=1}^{p} \frac{(n_j - n\theta_{j0})^2}{n_j} = \sum_{j=1}^{p} \frac{(O_j - E_j)^2}{O_j}. \tag{2.43}$$

The equivalence of the score and Pearson's tests and their local optimality has not been fully recognized in the statistics literature. Many researchers considered the LR statistic to be superior to P. Asymptotically, both statistics are locally optimal and equivalent, and, in terms of finite sample performance, P performs better [see for example Rayner and Best, 1989, pp. 26–7].

The three tests LR, W, and RS are based on the (efficient) maximum likelihood estimates. When consistent (rather than efficient) estimators are used there is another attractive way to construct a score-type test, which is due to Neyman (1954, 1959). In the literature this is known as the $C(\alpha)$, or effective score or Neyman–Rao test. To follow Neyman (1959), let us partition θ as $\theta = [\theta_1', \theta_2]'$, where θ_2 is a scalar and test $H_0 : \theta_2 = \theta_{20}$. Therefore, θ_1 is the nuisance parameter with dimension $(p - 1) \times 1$. Neyman's fundamental contribution is the *derivation* of an asymptotically optimal test using consistent estimators of the nuisance parameters. He achieved this in two steps. First he started with a class of function $g(y; \theta_1, \theta_2)$ satisfying regularity condition of Cramér (1946, p. 500).[4]

For simplicity let us start with a normed Cramér function, that is, $g(y; \theta_1, \theta_2)$ has zero mean and unit variance. We denote $\sqrt{n}$-consistent estimator of θ under H_0 by $\theta^+ = (\theta_1^{+'}, \theta_{20})'$. Neyman asked the question what should be the property of $g(\cdot)$ such that replacing θ by θ^+ in the test statistic would not make any difference asymptotically, and his Theorem 1 proved that $g(\cdot)$ must satisfy

$$\text{Cov}[g(y; \theta_1, \theta_{20}), s_{1j}(y; \theta_1, \theta_{20})] = 0, \tag{2.44}$$

where $s_{1j} = \frac{\partial l(\theta)}{\partial \theta_{1j}}$, i.e. the score for jth component of θ_1, $j = 1, 2, \ldots, p - 1$. In other words, the function $g(y; \theta)$ should be orthogonal to $s_1 = \frac{\partial l(\theta)}{\partial \theta_1}$. Starting from a normed Cramér function let us construct

$$\bar{g}(y; \theta_1, \theta_{20}) = g(y; \theta_1, \theta_{20}) - \sum_{j=1}^{p-1} b_j s_{1j}(\theta_1, \theta_{20}), \tag{2.45}$$

where b_j, $j = 1, 2, \ldots, p - 1$, are the regression coefficients of regressing $g(y; \theta_1, \theta_{20})$ on $s_{11}, s_{12}, \ldots, s_{1p-1}$. Denote by $\sigma^2(\theta_1, \theta_{20})$ the minimum variance of $\bar{g}(y; \theta_1, \theta_{20})$, and define

John Maynard Keynes was skeptical about applying statistical techniques to economic data, as can be seen in his review of Tinbergen's book. It was left to Haavelmo (1944) to successfully defend the application of statistical methodologies to economic data within the framework of the *joint* probability distribution of variables. Trygve Haavelmo was clearly influenced by Jerzy Neyman,[6] and Haavelmo (1944) contains a seven page account of the Neyman–Pearson theory. He clearly stated the limitation of the standard hypothesis testing approach and explicitly mentioned that a test is, in general, constructed on the basis of a given fixed set of possible alternatives that he called a priori admissible hypotheses. And whenever this priori admissible set deviates from the data generating process, the test loses its optimality [for more on this see (Bera and Yoon, 1993) and (Bera, 2000)]. Haavelmo, however, did not himself formally apply the Neyman–Pearson theory to econometric testing problems. That was left to Anderson (1948) and Durbin and Watson (1950).

3.1   The Neyman–Pearson lemma and the Durbin–Watson test

The *first* formal specification test in econometrics, the Durbin–Watson (DW) (1950) test for autocorrelation in the regression model has its foundation in the UMP test principle via a theorem of Anderson (1948). Most econometrics textbooks provide a detail discussion of the DW test but do not mention its origin. Let us consider the standard linear regression model with autocorrelated errors:

$$y_t = x_t'\beta + \varepsilon_t \tag{2.54}$$

$$\varepsilon_t = \rho\varepsilon_{t-1} + u_t, \tag{2.55}$$

where y_t is the tth observation on the dependent variable, x_t is the tth observation on k strictly exogenous variables, $|\rho| < 1$ and $u_t \sim \text{iid}N(0, \sigma^2)$, $t = 1, 2, \ldots, n$. The problem is testing $H_0 : \rho = 0$. Using the N–P lemma, Anderson (1948) showed that UMP tests for serial correlation can be obtained against one-sided alternatives.[7] A special case of Anderson's lemma is as follows:

If the probability density of ε can be written in the form,

$$f(\varepsilon) = \text{const. } \exp\left[-\frac{1}{2\sigma^2}\{(1 + \rho^2)\varepsilon'\varepsilon - 2\rho\varepsilon'D\varepsilon\}\right], \tag{2.56}$$

where $\varepsilon = (\varepsilon_1, \varepsilon_2, \ldots, \ldots \varepsilon_n)'$ and columns of $X = (x_1, x_2, \ldots, x_n)$ are generated by k eigen-vectors of D, the UMP test of $H_0 : \rho = 0$ against $H_1 : \rho > 0$ is given by $a > a_0$, where

$$a = \frac{\hat{\varepsilon}'D\hat{\varepsilon}}{\hat{\varepsilon}'\hat{\varepsilon}}, \tag{2.57}$$

and a_0 is such that $\Pr[a > a_0 \mid \rho = 0] = \alpha$, the size of the test. Here $\hat{\varepsilon} = (\hat{\varepsilon}_1, \hat{\varepsilon}_2, \ldots, \hat{\varepsilon}_n)'$ with $\hat{\varepsilon}_t = y_t - x_t \hat{\beta}$ and $\hat{\beta}$ is the ordinary least squares (OLS) residual vector.

For the model given in (2.54) and (2.55), the probability distribution of ε, that is, the likelihood function is given by[8]

$$\text{const. } \exp\left[-\frac{1}{2\sigma^2}\left\{ (1 + \rho^2)\varepsilon'\varepsilon - \rho^2(\varepsilon_1^2 + \varepsilon_n^2) - 2\rho \sum_{t=2}^{n} \varepsilon_t \varepsilon_{t-1} \right\} \right]. \tag{2.58}$$

Comparing (2.56) and (2.58), we see that the latter cannot be written in the form of the former. Durbin and Watson (1950) approached the problem from the opposite direction and selected a form of D in such a way that (2.56) becomes "close" to (2.58). They chose $D = I_n - \frac{1}{2}A$, where

$$A = \begin{bmatrix} 1 & -1 & 0 & 0 & \cdots & 0 & 0 & 0 \\ -1 & 2 & -1 & 0 & \cdots & 0 & 0 & 0 \\ 0 & -1 & 2 & -1 & \cdots & 0 & 0 & 0 \\ \vdots & \vdots & \vdots & \vdots & \cdots & \vdots & \vdots & \vdots \\ 0 & 0 & 0 & 0 & \cdots & -1 & 2 & -1 \\ 0 & 0 & 0 & 0 & \cdots & 0 & -1 & 1 \end{bmatrix} \tag{2.59}$$

so that

$$\varepsilon'D\varepsilon = \sum_{t=1}^{n} \varepsilon_t^2 - \frac{1}{2}\sum_{t=2}^{n} (\varepsilon_t - \varepsilon_{t-1})^2$$

$$= \frac{1}{2}(\varepsilon_1^2 + \varepsilon_n^2) + \sum_{t=2}^{n} \varepsilon_t \varepsilon_{t-1}. \tag{2.60}$$

Then, the density (2.56) reduces to

$$f(\varepsilon) = \text{const. } \exp\left[-\frac{1}{2\sigma^2}\left\{ (1 + \rho^2)\varepsilon'\varepsilon - \rho(\varepsilon_1^2 + \varepsilon_n^2) - 2\rho \sum_{t=2}^{n} \varepsilon_t \varepsilon_{t-1} \right\} \right]. \tag{2.61}$$

Now the only difference between the likelihood function (2.58) and (2.61) is on the middle terms involving ρ^2 and ρ, and the difference can be neglected. Anderson's theorem suggests that a UMP test should be based on

$$a = \frac{\hat{\varepsilon}'D\hat{\varepsilon}}{\hat{\varepsilon}'\hat{\varepsilon}} = \frac{\hat{\varepsilon}'\hat{\varepsilon} - \frac{1}{2}\hat{\varepsilon}'A\hat{\varepsilon}}{\hat{\varepsilon}'\hat{\varepsilon}}$$

$$= 1 - \frac{1}{2}\frac{\hat{\varepsilon}'A\hat{\varepsilon}}{\hat{\varepsilon}'\hat{\varepsilon}}. \tag{2.62}$$

Durbin and Watson (1950) used a slight transformation of "a" to form their test statistic, namely,

$$d = 2(1 - a)$$

$$= \frac{\hat{\varepsilon}'A\hat{\varepsilon}}{\hat{\varepsilon}'\hat{\varepsilon}} = \frac{\sum_{t=2}^{n}(\hat{\varepsilon}_t - \hat{\varepsilon}_{t-1})^2}{\sum_{t=1}^{n}\hat{\varepsilon}_t^2}. \tag{2.63}$$

Note that "a" in (2.62) is approximately equal to the estimate $\hat{\rho} = \sum_{t=2}^{n}\hat{\varepsilon}_t\hat{\varepsilon}_{t-1}/\sum_{t=1}^{n}\hat{\varepsilon}_t^2$, whereas $d \simeq 2(1 - \hat{\rho})$. Most econometrics textbooks discuss in details about tables of bounds for the DW test, and we will not cover that here. Our main purpose is to trace the origin of the DW test to the N–P lemma. For a historical account of the DW test, see (King, 1987). In spatial econometrics, Moran's (1950) test for spatial dependence has the similar form

$$I = \frac{\hat{\varepsilon}'W\hat{\varepsilon}}{\hat{\varepsilon}'\hat{\varepsilon}}, \tag{2.64}$$

where W is a spatial weight matrix that represents "degree of potential interaction" among neighboring locations. Using the above analysis it is easy to link I to the N–P lemma and demonstrate its optimality [for more on this, see (Anselin and Bera, 1998)].

3.2   Use of score test in econometrics

In the econometrics literature, Rao's score test is known as the Lagrange multiplier test. This terminology came from Silvey (1959). Note that the restricted MLE of θ under the restriction $H_0 : h(\theta) = c$ can be obtained from the first order condition of the Lagrangian function

$$\mathcal{L} = l(\theta) - \lambda'[h(\theta) - c], \tag{2.65}$$

where λ is an $r \times 1$ vector of Lagrange multipliers. The first order conditions are

$$s(\tilde{\theta}) - H(\tilde{\theta})\tilde{\lambda} = 0 \tag{2.66}$$

$$h(\tilde{\theta}) = c, \tag{2.67}$$

where $H(\theta) = \frac{\partial h(\theta)}{\partial \theta}$. Therefore, we have $s(\tilde{\theta}) = H(\tilde{\theta})\tilde{\lambda}$. Given that $H(\tilde{\theta})$ has full rank, $s(\tilde{\theta}) = 0$ is equivalent to $\tilde{\lambda} = 0$, that is, the Lagrange multipliers vanish. These multipliers can be interpreted as the implicit cost (shadow prices) of imposing the restrictions. It can be shown that

$$\tilde{\lambda} = \frac{\partial l(\tilde{\theta})}{\partial c}, \tag{2.68}$$

that is, the multipliers give the rate of change of the maximum attainable value with respect to the change in the constraints. If $H_0 : h(\theta) = c$ is true and $l(\tilde{\theta})$ gives the optimal value, $\tilde{\lambda}$ should be close to zero. Given this "economic" interpretation in terms of multipliers, it is not surprising that econometricians prefer the term LM rather than RS. In terms of Lagrange multipliers, (2.39) can be expressed as

$$\text{RS} = \text{LM} = \tilde{\lambda}'H(\tilde{\theta})'I(\tilde{\theta})^{-1}H(\tilde{\theta})\tilde{\lambda}. \tag{2.69}$$

Byron (1968), probably the first to apply the RS test in econometrics, used the version (2.69) along with the LR statistic for testing homogeneity and symmetry restrictions in demand equations. It took another decade for econometricians to realize the potential of the RS test. In this regard, the work of Breusch and Pagan (1980) has been the most influential. They collected relevant research reported in the statistics literature, presented the RS test in a general framework in the context of evaluating econometric models, and discussed many applications. Since the late 1970s, econometricians have applied the score principle to a variety of econometric testing problems and studied the properties of the resulting tests. Now the RS tests are the most common items in the econometricians' kit of testing tools. We will make no attempt to provide a test of all applications of the RS test in econometrics for these are far too many. For example, consider the linear regression model (2.54). The OLS analysis of this model is based on four basic assumptions: correct linear functional form; the assumptions of disturbance normality; homoskedasticity; and serial independence. Violation of these affects both estimation and inference results. With the aid of the RS principle, many procedures have been proposed to test the above assumptions and these are now routinely reported in most of the standard econometric software packages. In most cases, the algebraic forms of the LR and W tests can hardly be simplified beyond their original formulae (2.12) and (2.40). On the other hand, in many cases the RS test statistics, apart from its computational ease, can be reduced to neat and elegant formulae enabling its easy incorporation into computer software. Breusch and Pagan (1980), Godfrey (1988), Bera and Ullah (1991), Davidson and MacKinnon (1993), and Bera and Billias (2000) discussed many applications of the score tests in econometrics and demonstrated that many of the old and new econometric tests could be given a score-test interpretation. For example, test procedures developed in Hausman (1978), Newey (1985), Tauchen (1985), and White (1982) could be put in the framework of the score test. To see this, let us consider the Newey (1985) and Tauchen (1985) moment test and write the moment restriction as

$$E_f[m(y; \theta)] = 0, \tag{2.70}$$

where E_f means that (2.70) is true only when $f(y; \theta)$ is the correct p.d.f. A test for this hypothesis can be based on the estimate of the sample counterpart of (2.70), namely,

$$\frac{1}{n}\sum_{i=1}^{n} m(y_i; \theta). \tag{2.71}$$

suggestions on an earlier draft of this chapter. We, however, retain the responsibility for any remaining errors. Financial support from the Research Board of the University of Illinois at Urbana-Champaign and the Office of Research, College of Commerce and Business Administration, University of Illinois at Urbana-Champaign are gratefully acknowledged.

1   Neyman (1980, p. 6) stated their intuition as, "The intuitive background of the likelihood ratio test was simply as follows: if among the contemplated admissible hypotheses there are some that ascribe to the facts observed probabilities much larger than that ascribed by the hypothesis tested, then it appears 'reasonable' to reject the hypothesis."

2   This result follows from the generalized Cauchy–Schwarz inequality (Rao, 1973, p. 54)

$$(u'v)^2 \leq (u'Au)(v'A^{-1}v),$$

where u and v are column vectors and A is a non-singular matrix. Equality holds when $u = A^{-1}v$.

3   The interrelationships among these three tests can be brought home to students through an amusing story. Once around 1946 Ronald Fisher invited Jerzy Neyman, Abraham Wald, and C.R. Rao to his lodge for afternoon tea. During their conversation, Fisher mentioned the problem of deciding whether his dog, who had been going to an "obedience school" for some time, was disciplined enough. Neyman quickly came up with an idea: leave the dog free for some time and then put him on his leash. If there is not much difference in his behavior, the dog can be thought of as having completed the course successfully. Wald, who lost his family in the concentration camps, was adverse to any restrictions and simply suggested leaving the dog free and seeing whether it behaved properly. Rao, who had observed the nuisances of stray dogs in Calcutta streets, did not like the idea of letting the dog roam freely and suggested keeping the dog on a leash at all times and observing how hard it pulls on the leash. If it pulled too much, it needed more training. That night when Rao was back in his Cambridge dormitory after tending Fisher's mice at the genetics laboratory, he suddenly realized the connection of Neyman and Wald's recommendations to the Neyman–Pearson LR and Wald tests. He got an idea and the rest is history.

4   In the $C(\alpha)$ test the letter "C" refers to Cramér and "α" to the level of significance. Neyman (1959) was published in a Festschrift for Harald Cramér. Neyman frequently referred to this work as his "last performance." He was, however, disappointed that the paper did not attract as much attention as he had hoped for, and in later years, he regretted publishing it in a Festschrift as not many people read Festschrifts.

5   In the introduction (p. 11), Tinbergen stated,

> The purpose of this series of studies is to submit to statistical test some of the theories which have been put forward regarding the character and causes of cyclical fluctuation in business activity. Many of these theories, however, do not exist in a form immediately appropriate for statistical testing while most of them take account of the same body of economic phenomena – viz., the behavior of investment, consumption, incomes, prices, etc. Accordingly, the method of procedure here adopted is not to test the various theories one by one (a course which would involve much repetition), but to examine in succession, in the light of the various explanations which have been offered, the relation between certain groups of economic phenomena.

He, however, cautioned against relying too much on the test results, "for no statistical test can prove a theory to be correct" (p. 12). For more on this see (Duo, 1993, Chapter 5).

6   In his Nobel lecture he stated (Haavelmo, 1997),

> "For my own part I was lucky enough to be able to visit the United States in 1939 on a scholarship. . . . I then had the privilege of studying with the world famous statistician Jerzy Neyman in California for a couple of months. At that time, young and naive, I thought I knew something about econometrics. I exposed some of my thinking on the subject to Professor Neyman. Instead of entering into a discussion with me, he gave me two or three exercises for me to work out. He said he would talk to me when I had done these exercises. When I met him for the second talk, I had lost most of my illusions regarding the understanding of how to do econometrics. But Professor Neyman also gave me hopes that there might be other more fruitful ways to approach the problem of econometric methods than those which had so far caused difficulties and disappointments."

7   Technically speaking, this model does not fit in our earlier framework due to the dependence structure. However, once a proper likelihood function is defined we can derive our earlier test statistics.

8   Instead of dealing with the joint distribution conditional on the explanatory variables in all time periods, a better approach would be to consider sequential conditional distribution under much weaker assumptions. Wooldridge (1994) discusses the merits of modeling sequential distributions.

9   We should, however, note that econometricians have developed a number of procedures to estimate a consistent variance–covariance matrix to take account of the unknown form of dependence; for a discussion of this and other robust procedures see (Bera, 2000) and (Wooldridge, 2000).

References

Aigner, D.J., C.A.K. Lovell, and P. Schmidt (1977). Formulation and estimation of stochastic frontier production function model. *Journal of Econometrics* 6, 21–37.

Anderson, T.W. (1948). On the theory of testing serial correlation. *Skandinavisk Aktuarietidskrift* 31, 88–116.

Anselin, L., and A.K. Bera (1998). Spatial dependence in linear regression models with an introduction to spatial econometrics. In A. Ullah and D.E.A. Giles (eds.), *Handbook of Applied Economic Statistics*. New York: Marcel Dekker, 237–89.

Bayes, Rev. T. (1763). An essay toward solving a problem in the doctrine of chances. *Philosophical Transactions of the Royal Society* 53, 370–418.

Bera, A.K. (2000). Hypothesis testing in the 20th century with a special reference to testing with misspecified models. In C.R. Rao and G. Szekely (eds.), *Statistics for the 21st Century*. New York: Marcel Dekker, 33–92.

Bera, A.K., and Y. Billias (2000). Rao's score, Neyman's C(α) and Silvey's LM test: An essay on historical developments and some new results. *Journal of Statistical Planning and Inference* Forthcoming.

Bera, A.K., and C.M. Jarque (1981). An efficient large-sample test for normality of observations and regression residuals. Working Paper in Economics and Econometrics, Number 40, The Australian National University, Canberra.

Bera, A.K., and A. Ullah (1991). Rao's score test in econometrics. *Journal of Quantitative Economics* 7, 189–220.

Bera, A.K., and M.J. Yoon (1993). Specification testing with locally misspecified alternatives. *Econometric Theory* 9, 649–58.

Bera, A.K., S.-S. Ra, and N. Sarkar (1998). Hypothesis testing for some nonregular cases in econometrics. In S. Chakravarty, D. Coondoo, and R. Mukherjee (eds.), *Econometrics: Theory and Practice*, New Delhi: Allied Publishers, 319–51.

Beran, R.J., and N.I. Fisher (1998). A conversation with Geoff Watson. *Statistical Science* 13, 75–93.

Breusch, T.S., and A.R. Pagan (1980). The Lagrange multiplier test and its applications to model specification in econometrics. *Review of Economic Studies* 47, 239–53.

Byron, R.P. (1968). Methods for estimating demand equations using prior information: A series of experiments with Australian data. *Australian Economic Papers* 7, 227–48.

Cameron, A.C., and P.K. Trivedi (1990). Conditional moment tests and orthogonal polynomials, Working Paper in Economics, Number 90–051, Indiana University.

Chesher, A., and R. Smith (1997). Likelihood ratio specification tests. *Econometrica* 65, 627–46.

Cramér, H. (1946). *Mathematical Methods of Statistics*. New Jersey: Princeton University Press.

Dagenais, M.G., and J.-M. Dufour (1991). Invariance, nonlinear models, and asymptotic tests. *Econometrica* 59, 1601–15.

Davidson, R., and J.G. MacKinnon (1993). *Estimation and Inference in Econometrics*. Oxford: Oxford University Press.

Diebold, F.X., T.A. Gunther, and A.S. Tay (1998). Evaluating density forecasts with application to financial risk management. *International Economic Review*, 39, 863–905.

Duo, Q. (1993). *The Foundation of Econometrics: A Historical Perspective*. Oxford: Clarendon Press.

Durbin, J., and G.S. Watson (1950). Testing for serial correlation in least squares regression I. *Biometrika* 37, 409–28.

Fisher, R.A. (1922). On the mathematical foundations of theoretical statistics. *Philosophical Transaction of the Royal Society* A222, 309–68.

Godfrey, L.G. (1988). *Misspecification Tests in Econometrics, The Lagrange Multiplier Principle and Other Approaches*. Cambridge: Cambridge University Press.

Gouriéroux, C., and A. Monfort (1995). *Statistics and Econometric Models 2*. Cambridge: Cambridge University Press.

Gregory, A.W., and M.R. Veal (1985). Formulating Wald tests of nonlinear restrictions. *Econometrica* 53, 1465–8.

Haavelmo, T. (1944). The probability approach in econometrics. *Supplements to Econometrica* 12.

Haavelmo, T. (1997). Econometrics and the welfare state: Nobel lecture, December 1989. *American Economic Review* 87, 13–5.

Hausman, J.J. (1978). Specification tests in econometrics. *Econometrica* 46, 1215–72.

Jarque, C.M., and A.K. Bera (1980). Efficient tests for normality, homoskedasticity and serial independence of regression residuals. *Economics Letters* 6, 255–9.

King, M.L. (1987). Testing for autocorrelation in linear regression models: A survey. In M.L. King and D.E.A. Giles (eds.), *Specification Analysis in the Linear Model*. London: Routledge and Kegan Paul, 19–73.

Klein, L. (1991). The statistics seminar, MIT, 1942–1943. *Statistical Science* 6, 320–30.

Lee, L.F., and A. Chesher (1986). Specification testing when score test statistics are individually zero. *Journal of Econometrics* 31, 121–49.

Lehmann, E.L. (1986). *Testing Statistical Hypotheses*. New York: John Wiley & Sons.

Lehmann, E.L. (1999). *Elements of Large Sample Theory*. New York: Springer-Verlag.

Moran, P.A.P. (1950). A test for the serial independence of residuals. *Biometrika* 37, 178–81.

Newey, W. (1985). Maximum likelihood specification testing and conditional moment tests. *Econometrica* 53, 1047–70.

Neyman, J. (1937). "Smooth test" for goodness of fit. *Skandinavisk Akturarietidskrift* 20, 150–99.

Neyman, J. (1954). Sur une famille de tests asymptotiques des hypothèses statistiques compasées. *Trabajos de Estadistica* 5, 161–8.

Neyman, J. (1959). Optimal asymptotic test of composite statistical hypothesis. In U. Grenander (ed.), *Probability and Statistics, the Harald Cramér Volume*. Uppsala: Almqvist and Wiksell, 213–34.

Neyman, J. (1980). Some memorable incidents in probabilistic/statistical studies. In I.M. Chakravarti (ed.), *Asymptotic Theory of Statistical Tests and Estimation*, New York: Academic Press, 1–32.

Neyman, J., and E.S. Pearson (1928). On the use and interpretation of certain test criteria for purpose of statistical inference. *Biometrika* 20, 175–240.

Neyman, J., and E.S. Pearson (1933). On the problem of the most efficient tests of statistical hypothesis. *Philosophical Transactions of the Royal Society, Series A* 231, 289–337.

Neyman, J., and E.S. Pearson (1936). Contribution to the theory of testing statistical hypothesis I: Unbiased critical regions of type A and type A_1. *Statistical Research Memoirs* 1, 1–37.

Pearson, K. (1900). On the criterion that a given system of deviations from the probable in the case of a correlated system of variables is such that it can be reasonably supposed to have arisen from random sampling. *Philosophical Magazine Series 5*, 50, 157–75.

Rao, C.R. (1948). Large sample tests of statistical hypotheses concerning several parameters with applications to problems of estimation. *Proceedings of the Cambridge Philosophical Society* 44, 50–7.

Rao, C.R. (1973). *Linear Statistical Inference and Its Applications*. New York: John Wiley and Sons.

Rao, C.R. (2000). Two score and ten years of score tests. *Journal of Statistical Planning and Inference*.

Rao, C.R., and S.J. Poti (1946). On locally most powerful tests when alternatives are one sided. *Sankhyā* 7, 439–40.

Rayner, J.C.W., and D.J. Best (1989). *Smooth Tests of Goodness of Fit*. New York: Oxford University Press.

Serfling, R.J. (1980). *Approximation Theorems of Mathematical Statistics*. New York: John Wiley and Sons.

Silvey, S.D. (1959). The Lagrange multiplier test. *Annals of Mathematical Statistics* 30, 389–407.

Smith, R. (1989). On the use of distributional mis-specification checks in limited dependent variable models. *Economic Journal* 99, 178–92.

Tauchen, G. (1985). Diagnostic testing and evaluation of maximum likelihood models. *Journal of Econometrics* 30, 415–43.

Vaeth, M. (1985). On the use of Wald's test in exponential families. *International Statistical Review* 53, 199–214.

Wald, A. (1943). Tests of statistical hypothesis concerning several parameters when the number of observations is large. *Transactions of the American Mathematical Society* 54, 426–82.

White, H. (1982). Maximum likelihood estimation of misspecified models. *Econometrica* 50, 1–25.

White, H. (1984). Comment on "Tests of specification in econometrics." *Econometric Reviews* 3, 261–7.

Wooldridge, J.M. (1994). Estimation and inference for dependent processes. In R.F. Engle and D.L. McFadden (eds.), *Handbook of Econometrics* Vol. 4. Amsterdam: North-Holland, 2639–738.

Wooldridge, J.M. (2000). Diagnostic testing. Chapter 9 this volume.

This implies that the AR(1) process has an autocorrelation function of the form

$$\rho_{(i)} = \text{cov}(y_t, y_{t-i})/(\text{var}(y_t)\,\text{var}(y_{t-i}))^{1/2} = \rho^i$$

which declines at an exponential rate as i increases.

Another simple model is the first-order moving average (MA(1)) process which can be written as

$$y_t = \varepsilon_t + \gamma\varepsilon_{t-1}, \quad \varepsilon_t \sim \text{iid}(0, \sigma^2) \tag{3.2}$$

where ε_t is defined as in (3.1). The $n \times 1$ vector $\mathbf{y}$ has mean zero and covariance matrix

$$\text{var}(\mathbf{y}) = \sigma^2 \begin{bmatrix} 1+\gamma^2 & \gamma & 0 & \cdots & \cdots & \cdots & 0 \\ \gamma & 1+\gamma^2 & \gamma & & & & 0 \\ 0 & \gamma & 1+\gamma^2 & & & & 0 \\ \vdots & & & \ddots & & & \vdots \\ \vdots & & & & \ddots & & \vdots \\ \vdots & & & & & 1+\gamma^2 & \gamma \\ 0 & 0 & \cdots & \cdots & \cdots & \gamma & 1+\gamma^2 \end{bmatrix}. \tag{3.3}$$

Note that $\text{var}(y_t) = \sigma^2(1 + \gamma^2)$ and the autocorrelation function of an MA(1) process is

$$\rho_{(i)} = \gamma/(1 + \gamma^2), \quad i = 1$$
$$= 0, \qquad\qquad i > 1.$$

We usually assume $|\gamma| \le 1$ although it is possible to have an MA(1) process with $|\gamma| > 1$, but for normally distributed errors, it is impossible to distinguish between the likelihood function for (3.2) with $(\gamma^*, \sigma^{*2}) = (\gamma, \sigma^2)$ and $(\gamma^*, \sigma^{*2}) = (1/\gamma, \sigma^2\gamma^2)$ because (3.3) takes the same value for these two sets of parameter values. The standard solution to this minor identification problem is to restrict γ to the interval $|\gamma| \le 1$. This is known as the invertibility condition. An MA(1) process is stationary because y_t is a simple weighted sum of the innovations ε_t, ε_{t-1}, so no condition is required for stationarity.

If we combine (3.1) and (3.2), we get an autoregressive moving average (ARMA(1, 1)) process which can be written as

$$y_t = \rho y_{t-1} + \varepsilon_t + \gamma\varepsilon_{t-1}, \quad |\rho| < 1, \quad \varepsilon_t \sim \text{iid}(0, \sigma^2). \tag{3.4}$$

Note that

$$\text{var}(y_t) = \sigma^2\{(1 + \gamma^2) + 2\gamma\rho\}/(1 - \rho^2)$$

$$\text{cov}(y_t, y_{t-i}) = \rho\,\text{var}(y_t) + \gamma\sigma^2, \quad \text{for } i = 1$$
$$= \rho^i\text{var}(y_t), \qquad\qquad \text{for } i \ge 2.$$

It is also worth observing that if

$$y_t = \varepsilon_t, \tag{3.5}$$

i.e., we have a white noise model for y_t with no serial correlation, then by lagging (3.5) one period, multiplying it by ρ and subtracting from (3.5) we get

$$y_t = \rho y_{t-1} + \varepsilon_t - \rho \varepsilon_{t-1}$$

which is (3.4) with $\gamma = -\rho$. This is known as a model with a common factor. It appears to be an ARMA(1, 1) model but it is in fact a white noise model.

As in the AR(1) case, (3.4) is not complete until we have made an assumption about y_0. Again the usual assumption is stationarity, i.e. to assume that (3.4) is a process that has been going on forever.

The pth order autoregressive process (AR(p)) is a generalization of (3.1) and can be written as

$$y_t = \rho_1 y_{t-1} + \rho_2 y_{t-2} + \ldots + \rho_p y_{t-p} + \varepsilon_t, \quad \varepsilon_t \sim \text{iid}(0, \sigma^2). \tag{3.6}$$

The stationarity condition generalizes to the requirement that the roots of the polynomial equation

$$1 - \rho_1 z - \rho_2 z^2 - \ldots - \rho_p z^p = 0 \tag{3.7}$$

lie outside the unit circle. In other words, all the roots of (3.7) must be larger than one in absolute value. For an AR(2) process, this requires

$$\rho_1 + \rho_2 < 1, \quad \rho_2 - \rho_1 < 1 \quad \text{and} \quad \rho_2 > -1.$$

In a similar way, the qth order moving average process (MA(q)) is a generalization of (3.2) and has the form

$$y_t = \varepsilon_t + \gamma_1 \varepsilon_{t-1} + \ldots + \gamma_q \varepsilon_{t-q}, \quad \varepsilon_t \sim \text{iid}(0, \sigma^2). \tag{3.8}$$

The invertibility condition now becomes such that the roots of the polynomial equation

$$1 + \gamma_1 z + \gamma_2 z^2 + \ldots + \gamma_q z^q = 0$$

lie outside the unit circle. Again no further condition is required for stationarity.

Observe that

$$\text{var}(y_t) = \sigma^2(1 + \gamma_1^2 + \ldots + \gamma_q^2)$$

$$\text{cov}(y_t y_{t-i}) = \sigma^2(\gamma_i + \gamma_1 \gamma_{i+1} + \ldots + \gamma_{q-i} \gamma_q), \quad \text{for } i = 1, \ldots, q,$$

$$= 0, \quad \text{for } i > q.$$

previous period as well as on other independent variables. This leads naturally to the dynamic linear regression model, the simplest version of which is

$$y_t = \alpha_1 y_{t-1} + x_t'\beta + u_t, \quad t = 1, \ldots, n, \tag{3.18}$$

where α_1 is a scalar, β is a $k \times 1$ parameter vector, x_t is a $k \times 1$ vector of exogenous variables and u_t is the disturbance term. A more general model is

$$y_t = \alpha_1 y_{t-1} + \ldots + \alpha_p y_{t-p} + x_t'\beta + u_t, \quad t = 1, \ldots, n. \tag{3.19}$$

For completion, we need to also provide an assumption on the generation of $y_0, y_{-1}, \ldots, y_{1-p}$. One approach is to treat $y_0, y_{-1}, \ldots, y_{1-p}$ as constants. Another is to assume they each have a constant mean equal to $E(y_1)$ and that $v_t = y_t - E(y_t)$ follows the stationary AR(p) process

$$v_t = \alpha_1 v_{t-1} + \alpha_2 v_{t-2} + \ldots + \alpha_p v_{t-p} + u_t$$

in which u_t is the error term in (3.19). The former assumption is appropriate if we wish to make inferences conditional on the values taken by $y_0, y_{-1}, \ldots, y_{1-p}$ while the latter assumption has been made by Tse (1982) and Inder (1985, 1986).

In some circumstances, there is not much difference between the linear regression (3.12) with AR(1) errors and the first-order dynamic regression model (3.18). To see this, suppose x_t is made up of a constant intercept regressor and the time trend, i.e. $x_t = (1, t)'$. Consider

$$y_t = x_t'\beta + u_t \tag{3.20}$$

in which u_t follows the AR(1) process (3.13). If we lag (3.20) one period, multiply it by ρ and subtract from (3.20), we get

$$y_t = \rho y_{t-1} + x_t'\beta - \rho x_{t-1}'\beta + \varepsilon_t. \tag{3.21}$$

Observe that (3.21) is a regression with a well-behaved error term and five regressors. Because when x_t is lagged, it remains a constant regressor and a linear trend regressor, there is perfect multicollinearity between the regressors of x_t and x_{t-1}. This problem can be solved by dropping the $\rho x_{t-1}'\beta$ term, in which case (3.21) becomes the simple dynamic linear model (3.18) with $u_t \sim \text{iid}(0, \sigma^2)$. Thus in the general case of a linear regression model of the form of (3.20), if x_t is "lag invariant" in the sense that all regressors in x_{t-1} can be written as linear combinations of the regressors purely from x_t, then (3.18) and (3.20) are equivalent. This simple analysis has ignored the first observation. Any difference between the two models could depend largely on what is assumed about the first observation in each model.

3   ESTIMATION

This section discusses the problem of estimation for the models of the previous section. Recall that subsection 2.1 considered models with mean zero. These can be readily generalized to models in which y_t has a constant but unknown mean, say β_1. Such models can be written as a special case of a regression model (3.12) in which X is the vector of ones. It is very rare that the mean of y_t is known to be zero, so models which allow for nonzero means are more realistic. Thus in this section, we shall restrict our attention to the estimation of the linear regression model (3.12) with various ARMA-type disturbance processes.

3.1   Maximum likelihood estimation

An $n \times 1$ vector y generated by the linear regression model (3.12) with an ARMA(p, q) disturbance process with normal errors, i.e. $\varepsilon_t \sim IN(0, \sigma^2)$, can be shown to be distributed as

$$y \sim N(X\beta, \sigma^2\Omega(\rho, \gamma)) \tag{3.22}$$

where $\sigma^2\Omega(\rho, \gamma)$ is the covariance matrix of the ARMA(p, q) process in which $\rho = (\rho_1, \ldots, \rho_p)'$ and $\gamma = (\gamma_1, \ldots, \gamma_q)'$ are parameter vectors. The loglikelihood function of this model is

$$f(\beta, \sigma^2, \rho, \gamma \mid y) = -\frac{n}{2}\log(2\pi\sigma^2) - \frac{1}{2}\log|\Omega(\rho, \gamma)|$$

$$-\frac{1}{2\sigma^2}(y - X\beta)'\Omega(\rho, \gamma)^{-1}(y - X\beta). \tag{3.23}$$

For any given values of ρ and γ, the values of β and σ^2 that maximize (3.23) are

$$\tilde{\beta}_{\rho,\gamma} = (X'\Omega(\rho, \gamma)^{-1}X)^{-1}X'\Omega(\rho, \gamma)^{-1}y \tag{3.24}$$

and

$$\tilde{\sigma}^2_{\rho,\gamma} = (y - X\tilde{\beta}_{\rho,\gamma})'\Omega(\rho, \gamma)^{-1}(y - X\tilde{\beta}_{\rho,\gamma})/n. \tag{3.25}$$

If these estimators of β and σ^2 are substituted back into (3.23), we get the profile or concentrated loglikelihood:

$$f_p(\rho, \gamma \mid y) = -\frac{n}{2}\log(2\pi\tilde{\sigma}^2_{\rho,\gamma}) - \frac{1}{2}\log|\Omega(\rho, \gamma)| - \frac{n}{2}. \tag{3.26}$$

Full maximum likelihood estimates of the parameters in this model are therefore obtained by first finding the values of the ρ and γ vectors which maximize (3.26). These values of ρ and γ, denoted $\tilde{\rho}$ and $\tilde{\gamma}$, are then used in (3.24) and (3.25) to find $\tilde{\beta}$ and $\tilde{\sigma}^2$, the maximum likelihood estimates.

There are a number of practical issues in this process worthy of discussion. The first involves exploiting the Cholesky decomposition of $\Omega(\rho, \gamma)$ denoted $L(\rho, \gamma)$ such that

$$L(\rho, \gamma)L(\rho, \gamma)' = \Omega(\rho, \gamma)$$

where $L(\rho, \gamma)$ is a lower triangular matrix. If we denote

$$y^*(\rho, \gamma) = L(\rho, \gamma)^{-1}y \tag{3.27}$$

$$X^*(\rho, \gamma) = L(\rho, \gamma)^{-1}X, \tag{3.28}$$

then (3.24) becomes

$$\tilde{\beta}_{\rho,\gamma} = (X^*(\rho, \gamma)'X^*(\rho, \gamma))^{-1}X^*(\rho, \gamma)'y^*(\rho, \gamma), \tag{3.29}$$

the ordinary least squares (OLS) estimator from the regression of $y^*(\rho, \gamma)$ on $X^*(\rho, \gamma)$, and (3.25) becomes

$$\tilde{\sigma}^2_{\rho,\gamma} = e^*(\rho, \gamma)'e^*(\rho, \gamma)/n, \tag{3.30}$$

the sum of squared residuals from this regression divided by n, where

$$e^*(\rho, \gamma) = y^*(\rho, \gamma) - X^*(\rho, \gamma)\tilde{\beta}_{\rho,\gamma}. \tag{3.31}$$

The problem of maximizing (3.26) with respect to ρ and γ now reduces to one of maximizing

$$-\frac{n}{2} \log{(e^*(\rho, \gamma)'e^*(\rho, \gamma))} - \log{|L(\rho, \gamma)|} = -\frac{n}{2} \log{(\tilde{e}^*(\rho, \gamma)'\tilde{e}^*(\rho, \gamma))}$$

where

$$\tilde{e}^*(\rho, \gamma) = e^*(\rho, \gamma)|L(\rho, \gamma)|^{1/n}.$$

Thus the estimation problem reduces to minimizing the sum of squares

$$\tilde{s} = \sum_{i=1}^{n} \tilde{e}^*(\rho, \gamma)^2_i \tag{3.32}$$

with respect to ρ and γ. This may be achieved by applying a standard non-linear least squares algorithm to $\tilde{s}$ and then using the resultant $\tilde{\rho}$ and $\tilde{\gamma}$ in (3.29) and (3.30) to obtain $\tilde{\beta}$ and $\tilde{\sigma}^2$. Also observe that because $L(\rho, \gamma)$ is a lower triangular matrix, its determinant is easily calculated as the product of the diagonal elements, i.e.

$$|L(\rho, \gamma)| = \prod_{i=1}^{n} L(\rho, \gamma)_{ii}. \tag{3.33}$$

The remaining issue is the construction of $\Omega(\rho, \gamma)$ or more importantly $L(\rho, \gamma)$ or $L^{-1}(\rho, \gamma)$. Note that through (3.27), (3.28), (3.29), (3.30), and (3.32), maximum likelihood estimates can be obtained without the need to calculate $\Omega(\rho, \gamma)$ or $\Omega^{-1}(\rho, \gamma)$. In the case of AR(1) disturbances

$$L^{-1}(\rho, \lambda) = \begin{bmatrix} (1 - \rho^2)^{1/2} & 0 & \cdots & \cdots & \cdots & 0 & 0 \\ -\rho & 1 & & & & & \vdots \\ \vdots & & \ddots & & & & \vdots \\ \vdots & & & \ddots & & & \vdots \\ \vdots & & & & \ddots & & \vdots \\ 0 & & & & & 1 & 0 \\ 0 & \cdots & \cdots & \cdots & \cdots & -\rho & 1 \end{bmatrix}$$

which was first derived by Prais and Winsten (1954) and is also known as the Prais–Winsten transformation.

For AR(p) disturbances, van der Leeuw (1994) has shown that

$$\Omega(\rho, \gamma) = [P'P - NN']^{-1}$$

where P is the $n \times n$ triangular matrix

$$P = \begin{bmatrix} 1 & 0 & 0 & \cdots & \cdots & \cdots & 0 & 0 & \cdots & \cdots & \cdots & \cdots & 0 & 0 \\ -\rho_1 & 1 & 0 & & & & \vdots & & & & & & & 0 \\ -\rho_2 & -\rho_1 & 1 & & & & \vdots & & & & & & & \vdots \\ & & & \ddots & & & \vdots & & & & & & & \vdots \\ & & & & \ddots & & \vdots & & & & & & & \vdots \\ & & & & & \ddots & \vdots & & & & & & & \vdots \\ -\rho_p & -\rho_{p-1} & \cdots & \cdots & \cdots & \cdots & 1 & 0 & \cdots & \cdots & \cdots & \cdots & \cdots & 0 \\ 0 & -\rho_p & \cdots & \cdots & \cdots & \cdots & -\rho_1 & 1 & & & & & & 0 \\ \vdots & & & & & & & & \ddots & & & & & \vdots \\ \vdots & & & & & & \vdots & & & \ddots & & & & \vdots \\ \vdots & & & & & & \vdots & & & & \ddots & & & \vdots \\ \vdots & & & & & & \vdots & & & & & \ddots & & \vdots \\ \vdots & & & & & & \vdots & & & & & & 1 & 0 \\ 0 & 0 & \cdots & \cdots & \cdots & \cdots & 0 & 0 & \cdots & -\rho_p & \cdots & \cdots & -\rho_1 & 1 \end{bmatrix}$$

and N is an $n \times p$ matrix that has all elements zero except for its top $p \times p$ block which has the triangular form

$$
\begin{bmatrix}
-\rho_p & -\rho_{p-1} & \cdots & \cdots & \cdots & \cdots & -\rho_1 \\
0 & -\rho_p & & & & & -\rho_2 \\
0 & 0 & & & & & \\
& & & \ddots & & & \\
& & & & \ddots & & \\
& & & & & \ddots & \\
0 & 0 & & & & 0 & -\rho_p
\end{bmatrix}
$$

As noted by Ara (1995), in this case $L(\rho, \gamma)^{-1}$ has the same form as P but with the top left $p \times p$ block replaced by the lower triangular matrix

$$
\begin{bmatrix}
a_{11} & 0 & \cdots & \cdots & \cdots & 0 \\
a_{21} & a_{22} & & & & 0 \\
\vdots & & \ddots & & & \vdots \\
\vdots & & & \ddots & & \vdots \\
\vdots & & & & \ddots & \vdots \\
a_{p1} & a_{p2} & \cdots & \cdots & \cdots & a_{pp}
\end{bmatrix}.
$$

The a_{ij} values can be calculated recursively in the following order

$$
a_{pp} = (1 - \rho_p^2)^{1/2},
$$

$$
a_{p,p-i} = (-\rho_i - \rho_{p-i}\rho_p)/a_{pp}, \quad i = 1, \ldots, p - 1,
$$

for $j = p - 1, p - 2, \ldots, 2$ with $m = p - j$

$$
a_{jj} = \left(1 + \sum_{i=1}^{j-1} \rho_i^2 - \sum_{i=m+1}^{p} \rho_i^2 - \sum_{i=1}^{m} a_{j+i,j}^2 \right)^{1/2},
$$

for $\ell = 1, \ldots, j - 2$

$$
a_{j,j-\ell} = \left(-\rho_\ell - \sum_{i=1}^{j-\ell-1} \rho_i\rho_{i+\ell} - \sum_{i=j+1}^{p} a_{ij}a_{i,j-\ell} \right) \Big/ a_{jj}
$$

and

$$
a_{j1} = \left(-\rho_{j-1} - \rho_{m+1}\rho_p - \sum_{i=j+1}^{p} a_{ij}a_{i1} \right) \Big/ a_{jj};
$$

and

$$a_{11} = \left(1 - \rho_p^2 - \sum_{i=1}^{p-1} a_{i+1,1}^2\right)^{1/2}.$$

Note that in this case

$$|L(\rho, \gamma)|^{-1} = \prod_{i=1}^{p} a_{ii}.$$

For MA(q) disturbances, it is more convenient to construct $L(\rho, \gamma)$ which is the band triangular matrix:

$$L(\rho, \gamma) = \begin{bmatrix} a_{11} & 0 & 0 & \cdots & \cdots & \cdots & \cdots & & 0 \\ a_{21} & a_{22} & 0 & & & & & & 0 \\ a_{31} & a_{32} & a_{33} & & & & & & 0 \\ \vdots & \vdots & \vdots & \ddots & & & & & \vdots \\ \vdots & \vdots & \vdots & & \ddots & & & & \vdots \\ \vdots & \vdots & \vdots & & & \ddots & & & \vdots \\ a_{q+1,1} & a_{q+1,2} & a_{q+1,3} & & & a_{q+1,q+1} & & & 0 \\ 0 & a_{q+2,2} & a_{q+2,3} & & & & & & 0 \\ \vdots & & & & & & \ddots & & \vdots \\ 0 & & & & & & & \ddots & 0 \\ 0 & 0 & 0 & \cdots & \cdots & \cdots & & a_{n,n-q} & \cdots & \cdots & a_{nn} \end{bmatrix}.$$

$$(3.34)$$

We solve for the nonzero elements of this matrix recursively via

$$w_0 = (1 + \gamma_1^2 + \ldots + \gamma_q^2)$$

$$w_i = (\gamma_i + \gamma_1 \gamma_{i+1} + \ldots + \gamma_{q-i} \gamma_q), \quad i = 1, \ldots, q,$$

$$a_{11} = w_0^{1/2}$$

$$a_{i+1,1} = w_i / a_{11}, \quad i = 1, \ldots, q,$$

$$a_{jj} = \left(w_0 - \sum_{i=1}^{j-1} a_{ji}^2\right)^{1/2}$$

$$a_{i-j} = \left(w_{i-j} - \sum_{\ell=1}^{j-1} a_{j\ell} a_{i\ell}\right) \Big/ a_{jj}, \quad i = j+1, \ldots, q+j,$$

for $j = 2, \ldots, q - 1$ (using $a_{ij} = 0$ for all zero values of the elements of the above matrix in these formulae). For $i = q, \ldots, n$

$$a_{ii} = \left(w_0 - \sum_{j=1}^{q-1} a_{i,i-j}^2 \right)^{1/2}$$

and

$$a_{ji} = \left(w_{j-i} - \sum_{\ell=i+1}^{j-q+1} a_{i\ell} a_{j\ell} \right) \Big/ a_{ii}, \quad j = i + 1, \ldots, i + q.$$

Observe that given the band triangular nature of (3.34), the transformation of z to $z^* = L(\rho, \gamma)^{-1} z$, where z denotes an $n \times 1$ vector (either y in order to get $y^*(\rho, \gamma)$ or a column of X in order to compute $X^*(\rho, \gamma)$) can be performed recursively by

$$z_1^* = z_1 / a_{11}$$

$$z_i^* = \left(z_i - \sum_{j=1}^{i-1} a_{ij} z_j^* \right) \Big/ a_{ii}, \quad i = 2, \ldots, q,$$

$$z_i^* = \left(z_i - \sum_{j=i-q+1}^{i-1} a_{ij} z_j^* \right) \Big/ a_{ii}, \quad i = q + 1, \ldots, n.$$

The generalization of this approach to ARMA(p, q) disturbances is discussed by Ansley (1979) and in the special case of ARMA(1, 1) disturbances, is outlined by Rahman and King (1993). The above approach to maximum likelihood estimation is a general approach which requires numerical methods for optimization of the profile or concentrated loglikelihood. In the special cases of AR(1) disturbances and AR(2) disturbances, Beach and MacKinnon (1978a, 1978b) have derived an iterative method for solving the first-order conditions for the full maximum likelihood estimates. For further discussion of this and other methods, also see Davidson and MacKinnon (1993).

3.2 Maximum marginal likelihood estimation

There is a mounting literature that suggests that the method of maximum likelihood estimation as outlined in Section 3.1 can lead to biased estimates and inaccurate asymptotic test procedures based on these estimates. The problem is that, for the purpose of estimating ρ and γ, β and σ^2 are nuisance parameters. An early contribution on methods of overcoming the problems of nuisance parameters was made by Kalbfleisch and Sprott (1970) who proposed the use of marginal likelihood estimation. This approach does not work for all cases of nuisance parameters but fortunately works very well for our problem of estimating ρ and γ in the presence of β and σ^2.

An important contribution to this literature was made by Tunnicliffe Wilson (1989) who showed that the marginal loglikelihood for ρ and γ in (3.22) is

$$f_m(\rho, \gamma) = -\frac{1}{2}\log|\Omega(\rho, \gamma)| - \frac{1}{2}\log|X^*(\rho, \gamma)'X^*(\rho, \gamma)| - \frac{n-k}{2}\log e^*(\rho, \gamma)'e^*(\rho, \gamma)$$

(3.35)

where $X^*(\rho, \gamma)$ and $e^*(\rho, \gamma)$ are given by (3.28) and (3.31), respectively. Maximum marginal likelihood (MML) estimates can be obtained from maximizing (3.35) with respect to ρ and γ. The various tricks outlined in Section 3.1 can be used to evaluate (3.35) for given ρ and γ in an efficient manner.

Levenbach (1972) considered MML estimation for the AR(1) model and Cooper and Thompson (1977) demonstrated its use reduces estimation bias for γ_1 in the MA(1) model. Corduas (1986) demonstrated that MML estimation removes estimation bias in estimates of ρ_1 when estimating regressions with trending regressors and an AR(1) error term. Tunnicliffe Wilson (1989) also presented evidence that the MML reduces estimation bias. In addition, see Rahman and King (1998) and Laskar and King (1998). The evidence is clear. In order to reduce estimation bias in estimates of ρ and γ, it is better to use the MML rather than the profile or concentrated likelihood.

4   HYPOTHESIS TESTING

Much has been written on the problem of testing for serial correlation, particularly in the disturbances of the linear regression model. Given the nonexperimental nature of almost all economic data and also the strong potential for disturbances to be autocorrelated in economic time series applications, it is extremely important to test for autocorrelation in this context.

4.1   The Durbin–Watson test

The von Neumann (1941, 1942) ratio is an important test of the independence of successive Gaussian time series observations, with unknown but constant mean. Its test statistic is of the form

$$\eta = \frac{n\sum_{t=2}^{n}(y_t - y_{t-1})^2}{(n-1)\sum_{t=1}^{n}(y_t - \bar{y})^2}$$

where $\bar{y}$ is the sample mean. Hart (1942a, 1942b) tabulated the distribution and critical values of η under the null hypothesis of independent Gaussian y_ts.

The most well known test for autocorrelation in regression disturbances is the Durbin–Watson (DW) test. Durbin and Watson (1950, 1951, 1971) considered the problem of testing $H_0 : \rho = 0$ in the linear regression model (3.12) with stationary AR(1) disturbances (3.13) and Gaussian errors, i.e. $\varepsilon_t \sim IN(0, \sigma^2)$. The Durbin–Watson test statistic is of the form

$$d_1 = \sum_{t=2}^{n} (e_t - e_{t-1})^2 \bigg/ \sum_{t=1}^{n} e_t^2$$

where e is the OLS residual vector from (3.12). Unfortunately the null distribution of d_1 is a function of the X matrix through the projection matrix $M = I_n - X(X'X)^{-1}X'$. This meant that a single set of critical values could not be tabulated as was the case for the von Neumann ratio.

Durbin and Watson (1951) overcame this problem by tabulating bounds for the critical values. When the calculated value of the test statistic is between the two bounds, the test is inconclusive. A number of approximations to the DW critical values have been suggested, see King (1987). There are also extensive alternative tables of bounds, see Savin and White (1977), Farebrother (1980) and King (1981). These days computer methods such as simulation or Imhof's (1961) algorithm allow p-values for the test to be calculated as a matter of routine.

The Durbin–Watson test has a number of remarkable small sample power properties. The test is approximately uniformly most powerful invariant (UMPI) when the column space of X is spanned by k of the eigenvectors of the tridiagonal matrix,

$$A_1 = \begin{bmatrix} 1 & -1 & 0 & \cdots & \cdots & \cdots & 0 & 0 \\ -1 & 2 & -1 & & & & & 0 \\ 0 & -1 & 2 & & & & & 0 \\ \vdots & & & \ddots & & & & \vdots \\ \vdots & & & & \ddots & & & \vdots \\ \vdots & & & & & \ddots & & \vdots \\ \vdots & & & & & & 2 & -1 \\ 0 & 0 & 0 & & & & -1 & 1 \end{bmatrix}$$

and approximately locally best invariant (LBI) against AR(1) disturbances. The exact LBI test can be obtained by adding the first and last OLS residual squared to the numerator of the DW statistic. This is known as the modified DW test. The modified DW test is also LBI against MA(1) errors and is uniformly LBI against ARMA(1, 1) disturbances and sums of independent ARMA(1, 1) error components. Consequently, the DW test is approximately LBI or approximately uniformly LBI against these disturbance processes (see King and Evans, 1988). In summary, the literature suggests that the DW test generally has good power against any form of serial correlation provided there is a strong first-order component present.

4.2 Some other tests

The DW test has low power when testing against the simple AR(4) disturbance process given by (3.14) with Gaussian errors. Wallis (1972) and Vinod (1973) separately developed the fourth-order analogue to the DW test which has the test statistic

$$d_4 = \sum_{t=5}^{n} (e_t - e_{t-4})^2 \Big/ \sum_{t=1}^{n} e_t^2.$$

This has been a popular test for use with quarterly time series data and, as Vinod (1973) demonstrated, can be easily generalized to test against any simple AR(p) disturbance process.

Another weakness of the DW test against AR(1) disturbances is the potential for its power to decline to zero as ρ_1 tends to one. This was first noted by Tillman (1975) and explained convincingly by Bartels (1992). It means that the DW test can be at its weakest (in terms of power) just when it is needed most. The class of point optimal tests (King, 1985) provide a solution to this problem. They allow the researcher to fix a value of ρ_1 at which power is optimized. For some X matrices (similar to those for the DW test), this test is approximately UMPI, so optimizing power at a particular ρ_1 value does not mean the test has low power for other ρ_1 values.

The Lagrange multiplier (LM) test is a popular test for AR(p), MA(q) or ARMA(p, q) regression disturbances. A strength of the DW test is that it is one-sided in the sense that it can be applied to test for either positive or negative autocorrelation by use of the appropriate tail of the distribution of d_1 under H_0. The LM test is a general two-sided test and therefore cannot be expected to be as powerful against specific forms of autocorrelation. For further discussion, see Godfrey (1988) and the references therein.

Of course any of the classical tests, such as the likelihood ratio, Wald, and LM tests, can be applied to these testing problems. They can also be used to test one form of disturbance process against a more general form. Again there is mounting evidence to suggest that in terms of accuracy (more accurate sizes and better centered power curves), it is better to construct these tests using the marginal likelihood rather than the full likelihood function (see Rahman and King, 1998; Laskar and King, 1998).

With respect to non-nested testing of disturbance processes, there is a growing literature on testing MA(1) disturbances against AR(1) disturbances and vice versa. See for example King and McAleer (1987), Godfrey and Tremayne (1988) and Silvapulle and King (1991).

4.3 Testing disturbances in the dynamic linear regression model

Finally we turn our attention to the problem of testing for autocorrelation in the disturbances of the dynamic regression model (3.19). Whether the DW test can be used in these circumstances has been an area of controversy in the literature. Durbin and Watson (1950) and others have warned against its use in the dynamic model and this is a theme taken up by many textbooks until recently. The problem has been one of finding appropriate critical values.

Based on the work of Inder (1985, 1986), King and Wu (1991) observed that the small disturbance distribution (the limiting distribution as $\sigma^2 \to 0$) of the DW statistic is the exact distribution of d_1 for the corresponding regression with the lagged dependent variables replaced by their expected values. This provides a justification for the use of the familiar tables of bounds when the DW test is applied to a dynamic regression model. It also highlights a further difficulty. Because $E(y_{t-1})$ is a function of the regression parameters, it is clear the null distribution of the DW test also depends on these parameters, so the test can have different sizes for different parameter values under the null hypothesis. It appears this is a property shared by many alternative tests.

Durbin (1970) suggested his h-test and t-test as alternatives to the DW test. The h-test can suffer from problems in small samples caused by the need to take the square root of what can sometimes be a negative estimate of a variance. The t-test appears more reliable and can be conducted in a simple manner. Let $e_1, \ldots, e_n$ be the OLS residuals from (3.19). $H_0 : \rho = 0$ can be tested using OLS regression to test the significance of the coefficient of e_{t-1} in the regression of e_t on $e_{t-1}, y_{t-1}, y_{t-2} \ldots, x_t$.

That this can be a difficult testing problem is best illustrated by considering (3.18) and (3.13). If x_t is lag invariant then if we switch ρ and α_1, we will end up with the same value of the likelihood function which indicates a local identification problem. For near lag invariant x_t vectors, it is therefore difficult to distinguish between ρ and α_1. This causes problems for the small-sample properties of asymptotic tests in this case and explains why it has been difficult to find a satisfactory test for this testing problem.

5   MODEL SELECTION

A difficult question when modeling economic behavior is to decide on what lags should be in the ARIMA model, the ARMA disturbance model, or the dynamic regression model. It is tempting to use hypothesis testing to help make model specification decisions based on the data, but as discussed by Granger, King, and White (1995), there are disadvantages in doing so. They and others recommend the use of a model selection procedure to make these decisions, the most common of which are information criteria (IC). For each of the models under consideration, one calculates the maximized loglikelihood and then penalizes this value to take account of the number of free parameters in the model which we will denote by j. Akaike's (1973) IC (AIC) uses j as the penalty whereas Schwarz's (1978) Bayesian IC (BIC) uses $j \log(n)/2$. There are a range of other IC procedures, but these two have become the most popular.

These days, BIC seems to be the favored procedure because it is consistent, which means that as the sample size goes to infinity, the probability that it will choose the correct model from a finite number of models goes to one. An unfortunate consequence of this property is that in small samples, BIC tends to wrongly choose underfitting models and can have very low probabilities of correctly selecting a model which has a large number of free parameters. AIC seems more balanced in this regard in small samples, but can suffer from a tendency to overfit in larger samples.

References

Akaike, H. (1973). Information theory and an extension of the maximum likelihood principle. In B.N. Petro and F. Csaki (eds.) *2nd International Symposium on Information Theory*. Budapest: Akademiai Kiado, 267–81.

Ansley, C.F. (1979). An algorithm for the exact likelihood of a mixed autoregressive – moving average process. *Biometrika* 66, 59–65.

Ara, I. (1995). Marginal likelihood based tests of regression disturbances. Unpublished Ph.D. thesis, Monash University.

Baillie, R.T. (1996). Long memory processes and fractional integration in econometrics. *Journal of Econometrics* 73, 5–59.

Bartels, R. (1992). On the power function of the Durbin–Watson test. *Journal of Econometrics* 51, 101–12.

Beach, C.M., and J. MacKinnon (1978a). Full maximum likelihood procedure for regression with autocorrelated errors. *Econometrica* 46, 51–8.

Beach, C.M., and J. MacKinnon (1978b). Full maximum likelihood estimation of second-order autoregressive error models. *Journal of Econometrics* 7, 187–98.

Box, G.E.P., and G.M. Jenkins (1970). *Time Series Analysis, Forecasting and Control*. San Francisco: Holden-Day.

Box, G.E.P., and G.M. Jenkins (1976). *Time Series Analysis, Forecasting and Control*, 2nd edn. San Francisco: Holden-Day.

Cochrane, D., and G. Orcutt (1949). Application of least squares regression to relationships containing autocorrelated error terms. *Journal of the American Statistical Association* 44, 32–61.

Cooper, D.M., and R. Thompson (1977). A note on the estimation of parameters of the autoregressive-moving average process. *Biometrika* 64, 625–8.

Corduas, M. (1986). The use of the marginal likelihood in testing for serial correlation in time series regression. Unpublished M.Phil. thesis, University of Lancaster.

Davidson, R., and J.G. MacKinnon (1993). *Estimation and Inference in Econometrics*. Oxford: Oxford University Press.

Durbin, J. (1970). Testing for serial correlation in least squares regression when some of the regressors are lagged dependent variables. *Econometrica* 38, 410–21.

Durbin, J., and G.S. Watson (1950). Testing for serial correlation in least squares regression I. *Biometrika* 37, 409–28.

Durbin, J., and G.S. Watson (1951). Testing for serial correlation in least squares regression II. *Biometrika* 38, 159–78.

Durbin, J., and G.S. Watson (1971). Testing for serial correlation in least squares regression III. *Biometrika* 58, 1–19.

Farebrother, R.W. (1980). The Durbin–Watson test for serial correlation when there is no intercept in the regression. *Econometrica* 48, 1553–63 and 49, 227.

Godfrey, L.G. (1988). *Misspecification Tests in Econometrics: The Lagrange Multiplier Principle and Other Approaches*. Cambridge: Cambridge University Press.

Godfrey, L.G., and A.R. Tremayne (1988). Checks of model adequacy for univariate time series models and their application to econometric relationships. *Econometric Reviews* 7, 1–42.

Granger, C.W.J., M.L. King, and H. White (1995). Comments on testing economic theories and the use of model selection criteria. *Journal of Econometrics* 67, 173–87.

Hart, B.I. (1942a). Tabulation of the probabilities for the ratio of the mean square successive difference to the variance. *Annals of Mathematical Statistics* 13, 207–14.

Hart, B.I. (1942b). Significance levels for the ratio of the mean square successive difference to the variance. *Annals of Mathematical Statistics* 13, 445–7.

Imhof, P.J. (1961). Computing the distribution of quadratic forms in normal variables. *Biometrika* 48, 419–26.

Inder, B.A. (1985). Testing for first-order autoregressive disturbances in the dynamic linear regression model. Unpublished Ph.D. thesis, Monash University.

Inder, B.A. (1986). An approximation to the null distribution of the Durbin–Watson statistic in models containing lagged dependent variables. *Econometric Theory* 2, 413–28.

Johnston, J. (1972). *Econometric Methods*, 2nd edn. New York: McGraw-Hill.

Kalbfleisch, J.D., and D.A. Sprott (1970). Application of likelihood methods to models involving large numbers of parameters. *Journal of the Royal Statistical Society* B 32, 175–94.

King, M.L. (1981). The Durbin–Watson test for serial correlation: Bounds for regressions with trend and/or seasonal dummy variables. *Econometrica* 49, 1571–81.

King, M.L. (1985). A point optimal test for autoregressive disturbances. *Journal of Econometrics* 27, 21–37.

King, M.L. (1987). Testing for autocorrelation in linear regression models: A survey. In M.L. King and D.E.A. Giles (eds.) *Specification Analysis in the Linear Model*, London: Routledge and Kegan Paul, 19–73.

King, M.L., and M.A. Evans (1988). Locally optimal properties of the Durbin–Watson test. *Econometric Theory* 4, 509–16.

King, M.L., and M. McAleer (1987). Further results on testing AR(1) against MA(1) disturbances in the linear regression model. *Review of Economic Studies* 54, 649–63.

King, M.L., and P.X. Wu (1991). Small-disturbance asymptotics and the Durbin–Watson and related tests in the dynamic regression model. *Journal of Econometrics* 47, 145–52.

Laskar, M.R., and M.L. King (1998). Estimation and testing of regression disturbances based on modified likelihood functions. *Journal of Statistical Planning and Inference* 71, 75–92.

Levenbach, H. (1972). Estimation of autoregressive parameters from a marginal likelihood function. *Biometrika* 59, 61–71.

Nichols, D.F., A.R. Pagan, and R.D. Terrell (1975). The estimation and use of models with moving average disturbance terms: A survey. *International Economic Review* 16, 113–34.

Prais, S.J., and C.B. Winsten (1954). Trend estimators and serial correlation. Unpublished Cowles Commission Discussion Paper, University of Chicago.

Rahman, S., and M.L. King (1993). Testing for ARMA(1, 1) disturbances in the linear regression model. *Australian Economic Papers* 32, 284–98.

Rahman, S., and M.L. King (1998). Marginal-likelihood score-based tests of regression disturbances in the presence of nuisance parameters. *Journal of Econometrics* 82, 81–106.

Savin, N.E., and K.J. White (1977). The Durbin–Watson test for serial correlation with extreme sample sizes or many regressors. *Econometrica* 45, 1989–96.

Schwarz, G.W. (1978). Estimating the dimension of a model. *Annals of Statistics* 6, 461–4.

Silvapulle, P., and M.L. King (1991). Testing moving average against autoregressive disturbances in the linear regression model. *Journal of Business and Economic Statistics* 9, 329–35.

Thomas, J.J., and K.F. Wallis (1971). Seasonal variation in regression analysis. *Journal of the Royal Statistical Society* A 134, 57–72.

Tillman, J.A. (1975). The power of the Durbin–Watson test. *Econometrica* 43, 959–74.

Tse, Y.K. (1982). Edgeworth approximations in first-order stochastic difference equations with exogenous variables. *Journal of Econometrics* 20, 175–95.

Tunnicliffe Wilson, G. (1989). On the use of marginal likelihood in time series model estimation. *Journal of the Royal Statistical Society* B 51, 15–27.

Van der Leeuw, J. (1994). The covariance matrix of ARMA errors in closed form. *Journal of Econometrics* 63, 397–405.

Vinod, H.D. (1973). Generalization of the Durbin–Watson statistic for higher order autoregressive processes. *Communications in Statistics* 2, 115–44.

Von Neumann, J. (1941). Distribution of the ratio of the mean square successive difference to the variance. *Annals of Mathematical Statistics* 12, 367–95.

Von Neumann, J. (1942). A further remark concerning the distribution of the ratio of the mean square successive difference to the variance. *Annals of Mathematical Statistics* 13, 86–8.

Wallis, K.F. (1972). Testing for fourth order autocorrelation in quarterly regression equations. *Econometrica* 40, 617–36.

Heteroskedasticity

William E. Griffiths*

1   INTRODUCTION

A random variable y is said to be heteroskedastic if its variance can be different for different observations. Conversely, it is said to be homoskedastic if its variance is constant for all observations. The most common framework in which heteroskedasticity is studied in econometrics is in the context of the general linear model

$$y_i = x_i'\beta + e_i, \tag{4.1}$$

where x_i is a K-dimensional vector of observations on a set of explanatory variables, β is a K-dimensional vector of coefficients which we wish to estimate and y_i denotes the ith observation $(i = 1, 2, \ldots, N)$ on a dependent variable. In a heteroskedastic model the error term e_i is assumed to have zero-mean and variance σ_i^2, the i subscript on σ_i^2 reflecting possibly different variances for each observation. Conditional on $x_i'\beta$, the dependent variable y_i has mean $x_i'\beta$ and variance σ_i^2. Thus, in the heteroskedastic general linear model, the mean and variance of the random variable y can both change over observations.

Heteroskedasticity can arise empirically, through theoretical considerations and from model misspecification. Empirically, heteroskedasticity is often encountered when using cross-sectional data on a number of microeconomic units such as firms or households. A common example is the estimation of household expenditure functions. Expenditure on a commodity is more easily explained by conventional variables for households with low incomes than it is for households with high incomes. The lower predictive ability of the model for high incomes can be captured by specifying a variance σ_i^2 which is larger when income is larger. Data on firms invariably involve observations on economic units of varying sizes. Larger firms are likely to be more diverse and flexible with respect to the way in which values for y_i are determined. This additional diversity is captured through an error term with a larger variance. Theoretical considerations, such as randomness in behavior, can also lead to heteroskedasticity. Brown and Walker (1989, 1995) give examples of how it arises naturally in demand and production models. Moreover, as chapter 19 in this volume (by Swamy and Tavlas) illustrates, heteroskedasticity exists in all models with random coefficients. Misspecifications such as incorrect functional form, omitted variables and structural change are other reasons that a model may exhibit heteroskedasticity.

In this chapter we give the fundamentals of sampling theory and Bayesian estimation, and sampling theory hypothesis testing, for a linear model with heteroskedasticity. For sampling theory estimation it is convenient to first describe estimation for a known error covariance matrix and to then extend it for an unknown error covariance matrix. No attempt is made to give specific details of developments beyond what we consider to be the fundamentals. However, references to such developments and how they build on the fundamentals are provided. Autoregressive conditional heteroskedasticity (ARCH) which is popular for modeling volatility in time series is considered elsewhere in this volume and not discussed in this chapter.

2 Sampling Theory Inference with Known Covariance Matrix

Writing $y_i = x_i'\beta + e_i$ so that all N observations are included yields the familiar matrix expression

$$y = X\beta + e, \tag{4.2}$$

where y and e are of dimension $(N \times 1)$ and X is of dimension $(N \times K)$, and rank K. The assumption of heteroskedastic y can be written as

$$E[(y - X\beta)(y - X\beta)'] = E[ee'] = V = \sigma^2\Lambda, \tag{4.3}$$

where

$$V = \text{diagonal}(\sigma_1^2, \sigma_2^2, \ldots, \sigma_N^2)$$
$$= \sigma^2 \text{diagonal}(\lambda_1, \lambda_2, \ldots, \lambda_N)$$
$$= \sigma^2\Lambda. \tag{4.4}$$

In equation (4.4) a constant σ^2 has been factored out of V yielding a matrix Λ of ratios $\lambda_i = \sigma_i^2/\sigma^2$. This factoring device is useful (i) when Λ is known, but σ^2 is not, and (ii) if a heteroskedastic specification has a constant component (σ^2 in this case) and a component that varies over observations. The constant that is factored out is arbitrary, and, in practice, is chosen for convenience.

The generalized least squares estimator for β which, from the Gauss–Markov Theorem is known to be the best linear unbiased estimator, is given by

$$\hat{\beta} = (X'V^{-1}X)^{-1}X'V^{-1}y = \left(\sum_{i=1}^{N} \frac{x_i x_i'}{\sigma_i^2}\right)^{-1} \sum_{i=1}^{N} \frac{x_i y_i}{\sigma_i^2}$$

$$= (X'\Lambda^{-1}X)^{-1}X'\Lambda^{-1}y = \left(\sum_{i=1}^{N} \frac{x_i x_i'}{\lambda_i}\right)^{-1} \sum_{i=1}^{N} \frac{x_i y_i}{\lambda_i}. \tag{4.5}$$

The right-hand expressions in equations (4.4) emphasize the *weighted* nature of the generalized least squares estimator. Each observation (x_i and y_i) is weighted by the inverse standard deviation σ_i^{-1}, or a quantity proportional to it, $\lambda_i^{-1/2}$. Observations that are less reliable because they come from a distribution with a large variance are weighted less than more reliable observations where σ_i^2 is smaller. The mean and covariance matrix of the generalized least squares estimator are given by $E[\hat{\beta}] = \beta$ and $V_{\hat{\beta}}$, respectively, where

$$V_{\hat{\beta}} = (X'V^{-1}X)^{-1} = \left(\sum_{i=1}^{N} \frac{x_i x_i'}{\sigma_i^2}\right)^{-1} = \sigma^2 (X'\Lambda^{-1}X)^{-1} = \sigma^2 \left(\sum_{i=1}^{N} \frac{x_i x_i'}{\lambda_i}\right)^{-1}. \tag{4.6}$$

Practical application of (4.5) and (4.6) requires knowledge of at least Λ. For inference purposes, an unbiased estimator for σ^2 can be found from

$$\hat{\sigma}^2 = \frac{(y - X\hat{\beta})'\Lambda^{-1}(y - X\hat{\beta})}{N - K}. \tag{4.7}$$

Although most applications proceed by refining the specification of Λ into one that contains a reduced number of parameters that is constant for changing sample size, there are some scenarios where knowledge of Λ is a reasonable assumption. To illustrate one such example, suppose that we are interested in an industry cost function that can be written as

$$y_{ij} = x_{ij}'\beta + e_{ij}, \tag{4.8}$$

where the double subscript (i, j) refers to the jth firm in the ith industry. Suppose also that the e_{ij} are independent with $\mathrm{var}(e_{ij}) = \sigma^2$ (a constant) and that there are n_i firms in the ith industry. A model for data obtained by averaging over all firms in each industry is given by

$$\frac{1}{n_i}\sum_{j=1}^{n_i} y_{ij} = \frac{1}{n_i}\sum_{j=1}^{n_i} x_{ij}'\beta + \frac{1}{n_i}\sum_{j=1}^{n_i} e_{ij}$$

or

$$\bar{y}_i = \bar{x}_i'\beta + \bar{e}_i. \tag{4.9}$$

The variance of the error term is

$$\text{var}(\bar{e}_i) = \frac{1}{n_i^2} \sum_{j=1}^{n_i} \text{var}(e_{ij}) = \frac{1}{n_i^2} n_i \sigma^2 = \frac{\sigma^2}{n_i}.$$

That is, $\bar{e}_i$ is heteroskedastic with its variance depending on the number of firms used to compute the average industry data. Providing this number is available, the matrix Λ is known with its inverse given by

$$\Lambda^{-1} = \text{diagonal}(n_1, n_2, \ldots, n_N).$$

The generalized least squares procedure can be applied. It recognizes that industry observations obtained by averaging a large number of firms are more reliable than those obtained by averaging a small number of firms.

To construct confidence intervals for the elements in β or to test hypotheses about the elements in β, one can assume the error vector e is normally distributed and proceed with finite sample inference procedures, or one can use large sample approximate inference procedures without the assumption of normally distributed errors. When the errors are normally distributed the following results hold:

$$\frac{(N - K)\hat{\sigma}^2}{\sigma^2} \sim \chi^2_{(N-K)} \tag{4.10}$$

$$R\hat{\beta} \sim N[R\beta, \sigma^2 R(X'\Lambda^{-1}X)^{-1}R'] \tag{4.11}$$

$$\frac{(R\hat{\beta} - R\beta)'[R(X'\Lambda^{-1}X)^{-1}R']^{-1}(R\hat{\beta} - R\beta)}{\sigma^2} \sim \chi^2_{(J)} \tag{4.12}$$

$$F = \frac{(R\hat{\beta} - R\beta)'[R(X'\Lambda^{-1}X)^{-1}R']^{-1}(R\hat{\beta} - R\beta)/J}{\hat{\sigma}^2} \sim F_{[J,(N-K)]}. \tag{4.13}$$

In the above expressions R is a $(J \times K)$ matrix of rank J whose elements define the quantity for which inference is sought. These results parallel those for the general linear model with independent, identically distributed error terms, and can be derived from them by using a straightforward transformation. For details of the transformation, and more details of how equations (4.10)–(4.13) are used for hypothesis testing and interval estimation, see, for example, Judge et $al.$ (1988, ch. 8). When the errors are not assumed to be normally distributed, approximate large sample inference is based on equation (4.12) with σ^2 replaced by $\hat{\sigma}^2$.

For inferences about nonlinear functions of the elements of β that cannot be written as $R\beta$, we consider functions of the form $g(\beta) = 0$ where $g(\cdot)$ is a J-dimensional vector function. Inference can be based on the approximate result

$$\frac{g(\hat{\beta})'[G(X'\Lambda^{-1}X)^{-1}G']^{-1}g(\hat{\beta})}{\hat{\sigma}^2} \sim \chi^2_{(J)}, \tag{4.14}$$

where G is the $(J \times K)$ matrix of partial derivatives, with rank J,

$$G = \frac{\partial g(\beta)}{\partial \beta'}\bigg|_{\hat{\beta}}. \tag{4.15}$$

Three categories of tests frequently used in econometrics are the Wald, Lagrange multiplier, and likelihood ratio tests. In the context of the scenarios discussed so far (hypothesis tests about β in a model with covariance matrix $\sigma^2\Lambda$, with Λ known), all three testing principles lead to the results given above. The only difference is that, in a Lagrange multiplier test, the estimate for σ^2 is based on the restricted rather than unrestricted generalized least squares residuals.

Further details on estimation and hypothesis testing for the case of a known error covariance matrix can be found in standard textbooks such as Judge *et al.* (1988, chs. 8, 9), Greene (1997, ch. 12) and Baltagi (1998, chs. 5, 9). Of particular interest might be the consequences of using the ordinary least squares (OLS) estimator $b = (X'X)^{-1}X'y$ in the presence of heteroskedastic errors. It is well known that, under these circumstances, the OLS estimator is inefficient and that the estimated covariance matrix $\hat{\sigma}^2(X'X)^{-1}$ is a biased estimate of the true covariance matrix $\sigma^2(X'X)^{-1}X'\Lambda X(X'X)^{-1}$. Examples of inefficiencies and bias are given in most textbook treatments.

3   SAMPLING THEORY ESTIMATION AND INFERENCE WITH UNKNOWN COVARIANCE MATRIX

Consider again the linear model $y = X\beta + e$ with error-covariance matrix $V = \sigma^2\Lambda$. In this section we relax the assumption that Λ is known. As we saw in the previous section, there are some circumstances where such an assumption is reasonable. However, there are also many where it is not. For example, in a household expenditure function, we may be willing to assume the variance of expenditure depends on total expenditure and the demographic composition of the household, but not willing to specify the values of parameters that describe the dependence. Thus, we could write, for example,

$$\sigma_i^2 = \theta_0 + \theta_1 z_{1i} + \theta_2 z_{2i}, \tag{4.16}$$

where z_{1i} and z_{2i} are total expenditure and demographic composition, respectively, and $(\theta_0, \theta_1, \theta_2)$ are unknown parameters. If $(\sigma_1^2, \sigma_2^2, \ldots, \sigma_N^2)$ are not known, then some kind of reparameterization such as that in (4.16) is necessary to reduce the number of parameters to a manageable number that does not increase with sample size. We will work in terms of the general notation

$$\sigma_i^2 = \sigma^2 h_i(\alpha) = \sigma^2 h(z_i'\alpha), \tag{4.17}$$

where α is an $(S \times 1)$ vector of unknown parameters, and $h_i(\cdot)$ is a differentiable function of those parameters and an $(S \times 1)$ vector z_i which could be identical to or different from x_i. To write (4.16) in terms of the general notation in (4.17), we re-express it as

$$\sigma_i^2 = \theta_0 \left(1 + \frac{\theta_1}{\theta_0} z_{1i} + \frac{\theta_2}{\theta_0} z_{2i} \right) = \sigma^2 (1 + \alpha_1 z_{1i} + \alpha_2 z_{2i}) = \sigma^2 h_i(\alpha). \qquad (4.18)$$

In this example, and others which we consider, $h_i(0) = 1$, implying that $\alpha = 0$ describes a model with homoskedastic errors.

Several alternative specifications of $h_i(\alpha)$ have been suggested in the literature. See Judge *et al.* (1985, p. 422) for a review. One of these is that given in (4.18), namely

$$h_i(\alpha) = 1 + \alpha_1 z_{1i} + \ldots + \alpha_S z_{Si}. \qquad (4.19)$$

This model has been considered by, among others, Goldfeld and Quandt (1972) and Amemiya (1977), and, in the context of a random coefficient model, by Hildreth and Houck (1968) and Griffiths (1972). Note that, if $(z_{1i}, \ldots, z_{Si})$ are non-overlapping dummy variables, then the specification in (4.19) describes a partition of the sample into $(S + 1)$ subsamples, each one with a different error variance. Such a model could be relevant if parts of the sample came from different geographical regions or there exists some other way of naturally creating sample separations. Examples where estimation within this framework has been considered are Griffiths and Judge (1992) and Hooper (1993).

One potential difficulty with the specification in (4.19) is that the requirement $h_i(\alpha) > 0$ can mean that restrictions must be placed on α to ensure that negative variances are not possible. Two possible specifications which avoid this problem are

$$h_i(\alpha) = (1 + \alpha_1 z_{1i} + \ldots + \alpha_S z_{Si})^2 \qquad (4.20)$$

and

$$h_i(\alpha) = \exp(\alpha_1 z_{1i} + \ldots + \alpha_S z_{Si}). \qquad (4.21)$$

The specification in (4.20) has received attention from Rutemiller and Bowers (1968) and Jobson and Fuller (1980). The specification in (4.21) was introduced by Harvey (1976) under the heading "multiplicative heteroskedasticity." For applications and extensions, see Griffiths and Anderson (1982), and Hill *et al.* (1997).

A class of models which has been popular, but which does not fit within the framework of equation (4.17), is that where the location parameter vector β also appears within the variance function. Authors who have considered this class of models under varying degrees of generality include Amemiya (1973), Jobson and Fuller (1980), and Welsh *et al.* (1994).

3.1 Maximum likelihood estimation

Two-step estimation of heteroskedastic error models was popular prior to the development of modern software. These techniques use the residuals from least squares estimation to estimate α, and then use the estimate of α in a generalized least squares estimator. See Judge *et al.* (1985, pp. 431–41) for details. However, it is now more common to assume normally distributed errors and proceed with maximum likelihood estimation. Working in this direction, the loglikelihood function can be written as

$$L = -\frac{N}{2}\ln(2\pi) - \frac{N}{2}\ln(\sigma^2) - \frac{1}{2}\sum_{i=1}^{N}\ln(h_i(\alpha)) - \frac{1}{2\sigma^2}\sum_{i=1}^{N}\frac{(y_i - x_i'\beta)^2}{h_i(\alpha)}$$

$$= -\frac{N}{2}\ln(2\pi) - \frac{N}{2}\ln(\sigma^2) - \frac{1}{2}\ln|\Lambda| - \frac{1}{2\sigma^2}(y - X\beta)'\Lambda^{-1}(y - X\beta). \quad (4.22)$$

Differentiating this function with respect to σ^2 and β and setting these derivatives equal to zero gives the results

$$\hat{\beta}(\alpha) = (X'\Lambda^{-1}X)^{-1}X'\Lambda^{-1}y \quad (4.23)$$

$$\hat{\sigma}^2(\alpha) = \frac{1}{N}(y - X\hat{\beta}(\alpha))'\Lambda^{-1}(y - X\hat{\beta}(\alpha)). \quad (4.24)$$

Since these estimators are conditional on knowing α, they resemble those provided in the previous section, the only difference being the divisor N, instead of $(N - K)$, in equation (4.24).

Differentiating L with respect to α yields

$$\frac{\partial L}{\partial \alpha} = -\frac{1}{2}\sum_{i=1}^{N}\frac{1}{h_i(\alpha)}\frac{\partial h_i}{\partial \alpha} + \frac{1}{2\sigma^2}\sum_{i=1}^{N}\frac{(y_i - x_i'\beta)^2}{[h_i(\alpha)]^2}\frac{\partial h_i}{\partial \alpha}. \quad (4.25)$$

Setting this derivative equal to zero does not yield a convenient solution for α, although it does simplify for specific definitions of $h_i(\alpha)$. For example, for the specification in equation (4.21), written in matrix algebra notation as $h_i(\alpha) = \exp\{z_i'\alpha\}$, equating (4.25) to zero yields

$$\sum_{i=1}^{N}\frac{(y_i - x_i'\beta)^2}{\exp(z_i'\alpha)}z_i = \sigma^2\sum_{i=1}^{N}z_i. \quad (4.26)$$

Substituting (4.23) and (4.24) into (4.22) yields the concentrated loglikelihood function

$$L^*(\alpha) = \text{constant} - \frac{N}{2}\ln[(y - X\hat{\beta}(\alpha))'\Lambda^{-1}(y - X\hat{\beta}(\alpha))] - \frac{1}{2}\ln|\Lambda|. \quad (4.27)$$

Thus, maximum likelihood estimation can proceed by numerically finding the value of $\hat{\alpha}$ that maximizes L^*, and then substituting that value into equations (4.23) and (4.24).

The information matrix is given by

$$
I(\beta, \alpha, \sigma^2) = -E
\begin{bmatrix}
\dfrac{\partial^2 L}{\partial\beta\,\partial\beta'} & \dfrac{\partial^2 L}{\partial\beta\,\partial\alpha'} & \dfrac{\partial^2 L}{\partial\beta\,\partial\sigma^2} \\[2ex]
\dfrac{\partial^2 L}{\partial\alpha\,\partial\beta'} & \dfrac{\partial^2 L}{\partial\alpha\,\partial\alpha'} & \dfrac{\partial^2 L}{\partial\alpha\,\partial\sigma^2} \\[2ex]
\dfrac{\partial^2 L}{\partial\sigma^2\,\partial\beta'} & \dfrac{\partial^2 L}{\partial\sigma^2\,\partial\alpha'} & \dfrac{\partial^2 L}{\partial(\sigma^2)^2}
\end{bmatrix}
$$

$$
=
\begin{bmatrix}
\dfrac{X'\Lambda^{-1}X}{\sigma^2} & 0 & 0 \\[2ex]
0 & \dfrac{1}{2}\displaystyle\sum_{i=1}^{N}\dfrac{1}{[h_i(\alpha)]^2}\dfrac{\partial h_i}{\partial\alpha}\dfrac{\partial h_i}{\partial\alpha'} & \dfrac{1}{\partial\sigma^2}\displaystyle\sum_{i=1}^{N}\dfrac{1}{h_i(\alpha)}\dfrac{\partial h_i}{\partial\alpha} \\[2ex]
0 & \dfrac{1}{2\sigma^2}\displaystyle\sum_{i=1}^{N}\dfrac{1}{h_i(\alpha)}\dfrac{\partial h_i}{\partial\alpha'} & \dfrac{N}{2\sigma^4}
\end{bmatrix}
\qquad (4.28)
$$

The inverse of this matrix is the asymptotic covariance matrix for the maximum likelihood estimators of β, α and σ^2. Its block-diagonal nature means the asymptotic covariance matrix for the maximum likelihood estimator $\hat{\beta}$ is given by the familiar expression

$$
V_{\hat{\beta}} = \sigma^2(X'\Lambda^{-1}X)^{-1}.
$$

Equation (4.28) can be simplified considerably once $h_i(\alpha)$ is specified explicitly. For example, for the case where $h_i(\alpha) = \exp\{z_i'\alpha\}$,

$$
I(\beta, \alpha, \sigma^2) =
\begin{bmatrix}
\dfrac{X'\Lambda^{-1}X}{\sigma^2} & 0 & 0 \\[2ex]
0 & \dfrac{1}{2}Z'Z & \dfrac{1}{\partial\sigma^2}\displaystyle\sum z_i \\[2ex]
0 & \dfrac{1}{2\sigma^2}\displaystyle\sum z_i' & \dfrac{N}{2\sigma^4}
\end{bmatrix}
\qquad (4.29)
$$

where $Z' = (z_1, z_2, \ldots, z_N)$.

3.2   Testing hypotheses about β

To test hypotheses about β, the large sample result given in equation (4.12) can be used. The only differences are that $\hat{\beta}$ becomes the maximum likelihood estimator, and σ^2 and Λ are replaced by their maximum likelihood estimators.

Using the maximum likelihood estimator for β and its corresponding covariance matrix to test hypotheses about β requires knowledge of the function $h_i(\alpha)$. That is, the form of the heteroskedasticity is required. As an alternative, tests can be based on the ordinary least squares estimator for β and an estimate of its covariance matrix. Specifically, the least squares estimator $b = (X'X)^{-1}X'y$ has covariance matrix

$$V_b = (X'X)^{-1}X'VX(X'X)^{-1},$$

which White (1980) has shown can be consistently estimated by

$$\hat{V}_b = (X'X)^{-1}X'\hat{V}X(X'X)^{-1},$$

where $\hat{V}$ is a diagonal matrix containing the squares of the ordinary least squares residuals. Thus, the result

$$(Rb - R\beta)'(R\hat{V}_bR')^{-1}(Rb - R\beta) \overset{a}{\sim} \chi^2_{(J)}$$

can be used to make approximate inferences about β. The finite sample properties of such inferences have been questioned however and ways for improving the test have been investigated. For access to the literature on this issue see Keener et al. (1991) and Davidson and MacKinnon (1993).

3.3   Testing for heteroskedasticity

Assuming that $h_i(\alpha)$ is such that $h_i(0) = 1$, tests for heteroskedasticity can be formulated in terms of the hypotheses

$$H_0 : \alpha = 0 \qquad H_1 : \alpha \neq 0.$$

We will describe the likelihood ratio, Wald, and Lagrange multiplier test statistics for these hypotheses, and then refer to other tests and evaluations that have appeared in the literature.

Using equation (4.27), the *likelihood ratio (LR) test* statistic is given by

$$\gamma_{LR} = 2[L(\hat{\alpha}) - L(0)]$$

$$= N\ln\left(\frac{\hat{e}_0'\hat{e}_0}{\hat{e}'\hat{\Lambda}^{-1}\hat{e}}\right) - \sum_{i=1}^{N} \ln[h_i(\hat{\alpha})], \qquad (4.30)$$

where $\hat{e}_0 = y - Xb$ are the OLS residuals and $\hat{e} = y - X\hat{\beta}(\hat{\alpha})$ are the maximum likelihood residuals. When the null hypothesis of homoskedasticity holds, γ_{LR} has an approximate $\chi^2_{(s)}$ distribution.

The *Wald (W) test* statistic is given by

$$\gamma_W = \hat{\alpha}'\hat{V}_{\hat{\alpha}}^{-1}\hat{\alpha}, \qquad (4.31)$$

where, applying partitioned-inverse results to equation (4.28), it can be shown that

$$V_{\hat{\alpha}}^{-1} = \frac{1}{2} \sum_{i=1}^{N} \frac{1}{[h_i(\alpha)]^2} \frac{\partial h_i}{\partial \alpha} \frac{\partial h_i}{\partial \alpha'} - \frac{1}{2N} \left(\sum_{i=1}^{N} \frac{1}{h_i(\alpha)} \frac{\partial h_i}{\partial \alpha} \right) \left(\sum_{i=1}^{N} \frac{1}{h_i(\alpha)} \frac{\partial h_i}{\partial \alpha'} \right). \tag{4.32}$$

The statistic γ_W has an approximate $\chi^2_{(S)}$ distribution when $\alpha = 0$.

The *Lagrange multiplier* (LM) *test* statistic is given by

$$\gamma_{LM} = s_0' I_0^{-1}(\alpha, \sigma^2) s_0, \tag{4.33}$$

where

$$s_0 = \begin{pmatrix} \partial L/\partial \alpha \\ \partial L/\partial \sigma^2 \end{pmatrix} \text{ is evaluated at } \alpha = 0, \sigma^2 = \hat{\sigma}^2(0) \text{ and } \beta = b.$$

$I_0^{-1}(\alpha, \sigma^2)$ is the inverse of the bottom-right block in equation (4.28), evaluated at

$$\alpha = 0 \text{ and } \sigma^2 = \hat{\sigma}^2(0).$$

Recognizing that $\partial h_i/\partial \alpha$ evaluated at $\alpha = 0$ is equal to z_i, equation (4.25) can be used to yield

$$s_0 = \begin{pmatrix} \dfrac{1}{2} \sum_{i=1}^{N} z_i \left(\dfrac{\hat{e}_{0i}^2}{\hat{\sigma}_0^2} - 1 \right) \\ 0 \end{pmatrix} \tag{4.34}$$

where $\hat{\sigma}_0^2 = \sum_{i=1}^{N} \hat{e}_{0i}^2 / N = \hat{\sigma}^2(0)$.

Then, utilizing (4.32) evaluated at $\alpha = 0$, the Lagrange multiplier statistic becomes

$$\gamma_{LM} = \frac{\sum_{i=1}^{N} z_i'(\hat{e}_{0i}^2 - \hat{\sigma}_0^2) \left(\sum_{i=1}^{N} (z_i - \bar{z})(z_i - \bar{z})' \right)^{-1} \sum_{i=1}^{N} z_i(\hat{e}_{0i}^2 - \hat{\sigma}_0^2)}{2\hat{\sigma}_0^4}.$$

This statistic is conveniently calculated as one-half of the regression sum-of-squares of $\hat{e}_{0i}^2/\hat{\sigma}_0^2$ on z_i and a constant term. It has an approximate $\chi^2_{(S)}$ distribution under $H_0 : \alpha = 0$. The Lagrange multiplier test statistic was derived by Breusch and Pagan (1979) and Godfrey (1978). To make it more robust to departures from normality, replacement of the denominator $2\hat{\sigma}_0^4$ by $N^{-1} \sum_{i=1}^{N} (\hat{e}_{0i}^2 - \hat{\sigma}_0^2)^2$ has been suggested (Koenker and Bassett, 1982).

Many more tests for heteroskedasticity have been suggested in the literature. See Pagan and Pak (1993) for a review and for details on how the various tests can be classified as conditional moment tests. One popular test that we have not yet mentioned is the Goldfeld–Quandt (1965) test which uses the error variances from two separate least squares regressions to construct a finite sample F-statistic. Other classes of tests have been described by Szroeter (1978) and Farebrother (1987). Lee (1992) suggests a test where the mean function is estimated nonparametrically and hence does not have to be precisely specified. Orme (1992) describes tests in the context of censored and truncated regression models. Also, tests for heteroskedasticity in these and other nonlinear models, such as discrete choice models and count data models, are reviewed by Pagan and Pak (1993). Numerous Monte Carlo studies have compared the finite sample size and power of existing and new test statistics. Typically, authors uncover problems with existing test statistics such as poor finite sample size or power, or lack of robustness to misspecification and nonnormality, and suggest alternatives to correct for such problems. A study by Godfrey and Orme (1999) suggests that bootstrapping leads to favorable outcomes. Other examples of Monte Carlo studies that have appeared are Evans and King (1988), Griffiths and Surekha (1986), Griffiths and Judge (1992) and Godfrey (1996). See Farebrother (1987) for some insightful comments on the results of Griffiths and Surekha (1986).

3.4 Estimation with unknown form of heteroskedasticity

The work of White (1980) on testing for heteroskedasticity and testing hypotheses about β without specifying the precise form of the heteroskedasticity motivated others to seek *estimators* for β that did not require specification of the form of heteroskedasticity. Attempts have been made to specify estimators which are more efficient than OLS, while at the same time recognizing that the efficiency of GLS may not be achievable (Cragg, 1992; Amemiya, 1983). Carroll (1982) and Robinson (1987) develop adaptive estimators that assume no particular form of heteroskedasticity but nevertheless have the same asymptotic distribution as the generalized least squares estimator that uses a correct parametric specification. These adaptive estimators have been evaluated in terms of a second-order approximation by Linton (1996) and extended to time series models by Hidalgo (1992), to nonlinear multivariate models by Delgado (1992), and to panel data by Li and Stengos (1994). Szroeter (1994) suggests weighted least squares estimators that have better finite sample efficiency than OLS when the observations can be ordered according to increasing variances but no other information is available.

3.5 Other extensions

Rilestone (1991) has compared the relative efficiency of semiparametric and parametric estimators of β under different types of heteroskedasticity, whereas Surekha and Griffiths (1984) compare the relative efficiency of some Bayesian and sampling theory estimators using a similar Monte Carlo setup. Donald (1995) examines heteroskedasticity in sample selection models, and provides access to that literature. In truncated and censored models heteroskedasticity impacts on the consistency of estimators, not just their efficiency. Heteroskedasticity in the context of seemingly unrelated regressions has been studied by Mandy and Martins-Filho (1993). Further details appear in chapter 5 by Fiebig. A useful reference that brings together much of the statistical literature on heteroskedasticity is Carroll and Ruppert (1988).

4 Bayesian Inference

With Bayesian inference post-sample information about unknown parameters is summarized via posterior probability density functions (pdfs) on the parameters of interest. Representing parameter uncertainty in this way is (arguably) more natural than the point estimates and standard errors produced by sampling theory, and provides a flexible way of including additional prior information. In the heteroskedastic model that we have been discussing, namely, $y_i = x_i'\beta + e_i$, with var$(e_i) = \sigma^2 h_i(\alpha)$, the parameters of interest are β, α, and σ, with particular interest usually centering on β. The starting point for Bayesian inference is the specification of prior pdfs for β, σ, and α. Since noninformative prior pdfs carry with them the advantage of objective reporting of results, we adopt the conventional ones for β and σ (see Zellner, 1971)

$$f(\beta, \sigma) = f(\beta)f(\sigma) \propto \text{constant}\,\frac{1}{\sigma}. \tag{4.35}$$

The choice of prior for α is likely to depend on the function $h(\cdot)$. Possible choices are a uniform prior or a prior based on the information matrix. See Zellner (1971, p. 47) for details on the latter. Leaving the precise nature of the prior for α unspecified, the joint prior pdf for all unknown parameters can be written as

$$f(\beta, \sigma, \alpha) = f(\beta, \sigma)f(\alpha) \propto \frac{f(\alpha)}{\sigma}. \tag{4.36}$$

Assuming normally distributed observations, the likelihood function can be written as

$$f(y|\beta, \sigma, \alpha) \propto \frac{1}{\sigma^N}|\Lambda|^{-1/2}\exp\left\{-\frac{1}{2\sigma^2}(y - X\beta)'\Lambda^{-1}(y - X\beta)\right\}. \tag{4.37}$$

The joint posterior pdf for (β, σ, α) is

$$f(\beta, \sigma, \alpha|y) \propto f(y|\beta, \sigma, \alpha)f(\beta, \sigma, \alpha)$$

$$\propto \frac{f(\alpha)}{\sigma^{N+1}}|\Lambda|^{-1/2}\exp\left\{-\frac{1}{2\sigma^2}(y - X\beta)'\Lambda^{-1}(y - X\beta)\right\}. \tag{4.38}$$

Once this joint posterior pdf for all parameters has been obtained, the major task is to derive marginal posterior pdfs for each single parameter. The information in a marginal posterior pdf can then be represented in a diagram or summarized via the moments of the pdf. Where possible, marginal posterior pdfs are obtained by integrating out the remaining parameters. Where analytical integration is not possible, numerical methods are used to estimate the marginal posterior pdfs. There are a variety of ways in which one could proceed with respect to equation (4.38). The steps for one way that is likely to work well are:

1. Integrate σ out to obtain the joint posterior pdf $f(\beta, \alpha | y)$.
2. Integrate β out of the result in step 1 to obtain the posterior pdf $f(\alpha | y)$.
3. Use a Metropolis algorithm to draw observations from the density $f(\alpha | y)$.
4. Construct the conditional posterior pdf $f(\beta | \alpha, y)$ from the joint posterior pdf that was obtained in step 1; note the conditional mean $E[\beta | \alpha, y]$ and conditional variance $\text{var}[\beta | \alpha, y]$.
5. From step 4, note the conditional posterior pdf and corresponding moments for each element, say β_k, in the vector β.
6. Find estimates of the marginal posterior pdf for β_k, ($k = 1, 2, \ldots, K$), and its moments, by averaging the conditional quantities given in step 5, over the conditioning values of α drawn in step 3.

We will consider each of these steps in turn.

Step 1

The joint posterior pdf for (β, α) is given by

$$f(\beta, \alpha | y) = \int f(\beta, \alpha, \sigma | y) d\sigma$$

$$\propto f(\alpha) |\Lambda|^{-1/2} [N\hat{\sigma}^2(\alpha) + (\beta - \hat{\beta}(\alpha))'X'\Lambda^{-1}X(\beta - \hat{\beta}(\alpha))]^{-N/2} \quad (4.39)$$

where $\hat{\sigma}^2(\alpha)$ and $\hat{\beta}(\alpha)$ are defined in equations (4.23) and (4.24). The pdf in (4.39) is not utilized directly; it provides an intermediate step for obtaining $f(\alpha | y)$ and $f(\beta | \alpha, y)$.

Step 2

The marginal posterior pdf for the parameters in the variance function is given by

$$f(\alpha | y) = \int f(\beta, \alpha | y) d\beta$$

$$\propto f(\alpha) |\Lambda|^{-1/2} [\hat{\sigma}(\alpha)]^{-(N-K)} |X'\Lambda^{-1}X|^{-1/2} \quad (4.40)$$

STEP 3

The pdf in equation (4.40) is not of a recognizable form, even when imaginative choices for the prior $f(\alpha)$ are made. Thus, it is not possible to perform further analytical integration to isolate marginal posterior pdfs for single elements such as α_s. Instead, a numerical procedure, the Metropolis algorithm, can be used to indirectly draw observations from the pdf $f(\alpha \mid y)$. Once such draws are obtained, they can be used to form histograms as estimates of the posterior pdfs for single elements in α. As we shall see, the draws are also useful for obtaining the posterior pdfs for the β_k.

The random walk Metropolis algorithm which we describe below in the context of the heteroskedastic model is one of many algorithms which come under the general heading of Markov Chain Monte Carlo (MCMC). A recent explosion of research in MCMC has made Bayesian inference more practical for models that were previously plagued by intractable integrals. For access to this literature, see Geweke (1999).

The first step towards using a convenient random walk Metropolis algorithm is to define a suitable "candidate generating function." Assuming that the prior $f(\alpha)$ is relatively noninformative, and not in conflict with the sample information, the maximum likelihood estimate $\hat{\alpha}$ provides a suitable starting value $\alpha_{(0)}$ for the algorithm; and the maximum likelihood covariance matrix $V_{\hat{\alpha}}$ provides the basis for a suitable covariance matrix for the random walk generator function. The steps for drawing the $(m + 1)$th observation $\alpha_{(m+1)}$ are as follows:

1. Draw $\alpha^* = \alpha_{(m)} + \varepsilon$ where $\varepsilon \sim N(0, cV_{\hat{\alpha}})$ and c is scalar set so that α^* is accepted approximately 50 percent of the time.
2. Compute

$$r = \frac{f(\alpha^* \mid y)}{f(\alpha_{(m)} \mid y)}$$

Note that this ratio can be computed without knowledge of the normalizing constant for $f(\alpha \mid y)$.
3. Draw a value u for a uniform random variable on the interval $(0, 1)$.
4. If $u \leq r$, set $\alpha_{(m+1)} = \alpha^*$.
   If $u > r$, set $\alpha_{(m+1)} = \alpha_{(m)}$.
5. Return to step 1, with m set to $m + 1$.

By following these steps, one explores the posterior pdf for α, generating larger numbers of observations in regions of high posterior probability and smaller numbers of observations in regions of low posterior probability. Markov Chain Monte Carlo theory suggests that, after sufficient observations have been drawn, the remaining observations are drawn from the pdf $f(\alpha \mid y)$. Thus, by drawing a large number of values, and discarding early ones, we obtain draws from the required pdf.

Step 4

The conditional posterior pdf $f(\beta \mid \alpha, y)$ is obtained from the joint pdf $f(\beta, \alpha \mid y)$ by simply treating α as a constant in equation (4.39). However, for later use we also need to include any part of the normalizing constant that depends on α. Recognizing that, when viewed only as a function of β, equation (4.39) is in the form of a multivariate student-t pdf (Judge et al., 1988, p. 312), we have

$$f(\beta \mid \alpha, y) \propto |X'\Lambda^{-1}X|^{1/2}[\hat{\sigma}(\alpha)]^{N-K}[N\hat{\sigma}^2(\alpha) + (\beta - \hat{\beta}(\alpha))'X'\Lambda^{-1}X(\beta - \hat{\beta}(\alpha))]^{-N/2}$$

$$(4.41)$$

This pdf has

$$\text{mean} = E(\beta \mid \alpha, y) = \hat{\beta}(\alpha) = (X'\Lambda^{-1}X)^{-1}X'\Lambda^{-1}y \tag{4.42}$$

$$\text{covariance matrix} = \left(\frac{N}{N-K-2}\right)\hat{\sigma}^2(\alpha)(X'\Lambda^{-1}X)^{-1} \tag{4.43}$$

$$\text{degrees of freedom} = N - K.$$

Step 5

Let $a^{kk}(\alpha)$ be the kth diagonal element of $(X'\Lambda^{-1}X)^{-1}$, and $\hat{\beta}_k(\alpha)$ be the kth element of $\hat{\beta}(\alpha)$. The conditional marginal posterior pdf for β_k given α is the univariate-t pdf

$$f(\beta_k \mid \alpha, y) = k^*[\hat{\sigma}(\alpha)]^{N-K}[a^{kk}(\alpha)]^{(N-K)/2}[N\hat{\sigma}^2(\alpha)a^{kk}(\alpha) + (\beta_k - \hat{\beta}_k(\alpha))^2]^{-(N-K+1)/2}$$

$$(4.44)$$

where k^* is a normalizing constant independent of α. This pdf has

$$\text{mean} = E(\beta_k \mid \alpha, y) = \hat{\beta}_k(\alpha) \tag{4.45}$$

$$\text{variance} = \left(\frac{N}{N-K+2}\right)\hat{\sigma}^2(\alpha)a^{kk}(\alpha) \tag{4.46}$$

$$\text{degrees of freedom} = N - K.$$

Equations (4.42) and (4.45) provide Bayesian quadratic-loss point estimates for β given α. Note that they are identical to the generalized least squares estimator for known α. It is the unknown α case where sampling theory and Bayesian inference results for point estimation of β diverge. The sampling theory point estimate in this case is $\hat{\beta}(\hat{\alpha})$. The Bayesian point estimate is the mean of the marginal posterior pdf $f(\beta \mid y)$. It can be viewed as a weighted average of the $\hat{\beta}(\alpha)$ over all α with $f(\alpha \mid y)$ used as the weighting pdf. The mechanics of this procedure are described in the next step.

STEP 6

An estimate of the marginal posterior pdf $f(\beta_k \mid y)$ is given by

$$\hat{f}(\beta_k \mid y) = \frac{1}{M} \sum_{m=1}^{M} f(\beta_k \mid \alpha_{(m)}, y)$$

$$= \frac{k^*}{M} \sum_{m=1}^{M} ([\hat{\sigma}(\alpha_{(m)})]^{N-K} [a^{kk}(\alpha_{(m)})]^{(N-K)/2}$$

$$\times [N\hat{\sigma}^2(\alpha_{(m)}) a^{kk}(\alpha_{(m)}) + (\beta_k - \hat{\beta}_k(\alpha_{(m)}))^2]^{-(N-K+1)/2}) \qquad (4.47)$$

where $\alpha_{(1)}, \alpha_{(2)}, \ldots, \alpha_{(M)}$ are the draws from $f(\alpha \mid y)$ that were obtained in step 3. To graph $\hat{f}(\beta_k \mid y)$ a grid of values of β_k is chosen and the average in equation (4.47) is calculated for each value of β_k in the grid. The mean and variance of the marginal posterior pdf $f(\beta_k \mid y)$ can be estimated in a similar way. The mean is given by the average of the conditional means

$$\bar{\beta} = \hat{E}(\beta \mid y) = \frac{1}{M} \sum_{m=1}^{M} \hat{\beta}_k(\alpha_{(m)}). \qquad (4.48)$$

The variance is given by the average of the conditional variances plus the variance of the conditional means. That is,

$$\text{vâr}(\beta \mid y) = \left(\frac{N}{N-K+2}\right) \frac{1}{M} \sum_{m=1}^{M} \hat{\sigma}^2(\alpha_{(m)}) a^{kk}(\alpha_{(m)}) + \frac{1}{M-1} \sum_{m=1}^{M} (\hat{\beta}_k(\alpha_{(m)}) - \bar{\beta})^2$$

$$(4.49)$$

Presenting information about parameters in terms of posterior pdfs rather than point estimates provides a natural way of representing uncertainty. In the process just described, the marginal posterior pdfs also provide a proper reflection of finite sample uncertainty. Maximum likelihood estimates (or posterior pdfs conditional on $\hat{\alpha}$) ignore the additional uncertainty created by not knowing α.

There are, of course, other ways of approaching Bayesian inference in heteroskedastic models. The approach will depend on specification of the model and prior pdf, and on the solution to the problem of intractable integrals. Gibbs sampling is another MCMC technique that is often useful; and importance sampling could be used to obtain draws from $f(\alpha \mid y)$. However, the approach we have described is useful for a wide range of problems, with specific cases defined by specification of $h_i(\alpha)$ and $f(\alpha)$. Other studies which utilize Bayesian inference in heteroskedastic error models include Griffiths, Drynan, and Prakash (1979) and Boscardin and Gelman (1996).

5 CONCLUDING REMARKS

Recent sampling theory research on heteroskedastic models seems to be concentrated on methods for estimation and hypothesis testing that do not require specification of a particular parametric form of heteroskedasticity. They are motivated by our inability to be certain about the most appropriate variance specification. However, methodology suggested along these lines is generally asymptotic and may not perform well in finite samples. What is likely to be important, and what seems to have been neglected, is whether the types of inferences we make in practice are very sensitive to the assumed form of hetero-skedasticity. If they are not, then efforts to develop alternative methods, that do not require an explicit variance function, may be misplaced.

Bayesian estimation has several advantages. Results are presented in terms of intuitively meaningful posterior pdfs. Marginal posterior pdfs reflect all the parameter uncertainty in a model and do not condition on point estimates of nuisance parameters. Predictive pdfs for future values can also be constructed without conditioning on point estimates (Boscardin and Gelman, 1996). The advent of MCMC techniques means that many more practical applications of Bayesian inference to heteroskedastic models are now possible.

Note

*   The author acknowledges valuable comments on an earlier version by three anonymous reviewers.

References

Amemiya, T. (1973). Regression analysis when the variance of the dependent variable is proportional to the square of its expectation. *Journal of the American Statistical Association* 68, 928–34.

Amemiya, T. (1977). A note on a heteroscedastic model. *Journal of Econometrics* 6, 365–70; and Corrigenda. *Journal of Econometrics* 8, 275.

Amemiya, T. (1983). Partially generalized least squares and two-stage least squares estimators. *Journal of Econometrics* 23, 275–83.

Baltagi, B.H. (1998). *Econometrics*. New York: Springer-Verlag.

Boscardin, W.J., and A. Gelman (1996). Bayesian computation for parametric models of heteroscedasticity in the linear model. In R.C. Hill (ed.) *Advances in Econometrics Volume 11A: Bayesian Computational Methods and Applications*. Greenwich: JAI Press.

Breusch, T.S., and A.R. Pagan (1979). A simple test for heteroscedasticity and random coefficient variation. *Econometrica* 47, 1287–94.

Brown, B.W., and M.B. Walker (1989). The random utility hypothesis and inference in demand systems. *Econometrica* 57, 815–29.

Brown, B.W., and M.B. Walker (1995). Stochastic specification in random production models of cost minimizing firms. *Journal of Econometrics* 66, 175–205.

Carroll, R.J. (1982). Adapting for heteroscedasticity in linear models. *Annals of Statistics* 10, 1224–33.

Carroll, R.J., and D. Ruppert (1988). *Transformation and Weighting in Regression*. New York: Chapman and Hall.

Cragg, J.G. (1992). Quasi-Aitken estimation for heteroskedasticity of unknown form. *Journal of Econometrics* 54, 179–202.

Davidson, R., and J.G. MacKinnon (1993). *Estimation and Inference in Econometrics*. New York: Oxford University Press.

Delgado, M.A. (1992). Semiparametric generalized least squares in the multivariate non-linear regression model. *Econometric Theory* 8, 203–22.

Donald, S.G. (1995). Two-step estimation of heteroskedastic sample selection models. *Journal of Econometrics* 65, 347–80.

Evans, M.A., and M.L. King (1988). A further class of tests for heteroscedasticity. *Journal of Econometrics* 37, 265–76.

Farebrother, R.W. (1987). The statistical foundations of a class of parametric tests for heteroskedasticity. *Journal of Econometrics* 36, 359–68.

Geweke, J. (1999). Using simulation methods for Bayesian econometric models: inference, development and communication. *Econometric Reviews* 18, 1–74.

Godfrey, L.G. (1978). Testing for multiplicative heteroskedasticity. *Journal of Econometrics* 8, 227–36.

Godfrey, L.G. (1996). Some results on the Glejser and Koenker tests for heteroskedasticity. *Journal of Econometrics* 72, 275–99.

Godfrey, L.G., and C.D. Orme (1999). The robustness, reliability and power of hetero-skedasticity tests. *Econometric Reviews* 18, 169–94.

Goldfeld, S.M., and R.E. Quandt (1965). Some tests for homoscedasticity. *Journal of the American Statistical Association* 60, 539–47.

Goldfeld, S.M., and R.E. Quandt (1972). *Nonlinear Methods in Econometrics*. Amsterdam: North-Holland.

Greene, W. (1997). *Econometric Analysis*, 3rd edn. Upper Saddle River: Prentice Hall.

Griffiths, W.E. (1972). Estimation of actual response coefficients in the Hildreth–Houck random coefficient model. *Journal of the American Statistical Association* 67, 633–5.

Griffiths, W.E., and J.R. Anderson (1982). Using time-series and cross-section data to estimate a production function with positive and negative marginal risks. *Journal of the American Statistical Association* 77, 529–36.

Griffiths, W.E., and G.G. Judge (1992). Testing and estimating location vectors when the error covariance matrix is unknown. *Journal of Econometrics* 54, 121–38.

Griffiths, W.E., and K. Surekha (1986). A Monte Carlo evaluation of the power of some tests for heteroscedasticity. *Journal of Econometrics* 31, 219–31.

Griffiths, W.E., R.G. Drynan, and S. Prakash (1979). Bayesian estimation of a random coefficient model. *Journal of Econometrics* 10, 201–20.

Harvey, A.C. (1976). Estimating regression models with multiplicative heteroscedasticity. *Econometrica* 44, 461–5.

Hidalgo, J. (1992). Adaptive estimation in time series regression models with hetero-skedasticity of unknown form. *Econometric Theory* 8, 161–87.

Hildreth, C., and J.P. Houck (1968). Some estimators for a linear model with random coefficients. *Journal of the American Statistical Association* 63, 584–95.

Hill, R.C., J.R. Knight, and C.F. Sirmans (1997). Estimating capital asset price indexes. *Review of Economics and Statistics* 80, 226–33.

Hooper, P.M. (1993). Iterative weighted least squares estimations in heteroscedastic linear models. *Journal of the American Statistical Association* 88, 179–84.

Jobson, J.D., and W.A. Fuller (1980). Least squares estimation when the covariance matrix and parameter vector are functionally related. *Journal of the American Statistical Association* 75, 176–81.

Judge, G.G., W.E. Griffiths, R.C. Hill, and T.-C. Lee (1985). *The Theory and Practice of Econometrics*. New York: John Wiley and Sons.

Judge, G.G., R.C. Hill, W.E. Griffiths, H. Lütkepohl, and T.-C. Lee (1988). *An Introduction to the Theory and Practice of Econometrics*. New York: John Wiley and Sons.

Keener, R.W., J. Kmenta, and N.C. Weber (1991). Estimation of the covariance matrix of the least-squares regression coefficients when the disturbance covariance matrix is of unknown form. *Econometric Theory* 7, 22–43.

Koenker, R., and G. Bassett, Jr. (1982). Robust tests for heteroscedasticity based on regression quantiles. *Econometrica* 50, 43–61.

Lee, B.-J. (1992). A heteroskedasticity test robust to conditional mean specification. *Econometrica* 60, 159–72.

Li, Q., and T. Stengos (1994). Adaptive estimation in the panel data error model with heteroskedasticity of unknown form. *International Economic Review* 35, 981–1000.

Linton, O.B. (1996). Second order approximation in a linear regression with the heteroskedasticity of unknown form. *Econometric Reviews* 15, 1–32.

Mandy, D.M., and C. Martins-Filho (1993). Seemingly unrelated regressions under additive heteroscedasticity: theory and share equation applications. *Journal of Econometrics* 58, 315–46.

Orme, C. (1992). Efficient score tests for heteroskedasticity in microeconometrics. *Econometric Reviews* 11, 235–52.

Pagan, A., and Y. Pak (1993). Testing for heteroskedasticity. In G.S. Maddala, C.R. Rao, and H.D. Vinod (eds.) *Handbook of Statistics II: Econometrics*. Amsterdam: North-Holland, 489–518.

Rilestone, P. (1991). Some Monte Carlo evidence on the relative efficiency of parametric and semiparameteric EGLS estimators. *Journal of Business and Economic Statistics* 9, 179–87.

Robinson, P.M. (1987). Asymptotically efficient estimation in the presence of heteroscedasticity of unknown form. *Econometrica* 55, 875–91.

Rutemiller, H.C., and D.A. Bowers (1968). Estimation in a heteroscedastic regression model. *Journal of the American Statistical Association* 63, 552–7.

Surekha, K., and W.E. Griffiths (1984). A Monte Carlo comparison of some Bayesian and sampling theory estimators in two heteroscedastic error models. *Communications in Statistics B* 13, 85–105.

Szroeter, J. (1978). A class of parametric tests for heteroskedasticity in linear econometric models. *Econometrica* 46, 1311–28.

Szroeter, J. (1994). Exact finite-sample relative efficiency of sub-optimality weighted least squares estimators in models with ordered heteroscedasticity. *Journal of Econometrics* 64, 29–44.

Welsh, A.H., R.J. Carroll, and D. Ruppert (1994). Fitting heteroscedastic regression models. *Journal of the American Statistical Association* 89, 100–16.

White, H. (1980). A heteroscedasticity-consistent covariance matrix estimators and a direct test for heteroscedasticity. *Econometrica* 48, 817–38.

Zellner, A. (1971). *An Introduction to Bayesian Inference in Econometrics*. New York: John Wiley and Sons.

Seemingly Unrelated Regression

*Denzil G. Fiebig**

1   INTRODUCTION

Seemingly unrelated regression (SUR) is one of the econometric developments that has found considerable use in applied work. Not all theoretical developments find their way immediately into the toolkit of the practitioner, but SUR is one of those which has. The popularity of the model is related to its applicability to a large class of modeling and testing problems and also the relative ease of estimation. Empirical studies that utilize SUR have been supported by a considerable amount of theoretical development; consequently much is known about the basic model and the extensions needed to accommodate more complex problems.

As noted by Griliches and Intriligator (1983, p. xiii) "The historical evolution of econometrics was driven both by the increased availability of data and by the desire of generations of scientists to analyze such data in a rigorous and coherent fashion." SUR falls neatly into this characterization. The increased availability of data representing a sample of cross-sectional units observed over several time periods provides researchers with a potentially rich source of information. At the same time, the nature of the data necessitates careful consideration of how regression parameters vary (if at all) over the cross-sectional and time series dimensions and the appropriate specification of the disturbance covariance matrix. SUR is able to provide estimates of how relationships can potentially vary over the data dimensions as well as providing a convenient vehicle for testing hypotheses about these relationships. The specification of the basic SUR model as first introduced by Zellner (1962) remains an important option in any modeling exercise using pooled data.

Given the voluminous growth in the SUR literature, this chapter is necessarily selective. Material found in the survey paper of Srivastava and Dwivedi (1979) and the book by Srivastava and Giles (1987) serve to provide a good coverage of the literature until the mid to late 1980s. We concentrate on the more recent developments. While the SUR model has had a significant impact outside economics and business, these studies have largely been ignored to provide further focus for this current chapter.

2   Basic Model

Suppose we have a set of N cross-sections with T time series observations on each. The classic data introduced in Zellner's (1962) initial work comprised firm-level investment data collected annually for 20 years. More recently Batchelor and Gulley (1995) analysed the determinants of jewelry demand for a sample of six countries over 16 years. In both cases, the disturbances from different regression equations, at a given point in time, were correlated because of common unobservable factors.

It is convenient to continue with the cross-section, time series characterization of the data, but clearly what is distinctive is that the data have two dimensions. In general we are dealing with data fields. Often in demand studies a system of demand equations is specified to explain household level consumption of several commodities. Here the disturbance covariances arise because of potential correlations between household specific unobservables associated with each household's commodity demand. In the area of energy demand Bartels, Fiebig, and Plumb (1996) consider household expenditures on gas, and two types of electricity, while Fiebig, Bartels, and Aigner (1991) and Henley and Peirson (1994) consider electricity demands at different times of the day.

The structure of the multi-dimensional data focuses attention on two important specification issues: (i) what should be the appropriate parameter variation across the two dimensions, and (ii) what should be the appropriate stochastic specification. In the case of the basic SUR model these specification issues are resolved by forming a system of N equations each containing T observations:

$$y_i = X_i\beta_i + u_i \quad i = 1, \ldots, N \tag{5.1}$$

where y_i and u_i are T-dimensional vectors, X_i is $T \times K_i$ and β_i is a K_i-dimensional vector. Stacking all N equations yields:

$$\begin{bmatrix} y_1 \\ y_2 \\ \vdots \\ y_N \end{bmatrix} = \begin{bmatrix} X_1 & 0 & \cdots & 0 \\ 0 & X_2 & \cdots & 0 \\ \vdots & \vdots & \ddots & \vdots \\ 0 & 0 & \cdots & X_N \end{bmatrix} \begin{bmatrix} \beta_1 \\ \beta_2 \\ \vdots \\ \beta_N \end{bmatrix} + \begin{bmatrix} u_1 \\ u_2 \\ \vdots \\ u_N \end{bmatrix}$$

which can be written compactly as:

$$y = X\beta + u \tag{5.2}$$

where β is a K-dimensional vector of unknown parameters that needs to be estimated and $K = \sum_{i=1}^{N} K_i$. For the $NT \times 1$ vector of stacked disturbances the assumptions are (i) $E(u) = 0$, and (ii) the $NT \times NT$ covariance matrix is comprised of N^2 blocks of the form $E(u_i u_j') = \sigma_{ij} I_T$ where I_T is a $T \times T$ identity matrix. These assumptions mean that the T disturbances in each of the N equations have zero mean, equal variance, and are uncorrelated and that covariances between contemporaneous disturbances for a pair of equations are potentially nonzero but equal, while non-contemporaneous covariances are all zero. Thus the full covariance matrix of u is given by $\Omega = \Sigma \otimes I_T$ where $\Sigma = [\sigma_{ij}]$ is the $N \times N$ contemporaneous covariance matrix and $\otimes$ denotes the Kronecker product.

Each of the N equations is individually assumed to satisfy the classical assumptions associated with the linear regression model and can be estimated separately. Of course this ignores the correlation between the disturbances of different equations, which can be exploited by joint estimation. The individual equations are related, even though superficially they may not seem to be; they are only seemingly unrelated. The GLS (generalized least squares) estimator is readily defined as

$$\hat{\beta}(\Sigma) = [X'(\Sigma^{-1} \otimes I_T)X]^{-1} X'(\Sigma^{-1} \otimes I_T)y \qquad (5.3)$$

with a covariance matrix given by

$$\text{var}[\hat{\beta}(\Sigma)] = [X'(\Sigma^{-1} \otimes I_T)X]^{-1}. \qquad (5.4)$$

It is well known that the GLS estimator reduces to OLS (ordinary least squares) when: (i) there is an absence of contemporaneous correlations ($\sigma_{ij} = 0$, $i \neq j$); or (ii) the same set of explanatory variables are included in each equation ($X_1 = X_2 = \ldots = X_N$). A more complete characterization of when OLS is equivalent to GLS is given in Baltagi (1989) and Bartels and Fiebig (1991).

In his original article, Zellner (1962) recognized that the efficiency gains resulting from joint estimation tended to be larger when the explanatory variables in different equations were not highly correlated but the disturbances from these equations were highly correlated. Work by Binkley (1982) and Binkley and Nelson (1988) has led to an important qualification to this conventional wisdom. They show that even when correlation among variables across equations is present, efficiency gains from joint estimation can be considerable when there is multicollinearity within an equation.

Consider the class of feasible GLS (FGLS) estimators that differ only in the choice of the estimator used for the contemporaneous covariance matrix, say $\hat{\beta}(\hat{\Sigma})$. The estimator is given by:

$$\hat{\beta}(\hat{\Sigma}) = [X'(\hat{\Sigma}^{-1} \otimes I_T)X]^{-1} X'(\hat{\Sigma}^{-1} \otimes I_T)y, \qquad (5.5)$$

and inferences are based on the estimator of the asymptotic covariance matrix of $\hat{\beta}(\hat{\Sigma})$ given by:

$$\text{a var}[\hat{\beta}(\hat{\Sigma})] = [X'(\hat{\Sigma}^{-1} \otimes I_T)X]^{-1}. \qquad (5.6)$$

There are many variants of this particular FGLS estimator. Obviously, OLS belongs to the class with $\hat{\Sigma} = I_N$, but Zellner (1962) proposed the first operational estimator that explicitly utilized the SUR structure. He suggested an estimated covariance matrix calculated from OLS residuals obtained from (5.1); namely $S = (s_{ij})$ where $s_{ij} = (y_i - X_i b_i)'(y_j - X_j b_j)/\tau$ and b_i is the OLS estimator of β_i. For consistent estimation division by $\tau = T$ suffices but other suggestions have also been made; see for example Srivastava and Giles (1987).

S has been referred to as the restricted estimator of Σ, but estimation can also be based on the unrestricted residuals derived from OLS regressions which include all explanatory variables from the SUR system. Considerable theoretical work has been devoted to the comparison of respective finite sample properties of the restricted and unrestricted SUR estimators associated with the different estimators of Σ. All of the results discussed in Srivastava and Giles (1987) were based on the assumption of normally distributed disturbances. More recently, Hasegawa (1995) and Srivastava and Maekawa (1995) have presented comparisons between the restricted and unrestricted estimators allowing for nonnormal errors. None of this work produces a conclusive choice between the two alternative estimators.

While theoretical work continues on both restricted and unrestricted estimators, software designers typically make the choice for practitioners. SAS, SHAZAM, TSP, and LIMDEP all use restricted residuals in the estimation of Σ. Moreover, there is limited scope to opt for alternatives with only LIMDEP and TSP allowing one to input their own choice of estimator for Σ. Where the software packages do vary is in the default choice of τ and whether to iterate or not. See Silk (1996) for further discussion of software comparisons between SAS, SHAZAM, and TSP in terms of systems estimation.

3   Stochastic Specification

Many of the recent developments in estimation of the parameters of the SUR model have been motivated by the need to allow for more general stochastic specifications. These developments are driven in part by the usual diagnostic procedures of practitioners, but also by the strong theoretical arguments that have been presented for behavioral models of consumers and producers. Chavas and Segerson (1987) and Brown and Walker (1989, 1995) argue that behavioral models should include a stochastic component as an integral part of the model. When this is done, however, each equation in the resultant input share system or system of demand equations will typically exhibit heteroskedasticity. The basic SUR specification allows for heteroskedasticity across but not within equations and thus will be inappropriate for these systems.

Examples of where heteroskedastic SUR specifications have been discussed include the share equations system of Chavas and Segerson (1987); the SUR random coefficients model of Fiebig *et al.* (1991); and the groupwise heteroskedasticity model described in Bartels *et al.* (1996). Each of these examples are members of what Bartels and Fiebig (1992) called generalized SUR (GSUR).

Recall that the covariance matrix of the basic SUR model is $\Omega = \Sigma \otimes I_T$. GSUR allows for a covariance matrix with the following structure:

$$\Omega \equiv \Omega(\theta, \Sigma) = R(\Sigma \otimes I_T)R', \tag{5.7}$$

where $R = R(\theta)$ is block-diagonal, non-singular, and the parameters θ and Σ are assumed to be separable. With this specification, GLS estimation can be viewed as proceeding in two stages: the first stage involves transforming the GSUR model on an equation-by-equation basis so that the classical SUR structure appears as the transformed model; and in the second stage the usual SUR estimator is applied to the transformed model.

The distinguishing feature of the GSUR class of models is the convenience of estimating θ and Σ in separate stages with both stages involving familiar estimation techniques. Bollerslev (1990) also notes the computational convenience of this type of simplification for an SUR model that allows for time varying conditional variances and covariances. In this case estimation by maximum likelihood is proposed.

While computational convenience is important, this attractive feature of GSUR must be weighed against the potentially restrictive covariance structure shown in (5.7). While any symmetric, non-singular matrix Ω can be written as $R(\Sigma \otimes I_T)R'$, the matrix R will in general depend on Σ as well as θ and/or R may not be block diagonal. Ultimately, the validity of the assumption regarding the structure of the covariance matrix remains an empirical matter.

Mandy and Martins-Filho (1993) extended the basic SUR specification by assuming a contemporaneous covariance matrix that varies across observations within an equation. If we collect the N disturbances associated with the tth time period into the vector $u_{(t)} = (u_{1t}, \ldots, u_{Nt})'$, they assume

$$E(u_{(t)}u'_{(t)}) = \Omega_t = \begin{bmatrix} \sigma^t_{11} & \sigma^t_{12} & \cdots & \sigma^t_{1N} \\ \sigma^t_{21} & \sigma^t_{22} & \cdots & \sigma^t_{2N} \\ \vdots & \vdots & \ddots & \vdots \\ \sigma^t_{N1} & \sigma^t_{N2} & \cdots & \sigma^t_{NN} \end{bmatrix}. \tag{5.8}$$

Specifically, they consider an SUR model subject to additive heteroskedasticity of the form

$$\sigma^t_{ij} = \alpha'_{ij}z^t_{ij} \tag{5.9}$$

where α_{ij} is a vector of unknown parameters and z^t_{ij} a conformable vector of explanatory variables.

The framework of Mandy and Martins-Filho (1993) is less restrictive than GSUR but in general does not have the simplified estimation solutions of GSUR. Instead they develop an FGLS procedure that represents an SUR generalization of Amemiya's (1977) efficient estimator for the parameters of the covariance matrix in a single-equation additive heteroskedastic model. A practical problem with this class of estimators is the appearance of estimated covariance matrices which are not positive definite. Such problems should disappear with large enough samples but for any particular data set there are no guarantees. With some specifications, such as SUR with groupwise heteroskedasticity, the structure ensures that nonnegative variance estimates are obtained. Alternatively, for their SUR random coefficients model, Fiebig *et al.* (1991) employ an estimation procedure that automatically ensures the same result.

When the observations within an equation have a grouped structure it is reasonable to consider a random effects specification for each equation of the SUR system. Avery (1977) and Baltagi (1980) undertook the initial work on SUR models with error component disturbances. An extension allowing for the error components to be heteroskedastic has recently been proposed by Wan, Griffiths, and Anderson (1992) in their study of rice, maize, and wheat production in 28 regions of China over the period 1980–83. In another application, Kumbhakar and Heshmati (1996) consider a system comprising a cost equation and several cost share equations estimated using 26 annual observations for several Swedish manufacturing industries. For the cost equation, but not the share equations, they also specify disturbances comprising heteroskedastic error components. Estimation proceeds along the same lines as discussed in the context of GSUR. The cost equation is first transformed, and the usual SUR estimation can proceed for the share equations and the transformed cost equation.

As has been apparent from the discussion, a major use of SUR is in the estimation of systems of consumer or factor demands. Often these are specified in share form which brings with it special problems. In particular the shares should be restricted to lie between zero and one and should sum to unity. By far the most common approach to the specification of the stochastic component in such models is to append an additive error term to the deterministic component of the model that is obtained from economic theory. Typically the error term is assumed to be multivariate normal. Even if the deterministic component respects the constraint of lying between zero and one, it is clear that assuming normality for the stochastic component means that the modeled share can potentially violate the constraint. One approach is to choose a more appropriate distribution. Woodland (1979), who chose the Dirichlet distribution, seems to be the only example of this approach. An alternative approach advocated by Fry, Fry, and McLaren (1996) is to append a multivariate normal error after performing a logratio transformation of the observed shares.

A second property of share equations, that of adding up, implies that additive errors sum identically to zero across equations. The induced singularity of the covariance matrix is typically accommodated in estimation by deleting one of the equations. Conditions under which the resultant estimators are invariant to the equation that is dropped have long been known; see Bewley (1986) for a summary of these early contributions. More recently, McLaren (1990) and Dhrymes (1994) have provided alternative treatments, which they argue, provide a more transparent demonstration of the conditions for invariance. Dhrymes (1994) is the more general discussion as it allows for the added complication of autocorrelated errors.

Singularity of the disturbance covariance matrix places strong restrictions on any autocorrelation structure that is specified. If we consider the N-vector of disturbances associated with the tth time period then adding-up implies $\iota' u_{(t)} = 0$ where ι is a vector of ones. If a first order autoregressive process is assumed, i.e.

$$u_{(t)} = A u_{(t-1)} + \varepsilon_{(t)} \qquad (5.10)$$

then adding up requires that $\iota' \varepsilon_{(t)} = 0$ and $\iota' A = k\iota'$ where k is a scalar constant, implying that the columns of A sum to the same constant. If A is specified to be diagonal, all equations will need to have the same autocorrelation parameter. At the other extreme, A is a full matrix with $(N - 1)^2$ identifiable parameters. A series of contributions by Moschini and Moro (1994), McLaren (1996) and Holt (1998) have suggested alternative specifications involving $(N - 1)$ parameters, and hence represent a compromise between the very restrictive one-parameter specification and the computationally demanding full specification.

It is not unusual to observe empirical results where systems of static equations have been estimated to yield results that exhibit serially correlated residuals. Common advice that is often followed is to re-estimate assuming an autoregressive error structure. For example, Judge *et al.* (1985, p. 497) conclude that: "as a general recommendation for a researcher estimating a set of equations, we suggest that possible contemporaneous correlation should always be allowed for and, if the number of observations is sufficient, some kind of autocorrelation process could also be assumed."

In the single equation context there has been a movement away from the simple to specific modeling approach, involving correcting for autocorrelation in the errors of static regression models. For example, Anderson and Blundell (1982, p. 1560) note that: "in the context of a single equation model, it has been argued that an autoregressive error specification whilst being a convenient simplification, when appropriate, may be merely accommodating a dynamic structure in the model which could be better represented by a general unrestricted dynamic formulation." Mizon (1995) is even more forceful as evidenced by his paper's title: "A simple message for autocorrelation correctors: Don't." Such advice has largely gone unheeded in the SUR literature where there has been little work on dynamic SUR models. Support for this contention is provided by Moschini and Moro (1994) who report that they found 24 papers published over the period 1988–92 that estimated singular systems with autocorrelated disturbances and that out of these only three did so as special cases of the general dynamic model of Anderson and Blundell (1982).

Deschamps (1998) is one exception where a general dynamic model has been used. He proposes and illustrates a methodology for estimating long-run demand relationships by maximum likelihood. Unlike previous work such as Anderson and Blundell (1982), Deschamps formulates the full likelihood function that is not conditional on the first observations of the dependent variables.

One other contribution that recognizes the need for more work in the area of dynamic systems is that of Kiviet, Phillips, and Schipp (1995). They employ asymptotic expansions to compare the biases of alternative estimators of an SUR model comprised of dynamic regression equations.

As we have previously noted, the GLS estimator of a basic SUR model reduces to OLS when the design matrices are the same in each equation. Baltagi (1980), Bartels and Fiebig (1992) and Mandy and Martins-Filho (1993) all mention that this well known result needs modification when dealing with more general stochastic structures. The fact that each equation contains an identical set of explanatory variables is not a sufficient condition for joint GLS to collapse to OLS performed on each equation separately. The two-stage estimation process of GSUR highlights the intuition. The first stage involves transforming the GSUR model on an equation-by-equation basis so that the classical SUR structure appears as the transformed model. Even if the original explanatory variables were the same in each equation, the explanatory variables to be used in the second stage are generally not identical after being transformed. A related question is under what conditions does joint GLS collapse to GLS performed on each equation separately. Bartels and Fiebig (1992) provide necessary and sufficient conditions for the first-stage GLS estimates to be fully efficient. Lee (1995) provides some specific examples where this occurs in the estimation of singular systems with autoregressive errors.

4 TESTING

4.1 Testing linear restrictions

Under the standard assumptions of the basic SUR model, Atkinson and Wilson (1992) prove that:

$$\text{var}[\hat{\beta}(\tilde{\Sigma})] \geq \text{var}[\hat{\beta}(\Sigma)] \geq E[X'(\tilde{\Sigma}^{-1} \otimes I_T)X]^{-1} \tag{5.11}$$

where $\tilde{\Sigma}$ is any unbiased estimator of Σ and the inequalities refer to matrix differences. The first inequality indicates that FGLS is inefficient relative to GLS. The second inequality provides an indication of the bias in the conventional estimator of the asymptotic covariance matrix of FGLS. While the result requires unbiased estimation of Σ, which does not hold for most conventional estimators of SUR models, it conveniently highlights an important testing problem in SUR models. Asymptotic Wald (W), Lagrange multiplier (LM), and likelihood ratio (LR) tests are prone to be biased towards overrejection.

Fiebig and Theil (1983) and Freedman and Peters (1984) reported Monte Carlo work and empirical examples where the asymptotic standard errors tended to understate the true variability of FGLS. Rosalsky, Finke, and Theil (1984), and Jensen (1995) report similar understatement of asymptotic standard errors for maximum likelihood estimation of nonlinear systems. Work by Laitinen (1978), Meisner (1979), and Bewley (1983) alerted applied researchers to the serious size problems of testing cross-equation restrictions in linear demand systems especially when the number of equations specified was large relative to the available number of observations. Similar problems have been observed in finance in relation to testing restrictions associated with the CAPM (capital asset pricing model); see for example MacKinlay (1987).

In some special cases exact tests have been provided. For example, Laitinen (1978) derived an exact test based on Hotelling's T^2 statistic for testing homogeneity in demand systems. Bewley (1983), de Jong and Thompson (1990), and Stewart (1997) discuss a somewhat wider class of problems where similar results are available but these are very special cases and the search for solutions that involve test statistics with tractable distributions remains an open area. One contribution to this end is provided by Hashimoto and Ohtani (1990) who derive an exact test for linear restrictions on the regression coefficients in an SUR model. Apart from being confined to an SUR system with the same regressors appearing in each equation, the practical drawbacks of this test are that it is computationally complicated, has low power, and to be feasible requires a large number of observations. This last problem is especially troublesome, as this is exactly the situation where the conventional asymptotic tests are the most unreliable.

One approach designed to produce tests with improved sampling properties is to use bootstrap methods. Following the advice of Freedman and Peters (1984), the studies by Williams (1986) and Eakin, McMillen, and Buono (1990) both used bootstrap methods for their estimation of standard errors. Unconditional acceptance of this advice was questioned by Atkinson and Wilson (1992) who compared the bias in the conventional and bootstrap estimators of coefficient standard errors in SUR models. While their theoretical results were inconclusive, their simulation results cautioned that neither of the estimators uniformly dominated and hence bootstrapping provides little improvement in the estimation of standard errors for the regression coefficients in an SUR model.

Rilstone and Veall (1996) argue that an important qualification needs to be made to this somewhat negative conclusion of Atkinson and Wilson (1992). They demonstrated that bootstrapping could result in an improvement in inferences. Rather than using the bootstrap to provide an estimate of standard errors, Rilstone and Veall (1996) recommend bootstrapping the t-ratios. The appropriate percentiles of the bootstrap distribution of standardized FGLS estimators are then used to construct the bootstrap percentile-t interval. This is an example of what are referred to as pivotal methods. A statistic is (asymptotically) pivotal if its "limiting" distribution does not depend on unknown quantities. Theoretical work indicates that pivotal bootstrap methods provide a higher order of accuracy compared to the basic non-pivotal methods and, in particular, provide confidence intervals with superior coverage properties; see, for example, work cited in Jeong and Maddala (1993). This is precisely what Rilstone and Veall (1996) found.

Another potential approach to providing better inferences, involves the use of improved estimators for the disturbance covariance matrix. Fiebig and Theil (1983) and Ullah and Racine (1992) use nonparametric density estimation as an alternative source of moment estimators. In the tradition of the method of moments, the covariance matrix of a nonparametric density estimator is advocated as an estimator of the population covariance matrix. The proposed SUR estimators have the same structure as the FGLS estimator of equation (5.5) differing only in the choice of estimator for Σ. Ullah and Racine (1992) prove that their nonparametric density estimator of Σ can be expressed as the usual estimator S plus a *positive definite* matrix that depends on the smoothing parameter chosen for the density estimation. It is this structure of the estimator that suggests the approach is potentially useful in large equation systems.

Fiebig and Kim (2000) investigate the combination of both approaches, bootstrapping and the improved estimation of the covariance matrix especially in the context of large systems. They conclude that using the percentile-t method of bootstrapping in conjunction with the kernel-based estimator introduced by Ullah and Racine (1992) provides a very attractive estimator for large SUR models.

These studies that evaluate the effectiveness of the bootstrap typically rely on Monte Carlo simulations to validate the procedure and hence require large amounts of computations. Hill, Cartwright, and Arbaugh (1997) investigate the possibility of using Efron's (1992) jackknife-after-bootstrap as an alternative approach. Unfortunately their results indicate that the jackknife-after-bootstrap substantially overestimates the standard deviation of the bootstrap standard errors.

Yet another approach to the testing problem in SUR models is the use of Bartlett-type corrections. For the basic SUR model, Attfield (1998) draws on his earlier work in Attfield (1995) to derive a Bartlett adjustment to the likelihood ratio test statistic for testing linear restrictions. Since the derivations require the assumption of normality, and the absence of lagged dependent variables, the approach of Rocke (1989) may be a useful alternative. He suggests a computational rather than analytical approach for calculating the Bartlett adjustment using the bootstrap. In conclusion Rocke (1989) indicates that while his approach "achieves some improvement, this behavior is still not satisfactory when the sample size is small relative to the number of equations". But as we have observed, this is exactly the situation where the adjustment is most needed.

Silver and Ali (1989) also consider corrections that are derived computationally for the specific problem of testing Slutsky symmetry in a system of demand equations. On the basis of extensive Monte Carlo simulations they conclude that the covariance structure and the form of the regressors are relatively unimportant in describing the exact distribution of the F-statistic. Given this they use their simulation results to suggest "average" corrections that are only based on the sample size, T, and the number of equations, N. A second approach they consider is approximating the exact distribution of the F-statistic for symmetry using the Pearson class of distributions.

In many modeling situations it is difficult to confidently specify the form of the error covariance matrix. In the single equation context it has become very popular amongst practitioners to construct tests based on the OLS parameter estimators combined with a heteroskedastic and autocorrelation consistent (HAC) or "robust" covariance matrix estimator. Creel and Farell (1996) have considered extensions of this approach to the SUR model. They argue that in many applications the basic SUR stochastic specification will provide a reasonable approximation to a more general error structure. Proceeding in this manner, the usual estimator will be quasi-FGLS and will require a HAC covariance matrix to deal with the remaining heteroskedasticity and serial correlation.

Dufour and Torres (1998) are also concerned with obtaining robust inferences. They show how to use union-intersection techniques to combine tests or confidence intervals, which are based on different subsamples. Amongst their illustrations is an example showing how to test the null hypothesis that coefficients from different equations are equal without requiring any assumptions on how the equations are related as would be needed in the basic SUR specification.

4.2 Diagnostic testing

A cornerstone of the SUR model is the presence of contemporaneous correlation. When Σ is diagonal, joint estimation is not required, which simplifies computations. Shiba and Tsurumi (1988) provide a complete set of LM, W, and LR tests of the null hypothesis that Σ is block diagonal. When there are only two equations their LM test reduces to the popular test proposed by Breusch and Pagan (1980). They also derive a Bayesian test.

Classical tests such as the Breusch and Pagan (1980) LM test rely on large-T asymptotics. Frees (1995) recognizes that such tests may be inappropriate with other data configurations and explores alternative tests concentrating on issues that arise when N and possibly T are large.

Work in urban and regional economics is distinguished by consideration of spatial aspects. In SUR models where the observations within equations refer to regions, careful consideration needs to be given to the potential for spatial autocorrelation. Anselin (1990) stresses this point in the context of tests for regional heterogeneity. Neglecting the presence of spatial autocorrelation is shown to distort the size and power of conventional Chow-type tests of parameter constancy across equations. On the basis of his Monte Carlo simulations Anselin (1990) advocates a pre-test approach where the first step involves testing for spatial autocorrelation using the LM test proposed in Anselin (1988).

5 OTHER DEVELOPMENTS

5.1 Unequal observations and missing data

Extending the standard SUR model to allow for an unequal number of observations in different equations causes some problems for estimation of the disturbance covariance matrix. (Problems associated with sample selection bias are avoided by assuming that data are missing at random.) If there are at least $T_0 < T$ observations available for all equations then the key issue is how to utilize the "extra" observations in the estimation of the disturbance covariance matrix. Monte Carlo comparisons between alternative estimators led Schmidt (1977) to conclude that estimators utilizing less information did not necessarily perform poorly relative to those using more of the sample information. Baltagi, Garvin, and Kerman (1989) provide an extensive Monte Carlo evaluation of several alternative covariance matrix estimators and the associated FGLS estimators of β, attempting to shed some further light on conclusions made by Schmidt (1977). They conclude that while the use of extra observations may lead to better estimates of Σ

and Σ^{-1}, this does not necessarily translate into better estimates of β. Baltagi *et al.* (1989) considered both Σ and Σ^{-1} because of Hwang (1990) who noted that the mathematical form of the alternative estimators of Σ gave a misleading impression of their respective information content. This was clarified by considering the associated estimators of Σ^{-1}. Hwang (1990) also proposes a modification of the Telser (1964) estimator, which performs well when the contemporaneous correlation is high.

When there are unequal observations in equations, concern with the use of the "extra" observations arises because of two types of restrictions: (i) imposing equality of variances across groups defined by complete and incomplete observations; and (ii) the need to maintain a positive definite estimate of the covariance matrix. In the groupwise heteroskedasticity model employed by Bartels *et al.* (1996) the groupings corresponded to the divisions between complete and incomplete observations, and, provided that there are no across group restrictions on the parameters of the variance–covariance matrices, positive definite covariance matrix estimates can be readily obtained by applying a standard SUR estimation to each group of data separately.

Consider a two-equation SUR system of the form

$$y_i = X_i\beta_i + u_i \quad i = 1, 2 \tag{5.12}$$

where y_1 and u_1 are T-dimensional vectors, X_1 is $T \times k$, β_i are k-dimensional vectors and

$$y_2 = \begin{bmatrix} y_{21} \\ y_{2e} \end{bmatrix}, \, X_2 = \begin{bmatrix} X_1 \\ X_e \end{bmatrix}, \, u_2 = \begin{bmatrix} u_{21} \\ u_{2e} \end{bmatrix},$$

where the e subscript denotes m extra observations that are available for the second equation. If $m = 0$ there will be no gain from joint estimation because the system reduces to a basic SUR model with each equation containing an equal number of observations and common regressors. Conniffe (1985) and Im (1994) demonstrate that this conclusion no longer holds when there are an unequal number of observations, because y_{2e} and X_e are available. OLS for the second equation is the best linear unbiased estimator (BLUE) as one would expect but joint estimation delivers a more efficient estimator of β_1 than OLS applied to the first equation.

Suppose that y_2 and X are fully observed but y_1 is not. Instead, realizations of a dummy variable D are available where $D = 1$ if $y_1 > 0$ and otherwise $D = 0$. Under an assumption of bivariate normality, a natural approach is to estimate the first equation by probit and the second by OLS. Chesher (1984) showed that joint estimation can deliver more efficient estimates than the "single-equation" probit, but, again as you would expect, there is no gain for the other equation. What if these two situations are combined? Conniffe (1997) examines this case, where the system comprises of a probit and a regression equation, but where there are more observations available for the probit equation. In this case estimates for both equations can be improved upon by joint estimation.

Meng and Rubin (1996) were also concerned with SUR models containing latent variables. They use an extension of the expectation maximization (EM) algorithm called the expectation conditional maximization (ECM) algorithm to discuss estimation and inference in SUR models when latent variables are present or when there are observations missing because of nonresponse. One application of this work is to seemingly unrelated tobit models; see Hwang, Sloan, and Adamache (1987) for an example.

5.2 Computational matters

With the continuing increase in computer power it may appear strange to be concerned with computational matters. However, the need to use computationally intensive methods, such as the bootstrap, in conjunction with regular estimation procedures, provides an incentive to look for computational efficiencies of the type discussed by Hirschberg (1992) and Kontoghiorghes and Clarke (1995). Hirschberg (1992) provides a simplified solution to the Liapunov matrix equation proposed by Byron (1982) to estimate a class of SUR models that are often encountered in demand modeling. Kontoghiorghes and Clarke (1995) propose an alternative numerical procedure for generating SUR estimators that avoids directly computing the inverse of Σ.

When some structure is assumed for the disturbance covariance matrix, or when there are particular patterns in the regressors, general results may be simplified to yield computational gains. For example, Kontoghiorghes and Clarke (1995) develop their approach for the case where the regressors in each equation contain the regressors from the previous equations as a proper subset. Also Seaks (1990) reminds practitioners of the computational simplifications available when cross-equation restrictions need to be tested in SUR models which contain the same set of regressors in each equation.

5.3 Bayesian methods

While increased computational power has had important implications for many areas of econometrics, the impact has probably been most dramatic in the area of Bayesian econometrics. It has long been accepted that the implementation of Bayesian methods by practitioners has been hindered by the unavailability of flexible prior densities that admit analytical treatment of exact posterior and predictive densities. For the SUR model, the problem is that the joint posterior distribution, $f(\beta, \Sigma^{-1} \mid y, X)$, has complicated marginal posteriors. Approximate inferences can be based on a conditional posterior, $f(\beta \mid \Sigma^{-1} = \hat{\Sigma}^{-1}, y, X)$, but exact inferences using the marginal posterior distribution, $f(\beta \mid y, X)$, are problematic.

Richard and Steel (1988) and Steel (1992) have been somewhat successful in extending the exact analytical results that are available for SUR models. Steel (1992) admits, these extensions fall short of providing models that would be of interest to practitioners, but suggests ways in which their analytical results may be effectively used in conjunction with numerical methods.

A better understanding and availability of computational approaches has meant that there are fewer impediments to the routine use of Bayesian methods amongst practitioners. Percy (1992) demonstrated how Gibbs sampling could be used to approximate the predictive density for a basic SUR model. This and other work on Bayesian approaches to SUR estimation is briefly reviewed in Percy (1996).

More recently, Markov chain Monte Carlo methods have enabled Bayesian analyses of even more complex SUR models. Chib and Greenberg (1995) consider a Bayesian hierarchical SUR model and allow the errors to follow a vector autoregressive or vector moving average process. Their contribution aptly illustrates the power of Markov chain Monte Carlo methods in evaluating marginal posterior distributions, which previously have been intractable.

Joint estimation of a SUR model is typically motivated by the presence of disturbance covariation. Blattberg and George (1991) suggest that joint estimation may also be justified in the absence of such dependence if one feels that there are similarities between the regression parameters. When individual estimation leads to nonsensical parameter estimates, they suggest the use of a Bayesian hierarchical model to shrink estimates across equations toward each other thereby producing less estimator variation. They refer to seemingly unrelated equations, SUE rather than SUR.

With these kinds of developments it is not surprising to see more Bayesian applications of SUR models. Examples include Bauwens, Fiebig, and Steel (1994), Griffiths and Chotikapanich (1997) and Griffiths and Valenzuela (1998).

5.4   Improved estimation

In a series of papers Hill, Cartwright, and Arbaugh (1990, 1991, 1992) consider the performance of conventional FGLS compared to various improved estimators when applied to a basic SUR model. The improved estimators include several variants of the Stein-rule family and the hierarchical Bayes estimator of Blattberg and George (1991). The primary example is the estimation of a price-promotion model, which captures the impact of price reductions and promotional activities on sales.

In Hill, Cartwright, and Arbaugh (1996) they extend their previous work on estimator performance by investigating the possibility of estimating the finite sample variability of these alternative estimators using bootstrap standard errors. Conclusions based on their Monte Carlo results obtained for conventional FGLS are found to be somewhat contrary to those of Atkinson and Wilson (1992) that we discussed previously. Hill *et al.* (1996, p. 195) conclude, "the bootstrap standard errors are generally less downward biased than the nominal standard errors" concluding that the former are more reliable than the latter. For the Stein-rule estimators they find that the bootstrap may either overestimate or underestimate the estimator variability depending on whether the specification errors in the restrictions are small or not.

An SUR pre-test estimator can be readily defined based on an initial test of the null hypothesis that Σ is diagonal. Ozcam, Judge, Bera, and Yancey (1993) define such an estimator for a two-equation system using the Lagrange multiplier test of Breusch and Pagan (1980) and Shiba and Tsurumi (1988) and evaluate its risk properties under squared error loss.

5.5 Misspecification

Green, Hassan, and Johnson (1992) and Buse (1994) investigate the impact of model misspecification on SUR estimation. In the case of Green *et al.* (1992) it is the omission of income when estimating demand functions, the motivating example being the use of scanner data where demographic information such as income is not typically available. They conclude that anomalous estimates of own-price elasticities are likely due to this misspecifiaction. Buse (1994) notes that the popular linearization of the almost ideal demand system introduces an errors-in-variables problem, which renders the usual SUR estimator inconsistent.

5.6 Robust estimation

In the context of single-equation modeling there has been considerable work devoted to the provision of estimators that are robust to small perturbations in the data. Koenker and Portnoy (1990) and Peracchi (1991) extend this work by proposing robust alternatives to standard FGLS estimators of the basic SUR model. Both papers illustrate how their estimators can guard against the potential sensitivity due to data contamination. Neither paper addresses the equally important issue of drawing inferences from their robust estimators.

5.7 Model extensions

A natural extension to the basic SUR model is to consider systems that involve equations which are not standard regression models. In the context of time series modeling Fernandez and Harvey (1990) consider a multivariate structural time series model comprised of unobserved components that are allowed to be contemporaneously correlated. King (1989) and Ozuna and Gomez (1994) develop a seemingly unrelated Poisson regression model, which somehow is given the acronym SUPREME. Both applications were to two-equation systems, with extensions to larger models not developed. King (1989) analyses the number of presidential vetoes per year for the period 1946–84 allowing for different explanations to be relevant for social welfare and defense policy vetoes. Ozuna and Gomez (1994) apply the approach to estimate the parameters of a two-equation system of recreation demand functions representing the number of visits to one of two sites.

6 CONCLUSION

The SUR model has been the source of much interest from a theoretical standpoint and has been an extremely useful part of the toolkit of applied econometricians and applied statisticians in general. According to Goldberger (1991, p. 323), the SUR model "plays a central role in contemporary econometrics." This is evidenced in our chapter by the breadth of the theoretical and applied work that has appeared since the major surveys of Srivastava and Dwivedi (1979) and Srivastava and Giles (1987). Hopefully this new summary of recent research will provide a useful resource for further developments in the area.

Note

*   I gratefully acknowledge the excellent research assistance of Hong Li and Kerri Hoffman. Badi Baltagi, Bob Bartels, Mike Smith, and three anonymous referees also provided helpful comments.

References

Amemiya, T. (1977). A note on a heteroscedastic model. *Journal of Econometrics* 6, 365–70.

Anderson, G.J., and R.W. Blundell (1982). Estimation and hypothesis testing in dynamic singular equation systems. *Econometrica* 50, 1559–72.

Anselin, L. (1988). A test for spatial autocorrelation in seemingly unrelated regressions. *Economics Letters* 28, 335–41.

Anselin, L. (1990). Spatial dependence and spatial structural instability in applied regression analysis. *Journal of Regional Science* 30, 185–207.

Atkinson, S.E., and P.W. Wilson (1992). The bias of bootstrapped versus conventional standard errors in the general linear and SUR models. *Econometric Theory* 8, 258–75.

Attfield, C.L.F. (1995). Bartlett adjustment to the likelihood ratio test for a system of equations. *Journal of Econometrics* 66, 207–24.

Attfield, C.L.F. (1998). Bartlett adjustments for systems of linear equations with linear restrictions. *Economics Letters* 60, 277–83.

Avery, R. (1977). Error components and seemingly unrelated regressions. *Econometrica* 45, 199–209.

Baltagi, B.H. (1980). On seemingly unrelated regressions with error components. *Econometrica* 48, 1547–51.

Baltagi, B.H. (1989). Applications of a necessary and sufficient condition for OLS to be BLUE. *Statistics and Probability Letters* 8, 457–61.

Baltagi, B.H., S. Garvin, and S. Kerman (1989). Further evidence on seemingly unrelated regressions with unequal number of observations. *Annales D'Economie et de Statistique* 14, 103–15.

Bartels, R., and D.G. Fiebig (1991). A simple characterization of seemingly unrelated regressions models in which OLS is BLUE. *American Statistician* 45, 137–40.

Bartels, R., and D.G. Fiebig (1992). Efficiency of alternative estimators in generalized seemingly unrelated regression models. In R. Bewley, and T.V. Hao (eds.) *Contributions to Consumer Demand and Econometrics: Essays in Honour of Henri Theil*. London: Macmillan Publishing Company, 125–39.

Bartels, R., D.G. Fiebig, and M. Plumb (1996). Gas or electricity, which is cheaper? An econometric approach with application to Australian expenditure data. *Energy Journal* 17, 33–58.

Batchelor, R., and D. Gulley (1995). Jewellery demand and the price of gold. *Resources Policy* 21, 37–42.

Bauwens, L., D.G. Fiebig, and M.F.J. Steel (1994). Estimating end-use demand: A Bayesian approach. *Journal of Business and Economic Statistics* 12, 221–31.

Bewley, R.A. (1983). Tests of restrictions in large demand systems. *European Economic Review* 20, 257–69.

Bewley, R.A. (1986). *Allocation Models: Specification, Estimation and Applications.* Cambridge, MA: Ballinger Publishing Company.

Binkley, J.K. (1982). The effect of variable correlation on the efficiency of seemingly unrelated regression in a two equation model. *Journal of the American Statistical Association* 77, 890–5.

Binkley, J.K., and C.H. Nelson (1988). A note on the efficiency of seemingly unrelated regression. *American Statistician* 42, 137–9.

Blattberg, R.C., and E.I. George (1991). Shrinkage estimation of price and promotional elasticities: Seemingly unrelated equations. *Journal of the American Statistical Association* 86, 304–15.

Bollerslev, T. (1990). Modeling the coherence in short-run nominal exchange rates: A multivariate generalized ARCH model. *Review of Economics and Statistics* 72, 498–505.

Breusch, T.S., and A.R. Pagan (1980). The Lagrange multiplier test and its applications to model specification in econometrics. *Review of Economic Studies* 47, 239–53.

Brown, B.W., and M.B. Walker (1989). The random utility hypothesis and inference in demand systems. *Econometrica* 57, 815–29.

Brown, B.W., and M.B. Walker (1995). Stochastic specification in random production models of cost minimizing firms. *Journal of Econometrics* 66, 175–205.

Buse, A. (1994). Evaluating the linearized almost ideal demand system. *American Journal of Agricultural Economics* 76, 781–93.

Byron, R.P. (1982). A note on the estimation of symmetric systems. *Econometrica* 50, 1573–5.

Chavas, J.-P., and K. Segerson (1987). Stochastic specification and estimation of share equation systems. *Journal of Econometrics* 35, 337–58.

Chesher, A. (1984). Improving the efficiency of probit estimators. *Review of Economics and Statistics* 66, 523–7.

Chib, S., and E. Greenberg (1995). Hierarchical analysis of SUR models with extensions to correlated serial errors and time-varying parameter models. *Journal of Econometrics* 68, 339–60.

Conniffe, D. (1985). Estimating regression equations with common explanatory variables but unequal numbers of observations. *Journal of Econometrics* 27, 179–96.

Conniffe, D. (1997). Improving a linear regression through joint estimation with a probit model. *The Statistician* 46, 487–93.

Creel, M., and M. Farell (1996). SUR estimation of multiple time-series models with heteroscedasticity and serial correlation of unknown form. *Economic Letters* 53, 239–45.

de Jong, P., and R. Thompson (1990). Testing linear hypothesis in the SUR framework with identical explanatory variables. *Research in Finance* 8, 59–76.

Deschamps, P.J. (1998). Full maximum likelihood estimation of dynamic demand models. *Journal of Econometrics* 82, 335–59.

Dhrymes, P.J. (1994). Autoregressive errors in singular systems of equations. *Econometric Theory* 10, 254–85.

Dufour, J.M., and O. Torres (1998). Union-intersection and sample-split methods in econometrics with applications to MA and SURE models. In A. Ullah, and D.E.A. Giles (eds.) *Handbook of Applied Economic Statistics.* New York: Marcel Dekker, 465–505.

Eakin, B.K., D.P. McMillen, and M.J. Buono (1990). Constructing confidence intervals using the bootstrap: An application to a multi-product cost function. *Review of Economics and Statistics* 72, 339–44.

Efron, B. (1992). Jackknife-after-bootstrap standard errors and influence functions. *Journal of the Royal Statistical Society, B* 54, 83–127.

Fernandez, F.J., and A.C. Harvey (1990). Seemingly unrelated time series equations and a test for homogeneity. *Journal of Business and Economic Statistics* 8, 71–82.

Fiebig, D.G., and J.H. Kim (2000). Estimation and inference in SUR models when the number of equations is large. *Econometric Reviews* 19, 105–130.

Fiebig, D.G., and Theil, H. (1983). The two perils of symmetry-constrained estimation of demand systems. *Economics Letters* 13, 105–11.

Fiebig, D.G., R. Bartels, and D.J. Aigner (1991). A random coefficient approach to the estimation of residential end-use load profiles. *Journal of Econometrics* 50, 297–327.

Freedman, D.A., and S.C. Peters (1984). Bootstrapping a regression equation: Some empirical results. *Journal of the American Statistical Association* 79, 97–106.

Frees, E.W. (1995). Assessing cross-sectional correlation in panel data. *Journal of Econometrics* 69, 393–414.

Fry, J.M., T.R.L. Fry, and K.R. McLaren (1996). The stochastic specification of demand share equations: Restricting budget shares to the unit simplex. *Journal of Econometrics* 73, 377–86.

Goldberger, A.S. (1991). *A Course in Econometrics*. Cambridge, MA: Harvard University Press.

Green, R., Z.A. Hassan, and S.R. Johnson (1992). The bias due to omitting income when estimating demand functions. *Canadian Journal of Agricultural Economics* 40, 475–84.

Griffiths, W.E., and D. Chotikapanich (1997). Bayesian methodology for imposing inequality constraints on a linear expenditure system with demographic factors. *Australian Economic Papers* 36, 321–41.

Griffiths, W.E., and R. Valenzuela (1998). Missing data from infrequency of purchase: Bayesian estimation of a linear expenditure system. In T.B. Fomby, and R.C. Hill (eds.) *Advances in Econometrics, 13: Messy Data – Missing Observations, Outliers and Mixed-Frequency Data*. Greenwich CT: JAI Press, 47–74.

Griliches, Z., and M.D. Intriligator (1983). Preface. In Z. Griliches, and M.D. Intriligator (eds.) *Handbook of Econometrics*. Amsterdam: Elsevier Science Publishers B.V., xi–xvii.

Hasegawa, H. (1995). On small sample properties of Zellner's estimator for the case of two SUR equations with compound normal disturbances. *Communications in Statistics, Simulation and Computation* 24, 45–59.

Hashimoto, N., and K. Ohtani (1990). An exact test for linear restrictions in seemingly unrelated regressions with the same regressors. *Economics Letters* 32, 243–6.

Henley, A., and J. Peirson (1994). Time-of-use electricity pricing: Evidence from a British experiment. *Economics Letters* 45, 421–6.

Hill, R.C., P.A. Cartwright, and J.F. Arbaugh (1990). Using aggregate data to estimate micro-level parameters with shrinkage rules. *American Statistical Association: Proceedings of the Business and Economic Statistics Section* 339–44.

Hill, R.C., P.A. Cartwright, and J.F. Arbaugh (1991). Using aggregate data to estimate micro-level parameters with shrinkage rules: More results. *American Statistical Association: Proceedings of the Business and Economic Statistics Section* 155–60.

Hill, R.C., P.A. Cartwright, and J.F. Arbaugh (1992). The finite sample properties of shrinkage estimators applied to seemingly unrelated regressions. *American Statistical Association: Proceedings of the Business and Economic Statistics Section* 17–21.

Hill, R.C., P.A. Cartwright, and J.F. Arbaugh (1996). Bootstrapping estimators for the seemingly unrelated regressions model. *Journal of Statistical Computation and Simulation* 54, 177–96.

Hill, R.C., P.A. Cartwright, and J.F. Arbaugh (1997). Jackknifing the bootstrap: Some Monte Carlo evidence. *Communications in Statistics, Simulation and Computation* 26, 125–239.

Hirschberg, J.G. (1992). A computationally efficient method for bootstrapping systems of demand equations: A comparison to traditional techniques. *Statistics and Computing* 2, 19–24.

Holt, M.T. (1998). Autocorrelation specification in singular equation systems: A further look. *Economics Letters* 58, 135–41.

Hwang, H.S. (1990). Estimation of a linear SUR model with unequal numbers of observations. *Review of Economics and Statistics* 72, 510–15.

Hwang, C.J., F.A. Sloan, and K.W. Adamache (1987). Estimation of seemingly unrelated Tobit regressions via the EM algorithm. *Journal of Business and Economic Statistics* 5, 425–30.

Im, E.I. (1994). Unequal numbers of observations and partial efficiency gain. *Economics Letters* 46, 291–4.

Jensen, M.J. (1995). A Monte Carlo study on two methods of calculating the MLE's covariance matrix in a seemingly unrelated nonlinear regression. *Econometric Reviews* 14, 315–30.

Jeong, J., and G.S. Maddala (1993). A perspective on application of bootstrap methods in econometrics. In G.S. Maddala, C.R. Rao, and H.D. Vinod (eds.) *Handbook of Statistics, Volume 11*. Amsterdam: Elsevier Science Publishers B.V., 573–610.

Judge G.G., W.E. Griffiths, R.C. Hill, H. Lütkepohl, and T.-C. Lee (1985). *The Theory and Practice of Econometrics*, 2nd edn. New York: John Wiley and Sons.

King, G. (1989). A seemingly unrelated Poisson regression model. *Sociological Methods and Research* 17, 235–55.

Kiviet, J.F., G.D.A. Phillips, and B. Schipp (1995). The bias of OLS, GLS and ZEF estimators in dynamic SUR models. *Journal of Econometrics* 69, 241–66.

Koenker, R., and S. Portnoy (1990). M estimation of multivariate regressions. *Journal of the American Statistical Association* 85, 1060–8.

Kontoghiorghes, E.J. and M.R.B. Clarke (1995). An alternative approach to the numerical solution of seemingly unrelated regression equation models. *Computational Statistics and Data Analysis* 19, 369–77.

Kumbhakar, S.C., and A. Heshmati (1996). Technical change and total factor productivity growth in Swedish manufacturing industries. *Econometric Reviews* 15, 275–98.

Laitinen, K. (1978). Why is demand homogeneity so often rejected? *Economics Letters* 1, 187–91.

Lee, B.-J. (1995). Seemingly unrelated regression on the autoregressive (AR(p)) singular equation system. *Econometric Reviews* 14, 65–74.

MacKinley, A.C. (1987). On multivariate tests of the CAPM. *Journal of Financial Economics* 18, 341–71.

Mandy, D.M., and C. Martins-Filho (1993). Seemingly unrelated regressions under additive heteroscedasticity. *Journal of Econometrics* 58, 315–46.

McLaren, K.R. (1990). A variant on the arguments for the invariance of estimators in a singular system of equations. *Econometric Reviews* 9, 91–102.

McLaren, K.R. (1996). Parsimonious autocorrelation corrections for singular demand systems. *Economics Letters* 53, 115–21.

Meisner, J.F. (1979). The sad fate of the asymptotic Slutsky symmetry test for large systems. *Economics Letters* 2, 231–3.

Meng, X.L., and D.B. Rubin (1996). Efficient methods for estimation and testing with seemingly unrelated regressions in the presence of latent variables and missing observations. In D.A. Berry, K.M. Chaloner, and J.K. Geweke (eds.) *Bayesian Analysis in Statistics and Econometrics: Essays in Honor of Arnold Zellner*. New York: John Wiley and Sons, 215–27.

Mizon, G.E. (1995). A simple message for autocorrelation correctors: Don't. *Journal of Econometrics* 69, 267–88.

Moschini, G., and D. Moro (1994). Autocorrelation specification in singular equation systems. *Economics Letters* 46, 303–9.

Ozcam, A., G. Judge, A. Bera, and T. Yancey (1993). The risk properties of a pre-test estimator for Zellner's seemingly unrelated regression model. *Journal of Quantitative Economics* 9, 41–52.

Ozuna, T., and I.A. Gomez (1994). Estimating a system of recreation demand functions using a seemingly unrelated Poisson regression approach. *Review of Economics and Statistics* 76, 356–60.

Peracchi, F. (1991). Bounded-influence estimators for the SURE model. *Journal of Econometrics* 48, 119–34.

Percy, D.F. (1992). Prediction for seemingly unrelated regressions. *Journal of the Royal Statistical Society, B* 54, 243–52.

Percy, D.F. (1996). Zellner's influence on multivariate linear models. In D.A. Berry, K.M. Chaloner, and J.K. Geweke (eds.) *Bayesian Analysis in Statistics and Econometrics: Essays in Honor of Arnold Zellner*. New York: John Wiley and Sons, 203–13.

Richard, J.F., and M.F.J. Steel (1988). Bayesian analysis of systems of seemingly unrelated regression equations under a recursive extended natural conjugate prior density. *Journal of Econometrics* 38, 7–37.

Rilstone, P., and M. Veall (1996). Using bootstrapped confidence intervals for improved inferences with seemingly unrelated regression equations. *Econometric Theory* 12, 569–80.

Rocke, D.M. (1989). Bootstrap Bartlett adjustment in seemingly unrelated regression. *Journal of the American Statistical Association* 84, 598–601.

Rosalsky, M.C., R. Finke, and H. Theil (1984). The downward bias of asymptotic standard errors of maximum likelihood estimates of non-linear systems. *Economics Letters* 14, 207–11.

Schmidt, P. (1977). Estimation of seemingly unrelated regressions with unequal numbers of observations. *Journal of Econometrics* 5, 365–77.

Seaks, T.G. (1990). The computation of test statistics for multivariate regression models in event studies. *Economics Letters* 33, 141–5.

Shiba, T., and H. Tsurumi (1988). Bayesian and non-Bayesian tests of independence in seemingly unrelated regressions. *International Economic Review* 29, 377–95.

Silk, J. (1996). Systems estimation: A comparison of SAS, SHAZAM and TSP. *Journal of Applied Econometrics* 11, 437–50.

Silver, J.L., and M.M. Ali (1989). Testing Slutsky symmetry in systems of linear demand equations. *Journal of Econometrics* 41, 251–66.

Srivastava, V.K., and T.D. Dwivedi (1979). Estimation of seemingly unrelated regression equations: a brief survey. *Journal of Econometrics* 10, 15–32.

Srivastava, V.K., and D.E.A. Giles (1987). *Seemingly Unrelated Regression Models: Estimation and Inference*. New York: Marcel Dekker.

Srivastava, V.K., and K. Maekawa (1995). Efficiency properties of feasible generalized least squares estimators in SURE models under non-normal disturbances. *Journal of Econometrics* 66, 99–121.

Steel, M.F. (1992). Posterior analysis of restricted seemingly unrelated regression equation models: A recursive analytical approach. *Econometric Reviews* 11, 129–42.

Stewart, K.G. (1997). Exact testing in multivariate regression. *Econometric Reviews* 16, 321–52.

Telser, L.G. (1964). Iterative estimation of a set of linear regression equations. *Journal of the American Statistical Association* 59, 845–62.

Ullah, A., and J. Racine (1992). Smooth improved estimators of econometric parameters. In W.E. Griffiths, H. Lütkepohl, and M.E. Bock (eds.) *Readings in Econometric Theory and Practice*. Amsterdam: Elsevier Science Publishers B.V., 198–213.

Wan, G.H., W.E. Griffiths, and J.R. Anderson (1992). Using panel data to estimate risk effects in seemingly unrelated production functions. *Empirical Economics* 17, 35–49.

Williams, M.A. (1986). An economic application of bootstrap statistical methods: Addyston Pipe revisited. *American Economist* 30, 52–8.

Woodland, A.D. (1979). Stochastic specification and the estimation of share equations. *Journal of Econometrics* 10, 361–83.

Zellner, A. (1962). An efficient method of estimating seemingly unrelated regressions and tests of aggregation bias. *Journal of the American Statistical Association* 57, 348–68.

Simultaneous Equation Model Estimators: Statistical Properties and Practical Implications

Roberto S. Mariano

1 THE LINEAR SIMULTANEOUS EQUATIONS MODEL

This chapter deals with the statistical properties of estimators in simultaneous equation models. The discussion covers material that extends from the standard large sample asymptotics and the early works on finite-sample analysis to recent work on exact small-sample properties of IV (instrumental variable) estimators and the behavior of IV estimators when instruments are weak. This section introduces the linear simultaneous equations model and the notation for the rest of the chapter. Sections 2 and 3 then cover limited information and full information estimators of structural parameters. Section 4 moves on to large sample properties of the estimators while Sections 5 and 6 summarize results obtained in finite sample analysis. Section 7 ends the chapter with a summary of practical implications of the finite sample results and alternative asymptotics that involve increasing the number of instruments or reducing the correlation between instruments and endogenous regressors in instrumental variable estimation.

Consider the classical linear simultaneous equations model (SEM) of the form:

$$By_t + \Gamma x_t = u_t; \quad t = 1, 2, \ldots, T \quad \text{or} \quad YB' + X\Gamma' = U, \tag{6.1}$$

where

$B = G \times G$ matrix of fixed parameters (some of which are unknown),
$\Gamma = G \times K$ matrix of fixed parameters (some unknown),
$y_t = G \times 1$ vector of observations on endogenous variables at "time" t,
$x_t = K \times 1$ vector of observations on exogenous variables at "time" t,
$u_t = G \times 1$ vector of structural disturbances in "time" t,
$Y = T \times G$ matrix whose tth row is y_t',
$X = T \times K$ matrix whose tth row is x_t',
$U = T \times G$ matrix whose tth row is u_t',
$T =$ sample size.

The system described in (6.1) consists of G linear equations. Each equation is linear in the components of y_t, with a particular row of B and Γ containing the coefficients of an equation in the system. Each equation may be stochastic or nonstochastic depending on whether or not the corresponding component of the disturbance vector u_t has a nondegenerate probability distribution.

The following assumptions together with (6.1) comprise the *classical linear simultaneous equations model*:

A1. B is nonsingular. Thus, the model is complete in the sense that we can solve for y_t in terms of x_t and u_t.
A2. X is exogenous. That is, X and U are independently distributed of each other.
A3. X is of full column rank with probability 1.
A4. The disturbances u_t, for $t = 1, 2, \ldots, T$, are uncorrelated and identically distributed with mean zero and positive definite covariance matrix Σ.

At certain times, we will replace A4 with the stronger assumption,

A4′. The disturbances u_t are independent and identically distributed as multivariate normal with mean zero and covariance matrix Σ.

We refer to the G equations in (6.1) as being structural in that they comprise a simultaneous system which explains the mutual interdependence among G endogenous variables and their relationship to K exogenous variables whose behavior, by assumption A2, is in turn explained by factors outside the system.

This model differs from the standard multivariate linear regression model in the statistics literature to the extent that B is generally not diagonal and Y and U are correlated. Under these conditions, the structural equations are such that, after normalization, some explanatory or right-hand side variables are correlated with the disturbance terms. (One can thus claim that the canonical equivalence is between this structural system and a multivariate linear regression model with measurement errors.)

The structural system in (6.1) also leads to a multivariate linear regression system with coefficient restrictions. Premultiplying (6.1) by B^{-1}, we get the so-called reduced form equations of the model:

$$y_t = -B^{-1}\Gamma x_t + B^{-1}u_t = \Pi x_t + v_t \quad \text{or} \quad Y = -X\Gamma'B'^{-1} + UB'^{-1} = X\Pi' + V \quad (6.2)$$

where $\Pi = -B^{-1}\Gamma$, $v_t = B^{-1}u_t$, and $V = UB'^{-1}$.

It follows from A2 and (6.2) that X and V are independently distributed of each other and that, for $\Omega = B^{-1}\Sigma B'^{-1}$, $v_t \sim$ uncorrelated $(0, \Omega)$, if A4 holds; and $v_t \sim$ iid $N(0, \Omega)$ if A4' holds. Thus, $y_t | X \sim$ uncorrelated $(\Pi x_t, \Omega)$ under A4 and $y_t | X \sim$ independent $N(\Pi x_t, \Omega)$ under A4'.

The standard literature on identification of simultaneous equations models shows that identification of (6.1) through prior restrictions on the structural parameters (B, Γ, Σ) generally will imply restrictions on the matrix Π of reduced form coefficients. For more details on identification of simultaneous equations models, see Hsiao (1983), Bekker and Dijkstra (1990), and Bekker and Wansbeek (chapter 7) in this volume.

2   LIMITED-INFORMATION ESTIMATORS OF STRUCTURAL PARAMETERS

We now consider the estimation of an equation in the linear simultaneous system. Note that the ith rows of B and Γ contain the coefficients in the ith structural equation of the system. For the moment, let us consider the first equation of the system and, after imposing zero restrictions and a normalization rule, write it as

$$y_{t1} = -\sum_{i=2}^{G_1} \beta_{1i}y_{ti} - \sum_{j=1}^{K_1} \gamma_{1j}x_{tj} + u_{t1} \quad \text{or} \quad y_1 = Y_1\beta + X_1\gamma + u_1 = Z\delta + u_1, \quad (6.3)$$

where $y_{ti} = (t, i)$ element of the observation matrix Y, $x_{tj} = (t, j)$ element of X, $u_{ti} = (t, i)$ element of U, $\beta_{ij} = (i, j)$ element of B, $\gamma_{ij} = (i, j)$ element of Γ, $u_1 = $ 1st column of U, $X = (X_1, X_2)$, $Y = (y_1, Y_1, Y_2)$, $Z = (Y_1, X_1)$, $\delta' = (\beta', \gamma')$, $-\beta' = (\beta_{12}, \beta_{13}, \ldots, \beta_{1G_1})$, and $-\gamma' = (\gamma_{11}, \gamma_{12}, \ldots, \gamma_{1K_1})$.

Thus, the normalization rule is $\beta_{11} = 1$ and the prior restrictions impose the exclusion of the last $G - G_1$ endogenous variables and the last $K - K_1$ exogenous variables from the first equation.

From assumption A4 it follows that $u_1 \sim (0, \sigma_{11}I)$ where σ_{11} is the $(1, 1)$ element of Σ. By assumption A2, X_1 and u_1 are independent of each other. However, in general Y_1 and u_1 will be correlated.

We shall consider two general categories of estimators of (6.3):

1. limited information or single equation methods, and
2. full information or system methods.

Together with the specification (6.3) for the first equation, all that is needed for the limited information estimators are the reduced form equations for the "included endogenous variables," namely; (y_1, Y_1). Under the classical assumptions we have listed for the linear SEM (including A4'), this requirement reduces to a specification of the exogenous variables in the system since reduced form equations are linear in the exogenous variables with additive disturbances which are identically distributed as mutually independent multivariate Gaussian across sample observations. Full information methods, on the other hand, require the exact specification of the other structural equations composing the system.

In (6.3), the *ordinary least squares* (OLS) estimator of δ is obtained directly from the linear regression of y_1 on Z:

$$\hat{\delta}_{OLS} = (Z'Z)^{-1}Z'y_1 = \delta + (Z'Z)^{-1}Z'u_1. \tag{6.4}$$

Because of the nonzero covariance between Y_1 and u_1, this estimator is inconsistent, in general:

$$\begin{aligned}
\text{plim } \hat{\delta}_{OLS} - \delta &= \text{plim } [(Z'Z/T)^{-1}(Z'\mathbf{u}_1/T)] \\
&= [\text{plim } (Z'Z/T)^{-1}][\text{plim } (Z'\mathbf{u}_1/T)] \\
&= [\text{plim } (Z'Z/T)^{-1}] \begin{pmatrix} \Omega_{21} - \Omega_{22}\beta \\ 0 \end{pmatrix}
\end{aligned}$$

where Ω_{22} is the covariance matrix of tth row of Y_1 and Ω_{21} is the covariance vector between the tth rows of Y_1 and y_1.

A generic class of estimators of δ in (6.4) can be obtained by using an instrument matrix, say W, of the same size as Z to form the so-called *limited information instrumental variable* (IV) estimator satisfying the modified normal equations

$$W'y_1 = W'Z\hat{\delta}_{IV} \quad \text{or} \quad \hat{\delta}_{IV} = (W'Z)^{-1}W'y_1. \tag{6.5}$$

The minimal requirements on the instrument matrix W, which can be either stochastic or not, are

$$|W'Z| \neq 0 \text{ for any T and plim } (W'Z/T) \text{ is nonsingular.} \tag{6.6}$$

The ordinary least squares estimator belongs to this class – with the instrument matrix, say W_{OLS}, equal to Z itself.

With (6.6) satisfied, a necessary and sufficient condition for $\hat{\delta}_{IV}$ to be consistent is

$$\text{plim } (W'u_1/T) = 0. \tag{6.7}$$

Condition (6.7) is not satisfied in the case of OLS and hence OLS would be inconsistent in general. Note that a nonstochastic matrix W satisfying (6.6) will satisfy (6.7) as well.

The limited information estimators which we discuss presently and which have been developed as alternatives to OLS, can be interpreted as members of this class of IV estimators corresponding to stochastic matrices. First of all, since

X_1 is exogenous, we have plim $X_1'u_1/T = 0$ and so, for consistency, we can take an instrument matrix of the form

$$W = (W_y, X_1), \tag{6.8}$$

where W_y is the instrument matrix for Y_1 chosen so that

$$\text{plim } W_y'u_1/T = 0. \tag{6.9}$$

One possibility is to use $E(Y_1)$ for W_y, since $E(Y_1) = X\Pi_1'$ and hence plim $(\Pi_1 X'u_1/T) = \Pi_1 \text{ lim } (X'u_1/T) = 0$. However, there is still one problem: Π_1 is not known and $E(Y_1)$ is not observable. To remedy this, we can use an estimate of Π_1, say $\hat{\Pi}_1$ and as long as plim $\hat{\Pi}_1$ is finite, we get plim $(\hat{\Pi}_1 X'u_1/T) = (\text{plim } \hat{\Pi}_1) [\text{plim } (X'u_1/T)] = 0$, and consequently, the instrument matrix $(X\hat{\Pi}_1', X_1)$ provides a subclass of consistent instrumental variable estimators of δ. Note in this discussion that $\hat{\Pi}_1$ need not be consistent for Π_1; all that is needed is that $\hat{\Pi}_1$ have a finite probability limit and produces instruments that satisfy (6.6).

One member of this subclass is the *two-stage least squares* (2SLS) estimator where Π_1 is estimated from the unrestricted least squares regression of Y_1 on X; that is, $\hat{\Pi}_1' = (X'X)^{-1}X'Y_1$ and the instrument matrix for Z is the regression of Z on X:

$$W_{2SLS} = (X(X'X)^{-1}X'Y_1, X_1) = P_X Z. \tag{6.10}$$

The terminology for this estimator derives from the fact that it can be interpreted as least squares applied twice. The procedure, which first regresses Y_1 on X to get $P_x Y_1$ and then regresses y_1 on $P_x Y_1$ and X_1, produces in the second-step regression exactly the 2SLS estimator which we have defined above.

The 2SLS estimator also can be interpreted as a *generalized least squares* (GLS) estimator in the linear model obtained by premultiplying (6.3) by X'.

Other alternative preliminary estimates of Π_1 also have been proposed in the literature. One alternative is to estimate each structural equation by ordinary least squares, thus obtaining $\hat{B}_{OLS}$ and $\hat{\Gamma}_{OLS}$ and then using the appropriate sub-matrix of the derived reduced form coefficient matrix $\hat{\Pi} = -(\hat{B}_{OLS})^{-1}\hat{\Gamma}_{OLS}$, say, $\hat{\Pi}^{(0)}$, to construct the instrument matrix

$$(X\hat{\Pi}_1^{(0)'}, X_1). \tag{6.11}$$

Although $\hat{\Pi}_1^{(0)}$ itself is inconsistent, the IV estimate of δ based on (6.11) as instrument for Z will be consistent since (6.9) is satisfied.

The *limited information instrumental variable efficient* (LIVE) estimator is based on the instrument matrix

$$W_{LIVE} = (X\hat{\Pi}_1^{(1)'}, X_1),$$

where $\hat{\Pi}_1^{(1)}$ is a consistent estimator of Π_1 derived from some initial consistent estimates of B and Γ. This would be a two-step procedure if the initial consistent estimates of B and Γ are themselves obtained by an instrumental variable procedure. In fact, one way of getting these initial consistent estimates of B and Γ is by using $\hat{\Pi}^{(0)}$, as in (6.11), to generate instruments for the first-step consistent estimation of B and Γ. Further iteration of this sequential procedure leads to the so-called *iterated instrumental variable* (IIV) procedure.

Yet another alternative to 2SLS is the so-called modified two-stage least squares (M2SLS). Like 2SLS, this is a two-step regression procedure; but here, in the first stage, we would regress Y_1 on H instead of X, where H is a $T \times h$ data matrix of full column rank and rank $(\bar{P}_{X_1}H) \geq G - 1$ for $\bar{P}_{X_1} = I - P_{X_1}$. We can further show that this estimator will be exactly equivalent to the instrumental variable method with $(P_H Y_1, X_1)$ as the instrument matrix if the column space of H contains the column space of X_1 (see Mariano, 1977). Because of this, a suggested manner of constructing H is to start with X_1 and then add at least $(G_1 - 1)$ more of the remaining K_2 exogenous variables or, alternatively, the first $G_1 - 1$ principal components of $\bar{P}_{X_1} X_2$.

Another instrumental variable estimator is Theil's *k-class* estimator. In this estimator, the instrument matrix is a linear combination of the instrument matrices for OLS and 2SLS. Thus, for $W_{(k)} = k W_{2SLS} + (1 - k) W_{OLS} = k P_x Z + (1 - k)Z$, the *k*-class estimator of δ is

$$\hat{\delta}_{(k)} = (W'_{(k)}Z)^{-1}W'_{(k)}y_1 = \delta + (W'_{(k)}Z)^{-1}W'_{(k)}u_1. \tag{6.12}$$

For consistency, we see from (6.12) that

$$\text{plim } W'_{(k)}u_1/T = [\text{plim } (1 - k)] [\text{plim } Z'u_1/T], \tag{6.13}$$

assuming that plim k is finite. Thus, for (6.13) to be equal to zero (and consequently, the consistency of *k*-class), a necessary and sufficient condition is plim $(1 - k) = 0$.

The *limited information maximum likelihood* (LIML) estimator, though based, as the term connotes, on the principle of maximizing a certain likelihood function, can also be given an instrumental variable interpretation. In fact as we shall show presently, it is a member of the *k*-class of estimators in (6.12). Essentially, the LIML estimator of β and γ maximizes the likelihood of the included endogenous variables subject to the identifiability restrictions imposed on the equation being estimated. This is limited information (rather than full information) maximum likelihood in the sense that the likelihood function considered pertains only to those endogenous variables appearing in the estimated equation; endogenous variables excluded from this equation are thus disregarded. Also, identifiability restrictions on other equations in the system are not taken into account in the constrained maximization of the appropriate likelihood function.

For an explicit development of the LIML estimator, we start with the nonnormalized version of the equation to be estimated; $Y_1^* \beta^* = (y_1, Y_1)\beta^* = X_1\gamma + u_1$. Thus, for the moment, we take the first row of B as $(\beta^{*\prime}, 0')$. The reduced form equations for Y_1^* are $Y_1^* = X\Pi_1^{*\prime} + V_1^* = X_1\Pi_{11}^* + X_2\Pi_{12}^* + V_1^*$. From the relationship

$B\Pi = -\Gamma$, we get $\Pi_{11}^{*\prime}\beta^* = \gamma$ and $\Pi_{12}^{*\prime}\beta^* = 0$. For identifiability of the first equation, a necessary and sufficient condition is rank $\Pi_{12}^* = G_1 - 1$.

The LIML estimator thus maximizes the likelihood function for Y_1^* subject to the restriction that $\Pi_{12}^{*\prime}\beta^* = 0$. This constrained maximization process reduces to the minimization of

$$v = (\beta^{*\prime}A\beta^*)/(\beta^{*\prime}S\beta^*) = 1 + (\beta^{*\prime}W\beta^*)/(\beta^{*\prime}S\beta^*) \tag{6.14}$$

with respect to β^*, for

$$S = Y_1^{*\prime}\bar{P}_X Y_1^*, \ W = Y_1^{*\prime}(P_X - P_{X_1})Y_1^*, \ A = S + W = Y_1^{*\prime}\bar{P}_{X_1}Y_1^*. \tag{6.15}$$

Solving this minimization problem we get $\hat{\beta}_{\text{LIML}}^* = $ a characteristic vector of A (with respect to S) corresponding to h, where h is the smallest root of $|A - vS| = 0$ and is equal to $(\hat{\beta}_{\text{LIML}}^{*\prime}A\hat{\beta}_{\text{LIML}}^*)/(\hat{\beta}_{\text{LIML}}^{*\prime}S\hat{\beta}_{\text{LIML}}^*)$.

The above derivation of LIML also provides a least variance ratio interpretation for it. In (6.14), $\beta^{*\prime}W\beta^*$ is the marginal contribution (regression sum of squares) of X_2, given X_1, in the regression of $Y_1^*\beta$ on X, while $E\{\beta^{*\prime}S\beta^*/(T - K)\} = \sigma_{11}$.

Thus, LIML minimizes the explained sum of squares of $Y_1^*\beta^*$ due to X_2 given X_1, relative to a stochastic proxy for σ_{11}. On the other hand, $\hat{\beta}_{\text{2SLS}}^*$ simply minimizes $\beta^{*\prime}W\beta^*$ in absolute terms.

For the estimator $\hat{\beta}_{\text{LIML}}^*$ as described above to be uniquely determined, a normalization rule needs to be imposed. We shall use the normalization that the first element of $\hat{\beta}_{\text{LIML}}^*$ is equal to unity as in the case of all the limited information estimators which we have discussed so far. In this case, it can be easily shown that the LIML estimator of β and γ in the normalized equation (6.3) is a k-class estimator. The value of k which gives the LIML estimator is h, where h is the smallest characteristic root of A with respect to S. Note that because A = S + W, we also have $h = 1 + \ell$ where ℓ is the smallest characteristic root of W (wrt S). Thus we can interpret LIML as a linear combination of OLS and 2SLS, with $k > 1$. Indeed, it can be shown formally that the 2SLS estimate of β lies between the OLS and LIML estimates.

Also note that $\hat{\beta}_{\text{LIML}}^*$ and $\hat{\gamma}_{\text{LIML}}^*$ can be characterized equivalently as the maximum likelihood estimates of β and γ based on the "limited information" model

$$y_1 = Y_1\beta + X_1\gamma + u_1$$

$$Y_1 = X\Pi_1' + V_1.$$

If the equation being estimated is exactly identified by zero restrictions, then the *indirect least squares* (ILS) estimator of β and γ is well-defined. This is obtained directly from the unrestricted least squares estimate $\tilde{\Pi}_1^*$ and is the solution to the system of equations taken from $\tilde{\Pi}_{12}^{*\prime}\beta^* = 0$ and $\tilde{\Pi}_{11}^{*\prime}\beta^* = \gamma$ after setting $\beta^{*\prime} = (1, \beta')$. We can further verify that if the equation being estimated is exactly identified, then the following estimators are exactly equivalent: 2SLS, LIML, ILS, and IV using (X_1, X_2) as the instrument matrix for the regressors (X_1, Y_1).

3   FULL INFORMATION METHODS

In this section, we change the notation somewhat and write the jth equation as

$$y_j = Y_j\beta_j + X_j\gamma_j + u_j = Z_j\delta_j + u_j. \tag{6.16}$$

Here, y_j is $T \times 1$, Y_j is $T \times (G_j - 1)$, X_j is $T \times K_j$, and Z_j is $T \times (G_j + K_j - 1)$.

We can further write the whole linear simultaneous system in "stacked" form as

$$y = Z\delta + u, \tag{6.17}$$

where, now, y, Z, δ, and u are defined differently from previous sections. If we start with Y and U as defined in Section 1, then $y' = (\text{vec } Y)' = (y_1', y_2', \dots, y_G')$, $y_j = j$th column of Y, $u' = (\text{vec } U)' = (u_1', u_2', \dots, u_G')$, $u_j = j$th column of U, $\delta' = (\delta_1', \delta_2', \dots, \delta_G')$, $\delta_j' = (\beta_j', \gamma_j')$, $Z_j = (Y_j, X_j)$, and $Z = \text{diagonal } (Z_j)$.

Premultiplying both sides of (6.16) by X', we get

$$X'y_j = X'Z_j\delta_j + X'u_j; \quad j = 1, 2, \dots, G \tag{6.18}$$

or, for the whole system,

$$(I \otimes X')y = (I \otimes X')Z\delta + (I \otimes X')u. \tag{6.19}$$

Recall that the application of generalized least squares to equation (6.18) separately for each j, with $X'u_j \sim (0, \sigma_{jj}X'X)$ produces the 2SLS estimator of δ_j. On the other hand, feasible generalized least squares applied to the whole system in (6.19), with $(I \otimes X')u \sim (0, \Sigma \otimes X'X)$, leads to the *three-stage least squares* (3SLS) estimator of δ:

$$\hat{\delta}_{3SLS} = (Z'(\hat{\Sigma}^{-1} \otimes P_X)Z)^{-1}(Z'(\hat{\Sigma}^{-1} \otimes P_X)y), \tag{6.20}$$

where $\hat{\Sigma}$ is estimated from calculated 2SLS structural residuals.

In contrast, note that the 2SLS estimator of δ, obtained by applying 2SLS separately to each equation, is $\hat{\delta}_{2SLS} = (Z'(I \otimes P_X)Z)^{-1}(Z'(I \otimes P_X)y)$. Thus 2SLS is a special case of 3SLS where I is taken to be the estimate of Σ. Also, 2SLS and 3SLS would be exactly equivalent if Σ is diagonal.

Being a generalized least squares estimator, 3SLS also can be interpreted as an IV estimator of δ in (6.17), where the instrument matrix for Z is

$$W_{3SLS} = (\hat{\Sigma}^{-1} \otimes P_X)Z. \tag{6.21}$$

The (i, j)th block of W_{3SLS} can be written further as

$$\hat{\sigma}^{ij}(P_X Y_j, X_j) = \hat{\sigma}^{ij}(X\tilde{\Pi}_j', X_j), \tag{6.22}$$

where $\tilde{\Pi}_j$ is the unrestricted least squares estimate of Π_j.

As in the limited information case, instrumental variable procedures have been developed as alternatives to 3SLS. One method is the *full information instrumental variables efficient* estimator (FIVE). In this procedure, instead of (6.21), the instrument matrix for Z would be $s^{ij} (X\tilde{\Pi}'_j, X_j)$. As in the case of LIVE, $\tilde{\Pi}_j$ is the appropriate sub-matrix of the restricted reduced form estimate $\hat{\Pi} = -\hat{B}^{-1}\hat{\Gamma}$ based on some preliminary consistent estimates $\hat{B}$ and $\hat{\Gamma}$, and s^{ij} is the (i, j)th element of the inverse of $\hat{S} = \hat{U}'\hat{U}/T = (Y\hat{B}' + X\hat{\Gamma}')'(Y\hat{B}' + X\hat{\Gamma}')/T$.

Note that FIVE utilizes all the restrictions in the system to construct the instrument matrix. 3SLS, on the other hand, does not, in the sense that no restrictions on Π are imposed in the calculation of $X\tilde{\Pi}'_j$ in (6.22).

Another system method is the full information maximum likelihood (FIML) estimator. This is obtained by maximizing the likelihood of y defined in (6.17) subject to all prior restrictions in the model.

Solving $\partial \log L / \partial \Sigma^{-1} = 0$ yields the FIML estimate of Σ : $\hat{\Sigma} = (Y\hat{B}' + X\hat{\Gamma}')'(Y\hat{B}' + X\hat{\Gamma}')/T$. Thus, the concentrated loglikelihood with respect to Σ is $\log L_C = C + T \log \| B \| - T/2 \log | (YB' + X\Gamma')'(YB' + X\Gamma') |$, where $C = -GT/2(1 + \log 2\pi)$. The FIML estimate of B and Γ are then solutions to $0 = \partial \log L_C / \partial \delta = f(\hat{\delta}_{FIML})$, say.

A Taylor series expansion of $f(\hat{\delta}_{FIML})$ around some consistent estimator $\tilde{\delta}$ to get

$$0 = f(\hat{\delta}_{FIML}) \approx f(\tilde{\delta}) + (H(\tilde{\delta}))(\hat{\delta} - \tilde{\delta}) \tag{6.23}$$

gives the *linearized FIML* estimator:

$$\hat{\delta}_{LFIML} = \tilde{\delta} - (H(\tilde{\delta}))^{-1} f(\tilde{\delta}), \tag{6.24}$$

where H is the Hessian matrix (of second order partial derivatives) of $\log L_C$ with respect to δ.

This linearized FIML estimator provides one way of numerically approximating $\hat{\delta}_{FIML}$. Such a procedure, as we shall see in the next section, will be asymptotically equivalent to FIML under certain regularity conditions. If carried through to convergence, linearized FIML, if it converges, will coincide exactly with FIML. Furthermore, at convergence, $(H(\tilde{\delta}))^{-1}$ provides an estimate of the asymptotic covariance matrix of $\hat{\delta}_{FIML}$.

Other iterative procedures also have been devised for the numerical calculation of the FIML estimator. One such algorithm proceeds from a given estimate of δ, say $\hat{\delta}_{(p)}$ at the pth iteration:

$$\hat{\sigma}_{ij(p)} = (y_i - Z_i\hat{\delta}_{i(p)})'(y_j - Z\hat{\delta}_{j(p)})/T \quad \text{and} \quad \hat{\Sigma}_{(p)} = (\hat{\sigma}_{ij(p)}),$$

where $\hat{Z}_{(p)} = \text{diag}(\hat{Z}_1, \dots, \hat{Z}_G)$, $\hat{Z}_j = (\hat{Y}_j, X_j)$ and $\hat{Y}_j$ comes from the solution values of the estimated system based on the estimate $\hat{\delta}_{(p)}$.

The formula for $\hat{\delta}_{p+1}$ follows the 3SLS formula in (6.20) with the following major differences:

1. $\hat{\Sigma}$ is updated through the iteration rounds.
2. The endogenous components $\hat{Y}_j$ in $\hat{Z}_{(p)}$ are constructed as *solutions* to the structural system (as in FIVE) and not as in 3SLS.

We end this section with some additional algebraic relationships among the estimators.

1. 3SLS reduces to 2SLS when Σ is diagonal or when all equations are just identified.
2. If some equations are overidentified and some are just identified, then
    (a) the 3SLS estimates of the overidentified equations can be obtained by the application of 3SLS to the set of over identified equations, ignoring all just identified equations.
    (b) the 3SLS estimate of each just identified equation differs from the 2SLS estimate by a vector which is a linear function of the 3SLS residuals of the overidentified equations. In particular, if we are dealing with a system consisting of one just identified equation and one overidentified, then 2SLS and 3SLS will be exactly equivalent for the overidentified but not for the just identified equation.

4   LARGE SAMPLE PROPERTIES OF ESTIMATORS

The statistical behavior of these estimators has been analyzed in finite samples and in the following alternative parameter sequences:

1. Sample size $T \to \infty$ – the standard asymptotic analysis.
2. Concentration parameter $\to \infty$ with T fixed. For example, see Basmann (1961), Mariano (1975), Anderson (1977) and Staiger and Stock (1997). The concentration parameter is defined in Section 6.2 of this chapter.
3. Structural error variances go to zero – the so-called small-σ asymptotics discussed in Kadane (1971), and Morimune (1978).
4. Number of instruments, L, goes to infinity with sample size such that $L/T \to \alpha$ $(0 < \alpha < \infty)$. See Anderson (1977), Kunitomo (1980), Morimune and Kunitomo (1980), Morimune (1983), and Bekker (1994).
5. Weak instrument asymptotics. Here L is fixed and the coefficients of instruments in the first stage regression in IV or modified 2SLS estimators are assumed to be O $(T^{-1/2})$ as a way of representing weak correlation between the instruments and the endogenous explanatory variables – see Staiger and Stock (1997), and Bound, Jager and Baker (1995). Related discussion of structural testing, model diagnostics and recent applications is in Wang and Zivot (1998), Angrist (1998), Angrist and Krueger (1992), Donald and Newey (1999), and Hahn and Hausman (1999).

In this section, we summarize results under large sample asymptotics, then consider finite sample properties and end with a discussion of the practical implications of the analysis based on these alternative approaches.

4.1   Large sample properties of limited information estimators

We now consider the large sample asymptotic behavior of the limited information estimators described in Section 2. Because of space limitation, theorems are stated without proof. We start with a theorem for limited information instrumental variable estimators in general.

Thus, first consider the IV estimator defined in (6.5): $\hat{\delta}_{IV} = (W'Z)^{-1}W'y_1$, where the instrument matrix W is of the same dimension as $Z \equiv (Y_1, X_1)$ such that

(1)   plim $W'u_1/T = 0$ (6.25)

(2)   plim $W'W/T = Q_W$, positive definite and finite (6.26)

(3)   plim $W'Z/T = M'$, nonsingular (6.27)

(4) $W'u_1/\sqrt{T}$ converges in distribution to $N(0, \sigma^2 Q_w)$. (6.28)

Note that (6.25) together with (6.27) implies that $\hat{\delta}_{IV}$ is consistent. Also, (6.25) is a consequence of (6.28) and hence (6.25) would be unnecessary if (6.28) is assumed. (6.26) is not necessarily satisfied by the original model; for example, when X contains a trending variable. For cases like these, the theorems we discuss presently will require further modifications. Both (6.26) and (6.27) will need minimally the assumption that $(X'X/T)$ has a finite positive definite limit as T approaches infinity. (6.28) depends on a multivariate version (e.g. Lindeberg–Feller) of the central limit theorem for independent but nonidentically distributed random vectors.

Assuming that the instrument matrix W satisfies the three properties (6.26)–(6.28), we have

Theorem 1.

1. $\sqrt{T}(\hat{\delta}_{IV} - \delta) \xrightarrow{d} N(0, \sigma^2(MQ_W^{-1}M')^{-1}) \equiv N[0, \sigma^2 \text{plim}(Z'P_WZ/T)^{-1}]$
2.   A consistent estimator of σ^2 is $(y_1 - Z\hat{\delta}_{IV})'(y_1 - Z\hat{\delta}_{IV})/T$.

Applying the above result to two-stage least squares, we get

Theorem 2. $\sqrt{T}(\hat{\delta}_{2SLS} - \delta) \xrightarrow{d} N(0, \sigma^2(RQ^{-1}R')^{-1}) \equiv N[0, \sigma^2 \text{plim}(Z'P_XZ/T)^{-1}]$, where $R = \text{plim}(Z'X/T)$ and $Q = \text{plim}(X'X/T)$, under the assumptions that

1. R exists, is finite, and has full row rank,
2. Q exists and is finite and positive definite,
3. $X'u_1/(T^{1/2}) \to N(0, \sigma^2 Q)$.

Corollary 1.   A consistent estimator of σ^2 is $(y_1 - Z\hat{\delta}_{2SLS})'(y_1 - Z\hat{\delta}_{2SLS})/T$.

For the k-class estimator, we have already indicated that plim $k = 1$ is a sufficient condition for consistency. A sharper result derives from the two previous theorems.

Theorem 3.   If k is such that plim $T^{1/2}(k - 1) = 0$, then $T^{1/2}(\hat{\delta}_{2SLS} - \delta)$ and $T^{1/2}(\hat{\delta}_{(k)} - \delta)$ are asymptotically equivalent.

For the LIML estimator, we have the following result as a consequence of the preceding theorem.

Theorem 4. If the data matrix X is such that $(X'X/T)$ has a finite positive definite limit, then, under assumptions A1, A2, and A4' in Section 1, LIML is consistent and asymptotically equivalent to 2SLS; that is $\sqrt{T}(\delta_{\text{LIML}} - \delta) \to N(0, \sigma^2(RQ^{-1}R')^{-1})$ where R and Q are as defined in Theorem 2.

Under the conditions of the theorem, it can be shown that plim $\sqrt{T}\,\ell = 0$ where ℓ is the smallest characteristic root of $|W - \lambda S| = 0$, where W and S are the second moment residual matrices defined in (6.15). Thus, Theorem 4 now follows directly from Theorem 3 and the fact that LIML is equivalent to k-class with k equal to $1 + \ell$.

Note that $\sqrt{T}\ell \xrightarrow{p} 0$ is a consequence of the stronger result that $T\ell$ converges in distribution to a central chi-squared distribution with degrees of freedom equal to the number of overidentifying restrictions.

If the structural errors u_t are normally distributed, then LIML is asymptotically efficient among all consistent and uniformly asymptotic normal (CUAN) estimators of β and γ based on the "limited information" model discussed in the preceding section. By Theorem 4, under normality assumptions, 2SLS shares with LIML this property of being asymptotically efficient within this class of CUAN estimators of β and γ.

Theorem 5. Let $\hat{\delta}_{\text{LIVE}}$ be the IV estimator of δ based on the instrument matrix $W_L = (X\hat{\Pi}_1', X_1)$, where $\hat{\Pi}_1$ is *any* consistent estimator of Π_1. Then $\hat{\delta}_{\text{LIVE}}$ is asymptotically equivalent to $\hat{\delta}_{2\text{SLS}}$.

Theorem 6. Consider the class of IV estimators of the first equation where instruments are of the form $W = XF$, where F is either stochastic or nonstochastic and of size $K \times (K_1 + G_1 - 1)$ and of full rank. Within this class, two-stage least squares is asymptotically efficient.

Theorem 7. For the modified 2SLS estimator $\hat{\delta}_{\text{M2SLS}}$, where the first stage regressor matrix is H instead of X,

1. $\hat{\delta}_{\text{M2SLS}}$ is exactly equivalent to the IV estimator of δ using the instrument matrix $(P_H Y_1, X_1)$ if X_1 is contained in the column space of H.
2. $\hat{\delta}_{\text{M2SLS}}$ is consistent if and only if the column space of H contains the column space of X_1.

4.2 Large sample properties of full information estimators

Theorem 8. For a linear simultaneous equations model satisfying the assumptions in Theorem 2 and with a nonsingular error covariance matrix, the following asymptotic properties of the 3SLS estimator hold:

$$(a) \quad \sqrt{T}(\hat{\delta}_{3\text{SLS}} - \delta) \xrightarrow{d} N(0, V_{3\text{SLS}})$$

$$(b) \quad V_{3\text{SLS}} \leq V_{2\text{SLS}}$$

where

$$V_{3SLS} = \text{plim} \, (Z'(\Sigma^{-1} \otimes P_X)Z/T)^{-1}$$

$$V_{2SLS} = \text{plim} \, \{1/T(Z'(I \otimes P_X)Z)^{-1}(Z'(\Sigma^{-1} \otimes P_X)Z)(Z'(I \otimes P_X)Z)^{-1}\}.$$

Theorem 9. Under regularity conditions which are satisfied by the classical simultaneous equations model

$$\sqrt{T}(\hat{\delta}_{FIML} - \delta) \xrightarrow{d} N \{0, \, \text{plim} \, [(1/T)(\partial^2 \log L/\partial\delta\partial\delta')]^{-1}\}.$$

Furthermore, if there are no restrictions on Σ, then the asymptotic covariances of the 3SLS and FIML estimators coincide and thus, 3SLS and FIML are asymptotically equivalent. Finally, FIML and 3SLS are asymptotically efficient within the class of all consistent, uniformly asymptotically Gaussian estimators of δ.

Theorem 10. FIML and linearized FIML are asymptotically equivalent.

For the instrumental variable method, suppose the instrument matrix for Z in $y = Z\delta + u$ is $\hat{Z}$, of the form

$$\hat{Z} = \begin{pmatrix} \hat{Z}_{11} & \hat{Z}_{12} & \cdots & \hat{Z}_{1G} \\ \hat{Z}_{21} & \hat{Z}_{22} & \cdots & \hat{Z}_{2G} \\ \hat{Z}_{G1} & \hat{Z}_{G2} & \cdots & \hat{Z}_{GG} \end{pmatrix}.$$

Recall that the data matrix Z is diagonal $(Z_1, Z_2, \ldots, Z_G)$.

Following the partitioning of Z_j into (Y_j, X_j), we can further decompose each submatrix

$$\hat{Z} \text{ as } \hat{Z}_{ij} = (\hat{Z}_{ij1}, \hat{Z}_{ij2})$$

where $\hat{Z}_{ij1}$ and $\hat{Z}_{ij2}$ are parts of the instrument matrices for the right-hand side endogenous and exogenous variables, respectively, appearing in the jth equation with respective dimensions $T \times (G_j - 1)$ and $T \times K_j$.

Theorem 11. For the simultaneous system $y = Z\delta + u$, let $\hat{\delta}_{IV} = (\hat{Z}'Z)^{-1}\hat{Z}'y$, where $\hat{Z}$ is defined in the preceding paragraph. Suppose

1. $\text{Pr} \, (|\hat{Z}'Z| \neq 0) = 1$
2. $\text{plim} \, (\hat{Z}'u/T) = 0$
3. $\text{plim} \, (\hat{Z}'Z/T)$ is nonsingular and finite
4. $\text{plim} \, (\hat{Z}'Z/T) = \text{plim} \, (\hat{Z}'(\Sigma \otimes I)\hat{Z}/T).$

Then $\hat{\delta}_{IV}$ and $\hat{\delta}_{3SLS}$ are asymptotically equivalent if and only if the following two conditions hold:

1. $\text{plim} \, (\hat{Z}'_{ij1}X/T) = \sigma^{ii}\Pi_j \, \text{plim} \, (X'X/T)$
2. $\text{plim} \, (\hat{Z}'_{ij2}X/T) = \sigma^{ij} \, \text{plim} \, (X'_jX/T).$

5   Structure of Limited Information Estimators as Regression Functions

The structure of the SEM estimators is discussed at length in Hendry (1976) and Hausman (1983), and Phillips (1983). In this section, we develop a perspective on the structure of limited information estimators which is particularly helpful in the finite sample analysis of these procedures.

Most of the limited information estimators we have discussed so far can be related to the regression moment matrices S, W, and A defined in (6.15):

$$\hat{\beta}_{2SLS} = \arg \min \beta_*' W \beta_*$$

$$\hat{\beta}_{OLS} = \arg \min \beta_*' A \beta_*$$

$$\hat{\beta}_{LIML} = \arg \min (\beta_*' W \beta_* / \beta_*' S \beta_*).$$

If we partition S (and A and W similarly) as

$$S = \begin{pmatrix} s_{11} & S_{12} \\ S_{21} & S_{22} \end{pmatrix},$$

we then have

$$\hat{\beta}_{OLS} = A_{22}^{-1} A_{21}$$

$$\hat{\beta}_{2SLS} = W_{22}^{-1} W_{21} \tag{6.29}$$

and for the k-class estimator, with $\bar{k} = 1 - k$,

$$\hat{\beta}_{(k)} = (W_{22} + \bar{k} S_{22})^{-1} (W_{21} + \bar{k} S_{21}). \tag{6.30}$$

Thus, we also have

$$\hat{\beta}_{LIML} = (W_{22} - \ell S_{22})^{-1} (W_{21} - \ell S_{21}), \tag{6.31}$$

where ℓ = smallest eigenvalue of $S^{-1}W$.

We can also give a similar characterization to the modified 2SLS estimator where the data matrix for the first stage regressor is H (constrained to contain X_1) instead of X. Equivalently, this is the IV estimator using $P_H Y_1$ as the instrument matrix for Y_1 and its characterization is $\hat{\beta}_{M2SLS} = F_{22}^{-1} F_{21}$, where $F = Y_1'(P_H - P_{X_1}) Y_1$. Thus $\hat{\beta}_{OLS}$, $\hat{\beta}_{2SLS}$ and $\hat{\beta}_{M2SLS}$ are regression functions of moment matrices in Y_1 – namely, A, W, and F, which differ among themselves only in their associated projection matrices.

In the scalar Gaussian case, A, W, and F are all proportional to noncentral Chi-squared variates with different degrees of freedom. In higher dimensional cases, they would have a so-called noncentral Wishart distribution which is indexed by the following parameters:

1. the order or size of the matrix (in our case $G_1 + 1$),
2. the degrees of freedom or rank of the associated matrix Q (say q),
3. the common covariance matrix of the rows of Y (say Ω),
4. the so-called means–sigma matrix, which is the generalization of the non-centrality parameter and is equal to $(E(Y))'Q(E(Y)) = M$, and
5. the rank of the means–sigma matrix, say m.

The Wishart distributions of A, W, and F differ in their degrees of freedom. The means–sigma matrices for A and W are identical; that for F takes a different expression but it has the same rank as the first – one less than the order of the matrices (see Mariano, 1977). Consequently, the probability density functions for A, W, and F are all of the same form. Because of this, we can say that OLS, 2SLS, and M2SLS are "distributionally equivalent" in the sense that the problem of deriving analytical results for one is of the same mathematical form as for the other two.

Distributional equivalence in the same vein exists between two-stage least squares in the just identified case and the instrumental variable estimator based on nonstochastic instruments for Y_1 (see Mariano, 1977, 1982). The argument turns on the fact that 2SLS applied to a just identified equation can be interpreted as an IV estimator that uses the excluded exogenous variables as instruments for Y_1.

Expressions (6.29), (6.30), and (6.31) of the k-class estimators in terms of the matrices S, A, and W also lead to a generalized method-of-moments (GMM) interpretation for these estimators. The moment conditions come from the asymptotic orthogonality of the instruments relative to the structural disturbances. Under standard large-sample asymptotics, these moment conditions are satisfied by 2SLS, LIML and the k-class with k converging to 1 in probability.

Moment conditions can also be derived by expressing β in terms of expectations of the matrices A, W, and S; see Bekker (1994). Under Bekker's (1994) alternative asymptotics, where the number of instruments increases with sample size, LIML satisfies these moment conditions; but 2SLS and OLS do not. Consequently, under this alternative asymptotics LIML remains consistent while 2SLS and OLS are both inconsistent. This result provides a partial intuitive explanation for better LIML finite sample properties than 2SLS under conditions given in Section 7 of this chapter.

6 FINITE SAMPLE PROPERTIES OF ESTIMATORS

6.1 Arbitrary number of included endogenous variables

Let us first consider the available results dealing with the general case where there are no further restrictions on the linear system nor on the equation being estimated apart from the condition of identifiability and the classical Gaussian assumptions. The characterization in (6.29)–(6.31) is the starting point of the analysis.

The first group of results here deals with the existence and nonexistence of moments of various estimators and is best summarized in the following theorem.

Theorem 12.   In an identified equation in a linear simultaneous system satisfying assumptions A1–A4′, absolute moments of positive order for indicated estimators of coefficients in this structural equation are finite up to (and including) order

1. $K_2 - G_1$ for 2SLS and 3SLS;
2. $h - K_1 - G_1$, for modified 2SLS (the class of stochastic IV estimators) where h is the number of linearly independent first-stage regressors;
3. $T - K_1 - G_1$, for the k-class estimators with k nonstochastic and $0 \leq k < 1$;
4. 0, for the k-class with nonstochastic k exceeding 1;
5. 0, for instrumental variable estimators with nonstochastic instruments; and
6. 0, for LIML and FIML.

Because of the distributional equivalence results discussed in the preceding section, (2) follows from (1). As a corollary to (1), 2SLS in the just identified case will have no finite absolute moments of positive order; as a consequence (5) also follows from (1).

References to specific authors who derived these results are given in Mariano (1982) and Phillips (1983).

From Theorem 12, we see that the LIML and FIML estimators (as well as 2SLS if the degree of over-identification is less than two) are inadmissible under a strictly quadratic loss function. Of course, admissibility comparisons may change under alternative loss functions with finite risks for the estimators. Such alternatives could be based on probability concentration around the true parameter value or other loss functions that increase at a slower rate than quadratic.

Beyond these moment existence results, various authors have derived closed-form expressions for the exact moments and probability density functions of these estimators – see Phillips (1983) for specific references. The expressions are rather complicated, in terms of zonal polynomials.

Another class of results in the general case deals with asymptotic expansions for the estimators themselves – namely, expressions of the type

$$\hat{\alpha} = \sum_{j=0}^{r} a_j + O_p(N^{-(r+1)/2}),$$

where $a_j = O_p(N^{-j/2})$ and a_0 is the probability limit of $\hat{\alpha}$ as $N \to \infty$. See Rothenberg (1984) for an extensive review. For the k-class estimator, such an expansion can be obtained by noting that we can write $\hat{\beta}_{(k)} - \beta = H(I + \Delta)^{-1}\eta$, where H is nonstochastic, $\Delta = O_p(N^{-1/2})$ and $\eta = O_p(1)$ and then applying an infinite series expansion for the matrix inverse. One of the earliest papers on this in the econometric literature is Nagar (1959), where expansions of this type are formally obtained for the k-class estimator when k is of the form $1 + c/T$ where c is nonstochastic.

Given an asymptotic expansion like

$$\hat{\beta}_{(k)} - \beta = F_0 + F_{-1/2} + F_{-1} + O_p(T^{-3/2}) = F + O_p(T^{-3/2}),$$

we can then proceed to define the "asymptotic moments" of $(\hat{\beta}_{(k)} - \beta)$ to be the moments of the stochastic approximation up to a certain order; for example, the moments of F. Thus, asymptotic moments determined this way relate directly to the moments of an approximation to the estimator itself and will not necessarily be approximations to the exact moments of $\hat{\beta}_{(k)}$. For example, this will not hold for LIML and other estimators for which moments of low positive order do not exist. In cases where moments do exist, Sargan (1974, 1976) gives conditions under which these asymptotic moments are valid approximations to the moments of the estimator.

6.2   The case of two included endogenous variables

For a more concrete discussion, let us assume now that the equation being estimated contains only two endogenous variables. The early work on the analytical study of finite sample properties of SEM estimators dealt with this case. The equation now takes the following form:

$$y_1 = y_2\beta + X_1\gamma + u_1, \tag{6.32}$$

where β is scalar and y_2 is $T \times 1$. The characterization of the limited information estimators in (6.29)–(6.31) can be reduced further to canonical form for a better understanding of how parameter configurations affect the statistical behavior of the estimators (for example, see Mariano, 1977 and 1982). One reduction to canonical form simplifies in the case of two included endogenous variables to

$$\hat{\beta}_{(k)} - \beta = (\sigma/\omega)\sqrt{1 - \rho^2} \, (\hat{\beta}^*_{(k)} - \lambda), \tag{6.33}$$

where σ^2 = variance of the structural disturbance u_{t1}, ω^2 = variance of y_{t2}, ρ = correlation coefficient between y_{t2} and u_{t1}, $\lambda = \rho/\sqrt{1 - \rho^2}$, and

$$\hat{\beta}^*_{(k)} = (x'y + \bar{k}u'v)/(y'y + \bar{k}v'v). \tag{6.34}$$

The vectors x, y, u, and v are mutually independent multivariate normal (the first two are $K_2 \times 1$ and the last two are $(T - K) \times 1$) with unit variances, mean vector equal to zero for u and v and equal to $\alpha_x = (0, \ldots, 0, \mu\lambda)'$ and $\alpha_y = (0, \ldots, 0, \mu)'$ for x and y, with $\mu^2 = [(E(y_2))'(P_X - P_{X_1})(E(y_2))]/\omega^2$.

The last quantity, μ^2, has been called the "concentration parameter" in the literature. This derives from the fact that as this parameter increases indefinitely, with sample size staying fixed, for k nonstochastic as well as for LIML, $\hat{\beta}_{(k)}$ converges in probability to the true parameter value β; Basmann (1961) and Mariano (1975). Also, in large sample asymptotics with the usual assumption that $X'X/T$ tends to a finite, positive definite limit, the variance in the limiting normal distribution of $\sqrt{T} (\hat{\beta}_{2SLS} - \beta)$ is inversely proportional to the limit of μ^2/T. (The asymptotic variance is $(\sigma^2/\omega^2) (\lim (\mu^2/T))^{-1}$.)

One can then use (6.34) to derive exact expressions for moments and probability distributions of the k-class estimator – e.g. see Mariano (1982) and Phillips

(1983) for a more detailed survey. The critical parameters are the correlation between error and endogenous regressor, the concentration parameter, the degree of over-identification, the difference between sample size and number of exogenous variables, and the size of structural error variance relative to the variance of the endogenous regressor.

7   PRACTICAL IMPLICATIONS

Instead of going into more complicated formulas for pdfs or cdfs or moments of estimators, we devote this section to a discussion of the practical implications of the finite sample results and alternative asymptotics – covering material that extends from the early works in the 1960s to the recent results on exact small sample properties of IV estimators and the behavior of IV estimators when instruments are weak. For finite sample results, most of the conclusions come from the study of the case of two included endogenous variables.

1. For the k-class estimator (nonstochastic $k \in [0, 1]$) bias is zero if and only if ρ, the correlation between the structural error and the endogenous regressor, is equal to zero. The direction of bias is the same for all k and it follows the direction of ρ. Negative correlation implies a downward bias; positive correlation implies an upward bias.

2. Absolute bias is an increasing function of the absolute value of ρ, a decreasing function of the concentration parameter μ^2 and a decreasing concave function of k. Thus, whenever both exist, OLS bias is always greater in absolute value than 2SLS bias. Of course, if the equation is just identified, then 2SLS bias does not exist while OLS bias is finite.

3. For two-stage least squares, absolute bias is an increasing function of the degree of over-identification. Since the 2SLS probability distribution depends on sample size only through the concentration parameter and since the value of the concentration parameter increases with additional observations, then 2SLS bias in absolute value decreases upon inclusion of more observations in the sample. The total effect of additional observations on OLS bias, on the other hand, is indeterminate. An increase in sample size produces a positive effect on absolute OLS bias (because of the increase in degrees of freedom) and a negative indirect effect through the increase in the concentration parameter.

4. The size of the OLS bias relative to 2SLS gets larger with higher μ^2, lower degree of overidentification, bigger sample size, and higher absolute ρ.

5. For the k-class, the optimal value of nonstochastic k over [0, 1] for minimizing mean squared error varies over a wide range according to slight changes in parameter values and the sample size.

6. For the whole k-class, k nonstochastic and in [0, 1], exact mean squared error is a decreasing function of the concentration parameter, an increasing function of the absolute value of ρ and an indefinite function of the degrees of freedom parameter ($K_2 - 1$ or the degree of overidentification for 2SLS, $T - K_1$ for OLS, $h - K_1 - 1$ for M2SLS). Interpreting M2SLS as an IV method, keep in mind that h represents the number of instruments. Note also the *ceteris paribus* conditions here: all other parameters are kept fixed as a specific one, say the concentration

parameter, changes. Furthermore, because the 2SLS distribution depends on sample size only through the concentration parameter (see item 3), it follows that the exact mean squared error for 2SLS is a nonincreasing function of sample size. This does not apply, however, to the other k-class estimators; for them the net effect of increasing sample size is indefinite.

7. In terms of relative magnitudes of MSE, large values of μ^2 and large T favor 2SLS over OLS. One would expect this since the usual large-sample asymptotics would be taking effect and the dominant term would be the inconsistency in OLS. However, there are cases (small values of ρ and T) where OLS would dominate 2SLS even for large values of μ^2.

8. When the degree of overidentification gets large, the 2SLS and OLS distributions tend to be similar. This follows from the fact that the only difference in the distributions of 2SLS and OLS lies in the degrees of freedom parameter. These are the degree of overidentification for 2SLS and sample size less $(K_1 + 1)$ for OLS so that the smaller $(T - K)$ is, the more similar the 2SLS and OLS distributions will be. Of course, there will be no perfect coincidence since sample size is strictly greater than K.

9. The OLS and 2SLS distributions are highly sensitive to ρ and the 2SLS distribution is considerably asymmetric while the OLS distribution is almost symmetric.

10. The extensive tabulations of the 2SLS distribution function in Anderson and Sawa (1979) provide considerable insight into the degree of asymmetry and skewness in the 2SLS distribution. Bias in the direction of ρ is quite pronounced. For some combinations of parameter values (such as $K_2 \geq 20$, low concentration parameter and high numerical value of ρ), the probability is close to 1 that the 2SLS estimator will be on one side of the true value: e.g. less than the true value if ρ is negative. With regard to convergence to normality, when either ρ or K_2 or both are large, the 2SLS distribution tends to normality quite slowly. In comparison with 2SLS, the LIML distribution is far more symmetric though more spread out and it approaches normality faster.

11. Up to terms of order T^{-1}, the approximate LIML distribution (obtained from large sample asymptotic expansions) is median unbiased. For 2SLS, the median is β only if the equation is just identified or if $\rho = 0$. Up to order $T^{-1/2}$, the approximate distribution functions for both 2SLS and LIML assign the same probability as the normal to an interval which is symmetric about β. Also, the asymptotic mean squared errors, up to $T^{-1/2}$, reproduce that implied by the limiting normal distribution.

12. Anderson (1974) compares asymptotic mean squared errors of 2SLS and LIML up to order T^{-1} and finds that for a degree of overidentification (ν) strictly less than 7, 2SLS would have a smaller asymptotic mean squared error than LIML. For ν greater than or equal to 7 and for $\alpha^2 = \rho^2\omega^2\sigma^2/(\omega_{11}\omega^2 - \omega_{12})$ not too small, LIML will have the smaller AMSE. Calculation of probabilities of absolute deviations around β leads to the same conclusion: small ρ^2 or little simultaneity favors 2SLS while a high degree of over-identification favors LIML. The condition for 2SLS to have the advantage over LIML in this case is

$$\alpha^2 \leq 2/(K_2 - 1) = 2/v.$$

13. In dealing with the case of one explanatory endogenous variable and one instrument (the just-identified case), Nelson and Startz (1990) find that

1. the probability distribution of the IV estimator can be bimodal. Maddala and Jeong (1992) show that this is a consequence of near singularity of reduced form error covariance matrices but not necessarily of poor instruments.
2. The asymptotic distribution of the IV estimator is a poor approximation to the exact distribution when the instrument has low correlation with the regressor and when the number of observations is small.

14. As a further amplification of item 2, in dealing with the bias of instrumental variable estimators, Buse (1992) derives conditions under which Phillips' (1980, 1983) observation would hold – that $\hat{\beta}_{IV}$ would display more bias as the number of instruments increases. Buse shows that IV bias would increase or decrease with increased number of IV instruments depending on an inequality based on quadratic forms of incremental regression moment matrices of the right-hand side endogenous variables. In the case where there is only one right-hand side endogenous variable, the result simplifies to the conclusion that the estimated IV bias will increase with the number of excess instrumental variables "only if the proportional increase in the instruments is faster than the rate of increase in R^2 measured relative to the fit of Y_1 on X_1." Thus, adding less important instrumental variables later will add little to R^2 and increase IV bias. On the other hand, one could start with weak instruments and find that R^2 rises dramatically (with a decline in IV bias) as important instruments are added. Consequently, whether or not there is an improvement in efficiency tradeoff between bias and variability in IV as more instruments are added depends on the IV selection sequence.

15. In Bekker's (1994) asymptotic analysis where the number of instruments increases at the same rate as sample size, there is numerical evidence that approximations to distributions of IV estimators under this parameter sequence are more accurate than large sample approximations, even if the number of instruments is small. Confidence regions based on this alternative asymptotic analysis also produce more accurate coverage rates when compared to standard IV confidence regions. Under this alternative asymptotics, 2SLS becomes inconsistent while LIML remains consistent. The asymptotic Gaussian distribution of LIML depends on α, the limit of L/T, but the LIML asymptotic covariance matrix can be estimated by a strictly positive definite matrix without estimating α or specifying L – see Bekker (1994). Bekker's numerical analysis shows that inference based on this estimated limiting distribution is more accurate than that based on large sample asymptotics (where $\alpha = 0$).

16. From their weak-instrument asymptotics (number of instruments is fixed, coefficients of instruments in the first stage regression go to zero at the rate of $T^{-1/2}$), Staiger and Stock (1997) conclude that

1. Conventional asymptotic results are invalid, even when sample size is large. The k-class estimator is not consistent and has a nonstandard asymptotic

distribution. Similarly, Bound *et al.* (1995) find large inconsistencies in IV estimates when instruments are weak.

2. 2SLS and LIML are not asymptotically equivalent. 2SLS can be badly biased and can produce confidence intervals with severely distorted coverage rates. In light of this, nonstandard methods for interval estimation should be considered.

3. Estimator bias is less of a problem for LIML than 2SLS (when there are two included endogenous variables).

4. When doing IV estimation, the R^2 or F-statistic in the first stage regression should be reported. Bound *et al.* (1995) also recommend this as a useful indicator of the quality of IV estimates.

References

Anderson, T.W. (1974). An asymptotic expansion of the distribution of the limited information maximum likelihood estimate of a coefficient in a simultaneous equation system. *Journal of the American Statistical Association* 69, 565–73.

Anderson, T.W. (1977). Asymptotic expansions of the distributions of estimates in simultaneous equations for alternative parameter sequences. *Econometrica* 45, 509–18.

Anderson, T.W., and T. Sawa (1979). Evaluation of the distribution function of the two-stage least squares estimate. *Econometrica* 47, 163–82.

Angrist, J. (1998). Estimating the labor market impact of voluntary military service using social security data on military applicants. *Econometrica* 66, 249–88.

Angrist, J., and A. Krueger (1992). The effect of age of school entry on educational attainment: An application of instrumental variables with moments from two samples. *Journal of the American Statistical Association* 87, 328–36.

Basmann, R.L. (1961). A note on the exact finite sample frequency functions of GCL estimators in two leading over-identified cases. *Journal of the American Statistical Association* 56, 619–36.

Bekker, P.A. (1994). Alternative approximations to the distribution of instrumental variable estimators. *Econometrica* 62, 657–81.

Bekker, P.A., and T.K. Dijkstra (1990). On the nature and number of constraints on the reduced form as implied by the structural form. *Econometrica* 58, 507–14.

Bound, J., D.A. Jaeger, and R.M. Baker (1995). Problems with instrumental variables estimation when the correlation between the instruments and the endogenous explanatory variable is weak. *Journal of the American Statistical Association* 90, 443–50.

Buse, A. (1992). The bias of instrumental variable estimators. *Econometrica* 60, 173–80.

Donald, S., and W. Newey (1999). Choosing the number of instruments. M.I.T. Working Paper, Department of Economics.

Hahn, J., and J. Hausman (1999). A new specification test for the validity of instrumental variables. M.I.T. Working Paper, Department of Economics.

Hausman, J. (1983). Specification and estimation of simultaneous equation models. *The Handbook of Econometrics, Volume I* pp. 393–448. North-Holland Publishing Company.

Hendry, D.F. (1976). The structure of simultaneous equations estimators. *Journal of Econometrics* 4, pp. 51–88.

Hsiao, C. (1983). Identification. *The Handbook of Econometrics, Volume I* pp. 223–83. North-Holland Publishing Company.

Kadane, J. (1971). Comparison of *k*-class estimators when the disturbances are small. *Econometrica* 39, 723–37.

Kunitomo, N. (1980). Asymptotic expansions of the distributions of estimators in a linear functional relationship and simultaneous equations. *Journal of the American Statistical Association* 75, 693–700.

Maddala, G.S., and J. Jeong (1992). On the exact small sample distribution of the instrumental variable estimator. *Econometrica* 60, 181–3.

Mariano, R.S. (1982). Analytical small-sample distribution theory in econometrics: The simultaneous-equations case. *International Economic Review* 23, 503–34.

Mariano, R.S. (1975). Some large-concentration-parameter asymptotics for the k-class estimators. *Journal of Econometrics* 3, 171–7.

Mariano, R.S. (1977). Finite-sample properties of instrumental variable estimators of structural coefficients. *Econometrica* 45, 487–96.

Morimune, K. (1978). Improving the limited information maximum likelihood estimator when the disturbances are small. *Journal of the American Statistical Association* 73, 867–71.

Morimune, K. (1983). Approximate distribution of k-class estimators when the degree of overidentifiability is large compared with the sample size. *Econometrica* 51, 821–41.

Morimune, K., and N. Kunitomo (1980). Improving the maximum likelihood estimate in linear functional relationships for alternative parameter sequences. *Journal of the American Statistical Association* 75, 230–7.

Nagar, A.L. (1959). The bias and moment matrix of the general k-class estimators of the parameters in structural equations. *Econometrica* 27, 575–95.

Nelson, C.R., and R. Startz (1990). Some further results on the exact small sample properties of the instrumental variable estimator. *Econometrica* 58, 967–76.

Phillips, P.C.B. (1980). The exact finite-sample density of instrumental variable estimators in an equation with $n + 1$ endogenous variables. *Econometrica* 48, 861–78.

Phillips, P.C.B. (1983). Exact small sample theory in the simultaneous equations model. *The Handbook of Econometrics, Volume I* pp. 449–516. North-Holland Publishing Company.

Rothenberg, T. (1984). Approximating the distributions of econometric estimators and test statistics. *Handbook of Econometrics, Volume II* pp. 881–935. Elsevier Science Publishers.

Sargan, J.D. (1974). The validity of Nagar's expansion for the moments of econometric estimators. *Econometrica* 42, 169–76.

Sargan, J.D. (1976). Econometric estimators and the Edgeworth approximation. *Econometrica* 44, 421–48.

Staiger, D., and J. Stock (1997). Instrumental variables regression with weak instruments. *Econometrica* 65, 557–86.

Wang, J., and E. Zivot (1998). Inference on structural parameters in instrumental variables regression with weak instruments. *Econometrica* 66, 1389–404.

Identification in Parametric Models

Paul Bekker and Tom Wansbeek*

1   INTRODUCTION

Identification is a notion of essential importance in quantitative empirical branches of science like economics and the social sciences. To the extent that statistical inference in such branches of science extends beyond a mere exploratory analysis, the generic approach is to use the subject matter theory to construct a stochastic model where the parameters in the distributions of the various random variables have to be estimated from the available evidence. Roughly stated, a model is then called identified when meaningful estimates for these parameters can be obtained. If that is not the case, the model is called underidentified. In an underidentified model different sets of parameter values agree equally well with the statistical evidence. Hence, preference of one set of parameter values over other ones is arbitrary. Scientific conclusions drawn on the basis of such arbitrariness are in the best case void and in the worst case dangerous.

So assessing the state of identification of a model is crucial. In this chapter we present a self-contained treatment of identification in parametric models. Some of the results can also be found in e.g. Fisher (1966), Rothenberg (1971), Bowden (1973), Richmond (1974), and Hsiao (1983, 1987). The pioneering work in the field is due to Haavelmo (1943), which contained the first identification theory for stochastic models to be developed in econometrics; see Aldrich (1994) for an extensive discussion.

The set-up of the chapter is as follows. In Section 2 we introduce the basic concepts of observational equivalence of two parameter points, leading to the definitions of local and global identification. The motivating connection between the notions of identification on the one hand and the existence of a consistent estimator on the other hand is discussed. In Section 3 an important theorem is presented that can be employed to assess the identification of a particular model.

It provides the link between identification and the rank of the information matrix. A further step towards practical usefulness is taken in Section 4, where the information matrix criterion is elaborated and an identification criterion is presented in terms of the rank of a Jacobian matrix. In Section 5 the role played by additional restrictions is considered.

All criteria presented have the practical drawback that they involve the rank evaluation of a matrix whose elements are functions of the parameters. The relevant rank is the rank for the true values of the parameters. These, however, are obviously unknown. Section 6 shows that this is fortunately not a matter of great concern due to considerations of rank constancy.

Up till then, the discussion involved the identification of the whole parameter vector. Now it may happen that the latter is not identified but some individual elements are. How to recognize such a situation is investigated in Section 7. The classical econometric context in which the identification issue figures predominantly is the simultaneous equations model. This issue has become a standard feature of almost every econometric textbook. See, e.g., Pesaran (1987) for a brief overview. In Section 8 we give the relevant theory for the classical simultaneous equations model. Section 9 concludes.

As the title shows, the chapter is restricted to identification in parametric models.[1] It is moreover limited in a number of other respects. It essentially deals with the identification of "traditional" models, i.e. models for observations that are independently identically distributed (iid). Hence, dynamic models, with their different and often quite more complicated identification properties, are not discussed. See, e.g., Deistler and Seifert (1978), Hsiao (1983, 1997), Hannan and Deistler (1988), and Johansen (1995). Also, the models to be considered here are linear in the variables. For a discussion of nonlinear models, which in general have a more favorable identification status, see, e.g., McManus (1992).

We consider identification based on sample information and on exact restrictions on the parameters that may be assumed to hold. We do not pay attention to a Bayesian approach where non-exact restrictions on the parameters in the form of prior distributions are considered. For this approach, see, e.g., Zellner (1971), Drèze (1975), Kadane (1975), Leamer (1978), and Poirier (1998).

As to notation, we employ the following conventions. A superscript 0, as in β^0, indicates the "true" value of a parameter, i.e. its value in the data generating process. When no confusion is possible, however, we may omit this superscript. We use the semicolon in stacking subvectors or submatrices, as the horizontal delimiter of subvectors and submatrices:

$$(A_1; A_2) \equiv (A_1', A_2')' = \begin{bmatrix} A_1 \\ A_2 \end{bmatrix}.$$

We will use this notation in particular for a_1 and a_2 being vectors. Covariance matrices are indicated by Σ. When it has a single index, Σ is the variance–covariance matrix of the vector in the subscript. When it has a double subscript, Σ is the matrix of covariances between two random vectors, as indicated by the subscripts.

2 BASIC CONCEPTS

Consider a structure s that describes the probability distribution function $P_s(y)$ of a random vector Y. The set of all a priori possible structures is called a model. We assume that Y is generated by a known parametric probability function $P(\cdot)$ conditional on a parameter vector $\theta \in S$, where S is an open subset of $\mathbf{R}^l$. So a structure is described by a parameter point θ and a model is defined by a set $\{P(y, \theta) \mid \theta \in S\}$. Submodels $\{P(y, \theta) \mid \theta \in \mathcal{H}\}$ are defined by sets of structures $\mathcal{H}$ that are subsets of S: $\mathcal{H} \subset S$. Hence, a structure is described by a parametric point θ, and a model is a set of points $\mathcal{H} \subset \mathbf{R}^l$. So the problem of distinguishing between structures is reduced to the problem of distinguishing between parameter points.

Definition 1. The sets of structures S_1 and S_2 are *observationally equivalent* if $\{P(y, \theta) \mid \theta \in S_1\} = \{P(y, \theta) \mid \theta \in S_2\}$. In particular, two parameter points θ_1 and θ_2 are observationally equivalent if $P(y, \theta_1) = P(y, \theta_2)$ for all y.

Definition 2. The element θ_k^0 of the parameter vector $\theta^0 \in S$ is said to be *locally identified* in S if there exists an open neighborhood of θ^0 containing no point $\theta \in S$, with $\theta_k \neq \theta_k^0$, that is observationally equivalent to θ^0.

The notion of identification is related to the existence of an unbiased or consistent estimator. That is, if θ_k^0 is locally not identified, there exist points θ arbitrarily close to θ^0 with $\theta_k^0 \neq \theta_k$ and $P(y, \theta) = P(y, \theta^0)$. Hence exact knowledge of $P(y, \theta^0)$ is not sufficient to distinguish between θ_k^0 and θ_k.[2]

Now consider an estimator $\hat{\theta}_k$ of θ_k. Its distribution function is a function of $P(y, \theta^0)$ so that, again, exact knowledge of this distribution function is not sufficient to distinguish between θ_k^0 and θ_k. Asymptotically the same holds with respect to the limit distribution of $\hat{\theta}_k$. In that case θ_k^0 cannot be expressed as a function of the small- or large-sample distribution of $\hat{\theta}_k$. In particular, θ_k^0 cannot be expressed as the expectation or probability limit of $\hat{\theta}_k$.

On the other hand, if θ_k^0 is locally identified and if we restrict the parameter space to a sufficiently small open neighborhood of θ^0, we find that $P(y, \theta^0)$ corresponds uniquely to a single value $\theta_k = \theta_k^0$. In fact we have the following theorem.

Theorem 1. Let $P(y, \theta)$ be a continuous function of $\theta \in S$ for all y, then θ_k^0 is locally identified (in S) if and only if there exists an open neighborhood O_{θ^0} of θ^0 such that any sequence θ^i, $i = 1, 2, \ldots$ in $S \cap O_{\theta^0}$ for which $P(y, \theta^i) \to P(y, \theta^0)$, for all y, also satisfies $\theta_k^i \to \theta_k^0$.

Proof. The proof is in two parts.

Necessity. If θ_k^0 is locally not identified, then for any open neighborhood O_{θ^0} there exists a point $\theta \in S \cap O_{\theta^0}$ with $P(y, \theta) = P(y, \theta^0)$ and $\theta_k \neq \theta_k^0$. Thus if we take $\theta^i = \theta$, $i = 1, 2, \ldots$ we find $\theta_k^i = \theta_k \neq \theta_k^0$.

Sufficiency. If for any open neighborhood O_{θ^0} there exists a sequence θ^i, $i = 1$, $2, \ldots$ in $S \cap O_{\theta^0}$ for which $P(y, \theta^i) \to P(y, \theta^0)$ and θ_k^i does not converge to θ_k^0, we may consider converging subsequences in compact neighborhoods with $\theta_k^i \to \theta_k^*$ $\neq \theta_k^0$. Due to the continuity we find that $P(y, \theta^*) = P(y, \theta^0)$ so that θ_k^0 is locally not identified. ∎

Hence, if $P(y, \theta^0)$ can be consistently estimated, for example in the case of iid observations, then $\theta_{k'}^0$ the kth element of $\theta^0 \in O_{\theta^0}$, can be consistently estimated if and only if it is identified. Thus, if one considers a sample as a single observation on a random vector with probability distribution $P(y, \theta^0)$ and uses an asymptotic parameter sequence consisting of repeated samples, i.e. iid observations on this random vector, then θ_k^0 can be consistently estimated if and only if it is identified.[3]

So far for the identification of a single parameter. Definition 2 can be extended to the definition of the whole parameter vector straightforwardly.

Definition 3. If all elements of θ^0 are locally identified then θ^0 is said to be locally identified.

Although the notion of *local* identification plays the predominant role, we will occasionally refer to *global* identification.

Definition 4. If the open neighborhood referred to in definition 2 is equal to S, then the identification is said to be *global* in S.

Definitions 2 and 3 are obviously difficult to apply in practice. In the following section we present a much more manageable tool for the characterization of local identification.

3 IDENTIFICATION AND THE RANK OF THE INFORMATION MATRIX

When analyzing local identification of a model, the information matrix can be used conveniently. The following theorem, due to Rothenberg (1971) but with a slightly adapted proof, contains the essential result.

Definition 5. Let $M(\theta)$ be a continuous matrix function of $\theta \in \mathbf{R}^l$ and let $\theta^0 \in \mathbf{R}^l$. Then θ^0 is a *regular point* of $M(\theta)$ if the rank of $M(\theta)$ is constant for points in $\mathbf{R}^l$ in an open neighborhood of θ^0.

Theorem 2. Let θ^0 be a regular point of the information matrix $\Psi(\theta)$. Assume that the distribution of y has a density function $f(y, \theta)$, and assume that $f(y, \theta)$ and $\log f(y, \theta)$ are continuously differentiable in θ for all $\theta \in S$ and for all y. Then θ^0 is locally identified if and only if $\Psi(\theta^0)$ is nonsingular.

Proof. Let

$$g(y, \theta) \equiv \log f(y, \theta)$$

$$h(y, \theta) \equiv \partial \log f(y, \theta)/\partial\theta.$$

Then the mean value theorem implies

$$g(y, \theta) - g(y, \theta^0) = h(y, \theta^*)'(\theta - \theta^0), \tag{7.1}$$

for all θ in a neighborhood of θ^0, for all y, and with θ^* between θ and θ^0 (although θ^* may depend on y). Now suppose that θ^0 is *not* locally identified. Then any open neighborhood of θ^0 will contain parameter points that are observationally equivalent to θ^0. Hence we can construct an infinite sequence $\theta^1, \theta^2, \ldots, \theta^k, \ldots$, such that $\lim_{k \to \infty} \theta^k = \theta^0$, with the property that $g(y, \theta^k) = g(y, \theta^0)$, for all k and all y. It then follows from (7.1) that for all k and all y there exist points θ^{*k} (which again may depend on y), such that

$$h(y, \theta^{*k})'\delta^k \equiv h(y, \theta^{*k})'(\theta^k - \theta^0)/\|\theta^k - \theta^0\| = 0, \tag{7.2}$$

with θ^{*k} between θ^k and θ^0.

Since $\theta^k \to \theta^0$, there holds $\theta^{*k} \to \theta^0$ for all y. Furthermore, the sequence δ^1, $\delta^2, \ldots, \delta^k, \ldots$ is an infinite sequence on the unit sphere, so there must be at least one limit point. Let δ^0 be such a limit point. Then (7.2) implies $h(y, \theta^0)'\delta^0 = 0$ for all y. This gives for the information matrix

$$E\{(h(y, \theta^0)'\delta^0)^2\} = \delta^{0'}E\{h(y, \theta^0)h(y, \theta^0)'\}\delta^0 = \delta^{0'}\Psi(\theta^0)\delta^0 = 0,$$

so that indeed nonidentification of θ^0 implies singularity of the information matrix.

Conversely, if θ^0 is a regular point but $\Psi(\theta^0)$ is singular, then there exists a vector $c(\theta)$ such that in an open neighborhood of θ^0

$$c(\theta)'\Psi(\theta)c(\theta) = E\{(h(y, \theta)'c(\theta))^2\} = 0.$$

This implies, for all θ in this neighborhood, that $h(y, \theta)'c(\theta) = 0$ for all y. Since $\Psi(\theta)$ is continuous and of constant rank, $c(\theta)$ can be chosen to be continuous in a neighborhood of θ^0. We use this property to define a curve $\theta(t)$ which solves for $0 \le t \le t_*$ the differential equation d $\theta(t)/dt = c(\theta)$, $\theta(0) = \theta^0$. This gives

$$\frac{dg(y, \theta)}{dt} = h(y, \theta)'\frac{d\theta}{dt} = h(y, \theta)'c(\theta) = 0$$

for all y. So $g(y, \theta)$ is constant along the curve for $0 \le t \le t_*$, hence θ^0 is not identified. ∎

4   The Jacobian Matrix Criterion

The advantage of Theorem 2 is that we do not have to operate on the joint probability distribution of the underlying random variables directly when analyzing the identification of a particular model. It suffices to consider the information matrix. There is a further simplification possible when the underlying distribution admits a sufficient statistic (of a size that does not depend on the sample size). Under suitable regularity conditions, which are essentially those for the Cramér–Rao theorem, such a sufficient statistic exists if and only if the distribution belongs to the exponential family. Then, its density function can be written as

$$f(y, \theta) = a(y)e^{b(y)'\tau(\theta)+c(\theta)},$$

for a suitable choice of functions $a(\cdot)$, $b(\cdot)$, $c(\cdot)$ and $\tau(\cdot)$, where $\tau(\cdot)$ and $b(\cdot)$ are vector functions. Without loss of generality we assume that the covariance matrix of $b(y)$ is nonsingular.

When $y_1, \ldots, y_n$ denote the vectors of observations, a sufficient statistic is given by $s(y) \equiv \sum_{i=1}^{m} b(y_i)$, as follows from the factorization theorem for jointly sufficient statistics. The first-order derivative of the loglikelihood is

$$\frac{\partial \log l(\theta)}{\partial \theta} = Q(\theta)s(y) + n\frac{\partial c(\theta)}{\partial \theta},$$

where

$$Q(\theta) \equiv \frac{\partial \tau(\theta)'}{\partial \theta}. \tag{7.3}$$

Since $E\{\partial \log l(\theta)/\partial \theta\} = 0$, the information matrix is given by the variance of the derivative of the loglikelihood:

$$\Psi(\theta) = Q(\theta)\Sigma_{s(y)}Q(\theta)'.$$

Since $\Sigma_{s(y)}$ is of full rank, the information matrix is of full rank if and only if $Q(\theta)$ is of full row rank. So we have established the following result.

Theorem 3. Let $f(y, \theta)$ belong to the exponential family. Let θ^0 be a regular point of the information matrix $\Psi(\theta)$. Let $Q(\cdot)$ be as defined in (7.3). Then θ^0 is locally identified if and only if $Q(\theta^0)$ has full row rank.

As a byproduct of this theorem, we note that $\tau(\theta)$ (sometimes called the canonical or natural parameter) is identified since the corresponding information matrix is simply the covariance matrix of $s(y)$, assumed to be of full rank.

A major application of Theorem 3 concerns the k-dimensional normal distribution with parameters μ and Σ whose elements are functions of a parameter vector θ. For the normal we can write

$$f(y, \theta) = (2\pi)^{-k/2}|\Sigma|^{-\frac{1}{2}}e^{-\frac{1}{2}(y-\mu)'\Sigma^{-1}(y-\mu)}$$
$$= (2\pi)^{-k/2}e^{(y', -\frac{1}{2}y'\otimes y')(\Sigma^{-1}\mu; \text{vec}\Sigma^{-1}) + \log|\Sigma|^{-1/2} - \frac{1}{2}\mu'\Sigma^{-1}\mu}.$$

This gives the normal distribution in the form of the exponential family but the term $y \otimes y$ contains redundant elements and hence its covariance matrix is singular. To eliminate this singularity, let N_k (of order $k^2 \times k^2$), D_k (of order $k^2 \times \frac{1}{2}k(k+1)$), and L_k (of order $\frac{1}{2}k(k+1) \times k^2$) be matrices with properties

$$N_k\mathrm{vec}A = \mathrm{vec}\tfrac{1}{2}(A + A'), \quad D_k\mathrm{v}(A) = \mathrm{vec}A, \quad L_k'\mathrm{v}(B) = \mathrm{vec}B$$

for every $k \times k$-matrix A and for every lower triangular $k \times k$-matrix B, and the $\frac{1}{2}k(k+1)$-vector $\mathrm{v}(A)$ is the vector obtained from $\mathrm{vec}A$ by eliminating all supradiagonal elements of A. Then $D_kL_kN_k = N_k$ (Magnus, 1988, theorem 5.5(ii)), and

$$\begin{aligned}
(y \otimes y)'\mathrm{vec}\Sigma^{-1} &= (y \otimes y)'N_k\mathrm{vec}\Sigma^{-1} \\
&= (y \otimes y)'N_kL_k'D_k'\mathrm{vec}\Sigma^{-1} \\
&= (y \otimes y)'L_k'D_k'\mathrm{vec}\Sigma^{-1} \\
&= (L_k(y \otimes y))'D_k'\mathrm{vec}\Sigma^{-1}.
\end{aligned}$$

So the normal density fits in the k-dimensional exponential family with

$$b(y) = (y; -\tfrac{1}{2}L_k(y \otimes y)), \quad \tau(\theta) = (\Sigma^{-1}\mu; D_k'\mathrm{vec}\Sigma^{-1}).$$

The identification of a normality-based model with parameterized mean and variance hence depends on the column rank of the matrix of derivatives of $\tau(\theta)$ with respect to θ', or equivalently on the column rank of the matrix of derivatives of

$$\sigma(\theta) \equiv (\mu; \mathrm{v}(\Sigma)). \tag{7.4}$$

The equivalence is due to the fact that the Jacobian matrix of the transformation from $\tau(\theta)$ to $\sigma(\theta)$ is equal to

$$\begin{bmatrix} \Sigma^{-1} & -(\mu'\Sigma^{-1} \otimes \Sigma^{-1})D_k \\ 0 & -D_k'(\Sigma^{-1} \otimes \Sigma^{-1})D_k \end{bmatrix}$$

and is hence nonsingular. If, as is often the case in practice, the mean of the distribution is zero, (7.4) reduces to $\sigma(\theta) = \mathrm{v}(\Sigma)$. So, the identification of a model when the underlying distribution is multivariate normal with zero means depends on the structure of the covariance matrix only.

While frequently normality is an assumption of convenience, not justified by theory or data, it should be stressed that, when dealing with problems of identification, it is also a conservative assumption (cf. Aigner et al., 1984; Bekker, 1986). When the underlying distribution is nonnormal, models that are not identified under normality may as yet be identified since higher order moments can then be added to $\sigma(\theta)$, which either leaves the rank of the Jacobian matrix unaffected or increases it.

For the remainder of this chapter we do not make a specific assumption as to the form of the distribution. We merely assume in generality that there exists a vector function σ of order n, $\sigma(\theta) : \mathbf{R}^l \to \mathbf{R}^n$, such that there exists a one-to-one relation between the elements of $\{P(y, \theta) \mid \theta \in \mathbf{R}^l\}$ and $\{\sigma(\theta) \mid \theta \in \mathbf{R}^l\}$; the identification of the parameters from the underlying distribution is "transmitted" through $\sigma(\theta)$.

5 PRIOR INFORMATION

The information on the parameters can come from two sources. One is from the observations, which are informative about $\sigma(\theta)$. But we may also have a priori information. Let this be of the following form: θ^0 satisfies $\rho(\theta^0) = 0$, where $\rho(\cdot)$ is an r-dimensional vector function. Therefore we study the submodel $\mathcal{H} \subset \mathcal{S}$, where

$$\mathcal{H} = \{\theta \mid \theta \in \mathcal{S} \subset \mathbf{R}^l, \rho(\theta) = 0\}. \tag{7.5}$$

Now the problem of local identification of the parameter vector θ^0 reduces to the problem of verifying whether the equations system

$$f(\theta) \equiv \begin{bmatrix} \sigma(\theta) \\ \rho(\theta) \end{bmatrix} - \begin{bmatrix} \sigma(\theta^0) \\ \rho(\theta^0) \end{bmatrix} = 0 \tag{7.6}$$

has a locally unique solution: if we can find parameter points θ arbitrarily close to θ^0 for which $f(\theta) = 0$, then θ^0 is locally not identified. In order to find out whether θ^0 is locally identified we will apply the implicit function theorem. We will now first discuss this theorem.

Let C^r be the class of functions that are r times continuously differentiable in θ^0. Furthermore a C^∞ function is analytic if the Taylor series expansion of each component converges to that function. In practice most functions are analytic. They share the important quality of being either equal to zero identically or equal to zero only on a set of Lebesgue measure zero. We can now formulate the implicit function theorem.

Theorem 4. *Implicit function theorem. Let $f(\theta) = f(\theta_I; \theta_{II})$ be a C^p function ($p \geq 1$), $f : \mathbf{R}^{n+m} \to \mathbf{R}^n$; $\theta_I \in \mathbf{R}^n$, $\theta_{II} \in \mathbf{R}^m$ such that $f(\theta_I^0; \theta_{II}^0) = 0$ and the $n \times n$-matrix $\partial f(\theta)/\partial \theta_I' \mid \theta^0$ is nonsingular, then there exists an open neighborhood $\mathcal{U} \subset \mathbf{R}^n$ of θ_I^0 and an open neighborhood $\mathcal{V} \subset \mathbf{R}^m$ of θ_{II}^0 such that there exists a unique C^p function $g : \mathcal{V} \to \mathcal{U}$ with $g(\theta_{II}^0) = \theta_I^0$ and $f(g(\theta_{II}); \theta_{II}) = 0$ for all $\theta_{II} \in \mathcal{V}$.*

If indeed $\partial f(\theta)/\partial \theta_I' \mid \theta^0$ is nonsingular, so that $f(g(\theta_{II}); \theta_{II}) = 0$ for all $\theta_{II} \in \mathcal{V}$, then we also have for points $(\theta_I; \theta_{II}) = (g(\theta_{II}); \theta_{II})$ with $\theta_{II} \in \mathcal{V}$:

$$\frac{\partial f}{\partial \theta_{II}'} + \frac{\partial f}{\partial g'} \frac{\partial g}{\partial \theta_{II}'} = 0.$$

Returning to the question of identification of θ^0 a first important result is easily derived if we assume that $f(\theta)$, as defined in (7.6), is continuously differentiable in θ^0. Let the Jacobian matrix $J(\theta)$ be

$$J(\theta) \equiv \frac{\partial f(\theta)}{\partial \theta'}.$$

Now assume that $J(\theta^0)$ has full column rank. Then, possibly after a rearrangement of elements of $f(\theta) = (f_1(\theta); f_2(\theta))$, we have

$$J(\theta) = \begin{bmatrix} J_1(\theta) \\ J_2(\theta) \end{bmatrix} = \begin{bmatrix} \partial f_1(\theta)/\partial \theta' \\ \partial f_2(\theta)/\partial \theta' \end{bmatrix}, \tag{7.7}$$

where $J_2(\theta^0)$ is nonsingular. If we consider the function $h(\theta; v) \equiv f_2(\theta) + 0 \cdot v$, we find, by using the implicit function theorem, that the function $g(v) = \theta^0$, for which $h(g(v); v) = 0$, is unique. Consequently, there is an open neighborhood of θ^0 where $\theta = \theta^0$ is the only solution of $f_2(\theta) = 0$, or $f(\theta) = 0$. Thus, if $J(\theta^0)$ has full column rank, then θ^0 is locally identified.

Now assume that $J(\theta^0)$ is not of full column rank. Does this imply that θ^0 is not locally identified? The answer is negative. For example, consider the special case where $f(\theta) = \theta_1^2 + \theta_2^2$, and $\theta^0 = (0, 0)$. Here the Jacobian matrix $J(\theta)$ is given by $(2\theta_1, 2\theta_2)$ and $J(\theta^0) = (0, 0)$, which is clearly not of full column rank. However, θ^0 is the only point in $\mathbf{R}^2$ for which $f(\theta) = 0$, so that θ^0 is, in fact, globally identified.

This may seem a pathological case since the (row) rank of the Jacobian matrix simply was 0. What can we say if $J(\theta^0)$ is not of full column rank while it is of full row rank? In that case θ^0 will not be identified as a direct consequence of the implicit function theorem. And so we are left with the general case where $J(\theta^0)$ has both a deficient column rank and a deficient row rank. Without loss of generality we can rearrange the rows of $J(\theta)$ as in (7.7) where rank$\{J(\theta^0)\}$ = rank$\{J_2(\theta^0)\}$ while now $J_2(\theta^0)$ has full row rank. According to the implicit function theorem we can rearrange the elements of $\theta = (\theta_I; \theta_{II})$ so that locally there exists a unique function $g(\theta_{II})$ so that $f_2(g(\theta_{II}); \theta_{II}) = 0$. However, $f_1(g(\theta_{II}); \theta_{II}) = 0$ does not necessarily hold, and we have not yet established a lack of identification.

Let $h(\theta_{II}) = f(g(\theta_{II}); \theta_{II})$. Then we have locally

$$\frac{\partial h(\theta_{II})}{\partial \theta'_{II}} = \frac{\partial f}{\partial \theta'_{II}} + \frac{\partial f}{\partial g'} \frac{\partial g}{\partial \theta'_{II}}$$

$$= \begin{bmatrix} J_1(g(\theta_{II}); \theta_{II}) \\ J_2(g(\theta_{II}); \theta_{II}) \end{bmatrix} \begin{bmatrix} \partial g/\partial \theta'_{II} \\ I_k \end{bmatrix}$$

$$= \begin{bmatrix} J_1(g(\theta_{II}); \theta_{II}) \begin{bmatrix} \partial g/\partial \theta'_{II} \\ I_k \end{bmatrix} \\ 0 \end{bmatrix},$$

where $k \equiv l - \text{rank}\{J(\theta^0)\}$. If it can be established that the rows of $J_1(g(\theta_{II}); \theta_{II})$ are linearly dependent on the rows of $J_2(g(\theta_{II}); \theta_{II})$ for all θ_{II} in an open neighborhood of $\theta_{II}^0 \in \mathbf{R}^k$, then $\partial h(\theta_{II})/\partial\theta_{II}' = 0$ in that neighborhood, which can be taken to be convex, so that $f(g(\theta_{II}); \theta_{II}) = h(\theta_{II}) = h(\theta_{II}^0) = 0$ in an open neighborhood of θ_{II}^0. As a result θ^0 will not be locally identified.

Notice that θ^0 is a regular point of $J(\theta)$ if $J(\theta^0)$ has full row (or column) rank since in that case $|J(\theta^0)J(\theta^0)'| \neq 0$ (or $|J(\theta^0)'J(\theta^0)| \neq 0$) so that $J(\theta)$ will have full row (or column) rank for points close enough to θ^0. If θ^0 is a regular point of $J(\theta)$ and $\text{rank}\{J(\theta^0)\} = \text{rank}\{J_2(\theta^0)\}$, where $J(\theta)$ has been partitioned as in (7.7), and $J_2(\theta^0)$ is of full row rank, then θ^0 is a regular point of both $J(\theta)$ and $J_2(\theta)$. So $\text{rank}\{J(\theta)\} = \text{rank}\{J_2(\theta)\}$ in an open neighborhood of θ^0. In other words, for all points in an open neighborhood of θ^0 the rows of $J_1(\theta)$ will depend linearly on the rows of $J_2(\theta)$.

Summarizing these results we may give the following theorem, which is also given by Fisher (1966, theorem 5.9.2).

Theorem 5. Let $J(\theta)$ be the Jacobian matrix of order $(n + r) \times l$ formed by taking partial derivatives of $(\sigma(\theta); \rho(\theta))$ with respect to θ,

$$J(\theta) \equiv \begin{bmatrix} \partial\sigma(\theta)/\partial\theta' \\ \partial\rho(\theta)/\partial\theta' \end{bmatrix}.$$

If θ^0 is a regular point of $J(\theta)$, then a necessary and sufficient condition for θ^0 to be locally identified is that $J(\theta)$ has rank l at θ^0.

6 HANDLING THE RANK IN PRACTICE

The question is how one should apply this theorem in practice. Since θ^0 is an unknown parameter vector it is not yet clear how one should compute the rank of $J(\theta^0)$. Furthermore, a question can be raised as to the restrictiveness of the assumption of regularity of θ^0. It appears that these problems are related. That is, if θ^0 is a regular point of $J(\theta)$, then the rank of $J(\theta^0)$ can be computed even though θ^0 itself is unknown. On the other hand, the assumption of regularity of θ^0, as it is stated in Theorem 5, is unnecessarily restrictive.

The assumption of regularity of θ^0 makes it possible to compute the rank of $J(\theta^0)$. In the sequel we assume that $f(\theta)$ is an analytic function, in which case almost all points $\theta \in S$ are regular points: the irregular points constitute a set in $\mathbf{R}^l$ of Lebesgue measure zero. The proof of this statement is as follows. Let

$$\tilde{\theta} \equiv \underset{\theta \in \mathbf{R}^l}{\text{argmax}}\{\text{rank}\{J(\theta)\}\},$$

and let

$$J(\tilde{\theta}) \equiv \begin{bmatrix} J_1(\tilde{\theta}) \\ J_2(\tilde{\theta}) \end{bmatrix},$$

so that $\text{rank}\{J(\tilde{\theta})\} = \text{rank}\{J_2(\tilde{\theta})\}$ and $J_2(\tilde{\theta})$ is of full row rank. Then, due to continuity, $|J_2(\theta)J_2(\theta)'| > 0$ in an open neighborhood of $\tilde{\theta}$. That is, the analytic function $|J_2(\theta)J_2(\theta)'|$ is not equal to zero on a set of positive Lebesgue measure. Hence $|J_2(\theta)J_2(\theta)'| > 0$ almost everywhere, since an analytic function is either identical to zero or equal to zero on a set of Lebesgue measure zero only. Thus $J_2(\theta)$ will have full row rank almost everywhere in S so that $\text{rank}\{J(\theta)\} = \max_{\theta \in \mathbf{R}^l}\{\text{rank}\{J(\theta)\}\}$ almost everywhere. Consequently, if θ^0 is a regular point of $J(\theta)$, then $\text{rank}\{J(\theta)\} = \text{rank}\{J(\theta^0)\}$ for points θ in a neighborhood with positive Lebesgue measure. Hence, $\text{rank}\{J(\theta^0)\} = \max_{\theta \in \mathbf{R}^l}\{\text{rank}\{J(\theta)\}\}$, which can be computed without knowing θ^0. We thus have shown the following result, see also Johansen (1995, theorem 2).

Theorem 6. Let $\sigma(\cdot)$ and $\rho(\cdot)$ be analytic functions. Then θ^0 is a regular point of $J(\theta)$ if and only if

$$\text{rank}\{J(\theta^0)\} = \max_{\theta \in \mathbf{R}^l}\{\text{rank}\{J(\theta)\}\},$$

which holds for almost all $\theta^0 \in \mathbf{R}^l$.

Thus if we know nothing about θ^0 except that $\theta^0 \in S \subset \mathbf{R}^l$, where S is some open set in $\mathbf{R}^l$, then it would make sense to assume that θ^0 is a regular point, since almost all points of S are regular points. However, when doing so we would ignore the prior information contained in $\rho(\theta^0) = 0$. The set $\mathcal{H}$ (cf. (7.5)) constitutes a manifold of dimension $l - r$ in $\mathbf{R}^l$, where we assume that $\partial\rho(\theta)/\partial\theta'$ has full row rank in θ^0. Let

$$R(\theta) \equiv \frac{\partial\rho(\theta)}{\partial\theta'},$$

then $\text{rank}\{R(\theta^0)\} = r$. The set $\mathcal{H}$ is locally homeomorphic to an open set in $\mathbf{R}^{l-r}$: r elements of θ, collected in the vector θ_I, say, are locally unique functions of the remaining elements collected in θ_{II}: $\theta_I = g(\theta_{II})$, say. Without loss of generality we assume that θ_I constitutes the first r elements of θ. Now it does make sense to assume that θ_{II}^0 is a regular point of $J(g(\theta_{II}); \theta_{II})$ since almost all points in $\mathbf{R}^{l-r}$ are regular points and we do not have any further relevant prior information with respect to θ_{II}^0. This assumption is less restrictive than the assumption in Theorem 5 since the constancy of $\text{rank}\{J(\theta)\}$ in an open neighborhood of θ^0 implies the constancy of this rank for points close to θ^0 that satisfy $\theta_I = g(\theta_{II})$. Moreover, the rank of $J(\theta^0)$ should be computed by $\text{rank}\{J(\theta^0)\} = \max_{\theta \in \mathcal{H}}\{\text{rank}\{J(\theta)\}\}$, which may be less than the maximum over $\theta \in \mathbf{R}^l$. To formalize this, we generalize Definition 5 and generalize Theorem 5.

Definition 6. Let $M(\theta)$ be a continuous matrix function and let $\theta^0 \in \mathcal{H} \subset \mathbf{R}^l$. Then θ^0 is a *regular point* of $M(\theta) | \mathcal{H}$ if the rank of $M(\theta)$ is constant for points in $\mathcal{H}$ in an open neighborhood of θ^0.

Theorem 7.   Let $J(\theta)$ be the Jacobian matrix of order $(n + r) \times l$ formed by taking the partial derivatives of $(\sigma(\theta); \rho(\theta))$ with respect to $\theta \in \mathcal{S} \subset \mathbf{R}^l$:

$$J(\theta) \equiv \begin{bmatrix} \partial\sigma(\theta)/\partial\theta' \\ R(\theta) \end{bmatrix}. \tag{7.8}$$

Let rank$\{R(\theta^0)\} = r$. If θ^0 is a regular point of $J(\theta) \mid \mathcal{H}$, then θ^0 is locally identified in $\mathcal{H}$ if and only if $\max_{\theta \in \mathcal{H}}\{\text{rank}\{J(\theta)\}\} = l$.

Proof.   Since θ^0 is a regular point of $J(\theta) \mid \mathcal{H}$, the rank of $J(\theta^0)$ is equal to $\max_{\theta \in \mathcal{H}}\{\text{rank}\{J(\theta)\}\}$. So if the latter rank is equal to l, then $J(\theta^0)$ has full column rank and θ^0 is identified. If rank$\{J(\theta^0)\} < l$, then there is a partitioning as in (7.7), where the elements of $\rho(\theta)$ are elements of $f_2(\theta)$ and $J_2(\theta^0)$ has full row rank and a deficient column rank. Hence we may apply the implicit function theorem to show that there exist points $\theta = (g(\theta_{II}); \theta_{II})$ arbitrarily close to θ^0 so that $f_2(\theta) = f_2(\theta^0)$. Since the elements of $\rho(\theta)$ are also elements of $f_2(\theta)$, these points θ satisfy $\rho(\theta) = \rho(\theta^0)$, so that they are elements of $\mathcal{H}$.

Since θ^0 is a regular point of $J(\theta) \mid \mathcal{H}$ and the points $\theta = (g(\theta_{II}); \theta_{II})$ are located in $\mathcal{H}$, θ^0_{II} is a regular point of $J(g(\theta_{II}); \theta_{II})$, so that close to θ^0_{II} the rows of $J_1(g(\theta_{II}); \theta_{II})$ are linearly dependent on the rows of $J_2(g(\theta_{II}); \theta_{II})$ and so, by the same argument as in the proof of Theorem 5, $f_1(g(\theta_{II}); \theta_1) = f_1(\theta^0)$. As a result, θ^0 will not be locally identified in $\mathcal{H}$.   ■

It should be noted that, if $\sigma(\theta)$ and $\rho(\theta)$ are linear functions, so that $J(\theta) = J$ does not depend on θ and $f(\theta) - f(\theta^0) = J \cdot (\theta - \theta^0)$, then θ^0 is globally identified if and only if $J(\theta^0) = J$ is of full column rank.

7   PARTIAL IDENTIFICATION

Up till now we have been concerned with identification of θ^0 as a whole. However, if θ^0 is locally not identified, it may still be the case that some separate elements of θ^0 are identified. If, for example, the ith element of θ^0 is identified, this means that for a point θ observationally equivalent to θ^0 there holds $\theta_i = \theta^0_i$ if θ is close enough to θ^0.

Insight into such partial identification could be relevant for estimation purposes, if one is interested in estimating the single parameter θ^0_i. It could also be relevant for the purpose of model specification in the sense that it may suggest a further restriction of the parameter space such that θ^0 is identified as yet.

In order to describe conditions for the local identification of single parameters we denote by

$$\mathcal{A}_{(i)} \equiv \{\theta \mid \theta \in \mathcal{H}, \theta_i = \theta^0_i\}$$

the restricted parameter space whose elements satisfy the a priori restrictions $\rho(\theta) = 0$ and $\theta_i = \theta^0_i$, cf. (7.5). Furthermore, let $J_{(i)}(\theta)$ consist of the columns of $J(\theta)$

except the ith one, so that derivatives have been taken with respect to all elements of θ apart from the ith one. The main results on the identification of single parameters are contained in the following two theorems.

Theorem 8. Let $\mathcal{A}_{(i)} \equiv \{\theta \mid \theta \in \mathcal{H}, \theta_i = \theta_i^0\}$. If θ^0 is a regular point of $J(\theta) \mid \mathcal{H}$ and rank$\{J_{(i)}(\theta^0)\} = $ rank$\{J(\theta^0)\}$, then θ_i^0 is locally *not* identified in $\mathcal{H}$.

Proof. Let the rows of $J(\theta)$ be rearranged and partitioned as in (7.7) so that $J_2(\theta^0)$ is of full row rank equal to the rank of $J(\theta^0)$. Furthermore let the columns be rearranged so that

$$J_2(\theta) = (J_{21}(\theta), J_{22}(\theta)) = (\partial f_2/\partial \theta_I', \partial f_2/\partial \theta_{II}'),$$

where $J_{21}(\theta^0)$ is nonsingular. Now, if rank$\{J(\theta^0)\} = $ rank$\{J_{(i)}(\theta^0)\}$, then θ_{II} can be taken such that θ_i is an element of θ_{II}. Application of the implicit function theorem shows that there is a unique function $\theta_I = g(\theta_{II})$ so that $f_2(g(\theta_{II}); \theta_{II}) = 0$ for all θ_{II} in an open neighborhood of θ_{II}^0. Since the elements of $\rho(\theta)$ are elements of $f_2(\theta)$, the points $(g(\theta_{II}); \theta_{II})$ are located in $\mathcal{H}$. Furthermore, since θ^0 is a regular point of $J(\theta) \mid \mathcal{H}$, it follows, by the same argument as in the proof of Theorem 5, that also $f_1(g(\theta_{II}), \theta_{II}) = 0$. Hence all elements of θ_{II}, including θ_i, are locally not identified in $\mathcal{H}$. ■

We assume that rank$\{\partial \rho(\theta)/\partial \theta' \mid \theta^0\} = $ rank$\{R(\theta^0)\} = $ rank$\{R_{(i)}(\theta^0)\} = r$ so that θ_i^0 is locally not identified by the a priori restrictions $\rho(\theta^0) = 0$ alone. In other words, $\mathcal{H} = \{\theta \mid \theta \in S, \rho(\theta) = 0\}$ constitutes a manifold of dimension $l - r$ in $\mathbf{R}^l$ and $\mathcal{A}_{(i)} = \{\theta \in \mathcal{H}, \theta_i = \theta_i^0\}$ constitutes a manifold of dimension $l - r - 1$ in $\mathbf{R}^l$.

Theorem 9. Let $\mathcal{A}_{(i)} \equiv \{\theta \mid \theta \in \mathcal{H}, \theta_i = \theta_i^0\}$. If θ^0 is a regular point of $J_{(i)}(\theta) \mid \mathcal{A}_{(i)}$ and rank$\{J_{(i)}(\theta^0)\} < $ rank$\{J(\theta^0)\}$, then θ_i^0 is locally identified in $\mathcal{H}$.

Proof. Applying the same rearrangement and partitioning of $J(\theta)$ as in the proof of Theorem 8, we find that θ_i is an element of θ_I. Again there is a unique function so that $f_2(g(\theta_{II}), \theta_{II}) = 0$ for θ_{II} close to θ_{II}^0. Now, if we let $\theta_i = \theta_i^0$ and differentiate f_2 with respect to the remaining elements of θ, we get the Jacobian matrix $J_{2(i)}(\theta)$. Since rank$\{J_{(i)}(\theta^0)\} < $ rank$\{J(\theta^0)\}$, the matrix $J_{2(i)}(\theta^0)$ is not of full row rank and the rank of $\{J_{2(i)}(\theta^0)\}$ equals the rank of $\{J_{2(i)}(\theta^0)\}$. So if θ^0 is a regular point of $J_{(i)}(\theta) \mid \mathcal{A}_{(i)}$ it is also a regular point of $J_{2(i)}(\theta) \mid \mathcal{A}_{(i)}$. So we may use the same argument as in the proof of Theorem 8, where we assume that rank$\{R_{(i)}(\theta^0)\} = r$, to verify that if $\theta_i = \theta_i^0$, then there exist unique functions $\theta_j = h_j(\theta_{II})$, $j \neq i$, so that, if we write $h_i(\theta_{II}) \equiv \theta_i^0$, $f_2(h(\theta_{II}), \theta_{II}) = 0$ for θ_{II} close to θ_{II}^0. However, we already verified that $g(\theta_{II})$ is a unique function, so $g_i(\theta_{II}) = \theta_i^0$. Consequently θ_i^0 is locally identified. ■

Again the ranks that occur in these theorems can be evaluated by computing the maximum rank over the relevant parameter space (or manifold), which is $\mathcal{H}$ in Theorem 8 and $\mathcal{A}_{(i)}$ in Theorem 9.

The importance of these two theorems in practice is best brought out by the following reformulation.

Corollary 1. Let the regularity assumptions of Theorems 8 and 9 be satisfied (which holds for almost all $\theta^0 \in \mathcal{H}$). Let $N(\theta^0)$ be a basis for the null-space of $J(\theta^0)$, i.e. $J(\theta^0)N(\theta^0) = 0$ and let e_i be the ith unit vector. Then θ_i^0 is locally identified if and only if $e_i'N(\theta^0) = 0$.

So a zero-row in a null-space indicates an identified parameter.

8 THE CLASSICAL SIMULTANEOUS EQUATIONS MODEL

We now turn to identification in the classical simultaneous equations model. Estimation in this model is comprehensively reviewed in chapter 6 by Mariano. The model is

$$By + \Gamma x = \zeta, \tag{7.9}$$

where y is an m-vector of endogenous variables, x is a stochastic k-vector of exogenous variables, and ζ is an m-vector of disturbances. It is assumed that $E(\zeta) = 0$ and $E(x\zeta') = 0$, so that x and ζ are uncorrelated, and $\Sigma_x \equiv E(xx')$ is nonsingular. The coefficient matrices B and Γ are of order $m \times m$ and $m \times k$, respectively, and B is nonsingular.

Under normality, the distribution of the observations $(y; x)$ is uniquely determined by the first two moments. Since model (7.9) can be rewritten as

$$(y', x') = (\zeta', x') \begin{bmatrix} B' & 0 \\ \Gamma' & I_k \end{bmatrix}^{-1},$$

the moment equations are given by

$$(\mu_y', \mu_x') \equiv E(y', x') = (0', \mu_x') \begin{bmatrix} B' & 0 \\ \Gamma' & I_k \end{bmatrix}^{-1} \tag{7.10}$$

$$\begin{bmatrix} \Sigma_y & \Sigma_{yx} \\ \Sigma_{xy} & \Sigma_x \end{bmatrix} \equiv E\left\{ \begin{bmatrix} y \\ x \end{bmatrix} (y', x') \right\}$$

$$= \begin{bmatrix} B & \Gamma \\ 0 & I_k \end{bmatrix}^{-1} \begin{bmatrix} \Sigma_\zeta & 0 \\ 0 & \Sigma_x \end{bmatrix} \begin{bmatrix} B' & 0 \\ \Gamma' & I_k \end{bmatrix}^{-1}. \tag{7.11}$$

Thus, equations (7.10) and (7.11) contain all observational information with regard to the structural parameter matrices B, Γ and $\Sigma_\zeta \equiv E(\zeta\zeta')$.

However, for the identification of the structural parameter matrices we need only consider a subset of the equations in (7.10) and (7.11). The equations in (7.11) can be separated into

$$(B, \Gamma) \begin{bmatrix} \Sigma_y & \Sigma_{yx} \\ \Sigma_{xy} & \Sigma_x \end{bmatrix} \begin{bmatrix} B' \\ \Gamma' \end{bmatrix} - \Sigma_\zeta = 0 \tag{7.12}$$

$$(\Sigma_{xy}, \Sigma_x) \begin{bmatrix} B' \\ \Gamma' \end{bmatrix} = 0, \tag{7.13}$$

and, in fact, these equations contain all observational information relevant for the identification of B, Γ and Σ_ζ. That is to say, since the equations (7.10) and (7.11) are satisfied by the true parameter point, we find that $(\mu_y', \mu_x') = \mu_x' \Sigma_x^{-1}(\Sigma_{xy}, \Sigma_x)$ so that, if any matrices B and Γ satisfy (7.13), they will also satisfy (7.10). The first moment equations do not provide additional information.

Now let prior information be given by a set of restrictions on the coefficient matrices B and Γ:

$$\rho(B, \Gamma) = 0, \tag{7.14}$$

where $\rho(B, \Gamma)$ is a vector function of the matrices B and Γ. The parameter matrix Σ_ζ is assumed to be unrestricted. In that case all information relevant for the identification of B and Γ is given by equation (7.13), which after stacking in a vector can be written as

$$\sigma(B, \Gamma) \equiv (I_m \otimes \Sigma_{xy}) \mathrm{vec}(B') + (I_m \otimes \Sigma_x) \mathrm{vec}(\Gamma') = 0,$$

and by equation (7.14). The Jacobian matrix is

$$J(B, \Gamma) = \frac{\partial(\sigma(B, \Gamma); \rho(B, \Gamma))}{\partial(\mathrm{vec}'(B'), \mathrm{vec}'(\Gamma'))} = \begin{bmatrix} (I_m \otimes \Sigma_{xy}, I_m \otimes \Sigma_x) \\ R_{B\Gamma} \end{bmatrix},$$

where $R_{B\Gamma}$ is defined implicitly and is assumed to be of full row rank. Postmultiplication of the Jacobian by a conveniently chosen nonsingular matrix:

$$J(B, \Gamma) \begin{bmatrix} I_m \otimes B' & 0 \\ I_m \otimes \Gamma' & I_{mk} \end{bmatrix} = \begin{bmatrix} 0 & I_m \otimes \Sigma_x \\ R_{B\Gamma} \begin{bmatrix} I_m \otimes B' \\ I_m \otimes \Gamma' \end{bmatrix} & R_{B\Gamma} \begin{bmatrix} 0 \\ I_{mk} \end{bmatrix} \end{bmatrix}$$

shows that $J(B, \Gamma)$ has full column rank if and only if

$$\tilde{J}(B, \Gamma) \equiv R_{B\Gamma} \begin{bmatrix} I_m \otimes B' \\ I_m \otimes \Gamma' \end{bmatrix} \tag{7.15}$$

has full column rank. Furthermore $J(B, \Gamma)$ and $\tilde{J}(B, \Gamma)$ share regular points. Thus, by Theorem 7 we have the following result.

Theorem 10.   Let $\mathcal{H} \equiv \{(B, \Gamma) \mid (B, \Gamma) \in \mathbf{R}^{m^2+mk}, \rho(B, \Gamma) = 0\}$ and let $(B, \Gamma)^0$ be a regular point of $\tilde{J}(B, \Gamma) \mid \mathcal{H}$. Then $(B, \Gamma)^0$ is locally identified if and only if $\tilde{J}(B^0, \Gamma^0)$ has full row rank m^2.

This result corresponds to the classical condition for identification in a simultaneous equation model. If the restrictions on (B, Γ) are linear, i.e. when $\rho(B, \Gamma)$ is a linear function, for example when separate elements of (B, Γ) are restricted to be fixed, then both sets of identifying equations (7.13) and (7.14) are linear so that $J(B, \Gamma)$ is constant over the parameter space. In that case local identification implies global identification and we have the following corollary.

Corollary 2.   Let $\rho(B, \Gamma)$ be linear, then $(B, \Gamma)^0$ is globally identified if and only if $\text{rank}\{\tilde{J}(B, \Gamma)\} = m^2$.

This constitutes the well-known rank condition for identification in simultaneous equations models, as developed in the early work of the Cowles Commission, e.g. Koopmans, Rubin, and Leipnik (1950), Koopmans (1953), and Koopmans and Hood (1953). Johansen (1995, theorem 3) gives an elegant formulation of the identification of the coefficients of a single equation.

9   CONCLUDING REMARKS

In this chapter we have presented a rigorous, self-contained treatment of identification in parametric models with iid observations. The material is essentially from the book by Bekker, Merckens, and Wansbeek (1994); see Rigdon (1997) for an extended review. The reader is referred to this book for a number of further topics. For example, it discusses identification of two extensions of the classical simultaneous equations model in two directions, viz. restrictions on the covariance matrix of the disturbances, and the measurement error in the regressors. It also discusses local identification of the equally classical factor analysis model.[4] These two models have been integrated in the literature through the hugely popular Lisrel model, which however often confronts researchers with identification problems which are hard to tackle analytically since, in the rank condition for identification, inverse matrices cannot be eliminated as in the classical simultaneous equations model. The book tackles this issue by parameterizing the restrictions on the reduced form induced by the restrictions on the structural form.

A distinctive feature of the book is its use of symbolic manipulation of algebraic structures by the computer. Essentially, all identification and equivalence results are couched in terms of ranks of structured matrices containing unknown parameters. To assess such ranks has become practically feasible by using computer algebra. The book contains a diskette with a set of computer algebra programs that can be used for rank evaluation of parameterized matrices for the models discussed.

Notes

*   This chapter is largely based on material adapted from P.A. Bekker, A. Merckens, and T.J. Wansbeek, *Identification, Equivalent Models and Computer Algebra* (Orlando: Academic Press, 1994). Reproduced by kind permission of the publisher. We are grateful to Badi Baltagi, Bart Boon, and an anonymous referee for their useful comments.

1   Identification in nonparametric models is a much different field, see, e.g., Prakasa Rao (1992).

2   Of course, it may be the case that exact knowledge of $P(y, \theta^0)$ is sufficient to derive bounds on θ^0_k (see, e.g., Bekker *et al.*, 1987; Manski, 1989; Manski, 1995). In such a case the sample information can be used to increase knowledge about θ^0_k even though this parameter is not locally identified.

3   However, if one uses a "natural" parameter sequence, it may happen that θ^0_k is identified, whereas no estimator converges in probability to θ^0_k. For example, Gabrielsen (1978) discussed the model $y_i = \beta r^i + u_i$, $i = 1, \ldots, n$, where the u_i are iid $N(0, 1)$, r is known and $|r| < 1$, and β is an unknown parameter. Here the OLS estimator $\hat{\beta} \sim N(\beta, (1 - r^2)/(r^2(1 - r^{2n})))$ is unbiased, so clearly β is identified, but it is not consistent in the natural sequence defined by the model where $n \to \infty$. Since $\hat{\beta}$ is efficient, there does not exist a consistent estimator.

4   For a discussion of global identification in factor analysis see Bekker and ten Berge (1997).

References

Aigner D.J., C. Hsiao, A. Kapteyn, and T.J. Wansbeek (1984). Latent variable models in econometrics. In Z. Griliches and M.D. Intriligator (eds.) *Handbook of Econometrics volume 2*. Amsterdam: North-Holland.

Aldrich, J. (1994). Haavelmo's identification theory. *Econometric Theory* 10, 198–219.

Bekker, P.A. (1986). Comment on identification in the linear errors in variables model. *Econometrica* 54, 215–17.

Bekker, P.A., A. Kapteyn, and T.J. Wansbeek (1987). Consistent sets of estimates for regressions with correlated or uncorrelated measurement errors in arbitrary subsets of all variables. *Econometrica* 55, 1223–30.

Bekker, P.A., A. Merckens, and T.J. Wansbeek (1994). *Identification, Equivalent Models and Computer Algebra*. Orlando: Academic Press.

Bekker, P.A., and J.M.F. ten Berge (1997). Generic global identification in factor analysis. *Linear Algebra and its Applications* 264, 255–63.

Bowden, R. (1973). The theory of parametric identification. *Econometrica* 41, 1069–74.

Deistler, M., and H.-G. Seifert (1978). Identifiability and consistent estimability in econometric models. *Econometrica* 46, 969–80.

Drèze, J. (1975). Bayesian theory of identification in simultaneous equations models. In S.E. Fienberg and A. Zellner (eds.) *Studies in Bayesian Econometrics and Statistics*. Amsterdam: North-Holland.

Fisher, F.M. (1966). *The Identification Problem in Econometrics*. New York: McGraw-Hill.

Gabrielsen, A. (1978). Consistency and identifiability. *Journal of Econometrics* 8, 261–3.

Haavelmo, T. (1943). The statistical implications of a system of simultaneous equations. *Econometrica* 11, 1–12.

Hannan, E.J., and M. Deistler (1988). *The Statistical Theory of Linear Systems*. New York: Wiley.

Hsiao, C. (1983). Identification. In Z. Griliches and M.D. Intriligator (eds.) *Handbook of Econometrics Volume 1*. Amsterdam: North-Holland.

Hsiao, C. (1987). Identification. In J. Eatwell, M. Millgate, and P. Newman (eds.) *The New Palgrave: A Dictionary of Economics*. London: Macmillan.

Hsiao, C. (1997). Cointegration and dynamic simulatneous equations model. *Econometrica* 65, 647–70.

Johansen, S. (1995). Identifying restrictions of linear equations with applications to simultaneous equations and cointegration. *Journal of Econometrics* 69, 111–32.

Kadane, J.B. (1975). The role of identification in Bayesian theory. In S.E. Fienberg and A. Zellner (eds.) *Studies in Bayesian Econometrics and Statistics*. Amsterdam: North-Holland.

Koopmans, T.C., H. Rubin, and R.B. Leipnik (1950). Measuring the equation systems of dynamic economics. In T.C. Koopmans (ed.) *Statistical Inference in Dynamic Economic Models*. New York: Wiley.

Koopmans, T.C. (1953). Identification problems in economic model construction. In W.C. Hood and T.C. Koopmans (eds.) *Studies in Econometric Methods*. New York: Wiley.

Koopmans, T.C., and W.C. Hood (1953). The estimation of simultaneous linear economic relationships. In W.C. Hood and T.C. Koopmans (eds.) *Studies in Econometric Methods*. New York: Wiley.

Leamer, E.E. (1978). *Specification Searches, ad hoc Inference with Nonexperimental Data*. New York: Wiley.

Magnus, J.R. (1988). *Linear Structures*. London: Griffin.

Manski, C.F. (1989). Anatomy of the selection problem. *The Journal of Human Resources* 24, 343–60.

Manski, C.F. (1995). *Identification Problems in the Social Sciences*. Cambridge, MA: Harvard University Press.

McManus, D.A. (1992). How common is identification in parametric models? *Journal of Econometrics* 53, 5–23.

Pesaran, M.H. (1987). Econometrics. In J. Eatwell, M. Millgate, and P. Newman (eds.) *The New Palgrave: A Dictionary of Economics*. London: Macmillan.

Poirier, D.J. (1998). Revising beliefs in nonidentified models. *Econometric Theory* 14, 483–509.

Prakasa Rao, B.L.S. (1992). *Identifiability in Stochastic Models: Characterization of Probability Distributions*. Boston: Academic Press.

Richmond, J. (1974). Identifiability in linear models. *Econometrica* 42, 731–6.

Rigdon, E.E. (1997). Identification of structural equation models with latent variables: a review of contributions by Bekker, Merckens, and Wansbeek. *Structural Equation Modeling* 4, 80–5.

Rothenberg, T.J. (1971). Identification in parametric models. *Econometrica* 39, 577–92.

Zellner, A. (1971). *An Introduction to Bayesian Inference in Econometrics*. New York: Wiley.

Measurement Error and Latent Variables

Tom Wansbeek and Erik Meijer*

1   INTRODUCTION

Traditionally, an assumption underlying econometric models is that the regressors are observed without measurement error. In practice, however, economic observations, micro and macro, are often imprecise (Griliches, 1986). This may be due to clearly identifiable factors. If these are known, we may apply a better measurement procedure on a later occasion. However, it may also be the case that no better procedure is possible, not even in a perfect world. The variable concerned may be a purely mental construct that does not correspond to a variable that can, at least in principle, be observed in practice. In fact, quite often economic theorizing involves such *latent* variables.

Typical examples of latent variables appearing in economic models are utility, the productivity of a worker, permanent income, consumer satisfaction, financial health of a firm, the weather condition in a season, socioeconomic status, or the state of the business cycle. Although we use the epithet "latent" for these variables, we can, for each of these examples, think of related *observable* variables, so some kind of indirect measurement is possible. In this sense the latency of variables is a generalization of measurement error, where the relation between the observed variable and its true or latent counterpart is just of the simple kind: observed = true + measurement error.

Clearly, many variables economists work with are latent, due to measurement error or intrinsically so. In this chapter, we will discuss the problems that are invoked by the presence of measurement error and latent variables in econometric models, possible solutions to these problems, and the opportunities offered by latent variable models. Related references are Aigner, Hsiao, Kapteyn, and Wansbeek (1984), who give an extensive overview of latent variable models, and Fuller (1987) and Cheng and Van Ness (1999), which are book-length treatments of measurement error models.

2 THE LINEAR REGRESSION MODEL WITH MEASUREMENT ERROR

The standard linear multiple regression model can be written as

$$y = \Xi\beta + \varepsilon, \tag{8.1}$$

where y is an observable N-vector, ε an unobservable N-vector of random variables, the elements of which are independently identically distributed (iid) with zero expectation and variance σ_ε^2, and N is the sample size. The g-vector β is fixed but unknown. The $N \times g$-matrix Ξ contains the regressors, which are assumed to be independent of ε. For simplicity, variables are assumed to be measured in deviations from their means.[1]

If there are measurement errors in the explanatory variables, Ξ is not observed. Instead, we observe the matrix X:

$$X = \Xi + V, \tag{8.2}$$

where V $(N \times g)$ is a matrix of measurement errors. Its rows are assumed to be iid with zero expectation and covariance matrix Ω $(g \times g)$ and independent of Ξ and ε. Columns of V (and corresponding rows and columns of Ω) are zero when the corresponding regressors are measured without error.

We consider the consequences of neglecting the measurement errors. Let

$$b \equiv (X'X)^{-1}X'y$$

$$s_\varepsilon^2 \equiv \frac{1}{N-g}(y - Xb)'(y - Xb) = \frac{1}{N-g}y'(I_N - X(X'X)^{-1}X')y$$

be the ordinary least squares (OLS) estimators of β and σ_ε^2. Substitution of (8.2) into (8.1) yields

$$y = (X - V)\beta + \varepsilon = X\beta + u, \tag{8.3}$$

with $u \equiv \varepsilon - V\beta$. This means that (8.3) has a disturbance term which shares a stochastic term (V) with the regressor matrix. Thus, u is correlated with X and $E(u \mid X) \neq 0$. This lack of orthogonality means that a crucial assumption underlying the use of ordinary least squares regression is violated. As we shall see below, the main consequence is that b and s_ε^2 are no longer consistent estimators of β and σ_ε^2. In order to analyze the inconsistency, let $S_\Xi \equiv \Xi'\Xi/N$ and $S_X \equiv X'X/N$. Note that S_X is observable but S_Ξ is not.

We can interpret (8.1) in two ways. It is either a *functional* or a *structural* model. Under the former interpretation, we do not make explicit assumptions regarding the distribution of Ξ, but consider its elements as unknown fixed parameters. Under the latter interpretation, the elements of Ξ are supposed to be random variables. For both cases, we assume $\operatorname{plim}_{N\to\infty} S_\Xi = \Sigma_\Xi$ with Σ_Ξ a positive definite $g \times g$-matrix. Hence,

$$\Sigma_X \equiv \operatorname*{plim}_{N\to\infty} \frac{1}{N} X'X = \operatorname*{plim}_{N\to\infty} S_X = \Sigma_\Xi + \Omega.$$

Note that since Σ_Ξ is positive definite and Ω is positive semidefinite, Σ_X is also positive definite.

2.1   Inconsistency and bias of the OLS estimators

Given the setup, the probability limits of b and s_ε^2, for both the structural and the functional model, are

$$\kappa \equiv \plim_{N\to\infty} b = \beta - \Sigma_X^{-1}\Omega\beta = \Sigma_X^{-1}\Sigma_\Xi\beta. \tag{8.4}$$

$$\gamma \equiv \plim_{N\to\infty} s_\varepsilon^2 = \sigma_\varepsilon^2 + \beta'(\Sigma_\Xi - \Sigma_\Xi\Sigma_X^{-1}\Sigma_\Xi)\beta \geq \sigma_\varepsilon^2. \tag{8.5}$$

Hence b is inconsistent, with inconsistency equal to $\kappa - \beta = -\Sigma_X^{-1}\Omega\beta$, and s_ε^2 is also inconsistent, the inconsistency being nonnegative since $\Sigma_\Xi - \Sigma_\Xi\Sigma_X^{-1}\Sigma_\Xi = \Omega - \Omega\Sigma_X^{-1}\Omega \geq 0$.

Consider the case that there is only one regressor ($g = 1$), which is measured with error. Then $\Sigma_X > \Sigma_\Xi > 0$ are scalars and $\kappa/\beta = \Sigma_X^{-1}\Sigma_\Xi\beta/\beta$ is a number between 0 and 1. So asymptotically the regression coefficient estimate is biased towards zero. This phenomenon is called *attenuation*. The size of the effect of the regressor on the dependent variable is underestimated.

In the multiple regression case the characterization of the attenuation is slightly more complicated. The inequality $\Sigma_\Xi - \Sigma_\Xi\Sigma_X^{-1}\Sigma_\Xi \geq 0$ and (8.4) together imply

$$\beta'\Sigma_\Xi\beta \geq \kappa'\Sigma_X\kappa \tag{8.6}$$

or, using $\Sigma_X\kappa = \Sigma_\Xi\beta$, $(\beta - \kappa)'\Sigma_X\kappa \geq 0$. This generalizes $\beta - \kappa \geq 0$ for the case $g = 1$ (assuming $\kappa > 0$). So, given β, κ is located in the half space bounded by the hyperplane $\beta'c = \kappa'c$ that includes the origin, where $c \equiv \Sigma_\Xi\beta = \Sigma_X\kappa$, which is a hyperplane through β perpendicular to c. It is, however, possible that κ is farther from the origin than β.

The term $\beta'\Sigma_\Xi\beta$ in (8.6) is the variance of the systematic part of the regression. The term $\kappa'\Sigma_X\kappa$ is its estimate if measurement error is neglected. Thus the variance of the systematic part is underestimated. This also has a direct bearing on the properties of $R^2 \equiv (b'S_Xb)/\frac{1}{N}y'y$. This statistic converges to ρ^2, where

$$\rho^2 \equiv \frac{\kappa'\Sigma_X\kappa}{\sigma_\varepsilon^2 + \beta'\Sigma_\Xi\beta} \leq \frac{\beta'\Sigma_\Xi\beta}{\sigma_\varepsilon^2 + \beta'\Sigma_\Xi\beta},$$

and the right-hand side is the "true" R^2. So the explanatory power of the model is underestimated.

When there is more than one regressor, but only one is measured with error, generally the estimators of all regression coefficients are biased. The coefficient of the error-ridden regressor (the first one, say) is biased towards zero, and the sign of the biases of the other parameters can be estimated consistently. Let e_i denote the ith unit vector, $\beta_1 = e_1'\beta$ (assumed positive), and $\psi \equiv e_1'\Omega e_1 > 0$, then the bias of the ith element of the estimator of β is $e_i'(\kappa - \beta) = -e_i'\Sigma_X^{-1}\Omega\beta = -\psi\beta_1 \cdot e_i'\Sigma_X^{-1}e_1$. Thus, the first regression coefficient is underestimated whereas the signs of the biases in the other coefficients depend on the sign of the elements of the first column of Σ_X^{-1}. Even when Ω is unknown, these signs can be consistently estimated from the signs of the corresponding elements of S_X^{-1}.

2.2 Bounds on the parameters

Let us return to the bivariate regression model (no intercept, all variables having mean zero), written in scalar notation:

$$y_n = \beta \xi_n + \varepsilon_n \tag{8.7a}$$

$$x_n = \xi_n + v_n, \tag{8.7b}$$

where n denotes a typical element and the other notation is obvious. Assume for simplicity that $\beta > 0$ (the case with $\beta < 0$ is similar). OLS yields

$$\plim_{N \to \infty} (x'x)^{-1}x'y = \beta(1 - \sigma_v^2/\sigma_x^2) = \kappa < \beta, \tag{8.8}$$

the well known bias towards zero. But it also holds that

$$\plim_{N \to \infty} (x'y)^{-1}y'y = \beta + \frac{\sigma_\varepsilon^2}{\beta \sigma_\xi^2} > \beta. \tag{8.9}$$

The left-hand side of (8.9) is the probability limit of the inverse of the coefficient of the regression of x on y (the "reverse regression"). This regression also gives an inconsistent estimator of β, but with a bias away from zero. Thus, (8.8) and (8.9) bound the true β from below and above, respectively. Since these bounds can be estimated consistently, by the regression and the reverse regression, we can take $(x'x)^{-1}x'y$ and $(x'y)^{-1}y'y$ as bounds between which β should lie in the limit. The bounds are obtained without making assumptions about the size of the measurement error.

These results on bounds without additional information carry over to the multiple regression case to a certain limited extent only: β lies anywhere in the convex hull of the elementary regression vectors if these are all positive, where the $g + 1$ *elementary* regression vectors are defined as the regression vectors of each of the $g + 1$ variables on the g other variables (scaled properly). This condition can be formulated slightly more generally by saying that it suffices that all regression vectors are in the same orthant since by changing signs of variables this can simply be translated into the previous condition (see Bekker, Wansbeek, and Kapteyn, 1985, for a discussion).

Reverse regression has drawn much attention in the context of the analysis of discrimination; see, e.g., Goldberger (1984a, 1984b). In its simplest form, the model is an extension of (8.7):

$$y_n = \beta \xi_n + \alpha d_n + \varepsilon_n$$

$$x_n = \xi_n + v_n,$$

$$\xi_n = \mu d_n + \zeta_n,$$

where y_n is wage, d_n is a dummy indicating race or gender, and ξ_n is productivity. This variable can only be measured imperfectly through the indicator x_n. The last equation in this model reflects the different average level of productivity between race or gender groups. The crucial parameter is α, since a nonzero value (i.e. a wage differential even after controlling for productivity) may be interpreted as a sign of discrimination. Regressing y on x and d can be shown to give an overestimate of α. Reverse regression, i.e. regressing x on y and d, is a useful technique here, since it can be shown to give an underestimate of α. The primary research question then is whether the two estimates have the same sign.

3   Solutions to the Measurement Error Problem

In Section 2, it was shown that in the linear regression model with measurement errors, the OLS estimators are biased and inconsistent. There is no "quick fix" since the inconsistency is due to an identification problem. Essentially, identification is equivalent to the existence of a consistent estimator; see Bekker, Merckens, and Wansbeek (1994, p. 18), and in a generic case the measurement error model given by (8.1) and (8.2) is not identified if all random variables are jointly normally distributed or attention is confined to the first and second order moments of the observed variables only.

Let the elements of ε and the rows of V be iid normal. We consider first the case of a structural model. Then, according to Bekker (1986), β is identified if and only if there does not exist a nonsingular matrix $A = (a_1, A_2)$ such that $\xi'a_1$ is distributed normally and independently of $\xi'A_2$, where ξ' is a typical row of Ξ. In particular, this implies that if ξ is normally distributed, β is not identified. Due to a result by Wald (1940) this result applies in the functional case as well (cf. Aigner *et al.*, 1984, p. 1335). This means that, when searching for consistent estimators, additional information, instruments, nonnormality, or additional structure (typically through panel data) are desirable. In this section we consider these cases in turn. In a Bayesian context, incidentally, the outlook is different and inference on β is possible without identifying information, see, e.g., Poirier (1998).

3.1   Restrictions on the parameters

Equations (8.4) and (8.5) show that the inconsistency of b and s_ε^2 could be removed if Ω were known. For example, rather than b we would take $(I_g - S_X^{-1}\Omega)^{-1}b$ as an estimator of β, and from (8.4) it is clear this estimator is consistent. In general, Ω is unknown. If, however, we have a consistent estimator of Ω, we can replace Ω by its consistent estimate and obtain an estimator of β that by virtue of Slutsky's theorem is consistent. The resulting statistic is then a least squares estimator that is adjusted to attain consistency.

As a generalization, assume that a system of just identifying restrictions on the unknown parameters β, σ_ε^2, and Ω is available:

$$F(\beta, \sigma_\varepsilon^2, \Omega) = 0, \qquad (8.10)$$

with F a totally differentiable vector-function of order g^2. In view of the symmetry of Ω, $\frac{1}{2}g(g-1)$ of the restrictions in (8.10) are of the form $\Omega_{ij} - \Omega_{ji} = 0$.

If we combine the sample information with the prior information and add hats to indicate estimators we obtain the following system of equations:

$$(I_g - S_X^{-1}\hat{\Omega})\hat{\beta} - b = 0, \tag{8.11a}$$

$$\hat{\sigma}_\varepsilon^2 + \hat{\beta}'\hat{\Omega}b - s_\varepsilon^2 = 0, \tag{8.11b}$$

$$F(\hat{\beta}, \hat{\sigma}_\varepsilon^2, \hat{\Omega}) = 0. \tag{8.11c}$$

When F is such that this system admits a unique solution for $\hat{\beta}$, $\hat{\sigma}_\varepsilon^2$, and $\hat{\Omega}$, this solution will be a consistent estimator of β, σ_ε^2, and Ω since, asymptotically, S_X tends to Σ_X and the system then represents the relationship between the true parameters on the one hand and plim b and plim s_ε^2 on the other. This solution is called the *consistent adjusted least squares* (CALS) estimator (Kapteyn and Wansbeek, 1984).

The CALS estimator is easy to implement. One can use a standard regression program to obtain b and s_ε^2 and then employ a computer program for the solution of a system of nonlinear equations. In many cases it will be possible to find an explicit solution for (8.11), which then obviates the necessity of using a computer program for the solution of nonlinear equations.

It can be shown that, in both the structural model and the functional model, the CALS estimator has asymptotic distribution

$$\sqrt{N}(\hat{\theta}_{\text{CALS}} - \theta) \xrightarrow{\mathcal{L}} \mathcal{N}(0, H_\theta^{-1}H_\delta \Delta H_\delta'(H_\theta^{-1})'),$$

where $\theta = (\beta', \sigma_\varepsilon^2, (\text{vec }\Omega)')'$ and $\hat{\theta}_{\text{CALS}}$ is the CALS estimator of θ,

$$H_\theta \equiv \begin{bmatrix} \Sigma_X^{-1}\Sigma_\Xi & 0 & -\beta' \otimes \Sigma_X^{-1} \\ \kappa'\Omega & 1 & \kappa' \otimes \beta' \\ \dfrac{\partial F}{\partial \beta'} & \dfrac{\partial F}{\partial \sigma_\varepsilon^2} & \dfrac{\partial F}{\partial(\text{vec }\Omega)'} \end{bmatrix}$$

$$H_\delta \equiv \begin{bmatrix} -I_g & 0 & (\beta'\Omega \otimes I_g)(\Sigma_X^{-1} \otimes \Sigma_X^{-1})Q_g \\ \beta'\Omega & -1 & 0 \\ 0 & 0 & 0 \end{bmatrix}$$

$$\Delta \equiv \begin{bmatrix} \gamma\Sigma_X^{-1} & 0 & 0 \\ 0 & 2\gamma^2 & 0 \\ 0 & 0 & 2Q_g(\Sigma_X \otimes \Sigma_X) \end{bmatrix},$$

and $Q_g \equiv \frac{1}{2}(I_{g^2} + P_g)$, where P_g is the *commutation matrix* (Wansbeek, 1989).

Let us now consider the case in which inexact information on the measurement error variances is available of the following form:

$$0 \leq \Omega \leq \Omega^* \leq \Sigma_X,$$

with Ω^* given. The motivation behind such a bound is that researchers who have reason to suppose that measurement error is present may not know the actual size of its variance but may have an idea of an upper bound to that variance. This makes it possible to derive a bound on β that can be consistently estimated. If $\Omega > 0$, i.e. there is measurement error in all variables, β should satisfy the inequality

$$(\beta - \tfrac{1}{2}(\kappa + \kappa^*))'\Sigma_X(\Omega^{*-1} - \Sigma_X^{-1})\Sigma_X(\beta - \tfrac{1}{2}(\kappa + \kappa^*)) \leq \tfrac{1}{4}(\kappa^* - \kappa)'\Sigma_X\kappa,$$

where $\kappa^* \equiv (\Sigma_X - \Omega^*)^{-1}\Sigma_X\kappa$ is the probability limit of the estimator under the assumption that $\Omega = \Omega^*$. This is an ellipsoid with midpoint $\tfrac{1}{2}(\kappa + \kappa^*)$, passing through κ and κ^* and tangent to the hyperplane $\kappa'\Sigma_X(\beta - \kappa) = 0$. If Ω is singular (some variables are measured without error), a similar but more complicated inequality can be derived, see Bekker, Kapteyn, and Wansbeek (1984, 1987). In practical cases such ellipsoid bounds will be hard to use and bounds on the elements of β separately will be of more interest. Let a be an arbitrary g-vector. The ellipsoid bound implies for the linear combination $a'\beta$ that

$$\tfrac{1}{2}a'(\kappa + \kappa^*) - \tfrac{1}{2}\sqrt{c} \leq a'\beta \leq \tfrac{1}{2}a'(\kappa + \kappa^*) + \tfrac{1}{2}\sqrt{c},$$

with $c \equiv (\kappa^* - \kappa)'\Sigma_X\kappa \cdot a'F^*a$ and $F^* \equiv (\Sigma_X - \Omega^*)^{-1} - \Sigma_X^{-1}$. Bounds on separate elements of β are obtained when a is set equal to any of the g unit vectors. Erickson (1993) derived similar results by bounding the error *correlation* matrix, rather than the error covariance matrix. Bounds on quantities that are not identified are not often considered in econometrics and run against conventional wisdom. Yet, their usefulness has been recently advocated in the monograph by Manski (1995).

3.2   Instrumental variables

To introduce the notion of instrumental variables, we start from (8.3): $y = X\beta + u$, where consistent estimation was hampered by the correlation between X and u. If there are observations on variables, collected in Z, say, that correlate with the variables measured in X but do not correlate with u we have that the last term in $Z'y/N = (Z'X/N)\beta + Z'u/N$ vanishes asymptotically and hence may lead to consistent estimation of β. This is the idea behind *instrumental variables* (IV) estimation, Z being the matrix of instrumental variables. Of all the methods used to obtain consistent estimators in models with measurement error or with endogenous regressors in general, this is undisputably the most popular one.

If Z is of the same order as X and $Z'X/N$ converges to a finite, nonsingular matrix, the IV estimator b_{IV} of β, defined as

$$b_{IV} \equiv (Z'X)^{-1}Z'y, \tag{8.12}$$

is consistent. When Z has $h > g$ columns, the IV estimator is

$$b_{IV} = (X'P_Z X)^{-1}X'P_Z y,$$

where $P_Z \equiv Z(Z'Z)^{-1}Z'$. For $h = g$ this reduces to (8.12). Letting $\hat{X} \equiv P_Z X$, we have alternatively $b_{IV} = (\hat{X}'\hat{X})^{-1}\hat{X}'y$, so it can be computed by OLS after transforming X, which comes down to computing the predicted value of X after regressing each of its columns on Z. Therefore, b_{IV} is also called the two-stage least squares (2SLS) estimator.

Under some standard regularity conditions, b_{IV} is asymptotically normally distributed (Bowden and Turkington, 1984, p. 26):

$$\sqrt{N}(b_{IV} - \beta) \xrightarrow{\mathcal{L}} \mathcal{N}(0, \sigma_u^2(\Sigma_{ZX}'\Sigma_{ZZ}^{-1}\Sigma_{ZX})^{-1}),$$

where $\sigma_u^2 \equiv \sigma_\varepsilon^2 + \beta'\Omega\beta$, $\Sigma_{ZX} \equiv \text{plim}_{N\to\infty} Z'X/N$, and $\Sigma_{ZZ} \equiv \text{plim}_{N\to\infty} Z'Z/N$. The asymptotic covariance matrix can be consistently estimated by inserting $Z'X/N$ for Σ_{ZX}, $Z'Z/N$ for Σ_{ZZ}, and the consistent estimator $\hat{\sigma}_u^2 = (y - Xb_{IV})'(y - Xb_{IV})/N$ for σ_u^2. The residual variance σ_ε^2 can be consistently estimated by $\hat{\sigma}_\varepsilon^2 = y'(y - Xb_{IV})/N$, which differs from $\hat{\sigma}_u^2$ because, in contrast to the OLS case, the residuals $y - Xb_{IV}$ are not perpendicular to X. The matrix Ω cannot be estimated consistently unless additional assumptions are made. For example, if it is assumed that Ω is diagonal, a consistent estimator of Ω can be obtained.

The availability of instrumental variables is not only useful for consistent estimation in the presence of measurement error, it can also offer the scope for testing whether measurement error is present. An obvious testing strategy is to compare b from OLS with b_{IV} and to see whether they differ significantly. Under the null hypothesis of no measurement error, the difference between the two will be purely random, but since they have different probability limits under the alternative hypothesis, a significant difference might be indicative of measurement error.

If normality of the disturbance term u is assumed, a test statistic for the null hypothesis of no measurement error is (Bowden and Turkington, 1984, p. 51)

$$\frac{q/g}{(q^* - q)/(N - 2g)},$$

assuming X and Z do not share columns, where

$$q = (b - b_{IV})'((X'P_Z X)^{-1} - (X'X)^{-1})^{-1}(b - b_{IV})$$
$$q^* = (y - Xb)'(y - Xb)$$

and b is the OLS estimator $(X'X)^{-1}X'y$. Under the null hypothesis, this test statistic follows an F-distribution with g and $N - 2g$ degrees of freedom. If the disturbances are not assumed to be normally distributed, a test statistic for no measurement error is $q/\hat{\sigma}_u^2$, which under the null hypothesis converges in distribution to a chi-square variate with g degrees of freedom (Bowden and Turkington, 1984, p. 51).

Most of the above discussion has been asymptotic. It appears that in finite samples, instrumental variables estimators do not possess the desirable properties they have asymptotically, especially when the instruments correlate only weakly with the regressors (e.g. Nelson and Startz, 1990a, 1990b; Bound, Jaeger, and Baker, 1995; Staiger and Stock, 1997). This happens often in practice, because good instruments are frequently hard to find. Consider, for example, household income. If that is measured with error, typical instruments may be years of schooling or age of the head of the household. While these are obviously correlated with income, the relation will generally be relatively weak. Bekker (1994) proposed an alternative estimator that has better small sample properties than the standard IV estimator. His method of moments (MM) estimator is a generalization of the well known LIML estimator for simultaneous equations models. Its formula is given by

$$b_{MM} \equiv (X'P_Z^* X)^{-1} X'P_Z^* y, \tag{8.13}$$

where $P_Z^* \equiv P_Z + \lambda_{MM}(I_N - P_Z)$ and λ_{MM} is the smallest solution λ of the generalized eigenvalue equation

$$(\bar{S} - \lambda S^\perp) \begin{bmatrix} 1 \\ -\beta \end{bmatrix} = 0, \tag{8.14}$$

where $\bar{S} \equiv (y, X)'P_Z(y, X)$ and $S^\perp \equiv (y, X)'(I_N - P_Z)(y, X)$. Equivalently, λ_{MM} is the minimum of

$$\lambda \equiv \frac{(y - X\beta)'P_Z(y - X\beta)}{(y - X\beta)'(I_N - P_Z)(y - X\beta)}. \tag{8.15}$$

The solution vector β in (8.14) or (8.15) is equivalent to the estimator b_{MM} in (8.13). Under the usual assumptions of $N \to \infty$ and g constant, $\lambda_{MM} \to 0$ and, consequently, $P_Z^* \to P_Z$ and the IV estimator and MM estimator are asymptotically equivalent. In finite samples, however, MM performs better than IV.

Other proposals for alternative estimators that should have better small sample properties than standard IV estimators can, for example, be found in Alonso-Borrego and Arellano (1999) and Angrist, Imbens, and Krueger (1999).

3.3   Nonnormality

Consider the bivariate regression model with measurement errors (8.7). Further, assume that $\phi_3 \equiv E(\xi_n^3) \neq 0$ and that ξ_n, ε_n, and v_n are independently distributed (similar assumptions can be formulated for the functional model). Now,

$$\plim_{N\to\infty}\left(\frac{1}{N}\sum_{n=1}^{N}y_n^2x_n\middle/\frac{1}{N}\sum_{n=1}^{N}y_nx_n^2\right)=\frac{\beta^2\phi_3}{\beta\phi_3}=\beta. \tag{8.16}$$

This illustrates that nonnormality may be exploited to obtain consistent estimators. It was first shown by Reiersøl (1950) that the model is identified under nonnormality. The precise condition, as stated at the beginning of Section 3, was derived by Bekker (1986).

There are many ways in which nonnormality can be used to obtain a consistent estimator of β. The estimator (8.16) will generally not be efficient and its small sample properties are usually not very good. Asymptotically more efficient estimators may be obtained by combining the equations for the covariances and several higher order moments and then using a nonlinear GLS procedure (see Section 4). If $E(\xi_n^3) = 0$, the third order moments do not give information about β and fourth order or higher order moments may be used. An extensive discussion of the ways in which higher order moments can be used to obtain consistent estimators of β is given by Van Montfort, Mooijaart, and De Leeuw (1987).

3.4   Panel data

Panel data are repeated measurements over time for a set of cross-sectional units (e.g. households, firms, regions). The additional time dimension allows for consistent estimation when there is measurement error. As a start, consider the simple case with a single regressor and consider the impact of measurement error. For a typical observation indexed by n, $n = 1, \ldots, N$, the model is

$$y_n = \xi_n\beta + \iota_T \cdot \alpha_n + \varepsilon_n$$
$$x_n = \xi_n + v_n,$$

where y_n, ξ_n, ε_n, and v_n are vectors of length T and T is the number of observed time points; ξ_n, ε_n, and v_n are mutually independent, and their distributions are independent of α_n, which is the so-called individual effect, a time-constant latent characteristic (fixed or random) of the cross-sectional units commonly included in a panel data model; see, e.g., Baltagi (1995) for an overview. The vector ι_T is a T-vector of ones. The random vectors ξ_n, ε_n and v_n are iid with zero expectation and variances $E(\xi_n\xi_n') = \Sigma_\xi$, $E(\varepsilon_n\varepsilon_n') = \sigma_\varepsilon^2 I_T$, and $E(v_nv_n') = \Sigma_v$, respectively. Consequently, $E(x_nx_n') \equiv \Sigma_x = \Sigma_\xi + \Sigma_v$. Eliminating ξ_n gives $y_n = x_n\beta + \iota_T \cdot \alpha_n + u_n$, where $u_n \equiv \varepsilon_n - v_n\beta$.

Let Q be a symmetric $T \times T$-matrix which is as yet unspecified apart from the property $Q\iota_T = 0$, so that Qy_n does not contain the individual effect α_n anymore. We consider estimators of β of the form

$$\hat\beta = \frac{\sum_n x_n'Qy_n}{\sum_n x_n'Qx_n}. \tag{8.17}$$

This general formulation includes the so-called within-estimator when $Q = I_T - \iota_T \iota_T'/T$ is the centering operator and the first-difference estimator when $Q = RR'$, where R' is the matrix taking first differences. Now,

$$\plim_{N \to \infty} \hat{\beta} = \beta - \beta \frac{\operatorname{tr} Q\Sigma_v}{\operatorname{tr} Q\Sigma_x}.$$

Again we have an estimator that is asymptotically biased towards zero. Whatever the precise structure of Σ_v and Σ_x, it seems reasonable to assume that the true regressor values ξ will be much stronger correlated over time than the measurement errors v. Therefore, x will also have a stronger correlation over time. Hence the variance matrix Σ_x will be more reduced than Σ_v by eliminating the means over time by the Q matrix and the bias of the estimator (8.17) will be worse than the bias of the OLS estimator.

The main virtue of the panel data structure is, however, that in some cases, several of these estimators (with different Q matrices) can be combined into a consistent estimator. The basic results on measurement error in panel data are due to Griliches and Hausman (1986); see also Wansbeek and Koning (1991). Further elaboration for a variety of cases is given by Biørn (1992a, 1992b).

4　LATENT VARIABLE MODELS

Consider again the bivariate measurement error model (8.7), where the unobservable random variables ξ_n, ε_n, and v_n are assumed to be mutually independent with expectation zero. The variables y_n and x_n are observable. Now let us assume that there is a third observable variable, z_n, say, that is linearly related to ξ_n in the same way as y_n is:

$$z_n = \gamma \xi_n + u_n, \tag{8.18}$$

where u_n is independent of ξ_n, ε_n, and v_n, and has also mean zero. From this extended model, we obtain the following equations for the variances and covariances of the observable variables (the "covariance" equations):

$$\sigma_y^2 = \sigma_\xi^2 \beta^2 + \sigma_\varepsilon^2 \quad \sigma_{yx} = \sigma_\xi^2 \beta \quad\quad \sigma_{yz} = \sigma_\xi^2 \beta\gamma$$
$$\sigma_x^2 = \sigma_\xi^2 + \sigma_v^2 \quad \sigma_{xz} = \sigma_\xi^2 \gamma$$
$$\sigma_z^2 = \sigma_\xi^2 \gamma^2 + \sigma_u^2.$$

This system of six equations in six unknown parameters can be solved uniquely for the unknown parameters. Since the left-hand variables are consistently estimated by their sample counterparts consistent estimators for the parameters follow immediately. For example, the estimator of β is $\hat{\beta} = \hat{\sigma}_{yz}/\hat{\sigma}_{xz} = y'z/x'z$, which is equivalent to the IV estimator with z as instrumental variable.

4.1　Factor analysis

A generalization of the model discussed above is the *factor analysis* model. It is written, in a somewhat different notation, as

$$y_n = \Lambda \xi_n + \varepsilon_n,$$

where ξ_n is a vector of (common) *factors*, y_n is a vector of M *indicators* of these factors, Λ is an $M \times k$ matrix of *factor loadings*, and ε_n is a vector of M errors. It is assumed that $E(\xi_n) = 0$, $E(\xi_n \xi_n') \equiv \Phi$, $E(\varepsilon_n) = 0$, $\Psi \equiv E(\varepsilon_n \varepsilon_n')$ is diagonal, and $E(\xi_n \varepsilon_n') = 0$. Under this model, the covariance matrix of the observations is

$$\Sigma \equiv E(y_n y_n') = \Lambda \Phi \Lambda' + \Psi.$$

The diagonality of Ψ implies that any correlation that may exist between different elements of y is solely due to the common factors ξ.

　　The unrestricted model is not identified, but frequently, identifying restrictions on the parameters are available from substantive theory. This is the case when an economic theory forms the base of the model and for every concept in that theory (e.g. productivity of a worker) several well-chosen variables are used that should reflect the concept in question as well as possible. In that case, the loadings of the indicators with respect to the factors (concepts) that they are supposed to reflect are free parameters, whereas the other loadings are fixed to zero. For a given set of restrictions (i.e. a given model), the program IDFAC of Bekker *et al.* (1994) can be used to check whether the model is identified.

4.2　MIMIC and reduced rank regression

Above, we considered elaborations of equation (8.18), which offered additional information about the otherwise unidentified parameters in the form of an additional indicator. The latent variable appeared once more as the exogenous variable in yet another regression equation. Another way in which additional information may be available is in the form of a regression equation with the latent variable as the endogenous variable:

$$\xi_n = w_n' \alpha + u_n, \qquad (8.19)$$

where w_n is an l-vector of observable variables that "cause" ξ, α is an l-vector of regression coefficients and u_n is an iid disturbance term with mean zero and variance σ_u^2. Note that in this case, w_n can also be used as a vector of instrumental variables.

　　We now show that an additional relation of the form (8.19) can help identification. To that end, it is convenient to write the model in matrix format. For (8.19) this gives $\xi = W\alpha + u$ and for the factor analysis structure $Y = \xi \lambda' + E$ in self-evident notation. The model consisting of these two elements is known as the *multiple indicators-multiple causes* (MIMIC) model (Jöreskog and Goldberger, 1975) and relates a number of exogenous variables (causes) to a number of endogenous variables (indicators) through a single latent variable. In reduced form, it is

$$Y = W\alpha\lambda' + (E + u\lambda').$$

This multivariate regression system has two kinds of restriction on its parameters. First, the matrix of regression coefficients $\alpha\lambda'$, which is of order $l \times M$, has rank one. Second, the disturbance vector has a covariance matrix of the form $\Sigma \equiv \Psi + \sigma_u^2\lambda\lambda'$, with Ψ diagonal, which is a one-factor FA structure. One normalization on the parameters α, λ, and σ_u^2 is required since, for any $c > 0$, multiplying α by c, dividing λ by c and multiplying σ_u^2 by c^2 has no observable implications. Under this normalization, the model is identified.

A frequently used generalization of the MIMIC model is the *reduced rank regression* (RRR) model. It extends MIMIC in two ways. First, the rank of the coefficient matrix can be larger than one, and the error covariance matrix need not be structured. Then

$$Y = WA\Lambda' + F,$$

where A and Λ are $l \times r$ and $M \times r$ matrices, respectively, both of full column rank $r < \min(M, l)$, and F has iid rows with expectation zero and unrestricted covariance matrix Ψ. See, e.g., Cragg and Donald (1997), for tests of the rank r of the matrix of regression coefficients. Bekker, Dobbelstein, and Wansbeek (1996) showed that the *arbitrage pricing theory* model can be written as an RRR model with rank one. In its general form, A and Λ are not identified, because $A^*\Lambda^{*'} \equiv (AT)(T^{-1}\Lambda') = A\Lambda'$ for every nonsingular $r \times r$ matrix T. In some cases, the identification problem may be resolved by using restrictions derived from substantive theory, whereas in others an arbitrary normalization can be used. Ten Berge (1993, section 4.6) and Reinsel and Velu (1998) give an extensive discussion of the reduced rank regression model and its relations to other multivariate statistical methods.

4.3   General linear structural equation models

Up till now, we have discussed several models that specify linear relations among observed and/or latent variables. Such models are called (linear) *structural equation models*. A general formulation of structural equation models can be given by the following equations.

$$x_n = \Lambda_x\xi_n + \delta_n \tag{8.20a}$$

$$y_n = \Lambda_y\eta_n + \varepsilon_n, \tag{8.20b}$$

$$\eta_n = B\eta_n + \Gamma\xi_n + \zeta_n, \tag{8.20c}$$

where η_n is a vector of latent endogenous variables for subject n, ξ_n is a vector of latent exogenous variables for subject n, ζ_n is a vector of random residuals, B and Γ are matrices of regression coefficients, Λ_x and Λ_y are matrices of factor loadings, and δ_n and ε_n are vectors of errors. The random vectors δ_n, ε_n, ζ_n, and ξ_n are assumed mutually independent. The formulation (8.20) is known as the LISREL model, named after the widely used LISREL program in which it was implemented (Jöreskog and Sörbom, 1996) and consists of a simultaneous equations system in latent endogenous and exogenous variables (8.20c), where (8.20a) and (8.20b) relate the latent variables to observable variables through an FA structure. The theory of structural equation modeling is discussed by Bollen (1989) and Hoyle (1995), which also contains some applications and practicalities. An overview with more recent topics is given by Bentler and Dudgeon (1996).

It turns out that it is possible to write a large number of models as submodels of this model. Examples of submodels are standard linear regression models, simultaneous equations linear regression models, linear regression models with measurement errors, MANOVA, factor analysis, MIMIC. The general model is, of course, highly underidentified. In practice, many restrictions are imposed on the parameters, for example many loadings and regression coefficients are fixed to zero, the scales of the latent variables are fixed by setting a factor loading or a variance parameter to one. The advantage of the general formulation is that all restricted models can be easily estimated by the same computer program and that theoretical properties of estimators can be derived for a large class of models at the same time. For a given set of restrictions (i.e. a given model), the identification of the model can be checked by the program IDLIS (Bekker *et al.*, 1994). For the important special case of simultaneous equations with measurement error (i.e. x_n and ξ_n of the same order, $\Lambda_x = I$, and analogously for y_n, η_n, and Λ_y), identification conditions are given by Merckens and Bekker (1993) and estimation is discussed by Wooldridge (1996).

The most well known software packages for structural equation modeling are LISREL, including the preprocessor PRELIS (Jöreskog and Sörbom, 1996), EQS (Bentler, 1995), AMOS (Arbuckle, 1997), and SAS/CALIS. A new software package, which can also estimate latent class models, is M*plus* (Muthén and Muthén, 1998).

ESTIMATION

If a specific distribution of the observed variables is assumed, typically the normal distribution, the model can be estimated with maximum likelihood (ML). An alternative estimation method is (nonlinear) generalized least squares (GLS). Assume that we have a vector of sample statistics s_N, which usually consists of the diagonal and subdiagonal elements of the sample covariance matrix S_N of $z_n \equiv (x_n', y_n')'$. Further, assume that

$$\sqrt{N}(s_N - \sigma(\theta)) \overset{d}{\to} \mathcal{N}(0, \Upsilon),$$

where the vector $\sigma(\theta) = \text{plim } s_N$ and θ is the vector of free parameters. This assumption is usually satisfied under very mild regularity conditions. The estimator is obtained by minimizing the function

$$F(\theta) = (s_N - \sigma(\theta))'W(s_N - \sigma(\theta)), \tag{8.21}$$

where W is a symmetric positive definite matrix. If plim $W^{-1} = Y$, W is optimal in the sense that the estimator has the smallest asymptotic covariance matrix in the Löwner sense.

If s_N consists of the nonduplicated elements of the sample covariance matrix, the elements of the matrix Y are given by the formula $Y_{ij,kl} = \sigma_{ijkl} - \sigma_{ij}\sigma_{kl}$, where $Y_{ij,kl}$ is the asymptotic covariance between the (i, j)th and (k, l)th elements of $\sqrt{N}s_N$, $\sigma_{ijkl} \equiv E(z_{ni}z_{nj}z_{nk}z_{nl})$ and $\sigma_{ij} \equiv E(z_{ni}z_{nj})$. An asymptotically optimal W is given by letting W^{-1} have elements $s_{ijkl} - s_{ij}s_{kl}$. This estimator is called the *asymptotically distribution free* (ADF) estimator (Browne, 1984), denoted by $\hat{\theta}_{\text{ADF}}$ (although in EQS this is called AGLS and in LISREL it is called WLS). The asymptotic distribution of the ADF estimator is given by

$$\sqrt{N}(\hat{\theta} - \theta) \xrightarrow{L} \mathcal{N}(0, (\Delta'Y^{-1}\Delta)^{-1}),$$

where $\Delta \equiv \partial\sigma/\partial\theta'$, evaluated in the true value of θ. The asymptotic covariance matrix can be consistently estimated by evaluating Δ in $\hat{\theta}$ and inserting W for Y^{-1}. Note that ADF, as well as all estimators discussed before, are all special cases of *generalized method of moments* (GMM) estimators, see Hall (2001).

Model fit

If a structural equation model has been estimated, it is important to assess the *fit* of the model, i.e. whether the model and the data agree. Many statistics have been proposed for assessing model fit. Most of these are functions of $\hat{F} = F(\hat{\theta})$, where F denotes the function (8.21) that is minimized. In this section, it is assumed that plim $W^{-1} = Y$. The statistic most frequently used is the *chi-square statistic* $\chi^2 \equiv N\hat{F}$, which is a formal test statistic for the null hypothesis that the model is correct in the population against the alternative hypothesis that the model is not correct in the population. Under the null hypothesis, this test statistic converges to a chi-square variate with df $\equiv p^* - q$ degrees of freedom, where p^* is the number of elements of $\sigma(\theta)$ and q is the number of elements of θ.

In practice, however, models are obviously rarely entirely correct in the population. For the GLS estimators, $\hat{F}$ converges to $F_+ = (\sigma_+ - \sigma(\theta_+))'Y^{-1}(\sigma_+ - \sigma(\theta_+))$ for some θ_+, where $\sigma_+ = $ plim s_N. If the model is correct in the population, $\sigma_+ = \sigma(\theta_+)$ and $F_+ = 0$. If the model is not entirely correct in the population, $\sigma_+ \neq \sigma(\theta_+)$ and $F_+ > 0$. Hence, $\chi^2 \to NF_+ \to +\infty$. This illustrates the empirical finding that for large sample sizes, nonsaturated models (i.e. models with df > 0) tend to be rejected, although they may describe the data very well. Therefore, alternative measures of fit have been developed. The quality of the model may be defined by the quantity

$$\frac{F_0 - F_1}{F_0}, \tag{8.22}$$

where F_0 is defined similar to F_+, but for a highly restrictive baseline model or *null model* and F_1 is F_+ for the *target model*. It is customary to use the independence model, in which all variables are assumed to be independently distributed, as the null model. Clearly, (8.22) is very similar to R^2. It is always between zero and one, higher values indicating better fit. It may be estimated by the (Bentler–Bonett) *normed fit index* $\text{NFI} = (\hat{F}_0 - \hat{F}_1)/\hat{F}_0$. The NFI has been widely used since its introduction by Bentler and Bonett (1980).

However, simulation studies and theoretical derivations have shown that NFI is biased in finite samples and that its mean is generally an increasing function of N. By approximating the distribution of $N\hat{F}$ by a noncentral chi-square distribution, a better estimator of (8.22) has been derived. This is the *relative noncentrality index* (RNI)

$$\text{RNI} \equiv \frac{\hat{\delta}_0 - \hat{\delta}_1}{\hat{\delta}_0},$$

where $\hat{\delta}_i \equiv \hat{F}_i - \text{df}_i/N$ (McDonald and Marsh, 1990). A disadvantage of RNI is that it is not necessarily between zero and one, although usually it is. This disadvantage is overcome by the *comparative fit index* (CFI; Bentler, 1990), which is generally equal to the RNI, but if RNI > 1, CFI = 1, and if RNI < 0, CFI = 0, provided $\hat{\delta}_0 > 0$, which is usually the case.

Notes

* The authors would like to thank Anne Boomsma, Bart Boon, Jos ten Berge, Michel Wedel, and an anonymous referee for their helpful comments on an earlier version of this paper.
1 Strictly speaking, this violates the iid assumptions used in this chapter. It would be theoretically better to specify the model with nonzero means and intercepts. The practical consequences of this violation are, however, negligible, whereas the formulas are considerably less complicated. Therefore, in this chapter we ignore the resulting theoretical subtleties.

References

Aigner, D.J., C. Hsiao, A. Kapteyn, and T.J. Wansbeek (1984). Latent variable models in econometrics. In Z. Griliches and M.D. Intriligator (eds.) *Handbook of Econometrics, Volume 2.* pp. 1321–93. Amsterdam: North-Holland.

Alonso-Borrego, C., and M. Arellano (1999). Symmetrically normalized instrumental-variable estimation using panel data. *Journal of Business & Economic Statistics* 17, 36–49.

Angrist, J.D., G.W. Imbens, and A.B. Krueger (1999). Jackknife instrumental variables estimation. *Journal of Applied Econometrics* 14, 57–67.

Arbuckle, J.L. (1997). *Amos User's Guide. Version 3.6.* Chicago: Smallwaters.

Baltagi, B.H. (1995). *Econometric Analysis of Panel Data.* Chichester: Wiley.

Bekker, P.A. (1986). Comment on identification in the linear errors in variables model. *Econometrica* 54, 215–17.

Bekker, P.A. (1994). Alternative approximations to the distributions of instrumental variable estimators. *Econometrica* 62, 657–81.

Bekker, P.A., P. Dobbelstein, and T.J. Wansbeek (1996). The APT model as reduced rank regression. *Journal of Business & Economic Statistics* 14, 199–202.

Bekker, P.A., A. Kapteyn, and T.J. Wansbeek (1984). Measurement error and endogeneity in regression: bounds for ML and 2SLS estimates. In T.K. Dijkstra (ed.) *Misspecification Analysis*. pp. 85–103. Berlin: Springer.

Bekker, P.A., A. Kapteyn, and T.J. Wansbeek (1987). Consistent sets of estimates for regressions with correlated or uncorrelated measurement errors in arbitrary subsets of all variables. *Econometrica* 55, 1223–30.

Bekker, P.A., A. Merckens, and T.J. Wansbeek (1994). *Identification, Equivalent Models, and Computer Algebra*. Boston: Academic Press.

Bekker, P.A., T.J. Wansbeek, and A. Kapteyn (1985). Errors in variables in econometrics: New developments and recurrent themes. *Statistica Neerlandica* 39, 129–41.

Bentler, P.M. (1990). Comparative fit indexes in structural models. *Psychological Bulletin* 107, 238–46.

Bentler, P.M. (1995). *EQS Structural Equations Program Manual*. Encino, CA: Multivariate Software.

Bentler, P.M., and D.G. Bonett (1980). Significance tests and goodness of fit in the analysis of covariance structures. *Psychological Bulletin* 88, 588–606.

Bentler, P.M., and P. Dudgeon (1996). Covariance structure analysis: Statistical practice, theory, and directions. *Annual Review of Psychology* 47, 563–92.

Biørn, E. (1992a). The bias of some estimators for panel data models with measurement errors. *Empirical Economics* 17, 51–66.

Biørn, E. (1992b). Panel data with measurement errors. In L. Mátyás and P. Sevestre (eds.) *The Econometrics of Panel Data*. Dordrecht: Kluwer.

Bollen, K.A. (1989). *Structural Equations with Latent Variables*. New York: Wiley.

Bound, J., D.A. Jaeger, and R.M. Baker (1995). Problems with instrumental variables estimation when the correlation between the instruments and the endogenous explanatory variable is weak. *Journal of the American Statistical Association* 90, 443–50.

Bowden, R.J., and D.A. Turkington (1984). *Instrumental Variables*. Cambridge, UK: Cambridge University Press.

Browne, M.W. (1984). Asymptotically distribution-free methods for the analysis of covariance structures. *British Journal of Mathematical and Statistical Psychology* 37, 62–83.

Cheng, C.-L., and J.W. Van Ness (1999). *Statistical Regression with Measurement Error*. London: Arnold.

Cragg, J.G., and S.G. Donald (1997). Inferring the rank of a matrix. *Journal of Econometrics* 76, 223–50.

Erickson, T. (1993). Restricting regression slopes in the errors-in-variables model by bounding the error correlation. *Econometrica* 61, 959–69.

Fuller, W.A. (1987). *Measurement Error Models*. New York: Wiley.

Goldberger, A.S. (1984a). Redirecting reverse regression. *Journal of Business & Economic Statistics* 2, 114–16.

Goldberger, A.S. (1984b). Reverse regression and salary discrimination. *The Journal of Human Resources* 19, 293–319.

Griliches, Z. (1986). Economic data issues. In Z. Griliches and M.D. Intriligator (eds.) *Handbook of Econometrics, Volume 3*. Amsterdam: North-Holland.

Griliches, Z., and J.A. Hausman (1986). Errors in variables in panel data. *Journal of Econometrics* 32, 93–118.

Hall, A.R. (2001). Generalized method of moments. In B.H. Baltagi (ed.) *A Companion to Theoretical Econometrics*. Oxford: Blackwell Publishing. (this volume)

Hoyle, R. (ed.). (1995). *Structural Equation Modeling: Concepts, Issues, and Applications*. Thousand Oaks, CA: Sage.

Jöreskog, K.G., and A.S. Goldberger (1975). Estimation of a model with multiple indicators and multiple causes of a single latent variable. *Journal of the American Statistical Association* 70, 631–9.

Jöreskog, K.G., and D. Sörbom (1996). *LISREL 8 User's Reference Guide*. Chicago: Scientific Software International.

Kapteyn, A., and T.J. Wansbeek (1984). Errors in variables: Consistent Adjusted Least Squares (CALS) estimation. *Communications in Statistics – Theory and Methods* 13, 1811–37.

Manski, C.F. (1995). *Identification Problems in the Social Sciences*. Cambridge, MA: Harvard University Press.

McDonald, R.P., and H.W. Marsh (1990). Choosing a multivariate model: Noncentrality and goodness of fit. *Psychological Bulletin* 107, 247–55.

Merckens, A., and P.A. Bekker (1993). Identification of simultaneous equation models with measurement error: A computerized evaluation. *Statistica Neerlandica* 47, 233–44.

Muthén, B.O., and L.K. Muthén (1998). *Mplus User's Guide*. Los Angeles: Muthén & Muthén.

Nelson, C.R., and R. Startz (1990a). Some further results on the exact small sample properties of the instrumental variables estimator. *Econometrica* 58, 967–76.

Nelson, C.R., and R. Startz (1990b). The distribution of the instrumental variables estimator and its *t*-ratio when the instrument is a poor one. *Journal of Business* 63, 125–40.

Poirier, D.J. (1998). Revising beliefs in nonidentified models. *Econometric Theory* 14, 483–509.

Reiersøl, O. (1950). Identifiability of a linear relation between variables which are subject to error. *Econometrica* 18, 375–89.

Reinsel, G.C., and R.P. Velu (1998). *Multivariate Reduced Rank Regression: Theory and Applications*. New York: Springer.

Staiger, D., and J.H. Stock (1997). Instrumental variables regression with weak instruments. *Econometrica* 65, 557–86.

Ten Berge, J.M.F. (1993). *Least Squares Optimization in Multivariate Analysis*. Leiden, The Netherlands: DSWO Press.

Van Montfort, K., A. Mooijaart, and J. De Leeuw (1987). Regression with errors in variables: Estimators based on third order moments. *Statistica Neerlandica* 41, 223–39.

Wald, A. (1940). The fitting of straight lines if both variables are subject to error. *Annals of Mathematical Statistics* 11, 284–300.

Wansbeek, T.J. (1989). Permutation matrix – II. In S. Kotz and N.L. Johnson (eds.) *Encyclopedia of Statistical Sciences, Supplement Volume*. pp. 121–2. New York: Wiley.

Wansbeek, T.J., and R.H. Koning (1991). Measurement error and panel data. *Statistica Neerlandica* 45, 85–92.

Wooldridge, J.M. (1996). Estimating systems of equations with different instruments for different equations. *Journal of Econometrics* 74, 387–405.

CHAPTER NINE

Diagnostic Testing

Jeffrey M. Wooldridge*

1   INTRODUCTION

Diagnostic testing has become an integral part of model specification in econometrics, with several important advances over the past 20 years. Some of these advances involve new insights into older diagnostics, such as the Durbin–Watson (1950) statistic, Ramsey's (1969) regression error specification test (RESET), general Lagrange multiplier (LM) or score statistics, and White's (1982, 1994) information matrix (IM) test. Other advances have focused on the implicit alternatives of a diagnostic test (Davidson and MacKinnon, 1987) and the related topic of the robustness of diagnostic tests to auxiliary assumptions – that is, assumptions that are imposed under the null but which are not being tested (Wooldridge, 1990a, 1991a, 1991b).

How does diagnostic testing, which is also called *specification testing* (and sometimes *misspecification testing*), differ from classical testing? The difference is arguably a matter of perspective. In classical hypothesis testing we typically assume that we have, in an appropriate sense, a correctly specified parametric model. This could either be a model for a conditional mean, a conditional median, or a fully specified conditional distribution. We then use standard statistics, such as Wald, Lagrange multiplier, and likelihood (or quasi-likelihood) ratio statistics to test restrictions on the parameters.

With diagnostic testing our concern is with testing our maintained model for various misspecifications. We can do this by nesting the model within a more general model, testing it against a nonnested alternative, or using an omnibus test intended to detect a variety of misspecifications.

The purpose of this chapter is to develop diagnostic testing from a modern perspective, omitting some of the intricacies of large sample theory. Rather than considering a general, abstract setting and a unified approach to diagnostic testing – such as in Newey (1985), Tauchen (1985), Pagan and Vella (1989), Wooldridge (1990a), and White (1994) – I instead consider diagnostic testing in relatively simple settings that nevertheless arise often in applied work.

It is useful to organize our thinking on diagnostic testing before jumping into any analysis. The following questions arise, and, ideally, are answered, when devising and analyzing a diagnostic test:

1. What null hypothesis is the statistic intended to test?
2. What auxiliary assumptions are maintained under H_0? If an auxiliary assumption fails, does it cause the test to simply have the wrong null limiting distribution, or does the statistic reject with probability approaching one as the sample size grows?
3. Against which alternatives is the test consistent? (That is, against which alternatives does the test have unit asymptotic power?)
4. Against which local alternatives does the test have asymptotic power greater than asymptotic size?
5. Are unusual regularity conditions needed for the test to have a standard (i.e. normal or chi-square) limiting distribution under H_0?
6. In problems with a time dimension, what do we need to assume about stability and weak dependence of the time series processes? For example, when are unit roots allowed? How does the presence or absence of unit roots and cointegrating relationships affect the limiting distributions?

This chapter is broken down by the two most popular kinds of data sets used in econometrics. Section 2 covers cross section applications and Section 3 treats time series. Section 4 contains some concluding remarks, including a brief summary of some topics we did not discuss, some of which are fruitful areas for further research.

2 DIAGNOSTIC TESTING IN CROSS SECTION CONTEXTS

To obtain a unified view of diagnostic testing, it is important to use a modern perspective. This requires facility with concepts from basic probability, such as conditional expectations and conditional variances, and application of tools such as the law of iterated expectations. While sloppiness in stating assumptions is often innocuous, in some cases it is not. In the following sections we show how to properly state the null hypothesis for diagnostic testing in cross section applications.

2.1 Diagnostic tests for the conditional mean in the linear regression model

We begin with the standard linear regression model because it is still the workhorse in empirical economics, and because it provides the simplest setting for a modern approach to diagnostic testing. Even in this basic setup, we must be careful in stating assumptions. The following statement, or a slight variant on it, appears in numerous textbooks and research papers:

Consider the model

$$y_i = \beta_0 + x_i\beta + u_i, \quad i = 1, 2, \ldots, N, \tag{9.1}$$

where x_i is a $1 \times k$ vector of explanatory variables and the u_i are iid zero-mean errors.

This formulation may be so familiar that we do not even think to question it. Unfortunately, for econometric analysis, the statement of the model and assumptions is almost useless, as it omits the most important consideration: What is the relationship between the error, u_i, and the explanatory variables, x_i? If we assume random sampling, the errors *must* be independent and identically distributed because u_i is a function of y_i and x_i. But this tells us nothing of value for estimating β.

Often, the explanatory variables in (9.1) are assumed to be fixed or nonrandom. Then we can obtain an unbiased estimator of β because the model satisfies the Gauss–Markov assumptions. But assuming fixed regressors assumes away the interesting problems that arise with analyzing nonexperimental data.

What is a better model formulation? For most cross section applications it is best to start with a *population model*, which in the linear regression case is written as

$$y = \beta_0 + x\beta + u, \tag{9.2}$$

where $\mathbf{x}$ is a $1 \times k$ vector of explanatory variables and u is the error. If we supplement this model with random sampling – which, for econometric applications with cross section data, is more realistic than the fixed regressor assumption – we can forget about the realizations of the random variables in (9.2) and focus entirely on the assumptions in the population.

In order to consistently estimate β by OLS (ordinary least squares), we need to make assumptions about the relationship between u and x. There are several possibilities. The weakest useful assumptions are

$$E(u) = 0 \tag{9.3}$$

$$E(x'u) = 0, \tag{9.4}$$

where we assume throughout that all expectations are well-defined.

Assumption (9.3) is for free because we have included an intercept in the model. Assumption (9.4) is equivalent to assuming u is uncorrelated with each x_j. Under (9.3), (9.4), random sampling, and the assumption that var(x) has full rank – i.e. there is no perfect collinearity in the population – the OLS estimator is consistent and $\sqrt{N}$-asymptotically normal for β_0 and β.

As a minimal set of assumptions, (9.4) is fine. But it is not generally enough to interpret the β_j as the partial effect of x_j on the expected value of y. A stronger assumption is that u has a zero conditional mean:

$$E(u \mid x) = 0, \tag{9.5}$$

which implies that the population regression function, $E(y \mid x)$, is linear:

$$E(y \mid x) = \beta_0 + x\beta. \tag{9.6}$$

Under (9.6), no additional functions of x appear in a linear regression model. More formally, if for any $1 \times h$ function g(x) we write

$$y = \beta_0 + x\beta + g(x)\gamma + u,$$

and (9.5) holds, then $\gamma = 0$. Tests for functional form always maintain (9.6) as the null hypothesis. If we assume only (9.3) and (9.4), there is nothing to test: by definition, β_0 and β appear in the linear projection of y on x.

In testing for omitted variables, z, that are not exact functions of x, the null hypothesis in (9.2) is

$$E(u \mid x, z) = 0, \tag{9.7}$$

which is equivalent to

$$E(y \mid x, z) = E(y \mid x) = \beta_0 + x\beta. \tag{9.8}$$

The first equality in equation (9.8) has a very natural interpretation: once x has been controlled for, z has no effect on the mean value of y. The most common way to test (9.8) is to specify the extended model

$$y = \beta_0 + x\beta + z\gamma + u \tag{9.9}$$

and to test $H_0 : \gamma = 0$.

Similar considerations arise when we test a maintained model against a nonnested alternative. One use of nonnested tests is to detect misspecified functional form. A traditional way of specifying competing models that are linear in parameters is

$$y = \beta_0 + a(x)\beta + u \tag{9.10}$$

and

$$y = \gamma_0 + h(x)\gamma + v, \tag{9.11}$$

where a(x) and h(x) are row-vectors of functions of x that may or may not contain elements in common and can be of different dimensions. For example, in (9.10), all explanatory variables may be in level or quadratic form and in (9.11) some or all may be in logarithmic form. When we take the null to be (9.10), assumption (9.5) is the weakest assumption that makes sense: we are testing $H_0 : E(y \mid x) = \beta_0 + a(x)\beta$ against the alternative $H_1 : E(y \mid x) = \gamma_0 + h(x)\gamma$. Of course, there are different methods of testing H_0 against H_1, but before we choose a test we must agree on the proper statement of the null.

Stating the proper null requires even more care when using nonnested tests to choose between models with explanatory variables that are not functionally related to one another. If we agree to treat explanatory variables as random and focus on conditional expectations, no confusion can arise. The traditional approach to specifying the competing models is

$$y = \beta_0 + x\beta + u \tag{9.12}$$

and

$$y = \gamma_0 + z\gamma + v. \tag{9.13}$$

We are thinking of cases where not all elements of z are functionally related to x, and vice versa. For example, in an equation to explain student performance, x contains one set of school and family characteristics and z contains another set (where there might be some overlap). Specifying (9.12) as the null model gives us nothing to test, as we have assumed nothing about how u relates to x and z. Instead, the null hypothesis is exactly as in equation (9.8): once the elements of x have been controlled for, z has no effect on y. This is the sense in which (9.12) is the correct model, and (9.13) is not. Similarly, if (9.13) is the null model, we are really saying $E(y \mid x, z) = E(y \mid z) = \gamma_0 + z\gamma$.

It may be tempting to specify the null model as $E(y \mid x) = \beta_0 + x\beta$ and the competing model as $E(y \mid z) = \gamma_0 + z\gamma$, but then we have nothing to test. Both of these hypotheses can be true, in which case it makes no sense to test one against the other.

So far, we have said nothing about actually computing conditional mean diagnostics. A common method is based on *variable addition statistics* or *artificial regressions*. (See Davidson and MacKinnon, Chapter 1 this volume, for a survey of artificial regressions.) A general variable addition statistic is obtained by regressing the OLS residuals obtained under the null on the x_i and some additional test variables. In particular, the statistic is $N \cdot R_u^2$ from the regression

$$\hat{u}_i \text{ on } 1, \quad x_i, \hat{g}_i, \quad i = 1, 2, \ldots, N, \tag{9.14}$$

where $\hat{u}_i \equiv y_i - \hat{\beta}_0 - x_i\hat{\beta}$ are the OLS residuals and $\hat{g}_i \equiv g(x_i, z_i, \hat{\delta})$ is a $1 \times q$ vector of *misspecification indicators*. Notice that $\hat{g}_i$ is allowed to depend on some estimated *nuisance parameters*, $\hat{\delta}$, an $r \times 1$ vector.

When testing for misspecified functional form in (9.6), $\hat{g}_i$ depends only on x_i (and possible nuisance parameter estimates). For example, we can take $\hat{g}_i = g_i = g(x_i)$, where $g(x)$ is a row vector of nonlinear functions of x. (Squares and cross products are common, but we can use more exotic functions, such as $g_j(x) = \exp(x_j)/(1 + \exp(x_j))$.) For RESET, $\hat{g}_i$ consists of powers of the OLS fitted values, $\hat{y}_i = \hat{\beta}_0 + x_i\hat{\beta}$, usually $\hat{y}_i^2, \hat{y}_i^3$, and possibly $\hat{y}_i^4$. The Davidson–MacKinnon (1981) test of (9.6) against the nonnested alternative (9.11) takes $\hat{g}_i$ to be the scalar $\hat{\gamma}_0 + h(x_i)\hat{\gamma}$, the fitted values from an OLS regression of y_i on 1, $h(x_i)$, $i = 1, 2, \ldots, N$. Wooldridge (1992a), obtains the LM test of $\lambda = 1$ in the more general model $E(y \mid x) = (1 + \lambda(\beta_0 + x\beta))^{1/\lambda}$ when $y \geq 0$. Then, $\hat{g}_i = \hat{y}_i \log(\hat{y}_i)$, assuming that $\hat{y}_i > 0$ for all i.

As discussed above, the null hypothesis we are testing is given by (9.6). What auxiliary assumptions are needed to obtain a usable limiting distribution for

$LM \equiv N \cdot R_u^2$? (We denote this statistic by LM because, when we are testing the null model against a more general alternative, it is the most popular form of the LM statistic.) By auxiliary assumptions we do not mean regularity conditions. In this setup, regularity conditions consist of assuming enough finite moments on the elements of x_i, $g_i = g(x_i, \delta)$, and u_i, sufficient differentiability of $g(x, \cdot)$ over the interior of the nuisance parameter space, and $\sqrt{N}$-consistency of $\hat{\delta}$ for δ in the interior of the nuisance parameter space. We will say no more about these kinds of assumptions because they are rarely checked.

The key auxiliary assumption when testing for functional form, using the standard $N\text{-}R^2$ statistic, is homoskedasticity (which, again, is stated in terms of the population):

$$\text{var}(y \mid x) = \text{var}(u \mid x) = \sigma^2. \qquad (9.15)$$

(Notice how we do not restrict the variance of u given explanatory variables that do not appear in x, as no such restrictions are needed.) It follows from Wooldridge (1991a) that, under (9.6) and (9.15),

$$N \cdot R_u^2 \overset{a}{\sim} \chi_q^2, \qquad (9.16)$$

where we assume that there are no redundancies in $g(x_i, \delta)$. (Technically, the population residuals from the population regression of $g(x, \delta)$ on 1, x must have variance matrix with full rank.)

When we test for omitted variables in equation (9.9), $\hat{g}_i = z_i$. If we test (9.8) against the nonnested alternative $E(y \mid x, z) = \gamma_0 + z\gamma$, there are two popular tests. Let w be the elements of z not in x. The $N\text{-}R^2$ version of the F-statistic proposed by Mizon and Richard (1986) simply takes $\hat{g}_i = w_i$. In other words, we consider a composite model that contains all explanatory variables, and then test for joint significance of those variables not in x. The Davidson–MacKinnon test again takes $\hat{g}_i$ to be the fitted values from the alternative model. In these cases, the auxiliary assumption under H_0 is

$$\text{var}(y \mid x, z) = \text{var}(u \mid x, z) = \sigma^2. \qquad (9.17)$$

Note that (9.15) is no longer sufficient.

Rather than use an $N\text{-}R^2$ statistic, an F-test is also asymptotically valid. We simply obtain the F-statistic for significance of $\hat{g}_i$ in the artificial model

$$y_i = \beta_0 + x_i\beta + \hat{g}_i\gamma + error_i. \qquad (9.18)$$

The F-statistic is asymptotically valid in the sense that $q \cdot F \overset{a}{\sim} \chi_q^2$ under H_0 and the appropriate homoskedasticity assumption ((9.15) or (9.17)). From now on we focus on the LM form of the statistic.

Interestingly, when we test for omitted variables, the asymptotic result in (9.16) does not generally hold under (9.17) if we only assume u and z (and u and x) are uncorrelated under H_0. To see this, as well as gain other insights into the asymptotic behavior of the LM statistic, it is useful to sketch the derivation of (9.16). First, straightforward algebra shows that LM can be written as

$$LM = \left(N^{-1/2}\sum_{i=1}^{N}\hat{g}_i'\hat{u}_i\right)'\left[\hat{\sigma}^2\left(N^{-1}\sum_{i=1}^{N}\hat{r}_i'\hat{r}_i\right)\right]^{-1}\left(N^{-1/2}\sum_{i=1}^{N}\hat{g}_i'\hat{u}_i\right), \qquad (9.19)$$

where $\hat{\sigma}^2 = N^{-1}\sum_{i=1}^{N}\hat{u}_i^2$ and $\hat{r}_i \equiv \hat{g}_i - \hat{\pi}_0 - x_i\hat{\Pi}$ are the OLS residuals from a multivariate regression of $\hat{g}_i$ on $1, x_i, i = 1, 2, \ldots, N$. Equation (9.19) makes it clear that the statistic is based on the sample covariance between $\hat{g}_i$ and $\hat{u}_i$. From (9.19), we see that the asymptotic distribution depends on the asymptotic distribution of

$$N^{-1/2}\sum_{i=1}^{N}\hat{g}_i'\hat{u}_i.$$

As shown in Wooldridge (1990a, 1991a), under H_0 (either (9.6) or (9.8)),

$$N^{-1/2}\sum_{i=1}^{N}\hat{g}_i'\hat{u}_i = N^{-1/2}\sum_{i=1}^{N}r_i'u_i + o_p(1) \qquad (9.20)$$

where $r_i \equiv g_i - \pi_0 - x_i\Pi$ are the population residuals from the population regression of g_i on $1, x_i$. Under H_0, $E(u_i \mid r_i) = 0$ (since r_i is either a function of x_i or of (x_i, z_i)), and so $E(r_i'u_i) = 0$. It follows that the second term in (9.20) has a limiting q-variate normal distribution. Therefore, whether LM has a limiting chi-square distribution under H_0 hinges on whether $\hat{\sigma}^2(N^{-1}\sum_{i=1}^{N}\hat{r}_i'\hat{r}_i)$ is a consistent estimator of $\mathrm{var}(r_i'u_i) = E(u_i^2 r_i'r_i)$. By the law of iterated expectations,

$$E(u_i^2 r_i'r_i) = E[E(u_i^2 \mid r_i) \mid r_i'r_i] = \sigma^2 E(r_i'r_i), \qquad (9.21)$$

where the second equality holds provided $E(u_i^2 \mid r_i) = E(u_i^2) = \sigma^2$. For testing (9.8) under (9.17), $E(u_i^2 \mid x_i, z_i) = \mathrm{var}(u_i \mid x_i, z_i) = \sigma^2$, and r_i is a function of (x_i, z_i), so $E(u_i^2 \mid r_i) = \sigma^2$.

If we only assume $E(r_i'u_i) = 0$ – for example, $E(u) = 0$, $E(x'u) = 0$, and $E(z'u) = 0$ in (9.9) – then $E(u^2 \mid r)$ and $\mathrm{var}(u \mid r)$ are not necessarily the same, and (9.17) is no longer enough to ensure that LM has an asymptotic chi-square distribution.

We can also use (9.19) and (9.20) to see how LM behaves when the conditional mean null hypothesis holds but the auxiliary homoskedasticity assumption does not. An important point is that the representation in (9.20) holds with or without homoskedasticity, which implies that LM has a well-defined limiting distribution even if the conditional variance is not constant. Therefore, the rejection frequency tends to some number strictly less than one (typically, substantially below one), which means that a diagnostic test for the conditional mean has no systematic power to detect heteroskedasticity. Intuitively, it makes sense that a conditional mean test makes a poor test for heteroskedasticity. However, some authors have claimed that conditional mean diagnostics, such as RESET, have the ability to detect heteroskedasticity; the previous argument shows this simply is not true.

Without (9.21), the matrix in the quadratic form is not a consistent estimator of $\text{var}(r_i'u_i)$, and so the limiting distribution of LM is not chi-square. The resulting test based on chi-square critical values may be asymptotically undersized or oversized, and it is difficult to know which is the case.

It is now fairly well known how to adjust the usual LM statistic to allow for heteroskedasticity of unknown form under H_0. A computationally simple regression-based test has its roots in the Messer and White (1984) method for obtaining the heteroskedasticity-robust variance matrix of the OLS estimator, and was first proposed by Davidson and MacKinnon (1985). Subsequently, it was shown to be valid quite generally by Wooldridge (1990a). The simplest way to derive a heteroskedasticity-robust test is to note that a consistent estmator of $\text{var}(r_i'u_i)$, with or without homoskedasticity, is $N^{-1}\sum_{i=1}^{N}\hat{u}_i^2\hat{r}_i'\hat{r}_i$. A useful agebraic fact is

$$\sum_{i=1}^{N}\hat{g}_i'\hat{u}_i = \sum_{i=1}^{N}\hat{r}_i'\hat{u}_i,$$

because the $\hat{r}_i$ are residuals from an OLS regression of $\hat{g}_i$ on 1, x_i and x_i is orthogonal to $\hat{u}_i$ in sample. Therefore, the robust LM statistic is

$$\left(N^{-1/2}\sum_{i=1}^{N}\hat{r}_i'\hat{u}_i\right)'\left(N^{-1}\sum_{i=1}^{N}\hat{u}_i^2\hat{r}_i'\hat{r}_i\right)^{-1}\left(N^{-1/2}\sum_{i=1}^{N}\hat{r}_i'\hat{u}_i\right). \tag{9.22}$$

As a computational device, this can be obtained as $N \cdot R_0^2 = N - SSR_0$ from the regression

$$1 \text{ on } \hat{u}_i\hat{r}_i, \quad i = 1, 2, \ldots, N, \tag{9.23}$$

where R_0^2 is now the uncentered R^2 and SSR_0 is the usual sum of squared residuals. Under (9.6) or (9.8), the heteroskedasticity-robust LM statistic has an asymptotic χ_q^2 distribution.

As we mentioned in the introduction, for any diagnostic test it is important to know the alternatives against which it is consistent. Before we leave this subsection, we provide an example of how the previous tools can be used to shed light on conflicting claims about specification tests in the literature. Ramsey's RESET has often been touted as a general diagnostic that can detect, in addition to functional form problems, omitted variables. (See, e.g., Thursby (1979, 1989) and Godfrey (1988, section 4.2.2).) In fact, RESET, or any other test where the mis-specification indicators are functions of x_i (and possibly nuisance parameters) make poor tests for omitted variables. To see why, suppose that $E(y\,|\,x, q) = \beta_0 + x\beta + \gamma q$, where $\gamma \neq 0$. We start with this model to emphasize that we are interested in the partial effect of each x_j, holding q, and the other elements of x, fixed. Now, suppose that q is not observed. If q is correlated with one or more elements of x, the OLS regression y on 1, x, using a random sample of data, is biased and inconsistent for the β_j. What happens if we apply RESET or some other functional form test? Suppose that q has a linear conditional expectation given x: $E(q \mid x) = \pi_0 + x\pi$. This is certainly the leading case; after all, we started with a linear model for $E(y \mid x, q)$. Then, by iterated expectations,

$$E(y \mid x) = E[E(y \mid x, q) \mid x] = \beta_0 + x\beta + \gamma E(q \mid x)$$
$$= (\beta_0 + \gamma\pi_0) + x(\beta + \gamma\pi) \equiv \theta_0 + x\theta.$$

In other words, regardless of the size of γ or the amount of correlation between q and x, $E(y \mid x)$ is linear in x, and so RESET generally converges in distribution to a quadratic form in a normal random vector. This means it is inconsistent against the omitted variable alternative. If $\text{var}(y \mid x)$ is constant, as is the case if $\text{var}(y \mid x, q)$ is constant and $\text{var}(q \mid x)$ is constant, then RESET has a limiting chi-square distribution: its asymptotic power is equal to its asymptotic size. RESET would only detect the omission of q if $E(q \mid x)$ is nonlinear. But then we could never distinguish between $\gamma \neq 0$ and $E(y \mid x)$ being nonlinear in x.

Finally, we can compare (9.19) and (9.22) to see that, when the homoskedasticity assumption holds, the statistics have the same limiting distribution under local alternatives. (See Davidson and MacKinnon (1993, section 12.2) for a discussion of local alternatives.) The statistics only differ in the $q \times q$ matrix in the quadratic form. Under homoskedasticity, these both converge in probability to $\sigma^2 E(r'r)$ under local alternatives. See Wooldridge (1990a) for a more general discussion.

2.2 Testing for heteroskedasticity

If we only care about the conditional mean, it makes sense to make conditional mean diagnostics robust to arbitrary forms of heteroskedasticity. (Just as it is very common now in microeconometric studies to report heteroskedasticity-robust standard errors and t-statistics.) Some researchers prefer to compute nonrobust conditional mean diagnostics and then later test the homoskedasticity assumption. There are some drawbacks to such a strategy. If there is hetero-skedasticity, then the conditional mean tests were carried out at the incorrect size, and so the overall size of the testing procedure is difficult to determine. Plus, the standard regression-based tests for heteroskedasticity impose their own auxiliary assumptions.

Wooldridge (1991a) suggests first testing the conditional mean, making any conditional mean diagnostics robust to arbitrary heteroskedasticity. Then, if we are still interested in knowing whether homoskedasticity is violated, we can test that subsequently.

An alternative to sequentially testing the mean and variance is to test them jointly. Devising such a test is a good illustration of the role auxiliary assumptions play in obtaining a valid test statistic. For concreteness, consider a joint test of (9.6) and (9.15). (If we were testing for additional variables in the mean or variance function, the analysis would be essentially the same.) A general class of diagnostics is based on sample averages of the form $N^{-1}\sum_{i=1}^{N} \hat{g}_i'\hat{u}_i$ and $N^{-1}\sum_{i=1}^{N} \hat{h}_i'(\hat{u}_i^2 - \hat{\sigma}^2)$, where the first of these is familiar from the conditional mean tests in Section 2.1, and the second is intended to test (9.15). Like $\hat{g}_i$, $\hat{h}_i$ is a function of x_i and possibly some nuisance parameter estimates. For the Breusch–Pagan (1979) test for heteroskedasticity, $\hat{h}_i = x_i$. For the White (1980) test, $\hat{h}_i$ consists of x_i and all nonredundant squares and cross products of elements of x_i. A useful special case of the White test is when $\hat{h}_i = (\hat{y}_i, \hat{y}_i^2)$, where the $\hat{y}_i$ are the OLS fitted values. For concreteness, let $\hat{g}_i$ be $1 \times q$ and let $\hat{h}_i$ be $1 \times p$. Following Wooldridge (1991a), we can show that, under (9.6) and (9.15), equation (9.20) holds and

$$N^{-1/2} \sum_{i=1}^{N} \hat{h}_i'(\hat{u}_i^2 - \hat{\sigma}^2) = N^{-1/2} \sum_{i=1}^{N} (h_i - \mu_h)'(u_i^2 - \sigma^2) + o_p(1), \qquad (9.24)$$

where $\mu_h = E(h_i)$. Therefore, we need to obtain the limiting distribution of

$$N^{-1/2} \begin{pmatrix} \sum\limits_{i=1}^{N} r_i' u_i \\ \sum\limits_{i=1}^{N} c_i' v_i \end{pmatrix}, \qquad (9.25)$$

where $c_i \equiv (h_i - \mu_h)$ and $v_i \equiv (u_i^2 - \sigma^2)$. The limiting distribution is, of course, multivariate normal; what we need is to obtain the $(q + p) \times (q + p)$ variance–covariance matrix. Under (9.6) and (9.15), this is easily done. We already obtained the upper $q \times q$ block: $\sigma^2 E(r_i' r_i)$ (because we are maintaining homoskedasticity under H_0). The lower $p \times p$ block is simply

$$E(v_i^2 c_i' c_i) = E((u_i^2 - \sigma^2)^2 c_i' c_i). \qquad (9.26)$$

The $q \times p$ upper right block is

$$E(u_i v_i r_i' c_i) = E(u_i^3 r_i' c_i), \qquad (9.27)$$

where we use the fact that $E(u_i \mid x_i) = 0$ under (9.6) and r_i and c_i are both functions of x_i.

From (9.26) and (9.27), we see immediately that there are some convenient simplifications if we make standard auxiliary assumptions. First, if we assume *conditional symmetry*, then $E(u_i^3 \mid x_i) = 0$, and so $E(u_i^3 r_i' c_i) = 0$ by the usual iterated expectations argument. This means that the variance–covariance matrix of (9.25) is block diagonal, which has the important implication that the conditional mean and conditional variance tests are asymptotically independent. If our estimate of the asymptotic variance imposes block diagonality, the joint test statistic is simply the sum of the conditional mean and conditional variance statistics.

If we impose the *homokurtosis* assumption, that is, $E(u^4 \mid x) = \tau^2$, then $E((u^2 - \sigma^2)^2 \mid x)$ is constant, say κ^2, and the diagnostic for heteroskedasticity simplifies. A consistent estimator of the lower $p \times p$ block of the asymptotic variance matrix is $\hat{\kappa}^2(N^{-1}\sum_{i=1}^{N}(\hat{h}_i - \bar{h})'(\hat{h}_i - \bar{h}))$, where $\bar{h}$ is the sample average of $\hat{h}_i$ and $\hat{\kappa}^2 = N^{-1}\sum_{i=1}^{N}(\hat{u}_i^2 - \hat{\sigma}^2)^2$. The test for heteroskedasticity can be computed as $N \cdot R_v^2$ from the regression

$$\hat{u}_i^2 \text{ on } 1, \hat{h}_i, \quad i = 1, 2, \ldots, N, \tag{9.28}$$

where R_v^2 is the usual R^2. Under (9.6), (9.15), and the auxiliary homokurtosis assumption, $N \cdot R_v^2 \overset{a}{\sim} \chi_p^2$. (This is true whether or not the symmetry condition holds.)

We can easily relax the homokurtosis assumption in testing for heteroskedasticity. As shown in Wooldridge (1991a), or as can be derived from the above representations, a robust test for heteroskedasticity is obtained as $N \cdot R_1^2 = N - \text{SSR}_1$ from the regression

$$1 \text{ on } (\hat{u}_i^2 - \hat{\sigma}^2)(\hat{h}_i - \bar{h}), \quad i = 1, 2, \ldots, N, \tag{9.29}$$

where R_1^2 is the uncentered R^2 and SSR_1 is the sum of squared residuals. Under (9.6) and (9.15), $N \cdot R_1^2 \overset{a}{\sim} \chi_p^2$.

In some cases, we may want to test $\text{var}(y \mid x, z) = \sigma^2$, where z is an additional set of variables that does not show up in the mean equation. However, the test for heteroskedasticity only makes sense if $E(y \mid x, z) = E(y \mid x)$. The misspecification indicator $\hat{h}_i$ would depend on z_i as well as on x_i. When $E(y \mid x, z) = E(y \mid x)$, heteroskedasticity that depends only on z does not invalidate the usual OLS inference procedures.

Now we can combine various sets of auxiliary assumptions to find when different statistics for testing the joint null are valid. If (9.6), (9.15), symmetry, and homokurtosis all hold, then

$$N \cdot R_u^2 + N \cdot R_v^2 \sim \chi_{q+p}^2. \tag{9.30}$$

Notice that assuming u is independent of x and normally distributed is sufficient, but not necessary, for the auxiliary assumptions. (See Bera and Jarque (1982) for a similar test under normality.) If we maintain symmetry but relax homokurtosis, $N \cdot R_u^2 + N \cdot R_1^2 \overset{a}{\sim} \chi_{q+p}^2$; this appears to be a new result.

If we relax symmetry, there are no simple versions of the joint test statistic because the mean and variance tests are asymptotically correlated. To obtain a fully robust test – that is, a test that maintains only (9.6) and (9.15) under H_0 – we need to obtain the quadratic form with a general asymptotic variance estimator. For example, the upper $q \times p$ off-diagonal block can be estimated as $N^{-1}\sum_{i=1}^{N}\hat{u}_i^3 \hat{r}_i'(\hat{h}_i - \bar{h})$.

A joint test of the conditional mean and conditional variance is an example of an *omnibus test*. Such tests must be used with caution because it is difficult to know where to look if a statistic rejects. More importantly, it gives relatively unimportant forms of misspecification, such as the existence of heteroskedasticity, parity with important forms of misspecification, such as misspecification of the conditional mean.

2.3 Diagnostic testing in nonlinear models of conditional means

Much of what we discussed in Section 2.1 carries over to nonlinear models. With a nonlinear conditional mean function, it becomes even more important to state hypotheses in terms of conditional expectations; otherwise the null model has no interesting interpretation. For example, if y is a nonnegative response, a convenient regression function is exponential:

$$E(y \mid x) = \exp(x\beta), \tag{9.31}$$

where, for simplicity, unity is included in the $1 \times k$ vector x. Importantly, (9.31) puts no restrictions on the nature of y other than that it is nonnegative. In particular, y could be a count variable, a continuous variable, or a variable with discrete and continuous characteristics. We can construct a variety of alternatives to (9.31). For example, in the more general model

$$E(y \mid x) = \exp(x\beta + \delta_1(x\beta)^2 + \delta_2(x\beta)^3), \tag{9.32}$$

we can test $H_0 : \delta_1 = 0, \delta_2 = 0$.

Generally, if we nest $E(y \mid x) = m(x, \beta)$ in the model $\mu(x, \beta, \delta)$, where $m(x, \beta) = \mu(x, \beta, \delta_0)$, for a known value δ_0, then the LM statistic is easy to compute: $LM = N \cdot R_u^2$ from the regression

$$\hat{u}_i \text{ on } \nabla_\beta \hat{m}_i, \nabla_\delta \hat{\mu}_i, \quad i = 1, 2, \ldots, N, \tag{9.33}$$

where $\hat{u}_i = y_i - m(x_i, \hat{\beta})$, $\nabla_\beta \hat{m}_i = \nabla_\beta m(x_i, \hat{\beta})$, and $\nabla_\delta \hat{\mu}_i = \nabla_\delta \mu(x_i, \hat{\beta}, \delta_0)$; $\hat{\beta}$ is the nonlinear least squares (NLS) estimator obtained under H_0. (The R^2 is generally the uncentered R^2.) Under $H_0 : E(y \mid x) = m(x, \beta)$ and the homoskedasticity assumption (9.15), $LM \overset{a}{\sim} \chi_q^2$, where q is the dimension of δ. For testing (9.31) against (9.32), $\nabla_\beta \hat{m}_i = x_i \exp(x_i \hat{\beta})$ and $\nabla_\delta \hat{\mu}_i = ((x_i \hat{\beta})^2 \exp(x_i \hat{\beta}), (x_i \hat{\beta})^3 \exp(x_i \hat{\beta}))$; the latter is a 1×2 vector.

Davidson and MacKinnon (1985) and Wooldridge (1991a) show how to obtain a heteroskedasticity-robust form of the LM statistic by first regressing $\nabla_\delta \hat{\mu}_i$ on $\nabla_\beta \hat{m}_i$ and obtaining the $1 \times q$ residuals, $\hat{r}_i$, and then computing the statistic exactly as in (9.23).

For more general tests, $\nabla_\delta \hat{\mu}_i$ is replaced by a set of misspecification indicators, say $\hat{g}_i$. For example, if we are testing $H_0 : E(y \mid x) = m(x, \beta)$ against $H_1 : E(y \mid x) = \mu(x, \gamma)$, the Davidson–MacKinnon (1981) test takes $\hat{g}_i = \hat{\mu}_i - \hat{m}_i$, the difference in the fitted values from the two models. Wooldridge's (1990b) conditional mean encompassing (CME) test takes $\hat{g}_i = \nabla_\gamma \hat{\mu}_i = \nabla_\gamma \mu(x_i, \hat{\gamma})$, the $1 \times q$ estimated gradient from the alternative mean function.

It is straightforward to obtain conditional mean tests in the context of maximum likelihood or quasi-maximum likelihood estimation for densities in the linear exponential family (LEF). As shown by Gouriéroux, Monfort, and Trognon

(1984), the quasi-MLE is consistent and asymptotically normal provided only that the conditional mean is correctly specified. The tests have the same form as those for nonlinear regression, except that all quantities are weighted by the inverse of the estimated conditional standard deviation – just as in weighted nonlinear least squares. So, in (9.33), we would divide each quantity by $\hat{v}_i^{1/2}$, where $\hat{v}_i \equiv v(x_i, \hat{\beta})$ is the estimated conditional variance function from the LEF density, under H_0. For example, in the case of the binary response density, $\hat{v}_i = \hat{m}_i(1 - \hat{m}_i)$, where $\hat{m}_i$ would typically be the logit or probit function. (See Moon (1988) for some examples of alternative conditional mean functions for the logit model.) For Poisson regression, $\hat{v}_i = \hat{m}_i$, where $\hat{m}_i = \exp(x_i\hat{\beta})$ is the usual conditional mean function under H_0 (see Wooldridge (1997) for further discussion). The statistic from (9.33), after quantities have been appropriately weighted, is valid when $\text{var}(y_i \mid x_i)$ is proportional to the variance implied by the LEF density. The statistic obtained from (9.23) is robust to arbitrary variance misspecification, provided $\hat{u}_i$ is replaced with $\hat{u}_i/\hat{v}_i^{1/2}$ and $\hat{r}_i$ is replaced with the residuals from the multivariate regression $\nabla_\delta \hat{u}_i/\hat{v}_i^{1/2}$ on $\nabla_\beta \hat{m}_i/\hat{v}_i^{1/2}$; see Wooldridge (1991b, 1997) for details.

3 DIAGNOSTIC TESTING IN TIME SERIES CONTEXTS

All of the tests we covered in Section 2 can be applied in time series contexts. However, because we can no longer assume that the observations are independent of one another, the discussion of auxiliary assumptions under H_0 is more complicated. We assume in this section that the weak law of large numbers and central limit theorems can be applied, so that standard inference procedures are available. This rules out processes with unit roots, or fractionally integrated processes. (See Wooldridge (1994) or Pötscher and Prucha (chapter 10 in this volume) for a discussion of the kinds of dependence allowed.) For notational simplicity, we assume that the process is strictly stationary so that moment matrices do not depend on t.

3.1 Conditional mean diagnostics

To illustrate the issues that arise in obtaining conditional mean diagnostics for time series models, let x_t be a vector of conditioning variables, which can contain contemporaneous variables, z_t, as well as lagged values of y_t and z_t. Given x_t, we may be interested in testing linearity of $E(y_t \mid x_t)$, which is stated as

$$E(y_t \mid x_t) = \beta_0 + x_t\beta \tag{9.34}$$

for some $\beta_0 \in \mathbb{R}$ and $\beta \in \mathbb{R}^k$. For example, y_t might be the return on an asset, and x_t might contain lags of y_t and lagged economic variables. The same kinds of tests we discussed in Section 2.1 can be applied here, including RESET, the Davidson–MacKinnon test, and LM tests against a variety of nonlinear alternatives. Let $\hat{g}_t = g(x_t, \hat{\delta})$ be the $1 \times q$ vector of misspecification indicators. The *LM* statistic is obtained exactly as in (9.14), with standard notational changes (the t subscript replaces i and the sample size is denoted T rather than N). Just as in the cross section case, we need to assume homoskedasticity conditional on x_t:

$$\text{var}(y_t \mid x_t) = \sigma^2. \tag{9.35}$$

If x_t contains lagged y_t, this rules out dynamic forms of heteroskedasticity, such as ARCH (Engle, 1982) and GARCH (Bollerslev, 1986), as well as static forms of heteroskedasticity if x_t contains z_t.

Because of the serial dependence in time series data, we must add another auxiliary assumption in order for the usual LM statistic to have an asymptotic χ^2_q distribution. If we write the model in error form as

$$y_t = \beta_0 + x_t \beta + u_t, \tag{9.36}$$

then a useful auxiliary assumption is

$$E(u_t \mid x_t, u_{t-1}, x_{t-1}, \dots) = 0. \tag{9.37}$$

Assumption (9.37) implies that $\{u_t\}$ is serially uncorrelated, but it implies much more. For example, u_t and u_s are uncorrelated conditional on (x_t, x_s), for $t \neq s$. Also, u_t is uncorrelated with any function of $(x_t, u_{t-1}, x_{t-1}, \dots)$.

We can easily see why (9.37) is sufficient, along with (9.35), to apply the usual LM test. As in the cross section case, we can show under (9.34) that (9.20) holds with the obvious changes in notation. Now, for (9.19) to have an asymptotic chi-square distribution, we need $\hat{\sigma}^2(T^{-1}\sum_{t=1}^{T} r_t' \hat{r}_t)$ to consistently estimate

$$\lim_{T \to \infty} \text{var}\left(T^{-1/2} \sum_{t=1}^{T} r_t' u_t\right). \tag{9.38}$$

Assumption (9.37) ensures that all of the covariance terms in this asymptotic variance are zero. For $s < t$, $E(u_t u_s r_t' r_s) = E[E(u_t \mid r_t, u_s, r_s) u_s r_t' r_s] = 0$ because $E(u_t \mid r_t, u_s, r_s) = 0$ under (9.37). The last statement follows because (r_t, u_s, r_s) is a function of $(x_t, u_{t-1}, x_{t-1}, \dots)$. When we add the homoskedasticity assumption, we see that the usual T-R-squared statistic is asymptotically valid.

It is easily seen that (9.37) is equivalent to

$$E(y_t \mid x_t, y_{t-1}, x_{t-1}, y_{t-2}, \dots) = E(y_t \mid x_t) = \beta_0 + x_t \beta, \tag{9.39}$$

which we call *dynamic completeness* of the conditional mean. Under (9.39), all of the dynamics are captured by what we have put in x_t. For example, if $x_t = (y_{t-1}, z_{t-1})$, then (9.39) becomes

$$E(y_t \mid y_{t-1}, z_{t-1}, y_{t-2}, z_{t-2} \dots) = E(y_t \mid y_{t-1}, z_{t-1}), \tag{9.40}$$

which means at most one lag each of y_t and z_t are needed to fully capture the dynamics. (Because z_t is not in x_t in this example, (9.40) places no restrictions on any contemporaneous relationship between y_t and z_t.) Generally, if x_t contains lags of y_t and possibly lags of other variables, we are often willing to assume dynamic completeness of the conditional mean when testing for nonlinearities. In any case, we should know that the usual kind of test essentially requires this assumption.

If $x_t = z_t$ for a vector of contemporaneous variables, (9.39) is very strong:

$$E(y_t \,|\, z_t, y_{t-1}, z_{t-1}, y_{t-2}, \dots) = E(y_t \,|\, z_t), \tag{9.41}$$

which means that once contemporaneous z_t has been controlled for, lags of y_t and z_t are irrelevant. If we are just interested in testing for nonlinearities in a static linear model for $E(y_t \,|\, z_t)$, we might not want to impose dynamic completeness.

Relaxing the homoskedasticity assumption is easy: the same heteroskedasticity-robust statistic from regression (9.23) is valid, provided (9.39) holds. This statistic is not generally valid in the presence of serial correlation.

Wooldridge (1991a) discusses different ways to make conditional mean diagnostics robust to serial correlation (as well as to heteroskedasticity). One approach is to obtain an estimator of (9.38) that allows general serial correlation; see, for example, Newey and West (1987) and Andrews (1991). Perhaps the simplest approach is to prewhiten $\hat{k}_t \equiv \hat{u}_t \hat{r}_t$, where the $\hat{u}_t$ are the OLS residuals from estimating the null model and the $\hat{r}_t$ are the $1 \times q$ residuals from the multivariate regression of $\hat{g}_t$ on $1, x_t, t = 1, 2, \dots, T$. If $\hat{e}_t, t = (p+1), \dots, T$ are the $1 \times q$ residuals from a vector autoregression (VAR) of $\hat{k}_t$ on $1, \hat{k}_t, \dots, \hat{k}_{t-p}$, then the test statistic is

$$\left(\sum_{t=p+1}^{T} \hat{e}_t \right) \left(\sum_{t=p+1}^{T} \hat{e}_t' \hat{e}_t \right)^{-1} \left(\sum_{t=p+1}^{T} \hat{e}_t' \right);$$

under (9.34), the statistic has an asymptotic χ_q^2 distribution, provided the VAR adequately captures the serial correlation in $\{k_t \equiv u_t r_t\}$.

We can gain useful insights by studying the appropriate asymptotic representation of the LM statistic. Under (9.34), regularity conditions, and strict stationarity and weak dependence, we can write the T-R^2 LM statistic as

$$LM = \left(T^{-1/2} \sum_{t=1}^{T} r_t' u_t \right)' \left(\sigma^2 E(r_t' r_t) \right)^{-1} \left(T^{-1/2} \sum_{t=1}^{T} r_t' u_t \right) + o_p(1). \tag{9.42}$$

This representation does not assume either (9.35) or (9.37), but if either fails then $\sigma^2 E(r_t' r_t)$ does not generally equal (9.38). This is why, without (9.35) and (9.37), the usual LM statistic does not have a limiting chi-square distribution.

We can use (9.42) to help resolve outstanding debates in the literature. For example, there has long been a debate about whether RESET in a model with strictly exogenous explanatory variables is robust to serial correlation (with homoskedasticity maintained). The evidence is based on simulation studies. Thursby (1979) claims that RESET is robust to serial correlation; Porter and Kashyap (1984) find that it is not. We can help reconcile the disagreement by studying (9.42). With strictly exogenous regressors, $\{u_t\}$ is independent of $\{x_t\}$, and the $\{u_t\}$ are always assumed to have a constant variance (typically, $\{u_t\}$ follows a stable AR(1) model). Combined, these assumptions imply (9.35). Therefore, RESET will have a limiting chi-square distribution when the covariance terms in (9.38) are all zero, that is,

$$E(u_t u_s r_t' r_s) = 0, \quad t \neq s. \tag{9.43}$$

When $\{x_t\}$ is independent of $\{u_t\}$,

$$E(u_t u_s r_t' r_s) = E(u_t u_s)E(r_t' r_s),$$

because r_t is a function of x_t. Recall that r_t is a population residual from a regression that includes an intercept, and so it has zero mean. Here is the key: if $\{x_t\}$ is an independent sequence, as is often the case in simulation studies, then $E(r_t' r_s) = 0$, $t \neq s$. But then (9.43) holds, regardless of the degree of serial correlation in $\{u_t\}$. Therefore, if $\{x_t\}$ is generated to be strictly exogenous and serially independent, RESET is asymptotically robust to arbitrary serial correlation in the errors. (We have also shown that (9.37) is not necessary for the T-R^2 LM statistic to have a limiting chi-square distribution, as (9.37) is clearly false when $\{u_t\}$ is serially correlated. Instead, strict exogeneity and serial independence of $\{x_t\}$ are sufficient.)

If $\{x_t\}$ is serially correlated, the usual RESET statistic is not robust. However, what matters is serial correlation in r_t, and this might be small even with substantial serial correlation in $\{x_t\}$. For example, x_t^2 net of its linear projection on to $(1, x_t)$ might not have much serial correlation, even if $\{x_t\}$ does.

Earlier we emphasized that, in general, the usual LM statistic, or its heteroskedasticity-robust version, maintain dynamic completeness under H_0. Because dynamic completeness implies that the errors are not serially correlated, serially correlated errors provide evidence against (9.39). Therefore, testing for serial correlation is a common specification test.

The most common form of the LM statistic for AR(p) serial correlation – see, e.g., Breusch (1978), Godfrey (1978), or Engle (1984) – is $LM = (T - p)R_u^2$, where R_u^2 is the usual R^2 from the regression

$$\hat{u}_t \text{ on } 1, x_t, \hat{u}_{t-1}, \hat{u}_{t-2}, \ldots, \hat{u}_{t-p}, \quad t = (p + 1), \ldots, T. \tag{9.44}$$

Under what assumptions is LM asymptotically χ_q^2? In addition to (9.39) (equivalently, (9.37)), sufficient is the homoskedasticity assumption

$$\text{var}(u_t \mid x_t, u_{t-1}, \ldots, u_{t-p}) = \sigma^2. \tag{9.45}$$

Notice that (9.35) is no longer sufficient; we must rule out heteroskedasticity conditional on lagged u_t as well.

More generally, we can test for misspecified dynamics, misspecified functional form, or both, by using specification indicators $g(w_t, \hat{\delta})$, where w_t is a subset of

$(x_t, y_{t-1}, x_{t-1}, \dots)$. If we want to ensure the appropriate no serial correlation assumption holds, we take the null to be (9.39), which implies that $E(y_t | x_t, w_t) = E(y_t | x_t) = \beta_0 + x_t\beta$. The homoskedasticity assumption is $\text{var}(y_t | x_t, w_t) = \sigma^2$. The adjustment for heteroskedasticity is the same as described for pure functional form tests (see equation (9.23)).

In this section we have focused on a linear null model. Once we specify hypotheses in terms of conditional means, there are no special considerations for nonlinear regression functions with weakly dependent data. All of the tests we discussed for cross section applications can be applied. The statement of homoskedasticity is the same in the linear case, and the dynamic completeness assumption is stated as in (9.39) but with the linear regression function replaced by $m(x_t, \beta)$. The standard LM test discussed in Section 2.3 is valid, and both heteroskedasticity and serial correlation robust forms are easily computed (see Wooldridge (1991a) for details).

3.2   Testing for heteroskedasticity

As the discussion of testing for serial correlation in Section 3.1 suggests, different kinds of heteroskedasticity have different implications in time series models. Suppose we start with the linear model written in error form as in (9.36). The weakest useful homoskedasticity assumption is

$$H_0 : \text{var}(u_t | x_t) = \sigma^2, \tag{9.46}$$

which only makes sense once we have maintained $E(u_t | x_t) = 0$. Then, the conditional mean is correctly specified as $E(y_t | x_t) = \beta_0 + x_t\beta$. A popular class of test statistics for heteroskedasticity is based $T \cdot R_v^2$, where R_v^2 is the usual R^2 from the regression

$$\hat{u}_t^2 \text{ on } 1, \hat{h}(x_t), \quad t = 1, 2, \dots, T, \tag{9.47}$$

which is exactly the kind of statistic we covered for testing the homoskedasticity assumption in a cross section application. For the $T \cdot R_v^2$ statistic to be valid, we need the homokurtosis assumption $E(u_t^4 | x_t) = \kappa^2$, just as in Section 2.2. However, we need more. While the statistic from (9.47) clearly only has power against violations of (9.46), we need to rule out serial correlation in $\{u_t^2\}$. In particular, it suffices that $E((u_t^2 - \sigma^2)(u_s^2 - \sigma^2) | x_t, x_s) = 0$, $t \neq s$. Sufficient for this is dynamic completeness of the conditional mean, (9.39), along with the dynamic homoskedasticity assumption

$$\text{var}(y_t | x_t, y_{t-1}, x_{t-1}, \dots) = \sigma^2. \tag{9.48}$$

While (9.48) is not technically necessary, it would be weird to have (9.48) fail but have $T \cdot R_v^2 \stackrel{a}{\sim} \chi_q^2$. Thus, in time series contexts, the usual Breusch–Pagan and White-type tests for heteroskedasticity essentially maintain dynamic completeness of the variance under the null in order to obtain a limiting chi-square statistic.

Sometimes we want to test for dynamic heteroskedasticity even if the conditional mean is static. Consider, for example, (9.41), where the conditional mean model is linear. Then (9.47) becomes $\text{var}(u_t \mid z_t) = \sigma^2$, which does not restrict the variance conditional on past values. It could be that (9.46) holds, which, along with (9.8), means that the usual inference procedures are asymptotically valid. However, we might want to know if $\text{var}(u_t \mid z_t, u_{t-1}, z_{t-1}, \dots)$ depends on, say, u_{t-1}.

With general x_t under (9.39), Engle's (1982) ARCH model of order one implies

$$\text{var}(u_t \mid x_t, u_{t-1}, x_{t-1}, \dots) = \text{var}(u_t \mid u_{t-1}) = \delta_0 + \delta_1 u_{t-1}^2 \tag{9.49}$$

The ARCH(p) model has p lags of u_t^2, and the LM test for ARCH is obtained as $(T - p)R_v^2$ from the regression

$$\hat{u}_t^2 \text{ on } 1, \hat{u}_{t-1}^2, \dots, \hat{u}_{t-p}^2, \quad t = p + 1, \dots, T. \tag{9.50}$$

As with other tests for heteroskedasticity, this statistic uses an auxiliary homokurtosis assumption, in this case, $E(u_t^4 \mid x_t, u_{t-1}, x_{t-1}, \dots) = \kappa^2$. The regression in equation (9.29), which makes the test robust to heterokurtosis, is valid here as well.

3.3   Omnibus tests on the errors in time series regression models

Omnibus tests on the errors in time series regression models have recently become popular. A good example is the so-called BDS test (Brock, Dechert, LeBaron, and Scheinkman, 1996), which has been viewed as a general test for "nonlinearity." The null hypothesis for the BDS test is that the errors are independent and identically distributed, and the test has power against a variety of departures from the iid assumption, including neglected nonlinearities in the conditional mean, dynamic forms of heteroskedasticity, and even dynamics in higher order moments. Unfortunately, no economic theory implies that errors are iid. In many applications, especially in finance, it is often easy to reject the iid assumption using a simple test for dynamic heteroskedasticity, such as ARCH.

As with other omnibus tests, BDS gives equal weight to hypotheses that have very different practical importance. Finding that the errors in, say, an asset pricing equation are serially correlated – which usually means a violation of the efficient markets hypothesis – is more important than finding dynamic heteroskedasticity, which in turn is more important than finding, say, a nonconstant conditional fourth moment.

4   FINAL COMMENTS

Our focus in this chapter has been on the most common setting for diagnostic tests, namely, in univariate parametric models of conditional means and conditional variances. Recently, attention has turned to testing when some aspect of the estimation problem is nonparametric. For example, we might wish to construct a test of a parametric model that has unit asymptotic power against all alternatives that satisfy fairly weak regularity conditions. Bierens (1990), Wooldridge (1992b), Hong and White (1995), de Jong (1996), Fan and Li (1996), and Zheng (1996) are some examples. Or, the estimated model may be semiparametric in nature, depending on an infinite dimensional parameter in addition to a finite dimensional parameter (Stoker, 1992; Fan and Li, 1996). The alternative is an infinite dimensional parameter space. In some cases the null model may be fully nonparametric, in which case the alternative is also nonparametric (e.g. Lewbel, 1995; and Fan and Li, 1996).

For diagnostic testing in time series contexts, we assumed that the underlying stochastic processes were weakly dependent. Currently, there is no general theory of diagnostic testing when the processes are not weakly dependent. Wooldridge (1999) considers a particular class of diagnostic tests in linear models with integrated processes and shows that, when the misspecification indicator is cointegrated, in a generalized sense, with the included explanatory variables, LM-type statistics have asymptotic chi-square distributions.

Another important topic we have omitted is diagnostic testing for panel data models. Panel data raises some additional important considerations, most of which revolve around our ability to control, to some extent, for time-constant heterogeneity. Strict exogeneity assumptions on the regressors, especially conditional on the unobserved effect, are important. Dynamic models with unobserved effects raise even more issues for estimation and diagnostic testing. (See Hsiao (1986) and Baltagi (1995) for discussions of these issues.)

Note

*   Two anonymous referees and Badi Baltagi provided helpful, timely comments on the first draft.

References

Andrews, D.W.K. (1991). Heteroskedasticity and autocorrelation consistent covariance matrix estimation. *Econometrica* 59, 817–58.

Baltagi, B.H. (1995). *Econometric Analysis of Panel Data*. New York: Wiley.

Bera, A.K., and C.M. Jarque (1982). Model specification tests: A simultaneous approach. *Journal of Econometrics* 20, 59–82.

Bierens, H.J. (1990). A conditional moment test of functional form. *Econometrica* 58, 1443–58.

Bollerslev, T. (1986). Generalized autoregressive conditional heteroskedasticity. *Journal of Econometrics* 31, 307–27.

Breusch, T.S. (1978). Testing for autocorrelation in dynamic linear models. *Australian Economic Papers* 17, 334–55.

Breusch, T.S., and A.R. Pagan (1979). A simple test for heteroskedasticity and random coefficient variation. *Econometrica* 50, 987–1007.

Brock, W., W.D. Dechert, B. LeBaron, and J. Scheinkman (1996). A test for independence based on the correlation dimension. *Econometric Reviews* 15, 197–235.

Davidson, R., and J.G. MacKinnon (1981). Several tests of model specification in the presence of alternative hypotheses. *Econometrica* 49, 781–93.

Davidson, R., and J.G. MacKinnon (1985). Heteroskedasticity-robust tests in regression directions. *Annales de l'INSÉÉ* 59/60, 183–218.

Davidson, R., and J.G. MacKinnon (1987). Implicit alternatives and the local power of test statistics. *Econometrica* 55, 1305–29.

Davidson, R., and J.G. MacKinnon (1993). *Estimation and Inference in Econometrics*. New York: Oxford University Press.

de Jong, R.M. (1996). The Bierens test under data dependence. *Journal of Econometrics* 72, 1–32.

Durbin, J., and G.S. Watson (1950). Testing for serial correlation in least squares regressions I. *Biometrika* 37, 409–28.

Engle, R.F. (1982). Autoregressive conditional heteroskedasticity with estimates of the variance of United Kingdom inflation. *Econometrica* 50, 987–1008.

Engle, R.F. (1984). Wald, likelihood, ratio, and Lagrange multiplier tests in econometrics. In Z. Griliches and M. Intriligator, eds., *Handbook of Econometrics*, vol. 2, Amsterdam: North-Holland.

Fan, Y., and Q. Li (1996). Consistent model specification tests: Omitted variables and semiparametric functional forms. *Econometrica* 64, 865–90.

Godfrey, L.G. (1978). Testing for higher order serial correlation in regression equations when the regressors include lagged dependent variables. *Econometrica* 46, 1303–10.

Godfrey, L.G. (1988). *Misspecification Tests in Econometrics*. Cambridge: Cambridge University Press.

Gouriéroux, C., A. Monfort, and C. Trognon (1984). Pseudo-maximum likelihood methods: Theory. *Econometrica* 52, 681–700.

Hong, Y., and H. White (1995). Consistent specification testing via nonparametric series regression. *Econometrica* 63, 1133–59.

Hsiao, C. (1986). *Analysis of Panel Data*. Cambridge: Cambridge University Press.

Lewbel, A. (1995). Consistent nonparametric hypothesis tests with an application to Slutsky symmetry. *Journal of Econometrics* 67, 379–401.

Messer, K., and H. White (1984). A note on computing the heteroskedasticity consistent covariance matrix using instrumental variable techniques. *Oxford Bulletin of Economics and Statistics* 46, 181–4.

Mizon, G.E., and J.-F. Richard (1986). The encompassing principle and its application to testing non-nested hypotheses. *Econometrica* 54, 657–78.

Moon, C.-G. (1988). Simultaneous specification test in a binary logit model: Skewness and heteroskedasticity. *Communications in Statistics* 17, 3361–87.

Newey, W.K. (1985). Maximum likelihood specification testing and conditional moment tests. *Econometrica* 53, 1047–70.

Newey, W.K., and K.D. West (1987). A simple positive semi-definite heteroskedasticity and autocorrelation consistent covariance matrix. *Econometrica* 55, 703–8.

Pagan, A.R., and F. Vella (1989). Diagnostic tests for models based on individual data: A survey. *Journal of Applied Econometrics* 4, S29–59.

Porter, R.D., and A.K. Kashyap (1984). Autocorrelation and the sensitivity of RESET. *Economics Letters* 14, 229–33.

Ramsey, J.B. (1969). Tests for specification errors in the classical linear least squares regression analysis. *Journal of the Royal Statistical Society Series B* 31, 350–71.

Stoker, T.M. (1992). *Lectures on Semiparametric Econometrics*. Louvain-la-Neuve, Belgium: CORE Lecture Series.

Tauchen, G. (1985). Diagnostic testing and evaluation of maximum likelihood models. *Journal of Econometrics* 30, 415–43.

Thursby, J.G. (1979). Alternative specification error tests: A comparative study. *Journal of the American Statistical Association* 74, 222–5.

Thursby, J.G. (1989). A comparison of several specification error tests for a general alternative. *International Economic Review* 30, 217–30.

White, H. (1980). A heteroskedasticity-consistent covariance matrix estimator and a direct test for heteroskedasticity. *Econometrica* 48, 817–38.

White, H. (1982). Maximum likelihood estimation of misspecified models. *Econometrica* 50, 1–26.

White, H. (1994). *Estimation, Inference and Specification Analysis*. Cambridge: Cambridge University Press.

Wooldridge, J.M. (1990a). A unified approach to robust, regression-based specification tests. *Econometric Theory* 6, 17–43.

Wooldridge, J.M. (1990b). An encompassing approach to conditional mean tests with applications to testing nonnested hypotheses. *Journal of Econometrics* 45, 331–50.

Wooldridge, J.M. (1991a). On the application of robust, regression-based diagnostics to models of conditional means and conditional variances. *Journal of Econometrics* 47, 5–46.

Wooldridge, J.M. (1991b). Specification testing and quasi-maximum likelihood estimation. *Journal of Econometrics* 48, 29–55.

Wooldridge, J.M. (1992a). Some alternatives to the Box–Cox regression model. *International Economic Review* 33, 935–55.

Wooldridge, J.M. (1992b). A test for functional form against nonparametric alternatives. *Econometric Theory* 8, 452–75.

Wooldridge, J.M. (1994). Estimation and inference for dependent processes. In R.F. Engle and D.L. McFadden (eds.) *Handbook of Econometrics*, Volume 4. pp. 2639–2738. Amsterdam: North-Holland.

Wooldridge, J.M. (1997). Quasi-likelihood methods for count data. In M.H. Pesaran and P. Schmidt (eds.) *Handbook of Applied Econometrics*, Volume 2. pp. 352–406. Oxford: Blackwell.

Wooldridge, J.M. (1999). Asymptotic properties of some specification tests in linear models with integrated processes. In R.F. Engle and H. White (eds.) *Cointegration, Causality, and Forecasting*. Oxford: Oxford University Press.

Zheng, J.X. (1996). A consistent test of functional form via nonparametric estimation techniques. *Journal of Econometrics* 75, 263–89.

CHAPTER TEN

Basic Elements of Asymptotic Theory

Benedikt M. Pötscher and Ingmar R. Prucha

1   INTRODUCTION

Consider the estimation problem where we would like to estimate a parameter vector θ from a sample $Y_1, \ldots, Y_n$. Let $\hat{\theta}_n$ be an estimator for θ, i.e. let $\hat{\theta}_n = h(Y_1, \ldots, Y_n)$ be a function of the sample.[1] In the important special case where $\hat{\theta}_n$ is a *linear* function of $Y_1, \ldots, Y_n$, i.e. $\hat{\theta}_n = Ay$, where A is a nonrandom matrix and $y = (Y_1, \ldots, Y_n)'$, we can easily express the expected value and the variance–covariance matrix of $\hat{\theta}_n$ in terms of the first and second moments of y (provided those moments exist). Also, if the sample is normally distributed, so is $\hat{\theta}_n$. Well known examples of linear estimators are the OLS- and the GLS-estimator of the linear regression model. Frequently, however, the estimator of interest will be a *nonlinear* function of the sample. In principle, the distribution of $\hat{\theta}_n$ can then be found from the distribution of the sample, if the model relating the parameter θ to the observables $Y_1, \ldots, Y_n$ fully specifies the distribution of the sample. For example in a linear regression model with independently and identically distributed errors this would require assuming a specific distribution for the errors. However, even if the researcher is willing to make such a specific assumption, it will then still often be impossible – for all practical purposes – to obtain an exact expression for the distribution of $\hat{\theta}_n$ because of the complexity of the necessary calculations. (Even if $\hat{\theta}_n$ is linear, but the distribution of y is nonnormal, it will typically be difficult to obtain the exact distribution of $\hat{\theta}_n$.) Similarly, obtaining expressions for, say, the first and second moments of $\hat{\theta}_n$ will, for practical purposes, typically be unfeasible for nonlinear estimators; and even if it is feasible, the resulting expressions will usually depend on the entire distribution of the sample, and not only on the first and second moments as in the case of a linear estimator. A further complication arises in case the model relating θ to the observables $Y_1, \ldots, Y_n$ does not fully specify the distribution of $Y_1, \ldots, Y_n$. For example in a linear regression model the errors may only be assumed to be identically and independently distributed with zero mean and finite variance, without putting any further restrictions on the distribution function of the disturbances. In this case we obviously cannot get a handle on the distribution of $\hat{\theta}_n$ (even if $\hat{\theta}_n$ is linear), in the sense that this distribution will depend on the unknown distribution of the errors.

In view of the above discussed difficulties in obtaining *exact* expressions for characteristics of estimators like their moments or distribution functions we will often have to resort to *approximations* for these exact expressions. Ideally, these approximations should be easier to obtain than the exact expressions and they should be of a simpler form. Asymptotic theory is one way of obtaining such approximations by essentially asking what happens to the exact expressions as the sample size tends to infinity. For example, if we are interested in the expected value of $\hat{\theta}_n$ and an exact expression for it is unavailable or unwieldy, we could ask if the expected value of $\hat{\theta}_n$ converges to θ as the sample size increases (i.e. if $\hat{\theta}_n$ is "asymptotically unbiased"). One could try to verify this by first showing that the estimator $\hat{\theta}_n$ itself "converges" to θ in an appropriate sense, and then by attempting to obtain the convergence of the expected value of $\hat{\theta}_n$ to θ from the "convergence" of the estimator. In order to properly pose and answer such questions we need to study various notions of convergence of random vectors.

The article is organized as follows: in Section 2 we define various modes of convergence of random vectors, and discuss the properties of and the relationships between these modes of convergence. Sections 3 and 4 provide results that allow us to deduce the convergence of certain important classes of random vectors from basic assumptions. In particular, in Section 3 we discuss laws of large numbers, including uniform laws of large numbers. A discussion of central limit theorems is given in Section 4. In Section 5 we suggest additional literature for further reading.

We emphasize that the article only covers material that lays the foundation for asymptotic theory. It does not provide results on the asymptotic properties of estimators for particular models; for references see Section 5. All of the material presented here is essentially textbook material. We provide proofs for some selected results for the purpose of practice and since some of the proofs provide interesting insights. For most results given without a proof we provide references to widely available textbooks. Proofs for some of the central limit theorems presented in Section 4 are given in a longer mimeographed version of this article, which is available from the authors upon request.

We adopt the following notation and conventions: throughout this chapter Z_1, $Z_2, \ldots$, and Z denote random vectors that take their values in a Euclidean space R^k, $k \geq 1$. Furthermore, all random vectors involved in a particular statement are assumed to be defined on a common probability space $(\Omega, \mathcal{F}, P)$, except when noted otherwise. With $|.|$ we denote the absolute value and with $\|.\|$ the Euclidean norm. All matrices considered are real matrices. If A is a matrix, then A' denotes its transpose; if A is a square matrix, then A^{-1} denotes the inverse of A. The norm of a matrix A is denoted by $\|A\|$ and is taken to be $\|\text{vec}(A)\|$, where vec(A) stands for the columnwise vectorization of A. If C_n is a sequence of sets, then $C_n \uparrow C$ stands for $C_n \subseteq C_{n+1}$ for all $n \in \mathbb{N}$ and $C = \bigcup_{n=1}^{\infty} C_n$. Similarly, $C_n \downarrow C$ stands for $C_n \supseteq C_{n+1}$ for all $n \in \mathbb{N}$ and $C = \bigcap_{n=1}^{\infty} C_n$. Furthermore, if B is a set, then $\mathbf{1}(B)$ denotes the indicator function of B.

2   MODES OF CONVERGENCE FOR SEQUENCES OF RANDOM VECTORS

In this section we define and discuss various modes of convergence for sequences of random vectors taking their values in $\mathbb{R}^k$.

2.1   Convergence in probability, almost surely, and in rth mean

We first consider the case where $k = 1$, i.e. the case of real valued random variables. Extension to the vector case are discussed later. We start by defining convergence in probability.

Definition 1.   (Convergence in probability) The sequence of random variables Z_n converges in probability (or stochastically) to the random variable Z if for every $\varepsilon > 0$

$$\lim_{n \to \infty} P(|Z_n - Z| \le \varepsilon) = 1. \tag{10.1}$$

We then write $\underset{n \to \infty}{\operatorname{plim}} Z_n = Z$, or $Z_n \xrightarrow{p} Z$, or $Z_n \to Z$ i.p. as $n \to \infty$.

We next define almost sure convergence.

Definition 2.   (Almost sure convergence) The sequence of random variables Z_n converges almost surely (or strongly or with probability one) to the random variable Z if there exists a set $N \in \mathcal{F}$ with $P(N) = 0$ such that $\lim_{n \to \infty} Z_n(\omega) = Z(\omega)$ for every $\omega \in \Omega - N$, or equivalently

$$P(\{\omega \in \Omega : \lim_{n \to \infty} Z_n(\omega) = Z(\omega)\}) = 1. \tag{10.2}$$

We then write $Z_n \xrightarrow{a.s.} Z$, or $Z_n \to Z$ a.s., or $Z_n \to Z$ w.p.1 as $n \to \infty$.

The following theorem provides an alternative characterization of almost sure convergence.

Theorem 1.   The sequence of random variables Z_n converges almost surely to the random variable Z if and only if

$$\lim_{n \to \infty} P(\{|Z_i - Z| \le \varepsilon \text{ for all } i \ge n\}) = 1 \tag{10.3}$$

for every $\varepsilon > 0$.

Proof. Let

$$A = \{\omega \in \Omega : \lim_{n \to \infty} Z_n(\omega) = Z(\omega)\}$$

and

$$A_n^\varepsilon = \{\omega \in \Omega : |Z_i(\omega) - Z(\omega)| \leq \varepsilon \text{ for all } i \geq n\},$$

then (10.2) and (10.3) can be written equivalently as $P(A) = 1$ and $\lim_{n \to \infty} P(A_n^\varepsilon) = 1$. Next define $A^\varepsilon = \bigcup_{n=1}^\infty A_n^\varepsilon$ and observe that $A_n^\varepsilon \uparrow A^\varepsilon$. By construction A^ε is the set of all $\omega \in \Omega$ for which there exists some finite index $n_\varepsilon(\omega)$ such that $|Z_i(\omega) - Z(\omega)| \leq \varepsilon$ for all $i \geq n_\varepsilon(\omega)$. Consequently $A \subseteq A^\varepsilon$; in fact $A = \bigcap_{\varepsilon > 0} A^\varepsilon$. Now suppose (10.2) holds, i.e. $P(A) = 1$. Then, using the continuity theorem for probability measures given, e.g., in Billingsley (1979, p. 21), we have $P(A^\varepsilon) = \lim_{n \to \infty} P(A_n^\varepsilon) \geq P(A) = 1$, i.e. (10.3) holds. Conversely, suppose (10.3) holds, then $P(A^\varepsilon) = 1$. Observe that $A^\varepsilon \downarrow A$ as $\varepsilon \downarrow 0$. Choosing $\varepsilon = 1/k$ we have $A = \bigcap_{k=1}^\infty A^{1/k}$ and, using again the continuity theorem for probability measures, $P(A) = \lim_{k \to \infty} P(A^{1/k}) = 1$. ∎

The above theorem makes it evident that almost sure convergence implies convergence in probability.

Theorem 2. If $Z_n \xrightarrow{a.s.} Z$, then $Z_n \xrightarrow{p} Z$.

Proof. Obviously the event $B_n^\varepsilon = \{\omega \in \Omega : |Z_n(\omega) - Z(\omega)| \leq \varepsilon\}$ contains the event $A_n^\varepsilon = \{\omega \in \Omega : |Z_i(\omega) - Z(\omega)| \leq \varepsilon \text{ for all } i \geq n\}$. Hence Theorem 1 implies that $\lim_{n \to \infty} P(B_n^\varepsilon) = 1$, i.e. that (10.1) holds. ∎

The converse of the above theorem does not hold. That is, in general, convergence in probability does not imply almost sure convergence as is demonstrated by the following well known example.

Example 1.[2] Let $\Omega = [0, 1)$, let $\mathcal{F}$ be the corresponding Borel σ-field, and let $P(.)$ be the uniform distribution on Ω, i.e. $P([a, b]) = b - a$. Define

$$Z_n(\omega) = \begin{cases} 1 & \text{if } \omega \in [m_n 2^{-k_n}, (m_n + 1) 2^{-k_n}) \\ 0 & \text{otherwise} \end{cases}$$

where the integers m_n and k_n satisfy $n = m_n + 2^{k_n}$ and $0 \leq m_n < 2^{k_n}$. That is, k_n is the largest integer satisfying $2^{k_n} \leq n$. Let $Z = 0$ and let A_n^ε and B_n^ε be defined as above. Then for $\varepsilon < 1$ we have $B_n^\varepsilon = \Omega - [m_n 2^{-k_n}, (m_n + 1) 2^{-k_n})$ and hence $P(B_n^\varepsilon) = 1 - 2^{-k_n} \to 1$ as $n \to \infty$. This establishes that Z_n converges to zero in probability. Observe further that $A_n^\varepsilon = \bigcap_{i=n}^\infty B_i^\varepsilon = \emptyset$. Consequently Z_n does not converge to zero almost surely. In fact, in this example $Z_n(\omega)$ does not converge to 0 for any $\omega \in \Omega$, although $Z_n \xrightarrow{p} 0$.

We next define convergence in rth mean.

Definition 3. (Convergence in rth mean) The sequence of random variables Z_n converges in rth mean to the random variable Z, $0 < r < \infty$, if

$$\lim_{n \to \infty} E |Z_n - Z|^r = 0.$$

We then write $Z_n \xrightarrow{\text{rth}} Z$. For $r = 2$ we say the sequence converges in quadratic mean or mean square.[3]

Remark 1. For all three modes of convergence introduced above one can show that the limiting random variable Z is unique up to null sets. That is, suppose Z and Z^* are both limits of the sequence Z_n, then $P(Z = Z^*) = 1$.

Lyapounov's inequality implies that $E|Z_n - Z|^s \le \{E|Z_n - Z|^r\}^{s/r}$ for $0 < s \le r$. As a consequence we have the following theorem, which tells us that the higher the value of r, the more stringent the condition for convergence in rth mean.

Theorem 3. $Z_n \xrightarrow{\text{rth}} Z$ implies $Z_n \xrightarrow{\text{sth}} Z$ for $0 < s \le r$.

The following theorem gives conditions under which convergence in rth mean implies convergence of the rth moments.

Theorem 4.[4] Suppose $Z_n \xrightarrow{\text{rth}} Z$ and $E|Z|^r < \infty$. Then $E|Z_n|^r \to E|Z|^r$. If, furthermore, Z_n^r and Z^r are well-defined for all n (e.g. if $Z_n \ge 0$ and $Z \ge 0$, or if r is a natural number), then also $EZ_n^r \to EZ^r$.

By Chebyshev's inequality we have $P\{|Z_n - Z| \ge \varepsilon\} \le E|Z_n - Z|^r/\varepsilon^r$ for $r > 0$. As a consequence, convergence in rth mean implies convergence in probability, as stated in the following theorem.

Theorem 5. If $Z_n \xrightarrow{\text{rth}} Z$ for some $r > 0$, then $Z_n \xrightarrow{p} Z$.

The corollary below follows immediately from Theorem 5 with $r = 2$ by utilizing the decomposition $E|Z_n - c|^2 = \text{var}(Z_n) + (EZ_n - c)^2$.

Corollary 1. Suppose $EZ_n \to c$ and $\text{var}(Z_n) \to 0$, then $Z_n \xrightarrow{p} c$.

The corollary is frequently used to show that for an estimator $\hat{\theta}_n$ with $E\hat{\theta}_n \to \theta$ (i.e. an asymptotically unbiased estimator) and with $\text{var}(\hat{\theta}_n) \to 0$ we have $\hat{\theta}_n \xrightarrow{p} \theta$.

Example 2. Let y_t be a sequence of iid distributed random variables with $Ey_t = \theta$ and $\text{var}(y_t) = \sigma^2 < \infty$. Let $\hat{\theta}_n = n^{-1} \sum_{t=1}^{n} y_t$ denote the sample mean. Then $E\hat{\theta}_n = \theta$ and $\text{var}(\hat{\theta}_n) = \sigma^2/n \to 0$, and hence $\hat{\theta}_n \xrightarrow{p} \theta$.

Theorem 5 and Corollary 1 show how convergence in probability can be implied from the convergence of appropriate moments. The converse is not true in general, and in particular $Z_n \xrightarrow{p} Z$ does not imply $Z_n \xrightarrow{\text{rth}} Z$. In fact even $Z_n \xrightarrow{a.s.} Z$ does not imply $Z_n \xrightarrow{\text{rth}} Z$. These claims are illustrated by the following example.

Example 3. Let Ω, $\mathcal{F}$, and P be as in Example 1 and define

$$Z_n(\omega) = \begin{cases} 0 & \text{for } \omega \in [0, 1 - 1/n), \\ n & \text{for } \omega \in [1 - 1/n, 1). \end{cases}$$

Then $Z_n(\omega) \to 0$ for all $\omega \in \Omega$ and hence $Z_n \xrightarrow{a.s.} 0$. However, $E|Z_n| = 1$ for all n and hence Z_n does not converge to 0 in rth mean with $r = 1$.

The above example shows in particular that an estimator that satisfies $\hat{\theta}_n \xrightarrow{p} \theta$ (or $\hat{\theta}_n \xrightarrow{a.s.} \theta$) need not satisfy $E\hat{\theta}_n \to \theta$, i.e. need not be asymptotically unbiased. Additional conditions are needed for such a conclusion to hold. Such conditions are given in the following theorem. The theorem states that convergence in probability implies convergence in rth mean, given that the convergence is dominated.

Theorem 6.[5]   (Dominated convergence theorem) Suppose $Z_n \xrightarrow{p} Z$, and there exists a random variable Y satisfying $|Z_n| \leq Y$ a.s. for all n and $EY^r < \infty$. Then $Z_n \xrightarrow{rth} Z$ and $E|Z|^r < \infty$. (Of course, the theorem also holds if $Z_n \xrightarrow{p} Z$ is replaced by $Z_n \xrightarrow{a.s.} Z$, since the latter implies the former.)

Under the assumptions of the above theorem also convergence of the rth moments follows in view of Theorem 4. We also note that the existence of a random variable Y satisfying the requirements in Theorem 6 is certainly guaranteed if there exists a real number M such that $|Z_n| \leq M$ a.s. for all n (choose $Y = M$).

Now let Z_n be a sequence of random vectors taking their values in R^k. Convergence in probability, almost surely, and in the rth mean are then defined exactly as in the case $k = 1$ with the only difference that the absolute value $|.|$ has to be replaced by $\|.\|$, the Euclidean norm on R^k. Upon making this replacement all of the results presented in this subsection generalize to the vector case with two obvious exceptions: first, in Corollary 1 the condition $\text{var}(Z_n) \to 0$ has to be replaced by the conditions that the variances of the components of Z_n converge to zero, or equivalently, that the variance–covariance matrix of Z_n converges to zero. Second, the last claim in Theorem 4 continues to hold if the symbol Z_n^r is interpreted so as to represent the vector of the rth power of the components of Z_n. Instead of extending the convergence notions to the vector case by replacing the absolute value $|.|$ by the norm $\|.\|$, we could have defined convergence in probability, almost surely and in rth mean for sequences of random vectors by requiring that each component of Z_n satisfies Definition 1, 2, or 3, respectively. That this leads to an equivalent definition is shown in the following theorem.

Theorem 7.   Let Z_n and Z be random vectors taking their values in R^k, and let $Z_n^{(i)}$ and $Z^{(i)}$ denote their ith component, respectively. Then $Z_n \xrightarrow{p} Z$ if and only if $Z_n^{(i)} \xrightarrow{p} Z^{(i)}$ for $i = 1, \ldots, k$. An analogous statement holds for almost sure convergence and for convergence in rth mean.

The theorem follows immediately from the following simple inequality:

$$|Z_n^{(i)} - Z^{(i)}| \leq \|Z_n - Z\| \leq \sqrt{k} \max_{i=1,\ldots,k} (|Z_n^{(i)} - Z^{(i)}|).$$

For sequences of random $k \times l$-matrices W_n convergence in probability, almost surely, and in rth mean is defined as the corresponding convergence of the sequence $\text{vec}(W_n)$.

We finally note the following simple fact: Suppose $Z_1, Z_2, \ldots$, and Z are nonrandom vectors, then $Z_n \xrightarrow{p} Z$, $Z_n \xrightarrow{a.s.} Z$, and $Z_n \xrightarrow{r\text{th}} Z$ each hold if and only if $Z_n \to Z$ as $n \to \infty$. That is, in this case all of the concepts of convergence of random vectors introduced above coincide with the usual convergence concept for sequences of vectors in $\mathbf{R}^k$.

2.2   Convergence in distribution

Let $\hat{\theta}_n$ be an estimator for a real-valued parameter θ and assume $\hat{\theta}_n \xrightarrow{p} \theta$. If G_n denotes the cumulative distribution function (CDF) of $\hat{\theta}_n$, i.e., $G_n(z) = P(\hat{\theta}_n \leq z)$, then as $n \to \infty$

$$G_n(z) \to \begin{cases} 0 & \text{for } z < \theta \\ 1 & \text{for } z > \theta. \end{cases} \tag{10.4}$$

To see this observe that $P(\hat{\theta}_n \leq z) = P(\hat{\theta}_n - \theta \leq z - \theta) \leq P(|\hat{\theta}_n - \theta| \geq \theta - z)$ for $z < \theta$, and $P(\hat{\theta}_n \leq z) = 1 - P(\hat{\theta}_n > z) = 1 - P(\hat{\theta}_n - \theta > z - \theta) \geq 1 - P(|\hat{\theta}_n - \theta| > z - \theta)$ for $z > \theta$. The result in (10.4) shows that the distribution of $\hat{\theta}_n$ "collapses" into the degenerate distribution at θ, i.e., into

$$G(z) = \begin{cases} 0 & \text{for } z < \theta \\ 1 & \text{for } z \geq \theta. \end{cases} \tag{10.5}$$

Consequently, knowing that $\hat{\theta}_n \xrightarrow{p} \theta$ does not provide information about the shape of G_n. As a point of observation note that $G_n(z) \to G(z)$ for $z \neq \theta$, but $G_n(z)$ may not converge to $G(z) = 1$ for $z = \theta$. For example, if $\hat{\theta}_n$ is distributed symmetrically around θ, then $G_n(\theta) = 1/2$ and hence does not converge to $G(\theta) = 1$.

This raises the question of how we can obtain information about G_n based on some limiting process. Consider, for example, the case where $\hat{\theta}_n$ is the sample mean of iid random variables with mean θ and variance $\sigma^2 > 0$. Then $\hat{\theta}_n \xrightarrow{p} \theta$ in light of Corollary 1, since $E\hat{\theta}_n = \theta$ and $\text{var}(\hat{\theta}_n) = \sigma^2/n \to 0$. Consequently, as discussed above, the distribution of $\hat{\theta}_n$ "collapses" into the degenerate distribution at θ. Observe, however, that the rescaled variable $\sqrt{n}\,(\hat{\theta}_n - \theta)$ has mean zero and variance σ^2. This indicates that the distribution of $\sqrt{n}\,(\hat{\theta}_n - \theta)$ will *not* collapse to a degenerate distribution. Hence, if $\sqrt{n}\,(\hat{\theta}_n - \theta)$ "converges," the limiting CDF can be expected to be non-degenerate. To formalize these ideas we need to define an appropriate notion of convergence of CDFs.[6]

Definition 4.   (Convergence in distribution) Let $F_1, F_2, \ldots$, and F denote CDFs on R. Then F_n converges weakly to F if

$$\lim_{n \to \infty} F_n(z) = F(z)$$

for all $z \in \mathbf{R}$ that are continuity points of F.

Let Z_1, Z_2, ..., and Z denote random variables with corresponding CDFs F_1, F_2, ..., and F, respectively. We then say that Z_n converges in distribution (or in law) to Z, if F_n converges weakly to F. We write $Z_n \overset{d}{\to} Z$ or $Z_n \overset{L}{\to} Z$.

Consider again the sample mean $\hat{\theta}_n$ of iid random variables with mean θ and variance $\sigma^2 > 0$. As demonstrated above, $\hat{\theta}_n \overset{p}{\to} \theta$ only implies weak convergence of the CDF of $\hat{\theta}_n$ to a degenerate distribution, which is not informative about the shape of the distribution function of $\hat{\theta}_n$. In contrast the limiting distribution of $\sqrt{n}\,(\hat{\theta}_n - \theta)$ is found to be non-degenerate. In fact, using Theorem 24 below, it can be shown that $\sqrt{n}\,(\hat{\theta}_n - \theta)$ converges in distribution to a $N(0, \sigma^2)$ distributed random variable. As a result we can take $N(0, \sigma^2)$ as an approximation for the finite sample distribution of $\sqrt{n}\,(\hat{\theta}_n - \theta)$, and consequently take $N(\theta, \sigma^2/n)$ as an approximation for the finite sample distribution of $\hat{\theta}_n$.

Remark 2

(a) The reason for requiring in the above definition that $F_n(z) \to F(z)$ converges only at the continuity points of F is to accommodate situations as, e.g., in (10.4). Of course, if F is continuous, then F_n converges weakly to F if and only if $F_n(z) \to F(z)$ for all $z \in \mathbb{R}$.

(b) As is evident from the definition, the concept of convergence in distribution is defined completely in terms of the convergence of distribution functions. In fact, the concept of convergence in distribution remains well defined even for sequences of random variables that are not defined on a common probability space.

(c) To further illustrate what convergence in distribution does not mean consider the following example: Let Y be a random variable that takes the values $+1$ and -1 with probability $1/2$. Define $Z_n = Y$ for $n \geq 1$ and $Z = -Y$. Then clearly $Z_n \overset{d}{\to} Z$ since Z_n and Z have the same distribution, but $|Z_n - Z| = 2$ for all $n \geq 1$. That is, convergence in distribution does not necessarily mean that the difference between random variables vanishes in the limit. More generally, if $Z_n \overset{d}{\to} Z$ and one replaces the sequence Z_n by a sequence Z_n^* that has the same marginal distributions, then also $Z_n^* \overset{d}{\to} Z$.

The next theorem provides several equivalent characterizations of weak convergence.

Theorem 8.[7]   Consider the cumulative distribution functions F, F_1, F_2, ... Let Q, Q_1, Q_2, ... denote the corresponding probability measures on $\mathbb{R}$, and let ϕ, ϕ_1, ϕ_2, ... denote the corresponding characteristic functions. Then the following statements are equivalent:

(a) F_n converges weakly to F.

(b) $\lim_{n \to \infty} Q_n(A) = Q(A)$ for all Borel sets $A \subseteq \mathbb{R}$ that are Q-continuous, i.e. for all Borel sets A whose boundary ∂A satisfies $Q(\partial A) = 0$.

(c) $\lim_{n \to \infty} \int f dF_n = \int f dF$ for all bounded and continuous real valued functions f on $\mathbb{R}$.

(d) $\lim_{n \to \infty} \phi_n(t) = \phi(t)$ for all $t \in \mathbb{R}$.

If, furthermore, the cumulative distribution functions $F, F_1, F_2, \ldots$ have moment generating functions $M, M_1, M_2, \ldots$ in some common interval $[-t_*, t_*]$, $t_* > 0$, then (a), (b), (c) or (d) are, respectively, equivalent to

(e) $\lim_{n \to \infty} M_n(t) = M(t)$ for all $t \in [-t_*, t_*]$.

Remark 3.   The equivalence of (a) and (b) of Theorem 8 can be reformulated as $Z_n \overset{d}{\to} Z \Leftrightarrow P(Z_n \in A) \to P(Z \in A)$ for all Borel sets A with $P(Z \in \partial A) = 0$. The equivalence of (a) and (c) can be expressed equivalently as $Z_n \overset{d}{\to} Z \Leftrightarrow Ef(Z_n) \to Ef(Z)$ for all bounded and continuous real valued functions f on R.

The following theorem relates convergence in probability to convergence in distribution.

Theorem 9. $Z_n \overset{p}{\to} Z$ implies $Z_n \overset{d}{\to} Z$. (Of course, the theorem also holds if $Z_n \overset{p}{\to} Z$ is replaced by $Z_n \overset{a.s.}{\to} Z$ or $Z_n \overset{rth}{\to} Z$, since the latter imply the former.)

Proof.   Let $f(z)$ be any bounded and continuous real valued function, and let C denote the bound. Then $Z_n \overset{p}{\to} Z$ implies $f(Z_n) \overset{p}{\to} f(Z)$ by the results on convergence in probability of transformed sequences given in Theorem 14 in Section 2.3. Since $|f(Z_n(\omega))| \leq C$ for all n and $\omega \in \Omega$ it then follows from Theorems 6 and 4 that $Ef(Z_n) \to Ef(Z)$, and hence $Z_n \overset{d}{\to} Z$ by Theorem 8.   ∎

The converse of the above theorem does not hold in general, i.e. $Z_n \overset{d}{\to} Z$ does not imply $Z_n \overset{p}{\to} Z$. To see this consider the following example: let $Z \sim N(0, 1)$ and put $Z_n = (-1)^n Z$. Then Z_n does not converge almost surely or in probability. But since each $Z_n \sim N(0, 1)$, evidently $Z_n \overset{d}{\to} Z$.

Convergence in distribution to a constant is, however, equivalent to convergence in probability to that constant.

Theorem 10.   Let $c \in$ R, then $Z_n \overset{d}{\to} c$ is equivalent to $Z_n \overset{p}{\to} c$.

Proof.   Because of Theorem 9 we only have to show that $Z_n \overset{d}{\to} c$ implies $Z_n \overset{p}{\to} c$. Observe that for any $\varepsilon > 0$

$$P(|Z_n - c| > \varepsilon) = P(Z_n - c < -\varepsilon) + P(Z_n - c > \varepsilon)$$
$$\leq P(Z_n \leq c - \varepsilon) - P(Z_n \leq c + \varepsilon) + 1$$
$$= F_n(c - \varepsilon) - F_n(c + \varepsilon) + 1$$

where F_n is the CDF of Z_n. The CDF of $Z = c$ is

$$F(z) = \begin{cases} 0 & z < c \\ 1 & z \geq c \end{cases}.$$

Hence, $c - \varepsilon$ and $c + \varepsilon$ are continuity points of F. Since $Z_n \xrightarrow{d} Z$ it follows that $F_n(c - \varepsilon) \to F(c - \varepsilon) = 0$ and $F_n(c + \varepsilon) \to F(c + \varepsilon) = 1$. Consequently,

$$0 \leq P(|Z_n - c| > \varepsilon) \leq F_n(c - \varepsilon) + 1 - F_n(c + \varepsilon) \to 0 + 1 - 1 = 0.$$

This shows $Z_n \xrightarrow{p} Z = c$. ∎

In general convergence in distribution does not imply convergence of moments; in fact the moments may not even exist. However, we have the following result.

Theorem 11.[8]   Suppose $Z_n \xrightarrow{d} Z$ and suppose that $\sup_n E|Z_n|^r < \infty$ for some $0 < r < \infty$. Then for all $0 < s < r$ we have $E|Z|^s < \infty$ and $\lim_{n \to \infty} E|Z_n|^s = E|Z|^s$. If, furthermore, Z^s and Z_n^s are well-defined for all n, then also $\lim_{n \to \infty} EZ_n^s = EZ^s$.

Remark 4.   Since $Z_n \xrightarrow{p} Z$ and $Z_n \xrightarrow{a.s.} Z$ imply $Z_n \xrightarrow{d} Z$, Theorem 11 provides sufficient conditions under which $Z_n \xrightarrow{p} Z$ and $Z_n \xrightarrow{a.s.} Z$ imply convergence of moments. These conditions are an alternative to those of Theorems 6 and 4.

The concept of convergence in distribution can be generalized to sequences of random vectors Z_n taking their values in R^k. Contrary to the approach taken in generalizing the notions of convergence in probability, almost surely, and in rth mean to the vector case, the appropriate generalization is here *not* obtained by simply requiring that the component sequences $Z_n^{(i)}$ converge in distribution for $i = 1, \ldots, k$. Such an attempt at generalizing the notion of convergence in distribution would yield a nonsensical convergence concept as is illustrated by Example 4 below. The proper generalization is given in the following definition.

Definition 5.   Let $F_1, F_2, \ldots,$ and F denote CDFs on R^k. Then F_n converges weakly to F if

$$\lim_{n \to \infty} F_n(z) = F(z)$$

for all $z \in R^k$ that are continuity points of F.

Let $Z_1, Z_2, \ldots,$ and Z denote random vectors taking their values in R^k with corresponding CDFs $F_1, F_2, \ldots,$ and F, respectively. We then say that Z_n converges in distribution (or in law) to Z, if F_n converges weakly to F. We write $Z_n \xrightarrow{d} Z$ or $Z_n \xrightarrow{L} Z$.

All the results presented in this subsection so far also hold for the multivariate case (with R^k replacing R). Convergence in distribution of a sequence of random matrices W_n is defined as convergence in distribution of $\text{vec}(W_n)$.

The next theorem states that weak convergence of the joint distributions implies weak convergence of the marginal distributions.

Theorem 12.   Weak convergence of F_n to F implies weak convergence of $F_n^{(i)}$ to $F^{(i)}$ and $Z_n \xrightarrow{d} Z$ implies $Z_n^{(i)} \xrightarrow{d} Z^{(i)}$, where $F_n^{(i)}$ and $F^{(i)}$ denote the ith marginal distribution of F_n and F, and $Z_n^{(i)}$ and $Z^{(i)}$ denote the ith component of Z_n and Z, respectively.

Proof. The result follows from Theorem 14 below, since projections are continuous. ∎

However, as alluded to in the above discussion, the converse of Theorem 12 is not true. That is, weak convergence of the marginal distributions is not equivalent to weak convergence of the joint distribution, as is illustrated by the following counter example.

Example 4. Let $Z \sim N(0, 1)$ and let

$$Z_n = \begin{pmatrix} Z \\ (-1)^n Z \end{pmatrix}.$$

Clearly, the marginal distributions of each component of Z_n converge weakly to $N(0, 1)$. However, for n even the distribution of Z_n is concentrated on the line $\{(z, z) : z \in R\}$, whereas for n odd the distribution of Z_n is concentrated on the line $\{(z, -z) : z \in R\}$. Consequently, the random vectors Z_n do not converge in distribution, i.e. the distributions of Z_n do not converge weakly.

The following result is frequently useful in reducing questions about convergence in distribution of random vectors to corresponding questions about convergence in distribution of random variables.

Theorem 13. (Cramér–Wold device) Let $Z_1, Z_2, \ldots$, and Z denote random vectors taking their values in R^k. Then the following statements are equivalent:

(a) $Z_n \xrightarrow{d} Z$
(b) $\alpha' Z_n \xrightarrow{d} \alpha' Z$ for all $\alpha \in R^k$.
(c) $\alpha' Z_n \xrightarrow{d} \alpha' Z$ for all $\alpha \in R^k$ with $\| \alpha \| = 1$.

Proof. The equivalence of (b) and (c) is obvious. We now prove the equivalence of (a) with (c). Let $\phi_n(t)$ and $\phi(t)$ denote, respectively, the characteristic functions of Z_n and Z. According to the multivariate version of Theorem 8 we have $Z_n \xrightarrow{d} Z$ if and only if $\phi_n(t) \to \phi(t)$ for all $t = (t_1, \ldots, t_k)' \in R^k$. Let $\phi_n^\alpha(s)$ and $\phi^\alpha(s)$ denote the characteristic functions of $\alpha' Z_n$ and $\alpha' Z$, respectively. Again, $\alpha' Z_n \xrightarrow{d} \alpha' Z$ if and only if $\phi_n^\alpha(s) \to \phi^\alpha(s)$ for all $s \in R$. Observe that for $t \neq 0$ we have

$$\phi_n(t) = E(\exp(it' Z_n)) = E(\exp(is\alpha' Z_n)) = \phi_n^\alpha(s)$$

with $\alpha = t / \| t \|$ and $s = \| t \|$. Note that $\| \alpha \| = 1$. Similarly, $\phi(t) = \phi^\alpha(s)$. Consequently, $\phi_n(t) \to \phi(t)$ for all $t \neq 0$ if and only if $\phi_n^\alpha(s) \to \phi^\alpha(s)$ for all $s \neq 0$ and all α with $\| \alpha \| = 1$. Since $\phi_n(0) = \phi(0) = 1$ and $\phi_n^\alpha(0) = \phi^\alpha(0) = 1$, the proof is complete observing that $t = 0$ if and only if $s = 0$. ∎

2.3 Convergence properties and transformations

We are often interested in the convergence properties of transformed random vectors or variables. In particular, suppose Z_n converges to Z in a certain mode, then given a function g we may ask the question whether or not $g(Z_n)$ converges to $g(Z)$ in the same mode. The following theorem answers the question in the affirmative, provided g is continuous (in the sense specified below). Part (a) of the theorem is commonly referred to as Slutsky's theorem.

Theorem 14.[9] Let $Z_1, Z_2, \ldots$, and Z be random vectors in R^k. Furthermore, let $g : R^k \to R^s$ be a Borel-measurable function and assume that g is continuous with P_Z-probability one (where P_Z denotes the probability measure induced by Z on R^k).[10] Then

(a) $Z_n \overset{p}{\to} Z$ implies $g(Z_n) \overset{p}{\to} g(Z)$,
(b) $Z_n \overset{a.s.}{\to} Z$ implies $g(Z_n) \overset{a.s.}{\to} g(Z)$,
(c) $Z_n \overset{d}{\to} Z$ implies $g(Z_n) \overset{d}{\to} g(Z)$.

In the special case where $Z = c$ is a constant or a vector of constants, the continuity condition on g in the above theorem only requires that the function g is continuous at c.

As special cases of Theorem 14 we have, for example, the following corollaries.

Corollary 2. Let W_n and V_n be sequences of k-dimensional random vectors. Suppose $W_n \to W$ and $V_n \to V$ i.p. [a.s.], then

$$W_n \pm V_n \to W \pm V \quad \text{i.p. [a.s.],}$$
$$W_n' V_n \to W' V \quad \text{i.p. [a.s.].}$$

In case $k = 1$,

$$W_n / V_n \to W/V \quad \text{i.p. [a.s.]}$$

if $V \neq 0$ with probability one, and where W_n / V_n is set to an arbitrary value on the event $\{V_n = 0\}$.[11]

Proof. The assumed convergence of W_n and V_n implies that $Z_n = (W_n', V_n')'$ converges to $Z = (W', V')'$ i.p. [a.s.] in view of Theorem 7. The corollary then follows from Theorem 14(a), (b) since the maps $g_1(w, v) = w + v$, $g_2(w, v) = w - v$, $g_3(w, v) = w'v$ are continuous on all of R^{2k}, and since the map $g_4(w, v) = w/v$ if $v \neq 0$ and $g_4(w, v) = c$ for $v = 0$ (with c arbitrary) is continuous on $A = R \times (R - \{0\})$, observing furthermore that $P_Z(A) = 1$ provided $V \neq 0$ with probability 1. ∎

The proof of the following corollary is completely analogous.

Corollary 3. Let W_n and V_n be sequences of random matrices of fixed dimension. Suppose $W_n \to W$ and $V_n \to V$ i.p. [a.s.], then

$$W_n \pm V_n \to W \pm V \quad \text{i.p. [a.s.]},$$
$$W_n V_n \to WV \quad \text{i.p. [a.s.]}.$$

Furthermore

$$W_n V_n^{-1} \to WV^{-1} \quad \text{and} \quad V_n^{-1} W_n \to V^{-1} W \quad \text{i.p. [a.s.]}$$

if V is nonsigular with probability one, and where $W_n V_n^{-1}$ and $V_n^{-1} W_n$ are set to an arbitrary matrix of appropriate dimension on the event $\{V_n \text{ singular}\}$. (The matrices are assumed to be of conformable dimensions.)

The following example shows that convergence in probability or almost surely in Corollaries 2 and 3 *cannot* be replaced by convergence in distribution.

Example 5. Let $U \sim N(0, 1)$ and define $W_n = U$ and $V_n = (-1)^n U$. Then

$$W_n + V_n = \begin{cases} 2U \sim N(0, 4) & \text{if } n \text{ is even} \\ 0 & \text{if } n \text{ is odd.} \end{cases}$$

Clearly, $W_n + V_n$ does not converge in distribution, although $W_n \overset{d}{\to} U$ and $V_n \overset{d}{\to} U$.

The reason behind this negative result is again the fact that convergence in distribution of the components of a random vector does in general not imply convergence in distribution of the entire random vector. Of course, if the entire random vector $Z_n = (W_n', V_n')'$ converges in distribution to $Z = (W', V')'$ then $W_n \pm V_n \overset{d}{\to} W \pm V$, $W_n' V_n \overset{d}{\to} W'V$ as a consequence of Theorem 14; also, if $k = 1$ and $V \neq 0$ with probability 1, then $W_n / V_n \overset{d}{\to} W/V$.

However, there is an important special case in which we can conclude that $Z_n = (W_n', V_n')' \overset{d}{\to} Z = (W', V')'$ from knowing that $W_n \overset{d}{\to} W$ and $V_n \overset{d}{\to} V$: this is the case where $V = c$ and c is a constant vector.

Theorem 15. Let W_n and V_n be sequences of $k \times 1$ and $l \times 1$ random vectors, respectively. Let W be a $k \times 1$ random vector and let $V = c$ be a constant vector in R^l. Suppose $W_n \overset{d}{\to} W$ and $V_n \overset{d}{\to} c$ (or equivalently $V_n \overset{p}{\to} c$ in light of Theorem 10). Then $Z_n = (W_n', V_n')' \overset{d}{\to} Z = (W', V')' = (W', c')'$.

Proof. Let $\phi_n(t)$ and $\phi(t)$ denote, respectively, the characteristic function of Z_n and Z. To show that $Z_n \overset{d}{\to} Z$ it suffices to show that $\phi_n(t) \to \phi(t)$ for all $t \in R^{k+l}$ in light of the multivariate version of Theorem 8. Let $t = (s', u')'$ with $s \in R^k$ and $u \in R^l$ arbitrary. Observing that $|\exp(is'W_n)| = 1 = |\exp(iu'c)|$, we have

$$|\phi_n(t) - \phi(t)| = |E(e^{is'W_n}e^{iu'V_n} - e^{is'W}e^{iu'c})| \tag{10.6}$$

$$\leq E[|e^{is'W_n}||e^{iu'V_n} - e^{iu'c}|] + |e^{iu'c}||E(e^{is'W_n} - e^{is'W})|$$

$$\leq E|e^{iu'V_n} - e^{iu'c}| + |E(e^{is'W_n} - e^{is'W})|$$

$$= E|e^{iu'V_n} - e^{iu'c}| + |\phi_n^W(s) - \phi^W(s)|,$$

where $\phi_n^W(s)$ and $\phi^W(s)$ denote, respectively, the characteristic function of W_n and W. Since $V_n \xrightarrow{p} c$ it follows from Theorem 14 that $\exp(iu'V_n) - \exp(iu'c) \xrightarrow{p} 0$. Observing that $|\exp(iu'V_n) - \exp(iu'c)| \leq 2$ it follows furthermore from Theorem 6 that $E|\exp(iu'V_n) - \exp(iu'c)| \to 0$. By assumption $W_n \xrightarrow{d} W$. It then follows again from the multivariate version of Theorem 8 that $\phi_n^W(s) \to \phi^W(s)$. Thus both terms in the last line of (10.6) converge to zero, and hence $\phi_n(t) \to \phi(t)$. ∎

Given Theorem 15 the following result follows immediately from Theorem 14.

Corollary 4. Let W_n and V_n be sequences of $k \times 1$ and $l \times 1$ random vectors, respectively. Let W be a $k \times 1$ random vector and c a constant vector in $\mathbb{R}^l$. Suppose $W_n \xrightarrow{d} W$ and $V_n \xrightarrow{d} c$ (or equivalently $V_n \xrightarrow{p} c$). Let $g : \mathbb{R}^k \times \mathbb{R}^l \to \mathbb{R}^s$ be a Borel measurable function and assume that g is continuous in every point of $A \times \{c\}$ where $A \subseteq \mathbb{R}^k$ satisfies $P(W \in A) = 1$. Then $g(W_n, V_n) \xrightarrow{d} g(W, c)$.

As a further corollary we have the following useful results.

Corollary 5. Let W_n and V_n be sequences of $k \times 1$ and $l \times 1$ random vectors, let A_n and B_n be sequences of $l \times k$ and $k \times k$ random matrices, respectively. Furthermore, let W be a $k \times 1$ random vector, let c be a $l \times 1$ nonstochastic vector, and let A and B be some nonstochastic $l \times k$ and $k \times k$ matrices.

(a) For $k = l$

$$W_n \xrightarrow{d} W, \ V_n \xrightarrow{p} c \ \text{ implies } \ W_n \pm V_n \xrightarrow{d} W \pm c$$

$$W_n'V_n \xrightarrow{d} W'c.$$

(If $c = 0$, then $W_n'V_n \xrightarrow{d} 0$ and hence also $W_n'V_n \xrightarrow{p} 0$).

(b) For $k = l = 1$

$$W_n \xrightarrow{d} W, \ V_n \xrightarrow{p} c \ \text{ implies } \ W_n/V_n \xrightarrow{d} W/c \quad \text{if } c \neq 0,$$

$$V_n/W_n \xrightarrow{d} c/W \quad \text{if } P(W = 0) = 0.$$

(c) $W_n \xrightarrow{d} W, \ V_n \xrightarrow{p} c, \ A_n \xrightarrow{p} A \ \text{ implies } \ A_nW_n + V_n \xrightarrow{d} AW + c,$

(d) $W_n \xrightarrow{d} W, \ B_n \xrightarrow{p} B \ \text{ implies } \ W_n'B_nW_n \xrightarrow{d} W'BW.$

Of course, if in the above corollary $W \sim N(\mu, \Sigma)$, then $AW + c \sim N(A\mu + c, A\Sigma A')$. If $W \sim N(0, I_k)$ and B is idempotent of rank p, then $W'BW \sim \chi^2(p)$.

2.4   Orders of magnitude

In determining the limiting behavior of sequences of random variables it is often helpful to employ notions of orders of relative magnitudes. We start with a review of the concepts of order of magnitudes for sequences of real numbers.

Definition 6.   (Order of magnitude of a sequence of real numbers) Let a_n be a sequence of real numbers and let c_n be a sequence of positive real numbers. We then say a_n is at most of order c_n, and write $a_n = O(c_n)$, if there exists a constant $M < \infty$ such that $c_n^{-1}|a_n| \leq M$ for all $n \in N$. We say a_n is of smaller order than c_n, and write $a_n = o(c_n)$, if $c_n^{-1}|a_n| \to 0$ as $n \to \infty$. (The definition extends to vectors and matrices by applying the definition to their norm.)

The following results concerning the algebra of order in magnitude operations are often useful.

Theorem 16.   Let a_n and b_n be sequences of real numbers, and let c_n and d_n be sequences of positive real numbers.

(a)   If $a_n = o(c_n)$ and $b_n = o(d_n)$, then $a_n b_n = o(c_n d_n)$, $|a_n|^s = o(c_n^s)$ for $s > 0$,
   $a_n + b_n = o(\max\{c_n, d_n\}) = o(c_n + d_n)$.

(b)   If $a_n = O(c_n)$ and $b_n = O(d_n)$, then $a_n b_n = O(c_n d_n)$, $|a_n|^s = O(c_n^s)$ for $s > 0$,
   $a_n + b_n = O(\max\{c_n, d_n\}) = O(c_n + d_n)$.

(c)   If $a_n = o(c_n)$ and $b_n = O(d_n)$, then $a_n b_n = o(c_n d_n)$.

We now generalize the concept of order of magnitude from sequences of real numbers to sequences of random variables.

Definition 7.   (Order in probability of a sequence of random variables) Let Z_n be a sequence of random variables, and let c_n be a sequence of positive real numbers. We then say Z_n is at most of order c_n in probability, and write $Z_n = O_p(c_n)$, if for every $\varepsilon > 0$ there exists a constant $M_\varepsilon < \infty$ such that $P(c_n^{-1}|Z_n| \geq M_\varepsilon) \leq \varepsilon$. We say Z_n is of smaller order in probability than c_n, and write $Z_n = o_p(c_n)$, if $c_n^{-1}|Z_n| \xrightarrow{p} 0$ as $n \to \infty$. (The definition extends to vectors and matrices by applying the definition to their norm.)

The algebra of order in probability operations O_p and o_p is identical to that of order in magnitude operations O and o presented in the theorem above; see, e.g., Fuller (1976, p. 184).
   A sequence of random variables Z_n that is $O_p(1)$ is also said to be "stochastically bounded" or "bounded in probability". The next theorem gives sufficient conditions for a sequence to be stochastically bounded.

Theorem 17.

(a)   Suppose $E|Z_n|^r = O(1)$ for some $r > 0$, then $Z_n = O_p(1)$.
(b)   Suppose $Z_n \xrightarrow{d} Z$, then $Z_n = O_p(1)$.

Proof.   Part (a) follows readily from Markov's inequality. To prove part (b) fix $\varepsilon > 0$. Now choose M_ε^* such that F is continuous at $-M_\varepsilon^*$ and M_ε^*, and $F(-M_\varepsilon^*) \leq \varepsilon/4$ and $F(M_\varepsilon^*) \geq 1 - \varepsilon/4$. Since every CDF has at most a countable number of discontinuity points, such a choice is possible. By assumption $F_n(z) \to F(z)$ for all continuity points of F. Let n_ε be such that for all $n \geq n_\varepsilon$

$$| F_n(-M_\varepsilon^*) - F(-M_\varepsilon^*) | \leq \varepsilon/4$$

and

$$| F_n(M_\varepsilon^*) - F(M_\varepsilon^*) | \leq \varepsilon/4.$$

Then for $n \geq n_\varepsilon$

$$P(| Z_n | \geq M_\varepsilon^*) \leq F_n(-M_\varepsilon^*) - F_n(M_\varepsilon^*) + 1$$
$$\leq F(-M_\varepsilon^*) - F(M_\varepsilon^*) + 1 + \varepsilon/2 \leq \varepsilon.$$

Since $\lim_{M \to \infty} P(| Z_i | \geq M) = 0$ for each $i \in \mathbb{N}$ we can find an M_ε^{**} such that $P(| Z_i | \geq M_\varepsilon^{**}) \leq \varepsilon$ for $i = 1, \ldots, n_\varepsilon - 1$. Now let $M_\varepsilon = \max\{M_\varepsilon^*, M_\varepsilon^{**}\}$. Then $P(| Z_n | \geq M_\varepsilon) \leq \varepsilon$ for all $n \in \mathbb{N}$. ∎

3   LAWS OF LARGE NUMBERS

Let Z_t, $t \in \mathbb{N}$, be a sequence of random variables with $EZ_t = \mu_t$. Furthermore let $\bar{Z}_n = n^{-1} \sum_{t=1}^n Z_t$ denote the sample mean, and let $\bar{\mu}_n = E\bar{Z}_n = n^{-1} \sum_{t=1}^n \mu_t$. A law of large numbers (LLN) then specifies conditions under which

$$\bar{Z}_n - E\bar{Z}_n = n^{-1} \sum_{t=1}^n (Z_t - \mu_t)$$

converges to zero either in probability or almost surely. If the convergence is in probability we speak of a weak LLN, if the convergence is almost surely we speak of a strong LLN. We note that in applications the random variables Z_t may themselves be functions of other random variables.

The usefulness of LLNs stems from the fact that many estimators can be expressed as (continuous) functions of sample averages of random variables, or differ from such a function only by a term that can be shown to converge to zero i.p. or a.s. Thus to establish the probability or almost sure limit of such an estimator we may try to establish in a first step the limits for the respective averages by means of LLNs. In a second step we may then use Theorem 14 to derive the actual limit for the estimator.

Example 6.   As an illustration consider the linear regression model $y_t = x_t\theta + \varepsilon_t$, $t = 1, \ldots, n$, where y_t, x_t and ε_t are all scalar and denote the dependent variable, the independent variable, and the disturbance term in period t. The ordinary least squares estimator for the parameter θ is then given by

$$\hat{\theta}_n = \frac{\sum\limits_{t=1}^{n} x_t y_t}{\sum\limits_{t=1}^{n} x_t^2} = \theta + \frac{n^{-1}\sum\limits_{t=1}^{n} x_t \varepsilon_t}{n^{-1}\sum\limits_{t=1}^{n} x_t^2}$$

and thus $\hat{\theta}_n$ is seen to be a function of the sample averages of $x_t\varepsilon_t$ and x_t^2.

3.1   Independent processes

In this subsection we discuss LLNs for independent processes.

Theorem 18.[12]   (Kolmogorov's strong LLN for iid random variables) Let Z_t be a sequence of identically and independently distributed (iid) random variables with $E|Z_1| < \infty$ and $EZ_1 = \mu$. Then $\bar{Z}_n \xrightarrow{a.s.} \mu$ (and hence $\bar{Z}_n \xrightarrow{i.p.} \mu$) as $n \to \infty$.

We have the following trivial but useful corollary.

Corollary 6.   Let Z_t be a sequence of iid random variables, and let f be a Borel-measurable real function satisfying $E|f(Z_1)| < \infty$, then $n^{-1}\sum_{t=1}^{n} f(Z_t) \xrightarrow{a.s.} Ef(Z_1)$ as $n \to \infty$.

The corollary can, in particular, be used to establish convergence of sample moments of, say, order p to the corresponding population moment by choosing $f(Z_t) = Z_t^p$.
   We now derive the probability limit of the ordinary least squares estimator considered in Example 6 as an illustration.

Example 7.   Assume the setup of Example 6. Assume furthermore that the processes x_t and ε_t are iid with $Ex_t^2 = Q_x$, $0 < Q_x < \infty$, $E|\varepsilon_t| < \infty$, and $E\varepsilon_t = 0$, and that the two processes are independent of each other. Then $x_t\varepsilon_t$ is iid, has finite expectation and satisfies $Ex_t\varepsilon_t = Ex_t E\varepsilon_t = 0$. Hence it follows from Theorem 18 that $n^{-1}\sum_{t=1}^{n} x_t\varepsilon_t \xrightarrow{a.s.} 0$. Corollary 6 implies $n^{-1}\sum_{t=1}^{n} x_t^2 \xrightarrow{a.s.} Q_x$. Applying Theorem 14 then yields $\hat{\theta}_n \xrightarrow{a.s.} \theta + 0/Q_x = \theta$.

The assumption in Theorem 18 that the random variables are identically distributed can be relaxed at the expense of maintaining additional assumptions on the second moments.

Theorem 19.[13]   (Kolmogorov's strong LLN for ID random variables) Let Z_t be a sequence of independently distributed (ID) random variables with $EZ_t = \mu_t$ and $\mathrm{var}(Z_t) = \sigma_t^2 < \infty$. Suppose $\sum_{t=1}^{\infty} \sigma_t^2/t^2 < \infty$. Then $\bar{Z}_n - \bar{\mu}_n \xrightarrow{a.s.} 0$ as $n \to \infty$.

The condition $\sum_{t=1}^{n} \sigma_t^2/t^2 < \infty$ puts a restriction on the permissible variation in the σ_t^2. For example, it is satisfied if the sequence σ_t^2 is bounded.

3.2 Dependent processes

The following weak LLN follows immediately from Corollary 1. In contrast to the above LLNs this theorem does not require the variables to be independently distributed, but only requires uncorrelatedness.

Theorem 20. (Chebychev's weak LLN for uncorrelated random variables) Let Z_t be a sequence of uncorrelated random variables with $EZ_t = \mu_t$ and var$(Z_t) = \sigma_t^2 < \infty$. Suppose var$(\bar{Z}_n) = n^{-2} \sum_{t=1}^{n} \sigma_t^2 \to 0$ as $n \to \infty$, then $\bar{Z}_n - \bar{\mu}_n \overset{p}{\to} 0$.

The condition on the variance in Theorem 20 is weaker than the corresponding condition in Theorem 19 in view of Kronecker's lemma; see, e.g., Shiryayev (1984, p. 365). The condition is clearly satisfied if the sequence σ_t^2 is bounded.

A class of dependent processes that is important in econometrics and statistics is the class of martingale difference sequences. For example, the score of the maximum likelihood estimator evaluated at the true parameter value represents (under mild regularity conditions) a martingale difference sequence.

Definition 8. (Martingale difference sequence) Let $\mathcal{F}_t$, $t \geq 0$, be a sequence of σ-fields such that $\mathcal{F}_0 \subseteq \mathcal{F}_1 \subseteq \dots \subseteq \mathcal{F}$. Let Z_t, $t \geq 1$, be a sequence of random variables, then Z_t is said to be a martingale difference sequence (wrt the sequence $\mathcal{F}_t$), if Z_t is $\mathcal{F}_t$-measurable, $E|Z_t| < \infty$ and

$$E(Z_t \mid \mathcal{F}_{t-1}) = 0$$

for all $t \geq 1$.

We note that if Z_t is a martingale difference sequence then $E(Z_t) = E(E(Z_t \mid \mathcal{F}_{t-1})) = 0$ by the law of iterated expectations. Furthermore, since $E(Z_t Z_{t+k}) = E(Z_t E(Z_{t+k} \mid \mathcal{F}_{t+k-1})) = 0$ for $k \geq 1$, we see that every martingale difference sequence is uncorrelated, provided the second moments are finite. We also note, if Z_t is a martingale difference sequence wrt the σ-fields $\mathcal{F}_t$, then it is also a martingale difference sequence wrt the σ-fields $\mathcal{R}_t$ where $\mathcal{R}_t$ is generated by $\{Z_t, Z_{t-1}, \dots, Z_1\}$ and $\mathcal{R}_0 = \{\emptyset, \Omega\}$.

We now present a strong LLN for martingale difference sequences.

Theorem 21.[14] Let Z_t be a martingale difference sequence with var$(Z_t) = \sigma_t^2 < \infty$. Suppose $\sum_{t=1}^{n} \sigma_t^2 / t^2 < \infty$. Then $\bar{Z}_n \overset{a.s.}{\longrightarrow} 0$ as $n \to \infty$.

The above LLN contains Kolmogorov's strong LLN for independent random variables as a special case (with Z_t replaced by $Z_t - \mu_t$).

Many processes of interest in econometrics and statistics are correlated, and hence are not covered by the above LLNs. In the following we present a strong LLN for strictly stationary processes, which allows for a wide range of correlation structures.

Definition 9. (Strict stationarity) The sequence of random variables Z_t, $t \geq 1$, is said to be strictly stationary if $(Z_1, Z_2, \ldots, Z_n)$ has the same distribution as $(Z_{1+k}, Z_{2+k}, \ldots, Z_{n+k})$ for all $k \geq 1$ and $n \geq 1$.

Definition 10.[15] (Invariance and ergodicity of strictly stationary sequences) Let Z_t, $t \geq 1$, be a strictly stationary sequence.

(a) Consider the event

$$A = \{\omega \in \Omega : (Z_1(\omega), Z_2(\omega), \ldots) \in B\}$$

with $B \in \mathcal{B}^\infty$, where $\mathcal{B}^\infty$ are the Borel sets of R^∞. Then A is said to be invariant if

$$A = \{\omega \in \Omega : (Z_{1+k}(\omega), Z_{2+k}(\omega), \ldots) \in B\}$$

for all $k \geq 1$.

(b) The sequence Z_t is ergodic if every invariant event has probability one or zero.

We note that every iid sequence of random variables is strictly stationary and ergodic. Furthermore, if Z_t is strictly stationary and ergodic, and $g : R^\infty \to R$ is measurable, then the sequence Y_t with $Y_t = g(Z_t, Z_{t+1}, \ldots)$ is again strictly stationary and ergodic.

We can now give the following strong LLN, which is often referred to as the Ergodic Theorem. This theorem contains Kolmogorov's strong LLN for iid random variables as a special case.

Theorem 22.[16] Let Z_t be a strictly stationary and ergodic sequence with $E|Z_1| < \infty$ and $EZ_1 = \mu$. Then $\bar{Z}_n \overset{a.s.}{\longrightarrow} \mu$ as $n \to \infty$.

There is a large literature on LLNs for dependent processes beside the LLNs presented above. LLNs for weakly stationary processes, including linear processes and ARMA (autoregressive moving average) processes, can be found in Hannan (1970, ch. IV.3); see also Phillips and Solo (1992). Important classes of dependent processes considered in econometrics and statistics are α-mixing, ϕ-mixing, near epoch dependent and L_p-approximable processes. LLNs for such processes are discussed in some detail in, e.g., Davidson (1994, Part IV) and Pötscher and Prucha (1997, ch. 6), and in the references given therein; see also Davidson and de Jong (1997) for recent extensions.

3.3 Uniform laws of large numbers

In the previous sections we have been concerned with various notions of convergence for sequences of random variables and random vectors. Sometimes one is confronted with sequences of random functions, say $Q_n(\theta)$, that depend on a parameter vector θ contained in some parameter space Θ. That is, $Q_n(\theta)$ is a random variable for each fixed $\theta \in \Theta$.[17] As an example of a random function consider, for example, the loglikelihood function of iid random variables $Z_1, \ldots,$ Z_n with a density that depends on a parameter vector θ:

$$Q_n(\theta) = \frac{1}{n} \sum_{t=1}^{n} q(Z_t, \theta) \tag{10.7}$$

where q is the logarithm of the density of $\mathbf{Z}_t$. Clearly, for every fixed $\theta \in \Theta$ we can apply the notions of convergence for random variables discussed above to $Q_n(\theta)$. However, for many purposes these notions of "pointwise" convergence are not sufficient and stronger notions of convergence are needed. For example, those stronger notions of convergence are often useful in proving consistency of maximum likelihood estimators: in many cases an explicit expression for the maximum likelihood estimator will not be available. In those cases one may try to deduce the convergence behavior of the estimator from the convergence behavior of the loglikelihood objective function $Q_n(\theta)$. By Kolmogorov's LLN we have

$$Q_n(\theta) \xrightarrow{a.s.} Q(\theta) \text{ for all } \theta \in \Theta, \tag{10.8}$$

where $Q(\theta) = Eq(Z_t, \theta)$, provided $E|q(Z_t, \theta)| < \infty$. A well-established result from the theory of maximum likelihood estimation tells us furthermore that the limiting objective function $Q(\theta)$ is uniquely maximized at the true parameter value, say θ_0, provided θ_0 is identified. It is tempting to conclude that these two facts imply a.s. convergence of the maximum likelihood estimators, i.e. of the maximizers of the objective functions $Q_n(\theta)$, to θ_0. Unfortunately, this line of reasoning is not conclusive in general, as can be seen from counter examples; see, e.g., Amemiya (1985, p. 109). However, this line of reasoning can be salvaged if we can establish not only "pointwise" convergence a.s., i.e. (10.8), but even uniform convergence a.s., i.e.,

$$\sup_{\theta \in \Theta} |Q_n(\theta) - Q(\theta)| \xrightarrow{a.s.} 0, \tag{10.9}$$

and if, for example, Θ is compact and Q is continuous.[18]

The above discussion motivates interest in results that establish uniform convergence of random functions $Q_n(\theta)$. In the important special case where $Q_n(\theta) = n^{-1} \sum_{t=1}^{n} q(Z_t, \theta)$ and $Q(\theta) = EQ_n(\theta)$ such results are called uniform laws of large numbers (ULLNs). We next present an ULLN for functions of iid random variables.

Theorem 23.[19] Let Z_t be a sequence of identically and independently distributed $k \times 1$ random vectors, let Θ be a compact subset of R^p, and let q be a real valued function on $R^k \times \Theta$. Furthermore, let $q(., \theta)$ be Borel-measurable for each $\theta \in \Theta$, and let $q(z, .)$ be continuous for each $z \in R^k$. If $E \sup_{\theta \in \Theta} |q(Z_t, \theta)| < \infty$, then

$$\sup_{\theta \in \Theta} \left| \frac{1}{n} \sum_{t=1}^{n} [q(Z_t, \theta) - Eq(Z_t, \theta)] \right| \xrightarrow{a.s.} 0 \text{ as } n \to \infty,$$

i.e. $Q_n(\theta) = n^{-1} \sum_{t=1}^{n} q(Z_t, \theta)$ satisfies a ULLN.

The theorem also holds if the assumption that Z_t is iid is replaced by the assumption that Z_t is stationary and ergodic; see, e.g., Pötscher and Prucha (1986, Lemma A.2). Uniform laws of large numbers that also cover functions of dependent and heterogeneous random vectors are, for example, given in Andrews (1987) and Pötscher and Prucha (1989); for additional references see Pötscher and Prucha (1997, ch. 5).

4 CENTRAL LIMIT THEOREMS

Let Z_t, $t \in \mathbb{N}$, be a sequence of iid random variables with $EZ_t = \mu$ and $\mathrm{var}(Z_t) = \sigma^2$, $0 < \sigma^2 < \infty$. Let $\bar{Z}_n = n^{-1}\sum_{t=1}^{n} Z_t$ denote the sample mean. By Kolmogorov's strong LLN for iid random variables (Theorem 18) it then follows that $\bar{Z}_n - E\bar{Z}_n$ converges to zero a.s. and hence i.p. This implies that the limiting distribution of $\bar{Z}_n - E\bar{Z}_n$ is degenerate at zero, and thus no insight is gained from this limiting distribution regarding the shape of the distribution of the sample mean for finite n; compare the discussion at the beginning of Section 2.2. Suppose we consider the rescaled quantity

$$\sqrt{n}\,(\bar{Z}_n - E\bar{Z}_n) = n^{-1/2}\sum_{t=1}^{n}(Z_t - \mu). \tag{10.10}$$

Then the variance of the rescaled expression is $\sigma^2 > 0$ for all n, indicating that its limiting distribution will not be degenerate. Theorems that provide results concerning the limiting distribution of expressions like (10.10) are called central limit theorems (CLTs). Rather than to center the respective random variables, as is done in (10.10), we assume in the following, without loss of generality, that the respective random variables have mean zero.

4.1 Independent processes

SOME CLASSICAL CLTS
In this subsection we will present several classical CLTs, starting with the Lindeberg–Lévy CLT.

Theorem 24.[20] (Lindeberg–Lévy CLT) Let Z_t be a sequence of iid random variables with $EZ_t = 0$ and $\mathrm{var}(Z_t) = \sigma^2 < \infty$. Then $n^{-1/2}\sum_{t=1}^{n} Z_t \xrightarrow{d} N(0, \sigma^2)$. (In case $\sigma^2 = 0$ the limit $N(0, 0)$ should be interpreted as the degenerate distribution having all its probability mass concentrated at zero.[21])

Of course, if $\sigma^2 > 0$ the conclusion of the theorem can be written equivalently as $n^{-1/2}\sum_{t=1}^{n} Z_t/\sigma \xrightarrow{d} N(0, 1)$. Extensions of Theorem 24 and of any of the following central limit theorems to the vector case are readily obtained using the Cramér–Wold device (Theorem 13). To illustrate this we exemplarily extend Theorem 24 to the vector case.

Example 8. Let Z_t be a sequence of iid k-dimensional random vectors with zero mean and finite variance covariance matrix Σ. Let $\xi_n = n^{-1/2} \sum_{t=1}^{n} Z_t$, let $\xi \sim N(0, \Sigma)$ (where $N(0, \Sigma)$ denotes a singular normal distribution if Σ is singular), and let α be some element of $\mathbb{R}^k$. Now consider the scalar random variables $\alpha' \xi_n = n^{-1/2} \sum_{t=1}^{n} \alpha' Z_t$. Clearly the summands $\alpha' Z_t$ are iid with mean zero and variance $\alpha' \Sigma \alpha$. It hence follows from Theorem 24 that $\alpha' \xi_n$ converges in distribution to $N(0, \alpha' \Sigma \alpha)$. Of course $\alpha' \xi \sim N(0, \alpha' \Sigma \alpha)$, and hence $\alpha' \xi_n \xrightarrow{d} \alpha' \xi$. Since α was arbitrary it follows from Theorem 13 that $\xi_n \xrightarrow{d} \xi$, which shows that the random vector $n^{-1/2} \sum_{t=1}^{n} Z_t$ converges in distribution to $N(0, \Sigma)$.

Theorem 24 postulates that the random variables Z_t are iid. The following theorems relax this assumption to independence. It proves helpful to define

$$\sigma_{(n)}^2 = \sum_{t=1}^{n} \sigma_t^2 \qquad (10.11)$$

where $\sigma_t^2 = \text{var}(Z_t)$. For independent Z_ts clearly $\sigma_{(n)}^2 = n^2 \text{var}(\bar{Z}_n)$, and in case the Z_ts are iid with variance σ^2 we have $\sigma_{(n)}^2 = n\sigma^2$. To connect Theorem 24 with the subsequent CLTs observe that within the context of Theorem 24 we have $n^{-1/2} \sum_{t=1}^{n} Z_t / \sigma = \sum_{t=1}^{n} Z_t / \sigma_{(n)}$ (given $\sigma^2 > 0$).

Theorem 25.[22] (Lindeberg–Feller CLT) Let Z_t be a sequence of independent random variables with $EZ_t = 0$ and $\text{var}(Z_t) = \sigma_t^2 < \infty$. Suppose that $\sigma_{(n)}^2 > 0$, except for finitely many n. If for every $\varepsilon > 0$

$$\lim_{n \to \infty} \frac{1}{\sigma_{(n)}^2} \sum_{t=1}^{n} E[\,|Z_t|^2 \, 1\,(\,|Z_t| \geq \varepsilon \sigma_{(n)})\,] = 0, \qquad (L)$$

then $\sum_{t=1}^{n} Z_t / \sigma_{(n)} \xrightarrow{d} N(0, 1)$.

Condition (L) is called the Lindeberg condition. The next theorem employs in place of the Lindeberg condition a condition that is stronger but easier to verify.

Theorem 26.[23] (Lyapounov CLT) Let Z_t be a sequence of independent random variables with $EZ_t = 0$ and $\text{var}(Z_t) = \sigma_t^2 < \infty$. Suppose that $\sigma_{(n)}^2 > 0$, except for finitely many n. If for some $\delta > 0$

$$\lim_{n \to \infty} \sum_{t=1}^{n} E|Z_t / \sigma_{(n)}|^{2+\delta} = 0, \qquad (P)$$

then $\sum_{t=1}^{n} Z_t / \sigma_{(n)} \xrightarrow{d} N(0, 1)$.

Condition (P) is called the Lyapounov condition. Condition (P) implies condition (L). It is readily seen that a sufficient condition for (P) is that

$$n^{-1}\sigma_{(n)}^2 = n^{-1}\sum_{t=1}^{n}\sigma_t^2 \geq \text{const} > 0$$

for n sufficiently large and that

$$\lim_{n\to\infty}\sum_{t=1}^{n}E\left|Z_t/\sqrt{n}\right|^{2+\delta} = 0.$$

In turn, sufficient conditions for those two conditions are, respectively,

$$\lim_{n\to\infty} n^{-1}\sigma_{(n)}^2 = \psi, \quad 0 < \psi < \infty, \tag{10.12}$$

and

$$\sup_{n} n^{-1}\sum_{t=1}^{n}E|Z_t|^{2+\delta} < \infty. \tag{10.13}$$

We note that the conclusions of Theorems 25 and 26 can be stated equivalently as $n^{-1/2}\sum_{t=1}^{n}Z_t \xrightarrow{d} N(0, \psi)$, whenever (10.12) holds. In this context we also make the trivial observation, that for a sequence of independent random variables Z_t with zero mean and finite variances $\sigma_t^2 \geq 0$ the condition $n^{-1}\sigma_{(n)}^2 \to \psi = 0$ implies $n^{-1/2}\sum_{t=1}^{n}Z_t \xrightarrow{p} 0$ (Corollary 1), which can also be rewritten as $n^{-1/2}\sum_{t=1}^{n}Z_t \xrightarrow{d} N(0, \psi)$, $\psi = 0$.

The above CLTs were given for sequences of random variables $(Z_t, t \geq 1)$. They can be readily generalized to cover triangular arrays of random variables $(Z_{tn}, 1 \leq t \leq n, n \geq 1)$. In fact Theorems 25 and 26 hold with Z_t replaced by Z_{tn} and σ_t^2 replaced by σ_{tn}^2; see, e.g., Billingsley (1979, pp. 310–12).

The need for CLTs for triangular arrays arises frequently in econometrics. One example is the derivation of the limiting distribution of the least squares estimator when different regressors grow at different rates. In this case one can still obtain a limiting normal distribution for the least squares estimator if the usual $\sqrt{n}$-norming is replaced with a normalization by an appropriate diagonal matrix. In essence, this entails renormalizing the ith regressor by the square root of $\sum_{t=1}^{n}x_{ti}^2$, whose obvious dependence on n leads to the consideration of a CLT for quantities of the form $\sum_{t=1}^{n}c_{tn}u_t$ with u_t iid; see Theorem 28 below.

CLTs FOR REGRESSION ANALYSIS

In this subsection we present some CLTs that are geared towards regression analysis. As discussed above, within this context we will often need CLTs for a sequence of iid random variables multiplied by some time-varying scale factors, that may also depend on the sample size. We first give a general CLT that covers such situations as a corollary to the Lindeberg–Feller CLT.

Theorem 27.[24] Let $\underline{Z}_t$ be a sequence of iid random variables with $E\underline{Z}_t = 0$ and $\text{var}(\underline{Z}_t) = 1$. Furthermore, let $(\sigma_{tn}, 1 \leq t \leq n, n \geq 1)$ be a triangular array of real numbers, and define the triangular array Z_{tn} by $Z_{tn} = \sigma_{tn} \underline{Z}_t$. Suppose that $\sigma_{(n)}^2 = \sum_{t=1}^{n} \sigma_{tn}^2 > 0$, except for finitely many n. If

$$\lim_{n \to \infty} \frac{\max_{1 \le t \le n} \sigma_{tn}^2}{\sum_{t=1}^{n} \sigma_{tn}^2} = 0, \tag{M}$$

then $\sum_{t=1}^{n} Z_{tn} / \sigma_{(n)} \xrightarrow{d} N(0, 1)$.

All of the subsequent CLTs in this section are based on Theorem 27. Explicit proofs are given in a longer mimeographed version of this article, which is available from the authors upon request.

Theorem 28. Let u_t, $t \ge 1$, be a sequence of iid random variables with $Eu_t = 0$ and $Eu_t^2 = \sigma^2 < \infty$. Let X_n, $n \ge 1$, with $X_n = (x_{ti})$ be a sequence of real non-stochastic $n \times k$ matrices with

$$\lim_{n \to \infty} \frac{\max_{1 \le t \le n} x_{ti}^2}{\sum_{t=1}^{n} x_{ti}^2} = 0 \quad for \ i = 1, \ldots, k, \tag{10.14}$$

where it is assumed that $\sum_{t=1}^{n} x_{ti}^2 > 0$ for all but finitely many n. Define $W_n = X_n S_n^{-1}$ where S_n is a $k \times k$ diagonal matrix with the ith diagonal element equal to $[\sum_{t=1}^{n} x_{ti}^2]^{1/2}$, and assume that $\lim_{n \to \infty} W_n' W_n = \Phi$ is finite. Let $\mathbf{u}_n = [u_1, \ldots, u_n]'$, then $W_n' \mathbf{u}_n \xrightarrow{d} N(0, \sigma^2 \Phi)$.

The above theorem is given in Amemiya (1985, p. 97), for the case of nonsingular $\sigma^2 \Phi$.[25] The theorem allows for trending (nonstochastic) regressors. For example, (10.14) holds for $x_{ti} = t^p$, $p > 0$. We note that in case of a single regressor $W_n' W_n = \Phi = 1$.

Theorem 29. Let u_t, $t \ge 1$, be a sequence of iid random variables with $Eu_t = 0$ and $Eu_t^2 = \sigma^2 < \infty$. Let X_n, $n \ge 1$, with $X_n = (x_{ti})$ be a sequence of real nonstochastic $n \times k$ matrices with $\lim_{n \to \infty} n^{-1} X_n' X_n = Q$ finite. Let $\mathbf{u}_n = [u_1, \ldots, u_n]'$, then $n^{-1/2} X_n' \mathbf{u}_n \xrightarrow{d} N(0, \sigma^2 Q)$.

The theorem is, for example, given in Theil (1971, p. 380), for the case of nonsingular $\sigma^2 Q$. The theorem does not require that the elements of X_n are bounded in absolute value, as is often assumed in the literature.

We now use Theorems 28 and 29 to exemplarily give two asymptotic normality results for the least squares estimator.

Example 9. (Asymptotic normality of the least squares estimator) Consider the linear regression model

$$y_t = \sum_{i=1}^{k} x_{ti} \beta_i + u_t, \quad t \ge 1.$$

Suppose u_t and $X_n = (x_{ti})$ satisfy the assumption of Theorem 28. Assume furthermore that the matrix Φ in Theorem 28 is nonsingular. Then rank $(X_n) = k$ for large n and the least squares estimator for $\beta = (\beta_1, \ldots, \beta_k)'$ is then given by $\hat{\beta}_n = (X_n'X_n)^{-1}X_n'y_n$ with $y_n = (y_1, \ldots, y_n)'$. Since $\hat{\beta}_n - \beta = (X_n'X_n)^{-1}X_n'u_n$ we have

$$S_n(\hat{\beta}_n - \beta) = S_n(X_n'X_n)^{-1}S_n'S_n'^{-1}X_n'u_n = (W_n'W_n)^{-1}W_n'u_n,$$

where S_n is defined in Theorem 28. Since $\lim_{n\to\infty} W_n'W_n = \Phi$ and Φ is assumed to be nonsingular, we obtain

$$S_n(\hat{\beta}_n - \beta) \xrightarrow{d} N(0, \sigma^2\Phi^{-1})$$

as a consequence of Theorem 28. Note that this asymptotic normality result allows for trending regressors.

Now suppose that u_t and $X_n = (x_{ti})$ satisfy the assumptions of Theorem 29 and that furthermore Q is nonsingular. Then we obtain by similar argumentation

$$\sqrt{n}\,(\hat{\beta}_n - \beta) = (n^{-1}X_n'X_n)^{-1}(n^{-\frac{1}{2}}X_n'u_n) \xrightarrow{d} N(0, \sigma^2 Q^{-1}).$$

We note that Theorem 29 does not hold in general if the regressors are allowed to be triangular arrays, i.e. the elements are allowed to depend on n. For example, suppose $k = 1$ and $X_n = [x_{11,n}, \ldots, x_{n1,n}]'$ where

$$x_{t1,n} = \begin{cases} 0 & t < n \\ \sqrt{n} & t = n, \end{cases}$$

then $n^{-1}X_n'X_n = 1$ and $n^{-1/2}X_n'u_n = u_n$. The limiting distribution of this expression is just the distribution of the u_ts, and hence not necessarily normal, violating the conclusion of Theorem 29.

We now give a CLT where the elements of X_n are allowed to be triangular arrays, but where we assume additionally that the elements of the X_n matrices are bounded in absolute value.

Theorem 30. Let u_t, $t \geq 1$, be a sequence of iid random variables with $Eu_t = 0$ and $Eu_t^2 = \sigma^2 < \infty$. Let $(x_{ti,n}, 1 \leq t \leq n, n \geq 1)$, $i = 1, \ldots, k$, be triangular arrays of real numbers that are bounded in absolute value, i.e. $\sup_n \sup_{1\leq t\leq n, 1\leq i\leq k} |x_{ti,n}| < \infty$. Let $X_n = (x_{ti,n})$ denote corresponding sequences of $n \times k$ real matrices and let $\lim_{n\to\infty} n^{-1}X_n'X_n = Q$ be finite. Furthermore, let $u_n = [u_1, \ldots, u_n]'$, then $n^{-1/2}X_n'u_n \xrightarrow{d} N(0, \sigma^2 Q)$.

Inspection of the proof of Theorem 30 shows that the uniform boundedness condition is stronger than is necessary and that it can be replaced by the condition $\max_{1\leq t\leq n} |x_{ti,n}| = o\,(n^{1/2})$ for $i = 1, \ldots, k$.

4.2   Dependent processes

There is a large literature on CLTs for dependent processes. Due to space limitation we will only present here – analogously as in our discussion of LLNs – two
CLTs for dependent processes. Both CLTs are given for martingale difference
sequences. As discussed, martingale difference sequences represent an important
class of stochastic processes in statistics. The first of the subsequent two theorems
assumes that the process is strictly stationary.

Theorem 31.[26]   Let Z_t be a strictly stationary and ergodic martingale difference
sequence with $\mathrm{var}(Z_t) = \sigma^2 < \infty$. Then $n^{-1/2} \sum_{t=1}^{n} Z_t \xrightarrow{d} N(0, \sigma^2)$. (In case $\sigma^2 = 0$, the
limit $N(0, 0)$ should be interpreted as the degenerate distribution having all its
probability mass concentrated at zero.[27])

The above theorem contains the Lindeberg–Lévy CLT for iid random variables
as a special case. The usefulness of Theorem 31 is illustrated by the following
example.

Example 10.   Suppose y_t is a stationary autoregressive process of order one
satisfying

$$y_t = a y_{t-1} + \varepsilon_t,$$

where $|a| < 1$ and the ε_ts are iid with mean zero and variance $\sigma^2, 0 < \sigma^2 < \infty$. Then
$y_t = \sum_{j=0}^{\infty} a^j \varepsilon_{t-j}$ is strictly stationary and ergodic. The least squares estimator calculated from a sample $y_0, y_1, \ldots, y_n$ is given by $\hat{a}_n = \sum_{t=1}^{n} y_t y_{t-1} / \sum_{t=1}^{n} y_{t-1}^2$ (with the
convention that we set $\hat{a} = 0$ on the event $\{ \sum_{t=0}^{n} y_{t-1}^2 = 0 \}$). Thus

$$n^{1/2}(\hat{a}_n - a) = \left(n^{-1/2} \sum_{t=1}^{n} \varepsilon_t y_{t-1} \right) \bigg/ \left(n^{-1} \sum_{t=1}^{n} y_{t-1}^2 \right).$$

The denominator converges a.s. to $E(y_{t-1}^2) = \sigma^2/(1-a^2) > 0$ by the Ergodic Theorem
(Theorem 22). Observe that $Z_t = \varepsilon_t y_{t-1}$ satisfies $E(Z_t | \varepsilon_{t-1}, \varepsilon_{t-2}, \ldots) = y_{t-1} E(\varepsilon_t | \varepsilon_{t-1},
\varepsilon_{t-2}, \ldots) = y_{t-1} E(\varepsilon_t) = 0$ since y_{t-1} is a (linear) function of $\varepsilon_{t-1}, \varepsilon_{t-2}, \ldots$ and since ε_t is
independent of $\{\varepsilon_{t-1}, \varepsilon_{t-2}, \ldots\}$. Hence, Z_t is a martingale difference sequence wrt
$\mathcal{F}_t$, where $\mathcal{F}_t$ denotes the σ-field generated by $\varepsilon_t, \varepsilon_{t-1}, \ldots$. As a function of ε_t and
y_{t-1} the sequence Z_t is clearly strictly stationary and ergodic. Furthermore, $\mathrm{var}(Z_t)
= E(\varepsilon_t^2 y_{t-1}^2) = E(\varepsilon_t^2) E(y_{t-1}^2) = \sigma^4/(1-a^2) < \infty$. Theorem 31 then implies

$$n^{-1/2} \sum_{t=1}^{n} \varepsilon_t y_{t-1} \xrightarrow{d} N(0, \sigma^4/(1-a^2)).$$

Combining this with the already established convergence of the denominator
implies the asymptotic normality result

$$n^{1/2}(\hat{a}_n - a) \xrightarrow{d} N(0, 1-a^2).$$

Theorem 32.[28]   Let Z_t be a martingale difference sequence (wrt $\mathcal{F}_t$) with conditional variances $E(Z_t^2 \mid \mathcal{F}_{t-1}) = \sigma_t^2$. Let $\sigma_{(n)}^2 = \sum_{t=1}^n \sigma_t^2$. Suppose

$$n^{-1}\sigma_{(n)}^2 \overset{p}{\to} \psi, \quad 0 < \psi < \infty, \tag{10.15}$$

and

$$\sum_{t=1}^n E\left(\left|Z_t/\sqrt{n}\right|^{2+\delta} \mid \mathcal{F}_{t-1}\right) \overset{p}{\to} 0 \tag{10.16}$$

as $n \to \infty$ for some $\delta > 0$, then $n^{-1/2} \sum_{t=1}^n Z_t \overset{d}{\to} N(0, \psi)$.

Condition (10.16) is a conditional Lyapounov condition. A sufficient condition for (10.16) is

$$\sup_n n^{-1} \sum_{t=1}^n E(|Z_t|^{2+\delta} \mid \mathcal{F}_{t-1}) = O_p(1). \tag{10.17}$$

As mentioned above, there is an enormous body of literature on CLTs for dependent processes. For further CLTs for martingale difference sequences and related results see Hall and Heyde (1980). Central limit theorems for m-dependent and linear processes can, for example, be found in Hannan (1970, ch. IV.4), Anderson (1971, ch. 7.7), or Phillips and Solo (1992). Classical references to central limit theorems for mixingales (including α-mixing, ϕ-mixing, and near epoch dependent processes) are McLeish (1974, 1975). For additional discussions of CLTs see, e.g., Davidson (1994, Part V) and Pötscher and Prucha (1997, ch. 10) and the references given therein.

5   FURTHER READINGS

There is a large number of books available that provide further in-depth discussions of the material (or parts of the material) presented in this article. The list of such books includes texts by Billingsley (1968, 1979), Davidson (1994), Serfling (1980) and Shiryayev (1984), to mention a few. Hall and Heyde (1980) give a thorough discussion of martingale limit theory.

Recent books on asymptotic theory for least mean distance estimators (including maximum likelihood estimators) and generalized method of moments estimators for general classes of nonlinear models include texts by Bierens (1994), Gallant (1987), Gallant and White (1988), Pötscher and Prucha (1997), and White (1994). For recent survey articles see, e.g., Newey and McFadden (1994), and Wooldridge (1994).

Notes

1   Strictly speaking, $h(.)$ has to be Borel measurable; for a definition of Borel measurability see Billingsley (1979), section 13.

2   For an understanding of the example it proves helpful to plot $Z_1(\omega)$, $Z_2(\omega)$, . . . for $0 \leq \omega < 1$.

3   The space of all random variables with finite rth moment is often referred to as the space L^r. On this space convergence in rth mean is often referred to as L^r-convergence.

4   For a proof see, e.g., Serfling (1980, p. 15).

5   See Billingsley (1979, p. 180 and Example 21.21).

6   We note that the rescaled quantities like $\sqrt{n}\,(\hat{\theta}_n - \theta)$ typically do not converge a.s. or i.p., and thus a new notion of convergence is needed for these quantities.

7   See, e.g., Billingsley (1968, p. 12), Billingsley (1979, p. 345), and Serfling (1980, p. 16).

8   See, e.g., Serfling (1980, pp. 13–14).

9   See, e.g., Serfling (1980, p. 24).

10   That is, let $A \subseteq \mathbf{R}^k$ denote the set of continuity points of g, then $P_Z(A) = P(Z \in A) = 1$. Of course, if g is continuous on $\mathbf{R}^k$, then $A = \mathbf{R}^k$ and the condition $P_Z(A) = 1$ is trivially satisfied.

11   The event $\{V_n = 0\}$ has probability approaching zero, and hence it is irrelevant which value is assigned to W_n/V_n on this event.

12   See, e.g., Shiryayev (1984, p. 366).

13   See, e.g., Shiryayev (1984, p. 364).

14   See, e.g., Shiryayev (1984, p. 487), or Davidson (1994, p. 314).

15   See, e.g., Stout (1974, p. 180).

16   See, e.g., Stout (1974, p. 181).

17   More precisely, Q_n is a function from $\Omega \times \Theta$ into R such that $Q(., \theta)$ is $\mathcal{F}$-measurable for each $\theta \in \Theta$.

18   The same line of argument holds if (uniform) convergence a.s. is replaced by (uniform) convergence i.p.

19   For a proof see Jennrich (1969, Theorem 2).

20   See, e.g., Billingsley (1979, p. 308).

21   Of course, the case $\sigma^2 = 0$ is trivial since in this case $Z_t = 0$ a.s.

22   See, e.g., Billingsley (1979, p. 310).

23   See, e.g., Billingsley (1979, p. 312).

24   The theorem is given as Problem 27.6 in Billingsley (1979, p. 319).

25   The proof given in Amemiya seems not to be entirely rigorous in that it does not take into account that the elements of S_n and hence those of W_n depend on the sample size n.

26   See, e.g., Gänssler and Stute (1977, p. 372).

27   See footnote 21.

28   See, e.g., Gänssler and Stute (1977, p. 365 and 370).

References

Amemiya, T. (1985). *Advanced Econometrics*. Cambridge: Harvard University Press.

Anderson, T.W. (1971). *The Statistical Analysis of Time Series*. New York: Wiley.

Andrews, D.W.K. (1987). Consistency in nonlinear econometric models: A generic uniform law of large numbers. *Econometrica* 55, 1465–71.

Bierens, H.J. (1994). *Topics in Advanced Econometrics*. Cambridge: Cambridge University Press.

Billingsley, P. (1968). *Convergence of Probability Measures*. New York: Wiley.

Billingsley, P. (1979). *Probability and Measure*. New York: Wiley.

Davidson, J. (1994). *Stochastic Limit Theory*. Oxford: Oxford University Press.

Davidson, J., and R. de Jong (1997). Strong laws of large numbers for dependent heterogeneous processes: A synthesis of recent new results. *Econometric Reviews* 16, 251–79.

Fuller, W.A. (1976). *Introduction to Statistical Time Series*. New York: Wiley.

Gallant, A.R. (1987). *Nonlinear Statistical Models*. New York: Wiley.

Gallant, A.R., and H. White (1988). *A Unified Theory of Estimation and Inference in Nonlinear Dynamic Models*. New York: Basil Blackwell.

Gänssler, P., and W. Stute (1977). *Wahrscheinlichkeitstheorie*. New York: Springer Verlag.

Hall, P., and C.C. Heyde (1980). *Martingale Limit Theory and Its Application*. New York: Academic Press.

Hannan, E.J. (1970). *Multiple Time Series*. New York: Wiley.

Jennrich, R.I. (1969). Asymptotic properties of nonlinear least squares estimators. *Annals of Mathematical Statistics* 40, 633–43.

McLeish, D.L. (1974). Dependent central limit theorems and invariance principles. *Annals of Probability* 2, 620–8.

McLeish, D.L. (1975). Invariance principles for dependent variables. *Zeitschrift für Wahrscheinlichkeitstheorie und Verwandte Gebiete* 32, 165–78.

Newey, W.K., and D.L. McFadden (1994). Large sample estimation and hypothesis testing. In R.F. Engle, and D.L. McFadden (eds.) *Handbook of Econometrics, Volume 4*. pp. 2113–245, New York: Elsevier Science B.V.

Phillips, P.C.B., and V. Solo (1992). Asymptotics for linear processes. *Annals of Statistics* 20, 971–1001.

Pötscher, B.M., and I.R. Prucha (1986). A class of partially adaptive one-step M-estimators for the non-linear regression model with dependent observations. *Journal of Econometrics* 32, 219–51.

Pötscher, B.M., and I.R. Prucha (1989). A uniform law of large numbers for dependent and heterogeneous data processes. *Econometrica* 57, 675–83.

Pötscher, B.M., and I.R. Prucha (1997). *Dynamic Nonlinear Econometric Models, Asymptotic Theory*. New York: Springer Verlag.

Serfling, R.J. (1980). *Approximation Theorems of Mathematical Statistics*. New York: Wiley.

Shiryayev, A.N. (1984). *Probability*. New York: Springer Verlag.

Stout, W.F. (1974). *Almost Sure Convergence*. New York: Academic Press.

Theil, H. (1971). *Principles of Econometrics*. New York: Wiley.

White, H. (1994). *Estimation, Inference and Specification Analysis*. Cambridge: Cambridge University Press.

Wooldridge, J.M. (1994). Estimation and inference for dependent processes. In R.F. Engle and D.L. McFadden (eds.) *Handbook of Econometrics, Volume 4*. pp. 2641–738, New York: Elsevier Science B.V.

Generalized Method of Moments

Alastair R. Hall*

1   Introduction

Generalized method of moments (GMM) was first introduced into the econometrics literature by Lars Hansen in 1982. Since then, GMM has had considerable impact on the theory and practice of econometrics. For theoreticians, the main advantage is that GMM provides a very general framework for considering issues of statistical inference because it encompasses many estimators of interest in econometrics. For applied researchers, it provides a computationally convenient method of estimating nonlinear dynamic models without complete knowledge of the probability distribution of the data. These applications have been in very diverse areas spanning macroeconomics, finance, agricultural economics, environmental economics, and labour economics. Depending on the context, GMM has been applied to time series, cross-sectional, and panel data. In this chapter we provide a survey of the GMM estimation framework and its properties in correctly specified models.[1] Inevitably, GMM builds from earlier work, and its most obvious statistical antecedents are method of moments (Pearson, 1893, 1894, 1895) and instrumental variables estimation (Wright, 1925; Reiersol, 1941; Geary, 1942; Sargan, 1958).

To introduce the basic idea behind the GMM framework, it is useful to consider briefly the structure of method of moments (MM) estimation. Suppose that an economic and/or statistical model implies a vector of observed variables, v_t, and a $p \times 1$ vector of unknown parameters, θ_0, satisfy a $p \times 1$ vector of population moment conditions,

$$E[f(v_t, \theta_0)] = 0. \tag{11.1}$$

The MM estimator of θ_0, is found by solving the analogous sample moment condition. So if the MM estimator is denoted by $\hat{\theta}_T$ then it is defined by

$$g_T(\hat{\theta}_T) = T^{-1} \sum_{t=1}^{T} f(v_t, \hat{\theta}_T) = 0, \tag{11.2}$$

where T is the sample size. Notice that (11.2) represents a set of p equations in p unknowns and so has a unique solution under certain conditions. This approach has a natural appeal, and intuition suggests – correctly – that the solution to (11.2), $\hat{\theta}_T$, converges in probability to the solution to (11.1), θ_0, subject to appropriate regularity conditions. Now suppose that $f(\cdot)$ is a $q \times 1$ vector and that $q > p$. In this case (11.2) represents a set of q equations in $p < q$ unknowns. Such a system typically does not possess a solution and so MM estimation is rendered infeasible. *Generalized* method of moments circumvents this problem by choosing the value of θ which is closest to satisfying (11.2) as the estimator for θ_0. To make the approach operational, it is necessary to define a measure of how far $g_T(\theta)$ is from zero. In GMM, the measure of distance is

$$Q_T(\theta) = g_T(\theta)'W_T g_T(\theta), \tag{11.3}$$

where W_T is a $q \times q$ weighting matrix which must satisfy certain conditions that need not concern us for the moment. So the GMM estimator is defined to be

$$\hat{\theta}_T = \text{argmin}_{\theta \in \Theta} Q_T(\theta), \tag{11.4}$$

where Θ denotes the parameter space.

If it were always the case that $q = p$ in econometric applications then there would be no need for a separate GMM theory because GMM would reduce to MM. However, q is greater than p in many situations of interest, and it is this possibility which leads to the unique features of the GMM framework. In this chapter we concentrate on issues pertaining to estimation. This means we will largely ignore the considerable literature on hypothesis testing based on GMM estimators. However, the interested reader can find discussion of various aspects of hypothesis testing elsewhere in this volume.[2]

Throughout this chapter, the analysis abstracts to the general form of population moment condition given in (11.1). However, before we begin, it is useful to present two examples which help to illustrate both how population moment conditions arise and also the forms they can take. The first example is taken from a study in the education literature based on cross-sectional data. The second example is a study from the empirical finance and macroeconomic literatures based on time series data.

1. *Education example*: Angrist and Krueger (1992) investigate the impact of age at school entry on educational attainment using the model,

$$y_{i,n} = \alpha + \beta a_{i,n} + \varepsilon_{i,n}$$

where $y_{i,n}$ is the average number of years of education completed by students born in quarter i of year n, and $a_{i,n}$ is the average age of school entry for members of that cohort. Within this model, the marginal response of attainment to age of entry is captured by β, and so this represents the parameter of interest. Estimation of this parameter is complicated by a correlation between the explanatory variable and the error which arises because many children who start school at a younger age do so because they show above average learning potential. This correlation means the ordinary least squares estimator is inconsistent. However, the error is anticipated to be uncorrelated with the quarter of birth. This logic leads to the population moment condition $E[z_{i,n}(y_{i,n} - \alpha - \beta a_{i,n})] = 0$ where $z'_{i,n} = [Q_{1,i}, Q_{2,i}, Q_{3,i}, Q_{4,i}]$ and $Q_{j,i} = 1$ if $i = j$ and 0 otherwise.

2. *Empirical finance example*: Hansen and Singleton (1982) estimate a model which seeks to explain the relationship between asset prices and their returns via the decisions of a representative consumer.[3] Within this framework, a representative consumer makes consumption and investment decisions to maximize his or her expected discounted lifetime utility. If it is assumed that the agent possesses a constant relative risk aversion utility function and invests at time t in an asset which matures at time $t + 1$ then the asset return satisfies the equation

$$E[\delta(r_{t+1}/p_t)(c_{t+1}/c_t)^{\gamma-1} - 1 \mid \Omega_t] = 0 \qquad (11.5)$$

where r_{t+1} is the return on the asset in period $t + 1$, p_t is the price of the asset in period t, c_t is consumption in period t, Ω_t is the information set available to the agent in period t, γ is the agent's coefficient of relative risk aversion and δ is his or her discount factor. To use this model for asset pricing, it is necessary to estimate γ and δ. Unfortunately, the joint distribution of consumption growth and asset returns is unknown, and this makes maximum likelihood infeasible. However, (11.5) and an iterated expectations argument imply the population moment condition,

$$E[z_t(\delta(r_{t+1}/p_t)(c_{t+1}/c_t)^{\gamma-1} - 1)] = 0$$

where z_t is a vector of variables contained in Ω_t.

An overview of the chapter is as follows. To begin, we return to the basic definition of the GMM estimation principle, and consider formally certain issues which were swept aside in the heuristic discussion above. Most notably, the discussion was predicated on the assumption that the population moment condition provides sufficient information to uniquely determine θ_0. This need not be the case, and Section 2 introduces the concepts of global and local identification of the parameter vector. One important ramification of $q > p$ is that the estimation effects a decomposition on the population moment condition into so-called identifying and overidentifying restrictions. Section 3 describes this decomposition and shows how these components are linked to the parameter estimator and estimated sample moment, $g_T(\hat{\theta}_T)$. Section 4 considers the asymptotic properties of the estimator and the estimated sample moment. For the estimator, this discussion focuses on the consistency and asymptotic distribution of the estimator. The latter can be used to construct large sample confidence intervals for the elements of θ_0. In practice, these intervals depend on the long-run variance of the sample moment, and so we briefly consider how this variance can be estimated. For the estimated sample moment, the discussion concentrates on its asymptotic distribution. Up to this point the analysis only restricts the weighting matrix to be a member of a certain class. However, it will emerge that the choice of W_T impacts on the estimator via its asymptotic variance. Section 5 characterizes the optimal choice of W_T and discusses certain issues involved in the calculation of the associated "optimal" GMM estimator. Although we restrict attention to correctly specified models, a researcher can never be sure in practice that this is the case. Section 6 describes how the estimated sample moment can be used to construct the "overidentifying restrictions test" for the adequacy of the model specification. Throughout the first six sections, the population moment condition is taken as given. The next two sections explore issues related to the choice of $f(\cdot)$. Section 7 shows how various other econometric estimators can be considered special cases of GMM. Section 8 considers two extremes: the optimal choice of $f(\cdot)$ and what happens if the population moment condition provides no – or virtually no – information about θ_0. Finally Section 9 provides a brief review of the available evidence on the finite sample behavior of GMM.

Due to space constraints, we present only heuristic arguments for the main results and provide references to appropriate sources for more formal analyses. A rigorous treatment of the material in the chapter – and many other aspects of the GMM framework – can also be found in Hall (2000b).

2 THE POPULATION MOMENT CONDITION AND IDENTIFICATION

In this section, we consider the conditions under which the population moment provides sufficient information to determine uniquely θ_0 from all other elements in the parameter space $\Theta \subseteq \Re^p$. If this is the case then θ_0 is said to be *identified*. To begin, it is necessary to define formally the information contained in the population moment condition. From the heuristic discussion above, it is clear that the population moment condition is a statement about a $q \times 1$ vector of functions, $f(\cdot, \cdot)$, of the observable vector of random variables v_t and the unknown ($p \times 1$) parameter vector, θ_0. Certain restrictions must be placed on these constituents as we proceed with the analysis, and we shall impose the most important as they become necessary. However, space constraints forbid a complete accounting of all the required conditions; these can be found in Hansen (1982) or Wooldridge (1994). Throughout the chapter we follow Hansen's (1982) original framework and consider the following case.

Assumption 1. Strict Stationarity.   The ($r \times 1$) random vectors $\{v_t; -\infty < t < \infty\}$ form a strictly stationary process with sample space $V \subseteq \Re^r$.

Recall that this assumption implies all expectations of functions of v_t are independent of time.[4]

Assumption 2. Regularity Conditions for $f(\cdot, \cdot)$. The function $f: V \times \Theta \rightarrow \Re^q$ satisfies: (i) it is continuous on Θ for each $v \in V$; (ii) $E[f(v_t, \theta)]$ exists and is finite for every $\theta \in \Theta$; (iii) $E[f(v_t, \theta)]$ is continuous on Θ.

With these two assumptions in place, we can can now formally restate the population moment condition.

Assumption 3. Population Moment Condition. There exists $\theta_0 \in \Theta$ such that the following $(q \times 1)$ population moment condition holds: $E[f(v_t, \theta_0)] = 0$.

Throughout this chapter, we focus on the properties of the GMM estimator of θ_0 based on this population moment condition. However, by itself, Assumption 3 does not provide sufficient information to identify θ_0. This is only the case if there are no other values of θ at which the population moment condition is satisfied. This condition for parameter identification can be stated as follows.

Assumption 4. Global Identification. The parameter vector θ_0 is globally identified by the population moment condition in Assumption 3 if and only if $E[f(v_t, \bar{\theta})] \neq 0$ for all $\bar{\theta} \in \Theta$ such that $\bar{\theta} \neq \theta_0$.

The adjective "global" emphasizes that the population moment condition only holds at one value in the *entire* parameter space. While this condition is easily stated, it is often hard to verify a priori in nonlinear models. Identification can fail due to the properties of the data, v_t, or due to the properties of $f(\cdot)$ as a function of θ or due to an interaction of the two. Fortunately, a more useful condition can be found if attention is limited to some suitably defined neighborhood of θ_0. The price of this approach is that we are now deriving conditions for identification only within this neighborhood and so these are referred to as conditions for *local* identification. As the names suggest, local identification is necessary but not sufficient for global identification. Therefore, a more transparent condition for local identification is useful because it provides insights into the circumstances in which identification can fail.

The condition for local identification is based on a first order Taylor series expansion, and so it is necessary to introduce the following definition and assumption. An *ε-neighborhood* of θ_0 is defined to be the set N_ε which satisfies $N_\varepsilon = \{\theta; \|\theta - \theta_0\| < \varepsilon\}$ where $\|a\| = (a'a)^{1/2}$.

Assumption 5. Regularity Conditions on $\partial f(v_t, \theta)/\partial \theta'$. (i) The derivative matrix $\partial f(v, \theta)/\partial \theta'$ exists and is continuous on Θ for each $v \in V$; (ii) θ_0 is an interior point of Θ; (iii) $E[\partial f(v_t, \theta_0)/\partial \theta']$ exists and is finite.

To derive the condition for local identification, we restrict attention to a sufficiently small ε such that $f(\cdot)$ can be approximated by the following first order Taylor series expansion[5] in N_ε

$$f(v_t, \theta) \approx f(v_t, \theta_0) + \{\partial f(v_t, \theta_0)/\partial \theta'\} (\theta - \theta_0), \tag{11.6}$$

where $\partial f(v_t, \theta_0)/\partial \theta'$ is the $q \times p$ matrix with $i - j$th element $\partial f_i(v_t, \theta_0)/\partial \theta'_j$. Taking expectations on both sides of (11.6) and using Assumptions 3 and 5 yields

$$E[f(v_t, \theta)] \approx \{E[\partial f(v_t, \theta_0)/\partial \theta']\} (\theta - \theta_0). \tag{11.7}$$

Equation (11.7) states that in the neighborhood of θ_0, $E[f(v_t, \theta)]$ is essentially a linear function of $\theta - \theta_0$. This leads to the following condition for *local* identification.

Lemma 1. Local Identification. The parameter vector θ_0 is locally identified by the population moment condition in Assumption 3 if and only if $E[\partial f(v_t, \theta_0)/\partial \theta']$ is of rank p.

While this condition needs to be verified on a case by case basis, it does provide some general insights into identification in nonlinear models. First, the rank condition immediately implies identification fails if there are fewer moment conditions than parameters, i.e. $q < p$. Second, notice that the dependence of the partial derivative matrix on θ implies the population moment condition may provide enough information to identify the parameters at some values of θ_0 but not at others.

From this discussion, it is clear that the relationship between q and p is important. This has led to the introduction of the following terminology. If $p > q$ and hence the local identification condition is not satisfied then θ_0 is said to be *un*-identified. If $p = q$ and Assumption 4 is satisfied then θ_0 is said to *just*-identified. Finally, if $q > p$ and Assumption 4 is satisfied then θ_0 is said to be *over*-identified.

3   THE ESTIMATOR AND A FUNDAMENTAL DECOMPOSITION

The introduction provides the essence of GMM. In this section, we discuss the form of the estimator in more detail, and also describe how estimation effects a fundamental decomposition of the population moment condition.

Recall that the GMM estimator of θ_0 based on the population moment condition in Assumption 3 is:

$$\hat{\theta}_T = \text{argmin}_{\theta \in \Theta} Q_T(\theta), \tag{11.8}$$

where $Q_T(\theta) = g_T(\theta)'W_T g_T(\theta)$. For this approach to make sense, $Q_T(\theta)$ must be a meaningful measure of distance and hence the weighting matrix must possess certain properties. Specifically, W_T must be positive semi-definite for finite T so that $Q_T(\theta)$ is both nonnegative and equals zero if $g_T(\theta) = 0$. However, *semi*-definiteness leaves open the possibility that $Q_T(\theta) = 0$ without $g_T(\theta) = 0$. Since all our statistical analysis is based on asymptotic theory, it is only necessary to rule out this possibility in the limit. Accordingly, W_T is assumed to satisfy:

Assumption 6. Properties of the Weighting Matrix. W_T is a positive semi-definite matrix which converges in probability to the positive definite matrix of constants W.

If Assumption 5 holds, and in most cases of interest it will, then the first order conditions for this minimization imply $\partial Q_T(\hat{\theta}_T)/\partial\theta = 0$. This condition yields[6]

$$\left\{T^{-1}\sum_{t=1}^{T}\frac{\partial f(v_t, \hat{\theta}_T)}{\partial\theta'}\right\}' W_T \left\{T^{-1}\sum_{t=1}^{T}f(v_t, \hat{\theta}_T)\right\} = 0 \qquad (11.9)$$

However, there is typically no closed form solution for $\hat{\theta}_T$ and so the estimator must be obtained via numerical optimization techniques.[7]

This characterization of the estimator yields an interesting interpretation of GMM. Inspection of (11.9) reveals that the GMM estimator based on $E[f(v_t, \theta_0)] = 0$ can be interpreted as a method of moments estimator based on

$$\{E[\partial f(v_t, \theta_0)/\partial\theta']\}'WE[f(v_t, \theta_0)] = 0. \qquad (11.10)$$

Therefore, GMM is an MM estimator based on the information that the p linear combinations of $E[f(v_t, \theta_0)]$ in (11.10) are zero. Notice that if the assumptions behind Lemma 1 hold then these p linear combinations are linearly independent and so the MM interpretation emphasizes the fundamental connection between identification and estimation – that is, the p parameters are only *locally* identified if the estimation is based on p linearly independent equations. If $p = q$ then (11.10) is equivalent to $E[f(v_t, \theta_0)] = 0$, and we note parenthetically that this means the weighting matrix plays no role in the analysis. However, if $q > p$ then there is a difference between information used in estimation and the original population moment condition.

The advantage of this MM interpretation is that it makes explicit the information used in GMM information. However, it is not particularly amenable to the characterization of what information is left out because (11.10) is a system of $p < q$ equations. Sowell (1996) shows that this problem can be circumvented if (11.10) is interpreted in terms of the transformed moment condition $W^{1/2}E[f(v_t, \theta_0)]$. Equation (11.10) can then be rewritten as

$$F(\theta_0)'W^{1/2}E[f(v_t, \theta_0)] = 0, \qquad (11.11)$$

where $F(\theta_0) = W^{1/2}E[\partial f(v_t, \theta_0)/\partial\theta']$. Equation (11.11) states that $W^{1/2}E[f(v_t, \theta_0)]$ lies in the null space of $F(\theta_0)'$. Sowell (1996) shows that the information about θ_0 in (11.10) is equivalent to the information in

$$F(\theta_0)[F(\theta_0)'F(\theta_0)]^{-1}F(\theta_0)'W^{1/2}E[f(v_t, \theta_0)] = 0. \qquad (11.12)$$

Formally, (11.12) states that the least squares projection of $W^{1/2}E[f(v_t, \theta_0)]$ on to the column space of $F(\theta_0)$ is zero, and thereby places

$$\text{rank}\{F(\theta_0)[F(\theta_0)'F(\theta_0)]^{-1}F(\theta_0)'\} = p$$

restrictions on the transformed population moment condition. Sowell (1996) refers to (11.12) as the *identifying restrictions*.

The advantage of this alternative characterization is that (11.12) is a system of q equations and so it is now possible to characterize the part of $E[f(v_t, \theta_0)] = 0$ which is ignored in estimation. By definition, this remainder is

$$\{I_q - F(\theta_0)[F(\theta_0)'F(\theta_0)]^{-1}F(\theta_0)'\}W^{1/2}E[f(v_t, \theta_0)] = 0, \tag{11.13}$$

which represents what Hansen referred to as the *overidentifying restrictions* in his original article. Equation (11.13) states that the projection of $W^{1/2}E[f(v_t, \theta_0)]$ on to the orthogonal complement of $F(\theta_0)$ is zero, and thereby places $q - p$ restrictions on the transformed population moment condition.

Equations (11.12)–(11.13) indicate that GMM estimation effects a fundamental decomposition of the $q \times 1$ population moment condition into p identifying restrictions upon which estimation is based, and $q - p$ overidentifying restrictions which are ignored in estimation. Notice also that these two sets of restrictions are orthogonal due to the projection matrix structure.

The roles of the two sets of restrictions are reflected in their sample counterparts. Since the identifying restrictions represent the information used in estimation, their sample analogs are satisfied at $\hat{\theta}_T$ by construction. In contrast, the overidentifying restrictions are ignored in estimation and so their sample analog is not satisfied. However, they can be used to give a useful interpretation to the GMM minimand. From (11.9), it follows that

$$W_T^{1/2}T^{-1}\sum_{t=1}^T f(v_t, \hat{\theta}_T) = \{I_q - F_T(\hat{\theta}_T)[F_T(\hat{\theta}_T)'F_T(\hat{\theta}_T)]^{-1}F_T(\hat{\theta}_T)'\}$$

$$\times W_T^{1/2}T^{-1}\sum_{t=1}^T f(v_t, \hat{\theta}_T) \tag{11.14}$$

where $F_T(\theta) = T^{-1}\sum_{t=1}^T \partial f(v_t, \theta)/\partial \theta'$. Therefore, $Q_T(\hat{\theta}_T)$ can be interpreted as a measure of how far the sample is from satisfying the overidentifying restrictions.

4 ASYMPTOTIC PROPERTIES

At the beginning, we presented an intuitive justification for the GMM estimation framework. In this section, we provide a more rigorous argument by establishing the consistency and asymptotic normality of the estimator. The latter facilitates the construction of large sample confidence intervals for θ_0. These intervals depend on the long-run variance of the sample moment, and so we briefly discuss how this variance can be consistently estimated. We also derive the asymptotic distribution of the estimated sample moment. The latter analysis provides further evidence of the connection between $g_T(\hat{\theta}_T)$ and the overidentifying restrictions, and plays an important role in the model specification test discussed in Section 6.

The analysis rests on applications of the laws of large numbers (LLN) and the central limit theorem (CLT) to functions of v_t. So far, we have only restricted v_t to be stationary, and this is insufficient by itself to guarantee these limit theorems. Accordingly, we impose the following condition.

Assumption 7. Ergodicity. The random process $\{v_t; -\infty < t < \infty\}$ is ergodic.

A formal definition of ergodicity involves rather sophisticated mathematical ideas and is beyond the scope of this chapter. Instead we refer the interested reader to Davidson (1994, pp. 199–203). It is sufficient for ergodicity that the dependence between v_t and v_{t-m} decreases at a certain rate to zero as $m \to \infty$. If v_t satisfies this type of restriction then it is called a *mixing* process. Certain other regularity conditions must also be imposed but due to space constraints we shall not explore them here. Instead we refer the interested reader to Hansen's (1982) original article or the surveys by Newey and McFadden (1994) and Wooldridge (1994).

Recall that $\hat{\theta}_T$ is consistent for θ_0 if $\hat{\theta}_T \overset{p}{\to} \theta_0$. If there is a closed form solution for $\hat{\theta}_T$ then it is relatively straightforward to establish whether or not the estimator is consistent by examining the limiting behavior of appropriate functions of the data. Unfortunately, as remarked above, we do not have this luxury in most nonlinear models. However, although there is no closed form, $\hat{\theta}_T$ is clearly defined by (11.8). The key to a proof of consistency is the consideration of what happens if we perform a similar minimization on the population analog to $Q_T(\theta)$,

$$Q_0(\theta) = \{E[f(v_t, \theta)]\}' W \{E[f(v_t, \theta)]\} \tag{11.15}$$

The answer follows directly from our earlier assumptions. The population moment condition implies $Q_0(\theta_0) = 0$. The global identification condition and the positive definiteness of W, imply $Q_0(\theta) > 0$ for all $\theta \neq \theta_0$. Taken together these two properties imply $Q_0(\theta)$ has a unique minimum at $\theta = \theta_0$. Intuition suggests that if $\hat{\theta}_T$ minimizes $Q_T(\theta)$ and $Q_T(\theta)$ converges in probability to a function, $Q_0(\theta)$, with a unique minimum at θ_0, then $\hat{\theta}_T$ converges in probability to θ_0. In essence this intuition is correct but there is one mathematical detail which needs to be taken into account. It is not necessarily the case that the minimum of a sequence of functions converges to the minimum of the limit of the sequence of functions. For this to be the case, it is sufficient that $Q_T(\theta)$ converges *uniformly* to $Q_0(\theta)$.[8]

Assumption 8. Uniform Convergence in Probability of $Q_T(\theta)$.
$\sup_{\theta \in \Theta} |Q_T(\theta) - Q_0(\theta)| \overset{p}{\to} 0$.

Once uniform convergence is imposed, then consistency can be established along the lines described above; *e.g.* see Hansen (1982) or Wooldridge (1994).

Theorem 1. Consistency of the Parameter Estimator. If Assumptions 1–4, 6–8 and certain other regularity conditions hold then $\hat{\theta}_T \overset{p}{\to} \theta_0$.

To develop the asymptotic distribution of the estimator, we require an asymptotically valid closed form representation for $T^{1/2}(\hat{\theta}_T - \theta_0)$. This representation comes from an application of the Mean Value Theorem[9] which relates $f(\cdot)$ to its first derivatives $\partial f(v_t, \theta)/\partial \theta'$. So, to pursue this approach, it is necessary to impose Assumption 5. The Mean Value Theorem implies that

$$g_T(\hat{\theta}_T) = g_T(\theta_0) + G_T(\hat{\theta}_T, \theta_0, \lambda_T)(\hat{\theta}_T - \theta_0), \tag{11.16}$$

where $G_T(\hat{\theta}_T, \theta_0, \lambda)$ is the $(q \times p)$ matrix whose ith row is the corresponding row of $G_T(\bar{\theta}_T^{(i)})$ where $G_T(\theta) = T^{-1} \sum_{t=1}^{T} \partial f(v_t, \theta)/\partial \theta'$, $\bar{\theta}_T^{(i)} = \lambda_{i,T} \theta_0 + (1 - \lambda_{i,T}) \hat{\theta}_T$ for some $0 \le \lambda_{i,T} \le 1$, and λ_T is the $(q \times 1)$ vector with ith element $\lambda_{i,T}$. Premultiplication of (11.16) by $G_T(\hat{\theta}_T)'W_T$ yields

$$G_T(\hat{\theta}_T)'W_T g_T(\hat{\theta}_T) = G_T(\hat{\theta}_T)'W_T g_T(\theta_0) + G_T(\hat{\theta}_T)'W_T G_T(\hat{\theta}_T, \theta_0, \lambda_T)(\hat{\theta}_T - \theta_0). \tag{11.17}$$

Now the first order conditions in (11.9) imply the left-hand side of (11.17) is zero and so with some rearrangement it follows from (11.17) that

$$\begin{aligned} T^{1/2}(\hat{\theta}_T - \theta_0) &= -[G_T(\hat{\theta}_T)'W_T G_T(\hat{\theta}_T, \theta_0, \lambda_T)]^{-1} G_T(\hat{\theta}_T)'W_T T^{1/2} g_T(\theta_0) \\ &= \bar{M}_T T^{1/2} g_T(\theta_0) \text{ say.} \end{aligned} \tag{11.18}$$

Equation (11.18) implies that $T^{1/2}(\hat{\theta}_T - \theta_0)$ behaves like the product of a random matrix, $\bar{M}_T$, and a random vector, $T^{1/2} g_T(\theta_0)$. Therefore, we can derive the asymptotic distribution of the estimator from the limiting behavior of these two components. The asymptotic behavior of $T^{1/2} g_T(\theta_0)$ is given by a version of the CLT.

Assumption 9. Central Limit Theorem for $T^{1/2} g_T(\theta_0)$. $T^{1/2} g_T(\theta_0) \xrightarrow{d} N(0, S)$ where S is a positive definite matrix of constants.

Now consider $\bar{M}_T$. Since $\hat{\theta}_T \xrightarrow{p} \theta_0$ and $\bar{\theta}_T^{(i)}$ lies on the line segment between $\hat{\theta}_T$ and θ_0, then it follows that $\bar{\theta}_T^{(i)} \xrightarrow{p} \theta_0$ for $i = 1, 2 \ldots p$. Intuition suggests that this should imply both $G_T(\hat{\theta}_T)$ and $G_T(\hat{\theta}_T, \theta_0, \lambda_T)$ converge in probability to $G_0 = E[\partial f(v_t, \theta_0)/\partial \theta']$. In essence this is correct, but the argument can only be formally justified if $G_T(\theta)$ converges uniformly and certain other regularity conditions apply. For brevity, we adopt the high level assumption that the desired behavior occurs, and refer the interested reader to Newey and McFadden (1994) for the necessary underlying regularity conditions.

Assumption 10. Convergence of $G_T(\hat{\theta}_T)$ and $G_T(\hat{\theta}_T, \theta_0, \lambda_T)$. $G_T(\hat{\theta}_T) \xrightarrow{p} G_0$ and $G_T(\hat{\theta}_T, \theta_0, \lambda_T) \xrightarrow{p} G_0$.

Assumptions 6 and 10 can be combined with Slutsky's Theorem to deduce that $\bar{M}_T \xrightarrow{p} (G_0'WG_0)^{-1}G_0'W$. Therefore, $T^{1/2}(\hat{\theta}_T - \theta_0)$ is the product of a random matrix which converges in probability to a constant, and a random vector which converges to a normal distribution. This structure implies:[10]

Theorem 2. Asymptotic distribution of the estimator. If Assumptions 1–10 and certain other regularity conditions hold then: $T^{1/2}(\hat{\theta}_T - \theta_0) \xrightarrow{d} N(0, MSM')$ where $M = (G_0'WG_0)^{-1}G_0'W$.

Theorem 2 implies that an approximate $100(1 - \alpha)\%$ confidence interval for $\theta_{0,i}$ in large samples is given by

$$\hat{\theta}_{T,i} \pm z_{\alpha/2}\sqrt{\hat{V}_{T,ii}/T}, \qquad (11.19)$$

where $\hat{V}_{T,ii}$ is the $i - i$th element of a consistent estimator of MSM'. In practice, the asymptotic variance can be consistently estimated by $\hat{V}_T = \hat{M}_T\hat{S}_T\hat{M}_T'$ where $\hat{M}_T = [G_T(\hat{\theta}_T)'W_TG_T(\hat{\theta}_T)]^{-1}G_T(\hat{\theta}_T)'W_T$, and $\hat{S}_T$ is a consistent estimator of S. The construction of $\hat{S}_T$ depends on the time series properties of $f(v_t, \theta_0)$. With certain relatively mild additional conditions, it can be shown that[11]

$$S = \Gamma_0 + \sum_{i=1}^{\infty}(\Gamma_i + \Gamma_i'), \qquad (11.20)$$

where $\Gamma_j = E[((f_t - E[f_t])(f_{t-j} - E[f_{t-j}])']$ is known as the jth autocovariance matrix[12] of $f_t = f(v_t, \theta_0)$. For brevity, we distinguish only two cases of interest. First, if f_t is a martingale difference (MD) sequence and hence serially uncorrelated (that is, $\Gamma_i = 0$, $i \neq 0$) then S can be consistently estimated by[13]

$$\hat{S}_{MD} = T^{-1}\sum_{t=1}^{T} \hat{f}_t\hat{f}_t', \qquad (11.21)$$

where $\hat{f}_t = f(v_t, \hat{\theta}_T)$. It can be shown that $\hat{S}_{MD} \xrightarrow{p} S$ if the martingale difference assumption is valid; for example see White (1994, Theorem 8.27, p. 193). Second, and more generally, S can be estimated by a member of the class of *heteroskedasticity autocorrelation consistent covariance* (HACC) estimators,

$$\hat{S}_{HACC} = \hat{\Gamma}_0 + \sum_{i=1}^{b(T)} \omega_{iT}(\hat{\Gamma}_i + \hat{\Gamma}_i'), \qquad (11.22)$$

where $\hat{\Gamma}_i = T^{-1}\sum_{t=i+1}^{T}\hat{f}_t\hat{f}_{t-i}'$, $\{\omega_{iT}\}$ are known as weights and $b(T)$ is the bandwidth. The weights and bandwidth must satisfy certain conditions if $\hat{S}_{HACC}$ is to be both positive semi-definite[14] and consistent. Various combinations have been proposed in the literature.[15] One example is the "Bartlett" kernel proposed in this context by Newey and West (1987) for which $\omega_{i,T} = 1 - i/[b(T) + 1]$. Andrews (1991) shows that this choice yields a consistent estimator if $b(T) \to \infty$ and $b(T) = o(T^{1/2})$. In practice, the researcher must choose both the bandwidth and the weights. While this choice can be guided by asymptotic theory, there is no consensus to date upon what choice is best in the sample sizes encountered in economics and finance.[16] It should be noted that the consistency of both $\hat{S}_{MD}$ and $\hat{S}_{HACC}$ is predicated on $E[f(v_t, \theta_0)] = 0$. If the model is misspecified, and hence Assumption 3 is violated, then neither estimator is consistent. This inconsistency can have important consequences for the model specification test described in Section 6, and we return to this issue there.

Finally, we consider the asymptotic distribution of the estimated sample moment. It is most convenient to work with the transformed moment, $W_T^{1/2}T^{1/2}g_T(\hat{\theta}_T)$. Equation (11.16) implies

$$W_T^{1/2}T^{1/2}g_T(\hat{\theta}_T) = W_T^{1/2}T^{1/2}g_T(\theta_0) + W_T^{1/2}G_T(\hat{\theta}_T, \theta_0, \lambda_T)T^{1/2}(\hat{\theta}_T - \theta_0). \quad (11.23)$$

If we substitute for $T^{1/2}(\hat{\theta}_T - \theta_0)$ from (11.18) then (11.23) can be written as

$$W_T^{1/2}T^{1/2}g_T(\hat{\theta}_T) = N_T(\hat{\theta}_T)W_T^{1/2}T^{1/2}g_T(\theta_0), \quad (11.24)$$

where

$$N_T(\hat{\theta}_T) = I_q - W_T^{1/2}G_T(\hat{\theta}_T, \theta_0, \lambda_T)[G_T(\hat{\theta}_T)'W_T G_T(\hat{\theta}_T, \theta_0, \lambda_T)]^{-1}G_T(\hat{\theta}_T)'W_T^{1/2'}.$$

Equation (11.24) implies $W_T^{1/2}T^{1/2}g_T(\hat{\theta}_T)$ has the same generic structure as the expression for $T^{1/2}(\hat{\theta}_T - \theta_0)$ in (11.18) namely: a random matrix, which converges to a matrix of constants, times a random vector which converges to a normal distribution. Therefore, we can use the same logic as before to deduce the following result; see Hansen (1982).

Theorem 3. Asymptotic distribution of the estimated sample moment. If Assumptions 1–10 and certain other regularity conditions hold then: $W_T^{1/2}T^{1/2}g_T(\hat{\theta}_T) \xrightarrow{d} N(0, NSN')$ where $N = [I_q - P(\theta_0)]W^{1/2'}$ and $P(\theta_0) = F(\theta_0)[F(\theta_0)'F(\theta_0)]^{-1}F(\theta_0)'$.

The connection between the estimated sample moment and the overidentifying restrictions manifests itself in the asymptotic distribution. Equation (11.24) implies that

$$W_T^{1/2}T^{1/2}g_T(\hat{\theta}_T) = [I_q - P(\theta_0)]W^{1/2}T^{1/2}g_T(\theta_0) + o_p(1). \quad (11.25)$$

Inspection of (11.25) reveals that the asymptotic behavior of the estimated sample moment is governed by the function of the data which appears in the overidentifying restrictions. Therefore, the mean of the asymptotic distribution in Theorem 3 is zero because the overidentifying restrictions are satisfied at θ_0. This relationship also has an impact on the properties of the variance of the limiting distribution. Since $W^{1/2}$ and S are nonsingular, it follows that[17] rank$\{NSN'\}$ = rank$\{I_q - P(\theta_0)\} = q - p$, and so the covariance matrix is singular.[18] This rank is easily recognized to be the number of overidentifying restrictions.

5 THE OPTIMAL TWO-STEP OR ITERATED GMM ESTIMATOR

It is remarked in Section 3 that if $q = p$ then GMM is equivalent to the MM estimator based on $E[f(v_t, \theta_0)] = 0$ and so the estimator does not depend on the weighting matrix. However if $q > p$ then it is clear from Theorem 2 that the asymptotic variance of $\hat{\theta}_T$ depends on W_T via W.[19] This opens up the possibility that inferences may be sensitive to W. It is desirable to base inference on the most precise estimator and so the optimal choice of W is the one which yields the minimum variance in a matrix sense. This choice is given in the following theorem which was first proved by Hansen (1982).

Theorem 4. Optimal weighting matrix.   If Assumptions 1–10 and certain other regularity conditions hold then the minimum asymptotic variance of $\hat{\theta}_T$ is $(G_0'S^{-1}G_0)^{-1}$ and this can be obtained by setting $W = S^{-1}$.

Theorem 4 implies the optimal choice of W_T is $\hat{S}_T^{-1}$ where $\hat{S}_T$ is a consistent estimator of S. This appears to create a circularity because inspection of (11.21)–(11.22) reveals that $\hat{S}_T$ depends on $\hat{\theta}_T$ in general. However, this problem is easily resolved by using a two-step estimation. On the first step a sub-optimal choice of W_T is used to obtain a preliminary estimator, $\hat{\theta}_T(1)$. This estimator is used to obtain a consistent estimator of S, which is denoted $\hat{S}_T(1)$. On the second step θ_0 is re-estimated with $W_T = \hat{S}_T(1)^{-1}$. The resulting estimator, $\hat{\theta}_T(2)$, has the minimum asymptotic covariance matrix given in Theorem 4. However, this *two-step* estimator is based on a version of the optimal weighting matrix constructed using a sub-optimal estimator of θ_0. This suggests there may be finite sample gains from using $\hat{\theta}_T(2)$ to construct a new estimator of S, $\hat{S}_T(2)$ say, and then re-estimating θ_0 with $W_T = \hat{S}_T(2)^{-1}$. The resulting estimator, $\hat{\theta}_T(3)$, also has the same asymptotic distribution as $\hat{\theta}_T(2)$ but it is anticipated to be more efficient in finite samples. This potential finite sample gain in efficiency provides a justification for updating the estimate of S again and re-estimating θ_0. This process can be continued iteratively until the estimates converge; if this is done then it yields what has become known as the *iterated GMM estimator*.

The choice of $W = S^{-1}$ has a second important implication for the asymptotic behavior of the estimator which is presented in the following theorem.[20]

Theorem 5. Asymptotic independence of the estimator and estimated sample moment.   If (i) Assumptions 1–10 and certain other regularity conditions hold; (ii) $W = S^{-1}$; then $T^{1/2}(\hat{\theta}_T - \theta_0)$ and $S^{-1/2}T^{1/2}g_T(\hat{\theta}_T)$ are asymptotically independent.

Since both $T^{1/2}(\hat{\theta}_T - \theta_0)$ and $S^{-1/2}T^{1/2}g_T(\hat{\theta}_T)$ are asymptotically normally distributed, Theorem 5 is established by showing that these two statistics are asymptotically uncorrelated. The latter can be deduced from (11.18) and (11.25). Using Assumption 10 and putting $W = S^{-1}$, it follows from (11.18) and (11.25) that

$$T^{1/2}(\hat{\theta}_T - \theta_0) = H_{1,T} + o_p(1), \tag{11.26}$$

$$W_T^{1/2}T^{1/2}g_T(\hat{\theta}_T) = H_{2,T} + o_p(1), \tag{11.27}$$

where $H_{1,T} = -[F(\theta_0)'F(\theta_0)]^{-1}F(\theta_0)'S^{-1/2}T^{1/2}g_T(\theta_0)$ and $H_{2,T} = [I_q - P(\theta_0)]S^{1/2}T^{1/2}g_T(\theta_0)$. If we let $C = \lim_{T\to\infty} \text{cov}[H_{1,T}, H_{2,T}]$ then it follows from Theorems 2 and 3 that

$$C = \lim_{T\to\infty} E[H_{1,T}H_{2,T}']. \tag{11.28}$$

Using (11.25) and (11.26) in (11.28), we obtain

$$C = \lim_{T \to \infty} E[-[F(\theta_0)'F(\theta_0)]^{-1}F(\theta_0)'S^{-1/2}T^{1/2}g_T(\theta_0)T^{1/2}g_T(\theta_0)'S^{-1/2'}[I_q - P(\theta_0)]]$$

$$= -[F(\theta_0)'F(\theta_0)]^{-1}F(\theta_0)'S^{-1/2}\left\{\lim_{T \to \infty} \text{var}[T^{1/2}g_T(\theta_0)]\right\}S^{-1/2'}[I_q - P(\theta_0)]$$

$$= -[F(\theta_0)'F(\theta_0)]^{-1}F(\theta_0)'S^{-1/2}SS^{-1/2'}[I_q - P(\theta_0)]$$

$$= 0$$

because $S = S^{1/2'}S^{1/2}$ implies $S^{-1/2}SS^{-1/2'} = I_q$, and $F(\theta_0)'[I_q - P(\theta_0)] = 0$.

In contrast, if $W \neq S^{-1}$ then the same sequence of arguments yields the conclusion that $C \neq 0$. Therefore, Theorem 5 provides an interesting perspective on why this choice of W leads to an efficient estimator: $W = S^{-1}$ is the only choice of weighting matrix for which the estimator is statistically independent of the part of the moment condition unused in estimation. In other words, by making this choice of W, we have extracted all possible information about the parameters contained in the sample moment.

The estimators described in this section are often described as "the optimal two-step GMM" or "optimal iterated GMM" estimator. It is important to realize that this optimality only refers to the choice of weighting matrix. These are the most precise GMM estimators which can be constructed from the given population moment condition $E[f(v_t, \theta_0)] = 0$. It does not imply that there is anything optimal about the population moment condition itself. The optimal choice of moment condition is discussed in Section 8.

6 THE OVERIDENTIFYING RESTRICTIONS TEST

The asymptotic theory so far has been predicated on the assumption that the model is correctly specified in the sense that $E[f(v_t, \theta_0)] = 0$. If this assumption is false then the argument behind Theorem 1 breaks down, and it is no longer possible to establish the consistency of the estimator. Since the validity of the population moment condition is central to GMM, it is desirable to develop methods for testing whether the data are consistent with this assumption. If $p = q$ then it is not possible to examine this hypothesis directly because, as we have seen, $g_T(\hat{\theta}_T) = 0$. In this case, the validity of Assumption 3 can only be assessed indirectly using so called conditional moment tests; see Newey (1985) and Tauchen (1985). However, if $q > p$ then the estimator does not set the sample moment to zero and so this leaves scope for testing $E[f(v_t, \theta_0)] = 0$ directly. In Section 3, it is shown that GMM estimation effects a decomposition on the population moment condition into identifying and overidentifying restrictions. By definition, the estimator satisfies the sample analog to the identifying restrictions. However, the overidentifying restrictions are ignored in estimation and so are available as a basis for testing the validity of the population moment condition. This leads us to the overidentifying restrictions test, which is routinely reported in applications of GMM.

In practice, it is desirable to base inference on the the two-step (or iterated) estimator because it yields the most efficient GMM estimator based on $E[f(v_t, \theta_0)]$ $= 0$. Therefore, we restrict attention to this case and so substitute $W = S^{-1}$. In Section 3, it is shown that $Q_T(\hat\theta_T)$ can be interpreted as a measure of how close the sample is to satisfying the overidentifying restrictions. This motivated Sargan (1958) to propose using the statistic

$$J_T = TQ_T(\hat\theta_T) \tag{11.29}$$

to test whether the overidentifying restrictions are satisfied. His analysis is restricted to linear models estimated by instrumental variables. However, Hansen (1982) extends this approach to nonlinear models. The distribution is given in the following theorem.

Theorem 6. Asymptotic distribution of the overidentifying restrictions test. If Assumptions 1–10 and certain other regularity conditions hold and $W = S^{-1}$ then $J_T \overset{d}{\to} \chi^2_{q-p}$.

Notice that the degrees of freedom equal the number of overidentifying restrictions. The limiting distribution can be derived heuristically from our earlier analysis. From (11.25), we have that

$$
\begin{aligned}
TQ_T(\hat\theta_T) &= T^{1/2}g_T(\hat\theta_T)'\hat S_T^{-1} T^{1/2}g_T(\hat\theta_T) \\
&= T^{1/2}g_T(\theta_0)'S^{-1/2'}[I_q - P(\theta_0)]S^{-1/2}T^{1/2}g_T(\theta_0) + o_p(1) \tag{11.30}
\end{aligned}
$$

where we have used the fact that $I_q - P(\theta_0)$ is a projection matrix. Equation (11.30) implies J_T is asymptotically equivalent to a quadratic form in a random vector with an $N(0, I_q)$ distribution and a projection matrix with rank $q - p$. The result then follows directly from Rao (1973, p. 186).

To consider the power properties of the test, it is necessary to briefly consider what it means for the model to be misspecified in our context. Taken together, Assumptions 3 and 4 imply the population moment condition is satisfied at some unique value in Θ. Therefore, the model is misspecified if there is no value in Θ at which the population moment condition holds. Such a situation is captured by the following assumption.

Assumption 11. Misspecification. $E[f(v_t, \theta)] = \mu(\theta)$ where $\mu : \Theta \to \Re^q$ and $\|\mu(\theta)\| > 0$ for all $\theta \in \Theta$.

One important consequence of Assumption 11 is that the two covariance matrix estimators in (11.21)–(11.22) are inconsistent estimators of the long-run variance because they are calculated under the assumption that $E[f(v_t, \theta_0)] = 0$.[21] This inconsistency is not by itself a cause for concern provided $p\lim_{T\to\infty}\hat S_T^{-1}$ is a non-singular matrix. Such would be the case for the estimator $\hat S_{MD}$, and in consequence J_T is $O_p(T)$ and a consistent test versus the misspecification characterized in Assumption 11.[22] However, Hall (2000a) shows that $p \lim_{T \to \infty} \hat{S}_{\text{HACC}}^{-1}$ is a singular matrix, and that this causes J_T to be only $O_p(T/b(T))$ although still consistent. A more powerful test can be constructed by using a version of the HACC which is consistent under both null and alternative hypothesis. Hall (2000a) shows that such an estimator can be constructed by replacing $\hat{\Gamma}_i$ in (11.22) with

$$\tilde{\Gamma}_i = T^{-1} \sum_{t=i+1}^{T} [f(v_t, \hat{\theta}_T(1)) - g_T(\hat{\theta}_T(1))] [f(v_{t-i}, \hat{\theta}_T(1)) - g_T(\hat{\theta}_T(1))]'.$$

Once this change is made, the overidentifying restrictions test is consistent but now $O_p(T)$.

7   Other Estimators as Special Cases of GMM

It is remarked in the introduction that GMM estimation encompasses many estimators of interest in econometrics, and so provides a very convenient framework for the examination of various issues pertaining to inference. In this section, we justify this statement and illustrate it using maximum likelihood estimation.

Many econometric estimators are obtained by optimizing a scalar of the form

$$\sum_{t=1}^{T} N_t(\theta). \tag{11.31}$$

If $N_t(\theta)$ is differentiable then the estimator, $\tilde{\theta}$, is the value which solves the associated first order conditions

$$\sum_{t=1}^{T} \partial N_t(\tilde{\theta})/\partial \theta = 0. \tag{11.32}$$

Equation (11.32) implies that $\tilde{\theta}$ is equivalent to the MM estimator based on the population moment condition

$$E[\partial N_t(\theta_0)/\partial \theta] = 0. \tag{11.33}$$

Since $\partial N_t(\theta_0)/\partial \theta$ is a $(p \times 1)$ vector it can be recalled from Section 3 that $\tilde{\theta}$ is also the GMM estimator based on (11.33).

As an illustration, we now derive the population moment condition implicit in the GMM interpretation of maximum likelihood estimation. Suppose the conditional probability density function of the continuous stationary random vector v_t given $\{v_{t-1}, v_{t-2}, \ldots\}$ is $p(v_t; \theta_0, V_{t-1})$ where $V_{t-1} = (v_{t-1}', v_{t-2}', \ldots v_{t-k}')$. The maximum likelihood estimator (MLE) of θ_0 based on the conditional log likelihood function is the value of θ which maximizes,

$$L_T(\theta) = \sum_{t=1}^{T} \ln\{p(v_t; \theta, V_{t-1})\}. \tag{11.34}$$

This fits within our framework with $N_t(\theta) = \ln\{p(v_t; \theta, V_{t-1})\}$ and so the MLE can be interpreted as a GMM estimator based on the population moment condition

$$E[\partial \ln\{p(v_t; \theta, V_{t-1})\}/\partial \theta] = 0. \tag{11.35}$$

Since MLE is derived from a perfectly valid estimation principle in its own right, it is reasonable to question whether there is any value to this GMM interpretation. The advantage of the GMM interpretation is that it focuses attention specifically on the information used in estimation, and thereby facilitates an analysis of the consequences of misspecification. For example, the implementation of MLE requires a specific assumption about the distribution of the data. In many cases economic theory does not provide such information and so it is natural to be concerned about the consequences of choosing the wrong distribution. The GMM interpretation reveals that the estimator is still consistent provided (11.35) holds when expectations are taken with respect to the true distribution. Furthermore, Theorem 2 can be used to deduce the asymptotic distribution of the MLE in misspecified models[23] for which (11.35) holds.

8 OPTIMAL MOMENTS AND NEARLY UNINFORMATIVE MOMENTS

Throughout the analysis of the GMM estimator, we have taken the population moment condition as given. However, in practice, a researcher is typically faced with a large set of alternatives from which q elements are chosen to make up the population moment. In this section we consider the two extreme scenarios in which the "best" choice is made and the "worst" choice is made. To understand what best and worst mean in this context, it is useful to consider two ways in which the choice of population moment condition impacts on the asymptotic analysis. Theorem 1 establishes that the consistency of GMM depends crucially on the identification condition in Assumption 4. Theorem 2 reveals that the asymptotic variance of the estimator depends directly on the choice of moment condition via both S and G_0. Therefore, the best choice is the population moment condition which leads to the estimator with the smallest asymptotic variance. Section 8.1 summarizes the main results in the literature on the best or *optimal* choice of population moment condition. The worst case scenario is when the population moment condition does not or nearly does not provide enough information to identify θ_0. Section 8.2 describes both the consequences of (nearly) uninformative population moment conditions for the inference techniques discussed above and also how the problems can be circumvented.

8.1 The optimal choice

In its most general form, we have already answered this question in Section 7. It is shown there that MLE can be interpreted as a GMM estimator based on (11.35). Since the MLE is known to be asymptotically efficient in the class of consistent uniformly asymptotically normal estimators, the optimal choice of population moment condition is just the score function associated with the true probability distribution of the data. Unfortunately, in many cases of interest in economics, the true probability distribution is unknown. One solution is to choose a distribution arbitrarily but this strategy can have undesirable consequences if the wrong choice is made. In this case, the estimator is no longer asymptotically efficient and may also be inconsistent in nonlinear models.[24] In many cases where MLE is infeasible, GMM is applied using a population moment condition which takes the form

$$E[z_t \otimes u_t(\theta_0)] = 0, \tag{11.36}$$

where z_t is a vector of observable instruments and $u_t(\theta_0)$ is a vector of functions which depend on both the data and the unknown parameter vector. Hansen and Singleton (1982) refer to GMM estimation based on (11.36) as *generalized instrumental variables*. Notice that both our examples from the introduction fit into this class. Within this framework $u_t(\theta_0)$ is usually determined by the model, and so the only difference between choices of moment condition arises from the choice of instrument vector. Therefore, the optimal moment condition is characterized by finding the optimal choice of instrument vector.

In the literature on optimal instruments, it is customary to work with a slightly modified version of the population moment condition.[25] Instead of (11.36), the population moment condition takes the form

$$E[f(v_t, \theta_0)] = E[Z(v_{2t})u_t(\theta_0)] = 0, \tag{11.37}$$

where $u_t(\theta_0)$ is a $(s \times 1)$ vector of functions which satisfies $E[u_t(\theta_0) | \Omega_t] = 0$, Ω_t represents the information set at time t, $Z(v_{2t})$ is a $(q \times s)$ matrix whose elements are functions of $v_{2t} \in \Omega_t$, and we have partitioned $v_t = (v_{1t}, v_{2t})'$. The problem is then to find the optimal choice of $Z(v_{2t})$. This question is typically broken down into two parts: what is the optimal choice of $Z(\cdot)$ for a given choice of v_{2t}? and then what is the optimal choice of v_{2t}? The answer to the second question is going to depend on the model in question and so we do not address that here. Instead we focus entirely on the first question.

It turns out that the optimal instrument is relatively easy to characterize in static models, but is much more difficult in time series models. We therefore introduce the following restriction.

Assumption 12. Independence. $\{v_t; t = 1, 2 \ldots T\}$ forms an independent sequence.

Notice that Assumptions 1 and 12 imply v_t forms an iid process.

If GMM estimation is based on the population moment condition in (11.37) with the optimal choice of weighting matrix, then from Theorems 2 and 4 the asymptotic covariance matrix of the $\hat{\theta}_T$ is

$$V(Z) = \left\{ E\left[\left(\frac{\partial u_t(\theta_0)}{\partial \theta'} \right)' Z_t' \right] S_Z^{-1} E\left[Z_t \frac{\partial u_t(\theta_0)}{\partial \theta'} \right] \right\}^{-1}, \tag{11.38}$$

where for simplicity we have set $Z_t = Z(v_{2t})$ and $S_Z = E[Z_t u_t(\theta_0) u_t(\theta_0)' Z_t']$. The optimal choice of $Z(\cdot)$ given v_{2t} is the function which minimizes $V(Z)$ in a matrix sense, and this is given by the next theorem.[26]

Theorem 7. The optimal choice of instrument in static models. If
(i) Assumptions 1–10, 12 and certain other regularity conditions hold; (ii) the population moment condition is given by (11.37); then the optimal choice of $Z(\cdot)$ given v_{2t} is

$$Z^0(v_{2t}) = E[\partial u_t(\theta_0)/\partial\theta' \mid v_{2t}]' \Sigma_{u|v2}^{-1},$$

where $\Sigma_{u|v_2} = E[u_t(\theta_0) u_t(\theta_0)' \mid v_{2t}]$, and this choice leads to a GMM estimator with asymptotic covariance matrix

$$V(Z^0) = \{E[Z^0(v_{2t})]\Sigma_{u|v_2}E[Z^0(v_{2t})]'\}^{-1}.$$

An intuition for this result can be derived by relating the optimal estimator to the familiar case of two-stage least squares (2SLS) estimation in the linear model. For expositional simplicity, we consider the case in which $s = 1$, and so let $\Sigma_{u|v_2} = \sigma^2$. To set up the analogy to 2SLS, it is necessary to return to the asymptotic behavior of $T^{1/2}(\hat\theta_T - \theta_0)$. Our previous analysis indicates that $T^{1/2}(\hat\theta_T - \theta_0)$ is asymptotically equivalent to the function of the data in (11.26). Using (11.37), (11.26) becomes

$$T^{1/2}(\hat\theta_T - \theta_0) = -\{[T^{-1}D_T(\theta_0)'\tilde{Z}_T]W_T[T^{-1}\tilde{Z}_T'D_T(\theta_0)]\}^{-1}$$
$$\times [T^{-1}D_T(\theta_0)'\tilde{Z}_T]W_T T^{-1/2}\tilde{Z}_T'U_T(\theta_0) + o_p(1), \qquad (11.39)$$

where $D_T(\theta_0)$ is the $T \times p$ matrix with tth row $\partial u_t(\theta_0)/\partial\theta'$, $\tilde{Z}_T$ is the $T \times q$ matrix with tth row Z_t, and $U_T(\theta_0)$ is the $T \times 1$ vector with tth element $u_t(\theta_0)$. Assumption 12 implies that the optimal choice of weighting matrix is $S^{-1} = \sigma^{-2}\{E[Z_t Z_t']\}^{-1}$. Since the scaling factor σ^{-2} cancels out in the formula for the estimator, the two-step GMM estimator can be obtained by setting $W_T = (T^{-1}\tilde{Z}_T'\tilde{Z}_T)^{-1}$. Making this substitution in (11.39), we obtain

$$T^{1/2}(\hat\theta_T - \theta_0) = -\{[T^{-1}D_T(\theta_0)'\tilde{Z}_T][T^{-1}\tilde{Z}_T'\tilde{Z}_T]^{-1}[T^{-1}\tilde{Z}_T'D_T(\theta_0)]\}^{-1}$$
$$\times [T^{-1}D_T(\theta_0)'\tilde{Z}_T][T^{-1}\tilde{Z}_T'\tilde{Z}_T]^{-1}T^{-1/2}\tilde{Z}_T'U_T(\theta_0) + o_p(1). \qquad (11.40)$$

In the linear regression model, $u_t(\theta_0) = y_t - x_t'\theta_0$ and so $D_T(\theta_0) = -X$, the matrix of observations on x_t. In this case, (11.40) reduces to the formula for the linear IV estimator and the optimal instrument is $E[x_t|Z_t]$. If x_t is assumed to be a linear function of Z_t then the feasible optimal IV estimator is just the two-stage least squares estimator.[27]

Now let us return to the original nonlinear setting. By analogy to the linear model, (11.40) implies that $T^{1/2}(\hat\theta_T - \theta_0)$ behaves asymptotically like an IV estimator in a linear model with regressor vector, $x_t = -\partial u_t(\theta_0)/\partial\theta'$ and error, $u_t(\theta_0)$. Now we have just argued that the optimal instrument in a linear model is given by the conditional expectation of the regressor. Therefore, applying that logic here, the optimal instrument is given by $-E[\partial u_t(\theta_0)/\partial\theta'|Z_t]$, which is identical to the result in Theorem 7 except for the presence of the scaling factor, $-\sigma^2$. This difference is inconsequential because, as remarked above, the scaling factor cancels out and so does not effect the estimator. To construct a feasible optimal instrument, it is possible to follow a similar strategy to 2SLS and assume a model for $\partial u_t(\theta_0)/\partial\theta'$. However, this is likely to require an assumption about the distribution of v_{2t} in order to evaluate the expectation. This is undesirable here because it is the absence of this information which led us to generalized IV estimation in the first place. An alternative solution is to estimate $Z^0(v_{2t})$ nonparametrically, and Newey (1993) provides a survey of various methods which have been proposed in this context.

The above discussion gives an intuition for the part of $Z^0(v_{2t})$ involving the partial derivative, but does not explain the presence of $\Sigma_{u|v}^{-1}$ in the formula because the σ^2 factor canceled out. However, if $s > 1$ and $\Sigma_{u|v} \neq \sigma^2 I_s$ then it is necessary to employ a correction in the construction of the optimal instrument for either the unequal variances or any contemporaneous correlation (or both) of the elements of $u_t(\theta_0)$. It is for this reason that $Z^0(v_{2t})$ is transformed by $\Sigma_{u|v_2}^{-1}$.[28]

The matrix $V(Z^0)$ can be interpreted as a lower bound on the asymptotic covariance matrix for this class of estimators. It should be remembered that the optimal IV estimator is likely to be less efficient than maximum likelihood because (11.37) does not typically contain all the information in the true score function of the data. However, there is a sense in which $V(Z^0)$ is the best we can do given the information available. Chamberlain (1987) shows that $V(Z^0)$ is also the lower bound on the asymptotic covariance matrix of *any* consistent and asymptotically normal estimator of θ_0 in which the only substantive information used in estimation is the population moment condition in (11.39).[29]

It would be desirable to extend this theorem to time series, but so far there has only been limited success in this direction. Hansen and Singleton (1982), Hayashi and Sims (1983), Hansen (1985) and Hansen, Heaton, and Ogaki (1988) have all provided characterizations of a lower bound on the asymptotic variance under different assumptions about the functional form of $u_t(\theta_0)$ and its dynamic structure. However, as yet, these results have not been translated into general algorithms for the calculation of a feasible optimal instrument in dynamic non-linear models.[30]

8.2 Nearly uninformative moment conditions

While it is desirable to base estimation on the optimal moment conditions, this is not necessary. Even if the population moment condition is sub-optimal, the GMM framework can be used to obtain consistent, asymptotically normal estimators *provided* that the parameter is identified. In recent years, there has been a growing awareness that this proviso may not be so trivial in situations which arise in practice. In a very influential paper, Nelson and Startz (1990) drew attention to this potential problem and provided the first evidence of the problems it causes for the inference framework we have described above. Their paper has prompted considerable interest in the behavior of GMM in cases in which the population moment condition provided is nearly uninformative about θ_0. In this section we concentrate on illustrating the nature of the problem, and then briefly consider a potential solution.

For expositional simplicity, we restrict attention to the simple linear regression model,

$$y_t = x_t\theta_0 + u_t, \qquad (11.41)$$

in which u_t is an iid process with mean zero and variance σ^2. Suppose the scalar parameter θ_0 is estimated by instrumental variables which, as we have seen, is just GMM estimation based on the population moment condition

$$E[z_t u_t(\theta_0)] = 0, \qquad (11.42)$$

where z_t is a $q \times 1$ vector of instruments and $u_t(\theta_0) = y_t - x_t\theta_0$. From Lemma 1, θ_0 is identified[31] by (11.42) if rank$\{E[z_t x_t]\} = 1$. In this simple example, θ_0 is unidentified if $E[z_t x_t]$ is the null vector, which would occur if z_t and x_t are uncorrelated and both possess zero means. In practice, it is unlikely that $E[z_t x_t]$ is exactly zero. The contribution of Nelson and Startz's (1990) paper is to demonstrate that problems occur if $E[z_t x_t]$ is nonzero but small.[32] It is this scenario which we refer to as "nearly uninformative moment conditions."

To proceed, it is necessary to develop a model which can capture the idea of nearly uninformative moment conditions. Following Staiger and Stock (1997), we solve this problem by assuming that

$$x_t = z_t'\gamma_T + \varepsilon_t, \qquad (11.43)$$

where $\gamma_T = T^{-1/2}c$, c is a nonzero $q \times 1$ vector of constants, and ε_t is the unobserved error which has both a zero mean and is uncorrelated with z_t.[33] Notice that (11.43) implies that $E_T[z_t x_t] = E[z_t z_t']T^{-1/2}c$ and so is nonzero for finite T but zero in the limit as $T \to \infty$.[34] So the concept of nearly uninformative moment conditions is captured by assuming that $\{x_t; t = 1, 2, \ldots T\}$ is generated by a sequence of processes whose relationship to z_t disappears at rate $T^{1/2}$. This rate is chosen so that the effects of the nearly uninformative moment conditions manifest themselves in the limiting behavior of the estimator. Since $p = 1$, we have

$$\hat{\theta}_T - \theta_0 = \frac{x'Z(Z'Z)^{-1}Z'u}{x'Z(Z'Z)^{-1}Z'x}. \qquad (11.44)$$

To analyze the limiting behavior of $\hat{\theta}_T - \theta_0$ it is necessary to impose certain regularity conditions. We explicitly assume that z_t is independent of u_t, but leave the other necessary regularity conditions unstated for brevity. Using the weak law of large numbers and the central limit theorem respectively, it follows that: (i) $T^{-1}Z'Z = M_{zz}$, a positive definite matrix of constants; (ii) $T^{-1/2}Z'u \overset{d}{\to} N(0, \sigma^2 M_{zz})$. Notice that neither (i) nor (ii) involve the relationship between x_t and z_t

and so would equally hold if θ_0 is properly identified. The key difference comes in the behavior of $Z'x$. From (11.43), it follows that

$$Z'x = T^{-1/2}Z'Zc + Z'\varepsilon, \tag{11.45}$$

where ε is the $T \times 1$ vector with tth element ε_t. Therefore, $T^{-1}Z'x \xrightarrow{p} 0$ and $T^{-1/2}Z'x \xrightarrow{d} N(M_{zz}c, \sigma_\varepsilon^2 M_{zz})$. The nature of this limiting behavior means that,

$$\hat{\theta}_T - \theta_0 = \frac{T^{-1/2}x'Z(T^{-1}Z'Z)^{-1}T^{-1/2}Z'u}{T^{-1/2}x'Z(T^{-1}Z'Z)^{-1}T^{-1/2}Z'x}$$

$$\xrightarrow{d} \frac{\Psi_1' M_{zz}^{-1}\Psi_2}{\Psi_1' M_{zz}^{-1}\Psi_1} \tag{11.46}$$

where $\Psi_1 \sim N(M_{zz}c, \sigma_\varepsilon^2 M_{zz})$ and $\Psi_2 \sim N(0, \sigma_\varepsilon^2 M_{zz})$. Therefore, $\hat{\theta}_T$ converges to a random variable if the moment conditions are nearly uninformative in the sense of (11.43). This is in marked contrast to the case when θ_0 is identified in the sense of Assumption 4. In that case, Theorem 1 indicates $\hat{\theta}_T$ converges in probability to θ_0.

This analysis provides an indication that the asymptotic theory derived in Section 4 is inappropriate for the nearly uninformative moment condition case. It is unlikely to be known a priori if the population moment condition in question is informative – in the sense of Assumption 4 – or nearly uninformative. Therefore, it is useful to develop statistical tests to discriminate between the two cases. In our linear model example, a natural diagnostic is the F-statistic for the hypothesis x_t is linearly unrelated to z_t. If this hypothesis is not rejected then this can be interpreted as evidence that identification of θ_0 is suspect. Faced with an insignificant F-statistic, there are two possible responses. One strategy is to keep changing the instrument vector until the F-statistic is significant. However, Hall, Rudebusch and Wilcox (1996) report evidence that this approach does not solve the problem and in fact tends to make matters worse. A second, and more promising, strategy is to develop an inference theory which provides a better approximation in the nearly uninformative moment condition case. This line of research is still in its early stages but significant advances have been made by Staiger and Stock (1997), Stock and Wright (1997), and Wang and Zivot (1998).

9 FINITE SAMPLE BEHAVIOR

The foregoing discussion has rested upon asymptotic theory. In finite samples, such theory can only provide an approximation. It is therefore important to assess the quality of this approximation in the types of model and sample sizes that are encountered in economics and finance. Intuition suggests that the quality is going to vary from case to case depending on the form of the nonlinearity and the dynamic structure. A number of simulation studies have examined this question; see *inter alia* Tauchen (1986), Kocherlakota (1990) and the seven papers included in the July 1996 issue of *Journal of Business and Economics Statistics*. It is beyond the scope of this article to provide a comprehensive review of these studies.[35] However, it should be noted that in certain circumstances of interest the quality of the approximation is poor. In view of this evidence, it is desirable to develop methods which improve the quality of finite sample inferences. One such method is the bootstrap, and this has been explored in the context of GMM by Hall and Horowitz (1996).

Notes

* I am grateful to Atsushi Inoue, Fernanda Peixe, James Stock, and three anonymous reviewers for comments on an earlier draft of this paper.

1 Hall (1993) and Ogaki (1993) provide an overview of the areas in which GMM has been applied.

2 Also see Hall (1998) for a survey of hypothesis tests based specifically on GMM estimators.

3 This generic approach is known as the consumption based asset pricing model.

4 It is possible to generalize the arguments to allow for certain types of nonstationarity; see Gallant and White (1988), Pötscher and Prucha (1997).

5 E.g. see Apostol (1974, p. 361).

6 E.g. see Dhrymes (1984, Proposition 92, p. 111).

7 For example see Quandt (1983) or Gallant (1987, ch. 2).

8 This property is not guaranteed by pointwise convergence of $Q_T(\theta)$. See Apostol (1974, ch. 9) for a useful discussion of the difference between pointwise and uniform convergence.

9 E.g. see Apostol (1974, p. 355).

10 E.g. see Fuller (1976, p. 199). Hansen (1982) and Wooldridge (1994) provide formal proofs of the theorem.

11 For example see Hamilton (1994, pp. 279–80).

12 See Hamilton (1994, pp. 261–2) for a discussion of the properties of autocovariance matrices.

13 For example see White (1994, Theorem 8.27, p. 193).

14 The requirement that S_T be positive semi-definite (p.s.d.) is the matrix generalization of a nonnegative scalar variance. This property is not guaranteed for estimators of the generic form in (11.22). For example $\omega_{iT} = 1$ does not yield a p.s.d. matrix; see Newey and West (1987).

15 See *inter alia* Newey and West (1987), Gallant (1987), Andrews (1991), Andrews and Monahan (1992).

16 Andrews (1991) and Newey and West (1994) propose data-based methods for bandwidth selection.

17 See Dhrymes (1984, p. 17).

18 See Rao (1973, ch. 8) for a discussion of the singular normal distribution.

19 If $p = q$ then the asymptotic variance of $\hat{\theta}_T$ is $MSM' = (G_0'S^{-1}G_0)^{-1}$.

20 See Hall (2000b, ch. 3).

21 It is common to impose this assumption in both theoretical treatments and applications of these long-run variance estimators in the context of GMM.

22 See Hall (2000b, ch. 5).

23 White (1982) refers to such an estimator as *quasi*-maximum likelihood.

24 See Hansen and Singleton (1982).

25 This difference facilitates the analysis but makes no difference to the ultimate result.

26   See Newey (1993) for a formal proof.
27   See Hall (1993) or Theil (1971, pp. 451–3).
28   Notice that if $\Sigma_{u|v_2} = \sigma_2 I_s$ then the σ^2 factor cancels out as in our example.
29   Chamberlain's (1987) analysis is based on a form of semiparametric maximum likelihood subject to (11.37). Also see Newey (1993, pp. 423–4).
30   One exception is the case in which $u_t(\theta_0)$ is a martingale difference case for which Hansen (1985) shows Theorem 7 extends directly with only a slight modification to make allowance for conditional heteroskedasticity.
31   In the linear model, global and local identification are equivalent because (11.6) is no longer an approximation but is an identity which holds over Θ.
32   This terminology parallels the distinction between exact and near collinearity in the linear regression model.
33   Equation (11.43) implies the explanatory variable is a triangular array $\{x_{t,T}; t = 1, 2 \ldots T; T = 1, 2 \ldots\}$ but we suppress the second subscript for notational brevity.
34   Notice that the data generation process for x_t changes with T and it is for this reason that the expectations operator is indexed by T.
35   The interested reader is refered to Hall (1999b, ch. 6).

References

Andrews, D.W.K. (1991). Heteroscedasticity and autocorrelation consistent covariance matrix estimation. *Econometrica* 59, 817–58.

Andrews, D.W.K., and J.C. Monahan (1992). An improved heteroscedasticity and autocorrelation consistent covariance matrix. *Econometrica* 60, 953–66.

Angrist, J.D., and A.B. Krueger (1992). The effect of age at school entry on educational attainment: an application of instrumental variables with moments from two samples. *Journal of the American Statistical Association* 87, 328–36.

Apostol, T. (1974). *Mathematical Analysis*, 2nd edn. Reading, MA: Addison-Wesley.

Chamberlain, G. (1987). Asymptotic efficiency in estimation with conditional moment restrictions. *Journal of Econometrics* 34, 305–34.

Davidson, J. (1994). *Stochastic Limit Theory*. Oxford: Oxford University Press.

Dhrymes, P.J. (1984). *Mathematics for Econometrics*, 2nd edn. New York: Springer-Verlag.

Fuller, W.A. (1976). *Introduction to Statistical Time Series*. New York: Wiley.

Gallant, A.R. (1987). *Nonlinear Statistical Models*. New York: Wiley.

Gallant, A.R., and H. White (1988). *A Unified Theory of Estimation and Inference in Nonlinear Models*. Oxford: Basil Blackwell.

Geary, R.C. (1942). Inherent relations between random variables. *Proceedings of the Royal Irish Academy, Section A* 47, 63–76.

Hall, A.R. (1993). Some aspects of Generalized Method of Moments estimation. In G.S. Maddala, C.R. Rao, and H.D. Vinod (eds.) *Handbook of Statistics, Volume 11.* pp. 393–417. Amsterdam: Elsevier Science Publishers.

Hall, A.R. (1998). Hypothesis testing in models estimated by Generalized Method of Moments. In L. Mátyás (ed.) *Generalized Method of Moments.* pp. 75–101. Cambridge: Cambridge University Press.

Hall, A.R. (2000a). Covariance matrix estimation and the power of the overidentifying restrictions test. Discussion paper, Department of Economics, North Carolina State University, Raleigh NC.

Hall, A.R. (2000b). *Generalized Method of Moments*. Manuscript in preparation, Oxford: Oxford University Press.

Hall, A.R., G. Rudebusch, and D. Wilcox (1996). Judging instrument relevance in instrumental variables estimation. *International Economic Review* 37, 283–98.

Hall, P., and J.L. Horowitz (1996). Bootstrap critical values for tests based on generalized Method of Moments. *Econometrica* 64, 891–917.

Hamilton, J.D. (1994). *Time Series Analysis*. Princeton NJ: Princeton University Press.

Hansen, L.P. (1982). Large sample properties of Generalized Method of Moments estimators. *Econometrica* 50, 1029–54.

Hansen, L.P. (1985). A method of calculating bounds on the asymptotic covariance matrices of generalized method of moments estimators. *Journal of Econometrics* 30, 203–38.

Hansen, L.P., J. Heaton, and M. Ogaki (1988). Efficiency bounds implied by multi-period conditional moment restrictions. *Journal of the American Statistical Association* 83, 863–71.

Hansen, L.P., and K.S. Singleton (1982). Generalized instrumental variables estimation of nonlinear rational expectations models. *Econometrica* 50, 1269–86.

Hayashi, F., and C. Sims (1983). Nearly efficient estimation of time series models with predetermined, but not exogenous instruments. *Econometrica* 51, 783–98.

Kocherlakota, N.R. (1990). On tests of representative consumer asset pricing models. *Journal of Monetary Economics* 26, 285–304.

Nelson, C.R., and R. Startz (1990). The distribution of the instrumental variables estimator and its *t* ratio when the instrument in a poor one. *Journal of Business* 63, S125–S140.

Newey, W.K. (1985). Maximum likelihood specfifcation testing and instrumented score tests. *Econometrica* 53, 1047–70.

Newey, W.K. (1993). Efficient estimation of models with conditional moment restrictions. In G.S. Maddala, C.R. Rao, and H.D. Vinod (eds.) *Handbook of Statistics, Volume 2*. pp. 419–54. Amsterdam: Elsevier Science Publishers.

Newey, W.K., and D.L. McFadden (1994). Large sample estimation and hypothesis testing. In R. Engle and D.L. McFadden (eds.) *Handbook of Econometrics, Volume 4*. pp. 2113–247. Amsterdam: Elsevier Science Publishers.

Newey, W.K., and K.D. West (1987). A simple positive semi-definite heteroscedasticity and autocorrelation consistent covariance matrix. *Economentrica* 55, 703–8.

Newey, W.K., and K.D. West (1994). Automatic lag selection in covariance matrix estimation. *Review of Economic Studies* 61, 631–53.

Ogaki, M. (1993). Generalized Method of Moments: econometric applications. In G.S. Maddala, C.R. Rao, and H.D. Vinod (eds.) *Handbook of Statistics, Volume 11*. pp. 455–88. Amsterdam: Elsevier Science Publishers.

Pearson, K.S. (1893). Asymmetrical frequency curves. *Nature* 48: 615–16.

Pearson, K.S. (1894). Contributions to the mathematical theory of evolution. *Philosophical Transactions of the Royal Society of London (A)* 185, 71–110.

Pearson, K.S. (1895). Contributions to the mathematical theory of evolution, II: skew variation. *Philosophical Transactions of the Royal Society of London (A)* 186, 343–414.

Pötscher, B.M., and I.R. Prucha (1997). *Dynamic Nonlinear Econometric Models*. Berlin: Springer Verlag.

Quandt, R.E. (1983). Computational problems and methods. In Z. Grilliches and M.D. Intrilligator (eds.) *Handbook of Econometrics, Volume 1*. pp. 699–764. Amsterdam: Elsevier Science Publishers.

Rao, C.R. (1973). *Linear Statistical Inference and its Applications*, 2nd edn. New York: Wiley.

Reiersol (1941). Confluence analysis by means of lag moments and other methods of confluence analysis. *Econometrica* 9, 1–24.

Sargan, J.D. (1958). The estimation of economic relationships using instrumental variables. *Econometrica* 26, 393–415.

Sowell, F. (1996). Optimal tests of parameter variation in the Generalized Method of Moments framework. *Econometrica* 64, 1085–108.

Staiger, D., and J. Stock (1997). Instrumental variables regression with weak instruments. *Econometrica* 65, 557–86.

Stock, J., and J. Wright (1997). GMM with weak identification. Discussion paper, Kennedy School of Government, Harvard University, Cambridge, MA.

Tauchen, G. (1985). Diagnostic testing and evaluation of maximum likelihood models. *Journal of Econometrics* 30, 415–43.

Tauchen, G. (1986). Statistical properties of Generalized Method of Moments estimators of structural parameters obtained from financial market data. *Journal of Business and Economic Statistics* 4, 397–416.

Theil, H. (1971). *Principles of Econometrics*. New York: Wiley.

Wang, J. and E. Zivot (1998). Inference on structural parameters in instrumental variables regression with weak instruments. *Econometrica* 66, 1389–404.

White, H. (1982). Maximum likelihood in misspecified models. *Econometrica.* 50, 1–25.

White, H. (1994). *Estimation, Inference and Specification Analysis*. New York: Cambridge University Press.

Wooldridge, J.M. (1994). Estimation and inference for dependent processes. In R. Engle and D.L. McFadden (eds.) *Handbook of Econometrics, Volume 4.* pp. 2641–739. Amsterdam: Elsevier Science Publishers.

Wright, S. (1925). Corn and hog correlations. Discussion paper, US Department of Agriculture Bulletin No. 1300, Washington, DC.

CHAPTER TWELVE

Collinearity

R. Carter Hill and Lee C. Adkins*

Multicollinearity is God's will, not a problem
with OLS or statistical techniques in general.
Blanchard (1987, p. 49)

1   INTRODUCTION

Collinearity, a devilish problem to be sure, receives the blame for a substantial amount of inconclusive, weak, or unbelievable empirical work. Social scientists are, for the most part, nonexperimental scientists. We do not have the luxury of designing and carrying out the experiments that generate our data. Consequently our data are often weak and not up to the task of isolating the effect of changes in one economic variable upon another. In regression models the least squares estimates may have the wrong sign, be sensitive to slight changes in the data or the model specification, or may not yield statistically significant results for theoretically important explanatory variables. These symptoms may appear despite significant values for the overall F-test of model significance or high R^2 values. These are commonly cited consequences of a "collinearity problem."

In the context of the linear regression model, collinearity takes three distinct forms. First, an explanatory variable may exhibit little variability. Intuitively, this is a problem for regression because we are trying to estimate the effect of changes in the explanatory variable upon the dependent variable. If an explanatory variable does not vary much in our sample, it will be difficult to estimate its effect. Second, two explanatory variables may exhibit a large correlation. In this case, the attempt to isolate the effect of one variable, all other things held constant, is made difficult by the fact that in the sample the variable exhibits little *independent* variation. The correlation between two explanatory variables implies that changes in one are linked to changes in the other, and thus separating out their individual effects may be difficult. Third, and generally, there may be one, or more, nearly exact linear relationship among the explanatory variables. As in the case when two explanatory variables are correlated, such relationships obscure the effects of involved variables upon the dependent variable. These are the three faces of collinearity.

In this chapter we explore collinearity in linear and nonlinear models. In Section 2 we present the basics, examining the forms that collinearity may take and the damage it does to estimation. The variance decomposition of Belsley, Kuh, and Welsch (1980) (hereinafter BKW) is presented in Section 3, and other collinearity diagnostics and issues are considered in Section 4. Section 5 reviews suggested remedies for collinearity problems. In Section 6 we examine the problems of collinearity in nonlinear models. Summary remarks are contained in Section 7.

2   THE NATURE AND STATISTICAL CONSEQUENCES OF COLLINEARITY

Consider first a linear regression model with two explanatory variables,

$$y_t = \beta_1 + \beta_2 x_{t2} + \beta_3 x_{t3} + e_t. \tag{12.1}$$

Assume that the errors are uncorrelated, with mean zero and constant variance, σ^2, and that x_{t2} and x_{t3} are nonstochastic. Under these assumptions the least squares estimators are the best, linear, unbiased estimators of the regression parameters. The variance of the least squares estimator b_2 of β_2 is

$$\text{var}(b_2) = \frac{\sigma^2}{\sum_{t=1}^{T}(x_{t2} - \bar{x}_2)^2(1 - r_{23}^2)}, \tag{12.2}$$

where $\bar{x}_2$ is the sample mean of the T observations on x_{t2}, and r_{23} is the sample correlation between x_{t2} and x_{t3}. The formula for the variance of b_3, the least squares estimator of β_3, is analogous, but the variance of the intercept estimator is messier and we will not discuss it here. The covariance between b_2 and b_3 is

$$\text{cov}(b_2, b_3) = \frac{-r_{23}\sigma^2}{(1 - r_{23}^2)\sqrt{\sum_{t=1}^{T}(x_{t2} - \bar{x}_2)^2}\sqrt{\sum_{t=1}^{T}(x_{t3} - \bar{x}_3)^2}}. \tag{12.3}$$

The variance and covariance expressions reveal the consequences of two of the three forms of collinearity. First, suppose that x_{t2} exhibits little variation about its sample mean, so that $\sum(x_{t2} - \bar{x}_2)^2$ is small. The less the variation in the explanatory variable x_{t2} about its mean, the larger will be the variance of b_2, and the larger will be the covariance, in absolute value, between b_2 and b_3. Second, the larger the correlation between x_{t2} and x_{t3} the larger will be the variance of b_2, and the larger will be the covariance, in absolute value, between b_2 and b_3. If the correlation is positive the covariance will be negative. This is the source of another conventional observation about collinearity, namely that the coefficients of highly correlated variables tend to have opposite signs.

Exact, or perfect, collinearity occurs when the variation in an explanatory variable is zero, $\sum(x_{t2} - \bar{x}_2)^2 = 0$, or when the correlation between x_{t2} and x_{t3} is perfect, so that $r_{23} = \pm 1$. In these cases the least squares estimates are not unique, and, in absence of additional information, best linear unbiased estimators are not available for all the regression parameters. Fortunately, this extreme case rarely occurs in practice.

The commonly cited symptoms of collinearity, that least squares estimates have the wrong sign, are sensitive to slight changes in the data or the model specification, or are not statistically significant, follow from the large variances of the least squares estimators. The least squares estimators are unbiased under standard assumptions, so that $E[b_k] = \beta_k$, but how close an estimate might be to the true parameter value is determined by the estimator variance. Large variances for estimators imply that their sampling (probability) distributions are wide, meaning that in any particular sample the estimates we obtain may be far from the true parameter values.

2.1   Collinearity in the linear regression model

Denote the linear regression model as

$$y = X\beta + e, \qquad (12.4)$$

where y is a $T \times 1$ vector of observations on the dependent variable, X is a $T \times K$ non-stochastic matrix of observations on K explanatory variables, β is a $K \times 1$ vector of unknown parameters, and e is the $T \times 1$ vector of uncorrelated random errors, with zero means and constant variances, σ^2.

In the general linear model exact, or perfect, collinearity exists when the columns of X, denoted $x_i, i = 1, \ldots, K$, are linearly dependent. This occurs when there is at least one relation of the form $a_1 x_1 + a_2 x_2 + \ldots + a_K x_K = 0$, where the a_i are constants, not all equal to zero. In this case the column rank of X is less than K, the normal equations $X'X\beta = X'y$ do not have a unique solution, and least squares estimation breaks down. Unique best linear unbiased estimators do not exist for all K parameters. However, even in this most severe of cases, all is not lost. Consider equation (12.1), $y_t = \beta_1 + \beta_2 x_{t2} + \beta_3 x_{t3} + e_t$. Suppose that $a_2 x_2 + a_3 x_3 = 0$, or more simply, $x_2 = ax_3$. Substituting this into (12.1) we obtain $y_t = \beta_1 + \beta_2 (ax_3) + \beta_3 x_{t3} + e_t = \beta_1 + (a\beta_2 + \beta_3)x_{t3} + e_t = \beta_1 + \gamma x_{t3} + e_t$. Thus we *can* obtain a best linear unbiased estimator of $\gamma = a\beta_2 + \beta_3$, a linear combination of the parameters. The classic paper by Silvey (1969) provides expressions for determining which linear combinations of parameters are estimable.

Exact collinearity is rare, and easily recognized. More frequently, one or more linear combinations of explanatory variables are *nearly* exact, so that $a_1 x_1 + a_2 x_2 + \ldots + a_K x_K \approx 0$. We now examine the consequences of such near exact linear dependencies.

2.2 Diagnosing collinearity using the singular value decomposition

The singular-value decomposition is a factorization of X. The matrix X may be decomposed as $X = U\Lambda^{1/2}C'$, where $U'U = C'C = CC' = I_K$ and $\Lambda^{1/2}$ is a diagonal matrix with nonnegative diagonal values $\lambda_1^{1/2}, \lambda_2^{1/2}, \ldots, \lambda_K^{1/2}$, called the singular values of X. The relation to eigenanalysis is that the singular values are the positive square roots of the eigenvalues of $X'X$, and the $K \times K$ matrix C is the matrix whose columns contain the eigenvectors of $X'X$. Thus

$$C'X'XC = \Lambda, \tag{12.5}$$

where Λ is a diagonal matrix with the real values $\lambda_1, \lambda_2, \ldots, \lambda_K$ on the diagonal. The matrix U is $T \times K$, and its properties are discussed in Belsley (1991, pp. 42–3). The columns of the matrix C, denoted c_i, are the eigenvectors (or characteristic vectors) of the matrix $X'X$, and the real values λ_i are the corresponding eigenvalues (or characteristic roots). It is customary to assume that the columns of C are arranged so that the eigenvalues are ordered by magnitude, $\lambda_1 \geq \lambda_2 \geq \ldots \geq \lambda_K$.

If X is of full column rank K, so that there are no exact linear dependencies among the columns of X, then $X'X$ is a positive definite and symmetric matrix, and all its eigenvalues are not only real but also positive. If we find a "small" eigenvalue, $\lambda_i \approx 0$, then $c_i'X'Xc_i = (Xc_i)'(Xc_i) = \lambda_i \approx 0$ and therefore $Xc_i \approx 0$. Thus we have located a near exact linear dependency among the columns of X. If there is a single small eigenvalue, then the linear relation $Xc_i \approx 0$ indicates the form of the linear dependency, and can be used to determine which of the explanatory variables are involved in the relationship.

2.3 Collinearity and the least squares estimator

Using equation (12.5), and the orthogonality of C, $C'C = CC' = I_K$, we can write $X'X = C\Lambda C'$, and therefore

$$(X'X)^{-1} = C\Lambda^{-1}C' = \sum_{i=1}^{K} \lambda_i^{-1}c_ic_i'. \tag{12.6}$$

The covariance matrix of the least squares estimator b is $\text{cov}(b) = \sigma^2(X'X)^{-1}$, and using equation (12.6) the variance of b_j is

$$\text{var}(b_j) = \sigma^2 \left(\frac{c_{j1}^2}{\lambda_1} + \frac{c_{j2}^2}{\lambda_2} + \cdots + \frac{c_{jK}^2}{\lambda_K} \right), \tag{12.7}$$

where c_{jk} is the element in the jth row and ith column of C. The orthogonality of C implies that $\sum_{k=1}^{K} c_{jk}^2 = 1$. Thus the variance of b_j depends upon three distinct factors. First, the magnitude of the error variance, σ^2; second, the magnitudes of the constants c_{jk}; and third, the magnitude of the eigenvalues, λ_k. A small eigenvalue may cause a large variance for b_j if it is paired with a constant c_{jk} that is not close to zero. The constants $c_{jk} = 0$ when x_j and x_k, the jth and kth columns of X, respectively, are orthogonal, so that $x'_j x_k = 0$. This fact is an important one for it will allow us to determine which variables are "not" involved in collinear relationships.

Suppose β_j is a critical parameter in the model, and there is one small eigenvalue, $\lambda_K \approx 0$. If x_j is not involved in the corresponding linear dependency $Xc_K \approx 0$, then c_{jK} will be small, and the fact that $\lambda_K \approx 0$, i.e. the Kth eigenvalue is very small, will not adversely affect the precision of estimation of β_j. *The presence of collinearity in the data does not automatically mean that "all is lost."* If $X'X$ has one or more small eigenvalues, then you must think clearly about the objectives of your research, and determine if the collinearity reduces the precision of estimation of your key parameters by an unacceptable amount. We address the question What is a small eigenvalue? in Section 3. For more about the geometry of characteristic roots and vectors see Fomby, Hill, and Johnson (1984, pp. 288–93).

2.4   Collinearity and the least squares predictor

Another bit of conventional wisdom is that while collinearity may affect the precision of the least squares estimator, it need not affect the reliability of predictions based on it, *if* the collinearity in the sample extends to the forecast period. Suppose we wish to predict the value of y_0, given by $y_0 = x'_0\beta + e_0$, where x'_0 is a $1 \times K$ vector of regressor values, and e_0 is a random disturbance with zero-mean, constant variance σ^2, and which is uncorrelated with the regression disturbances. Using equation (12.6), the best linear unbiased predictor of $E(y_0)$, $\hat{y}_0 = x'_0 b$, has variance

$$\text{var}(\hat{y}_0) = \sigma^2 x'_0(X'X)^{-1}x_0 = \sigma^2 x'_0 C\Lambda^{-1}C'x_0 = \sigma^2\left(\frac{(x'_0 c_1)^2}{\lambda_1} + \frac{(x'_0 c_2)^2}{\lambda_2} + \cdots + \frac{(x'_0 c_K)^2}{\lambda_K}\right).$$

(12.8)

If, for example, there is a single linear dependence among the columns of X, then $\lambda_K \approx 0$, and $Xc_K \approx 0$. A small eigenvalue could make the last term of the sum in equation (12.8) large, producing a large prediction variance. However, *if* (and this is a big *if*) the new observation x'_0 obeys the same collinearity pattern as the sample data, then it may also be true that $x'_0 c_K \approx 0$, effectively negating the small eigenvalue.

3   The Variance Decomposition of Belsley, Kuh, and Welsch (1980)

A property of eigenvalues is that $\text{tr}(X'X) = \sum_{i=1}^{K} \lambda_i$. This implies that the sizes of the eigenvalues are determined in part by the scaling of the data. Data matrices

Table 12.1 Matrix of variance proportions

Condition index	Proportions of variances of least squares estimator			
	$var(b_1)$	$var(b_2)$	$\ldots$	$var(b_K)$
η_1	π_{11}	π_{12}	$\ldots$	π_{1K}
η_2	π_{21}	π_{22}	$\ldots$	π_{2K}
.	.	.		.
.	.	.	$\ldots$	.
.	.	.		.
η_K	π_{K1}	π_{K2}	$\ldots$	π_{KK}

consisting of large numbers will have larger eigenvalues, in total, than data matrices with small numbers. To remove the effect of scaling BKW, whose collinearity diagnostic procedure we recommend, suggest scaling the columns of X to unit length. Define $s_i = (\sum_{t=1}^{T} x_{ti}^2)^{1/2}$, and let $S = \text{diag}(s_1, s_2, \ldots, s_K)$. Then the scaled X matrix is XS^{-1}. This scaling is only for the purpose of diagnosing collinearity, not for model estimation or interpretation.

To diagnose collinearity, examine the proportion of the variance of each least squares coefficient contributed by each individual eigenvalue. Define $\phi_{jk} = \dfrac{c_{jk}^2}{\lambda_k}$, and let ϕ_j be the variance of b_j, apart from σ^2, $\phi_j = \left(\dfrac{c_{j1}^2}{\lambda_1} + \dfrac{c_{j2}^2}{\lambda_2} + \cdots + \dfrac{c_{jK}^2}{\lambda_K} \right)$. Then, the proportion of the variance of b_j associated with the kth eigenvalue λ_k is $\pi_{kj} = \dfrac{\phi_{jk}}{\phi_j}$, which appears in the kth row and the jth column of Table 12.1. The columns of the table correspond to the variances of individual least squares coefficients, and the sum of each column, because it contains the proportions π_{kj}, is one. The rows of this matrix correspond to the different eigenvalues, which have been scaled in a certain way. The "condition index" is the square root of the ratio of λ_1, the largest eigenvalue, to the kth largest, λ_k, that is, $\eta_k = \left(\dfrac{\lambda_1}{\lambda_k} \right)^{1/2}$. The condition indices are ordered in magnitude, with $\eta_1 = 1$ and η_K being the largest, since its denominator is λ_K, the smallest eigenvalue. The largest condition index is often called "the condition number of X" and denoted as $\eta_K = \left(\dfrac{\lambda_1}{\lambda_K} \right)^{1/2} = \kappa$.

Table 12.1 summarizes much of what we can learn about collinearity in data. BKW carried out extensive simulations to determine how large condition indexes affect the variances of the least squares estimators. Their diagnostic procedures, also summarized in Belsley (1991, ch. 5), are these:

Step 1

Begin by identifying large condition indices. A small eigenvalue and a near exact linear dependency among the columns of X is associated with each large condition index. BKW's experiments lead them to the general guidelines that indices in the range 0–10 indicate weak near dependencies, 10–30 indicate moderately strong near dependencies, 30–100 a strong near dependency, and indices in excess of 100 are very strong. Thus when examining condition indexes values of 30 and higher should immediately attract attention.

Step 2 (if there is a single large condition index)

Examine the variance–decomposition proportions. If there is a single large condition index, indicating a single near dependency associated with one small eigenvalue, collinearity adversely affects estimation when *two or more* coefficients each have 50 percent or more of their variance associated with the large condition index, in the last row of Table 12.1. The variables involved in the near dependency have coefficients with large variance proportions.

Step 2 (if there are two or more large condition indexes of relatively equal magnitude)

If there are $J \geq 2$ large and roughly equal condition indexes, then $X'X$ has J eigenvalues that are near zero and J near exact linear dependencies among the columns of X exist. Since the J corresponding eigenvectors span the space containing the coefficients of the true linear dependence, the "50 percent rule" for identifying the variables involved in the near dependencies must be modified.

If there are two (or more) small eigenvalues, then we have two (or more) near exact linear relations, such as $Xc_i \approx 0$ and $Xc_j \approx 0$. These two relationships do not, necessarily, indicate the form of the linear dependencies, since $X(a_1c_i + a_2c_j) \approx 0$ as well. In this case the two vectors of constants c_i and c_j define a two-dimensional vector space in which the two near exact linear dependencies exist. While we may not be able to identify the individual relationships among the explanatory variables that are causing the collinearity, we can identify the variables that appear in the two (or more) relations.

Thus variance proportions in a single row *do not* identify specific linear dependencies, as they did when there was but one large condition number. In this case, *sum* the variance proportions across the J large condition number rows in Table 12.1. The variables involved in the (set of) near linear dependencies are identified by summed coefficient variance proportions of greater than 50 percent.

Step 2 (if there are $J \geq 2$ large condition indexes, with one extremely large)

An extremely large condition index, arising from a very small eigenvalue, can "mask" the variables involved in other near exact linear dependencies. For example, if one condition index is 500 and another is 50, then there are two near exact linear dependencies among the columns of X. However, the variance decompositions associated with the condition index of 50 may not indicate that there are two or more variables involved in a relationship. Identify the variables involved in the set of near linear dependencies by summing the coefficient variance proportions in the last J rows of Table 12.1, and locating the sums greater than 50 percent.

STEP 3

Perhaps the most important step in the diagnostic process is determining which coefficients *are not* affected by collinearity. If there is a single large condition index, coefficients with variance proportions less than 50 percent in the last row of Table 12.1 are not adversely affected by the collinear relationship in the data. If there are $J \geq 2$ large condition indexes, then sum the last J rows of variance proportions. Coefficients with summed variance proportions of less than 50 percent are not adversely affected by the collinear relationships. If the parameters of interest have coefficients unaffected by collinearity, then small eigenvalues and large condition numbers *are not a problem*.

STEP 4

If key parameter estimates are adversely affected by collinearity, further diagnostic steps may be taken. If there is a single large condition index the variance proportions identify the variables involved in the near dependency. If there are multiple large condition indexes, auxiliary regressions may be used to further study the nature of the relationships between the columns of X. In these regressions one variable in a near dependency is regressed upon the other variables in the identified set. The usual t-statistics may be used as diagnostic tools to determine which variables are involved in specific linear dependencies. See Belsley (1991, p. 144) for suggestions. Unfortunately, these auxiliary regressions may also be confounded by collinearity, and thus they may not be informative.

4   OTHER DIAGNOSTIC ISSUES AND TOOLS

There are a number of issues related to the diagnosis of collinearity, and other diagnostic tools. In this section we summarize some of these.

4.1   The centering issue

Eigenvalue magnitudes are affected by the scale of the data. There is wide agreement that the X matrix should be scaled before analyzing collinearity, and scaling the columns of X to unit length is standard. A much more hotly debated issue, chronicled in Belsley (1984), is whether the data should be *centered*, and then scaled, prior to collinearity diagnosis. If the data are centered, by subtracting the mean, the origin is translated so that the regression, in terms of the centered data, has a y-intercept of zero. The least squares estimates of slopes are unaffected by centering. The least squares estimate of the intercept itself can be obtained after the slopes are estimated, as $b_1 = \bar{y} - b_2\bar{x}_2 - \ldots - b_K\bar{x}_K$. So nothing is really gained, or lost, by centering. Let X_c be the X matrix after centering, scaling to unit length, and deleting the first column of zeros. Then $X'_c X_c = R_c$ is the regressor correlation matrix.

The "pro-centering" point of view is summarized by Stewart (1987, p. 75), who suggests that the constant term is rarely of interest and its inclusion "masks" the real variables. "Centering simply shows the variable for what it is." The "anti-centering" viewpoint is based on several points. First, as a practical matter, centering lowers the condition number of the data (Belsley, 1991, p. 189), usually by a large amount, and thus makes it an unreliable diagnostic. Second, and more importantly, centering the data makes it impossible to identify collinearities caused by linear combinations of explanatory variables which exhibit little variation. If a variable, or a linear combination of variables, exhibits little variation, then it will be "collinear" with the constant term, the column of 1s in the first column of X. That is, suppose $a_2 x_{t2} + a_3 x_{t3} + \ldots + a_K x_{tK} \approx a$, where a is a constant. If $x_{t1} = 1$, then $a_2 x_{t2} + a_3 x_{t3} + \ldots + a_K x_{tK} - a x_{t1} \approx 0$.

The pro-centering view is that the constant term is not interesting, and therefore such linear dependencies are not important. The anti-centering group notes that such a collinear relationship affects not only the intercept, but also affects the coefficients of the variables in the collinear relationship, whether the intercept is of theoretical importance or not.

We fall squarely into the anti-centering camp. The data should be scaled to unit length, but not centered, prior to examining collinearity diagnostics. The interested reader should see Belsley (1984), including comments, for the complete, lively, debate.

4.2 Other diagnostics

The expression for the variance of the least squares estimator in equation (12.2), for the regression model with two explanatory variables, can be extended to the multiple regression context, for all coefficients except the intercept, as

$$\text{var}(b_j) = \frac{\sigma^2}{\sum_{t=1}^{T}(x_{tj} - \bar{x}_j)^2} \cdot \frac{1}{1 - R_j^2}, \tag{12.9}$$

where R_j^2 is the "R^2" goodness-of-fit measure from the auxiliary regression of x_{tj} on all other regressors. The second factor in (12.9) is called the *variance-inflation factor* (VIF), as it shows the effect of linear associations among the explanatory variables upon the variances of the least squares estimators, as measured by R_j^2. Stewart (1987) proposes collinearity indexes that are the square roots of the VIFs. Fox and Monette (1992) generalize VIFs to measure variance-inflation in a subset of coefficients. Auxiliary regressions and VIFs have the same strengths and weaknesses as collinearity diagnostics. Their strength is their intuitive appeal. If $R_j^2 \to 1$, then x_{tj} is in some collinear relationship. The weaknesses are, apart from the pro-centering–anti-centering debate, that we have no measure of how close R_j^2 must be to 1 to imply a collinearity problem, and these measures cannot determine the number of near linear dependencies in the data (Belsley, 1991, p. 30). Kennedy (1998, p. 90) suggests the rule of thumb that a VIF > 10, for scaled data, indicates severe collinearity. The same critiques apply to the strategy of looking at the matrix R_c of correlations among the regressors as a diagnostic tool.

Another diagnostic that is often mentioned, though recognized as deficient, is the determinant of $X'X$ (or $X_c'X_c = R_c$). One or more near exact collinearities among the columns of X drive this determinant to zero. The problems with measuring collinearity this way include deciding how small the determinant must be before collinearity is judged a problem, the fact that using this measure we determine neither the number nor form of the collinearities, and the ever-present centering debate. Soofi (1990) offers an information theory-based approach for diagnosing collinearity in which the log determinant plays an important role. Unfortunately, his measures reduce the diagnosis of collinearity to the examination of a single index, which has the same flaws as the determinant.

4.3 Collinearity-influential observations

One or two observations can make a world of difference in a data set, substantially improving, or worsening, the collinearity in the data. Can we find these "collinearity-influential" observations? If we do, what, if anything, do we do with them? The answer to the former question is "Maybe." The answer to the latter question is "It depends."

Influential-data diagnostics are designed to find "unusual" observations in a data set and evaluate their impact upon regression analysis. Standard references include BKW, Cook and Weisberg (1982) and Chatterjee and Hadi (1988). Mason and Gunst (1985) illustrate the effect that individual observations can have on data collinearity. Belsley (1991, pp. 245–70) reviews and illustrates diagnostics that may be useful for detecting collinearity-*inducing* observations, whose inclusion worsens collinearity in the data, and collinearity-*breaking* observations, whose inclusion lessens collinearity in the data. If $\kappa = (\lambda_1/\lambda_K)^{1/2}$ is the condition number of the X matrix, and if $\kappa_{(i)}$ denotes the condition index of the matrix X with row i (or set of rows) deleted, then one measure of the effect of an observation upon collinearity is

$$\delta_{(i)} = \frac{\kappa_{(i)} - \kappa}{\kappa}. \tag{12.10}$$

A large negative value of $\delta_{(i)}$ indicates a collinearity-inducing observation, while a positive value indicates a collinearity-breaking observation. Chatterjee and Hadi (1988), Hadi and Wells (1990) and Sengupta and Bhimasankaram (1997) study this measure and variations of it. See Belsley (1991, p. 251) for examples.

The question is what to do when collinearity-influential observations are found? As with all influential, or unusual, observations we must first determine if they are correct. If they are incorrect, then they should be corrected. If they are correct, then the observations deserve close examination, in an effort to determine why they are unusual, and exactly what effect their inclusion, or exclusion, has upon the signs, magnitudes, and significance of the coefficient estimates.

A second consideration concerns estimator choice. When collinearity is present, and deemed harmful to the least squares estimator, alternative estimators designed to improve the precision of estimation are sometimes suggested. We will review some of these estimators in Section 5. If collinearity is induced by a few influential observations, then a robust estimator may be an alternative to consider.

4.4   Detecting harmful collinearity

We can determine the number of collinear relations, their severity, and the variables involved using the diagnostics in Section 3. This does not end the diagnostic process, because we must still determine if the collinearity present is actually harmful to our regression. Whether the collinearity matters depends on the magnitude of the regression parameters. The parameters matter in two regards. First, from equations (12.2) and (12.9), it is clear that a small value of the error variance, σ^2, can offset the effects of high correlation between the regressors or low regressor variability.

Second, the magnitudes of the β_k matter. If the variance of b_k is $\sigma_{b_k}^2$, then $100(1 - \alpha)\%$ interval estimator for β_k is $b_k \pm t_c \hat{\sigma}_{b_k}$, where t_c is a critical value from the t-distribution. Suppose we diagnose severe collinearity affecting (and inflating) the variance of b_k and compute $t_c \hat{\sigma}_{b_k} = 3$. Is collinearity harmful when $\beta_k = 1$? What if $\beta_k = 1000$? If you answered "yes" to the first question, but "no" to the second, you are saying, and rightly so, that the magnitude of the parameter β_k also matters when determining if collinearity is harmful or not.

Belsley (1982) addresses these issues by developing tests for adequate "signal-to-noise," abbreviated s/n, in the regression model and data. For a single parameter Belsley defines an s/n parameter,

$$\tau = \frac{\beta_k}{\sigma_{b_k}}. \tag{12.11}$$

If τ is small, then the error variance σ^2 is not small enough, and/or β_k is not large enough, to offset the effects of collinearity and/or lack of regressor variability. Belsley proposes to test the hypothesis that $|\tau| > \tau_*$, where τ_* is an adequate magnitude. For details of this, and a more general multiparameter test, see Belsley (1982).

In the end, Belsley (1982, p. 225) proposes that investigators (i) examine collinearity using the diagnostics described in Section 3, and (ii) carry out the test for adequate s/n. The conclusions one can draw are summarized in Table 12.2.

The four possible outcomes are these: (I) negligible collinearity and adequate s/n; (II) collinearity present, but not harmful, since adequate s/n is present; (III) negligible collinearity, but inadequate s/n present, caused by lack of regressor variation; (IV) harmful collinearity, the joint occurrence of severe collinearity and inadequate s/n. In the next section we address what remedies are available in cases III and IV.

Table 12.2 Harmful collinearity decision matrix

| | | Collinearity present? | |
		no	*yes*
Inadequate	no	*I*	*II*
signal-to-noise present?	yes	*III*	*IV*

5   WHAT TO DO?

In this section we address the question of what to do when harmful collinearity is found with respect to the important parameters in a regression model. This section is like a minefield. There is danger all around, and but two safe paths. We will identify the safe paths, though these are the roads less traveled, and we will mention some potentially dangerous and self-defeating methods for dealing with collinearity.

Since the collinearity problem is actually one of insufficient independent variation in the data, the first and most desirable solution is to obtain more and *better* data. If the new data possess the same dependencies found in the original sample, then they are unlikely to be of much help. On the other hand, if new data can be found in, as Belsley (1991, p. 297) calls it, "novel or underrepresented portions" of the sample space, then the new observations may mitigate the ill-effects of collinearity. Unfortunately, nonexperimental empirical researchers seldom have much if any control over the design of the data generation process, and hence this advice is, for the most part, empty of practical content. Should the occasion arise, however, Silvey (1969, p. 545) discusses the optimal choice, for the purpose of improving the estimation of a linear combination of the parameters $c'\beta$, of the values of the explanatory variables in a new observation. This classic treatment has been extended by Sengupta (1995).

Blanchard (1987, p. 449) says, "Only use of more economic theory in the form of additional restrictions may help alleviate the multicollinearity problem." We agree that the only "cure" for collinearity, apart from additional data, is additional information about regression parameters. However, restrictions can come from economic theory or previous empirical research, which we collectively term *nonsample* sources. If harmful collinearity is present, we are admitting that the sample data are inadequate for the purpose of precisely estimating some or all of the regression parameters. Thus the second safe strategy for mitigating the effects of collinearity is to introduce *good* nonsample information about the parameters into the estimation process. When nonsample information is added during the estimation process, estimator variances are reduced, which is exactly what we want to happen in the presence of collinearity (and indeed, all the time.) The downside to using nonsample information is that estimator bias is introduced.

It is possible that small amounts of bias are acceptable in return for significant increases in precision. The most commonly used measure of the bias/precision tradeoff is mean-square-error (MSE),

$$\text{MSE}(\hat{\beta}) = E[(\hat{\beta} - \beta)'(\hat{\beta} - \beta)] = \sum_k \text{var}(\hat{\beta}_k) + \sum_k [E(\hat{\beta}_k) - \beta_k]^2, \qquad (12.12)$$

which combines estimator variances with squared biases. This measure is also known as estimator "risk" in decision theory literature (Judge *et al.*, 1988, pp. 807–12).

Our general objective is to introduce nonsample information that improves upon the MSE of the OLS estimator. This is much easier said than done, and there is a huge literature devoted to methods for obtaining MSE improvement. See Judge and Bock (1978, 1983). Suffice it to say that MSE improvements occur only when the nonsample information we employ is good. How do we know if the information we introduce is good enough? We do *not* know, and can *never* know, if our nonsample information is good enough to ensure an MSE reduction, since that would require us to know the true parameter values. This is our conundrum. Below we briefly survey alternative methods for introducing non-sample information, all of which can be successful in reducing MSE, if the nonsample information is good enough.

5.1 Methods for introducing exact nonsample information

The most familiar method for introducing nonsample information into a regression model is to use restricted least squares (RLS). The restricted least squares estimator, which we denote as b^*, is obtained by minimizing the sum of squared errors subject to J exact linear parameter restrictions, $R\beta = r$. Examples of linear restrictions are $\beta_2 + \beta_3 = 1$ and $\beta_5 = \beta_6$. The variances of the RLS estimator are smaller than those of the OLS estimator, but b^* is biased unless the parameter restrictions imposed are exactly true. As noted above, the restrictions do not have to be exactly true for RLS to be better than OLS under a criterion such as MSE, which trades off bias against variance reduction. A question that naturally arises is why such restrictions, if they exist, are not imposed at the outset. A classic example of RLS used to mitigate collinearity is the Almon (1965) polynomial distributed lag. To determine if the imposed restrictions improve the conditioning of X, substitute the restrictions into the model, via the method outlined in Fomby *et al.* (1984, p. 85), and apply the collinearity diagnostics.

Some familiar "tricks" employed in the presence of collinearity are, in fact, RLS estimators. The most common, and often ill-advised, strategy is to drop a variable if it is involved in a collinear relationship and its estimated coefficient is statistically insignificant. Dropping a variable, x_k, is achieved by imposing the linear constraint that $\beta_k = 0$. Unless $\beta_k = 0$, dropping x_k from the model generally biases *all* coefficient estimators. Similarly, two highly correlated variables are often replaced by their sum, say $z = x_k + x_m$. How is this achieved? By imposing the restriction that $\beta_k = \beta_m$. Once again, if this constraint is not correct, reductions in variance are obtained at the expense of biasing estimation of all regression coefficients. Kennedy (1983) detects the failure of a similar collinearity trick used by Buck and Hakim (1981) in the context of estimating and testing differences in parameters between two groups of observations.

Economists recognize the bias/precision tradeoff and wish to impose constraints that are "good." It is standard practice to check potential constraints against the data by testing them as if they were hypotheses. Should we drop x_k? Test the hypothesis that $\beta_k = 0$. Should we sum x_k and x_m? Test the hypothesis $\beta_k = \beta_m$. Belsley (1991, p. 212) suggests formally testing for MSE improvement. The MSE test amounts to comparing the usual F-statistic for a joint hypothesis to critical values tabled in Toro-Vizcarrondo and Wallace (1968). Following the tests a decision is made to abandon restrictions that are rejected, and use restrictions that are not rejected. Such a strategy prevents egregious errors, but actually defines a new, "pre-test" estimation rule. This rule, which chooses either the OLS or RLS estimator based on the outcome of a test, does not have desirable statistical properties, but it seems unlikely that this practice will be abandoned. See Judge *et al.* (1985, ch. 3).

Another alternative is the Stein-rule estimator, which is a "smart" weighted average of the OLS and RLS estimators, weighting the RLS estimator more when the restrictions are compatible with the data, and weighting the OLS estimator more when the restrictions are not compatible with the data. The Stein-rule usually provides an MSE gain over OLS, but it is not guaranteed to ameliorate the specific problems caused by collinearity. See Judge *et al.* (1985, ch. 22).

5.2 Methods for introducing inexact nonsample information

Economists usually bring general information about parameters to the estimation problem, but it is not like the exact restrictions discussed in the previous section. For example, we may know the signs of marginal effects, which translate into inequality restrictions on parameters. Or we may think that a parameter falls in the unit interval, and that there is a good chance it falls between 0.25 and 0.75. That is, we are able to suggest signs of parameters, and even perhaps ranges of reasonable values. While such information has long been available, it has been difficult to use in applications. Perhaps the biggest breakthrough in recent years has been the development of methods and the distribution of software that makes it feasible to estimate linear (and nonlinear) models subject to inequality restrictions, and to implement Bayesian statistical methods.

The theory of inequality restricted least squares was developed some time ago. See Judge and Yancey (1986). However, the numerical problems of minimizing the sum of squared regression errors or maximizing a likelihood function subject to general inequality restrictions are substantial. Recently major software packages (SAS, GAUSS, GAMS) have made algorithms for such constrained optimization much more accessible. With inequality restrictions, such as $\beta_k > 0$, MSE gains require only that the direction of the inequality be correct.

The Bayesian paradigm is an alternative mode of thought. See Zellner (1971). In it we represent our uncertainty about parameter values using probability distributions. Inexact nonsample information is specified up front in the Bayesian world, by specifying a "prior" probability distribution for each parameter (in general a joint prior). The prior density can be centered over likely values. It can be a truncated distribution, putting zero prior probability on parameter values we rule out on theoretical grounds, and so on. When prior beliefs are combined with data a multivariate probability distribution of the parameters is generated, called the posterior distribution, which summarizes all available information about the parameters.

As noted in Judge *et al.* (1985, p. 908), Bayesians have no special problem dealing with the singularity or near-singularity of $X'X$. Their approach to the collinearity problem is to combine the prior densities on the parameters, β with the sample information contained in the data to form a posterior density (see Zellner, 1971, pp. 75–81). The problem for Bayesians, as noted by Leamer (1978), is that when data are collinear the posterior distribution becomes very sensitive to changes in the prior. Small changes in the prior density result in large changes in the posterior, which complicates the use and analysis of the results in much the same way that collinearity makes inference imprecise in the classical theory of inference.

Bayesian theory is elegant, and logically consistent, but it has been a nightmare in practice. Suppose $g(\beta)$ is the multivariate posterior distribution for the vector of regression parameters β. The problem is how to extract the information about a single parameter of interest, say β_k. The brute force method is to obtain the posterior density for β_k by integrating all the other parameters out of $g(\beta)$. When the posterior distribution $g(\beta)$ is complicated, as it usually is, this integration is a challenging problem.

The Bayesian miracle has been the development of computationally intensive, but logically simple, procedures for deriving the posterior densities for individual parameters. These procedures include the Gibbs sampler, the Metropolis and Metropolis–Hastings algorithms (Dorfman, 1997). These developments will soon make Bayesian analysis feasible in many economic applications.

In passing we note that non-Bayesians have tried to achieve the incorporation of similar information by making the exact restrictions in Section 5.1 inexact (Theil and Goldberger, 1961). This is achieved by adding a random disturbance $v \sim (0, \Omega)$ to exact restrictions, to obtain $r = R\beta + v$. This additional information is combined with the linear model as

$$\begin{bmatrix} y \\ r \end{bmatrix} = \begin{bmatrix} X \\ R \end{bmatrix} \beta + \begin{bmatrix} e \\ v \end{bmatrix}. \tag{12.13}$$

The resulting model is estimated by generalized least squares, which is called "mixed estimation" in this context. The difficulty, of course, apart from specifying the constraints, is the specification of the covariance matrix Ω, reflecting parameter uncertainty.

Another estimation methodology has been introduced recently, based upon the maximum entropy principle (Golan, Judge, and Miller, 1996). This estimation method, instead of maximizing the likelihood function, or minimizing the sum of squared errors, maximizes the entropy function, subject to data and logical constraints. The method of maximum entropy is "nonparametric" in the sense that no specific probability distribution for the errors need be assumed. Like the Bayesian methodology, maximum entropy estimation requires the incorporation of prior information about the regression parameters at the outset. Golan, Judge and Miller find that the maximum entropy estimator, which like the Stein-rule is a shrinkage estimator, performs well in the presence of collinearity.

5.3 Estimation methods designed specifically for collinear data

A number of estimation methods have been developed to improve upon the least squares estimator when collinearity is present. We will briefly discuss two, ridge regression and principal components regression, if only to warn readers about their use.

The ridge family of estimators is

$$b(k) = (X'X + kI)^{-1}X'y, \tag{12.14}$$

where k is a suitably chosen constant. When $k = 0$ then the ridge estimator is just the OLS estimator of β. For nonstochastic values of $k > 0$ the ridge estimator is biased, but has smaller variances than the least squares estimator. It achieves the variance reduction by "shrinking" the least squares estimates towards zero. That is, the (Euclidean) length of the ridge estimator is smaller than that of the least squares estimator. Choosing k is important since some values result in reductions of overall mean square error and others do not. Unfortunately, picking a value of k that assures reduction in overall MSE requires knowledge of β and σ^2, the original object of the regression analysis. Numerous methods for selecting k based on the data have been proposed, but choosing k using data makes k random, and completely alters the statistical properties of the resulting "adaptive" ridge estimator (Hoerl, Kennard, and Baldwin, 1975; Lawless and Wang, 1976). Finite sample inference using the ridge estimator is hindered by dependence of its sampling distribution on unknown parameters. There is a huge statistics literature on the ridge estimator, but the fundamental problems remain and we cannot recommend this estimator.

Principal components regression (Fomby et al., 1984, pp. 298–300) is based upon eigenanalysis. Recall that the $(K \times K)$ matrix C, whose columns are the eigenvectors of $X'X$, is an orthogonal matrix, such that $C'C = CC' = I$. The $T \times K$ matrix $Z = XC$ is called the matrix of principal components of X. The ith column of Z, $z_i = Xc_i$, is called the ith principal component. From equation (12.5) z_i has the property that $z_i'z_i = \lambda_i$.

The "principal components" form of the linear regression model is

$$y = X\beta + e = XCC'\beta + e = Z\theta + e, \tag{12.15}$$

where $Z = XC$ and $\theta = C'\beta$. The new set of explanatory variables Z are linear transformations of the original variables, and have the property that $Z'Z = \Lambda = \text{diag}(\lambda_1, \lambda_2, \ldots, \lambda_K)$, where the λ_k are the ordered (in decreasing magnitude) eigenvalues of $X'X$. If we apply least squares to the transformed model we obtain $\hat{\theta} = (Z'Z)^{-1}Z'y$, which has covariance matrix $\text{cov}(\hat{\theta}) = \sigma^2(Z'Z)^{-1} = \sigma^2\Lambda^{-1}$, so that $\text{var}(\hat{\theta}_k) = \sigma^2/\lambda_k$. If the data are collinear then one or more of the eigenvalues will be near zero. If $\lambda_K \approx 0$ then the eigenvector $z_K \approx 0$, and consequently it is difficult to estimate θ_K precisely, which is reflected in the large variance of its estimator, $\text{var}(\hat{\theta}_K) = \sigma^2/\lambda_K$. Principal components regression deletes from equation (12.15) the z_k associated with small eigenvalues (usually based upon tests of significance, or some other model selection criterion, such as AIC or BIC). Partition the transformed model as $y = Z\theta + e = Z_1\theta_1 + Z_2\theta_2 + e$. Dropping Z_2, which contains the z_k to be deleted, and applying OLS yields $\hat{\theta}_1 = (Z_1'Z_1)^{-1}Z_1'y$. The principal components estimator of β is obtained by applying an inverse transformation

$$b_{pc} = C\theta = [C_1 \quad C_2]\begin{bmatrix} \hat{\theta}_1 \\ \theta_2 = 0 \end{bmatrix} = C_1\hat{\theta}_1. \tag{12.16}$$

The properties of this estimator follow directly from the observation that it is equivalent to the RLS estimator of β obtained by imposing the constraints $C_2'\beta = 0$. Thus the principal components estimator b_{pc} is biased, but has smaller variances than the OLS estimator. The data based constraints $C_2'\beta = 0$ generally have no economic content, and are likely to induce substantial bias. One positive use of principal components regression is as a benchmark. The J constraints $C_2'\beta = 0$ have the property that they provide the maximum variance reduction of any set of J linear constraints (Fomby, Hill, and Johnson, 1978). Thus researchers can measure the potential for variance reduction using linear constraints.

5.4   Artificial orthogonalization

Consider a regression model containing two explanatory variables,

$$y = \beta_1 + \beta_2 x_2 + \beta_3 x_3 + e, \tag{12.17}$$

where the regressors x_2 and x_3 are highly correlated. To "purge" the model of collinearity regress x_3 on x_2, and compute the residuals $x_3^* = x_3 - \hat{x}_3$. It is argued that x_3^* contains the information in the variable x_3 after the effects of collinearity are removed. Because least squares residuals are orthogonal to the regressors, x_3^* and x_2 are uncorrelated, and thus collinearity is eliminated! Substituting x_3^* into the model we obtain,

$$y = \beta_1 + \beta_2 x_2 + \beta_3^* x_3^* + e^*, \tag{12.18}$$

which is then estimated by OLS. Buse (1994) shows that the least squares estimates of β_1 and β_3 are unaffected by this substitution, as are their standard errors and t-statistics, and the residuals from (12.18) are identical to those from (12.17), hence statistics such as R^2, the Durbin–Watson d, and $\hat{\sigma}^2$ are unaffected by the substitution. But what about the estimator of β_2? Kennedy (1982) first points out the problems with this procedure, and Buse (1994) works out the details. Buse shows that the estimator of β_2 from (12.18) is biased. Furthermore, instead of gaining a variance reduction in return for this bias, Buse shows that the variance of $\hat{\beta}_2^*$ can be larger than the OLS variance of b_3, and he gives several examples. Thus artificial orthogonalization is not a cure for collinearity.

6 NONLINEAR MODELS

Assessing the severity and consequences of collinearity in nonlinear models is more complicated than in linear models. To illustrate, we first discuss its detection in nonlinear regression, and then in the context of maximum likelihood estimation.

6.1 The nonlinear regression model

Consider the nonlinear regression model

$$y = f(X,\beta) + e, \tag{12.19}$$

where $e \sim (0, \sigma^2 I)$ and $f(X,\beta)$ is some nonlinear function that relates the independent variables and parameters to form the systematic portion of the model. The nonlinear least squares estimator chooses $\hat{\beta}$ to minimize

$$S(\beta) = [y - f(X,\beta)]'[y - f(X,\beta)].$$

The first order conditions yield the least squares solution,

$$Z(\beta)'[y - f(X,\beta)] = 0, \tag{12.20}$$

where the $T \times K$ matrix $Z(\beta) = \partial f(X,\beta)/\partial \beta'$. Since equation (12.20) is nonlinear, the least squares estimates $\hat{\beta}$ must be obtained using numerical methods.

A useful algorithm for finding the minimum of $S(\beta)$ is the Gauss–Newton. The Gauss–Newton algorithm is based on a first order Taylor's series expansion of $f(X,\beta)$ around a starting value β_1. From that we obtain the linearized model

$$\bar{y}(\beta_1) = Z(\beta_1)\beta + e, \tag{12.21}$$

where $\bar{y}(\beta_1) = y - f(X, \beta_1) + Z(\beta_1)\beta_1$. In (12.21) the dependent variable and the "regressors" $Z(\beta_1)$ are completely determined given β_1. The next round estimate is obtained by applying least squares to (12.21), and in general the iterations are

$$\beta_{n+1} = [Z(\beta_n)'Z(\beta_n)]^{-1}Z(\beta_n)'\bar{y}(\beta_n). \tag{12.22}$$

The iterations continue until a convergence criterion is met, perhaps that $\beta_n \approx \beta_{n+1}$ $= \hat{\beta}$, which defines the nonlinear least squares estimates of β. Given that $f(X, \beta)$ is a nice function, then, asymptotically,

$$\hat{\beta} \sim N(\beta, \sigma^2[Z(\beta)'Z(\beta)]^{-1}) \tag{12.23}$$

and the asymptotic covariance matrix of $\hat{\beta}$ is estimated as

$$\mathrm{ac\hat{o}v}(\hat{\beta}) = \hat{\sigma}^2[Z(\hat{\beta})'Z(\hat{\beta})]^{-1}, \tag{12.24}$$

where $\hat{\sigma}^2 = S(\hat{\beta})/(T - K)$. Equations (12.21)–(12.23) show that $Z(\beta)$ in nonlinear regression plays the role of X in the linear regression model. Consequently, it is the columns of $Z(\beta)$, which we examine via the BKW diagnostics in Section 3, that we must consider when diagnosing collinearity in the nonlinear regression model.

6.2   Collinearity in nonlinear regression models

When examining $Z(\beta)$ for collinearity a problem arises. That is, $Z(\beta)$ depends not only on the data matrix X but also on the parameter values β. Thus collinearity changes from point to point in the parameter space, and the degree of collinearity among the columns of the data matrix X may or may not correspond to collinearity in $Z(\beta)$. This problem affects nonlinear regression in two ways. First, the Gauss–Newton algorithm itself may be affected by collinearity in $Z(\beta)$, because at each iteration the cross-product matrix $Z(\beta_n)'Z(\beta_n)$ must be inverted. If the columns of $Z(\beta_n)$ are highly collinear then the cross-product matrix may be difficult to invert, at which point the algorithm may fail. Second, the estimated asymptotic covariance matrix of the nonlinear least squares estimator, equation (12.24), contains the cross-product matrix $Z(\hat{\beta})'Z(\hat{\beta})$, and thus the estimated variances and covariances suffer from the usual consequences of collinearity, depending on the relationships between the columns of $Z(\hat{\beta})$. Computer software packages, such as SAS 6.12, compute and report the BKW diagnostics for the matrix $Z(\beta_n)'Z(\beta_n)$ when the Gauss–Newton algorithm fails, so that the user may try to determine the source of the very nearly exact collinearity that leads to the failure, and it also computes the conditioning diagnostics for $Z(\hat{\beta})'Z(\hat{\beta})$, upon convergence of the algorithm. There remains, of course, the collinearity among the columns of $Z(\beta)$, which enters the true asymptotic covariance matrix of the nonlinear least squares estimator in equation (12.23), and which remains unknown.

What do we do if collinearity, or ill-conditioning, of $Z(\beta_n)$ causes the Gauss–Newton algorithm to fail to converge? The conditioning of $Z(\beta_n)$ can be affected by scaling the data. One common problem is that the columns of $Z(\beta_n)$ have greatly different magnitudes. Recall that $Z(\beta_n)$ contains the first derivatives of the function evaluated at β_n, so magnitudes in $Z(\beta_n)$ are slopes of the functions $f(X,\beta)$. If these are greatly different then the function is steep in some directions and shallow in others. Such an irregular surface is difficult to work with. By rescaling the columns of X, it is sometimes possible to more nearly equalize the columns of $Z(\beta_n)$, meaning that the function $f(X, \beta)$ itself has been smoothed. This is usually advantageous.

When computing the BKW diagnostics the columns of $Z(\beta_n)$ should be scaled to unit length. If, after the data are scaled, the condition number of $Z(\beta_n)$ is still large, closer examination of the function, data, and parameter values are required. To illustrate, Greene (1997, p. 456) and Davidson and MacKinnon (1993, pp. 181–6) give the example of the nonlinear consumption function $C = \alpha + \beta Y^\gamma + e$, where C is consumption and Y is aggregate income. For this model the tth row of $Z(\beta)$ is [1 Y^γ $\beta Y^\gamma \ln Y$]. What happens if during the Gauss–Newton iterations the value of γ approached zero? The second column approaches 1, and is collinear with the first column. What happens if $\beta \to 0$? Then the third column approaches 0, making $Z(\beta)$ ill-conditioned. In these cases collinearity is avoided by avoiding these parameter values, perhaps by selecting starting values wisely. For a numerical example see Greene (1997, pp. 456–8). There are alternative algorithms to use when convergence is a problem in nonlinear least squares regression. It is very useful to be aware of the alternatives offered by your software, as some may perform better than others in any given problem. See Greene (1997, ch. 5).

6.3 Collinearity in maximum likelihood estimation

Collinearity in the context of maximum likelihood estimation is similarly diagnosed. Instead of minimizing the sum of squared errors we maximize the loglikelihood function. Standard gradient methods for numerical maximization use first and/or second derivatives. As in the Gauss–Newton algorithm for nonlinear least squares, these methods involve an inversion: the Hessian for the Newton–Raphson, the Information matrix for the method of scoring, and the cross-product matrix of first derivatives for the method of Berndt, Hall, Hall, and Hausman. In these algorithms if the matrix to be inverted becomes singular, or nearly so, estimation fails. In each case we can apply the BKW diagnostics to the matrix we are inverting at each step of the nonlinear optimization, and to the estimate of the asymptotic covariance matrix. The same difficulties arise in diagnosing collinearity here as in nonlinear least squares, only it is worse, because while the condition numbers provide a measure of how ill-conditioned the matrix is, the rows of Table 12.1 no longer provide any information about which variables are involved in collinear relations. Similar remarks hold for collinearity diagnosis in generalized least squares and simultaneous equations models.

Some common maximum likelihood estimators, among others, probit, logit, tobit, Poisson regression, and multiplicative heteroskedasticity, have information matrices of a common form,

$$I(\beta) = X'WX, \tag{12.25}$$

where W is a $T \times T$ diagonal weight matrix that often is a function of the unknown parameters, β, and the independent variables.

The class of generalized linear models (McCullagh and Nelder, 1989) contains many of these estimators as special cases, and have information matrices in the form of equation (12.25), thus collinearity diagnostics for these models are relevant. Weissfeld and Sereika (1991) explore the detection of collinearity in the class of generalized linear models (GLM). Segerstedt and Nyquist (1992) observe that ill-conditioning in these models can be due to collinearity of the variables, X, the influence of the weights, W, or both. Weissfeld and Sereika suggest applying the BKW diagnostics to the scaled information matrix. Lee and Weissfeld (1996) do the same for the Cox regression model. Once again, while the variance decompositions can be computed in these instances, their interpretation is not straightforward, since collinearity can be due to the weights, W.

Lesaffre and Marx (1993) also investigate the problem of ill-conditioning in GLM and take a slightly different approach. Following Mackinnon and Puterman (1989), they suggest that only the columns of X be standardized to unit length, forming X_1. Then, conditioning diagnostics are computed on $X_1' \hat{W} X_1$, where $\hat{W}$ is the estimated weight matrix based on the rescaled data. The square root of the ratio of the largest to smallest eigenvalue describes the worst relative precision with which linear combinations of the parameters can be estimated. Thus, this scaling gives a structural interpretation to the conditioning diagnostic. One problem with this scaling is that $X_1' \hat{W} X_1$ could be ill-conditioned because of the effects of $\hat{W}$.

7 CLOSING REMARKS

We conclude by pointing out the main lessons of this essay. First, we have tools, the Belsley, Kuh, and Welsch (1980) collinearity diagnostics, which allow us to determine the form and severity of collinearity in the linear regression model. Most importantly, we know which variables are involved in collinear relationships, and which variables are *not* involved in collinear relationships. If the least squares estimator is severely affected by collinearity, but the model's variables of interest are not involved in the collinear relationships, then there is no call for remedial actions. Such a conclusion requires us to think clearly about our models, and to pinpoint key variables.

Since new and better data are rarely available, the only practical approach to mitigating harmful collinearity is the introduction of nonsample information about the parameters, based on prior empirical research or economic theory. However the information is introduced, whether it be via restricted least squares, the Bayesian approach, or maximum entropy estimation, we must endeavor to introduce "good" nonsample information. The difficulty with this statement is that we never *truly* know whether the information we introduce is good enough to reduce estimator mean square error, or not.

The analysis of collinearity in nonlinear models is difficult. Collinearity (ill-conditioning) in asymptotic covariance matrices may arise from collinearity in the matrix of explanatory variables X, and/or particular parameter values and function values. Identifying the cause of the ill-conditioning may, or may not, be possible, but again the use of good nonsample information would seem the only remedy. In nonlinear models the problem of collinearity spills over into the estimation process, because the iterative algorithms used for numerical optimization may be sensitive to it. When this occurs, consider alternative algorithms, because *how* we find the maximum or minimum of our objective function is not important. Estimator properties only depend upon the successful location of the global maximum.

Note

* The authors wish to thank three anonymous referees for their helpful comments. All remaining errors are the authors' own.

References

Almon, S. (1965). The distributed lag between capital appropriations and expenditures. *Econometrica* 33, 178–96.

Belsley, D.A. (1982). Assessing the presence of harmful collinearity and other forms of weak data through a test for signal-to-noise. *Journal of Econometrics* 20, 211–53.

Belsley, D.A. (1984). Demeaning conditioning diagnostics through centering. *American Statistician* 38, 73–93.

Belsley, D.A. (1991). *Collinearity Diagnostics: Collinearity and Weak Data in Regression*. New York: Wiley.

Belsley, D.A., E. Kuh, and R.E. Welsch (1980). *Regression Diagnostics: Identifying Influential Data and Sources of Collinearity*. New York: Wiley.

Blanchard, O.J. (1987). Comment. *Journal of Business and Economic Statistics* 5, 449–51.

Buck, A.J., and S. Hakim (1981). Appropriate roles for statistical decision theory and hypothesis testing in model selection: An exposition. *Regional Science and Urban Economics* 11, 135–47.

Buse, A. (1994). Brickmaking and the collinear arts: a cautionary tale. *Canadian Journal of Economics* 27, 408–14.

Chatterjee, S. and A.S. Hadi (1988). *Sensitivity Analysis in Linear Regression*. New York: Wiley.

Cook, R.D. and S. Weisberg (1982). *Residuals and Influence in Regression*. London: Chapman & Hall.

Davidson, R. and J.G. MacKinnon (1993). *Estimation and Inference in Econometrics*. New York: Oxford University Press.

Dorfman, J.H. (1997). *Bayesian Economics through Numerical Methods: A Guide to Econometrics and Decision-Making with Prior Information*. New York: Springer.

Fomby, T.B., R.C. Hill, and S.R. Johnson (1978). An optimality property of principal components regression. *Journal of the American Statistical Association* 73, 191–3.

Fomby, T.B., R.C. Hill, and S.R. Johnson (1984). *Advanced Econometric Methods*. New York: Springer-Verlag.

Fox, J. and G. Monette (1992). Generalized collinearity diagnostics. *Journal of the American Statistical Association* 87, 178–83.

Golan, A., G.G. Judge, and D. Miller (1996). *Maximum Entropy Econometrics: Robust Estimation with Limited Data*. New York: John Wiley and Sons.

Greene, W. (1997). *Econometric Analysis*, 3rd edn. Upper Saddle River, NJ: Prentice Hall.

Hadi, A.S. and M.T. Wells (1990). Assessing the effects of multiple rows on the condition of a matrix. *Journal of the American Statistical Association* 85, 786–92.

Hoerl, A.E., R.W. Kennard, and K.F. Baldwin (1975). Ridge regression: Some simulations. *Communications in Statistics*, A, 4 105–23.

Judge, G.G. and M.E. Bock (1978). *Statistical Implications of Pretest and Stein-Rule Estimators in Econometrics*. Amsterdam: North-Holland.

Judge, G.G. and M.E. Bock (1983). Biased Estimation. In Z. Griliches and M.D. Intrilligator (eds.), *Handbook of Econometrics, Volume 1*. Amsterdam: North-Holland.

Judge, G.G., W.E. Griffiths, R.C. Hill, H. Lütkepohl, and T.C. Lee (1985). *The Theory and Practice of Econometrics*, 2nd edn. New York: John Wiley and Sons, Inc.

Judge, G.G., R.C. Hill, W.E. Griffiths, H. Lütkepohl, and T.C. Lee (1988). *Introduction to the Theory and Practice of Econometrics*, 2nd edn. New York: John Wiley and Sons, Inc.

Judge, G.G. and T.A. Yancy (1986). *Improved Methods of Inference in Econometrics*. Amsterdam: North-Holland.

Kennedy, P. (1982). Eliminating problems caused by multicollinearity: A warning. *Journal of Economic Education* 13, 62–4.

Kennedy, P. (1983). On an inappropriate means of reducing multicollinearity. *Regional Science and Urban Economics* 13, 579–81.

Kennedy, P. (1998). *A Guide to Econometrics*, 4th edn. Cambridge: MIT Press.

Lawless, J.F. and P. Wang (1976). A simulation study of ridge and other regression estimators. *Communications in Statistics* A 5, 307–23.

Leamer, E.E. (1978). *Specification Searches: Ad Hoc Inference with Nonexperimental Data*. New York: Wiley.

Lee, Kyung Yul and L.A. Weissfeld (1996). A multicollinearity diagnostic for the Cox model with time dependent covariates. *Communications in Statistics – Simulation* 25, 41–60.

Lesaffre, E. and B.D. Marx (1993). Collinearity in generalized linear regression. *Communications in Statistics – Theory and Methods* 22, 1933–52.

Mackinnon, M.J. and M.L. Puterman (1989). Collinearity in generalized linear models. *Communications in Statistics – Theory and Methods* 18, 3463–72.

McCullagh, P. and J.A. Nelder (1989). *Generalized Linear Models*, 2nd edn. London: Chapman and Hall.

Mason, R.L. and R.F. Gunst (1985). Outlier-induced collinearities. *Technometrics* 27, 401–7.

Segerstedt, B. and H. Nyquist (1992). On the conditioning problem in generalized linear models. *Journal of Applied Statistics* 19, 513–22.

Sengupta, D. (1995). Optimal choice of a new observation in a linear model. *Sankhya: The Indian Journal of Statistics* Series A 57, 137–53.

Sengupta, D. and P. Bhimasankaram (1997). On the roles of observations in collinearity in the linear model. *Journal of the American Statistical Association* 92, 1024–32.

Silvey, S. (1969). Multicollinearity and imprecise estimation. *Journal of the Royal Statistical Society* B 31, 539–52.

Soofi, E.S. (1990). Effects of collinearity on information about regression coefficients. *Journal of Econometrics* 43, 255–74.

Stewart, G.W. (1987). Collinearity and least squares regression. *Statistical Science* 1, 68–100.

Theil, H. and A. Goldberger (1961). On pure and mixed statistical estimation in economics. *International Economic Review* 2, 65–78.

Toro-Vizcarrondo, C. and T. Wallace (1968). A test of the mean square error criterion for restrictions in linear regression. *Journal of the American Statistical Association* 63, 558–76.

Weissfeld, L.A. and S.M. Sereika (1991). A multicollinearity diagnostic for generalized linear models. *Communications in Statistics* A 20, 1183–98.

Zellner, A. (1971). *An Introduction to Bayesian Inference in Econometrics*. New York: John Wiley and Sons.

Nonnested Hypothesis Testing: An Overview

M. Hashem Pesaran and Melvyn Weeks

1 INTRODUCTION

This chapter focuses on the hypotheses testing problem when the hypotheses or models under consideration are "nonnested" or belong to "separate" families of distributions, in the sense that none of the individual models may be obtained from the remaining either by imposition of parameter restrictions or through a limiting process.[1] In econometric analysis nonnested models arise naturally when rival economic theories are used to explain the same phenomenon such as unemployment, inflation, or output growth. Typical examples from the economics literature are Keynesian and new classical explanations of unemployment, structural, and monetary theories of inflation, alternative theories of investment, and endogenous and exogenous theories of growth.[2] Nonnested models could also arise when alternative functional specifications are considered such as multinomial probit and logit distribution functions used in the qualitative choice literature, exponential, and power utility functions used in the asset pricing models, and a variety of nonnested specifications considered in the empirical analysis of income and wealth distributions. Finally, even starting from the same theoretical paradigm, it is possible for different investigators to arrive at different models if they adopt different conditioning or follow different paths to a more parsimonious model using the general-to-specific specification search methodology, advocated, for example by Hendry (1993).

The concept of an econometric model is discussed in Section 2, where a distinction is made between conditional and unconditional models. This is an important distinction since most applied work in econometrics takes place within a modeling framework where the behavior of one or more "endogenous" variables is often explained *conditional* on a set of "exogenous" variables. This discussion also highlights the importance of conditioning in the process of model evaluation.

Examples of nonnested models are given in Section 3. Section 4 discusses the differences that lie behind model selection and hypotheses testing. Although this chapter is primarily concerned with hypotheses testing involving nonnested models, a discussion of the differences and similarities of the two approaches to model evaluation can serve an important pedagogic purpose in clarifying the conditions under which one approach rather than the other could be appropriate.

The literature on nonnested hypothesis testing in statistics was pioneered by the seminal contributions of Cox (1961), Cox (1962), and Atkinson (1970), and was subsequently applied to econometric models by Pesaran (1974) and Pesaran and Deaton (1978). The analysis of nonnested regression models was further considered by Davidson and MacKinnon (1981), Fisher and McAleer (1981), Dastoor (1983), Deaton (1982), Sawyer (1983), Gouriéroux, Monfort, and Trognon (1983), and Godfrey and Pesaran (1983).[3] This literature is reviewed in Section 5 where we examine a number of alternative approaches to testing nonnested hypotheses, including the encompassing approach advanced by Mizon and Richard (1986), Gouriéroux and Monfort (1995), and Smith (1993).

Generally speaking, two models, say H_f and H_g, are said to be nonnested if it is not possible to derive H_f (or H_g) from the other model either by means of an exact set of parametric restrictions or as a result of a limiting process. But for many purposes a more rigorous definition is needed. Section 6 examines this issue and focuses on the Kullback–Leibler divergence measure which has played a pivotal role in the development of a number of nonnested test statistics. The Vuong approach to model selection, viewed as a hypothesis testing problem is also discussed in this section (see Vuong, 1989). Section 7 deals with the practical problems involved in the implementation of the Cox procedure. Apart from a few exceptions, the centering of the loglikelihood ratio statistic required to construct the Cox statistic, will involve finding an estimate of the Kullback–Leibler measure of closeness of the alternative to the null hypothesis, which in most cases is not easy to compute using analytical techniques. Subsequently, we explore two methods which circumvent the problem. First, following work by Pesaran and Pesaran (1993), we examine the simulation approach which provides a consistent estimator of the KLIC measure. However, since this approach is predicated upon the adherence to a classical testing framework, we also examine the use of a parametric bootstrap approach. Whereas the use of simulation facilitates the construction of a pivotal test statistic with an asymptotically well-defined limiting distribution, the bootstrap procedure effectively replaces the theoretical distribution with the empirical distribution function. We also discuss the use of pivotal bootstrap statistics for testing nonnested models.

2 Models and Their Specification

Suppose the focus of the analysis is to consider the behavior of the $n \times 1$ vector of random variables $w_t = (w_{1t}, w_{2t}, \ldots, w_{nt})'$ observed over the period $t = 1, 2, \ldots, T$. A model of w_t, indexed by $\mathfrak{M}_i$, is defined by the joint probability distribution function (pdf) of the observations

$$W = (w_1', w_2', \ldots, w_T')'$$

$$\mathfrak{M}_i : f_i(w_1, w_2, \ldots, w_T \mid w_0, \varphi_i) = f_i(W \mid w_0, \varphi_i), \quad i = 1, 2, \ldots, m, \quad (13.1)$$

where $f_i(\cdot)$ is the probability density function of the model (hypothesis) $\mathfrak{M}_i$, and φ_i is a $p_i \times 1$ vector of unknown parameters associated with model $\mathfrak{M}_i$.[4]

The models characterized by $f_i(W \mid w_0, \varphi_i)$ are *unconditional* in the sense that probability distribution of w_t is fully specified in terms of some initial values, w_0, and for a given value of φ_i. In econometrics the interest often centers on conditional models, where a vector of "endogenous" variables, y_t, is explained (or modeled) *conditional* on a set of "exogenous", variables, x_t. Such conditional models can be derived from (13.1) by noting that

$$f_i(w_1, w_2, \ldots, w_T \mid w_0, \varphi_i) = f_i(y_1, y_2, \ldots, y_T \mid x_1, x_2, \ldots, x_T, \psi(\varphi_i))$$

$$\times f_i(x_1, x_2, \ldots, x_T \mid w_0, \kappa(\varphi_i)), \quad (13.2)$$

where $w_t = (y_t', x_t')$. The unconditional model $\mathfrak{M}_i$ is decomposed into a conditional model of y_t given x_t and a marginal model of x_t. Denoting the former by $\mathfrak{M}_{i,y \mid x}$ we have

$$\mathfrak{M}_{i,y \mid x} : f_i(y_1, y_2, \ldots, y_T \mid x_1, x_2, \ldots, x_T, w_0, \psi(\varphi_i)) = f_i(Y \mid X, w_0, \psi(\varphi_i)), \quad (13.3)$$

where $Y = (y_1', y_2', \ldots, y_T')'$ and $X = (x_1', x_2', \ldots, x_T')'$.

Confining attention to the analysis and comparison of conditional models is valid only if the variations in the parameters of the marginal model, $\kappa(\varphi_i)$, does not induce changes in the parameters of the conditional model, $\psi(\varphi_i)$. Namely $\partial \psi(\varphi_i)/\partial' \kappa(\varphi_i) = 0$. When this condition holds it is said that x_t is *weakly exogenous* for ψ_i. The parameters of the conditional model, $\psi_i = \psi(\varphi_i)$, are often referred to as the *parameters of interest*.[5]

The conditional models $\mathfrak{M}_{i,y \mid x}$ $i = 1, 2, \ldots, m$ all are based on the same conditioning variables, x_t, and differ only in so far as they are based upon different pdfs. We may introduce an alternative set of models which share the same pdfs but differ with respect to the inclusion of exogenous variables. For any model, $\mathfrak{M}_i$ we may partition the set of exogenous variables x_t according to a simple included/excluded dichotomy. Therefore $x_t = (x_{it}', x_{it}'^*)'$ writes the set of exogenous variables according to a subset x_{it} which are included in model $\mathfrak{M}_i$, and a subset x_{it}^* which are excluded. We may then write

$$f_i(Y \mid x_1, x_2, \ldots x_T, w_0, \varphi_i) = f_i(Y \mid x_{i1}, x_{i2} \ldots x_{iT}, x_{i1}^*, x_{i2}^*, \ldots, x_{iT}^*, w_0, \varphi_i)$$

$$= f_i(Y \mid X_i, w_0, \psi_i(\varphi_i)) \times f_i(X_i^* \mid X_i, w_0, c_i(\varphi_i)),$$

where $X_i = (x_{i1}', x_{i2}', \ldots, x_{iT}')'$ and $X_i^* = (x_{i1}'^*, x_{i2}'^*, \ldots, x_{iT}'^*)'$. As noted above in the case of models differentiated solely by different pdfs, a comparison of models based upon the partition of x_t into x_{it} and x_{it}^* should be preceded by determining whether $\partial \psi_i(\varphi_i)/\partial c_i'(\varphi_i) = 0$.

The above setup allows consideration of rival models that could differ in the conditioning set of variables, $\{x_{it}, i = 1, 2, \ldots, m\}$ and/or the functional form of their underlying probability distribution functions, $\{f_i(\cdot), i = 1, 2, \ldots, m\}$. In much of this chapter we will be concerned with two rival (conditional) models and for notational convenience we denote them by

$$H_f : \mathcal{F}_\theta = \{f(y_t \,|\, x_t, \Omega_{t-1}; \theta), \theta \in \Theta\}, \tag{13.4}$$

$$H_g : \mathcal{F}_\gamma = \{g(y_t \,|\, z_t, \Omega_{t-1}; \gamma), \gamma \in \Gamma\}, \tag{13.5}$$

where Ω_{t-1} denotes the set of all past observations on y, x and z, θ and γ are respectively k_f and k_g vectors of unknown parameters belonging to the non-empty compact sets Θ and Γ, and where x and z represent the conditioning variables. For the sake of notational simplicity we shall also often use $f_t(\theta)$ and $g_t(\gamma)$ in place of $f(y_t \,|\, x_t, \Omega_{t-1}; \theta)$ and $g(y_t \,|\, z_t, \Omega_{t-1}; \gamma)$, respectively.

Now given the observations $(y_t, x_t, z_t, t = 1, 2, \ldots, T)$ and conditional on the initial values w_0, the maximum likelihood (ML) estimators of θ and γ are given by

$$\hat{\theta}_T = \underset{\theta \in \Theta}{\arg\max}\, L_f(\theta), \quad \hat{\gamma}_T = \underset{\gamma \in \Gamma}{\arg\max}\, L_g(\gamma), \tag{13.6}$$

where the respective loglikelihood functions are given by:

$$L_f(\theta) = \sum_{t=1}^{T} \ln f_t(\theta), \quad L_g(\gamma) = \sum_{t=1}^{T} \ln g_t(\gamma). \tag{13.7}$$

Throughout we shall assume that the conditional densities $f_t(\theta)$ and $g_t(\gamma)$ satisfy the usual regularity conditions as set out, for example, in White (1982) and Smith (1993), needed to ensure that $\hat{\theta}_T$ and $\hat{\gamma}_T$ have asymptotically normal limiting distributions under the data generating process (DGP). We allow the DGP to differ from H_f and H_g, and denote it by H_h; thus admitting the possibility that both H_f and H_g could be misspecified and that both are likely to be rejected in practice. In this setting $\hat{\theta}_T$ and $\hat{\gamma}_T$ are referred to as quasi-ML estimators and their probability limits under H_h, which we denote by θ_{h*} and γ_{h*} respectively, are known as (asymptotic) pseudo-true values. These pseudo-true values are defined by

$$\theta_{h*} = \underset{\theta \in \Theta}{\arg\max}\, E_h\{T^{-1}L_f(\theta)\}, \quad \gamma_{h*} = \underset{\gamma \in \Gamma}{\arg\max}\, E_h\{T^{-1}L_g(\gamma)\}, \tag{13.8}$$

where $E_h(\cdot)$ denotes expectations are taken under H_h. In the case where w_t follows a strictly stationary process, (13.8) simplifies to

$$\theta_{h*} = \underset{\theta \in \Theta}{\arg\max}\, E_h\{\ln f_t(\theta)\}, \quad \gamma_{h*} = \underset{\gamma \in \Gamma}{\arg\max}\, E_h\{\ln g_t(\gamma)\}. \tag{13.9}$$

To ensure global identifiability of the pseudo-true values, it will be assumed that θ_{f*} and γ_{f*} provide *unique* maxima of $E_h\{T^{-1}L_f(\theta)\}$ and $E_h\{T^{-1}L_g(\gamma)\}$, respectively. Clearly, under H_f, namely assuming H_f is the DGP, we have $\theta_{f*} = \theta_0$, and $\gamma_{f*} = \gamma_*(\theta_0)$ where θ_0 is the "true" value of θ under H_f. Similarly, under H_g we have $\gamma_{g*} = \gamma_0$, and $\theta_{g*} = \theta_*(\gamma_0)$ with γ_0 denoting the "true" value of γ under H_g. The functions $\gamma_*(\theta_0)$, and $\theta_*(\gamma_0)$ that relate the parameters of the two models under consideration are called the *binding* functions. These functions do not involve the true model, H_h, and only depend on the models H_f and H_g that are under consideration. As we shall see later a formal definition of encompassing is given is terms of the pseudo-true values, θ_{h*} and γ_{h*}, and the binding functions $\gamma_*(\theta_0)$, and $\theta_*(\gamma_0)$.

Before proceeding further it would be instructive to consider some examples of nonnested models from the literature.

3 Examples of Nonnested Models

We start with examples of unconditional nonnested models. One such example, originally discussed by Cox (1961) is that of testing a lognormal versus an exponential distribution.

$$H_f : f(y_t \mid \theta) = f_t(\theta) = y_t^{-1}(2\pi\theta_2)^{-1/2} \exp\left\{-\frac{(\ln y_t - \theta_1)^2}{2\theta_2}\right\}, \ \infty > \theta_2 > 0, \ y_t > 0.$$

$$H_g : g(y_t \mid \gamma) = g_t(\gamma) = \gamma^{-1} \exp(-y_t/\gamma), \ \gamma > 0, \ y_t > 0.$$

These hypotheses (models) are globally nonnested, in the sense that neither can be obtained from the other either by means of suitable parametric restrictions or by a limiting process.[6] Under H_f the pseudo-true value of γ, denoted by γ_{f*} is obtained by solving the following maximization problem

$$\gamma_{f*} = \arg\max_{\gamma > 0} E_f\{\ln g_t(\gamma)\}.$$

But[7]

$$E_f\{\ln g_t(\gamma)\} = -\ln \gamma - E_f(y_t)/\gamma = -\ln \gamma - \exp(\theta_1 + 0.5\theta_2)/\gamma,$$

which yields

$$\gamma_{f*} = \gamma_*(\theta_0) = \exp(\theta_{10} + 0.5\theta_{20}).$$

Similarly, under H_g we have[8]

$$\theta_1^*(\lambda_0) = \ln \gamma_0 - 0.5772, \quad \theta_2^*(\gamma_0) = 1.6449.$$

Other examples of nonnested unconditional models include lognormal versus Weibull and Pereira (1984) and lognormal versus gamma distribution, Pesaran (1987).

The most prominent example of conditional nonnested models is linear normal regression models with "rival" sets of conditioning variables. As an example consider the following regression models:

$$H_f : y_t = \alpha' x_t + u_{tf}, \quad u_{tf} \sim N(0, \sigma^2), \quad \infty > \sigma^2 > 0, \tag{13.10}$$

$$H_g : y_t = \beta' z_t + u_{tg}, \quad u_{tg} \sim N(0, \omega^2), \quad \infty > \omega^2 > 0. \tag{13.11}$$

The conditional probability density associated with these regression models are given by

$$H_f : f(y_t \mid x_t; \theta) = (2\pi\sigma^2)^{-1/2} \exp\left\{\frac{-1}{2\sigma^2}(y_t - \alpha' x_t)^2\right\}, \tag{13.12}$$

$$H_g : g(y_t \mid z_t; \theta) = (2\pi\omega^2)^{-1/2} \exp\left\{\frac{-1}{2\omega^2}(y_t - \beta' z_t)^2\right\}, \tag{13.13}$$

where $\theta = (\alpha', \sigma^2)'$, and $\gamma = (\beta', \omega^2)'$. These regression models are nonnested if it is not possible to write x_t as an exact linear function of z_t and vice versa, or more formally if $x_t \not\subseteq z_t$ and $z_t \not\subseteq x_t$. Model H_f is said to be nested in H_g if $x_t \subset z_t$ and $z_t \not\subseteq x_t$. The two models are observationally equivalent if $x_t \subset z_t$ and $z_t \subset x_t$. Suppose now that neither of these regression models is true and the DGP is given by

$$H_h : y_t = \delta' w_t + u_{th}, \quad u_{th} \sim N(0, \upsilon^2), \quad \infty > \upsilon^2 > 0. \tag{13.14}$$

It is then easily seen that conditional on $\{x_t, z_t, w_t, t = 1, 2, \ldots, T\}$

$$E_h\{T^{-1}L_f(\theta)\} = -\frac{1}{2}\ln(2\pi\sigma^2) - \frac{\upsilon^2}{2\sigma^2} - \frac{\delta'\hat{\Sigma}_{ww}\delta - 2\delta'\hat{\Sigma}_{wx}\alpha + \alpha'\hat{\Sigma}_{xx}\alpha}{2\sigma^2},$$

where

$$\hat{\Sigma}_{ww} = T^{-1}\sum_{t=1}^{T} w_t w_t', \quad \hat{\Sigma}_{xx} = T^{-1}\sum_{t=1}^{T} x_t x_t', \quad \hat{\Sigma}_{wx} = T^{-1}\sum_{t=1}^{T} w_t x_t'.$$

Maximizing $E_h\{T^{-1}L_f(\theta)\}$ with respect to θ now yields the conditional pseudo-true values:

$$\theta_{h*} = \begin{pmatrix} \alpha_{h*} \\ \sigma^2_{h*} \end{pmatrix} = \begin{pmatrix} \hat{\Sigma}_{xx}^{-1}\hat{\Sigma}_{xw}\delta \\ \upsilon^2 + \delta'(\hat{\Sigma}_{ww} - \hat{\Sigma}_{wx}\hat{\Sigma}_{xx}^{-1}\hat{\Sigma}_{xw})\delta \end{pmatrix}. \tag{13.15}$$

Similarly,

$$\gamma_{h*} = \begin{pmatrix} \beta_{h*} \\ w^2_{h*} \end{pmatrix} = \begin{pmatrix} \hat{\Sigma}_{zz}^{-1}\hat{\Sigma}_{zw}\delta \\ \upsilon^2 + \delta'(\hat{\Sigma}_{ww} - \hat{\Sigma}_{wz}\hat{\Sigma}_{zz}^{-1}\hat{\Sigma}_{zw})\delta \end{pmatrix}, \tag{13.16}$$

where

$$\hat{\Sigma}_{zz} = T^{-1}\sum_{t=1}^{T} z_t z_t', \ \hat{\Sigma}_{wz} = T^{-1}\sum_{t=1}^{T} w_t z_t'.$$

When the regressors are stationary, the unconditional counterparts of the above pseudo-true values can be obtained by replacing $\hat{\Sigma}_{ww}$, $\hat{\Sigma}_{xx}$, $\hat{\Sigma}_{wx}$, etc. by their population values, namely $\Sigma_{ww} = E(w_t w_t')$, $\Sigma_{xx} = E(x_t x_t')$, $\Sigma_{wx} = E(w_t x_t')$, etc.

Other examples of nonnested regression models include models with endogenous regressors estimated by instrumental variables (see, for example, Ericsson, 1983; and Godfrey, 1983), nonnested nonlinear regression models and regression models where the left-hand side variables of the rival regressions are known transformations of a dependent variable of interest. One important instance of this last example is the problem of testing linear versus loglinear regression models and vice versa.[9] More generally we may have

$$H_f : f(y_t) = \alpha' x_t + u_{tf}, \quad u_{tf} \sim N(0, \sigma^2), \quad \infty > \sigma^2 > 0,$$

$$H_g : g(y_t) = \beta' z_t + u_{tg}, \quad u_{tg} \sim N(0, \omega^2), \quad \infty > \omega^2 > 0,$$

where $f(y_t)$ and $g(y_t)$ are known one-to-one functions of y_t. Within this more general regression framework testing a linear versus a loglinear model is characterized by $f(y_t) = y_t$ and $g(y_t) = \ln(y_t)$; a ratio model versus a loglinear model by $f(y_t) = y_t/q_t$ and $g(y_t) = \ln(y_t)$, where q_t is an observed regressor, and a ratio versus a linear model by $f(y_t) = y_t/q_t$ and $g(y_t) = y_t$. For example, in analysis of aggregate consumption a choice needs to be made between a linear and a loglinear specification of the aggregate consumption on the one hand, and between a loglinear and a saving rate formulation on the other hand. The testing problem is further complicated here due to the linear transformations of the dependent variable, and additional restrictions are required if the existence of pseudo-true values in the case of these models are to be ensured. For example, suitable truncation restrictions need to be imposed on the errors of the linear model when it is tested against a loglinear alternative.

Other examples where specification of an appropriate error structure plays an important role in empirical analysis include discrete choice and duration models used in microeconometric research. Although the analyst may utilize both prior knowledge and theory to select an appropriate set of regressors, there is generally little guidance in terms of the most appropriate probability distribution. Nonnested hypothesis testing is particularly relevant to microeconometric research where the same set of regressors are often used to explain individual decisions but based on different functional distributions, such as multinomial probit and logit specifications in the analysis of discrete choice, exponential and Weibull distributions in the analysis of duration data. In the simple case of a probit (H_f) versus a logit model (H_g) we have

$$H_f : \Pr(y_t = 1) = \Phi(\theta' x_t) = \int_{-\infty}^{\theta' x_t} \frac{1}{\sqrt{2\pi}} \exp\{-\tfrac{1}{2}v^2\} \, dv \qquad (13.17)$$

$$H_g : \Pr(y_t = 1) = \Lambda(\gamma' z_t) = \frac{e^{\gamma' z_t}}{1 + e^{\gamma' z_t}} \qquad (13.18)$$

where y_t, $t = 1, 2, \ldots, T$ are independently distributed binary random variables taking the value of 1 or 0. In practice the two sets of regressors x_t used in the probit and logit specifications are likely to be identical, and it is only the form of the distribution functions that separate the two models. Other functional forms can also be entertained. Suppose, for example, that the true DGP for this simple discrete choice problem is given by the probability distribution function $H(\delta' x_t)$, then pseudo-true values for θ and γ can be obtained as functions of δ, but only in an implicit form. We first note that the loglikelihood function under H_f, for example, is given by

$$L_f(\theta) = \sum_{t=1}^{T} y_t \log[\Phi(\theta' x_t)] + \sum_{t=1}^{T} (1 - y_t) \log[1 - \Phi(\theta' x_t)],$$

and hence under the assumed DGP we have

$$E_h\{T^{-1} L_f(\theta)\} = T^{-1} \sum_{t=1}^{T} H(\delta' x_t) \log[\Phi(\theta' x_t)]$$

$$+ T^{-1} \sum_{t=1}^{T} [1 - H(\delta' x_t)] \log[1 - \Phi(\theta' x_t)].$$

Therefore, the pseudo-true value of θ, namely $\theta_*(\delta)$ or simply θ_*, satisfies the following equation

$$T^{-1} \sum_{t=1}^{T} x_t \phi(\theta'_* x_t) \left\{ \frac{H(\delta' x_t)}{\Phi(\theta'_* x_t)} - \frac{1 - H(\delta' x_t)}{1 - \Phi(\theta'_* x_t)} \right\} = 0,$$

where $\phi(\theta'_* x_t) = (2\pi)^{-1/2} \exp[\frac{-1}{2}(\theta'_* x_t)^2]$. Using results in Amemiya (1985, pp. 271–2) it is easily established that the solution of θ_* in terms of δ is in fact unique, and $\theta_* = \delta$ if and only if $\Phi(\cdot) = H(\cdot)$. Similar results also obtain for the logistic specification.

4   MODEL SELECTION VERSUS HYPOTHESIS TESTING

Hypothesis testing and model selection are different strands in the model evaluation literature. However, these strands differ in a number of important respects which are worth emphasizing here.[10] Model selection begins with a given set of models, $\mathcal{M}$, characterized by the (possibly) conditional pdfs

$$\mathcal{M} = \{f_i(Y \mid X_i, \psi_i), i = 1, 2, \ldots, m\},$$

with the aim of *choosing* one of the models under consideration for a particular purpose with a specific loss (utility) function in mind. In essence model selection is a part of decision making and as argued in Granger and Pesaran (2000) ideally it should be fully integrated into the decision making process. However, most of the current literature on model selection builds on statistical measure of fit such as sums of squares of residuals or more generally maximized loglikelihood values, rather than economic value which one would expect to follow from a model choice.[11] As a result model selection seems much closer to hypothesis testing than it actually is in principle.

The model selection process treats all models under consideration symmetrically, while hypothesis testing attributes a different status to the null and to the alternative hypotheses and by design treats the models asymmetrically. Model selection always ends in a definite outcome, namely one of the models under consideration is selected for use in decision making. Hypothesis testing on the other hand asks whether there is any statistically significant evidence (in the Neyman–Pearson sense) of departure from the null hypothesis in the direction of one or more alternative hypotheses. Rejection of the null hypothesis does not necessarily imply acceptance of any one of the alternative hypotheses; it only warns the investigator of possible shortcomings of the null that is being advocated. Hypothesis testing does not seek a definite outcome and if carried out with due care need not lead to a favorite model. For example, in the case of nonnested hypothesis testing it is possible for all models under consideration to be rejected, or all models to be deemed as observationally equivalent.

Due to its asymmetric treatment of the available models, the choice of the null hypothesis plays a critical role in the hypothesis testing approach. When the models are nested the most parsimonious model can be used as the null hypothesis. But in the case of nonnested models (particularly when the models are globally nonnested) there is no natural null, and it is important that the null hypothesis is selected on a priori grounds.[12] Alternatively, the analysis could be carried out with different models in the set treated as the null. Therefore, the results of nonnested hypothesis testing is less clear cut as compared to the case where the models are nested.[13]

It is also important to emphasize the distinction between *paired* and joint nonnested hypothesis tests. Letting f_1 denote the null model and $f_i \in \mathcal{M}, i = 2, \ldots, m$ index a set of $m - 1$ alternative models, a paired test is a test of f_1 against a *single* member of $\mathcal{M}$, whereas a joint test is a test of f_1 against multiple alternatives in $\mathcal{M}$. McAleer (1995) is careful to highlight this distinction and in doing so points out a deficiency in many applied studies insofar as many authors have utilized a sequence of paired tests for problems characterized by multiple alternatives. Examples of studies which have applied nonnested tests to the choice between more than two models include Sawyer (1984), Smith and Maddala (1983) and Davidson and MacKinnon (1981). The paper by Sawyer is particularly relevant since he develops the multiple model equivalent of the Cox test.

The distinction between model selection and nonnested hypothesis tests can also be motivated from the perspective of Bayesian versus sampling-theory approaches to the problem of inference. For example, it is likely that with a large amount of data the posterior probabilities associated with a particular hypothesis will be close to one. However, the distinction drawn by Zellner (1971) between "comparing" and "testing" hypothesis is relevant given that within a Bayesian perspective the progression from a set of prior to posterior probabilities on $\mathcal{M}$, mediated by the Bayes factor, does not necessarily involve a decision to accept or reject the hypothesis. If a decision is required it is generally based upon minimizing a particular expected loss function. Thus, model selection motivated by a decision problem is much more readily reconcilable with the Bayesian rather than the classical approach to model selection.

Finally, the choice between hypothesis testing and model selection clearly depends on the primary objective of the exercise. There are no definite rules. Model selection is more appropriate when the objective is decision making. Hypothesis testing is better suited to inferential problems where the empirical validity of a theoretical prediction is the primary objective. A model may be empirically adequate for a particular purpose but of little relevance for another use. Only in the unlikely event that the true model is known or knowable will the selected model be universally applicable. In the real world where the truth is elusive and unknowable both approaches to model evaluation are worth pursuing.

5 Alternative Approaches to Testing Nonnested Hypotheses with Application to Linear Regression Models

To provide an intuitive introduction to concepts which are integral to an understanding of nonnested hypothesis tests we consider testing of linear regression models as a convenient starting point. In the ensuing discussion we demonstrate that despite its special features nonnested hypothesis testing is firmly rooted within the Neyman–Pearson framework.

There are three general approaches to nonnested hypothesis testing all discussed in the pioneering contributions of Cox (1961) and Cox (1962). (i) The modified (centered) loglikelihood ratio procedure, also known as the Cox test. (ii) The comprehensive model approach, whereby the nonnested models are tested against an artificially constructed general model that includes the nonnested models as special cases. This approach was advocated by Atkinson (1970) and was later taken up under a different guise by Davidson and MacKinnon (1981) in developing their J-test and by Fisher and McAleer (1981) who proposed a related alternative procedure known as the JA-test. (iii) A third approach, originally considered by Deaton (1982) and Dastoor (1983) and further developed by Gouriéroux et al. (1983) and Mizon and Richard (1986) is the encompassing procedure where the ability of one model to explain particular features of an alternative model is tested directly. The Wald and score encompassing tests (usually denoted by WET and SET) are typically constructed under the assumption that one of the rival models is correct. Encompassing tests when the true model does not necessarily lie in the set of models (whether nested or nonnested) under consideration are proposed by Gouriéroux and Monfort (1995) and Smith (1993).

We shall now illustrate the main features of these three approaches in the context of the classical linear normal regression models (13.10) and (13.11) set out above. Rewriting these models in familiar matrix notations we have:

$$H_f : y = X\alpha + u_f, \quad u_f \sim N(0, \sigma^2 I_T),$$
(13.19)

$$H_g : y = Z\beta + u_g, \quad u_g \sim N(0, \omega^2 I_T),$$
(13.20)

where y is the $T \times 1$ vector of observations on the dependent variable, X and Z are $T \times k_f$ and $T \times k_g$ observation matrices for the regressors of models H_f and H_g, α and β are the $k_f \times 1$ and $k_g \times 1$ unknown regression coefficient vectors, u_f and u_g are the $T \times 1$ disturbance vectors, and I_T is an identity matrix of order T. In addition, throughout this section we assume that

$$T^{-1}X'u_f \xrightarrow{p} 0, \quad T^{-1}X'u_g \xrightarrow{p} 0, \quad T^{-1/2}X'u_f \xrightarrow{a} N(0, \sigma^2 \Sigma_{xx}),$$

$$T^{-1}Z'u_g \xrightarrow{p} 0, \quad T^{-1}Z'u_f \xrightarrow{p} 0, \quad T^{-1/2}Z'u_g \xrightarrow{a} N(0, \omega^2 \Sigma_{zz}),$$

$$\hat{\Sigma}_{xx} = T^{-1}X'X \xrightarrow{p} \Sigma_{xx}, \quad \hat{\Sigma}_{zz} = T^{-1}Z'Z \xrightarrow{p} \Sigma_{zz}, \quad \hat{\Sigma}_{zx} = T^{-1}Z'X \xrightarrow{p} \Sigma_{zx},$$

where $\xrightarrow{p}$ denotes convergence in probability, the matrices $\hat{\Sigma}_{xx}, \Sigma_{xx}, \hat{\Sigma}_{zz}, \Sigma_{zz}$ are non-singular, $\Sigma_{zx} = \Sigma'_{xz} \neq 0$, and set

$$\Sigma_f = \Sigma_{xx} - \Sigma_{xz}\Sigma_{zz}^{-1}\Sigma_{zx}, \text{ and } \Sigma_g = \Sigma_{zz} - \Sigma_{zx}\Sigma_{xx}^{-1}\Sigma_{xz}.$$

5.1 Motivation for nonnested statistics

From a statistical view point the main difference between the nested and nonnested hypothesis testing lies in the fact that the usual loglikelihood ratio or Wald statistics used in the conventional hypothesis testing are automatically centered at zero under the null when the hypotheses under consideration are nested while this is not true in the case of nonnested hypotheses. However, once the conventional test statistics are appropriately centered (at least asymptotically) the same classical techniques can be applied to testing of nonnested hypotheses. Using the two nonnested linear regression models in (13.19) and (13.20) we first demonstrate the problems with standard test statistics by focusing on a simple comparison of sums of squared errors.

Consider the following test statistic:

$$\xi_T = \tilde{\sigma}_g^2 - \tilde{\sigma}_f^2,$$
(13.21)

where

$$\tilde{\sigma}_f^2 = e_f'e_f / (T - k_f)$$

$$\tilde{\sigma}_g^2 = e_g'e_g / (T - k_g),$$

and e_f is the OLS residual vector under H_f such that $e_f = M_f y$. Note that (13.21) represents a natural starting point being the difference between the mean sum of squared errors for the two models.

In general the exact distribution of ξ_T will depend on the unknown parameters. To see this, first note that under H_f, $e_f = M_f(u_f + X\alpha)$ therefore, (since $M_f X = 0$), we have

$$(T - k_f)\tilde{\sigma}_f^2 = u_f' M_f u_f. \tag{13.22}$$

Now under H_f,

$$e_g = M_g y = M_g(X\alpha + u_f),$$

or

$$e_g = M_g X\alpha + M_g u_f$$

and

$$\begin{aligned}
(T - k_g)\tilde{\sigma}_g^2 &= e_g' e_g \\
&= (u_f' + \alpha' X')M_g(X\alpha + u_f) \\
&= u_f' M_g u_f + 2\alpha' X' M_g u_f + \alpha' X' M_g X\alpha. \tag{13.23}
\end{aligned}$$

Using (13.22) and (13.23) in (13.21) and taking expectations (under H_f) we have

$$E(\xi_T) = \frac{\alpha' X' M_g X\alpha}{T - k_g} \geq 0, \tag{13.24}$$

which we denote by $\mu_T = (\alpha' X' M_g X\alpha)/(T - k_g)$. Since ξ_T does not have mean zero under the null hypothesis H_f, then ξ_T cannot provide us with a suitable *test-statistic*. Notice, however that when H_f is nested within H_g, then $M_g X = 0$ and ξ_T will have mean zero (exactly) under H_g. In this case, if we also assume that u_f is normally distributed, it can be easily shown that

$$\frac{(T - k_f)\xi_T}{r\tilde{\sigma}_g^2} = 1 - F_{r, T-k_g}$$

where $F_{r, T-k_g}$ is distributed as a (central) F with r and $T - k_g$ degrees of freedom; r here stands for the number of restrictions that we need to impose on H_g in order to obtain H_f.

A fundamental tenet of classical hypothesis testing is that the distribution of the test statistic is known under a well specified null hypothesis. Thus, in this context if H_f is nested within H_g then under the null of H_f the normalized difference between the sum of squared errors have a zero expectation. When H_f is not nested within H_g we may adopt a number of alternate approaches. First, a suitable test statistic that has zero mean asymptotically will be

$$z_T = \xi_T - \hat{\mu}_T$$

where $\hat{\mu}_T$ is a consistent estimator of μ_T under H_f. More specifically

$$z_T = \tilde{\sigma}_g^2 - \tilde{\sigma}_f^2 - \frac{\hat{\alpha}'X'M_gX\hat{\alpha}}{T - k_g}, \tag{13.25}$$

where $\hat{\alpha} = (X'X)^{-1}X'y$. Equation (13.25) represents an example of *centering* of a test statistic such that the distribution of z_T is known (asymptotically). Cox (1961, 1962) utilized this approach to center the loglikelihood ratio statistic for two nonnested models. When the models are nested the loglikelihood ratio statistic is properly centered (at least asymptotically). For example, if we let $L_f(\theta)$ and $L_g(\gamma)$ denote, respectively the loglikelihood functions for H_f and H_g, and we if assume that H_f is nested within H_g, then under H_f the loglikelihood ratio statistic, $2[L_g(\hat{\gamma}_T) - L_f(\hat{\theta}_T)]$, does not require any centering and the test defined by the critical region

$$2[L_g(\hat{\gamma}_T) - L_f(\hat{\theta}_T)] \geq \chi^2_{(1-\alpha)}(r),$$

where r is the number of parameter restrictions required to obtain H_f from H_g, asymptotically has the size α and is consistent. In the case of nonnested models the likelihood ratio statistic is not distributed as a chi-squared random variable. The reason for this is simple. The degrees of freedom of the chi-square statistic for the *LR* test is equal to the reduction in the size of the parameter space after imposing the necessary set of zero restrictions. Thus, if neither H_f nor H_g nests the other model, the attendant parameter spaces and hence the likelihoods are unrelated. In Section 5.2 we examine the application of centering (or mean adjustment) of the likelihood ratio statistic to obtain a test statistic that has a known asymptotic distribution. Given that in most instances the form of mean adjustment involves analytically intractable expectations in Section 7.1 we examine the use of simulation methods as a method of circumventing this problem.

Following seminal work by Efron (1979), an alternative approach conducts inference utilizing the empirical distribution function of the test statistic. In this instance there is, in general, no need to center ξ_T using $\hat{\mu}_T$. Instead we take ξ_T as the observed test statistic, and given a null hypothesis, we simulate a large number, say R, of the $\tilde{\sigma}_g^2$, $\tilde{\sigma}_f^2$ pairs. The empirical distribution function for ξ_T is then constructed based on $\hat{\sigma}_{gr}^2$ and $\hat{\sigma}_{fr}^2$, $r = 1, 2, \ldots, R$. In Section 7.2 we examine the use of bootstrap procedures for conducting nonnested hypothesis tests. We also consider the case for combining the type of mean adjustment in (13.25) with bootstrap procedures.

5.2   The Cox procedure

This procedure focuses on the loglikelihood ratio statistic, and in the case of the above regression models is given by (using the notations of Section 2):

$$LR_{fg} = L_f(\hat{\theta}_T) - L_g(\hat{\gamma}_T) = \frac{T}{2}\ln\left(\frac{\hat{\sigma}_T^2}{\hat{\omega}_T^2}\right),$$

where

$$\hat{\sigma}_T^2 = T^{-1}e_f'e_f, \quad \hat{\alpha}_T = (X'X)^{-1}X'y,$$

$$e_f = y - X\hat{\alpha}_T = M_x y, \quad M_x = I_T - X(X'X)^{-1}X', \tag{13.26}$$

and

$$\hat{\omega}_T^2 = T^{-1}e_g'e_g, \quad \hat{\beta}_T = (Z'Z)^{-1}Z'y,$$

$$e_g = y - Z\hat{\beta}_T = M_z y, \quad M_z = I_T - Z(Z'Z)^{-1}Z'. \tag{13.27}$$

In the general case where the regression models are nonnested the average loglikelihood ratio statistic, $\frac{1}{2}\ln(\hat{\sigma}_T^2/\hat{\omega}_T^2)$, does not converge to zero even if T is sufficiently large. For example, under H_f we have

$$\plim_{T \to \infty} (T^{-1}LR_{fg} \mid H_f) = \frac{1}{2}\ln\left(\frac{\sigma_0^2}{\omega_*^2(\theta_0)}\right) = \frac{1}{2}\ln\left(\frac{\sigma_0^2}{\sigma_0^2 + \alpha_0'\Sigma_f \alpha_0}\right),$$

and under H_g:

$$\plim_{T \to \infty} (T^{-1}LR_{fg} \mid H_g) = \frac{1}{2}\ln\left(\frac{\sigma_*^2(\gamma_0)}{\omega_0^2}\right) = \frac{1}{2}\ln\left(\frac{\omega_0^2 + \beta_0'\Sigma_g \beta_0}{\omega_0^2}\right).$$

The LR statistic is naturally centered at zero if one or the other of the above probability limits is equal to zero; namely if either $\Sigma_f = 0$ or $\Sigma_g = 0$.[14] When $\Sigma_f = 0$ then $X \subset Z$ and H_f is nested in H_g. Alternatively, if $\Sigma_g = 0$, then $Z \subset X$ and H_g is nested in H_f. Finally, if both $\Sigma_f = 0$ and $\Sigma_g = 0$ then the two regression models are observationally equivalent. In the nonnested case where both $\Sigma_f \neq 0$ or $\Sigma_g \neq 0$, the standard LR statistic will not be applicable and needs to be properly centered. Cox's contribution was to note that this problem can be overcome if a consistent estimate of $Plim_{T \to \infty}(T^{-1}LR_{fg} \mid H_f)$, which we denote by $\hat{E}_f(T^{-1}LR_{fg})$, is subtracted from $T^{-1}LR_{fg}$, which yields the new centered (modified) loglikelihood ratio statistic (also known as the Cox statistic) for testing H_f against H_g:

$$S_{fg} = T^{-1}LR_{fg} - \hat{E}_f(T^{-1}LR_{fg}) \tag{13.28}$$

$$= \frac{1}{2}\ln\left(\frac{\hat{\sigma}_T^2}{\hat{\omega}_T^2}\right) - \frac{1}{2}\ln\left(\frac{\sigma_T^2}{\hat{\sigma}_T^2 + \hat{\alpha}_T'\hat{\Sigma}_f \hat{\alpha}_T}\right)$$

$$= \frac{1}{2}\ln\left(\frac{\hat{\sigma}_T^2 + \hat{\alpha}_T'\hat{\Sigma}_f \hat{\alpha}_T}{\hat{\omega}_T^2}\right). \tag{13.29}$$

It is now clear that by construction the Cox statistic, S_{fg}, has asymptotically mean zero under H_f. As was pointed out earlier, since there is no natural null hypothesis in this setup, one also needs to consider the modified loglikelihood ratio statistic for testing H_g against H_f which is given by

$$S_{gf} = \frac{1}{2}\ln\left(\frac{\hat{\omega}_T^2 + \hat{\beta}_T'\hat{\Sigma}_g\hat{\beta}_T}{\hat{\sigma}_T^2}\right).$$

Both of these test statistics (when appropriately normalized by $\sqrt{T}$) are asymptotically normally distributed under their respective nulls with a zero mean and finite variances. For the test of H_f against H_g we have[15]

$$\widehat{\text{Asyvar}}(\sqrt{T}S_{fg}) = V_{fg} = \frac{\hat{\sigma}_T^2(\hat{\alpha}_T'X'M_zM_xM_zX\hat{\alpha}_T)}{T(\hat{\sigma}_T^2 + \hat{\alpha}_T'\hat{\Sigma}_f\hat{\alpha}_T)^2}.$$

The associated standardized Cox statistic is given by

$$N_{fg} = \frac{\sqrt{T}S_{fg}}{\sqrt{V_{fg}}} \overset{a}{\sim} N(0, 1). \tag{13.30}$$

By reversing the role of the null and the alternative hypothesis a similar standardized Cox statistic can be computed for testing H_g against H_f, which we denote by N_{gf}. Denote the $(1 - \alpha)$ percent critical value of the standard normal distribution by C_α, then four outcomes are possible:

1. Reject H_g but not H_f if $|N_{fg}| < C_\alpha$ and $|N_{gf}| \geq C_\alpha$,
2. Reject H_f but not H_g if $|N_{fg}| \geq C_\alpha$ and $|N_{gf}| < C_\alpha$,
3. Reject both H_f and H_g if $|N_{fg}| \geq C_\alpha$ and $|N_{gf}| \geq C_\alpha$,
4. Reject neither H_f nor H_g if $|N_{fg}| < C_\alpha$ and $|N_{gf}| < C_\alpha$.

These are to be contrasted to the outcomes of the nested hypothesis testing where the null is either rejected or not, which stem from the fact that when the hypotheses under consideration are nonnested there is no natural null (or maintained) hypothesis and one therefore needs to consider in turn each of the hypotheses as the null. So there are twice as many possibilities as there are when the hypotheses are nested. Note that if we utilize the information in the *direction of rejection*, that is instead of comparing the *absolute* value of N_{fg} with C_α we determine whether rejection is in the direction of the null or the alternative, there are a total of eight possible test outcomes (see the discussion in Fisher and McAleer (1979) and Dastoor (1981)). This aspect of nonnested hypothesis testing has been criticized by some commentators, pointing out the test outcome can lead to ambiguities. (See, for example, Granger, King, and White, 1995.) However, this is a valid criticism only if the primary objective is to *select* a specific model for forecasting or decision making, but not if the aim is to learn about the comparative strengths and weaknesses of rival explanations. What is viewed as a weakness from the perspective of model selection now becomes a strength when placed in the context of statistical inference and model building. For example, when both models are rejected the analysis points the investigator in the direction of developing a third model which incorporates the main desirable features of the original, as well as being theoretically meaningful. (See Pesaran and Deaton, 1978.)

5.3   The comprehensive approach

Another approach closely related to the Cox's procedure is the comprehensive approach advocated by Atkinson (1970) whereby tests of nonnested models are based upon a third comprehensive model, artificially constructed so that each of the nonnested models can be obtained from it as special cases. Clearly, there are a large number of ways that such a comprehensive model can be constructed. A prominent example is the exponential mixture, H_λ, which in the case of the nonnested models (13.4) and (13.5) is defined by

$$H_\lambda : c_\lambda(y_t | x_t, z_t, \Omega_{t-1}; \theta, \gamma) = \frac{f(y_t | x_t, \Omega_{t-1}; \theta)^{1-\lambda} g(y_t | z_t, \Omega_{t-1}; \gamma)^\lambda}{\int_{\mathcal{R}_y} f(y_t | x_t, \Omega_{t-1}; \theta)^{1-\lambda} g(y_t | z_t, \Omega_{t-1}; \gamma)^\lambda dy_t},$$

where $\mathcal{R}_y$ represents the domain of variations of y_t, and the integral in the denominator ensures that the combined function, $c_\lambda(y_t | x_t, z_t, \Omega_{t-1}; \theta, \gamma)$, is in fact a proper density function integrating to unity over $\mathcal{R}_y$. The "mixing" parameter λ varies in the range $[0, 1]$ and represents the weight attached to model H_f. A test of $\lambda = 0$ ($\lambda = 1$) against the alternative that $\lambda \neq 0$ ($\lambda \neq 1$) can now be carried out using standard techniques from the literature on nested hypothesis testing. (See Atkinson, 1970 and Pesaran, 1982a.) This approach is, however, subject to three important limitations. First, although the testing framework is nested, the test of $\lambda = 0$ is still *nonstandard* due to the fact that under $\lambda = 0$ the parameters of the alternative hypothesis, γ, disappear. This is known as the Davies problem. (See Davies, 1977.) The same also applies if the interest is in testing $\lambda = 1$. The second limitation is due to the fact that testing $\lambda = 0$ against $\lambda \neq 0$, is not equivalent to testing H_f against H_g, which is the problem of primary interest. This implicit change of the alternative hypothesis can have unfavorable consequences for the power of nonnested tests. Finally, the particular functional form used to combine the two models is arbitrary and does not allow identification of the mixing parameter, λ, even if θ and γ are separately identified under H_f and H_g respectively. (See Pesaran, 1981.)

The application of the comprehensive approach to the linear regression models (13.19) and (13.20) yields:

$$H_\lambda : y = \left\{ \frac{(1-\lambda)v^2}{\sigma^2} \right\} X\alpha + \left\{ \frac{\lambda v^2}{\omega^2} \right\} Z\beta + u, \quad u \sim N(0, v^2 I_T), \tag{13.31}$$

where $v^{-2} = (1 - \lambda)\sigma^{-2} + \lambda\omega^{-2}$. It is clear that the mixing parameter λ is not identified.[16] In fact setting $\kappa = \lambda v^2 / \omega^2$ the above "combined" regression can also be written as

$$H_\kappa : y = (1 - \kappa)X\alpha + \kappa Z\beta + u, \tag{13.32}$$

and a test of $\lambda = 0$ in (13.31) can be carried by testing $\kappa = 0$ in (13.32). Since the error variances σ^2 and ω^2 are strictly positive $\lambda = 0$ will be equivalent to testing $\kappa = 0$. The Davies problem, of course, continues to apply and under $H_f(\kappa = 0)$ the coefficients of the rival model, β, disappear from the combined model. To resolve this problem Davies (1977) proposes a two-stage procedure. First, for a given value of β a statistic for testing $\kappa = 0$ is chosen. In the present application this is given by the t-ratio of κ in the regression of y on X and $y_\beta = Z\beta$, namely

$$t_\kappa(Z\beta) = \frac{\beta'Z'M_xy}{\hat{v}(\beta'Z'M_xZ\beta)^{1/2}},$$

$$\hat{v}^2 = \frac{1}{T - k_f - 1}\left\{y'M_xy - \frac{(\beta'Z'M_xy)^2}{\beta'Z'M_xZ\beta}\right\},$$

and where M_x is already defined by (13.26). In the second stage a test is constructed based on the entire random function of $t_\kappa(Z\beta)$ viewed as a function of β. One possibility would be to construct a test statistic based on

$$F_\kappa = \underset{\beta}{\text{Max}}\{t_\kappa(Z\beta)\}.$$

Alternatively, a test statistic could be based on the average value of $t_\kappa(Z\beta)$ obtained using a suitable prior distribution for β. Following the former classical route it is then easily seen that F_κ becomes the standard F_{z^*} statistic for testing $b_2 = 0$, in the regression

$$y = Xb_1 + Z^*b_2 + v_f, \tag{13.33}$$

where Z^* is the set of regressors in Z but not in X, namely $Z^* = Z - X \cap Z$.[17] Similarly for testing H_g against H_f the comprehensive approach involves testing $c_1 = 0$, in the combined regression

$$y = X^*c_1 + Zc_2 + v_g, \tag{13.34}$$

where X^* is the set of variables in X but not in Z. Denoting the F-statistic for testing $c_1 = 0$ in this regression by F_{x^*}, notice that there are still four possible outcomes to this procedure; in line with the ones detailed above for the Cox test. This is because we have two F-statistics, F_{x^*} and F_{z^*}, with the possibility of rejecting both hypotheses, rejecting neither, etc.

An altogether different approach to the resolution of the Davies problem would be to replace the regression coefficients, β, in (13.32) by an estimate, say $\tilde{\beta}$, and then proceed as if $\tilde{y}_\beta = Z\tilde{\beta}$ is data. This is in effect what is proposed by Davidson and MacKinnon (1981) and Fisher and McAleer (1981). Davidson and MacKinnon suggest using the estimate of β under H_g, namely $\hat{\beta}_T = (Z'Z)^{-1}Zy$. This leads to the J-test which is the standard t-ratio of the estimate of κ in the artificial regression[18]

$$H_\kappa : y = X\alpha + \kappa Z\hat{\beta}_T + v_\kappa. \tag{13.35}$$

For testing H_g against H_f, the J-test will be based on the OLS regression of y on Z and $X\hat{\alpha}_T$, and the J-statistic is the t-ratio of the coefficient of $X\hat{\alpha}_T$ (which is the vector of fitted values under H_f) in this regression.

The test proposed by Fisher and McAleer (known as the JA-test) replaces β by the estimate of its pseudo-true value under H_f, given by $\beta_*(\hat{\alpha}_T)$

$$\hat{\beta}_*(\hat{\alpha}_T) = (Z'Z)^{-1}Z'\hat{\alpha}_T.$$

In short the JA-test of H_f against H_g is the t-ratio of the coefficient of $\hat{y}_{\beta\alpha} = Z(Z'Z)^{-1}Z'\hat{\alpha}_T$ in the OLS regression of y on X and $\hat{y}_{\beta\alpha}$. Similarly, a JA-test of H_g against H_f can be computed.

Both the J- and the JA-test statistics, as well as their various variations proposed in the literature can also be derived as linear approximations to the Cox test statistic. See (13.28).

Various extensions of nonnested hypothesis testing have also appeared in the literature. These include tests of nonnested linear regression models with serially correlated errors (McAleer *et al.*, 1990); models estimated by instrumental variables (Ericsson, 1983; Godfrey, 1983); models estimated by the generalized method of moments (Smith, 1992); nonnested Euler equations (Ghysels and Hall, 1990); autoregressive versus moving average models (Walker, 1967; King, 1983); the generalized autoregressive conditional heteroskedastic (GARCH) model against the exponential-GARCH model (McAleer and Ling, 1998); linear versus loglinear models (Aneuryn-Evans and Deaton, 1980; Davidson and MacKinnon, 1985; Pesaran and Pesaran, 1995); logit and probit models (Pesaran and Pesaran, 1993; Weeks, 1996; Duncan and Weeks, 1998); nonnested threshold autoregressive models (Altissimo and Violante, 1998; Pesaran and Potter, 1997; Kapetanios and Weeks, 1999).

5.4   The encompassing approach

This approach generalizes Cox's original idea and asks whether model H_f can explain one or more features of the rival model H_g. When *all* the features of model H_g can be explained by model H_f it is said that model H_f *encompasses* model H_g; likewise model H_g is said to encompass model H_f if all the features of model H_f can be explained by model H_g. A formal definition of encompassing can be given in terms of the pseudo-true parameters and the binding functions defined in Section 2.

Model H_g is said to encompass model H_f, respectively defined by (13.5) and (13.4), if and only if

$$H_g \mathcal{E} H_f : \theta_{h*} = \theta_*(\gamma_{h*}). \tag{13.36}$$

Similarly, H_f is said to encompass H_g (or H_g is encompassed by H_f) if and only if

$$H_f \mathcal{E} H_g : \gamma_{h*} = \gamma_*(\theta_{h*}).$$

Recall that θ_{h*} and γ_{h*} are the pseudo-true values of θ, and γ with respect to the true model H_h, and $\theta_*(\cdot)$ are $\gamma_*(\cdot)$ are the binding functions linking the parameters of the models H_f and H_g. For example, in the case of the linear rival regression models (13.10) and (13.11), and assuming that the true model is given by (13.14) then it is easily seen that the functions that bind the parameters of model H_g to that of H_f are

$$\theta_*(\gamma_{h*}) = \begin{pmatrix} \hat{\Sigma}_{xx}^{-1}\hat{\Sigma}_{xz}\beta_{h*} \\ \omega_{h*}^2 + \beta_{h*}'(\hat{\Sigma}_{zz} - \hat{\Sigma}_{zx}\hat{\Sigma}_{xx}^{-1}\hat{\Sigma}_{xz})\beta_{h*} \end{pmatrix}.$$

Using (13.16) to substitute for the pseudo-true values β_{h*} and ω_{h*}^2 we have

$$\theta_*(\gamma_{h*}) = \begin{pmatrix} \hat{\Sigma}_{xx}^{-1}\hat{\Sigma}_{xz}\hat{\Sigma}_{zz}^{-1}\hat{\Sigma}_{zw}\delta \\ \upsilon^2 + \delta'(\hat{\Sigma}_{ww} - \hat{\Sigma}_{wz}\hat{\Sigma}_{zz}^{-1}\hat{\Sigma}_{zw})\delta + \delta'\hat{\Sigma}_{wz}\hat{\Sigma}_{zz}^{-1}(\hat{\Sigma}_{zz} - \hat{\Sigma}_{zx}\hat{\Sigma}_{xx}^{-1}\hat{\Sigma}_{xz})\hat{\Sigma}_{zz}^{-1}\hat{\Sigma}_{zw}\delta \end{pmatrix}.$$

Therefore, conditional on the observation matrices X, Z, and W, model H_f encompasses model H_g if and only if

$$\begin{pmatrix} \hat{\Sigma}_{xx}^{-1}\hat{\Sigma}_{xw}\delta \\ \upsilon^2 + \delta'(\hat{\Sigma}_{ww} - \hat{\Sigma}_{wx}\hat{\Sigma}_{xx}^{-1}\hat{\Sigma}_{xw})\delta \end{pmatrix}$$

$$= \begin{pmatrix} \hat{\Sigma}_{xx}^{-1}\hat{\Sigma}_{xz}\hat{\Sigma}_{zz}^{-1}\hat{\Sigma}_{zw}\delta \\ \upsilon^2 + \delta'(\hat{\Sigma}_{ww} - \hat{\Sigma}_{wz}\hat{\Sigma}_{zz}^{-1}\hat{\Sigma}_{zw})\delta + \delta'\hat{\Sigma}_{wz}\hat{\Sigma}_{zz}^{-1}(\hat{\Sigma}_{zz} - \hat{\Sigma}_{zx}\hat{\Sigma}_{xx}^{-1}\hat{\Sigma}_{xz})\hat{\Sigma}_{zz}^{-1}\hat{\Sigma}_{zw}\delta \end{pmatrix}.$$

These conditions are simplified to

$$\hat{\Sigma}_{xw}\delta = \hat{\Sigma}_{xz}\hat{\Sigma}_{zz}^{-1}\hat{\Sigma}_{zw}\delta, \tag{13.37}$$

and

$$\delta'\hat{\Sigma}_{wx}\hat{\Sigma}_{xx}^{-1}\hat{\Sigma}_{xw}\delta = \delta'\hat{\Sigma}_{wz}\hat{\Sigma}_{zz}^{-1}\hat{\Sigma}_{zx}\hat{\Sigma}_{xx}^{-1}\hat{\Sigma}_{xz}\hat{\Sigma}_{zz}^{-1}\hat{\Sigma}_{zw}\delta. \tag{13.38}$$

But it is easily verified that (13.37) implies (13.38), namely encompassing with respect to the regression coefficients imply encompassing with respect to the error variances. Therefore, H_f is encompassed by H_g if and only if $(X'M_zW)\delta = 0$. This condition is clearly satisfied if either H_f is nested within H_g, $(X'M_z = 0)$, or if H_g contains the true model, $(M_zW = 0)$. The remaining possibility, namely when $(X'M_zW) = 0$, but the true value of δ, say δ_0, is such that $(X'M_zW)\delta_0 = 0$, is a rather a low probability event.

The encompassing hypothesis, $H_g \mathcal{E} H_f$, (or $H_f \mathcal{E} H_g$) can now be tested using the encompassing statistics, $\sqrt{T}[\hat{\theta}_T - \theta_*(\hat{\gamma}_T)]$, (or $\sqrt{T}[\hat{\gamma}_T - \gamma_*(\hat{\theta}_T)]$). Gouriéroux and Monfort (1995) show that under the encompassing hypothesis, $\theta_{h*} = \theta_*(\gamma_{h*})$, and assuming certain requilarity conditions are met, $\sqrt{T}[\hat{\theta}_T - \theta_*(\hat{\gamma}_T)]$ is asymptotically normally distributed with zero means and a variance covariance matrix that in general depends in a complicated way on the probability density functions of the rival models under consideration. Complications arise since H_g need not belong to H_h. Two testing procedures are proposed, the Wald encompassing test

(WET) and the score encompassing test (SET), both being difficult to implement. First, the binding functions $\theta_*(\cdot)$ and $\gamma_*(\cdot)$ are not always easy to derive. (But this problem also afflicts the implementation of the Cox procedure, see below.) Second, and more importantly, the variance–covariance matrices of $\sqrt{T}\,[\hat{\theta}_T - \theta_*(\hat{\gamma}_T)]$, (or $\sqrt{T}\,[\hat{\gamma}_T - \gamma_*(\hat{\theta}_T)]$), are, in general, non-invertible and the construction of WET and SET statistics involve the use of generalized inverse and this in turn requires estimation of the rank of these covariance matrices. Alternative ways of dealing with these difficulties are considered in Gouriéroux and Monfort (1995) and Smith (1993).

In the case of linear regression models full parameter encompassing (namely an encompassing exercise involving both regression coefficients and error variances) is unnecessary.[19] Focusing on regression coefficients the encompassing statistics for testing $H_g \mathcal{E} H_f$ are given by

$$\sqrt{T}\,[\hat{\alpha}_T - \alpha_*(\hat{\beta}_T)] = \sqrt{T}\,(X'X)^{-1}X'M_z y.$$

Under H_h, defined by (13.14),

$$\sqrt{T}\,[\hat{\alpha}_T - \alpha_*(\hat{\beta}_T)] = \sqrt{T}\,(X'X)^{-1}(X'M_z W)\delta + \sqrt{T}\,(X'X)^{-1}X'M_z u_h,$$

where $u_h \sim N(0, \upsilon^2 I_T)$.[20] Hence, under the encompassing hypothesis, $(X'M_z W)\delta = 0$, the encompassing statistic $\sqrt{T}\,[\hat{\alpha}_T - \alpha_*(\hat{\beta}_T)]$ is asymptotically normally distributed with mean zero and the covariance matrix $\upsilon^2 \Sigma_{xx}^{-1}(\Sigma_{xx} - \Sigma_{xz}\Sigma_{zz}^{-1}\Sigma_{zx})\Sigma_{xx}^{-1}$. Therefore, the construction of a standardized encompassing test statistic requires a consistent estimate of υ^2, the error variance of the true regression model, and this does not seem possible without further assumptions about the nature of the true model. In the literature it is often (implicitly) assumed that the true model is contained in the union intersection of the rival models under consideration (namely $W \equiv X \cup Z$) and υ^2 is then consistently estimated from a regression of y on $X \cup Z$. Under this additional assumption, the WET statistic for testing $H_g \mathcal{E} H_f$, is given by

$$\mathcal{E}_{gf} = \frac{y'M_z X(X'M_z \tilde{X})X'M_z y}{\hat{\upsilon}^2},$$

where $\hat{\upsilon}^2$ is the estimate of the error variance of the regression of y on $X \cup Z$, and $(X'M_z\tilde{X})$ is a generalized inverse of $X'M_z X$. This matrix is rank deficient whenever X and Z have variables in common, namely if $X \cap Z = Q \neq 0$. Let $X = (X_1, Q)$ and $Z = (Z_1, Q)$, then

$$X'M_z X = \begin{pmatrix} X_1'M_z X_1 & 0 \\ 0 & 0 \end{pmatrix}.$$

But it is easily seen that $\mathcal{E}_{gf}$ is invariant to the choice of the g-inverse used and is given by

$$\mathcal{E}_{gf} = \frac{y'M_z X_1(X_1'M_z X_1)^{-1}X_1'M_z y}{\hat{\upsilon}^2},$$

and is identical to the standard Wald statistic for testing the statistical significance of X_1 in the OLS regression of y on Z and X_1. This is perhaps not surprising, considering the (implicit) assumption concerning the true model being a union intersection of the rival regression models H_f and H_g.

Other encompassing tests can also be developed depending on the parameters of interest or their functions. For example, a *variance* encompassing test of $H_g \mathcal{E} H_f$ compares a consistent estimate of σ^2 with that of its pseudo-true value σ^2_{h*}, namely $\hat{\sigma}^2_T - \sigma^2_*(\hat{\gamma}_T) = \hat{\sigma}^2_T - [\hat{\omega}^2_T + T^{-1}\hat{\beta}'_T Z' M_x Z \hat{\beta}_T]$.[21] Under the encompassing hypothesis this statistic tends to zero, but its asymptotic distribution in general depends on H_h. In the case where H_g contains the true model the variance encompassing test will become asymptotically equivalent to the Cox and the J-tests discussed above.

The encompassing approach can also be applied to the loglikelihood functions. For example, to test $H_g \mathcal{E} H_f$ one could use the encompassing loglikelihood ratio statistic $T^{-1}\{L_f(\hat{\theta}_T) - L_f(\theta_*(\hat{\gamma}_T))\}$. This test can also be motivated using Cox's idea of a centered loglikelihood ratio statistic, with the difference that the centering is now carried out under H_h rather than under H_g (or H_f). See Gouriéroux and Monfort (1995) and Smith (1993) for details and difficulties involved in their implementation. Other relevant literature include Dastoor (1983), Gouriéroux *et al.* (1983) and Mizon and Richard (1986).

5.5 Power and finite sample properties

A number of studies have examined the small sample properties of nonnested tests. For a limited number of cases it is possible to determine the exact form of the test statistic and the sampling distribution. For example, Godfrey (1983) shows that under H_f if X and Z are non-stochastic with normal errors, then the JA-test has an exact $t(T - k_f - 1)$ distribution.[22] In the majority of cases the finite sample properties have been examined using Monte Carlo studies. A recurrent finding is that many Cox-type tests for nonnested regression models have a finite sample size which is significantly greater than the nominal level. Modifications based upon mean and variance adjustments have been proposed in Godfrey and Pesaran (1983), and are shown to affect a substantial improvement in finite sample performance. The authors demonstrate that in experimental designs allowing for nonnested models with either nonnormal errors, different number of regressors, or a lagged dependent variable, the adjusted Cox-test performs favorably relative to the J-test or F-test.[23] In the case of nonnested linear regression models, Davidson and MacKinnon (1982) compared a number of variants of the Cox-test with F-, JA- and J-test.

An analysis of the power properties of non-tested tests has been undertaken using a number of approaches. In the case of nested models local alternatives are readily defined in terms of parameters that link the null to the alternative. Obviously in the case of models that are globally nonnested (i.e. the exponential and lognormal) this procedure is not possible. In the case of regression models Pesaran (1982a) is able to develop a asymptotic distribution of Cox-type tests under a sequence of local alternatives defined in terms of the degree of multicollinearity of the regressors from the two rival models. Under this sequence of local alternatives he shows that the F-test based on the comprehensive model is less powerful than the Cox-type tests, unless the number of non-overlapping variables of the alternative over the null hypothesis is unity. An alternative approach to asymptotic power comparisons which does not require specification of local alternatives is advanced by Bahadur (1960) and Bahadur (1967) and holds the alternative hypothesis fixed but allows the size of the test to tend to zero as the sample size increases. Asymptotic power comparisons of nonnested tests by the Bahadur approach is considered in Gouriéroux (1982) and Pesaran (1984).

6   MEASURES OF CLOSENESS AND VUONG'S APPROACH

So far the concepts of nested and nonnested hypotheses have been loosely defined, but for a more integrated approach to nonnested hypothesis testing and model selection a more formal definition is required. This can be done by means of a variety of "closeness" criteria proposed in the literature for measuring the divergence of one distribution function with respect to another. A popular measure employed in Pesaran (1987) for this purpose is the Kullback–Leibler (Kullback, 1959) information criterion (KLIC). This criterion has been used extensively in the development of both nonnested hypotheses tests and model selection procedures. Given hypotheses H_f and H_g, defined by (13.4) and (13.5), the KLIC measure of H_g with respect to H_f is written as

$$I_{fg}(\theta, \gamma) = E_f\{\ln f_t(\theta) - \ln g_t(\gamma)\}$$

$$\int_{R_f} \ln\left\{\frac{f_t(\theta)}{g_t(\gamma)}\right\} f_t(\theta)dy. \tag{13.39}$$

It is important to note that $I_{fg}(\theta, \gamma)$ is not a distance measure. For example, in general $I_{fg}(\theta, \gamma)$ is not the same as $I_{gf}(\gamma, \theta)$, and KLIC does not satisfy the triangular inequality, namely $I_{fg} + I_{gh}$ need not exceed I_{fh} as required if KLIC were a distance measure. Nevertheless, KLIC has a number attractive properties: $I_{fg}(\theta, \gamma) \geq 0$, with the strict equality holding if and only if $f(\cdot) = g(\cdot)$. Assuming that observations on y_t are independently distributed then the KLIC measure is additive over sample observations.

To provide a formal definition of nonnested or nested hypothesis we define two "closeness" measures: one measuring the closeness of H_g to H_f (viewed from the perspective of H_f), and another the closeness measure of H_f to H_g. These are respectively given by $C_{fg}(\theta_0) = I_{fg}(\theta_0, \gamma_*(\theta_0))$, and $C_{gf}(\gamma_0) = I_{gf}(\gamma_0, \theta_*(\gamma_0))$, where, as before, $\gamma_*(\theta_0)$ is the pseudo-true value of γ under H_f, and $\theta_*(\gamma_0)$ is pseudo-true value of θ under H_g.

Definition 1. H_f is nested within H_g *if and only if* $C_{fg}(\theta_0) = 0$, for all values of $\theta_0 \in \Theta$, and $C_{gf}(\gamma_0) \neq 0$ for some $\gamma_0 \in \Gamma$.

Definition 2. H_f and H_g are globally nonnested *if and only if* $C_{fg}(\theta_0)$ and $C_{gf}(\gamma_0)$ are both non-zero for all values of $\theta_0 \in \Theta$ and $\gamma_0 \in \Gamma$.

Definition 3. H_f and H_g are partially nonnested if $C_{fg}(\theta_0)$ and $C_{gf}(\gamma_0)$ are both non-zero for some values of $\theta_0 \in \Theta$ and $\gamma_0 \in \Gamma$.

Definition 4. H_f and H_g are observationally equivalent *if and only if* $C_{fg}(\theta_0) = 0$ and $C_{gf}(\gamma_0) = 0$ for all values of $\theta_0 \in \Theta$ and $\gamma_0 \in \Gamma$.

Using the above definitions it is easily seen, for example, that linear or nonlinear rival regression models can at most be partially nonnested, but exponential and lognormal distributions discussed in Section 3 are globally nonnested. For further details see Pesaran (1987).

We may also define a closeness measure of H_g to H_f from the perspective of the true model H_h and in doing so are able to motivate Vuong's approach to hypothesis testing and model selection. (See Vuong, 1989.) The primary focus of Vuong's analysis is to test the hypothesis that the models under consideration are "equally" close to the true model. As Vuong (1989) notes "If the distance between a specified model and the true distribution is defined as the minimum of the KLIC over the distributions in the model, then it is natural to define the 'best' model among a collection of competing models to be the model that is closest to the true distribution". Thus, in contrast to the standard approach to model selection, a hypothesis testing framework is adopted and a *probabilistic* decision rule used to select a "best" model.

With our setup and notations the closeness of H_f to H_h viewed from the perspective of the true model, H_h is defined by

$$C_{hf}(\theta_{h*}) = E_h\{\ln h_t(\cdot) - \ln f_t(\theta_{h*})\}.$$

Similarly, the closeness of H_g to H_h is defined by

$$C_{hg}(\gamma_{h*}) = E_h\{\ln h_t(\cdot) - \ln g_t(\gamma_{h*})\}.$$

The null hypothesis underlying Vuong's approach is now given by

$$H_V : C_{hf}(\theta_{h*}) = C_{hg}(\gamma_{h*}),$$

which can also be written as

$$H_V : E_h\{\ln f_t(\theta_{h*})\} = E_h\{\ln g_t(\gamma_{h*})\}.$$

The quantity $E_h\{\ln f_t(\theta_{h*}) - \ln g_t(\gamma_{h*})\}$ is unknown and depends on the unknown true distribution H_h, but can be consistently estimated by the average loglikelihood ratio statistic, $T^{-1}\{L_f(\hat{\theta}_T) - L_g(\hat{\gamma}_T)\}$. Vuong derives the asymptotic distribution of the average loglikelihood ratio under H_V, and shows that it crucially depends on whether $f_t(\theta_{h*}) = g_t(\gamma_{h*})$, namely whether the distributions in H_f and H_g that are closest to the true model are observationally equivalent or not. In view of this a sequential approach to hypothesis testing is proposed. See Vuong (1989) for further details.

7   PRACTICAL PROBLEMS

In Section 5 we noted that the motivation for the Cox test statistic was based upon the observation that unless two models, say $f(\cdot)$ and $g(\cdot)$ are nonnested then the expectation

$$T^{-1}E_f[L_f(\theta) - L_g(\gamma)], \tag{13.40}$$

does not evaluate to zero and as a result standard likelihood ratio statistics are not appropriate. Cox (1961, 1962) proposed a procedure such that a centered (modified) loglikelihood ratio has a well-defined limiting distribution. In Section 5.1 we demonstrated that in the case of the linear regression we may obtain a closed form consistent estimate of (13.40). However, this is the exception rather than the rule and the use of the Cox test has been restricted to a relatively small number of applications due to problems in constructing a consistent estimate of the expected loglikelihood ratio statistic. There are two principal problems. First, in order to estimate (13.40) we require a consistent estimate of the pseudo-true value, $\gamma(\theta_0)$. Second, in most cases even given such an estimate, the expectation (13.40) will still be intractable. An exception is the application of the Cox test to both binary and multinomial probit and logit models. Independent of the dimension of the choice set, the expected difference between the two loglikelihoods under the null has a relatively simple, closed form expression (see Pesaran and Pesaran, 1993).

Following the work of Pesaran and Pesaran (1993, 1995) and Weeks (1996), a simulation-based application of the modified likelihood principle has been used to affect adjustments to the test statistic in order to improve the finite sample size and power properties. A drawback of this approach is that it is still reliant upon a reference distribution which is valid asymptotically. In addition, Orme (1994) attests to the existence of a large number of asymptotically equivalent (AE) variants of the Cox test statistic which represents a formidable menu of choices for the applied econometrician. In the case of the numerator, various test statistics are based upon the use of alternative consistent estimators of the Kullback–Leibler measure of closeness. An additional set of variants of the Cox test statistic depends upon the existence of a number of AE ways of estimating the variance of the test statistic.

An alternative approach based upon the seminal work of Efron (1979), with contributions by Hall (1986), Beran (1988), Hinkely (1988), and Coulibaly and Brorsen (1998), applies bootstrap-based procedures to directly evaluate the empirical distribution function of the loglikelihood ratio statistic. In this context the focus is upon correcting the reference distribution rather than centering the loglikelihood ratio statistic and utilizing limiting distribution arguments. This type of adjustment may, in a number of cases, be theoretically justified through Edgeworth expansions and can under certain conditions result in improvements over classical asymptotic inference. The existence of a large menu of broadly equivalent test statistics is also relevant in the context of bootstrap-based inference. Recent surveys by Vinod (1993), Jeong and Maddala (1993), and Li and

Maddala (1996), review a large number of variants including the double, recursive, and weighted bootstrap. Similarly, Hall (1988) notes that in many applications the precise nature of the bootstrap design is not stated.

7.1 A simulation application of the modified likelihood principle

The essence of the Cox nonnested test is that the mean adjusted ratio of the maximized loglikelihoods of two nonnested models has a well-defined *limiting* distribution under the null hypothesis. Using the notation set out in Section 2 above we may write the numerator of the Cox test statistic as

$$S_{fg} = T^{-1}LR_{fg} - C_{fg}(\hat{\theta}_T, \tilde{\gamma}). \tag{13.41}$$

The last term on the right-hand side of (13.41), $C_{fg}(\hat{\theta}_T, \tilde{\gamma})$, represents a consistent estimator of $C_{fg}(\theta_0, \gamma_*(\theta_0))$, the KLIC measure of closeness of $g(\cdot)$ to $f(\cdot)$. This may be written as $C_{fg}(\hat{\theta}_T, \tilde{\gamma}) = \hat{E}_f[T^{-1}(L_f(\hat{\theta}_T) - L_g(\tilde{\gamma}))]$, and is an estimator of the difference between the expected value of the two maximized loglikelihoods under the distribution given by $f(\cdot)$; $\tilde{\gamma}$ is any consistent estimator for $\gamma_*(\theta_0)$. Weeks (1996), in testing probit and logit models of discrete choice, distinguished between three variants, $\tilde{\gamma} = \{\hat{\gamma}_T, \gamma_R(\hat{\theta}_T), \tilde{\gamma}_T\}$. $\hat{\gamma}_T$ is the MLE of γ, $\tilde{\gamma}$ is due to Kent (1986) and is an estimator derived from maximizing the fitted loglikelihood, and $\gamma_{*R}(\hat{\theta}_T) = \frac{1}{R}\sum_{r=1}^{R}\gamma_*^r(\hat{\theta}_T)$ is a simulation-based estimator where $\gamma_*^r(\hat{\theta}_T)$ is the solution to

$$\arg\max_{\gamma}\left\{L_g^r(\gamma) = \sum_{t=1}^{T}\ln g(y_t^r(\hat{\theta}_T) \mid z_t, \Omega_{t-1}; \gamma)\right\}, \tag{13.42}$$

where $y_t^r(\hat{\theta}_T)$ is the rth draw of y_t under H_f using $\hat{\theta}_T$ and R is the number of simulations. Note that for both $R \to \infty$ and $T \to \infty$ then $\gamma_{*R}(\hat{\theta}_T) \to \gamma_*(\theta_0)$.

A simulation-based estimator of $C_{fg}(\theta_0, \gamma_*(\theta_0))$ has been suggested by Pesaran and Pesaran (1993) and is given by

$$C_{fg,R}(\hat{\theta}_T, \gamma_{*R}(\hat{\theta}_T)) = \frac{1}{TR}\sum_{r=1}^{R}[L_f^r(\hat{\theta}_T) - L_g^r(\gamma_{*R}(\hat{\theta}_T))]. \tag{13.43}$$

However (13.43) represents one approach to centering the loglikelihood ratio statistic, whereby both $\hat{\theta}_T$ and $\gamma_{*R}(\hat{\theta}_T)$ are treated as *fixed* parameters. An alternative method of mean adjustment is given by the following estimator of KLIC

$$C_{fg,R}(\hat{\theta}_T^1, \ldots, \hat{\theta}_T^R, \gamma_*^1(\hat{\theta}_T), \ldots, \gamma_*^R(\hat{\theta}_T)) = \frac{1}{TR}\sum_{r=1}^{R}[L_f^r(\hat{\theta}_T^r) - L_g^r(\gamma_*^r(\hat{\theta}_T))], \tag{13.44}$$

where the parameter arguments to both $L_f(\cdot)$ and $L_g(\cdot)$ are allowed to *vary* across each rth replication. (See Coulibaly and Brorsen, 1998.)

7.2   Resampling the likelihood ratio statistic: bootstrap methods

The bootstrap is a data based simulation method for statistical inference. The bootstrap approach involves approximating the distribution of a function of the observed data by the bootstrap distribution of the quantity. This is done by substituting the empirical distribution function for the unknown distribution and repeating this process many times to obtain a simulated distribution. Its recent development follows from the requirement of a significant amount of computational power. Obviously there is no advantage to utilizing bootstrap procedures when the exact sampling distribution of the test statistic is known. However, it has been demonstrated that when the sampling distribution is not known, the substitution of computational intensive bootstrap resampling can offer an improvement over asymptotic theory. The use of *non-pivotal* bootstrap testing procedures does not require the mean adjustment facilitated by (13.43) and (13.44). However, pivotal (or bootstrap-t) procedures require both mean and variance adjustments in order to guarantee asymptotic pivotalness.

Utilizing a parametric bootstrap we present below a simple algorithm for resampling the likelihood ratio statistic which we then use to construct the empirical distribution function of the test statistic. For the purpose of exposition the algorithm is presented for the non-pivotal bootstrap.

1. Generate R samples of size T by sampling from the *fitted* null model $f_t(\hat{\theta}_T)$.
2. For each rth simulated sample, the pair $(\hat{\theta}_T^r, \gamma_*^r(\hat{\theta}_T))$ represent the parameter estimates obtained by maximizing the loglikelihoods

$$L_f^r(\theta) = \sum_{t=1}^{T} \ln f_t(y_t^r(\hat{\theta}_T) \mid x_t, \Omega_{t-1}; \theta), \; L_g^r(\gamma) = \sum_{t=1}^{T} \ln g_t(y_t^r(\hat{\theta}_T) \mid z_t, \Omega_{t-1}; \gamma),$$

$$(13.45)$$

where $y_t^r(\hat{\theta}_T)$ denotes the rth bootstrap-sample conditional upon $\theta = \hat{\theta}_T$. We then compute the simulated loglikelihood ratio statistic

$$T_f^r = L_f(\hat{\theta}_T^r) - L_g(\gamma_*^r(\hat{\theta}_T)).$$

3. By constructing the empirical cdf of $\{T_f^r : 1 \le r \le R\}$, we can compare the *observed* test statistic, $T_f = L_f(\hat{\theta}_T) - L_g(\gamma_*(\hat{\theta}_T))$, with critical values obtained from the R independent (conditional) realizations of T_f^r. The p-value based upon the bootstrap procedure is given by[24]

$$P_R = \frac{\sum_{r=1}^{R} 1(T_f^r \ge T_f)}{R}, \qquad (13.46)$$

where $1(.)$ is the indicator function.

The bootstrap procedure outlined above simply resamples the likelihood ratio statistic *without* pivoting. There are a number of alternative test statistics which by using pivotal methods are conjectured to represent an improvement over classical first order methods (see for example, Beran (1988) and Hall (1988)). An evaluation of both the size and power properties of a number of simulation and bootstrap-based tests applied to linear versus loglinear regression models and a number of variants of threshold autoregressive models is provided in Kapetanios and Weeks (1999).

Notes

1 Therefore our focus is distinct from Chow (1981) who, in examining a similar problem, assumes that the set of models under consideration contains a general model from which all other competing models may be obtained by the imposition of suitable parameter restrictions.

2 See, for example, Friedman and Meiselman (1963) on alternative consumption models, Barro (1977), Pesaran (1982b) and McAleer, Pesaran, and Bera (1990) on alternative explanations of the unemployment rate; Jorgenson and Siebert (1968), Dixit and Pindyck (1994) and Bernanke, Bohn, and Reiss (1988) on alternative models of investment behavior; and McAleer, Fisher, and Volker (1982) and Smith and Smyth (1991) on nonnested money demand functions.

3 An excellent survey article on nonnested hypothesis testing can be found in Gouriéroux and Monfort (1994).

4 In cases where one or more elements of z_t are discrete, as in probit or tobit specifications cumulative probability distribution functions can be used instead of probability density functions.

5 See Engle, Hendry, and Richard (1983).

6 A formalization of the concept of globally nonnested models can be found in Pesaran (1987). Also see Section 6.

7 Note that under H_f, $E(y_t) = E\{\exp(\ln y_t)\} = \exp(\theta_1 + 0.5\theta_2)$.

8 See, Pesaran (1984, pp. 249–50).

9 There is substantial literature on nonnested tests of linear versus loglinear regression models. Earlier studies include Aneuryn-Evans and Deaton (1980), Godfrey and Wickens (1981) and Davidson and MacKinnon (1985). In a more recent study Pesaran and Pesaran (1995) have examined the properties of a simulation-based variant of the Cox test.

10 A review of the model selection literature is beyond the scope of the present paper. See, for example, Leamer (1983) for an excellent review. A recent review focusing upon the selection of regressors problems is to be found in Lavergne (1998). Two excellent texts are Grasa (1989) and Linhart and Zucchini (1986). Maddala (1981) edited a special issue of the *Journal of Econometrics* which focuses on model selection.

11 For the case of the classical linear regression model examples of model selection criteria include Theil's $\bar{R}^2$, with more general loss functions based upon information criteria including Akaike's (1973) information criteria and Schwarz's (1978) Bayesian information criterion.

12 The concepts of globally and partially nonnested models are defined in Pesaran (1987).

13 See also Dastoor (1981) for further discussion.

14 The cases where $\Sigma_f \neq 0$ (respectively $\Sigma_g \neq 0$) but nevertheless $\Sigma_f \alpha_0 = 0$ (respectively $\Sigma_g \beta_0 = 0$) are discussed in Pesaran (1987, p. 74).

15 See Pesaran (1974) for details of the derivations.

16 For example, it is not possible to test whether $\lambda = 1/2$, which could have been of interest in assessing the relative weights attached to the two rival models.

17 For a proof see McAleer and Pesaran (1986).

18 Chao and Swanson (1997) provide some asymptotic results for the J-test in the case of nonnested models with $I(1)$ regressors.

19 Recall that the encompassing condition (13.37) for the regression coefficients implies the condition (13.38) for error variance encompassing but not vice versa.

20 Notice that the normality assumption is not needed and can be relaxed.

21 Similarly, the variance encompassing statistic for testing $H_f \mathcal{E} H_g$ is given by $\hat{\omega}_T^2 - [\hat{\sigma}_T^2 + T^{-1}\hat{\alpha}_T' X' M_z X \hat{\alpha}_T']$.

22 See also McAleer (1983).

23 See McAleer and Pesaran (1986) for additional details.

24 If T is discrete then repeat values of T can occur requiring that we make an adjustment to (13.46).

References

Akaike, H. (1973). Information theory and an extension of the maximum likelihood principle. In N. Petrov and F. Csadki (eds.) *Proceedings of the 2nd International Symposium on Information Theory.* pp. 267–81. Budapest: Akademiai Kiado.

Altissimo, F., and G.L. Violante (1998). The nonlinear dynamics of output and unemployment in the US. *Journal of Applied Econometrics* (forthcoming).

Amemiya, T. (1985). *Advanced Econometrics.* Cambridge, MA: Harvard University Press.

Aneuryn-Evans, G., and A.S. Deaton (1980). Testing linear versus logarithmic regression models. *Review of Economic Studies* 47, 275–91.

Atkinson, A. (1970). A method for discriminating between models (with discussion). *Journal of the Royal Statistical Society, B* B32, 323–53.

Bahadur, R.R. (1960). Stochastic comparison of tests. *Annals of Mathematics and Statistics.* 31, 276–95.

Bahadur, R.R. (1967). Rates of convergence of estimates and test statistics. *Annals of Mathematics and Statistics* 38, 303–24.

Barro, R. (1977). Unanticipated money growth and unemployment in the United States. *American Economic Review* 67, 101–15.

Beran, R. (1988). Prepivoting test statistics: A bootstrap view of asymptotic refinements. *Journal of the American Statistical Association* 83, 403.

Bernanke, B., H. Bohn, and P. Reiss (1988). Alternative nonnested specification tests of time-series investment models. *Journal of Econometrics* 37, 293–326.

Chao, J.C., and N.R. Swanson (1997). Tests of nonnested hypotheses in nonstationary regressions with an application to modeling industrial production. Working Paper, Department of Economics, Pennsylvania State University.

Chow, G.C. (1981). A comparison of the information and posterior probability criteria for model selection. *Journal of Econometrics* 16, 21–33.

Coulibaly, N., and B. Brorsen (1998). A Monte Carlo sampling approach to testing nonnested hypotheses: Monte Carlo results. *Econometric Reviews* 195–209.

Cox, D. (1961). Tests of separate families of hypothesis. *Proceedings of the Fourth Berkeley Symposium on Mathematical Statistics and Probability.*

Cox, D. (1962). Further results on tests of separate families of hypothesis. *Journal of Royal Statistical Society* B24, 406–24.

Dastoor, N. (1981). A note on the interpretation of the Cox procedure for nonnested hypotheses. *Economics Letters* 8, 113–19.

Dastoor, N.K. (1983). Some aspects of testing nonnested hypotheses. *Journal of Econometrics* 21, 213–28.

Davidson, R., and J. MacKinnon (1981). Several tests for model specification in the presence of alternative hypotheses. *Econometrica* 49, 781–93.

Davidson, R., and J.G. MacKinnon (1982). Some nonnested hypothesis tests and the relations among them. *Review of Economic Studies* 49, 551–65.

Davidson, R., and J.G. MacKinnon (1985). Testing linear and loglinear regressions against Box–Cox alternatives. *Canadian Journal of Economics* 18, 499–517.

Davies, R.B. (1977). Hypothesis testing when a nuisance parameter is present only under the alternative. *Biometrika* 64(2), 247–54.

Deaton, A.S. (1982). Model selection procedures, or, does the consumption function exist? In G.C. Show, and P. Corsi (eds.) *Evaluating the Reliability of Macroeconomic Models*, pp. 43–65. New York: Wiley.

Dixit, A.V., and R.S. Pindyck (1994). *Investment Under Uncertainty*. Chichester, UK: Princeton University Press.

Duncan, A., and M. Weeks (1998). Nonnested models of labour supply with discrete choices. Working Paper, Department of Economics, University of York.

Efron, B. (1979). Bootstrap methods: Another look at the jackknife. *Annals of Statistics* 7, 1–26.

Engle, R., D. Hendry, and J. Richard (1983). Exogeneity. *Econometrica* 51, 277–304.

Ericsson, N. (1983). Asymptotic properties of instrumental variables statistics for testing nonnested hypotheses. *Review of Economic Studies* 50, 287–304.

Fisher, G., and M. McAleer (1979). On the interpretation of the Cox test in econometrics. *Economic Letters* 4, 145–50.

Fisher, G.R., and M. McAleer (1981). Alternative procedures and associated tests of significance for nonnested hypotheses. *Journal of Econometrics* 16, 103–19.

Friedman, M., and D. Meiselman (1963). The relative stability of monetary velocity and the investment multiplier in the United States 1897–1958. In *Stabilization Policies*. Englewood Cliffs, NJ: Commission on Money and Credit Research Study.

Ghysels, E., and A. Hall (1990). Testing nonnested Euler conditions with quadrature based method of approximation. *Journal of Econometrics* 46, 273–308.

Godfrey, L.G. (1983). Testing nonnested models after estimation by instrumental variables or least squares. *Econometrica* 51(2), 355–65.

Godfrey, L.G., and M.H. Pesaran (1983). Tests of nonnested regression models: Small sample adjustments and Monte Carlo evidence. *Journal of Econometrics* 21, 133–54.

Godfrey, L.G., and M. Wickens (1981). Testing linear and loglinear regressions for functional form. *Review of Economic Studies* 48, 487–96.

Gouriéroux, C. (1982). Asymptotic comparison of tests for nonnested hypotheses by Bahadur's A.R.E. Discussion Paper 8215, CEPREMAP, Paris.

Gouriéroux, C., and A. Monfort (1994). Testing nonnested hypotheses. In R.F. Engle, and D.L. McFadden (eds.) *Handbook of Econometrics, Volume 4*. Oxford: Elsevier.

Gouriéroux, C., and A. Monfort (1995). Testing, encompassing, and simulating dynamic econometric models. *Econometric Theory* 11, 195–228.

Gouriéroux, C., A. Monfort, and A. Trognon (1983). Testing nested or nonnested hypotheses. *Journal of Econometrics* 21, 83–115.

Granger, C.W.J., M.L. King, and H. White (1995). Comments on testing economic theories and the use of model selection criteria. *Journal of Econometrics* 67, 173–87.

Granger, C.W.J., and M.H. Pesaran (2000). A decision theoretic approach to forecast evaluation. In W.S. Chan, W.K. Li, and H. Tong (eds.), *Statistics and Finance: An Interface.* London: Imperial College Press.

Grasa, A.A. (1989). *Econometric Model Selection: A New Approach.* Spain: Kluwer Academic Publishers.

Hall, P. (1986). On the number of bootstrap simulations required to construct a confidence interval. *The Annals of Statistics* 14(4).

Hall, P. (1988). Theoretical comparison of bootstrap confidence intervals. *Annals of Statistics* 16, 927–53.

Hendry, D.F. (1993). *Econometrics: Alchemy or Science?* Oxford: Blackwell Publishers.

Hinkely, D. (1988). Bootstrap methods. *Journal of the Royal Statistical Society, Series B* 50, 321–37.

Jeong, J., and G. Maddala (1993). A perspective on application of bootstrap methods in econometrics. *Handbook of Statistics* 11, 573–605.

Jorgenson, D.W., and C.D. Siebert (1968). A comparison of alternative theories of corporate investment behavior. *American Economic Review* 58, 681–712.

Kapetanios, G., and M. Weeks (1999). Nonnested models and the likelihood ratio statistic: A comparison of simulation and bootstrap-based tests. Department of Applied Economics Working Paper, University of Cambridge.

Kent, J. (1986). The underlying structure of nonnested hypothesis tests. *Biometrika* 7, 333–43.

King, M.L. (1983). Testing for autoregressive against moving average errors in the linear regression model. *Journal of Econometrics* 21, 35–51.

Kullback, S. (1959). *Information Theory and Statistics.* New York: Wiley.

Lavergne, P. (1998). Selection of regressors in econometrics: Parametric and nonparametric methods. *Econometric Reviews* 17(3), 227–73.

Leamer, E.E. (1983). Model choice and specification analysis. In Z. Griliches, and M.D. Intriligator (eds.) *Handbook of Econometrics Volume 1.* University of California, LA: North-Holland Publishing Company.

Li, H., and G. Maddala (1996). Bootstrapping time series models. *Econometric Reviews* 15(2), 115–58.

Linhart, H., and W. Zucchini (1986). *Model Selection.* New York: Wiley and Sons.

Maddala, G.S.E. (1981). Model selection. Special Issue of *Journal of Econometrics* 16(1).

McAleer, M. (1983). Exact tests of a model against nonnested alternative. *Biometrika* 70, 285–88.

McAleer, M. (1995). The significance of testing empirical nonnested models. *Journal of Econometrics* 67, 149–71.

McAleer, M., and S. Ling (1998). A nonnested test for the GARCH and E-GARCH models. Working Paper, Department of Economics, University of Western Australia.

McAleer, M., and M.H. Pesaran (1986). Statistical inference in nonnested econometric models. *Applied Mathematics and Computation* 20, 271–311.

McAleer, M.G., G. Fisher, and P. Volker (1982). Separate misspecified regressions and U.S. long run demand for money function. *Review of Economics and Statistics* 64, 572–83.

McAleer, M.J., M.H. Pesaran, and A.K. Bera (1990). Alternative approaches to testing nonnested models with autocorrelated disturbances: An application to models of U.S. unemployment. *Communications in Statistics* series A(19), 3619–44.

Mizon, G.E., and J.F. Richard (1986). The encompassing principle and its application to nonnested hypotheses. *Econometrica* 54, 657–78.

Orme, C. (1994). Nonnested tests for discrete choice models. Working Paper, Department of Economics, University of York.

Pereira, B.D.B. (1984). On the choice of a Weibull model. *Journal of the Inter American Statistical Institute* 26, 157–63.

Pesaran, M.H. (1974). On the general problem of model selection. *Review of Economic Studies* 41, 153–71.

Pesaran, M.H. (1981). Pitfalls of testing nonnested hypotheses by the Lagrange multiplier method. *Journal of Econometrics* 17, 323–31.

Pesaran, M.H. (1982a). Comparison of local power of altenative tests of nonnested regression models. *Econometrica*.

Pesaran, M.H. (1982b). A critique of the proposed tests of the natural rate-rational expectations hypothesis. *The Economic Journal* 92, 529–54.

Pesaran, M.H. (1984). Asymptotic power comparisons of tests of separate parametric families by Bahadur's approach. *Biometrika* 71(2), 245–52.

Pesaran, M.H. (1987). Global and partial nonnested hypotheses and asymptotic local power. *Econometric Theory* 3, 69–97.

Pesaran, M.H., and S. Deaton (1978). Testing nonnested nonlinear regression models. *Econometrica* 46, 677–94.

Pesaran, M.H., and B. Pesaran (1993). A simulation approach to the problem of computing Cox's statistic for testing nonnested models. *Journal of Econometrics* 57, 377–92.

Pesaran, M.H., and B. Pesaran (1995). A nonnested test of level differences versus log-differenced stationary models. *Econometric Reviews* 14(2), 213–27.

Pesaran, M.H., and S. Potter (1997). A floor and ceiling model of US output. *Journal of Economic Dynamics and Control* 21(4–5), 661–96.

Sawyer, K.R. (1983). Testing separate families of hypotheses: An information criterion. *Journal of the Royal Statistical Society B* 45, 89–99.

Sawyer, K.R. (1984). Multiple hypothesis testing. *Royal Statistical Society B* 46(3), 419–24.

Schwarz, G. (1978). Estimating the dimension of a model. *Annals of Statistics* 6, 461–4.

Smith, M.A., and G.S. Maddala (1983). Multiple model testing for nonnested heteroskedastic censored regression models. *Journal of Econometrics* 21, 71–81.

Smith, M.D., and D.J. Smyth (1991). Multiple and pairwise nonnested tests of the influence of taxes on money demand. *Journal of Applied Econometrics* 6, 17–30.

Smith, R.J. (1992). Nonnested tests for competing models estimated by generalized method of moments. *Econometrica* 60, 973–80.

Smith, R.J. (1993). Consistent tests for the encompassing hypothesis. Document de Travail No. 9403, INSEE, Paris.

Vinod, H. (1993). Bootstrap methods: Applications in econometrics. *Handbook of Statistics* 11, 629–61.

Vuong, Q.H. (1989). Likelihood ratio tests for model selection and nonnested hypothesis. *Econometrica* 57(2), 307–33.

Walker, A.M. (1967). Some tests of separate families of hypotheses in time series analysis. *Biometrika* 54, 39–68.

Weeks, M. (1996). Testing the binomial and multinomial choice models using Cox's nonnested test. *Journal of the American Statistical Association (Papers and Proceedings)*.

White, H. (1982). Regularity conditions for Cox's test of nonnested hypothesis. *Journal of Econometrics* 19, 301–18.

Zellner, A. (1971). *An Introduction to Bayesian Inference in Econometrics*. New York: John Wiley and Sons.

Spatial Econometrics

*Luc Anselin**

1 Introduction

Spatial econometrics is a subfield of econometrics that deals with spatial interaction (*spatial autocorrelation*) and spatial structure (*spatial heterogeneity*) in regression models for cross-sectional and panel data (Paelinck and Klaassen, 1979; Anselin, 1988a). Such a focus on location and spatial interaction has recently gained a more central place not only in applied but also in theoretical econometrics. In the past, models that explicitly incorporated "space" (or geography) were primarily found in specialized fields such as regional science, urban, and real estate economics and economic geography (e.g. recent reviews in Anselin, 1992a; Anselin and Florax, 1995a; Anselin and Rey, 1997; Pace *et al.*, 1998). However, more recently, spatial econometric methods have increasingly been applied in a wide range of empirical investigations in more traditional fields of economics as well, including, among others, studies in demand analysis, international economics, labor economics, public economics and local public finance, and agricultural and environmental economics.[1]

This new attention to specifying, estimating, and testing for the presence of spatial interaction in the mainstream of applied and theoretical econometrics can be attributed to two major factors. One is a growing interest within theoretical economics in *models* that move towards an explicit accounting for the interaction of an economic agent with other heterogeneous agents in the system. These new theoretical frameworks of "interacting agents" model strategic interaction, social norms, neighborhood effects, copy-catting, and other peer group effects, and raise interesting questions about how the individual interactions can lead to emergent collective behavior and aggregate patterns. Models used to estimate such phenomena require the specification of how the magnitude of a variable of interest (say crime) at a given location (say a census tract) is determined by the values of the same variable at other locations in the system (such as neighboring census tracts). If such a dependence exists, it is referred to as spatial autocorrelation. A second driver behind the increased interest in spatial econometric techniques is the need to handle spatial *data*. This has been stimulated by the explosive diffusion of geographic information systems (GIS) and the associated availability of geocoded data (i.e. data sets that contain the location of the observational units). There is a growing recognition that standard econometric techniques often fail in the presence of spatial autocorrelation, which is commonplace in geographic (cross-sectional) data sets.[2]

Historically, spatial econometrics originated as an identifiable field in Europe in the early 1970s because of the need to deal with sub-country data in regional econometric models (e.g. Paelinck and Klaassen, 1979). In general terms, spatial econometrics can be characterized as the set of techniques to deal with methodological concerns that follow from the explicit consideration of *spatial effects*, specifically spatial autocorrelation and spatial heterogeneity. This yields four broad areas of interest: (i) the formal *specification* of spatial effects in econometric models; (ii) the *estimation* of models that incorporate spatial effects; (iii) specification *tests* and diagnostics for the presence of spatial effects; and (iv) spatial *prediction* (interpolation). In this brief review chapter, I will focus on the first three concerns, since they fall within the central preoccupation of econometric methodology.

The remainder of the chapter is organized as follows. In Section 2, I outline some foundations and definitions. In Section 3, the specification of spatial regression models is treated, including the incorporation of spatial dependence in panel data models and models with qualitative variables. Section 4 focuses on estimation and Section 5 on specification testing. In Section 6, some practical implementation and software issues are addressed. Concluding remarks are formulated in Section 7.

2   FOUNDATIONS

2.1   Spatial autocorrelation

In a regression context, spatial effects pertain to two categories of specifications. One deals with spatial dependence, or its weaker expression, *spatial autocorrelation*, and the other with *spatial heterogeneity*.[3] The latter is simply structural instability, either in the form of non-constant error variances in a regression model (heteroskedasticity) or in the form of variable regression coeffcients. Most of the methodological issues related to spatial heterogeneity can be tackled by means of the standard econometric toolbox.[4] Therefore, given the space constraints for this chapter, the main focus of attention in the remainder will be on spatial dependence.

The formal framework used for the statistical analysis of spatial autocorrelation is a so-called spatial stochastic process (also often referred to as a spatial random field), or a collection of random variables y, indexed by location i,

$$\{y_i, i \in D\}, \tag{14.1}$$

where the index set D is either a continuous surface or a finite set of discrete locations. (See Cressie (1993), for technical details.) Since each random variable is "tagged" by a location, spatial autocorrelation can be formally expressed by the moment condition,

$$cov[y_i, y_j] = E[y_i y_j] - E[y_i] \cdot E[y_j] \neq 0, \quad \text{for } i \neq j \qquad (14.2)$$

where i, j refer to individual observations (locations) and y_i (y_j) is the value of a random variable of interest at that location. This covariance becomes meaningful from a spatial perspective when the particular configuration of nonzero i, j pairs has an interpretation in terms of spatial structure, spatial interaction or the spatial arrangement of the observations. For example, this would be the case when one is interested in modeling the extent to which technological innovations in a county spill over into neighboring counties.

The spatial covariance can be modeled in three basic ways. First, one can specify a particular functional form for a spatial stochastic process generating the random variable in (14.1), from which the covariance structure would follow. Second, one can model the covariance structure directly, typically as a function of a small number of parameters (with any given covariance structure corresponding to a class of spatial stochastic processes). Third, one can leave the covariance unspecified and estimate it nonparametrically.[5] I will review each of these approaches in turn.

SPATIAL STOCHASTIC PROCESS MODELS

The most often used approach to formally express spatial autocorrelation is through the specification of a functional form for the spatial stochastic process (14.1) that relates the value of a random variable at a given location to its value at other locations. The covariance structure then follows from the nature of the process. In parallel to time series analysis, spatial stochastic processes are categorized as spatial autoregressive (SAR) and spatial moving average (SMA) processes, although there are several important differences between the cross-sectional and time series contexts.[6]

For example, for an $N \times 1$ vector of random variables, y, observed across space, and an $N \times 1$ vector of iid random errors ε, a simultaneous spatial autoregressive (SAR) process is defined as

$$(y - \mu i) = \rho W(y - \mu i) + \varepsilon, \quad \text{or} \quad (y - \mu i) = (I - \rho W)^{-1} \varepsilon, \qquad (14.3)$$

where μ is the (constant) mean of y_i, i is an $N \times 1$ vector of ones, and ρ is the spatial autoregressive parameter.

Before considering the structure of this process more closely, note the presence of the $N \times N$ matrix W, which is referred to as a *spatial weights matrix*. For each location in the system, it specifies which of the other locations in the system affect the value at that location. This is necessary, since in contrast to the unambiguous notion of a "shift" along the time axis (such as y_{t-1} in an autoregressive model), there is no corresponding concept in the spatial domain, especially when observations are located irregularly in space.[7] Instead of the notion of shift, a *spatial lag operator* is used, which is a weighted average of random variables at "neighboring" locations.[8]

The spatial weights crucially depend on the definition of a neighborhood set for each observation. This is obtained by selecting for each location i (as the row) the neighbors as the columns corresponding to nonzero elements w_{ij} in a fixed (nonstochastic) and positive $N \times N$ spatial weights matrix W.[9] A spatial lag for y at i then follows as

$$[Wy]_i = \sum_{j=1,\ldots,N} w_{ij} \cdot y_j, \tag{14.4}$$

or, in matrix form, as

$$Wy. \tag{14.5}$$

Since for each i the matrix elements w_{ij} are only nonzero for those $j \in S_i$ (where S_i is the neighborhood set), only the matching y_j are included in the lag. For ease of interpretation, the elements of the spatial weights matrix are typically row-standardized, such that for each i, $\Sigma_j w_{ij} = 1$. Consequently, the spatial lag may be interpreted as a weighted average (with the w_{ij} being the weights) of the neighbors, or as a spatial smoother.

It is important to note that the elements of the weights matrix are nonstochastic and exogenous to the model. Typically, they are based on the geographic arrangement of the observations, or contiguity. Weights are nonzero when two locations share a common boundary, or are within a given distance of each other. However, this notion is perfectly general and alternative specifications of the spatial weights (such as economic distance) can be considered as well (Anselin, 1980, ch. 8; Case, Rosen, and Hines, 1993; Pinkse and Slade, 1998).

The constraints imposed by the weights structure (the zeros in each row), together with the specific form of the spatial process (autoregressive or moving average) determine the variance–covariance matrix for y as a function of two parameters, the variance σ^2 and the spatial coefficient, ρ. For the SAR structure in (14.3), this yields (since $E[y - \mu i] = 0$)

$$\text{cov}[(y - \mu i), (y - \mu i)] = E[(y - \mu i)(y - \mu i)'] = \sigma^2[(I - \rho W)'(I - \rho W)]^{-1}. \tag{14.6}$$

This is a full matrix, which implies that shocks at any location affect all other locations, through a so-called *spatial multiplier* effect (or, global interaction).[10]

A major distinction between processes in space compared to the time domain is that even with iid error terms ε_i, the diagonal elements in (14.6) are not constant.[11] Furthermore, the heteroskedasticity depends on the neighborhood structure embedded in the spatial weights matrix W. Consequently, the process in y is not covariance-stationary. Stationarity is only obtained in very rare cases, for example on regular lattice structures when each observation has an identical weights structure, but this is of limited practical use. This lack of stationarity has important implications for the types of central limit theorems (CLTs) and laws of large numbers (LLNs) that need to be invoked to obtain asymptotic properties for estimators and specification test, a point that has not always been recognized in the literature.

Direct representation

A second commonly used approach to the formal specification of spatial autocorrelation is to express the elements of the variance–covariance matrix in a parsimonious fashion as a "direct" function of a small number of parameters and one or more exogenous variables. Typically, this involves an inverse function of some distance metric, for example,

$$\text{cov}[\varepsilon_i, \varepsilon_j] = \sigma^2 f(d_{ij}, \varphi), \tag{14.7}$$

where ε_i and ε_j are regression disturbance terms, σ^2 is the error variance, d_{ij} is the distance separating observations (locations) i and j, and f is a distance decay function such that $\frac{\partial f}{\partial d} < 0$ and $|f(d_{ij}, \varphi)| \leq 1$, with $\varphi \in \Phi$ as a $p \times 1$ vector of parameters on an open subset Φ of R^p. This form is closely related to the variogram model used in geostatistics, although with stricter assumptions regarding stationarity and isotropy. Using (14.7) for individual elements, the full error covariance matrix follows as

$$E[\varepsilon\varepsilon'] = \sigma^2 \Omega(d_{ij}, \varphi), \tag{14.8}$$

where, because of the scaling factor σ^2, the matrix $\Omega(d_{ij}, \varphi)$ must be a positive definite spatial correlation matrix, with $\omega_{ii} = 1$ and $|\omega_{ij}| \leq 1$, $\forall\ i, j$.[12] Note that, in contrast to the variance for the spatial autoregressive model, the direct representation model does not induce heteroskedasticity.

In spatial econometrics, models of this type have been used primarily in the analysis of urban housing markets, e.g. in Dubin (1988, 1992), and Basu and Thibodeau (1998). While this specification has a certain intuition, in the sense that it incorporates an explicit notion of spatial clustering as a function of the distance separating two observations (i.e. positive spatial correlation), it is also fraught with a number of estimation and identification problems (Anselin, 2000a).

Nonparametric approaches

A nonparametric approach to estimating the spatial covariance matrix does not require an explicit spatial process or functional form for the distance decay. This is common in the case of panel data, when the time dimension is (considerably) greater than the cross-sectional dimension ($T \gg N$) and the "spatial" covariance is estimated from the sample covariance for the residuals of each set of location pairs (e.g. in applications of Zellner's SUR estimator; see Chapter 5 by Fiebig in this volume).

Applications of this principle to spatial autocorrelation are variants of the well known Newey–West (1987) heteroskedasticity and autocorrelation consistent covariance matrix and have been used in the context of generalized methods of moments (GMM) estimators of spatial regression models (see Section 4.3). Conley (1996) suggested a covariance estimator based on a sequence of weighted averages of sample autocovariances computed for subsets of observation pairs that fall within a given distance band (or spatial window). Although not presented as such, this has a striking similarity to the nonparametric estimation of a semi-variogram in geostatistics (see, e.g. Cressie, 1993, pp. 69–70), but the assumptions of stationarity and isotropy required in the GMM approach are stricter than those needed in variogram estimation. In a panel data setting, Driscoll and Kraay (1998) use a similar idea, but avoid having to estimate the spatial covariances by distance bands. This is accomplished by using only the cross-sectional averages (for each time period) of the moment conditions, and by relying on asymptotics in the time dimension to yield an estimator for the spatial covariance structure.

2.2   Aymptotics in spatial stochastic processes

As in time series analysis, the properties of estimators and tests for spatial series are derived from the asymptotics for stochastic processes. However, these properties are not simply extensions to two dimensions of the time series results. A number of complicating factors are present and to date some formal results for the spatial dependence case are still lacking. While an extensive treatment of this topic is beyond the scope of the current chapter, three general comments are in order. First, the intuition behind the asymptotics is fairly straightforward in that regularity conditions are needed to limit the extent of spatial dependence (memory) and heterogeneity of the spatial series in order to obtain the proper (uniform) laws of large numbers and central limit theorems to establish consistency and asymptotic normality. In this context, it is important to keep in mind that both SAR and SMA processes yield heteroskedastic variances, so that the application of results for dependent *stationary* series are not applicable.[13] In addition to the usual moment conditions that are similar in spirit to those for heterogeneous dependent processes in time (e.g. Pötscher and Prucha, 1997), specific spatial conditions will translate into constraints on the spatial weights and on the parameter space for the spatial coefficients (for some specific examples, see, e.g. Anselin and Kelejian, 1997; Kelejian and Prucha, 1999b; Pinkse and Slade, 1998; Pinkse, 2000). In practice, these conditions are likely to be satisfied by most spatial weights that are based on simple contiguity, but this is not necessarily the case for general weights, such as those based on economic distance.

A second distinguishing characteristic of asymptotics in space is that the limit may be approached in two different ways, referred to as *increasing domain* asymptotics and *infill* asymptotics.[14] The former consists of a sampling structure where new "observations" are added at the edges (boundary points), similar to the underlying asymptotics in time series analysis. Infill asymptotics are appropriate when the spatial domain is bounded, and new observations are added in between existing ones, generating a increasingly denser surface. Many results for increasing domain asymptotics are not directly applicable to infill asymptotics (Lahiri, 1996). In most applications of spatial econometrics, the implied structure is that of an increasing domain.

Finally, for spatial processes that contain spatial weights, the asymptotics require the use of CLT and LLN for triangular arrays (Davidson, 1994, chs. 19, 24). This is caused by the fact that for the boundary elements the "sample" weights matrix changes as new data points are added (i.e. the new data points change the connectedness structure for existing data points).[15] Again, this is an additional degree of complexity, which is not found in time series models.

3   SPATIAL REGRESSION MODELS

3.1   Spatial lag and spatial error models

In the standard linear regression model, spatial dependence can be incorporated in two distinct ways: as an additional regressor in the form of a spatially lagged dependent variable (Wy), or in the error structure ($E[\varepsilon_i\varepsilon_j] \neq 0$). The former is referred to as a *spatial lag* model and is appropriate when the focus of interest is the assessment of the existence and strength of spatial interaction. This is interpreted as substantive spatial dependence in the sense of being directly related to a *spatial model* (e.g. a model that incorporates spatial interaction, yardstick competition, etc.). Spatial dependence in the regression disturbance term, or a *spatial error* model is referred to as nuisance dependence. This is appropriate when the concern is with correcting for the potentially biasing influence of the spatial autocorrelation, due to the use of *spatial data* (irrespective of whether the model of interest is spatial or not).

Formally, a spatial lag model, or a mixed regressive, spatial autoregressive model is expressed as

$$y = \rho Wy + X\beta + \varepsilon, \qquad (14.9)$$

where ρ is a spatial autoregressive coefficient, ε is a vector of error terms, and the other notation is as before.[16] Unlike what holds for the time series counterpart of this model, the spatial lag term Wy is correlated with the disturbances, even when the latter are iid. This can be seen from the reduced form of (14.9),

$$y = (I - \rho W)^{-1}X\beta + (I - \rho W)^{-1}\varepsilon, \qquad (14.10)$$

in which each inverse can be expanded into an infinite series, including both the explanatory variables and the error terms at all locations (the spatial multiplier). Consequently, the spatial lag term must be treated as an endogenous variable and proper estimation methods must account for this endogeneity (OLS will be biased and inconsistent due to the simultaneity bias).

A spatial error model is a special case of a regression with a non-spherical error term, in which the off-diagonal elements of the covariance matrix express the structure of spatial dependence. Consequently, OLS remains unbiased, but it is no longer efficient and the classical estimators for standard errors will be biased. The spatial structure can be specified in a number of different ways, and (except for the non-parametric approaches) results in a error variance–covariance matrix of the form

$$E[\varepsilon\varepsilon'] = \Omega(\theta), \qquad (14.11)$$

where θ is a vector of parameters, such as the coefficients in an SAR error process.[17]

3.2 Spatial dependence in panel data models

When observations are available across space as well as over time, the additional dimension allows the estimation of the full covariance of one type of association, using the other dimension to provide the asymptotics (e.g. in SUR models with $N \ll T$). However, as in the pure cross-sectional case, there is insufficient information in the NT observations to estimate the complete $(NT)^2$ covariance matrix $\mathrm{cov}[y_{it}, y_{js}] \neq 0$, (with $i \neq j$ and $t \neq s$) without imposing some structure. For small N and large T, the asymptotics in the time domain can be exploited to obtain a nonparametric estimate of cross-sectional dependence, while time dependence must be parameterized. Similarly, for large N and small T, the asymptotics in the spatial domain can be exploited to yield a nonparametric estimate of serial (time) dependence, while spatial dependence must be parameterized. As in the pure cross-sectional case, the latter requires the use of a spatial weights matrix. In each of these situations, asymptotics are only needed in one of the dimensions while the other can be treated as fixed.

When both spatial as well as serial dependence are parameterized, a range of specifications can be considered, allowing different combinations of the two. For ease of exposition, assume that the observations are stacked by time period, i.e. they can be considered as T time slices of N cross-sectional units. Restricting attention to "lag" dependence, and with $f(z)$ as a generic designation for the regressors (which may be lagged in time and/or space), four types of models can be distinguished.

1. *pure space-recursive*, in which the dependence pertains to neighboring locations in a different period, or,

$$y_{it} = \gamma[Wy_{t-1}]_i + f(z) + \varepsilon_{it}, \tag{14.12}$$

where, using the same notational convention as before, $[Wy_{t-1}]_i$ is the ith element of the spatial lag vector applied to the observations on the dependent variable in the previous time period (using an $N \times N$ spatial weights matrix for the cross-sectional units).

2. *time–space recursive*, in which the dependence relates to the same location as well as the neighboring locations in another period, or,

$$y_{it} = \lambda y_{it-1} + \gamma[Wy_{t-1}]_i + f(z) + \varepsilon_{it} \tag{14.13}$$

3. *time–space simultaneous*, with both a time-wise and a spatially lagged dependent variable, or,

$$y_{it} = \lambda y_{it-1} + \rho[Wy_t]_i + f(z) + \varepsilon_{it} \tag{14.14}$$

where $[Wy_t]_i$ is the ith element of the spatial lag vector in the same time period.

4. *time–space dynamic*, with all forms of dependence, or,

$$y_{it} = \lambda y_{it-1} + \rho[\mathbf{W}\mathbf{y}_t]_i + \gamma[\mathbf{W}\mathbf{y}_{t-1}]_i + f(z) + \varepsilon_{it}. \qquad (14.15)$$

In order to estimate the parameters of the time–space simultaneous model, asymptotics are needed in the cross-sectional dimension, while for the time–space dynamic model, asymptotics are needed in both dimensions. For the other models, the type of asymptotics required are determined by the dependence structure in the error terms. For example, the pure space-recursive model with iid errors satisfies the assumptions of the classical linear model and can be estimated by means of OLS.

Spatial lag and spatial error dependence can be introduced into the cross-sectional dimension of traditional panel data models in a straightforward way. For example, in a spatial SUR model, both autoregressive as well as regression parameters are allowed to vary by time period, in combination with a nonparametric serial covariance. The spatial lag formulation of such a model would be (in the same notation as before):

$$y_{it} = \rho_t[\mathbf{W}\mathbf{y}_t]_i + x'_{it}\beta_t + \varepsilon_{it} \qquad (14.16)$$

with $\text{var}[\varepsilon_{it}] = \sigma_t^2$ and $E[\varepsilon_{it}\varepsilon_{is}] = \sigma_{ts}$.[18]

An important issue to consider when incorporating spatial dependence in panel data models is the extent to which fixed effects may be allowed. Since the estimation of the spatial process models requires asymptotics in the cross-sectional domain ($N \rightarrow \infty$), fixed effects (i.e. a dummy variable for each location) would suffer from the incidental parameter problem and no consistent estimator exists. Hence, fixed cross-sectional effects are incompatible with spatial processes and instead a random effects specification must be considered.

3.3   Spatial dependence in models for qualitative data

Empirical analysis of interacting agents requires models that incorporate spatial dependence for discrete dependent variables, such as counts or binary outcomes (Brock and Durlauf, 1995). This turns out to be quite complex and continues to be an active area of research. While an extensive discussion of the technical aspects associated with spatial discrete choice models is beyond the scope of the current chapter, the salient issues may be illustrated with a spatial version of the probit model, which has recently received considerable attention.[19]

The point of departure is the familiar expression for a linear model in a latent (unobserved) dependent variable y_i^*

$$y_i^* = x'_i\beta + \varepsilon_i, \qquad (14.17)$$

where ε_i is a random variable for which a given distribution is assumed (e.g. the normal for the probit model). The realization of y_i^* is observed in the form of discrete events, $y_i = 1$ for $y_i^* \geq 0$, and $y_i = 0$ for $y_i^* < 0$. The discrete events are related to the underlying probability model through the error term, for example, $y_i^* \geq 0$ implies $-x_i'\beta < \varepsilon_i$, and, therefore,

$$E[y_i] = P[y_i = 1] = \Phi[x_i'\beta], \tag{14.18}$$

where Φ is the cumulative distribution function for the standard normal.

Spatial autocorrelation can be introduced into this model in the form of a spatial autoregressive process for the error term ε_i in (14.17), or

$$\varepsilon_i = \lambda \sum_j w_{ij}\varepsilon_j + u_i, \tag{14.19}$$

where λ is an autoregressive parameter, the w_{ij} are the elements in the ith row of a spatial weights matrix, and u_i may be assumed to be iid standard normal. As a consequence of the spatial multiplier in the autoregressive specification, the random error at each location now becomes a function of the random errors at all other locations as well. Its distribution is multivariate normal with $N \times N$ variance–covariance matrix

$$E[\varepsilon\varepsilon'] = [(I - \lambda W)'(I - \lambda W)]^{-1}. \tag{14.20}$$

As pointed out above, besides being nondiagonal, (14.20) is also heteroskedastic. Consequently, the usual inequality conditions that are at the basis of (14.18) no longer hold, since each location has a different variance. Moreover, $P[-x_i'\beta < \varepsilon_i]$ can no longer be derived from the univariate standard normal distribution, but rather must be expressed explicitly as the marginal distribution of a N-dimensional multivariate normal vector, whose variance–covariance matrix contains off-diagonal elements that are a function of the autoregressive parameter λ. This is non-standard and typically not analytically tractable, which greatly complicates estimation and specification testing. Similar issues are faced in the spatial lag model for a latent variable.[20]

4 ESTIMATION

4.1 Maximum likelihood estimation

Maximum likelihood (ML) estimation of spatial lag and spatial error regression models was first outlined by Ord (1975).[21] The point of departure is an assumption of normality for the error terms. The joint likelihood then follows from the multivariate normal distribution for y. Unlike what holds for the classic regression model, the joint loglikelihood for a spatial regression does not equal the sum of the loglikelihoods associated with the individual observations. This is due to the two-directional nature of the spatial dependence, which results in a Jacobian term that is the determinant of a full $N \times N$ matrix, e.g. $|I - \rho W|$.

For the SAR error model, the loglikelihood is based on the multivariate normal case, for example, as used in the general treatment of Magnus (1978). Since $\varepsilon \sim MVN(0, \Sigma)$, it follows that, with $\varepsilon = y - X\beta$ and $\Sigma = \sigma^2[(I - \lambda W)'(I - \lambda W)]^{-1}$,

$$\ln L = -(N/2) \ln (2\pi) - (N/2) \ln \sigma^2 + \ln |I - \lambda W|$$
$$-(1/2\sigma^2)(y - X\beta)'(I - \lambda W)'(I - \lambda W)(y - X\beta). \tag{14.21}$$

Closer inspection of the last term in (14.21) reveals that, conditional upon λ (the spatial autoregressive parameter), a maximization of the loglikelihood is equivalent to the minimization of the sum of squared residuals in a regression of a spatially filtered dependent variable $y^* = y - \lambda Wy$ on a set of spatially filtered explanatory variables $X^* = X - \lambda WX$. The first order conditions for $\hat{\beta}_{ML}$ indeed yield the familiar generalized least squares estimator:

$$\hat{\beta}_{ML} = [(X - \lambda WX)'(X - \lambda WX)]^{-1}(X - \lambda WX)'(y - \lambda Wy) \tag{14.22}$$

and, similarly, the ML estimator for σ^2 follows as:

$$\hat{\sigma}^2_{ML} = (e - \lambda We)'(e - \lambda We)/N \tag{14.23}$$

with $e = y - X\hat{\beta}_{ML}$. However, unlike the time series case, a consistent estimator for λ cannot be obtained from the OLS residuals and therefore the standard two-step FGLS approach does not apply.[22] Instead, the estimator for λ must be obtained from an explicit maximization of a concentrated likelihood function (for details, see Anselin, 1988a, ch. 6, and Anselin and Bera, 1998).

The loglikelihood for the spatial lag model is obtained using the same general principles (see Anselin, 1988, ch. 6 for details) and takes the form

$$\ln L = -(N/2) \ln (2\pi) - (N/2) \ln \sigma^2 + \ln |I - \rho W|$$
$$-(1/2\sigma^2)(y - \rho Wy - X\beta)'(y - \rho Wy - X\beta). \tag{14.24}$$

The minimization of the last term in (14.24) corresponds to OLS, but since this ignores the log Jacobian $\ln |I - \rho W|$, OLS is not a consistent estimator in this model. As in the spatial error model, there is no satisfactory two-step procedure and estimators for the parameters must be obtained from an explicit maximization of the likelihood. This is greatly simplified since both $\hat{\beta}_{ML}$ and $\hat{\sigma}^2_{ML}$ can be obtained conditional upon ρ from the first order conditions:

$$\hat{\beta}_{ML} = (X'X)^{-1}X'(y - \rho Wy), \tag{14.25}$$

or, with $\hat{\beta}_0 = (X'X)^{-1}X'y$, $e_0 = y - X\hat{\beta}_0$, $\hat{\beta}_L = (X'X)^{-1}X'Wy$, $e_L = y - X\hat{\beta}_L$,

$$\hat{\beta}_{ML} = \hat{\beta}_0 - \rho\hat{\beta}_L \tag{14.26}$$

and

$$\hat{\sigma}^2_{ML} = (e_0 - \rho e_L)'(e_0 - \rho e_L)/N. \tag{14.27}$$

This yields a concentrated loglikelihood in a single parameter, which is straightforward to optimize by means of direct search techniques (see Anselin (1980, 1988a) for derivations and details).

Both spatial lag and spatial error models are special cases of a more general specification that may include forms of heteroskedasticity as well. This also provides the basis for ML estimation of spatial SUR models with spatial lag or spatial error terms (Anselin, 1980, ch. 10). Similarly, ML estimation of error components models with spatial lag or spatial error terms can be implemented as well. Spatial models with discrete dependent variables are typically not estimated by means of ML, given the prohibitive nature of evaluating multiple integrals to determine the relevant marginal distributions.[23]

Finally, it is important to note that models with spatial dependence do not fit the classical framework (e.g. as outlined in Rao, 1973) under which the optimal properties (consistency, asymptotic efficiency, asymptotic normality) of ML estimators are established. This implies that these properties do not necessarily hold and that careful consideration must be given to the explicit formulation of regularity conditions. In general terms, aside from the usual restrictions on the variance and higher moments of the model variables, these conditions boil down to constraints on the range of dependence embodied in the spatial weights matrix.[24] In addition, to avoid singularity or explosive processes, the parameter space for the coefficient in a spatial process model is restricted to an interval other than the familiar −1, +1. For example, for an SAR process, the parameter space is $1/\omega_{min} < \rho < 1/\omega_{max}$, where ω_{min} and ω_{max} are the smallest (on the real line) and largest eigenvalues of the spatial weights matrix W. For row-standardized weights, $\omega_{max} = 1$, but $\omega_{min} > -1$, such that the lower bound on the parameter space is less than −1 (Anselin, 1980). This must be taken into account in practical implementations of estimation routines.

4.2   Spatial two-stage least squares

The endogeneity of the spatially lagged dependent variable can also be addressed by means of an instrumental variables or two-stage least squares (2SLS) approach (Anselin, 1980, 1988a, 1990; Kelejian and Robinson, 1993; Kelejian and Prucha, 1998). As demonstrated in Kelejian and Robinson (1993), the choice of an instrument for Wy follows from the conditional expectation in the reduced form (14.10),

$$E[y \mid X] = (I - \rho W)^{-1} X\beta = X\beta + \rho W X\beta + \rho^2 W^2 X\beta + \dots . \qquad (14.28)$$

Apart from the exogenous variables X (which are always instruments), this includes their spatial lags as well, suggesting WX as a set of instruments.

Under a set of reasonable assumptions that are easily satisfied when the spatial weights are based on contiguity, the spatial two-stage least squares estimator achieves the consistency and asymptotic normality properties of the standard 2SLS (see, e.g. the theorems spelled out in Schmidt, 1976).[25] A straightforward extension is the application of 3SLS to the spatial SUR model with a spatial lag (Anselin, 1988a, ch. 10).

4.3   Method of moments estimators

Recently, a number of approaches have been outlined to estimate the coefficients in a spatial error model as an application of general principles underlying the method of moments. Kelejian and Prucha (1999a) develop a set of moment conditions that yield estimation equations for the parameter of an SAR error model. Specifically, assuming an iid error vector u, the following three conditions readily follow

$$E[u'u/N] = \sigma^2$$

$$E[u'W'Wu/N] = \sigma^2(1/N)\text{tr}(W'W) \qquad (14.29)$$

$$E[u'Wu/N] = 0$$

where tr is the matrix trace operator. Replacing u by e − λWe (with e as the vector of OLS residuals) in (14.29) yields a system of three equations in the parameters λ, λ², and σ². Kelejian and Prucha (1999a) suggest the use of nonlinear least squares to obtain a consistent generalized moment estimator for λ from this system, which can then be used to obtain consistent estimators for the β in an FGLS approach. Since the λ is considered as a nuisance parameter, its significance (as a test for spatial autocorrelation) cannot be assessed, but its role is to provide a consistent estimator for the regression coefficients.[26]

A different approach is taken in the application of Hansen's (1982) generalized method of moments estimator (GMM) to spatial error autocorrelation in Conley (1996). This estimator is the standard minimizer of a quadratic form in the sample moment conditions, where the covariance matrix is obtained in nonparametric form as an application of the ideas of Newey and West (1987). Specifically, the spatial covariances are estimated from weighted averages of sample covariances for pairs of observations that are within a given distance band from each other. Note that this approach requires covariance stationarity, which is only satisfied for a restricted set of spatial processes (e.g. it does not apply to SAR error models).

Pinkse and Slade (1998) use a set of moment conditions to estimate a probit model with SAR errors. However, they focus on the induced heteroskedasticity of the process and do not explicitly deal with the spatial covariance structure.[27]

The relative efficiency of the new methods of moments approaches relative to the more traditional maximum likelihood techniques remains an area of active investigation.

4.4   Other estimation methods

A number of other approaches have been suggested to deal with the estimation of spatial regression models. An early technique is the so-called coding method, originally examined in Besag and Moran (1975).[28] This approach consists of selecting a subsample from the data such that the relevant neighbors are removed (a non-contiguous subsample). This in effect eliminates the simultaneity bias in the spatial lag model, but at the cost of converting the model to a conditional one and with a considerable reduction of the sample size (down to 20 percent of the original sample for irregular lattice data). The advantage of this approach is that standard methods may be applied (e.g. for discrete choice models). However, it is not an efficient procedure and considerable arbitrariness is involved in the selection of the coding scheme.

Another increasingly common approach consists of the application of computational estimators to spatial models. A recent example is the recursive importance sampling (RIS) estimator (Vijverberg, 1997) applied to the spatial probit model in Beron and Vijverberg (2000).

A considerable literature also exists on Bayesian estimation of spatial models, but a detailed treatment of this is beyond the current scope.

5   SPECIFICATION TESTS

5.1   Moran's I

The most commonly used specification test for spatial autocorrelation is derived from a statistic developed by Moran (1948) as the two-dimensional analog of a test for univariate time series correlation (see also Cliff and Ord, 1973). In matrix notation, Moran's I statistic is

$$I = [N/S_0)(e'We/e'e),\qquad(14.30)$$

with e as a vector of OLS residuals and $S_0 = \Sigma_i\Sigma_j w_{ij}$, a standardization factor that corresponds to the sum of the weights for the nonzero cross-products. The statistic shows a striking similarity to the familiar Durbin–Watson test.[29]

Moran's I test has been shown to be locally best invariant (King, 1981) and consistently outperforms other tests in terms of power in simulation experiments (for a recent review, see Anselin and Florax, 1995b). Its application has been extended to residuals in 2SLS regression in Anselin and Kelejian (1997), and to generalized residuals in probit models in Pinkse (2000). General formal conditions and proofs for the asymptotic normality of Moran's I in a wide range of regression models are given in Pinkse (1998) and Kelejian and Prucha (1999b). The consideration of Moran's I in conjunction with spatial heteroskedasticity is covered in Kelejian and Robinson (1998, 2000).

5.2   ML based tests

When spatial regression models are estimated by maximum likelihood, inference on the spatial autoregressive coefficients may be based on a Wald or asymptotic t-test (from the asymptotic variance matrix) or on a likelihood ratio test (see Anselin, 1988a, ch. 6; Anselin and Bera, 1998). Both approaches require that the alternative model (i.e. the spatial model) be estimated. In contrast, a series of test statistics based on the Lagrange Multiplier (LM) or Rao Score (RS) principle only require estimation of the model under the null. The LM/RS tests also allow for the distinction between a spatial error and a spatial lag alternative.[30]

An LM/RS test against a spatial error alternative was originally suggested by Burridge (1980) and takes the form

$$LM_{err} = [e'We/(e'e/N)]^2/[tr(W^2 + W'W)]. \qquad (14.31)$$

This statistic has an asymptotic $\chi^2(1)$ distribution and, apart from a scaling factor, corresponds to the square of Moran's I.[31] From several simulation experiments (Anselin and Rey, 1991; Anselin and Florax, 1995b) it follows that Moran's I has slightly better power than the LM_{err} test in small samples, but the performance of both tests becomes indistinguishable in medium and large size samples. The LM/RS test against a spatial lag alternative was outlined in Anselin (1988c) and takes the form

$$LM_{lag} = [e'Wy/(e'e/N)]^2/D, \qquad (14.32)$$

where $D = [(WX\beta)'(I - X(X'X)^{-1}X')(WX\beta)/\sigma^2] + tr(W^2 + W'W)$. This statistic also has an asymptotic $\chi^2(1)$ distribution.

Since both tests have power against the other alternative, it is important to take account of possible lag dependence when testing for error dependence and vice versa. This can be implemented by means of a joint test (Anselin, 1988c) or by constructing tests that are robust to the presence of local misspecification of the other form (Anselin et al., 1996).

The LM/RS principle can also be extended to more complex spatial alternatives, such as higher order processes, spatial error components and direct representation models (Anselin, 2000), to panel data settings (Anselin, 1988b), and to probit models (Pinkse, 1998, 2000; Pinkse and Slade, 1998). A common characteristic of the LM/RS tests against spatial alternatives is that they do not lend themselves readily to a formulation as an NR^2 expression based on an auxiliary regression. However, as recently shown in Baltagi and Li (2000a), it is possible to obtain tests for spatial lag and spatial error dependence in a linear regression model by means of Davidson and MacKinnon's (1988) double length artificial regression approach.

6   IMPLEMENTATION ISSUES

To date, spatial econometric methods are not found in the main commercial econometric and statistical software packages, although macro and scripting facilities may be used to implement some estimators (Anselin and Hudak, 1992). The only comprehensive software to handle both estimation and specification testing of spatial regression models is the special-purpose SpaceStat package (Anselin, 1992b, 1998). A narrower set of techniques, such as maximum likelihood estimation of spatial models is included in the Matlab routines of Pace and Barry (1998), and estimation of spatial error models is part of the S+Spatialstats add-on to S-Plus (MathSoft, 1996).[32]

In contrast to maximum likelihood estimation, method of moments and 2SLS can easily be implemented with standard software, provided that spatial lags can be computed. This requires the construction of a spatial weights matrix, which must often be derived from information in a geographic information system. Similarly, once a spatial lag can be computed, the LM/RS statistics are straightforward to implement.

The main practical problem is encountered in maximum likelihood estimation where the Jacobian determinant must be evaluated for every iteration in a nonlinear optimization procedure. The original solution to this problem was suggested by Ord (1975), who showed how the log Jacobian can be decomposed in terms that contain the eigenvalues of the weights matrix ω_i,

$$\ln|I - \rho W| = \sum_{i=1}^{n} \ln(1 - \rho\omega_i). \qquad (14.33)$$

This is easy to implement in a standard optimization routine by treating the individual elements in the sum as observations on an auxiliary term in the log-likelihood (see Anselin and Hudak, 1992). However, the computation of the eigenvalues quickly becomes numerically unstable for matrices of more than 1,000 observations. In addition, for large data sets this approach is inefficient in that it does not exploit the high degree of sparsity of the spatial weights matrix. Recently suggested solutions to this problem fall into two categories. Approximate solutions avoid the computation of the Jacobian determinant, but instead approximate it by a polynomial function or by means of simulation methods (e.g. Barry and Pace, 1999). Exact solutions are based on Cholesky or LU decomposition methods that exploit the sparsity of the weights (Pace and Barry, 1997a, 1997b), or use a characteristic polynomial approach (Smirnov and Anselin, 2000). While much progress has been made, considerable work remains to be done to develop efficient algorithms and data structures to allow for the analysis of very large spatial data sets.

7   CONCLUDING REMARKS

This review chapter has been an attempt to present the salient issues pertaining to the methodology of spatial econometrics. It is by no means complete, but it is hoped that sufficient guidance is provided to pursue interesting research directions. Many challenging problems remain, both methodological in nature as well as in terms of applying the new techniques to meaningful empirical problems. Particularly in dealing with spatial effects in models other than the standard linear regression, much needs to be done to complete the spatial econometric toolbox. It is hoped that the review presented here will stimulate statisticians and econometricians to tackle these interesting and challenging problems.

Notes

* This paper benefited greatly from comments by Wim Vijverberg and two anonymous referees. A more comprehensive version of this paper is available as Anselin (1999).

1 A more extensive review is given in Anselin and Bera (1998) and Anselin (1999).

2 An extensive collection of recent applications of spatial econometric methods in economics can be found in Anselin and Florax (2000).

3 In this chapter, I will use the terms spatial dependence and spatial autocorrelation interchangeably. Obviously, the two are not identical, but typically, the weaker form is used, in the sense of a moment of a joint distribution. Only seldom is the focus on the complete joint density (a recent exception can be found in Brett and Pinkse (1997)).

4 See Anselin (1988a), for a more extensive discussion.

5 One would still need to establish the class of spatial stochastic processes that would allow for the consistent estimation of the covariance; see Frees (1995) for a discussion of the general principles.

6 See Anselin and Bera (1998) for an extensive and technical discussion.

7 On a square grid, one could envisage using North, South, East and West as spatial shifts, but in general, for irregular spatial units such as counties, this is impractical, since the number of neighbors for each county is not constant.

8 In Anselin (1988a), the term spatial lag is introduced to refer to this new variable, to emphasize the similarity to a distributed lag term rather than a spatial shift.

9 By convention, $w_{ii} = 0$, i.e. a location is never a neighbor of itself. This is arbitrary, but can be assumed without loss of generality. For a more extensive discussion of spatial weights, see Anselin (1988a, ch. 3), Cliff and Ord (1981), Upton and Fingleton (1985).

10 See Anselin and Bera (1998) for further details.

11 See McMillen (1992) for an illustration.

12 The specification of spatial covariance functions is not arbitrary, and a number of conditions must be satisfied in order for the model to be "valid" (details are given in Cressie (1993, pp. 61–3, 67–8 and 84–6)).

13 Specifically, this may limit the applicability of GMM estimators that are based on a central limit theorem for stationary mixing random fields such as the one by Bolthausen (1982), used by Conley (1996).

14 Cressie (1993, pp. 100–1).

15 See Kelejian and Prucha (1999a, 1999b).

16 For ease of exposition, the error term is assumed to be iid, although various forms of heteroskedasticity can be incorporated in a straightforward way (Anselin, 1988a, ch. 6).

17 Details and a review of alternative specifications are given in Anselin and Bera (1998).

18 For further details, see Anselin (1988a, 1988b). A recent application is Baltagi and Li (2000b).

19 Methodological issues associated with spatial probit models are considered in Case (1992), McMillen (1992), Pinkse and Slade (1998) and Beron and Vijverberg (2000).

20 For an extensive discussion, see Beron and Vijverberg (2000).

21 Other classic treatments of ML estimation in spatial models can be found in Whittle (1954), Besag (1974), and Mardia and Marshall (1984).

22 For a formal demonstration, see Anselin (1988a) and Kelejian and Prucha (1997).

23 For details, see, e.g. McMillen (1992), Pinkse and Slade (1998), Beron and Vijverberg (2000), and also, for general principles, Poirier and Ruud (1988).

24 For a careful consideration of these issues, see Kelejian and Prucha (1999a).

25 For technical details, see, e.g. Kelejian and Robinson (1993), Kelejian and Prucha (1998).

26 A recent application of this method is given in Bell and Bockstael (2000). An extension of this idea to the residuals of a spatial 2SLS estimation is provided in Kelejian and Prucha (1998).

27 See also Case (1992) and McMillen (1992) for a similar focus on heteroskedasticity in the spatial probit model.

28 See also the discussion in Haining (1990, pp. 131–3).

29 For example, for row-standardized weights, $S_0 = N$, and $I = e'We/e'e$. See Anselin and Bera (1998) for an extensive discussion.

30 Moran's I is not based on an explicit alternative and has power against both (see Anselin and Rey, 1991).

31 As shown in Anselin and Kelejian (1997) these tests are asymptotically equivalent.

32 Neither of these toolboxes include specification tests. Furthermore, S+Spatialstats has no routines to handle the spatial lag model.

References

Anselin, L. (1980). *Estimation Methods for Spatial Autoregressive Structures*. Regional Science Dissertation and Monograph Series 8. Field of Regional Science, Cornell University, Ithaca, N.Y.

Anselin, L. (1988a). *Spatial Econometrics: Methods and Models*. Kluwer Academic, Dordrecht.

Anselin, L. (1988b). A test for spatial autocorrelation in seemingly unrelated regressions. *Economics Letters* 28, 335–41.

Anselin, L. (1988c). Lagrange multiplier test diagnostics for spatial dependence and spatial heterogeneity. *Geographical Analysis* 20, 1–17.

Anselin, L. (1990). Some robust approaches to testing and estimation in spatial econometrics. *Regional Science and Urban Economics* 20, 141–63.

Anselin, L. (1992a). Space and applied econometrics. Special Issue, *Regional Science and Urban Economics* 22.

Anselin, L. (1992b). *SpaceStat, a Software Program for the Analysis of Spatial Data*. National Center for Geographic Information and Analysis, University of California, Santa Barbara, CA.

Anselin, L. (1998). *SpaceStat Version 1.90*. http://www.spacestat.com.

Anselin, L. (1999). Spatial econometrics, An updated review. Regional Economics Applications Laboratory (REAL), University of Illinois, Urbana-Champaign.

Anselin, L. (2000). Rao's score test in spatial econometrics. *Journal of Statistical Planning and Inference* (forthcoming).

Anselin, L., and A. Bera (1998). Spatial dependence in linear regression models with an introduction to spatial econometrics. In A. Ullah and D.E.A. Giles (eds.) *Handbook of Applied Economic Statistics*, pp. 237–89. New York: Marcel Dekker.

Anselin, L., and R. Florax (1995a). Introduction. In L. Anselin and R. Florax (eds.) *New Directions in Spatial Econometrics*, pp. 3–18. Berlin: Springer-Verlag.

Anselin, L., and R. Florax (1995b). Small sample properties of tests for spatial dependence in regression models: some further results. In L. Anselin and R. Florax (eds.) *New Directions in Spatial Econometrics*, pp. 21–74. Berlin: Springer-Verlag.

Anselin, L., and R. Florax (2000). *Advances in Spatial Econometrics*. Heidelberg: Springer-Verlag.

Anselin, L., and S. Hudak (1992). Spatial econometrics in practice, a review of software options. *Regional Science and Urban Economics* 22, 509–36.

Anselin, L., and H.H. Kelejian (1997). Testing for spatial error autocorrelation in the presence of endogenous regressors. *International Regional Science Review* 20, 153–82.

Anselin, L., and S. Rey (1991). Properties of tests for spatial dependence in linear regression models. *Geographical Analysis* 23, 112–31.

Anselin, L., and S. Rey (1997). Introduction to the special issue on spatial econometrics. *International Regional Science Review* 20, 1–7.

Anselin, L., A. Bera, R. Florax, and M. Yoon (1996). Simple diagnostic tests for spatial dependence. *Regional Science and Urban Economics* 26, 77–104.

Baltagi, B., and D. Li (2000a). Double length artificial regressions for testing spatial dependence. *Econometric Review*, forthcoming.

Baltagi, B., and D. Li (2000b). Prediction in the panel data model with spatial correlation. In L. Anselin and R. Florax (eds.) *Advances in Spatial Econometrics*. Heidelberg: Springer-Verlag.

Barry, R.P., and R.K. Pace (1999). Monte Carlo estimates of the log determinant of large sparse matrices. *Linear Algebra and its Applications* 289, 41–54.

Basu, S., and T.G. Thibodeau (1998). Analysis of spatial autocorrelation in housing prices. *Journal of Real Estate Finance and Economics* 17, 61–85.

Bell, K.P., and N.E. Bockstael (2000). Applying the generalized moments estimation approach to spatial problems involving micro-level data. *Review of Economics and Statistics* 82, 72–82.

Beron, K.J., and W.P.M. Vijverberg (2000). Probit in a spatial context: a Monte Carlo approach. In L. Anselin and R. Florax (eds.) *Advances in Spatial Econometrics*. Heidelberg: Springer-Verlag.

Besag, J. (1974). Spatial interaction and the statistical analysis of lattice systems. *Journal of the Royal Statistical Society B* 36, 192–225.

Besag, J., and P.A.P. Moran (1975). On the estimation and testing of spatial interaction in Gaussian lattice processes. *Biometrika* 62, 555–62.

Bolthausen, E. (1982). On the central limit theorem for stationary mixing random fields. *Annals of Probability* 10, 1047–50.

Brett, C., and J. Pinkse (1997). Those taxes all over the map! A test for spatial independence of municipal tax rates in British Columbia. *International Regional Science Review* 20, 131–51.

Brock, W.A., and S.N. Durlauf (1995). Discrete choice with social interactions I: Theory. NBER Working Paper No. W5291. Cambridge, MA: National Bureau of Economic Research.

Burridge, P. (1980). On the Cliff–Ord test for spatial autocorrelation. *Journal of the Royal Statistical Society B* 42, 107–8.

Case, A. (1992). Neighborhood influence and technological change. *Regional Science and Urban Economics* 22, 491–508.

Case, A., H.S. Rosen, and J.R. Hines (1993). Budget spillovers and fiscal policy interdependence: evidence from the States. *Journal of Public Economics* 52, 285–307.

Cliff, A., and J.K. Ord (1973). *Spatial Autocorrelation*. London: Pion.

Cliff, A., and J.K. Ord (1981). *Spatial Processes: Models and Applications*. London: Pion.

Conley, T.G. (1996). *Econometric modelling of cross-sectional dependence*. Ph.D. dissertation. Department of Economics, University of Chicago, Chicago, IL.

Cressie, N. (1993). *Statistics for Spatial Data*. New York: Wiley.

Davidson, J. (1994). *Stochastic Limit Theory*. Oxford: Oxford University Press.

Davidson, R. and J.G. MacKinnon (1988). Double-length artificial regressions. *Oxford Bulletin of Economics and Statistics* 50, 203–17.

Driscoll, J.C., and A.C. Kraay (1998). Consistent covariance matrix estimation with spatially dependent panel data. *Review of Economics and Statistics* 80, 549–60.

Dubin, R. (1988). Estimation of regression coefficients in the presence of spatially autocorrelated error terms. *Review of Economics and Statistics* 70, 466–74.

Dubin, R. (1992). Spatial autocorrelation and neighborhood quality. *Regional Science and Urban Economics* 22, 433–52.

Frees, E.W. (1995). Assessing cross-sectional correlation in panel data. *Journal of Econometrics* 69, 393–414.

Haining, R. (1990). *Spatial Data Analysis in the Social and Environmental Sciences*. Cambridge: Cambridge University Press.

Hansen, L.P. (1982). Large sample properties of generalized method of moments estimators. *Econometrica* 50, 1029–54.

Kelejian, H., and I. Prucha (1997). Estimation of spatial regression models with autoregressive errors by two stage least squares procedures: a serious problem. *International Regional Science Review* 20, 103–11.

Kelejian, H., and I. Prucha (1998). A generalized spatial two stage least squares procedure for estimating a spatial autoregressive model with autoregressive disturbances. *Journal of Real Estate Finance and Economics* 17, 99–121.

Kelejian, H., and I. Prucha (1999a). A generalized moments estimator for the autoregressive parameter in a spatial model. *International Economic Review* 40, 509–33.

Kelejian, H.H., and I. Prucha (1999b). On the asymptotic distribution of the Moran I test statistic with applications. Working Paper, Department of Economics, University of Maryland, College Park, MD.

Kelejian, H.H., and D.P. Robinson (1993). A suggested method of estimation for spatial interdependent models with autocorrelated errors, and an application to a county expenditure model. *Papers in Regional Science* 72, 297–312.

Kelejian, H.H., and D.P. Robinson (1998). A suggested test for spatial autocorrelation and/or heteroskedasticity and corresponding Monte Carlo results. *Regional Science and Urban Economics* 28, 389–417.

Kelejian, H.H., and D.P. Robinson (2000). The influence of spatially correlated heteroskedasticity on tests for spatial correlation. In L. Anselin and R. Florax (eds.) *Advances in Spatial Econometrics*. Heidelberg: Springer-Verlag (forthcoming).

King, M. (1981). A small sample property of the Cliff–Ord test for spatial correlation. *Journal of the Royal Statistical Society B* 43, 263–4.

Lahiri, S.N. (1996). On the inconsistency of estimators under infill asymptotics for spatial data. *Sankhya A* 58, 403–17.

Magnus, J. (1978). Maximum likelihood estimation of the GLS model with unknown parameters in the disturbance covariance matrix. *Journal of Econometrics* 7, 281–312. (Corrigenda, *Journal of Econometrics* 10, 261).

Mardia, K.V., and R.J. Marshall (1984). Maximum likelihood estimation of models for residual covariance in spatial regression. *Biometrika* 71, 135–46.

MathSoft (1996). *S+SpatialStats User's Manual for Windows and Unix*. Seattle, WA: MathSoft, Inc.

McMillen, D.P. (1992). Probit with spatial autocorrelation. *Journal of Regional Science* 32, 335–48.

Moran, P.A.P. (1948). The interpretation of statistical maps. *Biometrika* 35, 255–60.

Newey, W.K., and K.D. West (1987). A simple, positive semi-definite, heteroskedasticity and autocorrelation consistent covariance matrix. *Econometrica* 55, 703–8.

Ord, J.K. (1975). Estimation methods for models of spatial interaction. *Journal of the American Statistical Association* 70, 120–6.

Pace, R.K., and R. Barry (1997a). Sparse spatial autoregressions. *Statistics and Probability Letters* 33, 291–7.

Pace, R.K., and R. Barry (1997b). Quick computation of spatial autoregressive estimators. *Geographical Analysis* 29, 232–46.

Pace, R.K., and R. Barry (1998). *Spatial Statistics Toolbox 1.0.* Real Estate Research Institute, Lousiana State University, Baton Rouge, LA.

Pace, R.K., R. Barry, C.F. Sirmans (1998). Spatial statistics and real estate. *Journal of Real Estate Finance and Economics* 17, 5–13.

Paelinck, J., and L. Klaassen (1979). *Spatial Econometrics.* Farnborough: Saxon House.

Pinkse, J. (1998). Asymptotic properties of the Moran and related tests and a test for spatial correlation in probit models. Working Paper, Department of Economics, University of British Columbia, Vancouver, BC.

Pinkse, J. (2000). Moran-flavored tests with nuisance parameters. In L. Anselin and R. Florax (eds.) *Advances in Spatial Econometrics.* Heidelberg: Springer-Verlag.

Pinkse, J., and M.E. Slade (1998). Contracting in space: an application of spatial statistics to discrete-choice models. *Journal of Econometrics* 85, 125–54.

Poirier, D.J., and P.A. Ruud (1988). Probit with dependent observations. *Review of Economic Studies* 55, 593–614.

Pötscher, B.M., and I.R. Prucha (1997). *Dynamic Nonlinear Econometric Models.* Berlin: Springer.

Rao, C.R. (1973). *Linear Statistical Inference and its Applications* (2nd edn). New York: Wiley.

Schmidt, P. (1976). *Econometrics.* New York: Marcel Dekker.

Smirnov, O., and L. Anselin (2000). Fast maximum likelihood estimation of very large spatial autoregressive models: a characteristic polynomial approach. Computational Statistics and Data Analysis.

Upton, G.J., and B. Fingleton (1985). *Spatial Data Analysis by Example. Volume 1: Point Pattern and Quantitative Data.* New York: Wiley.

Vijverberg, W. (1997). Monte Carlo evaluation of multivariate normal probabilities. *Journal of Econometrics* 76, 281–307.

Whittle, P. (1954). On stationary processes in the plane. *Biometrika* 41, 434–49.

Essentials of Count Data Regression

A. Colin Cameron and Pravin K. Trivedi

1 INTRODUCTION

In many economic contexts the dependent or response variable of interest (y) is a nonnegative integer or count which we wish to explain or analyze in terms of a set of covariates (x). Unlike the classical regression model, the response variable is discrete with a distribution that places probability mass at nonnegative integer values only. Regression models for counts, like other limited or discrete dependent variable models such as the logit and probit, are nonlinear with many properties and special features intimately connected to discreteness and nonlinearity.

Let us consider some examples from microeconometrics, beginning with samples of independent cross section observations. Fertility studies often model the number of live births over a specified age interval of the mother, with interest in analyzing its variation in terms of, say, mother's schooling, age, and household income (Winkelmann, 1995). Accident analysis studies model airline safety, for example, as measured by the number of accidents experienced by an airline over some period, and seek to determine its relationship to airline profitability and other measures of the financial health of the airline (Rose, 1990). Recreational demand studies seek to place a value on natural resources such as national forests by modeling the number of trips to a recreational site (Gurmu and Trivedi, 1996). Health demand studies model data on the number of times that individuals consume a health service, such as visits to a doctor or days in hospital in the past year (Cameron, Trivedi, Milne and Piggott, 1988), and estimate the impact of health status and health insurance.

Examples of count data regression based on time series and panel data are also available. A time series example is the annual number of bank failures over some period, which may be analyzed using explanatory variables such as bank profitability, corporate profitability, and bank borrowings from the Federal Reserve Bank (Davutyan, 1989). A panel data example that has attracted much attention in the industrial organization literature on the benefits of research and development expenditures is the number of patents received annually by firms (Hausman, Hall, and Griliches, 1984).

In some cases, such as number of births, the count is the variable of ultimate interest. In other cases, such as medical demand and results of research and development expenditure, the variable of ultimate interest is continuous, often expenditures or receipts measured in dollars, but the best data available are, instead, a count.

In all cases the data are concentrated on a few small discrete values, say 0, 1, and 2; skewed to the left; and intrinsically heteroskedastic with variance increasing with the mean. In many examples, such as number of births, virtually all the data are restricted to single digits, and the mean number of events is quite low. But in other cases, such as number of patents, the tail can be very long with, say, one-quarter of the sample being awarded no patents while one firm is awarded 400 patents.

These features motivate the application of special methods and models for count regression. There are two ways to proceed. The first approach is a fully parametric one that completely specifies the distribution of the data, fully respecting the restriction of y to nonnegative integer values. The second approach is a mean–variance approach, which specifies the conditional mean to be nonnegative, and specifies the conditional variance to be a function of the conditional mean.

These approaches are presented for cross section data in Sections 2 to 4. Section 2 details the Poisson regression model. This model is often too restrictive and other, more commonly-used, fully parametric count models are presented in Section 3. Less-used alternative parametric approaches for counts, such as discrete choice models and duration models, are also presented in this section. The partially parametric approach of modeling the conditional mean and conditional variance is detailed in Section 4. Extensions to other types of data, notably time series, multivariate and panel data, are given in Section 5. In Section 6 practical recommendations are provided. For pedagogical reasons the Poisson regression model for cross section data is presented in some detail. The other models, many superior to Poisson, are presented in less detail for space reasons. For more complete treatment see Cameron and Trivedi (1998) and the guide to further reading in Section 7.

2   POISSON REGRESSION

The Poisson is the starting point for count data analysis, though it is often inadequate. In Sections 2.1–2.3 we present the Poisson regression model and estimation by maximum likelihood, interpretation of the estimated coefficients, and extensions to truncated and censored data. Limitations of the Poisson model, notably overdispersion, are presented in Section 2.4.

2.1   Poisson MLE

The natural stochastic model for counts is a Poisson point process for the occurrence of the event of interest. This implies a Poisson distribution for the number of occurrences of the event, with density

$$\Pr[Y = y] = \frac{e^{-\mu}\mu^{y}}{y!}, \quad y = 0, 1, 2, \ldots, \tag{15.1}$$

where μ is the intensity or rate parameter. We refer to the distribution as $P[\mu]$. The first two moments are

$$E[Y] = \mu,$$

$$V[Y] = \mu. \tag{15.2}$$

This shows the well known equality of mean and variance property of the Poisson distribution.

By introducing the observation subscript i, attached to both y and μ, the framework is extended to non-iid data. The *Poisson regression model* is derived from the Poisson distribution by parameterizing the relation between the mean parameter μ and covariates (regressors) x. The standard assumption is to use the exponential mean parameterization,

$$\mu_{i} = \exp(x_{i}'\beta), \quad i = 1, \ldots, n, \tag{15.3}$$

where by assumption there are k linearly independent covariates, usually including a constant. Because $V[y_{i}|x_{i}] = \exp(x_{i}'\beta)$, by (15.2) and (15.3), the Poisson regression is intrinsically heteroskedastic.

Given (15.1) and (15.3) and the assumption that the observations $(y_{i}|x_{i})$ are independent, the most natural estimator is maximum likelihood (ML). The loglikelihood function is

$$\ln L(\beta) = \sum_{i=1}^{n} \{y_{i}x_{i}'\beta - \exp(x_{i}'\beta) - \ln y_{i}!\}. \tag{15.4}$$

The Poisson MLE (maximum likelihood estimation), denoted $\hat{\beta}_{P}$, is the solution to k nonlinear equations corresponding to the first-order condition for maximum likelihood,

$$\sum_{i=1}^{n} (y_{i} - \exp(x_{i}'\beta))x_{i} = 0. \tag{15.5}$$

If x_{i} includes a constant term then the residuals $y_{i} - \exp(x_{i}'\beta)$ sum to zero by (15.5). The loglikelihood function is globally concave; hence solving these equations by

Gauss–Newton or Newton–Raphson iterative algorithm yields unique parameters estimates.

By standard maximum likelihood theory of correctly specified models, the estimator $\hat{\beta}_P$ is consistent for β and asymptotically normal with the sample covariance matrix

$$V[\hat{\beta}_P] = \left(\sum_{i=1}^{n} \mu_i x_i x_i'\right)^{-1},$$
(15.6)

in the case where μ_i is of the exponential form (15.3). In practice an alternative more general form for the variance matrix should be used; see Section 4.1.

2.2 Interpretation of regression coefficients

For linear models, with $E[y|x] = x'\beta$, the coefficients β are readily interpreted as the effect of a one-unit change in regressors on the conditional mean. For nonlinear models this interpretation needs to be modified. For any model with exponential conditional mean, differentiation yields

$$\frac{\partial E[y|x]}{\partial x_j} = \beta_j \exp(x'\beta),$$
(15.7)

where the scalar x_j denotes the jth regressor. For example, if $\hat{\beta}_j = 0.25$ and $\exp(x_i'\hat{\beta}) = 3$, then a one-unit change in the jth regressor increases the expectation of y by 0.75 units. This partial response depends upon $\exp(x_i'\hat{\beta})$ which is expected to vary across individuals. It is easy to see that β_j measures the relative change in $E[y|x]$ induced by a unit change in x_j. If x_j is measured on log-scale, β_j is an elasticity.

For purposes of reporting a single response value, a good candidate is an estimate of the *average response*, $\frac{1}{n}\sum_{i=1}^{n}\partial E[y_i|x_i]/\partial x_{ij} = \hat{\beta}_j \times \frac{1}{n}\sum_{i=1}^{n}\exp(x_i'\hat{\beta})$. For Poisson regression models with intercept included, this can be shown to simplify to $\hat{\beta}_j\bar{y}$.

Another consequence of (15.7) is that if, say, β_j is twice as large as β_k, then the effect of changing the jth regressor by one unit is twice that of changing the kth regressor by one unit.

2.3 Truncation and censoring

In some studies, inclusion in the sample requires that sampled individuals have been engaged in the activity of interest. Then the count data are *truncated*, as the data are observed only over part of the range of the response variable. Examples of truncated counts include the number of bus trips made per week in surveys taken on buses, the number of shopping trips made by individuals sampled at a mall, and the number of unemployment spells among a pool of unemployed. In all these cases we do not observe zero counts, so the data are said to be zero-truncated, or more generally left-truncated. Right truncation results from loss of observations greater than some specified value.

Truncation leads to inconsistent parameter estimates unless the likelihood function is suitably modified. Consider the case of zero truncation. Let $f(y \mid \theta)$ denote the density function and $F(y \mid \theta) = \Pr[Y \leq y]$ denote the cumulative distribution function of the discrete random variable, where θ is a parameter vector. If realizations of y less than a positive integer 1 are omitted, the ensuing zero-truncated density is given by

$$f(y \mid \theta, y \geq 1) = \frac{f(y \mid \theta)}{1 - F(0 \mid \theta)}, \quad y = 1, 2, \ldots . \tag{15.8}$$

This specializes in the zero-truncated Poisson case, for example, to $f(y \mid \mu, y \geq 1) = e^{-\mu}\mu^{y}/[y!(1 - \exp(-\mu))]$. It is straightforward to construct a loglikelihood based on this density and to obtain maximum likelihood estimates.

Censored counts most commonly arise from aggregation of counts greater than some value. This is often done in survey design when the total probability mass over the aggregated values is relatively small. Censoring, like truncation, leads to inconsistent parameter estimates if the uncensored likelihood is mistakenly used.

For example, the number of events greater than some known value c might be aggregated into a single category. Then some values of y are incompletely observed; the precise value is unknown but it is known to equal or exceed c. The observed data has density

$$g(y \mid \theta) = \begin{cases} f(y \mid \theta) & \text{if } y < c, \\ 1 - F(c \mid \theta) & \text{if } y \geq c, \end{cases} \tag{15.9}$$

where c is known. Specialization to the Poisson, for example, is straightforward.

A related complication is that of *sample selection* (Terza, 1998). Then the count y is observed only when another random variable, potentially correlated with y, crosses a threshold. For example, to see a medical specialist one may first need to see a general practitioner. Treatment of count data with sample selection is a current topic of research.

2.4 Overdispersion

The Poisson regression model is usually too restrictive for count data, leading to alternative models as presented in Sections 3 and 4. The fundamental problem is that the distribution is parameterized in terms of a single scalar parameter (μ) so that all moments of y are a function of μ. By contrast the normal distribution has separate parameters for location (μ) and scale (σ^2). (For the same reason the one-parameter exponential is too restrictive for duration data and more general two-parameter distributions such as the Weibull are superior. Note that this complication does not arise with binary data. Then the distribution is clearly the one-parameter Bernoulli, as if the probability of success is p then the probability of failure must be $1 - p$. For binary data the issue is instead how to parameterize p in terms of regressors.)

One way this restrictiveness manifests itself is that in many applications a Poisson density predicts the probability of a zero count to be considerably less than is actually observed in the sample. This is termed the *excess zeros* problem, as there are more zeros in the data than the Poisson predicts.

A second and more obvious way that the Poisson is deficient is that for count data the variance usually exceeds the mean, a feature called *overdispersion*. The Poisson instead implies equality of variance of mean, see (15.2), a property called *equidispersion*.

Overdispersion has qualitatively similar consequences to the failure of the assumption of homoskedasticity in the linear regression model. Provided the conditional mean is correctly specified, that is (15.3) holds, the Poisson MLE is still consistent. This is clear from inspection of the first-order conditions (15.5), since the left-hand side of (15.5) will have an expected value of zero if $E[y_i | x_i] = \exp(x_i'\beta)$. (This consistency property applies more generally to the quasi-MLE when the specified density is in the linear exponential family (LEF). Both Poisson and normal are members of the LEF.) It is nonetheless important to control for overdispersion for two reasons. First, in more complicated settings such as with truncation and censoring, overdispersion leads to the more fundamental problem of inconsistency. Second, even in the simplest settings large overdispersion leads to grossly deflated standard errors and grossly inflated t-statistics in the usual ML output.

A statistical test of overdispersion is therefore highly desirable after running a Poisson regression. Most count models with overdispersion specify overdispersion to be of the form

$$V[y_i | x_i] = \mu_i + \alpha g(\mu_i), \tag{15.10}$$

where α is an unknown parameter and $g(\cdot)$ is a known function, most commonly $g(\mu) = \mu^2$ or $g(\mu) = \mu$. It is assumed that under both null and alternative hypotheses the mean is correctly specified as, for example, $\exp(x_i'\beta)$, while under the null hypothesis $\alpha = 0$ so that $V[y_i | x_i] = \mu_i$. A simple test statistic for $H_0 : \alpha = 0$ versus $H_1 : \alpha \neq 0$ or $H_1 : \alpha > 0$ can be computed by estimating the Poisson model, constructing fitted values $\hat{\mu}_i = \exp(x_i'\hat{\beta})$ and running the auxiliary OLS regression (without constant)

$$\frac{(y_i - \hat{\mu}_i)^2 - y_i}{\hat{\mu}_i} = \alpha \frac{g(\hat{\mu}_i)}{\hat{\mu}_i} + u_i, \tag{15.11}$$

where u_i is an error term. The reported t-statistic for α is asymptotically normal under the null hypothesis of no overdispersion. This test can also be used for *underdispersion*, in which case the conditional variance is less than the conditional mean.

3   OTHER PARAMETRIC COUNT REGRESSION MODELS

Various models that are less restrictive than Poisson are presented in this section.

First, overdispersion in count data may be due to unobserved heterogeneity. Then counts are viewed as being generated by a Poisson process, but the researcher is unable to correctly specify the rate parameter of this process. Instead the rate parameter is itself a random variable. This mixture approach, presented in Sections 3.1–3.2, leads to the widely-used negative binomial model.

Second, overdispersion, and in some cases underdispersion, may arise because the process generating the first event may differ from that determining later events. For example, an initial doctor consultation may be solely a patient's choice, while subsequent visits are also determined by the doctor. This leads to the hurdle model, presented in Section 3.3.

Third, overdispersion in count data may be due to failure of the assumption of independence of events which is implicit in the Poisson process. One can introduce dependence so that, for example, the occurrence of one doctor visit makes subsequent doctor visits more likely. This approach has not been widely used in count data analysis. (In duration data analysis this is called true state dependence, to be contrasted with the first approach of unobserved heterogeneity.) Particular assumptions again lead to the negative binomial; see also Winkelmann (1995). A discrete choice model that progressively models $\Pr[y = j \mid y \geq j - 1]$ is presented in Section 3.4, and issues of dependence also arise in Section 5 on time series.

Fourth, one can refer to the extensive and rich literature on univariate iid count distributions, which offers intriguing possibilities such as the logarithmic series and hypergeometric distribution (Johnson, Kotz, and Kemp, 1992). New regression models can be developed by letting one or more parameters be a specified function of regressors. Such models are not presented here. The approach has less motivation than the first three approaches and the resulting models may not be any better.

3.1   Continuous mixture models

The negative binomial model can be obtained in many different ways. The following justification using a mixture distribution is one of the oldest and has wide appeal.

Suppose the distribution of a random count y is Poisson, conditional on the parameter λ, so that $f(y \mid \lambda) = \exp(-\lambda)\lambda^y/y!$. Suppose now that the parameter λ is random, rather than being a completely deterministic function of regressors x. In particular, let $\lambda = \mu v$, where μ is a deterministic function of x, for example $\exp(x'\beta)$, and $v > 0$ is iid distributed with density $g(v \mid \alpha)$. This is an example of *unobserved heterogeneity*, as different observations may have different λ (heterogeneity) but part of this difference is due to a random (unobserved) component v.

The marginal density of y, unconditional on the random parameter v but conditional on the deterministic parameters μ and α, is obtained by integrating out v. This yields

$$h(y \mid \mu, \alpha) = \int f(y \mid \mu, \nu) g(\nu \mid \alpha) d\nu, \qquad (15.12)$$

where $g(\nu \mid \alpha)$ is called the *mixing distribution* and α denotes the unknown parameter of the mixing distribution. The integration defines an "average" distribution. For some specific choices of $f(\cdot)$ and $g(\cdot)$, the integral will have an analytical or closed-form solution.

If $f(y \mid \lambda)$ is the Poisson density and $g(\nu)$, $\nu > 0$, is the gamma density with $E[\nu] = 1$ and $V[\nu] = \alpha$ we obtain the negative binomial density

$$h(y \mid \mu, \alpha) = \frac{\Gamma(\alpha^{-1} + y)}{\Gamma(\alpha^{-1})\Gamma(y+1)} \left(\frac{\alpha^{-1}}{\alpha^{-1} + \mu}\right)^{\alpha^{-1}} \left(\frac{\mu}{\mu + \alpha^{-1}}\right)^{y}, \quad \alpha > 0, \qquad (15.13)$$

where $\Gamma(\cdot)$ denotes the gamma integral which specializes to a factorial for an integer argument. Special cases of the negative binomial include the Poisson ($\alpha = 0$) and the geometric ($\alpha = 1$).

The first two moments of the negative binomial distribution are

$$E[y \mid \mu, \alpha] = \mu,$$

$$V[y \mid \mu, \alpha] = \mu(1 + \alpha\mu). \qquad (15.14)$$

The variance therefore exceeds the mean, since $\alpha > 0$ and $\mu > 0$. Indeed it can be shown easily that overdispersion always arises if $y \mid \lambda$ is Poisson and the mixing is of the form $\lambda = \mu\nu$ where $E[\nu] = 1$. Note also that the overdispersion is of the form (15.10) discussed in Section 2.4.

Two standard variants of the negative binomial are used in regression applications. Both variants specify $\mu_i = \exp(x_i'\beta)$. The most common variant lets α be a parameter to be estimated, in which case the conditional variance function, $\mu + \alpha\mu^2$ from (15.14), is quadratic in the mean. The loglikelihood is easily obtained from (15.13), and estimation is by maximum likelihood.

The other variant of the negative binomial model has a linear variance function, $V[y \mid \mu, \alpha] = (1 + \delta)\mu$, obtained by replacing α by δ/μ throughout (15.13). Estimation by ML is again straightforward. Sometimes this variant is called negative binomial 1 (NB1) in contrast to the variant with a quadratic variance function which has been called negative binomial 2 (NB2) model (Cameron and Trivedi, 1998).

The negative binomial model with quadratic variance function has been found to be very useful in applied work. It is the standard cross section model for counts, which are usually overdispersed, along with the quasi-MLE of Section 4.1.

For mixtures other than Poisson-gamma, such as those that instead use as mixing distribution the lognormal distribution or the inverse-Gaussian distribution, the marginal distribution cannot be expressed in a closed form. Then one may have to use numerical quadrature or simulated maximum likelihood to estimate the model. These methods are entirely feasible with currently available computing power. If one is prepared to use simulation-based estimation methods, see Gouriéroux and Monfort (1997), the scope for using mixed-Poisson models of various types is very extensive.

3.2   Finite mixture models

The mixture model in the previous subsection was a continuous mixture model, as the mixing random variable v was assumed to have continuous distribution. An alternative approach instead uses a *discrete* representation of unobserved heterogeneity, which generates a class of models called *finite mixture models*. This class of models is a particular subclass of *latent class models*.

In empirical work the more commonly used alternative to the continuous mixture is in the class of modified count models discussed in the next section. However, it is more natural to follow up the preceding section with a discussion of finite mixtures. Further, the subclass of modified count models can be viewed as a special case of finite mixtures.

We suppose that the density of y is a linear combination of m different densities, where the jth density is $f_j(y \mid \lambda_j)$, $j = 1, 2, \ldots, m$. Thus an m-component finite mixture is

$$f_j(y \mid \lambda, \pi) = \sum_{j=1}^{m} \pi_j f_j(y \mid \lambda_j), \quad 0 < \pi_j < 1, \quad \sum_{j=1}^{m} \pi_j = 1. \tag{15.15}$$

For example, in a study of the use of medical services with $m = 2$, the first density may correspond to heavy users of the service and the second to relatively low users, and the fractions of the two types in the populations are π_1 and $\pi_2(= 1 - \pi_1)$ respectively.

The goal of the researcher who uses this model is to estimate the unknown parameters λ_j, $j = 1, \ldots, m$. It is easy to develop regression models based on (15.15). For example, if NB2 models are used then $f_j(y \mid \lambda_j)$ is the NB2 density (15.13) with parameters $\mu_j = \exp(x'\beta_j)$ and α_j, so $\lambda_j = (\beta_j, \alpha_j)$. If the number of components, m, is given, then under some regularity conditions maximum likelihood estimation of the parameters (π_j, λ_j), $j = 1, \ldots, m$, is possible. The details of the estimation methods, less straightforward due to the presence of the mixing parameters π_j, is omitted here because of space constraints. See Cameron and Trivedi (1998, ch. 4). It is possible also to probabilistically assign each case to a subpopulation (in the sense that the estimated probability of the case belonging to that subpopulation is the highest) *after* the model has been estimated.

3.3   Modified count models

The leading motivation for modified count models is to solve the so-called problem of excess zeros, the presence of more zeros in the data than predicted by count models such as the Poisson.

The *hurdle model* or *two-part model* relaxes the assumption that the zeros and the positives come from the same data generating process. The zeros are determined by the density $f_1(\cdot)$, so that $\Pr[y = 0] = f_1(0)$. The positive counts come from the truncated density $f_2(y \mid y > 0) = f_2(y)/(1 - f_2(0))$, which is multiplied by $\Pr[y > 0] = 1 - f_1(0)$ to ensure that probabilities sum to unity. Thus

$$
g(y) = \begin{cases} f_1(0) & \text{if } y = 0, \\ \dfrac{1 - f_1(0)}{1 - f_2(0)} f_2(y) & \text{if } y \geq 1. \end{cases} \tag{15.16}
$$

This reduces to the standard model only if $f_1(\cdot) = f_2(\cdot)$. Thus in the modified model the two processes generating the zeros and the positives are not constrained to be the same. While the motivation for this model is to handle excess zeros, it is also capable of modeling too few zeros.

Maximum likelihood estimation of the hurdle model involves separate maximization of the two terms in the likelihood, one corresponding to the zeros and the other to the positives. This is straightforward.

A hurdle model has the interpretation that it reflects a two-stage decision making process. For example, a patient may initiate the first visit to a doctor, but the second and subsequent visits may be determined by a different mechanism (Pohlmeier and Ulrich, 1995).

Regression applications use hurdle versions of the Poisson or negative binomial, obtained by specifying $f_1(\cdot)$ and $f_2(\cdot)$ to be the Poisson or negative binomial densities given earlier. In application the covariates in the hurdle part which models the zero/one outcome need not be the same as those which appear in the truncated part, although in practice they are often the same. The hurdle model is widely used, and the hurdle negative binomial model is quite flexible. Drawbacks are that the model is not very parsimonious, typically the number of parameters is doubled, and parameter interpretation is not as easy as in the same model without hurdle.

The conditional mean in the hurdle model is the product of a probability of positives and the conditional mean of the zero-truncated density. Therefore, using a Poisson regression when the hurdle model is the correct specification implies a misspecification which will lead to inconsistent estimates.

3.4   Discrete choice models

Count data can be modeled by discrete choice model methods, possibly after some grouping of counts to limit the number of categories. For example, the categories may be 0, 1, 2, 3, and 4 or more if few observations exceed four. Unordered models such as multinomial logit are not parsimonious and more importantly are inappropriate. Instead, one should use a sequential discrete choice model that recognizes the ordering of the data, such as ordered logit or ordered probit.

4 PARTIALLY PARAMETRIC MODELS

By partially parametric models we mean that we focus on modeling the data via the conditional mean and variance, and even these may not be fully specified. In Section 4.1 we consider models based on specification of the conditional mean and variance. In Section 4.2 we consider and critique the use of least squares methods that do not explicitly model the heteroskedasticity inherent in count data. In Section 4.3 we consider models that are even more partially parametric, such as incomplete specification of the conditional mean.

4.1 Quasi-ML estimation

In the econometric literature *pseudo-ML* (PML) or *quasi-ML* (QML) estimation refers to estimating by ML, under the assumption that the specified density is possibly incorrect (Gouriéroux *et al.*, 1984a). PML and QML are often used interchangeably. The distribution of the estimator is obtained under weaker assumptions about the data generating process than those that led to the specified likelihood function. In the statistics literature QML often refers to nonlinear generalized least squares estimation. For the Poisson regression QML in the latter sense is equivalent to standard maximum likelihood.

From (15.5), the Poisson PML estimator, $\hat{\beta}_P$, has first-order conditions $\sum_{i=1}^{n}(y_i - \exp(x_i'\beta))x_i = 0$. As already noted in Section 2.4, the summation on the left-hand side has an expectation of zero if $E[y_i \mid x_i] = \exp(x_i'\beta)$. Hence the Poisson PML is consistent under the weaker assumption of correct specification of the conditional mean – the data need not be Poisson distributed. Using standard results, the variance matrix is of the sandwich form, with

$$V_{\mathrm{PML}}[\hat{\beta}_P] = \left(\sum_{i=1}^{n}\mu_i x_i x_i'\right)^{-1}\left(\sum_{i=1}^{n}\omega_i x_i x_i'\right)\left(\sum_{i=1}^{n}\mu_i x_i x_i'\right)^{-1} \quad (15.17)$$

and $\omega_i = V[y_i \mid x_i]$ is the conditional variance of y_i.

Given an assumption for the functional form for ω_i, and a consistent estimate $\hat{\omega}_i$ of ω_i, one can consistently estimate this covariance matrix. We could use the Poisson assumption, $\omega_i = \mu_i$, but as already noted the data are often overdispersed, with $\omega_i > \mu_i$. Common variance functions used are $\omega_i = (1 + \alpha\mu_i)\mu_i$, that of the NB2 model discussed in Section 3.1, and $\omega_i = (1 + \alpha)\mu_i$, that of the NB1 model. Note that in the latter case (15.17) simplifies to $V_{\mathrm{PML}}[\hat{\beta}_P] = (1 + \alpha)\,(\sum_{i=1}^{n}\mu_i x_i x_i')^{-1}$, so with overdispersion ($\alpha > 0$) the usual ML variance matrix given in (15.6) is understating the true variance.

If $\omega_i = E[(y_i - x_i'\beta)^2 \mid x_i]$ is instead unspecified, a consistent estimate of $V_{\mathrm{PML}}[\hat{\beta}_P]$ can be obtained by adapting the Eicker–White robust sandwich variance estimate formula to this case. The middle sum in (15.17) needs to be estimated. If $\hat{\mu}_i \overset{p}{\to} \mu_i$ then $n^{-1}\sum_{i=1}^{n}(y_i - \hat{\mu}_i)^2 x_i x_i' \overset{p}{\to} \lim n^{-1}\sum_{i=1}^{n}\omega_i x_i x_i'$. Thus a consistent estimate of $V_{\mathrm{PML}}[\hat{\beta}_P]$ is given by (15.17) with ω_i and μ_i replaced by $(y_i - \hat{\mu}_i)^2$ and $\hat{\mu}_i$.

When doubt exists about the form of the variance function, the use of the PML estimator is recommended. Computationally this is essentially the same as Poisson ML, with the qualification that the variance matrix must be recomputed. The calculation of robust variances is often an option in standard packages.

These results for Poisson PML estimation are qualitatively similar to those for PML estimation in the linear model under normality. They extend more generally to PML estimation based on densities in the linear exponential family. In all cases consistency requires only correct specification of the conditional mean (Nelder and Wedderburn, 1972; Gouriéroux et al., 1984a). This has led to a vast statistical literature on *generalized linear models* (GLM), see McCullagh and Nelder (1989), which permits valid inference providing the conditional mean is correctly specified and nests many types of data as special cases – continuous (normal), count (Poisson), discrete (binomial) and positive (gamma). Many methods for complications, such as time series and panel data models, are presented in the more general GLM framework rather than specifically for count data.

Many econometricians find it more natural to use the *generalized method of moments* (GMM) framework rather than GLM. Then the starting point is the conditional moment $E[y_i - \exp(x_i'\beta) \mid x_i] = 0$. If data are independent over i and the conditional variance is a multiple of the mean it can be shown that the optimal choice of instrument is x_i, leading to the estimating equations (15.5); for more detail, see Cameron and Trivedi (1998, pp. 37–44). The GMM framework has been fruitful for panel data on counts, see Section 5.3, and for *endogenous* regressors. Fully specified simultaneous equations models for counts have not yet been developed, so instrumental variables methods are used. Given instruments z_i, $\dim(z) \geq \dim(x)$, satisfying $E[y_i - \exp(x_i'\beta) \mid z_i] = 0$, a consistent estimator of β minimizes

$$Q(\beta) = \left(\sum_{i=1}^{n} (y_i - \exp(x_i'\beta))z_i \right)' W \left(\sum_{i=1}^{n} (y_i - \exp(x_i'\beta))z_i \right),$$

where W is a symmetric weighting matrix.

4.2 Least squares estimation

When attention is focused on modeling just the conditional mean, least squares methods are inferior to the approach of the previous subsection.

Linear least squares regression of y on x leads to consistent parameter estimates if the conditional mean is linear in x. But for count data the specification $E[y \mid x] = x'\beta$ is inadequate as it permits negative values of $E[y \mid x]$. For similar reasons the linear probability model is inadequate for binary data.

Transformations of y may be considered. In particular the logarithmic transformation regresses $\ln y$ on x. This transformation is problematic if the data contain zeros, as is often the case. One standard solution is to add a constant term, such as 0.5, and to model $\ln(y + .5)$ by OLS. This method often produces unsatisfactory results, and complicates the interpretation of coefficients. It is also unnecessary as software to estimate basic count models is widely available.

4.3 Semiparametric models

By *semiparametric models* we mean partially parametric models that have an infinite-dimensional component.

One example is optimal estimation of the regression parameters β, when $\mu_i = \exp(x_i'\beta)$ is assumed but $V[y_i | x_i] = \omega_i$ is left unspecified. The infinite-dimensional component arises because as $n \to \infty$ there are infinitely many variance parameters ω_i. An optimal estimator of β, called an *adaptive estimator*, is one that is as efficient as that when ω_i is known. Delgado and Kniesner (1997) extend results for the linear regression model to count data with exponential conditional mean function, using kernel regression methods to estimate weights to be used in a second-stage nonlinear least squares regression. In their application the estimator shows little gain over specifying $\omega_i = \mu_i(1 + \alpha\mu_i)$, overdispersion of the NB2 form.

A second class of semiparametric models incompletely specifies the conditional mean. Leading examples are *single-index models* and *partially linear models*. Single-index models specify $\mu_i = g(x_i'\beta)$ where the functional form $g(\cdot)$ is left unspecified. Partially linear models specify $\mu_i = \exp(x_i'\beta + g(z_i))$ where the functional form $g(\cdot)$ is left unspecified. In both cases root-n consistent asymptotically normal estimators of β can be obtained, without knowledge of $g(\cdot)$.

5 TIME SERIES, MULTIVARIATE AND PANEL DATA

In this section we very briefly present extension from cross section to other types of count data (see Cameron and Trivedi, 1998, for further detail). For time series and multivariate count data many models have been proposed but preferred methods have not yet been established. For panel data there is more agreement in the econometrics literature on which methods to use, though a wider range of models is considered in the statistics literature.

5.1 Time series data

If a time series of count data is generated by a Poisson point process then event occurrences in successive time intervals are independent. Independence is a reasonable assumption when the underlying stochastic process for events, conditional on covariates, has no memory. Then there is no need for special time series models. For example, the number of deaths (or births) in a region may be uncorrelated over time. At the same time the population, which cumulates births and deaths, will be very highly correlated over time.

The first step for time series count data is therefore to test for serial correlation. A simple test first estimates a count regression such as Poisson, obtains the residual, usually $(y_t - \exp(x_t'\hat{\beta}))$ where x_t may include time trends, and tests for zero correlation between current and lagged residuals, allowing for the complication that the residuals will certainly be heteroskedastic.

Upon establishing the data are indeed serially correlated, there are several models to choose from. An aesthetically appealing model is the INAR(1) model (*integer autoregressive model* of order one and its generalization to the negative binomial and to higher orders of serial correlation. This model specifies $y_t = \rho_t \circ y_{t-1} + \varepsilon_t$, where ρ_t is a correlation parameter with $0 < \rho_t < 1$, for example $\rho_t = 1/[1 + \exp(-z_t'\gamma)]$. The symbol $\circ$ denotes the *binomial thinning* operator, whereby $\rho_t \circ y_{t-1}$ is the realized value of a binomial random variable with probability of success ρ_t in each of y_{t-1} trials. One may think of each event as having a replication or survival probability of ρ_t in the following period. As in a linear first-order Markov model, this probability decays geometrically. A Poisson INAR(1) model, with a Poisson marginal distribution for y_t arises when ε_t is Poisson distributed with mean, say, $\exp(x_t'\beta)$. A negative binomial INAR(1) model arises if ε_t is negative binomial distributed.

An *autoregressive model*, or *Markov model*, is a simple adjustment to the earlier cross section count models that directly enters lagged values of y into the formula for the conditional mean of current y. For example, we might suppose y_t conditional on current and past x_t and past y_t is Poisson distributed with mean $\exp(x_t'\beta + \rho \ln y_{t-1}^*)$, where y_{t-1}^* is an adjustment to ensure a nonzero lagged value, such as $y_{t-1}^* = (y_{t-1} + 0.5)$ or $y_{t-1}^* = \max(0.5, y_{t-1})$.

Serially correlated error models induce time series correlation by introducing unobserved heterogeneity, see Section 3.1, and allowing this to be serially correlated. For example, y_t is Poisson distributed with mean $\exp(x_t'\beta)v_t$ where v_t is a serially correlated random variable (Zeger, 1988).

State space models or *time-varying parameters models* allow the conditional mean to be a random variable drawn from a distribution whose parameters evolve over time. For example, y_t is Poisson distributed with mean μ_t where μ_t is a draw from a gamma distribution (Harvey and Fernandes, 1989).

Hidden Markov models specify different parametric models in different regimes, and induce serial correlation by specifying the stochastic process determining which regime currently applies to be an unobserved Markov process (MacDonald and Zucchini, 1997).

5.2   Multivariate data

In some data sets more than one count is observed. For example, data on the utilization of several different types of health service, such as doctor visits and hospital days, may be available. Joint modeling will improve efficiency and provide richer models of the data if counts are correlated.

Most parametric studies have used the *bivariate Poisson*. This model, however, is too restrictive as it implies variance–mean equality for the counts and restricts the correlation to be positive. Development of better parametric models is a current area of research.

5.3   Panel data

One of the major and earliest applications of count data methods in econometrics is to panel data on the number of patents awarded to firms over time (Hausman *et al.*, 1984). The starting point is the Poisson regression model with exponential conditional mean and multiplicative individual-specific term

$$y_{it} \sim P[\alpha_i \exp(x'_{it}\beta)], \quad i = 1, \dots, n, \quad t = 1, \dots, T, \quad (15.18)$$

where we consider a short panel with T small and $n \rightarrow \infty$. As in the linear case, both fixed effects and random effects models are possible.

The *fixed effects model* lets α_i be an unknown parameter. This parameter can be eliminated by quasi-differencing and modeling the transformed random variable $y_{it} - (\lambda_{it}/\bar{\lambda}_i)\bar{y}_i$, where $\bar{\lambda}_i$ and $\bar{y}_i$ denote the individual-specific means of λ_{it} and y_{it}. By construction this has zero mean, conditional on $x_{i1}, \dots, x_{iT}$. A moments-based estimator of β then solves the sample moment condition $\sum_{i=1}^{n} \sum_{t=1}^{T} x_{it}(y_{it} - (\lambda_{it}/\bar{\lambda}_i)\bar{y}_i) = 0$.

An alternative to the quasi-differencing approach is the conditional likelihood approach that was followed by Hausman *et al.* (1984). In this approach the fixed effects are eliminated by conditioning the distribution of counts on $\sum_{t=1}^{T} y_{it}$.

The *random effects model* lets α_i be a random variable with specified distribution that depends on parameters, say δ. The random effects are integrated out, in a similar way to the unobserved heterogeneity in Section 3.1, and the parameters β and δ are estimated by maximum likelihood. In some cases, notably when α_i is gamma distributed, a closed-form solution is obtained upon integrating out α_i. In other cases, such as normally distributed random effects, a closed-form solution is not obtained, but ML estimation based on numerical integration is feasible.

Dynamic panel data models permit the regressors x to include lagged values of *y*. Several studies use the fixed effects variant of (15.18), where x_{it} now includes, for example, y_{it-1}. This is an autoregressive count model, see Section 5.1, adapted to panel data. The quasi-differencing procedure for the nondynamic fixed effects case can be adapted to the dynamic case.

6 PRACTICAL CONSIDERATIONS

Those with experience of nonlinear least squares will find it easy to use packaged software for Poisson regression, which is a widely available option in popular econometrics packages like LIMDEP, STATA, and TSP. One should ensure, however, that reported standard errors are based on (15.17) rather than (15.6). Many econometrics packages also include negative binomial regression, also widely used for cross section count regression, and the basic panel data models. Statistics packages such as SAS and SPSS include count regression in a generalized linear models module. Standard packages also produce some goodness-of-fit statistics, such as the G^2-statistic and pseudo-R^2 measures, for the Poisson (see Cameron and Windmeijer, 1996).

More recently developed models, such as finite mixture models, most time series models and dynamic panel data models, require developing one's own programs. A promising route is to use matrix programming languages such as GAUSS, MATLAB, SAS/IML, or SPLUS in conjunction with software for implementing estimation based on user-defined objective functions. For simple models packages such as LIMDEP, STATA, and TSP make it possible to implement maximum likelihood estimation and (highly desirable) robust variance estimation for user-defined functions.

In addition to reporting parameter estimates it is useful to have an indication of the magnitude of the estimated effects, as discussed in Section 2.2. And as noted in Section 2.4, care should be taken to ensure that reported standard errors and t-statistics for the Poisson regression model are based on variance estimates robust to overdispersion.

In addition to estimation it is strongly recommended that specification tests are used to assess the adequacy of the estimated model. For Poisson cross section regression overdispersion tests are easy to implement. For time series regression tests of serial correlation should be used. For any parametric model one can compare the actual and fitted frequency distribution of counts. Formal statistical specification and goodness-of-fit tests based on actual and fitted frequencies are available.

In most practical situations one is likely to face the problem of model selection. For likelihood-based models that are nonnested one can use selection criteria, such as the Akaike and Schwarz criteria, which are based on the fitted loglikelihood but with degrees of freedom penalty for models with many parameters.

7 FURTHER READING

All the topics dealt with in this chapter are treated at greater length and depth in Cameron and Trivedi (1998) which also provides a comprehensive bibliography. Winkelmann (1997) also provides a fairly complete treatment of the econometric literature on counts. The statistics literature generally analyzes counts in the context of generalized linear models (GLM). The standard reference is McCullagh and Nelder (1989). The econometrics literature generally fails to appreciate the contributions of the GLM literature on generalized linear models. Fahrmeir and Tutz (1994) provide a recent and more econometric exposition of GLMs.

The material in Section 2 is very standard and appears in many places. A similar observation applies to the negative binomial model in Section 3.1. Cameron and Trivedi (1986) provide an early presentation and application. For the finite mixture approach of Section 3.2 see Deb and Trivedi (1997). Applications of the hurdle model in Section 3.3 include Mullahy (1986), who first proposed the model, Pohlmeier and Ulrich (1995), and Gurmu and Trivedi (1996). The quasi-MLE of Section 4.1 is presented in detail by Gouriéroux *et al.* (1984a, 1984b) and by Cameron and Trivedi (1986).

Regression models for the types of data discussed in Section 5 are in their infancy. The notable exception is that (static) panel data count models are well established, with the standard reference being Hausman *et al.* (1984). See also Brännäs and Johansson (1996). For reviews of the various time series models see MacDonald and Zucchini (1997, ch. 2) and Cameron and Trivedi (1998, ch. 7). Developing adequate regression models for multivariate count data is currently an active area. For dynamic count panel data models there are several recent references, including Blundell *et al.* (1995).

For further discussion of diagnostic testing, only briefly mentioned in Section 6, see Cameron and Trivedi (1998, ch. 5).

References

Blundell, R., R. Griffith, and J. Van Reenen (1995). Dynamic count data models of technological innovation. *Economic Journal* 105, 333–44.

Brännäs, K., and P. Johansson (1996). Panel data regression for counts. *Statistical Papers* 37, 191–213.

Cameron, A.C., and P.K. Trivedi (1986). Econometric models based on count data: Comparisons and applications of some estimators. *Journal of Applied Econometrics* 1, 29–53.

Cameron, A.C., and P.K. Trivedi (1998). *Regression Analysis of Count Data*. New York: Cambridge University Press.

Cameron, A.C., P.K. Trivedi, F. Milne, and J. Piggott (1988). A microeconometric model of the demand for health care and health insurance in Australia. *Review of Economic Studies* 55, 85–106.

Cameron, A.C., and F.A.G. Windmeijer (1996). R-squared measures for count data regression models with applications to health care utilization. *Journal of Business and Economic Statistics* 14, 209–20.

Davutyan, N. (1989). Bank failures as Poisson variates. *Economic Letters* 29, 333–8.

Deb, P., and P.K. Trivedi (1997). Demand for medical care by the elderly: A finite mixture approach. *Journal of Applied Econometrics* 12, 313–26.

Delgado, M.A., and T.J. Kniesner (1997). Count data models with variance of unknown form: An application to a hedonic model of worker absenteeism. *Review of Economics and Statistics* 79, 41–9.

Fahrmeir, L., and G.T. Tutz (1994). *Multivariate Statistical Modelling Based on Generalized Linear Models*. New York: Springer-Verlag.

Gouriéroux, C., and A. Monfort (1997). *Simulation Based Econometric Methods*. Oxford: Oxford University Press.

Gouriéroux, C., A. Monfort, and A. Trognon (1984a). Pseudo maximum likelihood methods: Theory. *Econometrica* 52, 681–700.

Gouriéroux, C., A. Monfort, and A. Trognon (1984b). Pseudo maximum likelihood methods: Applications to Poisson models. *Econometrica* 52, 701–20.

Gurmu, S., and P.K. Trivedi (1996). Excess zeros in count models for recreational trips. *Journal of Business and Economic Statistics* 14, 469–77.

Harvey, A.C., and C. Fernandes (1989). Time series models for count or qualitative observations (with discussion). *Journal of Business and Economic Statistics* 7, 407–17.

Hausman, J.A., B.H. Hall, and Z. Griliches (1984). Econometric models for count data with an application to the patents–R and D relationship. *Econometrica* 52, 909–38.

Johnson, N.L., S. Kotz, and A.W. Kemp (1992). *Univariate Distributions*, 2nd edn. New York: John Wiley.

MacDonald, I.L., and W. Zucchini (1997). *Hidden Markov and other Models for Discrete-valued Time Series*. London: Chapman and Hall.

McCullagh, P., and J.A. Nelder (1989). *Generalized Linear Models*, 2nd edn. London: Chapman and Hall.

Mullahy, J. (1986). Specification and testing of some modified count data models. *Journal of Econometrics* 33, 341–65.

Nelder, J.A., and R.W.M. Wedderburn (1972). Generalized linear models. *Journal of the Royal Statistical Society* A 135, 370–84.

Pohlmeier, W., and V. Ulrich (1995). An econometric model of the two-part decision-making process in the demand for health care. *Journal of Human Resources* 30, 339–61.

Rose, N. (1990). Profitability and product quality: Economic determinants of airline safety performance. *Journal of Political Economy* 98, 944–64.

Terza, J. (1998). Estimating count data models with endogenous switching: Sample selection and endogenous switching effects. *Journal of Econometrics* 84, 129–39.

Winkelmann, R. (1995). Duration dependence and dispersion in count-data models. *Journal of Business and Economic Statistics* 13, 467–74.

Winkelmann, R. (1997). *Econometric Analysis of Count Data*. Berlin: Springer-Verlag.

Zeger, S.L. (1988). A regression model for time series of counts. *Biometrika* 75, 621–9.

Panel Data Models

Cheng Hsiao*

1 INTRODUCTION

A panel (or longitudinal or temporal cross-sectional) data set is one which follows a number of individuals over time. By providing sequential observations for a number of individuals, panel data allow us to distinguish inter-individual differences from intra-individual differences, thus allow us to construct and test more complicated behavioral models than a single time series or cross section data set would allow. Moreover, panel data offer many more degrees of freedom, provide the possibility to control for omitted variable bias and reduce the problem of multicollinearity, hence improving the accuracy of parameter estimates and prediction (e.g. Baltagi, 1995; Chamberlain, 1984; Hsiao, 1985, 1986, 1995; Mátyás and Sevestre, 1996).

However, the emphasis of panel data is on individual outcomes. Factors affecting individual outcomes are numerous, yet a model is a simplification of the real world. It is neither feasible nor desirable to include all factors that affect the outcomes in the specification. If the specification of the relationships among variables appears proper, yet the outcomes conditional on the included explanatory variables cannot be viewed as random draws from a probability distribution, then standard statistical procedures will lead to misleading inferences. Therefore, the focus of panel data research is on controlling the impact of unobserved heterogeneity among cross-sectional units over time in order to draw inference about the population characteristics.

If heterogeneity among cross-sectional units over time cannot be captured by the explanatory variables, one can either let this heterogeneity be represented by the error term or let the coefficients vary across individuals and/or over time. For instance, for a panel of N individuals over T time periods, a linear model specification can take the form

$$y_{it} = \beta'_{it} x_{it} + u_{it}, \quad i = 1, \ldots, N$$
$$t = 1, \ldots, T, \tag{16.1}$$

where both the coefficients of x variables and the error of the equation vary across individuals and over time. However, model (16.1) only has descriptive value. One can neither estimate β_{it} nor use it to draw inference about the population if each individual is different and varies their behavioral patterns over time. In this chapter we will give a selected survey of panel data models.

For ease of exposition we shall assume that the unobserved heterogeneities vary across individuals but stay constant over time. We discuss linear models in Section 2, dynamic models in Section 3, nonlinear models in Section 4, sample attrition and sample selectivity in Section 5. Conclusions are in Section 6.

2   Linear Models

Suppose there are observations of $1 + k_1 + k_2$ variables $(y_{it}, x'_{it}, z'_{it})$ of N cross-sectional units over T time periods, where $i = 1, \ldots, N$, and $t = 1, \ldots, T$. Let $y = (y'_1, \ldots, y'_N)'$, $X = \text{diag}(X_i)$, $Z = \text{diag}(Z_i)$, where $y'_i = (y_{i1}, \ldots, y_{iT})$, X_i and Z_i are $T \times k_1$ and $T \times k_2$ matrices of T observed values of the explanatory variables x'_{it} and z'_{it} for $i = 1, \ldots, N$. If all the individuals in the panel data are different, we have the unconstrained linear model,

$$y = X\beta + Z\gamma + u, \tag{16.2}$$

where $\beta = (\beta'_1, \ldots, \beta'_N)'$ and $\gamma = (\gamma'_1, \ldots, \gamma'_N)'$ are $Nk_1 \times 1$ and $Nk_2 \times 1$ vector of constants, $u = (u'_1, \ldots, u'_N)$ is an $NT \times 1$ vector of the error term, β_i, γ_i and u_i denote the coefficients of X_i, Z_i and the error of the ith individual for $i = 1, \ldots, N$. We assume that u is independent of x and z and is multivariately normally distributed with mean 0 and covariance matrix C_1,[1]

$$u \sim N(0, C_1). \tag{16.3}$$

There is no particular advantage of pooling the panel data to estimate (16.2) except for the possibility of exploiting the common shocks in the error term if C_1 is not block diagonal by applying the Zellner's (1962) seemingly unrelated regression estimator. To take advantage of the panel data there must be constraints on (16.2). Two types of constraints are commonly imposed – stochastic and exact. We shall assume that the coefficients of x_{it} are subject to stochastic constraints and the coefficients of z_{it} are subject to exact constraints.

To postulate stochastic constraints, we let

$$\beta = \begin{pmatrix} \beta_1 \\ \vdots \\ \beta_N \end{pmatrix} = A_1 \bar{\beta} + \varepsilon, \tag{16.4}$$

where A_1 is an $Nk_1 \times m$ matrix with known elements, $\bar{\beta}$ is an $m \times 1$ vector of constants, and

$$\underline{\varepsilon} \sim N(\underline{0}, C_2). \tag{16.5}$$

The variance covariance matrix C_2 is assumed to be nonsingular. Furthermore, we assume that[2]

$$\text{cov}(\underline{\varepsilon}, \underline{u}) = 0, \text{cov}(\underline{\varepsilon}, X) = \underline{0} \quad \text{and} \quad \text{cov}(\underline{\varepsilon}, Z) = \underline{0}. \tag{16.6}$$

To postulate exact constraints, we let

$$\underline{\gamma} = \begin{pmatrix} \underline{\gamma}_1 \\ \vdots \\ \underline{\gamma}_N \end{pmatrix} = A_2 \bar{\underline{\gamma}}, \tag{16.7}$$

where A_2 is an $Nk_2 \times n$ matrix with known elements, and $\bar{\underline{\gamma}}$ is an $n \times 1$ vector of constants. Because A_2 is known, (16.2) is formally identical to

$$\underline{y} = X\underline{\beta} + \tilde{Z}\bar{\underline{\gamma}} + \underline{u}, \tag{16.8}$$

where $\tilde{Z} = ZA_2$.

Formulation (16.4)–(16.8) encompasses various linear panel data models as special cases. These include:

1. *A common model for all cross-sectional units* by letting $X = \underline{0}$, $A_2 = \underline{e}_N \otimes I_{k_2}$, where $\underline{e}_N$ is an $N \times 1$ vector of ones, I_p denotes a $p \times p$ identity matrix and $\otimes$ denotes Kronecker product.
2. *Different models for different cross-sectional units* by letting $X = 0$ and A_2 be an $Nk_2 \times Nk_2$ identity matrix.
3. *Variable intercept models* (e.g. Kuh, 1963; Mundlak, 1978) by letting $X = 0$, $Z_i = (\underline{e}_T, \tilde{Z}_i)$, $A_2 = (I_N \otimes \underline{i}_{k_2} \vdots \underline{e}_N \otimes I^*_{k_2-1})$ where $\underline{i}_{k_2}$ is a $k_2 \times 1$ vector of $(1, 0, \ldots, 0)'$ and $I^*_{k_2-1}$ is a $k_2 \times (k_2 - 1)$ matrix of $\begin{pmatrix} \underline{0}' \\ I_{k_2-1} \end{pmatrix}$.
4. *Error components model* (e.g. Balestra and Nerlove, 1966; Wallace and Hussain, 1969) by letting $X_i = \underline{e}_T$, $A_1 = \underline{e}_N$, $C_2 = \sigma_\beta^2 I_N$.
5. *Random coefficients models* (e.g. Hsiao, 1974, 1975; Swamy, 1970) by letting $Z = \underline{0}$, $A_1 = \underline{e}_N \otimes I_{k_1}$, $C_2 = I_N \otimes \Delta$, where $\Delta = E(\underline{\beta}_i - \bar{\underline{\beta}})(\underline{\beta}_i - \bar{\underline{\beta}})'$.
6. *Mixed fixed and random coefficients models* (e.g. Hsiao et al., 1989; Hsiao and Mountain, 1995; Hsiao and Tahmiscioglu, 1997) as postulated by (16.4)–(16.8).

Substituting (16.4) into (16.8), we have

$$\underline{y} = XA_1\bar{\underline{\beta}} + \tilde{Z}\bar{\underline{\gamma}} + \underline{u}^*, \tag{16.9}$$

with $\underline{u}^* = \underline{u} + X\underline{\varepsilon}$. The generalized least squares (GLS) estimator of (16.9) is

$$\begin{pmatrix} \hat{\beta}_{GLS} \\ \hat{\gamma}_{GLS} \end{pmatrix} = \begin{pmatrix} A_1'X'(C_1 + XC_2X')^{-1}XA_1 & A_1'X(C_1 + XC_2X')^{-1}\tilde{Z} \\ \tilde{Z}'(C_1 + X'C_2X')^{-1}XA_1 & \tilde{Z}'(C_1 + XC_2X')^{-1}\tilde{Z} \end{pmatrix}^{-1}$$

$$\begin{pmatrix} A_1'X'(C_1 + XC_2X')^{-1}\underset{\sim}{y} \\ \tilde{Z}'(C_1 + XC_2X')^{-1}\underset{\sim}{y} \end{pmatrix}. \tag{16.10}$$

The GLS estimator is also the Bayes estimator conditional on C_1 and C_2 with a diffuse prior for $\bar{\beta}$ and $\bar{\gamma}$ (Lindley and Smith, 1972; Hsiao, 1990). Moreover, if predicting individual β_i is of interest, the Bayes procedure predicts $\underset{\sim}{\beta_i}$ as a weighted average between the GLS estimator of $\bar{\beta}$ and the individual least squares estimator of $\hat{\underset{\sim}{\beta}}_i$ (Hsiao et al., 1993)

$$\hat{\underset{\sim}{\beta}}^* = \{X'DX + C_2^{-1}\}^{-1}\{X'DX\hat{\underset{\sim}{\beta}} + C_2^{-1}A_1\hat{\underset{\sim}{\beta}}\}, \tag{16.11}$$

where $D = [C_1^{-1} - C_1^{-1}\tilde{Z}(\tilde{Z}'C_1^{-1}\tilde{Z})^{-1}\tilde{Z}'C_1]$ and

$$\hat{\underset{\sim}{\beta}} = \{X'DX\}^{-1}\{X'D\underset{\sim}{y}\} \tag{16.12}$$

In other words, if cross-sectional units are similar as postulated in (16.4), there is an advantage of pooling since if there is not enough information about a cross-sectional unit, one can obtain a better prediction of that individual's outcome by learning from other cross section units that behave similarly.

The above formulation presupposes that which variables are subject to stochastic constraints and which variables are subject to deterministic constraints is known. In practice, there is very little knowledge about it. In certain special cases, formal statistical testing procedures have been proposed (e.g. Breusch and Pagan, 1980; Hausman, 1978). However, a typical test postulates a simple null versus a composite alternative. The distribution of a test statistic is derived under an assumed true null hypothesis. A rejection of a null hypothesis does not automatically imply the acceptance of a particular alternative. However, most of the tests of fixed versus random effects specification are indirect in the sense that they exploit a particular implication of the random effects formulation. For instance, the rejection of a null of homoskedasticity does not automatically imply the acceptance of a particular alternative of random effects. In fact, it would be more useful to view the above different formulations as different models and treat them as an issue of model selection. Various model selection criteria (e.g. Akaike, 1973; Schwarz, 1978) can be used. Alternatively, predictive density ratio (e.g. Hsiao and Tahmiscioglu, 1997; Min and Zellner, 1993) can be used to select the appropriate formulation. The predictive density ratio approach divides the time series observations into two periods, 1 to T_1, denoted by $\underset{\sim}{y_1^*}$ and $T_1 + 1$ to T, denoted by $\underset{\sim}{y_2^*}$. The first period observations, $\underset{\sim}{y_1^*}$, are used to derive the posterior probability distribution of θ_0 and θ_1 given hypothesis H_0 and H_1, $f(\theta_0 | \underset{\sim}{y_1^*})$ and $f(\theta | \underset{\sim}{y_1^*})$. The second period observations are used to compare how H_0 or H_1 predicts the outcome. The predictive density ratio is then computed as

$$\frac{\int f(y_2^* \mid \underset{\sim}{\theta}_0, y_1^*) f(\underset{\sim}{\theta}_0 \mid y_1^*) d\underset{\sim}{\theta}_0}{\int f(y_2^* \mid \underset{\sim}{\theta}_1, y_1^*) f(\underset{\sim}{\theta}_0 \mid y_1^*) d\underset{\sim}{\theta}_1},$$ (16.13)

where $f(y_2^* \mid \underset{\sim}{\theta}_1, y_1^*)$ and $f(y_2^* \mid \underset{\sim}{\theta}_2, y_2^*)$ are the conditional densities of y_2^* given y_1^* and $\underset{\sim}{\theta}_0$ or $\underset{\sim}{\theta}_1$. If (16.13) is greater than 1, then H_0 is favored. If (16.13) is less than 1, then H_1 is favored. When T is small, a recursive updating scheme of the posterior probability distribution of $\underset{\sim}{\theta}_0$ and $\underset{\sim}{\theta}_1$ each with additional observations can be used to balance the sample dependence of predictive outcome and informativeness of the conditional density of $\underset{\sim}{\theta}_i$ given observables. The Monte Carlo studies appear to indicate that the predictive density ratio performs well in selecting the appropriate formulation (e.g. Hsiao et al., 1995; Hsiao and Tahmiscioglu, 1997).

3   DYNAMIC MODELS

When $\underset{\sim}{x}_{it}$ and/or $\underset{\sim}{z}_{it}$ contain lagged dependent variables, because a typical panel contains a large number of cross-sectional units followed over a short period of time, it turns out that how the initial value of the dependent variable is modeled plays a crucial role with regard to the consistency and efficiency of an estimator (e.g. Anderson and Hsiao, 1981, 1982; Bhargava and Sargan, 1983; Blundell and Bond, 1998). Moreover, if there exists unobserved heterogeneity and the individual specific effects is more appropriately treated as random, the random effects and the lagged dependent variables are correlated, thus (16.6) is violated. If the individual effects are treated as fixed, then the number of individual specific parameters increases with the number of cross-sectional units, N. Contrary to the static case of Section 2, the estimation of the individual specific effects in a dynamic model is not independent of the estimation of the structural parameters that are common across N and T. Since for each individual there are only a finite number of observations, there is no way the individual specific parameters can be accurately estimated. The errors in the estimation of individual specific parameters will be transmitted into the estimation of the structural parameters if the two estimators are not independent. This is the classical incidental parameters problem (Neyman and Scott, 1948).

Consider a simple dynamic model with individual specific effects appearing in the intercepts only,

$$\underset{\sim}{y}_i = \underset{\sim}{e}_T \alpha_i + \underset{\sim}{y}_{i,-1} \gamma_1 + Z_i \underset{\sim}{\gamma}_2 + \underset{\sim}{u}_i$$ (16.14)

where $\underset{\sim}{z}_{it}$ is a $k_2 - 1$ dimensional exogenous variables, $\underset{\sim}{y}_{i,-1} = (y_{i,0}, \ldots, y_{i,T-1})$ and for ease of exposition, we assume that y_{i0} are observable. Let H be an $m \times T$ transformation matrix such that $H\underset{\sim}{e}_T = 0$. Multiplying H to (16.14), we eliminate the individual specific effects α_i from the specification,

$$H\underset{\sim}{y}_i = H\underset{\sim}{y}_{i,-1} \gamma_1 + HZ_i \underset{\sim}{\gamma}_2 + H\underset{\sim}{u}_i.$$ (16.15)

Since (16.15) does not depend on α_i, if we can find instruments that are correlated with the explanatory variables but uncorrelated with $H\underset{\sim}{u}_i$, we can apply the instrumental variable method to estimate γ_1 and γ_2 (e.g. Anderson and Hsiao, 1981, 1982). Let W_i be the $q \times m$ matrix of instrumental variables that satisfies

$$E(W_i H \underline{u}_i) = 0. \tag{16.16}$$

The generalized method of moments (GMM) estimator takes the form

$$\begin{pmatrix} \hat{\gamma}_1 \\ \hat{\gamma}_2 \end{pmatrix} = \left\{ \left[\sum_{i=1}^{N} \begin{pmatrix} y'_{i,-1} \\ Z'_i \end{pmatrix} H'W'_i \right] \left(\sum_{i=1}^{N} W_i \Phi W'_i \right)^{-1} \left[\sum_{i=1}^{N} W_i H(y_{i,-1}, Z_i) \right] \right\}^{-1}$$

$$\left\{ \left[\sum_{i=1}^{N} \begin{pmatrix} y'_{i,-1} \\ Z'_i \end{pmatrix} H'W'_i \right] \left(\sum_{i=1}^{N} W_i \Phi W'_i \right)^{-1} \left[\sum_{i=1}^{N} W_i H y_i \right] \right\}, \tag{16.17}$$

where $\Phi = E(H\underline{u}_i \underline{u}'_i H')$. In the case when the transformation matrix H takes the form of first differencing (16.14), H is a $(T - 1) \times T$ matrix with all the elements in the tth row equal to zero except for the tth and $(t + 1)$th element that takes the value of -1 and 1, respectively. If u_{it} is iid, then W_i takes the form (e.g. Ahn and Schmidt, 1995; Amemiya and MaCurdy, 1986; Arellano and Bover, 1995; Blundell and Bond, 1998)

$$W'_i = \begin{pmatrix} z'_i & 0' & 0' & 0 & 0 \\ 0 & y_{i0}, z'_i & 0' & 0 & 0 \\ 0 & 0 & y_{i0}, y_{i1}, z'_i & 0 & \cdot \\ \cdot & \cdot & \cdot & \cdot & \cdot \\ \cdot & \cdot & \cdot & \cdot & y_{i0}, y_{i1}, \ldots, y_{i,T-2}, z'_i \end{pmatrix}, \tag{16.18}$$

where $z'_i = (z'_{i1}, \ldots, z'_{iT})$.

GMM estimator (16.17) makes use of $\frac{T(T-1)}{2} + T(k_2 - 1)$ orthogonality conditions. Where $k_2 - 1$ denotes the dimension of z_{it}. In most applications, this is a large number. For instance, even in the case of $k_2 - 1 = 0$, there are still 45 orthogonality conditions for a model with only one lagged dependent variable when $T = 10$ which makes the implementation of the GMM estimator (16.17) nontrivial. Moreover, in finite sample, it suffers severe bias as demonstrated in a Monte Carlo study conducted by Ziliak (1997) because of the correlation between the estimated weight matrix and the sample moments and/or the weak instruments phenomena (Wansbeek and Knaap, 1999). The bias of the GMM estimator leads to poor coverage rates for confidence intervals based on asymptotic critical values. Hsiao, Pesaran and Tahmiscioglu (1998b) propose a transformed maximum likelihood estimator that maximizes the likelihood function of (16.15) and the initial value function

$$\nabla y_{i1} = \underline{\delta}' \nabla z_i + v_i, \tag{16.19}$$

where ∇z_i denotes the first difference of z_i. The transformed MLE is consistent and asymptotically normally distributed provided that the generating process of z_{it} is difference stationary, i.e. the data generating process of z_{it} is of the form

$$z_{it} = \mu_i + gt + \sum_{j=0}^{\infty} B_j \tau_{i,t-j}, \tag{16.20}$$

where τ_{it} is iid with constant mean and covariances, and $\Sigma \| B_j \| < \infty$. The transformed MLE is easier to implement than the GMM and is asymptotically more efficient because the GMM requires each instrument to be orthogonal to the transformed error while the transformed MLE only requires a linear combination of the instruments to be orthogonal to the transformed errors. The Monte Carlo studies conducted by Hsiao, Pesaran and Tahmiscioglu (1998) show that the transformed MLE performs very well even when T and N both are small.

Where individual heterogeneity cannot be completely captured by individual time-invariant effects, a varying parameter model is often used. However, while it may be reasonable to assume (16.5), (16.6) cannot hold if x_{it} contains lagged dependent variables. For instance, consider a simple dynamic model

$$\begin{aligned} y_{it} &= \beta_i y_{i,t-1} + \bar{\gamma} z_{it} + u_{it} \\ &= \bar{\beta} y_{i,t-1} + \bar{\gamma} z_{it} + v_{it}, \end{aligned} \tag{16.21}$$

where $v_{it} = \varepsilon_i y_{i,t-1} + u_{it}$. By continuous substitution, it can be shown that

$$y_{i,t-1} = \bar{\gamma} \sum_{j=0}^{\infty} \left(\bar{\beta} + \varepsilon_i \right)^j z_{i,t-j-1} + \sum_{j=0}^{\infty} \left(\bar{\beta} + \varepsilon_i \right)^j u_{i,t-j-1}. \tag{16.22}$$

It follows that $E(v_{it} \mid y_{i,t-1}) \neq 0$. Therefore, the least squares estimator is inconsistent. Neither is the instrumental variable estimator feasible because the instruments that are uncorrelated with v_{it} are most likely uncorrelated with z_{it} as well.

Noting that when $T \to \infty$, estimating the coefficients of each cross-sectional unit using the least squares method is consistent, Pesaran and Smith (1995) propose a mean group estimator that takes an average of the individual least squares estimated $\tilde{\beta}_i$,

$$\hat{\bar{\beta}} = \frac{1}{N} \sum_{i=1}^{N} \tilde{\beta}_i. \tag{16.23}$$

When both T and $N \to \infty$, (16.23) is consistent. However, the Monte Carlo studies conducted by Hsiao, Pesaran and Tahmiscioglu (1999) show that (16.23) does not perform well in finite sample.

Under (16.4), (16.5), conditional on y_{i0} being a fixed constant, the Bayes estimators of $\bar{\beta}$ and $\bar{\gamma}$ are identical to (16.10), conditional on C_1 and C_2 with diffuse priors for β and γ̄ (Hsiao, Pesaran and Tahmiscioglu, 1999). The Monte Carlo studies show that a hierarchical Bayesian approach (e.g. Lindley and Smith, 1972) performs fairly well even when T is small and better than other consistent estimators despite the fact that y_{i0} being a fixed constant is not justifiable. This makes Bayes' procedure particularly appealing. Moreover, the implementation of a Bayesian approach has been substantially simplified by the recent advance of Markov Chain Monte Carlo methods (e.g. Gelfand and Smith, 1990).

4 NONLINEAR MODELS

The existence of individual specific effects in nonlinear models is particularly difficult to handle. First, in general there is no simple transformation of the data to eliminate the individual specific effects. Second, the estimation of the individual specific parameters and the structural (or common) parameters are not independent of each other. When a panel contains a large number of individuals but only over a short time period, the error in the estimation of the individual specific coefficients is transmitted into the estimation of the structural parameters, and hence leads to inconsistency of the structural parameter estimation. If individual specific effects are treated as random, the estimation of the structural parameters often requires integrating out the individual effects. It is often computationally unwieldy (e.g. Hsiao, 1992).

Many approaches have been suggested for estimating nonlinear panel data models. One approach is the conditional maximum likelihood approach by conditioning the likelihood function on the minimum sufficient statistics for the incidental parameters to eliminate the individual specific parameters (Anderson, 1970; Chamberlain, 1980). For instance, consider a binary logit model in which the probability of $y_{it} = 1$ is given by

$$P(y_{it} = 1) = \frac{e^{\alpha_i + \gamma' z_{it}}}{1 + e^{\alpha_i + \gamma' z_{it}}} \tag{16.24}$$

For ease of exposition, we assume that $T = 2$. It can be shown that when $z_{i1} = 0$, $z_{i2} = 1$ the MLE of γ converges to 2γ as $N \to \infty$, which is not consistent (e.g. Hsiao, 1986). However, we may condition the likelihood function on the minimum sufficient statistic of α_i. We note that for those individuals that $y_{i1} + y_{i2} = 2$ or $y_{i1} + y_{i2} = 0$, they provide no information about γ since the former leads to $\hat{\alpha}_i = \infty$ and the latter leads to $\hat{\alpha}_i = -\infty$. Only those individuals that $y_{i1} + y_{i2} = 1$ provide information about γ. For individuals that $y_{i1} + y_{i2} = 1$, let $d_i = 1$ if $y_{i1} = 0$ and $y_{i2} = 1$ and $d_i = 0$ if $y_{i1} = 1$ and $y_{i2} = 0$, then

$$\text{prob}\,(d_i = 1 \mid y_{i1} + y_{i2} = 1) = \frac{e^{\gamma'(z_{i2} - z_{i1})}}{1 + e^{\gamma'(z_{i2} - z_{i1})}}. \tag{16.25}$$

Equation (16.25) no longer contains the individual effects α_i and is of the form of a standard logit model. Therefore, maximizing the conditional loglikelihood function on the subset of individuals with $y_{i1} + y_{i2} = 1$ is consistent and asymptotically normally distributed as N tends to infinity.

The problem becomes more complicated if lagged dependent variables representing state dependence also appear in z_{it} in the specification (16.24), Chamberlain (1984) shows that we need $T \geq 4$ for the identification of a logit model of the form

$$P(y_{it} = 1 \mid \alpha_i, y_{i1}, \dots, y_{i,t-1}) = \frac{e^{\alpha_i + \gamma_1 y_{i,t-1}}}{1 + e^{\alpha_i + \gamma_1 y_{i,t-1}}}. \tag{16.26}$$

When exogenous variables are also present, consider the events $A = \{y_{i1}, y_{i2} = 0, y_{i3} = 1, y_{i4}\}$ and $B = \{y_{i1}, y_{i2} = 1, y_{i3} = 0, y_{i4}\}$, where y_{i1} and y_{i4} are either 0 or 1. Then

$$P(A \mid z_i, \alpha_i) = P_1(z_i, \alpha_i)^{y_{i1}} (1 - P_1(z_i, \alpha_i))^{1-y_{i1}}$$

$$\cdot \frac{1}{1 + \exp(\gamma_1 y_{i1} + z'_{i2}\gamma_2 + \alpha_i)} \cdot \frac{\exp(z'_{i3}\gamma_2 + \alpha_i)}{1 + \exp(z'_{i3}\gamma_2 + \alpha_i)}$$

$$\cdot \frac{\exp y_{i4}(\gamma_1 + \gamma'_2 z_{i4} + \alpha_i)}{1 + \exp(\gamma_1 + \gamma'_2 z_{i4} + \alpha_i)}, \tag{16.27}$$

and

$$P(B \mid z_i, \alpha_i) = P_1(z_i, \alpha_i)^{y_{i1}} (1 - P_1(z_i, \alpha_i))^{1-y_{i1}}$$

$$\cdot \frac{\exp(\gamma_1 y_{i1} + z'_{i2}\gamma_2 + \alpha_i)}{1 + \exp(\gamma_1 y_{i1} + z'_{i2}\gamma_2 + \alpha_i)} \cdot \frac{1}{1 + \exp(\gamma_1 + \gamma'_2 z_{i3} + \alpha_i)}$$

$$\cdot \frac{\exp y_{i4}(\gamma'_2 z_{i4} + \alpha_i)}{1 + \exp(\gamma'_2 z_{i4} + \alpha_i)}, \tag{16.28}$$

where $P_1(z_i, \alpha_i)$ denotes the probability that $y_{i1} = 1$ given α_i and $z'_i = (z_{i1}, \dots, z_{iT})$ where z_{it} is a $k_2 - 1$ dimensional exogenous variables and $T = 4$ here. In general, $P(A \mid z_i, \alpha_i, A \cup B)$ will depend on α_i, hence the conditional method in general will not work with the presence of exogenous explanatory variables.

However, if $z_{i3} = z_{i4}$, then

$$P(A \mid z_i, \alpha_i, A \cup B, z_{i3} = z_{i4}) = \frac{1}{1 + \exp\left[(z_{i2} - z_{i3})'\gamma_2 + \gamma_1(y_{i4} - y_{i1})\right]} \tag{16.29}$$

will not depend on α_i. Thus, Honoré and Kyriazidou (1997), Chintagunta, Kyriazidou and Perktold (1998) suggest maximizing

$$\sum_{i=1}^{N} \sum_{1 \leq s < t \leq T-1} I(y_{is} + y_{it} = 1) K\left(\frac{z_{i,s+1} - z_{i,t+1}}{h_N}\right)$$

$$\cdot \ln\left[\frac{\exp[(z_{is} - z_{it})'\gamma_2 + \gamma_1(y_{i,s-1} - y_{i,t+1}) + \gamma_1(y_{i,s+1} - y_{i,t-1})]\mathbb{1}(t - s \geq 3)^{y_{is}}}{1 + \exp[(z_{is} - z_{it})'\gamma_2 + \gamma_1(y_{i,s-1} - y_{i,t+1}) + \gamma_1(y_{i,s+1} - y_{i,t-1})]\mathbb{1}(t - s \geq 3)}\right] \tag{16.30}$$

where $I(\cdot)$ denotes the indicator function, $K(\cdot)$ is a kernel function such that $K(v)$ $\to 0$ as $|v| \to \infty$, and h_N is a bandwidth which shrinks to zero as $N \to \infty$. Honoré and Kyriazidou (1997) show that the estimator is consistent and asymptotically normal, with the rate of convergence proportional to $\sqrt{Nh_N^{k_2-1}}$. (For additional discussion, see chapter 17 by Maddala and Flores-Lagunes in this volume.)

Another approach to estimating a nonlinear panel data model is to apply some data transformation to eliminate the individual effects if the nonlinear model is of the form of a single index model where the index possesses a linear structure. Some semiparametric methods can then be applied to the transformed data. For instance, a binary choice model can be written in the form $y_{it} = 1$ if $y_{it}^* > 0$ and $y_{it} = 0$ if $y_{it}^* \leq 0$, where

$$y_{it}^* = \alpha_i + \underline{\gamma}'\underline{z}_{it} + \varepsilon_{it}. \tag{16.31}$$

Thus, if ε_{it} follows a logistic distribution, we have a logit model (16.21). If $\underline{\varepsilon}_{it}$ is normally distributed, we have a probit model (e.g. Hsiao, 1992). Then

$$\underline{\gamma}'\underline{z}_{it} > \underline{\gamma}'\underline{z}_{i,t-1} \Leftrightarrow E(y_{it}\,|\,\underline{z}_{it}) > E(y_{i,t-1}\,|\,\underline{z}_{i,t-1}),$$
$$\underline{\gamma}'\underline{z}_{it} = \underline{\gamma}'\underline{z}_{i,t-1} \Leftrightarrow E(y_{it}\,|\,\underline{z}_{it}) = E(y_{i,t-1}\,|\,\underline{z}_{i,t-1}),$$
$$\underline{\gamma}'\underline{z}_{it} < \underline{\gamma}'\underline{z}_{i,t-1} \Leftrightarrow E(y_{it}\,|\,\underline{z}_{it}) < E(y_{i,t-1}\,|\,\underline{z}_{i,t-1}). \tag{16.32}$$

Rewriting (16.28) into the equivalent first difference form, Manski (1975) proposes a maximum score estimator (MS) that maximizes the sample average function

$$\frac{1}{N}\sum_{i=1}^{N}\sum_{t=2}^{T}\text{sgn}\,[(\underline{z}_{it} - \underline{z}_{i,t-1})'\underline{\gamma}](y_{it} - y_{i,t-1}), \tag{16.33}$$

where $\text{sgn}[(\underline{z}_{it} - \underline{z}_{i,t-1})'\underline{\gamma}] = 1$ if $(\underline{z}_{it} - \underline{z}_{i,t-1})'\underline{\gamma} \geq 0$ and $\text{sgn}[(\underline{z}_{it} - \underline{z}_{i,t-1})'\underline{\gamma}] = -1$ if $(\underline{z}_{it} - \underline{z}_{i,t-1})'\underline{\gamma} < 0$. The MS is consistent but is not root-n consistent, where $n = N(T-1)$. Its rate of convergence is $n^{\frac{1}{3}}$ and $n^{\frac{1}{3}}(\hat{\underline{\gamma}} - \underline{\gamma})$ converges to a nonnormal distribution.[3]

A third approach is to find an orthogonal reparameterization of the fixed effects for each individual, say α_i, to a new fixed effects, say g_i, which is independent of the structural parameters in the information matrix sense. The g_i are then integrated out of the likelihood with respect to an uninformative, uniform prior distribution which is independent of the prior distribution of the structural parameters. Lancaster (1998) uses a two period duration model to show that the marginal posterior density of the structural parameter possesses a mode which consistently estimates the true parameter.

While all these methods are quite ingenious, unfortunately, none of these approaches can claim general applicability. For instance, the conditional maximum likelihood cannot work for the probit model because there does not exist simple minimum sufficient statistics for the incidental parameters that are independent of the structural parameters. The data transformation approach cannot work if the model does not have a latent linear structure. The orthogonal reparameterization approach only works for some particular model. The general properties of such procedures remain unknown. In short, the method and consistency of nonlinear panel data estimators must be established case by case.

5 Sample Attrition and Sample Selection

Missing observations occur frequently in panel data. If individuals are missing randomly, most estimation methods for the balanced panel can be extended in a straightforward manner to the unbalanced panel (e.g. Hsiao, 1986). For instance, suppose that

$$d_{it}y_{it} = d_{it}[\alpha_i + \underline{\gamma}'z_{it} + u_{it}], \tag{16.34}$$

where d_{it} is an observable scalar indicator variable which denotes whether information about (y_{it}, z'_{it}) for the ith individual at tth time period is available or not. The indicator variable d_{it} is assumed to depend on a q-dimensional variables, $\underline{w}_{it}$, individual specific effects λ_i and an unobservable error term η_{it},

$$d_{it} = I(\lambda_i + \underline{\delta}'w_{it} + \eta_{it} > 0), \tag{16.35}$$

where $I(\cdot)$ is the indicator function that takes the value of 1 if $\lambda_i + \underline{\delta}'w_{it} + \eta_{it} > 0$ and 0 otherwise. In other words, the indicator variable d_{it} determines whether (y_{it}, z_{it}) in (16.34) is observed or not (e.g. Hausman and Wise, 1979).

Without sample selectivity, that is $d_{it} = 1$ for all i and t, (16.31) is the standard variable intercept (or fixed effects) model for panel data discussed in Section 2. With sample selection and if η_{it} and u_{it} are correlated, $E(u_{it} | z_{it}, d_{it} = 1) \neq 0$. Let $\theta(\cdot)$ denote the conditional expectation of u_{it} conditional on $d_{it} = 1$ and $\underline{w}_{it}$, then (16.31) can be written as

$$y_{it} = \alpha_i + \underline{\gamma}'z_{it} + \theta(\lambda_i + \underline{\delta}'w_{it}) + \varepsilon_{it}, \tag{16.36}$$

where $E(\varepsilon_{it} | z_{it}, d_{it} = 1) = 0$. The form of the selection function is derived from the joint distribution of u and η. For instance, if u and η are bivariate normal, then we have the Heckman (1979) sample selection model with $\theta(\lambda_i + \underline{\delta}'w_{it}) = \sigma_{u\eta} \dfrac{\phi(\lambda_i + \underline{\delta}'w_{it})}{\Phi(\lambda_i + \underline{\delta}'w_{it})}$, where $\sigma_{u\eta}$ denotes the covariance between u and η, $\phi(\cdot)$ and $\Phi(\cdot)$ are standard normal density and distribution, respectively, and the variance of η is normalized to be 1. Therefore, in the presence of sample attrition or selection, regressing y_{it} on z_{it} using only the observed information is invalidated by two problems. First, the presence of the unobserved effects α_i, and second, the "selection bias" arising from the fact that $E(u_{it} | z_{it}, d_{it} = 1) = \theta(\lambda_i + \underline{\delta}w_{it})$.

When individual effects are random and the joint distribution function of $(u, \eta, \gamma_i, \lambda_i)$ is known, both the maximum likelihood and two- or multi-step estimators can be derived (e.g. Heckman, 1979; and Ryu, 1998). The resulting estimators are consistent and asymptotically normally distributed. The speed of convergence is proportional to the square root of the sample size. However, if the joint distribution of u and η is misspecified, then even without the presence of

α_i, both the maximum likelihood and Heckman (1979) two-step estimators will be inconsistent. This sensitivity of parameter estimate to the exact specification of the error distribution has motivated the interest in semiparametric methods.

The presence of individual effects is easily solved by pairwise differencing those individuals that are observed for two time periods t and s, i.e. who has $d_{it} = d_{is} = 1$. However, the sample selectivity factors are not eliminated by pairwise differencing. The expected value of $y_{it} - y_{is}$ given $d_{it} = 1$ and $d_{is} = 1$ takes the form

$$E(y_{it} - y_{is} \mid d_{it} = 1, d_{is} = 1) = (z_{it} - z_{is})'\gamma + E[u_{it} - u_{is} \mid d_{it} = 1, d_{is} = 1]. \quad (16.37)$$

In general,

$$\theta_{its} = E(u_{it} - u_{is} \mid d_{it} = 1, d_{is} = 1) \neq 0 \quad (16.38)$$

and are different from each other. If (u_{it}, η_{it}) are independent, identically distributed (iid) and are independent of α_i, λ_i, z and w, then

$$\theta_{it} = E(u_{it} \mid d_{it} = 1, d_{is} = 1) = E(u_{it} \mid d_{it} = 1)$$

$$= E(u_{it} \mid \eta_{it} > -w_{it}'\delta - \lambda_i) = \theta(\delta'w_{it} + \lambda_i), \quad (16.39)$$

where the second equality is due to the independence over time assumption of the error vector and the third equality is due to the independence of the errors to the individual effects and the explanatory variables. The function $\theta(\cdot)$ of the single index, $\delta'w_{it} + \lambda_i$, is the same over i and t because of the iid assumption of (u_{it}, η_{it}), but in general, $\theta(\delta'w_{it} + \lambda_i) \neq \theta(\delta'w_{is} + \lambda_i)$ because of the time variation of the scalar index $\delta'w_{it}$. However, for an individual i that has $\delta'w_{it} = \delta'w_{is}$ and $d_{it} = d_{is} = 1$, the sample selection effect θ_{it} will be the same in the two periods. Therefore, for this particular individual, time differencing eliminates both the unobserved individual effect and the sample selection effect,

$$y_{it} - y_{is} = \gamma'(z_{it} - z_{is}) + (\varepsilon_{it} - \varepsilon_{is}). \quad (16.40)$$

This suggests estimating γ by the least squares from a subsample that consists of those observations that satisfy $\delta'w_{it} = \delta'w_{is}$ and $d_{it} = d_{is} = 1$,

$$\hat{\gamma} = \left[\sum_{i=1}^{N} \sum_{1 \leq s < t \leq T_i} (z_{it} - z_{is})(z_{it} - z_{is})' 1\{(w_{it} - w_{is})'\delta = 0\} d_{it} d_{is} \right]^{-1}$$

$$\left[\sum_{i=1}^{N} \sum_{1 \leq s < t \leq T_i} (z_{it} - z_{is})(y_{it} - y_{is}) 1\{(w_{it} - w_{is})'\delta\} d_{it} d_{is} \right] \quad (16.41)$$

where T_i denotes the number of ith individual's time series observations.

The estimator (16.41) cannot be directly implemented because δ is unknown. Moreover, the scalar index $\delta'w_{it}$ will typically be continuous if any of the variables in w_{it} is continuous. Ahn and Powell (1993) note that if θ is a sufficiently "smooth" function, and $\hat{\underline{\delta}}$ is a consistent estimator of $\underline{\delta}$, observations for which the difference $(w_{it} - w_{is})'\hat{\underline{\delta}}$ is close to zero should have $\theta_{it} - \theta_{is} \simeq 0$. They propose a two-step procedure. In the first step, consistent semiparameter estimates of the coefficients of the "selection" equation are obtained. The result is used to obtain estimates of the "single index, $w_{it}\hat{\underline{\delta}}$," variables characterizing the selectivity bias in the equation of index. The second step of the approach estimates the parameters of the equation of interest by a weighted instrumental variables regression of pairwise differences in dependent variables in the sample on the corresponding differences in explanatory variables; the weights put more emphasis on pairs with $w'_{it}\hat{\underline{\delta}} \simeq w'_{i,t-1}\hat{\underline{\delta}}$.

Kyriazidou (1997) and Honoré and Kyriazidou (1998) generalize this concept and propose to estimate the fixed effects sample selection models in two steps: In the first step, estimate $\underline{\delta}$ by either the Anderson (1970), Chamberlain (1980) conditional maximum likelihood approach or the Manski (1975) maximum score method. In the second step, the estimated $\hat{\underline{\delta}}$ is used to estimate γ, based on pairs of observations for which $d_{it} = d_{is} = 1$ and for which $(w_{it} - w_{is})'\hat{\underline{\delta}}$ is "close" to zero. This last requirement is operationalized by weighting each pair of observations with a weight that depends inversely on the magnitude of $(w_{it} - w_{is})'\hat{\underline{\delta}}$, so that pairs with larger differences in the selection effects receive less weight in the estimation. The Kyriazidou (1997) estimator takes the form:

$$\hat{\underline{\gamma}} = \left\{ \sum_{i=1}^{N} \sum_{1 \le s < t \le T_i} (\underline{z}_{it} - \underline{z}_{is})(\underline{z}_{it} - \underline{z}_{is})' K\left[\frac{(w_{it} - w_{is})'\hat{\underline{\delta}}}{h_N} \right] d_{it} d_{is} \right\}^{-1}$$

$$\left\{ \sum_{i=1}^{N} \sum_{1 \le s < t < T_i} (\underline{z}_{it} - \underline{z}_{is})(y_{it} - y_{is}) K\left[\frac{(w_{it} - w_{is})'\hat{\underline{\delta}}}{h_N} \right] d_{it} d_{is} \right\} \qquad (16.42)$$

where K is a kernel density function which tends to zero as the magnitude of its argument increases and h_N is a positive constant that decreases to zero as $N \to \infty$.

Under appropriate regularity conditions, Kyriazidou (1997) shows that $\underline{\tilde{\gamma}}$ (16.42) is consistent and asymptotically normally distributed. However, the rate of convergence is slower than the standard square root of the sample size.

6 CONCLUSIONS

There is an explosion of techniques and procedures for the analysis of panel data (e.g. Mátyás and Sevestre, 1996). In this chapter we have discussed some popular panel data models. We did not discuss issues of duration and count data models (e.g. Cameron and Trivedi, 1998; Heckman and Singer, 1984; Lancaster, 1990; Lancaster and Intrator, 1998), simulation-based inference (e.g. Gouriéroux and Monfort, 1993), specification analysis (e.g. Baltagi and Li, 1995; Lee, 1987; Li and Hsiao, 1998; Maddala, 1995; Wooldridge, 1995), measurement errors (e.g. Biorn, 1992; Griliches and Hausman, 1984; Hsiao, 1991; Hsiao and Taylor, 1991) pseudo panels or matched samples (e.g. Deaton, 1985; Moffit, 1993; Peracchi and Welsch,

1995; Verbeek, 1992), etc. In general, there does not exist a panacea for panel data analysis. It appears more fruitful to explicitly recognize the limitations of the data and focus attention on providing solutions for a specific type of model. A specific model often contains specific structural information that can be exploited. However, the power of panel data depends on the validity of the assumptions upon which the statistical methods have been built (e.g. Griliches, 1979).

Notes

*   This work was supported in part by National Science Foundation grant SBR96-19330. I would like to thank two referees for helpful comments.
1   Normality is made for ease of relating sampling approach and Bayesian approach estimators. It is not required.
2   See Chamberlain (1984), Hausman and Taylor (1981) for the approaches of estimating models when u and ε are correlated.
3   Under smooth conditions, Horowitz (1992) proposed a smoothed maximum score estimator that has a $n^{-2/5}$ rate of convergence. With even stronger conditions Lee (1999) is able to propose a root-n consistent semiparametric estimator.

References

Ahn, H., and J.L. Powell (1993). Semiparametric estimation of censored selection models with a nonparametric selection mechanism. *Journal of Econometrics* 58, 3–30.

Ahn, S.C., and P. Schmidt (1995). Efficient estimation of models for dynamic panel data. *Journal of Econometrics* 68, 29–52.

Akaike, H. (1973). Information theory and an extension of the maximum likelihood principle. In *Prac. 2nd Int. Symp. Information Theory*, pp. 267–81.

Amemiya, T., and T. MaCurdy (1986). Instrumental variable estimation of an error components model. *Econometrica* 54, 869–81.

Anderson, E.B. (1970). Asymptotic properties of conditional maximum likelihood estimators. *Journal of the Royal Statistical Society* series B 32, 283–301.

Anderson, E.B. (1973). *Conditional Inference and Models for Measuring*. Kobenbaun: Mentalhygiejnisk Forlag.

Anderson, T.W., and C. Hsiao (1981). Estimation of dynamic models with error components. *Journal of the American Statistical Association* 76, 598–606.

Anderson, T.W., and C. Hsiao (1982). Formulation and estimation of dynamic models using panel data. *Journal of Econometrics* 18, 47–82.

Arellano, M., and O. Bover (1995). Another look at the instrumental variable estimation of error-components models. *Journal of Econometrics* 68, 29–52.

Balestra, P., and M. Nerlove (1966). Pooling cross-section and time series data in the estimation of a dynamic model: The demand for natural gas. *Econometrica* 34, 585–612.

Baltagi, B.H. (1995). *Econometric Analysis of Panel Data*. New York: Wiley.

Baltagi, B.H., and Q. Li (1995). Testing AR(1) against MA(1) distrubances in an error components model. *Journal of Econometrics* 68, 133–52.

Biorn, E. (1992). Econometrics of panel data with measurement errors. In L. Mátyás and P. Sevestre (eds.) *Econometrics of Panel Data: Theory and Applications*, pp. 152–95. Kluwer.

Bhargava A., and J.D. Sargan (1983). Estimating dynamic random effects models from panel data covering short time periods. *Econometrica* 51, 1635–59.

Blundell, R., and S. Bond (1998). Initial conditions and moment restrictions in dynamic panel data models. *Journal of Econometrics* 87, 115–43.

Breusch, T.S., and A.R. Pagan (1979). A simple test for heteroscedasticity and random coefficient variation. *Econometrica* 47, 1287–94.

Cameron, A.C., and P.K. Trivedi (1998). *Regression Analysis of Count Data*. Cambridge: Cambridge University Press.

Chamberlain, G. (1980). Analysis of covariance with qualitative data. *Review of Economic Studies* 47, 225–38.

Chamberlain, G. (1984). Panel data. In Z. Griliches and M. Intriligator (eds.), *Handbook of Econometrics, Volume 2*. pp. 1247–1318. Amsterdam: North-Holland.

Chintagunta, P., E. Kyriazidou, and J. Perktold (1998). Panel data analysis of household brand choices. *Journal of Econometrics*.

Deaton, A. (1985). Panel data from time series of cross-sections. *Journal of Econometrics* 30, 109–26.

Gelfand, A.E., and A.F.M. Smith (1990). Sampling-based approaches to calculating marginal densities. *Journal of the American Statistical Association* 85, 398–409.

Gouriéroux, C., and A. Monfort (1993). Simulation based inference: A survey with special reference to panel data models. *Journal of Econometrics* 59, 5–34.

Griliches, Z. (1979). Sibling models and data in economics, beginning of a survey. *Journal of Political Economy* 87, supplement 2, S37–S64.

Griliches, Z., and J.A. Hausman (1984). Errors-in-variables in panel data. *Journal of Econometrics* 31, 93–118.

Hausman, J.A. (1978). Specification tests in econometrica. *Econometrica* 46, 1251–71.

Hausman, J.A., and W.E. Taylor (1981). Panel data and unobservable individual effects. *Econometrica* 49, 1377–98.

Hausman, J.A., and D.A. Wise (1979). Attrition bias in experimental and panel data: The Gary income maintenance experiment. *Econometrica* 47, 455–73.

Heckman, J. (1979). Sample selection bias as a specification error. *Econometrica* 47, 153–61.

Heckman, J.J., and B. Singer (1984). Econometric duration analysis. *Journal of Econometrics* 24, 63–132.

Honoré, B.E., and E. Kyriazidou (1997). Panel data discrete choice models with lagged dependent variables. Mimeo.

Honoré, B.E., and E. Kyriazidou (1998). Estimation of tobit-type models with individual specific effects. Mimeo.

Hsiao, C. (1974). Statistical inference for a model with both random cross-sectional and time effects. *International Economic Review* 15, 12–30.

Hsiao, C. (1975). Some estimation methods for a random coefficients model. *Econometrica* 43, 305–25.

Hsiao, C. (1985). Benefits and limitations of panel data. *Econometric Reviews* 4, 121–74.

Hsiao, C. (1986). *Analysis of Panel Data*. Econometric Society monographs No. 11, New York: Cambridge University Press.

Hsiao, C. (1989). Consistent estimation for some nonlinear errors-in-variables models. *Journal of Eocnometrics* 41, 159–85.

Hsiao, C. (1990). A mixed fixed and random coefficients framework for pooling cross-section and time series data. Paper presented at the Third Conference on Telecommunication Demand Analysis with Dynamic Regulation, Hilton Head, S. Carolina.

Hsiao, C. (1991). Indentification and estimation of latent binary choice models using panel data. *Review of Economic Studies* 58, 717–31.

Hsiao, C. (1992). Nonlinear latent variables models. In L. Matyas and P. Sevestre (eds.) *Econometrics of Panel Data*. pp. 242–61. Kluwer.

Hsiao, C. (1995). Panel analysis for metric data. G. Arminger, C.C. Clogg, and M.E. Sobel, *Handbook of Statistical Modelling in the Social and Behavioral Sciences*, (3rd edn). pp. 361–400. Plenum.

Hsiao, C., and D. Mountain (1995). A framework for regional modelling and impact analysis – an analysis of demand for electricity by large municipalities in Ontario, Canada. *Journal of Regional Science* 34, 361–85.

Hsiao, C., and A.K. Tahmiscioglu (1997). A panel analysis of liquidity constraints and firm investment. *Journal of the American Statistical Association* 92, 455–65.

Hsiao, C., and G. Taylor (1991). Some remarks on measurement errors and the identification of panel data models. *Statistical Neerlandica* 45, 187–94.

Hsiao, C., T.W. Applebe, and C.R. Dineen (1993). A general framework for panel data models – with an application to Canadian customer-dialed long distance telephone service. *Journal of Econometrics* 59, 63–86.

Hsiao, C., D.C. Mountain, K.Y. Tsui, and M.W. Luke Chan (1989). Modelling Ontario regional electricity system demand using a mixed fixed and random coefficients approach. *Regional Science and Urban Economics* 19, 567–87.

Hsiao, C., M.H. Pesaran, and A.K. Tahmiscioglu (1998). Maximum likelihood estimation of fixed effects dynamic panel data models covering short time periods. Mimeo, Cambridge University.

Hsiao, C., M.H. Pesaran, and A.K. Tahmiscioglu (1999). Bayes estimation of short-run coefficients in dynamic panel data models. In C. Hsiao, L.F. Lee, K. Lahiri, and M.H. Pesaran (eds.) *Analysis of Panels and Limited Dependent Variables Models*. Cambridge: Cambridge University Press, pp. 268–96.

Hsiao, C., B.H. Sun, and J. Lightwood (1995). Fixed vs. random effects specification for panel data analysis. Paper presented in International Panel Data Conference, Paris.

Horowitz, J. (1992). A smoothed maximum score estimator for the binary response model. *Econometrica* 60, 505–31.

Kuh, E. (1963). *Capital Stock Growth: A Micro-Econometric Approach*. Amsterdam: North-Holland.

Kyriazidou, E. (1997). Estimation of a panel data sample selection model. *Econometrica* 65, 1335–64.

Lancaster, T. (1990). *The Econometric Analysis of Transition Data*. Cambridge: Cambridge University Press.

Lancaster, T. (1998). Some econometrics of scarring. In C. Hsiao, K. Morimune, and J. Powell (eds.) *Nonlinear Statistical Inference*. Cambridge: Cambridge University Press.

Lancaster, T., and O. Intrator (1998). Panel data with survival: Hospitalization of HIV-positive patients. *Journal of the American Statistical Association* 93, 46–53.

Lee, L.F. (1987). Nonparametric testing of discrete panel data models. *Journal of Econometrics* 34, 147–78.

Lee, M.J. (1999). A root-n consistent semiparametric estimator for related effect binary response panel data. *Econometrica* 67, 427–33.

Li, Q., and C. Hsiao (1998). Testing serial correlation in semiparametric panel data models. *Journal of Econometrics* 87, 207–37.

Lindley, D.V., and A.F.M. Smith (1972). Bayes estimates for the linear model. *Journal of the Royal Statistical Society* B 34, 1–41.

Maddala, G.S. (1995). Specification tests in limited dependent variable models. In G.S. Maddala, P.C.B. Phillips, and T.N. Srinivasan (eds.) *Advances in Econometrics and Quantitative Economics: Essays in Honor of C.R. Rao*. Oxford: Blackwell. pp. 1–49.

Manski, C.F. (1975). Maximum score estimation of the stochastic utility model of choice. *Journal of Econometrics* 3, 205–28.

Mátyás, L., and P. Sevestre (1996). *The Econometrics of Panel Data – Handbook of Theory and Applications*, 2nd edn. Dordrecht: Kluwer.

Min, C.K., and A. Zellner (1993). Bayesian and non-Bayesian methods for combining models and forecasts with applications to forecasting international growth rate. *Journal of Econometrics* 56, 89–118.

Moffitt, R. (1993). Identification and estimation of dynamic models with a time series of repeated cross-sections. *Journal of Econometrics* 59, 99–123.

Mundlak, Y. (1978). On the pooling of time series and cross section data. *Econometrica* 46, 69–85.

Neyman, J., and E.L. Scott (1948). Consistent estimates based on partially consistent observations. *Econometrica* 16, 1–32.

Peracchi, F., and F. Welsch (1995). How representative are matched cross-sections? Evidence from the current population survey. *Journal of Econometrics* 68, 153–80.

Pesaran, M.H., and R. Smith (1995). Estimation of long-run relationships from dynamic heterogeneous panels. *Journal of Econometrics* 68, 79–114.

Ryu, K.K. (1998). New approach to attrition problem in longitudinal studies. In C. Hsiao, K. Morimune, and J. Powell (eds.) *Nonlinear Statistical Inference*. Cambridge University Press.

Schwarz, G. (1978). Estimating the dimension of a model. *Annals of Statistics* 6, 461–4.

Swamy, P.A.V.B. (1970). Efficient inference in a random coefficient regression model. *Econometrica* 38, 311–23.

Verbeek, M. (1992). The design of panel surveys and the treatment of missing observations. Ph.D. dissertation, Tilburg University.

Wallace, T.D., and A. Hussain (1969). The use of error components models in combining cross-section with time series data. *Econometrica* 37, 55–72.

Wansbeek, T., and T. Knaap (1999). Estimating a dynamic panel data model with heterogeneous trend. *Annales d'Economie et de Statistique* 55–6, 331–50.

Wooldridge, J.M. (1995). Selection corrections for panel data models under conditional mean independence assumptions. *Journal of Econometrics* 68, 115–32.

Zellner, A. (1962). An efficient method of estimating seemingly unrelated regressions and tests for aggregation bias. *Journal of the American Statistical Association* 57, 348–68.

Ziliak, J.P. (1997). Efficient estimation with panel data when instruments are predetermined: An empirical comparison of moment-condition estimators. *Journal of Business and Economic Statistics* 15, 419–31.

Qualitative Response Models

G.S. Maddala and A. Flores-Lagunes*

1   INTRODUCTION

This chapter deals with regression models when the dependent variable is qualitative. There are many situations in economics where the dependent variable takes discrete values, due to the qualitative nature of many behavioral responses. For instance, consider a worker deciding whether or not to participate in the labor force, a consumer deciding whether or not to buy a good, etc.

There are good reviews of qualitative response models (QRM) in the literature (Amemiya, 1981; McFadden, 1981, 1984; Maddala, 1983, chs. 2–5). Here we focus on some basic concepts about QRM, some topics not covered in the above reviews, and on some recent work in this area. We discuss binary and multinomial response models, specification tests, panel data with qualitative variables, semi-parametric estimation, and simulation methods.

Section 2 introduces some basic concepts about QRM, with an emphasis on univariate QRM and, in particular, on the estimation of binary and multinomial logit and probit models. A more in-depth review of all types of QRM, both univariate and multivariate, can be found in Maddala (1983, chs. 2–5).

Some concepts about specification tests in QRM are discussed in Section 3. Pagan and Vella (1989) argued that the use of specification tests in qualitative response models is not common since they are difficult to compute, but that has changed as computationally simpler specification tests have become available.

Sections 4 to 6 review some further topics in QRM. Panel data with qualitative variables (Section 4) has been an intensive area of research, both theoretical and applied, since the early reviews by Heckman (1981) and Chamberlain (1980, 1984). The principal issue in this literature is on controling for heterogeneity and state dependence.

The other two topics, semiparametric estimation (Section 5) and simulation methods (Section 6), correspond to two specific problems in qualitative response models: the inconsistency of estimators when the distributional assumption of the model is incorrect, and the computational problem of evaluating higher order integrals in multinomial qualitative response models.

2   BINARY AND MULTINOMIAL RESPONSE MODELS

In this section we present the basic analysis of models with a single explanatory variable that is observed as a dichotomous (binary or binomial) or polychotomous (multinomial) variable.

Both binary and multinomial response models are models in which the dependent variable assumes discrete values. The simplest of these models is that in which the dependent variable y is binary; for instance, y can be defined as 1 if the individual is in the labor force, 0 otherwise.

When a dependent variable y can assume more than two values it can be classified as (i) categorical variable and (ii) count (noncategorical) variable. For instance, a categorical variable y may be defined as: $y = 1$ if the individual earns less than \$10,000; $y = 2$ if the individual earns between \$10,000 and \$30,000; and $y = 3$ if the individual earns more than \$30,000. Note that, as the name indicates, the variable categorizes individuals into different categories. A count variable is discrete but it does not categorize, like the number of strikes on a country in a given year. The methods of analysis are different for models with categorical and count variables (see Cameron and Trivedi, Chapter 15 in this companion).

Categorical variables can be further classified as (i) unordered, (ii) ordered, and (iii) sequential. Unordered categorical variables can be defined in any order desired, for instance: $y = 1$ if occupation is lawyer; $y = 2$ if occupation is teacher; and $y = 3$ if occupation is doctor. An example of an ordered categorical variable is the one above concerning the level of earnings. Finally, a sequential categorical variable can be illustrated as: $y = 1$ if the individual has not completed high school; $y = 2$ if the individual has completed high school but not college; $y = 3$ if the individual has completed college but not a higher degree; and $y = 4$ if the individual has completed a professional degree.

Let us now turn our attention to binary response models. We motivate these models by introducing the linear probability model. This is a regression model in which the dependent variable y is a binary variable. The model can be written as:

$$y_i = \beta' x_i + u_i, \tag{17.1}$$

with $E(u_i) = 0$. The conditional expectation $E(y_i/x_i)$ is equal to $\beta' x_i$, which is interpreted as the probability that the event will occur given the x_i. The fitted value, $\hat{y}_i = \hat{\beta}' x_i$, will give the estimated probability that the event will occur given the particular value of x.

Since the model is heteroskedastic (the reader can easily check it), it has to be estimated by weighted least squares. However, the linear probability model is seldom used because the least squares method is not fully efficient due to the nonnormality of the residuals u_i, and more importantly, because in many cases $E(y_i/x_i)$, interpreted as a probability, can lie outside the limits $(0, 1)$.

Two alternative models that avoid the previous two problems are widely used for the estimation of binary response models: the probit and the logit. Both models assume that there is an underlying response variable y_i^* defined by the regression relationship $y_i^* = \beta'x_i + u_i$. In practice, y_i^* is unobservable but we observe a dummy variable defined by:

$$y_i = 1 \quad \text{if} \quad y_i^* > 0; \quad y_i = 0 \quad \text{otherwise.} \tag{17.2}$$

Note that in this formulation, $\beta'x_i$ is not $E(y_i/x_i)$ as in the linear probability model; it is $E(y_i^*/x_i)$. From the regression relationship for y_i^* and (17.2) we get:

$$P(y_i = 1) = P(u_i > -\beta'x_i) = 1 - F(-\beta'x_i), \tag{17.3}$$

where F is the cumulative distribution function for u_i.

In this case the observed values of y are just realizations of a binomial process with probabilities given by (17.3) and varying from trial to trial (depending on x_i). Hence, the loglikelihood function is:

$$\log L = \sum_{i=1}^{n} y_i \log F(\beta'x_i) + \sum_{i=1}^{n} (1 - y_i) \log [1 - F(\beta'x_i)]. \tag{17.4}$$

The functional form for F depends on the assumptions made about u_i. If the cumulative distribution assumed is the logistic we have the logit model, if it is assumed to be the normal distribution then we have the probit model. The logistic and the normal distributions are very close to each other, except at the tails; but even though the parameter estimates are usually close, they are not directly comparable because the logistic distribution has variance $\pi^2/3$ rather than normalized to 1 as for the normal. Amemiya (1981) suggests that the logit estimates be multiplied by 0.625, instead of the exact $3^{\frac{1}{2}}/\pi$, arguing that it produces a closer approximation.

For the purpose of predicting effects of changes in one of the independent variables on the probability of belonging to a group, the derivative of the probability with respect to the particular independent variable needs to be computed. Letting x_{ik} and β_k be the kth elements of the vector of explanatory variables and parameters, respectively, the derivatives for the logit and probit models are given by:

$$\frac{\partial}{\partial x_{ik}} L(x_i'\beta) = \frac{\exp(x_i'\beta)}{[1 + \exp(x_i'\beta)]^2} \beta_k = \beta_k P(y_i = 1) P(y_i = 0) \quad \text{for the logit, and}$$

$$\tag{17.5}$$

$$\frac{\partial}{\partial x_{ik}} \Phi(x_i'\beta) = \phi(x_i'\beta)\beta_k \quad \text{for the probit,} \tag{17.6}$$

where L, Φ, and ϕ are the logistic cdf, and the standard normal cdf and pdf, respectively. In both models, we need to calculate the derivatives at different levels of the explanatory variables to get an idea of the range of variation of the resulting changes in probabilities. A common practice in empirical work is to evaluate them at the mean of the vector of independent variables.

The estimation of logit and probit models is done by maximization of the log-likelihood function (17.4) after substituting either the logistic or normal distribution for the functional form F. Since the derivatives of the loglikelihood function are nonlinear in β, we have to use iterative methods like the Newton–Raphson or the scoring methods. The asymptotic covariance matrix, which can be used for hypothesis testing, is obtained by inverting the corresponding information matrix. In practice, the logit and probit models are readily available in statistical software. When dealing with multiple observations (as with grouped data), a general method based on weighted least squares, known as the minimum chi-square method, can be used (see Maddala, 1983, section 2.8).

Regarding multinomial response models, we will only cover the case of unordered categorical variables. The estimation of models with ordered and sequential categorical variables follow the same rationale. The reader is referred to sections 2.13 and 2.14 of Maddala (1983) for the particulars involved. Models with count data are often estimated using Poisson regression, which is covered in section 2.15 of the same monograph and in Cameron and Trivedi's chapter in this companion.

The multinomial logit (MNL) and probit (MNP) models are often used to estimate models with unordered categorical variables. The MNP model, however, involves the computation of multidimensional integrals which for models with variables taking more than 3 or 4 values are infeasible to compute by direct means. Nonetheless, we can use simulation methods to evaluate such integrals. These methods are reviewed in Section 6 below and in Chapter 22 by Geweke, Houser, and Keane in this companion.

Both MNL and MNP models can be motivated by a random utility formulation. Let $y_{ij}^*(i = 1, \ldots, n, j = 1, \ldots m)$ be the stochastic utility associated with the jth alternative for individual i, with

$$y_{ij}^* = \beta_j' x_i + u_{ij}, \tag{17.7}$$

where x_i are explanatory variables, β_j are unknown parameters and u_{ij} is an unobservable random variable. We assume that the individual chooses the alternative for which the associated utility is highest. Define a set of dummy variables $y_{ij} = 1$ if the ith individual chooses the jth alternative, $y_{ij} = 0$ otherwise. Then, for example, the probability that alternative 1 is chosen is given by:

$$P_{i1} = P(y_{i1} = 1) = \int_{-\infty}^{x_i'\beta_1 - x_i'\beta_2} \ldots \int_{-\infty}^{x_i'\beta_1 - x_i'\beta_m} f(\eta_{21}, \ldots, \eta_{m1})d\eta_{21} \ldots d\eta_{m1}, \tag{17.8}$$

where $\eta_{kj} = u_{ik} - u_{ij}$. Considering the observations as arising from a multinomial distribution with probabilities given by P_{ij}, the loglikelihood function for either the MNL or MNP models can be written as:

$$\log L = \sum_{i=1}^{n} \sum_{j=1}^{m} y_{ij} \log P_{ij}. \tag{17.9}$$

For the MNL model, we assume that the u_{ij}s follow independent extreme-value distributions. McFadden (1974) showed that the probabilities in (17.9) for the MNL model are given by:

$$P_{ij} = \frac{\exp(\beta'_j x_i)}{\sum_{j=1}^{m-1} \exp(\beta'_j x_i)}. \tag{17.10}$$

This model is computationally convenient since it avoids the problem of evaluating multidimensional integrals as opposed to the MNP model (see below). The estimation of the MNL model is through maximum likelihood (ML) using an iterative method (since again the derivatives are nonlinear in β). The asymptotic covariance matrix is also obtained by inverting the corresponding information matrix.

McFadden (1974) also suggested the conditional logit model. The main difference between this model and the MNL considered in (17.10) is that the former considers the effect of choice characteristics on the determinants of choice probabilities as well, whereas the MNL model makes the choice probabilities dependent on individual characteristics only. To illustrate this, let x_{ij} denote the vector of the values of the characteristics of choice j as perceived by individual i. Then, the probability that individual i chooses alternative j is

$$P_{ij} = \frac{\exp(\beta' x_{ij})}{\sum_{k=1}^{m} \exp(\beta' x_{ik})}. \tag{17.11}$$

Note that, as opposed to (17.10), P_{ij} does not have different coefficient vectors β_j. In (17.11) the vector β gives the vector of implicit prices for the characteristics.[1] The conditional logit model is similarly estimated by ML.

Both MNL and conditional logit models have the property referred to as "independence of irrelevant alternatives" (IIA). This is because the odds ratio for any two choices i and j is $\exp(\beta' x_i)/\exp(\beta' x_j)$, which is the same irrespective of the total number m of choices considered. If the individual is offered an expanded choice set, that does not change its odds ratio. This property is in fact a drawback in many applications. Debreu (1960) pointed out that these models predict too high a joint probability of selection for two alternatives that are in fact perceived as similar rather than independent by the individual. To see this, consider the following choices: (i) red bus, (ii) blue bus, and (iii) auto. Suppose that consumers treat the two buses as equivalent and are indifferent between auto and bus. Then, the relative odds of alternatives (i) and (iii) depend on the presence of alternative (ii). They are 1:1 if choice (ii) is not present. They are 1:2 if choice (ii) is present. However, this is inconsistent with the IIA property.

The MNP model does not have the IIA property and thus would be preferred to the MNL model when such property is inappropriate. Nonetheless, recall the

MNP model computational problems mentioned above. To illustrate this, consider only three alternatives in the formulation (17.7) (i.e. $j = 3$), and assume that the residuals have a trivariate normal distribution with mean vector zero and some covariance matrix Σ. Using the same definitions as above, to compute the corresponding probabilities as in (17.8), the η_{kj}'s will have a bivariate normal distribution with covariance matrix Ω_1 (that can be derived from Σ by standard formulae for normal densities), requiring thus the computation of bivariate integrals. It is easy to see that we must deal with trivariate integrals when considering four alternatives, and so on.

There are other models for the analysis of polychotomous variables. The elimination-by-aspects (EBA) model assumes that each alternative is described by a set of aspects (characteristics) and that at each stage of the process an aspect is selected. The selection of the aspect eliminates alternatives that do not contain the selected aspect, and the selection continues until a single alternative remains. Aspects common to all alternatives do not affect the choice probabilities avoiding thus the IIA property. Another model is the hierarchical elimination-by-aspects (HEBA) model. When aspects have a tree structure, the EBA model reduces to the HEBA model. McFadden (1981) introduced the generalized extreme value (GEV) and the nested multinomial logit (NMNL) models, which are models based on a random utility formulation where the error distribution is a multivariate generalization of the extreme-value distribution, and are formulated in such a way that the multivariate integrals analogous to (17.8) are analytically tractable. McFadden (1984) considers the GEV model as an elimination model that can be expressed in latent variable form and the NMNL model as a hierarchical elimination model based on the GEV structure. None of these models have the IIA property. References for the EBA, HEBA, GEV, and NMNL models are in Maddala (1983, ch. 3) and McFadden (1984).

So far, we have only discussed models with univariate qualitative variables. There are also models with multivariate qualitative variables in the literature. Among such models are, for instance, simultaneous equation models with qualitative variables, simultaneous equation models with qualitative variables and structural shift, and others. Multivariate qualitative response models are reviewed in Maddala (1983, ch. 5).

3 SPECIFICATION TESTS

The area of specification tests in QRM (in fact all limited dependent variable models) has been surveyed in Pagan and Vella (1989), and more exhaustively in Maddala (1995). Pagan and Vella argue that the use of specification tests in limited dependent variable models is not common because they are difficult to compute. They suggest a number of specification tests based on conditional moments that they argue are easier to use. Maddala (1995) discusses these tests and shows that they are equivalent to score tests.

Most of the specification tests for qualitative response models are Rao's score tests (known as LM tests in the econometric literature) but there are others which are Hausman (1978) type tests, White's (1982) IM (information matrix) tests, and CM (conditional moment) tests suggested by Newey (1985) and Tauchen (1985). A detailed description of all these categories of tests is in Maddala (1995, pp. 2–10).

The survey by Maddala also considers tests for a variety of specification errors as follows: tests for heteroskedasticity, tests for normality, tests for autocorrelation, tests for sample selection, tests for exogeneity, tests for omitted variables, tests for stability, and multinomial logit specification tests, which are tests for the IIA property. The reader is referred to that paper for a detailed review of all these tests and references to the literature. In the rest of this section, we will limit ourselves to provide some general ideas.

1. Most of the specification tests for qualitative response models use the concept of generalized residuals introduced by Gouriéroux, Monfort, and Trognon (1987). These are the counterpart for nonlinear models (such as probit and logit) of the usual residuals in linear regression, and are used as the latter in hypothesis testing.

2. On the different specification tests, one can use the information matrix or its sample estimates like the Hessian of the loglikelihood function for the model or the outer product gradient (OPG), to avoid evaluating expectations (which are often cumbersome). It is important to keep in mind that, whereas the OPG version is computationally simpler, it has been found to have bad small sample properties (see Davidson and MacKinnon, 1989; Orme, 1990; and the references in those papers). Tests based on the Hessian version have been found to perform only slightly better than the OPG (Taylor, 1991). Therefore, whenever possible, one should try to use the exact information matrix.[2]

3. Specification tests in qualitative response models are particularly useful when the unrestricted model is much more complicated to estimate than the restricted model, which is often the case. For instance, consider testing for sample selection in the following censored bivariate probit model:

$$y_{1i}^* = \beta_1' x_{1i} + u_{1i}$$

$$y_{2i}^* = \beta_2' x_{2i} + u_{2i},$$ (17.12)

where y_{1i}^* is censored by the second equation (selection equation). The estimation of this model under sample selection is not trivial (since it involves bivariate integrals). Hence, it is useful to have a test for the null of no sample selectivity, since univariate probit models can then be used.

The above reviews do not cover specification tests in panel data, a topic discussed in the following section, nor models estimated by semiparametric and simulation based methods, covered in Sections 5 and 6. Baltagi (1999) briefly mentions score type tests for fixed effects in logit and probit models with panel data (section 5 of his paper). Lee (1997) has an exhaustive discussion of all the specification errors discussed in Maddala's paper in the context of models estimated by simulation methods.

4 PANEL DATA WITH QUALITATIVE VARIABLES

Early reviews of models of panel data with qualitative variables are in Heckman (1981) and Chamberlain (1980, 1984). This work in the early 1980s is reviewed in Maddala (1987) which discusses fixed effects logit and probit models, random effects probit models, autoregressive logit models, autoregressive probit models, and the problems of serial correlation and state dependence.

The main issue in panel data models with qualitative response variables is that the presence of individual effects (heterogeneity) complicates the estimation. For instance, the fixed effects model for panel data does not give consistent estimates of the slope parameters. Chamberlain (1980) suggested a conditional ML approach in which the likelihood function of the model is conditioned on sufficient statistics of the incidental parameters α_i (i.e. the fixed effects), which in this case are $\sum_t y_{it}$. The method is illustrated in Maddala (1987) for the logit model. The probit model cannot be used with Chamberlain's method due to computational problems.

In contrast, when using the random effects approach, the probit model is about the only choice, since on the multivariate logistic distribution the correlations between the error term and the cross section units are all constrained to be $1/2$ (see Johnson and Kotz, 1972, pp. 293–4), which is implausible to assume in most applications. The random effects probit model implies serial correlation of a specific nature, the equicorrelation model, for which there is an efficient ML algorithm due to Butler and Moffitt (1982). For the case of a general type of serial correlation, the Avery, Hansen, and Hotz (1983) method of GMM was discussed in Maddala (1987).

An additional problem in panel data models with qualitative response variables occurs if there is "state dependence", which can be interpreted as a situation in which an individual's past state $y_{i,t-1}$ helps predict his or her current state $y_{i,t}$, after allowing for individual effects.

The problem of discrete choice panel data models with lagged dependent variables was first discussed in Chamberlain (1985). The model considered is a model with heterogeneity and state dependence. Heterogeneity is captured by the inclusion of individual specific effects α_i, and state dependence is captured by the inclusion of the lagged dependent variable $y_{i,t-1}$. The model considered by Chamberlain is:

$$P(y_{i0} = 1/\alpha_i) = P_0(\alpha_i)$$

$$P(y_{it} = 1/\alpha_i, y_{i0}, y_{i1}, \ldots, y_{i,t-1})$$

$$= \frac{\exp(\alpha_i + \gamma y_{i,t-1})}{1 + \exp(\alpha_i + \gamma y_{i,t-1})} \quad t = 1, 2 \ldots T, \quad T \geq 3. \tag{17.13}$$

The procedure used by Chamberlain (1985) is to derive a set of probabilities that do not depend on the individual effects. Let $T = 3$ and consider the events:

$$A = \{y_{i0} = d_0,\ y_{i1} = 0,\ y_{i2} = 1,\ y_{i3} = d_3\}$$

$$B = \{y_{i0} = d_0,\ y_{i1} = 1,\ y_{i2} = 0,\ y_{i3} = d_3\} \tag{17.14}$$

where d_0 and d_3 are either 0 or 1. Then the conditional probabilities $P(A/\alpha_i, A \cup B)$ and $P(B/\alpha_i, A \cup B)$ will not depend on α_i. However, this method will not work in the presence of explanatory variables.

Honoré and Kyriazidou (1998), to be referred to as H–K, consider a more general model with exogenous explanatory variables. Their model is:

$$P(y_{i0} = 1/x_i,\ \alpha_i) = P_0(x_i,\ \alpha_i)$$

$$P(y_{it} = 1/x_i,\ \alpha_i,\ y_{i0},\ y_{i1},\ \ldots,\ y_{i,t-1})$$

$$= \frac{\exp(x_{it}\beta + \gamma y_{i,t-1} + \alpha_i)}{1 + \exp(x_{it}\beta + \gamma y_{i,t-1} + \alpha_i)} \quad t = 1, 2 \ldots T, \quad T \geq 3 \tag{17.15}$$

H–K observe that if say $x_{i2} = x_{i3}$ then these conditional probabilities do not depend on α_i. In practice this is not a reasonable assumption. In the special case where all explanatory variables are discrete, and $P(x_{i2} = x_{i3}) > 0$, one may estimate β and γ by maximizing with respect to b and g the weighted likelihood function:

$$\sum_{i=1}^{N} I(y_{i1} + y_{i2} = 1)I(x_{i2} - x_{i3} = 0) \ln \frac{\exp\{(x_{i1} - x_{i2})b + g(y_{i0} - y_{i3})\}^{y_{i1}}}{1 + \exp\{(x_{i1} - x_{i2})b + g(y_{i0} - y_{i3})\}} \tag{17.16}$$

where $I(\cdot)$ are indicator functions. The resulting estimator will have all the usual properties (consistency and root-n asymptotic normality).

In the case where the xs are not discrete, H–K suggest replacing the indicator function $I(x_{i2} - x_{i3} = 0)$ by a weight function $k[(x_{i2} - x_{i3})/\sigma_n]$ with weights depending inversely on the magnitude of $x_{i2} - x_{i3}$ giving more weight to observations for which x_{i2} is "close" to x_{i3}. σ_n is a bandwidth that shrinks as n increases and $k(\cdot)$ is the kernel, chosen so that $k(v) \to 0$ as $v \to \infty$.

H–K show that the resultant estimators are consistent and asymptotically normal, although their rate of convergence will be slower than $n^{-\frac{1}{2}}$ and will depend on the number of covariates in x_{it}. Furthermore, for identification, their model requires that $x_{i2} - x_{i3}$ be continuously distributed with support in a neighborhood of 0, and that $x_{i1} - x_{i2}$ has sufficient variation conditional on the event $x_{i2} - x_{i3} = 0$. H–K also extend their model for the general case of M alternatives.

5   SEMIPARAMETRIC ESTIMATION

We have seen that in the estimation of QRM the assumption is made about the error term being distributed according to some known distribution (i.e. logistic or normal). The validity of this assumption may be rejected using appropriate specification tests, implying (if correct) the inconsistency of the estimators. For this reason, several semiparametric methods of estimation have been proposed in the literature, which, based on weaker assumptions about the error distribution, estimate the relevant parameters of the model.

In this section, we will consider four semiparametric estimators: the Maximum Score (MS) estimator (Manski, 1975, 1985; Manski and Thompson, 1986), the Quasi Maximum Likelihood (QML) estimator (Klein and Spady, 1993), the Generalized Maximum Likelihood (GML) estimator (Cosslett, 1983), and the semi-nonparametric (SNP) estimator (Gallant and Nychka, 1987). This is, by no means, an exhaustive review of the many existing semiparametric estimators for QRM. The interested reader is referred to the comprehensive review of semiparametric models in the context of limited dependent variables by Powell (1994).

Our main focus is on the binary response model, however, the MS and QML can be extended to multinomial response models. Other estimators for the multinomial response model have been developed by Thompson (1989a, 1989b) and Lee (1994).

Gabler, Laisney, and Lechner (1993) use a small-scale Monte Carlo study to conclude that the bias associated with incorrect distributional assumptions in the binary probit model can be substantial both in finite samples and asymptotically. Similar results for the binary logit model are shown by Horowitz (1993).

The MS estimator for the parameter vector β is intuitively obtained by maximizing the number of correct predictions of y (dependent variable) by the sign of the latent regression function $x'\beta$. More formally, this estimator maximizes the following score function over a suitable parameter space:

$$S_n(\beta) \equiv \sum_{i=1}^{N} [y_i I\{x_i'\beta > 0\} + (1 - y_i) I\{x_i'\beta < 0\}]. \tag{17.17}$$

The only restriction imposed on the distribution of the error term is to have conditional median zero, which ensures consistency of the estimator. Despite the fact that the MS estimator is consistent, it is not root-n consistent under standard regularity conditions, nor asymptotically normal. Its rate of convergence is $n^{\frac{1}{3}}$, and $n^{\frac{1}{3}}(\hat{\beta} - \beta_0)$ converges to a nonnormal distribution (Kim and Pollard, 1990).

The QML estimator, proposed by Klein and Spady (1993), is obtained as follows.[3] By the use of Bayes' theorem, we can write the probability of $y = 1$ given x as:

$$P\{y = 1/x\} = \frac{P\{y = 1\}g(x\beta/y = 1)}{g(x\beta)} \equiv p(x\beta). \tag{17.18}$$

The mean of y is a consistent estimator for $P\{y = 1\}$ above, and we can also obtain consistent estimators for $g(x\beta/y = 1)$ and $g(x\beta)$ using kernel estimates (for known β). Having those estimators, we can obtain consistent estimates $\hat{p}(x\beta)$ that are used to compute the QML estimator by substituting them for $F(\beta'x_i)$ on (17.4) and maximizing the expression.

This estimator is strongly consistent, asymptotically normal, and attains the semiparametric efficiency bound (Newey, 1990); however, it relies on the stringent assumption of independence between the error term and the regressors.

Cosslett's (1983) GML estimator uses the likelihood function for the binary choice model (17.4) and maximizes it with respect to the functional form F as well as β, subject to the condition that F is a distribution function. This maximization is done in two steps: first, β is fixed and (17.4) is maximized with respect to F to obtain $\hat{F}$; then, in the second step, $\hat{F}$ is used as the correct distribution and (17.4) is maximized with respect to β, obtaining $\hat{\beta}$. Cosslett (1983) derived the conditions under which this estimator is consistent; however, its asymptotic normality has not been proved yet, and the second step is computationally costly since the likelihood function at that stage varies in discrete steps over the parameter space.

The paper by Gabler, Laisney, and Lechner (1993), to be referred as GLL, is an application of the SNP estimator proposed by Gallant and Nychka (1987) to the binary choice model. In general, the term semi-nonparametric is used when the goal is to approximate a function of interest with a parametric approximation (in this case the distribution function of the errors). The larger the number of observations available to estimate the function, the larger the number of parameters to be used in approximating the function of interest and, as a result, the better the approximation.

Gallant and Nychka (1987) proposed the approximation of any smooth density that has a moment generating function with the Hermite form:[4]

$$h^*(u) = \sum_{i,j=0}^{K} \alpha_i \alpha_j u^{i+j} \exp\{-(u/\delta)^2\}. \tag{17.19}$$

The estimation method used by GLL is to fix K (the degree of the Hermite polynomial) in a somewhat optimal way and use the framework of pseudo maximum likelihood (PML).

For the binary choice model, we use the above approximation for the density F in the likelihood function (17.4). The likelihood function is then maximized taking into account two additional restrictions on α and δ: u has to have zero expectation, and the requirement of unit mass below the density F. Moreover, a condition for consistency in this approach is the degree K of the approximation to increase with the sample size.[5] For the details of the estimation method refer to GLL's paper.

The asymptotic normality of this SNP estimator follows from the asymptotic theory of PML estimation. References in this literature are White (1982, 1983) and Gouriéroux and Monfort (1995). This allows for hypothesis testing with the usual techniques. Note that the PML theory is being used for the asymptotic distribution of a potentially inconsistent estimator (due to the use of a fixed K).[6] In addition, let us note that this asymptotic normality result is not a standard asymptotic result, since the asymptotic variance is only approximated as $N \to \infty$, holding K at the fixed value chosen a priori.[7]

While all four estimators discussed above relax distributional assumptions about the error term, each of them shows drawbacks that are worth considering before their use in empirical applications. The MS estimator has been used more than the other estimators due to its computational feasibility (it is even available in some software packages, although with size limitations), but its asymptotic nonnormality is a drawback when hypothesis testing beyond parameter significance is needed since additional steps are required. This last drawback is shared with GML, which is also computationally costly. On the other hand, QML is asymptotically normal and efficient, but should not be used when dependence between the error term and the regressors is suspected, limiting its application considerably. Finally, the relatively new SNP estimator does not share the drawbacks of the MS and GML estimators, and the authors offer a GAUSS program upon request. However, the estimator is inconsistent if K is not chosen carefully, and the nonglobal concavity of its objective function require good starting values, which usually implies the estimation of a probit model. Besides, it shares QML's drawback regarding the dependence between the error term and the regressors. More evidence about the relative performance of these estimators is needed.

6 SIMULATION METHODS

In binary QRM there is little basis to choose between the logit and probit models because of the similarity of the cumulative normal and the logistic distributions. In the multinomial situation this is not the case. The multinomial logit (MNL) model has a closed form representation and is computationally tractable but lacks flexibility due to the IIA property. The multinomial probit (MNP) model gives flexibility but is computationally burdensome because of the need to evaluate multidimensional integrals. Another problem which involves high dimensional integrals is the probit (or tobit) model with serially correlated errors.

Until a few years ago, only 3 or 4 dimensional integrals could be evaluated. However, developments during the last decade on simulation based estimation allow us to estimate otherwise intractable models by approximating high-dimensional integrals. A simple exposition of the econometric literature on simulation methods can be found in Stern (1997).

The generic problem for simulation is to evaluate expressions like $E[g(x)] = \int g(x)f(x)dx$ where x is a random variable with density $f(x)$ and $g(x)$ is a function of x. The simulation method consists of drawing samples $x_1, x_2, \ldots, x_N$ from $f(x)$ and computing $g(x_i)$. Then, $\widehat{E[g(x)]} = \frac{1}{N}\sum_{i=1}^{N}g(x_i)$ is an unbiased estimator of $E[g(x)]$, and its variance is $\text{var}(g(x_i))/N$. As $N \to \infty$, the variance of the simulator goes to zero. $f(x)$ can be a discrete distribution.

Different applications of the simulation method depend on refinements in the way the sampling of $f(x)$ is done. These refinements in probability simulators fall into the following categories: importance sampling, GHK simulator, Gibbs sampling, and antithetic variables. Importance sampling involves oversampling some "important" parts of $f(x)$ from a well-chosen distribution $g(x)$ from which it is easy to sample. The GHK simulator algorithm decomposes the joint density of the errors into a product of conditional densities. It has been found to perform very well for simulating multinomial probit probabilities. Gibbs sampling is an iterative sampling method from conditional densities. Finally, the method of antithetic variables can be used on the above probability simulators to reduce sampling costs and the variance of the simulator through the sampling of pairs of random variables which are negatively correlated.[8]

The estimation methods commonly used are the method of simulated moments (MSM), the method of simulated likelihood (MSL), and the method of simulated scores (MSS). A detailed review of the above estimation methods can be found in Hajivassiliou and Ruud (1994) and in Geweke, Houser, and Keane, Chapter 22, in this companion.

The MSM is based on the GMM (generalized method of moments) method of estimation. The least squares method is a simple example of the method of moments. The GMM method depends on orthogonality conditions. For example, Avery, Hansen, and Hotz (1983) suggest how to estimate the multiperiod probit model by a set of within period orthogonality conditions that allows consistent estimation of the parameters and their standard errors under serial correlation. In many problems, the orthogonality conditions cannot be evaluated analytically. This is where simulation methods help. The resulting estimator is the MSM estimator. Let us illustrate this method with the MNP model. The loglikelihood function for a sample of size n with m alternatives is given by (17.9). The MSM consists of simulating $\tilde{P}(j/x, \beta)$ using the multivariate normal distribution and substituting it in the moment equation:

$$\sum_{i=1}^{n}\sum_{j=1}^{m} w_{ijk}[y_{ij} - P(j/x, \beta)] = 0, \tag{17.20}$$

for some weighting function w (k is an index taking on the values $1, \ldots, K$ where K is the dimension of β). The estimator $\hat{\beta}_{MSM}$ is obtained by solving (17.20).

The MSL is based on the maximum likelihood method of estimation and is useful when the likelihood function is not easily computed by analytical methods. In the context of multinomial choice models, MSL consists in simulating the actual choice probabilities given by $P_{ij}(x, \beta)$ in (17.9). $\hat{\beta}_{MSL}$ is obtained by maximizing (17.9) once the simulated choice probabilities are substituted.

The MSS is based on the idea that the score statistic (the derivative of the likelihood function) should have an expected value of zero at the true value of β. The potential advantage of the MSS relative to MSM is that it uses the efficiency properties of ML, but it is computationally more difficult than the MSM since the weight function itself has to be simulated, while it is analytically computed on the MSM. To see this, note that the MSS implies simulating $\tilde{P}(j/x, \beta)$ in the following expression:

$$\sum_{i=1}^{n}\sum_{j=1}^{m} \frac{1}{P(j/x, \beta)} \frac{\partial P(j/x, \beta)}{\partial \beta}[y_{ij} - P(j/x, \beta)] = 0, \tag{17.21}$$

which makes clear that the weight function itself has to be simulated.

There are several papers using simulation methods but there are very few that compare the different methods. Geweke, Keane, and Runkle (1994) compare different methods in the estimation of the multinomial probit model, based on two Monte Carlo experiments for a seven choice model. They compare the MSL estimator using the GHK recursive probability simulator, the MSM method using the GHK recursive probability simulator and kernel-smoothed frequency simulators, and Bayesian methods based on Gibbs sampling. Overall, the Gibbs sampling algorithm had a slight edge, while the relative performance of the MSM and MSL (based on the GHK simulator) was difficult to evaluate. The MSM with the kernel-smoothed frequency simulator was clearly inferior.

In another paper, Geweke, Keane, and Runkle (1997) again compare the Bayesian methods based on Gibbs sampling and the MSM and MSL methods based on the GHK simulator. They do Monte Carlo studies with AR(1) errors in the multinomial multiperiod probit model, finding that the Gibbs sampling algorithm performs better than the MSM and MSL, especially under strong serial correlation in the disturbances (e.g. an AR(1) parameter of 0.8). They also find that to have root mean squared errors (RMSEs) for MSL and MSM within 10 percent of the RMSEs by the Gibbs sampling method one needs samples of 160 and 80 draws respectively (much higher than the 20 draws normally used). Thus, with serially correlated errors, the performance ranking is Gibbs sampling first, MSM second, and MSL last.

Keane (1993) discusses in detail the MSM estimator of limited dependent variable models with general patterns of serial correlation. He uses the recursive GHK algorithm. He argues that the equicorrelation model (implicit in the random effects probit model), for which the Butler and Moffitt algorithm works, is not empirically valid.

Notes

*   We would like to thank three anonymous referees, the editor, Stephen Cosslett, and Kajal Lahiri for helpful comments. Remaining errors are our own. A. Flores-Lagunes gratefully acknowledges financial support from the National Council for Science and Technology of Mexico (CONACYT).
1   In (17.11) we need some normalization, like setting the first element of β to 1.
2   In the case of the binary choice models (logit and probit), Davidson and MacKinnon (1989) show that the score test statistic based on the exact information matrix can be computed easily using a particular artificial regression. See also Davidson and MacKinnon Chapter 1 in this companion.
3   We draw here from Gouriéroux (1989).
4   Note that the approximating density is positive for all u.
5   GLL suggest, based on simulations, that using $K = 3$ allows for considerable flexibility in the distribution.
6   The asymptotic bias of the estimator will become negligible as K increases. GLL suggest starting with $K = 3$ (see previous fn.) and use score tests to determine whether such a value of K is appropriate.
7   The corresponding theorems can be found in Gallant and Nychka (1987).
8   References on probability simulators are Geweke, Keane, and Runkle (1994, 1997), Stern (1997), and Tanner (1996). For the reader interested in applying these methods,

Vassilis Hajivassiliou offers GAUSS and FORTRAN routines for the GHK simulator and other simulators at the following electronic address: http://econ.lse.ac.uk/~vassilis/pub/simulation/gauss/

References

Amemiya, T. (1981). Qualitative response models: A survey. *Journal of Economic Literature* 19, 483–536.

Avery, R., L. Hansen, and V.J. Hotz (1983). Multiperiod probit models and orthogonality condition estimation. *International Economic Review* 24, 21–35.

Baltagi, B.H. (1999). Specification tests in panel data models using artificial regressions. *Annales d'Economie et de Statistique* 55–6, 277–98.

Butler, I., and R. Moffitt (1982). A computationally efficient procedure for the one factor multinomial probit model. *Econometrica* 50, 761–4.

Chamberlain, G. (1980). Analysis of covariance with qualitative data. *Review of Economic Studies*, 47, 225–38.

Chamberlain, G. (1984). Panel data. In Z. Griliches and M.D. Intrilligator (eds.) *Handbook of Econometrics*, Volume 2. Amsterdam and New York: North-Holland, ch. 22.

Chamberlain, G. (1985). Heterogeneity, omitted variable bias and duration dependence. In J.J. Heckman and B. Singer (eds.) *Longitudinal Analysis of Labor Market Data*. Cambridge: Cambridge University Press.

Cosslett, S.R. (1983). Distribution-free maximum likelihood estimator of the binary choice model. *Econometrica* 51, 765–82.

Davidson, R., and J.G. MacKinnon (1989). Testing for consistency using artificial regressions. *Econometric Theory* 50, 363–84.

Debreu, G. (1960). Review of R.D. Luce "Individual Choice Behavior". *American Economic Review* 50, 186–8.

Gabler, S., F. Laisney, and M. Lechner (1993). Seminonparametric estimation of binary-choice models with application to labor-force participation. *Journal of Business and Economic Statistics* 11, 61–80.

Gallant, R., and D.W. Nychka (1987). Seminonparametric maximum likelihood estimation. *Econometrica* 55, 363–90.

Geweke, J.F., M.P. Keane, and D.E. Runkle (1994). Alternative computational approaches to inference in the multinomial probit model. *Review of Economics and Statistics* 76, 609–32.

Geweke, J.F., M.P. Keane, and D.E. Runkle (1997). Statistical inference in the multinomial multiperiod probit model. *Journal of Econometrics* 80, 125–65.

Gouriéroux, C. (1989). *Econométrie des Variables Qualitatives*, 2nd edn. Paris: Economica.

Gouriéroux, C., and A. Monfort (1995). *Statistics and Econometrics Models*, Volume 1. Cambridge: Cambridge University Press.

Gouriéroux, C., A. Monfort, and A. Trognon (1987). Generalised residuals. *Journal of Econometrics* 34, 5–32.

Hajivassiliou, V.A., and P.A. Ruud (1994). Classical estimation methods for LDV models using simulation. In R.F. Engle and D.L. McFadden (eds.) *Handbook of Econometrics*, Volume 4. Amsterdam and New York: North-Holland, ch. 40.

Hausman, J. (1978). Specification tests in econometrics. *Econometrica* 46, 1251–71.

Heckman, J.J. (1981). Statistical models for discrete panel data. In C.F. Manski and D.L. McFadden (eds.) *Structural Analysis of Discrete Data with Econometric Applications*. Cambridge, MA: MIT Press.

Honoré, B.E., and E. Kyriazidou (2000). Panel data discrete choice models with lagged dependent variables. *Econometrica* 68, 839–74.

Horowitz, J.L. (1993). Semiparametric and nonparametric estimation of quantal response models. In G.S. Maddala, C.R. Rao, and H.D. Vinod (eds.) *Handbook of Statistics*, Volume 11. Amsterdam and New York: North-Holland, ch. 2.

Johnson, N.L. and S. Kotz (1972). *Continuous Multivariate Distributions*. New York: Wiley.

Keane, M.P. (1993). Simulation estimation for panel data models with limited dependent variables. In G.S. Maddala, C.R. Rao, and H.D. Vinod (eds.) *Handbook of Statistics*, Volume 11. Amsterdam and New York: North-Holland, ch. 20.

Kim, J., and D. Pollard (1990). Cube root asymptotics. *The Annals of Statistics* 18, 191–219.

Klein, R.W., and R.H. Spady (1993). An efficient semiparametric estimator for discrete choice models. *Econometrica* 61, 387–421.

Lee, L.F. (1994). Semiparametric instrumental variables estimation of simultaneous equation sample selection models. *Journal of Econometrics* 63, 341–88.

Lee, L.F. (1997). Some common structures of simulated specification tests in multinormal discrete and limited dependent variable models. Working Paper 97/04, Hong Kong University of Science and Technology.

Maddala, G.S. (1983). *Limited Dependent and Qualitative Variables in Econometrics*. Cambridge: Cambridge University Press.

Maddala, G.S. (1987). Limited dependent variable models using panel data. *Journal of Human Resources* 22, 307–38.

Maddala, G.S. (1995). Specification tests in limited dependent variable models. In G.S. Maddala, P.C.B. Phillips and T.N. Srinivasan (eds.) *Advances in Econometrics and Quantitative Economics: Essays in Honor of C.R. Rao*. pp. 1–49. Oxford: Blackwell.

Manski, C.F. (1975). Maximum score estimation of the stochastic utility model of choice. *Journal of Econometrics* 3, 205–28.

Manski, C.F. (1985). Semiparametric analysis of discrete response: Asymptotic properties of the maximum score estimator. *Journal of Econometrics* 27, 313–33.

Manski, C.F., and S. Thompson (1986). Operational characteristics of maximum score estimation. *Journal of Econometrics* 32, 85–108.

McFadden, D.L. (1974). Conditional logit analysis of qualitative choice behavior. In P. Zarembka (ed.) *Frontiers in Econometrics*. New York: Academic Press.

McFadden, D.L. (1981). Econometric models of probabilistic choice. In C.F. Manski and D.L. McFadden (eds.) *Structural Analysis of Discrete Data with Econometric Applications*. Cambridge, MA: MIT Press.

McFadden, D.L. (1984). Econometric analysis of qualitative response models. In Z. Griliches and M.D. Intrilligator (eds.) *Handbook of Econometrics*, Volume 2. Amsterdam and New York: North-Holland, ch. 24.

Newey, W.K. (1985). Maximum likelihood specification testing and conditional moment tests. *Econometrica* 53, 1047–70.

Newey, W.K. (1990). Semiparametric efficiency bounds. *Journal of Applied Econometrics* 5, 99–135.

Orme, C. (1990). The small-sample performance of the information matrix test. *Journal of Econometrics* 46, 309–31.

Pagan, A.R. and F. Vella (1989). Diagnostic tests for models based on unit record data: A survey. *Journal of Applied Econometrics* 4, 529–59.

Powell, J. (1994). Estimation of semiparametric models. In R.F. Engle and D.L. McFadden (eds.) *Handbook of Econometrics*, Volume 4. Amsterdam and New York: North-Holland, ch. 41.

Stern, S. (1997). Simulation-based estimation. *Journal of Economic Literature* 35, 2006–39.

Tanner, M.A. (1996). *Tools for Statistical Inference: Methods for the Exploration of Posterior Distributions and Likelihood Functions*. New York: Springer-Verlag.

Tauchen, G. (1985). Diagnostic testing and evaluation of maximum likelihood models. *Journal of Econometrics* 30, 415–43.

Taylor, L. (1991). Testing exclusion restrictions for misspecified tobit model. *Economics Letters* 37, 411–16.

Thompson, T.S. (1989a). Identification of semiparametric discrete choice models. Discussion Paper 249, Center for Economic Research, University of Minnesota.

Thompson, T.S. (1989b). Least squares estimation of semiparametric discrete choice models. Manuscript, Department of Economics, University of Minnesota.

White, H. (1982). Maximum likelihood estimation of misspecified models. *Econometrica* 50, 1–25.

White, H. (1983). Corrigendum. *Econometrica* 51, 513.

CHAPTER EIGHTEEN

Self-Selection

Lung-fei Lee*

1 INTRODUCTION

This paper provides some account on econometric models and analysis of sample selection problems. The paper is divided into three parts. The first part considers possible selection-bias issues in econometric data. Selection biases can occur as the observed outcomes are results of individual's self-selection. The second part points out some development on econometric models with sample selection. This part concentrates on the specification, estimation, and test problems for parametric models. The third part lists some of the development of semiparametric estimation of sample selection models. Related surveys on the earlier development on sample selection models are Maddala (1983) and Amemiya (1984), which concern mainly parametric specification and estimation. Recent developments of the subject concern semiparametric estimation methods. Surveys on the latter are Powell (1994), Vella (1998), and M.-J. Lee (1997). Powell's survey covers broad areas of semiparametric estimation methods for microeconometric models in addition to sample selection models. A large part of the survey in Vella (1998) concerns the recent development on sample selection panel models. Treatment effect models as compared with sample selection models have been discussed in M.-J. Lee (1997). Because of their coverage and many developments on panel and treatment effect models being currently in their development stages in working paper format and because of space limitation, we skip these topics in this survey.

2 SAMPLE SELECTION BIAS

2.1 Self-selection

The problem of selection bias in economics arises when sampling observations are generated from the population by rules other than simple random sampling. Consequently, the sample representation of a true population is distorted. This is the essence of the selection problem. Distorted sample generation may be the outcome of sample collection by surveyors. More importantly, distorted sample observations result from self-selection decisions by the agents being studied. A sample generated by self-selection may not represent the true population distribution of characteristics no matter how big the sample size. However, self-selection biases can be corrected to produce an accurate description of the underlying population if the underlying sampling generating processes can be understood and relevant identification conditions are available. Economic theories and institutional settings can provide guidance. It is for this reason that the econometrics of self-selection is, by and large, a subject of microeconometrics.

The issue of selectivity bias first arose in labor economics, namely, the determinants of occupational wages in Roy (1951) and labor supply behavior of females in Gronau (1974) and Heckman (1974). Consider the labor supply problem of females in a free society. In a population of women, each individual is characterized by her endowments of observable and unobservable characteristics. (All characteristics are, of course, known to an individual herself, but some may be unobservable to an investigator.) She has the freedom to engage in market activities. It may be observed that only a subsample of the population is engaged in market employment and reports wages. A researcher or a policy maker may be interested in identifying the determinants of wages for working women so as to understand the determinants of wages for all women. The decision to work or not to work is not random as it is made in accordance with an individual's own interest. Consequently, the working and nonworking samples may have different characteristics. Sample selection bias arises when some component of the work decision is relevant to the wage determining process or the (expected) wage is a factor in the working decision. When the relationship between the work decision and the wage is purely through the observables and those observable variables are exogenous, the sample selection bias is controlled for when all relevant exogenous variables are included in the equations. The possibility of sample selection bias arises when there are unobservable characteristics that influence both the observed outcomes and the decision process.

2.2   Some conventional sample selection models

The tobit model assumes that the censoring threshold is deterministic and known. A generalization of the tobit model assumes that the censoring threshold is an unobservable stochastic variable. This generalization consists of two latent regression functions defined on the population: $y_1^* = x_1\beta_1 + u_1$ and $y_2^* = x_2\beta_2 + u_2$. The sample observation is (Iy_1, I), where $y_1 = y_1^*$ and $I = 1$ if $y_1^* \geq y_2^*$, and $I = 0$ if $y_1^* < y_2^*$. An example of this model is a labor supply model (Gronau, 1974; Heckman, 1974; Nelson, 1977), where y_1^* is an offered wage and y_2^* is the reservation wage of an individual. In a labor supply model, the individual maximizes utility with respect to income and leisure time subject to income and time constraints: $\max\{U(t, c, u) : c = y_1^*(T - t) + c_0, t \leq T\}$, where T is the available time, c_0 is nonlabor income available, c is the total income, and u represents unobserved characteristics of an individual. The reservation wage y_2^* is $(\partial U/\partial t)/(\partial U/\partial c)|_{t=T}$. The market wage y_1^* can be observed only for the worker. This formulation can further be generalized to incorporate fixed costs of participation. A general framework for these models can be written as

$$y^* = x\beta + u, \quad \text{and} \quad I^* = z\gamma - \varepsilon, \tag{18.1}$$

where $y = y^*$ can be observed only if $I^* > 0$. This two-equation formulation provides the prototypical sample selection model in econometrics. The sample is censored if the sign of I^* is observable in addition to Iy. It is a truncated case if only the event $I = 1$ and its corresponding sample observations of y are available.

Sample data can be generated by individuals making choices of belonging to one or another group, i.e. by the self-selection of individuals. A prototypical choice theoretic model of self-selection is that of Roy (1951). Roy (1951) discussed the problem of individuals choosing between two professions, hunting and fishing, based on their productivity (income) in each. There is a latent population of skills. While every person can, in principle, do the work in each "occupation", self-interest drives individuals to choose the occupation that produces the highest income for them. Roy's model is special in that an individual chooses his occupation based on the highest income among occupations. A more general setting is that individuals choose between several alternatives based on their preferences and the (potential) outcomes can be factors in their utility functions (Lee, 1978; Willis and Rosen, 1979).

A self-selection model with two alternatives and a potential outcome equation for each alternative can be

$$y_1^* = x_1\beta_1 + u_1, \quad \text{and} \quad y_2^* = x_2\beta_2 + u_2, \tag{18.2}$$

with a choice equation

$$I^* = z\gamma - \varepsilon. \tag{18.3}$$

The sample observation (I, y) is $I = 1$ and $y = y_1^*$ if $I^* > 0$, and $I = 0$ and $y = y_2^*$ if $I^* \leq 0$. For cases with polychotomous choices, a self-selection model with m alternatives and m_1 potential outcome equations, where $0 < m_1 \leq m$, is

$$y_j = x_j\beta_j + u_j, \quad j = 1, \ldots, m_1, \tag{18.4}$$

and

$$U_j = z_j\gamma + v_j, \quad j = 1, \ldots, m. \tag{18.5}$$

The U_j represents the utility of the alternative j. Outcomes are available for some m_1 alternatives. The outcome y_j can be observed only if the alternative j is chosen by the individual. In a utility maximization framework, the alternative j will be chosen if $U_j > U_l$ for all $l \neq j, l = 1, \ldots, m$.

The selection equations in the preceding models provide discrete choices. In some cases, the selection equations may provide more sample information than discrete choices. A censored regression selection criterion is such a case. A model of female labor supply without participation cost is an example. The market wage can be observed when the hour of work of an individual is positive and the hours-of-work equation can be modeled by a tobit model. A sample selection model with a tobit (censored) selection rule can be specified as

$$y_1^* = x\gamma + u_1, \quad \text{and} \quad y_2^* = x\beta + u_2, \tag{18.6}$$

where (y_1, y_2) can be observed such that $(y_1, y_2) = (y_1^*, y_2^*)$ when $y_1^* > 0$. This model provides additional information in that positive values of y_1^* can be observed instead of just the sign of y_1^*. Other models that are of interest are simultaneous equation models and panel data models.

An important feature of a sample selection model is its usage to investigate potential outcomes or opportunity costs besides observed outcomes. For sectorial wage or occupational choices with self-selection, Roy's model (Roy, 1951; Heckman and Honoré, 1990) has emphasized comparative advantage in individuals and its effect on income distribution. For example, the comparative advantage measure of Sattinger (1978) involves the computation of opportunity costs for forgone choices (Lee, 1995). Opportunity costs are counterfactual outcomes. The evaluations of counterfactual outcomes are important in social welfare programs (Heckman and Robb, 1985; Bjorklund and Moffitt, 1987) because of their policy implications.

3 PARAMETRIC ESTIMATION

3.1 Two-stage estimation

Consider the estimation of the model (18.1). Assume that u and ε are jointly normally distributed with zero-means and the variance of ε being normalized to be a unity, i.e. $\text{var}(\varepsilon) = 1$. The least squares procedure applied to the observed y and x will give inconsistent estimates, if $E(u \mid x, z\gamma \geq \varepsilon)$ is not zero and is correlated with x. This omitted selection-bias term needs to be corrected for consistent estimation (Heckman, 1979). With normally distributed disturbances, $E(\varepsilon \mid x, z, I = 1) = -\sigma_{1\varepsilon} \frac{\phi(z\gamma)}{\Phi(z\gamma)}$, where ϕ and Φ denote, respectively, the standard normal density and distribution functions and $\sigma_{1\varepsilon}$ is the covariance of u and ε. The bias-corrected regression equation is $y = x\beta - \sigma_{1\varepsilon} \frac{\phi(z\gamma)}{\Phi(z\gamma)} + \eta$, where $E(\eta \mid x, z, I = 1) = 0$. A two-stage method can be applied to estimate the corrected equation for β (Heckman, 1979). In the first stage, γ is estimated by the probit maximum likelihood method. The least squares method can then be applied to estimate β and $\sigma_{1\varepsilon}$ in

$$y = x\beta + \sigma_{1\varepsilon}\left(-\frac{\phi(z\hat{\gamma})}{\Phi(z\hat{\gamma})}\right) + \tilde{\eta}, \tag{18.7}$$

with the observed subsample corresponding to $I = 1$, where $\hat{\gamma}$ is the probit maximum likelihood estimate of γ. The estimator is consistent but the asymptotic distribution of the two-stage estimator is not the conventional one of a linear regression model. The disturbances η and, hence, $\tilde{\eta}$ are heteroskedastic. The estimated bias corrected term is a generated regressor. The replacement of γ by the estimate $\hat{\gamma}$ introduces additional errors, which are correlated across different sample units. By taking into account the heteroskedasticity of disturbances but ignoring the randomness of $\hat{\gamma}$ in equation (18.7), the constructed asymptotic variance matrix of the two-stage estimates $\hat{\beta}$ and $\hat{\sigma}_{1\varepsilon}$ will underestimate the correct one unless $\sigma_{1\varepsilon} = 0$.

For the two-sector model (18.2)–(18.3), the expected observable outcome equation for y_1^* is $E(y_1 \mid x, I = 1) = x_1\beta_1 + \sigma_{1\varepsilon}(-\frac{\phi(z\gamma)}{\Phi(z\gamma)})$, and the expected observable outcome for y_2^* will be $E(y_2 \mid x, I = 0) = x_2\beta_2 + \sigma_{2\varepsilon}(\frac{\phi(z\gamma)}{1 - \Phi(z\gamma)})$. For this model, each bias-corrected equation can be either separately or jointly estimated by the two-stage method (Lee, 1978). While $\sigma_{1\varepsilon}$ is the covariance of u_1 and ε and $\sigma_{2\varepsilon}$ is the covariance of u_2 and ε, their signs may be of special interest for some empirical studies as they determine the direction of selection bias. When $\sigma_{1\varepsilon}$ is negative, the observed outcome y_1 is subject to positive selection as $\sigma_{1\varepsilon}(-\frac{\phi(z\gamma)}{\Phi(z\gamma)})$ is strictly positive. For example, for the study on the return to college education, if high school graduates with high unobserved ability are likely to go to college and that ability could increase earning, one might expect that the observed earning of college graduates would be subject to positive selection. In some situations, negative selection might also be meaningful. For example, from the view of comparative advantage, what matters is the sign of $\sigma_{2\varepsilon} - \sigma_{1\varepsilon}$. As the measure of expected unobservable comparative advantage is $E(u_1 - u_2 \mid x, I = 1) + E(u_2 - u_1 \mid x, I = 0) = (\sigma_{2\varepsilon} - \sigma_{1\varepsilon})(\frac{\phi(z\gamma)}{\Phi(z\gamma)} + \frac{\phi(z\gamma)}{1 - \Phi(z\gamma)})$, an individual has comparative advantage in his or her chosen task when $\sigma_{2\varepsilon} - \sigma_{1\varepsilon}$ is positive. The relevance of comparative advantage in self-selection has been explored in Lee (1978) and Willis and Rosen (1979). Heckman and Honoré (1990) provide an in-depth analysis of the implications of Roy's model.

The normal distribution is a common distributional assumption for sample selection models. For the simplicity of the two-stage estimation method, Olsen (1980) pointed out that the crucial property underlying the derivation of the bias correction is the linearity of the conditional expectation of u given ε. Based on that property, Olsen specified the potential outcome equation $y^* = x\beta + \lambda(\varepsilon - \mu_\varepsilon) + \eta$, where μ_ε is the mean of ε, as the basic structure and suggested a linear probability modification to correct for the selection bias in observed outcomes. This modification is useful as it provides an alternative parametric specification without being restricted to normal disturbances. The correction of selection bias is now dependent on the marginal distribution of ε. However, the selectivity bias terms may be sensitive to a specific choice probability model. Lee (1982) suggested the use of nonlinear transformations to overcome possible restrictions in Olsen's approach and suggested some flexible functional form and series expansion for the selection-bias correction. The dichotomous indicator I is determined by the selection decision such that $I = 1$ if and only if $z\gamma > \varepsilon$. Thus, for any strictly increasing transformation J, $I = 1$ if and only if $J(z\gamma) > J(\varepsilon)$. The Olsen specification was generalized into $y^* = x\beta + \lambda(J(\epsilon) - \mu_J) + \eta$, where $\mu_J = E(J(\epsilon))$. The selection bias term for the observed y is $E(\epsilon^* \mid J(z\gamma) \geq \epsilon^*) = \frac{\mu(J(z\gamma))}{F(J(z\gamma))}$ where F is the distribution of ϵ, $\epsilon^* = J(\epsilon)$ and $\mu(J(\epsilon)) = \int_{J(-\infty)}^{J(z\gamma)} \epsilon^* f_J(\epsilon^*) d\epsilon^*$ with f_J being the implied density function of ϵ^*. Conditional on y being observed, the outcome equation becomes $y = x\beta + \lambda(\frac{\mu(J(z\gamma))}{F(z\gamma)} - \mu_J) + \eta$, which can be estimated by a simple two-stage method. This approach generates a large class of models with selectivity while the probability choice model can be chosen to be a specific popular choice model and remains unchanged. The choice of different possible Js is, in general, a regressor selection problem in a linear regression model.

The specification of the conditional expectation of u on $J(\epsilon)$ being linear can be further relaxed by introducing a flexible expansion of distributions (Lee, 1982). It was noted that if the bivariate distribution of u^* and ϵ, where $u^* = u/\sigma_u$, could be represented by a bivariate Edgeworth expanded distribution, the conditional expectation of u^* conditional on ϵ would be $E(u^* \mid \epsilon) = \{\rho\epsilon + \sum_{r\geq3}^{\infty}[\rho A_{0r}H_{r+1}(\epsilon)/r! + A_{1,r-1}H_{r-1}(\epsilon)/(r-1)!]\}/D(\epsilon)$ where $D(\epsilon) = 1 + \sum_{r\geq3}^{\infty}A_{0r}H_r(\epsilon)/r!$, A_{rs} are functions of cumulants of u^* and ϵ, and $H_r(\epsilon)$ is the rth order Hermite polynomial. When the marginal distribution of ϵ is normal, $D(\epsilon) = 1$. Bias correction can be based on the expanded conditional expectation. With a normal ϵ (or a normally transformed ϵ^*) and expanded terms up to $r + s = 4$ (instead of an infinite series), the bias corrected outcome equation is

$$y = x\beta + \rho\sigma_u[-\phi(z\gamma)/\Phi(z\gamma)] + \mu_{12}\sigma_u[-(z\gamma)\phi(z\gamma)/(2\Phi(z\gamma))]$$
$$+ (\mu_{13} - 3\rho)\sigma_u[(1 - (z\gamma)^2)\phi(z\gamma)/(6\Phi(z\gamma))] + \eta. \tag{18.8}$$

The additional terms generalize the selection-bias correction of a normally distributed u to a flexible distributional one. The two-stage estimation can be applied to the estimation of equation (18.8). The correct variance matrix of the two-stage estimator shall take into account both the heteroskedasticity of the disturbance η and the distribution of the first-stage estimator of γ. For the model in (18.8), the exact expression of the heteroskedastic variance of η would be too complicated to be useful for estimation. To overcome that complication, Lee (1982) suggests the adoption of White's robust variance formulation. White's correction will estimate the first component of the correct variance matrix. The second component will be the variance and covariances due to the first stage estimate of γ. Equation (18.8) can also be used for the testing of normality disturbance by checking whether the coefficients of the last two terms are zero. A test of the presence of selection bias is to see whether the coefficients of all the (three) bias-correction terms are zero. In principle, it is possible to formulate the bias correction with more terms. However, with additional terms, one might quickly run into possible increasing multicollinearity in a regression framework. The proper selection of expanded terms is an issue on the selection of regressors or a model selection problem. One may think that it is sensible to incorporate more expanded terms as sample size increases. Such a strategy can be better justified in a semiparametric estimation framework (Newey, Powell, and Walker, 1990).

For the estimation of sample selection model, multicollinearity due to the addition of the bias-correction term in the observed outcome equation remains a serious point of contention. Olsen's specification with a linear probability choice equation highlights eloquently the multicollinearity issue at an early development stage of the literature. The linear choice probability corresponds to a uniform distribution for ε. With ε being a uniform random variable on $[0, 1]$, $E(\varepsilon \mid z\gamma > \varepsilon) = z\gamma/2$. If $z = x$ or z is a subvector of x, the bias-correction term will be perfectly multicollinear with the included x of the outcome equation. Consequently, the two-stage estimation method will break down completely. This multicollinearity issue is related to model identification. With normal disturbances, the bias-corrected term is a nonlinear function of z and, because of the nonlinearity, the two-stage method would not completely break down. However, severe multicollinearity might still be an issue for some samples. Nawata (1993) and Leung and Yu (1996) showed that $\phi(z\gamma)/\Phi(z\gamma)$ is almost linear in $z\gamma$ on a range of approximately $[-3, 3]$. The two-stage estimator would not be reliable under multicollinearity. Wales and Woodland (1980), Nelson (1984), Manning, Duan, and Rogers (1987), Nawata and Nagase (1996), and Leung and Yu (1996), among others, investigate this issue by several Monte Carlo studies. The overall conclusions from these Monte Carlo studies are that the effectiveness of the two-stage estimator depends on either exclusion restrictions whereby some relevant variables in z do not appear in x or on the fact that at least one of the relevant variables in z displays sufficient variation to make the nonlinearity effective. In a distribution-free sample selection model, the exclusion restriction is a necessary condition for identification as it needs to rule out the linear probability setting of Olsen.

The possible multicollinearity of the two-stage estimation procedure created a debate in the health economics literature on whether a sample selection model is a better model than multi-part models for modeling discrete choices with outcome equations. A multi-part model essentially assumes uncorrelated disturbances among outcomes and choice equations (Manning *et al.*, 1987; Maddala, 1985; Hay and Olsen, 1984; Leung and Yu, 1966). Hay and Olsen (1984) and Maddala (1985) point out an important feature of the sample selection model is its usage to investigate potential outcomes in addition to observed outcomes. For the normal distribution model, in the presence of severe multicollinearity, one has to resort to the method of maximum likelihood for a better inference.

3.2 Maximum likelihood estimation

Under the assumption that (ε_i, u_i), $i = 1, \ldots, n$, are iid normally distributed with zero means, a unit variance for ε, a variance σ^2 for u, and a correlation coefficient ρ_{12}, the loglikelihood function for the model (18.1) is

$$\ln L(\theta) = \sum_{i=1}^{n} \left\{ (1 - I_i) \ln (1 - \Phi(z_i\gamma)) - \frac{1}{2} I_i \ln (2\pi\sigma^2) - \frac{1}{2\sigma^2} I_i(y_i - x_i\beta)^2 \right.$$

$$\left. + I_i \ln \Phi\left[(z_i\gamma - \frac{\rho}{\sigma}(y_i - x_i\beta))/\sqrt{1 - \rho^2} \right] \right\}, \tag{18.9}$$

where $\theta = (\beta', \sigma^2, \gamma', \rho)'$. The use of the maximum likelihood method can be found, for example, in Heckman (1974), Nelson (1977), and Griliches, Hall, and Hausman (1978). The logarithmic likelihood function (18.9) may not have a unique maximum (Nelson, 1977; Olsen, 1982). However, Olsen (1982) showed that, for a given value of ρ, it has a unique maximum for the remaining parameter. Despite the latter property, the implementation of the maximum likelihood method of this model remains an overlooked issue. Nawata and Nagase (1996) pointed out that the maximum likelihood method implemented in several popular econometric packages by standard optimization methods may be incomplete. They recommended the use of scanning methods.

Under some regularity conditions, the maximum likelihood estimate (MLE) is, in general, consistent, asymptotically normal and efficient (Amemiya, 1973). But in some special cases, the loglikelihood function has irregularities at some parameter subspace. At $\rho = 0$, if x and $\phi(z\gamma)/\Phi(z\gamma)$ are linearly dependent, the information matrix will be singular. This follows because $\frac{\partial \ln L}{\partial \beta} = \frac{1}{\sigma^2} \sum_{i=1}^{n} I_i x_i' u_i$ and $\frac{\partial \ln L}{\partial \rho} = -\frac{1}{\sigma} \sum_{i=1}^{n} \frac{\phi(z_i\gamma)}{\Phi(z_i\gamma)} I_i u_i$ at $\rho = 0$. Singular information matrix in this sample selection model does not indicate that the parameter vector of interest is not identifiable. Lee and Chesher (1986) investigated the implications on the MLE under such an irregularity for a concrete case that x contains an intercept term and z contains only a constant term, namely, $y = x\beta + u$ and $y^* = \gamma - \varepsilon$, under the normal assumption, when the true but unknown ρ is zero. The asymptotic distribution can be analyzed by the Taylor series expansion of a concentrated likelihood function. It turns out that for some components of the parameter vector their MLEs are still consistent at the usual $1/\sqrt{n}$-rate of convergence and their distributions are asymptotically normal, but the MLEs of remaining parameters converge at much lower rates of convergence and are nonnormally distributed. The MLE $\hat{\rho}$ has the asymptotic property that $\sqrt{n}\,\hat{\rho}^3$ is asymptotically normal with zero mean and a finite variance. Hence, $\hat{\rho}$ converges at the rate of $n^{-1/6}$ and $n^{1/6}\hat{\rho}$ is asymptotically distributed as a cubic root of a normal variable. For the remaining estimates, let $\beta = (\beta_1, \beta_2)$ where β_1 is the unknown intercept and β_2 is the slope vector of regressors. The MLEs of β_2 and γ turn out to be $\sqrt{n}$-consistent and $\sqrt{n}\,(\hat{\beta}_2 - \beta_2)$ and $\sqrt{n}\,(\hat{\gamma} - \gamma)$ are asymptotically normal. However, $\hat{\beta}_1$ converges at the low $n^{-1/6}$-rate and $n^{1/6}(\hat{\beta}_1 - \beta_1)$ is asymptotically a cubic root of a normal variable. For σ^2, its MLE $\hat{\sigma}^2$ converges at an $n^{-1/3}$-rate and $n^{1/3}(\hat{\sigma}^2 - \sigma^2)$ is asymptotically the $2/3$ power of a normal variable.

3.3   Polychotomous choice sample selection models

A polychotomous choice model with m-alternatives specifies the latent utility values $U_j = z_j\gamma + v_j$, $j = 1, \ldots, m$, and the alternative j is chosen if and only if $U_j > \max\{U_k : k = 1, \ldots, m; k \neq j\}$. A specified joint distribution for $v = (v_1, \ldots, v_m)$ implies the choice probability G_j for the jth alternative, where $G_j(x\gamma) = P(z_j\gamma - z_k\gamma > v_k - v_j, k \neq j, k = 1, \ldots, m \mid x)$. Familiar parametric polychotomous choice models are the conditional logit model and the nested logit model of McFadden (1973, 1978) and the multinomial probit model. For a recent survey on qualitative response models, see Chapter 17 by Maddala and Flores-Lagunes in this volume. For a sample selection model, say, $y = x\beta + u$ for the alternative 1, a desirable specification will allow u to correlate with the disturbances in the utility equations. A traditional approach may specify a joint distribution for $v = (v_1, \ldots, v_m)$ and u. In such an approach, the marginal distributions for v and u are determined by the joint distribution. If they are jointly normally distributed, the implied choice model will be the multinomial probit model. However, it is less obvious how to incorporate selected outcome equations with other familiar choice models. Dubin and McFadden (1984) and Lee (1983) suggest alternative specification approaches. Dubin and McFadden (1984) suggest a linear conditional expectation specification in that $E(u \mid v, x)$ is a linear function of v. The distribution of v can be the one which generates the logit or nested logit choice component. They suggest two-stage estimation methods based on bias-corrected outcome equations. Lee (1983) suggests an approach based on order statistics and distributional transformations. The marginal distributions of v and u are first specified, and the model is then completed with a distribution with specified margins. From the choice equations, define a random variable ε_1 as $\varepsilon_1 = \max\{y_k^* : k = 2, \ldots, m\} - v_1$. The first alternative is chosen if and only if $z_1\gamma > \varepsilon_1$. In terms of ε_1, the choice inequality looks like a binary choice criterion for alternative 1. Given the distributions for v (and hence G_1), the implied distribution of ε_1 is $F_1(c \mid x) = G_1(c - z_2\gamma_2, \ldots, c - z_m\gamma_m)$. When u_1 is normally distributed, a normal-distribution transformation is suggested to transform ε_1 to a standard normal variable ε_1^* as $\varepsilon_1^* = \Phi^{-1}(F_1(\varepsilon_1 \mid x))$. The u and ε_1^* are then assumed to be jointly normally distributed with zero means and a covariance $\sigma_{u_1\varepsilon_1^*}$. Under such a specification, the bias-corrected outcome equation is similar to the familiar one as $E(y_1 \mid x, I_1 = 1) = x_1\beta_1 - \sigma_{u_1\varepsilon_1^*} \frac{\phi(\Phi^{-1}(G_1(z\gamma)))}{G_1(z\gamma)}$. If u were not normally distributed, other transformations rather than the normal distribution might be desirable. If the marginal distribution of u_1 were unknown, flexible functional specifications such as the bivariate Edgeworth expansion might be used. Under this approach, both a simple two-stage method and the method of maximum likelihood can be used. Schmertmann (1994) compares the advantages and disadvantages of the McFadden and Dubin, and Lee approaches. His conclusion is that the McFadden and Dubin specification can likely be affected by multicollinearity as several bias-correction terms may be introduced; and Lee's specification imposes restrictive covariance structures on u and v and may be sensitive to misspecification. On the latter, Lee (1995) derives some implications on comparative advantage measures.

3.4   Simulation estimation

The multinomial probit model has long been recognized as a useful discrete choice model. But, because its choice probability does not have a closed-form expression and its computation involves multiple integrals, it has not been a popular model for empirical studies until the 1990s. The advancement of computing technology and the recent development on simulation estimation techniques provide effective ways to implement this model. For a general description on various simulation methods, see Chapter 22 by Geweke, Houser, and Keane in this volume. Simulation estimation methods can be developed for the estimation of the multinomial probit sample selection model (Lee, 1996). The model can be estimated by two-stage methods and/or the method of maximum likelihood via Monte Carlo simulation. A simulated two-stage method is similar to the method of simulated moments (McFadden, 1989). For a two-stage method, the choice equations are first estimated. The likelihood function of the choice model can be simulated with the GHK (Geweke–Hajivassiliou–Keane) simulator. The probabilities of $U_j - U_l > 0$, $l = 1, \ldots, m$ but $l \neq j$ are determined by the normal distribution of $\varepsilon_j = (v_1 - v_j, \ldots, v_{j-1} - v_j, v_{j+1} - v_j, \ldots, v_m - v_j)$. Denote $w_j = (z_j - z_1, \ldots, z_j - z_{j-1}, z_j - z_{j+1}, \ldots, z_j - z_m)$. The ε_j can be represented as $\varepsilon_j = H_j \eta_j$, where H_j is a lower triangular matrix of the Cholesky decomposition of the variance of ε_j and $\eta_j = (\eta_{j1}, \ldots, \eta_{j,m-1})$ is a standard normal vector. Define $L_{j1} = w_{j1}\gamma/h_{j11}$ and $L_{jl} = [w_{jl}\gamma - \sum_{k=1}^{l-1} h_{jlk}\eta_k]/h_{jll}$ for $l = 2, \ldots, m - 1$. It follows that

$$P(I_j = 1) = \int_{-\infty}^{L_{j,m-1}} \cdots \int_{-\infty}^{L_{j1}} \prod_{l=1}^{m-1} \phi(\eta_{jl}) d\eta_{jl} = \int_{-\infty}^{\infty} \cdots \int_{-\infty}^{\infty} \prod_{l=1}^{m-1} \Phi(L_{jl})\phi_{(-\infty, L_{jl})}(\eta_{jl}) d\eta_{jl},$$

where $\phi_{(a,b)}$ is a truncated standard normal density with support on (a, b). The GHK sampler is to generate sequentially truncated standard normal variables from $\prod_{l=1}^{m-1} \phi_{(-\infty, L_{jl})}(\eta_{jl})$. With S simulation runs, the GHK likelihood simulator of the choice model is $\hat{L}_S^C(\bar{I}) = \prod_{j=1}^{m} \{\frac{1}{S}\sum_{s=1}^{S} \prod_{l=1}^{m-1} \Phi(L_{jl}^{(s)})\}^{I_j}$. The parameter γ can be estimated by maximizing this simulated likelihood function. With the first-stage estimate $\hat{\gamma}$, the outcome equation can be estimated by the method of simulated moments. Simulated moment equations can be derived from observed outcome equations. Consider the bias-corrected outcome equation $y = x\beta + E(u \mid x, I_1 = 1) + \eta$. As ε_1 has the Cholesky decomposition $\varepsilon_1 = H_1 \eta_1$,

$$E(u \mid x, I_1 = 1) = \frac{1}{P(I_1 = 1)} \int_{-\infty}^{\infty} \cdots \int_{-\infty}^{\infty} E(u \mid \varepsilon_1 = H_1 \eta_1) \prod_{l=1}^{m-1} \Phi(L_{1l})\phi_{(-\infty, L_{1l})}(\eta_{1l}) d\eta_{1l}. \tag{18.10}$$

The GHK sampler $\prod_{l=1}^{m-1} \phi_{(-\infty, L_{1l})}(\eta_{1l})$ can be used simultaneously to simulate both the numerator and denominator in (18.10). With S simulation runs from the GHK sampler, (18.10) can be simulated as $\hat{E}_S(u \mid I_1 = 1) = \sum_{s=1}^{S} E(u \mid \varepsilon_1 = H_1 \eta_1^{(s)})\omega^{(s)}$, where $\omega^{(s)} = \prod_{l=1}^{m-1} \Phi(L_{1l}^{(s)})/\sum_{r=1}^{S} \prod_{l=1}^{m-1} \Phi(L_{1l}^{(r)})$. $\hat{E}_S(u \mid I_1 = 1)$ is a consistent estimator of $E(u \mid I_1 = 1)$ when S goes to infinity. The simulated method of moments can then be applied to estimate the equation $y = x\beta + \hat{E}_S(u \mid I_1 = 1) + \tilde{\eta}$. The method of simulated moments is a generalized method of (simulated) moments. It is essentially an instrumental variable (IV) method. It is not desirable to apply a least squares procedure to the bias-corrected equation because $\hat{E}_S(u \mid I_1 = 1)$ with a finite S creates an error-in-variable (on regressors) problem.

The method of simulated maximum likelihood can be asymptotically efficient if the number of random draws S increases at a rate faster than the $\sqrt{n}$-rate

(Lee, 1992b). The likelihood function for an observation of the model with m-alternatives and with outcome for alternative 1 is

$$L(\tilde{I}, y) = \left[\int_{-\infty}^{L_{1,m-1}} \cdots \int_{-\infty}^{L_{11}} f(u \mid \varepsilon_1 = H_1 \eta_1) \prod_{l=1}^{m-1} \phi(\eta_{1l}) d\eta_{1l} \right]^{I_1} \prod_{j=2}^{m} P(I_j = 1)^{I_j},$$

where $u = y - x\beta$. Each of the likelihood components can be simulated without bias with a generalization of the GHK simulator. The likelihood function can be simulated as

$$\tilde{L}_S(\tilde{I}, y) = \left\{ \frac{1}{S} \sum_{s=1}^{S} f(u \mid \varepsilon_1 = H_1 \eta_1^{(s)}) \prod_{l=1}^{m-1} \Phi(L_{1l}^{(s)}) \right\}^{I_1} \prod_{j=2}^{m} \left\{ \frac{1}{S} \sum_{s=1}^{S} \prod_{l=1}^{m-1} \Phi(L_{jl}^{(s)}) \right\}^{I_j},$$

where the random variables are drawn from $\prod_{l=1}^{m-1} \phi_{(-\infty, L_{jl})}(\eta_{jl})$ for each $j = 1, \ldots, m$. Lee (1996) compares these simulation methods and finds that the simulated maximum likelihood method can indeed be more efficient with a moderate amount of simulation draws. One may expect that simulation methods may play an important role in the future development of sample selection models with dynamic structures.

3.5 Estimation of simultaneous equation sample selection model

A two-stage estimation method can be easily generalized for the estimation of a simultaneous equation model. Consider the linear simultaneous equation $y^* = y^* B + xC + u$, which can be observed only if $z\gamma > \varepsilon$. For the estimation of structural parameters, consider the first structural equation $y_1^* = y_{(1)}^* \beta_1 + x_1 \delta_1 + u_1$ where $y_{(1)}^*$ consists of included endogenous variables on the right-hand side of the structural equation. The bias-corrected structural equation is $y_1 = y_{(1)} \beta_1 + x_1 \delta_1 + \sigma_{1\varepsilon} \left(-\frac{\phi(z\hat{\gamma})}{\Phi(z\hat{\gamma})} \right) + \tilde{\eta}_1$. The system implies the reduced form equations $y^* = x\Pi + v$. Lee, Maddala, and Trost (1980) suggest the estimation of the reduced form parameters Π by the Heckman two-stage method, and used the predicted $y_{(1)}$ to estimate the bias-corrected structural equation similar to Theil's two-stage method for a conventional simultaneous equation model.

The structural parameters can also be estimated by a general minimum distance procedure (Amemiya, 1979). Amemiya's method is a systematic procedure for estimating structural parameters directly from estimated reduced form parameters. Let J_1 and J_2 be the selection matrices such that $y_{(1)}^* = y^* J_1$ and $x_1 = x J_2$. As $y_1^* = y^* J_1 \beta_1 + x J_2 \delta_1 + u_1 = x(\Pi J_1 \beta_1 + J_2 \delta_1) + v_1$, one has $\pi_1 = \Pi J_1 \beta_1 + J_2 \delta_1$. Let $\hat{\Pi}$ be the reduced form estimate from Heckman's two-stage estimation. Amemiya's minimum distance procedure is to estimate β_1 and δ_1 from the linear equation $\hat{\pi}_1 = \hat{\Pi} J_1 \beta_1 + J_2 \delta + \zeta_1$, where $\zeta_1 = (\hat{\pi}_1 - \pi_1) - (\hat{\Pi} - \Pi) J_1 \beta_1$ is the disturbance, by least squares or generalized least squares. The relative efficiency of an estimator from this minimum distance approach depends on the relative efficiency of the reduced form parameter estimates (Amemiya, 1983). Lee (1981), Amemiya (1983) and Newey (1987) compare various two-stage IV estimation methods with Amemiya's generalized minimum distance estimators. It was found that many two-stage IV estimators are special cases of Amemiya's minimum distance estimators depending on appropriate reduced form estimates. Lee (1992a) shows that the minimized generalized sum of squares residuals from Amemiya's generalized least-squares procedure also provides a test of overidentification restrictions of a linear structural equation. However, because Amemiya's approach relies on solving structural parameters from reduced form parameters, it cannot be generalized to the estimation of a nonlinear simultaneous equation system while many IV approaches can.

3.6   Misspecification and tests

In the sample selection model (18.1), the data on observed outcomes y are censored and least squares estimators of β obtained using y suffer from selectivity bias when the disturbances u and ε are correlated. But if they were independent, the model would have a simple structure and β and σ^2 could be estimated by applying ordinary least squares to the observed outcome equation and γ of the selection equation can be estimated by the probit MLE. To test whether there is selectivity for sample under normal disturbances, one may examine the hypothesis $H_0 : \rho = 0$. The score test statistic for this hypothesis is derived in Melino (1982). The score test statistic has the same asymptotic distribution as a t-statistic for testing the significance of the coefficient of the bias-corrected term in a two-stage estimation procedure. The simple t-statistic is an asymptotically efficient test statistic.

For special cases where the bias-corrected term is perfectly collinear with included regressors, these test statistics break down. The score vector evaluated at the restricted MLE under such a circumstance is identically zero and the corresponding information matrix is singular. Lee and Chesher (1986) suggest a generalization of the score test to extremum tests. The intuition behind the score test statistic is to ask whether the average loglikelihood of a model evaluated at the restricted MLE has a significantly nonzero gradient. When it does, we are led to reject the null hypothesis because by moving from the parameter vector under the null hypothesis, higher values of the loglikelihood can be achieved. The score test is exploiting the first-order derivative testing for a maximum. Thus, when the score test statistic is identically zero, one should consider tests for extremum based on higher-order derivatives as in calculus. For testing the presence of sample selection bias, the extremum test statistic is asymptotically equivalent to a test of skewness constructed from the statistic $\frac{1}{\sqrt{N}}\sum_{i=1}^{N} I_i e_i^3/(3\hat{\sigma}^3)$ where e_i is the least squares residual of the outcome equation. This statistic is intuitively appealing because, if $\rho \neq 0$, the disturbance of the observed outcome equation has nonzero mean and its distribution (conditional on selection) is not symmetric.

The normal distribution is a popular assumption in parametric sample selection models. Contrary to the standard linear regression model, the misspecification of normality of disturbances will, in general, provide inconsistent estimates under the two-stage or maximum likelihood methods. Theoretical consequences of misspecification are well presented for limited dependent variables models (Goldberger, 1983). For the sample selection model, investigations of sensitivity of distributional misspecification can be found in Olsen (1982), Lee (1982), Mroz (1987), and others. Diagnostic test statistics have been developed for detecting model misspecification. The computationally simple and motivating approach is the Lagrange multiplier (efficient score) approach. For various misspecifications such as omitted variables, heteroskedasticity, serial correlation, and normal disturbances, the Lagrange multiplier statistics have simple moment structures (see the survey by Pagan and Vella, 1989). This can be seen as follows. In an econometric model with latent variables, suppose that $g(y^*, y \mid \theta)$ is the joint density of latent variables y^* and observed sample y, where θ is a vector of possible parameters. Let $f(y \mid \theta)$ be the density of y, and $g(y^* \mid y, \theta)$ be the conditional density of y^* given y. Since $g(y^*, y \mid \theta) = g(y^* \mid y, \theta) f(y \mid \theta)$, $\ln f(y \mid \theta) = \ln g(y^*, y \mid \theta) - \ln g(y^* \mid y, \theta)$, and $\frac{\partial \ln f(y \mid \theta)}{\partial \theta} = \frac{\partial \ln g(y^*, y \mid \theta)}{\partial \theta} - \frac{\partial \ln g(y^* \mid y, \theta)}{\partial \theta}$. Integrating these expressions with respect to $g(y^* \mid y, \theta^+)$ where θ^+ is an arbitrary value of θ, it follows that $\ln f(y \mid \theta) = \int_{-\infty}^{\infty} [\ln g(y^*, y \mid \theta)] g(y^* \mid y, \theta^+) dy^* - \int_{-\infty}^{\infty} [\ln g(y^* \mid y, \theta)] g(y^* \mid y, \theta^+) dy^*$ and

$$\frac{\partial \ln f(y \mid \theta)}{\partial \theta} = \int_{-\infty}^{\infty} \frac{\partial \ln g(y^*, y \mid \theta)}{\partial \theta} g(y^* \mid y, \theta^+) dy^* - \int_{-\infty}^{\infty} \frac{\partial \ln g(y^* \mid y, \theta)}{\partial \theta} g(y^* \mid y, \theta^+) dy^*.$$

(18.11)

At $\theta^+ = \theta$, the first-order derivative of the loglikelihood (18.11) becomes $\frac{\partial \ln f(y \mid \theta)}{\partial \theta} = E_\theta \left(\frac{\partial \ln g(y^*, y \mid \theta)}{\partial \theta} \mid y \right)$, because $E_\theta \left(\frac{\partial \ln g(y^* \mid y, \theta)}{\partial \theta} \mid y \right) = 0$. A test statistic based on the score $\frac{\partial \ln f(y \mid \theta)}{\partial \theta}$ will be a conditional moment statistic of $\frac{\partial \ln g(y^*, y \mid \theta)}{\partial \theta}$ conditional on sample observations. For many specification tests of the sample selection model, the score test statistics are based on some simple conditional moments. Lee (1984) considered the efficient score test of normality of the sample selection model (18.1). The test statistic is derived within the bivariate Edgeworth series of distributions. For the truncated sample selection case, the test compares some sample moments of order (r, s) for which $r + s > 2$ with correspondingly estimated hypothesized conditional moments of disturbances. For the censored case, the test is equivalent to the testing of some sample semi-invariants for which $r + s > 2$ are zeros.

4 Semiparametric and Nonparametric Approaches

4.1 Semiparametric two-stage estimation

Manski (1975) showed that a parametric distribution is not necessary for consistent estimation of discrete choice models, and thus originated the semiparametric estimation literature in microeconometrics. Recognition of inconsistency of the maximum likelihood and two-stage estimation methods under a misspecified error distribution has speeded up the studies on semiparametric and nonparametric estimation methods. Cosslett (1991) initiated semiparametric estimation of the sample selection model with a binary selection equation. Based on a series approximation to an unknown density function, Gallant and Nychka (1987) have proposed a consistent semi-nonparametric maximum likelihood method. The asymptotic distributions of both the estimators of Cosslett and Gallant and Nychka are unknown. Robinson (1988) obtained a semiparametric estimator of parameters of the outcome equation and derived its asymptotic distribution. His method is based on a nonparametric kernel regression correction of the selection-bias term. Subsequent contributions have largely concentrated on index formulations for dimension reduction. Powell (1987) considered a single index case and Ichimura and Lee (1991) studied the general multiple index situation. Ahn and Powell (1993) considered a probability index formulation. The approaches in Robinson, Powell, and Ahn and Powell are single equation two-stage estimation methods with nonparametric kernel regression functions. The approach in Ichimura and Lee (1991) is a semiparametric nonlinear least squares method, which can also be used for truncated sample on outcome equations. Others (Newey, 1988; Andrews, 1991) have used series approximations for conditional expectations.

These two-stage estimation methods are motivated by the implied bias-corrected outcome equation having the form

$$y_i = x_i\beta + \psi(z_i\gamma) + \eta_i, \tag{18.12}$$

where $E(\eta_i \mid I_i = 1, x_i) = 0$ for cross-sectional data. For semiparametric models, ψ is an unknown function but can be estimated by some nonparametric estimators. The various semiparametric two-stage methods differ from each other on how ψ has been estimated. As ψ may be a linear function, it is essential that there is at least one variable which is in z but not in x for the identification of β in a semiparametric two-stage estimation procedure. If this exclusion condition does not hold for (18.12), some linear transformation of β, which creates the exclusion requirement, can still be identified and estimated (Chamberlain, 1986; Lee, 1994b). With the unknown ψ replaced by a nonparametric function $E_n(z_i, \theta)$ where $\theta = (\beta, \gamma)$, various suggested approaches amount to estimate unknown parameters of the equation $y_i = x_i\beta + E_n(z_i, \theta) + \tilde{\eta}_i$. In the index context, one only needs to know that $\psi(z\gamma) = E(y - x\beta \mid z\gamma)$ is a function of $z\gamma$. For a kernel type estimator, $\psi(z_i\gamma)$ can be estimated by a nonparametric regression estimator, $E_n(z_i, \theta) = \dfrac{\sum_{j\neq i}^{n}(y_j - x_j\beta)K(\frac{z_i\gamma - z_j\gamma}{a_n})}{\sum_{j\neq i}^{n}K(\frac{z_i\gamma - z_j\gamma}{a_n})}$,

where K is a kernel function and a_n is a bandwidth or window width. The consistency and asymptotic distribution of a derived estimator of β (and/or γ) depend on certain essential conditions on a selected sequence of bandwidths $\{a_n\}$. The bandwidth sequence is required to converge to zero as n goes to infinity, but its rate of convergence cannot be too fast. The rate of convergence of a nonparametric regression will, in general, depend on the degree of smoothness of underlying densities of disturbances and regressors of the model. For series approximations, the corresponding problem refers to the number of terms included in an approximation. For general issues on nonparametric regression, see Ullah, Chapter 20 in this volume.

The use of the kernel-type regression function (or series approximation) is valuable in that asymptotic properties of estimators can be established. The β can be consistently estimated and the semiparametric estimators are $\sqrt{n}$-consistent and asymptotic normal. For empirical applications, one has to be careful on selecting appropriate bandwidths. The bandwidth selection can be a complicated issue. In practice, one may hope that a bandwidth parameter can be automatically determined. The Cosslett two-stage approach has the latter feature. The implicit window widths in his approach are automatically determined. At the first stage, a semiparametric maximum likelihood procedure is used to estimate γ and the distribution F of choice equation disturbance ε under the assumption that ε and u are independent of all regressors. The estimator of F for each γ is $\hat{F}(\cdot \mid \gamma)$ derived by maximizing the loglikelihood function $\ln L(F, \gamma) = \sum_{i=1}^{n}[I_i \ln F(z_i\gamma) + (1 - I_i)\ln(1 - F(z_i\gamma))]$ with respect to F. The estimator of γ is then derived by maximizing $\ln L(\hat{F}(\cdot \mid \gamma), \gamma)$ with respect to γ. The estimator $\hat{F}$ is also used for the estimation of β in the second stage. The estimator $\hat{F}$ is a step function with steps located at some ε_j^*, $j = 1, \ldots, J$, where $\varepsilon_1^* < \varepsilon_2^* < \ldots < \varepsilon_J^*$. The number of steps, their locations and their heights are all determined in the first-stage estimation. The implicit bandwidths $\varepsilon_j^* - \varepsilon_{j-1}^*$ for $j = 1, \ldots, J$ with $\varepsilon_0^* = -\infty$ as a convention, are automatic. Under the assumption that u and ε are independent of x and z, $\psi(z_i\hat{\gamma})$ in (18.12) is $\psi(z\gamma) = \int_{-\infty}^{z\gamma} E(u \mid \varepsilon)dF(\varepsilon)/\int_{-\infty}^{z\gamma} dF(\varepsilon)$. With $\hat{F}$ replacing F, the estimated $\hat{\psi}(z\hat{\gamma})$ is a constant λ_j for all $z\gamma$ in the interval $(\varepsilon_{j-1}^*, \varepsilon_j^*)$, where $\lambda_j = \int_{-\infty}^{\varepsilon_{j-1}^*} E(u \mid \varepsilon)d\hat{F}(\varepsilon)/\int_{-\infty}^{\varepsilon_{j-1}^*} d\hat{F}(\varepsilon)$. Define the subset of sample observations $S_j = \{i \mid \varepsilon_{j-1}^* < z_i\hat{\gamma} < \varepsilon_j^* \text{ and } I_i = 1\}$ and the set indicator I_{S_j}. Cosslett's approach leads to the estimation of the regression equation with added dummy regressors: $y_i = x_i\beta + \sum_{j=1}^{J} \lambda_j I_{S_j}(i) + \eta_i$. Cosslett (1991) showed that the estimator is consistent. However, its asymptotic distribution remains unknown. The automatic window width in the approach may have induced complications for asymptotic analysis.

4.2 Semiparametric efficiency bound and semiparametric MLE

On asymptotic efficiency for semiparametric estimation, Chamberlain (1986) derived an asymptotically lower bound for variances of $\sqrt{n}$-consistent regular semiparametric estimators for the sample selection model (18.1). The notion of asymptotic efficiency for parameter estimators in a semiparametric model was originated in Stein (1956). The semiparametric asymptotic variance bound V for a semiparametric model is defined as the supremum of the Cramer–Rao bounds for all regular parametric submodels. The intuition behind this efficient criterion is that a parametric MLE for any parametric submodel should be at least as efficient as any semiparametric estimator. The class of estimators is restricted to regular estimators so as to exclude superefficient estimators and estimators using information that is not contained in a semiparametric model. Newey (1990) provides a useful characterization for a semiparametric estimator to be regular. A way to derive the semiparametric bound is to derive a relevant tangent set and its efficient score S. Let $\delta = (\theta', \eta')'$ be the parameters of a submodel and let $S_\delta = (S'_\theta, S'_\eta)'$ be the score vector. A tangent set I is defined as the mean-squares closure of all linear combinations of scores S_η for parameter models. The efficient score S is the unique vector such that $S_\theta - S \in I$ and $E(S't) = 0$, for all $t \in I$. The semiparametric variance bound is $V = (E[SS'])^{-1}$.

The sample selection model considered in Chamberlain (1986) is (18.1) under the assumption that ε and u are independent of all the regressors in the model. With a parametric submodel, the scores for (β, γ) of a single observation have the form $\frac{\partial \ln L(\beta, \gamma)}{\partial \beta} = a_1(y - x\beta, I, z\gamma)x$ and $\frac{\partial \ln L(\beta, \gamma)}{\partial \gamma} = a_2(y - x\beta, I, z\gamma)z$, for some functions a_1 and a_2. Chamberlain (1986) showed that the effective scores of the semiparametric sample selection model are simply the preceding scores with the factors x and z replaced, respectively, by $x - E(x \mid z\gamma)$ and $z - E(z \mid z\gamma)$, i.e.,

$$\frac{\partial \ln L(\beta, \gamma)}{\partial \beta} = a_1(y - x\beta, I, z\gamma)(x - E(x \mid z\gamma)), \quad \text{and}$$

$$\frac{\partial \ln L(\beta, \gamma)}{\partial \gamma} = a_2(y - x\beta, I, z\gamma)(z - E(z \mid z\gamma). \tag{18.13}$$

The information matrix of the semiparametric model is formed from these effective scores. The expressions in (18.13) provide insight into qualitative differences between parametric and semiparametric models. The information matrix of the semiparametric model is singular if there is no restriction on γ of the choice equation. This is so because $(z - E(z \mid z\gamma))\gamma = 0$. Furthermore, if z consists of all discrete variables, then $E(z \mid z\gamma)$ generally equals z. So, in order that the information matrix is nonsingular, one component of z must have a continuously distributed variable. If z were a subvector of x, the effective scores would also be linearly dependent and the information matrix would be singular. So an exclusion restriction on β is also needed. Chamberlain (1986) pointed out that if the information matrix of the semiparametric model is singular, then there are parameters for which no (regular) consistent estimator can converge at rate $n^{-1/2}$.

Ai (1997) and Chen and Lee (1998) proposed semiparametric scoring estimation methods based on index restriction and kernel regression functions. The approaches involve the construction of efficient score functions. Ai's estimator was defined by setting an estimated sample score equal to zero and involved solving nonlinear equations. Chen and Lee's approach was a two-step efficient scoring method. Given an initial $\sqrt{n}$-consistent estimator, the latter estimator has a closed form. Both the estimator of Ai and that of Chen and Lee were shown to be asymptotically efficient for model (18.1) under the independence assumption. Chen and Lee (1998) also derived the efficient bound for the polychotomous choice model with index restrictions and pointed out that their estimator attained that bound. As an index model with L choice alternatives, $P(I_l \mid x) = E(I_l \mid z\gamma)$ are functions of index $z\gamma$ of the choice equations and the density function of y

conditional on $I_1 = 1$ and all exogenous variables in the model is the conditional density function of $y - x\beta$ conditional on $I_1 = 1$ and $z\gamma$ at the true parameter vector (β_0, γ_0), i.e. $f(y \mid I_1 = 1, x, z) = f(y - x\beta_0 \mid I_1 = 1, z\gamma_0) = g(y - x\beta_0, x\gamma_0 \mid I_1 = 1)/p(x\gamma_0 \mid I_1 = 1)$, where $g(\varepsilon, x\gamma_0 \mid I_1 = 1)$ is the conditional density of ε and $x\gamma_0$ conditional on $I_1 = 1$, and $p(x\gamma_0 \mid I_1 = 1)$ is the conditional density of $x\gamma_0$. Given a random sample of size n, for any possible value θ, the probability function $E(I_l \mid z_i\gamma, \theta)$ of I_l conditional on $z\gamma$ evaluated at point $z_i\gamma$ can be estimated by $P_{nl}(x_i, \theta) = A_n(I_l \mid x_i, \theta)/A_n(1 \mid x_i, \theta)$, where $A_n(v \mid x_i, \theta) = \frac{1}{n-1}\sum_{j \neq i} v_j \frac{1}{a_{1,n}^m} K(\frac{z_i\gamma - z_j\gamma}{a_{1,n}})$ for $v = I_1, \ldots, I_K$, or 1, $K(\cdot)$ is a kernel function on R^m when $z\gamma$ is an m-dimensional vector of indices. On the other hand, $f(y - x\beta \mid I_1 = 1, z\gamma, \theta)$ evaluated at point $(y_i - x_i\beta, z_i\gamma)$ can be estimated by $f_n(y_i - x_i\beta \mid I_{1i} = 1, z_i\gamma) = C_n(x_i, y_i, \theta)/A_n(I_1 \mid x_i, \theta)$, where $C_n(x_i, y_i, \theta) = \frac{1}{n-1}\sum_{j \neq i} I_{1j} \frac{1}{a_{2,n}^{m+k}} J(\frac{(y_i - x_i\beta) - (y_j - x_j\beta)}{a_{2,n}}, \frac{z_i\gamma - z_j\gamma}{a_{2,n}})$ when $y - x\beta$ is a vector of dimension k. These nonparametric functions formulate a semiparametric loglikelihood function $\ln L_n(\theta) = \frac{1}{n}\sum_{i=1}^{n}\{I_{1i}\ln f_n(y_i - x_i\beta \mid I_{1i} = 1, z_i\gamma) + \sum_{l=1}^{L} I_{li} \ln P_{nl}(x_i, \theta)\}$. But, due to technical difficulties, this semiparametric likelihood function can hardly be used. Instead, one can work with its implied score function, i.e. the derivative of the semiparametric loglikelihood function with respect to θ. With an initial $\sqrt{n}$-consistent estimate of θ, the Chen–Lee estimator is a semiparametric two-step scoring estimator.

4.3   Semiparametric IV estimation and conditional moments restrictions

Simultaneous equation models with selectivity can also be estimated by semiparametric methods. Semiparametric IV methods for the estimation of sample selection models are considered in Powell (1987) and Lee (1994b). Powell (1987) has a interest in the asymptotic property of a general semiparametric IV estimator. Lee (1994b) follows the literature on classical linear simultaneous equation models by focusing on both the identification and estimation of a structural equation with sample selection. It considered possible generalizations of two-stage least squares methods and their possible optimum IV property. Consider a single linear structural equation

$$y_1^* = y_2^*\alpha + xJ\delta + u_1, \tag{18.14}$$

where y_1^* is a latent endogenous variable, y_2^* is a vector of latent endogenous variables not including y_1^*, x is a vector of exogenous variables in the system, and xJ, where J is a selection matrix, represents the subset of exogenous variables included in this structural equation. The reduced form equation of y_2^* is $y_2^* = x\Pi_2 + v_2$. The sample observations y_1 and y_2 of y_1^* and y_2^* are subject to selection. The selection equation is $I^* = x\gamma - \varepsilon$. y_1 and y_2 are observed if and only if $I^* > 0$. As in the index framework, the joint distribution of (u_1, v_2, ε) conditional on x is assumed to be a function of the index $x\gamma$. In this system with sample selection, the identification of structural parameters requires stronger conditions than the usual rank condition in the classical linear simultaneous equation model (without selectivity) and the parametric linear simultaneous equation sample selection model considered in Lee *et al.* (1980) and Amemiya (1983). Let $y_1^* = x\pi_1 + v_1$ be the implied reduced form equation for y_1^*. Conditional on x and $I = 1$, $E(y_1 \mid x, I = 1) = x\pi_1 + E(v_1 \mid x\gamma, x\gamma > \varepsilon)$ and $E(y_2 \mid x, I = 1) = x\Pi_2 + E(v_2 \mid x\gamma, x\gamma > \varepsilon)$. As in the classical linear simultaneous equation model, the identification of structural parameters is directly related to the reduced form parameters. However, contrary to the classical system, the reduced form parameter vectors π_1 and Π_2 are not identifiable because the same x appears in the selection equation. It turns out that some linear combinations of the reduced form parameters can be identified. As the selection equation is a single index model, a conventional normalization suggested by Ichimura (1993) is to set the coefficient of a continuous and exogenous variable to be unity, i.e. $x\gamma = x_{(1)} + x_{(2)}\zeta$, where $x_{(1)}$ is a relevant continuous and exogenous variable in $x = (x_{(1)}, x_{(2)})$. With the partition of x into $x_{(1)}$ and $x_{(2)}$, the above equations imply that the parameters $\pi_{(1)}^*$ and Π_2^* in $E(y_1 \mid x, I = 1) = x_{(2)}\pi_{(1)}^* + E(v_1^* \mid x\gamma, I = 1)$ and $E(y_2 \mid x, I = 1) = x_{(2)}\Pi_{(2)}^* + E(v_2^* \mid x\gamma, I = 1)$ are identifiable. The structural parameters are related to those identified reduced-form parameters as

$$\pi_1^* = \Pi_2^*\alpha - \delta_1\zeta + \delta_2. \qquad (18.15)$$

The identification of the structural parameters follows from this relation. With exclusion restrictions as in (18.14), one can see that the order identification condition for the semiparametric model corresponds to the overidentification condition of the classical linear simultaneous equation model. The stronger condition for the identification of the semiparametric model is due to the addition of a selection bias term with an unknown form in the bias-corrected structural equation. Exogenous variables excluded from the structural equation (18.14) before bias correction reappear in the selection bias term through the index $x\gamma$. Such exogenous variables identify the bias term. But, the bias-correction term introduces excluded exogenous variables back into the bias-corrected structural equation. It follows that the effective number of the included exogenous variables in this equation is the number of originally included exogenous variables plus one. Therefore, the order condition for identification requires stronger exclusion restrictions than the classical model or a parametric model. For a parametric model under normal disturbances, the bias-correction term has a known nonlinear form which can help identification.

The structural parameters α and δ can be estimated via (18.15) by Amemiya's minimum distance methods. But semiparametric least squares are relatively simple and illustrative. For the semiparametric estimation of the structural equation (18.14), let $w = (y_2, xJ)$ and $\beta = (\alpha, \delta)$. For any possible value (β, γ), $E(y_1 - w\beta \mid x\gamma, I = 1)$ evaluated at a point $x_i\gamma$ of $x\gamma$ can be estimated by a nonparametric kernel estimator $E_n(y_1 \mid x_i\hat{\gamma}) - E_n(w \mid x_i\hat{\gamma})\beta$, where $\hat{\gamma}$ is a consistent estimate of γ from the selection equation. The bias-corrected structural equation becomes

$$y_{1i} - E_n(y_1 \mid x_i\hat{\gamma}) = (w_i - E_n(w \mid x_i\hat{\gamma}))\beta + \hat{u}_{ni}. \qquad (18.16)$$

If p is a vector of instrumental variables for w, a semiparametric IV estimator of β can be

$$\hat{\beta}_p = \left(\sum_{i=1}^n t_n(x_i\hat{\gamma}) p_i'(w_i - E_n(w \mid x_i\hat{\gamma})) \right)^{-1} \sum_{i=1}^n t_n(x_i\hat{\gamma}) p_i'(y_{1i} - E_n(y_1 \mid x_i\hat{\gamma})),$$

where $t_n(x_i\hat{\gamma})$ is a weighting or trimming function. Powell (1987) used the denominator in the nonparametric kernel regression functions $E_n(w \mid x_i\hat{\gamma})$ and $E_n(y \mid x_i\hat{\gamma})$ as the weight so as to cancel the denominator in those kernel regression functions. This weighting plays the role of trimming and has nothing to do with the variance of disturbances $\hat{u}_{ni}$ in equation (18.16). Lee (1994b) suggested a semiparametric two-stage least squares estimator and a more efficient semiparametric generalized two-stage least squares estimator. The latter takes into account both the heteroskedasticity of disturbances and the variance and covariance due to $\hat{\gamma}$. The disturbance $\hat{u}_{ni}$ consists of three components as $\hat{u}_{ni} = (u_{1i} - E_n(u_1 \mid x_i\hat{\gamma})) = (u_{1i} - E(u_1 \mid x_i\gamma)) - (E_n(u_1 \mid x_i\hat{\gamma}) - E_n(u_1 \mid x_i\gamma)) - (E_n(u_1 \mid x_i\gamma) - E(u_1 \mid x_i\gamma))$. The first component represents the disturbance in the structural equation after the correction of selection bias. The second component represents the disturbance introduced in $E_n(u_1 \mid x_i\gamma)$ by replacing γ by the estimate $\hat{\gamma}$. These two components are asymptotically uncorrelated. The last component represents the error introduced by the nonparametric estimate of the conditional expectation of u_{1i}. The last component does not influence the asymptotic distribution of a semiparametric two-stage estimator due to an asymptotic orthogonality property of the index structure. As the variance of $u_{1i} - E(u_1 \mid x_i\gamma)$ is a function of $x_i\gamma$, it can be estimated by a nonparametric kernel estimator $\hat{\omega}_{ni}$. Let Σ be the variance matrix of the vector consisting of $\hat{u}_{ni}$, which is determined by the first two components of $\hat{u}_{ni}$. It captures the heteroskedastic variances of the first component and the covariance of the second component across sample observations due to $\hat{\gamma}$. A feasible semiparametric generalized two-stage least-squares estimator can either be $\hat{\beta} = [\hat{W}'\hat{X}_2(\hat{X}_2'\hat{X}_2)^{-1}\hat{X}_2'\hat{\Sigma}^{-1}\hat{W}]^{-1}\hat{W}'\hat{X}_2(\hat{X}_2'\hat{X}_2)^{-1}\hat{X}_2'\hat{\Sigma}^{-1}\hat{Y}$, or $\tilde{\beta} = [\hat{W}'\hat{\Sigma}^{-1}\hat{X}_2(\hat{X}_2'\hat{\Sigma}^{-1}\hat{X}_2)^{-1}\hat{X}_2'\hat{\Sigma}^{-1}\hat{W}]^{-1}\hat{W}'\hat{\Sigma}^{-1}\hat{X}_2(\hat{X}_2'\hat{\Sigma}^{-1}\hat{X}_2)^{-1}\hat{X}_2'\hat{\Sigma}^{-1}\hat{Y}$, where the elements of $\hat{X}_2$, $\hat{W}$ and $\hat{Y}$ are, respectively, $t_n(x_i\hat{\gamma})(x_{(2)i} - E_n(x_{(2)} \mid x_{1i}\hat{\gamma}))$, $t_n(x_i\hat{\gamma})(w_i - E_n(w \mid x_{1i}\hat{\gamma}))$ and $t_n(x_i\hat{\gamma})(y_{1i} - E_n(y_1 \mid x_{1i}\hat{\gamma}))$. These two estimators are asymptotically equivalent and are asymptotically efficient semiparametric IV estimators (conditional on the choice of first-stage estimator $\hat{\gamma}$ and the trimming function). These semiparametric methods are two-stage estimation methods in that the selection equation is separately estimated and its coefficient estimate $\hat{\gamma}$ is used for the estimation of the outcome equations.

Instead of two-stage methods, it is possible to estimate jointly the selection and structural outcome equations so as to improve efficiency (Lee, 1998). As a generalization, consider the estimation of a nonlinear simultaneous equation sample selection model: $g(y^*, x, \beta) = u$, where the vector y^* can be observed only if $x\gamma > \varepsilon$. Under the index assumption that the joint distribution of u and ε conditional on x may depend only on $x\gamma$, the bias-corrected structural system is $g(y, x, \beta) = E(g(y, x, \beta) \mid I = 1, x\gamma) + \eta$, where $\eta = u - E(u \mid I = 1, x\gamma)$ with its variance being a function of $x\gamma$. This system implies the moment equation $E(g(y, x, \beta) | I = 1, x) = E(g(y, x, \beta) | I = 1, x\gamma)$ at the true parameter vector. For a truncated sample selection model where only sample observations of y and the event $I = 1$ are available, this moment equation forms the system for estimation. For a (censored) sample selection model, the events of $I = 1$ or $I = 0$ are observed that introduces an additional moment equation $E(I | x) = E(I | x\gamma)$ at the true parameter vector. These moment equations can be used together for estimation. Suppose that these moment equations are combined and are written in a general format as $E(f(z, \beta) | x) = E(f(z, \beta) | x\gamma)$, where z includes all endogenous and exogenous variables in the model. The parameter vector β in the system can be estimated by semiparametric nonlinear two-stage least squares methods. $E(f(z, \beta) | x\gamma)$ can be estimated by a nonparametric regression function $E_n(f(z, \beta) | x\gamma)$. The relevant variance function can be estimated by $V_n(x\gamma) = E_n(f(z, \beta)f'(z, \beta) | x\gamma) - E_n(f(z, \beta) | x\gamma)E_n(f'(z, \beta) | x\gamma)$. Let $u_n(z, \theta) = f(z, \beta) - E_n(f(z, \beta) | x\gamma)$ and t_n be a proper trimming function. Let w be an IV vector. The semiparametric nonlinear weighted two-stage method with the IV w is

$$\min_{\theta} \sum_{i=1}^{n} t_{ni} u_n'(z_i, \theta) V_n^{-1}(x_i\hat{\gamma}) w_i \left(\sum_{i=1}^{n} t_{ni} w_i' V_n^{-1}(x_i\hat{\gamma}) w_i \right)^{-1} \sum_{i=1}^{n} t_{ni} w_i' V_n^{-1}(x_i\hat{\gamma}) u_n(z_i, \theta),$$

where $\hat{\gamma}$ is a consistent estimate of γ. Lee (1998) shows that an optimal IV is any consistent estimate of $G_{\theta'}(x, \theta)$ where $G_{\theta'}(x, \theta) = [E(\frac{\partial f(z, \beta)}{\partial \theta} | x) - E(\frac{\partial f(z, \beta)}{\partial \theta} | x\gamma)] - \nabla'E(f(z, \beta) | x\gamma))[\frac{\partial \gamma'(\theta)x'}{\partial \theta'} - E(\frac{\partial \gamma'(\theta)}{\partial \theta'}x' | x\gamma)]$, where $\nabla E(\cdot | x\gamma)$ denotes the gradient of $E(\cdot | x\gamma)$ with respect to the vector $x\gamma$. In Lee (1998), semiparametric minimum-distance methods have also been introduced. Semiparametric minimum-distance methods compare directly $E_n(f(z, \beta) | x)$ with $E_n(f(z, \beta) | x\gamma)$. A semiparametric minimum-distance method with weighting is

$$\min_{\theta} \sum_{i=1}^{n} t_{ni}[E_n(f(z, \beta) | x_i) - E_n(f(z, \beta) | x_i\gamma)]V_n^{-1}(x_i\hat{\delta})[E_n(f(z, \beta) | x_i) - E_n(f(z, \beta) | x_i\gamma)].$$

The semiparametric weighted minimum-distance estimator is asymptotically equivalent to the optimal IV estimator. The semiparametric minimum-distance method has a interesting feature of not emphasizing the construction of instrumental variables. As z in $f(z, \beta)$ may or may not contain endogenous variables, semiparametric minimum-distance methods can be applied to the estimation of regression models as well as simultaneous equation models in a single framework.

The efficiency of estimating a structural equation is related to the efficiency issue for semiparametric models with conditional moment restrictions. Chamberlain (1992) investigates semiparametric efficiency bounds for semiparametric models with conditional moment restrictions. The conditional moment restriction considered has the form $E[\rho(x, y, \beta_0, q_0(x_2)) | x] = 0$, where x_2 is a subvector of x, $\rho(x, y, \beta, \tau)$ is a known function, but $q(x_2)$ is an unknown mapping. Chamberlain (1992) derives an efficiency bound for estimators of β under the conditional moment restriction. Several concrete examples are provided. Among them is a sample selection model. The sample selection model considered in Chamberlain (1992) is $y^* = x_1\beta + x_2\delta + u$ and $I = 1$, if $g(x_2, \varepsilon) \geq 0$; 0, otherwise, where $x = (x_1, x_2)$ and $y = (y_1, I)$ with $y_1 = Iy^*$, are observed. The unknown function q depends on x only via x_2 but is otherwise unrestricted. The disturbances u and ε satisfy the restrictions that $E(u \mid x, \varepsilon) = E(u \mid \varepsilon)$ and ε is independent of x_1 conditional on x_2. It is a sample selection model with indices x_2. This model implies that $E(y_1 \mid x, I = 1)$ $= x_1\beta_0 + q_0(x_2)$, where $q_0(x_2) = x_2\delta_0 + E(u \mid x_2, I = 1)$, Thus $\rho(x, y, \beta, \tau) = I(y_1 - x_1\beta - \tau)$ in Chamberlain's framework for this sample selection model. Chamberlain pointed out that one might extend the ρ function to include the restriction that $E(I \mid x) = E(I \mid x_2)$, so that $\rho(x, y, \beta, \tau) = [I(y_1 - x_1\beta - \tau_1), I - \tau_2]$ but the efficiency bound for β is the same with either one of the above ρ. Let $\sigma^2(x)$ denote $\mathrm{var}(y_1 \mid x, I = 1)$. The efficient bound for β is $J = E\{E(I \mid x_2)[E(\frac{x_1'x_1}{\sigma^2(x)}) - E(\frac{x_1'}{\sigma^2(x)} \mid x_2)E(\frac{x_1}{\sigma^2(x)} \mid x_2)/E(\frac{1}{\sigma^2(x)} \mid x_2)]\}$. For the case where $\sigma^2(x)$ happens to depend on x only through x_2, the efficiency bound will be simplified to $J = E\{E(I \mid x_2)\sigma^{-2}(x_2)[x_1 - E(x_1 \mid x_2)][x_1 - E(x_1 \mid x_2)]'\}$. The semiparametric weighted minimum-distance method can be applied to estimate the sample selection model with $f'(z, \beta) = [I(y - x_1\beta), I]$. Lee (1998) showed that the semiparametric weighted minimum-distance estimator attains the efficiency bound if $\sigma^2(x)$ happens to depend only on x_2. It is of interest to note that if the moment equation $E(I \mid x) = E(I \mid x_2)$ were ignored and only the moment equation $E(I(y_1 - x_1\beta_0) \mid x] = E(I(y_1 - x_1\beta_0) \mid x_2]$ were used in the estimation, the resulting estimator will have a larger variance. The point is that even though the moment restriction $E(I \mid x) = E(I \mid x_2)$ does not contain β, it helps to improve the efficiency in estimating β (as in a seemingly unrelated regression framework). On the other hand, if the conditional moment restriction $E(y - x_1\beta_0 \mid x, I = 1) = E(y_1 - x_1\beta_0 \mid x\gamma_0, I = 1)$ is used for estimation, the resulted estimator will have the same smaller variance. This is so because $I - E(I \mid x)$ is uncorrelated with the disturbance $(y - x_1\beta_0) - E(y - x_1\beta_0 \mid x, I = 1)$.

4.4   Estimation of the intercept

The semiparametric estimation of sample selection models described has focused on the estimation of regression coefficients in outcome and selection equations. The intercept of the outcome equation has been absorbed in the unknown distribution of disturbances. For some empirical applications, one might be interested in estimating counterfactual outcomes and, hence, the intercept of an outcome equation. The semi-nonparametric likelihood approach of Gallant and Nychka (1987) based on series expansion can consistently estimate the unknown intercept but the asymptotic distribution of the estimator remains unknown. Instead of the likelihood approach, alternative approaches can be based on the observed outcome equation under the assumption that the underlying disturbances have zero-mean. One may imagine that the observed outcome equation is not likely to be subject to selection bias for individuals whose decisions of participation are almost certain, i.e. individuals with observed characteristics x such that $P(I = 1 \mid x) = 1$. This idea is in Olsen (1982), and has lately been picked up in

Heckman (1990) and Andrews and Schafgans (1998). Consider the sample selection model with outcome $y = \beta_1 + x\beta_2 + u$, which can be observed only if $z\gamma > \varepsilon$, where (u, ε) is independent of x and z. The β_2 and γ can be estimated by various semiparametric methods as described before. Let $\hat{\beta}_2$ and $\hat{\gamma}$ be, respectively, consistent estimates of β_2 and γ. Heckman (1990) suggests the estimator $\hat{\beta}_1 = \sum_{i=1}^n I_i(y_i - x_i\hat{\beta}_2) I_{(b_n, \infty)}(z_i\hat{\gamma})/\sum_{i=1}^n I_i I_{(b_n, \infty)}(z_i\hat{\gamma})$, where $\{b_n\}$ is supposed to be a sequence of bandwidth parameters depending on sample size n such that $b_n \to \infty$. The latter design is necessary as only the upper tails of $z\gamma$ would likely identify the individual with the choice probability close to one. Heckman did not provide an asymptotic analysis of his suggested estimator. Andrews and Schafgans (1998) suggest a smooth version by replacing $I_{(b_n, \infty)}(z_i\hat{\gamma})$ with a smooth distribution function. The later modification provides relatively easy asymptotic analysis of the estimator. The rate of convergence and possible asymptotic distribution of the estimator depend on some relative behaviors of the upper tail distributions of $z\gamma$ and ε. Andrews and Schafgans (1998) show that the intercept estimator can only achieve up to a cube-root-n rate of convergence when the upper tail of the distribution of $z\gamma$ has the same tail thickness as the upper tail of the distribution of ε. The rate of convergence can be up to square-root-n only when the upper tail of the distribution of $z\gamma$ is thicker than the upper tail of the distribution of ε. One may recall some similarity on the asymptotic behavior of order statistics for the estimation of the range of a distribution.

4.5   Sample selection models with a tobit selection rule

For the semiparametric estimation of a sample selection model with a discrete choice equation, the exclusion restriction of a relevant regressor in the choice equation from the outcome equation provides the crucial identification condition. Such an exclusion restriction will not be required when the selection criterion is a tobit rule. The identification and estimation of such a model are considered in Lee (1994a), Chen (1997), and Honoré, Kyriazidou, and Udry (1997). The model in Lee (1994a) assumes that the disturbances (u_1, u_2) in equation (18.6) are independent of the regressors x. With iid disturbances, model (18.6) implies two observable outcome equations: $E(y_{2i} \mid y_{1i} > 0, x_i) = x_i\beta + E(u_{2i} \mid y_{1i} > 0, x_i)$ and

$$E(y_2 \mid u_1 > -x_i\gamma, x\gamma > x_i\gamma, x_i) = E(x \mid x\gamma > x_i\gamma, x_i)\beta + E(u_2 \mid u_1 > -x_i\gamma, x\gamma > x_i\gamma, x_i).$$

As the disturbances are independent of x, the conditional moment restriction $E(u_2 \mid u_1 > -x_i\gamma, x\gamma > x_i\gamma, x_i) = E(u_{2i} \mid y_i > 0, x_i)$ provides the identification of β given γ from the tobit equation. The intuition behind these formulations is based on the fact that the density of (u_{1i}, u_{2i}) conditional on $y_{1i} > 0$ and x_i is the same as the density of any (u_{1j}, u_{2j}) conditional on $u_{1j} > -x_i\gamma$ and $x_j\gamma > x_i\gamma$ at the point $x_i\gamma$. The conditions $x_j\gamma > x_i\gamma$ and $u_{1j} > -x_i\gamma$ imply that $y_{1j} = x_j\gamma + u_{1j} > 0$ and, hence, the observability of (y_{1j}, y_{2j}). The $E(u_2 \mid u_1 > -x_i\gamma, x\gamma > x_i\gamma, x_i)$ can be estimated by $\sum_{j=1}^n u_{2j}I(u_{1j} > -x_{1i}\gamma, x_{1j}\gamma > x_{1i}\gamma)/\sum_{j=1}^n I(u_{1j} > -x_{1i}\gamma, x_{1j}\gamma > x_{1i}\gamma)$. Instead of this estimator,

Lee (1994a) suggests a kernel smoothing estimator $E_n(y_2 - x\beta \,|\, x_{1i}\hat{\gamma})$ where $\hat{\gamma}$ is a consistent estimator from first-stage semiparametric estimation of the tobit selection equation, and proposed a semiparametric least squares procedure: $\min_\beta \frac{1}{n}\sum_{i=1}^n I_X(x_i)(y_{2i} - x_i\beta - E_n(y_2 - x\beta \,|\, x_{1i}, \hat{\gamma}))$, where $I_X(x_i)$ is a trimming function on x. The two-stage estimator of β has a closed form expression and is $\sqrt{n}$-consistent and asymptotically normal. Chen (1997) proposed two estimation approaches for this model. One is similar to the semiparametric least squares procedure in Lee (1994a) except that the ratio of sample indicators is used without smoothing and the trimming function is replaced by the weighting function as in Powell (1987). The second estimation approach in Chen (1997) is $\min_{\beta,\alpha} \frac{1}{n}\sum_{i=1}^n I(y_{1i} - x_i\hat{\gamma} > 0, x_i\hat{\gamma} > 0)(y_{2i} - x_i\beta - \alpha)$. This approach utilizes a different portion of the observable disturbances where $E(u_{2i} \,|\, u_{1i} > 0, x_i\gamma > 0) = \alpha$ is a constant for all is under the independence assumption. Chen (1997) also derives the asymptotic efficiency bound for this semiparametric model. None of the estimators available in the literature (including the estimators in Honoré *et al.* (1997) discussed later) attain the efficiency bound. Honoré *et al.* (1997) propose two-stage estimators based on symmetry. They consider first the case that (u_1, u_2) is symmetrically distributed conditional on x (arbitrary heteroskedasticity is allowed), i.e. $(-u_1, -u_2)$ is distributed like (u_1, u_2) conditional on x. The property of symmetry in disturbances was first explored for estimating the censored and truncated regression models in Powell (1986). Even though the underlying disturbances are symmetrically distributed, the observable disturbances are no longer symmetrically distributed under sample selection. Honoré *et al.* (1997) restore the symmetric property by restricting the estimation of β with sample observations in the region where $-x\gamma < u_1 < x\gamma$ (equivalently, $0 < y_1 < 2x\gamma$). With sample observations in the restricted region, u_1 is symmetrically distributed around 0 and the proposed estimation procedures can be based on least absolute deviations or least squares, i.e. $\min_\beta \frac{1}{n}\sum_{i=1}^n I(0 < y_{1i} < 2x_i\hat{\gamma}) \,|\, y_{2i} - x_i\beta \,|$, or $\min_\beta \frac{1}{n}\sum_{i=1}^n I(0 < y_{1i} < 2x_i\hat{\gamma})(y_{2i} - x_i\beta)^2$, where $\hat{\gamma}$ is a first-stage estimator, e.g. semiparametric censored or truncated regression from Powell (1986). The restoration of symmetric region demonstrates elegantly the usefulness of observed residuals of u_1 from the tobit selection equation for estimation. Honoré *et al.* (1997) consider also the case that (u_1, u_2) is independent of x in the underlying equations. They suggest estimation approaches based on pairwise differences across sample observations. The pairwise difference approach is to create a possible symmetric property on the difference of disturbances. The difference of two iid random variables must be symmetrically distributed around zero if there is no sample selection. Under sample selection, one has to restore the symmetry property of the pairwise difference. Honoré *et al.* suggested the trimming of u_{1i} and u_{1j} identically so that $u_{1i} > \max\{-x_i\gamma, -x_j\gamma\}$ and $u_{1j} > \max\{-x_i\gamma, -x_j\gamma\}$ (equivalently, $y_{1j} > \max\{0, (x_i - x_j)\gamma\}$ and $y_{1i} > \max\{0, (x_j - x_i)\gamma\}$). On this trimmed region, the independence assumption implies that $u_{2i} - u_{2j}$ is distributed symmetrically around 0. Their suggested pairwise difference estimators are $\min_\beta \sum_{i<j} I(y_{1i} > \max\{0, (x_i - x_j)\hat{\gamma}\}, y_{1j} > \max\{0, (x_j - x_i)\hat{\gamma}\}) \,|\, y_{2i} - y_{2j} - (x_{2i} - x_{2j})\beta \,|$ or $\min_\beta \sum_{i<j} I(y_{1i} > \max\{0, (x_i - x_j)\hat{\gamma}\}, y_{1j} > \max\{0, (x_j - x_i)\hat{\gamma}\}) \,|\, y_{2i} - y_{2j} - (x_{2i} - x_{2j})\beta \,|^2$. Consistency and asymptotic normality of the estimators are derived by empirical process arguments from Pakes and Pollard (1989).

4.6 Identification and estimation of counterfactual outcomes

As counterfactual outcomes are important objects of inference, one may be interested in the identification and estimation of counterfactual outcomes. The possible identification of counterfactual outcomes follows from model structures and observed decisions and outcomes (Heckman, 1990; Lee, 1995). Observed outcomes and choice probabilities provide sample information. Latent variable models provide prior structural restrictions.

Professor C. Manski in a series of articles put aside the latent-variable model perspective to go back to probabilistic basics. His results are summarized in Manski (1994). The main findings provide informative bounds on some counterfactual outcomes. Without latent variable modeling, if one is not satisfied with just bounds, the identification and evaluation of a counterfactual outcome would require extra prior restrictions on some other counterfactual outcomes. Statisticians approach the selected sample as a mixture problem. A widely-used method of evaluation in statistics is the method of matching (Rubin, 1987). Heckman, Ichimura, and Todd (1998) show that the fundamental identification condition (or assumption) for the matching method is a condition imposed on a specific counterfactual outcome. Corresponding to the two-sector model in (18.2)–(18.3), this identification condition requires that $\sigma_{2\varepsilon} = 0$ (Heckman et al., 1998, pp. 268–9). Professor J. Heckman and his associates in a series of forthcoming papers contrast the econometrics and statistical approaches on program evaluation. Some preliminary review can be found in M.J. Lee (1997).

Note

* The author acknowledges research support from the Research Grants Council of Hong Kong under grant HKUST595/96H for his research.

References

Ahn, H., and J.L. Powell (1993). Semiparametric estimation of censored selection models with a nonparametric selection mechanism. *Journal of Econometrics* 58, 3–29.

Ai, C. (1997). A semiparametric maximum likelihood estimator. *Econometrica* 65, 933–63.

Amemiya, T. (1973). Regression analysis when the dependent variable is truncated normal. *Econometrica* 41, 997–1016.

Amemiya, T. (1974). Multivariate regression and simultaneous equation models when the dependent variables are truncated normal. *Econometrica* 42, 999–1012.

Amemiya, T. (1979). The estimation of a simultaneous equation tobit model. *International Economic Review* 20, 169–81.

Amemiya, T. (1983). A comparison of the Amemiya GLS and the Lee-Maddala-Trost G2SLS in a simultaneous equations tobit model. *Journal of Econometrics* 23, 295–300.

Amemiya, T. (1984). Tobit models: a survey. *Journal of Econometrics* 24, 3–61.

Andrews, D.W.K. (1991). Asymptotic normality of series estimators for nonparametric and semiparametric regression models. *Econometrica* 59, 307–45.

Andrews, D.W.K., and M.M.A. Schafgans (1998). Semiparametric estimation of the intercept of a sample selection model. *Review of Economic Studies* 65, 497–517.

Bjorklund, A., and R. Moffitt (1987). Estimation of wage gains and welfare gains in self-selection models. *Review of Economics and Statistics* 69, 42–9.

Chamberlain, G. (1986). Asymptotic efficiency in semiparametric models with censoring. *Journal of Econometrics* 32, 189–218.

Chamberlain, G. (1992). Efficiency bounds for semiparametric regression. *Econometrica* 60, 567–96.

Chen, S. (1997). Semiparametric estimation of the Type-3 tobit model. *Journal of Econometrics* 80, 1–34.

Chen, S., and L.F. Lee (1998). Efficient semiparametric scoring estimation of sample selection models. *Econometric Theory* 14, 423–62.

Cosslett, S.R. (1991). Semiparametric estimation of regression model with sample selectivity. In W.A. Barnett, J. Powell, and G. Tauchen (eds.) *Nonparametric and Semiparametric Methods in Econometrics and Statistics*. pp. 175–97. Cambridge: Cambridge University Press.

Dubin, J., and D. McFadden (1984). An econometric analysis of residential electric appliance holdings and consumption. *Econometrica* 52, 345–62.

Gallant, A.R., and D.W. Nychka (1987). Semiparametric maximum likelihood estimation. *Econometrica* 55, 363–93.

Goldberger, A.S. (1983). Abnormal selection bias. In S. Karlin, T. Amemiya, and L.A. Goodman (eds.) *Studies in Econometrics, Time Series and Multivariate Statistics*. New York: Wiley.

Griliches, Z., B.H. Hall, and J.A. Hausman (1978). Missing data and self-selection in large panels. *Annals de l'INSEE* 30–31, 137–76.

Gronau, R. (1974). Wage comparisons: a selectivity bias. *Journal of Political Economy* 82, 119–43.

Hay, J., and R.J. Olsen (1984). Let them eat cake: a note on comparing alternative models of the demand for medical care. *Journal of Business and Economic Statistics* 2, 279–82.

Heckman, J.J. (1974). Shadow prices, market wages, and labor supply. *Econometrica* 42, 679–94.

Heckman, J.J. (1979). Sample selection bias as specification error. *Econometrica* 47, 153–61.

Heckman, J.J. (1990). Varieties of selection bias. *American Economic Association Papers and Proceedings* 313–18.

Heckman, J.J., and R. Robb (1985). Alternative methods for evaluating the impact of interventions. In J. Heckman and B. Singer (eds.) *Longitudinal Analysis of Labor Market Data*. Cambridge: Cambridge University Press.

Heckman, J.J., and B.E. Honoré (1990). The empirical content of the Roy model. *Econometrica* 58, 1121–49.

Heckman, J.J., H. Ichimura, and P. Todd (1998). Matching as an econometric evaluation estimator. *Review of Economic Studies* 65, 261–94.

Honoré, B.E., E. Kyriazidou, and C. Udry (1997). Estimation of type 3 tobit models using symmetric trimming and pairwise comparisons. *Journal of Econometrics* 76, 107–28.

Ichimura, H. (1993). Semiparametric least squares estimation of single index models. *Journal of Econometrics* 58, 71–120.

Ichimura, H., and L.F. Lee (1991). Semiparametric estimation of multiple index models: single equation estimation. In W.A. Barnett, J. Powell, and G. Tauchen (eds.) *Nonparametric and Semiparametric Methods in Econometrics and Statistics*, ch. 1. New York: Cambridge University Press.

Lee, L.F. (1978). Unionism and wage rates: a simultaneous equation model with qualitative and limited dependent variables. *International Economic Review* 19, 415–33.

Lee, L.F. (1981). Simultaneous equations models with discrete endogenous variables. In C.F. Manski and D. McFadden (eds.) *Structural Analysis of Discrete Data and Econometric Applications*, ch. 9. Cambridge, MA: MIT Press.

Lee, L.F. (1982). Some approaches to the correction of selectivity bias. *Review of Economic Studies* 49, 355–72.

Lee, L.F. (1983). Generalized econometrics models with selectivity. *Econometrica* 51, 507–12.

Lee, L.F. (1984). Tests for the bivariate normal distribution in econometric models with selectivity. *Econometrica* 52, 843–63.

Lee, L.F. (1992a). Amemiya's generalized least squares and tests of overidentification in simultaneous equation models with qualitative or limited dependent variables. *Econometric Reviews* 11, 319–28.

Lee, L.F. (1992b). On efficiency of methods of simulated moments and maximum simulated likelihood estimation of discrete response models. *Econometric Theory* 8, 518–52.

Lee, L.F. (1994a). Semiparametric two-stage estimation of sample selection models subject to tobit-type selection rules. *Journal of Econometrics* 61, 305–44.

Lee, L.F. (1994b). Semiparametric instrumental variable estimation of simultaneous equation sample selection models. *Journal of Econometrics* 63, 341–88.

Lee, L.F. (1995). The computational of opportunity costs in polychotomous choice models with selectivity. *Review of Economics and Statistics* 77, 423–35.

Lee, L.F. (1996). Simulation estimation of sample selection models. Working Paper no. 96/97-4, Department of Economics, Hong Kong University of Science and Technology.

Lee, L.F. (1998). Semiparametric estimation of simultaneous-equation microeconometric models with index restrictions. *Japanese Economic Review* 49, 343–80.

Lee, L.F., and A. Chesher (1986). Specification testing when some test statistics are identically zero. *Journal of Econometrics* 31, 121–49.

Lee, L.F., G.S. Maddala, and R.P. Trost (1980). Asymptotic covariance matrices of two-stage probit and two-stage tobit methods for simultaneous equations models with selectivity. *Econometrica* 48, 491–503.

Lee, M.-J. (1997). Econometric methods for sample selection and treatment effect models. Manuscript, Institute of Policy and Planning Science, University of Tsukuba, Japan.

Leung, S.F., and S. Yu (1996). On the choice between sample selection and two-part models. *Journal of Econometrics* 72, 197–229.

Manning, W.G., N. Duan, and W.H. Rogers (1987). Monte Carlo evidence on the choice between sample selection and two-part models. *Journal of Econometrics* 35, 59–82.

Maddala, G.S. (1983). *Limited Dependent and Qualitative Variables in Econometrics*. Cambridge: Cambridge University Press.

Maddala, G.S. (1985). A survey of the literature on selectivity bias as it pertains to health care markets. *Advances in Health Economics and Health Services Research* 6, 3–18.

Manski, C. (1975). Maximum score estimation of the stochastic utility model of choice. *Journal of Econometrics* 3, 205–28.

Manski, C. (1994). The selection problem. In C. Sims (ed.) *Advances in Econometrics*, ch. 4, pp. 143–70. Cambridge: Cambridge University Press.

Melino, A. (1982). Testing for selection bias. *Review of Economic Studies* 49, 151–3.

McFadden, D. (1973). Conditional logit analysis of qualitative choice behavior. In P. Zarembka (ed.) *Frontiers in Econometrics*. New York: Academic Press.

McFadden, D. (1978). Modeling the choice of residential location. In A. Karlquist *et al.* (eds.) *Spatial Interaction Theory and Residential Location*. Amsterdam: North-Holland.

McFadden, D. (1989). A method of simulated moments for estimation of discrete response models without numerical integration, *Econometrica* 57, 995–1026.

Mroz, T.A. (1987). The sensitivity of empirical models with sample-selection biases. *Econometrica* 55, 765–99.

Nawata, K. (1993). A note on the estimation with sample-selection bias. *Economics Letters* 42, 15–24.

Nawata, K., and N. Nagase (1996). Estimation of sample selection bias models. *Econometric Reviews* 15, 387–400.

Nelson, F.D. (1977). Censored regression models with unobserved, stochastic censoring thresholds. *Journal of Econometrics* 6, 309–27.

Nelson, F. (1984). Efficiency of the two step estimator for models with endogenous sample selection. *Journal of Econometrics* 24, 181–96.

Newey, W.K. (1987). Efficient estimation of limited dependent variable models with endogenous explanatory variables. *Journal of Econometrics* 36, 231–50.

Newey, W.K. (1988). Two step estimation of sample selection models. Manuscript, Department of Economics, Princeton University.

Newey, W.K. (1990). Semiparametric efficiency bounds. *Journal of Applied Econometrics* 5, 99–135.

Newey, W.K., J.L. Powell, and J.R. Walker (1990). Semiparametric estimation of selection models: some empirical results. *AEA Papers and Proceedings* 80, 324–8.

Olsen, R. (1980). A least squares correction for selectivity bias. *Econometrica* 48, 1815–20.

Olsen, R. (1982). Distributional tests for selectivity bias and a more robust likelihood estimator. *International Economic Review* 23, 223–40.

Pagan, A., and F. Vella (1989). Diagnostic tests for models based on individual data: a survey. *Journal of Applied Econometrics* 4, S29–S59.

Pakes, A., and D. Pollard (1989). Simulation and the asymptotic of optimization estimators. *Econometrica* 57, 1027–57.

Powell, J.L. (1986). Symmetrically trimmed least squares estimation for tobit models. *Econometrica* 54, 1435–60.

Powell, J.L. (1987). Semiparametric estimation of bivariate latent variable models. Discussion paper no. 8704, Social Systems Research Institute, University of Wisconsin, Madison, WI.

Powell, J.L. (1994). Estimation of semiparametric models. In R.F. Engle and D.L. McFadden (eds.) *Handbook of Econometrics, Volume 4*, ch. 14. Amsterdam: North-Holland.

Robinson, P.M. (1988). Root-n-consistent semiparametric regression. *Econometrica* 56, 931–54.

Roy, A. (1951). Some thoughts on the distribution of earnings. *Oxford Economic Papers* 3, 135–46.

Rubin, D. (1987). *Multiple Imputation for Nonresponse in Surveys*. New York: John Wiley.

Sattinger, M. (1978). Comparative advantage in individuals. *Review of Economics and Statistics* 60, 259–67.

Schmertmann, C.P. (1994). Selectivity bias correction methods in polychotomous sample selection models. *Journal of Econometrics* 60, 101–32.

Stein, C. (1956). Efficient nonparametric testing and estimation. In *Proceedings of the Third Berkeley Symposium on Mathematical Statistics and Probability*, Volume 1 pp. 187–95. Berkeley: University of California Press.

Vella, F. (1998). Estimating models with sample selection bias: a survey. *Journal of Human Resources* 33, 127–69.

Wales, T.J., and A.D. Woodland (1980). Sample selectivity and the estimation of labour supply functions. *International Economic Review* 21, 437–68.

Willis, R.J., and S. Rosen (1979). Education and self-selection. *Journal of Political Economy* 87, S7–S36.

Random Coefficient Models

P.A.V.B. Swamy and George S. Tavlas*

1 INTRODUCTION

Random coefficient models (RCMs) grew out of Zellner's path-breaking article (1969) on aggregation and have undergone considerable modification over time.[1] Initially, RCMs were primarily concerned with relaxing an assumption typically made by researchers who use classical models. This assumption is that there is a constant vector of coefficients relating the dependent and independent variables. Unfortunately, as Keynes (Moggridge, 1973, p. 286) long ago observed, the assumption of constant coefficients is unlikely to be a reasonable one. Recent work on RCMs has focused on also relaxing the following assumptions frequently made by researchers in econometrics: (i) the true functional forms of the systematic components of economic relationships (whether linear or nonlinear) are known; (ii) excluded variables are proxied through the use of an additive error term and, therefore, have means equal to zero and are independent of the included explanatory variables; and (iii) variables are not subject to measurement error.

The purpose of this chapter is to provide an accessible description of RCMs. The chapter is divided into six sections, including this introduction. Section 2 discusses some characteristics of what we characterize as first-generation models. Essentially, these models attempt to deal with the problem that arises because aggregate time series data and cross-section data on micro units are unlikely to have constant coefficients. Thus, the focus of this literature is on relaxing the constant coefficient assumption. Section 3 describes a generalized RCM whose origins are in work by Swamy and Mehta (1975) and Swamy and Tinsley (1980). The generalized RCM, which relaxes the constant coefficient assumption and all three of the restrictions mentioned in the preceding paragraph, is referred to as a second-generation model. It is based on the assumptions that

1. any variable that is not mismeasured is true;
2. any economic equation with the correct functional form, without any omitted explanatory variable, and without mismeasured variables is true.

Economic theories are true if and only if they deal with the true economic relationships. They cannot be tested unless we know how to estimate the true economic relationships. The generalized RCM corresponds to the underlying true economic relationship if each of its coefficients is interpreted as the sum of three parts: (i) a direct effect of the true value of an explanatory variable on the true value of an explained variable; (ii) an indirect effect (or omitted-variable bias) due to the fact that the true value of the explanatory variable affects the true values of excluded variables and the latter values, in turn, affect the true value of the explained variable; and (iii) an effect of mismeasuring the explanatory variable. A necessary condition that a specified model coincides with the underlying true economic relationship is that each of its coefficients has this interpretation. Importantly, the second-generation models satisfy the conditions for observability of stochastic laws, defined by Pratt and Schlaifer (1988), whenever they coincide with the underlying true economic relationships. In order to enhance the relevance of the following discussion, the presentation of RCMs is made in the context of a money-demand model that has been extensively applied in the literature. Also, to heighten accessibility, the section does not attempt rigorous exposition of some technical concepts (e.g. stochastic laws), but refers the interested reader to the relevant literature. Section 4 applies five criteria to validate RCMs. Section 5 uses an example of a money demand model to illustrate application of the second-generation RCMs. Section 6 concludes.

2 SOME FIRST-GENERATION RCMs

When considering situations in which the parameters of a regression model are thought to change – perhaps as frequently as every observation – the parameter variation must be given structure to make the problem tractable. A main identifying characteristic of first-generation RCMs is that they are concerned with providing a structure to the process generating the coefficients. In other words, this class of models seeks to account for the process generating the coefficients of the regression model, but does not address specification issues related to functional form, omitted variables, and measurement errors.[2]

To explain, consider the following model:

$$m_t = x_{t1}\beta_{t1} + \sum_{j=2}^{K} x_{tj}\beta_{tj} = x_t'\beta_t \quad (t = 1, 2, \ldots, T), \qquad (19.1)$$

where m_t is the logarithm of real money balances (i.e. a measure of the money supply divided by a price-level variable); x_t' is a row vector of K elements having the jth explanatory variable x_{tj} as its jth element; $x_{t1} = 1$ for all t; the remaining x_{tj} $(j = 2, \ldots, K)$ are the variables thought to influence the demand for real money balances (such as the logarithms of real income and interest rates); β_t is a column vector of K elements having the jth coefficient β_{tj} as its jth element; the first coefficient β_{t1} combines the usual disturbance term and intercept and t indexes time series or cross section observations.

Since the model assumes that β_t is changing, we have to say something about how it is changing. That is, we have to introduce some structure into the process thought to be determining the coefficients. One simple specification is

$$\beta_t = \bar{\beta} + \varepsilon_t, \tag{19.2}$$

where $\bar{\beta} = (\bar{\beta}_1, \ldots, \bar{\beta}_K)'$ is the mean and the $\varepsilon_t = (\varepsilon_{t1}, \ldots, \varepsilon_{tK})'$ are the disturbance terms that are identically and independently distributed with $E(\varepsilon_t) = 0$. Basically, this equation says that the variations in all the coefficients of equation (19.1) are random unless shown otherwise by the real-world sources and interpretations of β_t and at any particular time period or for any one individual these coefficients are different from their means.[3] Assume further that the random components, $\varepsilon_{t1}, \ldots, \varepsilon_{tK}$, are uncorrelated,

$$E(\varepsilon_t \varepsilon_t') = \text{diag}[\sigma_{\varepsilon_1}^2, \sigma_{\varepsilon_2}^2, \ldots, \sigma_{\varepsilon_K}^2] \tag{19.3}$$

which is a $K \times K$ diagonal matrix whose ith diagonal element is $\sigma_{\varepsilon_i}^2$. This assumption stipulates that the random component of one coefficient is uncorrelated with that of another. We also assume that the x_t are independent of the β_t.[4] Correlations among the elements of ε_t will be introduced at the end of the section.

Since we have postulated that all the coefficients of equation (19.1) vary over time or across individuals according to equation (19.2), an issue that arises is how to test whether equations (19.1) and (19.2) are true. In order to answer this question, first substitute equation (19.2) into equation (19.1) to obtain

$$m_t = x_t'\bar{\beta} + \sum_{j=1}^{K} x_{tj}\varepsilon_{tj}. \tag{19.4}$$

Next, let w_t denote the combined disturbances (i.e. the sum of the products of x_{tj} and ε_{tj}), $w_t = \sum_{j=1}^{K} x_{tj}\varepsilon_{tj}$, so that $m_t = x_t'\bar{\beta} + w_t$, where $E(w_t | x_t) = 0$. Moreover, the conditional variance of the combined disturbance term of equation (19.4) is

$$E(w_t^2 | x_t) = x_{t1}^2 \sigma_{\varepsilon_1}^2 + \ldots + x_{tK}^2 \sigma_{\varepsilon_K}^2, \tag{19.5}$$

since w_t is a linear combination of uncorrelated random variables and the x_t are independent of the ε_t. For $t \neq s$, the covariance between w_t and w_s is zero. Let $v_t = w_t^2 - E(w_t^2 | x_t)$, where $E(w_t^2 | x_t)$ is given in (19.5). It is straightforward to show that the conditional mean of v_t given x_t is zero.

The definition of v_t can be rearranged to form a regression as

$$w_t^2 = E(w_t^2 | x_t) + v_t, \tag{19.6}$$

where $E(v_t | x_t)$, as pointed out, is zero. Accordingly, using equations (19.5) and (19.6), w_t^2 can be expressed as $w_t^2 = \sum_{j=1}^{K} x_{tj}^2 \sigma_{\varepsilon_j}^2 + v_t$, where for $t \neq s$, v_t and v_s are uncorrelated if the ε_{tj} are independent.

If our goal is to test whether equation (19.1) is the same as the fixed-coefficient model of the conventional type, then our null hypothesis is that the random components of all the coefficients on $x_{t2}, \ldots, x_{tK}$ are zero with probability 1. A complete statement of this hypothesis is

$$H_0: \text{For } i, j = 1, \ldots, K; t, s = 1, \ldots, T, \ E(\beta_{tj}) = \bar{\beta}_j \text{ and}$$

$$E(\varepsilon_{ti} \varepsilon_{sj}) = \begin{cases} \sigma_{\varepsilon_1}^2 > 0 & \text{if } i = j = 1 \text{ and } t = s \\ 0 & \text{otherwise} \end{cases}$$

such that $E(\varepsilon_{t1} | x_t) = E(\varepsilon_{t1}) = 0$ and ε_{t1} is normally distributed.

There are several alternatives to this hypothesis. One of them, provided by equations (19.1)–(19.3), is

$$H_1: \text{For } i, j = 1, \ldots, K; t, s = 1, \ldots, T, \ E(\beta_{tj}) = \bar{\beta}_j \text{ and}$$

$$E(\varepsilon_{ti} \varepsilon_{sj}) = \begin{cases} \sigma_{\varepsilon_j}^2 > 0 & \text{if } i = j \text{ and } t = s \\ 0 & \text{otherwise} \end{cases}$$

such that $E(\varepsilon_{tj} | x_t) = E(\varepsilon_{tj}) = 0$ and ε_{tj} is normally distributed.

The following steps lead to a test of H_0 against H_1: (i) obtain the ordinary least squares (OLS) estimate of β, denoted by $\bar{b}_{OLS}$, by running the classical least squares regression of m_t on x_t; (ii) in equation (19.4), replace β by $\bar{b}_{OLS}$ to calculate $\hat{w}_t = m_t - x_t'\bar{b}_{OLS}$; (iii) square $\hat{w}_t$ and run the classical least squares regression of $\hat{w}_t^2$ on $x_{t1}^2, \ldots, x_{tK}^2$;[5] the sum of squares of the residuals of this regression gives an unrestricted error sum of squares (ESS_U); and (iv) regress $\hat{w}_t^2$ only on x_{t1}^2; the sum of squares of the residuals of this regression gives a restricted error sum of squares (ESS_R) because all the $\sigma_{\varepsilon_j}^2$, $j = 2, \ldots, K$, are assumed to be zero (i.e. it is restrictive because it imposes the restrictions implied by H_0). Let $q(\tilde{w}) = (T/(K-1))(ESS_R - ESS_U)/ESS_U$ be a test statistic. Reject H_0 if the value $q(w)$ of $q(\tilde{w})$ obtained in a particular sample is greater than some critical value c and do not reject H_0 otherwise.

Although the foregoing testing methodology is characteristic of the first-generation literature, this test is misleading under the usual circumstances. Probabilities of false rejection of H_0 (Type I error) and false acceptance of H_1 (Type II error) associated with this test are unknown because both the exact finite sample (or asymptotic) distributions of $q(\tilde{w})$ when H_0 and H_1 are true are unknown. All that is known is that these probabilities are positive and less than 1. This is all that we need to show that the following argument is valid: Rejection of H_0 is not proof that H_0 is false or acceptance of H_0 is not proof that H_0 is true (Goldberger, 1991, p. 215). However, the occurrence of a real-world event does constitute strong evidence against H_0 if that event has a small probability of occurring whenever H_0 is true and a high probability of occurring whenever H_1 is true. This is an attractive definition of evidence, but finding such strong evidence is no easy task. To explain, we use the above test procedure. Note that there is no guarantee that one of H_0 and H_1 is true. When both H_0 and H_1 are false, observing a value of $q(\tilde{w})$ that lies in the critical region $\{q(\tilde{w}) > c\}$ is not equivalent to observing a real-world event because the critical region whose probability is calculated under H_0 (or H_1) to evaluate Type I error (or $1 -$ Type II error) probability is not the event of observing the actual data. Both H_0 and H_1 are false when, for example, the x_t are correlated with the β_t or when ε_t is not normal. We show in the next section that we need to assume that the x_t are correlated with the β_t if we want to make assumptions that are consistent with the real-world interpretations of the coefficients of equation (19.1). If our assumptions are inconsistent, then both H_0 and H_1 are false. In that event, finding the value $q(w) > c$ should not be taken as strong evidence against H_0 and for H_1, since the probabilities of the critical region $\{q(\tilde{w}) > c\}$ *calculated under H_0* and H_1 are incorrect. More generally, a test of a false null hypothesis against a false alternative hypothesis either rejects the false null hypothesis in favor of the false alternative hypothesis or accepts the false null hypothesis and rejects the false alternative hypothesis. Such tests continue to trap the unwary. We can never guarantee that one of H_0 and H_1 is true, particularly when the assumptions under which the test statistic $q(\tilde{w})$ is derived are inconsistent with the real-world interpretations of the coefficients of equation (19.1). We explain in the next section why such inconsistencies arise.[6]

At the very minimum, the above argument should indicate how difficult it is to produce strong evidence against hypotheses of our interest. For this reason, de Finetti (1974a, p. 128) says, "accept or reject is the unhappy formulation which I consider as the principal cause of the fogginess widespread all over the field of statistical inference and general reasoning." It is not possible to find useful approximations to reality by testing one false hypothesis against another false hypothesis. As discussed below, second-generation RCMs stress the importance of finding sufficient and logically consistent explanations of real phenomena (see, e.g., Zellner, 1988, p. 8) because of the limits to the usefulness of hypothesis testing.

In order to estimate the foregoing model, note that the error structure embedded in equation (19.4) is heteroskedastic. Specifically, the variance of the error at each sample point is a linear combination of the squares of the explanatory variables at that point (equation (19.5)). This suggests that this RCM can be estimated using a feasible generalized least squares estimation procedure that accounts for the heteroskedastic nature of the error process (Judge *et al.*, 1985, pp. 808–9).

In the case where t indexes time, a natural extension of this class of models is to incorporate serial correlation in the process determining the coefficients as follows: For $t = 1, 2, \ldots, T$,

$$\text{(a) } m_t = x_t'\beta_t, \text{ (b) } \beta_t = \bar{\beta} + \varepsilon_t, \text{ (c) } \varepsilon_t = \Phi\varepsilon_{t-1} + a_t. \tag{19.7}$$

This model differs from the previous model because it assumes that the process generating the coefficients is autoregressive, where Φ is a matrix with eigenvalues less than 1 in absolute value.

This discussion above has presented the basic building blocks of first-generation RCMs. These models have been extended in a number of directions. For example, the stochastic structure determining the coefficients can be made to vary as a function of some observable variables. A main difficulty in using such models, however, is that one must specify the structure explaining coefficient variations. Errors in specification will lead to familiar and unfortunate consequences. Further, the structures are usually specified in a mechanical manner. Accordingly, we now discuss the class of second-generation RCMs, which directly confront these and other specification errors, and can be shown to include the first-generation RCMs and several well-known fixed-coefficient models as special cases (Swamy and Tavlas, 1995).

3 SECOND-GENERATION RCMs

As previously noted, second-generation RCMs are concerned with relaxing the usual restrictions concerning the direct effects of explanatory variables on the explained variables, functional forms, measurement errors, and use of an additive error term to proxy excluded variables. If these restrictions are violated – for example, if there are measurement errors when no measurement errors are assumed or a specified functional form is incorrect – the resulting estimates are subject to specification errors. In two path-breaking papers, Pratt and Schlaifer (1984, 1988) have demonstrated that, in order to assess the plausibility of these restrictions, we need "real-world" interpretations of the coefficients in equation (19.1). In essence, two questions need to be addressed: (i) what are these real-world interpretations? (ii) are the above restrictions consistent with these interpretations? In what follows we show that any equation relating observable variables cannot coincide with the corresponding true economic relationship if each of its coefficients is not treated as the sum of three parts – one corresponding to a direct effect of the true value of a regressor on the true value of the dependent variable, a second part capturing omitted-variable biases, and a third part capturing the effect of mismeasuring the regressor. We also show that the true functional form of the equation is a member of a class of functional forms.

To explain, consider the following model of money demand:

$$m_t = \gamma_0 + \gamma_1 r_t + \gamma_2 y_t + u_t, \tag{19.8}$$

where r_t is the logarithm of an interest rate (i.e. opportunity cost) variable, y_t is the logarithm of real income, and u_t is an error term. It is assumed that the γs are constant and u_t has mean zero and is mean independent of r_t and y_t. As before, m_t is the logarithm of real money balances. Note that the variables in equation (19.8) are observed values. Because of measurement errors, they are unlikely to represent true values. Also, equation (19.8) is unlikely to coincide with the "true" money demand equation, as we now show.

Consider the implications arising from a typical errors-in-the-variables model. Thus, suppose that $m_t = m_t^* + v_{0t}$, $r_t = r_t^* + v_{1t}$, and $y_t = y_t^* + v_{2t}$, where m_t, r_t, and y_t are the observed values of the variables, the variables with an asterisk represent the true values, and the vs represent the errors made in the measurement of the variables. For example, y_t^* could be permanent income and r_t^* could be the opportunity cost of holding money that is implied by the definition of permanent income. One consequence of using the observed rather than the true values is that a set of random variables – the vs – is incorporated into the equation determining m_t. Additionally, we show below that the existence of measurement errors contradicts the assumption that the coefficients of equation (19.8) can be constants.

For the time being, suppose we are fortunate enough to know the true values of the variables. In that case, the true functional form of the money demand equation is a member of the class:

$$m_t^* = \alpha_{0t} + \alpha_{1t}r_t^* + \alpha_{2t}y_t^* + \sum_{j=3}^{n_t}\alpha_{jt}x_{jt}^* \quad (t = 1, \ldots, T), \quad (19.9)$$

where the x_{jt}^* are all the determinants of m_t^* other than r_t^* and y_t^* and where the αs and n_t are coefficients and the number of explanatory variables, respectively; they are time-varying, as indicated by their time subscripts. The variables r_t^* and y_t^* are called the included variables and the variables x_{jt}^* are called the excluded variables. Temporal changes in the set of excluded variables change n over time. Equation (19.9) is not necessarily linear, since the time-varying quality of the coefficients permits the equation to pass through every data point even when the number of observations on its variables exceeds $n_t + 1$. Thus, with time-varying coefficients the equation can be nonlinear. Equation (19.9) will have different functional forms for different sequences of its coefficients (or for different paths of variation in its coefficients) and the class of functional forms it represents is unrestricted as long as its coefficients are unrestricted. This lends support to our speculation that a member of this class is true. Equation (19.9) with unrestricted coefficients is more general than even the true money demand function, $m_t^* = f(r_t^*, y_t^*, x_{3t}^*, \ldots, x_{n_t t}^*)$, whose functional form is unknown. However, for a certain (unknown) pattern of variation in its coefficients, (19.9) coincides with the true equation. The essential feature of equation (19.9) is that, since it encompasses time-varying coefficients, the true values of variables, the correct functional form, and any omitted variables, it covers the true function determining money demand as a special case. The α coefficients that follow the true pattern of variation would represent the true elasticities of the determinants of money demand. We call α_{1t} and α_{2t} (representing the true pattern of variation) the direct effects on m_t^* of r_t^* and y_t^*, respectively, since they are not contaminated by any of the four specification errors discussed above.

Two fundamental problems are involved in any attempt to estimate equation (19.9). First, we may not know much (if anything) about the x_{jt}^*. Whatever we know may not be enough to prove that they are uncorrelated with the other explanatory variables in equation (19.9) (Pratt and Schlaifer, 1984, pp. 11–12). Second, the observed (as opposed to the true) values of the variables, are likely to contain measurement errors. A way to resolve the former problem is to assume that the x_{jt}^* are correlated with the other explanatory variables as follows:

$$x_{jt}^* = \psi_{0jt} + \psi_{1jt}r_t^* + \psi_{2jt}y_t^* \quad (j = 3, \ldots, n_t). \quad (19.10)$$

The coefficient ψ_{0jt} has a straightforward interpretation. It is the portion of x_{jt}^* (i.e. an excluded variable) remaining after the effects of the variables r_t^* and y_t^* have been removed. The remaining ψ coefficients represent the partial correlations between the excluded and the included variables. As with equation (19.9), the coefficients of equation (19.10) will not be constants unless this equation is known with certainty to be linear.

In order to take account of the correlations among the r_t^* and y_t^* and the x_{jt}^*, substitute equation (19.10) into equation (19.9):

$$ m_t^* = \left(\alpha_{0t} + \sum_{j=3}^{n_t} \alpha_{jt} \psi_{0jt} \right) + \left(\alpha_{1t} + \sum_{j=3}^{n_t} \alpha_{jt} \psi_{1jt} \right) r_t^* + \left(\alpha_{2t} + \sum_{j=3}^{n_t} \alpha_{jt} \psi_{2jt} \right) y_t^*. $$

(19.11)

Equation (19.11) expresses the time-varying relationship between the true values of the variables, where the time-varying effects of the excluded variables (i.e. the x_{jt}^*) are included in each coefficient on the right-hand side. For example, the remaining portion of x_{jt}^* after the effects of the variables r_t^* and y_t^* have been removed is captured in the first coefficient (via ψ_{0jt}), while the effects of r_t^* on the x_{jt}^* are captured in the second term (via ψ_{1jt}).

Equation (19.11) involves a relationship between the true variables, which are unobservable. Accordingly, to bring us closer to estimation substitute the observable counterparts of these variables into equation (19.11) to obtain:

$$ m_t = \gamma_{0t} + \gamma_{1t} r_t + \gamma_{2t} y_t, $$

(19.12)

where $\gamma_{0t} = (\alpha_{0t} + \sum_{j=3}^{n_t} \alpha_{jt} \psi_{0jt} + v_{0t})$, $\gamma_{1t} = (\alpha_{1t} + \sum_{j=3}^{n_t} \alpha_{jt} \psi_{1jt}) (1 - \frac{v_{1t}}{r_t})$, and $\gamma_{2t} = (\alpha_{2t} + \sum_{j=3}^{n_t} \alpha_{jt} \psi_{2jt}) (1 - \frac{v_{2t}}{y_t})$.

The coefficients of equation (19.12) have straightforward real-world interpretations corresponding to the direct effect of each variable and the effects of omitted variables and measurement errors. Consider, for example, the coefficient γ_{1t} on r_t. It consists of three parts: a direct effect, α_{1t}, of the true interest rate (r_t^*) on the true value of real money balances (m_t^*) given by equation (19.9); a term ($\sum_{j=3}^{n_t} \alpha_{jt} \psi_{1jt}$) capturing an indirect effect or omitted-variable bias (recall, α_{jt} with $j \geq 3$ is the effect of an omitted variable on m_t^*, and ψ_{1jt} is the effect of r_t^* on that omitted variable); and a term capturing the effect of measurement error, $-(\alpha_{1t} + \sum_{j=3}^{n_t} \alpha_{jt} \psi_{1jt})(v_{1t}/r_t)$ (recall that v_{1t} is the measurement error associated with the interest rate). The coefficient γ_{2t} can be interpreted analogously. The direct effects provide economic explanations. The term γ_{0t} also consists of three parts and these include the intercepts of equations (19.9) and (19.10), the effects of omitted variables on m_t^*, and the measurement error in m_t. It is the connection between γ_{0t} and the intercepts of equations (19.9) and (19.10) that demonstrates the real-world origin of γ_{0t}. In other words, all the coefficients in equation (19.12) have been derived on the basis of a set of realistic assumptions which directly confront the problems that arise because of omitted explanatory variables, their correlations with the included explanatory variables, measurement errors, and unknown functional forms. When these problems are present, as they usually are, a necessary condition for equation (19.12) to coincide with the true money demand function is that its coefficients are the sums of three parts stated below equation (19.12). At least two of these parts (omitted-variable biases and measurement error effects) cannot be constant and hence it may not be reasonable to assume that the constant coefficients of equation (19.8) are the sums of these three parts. Thus, equation (19.8)'s premises are inconsistent with the real-world interpretations of the coefficients of equation (19.12), and equation (19.8) cannot coincide with the true money demand function. These results are false if (i) v_{1t} and v_{2t} are equal to zero for all t (i.e. there are no measurement errors in r_t and y_t), (ii) ψ_{1jt} and ψ_{2jt} are equal to zero for all $j \geq 3$ and t (i.e. the included variables are independent of excluded variables), (iii) α_{1t} and α_{2t} are constant (i.e. the direct effects of r_t^* and y_t^* on m_t^* are constant), and (iv) $\gamma_{0t} = \gamma_0 + u_t$ (i.e. the intercept of equation (19.12) is equal to the intercept plus the error of equation (19.8)). Though under these conditions, equations (19.8) and (19.12) coincide with equation (19.9) and no inconsistencies arise, the difficulty is that these conditions are shown to be false by Pratt and Schlaifer (1984, pp. 11–12).

Equation (19.12) may be correct in theory, but we need to implement it empirically. Ideally, we would like to have empirical estimates of the direct effects, but as shown above, the direct effects are commingled with mismeasurement effects and omitted-variable biases. It should also be observed that equation (19.12) is more complicated than a structural equation without exogenous variables since γ_{0t}, γ_{1t}, and γ_{2t} are correlated both with each other and with the variables r_t and y_t. These correlations arise because γ_{1t} and γ_{2t} are functions of r_t and y_t, respectively, and γ_{0t}, γ_{1t}, and γ_{2t} have a common source of variation in α_{jt}, $j = 3, \ldots, n_t$. Instrumental variable estimation (IVE) – intended to deal with the problem of correlations between γ_{0t} and r_t and y_t when γ_{1t} and γ_{2t} are constant – of equation (19.12) does not "purge" its coefficients of mismeasurement effects and omitted-variable biases and, hence, cannot be used. IVE is designed neither to decompose the γs into direct, indirect, and mismeasurement effects nor to deal with the correlations between the included explanatory variables and their coefficients.

In an attempt to estimate α_{1t} and α_{2t}, we need to introduce some additional terminology.[7] To derive estimates of α_{1t} and α_{2t}, we will attempt to estimate the γs using concomitants. A formal definition of concomitants is provided in footnote 7. Intuitively, these may be viewed as variables that are not included in the equation used to estimate money demand, but help deal with the correlations between the γs and the explanatory variables (in this example, interest rates and real income). This notion can be stated more precisely in the form of the following two assumptions:

Assumption 1. The coefficients of equation (19.12) satisfy the stochastic equations

$$\gamma_{kt} = \pi_{k0} + \sum_{j=1}^{p} \pi_{kj} z_{jt} + \varepsilon_{kt} \quad (k = 0, 1, 2), \tag{19.13}$$

where the concomitants z_{jt} explain the variation in the γ_{kt}, $E(\varepsilon_{kt} \mid z_t) = E(\varepsilon_{kt}) = 0$ for all t and each k, and the ε_{kt} satisfy the stochastic equation

$$\varepsilon_{kt} = \varphi_{kk}\varepsilon_{k,t-1} + a_{kt}, \tag{19.14}$$

where for $k, k' = 0, 1, 2, -1 < \varphi_{kk} < 1$, and a_{kt} are serially uncorrelated with $E(a_{kt}) = 0$ and $E a_{kt} a_{k't} = \sigma_{kk'}$ for all t.

Assumption 2. The explanatory variables of equation (19.12) are independent of the ε_{kt}, given any values of the concomitants z_{jt}, and condition (iii) of footnote 7 holds.

Equation (19.14) is not needed if t indexes individuals and is needed if t indexes time and if the ε_{kt} in equation (19.13) are partly predictable. It can also be assumed that ε_{kt} and $\varepsilon_{k',t-1}$ with $k \neq k'$ are correlated. The explanatory variables of equation (19.12) can be independent of their coefficients conditional on a given value of the zs even though they are not unconditionally independent of their coefficients. This property provides a useful procedure for consistently estimating the direct effects contained in the coefficients of equation (19.12). The criticism of Assumption 1 contained in the last paragraph of Section 2 (or the errors in the specification of equation (19.13)) can be avoided by following the criteria laid out in Section 4.

To illustrate the procedure, suppose a money demand specification includes two explanatory variables – real income and a short-term interest rate. Also, suppose two concomitants (so that $p = 2$) are used to estimate the γs – a long-term interest rate (denoted as z_{1t}) and the inflation rate (denoted as z_{2t}). A straightforward interpretation of the use of these concomitants is the following. The direct effect (α_{1t}) component of the coefficient (i.e. γ_{1t}) on the short-term interest-rate variable r_t in equation (19.12) is represented by the linear function ($\pi_{10} + \pi_{11}z_{1t}$) of the long-term rate. The indirect and mismeasurement effects are captured by using a function ($\pi_{12}z_{2t} + \varepsilon_{1t}$) of the inflation rate and ε_{1t}. In this example, the measure of the direct effects (α_{2t}) contained in γ_{2t} (the coefficient on real income) is represented in ($\pi_{20} + \pi_{21}z_{1t}$); the measure of indirect and mismeasurement effects contained in γ_{2t} is represented in ($\pi_{22}z_{2t} + \varepsilon_{2t}$). These definitions do not impose any zero restrictions, but may need to be extended (see Section 4).

Substituting equation (19.13) into equation (19.12) gives an equation in estimable form:

$$m_t = \pi_{00} + \sum_{j=1}^{p} \pi_{0j}z_{jt} + \pi_{10}r_t + \sum_{j=1}^{p} \pi_{1j}z_{jt}r_t + \pi_{20}y_t$$

$$+ \sum_{j=1}^{p} \pi_{2j}z_{jt}y_t + \varepsilon_{0t} + \varepsilon_{1t}r_t + \varepsilon_{2t}y_t \quad (t = 1, 2, \ldots, T). \tag{19.15}$$

A computer program developed by Chang, Swamy, Hallahan and Tavlas (1999) can be used to estimate this equation. Note that equation (19.15) has three error terms, two of which are the products of εs and the included explanatory variables of equation (19.8). The sum of these three terms is both heteroskedastic and serially correlated. Under Assumptions 1 and 2, the right-hand side of equation (19.15) with the last three terms suppressed gives the conditional expectation of the left-hand side variable as a nonlinear function of the conditioning variables. This conditional expectation is different from the right-hand side of equation (19.8) with u_t suppressed. This result demonstrates why the addition of a single error term to a mathematical formula and the exclusion of the interaction terms on the right-hand side of equation (19.15) introduce inconsistencies in the usual situations where measurement errors and omitted-variable biases are present and the true functional forms are unknown.

In these usual situations, equation (19.8) can be freed of its inconsistencies by changing it to equation (19.12) and making Assumptions 1 and 2. A similar approach does not work for probit and logit models which are also based on assumptions that are inconsistent with the real-world interpretations of their coefficients. As regards switching regressions, Swamy and Mehta (1975) show that these regressions do not approximate the underlying true economic relationships better than random coefficient models.

Note the validity of our above remarks regarding IVE. There cannot be any instrumental variables that are uncorrelated with the error term of equation (19.15) and highly correlated with the explanatory variables of equation (19.12) because these explanatory variables also appear in the error term.

Second-generation RCMs have been applied in recent years to a wide variety of circumstances and with much success in terms of forecasting performance relative to models of the type in equation (19.8) (Akhavein, Swamy, Taubman, and Singamsetti, 1997; Leusner, Akhavein, and Swamy, 1998; Phillips and Swamy, 1998; and Hondroyiannis, Swamy, and Tavlas, 1999).

4   CRITERIA FOR CHOOSING CONCOMITANTS IN RCMS

Equations (19.9)–(19.12) incorporate in a consistent way all the prior information that is usually available about these equations. The most difficult step arises in the form of equation (19.13). Not much prior information is available about the proper concomitants that satisfy Assumptions 1 and 2. As a minimum exercise of caution, the applied econometrician who approaches the problem of estimating equation (19.15) should choose among various sets of concomitants after carefully examining their implications for the estimates of the direct effect components of the coefficients of equation (19.12). Different models of the form (19.15) are obtained by including different sets of concomitants in equation (19.13). The question we address in this section is the following: how can we validate these different models? In what follows, we briefly describe a set of validation criteria and relate them to the RCM described above.

A money demand model can be considered to be validated if (i) it fits within-sample values well; (ii) it fits out-of-sample values well; (iii) it has high explanatory power; (iv) it is derived from equation (19.12) by making assumptions that are consistent with the real-world interpretations of the coefficients of equation (19.12); (v) the signs and statistical significance of the estimates of direct effects remain virtually unchanged as one set of concomitants (other than the determinants of direct effects) after another is introduced into equation (19.13).

Condition (i) is used in almost all econometric work as a measure of fitted-model adequacy. The definition of the coefficient of determination (R^2) that is appropriate to a regression equation with nonspherical disturbances can be applied to equation (19.15). Such a definition is given in Judge *et al.* (1985, p. 32). The coefficient is a measure of the proportion of weighted variation in m_t, $t = 1$, $2, \ldots, T$, explained by the estimated equation (19.15). Within the RCM framework, a low R^2 implies that the set of concomitants included in equation (19.13) together with the explanatory variables of equation (19.12) do not adequately explain the weighted variation in m_t, $t = 1, 2, \ldots, T$. The problem with R^2, however, is that a high value can result by arbitrarily increasing the number of concomitants in equation (19.13), even if all these concomitants are not relevant for explaining the coefficients of equation (19.12).

Condition (ii) is based on cross validation, which is used to assess the ability of equation (19.15) to predict out-of-sample values of m_t. In this procedure, the data sample is divided into two subsamples. The choice of a model with a set of concomitants, including any necessary estimation, is based on one subsample and then its performance is assessed by measuring its prediction against the other subsample. This method is related to Stone's (1974) cross-validatory choice of statistical predictions.

The premise of this approach is that the validity of statistical estimates should be judged by data different from those used to derive the estimates (Mosteller and Tukey, 1977, pp. 36–40; Friedman and Schwartz, 1991, p. 47). Underlying this approach is the view that formal hypothesis tests of a model on the data that are used to choose its numerical coefficients are almost certain to overestimate performance. Also, statistical tests lead to false models with probability 1 if both the null and alternative hypotheses considered for these tests are false, as we have already shown in Section 2. This problem can arise in the present case because of the lack of any guarantee that either a null or an alternative hypothesis will be true if inconsistent restrictions are imposed on equation (19.9).

Predictive testing – extrapolation to data outside the sample – also has its limitations. All forecasts and forecast comparisons should take into account the result, due to Oakes (1985), that there is no universal algorithm to guarantee accurate forecasts forever. This result implies that equation (19.15) with a single set of concomitants cannot predict m_t well in all future periods. This is especially true when the set of x_{jt}^*s in equation (19.9) changes over time. Also, past success does not guarantee future success. That is, if all we knew about equation (19.15) was that it had produced accurate forecasts in the past, there would be no way we could guarantee that future forecasts of equation (19.15) would be sufficiently accurate, since there are some sets of concomitants (e.g. dummy (or shift) variables that are appropriate for a past period) for which past values do not control future values. Even false models based on contradictory premises can sometimes predict their respective dependent variables well. To satisfy a necessary condition under which models are true, de Finetti (1974b) sets up minimal coherence criteria that forecasts should satisfy based on data currently available. By these criteria, different forecasts are equally valid *now* if they all satisfy the requirements for coherence, given currently available knowledge. Thus, a forecast from equation (19.15) can at best represent a measure of the confidence with which one expects that equation to predict an event in the future, based on currently available evidence and not on information yet to be observed, provided that the forecast satisfies the requirements for coherence.[8]

To choose models that satisfy de Finetti's criteria of coherence, we impose the additional conditions (iii)–(v) on RCMs. As with de Finetti's concept of coherence, condition (iv) also explicitly prohibits the use of contradictory premises.[9] Together, conditions (i)–(v) provide an improved method of model validation.

Condition (iii) has also been advocated by Zellner (1988). If prediction were the only criterion of interest, there would be no need to separate direct effects from indirect and mismeasurement effects. But if we are interested in economic explanations – for example, a transmission mechanism of a particular policy action – we need to separate these effects. Equation (19.9) will have the highest explanatory power whenever it coincides with the true money demand function. It would be fortunate if $\sum_{j=3}^{n_t} \alpha_{jt} \psi_{0jt}$ were offset exactly by v_{0t} and if $\sum_{j=3}^{n_t} \alpha_{jt} \psi_{1jt}$ (or $\sum_{j=3}^{n_t} \alpha_{jt} \psi_{2jt}$) and $-(\alpha_{1t} + \sum_{j=3}^{n_t} \alpha_{jt} \psi_{1jt}) \frac{v_{1t}}{r_t}$ (or $-(\alpha_{2t} + \sum_{j=3}^{n_t} \alpha_{jt} \psi_{2jt}) \frac{v_{2t}}{y_t}$ canceled each other. In this case, $\gamma_{0t} = \alpha_{0t}$, $\gamma_{1t} = \alpha_{1t}$, $\gamma_{2t} = \alpha_{2t}$, and equation (19.12) has the same explanatory power as equation (19.9). Alternatively, when $\gamma_{1t} \neq \alpha_{1t}$ and $\gamma_{2t} \neq \alpha_{2t}$, equation (19.12) explains well if it is closer to the true money demand function than to any other equation and cannot provide the proper explanations otherwise. To discern which one of these cases is true given the data on m_t, r_t, and y_t, an accurate means for separating α_{1t} and α_{2t} from the other terms of γ_{1t} and γ_{2t} is needed. Equation (19.15) attempts to make such a separation.

Condition (iv) conforms to de Finetti's (1974b) requirement of coherence – namely, that statistical analysis applied to data should not violate probability laws. We apply this requirement in a somewhat different manner. To explain, consider the following example. Equation (19.12) represents a particular economic (i.e. money demand) relationship that we have in mind but cannot estimate. What we can estimate is equation (19.15). Underlying equation (19.15) are equation (19.12) and Assumptions 1 and 2. Thus, estimation requires that Assumptions 1 and 2 are consistent with the real-world interpretations of the coefficients of equation (19.12) so that de Finetti's condition is satisfied. Assumptions 1 and 2 are consistent with the real-world interpretations of the coefficients of equation (19.12) if the concomitants included in equation (19.13) satisfy Assumptions 1 and 2. For example, Assumptions 1 and 2 are satisfied if the correlations between $(\gamma_{0t}, \gamma_{1t}, \gamma_{2t})$ and (r_t, y_t) arise because of their dependence on a common third set of variables, z_{jt}, $j = 1, \ldots, p$, and if these zs together with $\varepsilon_{k,t-1}$, $k = 0, 1, 2$, capture all the variation in γ_{1t} and γ_{2t} and almost all the variation in γ_{0t}. An example of forecasts that do not satisfy de Finetti's requirement of coherence is a forecast of m_t from equation (19.8), since the premises of this equation are inconsistent with the real-world interpretations of the coefficients of equation (19.12).

Condition (v) concerns the sensitivity of the signs and magnitudes of direct effects to changes in the set of concomitants. Following Pratt and Schlaifer (1988,

p. 45), we state that the only convincing evidence that equation (19.12) under Assumptions 1 and 2 coincides with the true money demand function is of the following kind. It is found that the signs and statistical significance of the estimates of α_{1t} and α_{2t} remain virtually unchanged as one set of concomitants (other than those determining α_{1t} and α_{2t}) after another is introduced into equation (19.13), until finally it is easier to believe that r_t^* and y_t^* have the effects they seem to have on m_t^* than to believe that they are merely the proxies for some other, as yet undiscovered, variable or variables.

5 AN EMPIRICAL EXAMPLE

In this section, we use annual UK data to estimate the demand for money (i.e. equation (19.12) extended to include one additional explanatory variable), with and without concomitants, over the long period 1881–1990. The algebraic forms of these two models are given by the sets (19.12)–(19.14) and (19.7) of equations, respectively. Post-sample forecasts are generated over the period 1991–95. The dependent variable is the log of M3 (currency held by the public plus gross deposits at London and country joint stock and private banks divided by the implicit price deflator for net national product). One of the regressors is the log of per capita net national income, deflated by the implicit price deflator. The antilog of r_t is a short-term rate – the rate on three month bank bills. Following Friedman and Schwartz (1982), and others, we use the rate of change of nominal income as a regressor to proxy the nominal yield on physical assets – that is, as an additional opportunity cost variable. Two concomitants are used: (i) a long-term interest rate – the annual yield on consols; and (ii) the inflation rate, as measured by the rate of change of the implicit price deflator. All data are from Friedman and Schwartz (1982) and have been updated by the present authors.[10]

Table 19.1 presents the results.[11] RCM1 and RCM2 denote the above extended equation (19.12) without and with concomitants, respectively. The coefficient estimates are the average values of the individual time-varying coefficients. Point estimates of the elasticities of income and the interest rate in Table 19.1, but not their t-ratios, are within the range of those yielded in previous empirical studies of UK money demand (see, e.g. Hondroyiannis et al., 1999). Also, both RCM1 and RCM2 produce low root mean square errors (RMSEs). In this example, the equation without concomitants yields a lower RMSE over the post-sample period than does the equation with concomitants. An explanation of this result is that over the range of the values of its dependent and independent variables for the period 1991–95 the money demand function without concomitants seems to approximate the true money demand function better than the money demand function with concomitants. The specifications were also used to provide forecasts over various decades beginning with the 1930s. For this purpose, each specification was re-estimated using data prior to the decade for which it was used to forecast. The equation with concomitants produced lower RMSEs in four out of the six decades. For the sake of brevity, these results are not reported but are available from the authors.

Table 19.1 Long-run elasticities

	RCM1	RCM2
Intercept	−3.69	−3.19
	(−4.97)	(−4.03)
Short-term interest rate	−0.04	−0.01
	(−2.86)	(−0.51)
Real per capita income	0.74	0.67
	(6.03)	(4.98)
Nominal income growth	−0.41	−0.39
	(−4.15)	(−3.09)
RMSE	0.020	0.041

Estimation period is 1881–1990. Forecast period is 1991–95. Figures in parentheses are *t*-ratios.

Table 19.2 Long-run elasticities and direct effects from RCM2

Intercept	Interest rate		Real per capita income		Nominal income growth	
γ_{0t}	γ_{1t}	Direct effect	γ_{2t}	Direct effect	γ_{3t}	Direct effect
−3.19	−0.01	−0.007	0.67	0.68	−0.39	−0.42
(−4.0)	(−0.5)	(−0.4)	(5.0)	(5.1)	(−3.1)	(−3.1)

Figures in parentheses are *t*-ratios.

Table 19.2 reports the averages of the total and direct effect components of the coefficients from the equation with concomitants (i.e. RCM2). Recall, since this specification includes two concomitants, it is possible to extract the direct effects from the total effects, as shown in Section 3. (For the other specification, the indirect and mismeasurement effects in each coefficient are captured in the corresponding error term.) As shown in the table, the γ (i.e. total) coefficients and the direct-effect coefficients are very close to each other for all variables, as are the corresponding *t*-ratios. Figures 19.1 and 19.2 show the time profiles of the elasticity of the short-term interest rate in the absence of concomitants and with concomitants, respectively. The figures also include the time profile of the short-term interest rate. Without concomitants, the interest rate coefficients vary within extremely narrow ranges around their average values. To be exact, the elasticity of the short rate varies between −0.0422 (in 1976) and −0.0431 (in 1973). The narrow range of the interest rate elasticities is due to the specification of the coefficients

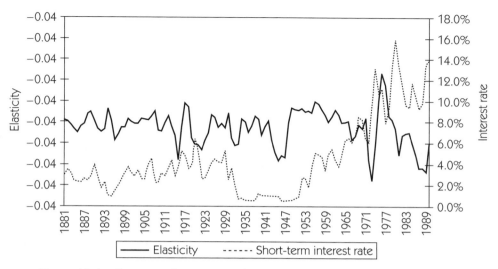

Figure 19.1 Short-term interest rate elasticity for RCM1 (without concomitants)

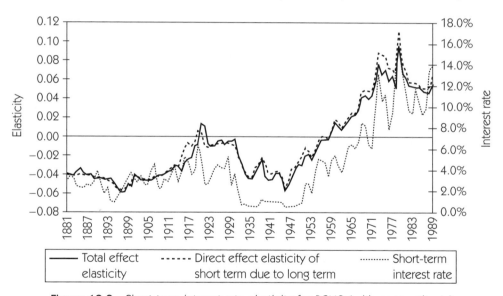

Figure 19.2 Short-term interest rate elasticity for RCM2 (with concomitants)

in the absence of concomitants. Without concomitants the coefficients are equal to a constant mean plus an error term. If the error term has a small variance and does not exhibit serial correlation, the coefficient itself will not vary very much. As shown in Figure 19.2, the coefficients with concomitants exhibit a wider variation than is the case in the specification estimated without concomitants.

The RCM procedure also provides the coefficients of the other regressors. To save space, we report only the time profiles of the interest rate elasticity to give a flavor of the results obtainable from the procedure. Obviously, a richer specification of concomitants might well have provided different results. Examples of the use of varying combinations of concomitants can be found in the papers cited at the end of Section 3.

6 Conclusions

This chapter has attempted to provide a basic introduction to the rationale underlying RCMs. The focus has been on what we characterized as second-generation RCMs, which have been developed to deal with four main problems frequently faced by researchers in applied econometrics. These second-generation RCMs aim to satisfy the conditions for observability of stochastic laws. The use of concomitants – variables that are not included as regressors in the economic relationship to be estimated, but which help deal with correlations between the explanatory variables and their coefficients – allows estimation of both direct and total effects. A set of model validation criteria have also been presented that can be used to discriminate among models and these criteria have been applied to RCMs.

Notes

* Views expressed in this chapter are those of the authors and do not necessarily reflect those of the Office of the Comptroller of the Currency, the Department of the Treasury, International Monetary Fund, or the Bank of Greece. We are grateful to Badi Baltagi for encouragement and guidance, and to four anonymous referees for helpful comments.
1 The suggestion that the coefficients of regression could be random was also made by Klein (1953).
2 An exposition of first-generation RCMs at text-book level has been provided by Judge, Griffiths, Hill, Lütkepohl and Lee (1985, chs 11, 13, and 19). See, also, Chow (1984) and Nicholls and Pagan (1985).
3 The discussion of the real-world sources and interpretations of β_t and their implications for its distribution is postponed until the next section.
4 We start with this assumption and, in the next section, detect departures from it that are warranted by the real-world sources and interpretations of the coefficients of equation (19.1).
5 For a derivation of $E(\hat{w}_t^2 | x_t)$, see Judge et al. (1985, p. 435).
6 The above argument is valid even when $q(\tilde{w})$ is replaced by the Breusch and Pagan (1979) or Judge et al. (1985, p. 436) test statistic.
7 We can write $p(m_t, r_t, y_t | z_t, \theta) = p(m_t | r_t, y_t, z_t, \theta_1)p(r_t, y_t | z_t, \theta_2)$, where $p(\cdot)$ is a probability density function, z_t is a vector of concomitants, and θ, θ_1, and θ_2 are the vectors of fixed parameters. Since γ_{0t}, γ_{1t}, γ_{2t}, r_t, and y_t are correlated with one another, the inferences about α_{1t} and α_{2t} can be drawn without violating probability laws by using the density $p(\gamma_{0t} + \gamma_{1t}r_t + \gamma_{2t}y_t | r_t, y_t, z_t, \theta_1)$ if the following three conditions are satisfied: (i) θ_1 and θ_2 are independent – a good discussion of parameter independence is given in Basu (1977); (ii) $(\gamma_{0t}, \gamma_{1t}, \gamma_{2t})$ are independent of (r_t, y_t), given a value of z_t – a good discussion of conditional independence is given in Dawid (1979, pp. 3–4); (iii) $pr(r_t \in S_r, y_t \in S_y | z_t, m_t) = pr(r_t \in S_r, y_t \in S_y | z_t)$, where the symbol pr is shorthand for probability, and S_r and S_y are the intervals containing the realized values of

r_t and y_t, respectively, to which the observed values of m_t are connected by a law – a definition of stochastic law is given in Pratt and Schlaifer (1988). When condition (ii) holds, $p(\gamma_{0t}, \gamma_{1t}, \gamma_{2t}, r_t, y_t | z_t, \pi) = p(\gamma_{0t}, \gamma_{1t}, \gamma_{2t} | z_t, \pi_1)p(r_t, y_t | z_t, \theta_2)$. This equation provides a formal definition of concomitants.

8 For further discussion of these points, see Schervish (1985).

9 With an inconsistently formulated model, even use of Bayesian methods will probably lead to incoherent forecasts (Pratt and Schlaifer, 1988, p. 49).

10 The data and their sources are available from the authors.

11 The t-ratios were computed by taking account of the correlations among the coefficients.

References

Akhavein, J.D., P.A.V.B. Swamy, S.B. Taubman, and R.N. Singamsetti (1997). A general method of deriving the inefficiencies of banks from a profit function. *Journal of Productivity Analysis* 8, 71–94.

Basu, D. (1977). On the elimination of nuisance parameters. *Journal of the American Statistical Association* 72, 355–66.

Breusch, T.S., and A.R. Pagan (1979). A simple test for heteroscedasticity and random coefficient variation. *Econometrica* 47, 1287–94.

Chang, I., P.A.V.B. Swamy, C. Hallahan, and G.S. Tavlas (1999). A computational approach to finding causal economic laws. *Computational Economics* forthcoming.

Chow, G.C. (1984). Random and changing coefficient models. In Z. Griliches and M.D. Intrilligator (eds.) *Handbook of Econometrics*, Volume 2, Amsterdam: North-Holland Publishing Company.

Dawid, A.P. (1979). Conditional independence in statistical theory. *Journal of the Royal Statistical Society* B, 41, 1–31.

de Finetti, B. (1974a). Bayesianism. *International Statistical Review* 42, 117–30.

de Finetti, B. (1974b). *The Theory of Probability*, Volume 1. New York: John Wiley & Sons.

Friedman, M., and A.J. Schwartz (1982). *Monetary Trends in the United States and the United Kingdom: Their Relation to Income, Prices, and Interest Rates, 1867–1975*. Chicago: University of Chicago Press.

Friedman, M., and A.J. Schwartz (1991). Alternative approaches to analyzing economic data. *American Economic Review* 81, 39–49.

Goldberger, A.S. (1991). *A Course in Econometrics*. Cambridge, MA: Harvard University Press.

Hondroyiannis, G., P.A.V.B. Swamy, and G.S. Tavlas (1999). Modelling the long-run demand for money in the United Kingdom: A random coefficient analysis. *Economic Modelling* forthcoming.

Judge, G.G., W.E. Griffiths, R. Carter Hill, H. Lütkepohl, and T. Lee (1985). *The Theory and Practice of Econometrics*, 2nd edn. New York: John Wiley and Sons.

Klein, L.R. (1953). *A Textbook of Econometrics*. Evanston: Row Peterson and Company.

Leusner, J., J.D. Akhavein, and P.A.V.B. Swamy (1998). Solving an empirical puzzle in the capital asset pricing model. In A.H. Chen (ed.) *Research in Finance*, Volume 16, Stamford, CT: JAI Press, Inc.

Moggridge, D. (1973). *The General Theory and After*. New York: Macmillan.

Mosteller, F., and J.W. Tukey (1977). *Data Analysis and Regression*. Reading, MA: Addison-Wesley Publishing Company.

Nicholls, D.F., and A.R. Pagan (1985). Varying coefficient regression. In E.J. Hannan, P.R. Krishnaiah, and M.M. Rao (eds.) *Handbook of Statistics*, Volume 5, New York: Elsevier Science Publishers.

Oakes, D. (1985). Self-calibrating priors do not exist. *Journal of the American Statistical Association* 80, 339.

Phillips, R.J., and P.A.V.B. Swamy (1998). Par clearance in the domestic exchanges: The impact of national bank notes. In A.J. Field, G. Clark, and W.A. Sundstrom (eds.) *Research in Economic History.* pp. 121–44. Stamford, CT: JAI Press, Inc.

Pratt, J.W., and R. Schlaifer (1984). On the nature and discovery of structure. *Journal of the American Statistical Association* 79, 9–21, 29–33.

Pratt, J.W., and R. Schlaifer (1988). On the interpretation and observation of laws. *Journal of Econometrics* 39, 23–52.

Schervish, M.J. (1985). Discussion of "Calibration-based empirical probability" by A.P. Dawid. *Annals of Statistics* 13, 1274–82.

Stone, M. (1974). Cross-validatory choice and assessment of statistical predictions. *Journal of the Royal Statistical Society* B, 36, 111–33.

Swamy, P.A.V.B., and J.S. Mehta (1975). Bayesian and non-Bayesian analysis of switching regressions and of random coefficient regression models. *Journal of the American Statistical Association* 70, 593–602.

Swamy, P.A.V.B., and G.S. Tavlas (1995). Random coefficient models: Theory and applications. *Journal of Economic Surveys* 9, 165–82.

Swamy, P.A.V.B., and P.A. Tinsley (1980). Linear prediction and estimation methods for regression models with stationary stochastic coefficients. *Journal of Econometrics* 12, 103–42.

Zellner, A. (1969). On the aggregation problem. In K.A. Fox, J.K. Sengupta, and G.V.L. Narasimham (eds.) *Economic Models, Estimation and Risk Programming: Essays in Honor of Gerhard Tintner.* pp. 365–74. New York: Springer-Verlag.

Zellner, A. (1988). Causality and causal laws in economics. *Journal of Econometrics* 39, 7–22.

Nonparametric Kernel Methods of Estimation and Hypothesis Testing

Aman Ullah*

1 INTRODUCTION

Over the last five decades much research in empirical and theoretical econometrics has been centered around the estimation and testing of various econometric functions. For example the regression functions studying the consumption and production functions, the heteroskedasticity functions studying the variability or volatility of financial returns, the autocorrelation function exploring the nature of the time series, and the density functions analyzing the shape of the residuals or any economic variable. A traditional approach to studying these functions has been to first impose a parametric functional form and then proceed with the estimation and testing of interest. A major disadvantage of this traditional approach is that the econometric analysis may not be robust to the slight data inconsistency with the particular parametric specification. Indeed any misspecification in the functional form may lead to erroneous conclusions. In view of these problems, recently a vast amount of literature has appeared on the nonparametric and semiparametric approaches to econometrics, see the books by Prakasa Rao (1983), Silverman (1986), Härdle (1990), Fan and Gijbels (1996) and Pagan and Ullah (1999). In fact a large number of papers continue to pour in to various journals of statistics and econometrics.

The basic point in the nonparametric approach to econometrics is to realize that, in many instances, one is attempting to estimate an expectation of one variable, y, conditional upon others, x. This identification directs attention to the need to be able to estimate the conditional mean of y given x from the data y_i and x_i, $i = 1, \ldots, n$. A nonparametric estimate of this conditional mean simply follows as a weighted average $\Sigma w(x_i, x)y_i$, where $w(x_i, x)$ are a set of weights that depend upon the distance of x_i from the point x at which the conditional expectation is to be evaluated. A kernel weight is considered and it is the subject of discussion in Section 2. This section also indicates how the procedures extend to the estimation of any higher order moments and the estimation of the derivatives of the function linking y and x. Finally, a detailed discussion of the existing and some new goodness-of-fit procedures for the nonparametric regression are presented; and their applications for determining the window width in the kernel weight, and the variables selection are discussed.

A problem with the a priori specified parametric function is that when it is misspecified, even in the small regions of the data, the parametric fit may be poor (biased) though it may be smooth (low variance). On the other hand the nonparametric functional estimation techniques, which totally depend on the data and have no a priori specified functional form may trace the irregular pattern in the data well (less bias) but may be more variable (high variance). A solution discussed in Section 3 is to use a combination of parametric and nonparametric regressions which can improve upon, in the mean squared error (MSE) sense, the drawbacks of each when used individually.

Perhaps the major complications in a purely nonparametric approach to estimation is the "curse of dimensionality", which implies that, if an accurate measurement of the function is to be made, the size of sample should increase rapidly with the number of variables involved in any relation. This problem has lead to the development of additive nonparametric regressions which estimate the regressions with the large numbers of x with a similar accuracy as the regression with one variable. This is discussed in Section 4. Another solution is to consider a linear relationship for some variables while allowing a much smaller number to have an unknown nonlinear relation. Accordingly, Section 4.1 deals with these and other related models which are referred to as the semiparametric models.

While the major developments in nonparametric and semiparametric research have been in the area of estimation, only recently have papers started appearing which deal with the hypothesis testing issues. The general question is how to deal with the traditional hypothesis testing problems – such as the test of functional forms, restrictions, heteroskedasticity – in the nonparametric and semiparametric models. This is explored in Section 5.

The plan of the paper is as follows. In Section 2 we present the estimation of nonparametric regression. Then in Section 3 we discuss the combined regressions. Section 4 deals with the additive regressions and the semiparametric models. Finally, in Section 5 we explore the issues in the nonparametric hypothesis testing.

2   Nonparametric Regression

Consider the regression model

$$y_i = m(x_i) + u_i,$$

where $i = 1, \ldots, n$, y_i is the dependent variable, $x_i = (x_{i1}, \ldots, x_{iq})$ are q regressors, $m(x_i) = E(y_i \mid x_i)$ is the true but unknown regression function, and u_i is the error term such that $E(u_i \mid x_i) = 0$ and $V(u_i \mid x_i) = \sigma^2(x_i)$.

If $m(x_i) = f(\beta, x_i)$ is a correctly specified family of parametric regression functions then $y_i = f(\beta, x_i) + u_i$ is a correct model and, in this case, one can construct a consistent least squares (LS) estimator of $m(x_i)$ given by $f(\hat{\beta}, x_i)$, where $\hat{\beta}$ is the LS estimator of the parameter vector β. This $\hat{\beta}$ is obtained by minimizing $\sum u_i^2 = \sum (y_i - f(\beta, x_i))^2$ with respect to β. For example, if $f(\beta, x_i) = \alpha + x_i \beta = X_i \delta$, $\delta = (\alpha, \beta')'$, is linear we can obtain the LS estimator of δ as $\hat{\delta} = (X'X)^{-1}X'y$, where X is a $n \times (q + 1)$ matrix with the ith row given by $X_i = (1, x_i)$. Further the predicted (fitted) values are $\hat{y}_i = X_i \hat{\delta} = X_i (X'X)^{-1}X'y$. In general, if the parametric regression $f(\beta, x)$ is incorrect or the form of $m(x)$ is unknown then the $f(\hat{\beta}, x)$ may not be a consistent estimate of $m(x)$.

An alternative approach is to use the nonparametric regression estimation of the unknown $m(x)$ by using techniques such as kernel, series, and spline, among others, see Newey (1997), Härdle (1990) and Pagan and Ullah (1999) for details. Here we consider the kernel estimation since it is simple to implement and its asymptotic properties are well established. Essentially the kernel estimator is a local LS (LLS) estimator obtained by minimizing $\sum u_i^2 K\left(\frac{x_i - x}{h}\right)$ where $u_i = y_i - f(\beta, x_i)$, $K_{i,x} = K\left(\frac{x_i - x}{h}\right)$ are a decreasing function of the distances of the regressor vector x_i from the point $x = (x_1, \ldots, x_q)$, and $h > 0$ is the window width (smoothing parameter) which determines how rapidly the weights decrease as the distance of x_i from x increases. When $h = \infty$, $K_{i,x} = K(0)$ is a constant so that the minimization of $K(0) \sum u_i^2$ is the same as the minimization of $\sum u_i^2$, that is the LLS estimator becomes the global LS estimator described above. In general, while the nonparametric LLS estimation fits $f(\beta, x_i)$ to the points in the interval of length h around x, the parametric LS estimator fits $f(\beta, x_i)$ globally to the entire scattering of the data.

When one treats $m(x_i) = f(\beta, x_i)$ locally (around x) as $X_i \delta(x)$, where $\delta(x) = (\alpha(x), \beta(x)')'$, an explicit expression of the LLS estimator of $\delta(x)$ is

$$\hat{\delta}(x) = (X'K(x)X)^{-1}X'K(x)y,$$

and the predicted values of $m(x)$ are

$$\hat{y}_i = \hat{m}(x_i) = X_i \hat{\delta}(x_i) = X_i(X'K(x_i)X)^{-1}X'K(x_i)y = w_i y$$

or $\hat{y} = Wy = \hat{m}$ where $w_i = X_i(X'K(x_i)X)^{-1}X'K(x_i)$ is an $n \times n$ ith row of W, $K(x)$ is the diagonal matrix with the diagonal elements $(K(\frac{x_i - x}{h})), \ldots,$ and $\hat{m} = [\hat{m}(x_1), \ldots,$

$\hat{m}(x_n)]'$. The estimator $\delta(x)$ is the local linear LS (LLLS) or simply the local linear (LL) estimator. One can consider $f(\beta, x_i)$ to be the polynomials in x_i of degree d, in which case the matrix X will contain polynomials and the estimator $\delta(x)$ will be the local polynomial LS (LPLS) estimator. For more details, see Fan and Gijbels (1996).

When one treats $m(x_i)$ locally (around x) as a scalar constant $\alpha(x)$, the LLS estimator of $\alpha(x)$ is

$$\hat{\alpha}(x) = (\iota'K(x)\iota)^{-1}\iota'K(x)y = \frac{\sum_i y_i K_{i,x}}{\sum_i K_{i,x}},$$

and the predicted values are $\hat{y}_i = \hat{m}(x_i) = \hat{\alpha}(x_i) = w_i y = \dfrac{\sum_j y_j K_{ji}}{\sum_j K_{ji}} = \sum_j y_j w_{ji}$, where ι is

an $n \times 1$ vector of unit elements, $K_{ji} = K(\frac{x_j - x_i}{h})$, $w_i = (\iota'K(x_i)\iota)^{-1}\iota'K(x_i)$ is the ith row of W, and $w_{ji} = K_{ji}/\sum_j K_{ji}$. The estimator $\hat{\alpha}(x)$ is the local constant LS (LCLS) estimator, and it was first introduced by Nadaraya (1964) and Watson (1964) (N–W).

The traditional approach to LLLS estimator (Fan and Gijbles, 1996) is to take a first-order Taylor series expansion of $m(x_i)$ around x so that $y_i = m(x_i) + u_i = m(x) + (x_i - x)m^{(1)}(x) + v_i = \alpha(x) + x_i\beta(x) + v_i = X_i\delta(x) + v_i$; where $m^{(1)}(x) = \beta(x) = \partial m(x)/\partial x$ is the first derivative of $m(x)$, $\alpha(x) = m(x) - x\beta(x)$ and X_i and $\delta(x)$ are as given above. The LLLS estimator $\hat{\delta}(x)$ is then obtained by minimizing $\sum v_i^2 K(\frac{x_i - x}{h})$, and it is equivalent to $\hat{\delta}(x)$ given above. Furthermore $\hat{m}(x_i) = \hat{\alpha}(x_i) + x_i\hat{\beta}(x_i) = X_i\hat{\delta}(x_i)$ is an estimator of $m(x_i) = \alpha(x_i) + X_i\beta(x_i) = X_i\delta(x_i)$. We note that while LLLS provides the estimates of the unknown function $m(x)$ and its derivative $\beta(x)$ simultaneously, LCLS estimator of N–W provides the estimator of $m(x)$ only. The first analytical derivative of $\hat{m}(x)$ is then taken to obtain $\hat{\beta}(x)$, see Pagan and Ullah (1999, ch. 4).

The LLS results provide the point-wise estimates of β which vary with x. In some situations one may be interested in knowing how the parameters change with respect to a vector of variables z_i which is not necessarily in the model. That is, the model to be estimated is, say, $y_i = f(\beta(z_i), x_i) + u_i$ or in the linear case $y_i = x_i\beta(z_i) + u_i$. This can be estimated by minimizing $\sum u_i^2 K(\frac{z_i - z}{h}) = \sum[y_i - x_i\beta]^2 K(\frac{z_i - z}{n})$ which gives $\hat{\beta}(z) = (X'K(z)X)^{-1}X'K(z)y$. For examples and applications of these models, see Cai, Fan, and Yao (1998), Robinson (1989) and Li, Huang, and Fu (1998).

The above results extend to the estimation of $E(g(y_i)|x_i)$ where $g(y_i)$ is a function of y_i such that $E|g(y_i)| < \infty$, for example, $E(y_i^2|x_i)$, where $g(y_i) = y_i^2$.

The asymptotic normality results of LLS and N–W (LCLS) estimators are similar and they are well established in the literature. But their finite sample approximate bias expressions to $O(h^2)$ are different while the variance expressions are the same. These are now well known, see Pagan and Ullah (1999, chs. 3 and 4) for details. These results accompanied by several simulation studies (see Fan and Gijbels, 1996) indicate that the MSE performance of the LLLS is much better than that of N–W estimator especially in the tails where data are fewer. In particular, the bias of the N–W estimator is much worse compared to LLLS in the tails, and while the LLLS is unbiased when the true regression function $m(x)$ is linear, the N–W estimator is biased. Intuitively this makes sense since while the N–W estimator fits a constant to the data around each point x the LLLS estimator fits a linear line around x. These properties and the fact that the LLLS estimator provides derivatives (elasticities) and the regression estimators simultaneously, and that it is simple to calculate, make LLLS an appealing estimation technique. In the future, however, more research is needed to compare the performances of LPLS and LLLS.

An important implication of the asymptotic results of LLS and N–W estimators of $m(x)$ and $\beta(x)$ is that the rate of convergence of $\hat{m}(x)$ is $(nh^q)^{1/2}$ and that of $\hat{\beta}(x)$ is $(nh^{q+2})^{1/2}$ which are slower than the parametric rate of $n^{1/2}$. In fact as the dimension of regressors q increases the rates become worse. This is the well known problem of the "curse of dimensionality" in the purely nonparametric regression. In recent years there have been several attempts to resolve this problem. One idea is to calculate the average regression coefficients, e.g. $\sum^n \hat{\beta}(x_i)/n$ or weighted average coefficients which give $n^{1/2}$ convergence rate. This, however, may not have much economic meaning in general, except in the case of single index models used in labor econometrics, see Powell, Stock, and Stoker (1989). Another solution is to use the additive regression models which improve the $(nh^q)^{1/2}$ rate to a univariate rate of $(nh)^{1/2}$. This is described in Section 4.

The asymptotic results described above are well established for the independently and identically distributed (iid) observations, and for the weakly dependent time series data. For the extensions of the results to nonparametric kernel estimation with nonstationary data, see Phillips and Park (1998), and for the case of a purely nonparametric single index model $y_i = m(x_i\beta) + u_i$, see Lewbel and Linton (1998).

2.1 Goodness of fit measures and choices of kernel and bandwidth

The LLS estimators are easy to implement. Once a window width and kernel are chosen, $K_{i,x} = K\left(\frac{x_i - x}{h}\right)$ can be computed for each value of the $x = x_j$, $j = 1, \ldots n$, in the sample and then substituted in the LLS, LLLS, and N–W (LCLS) estimators given above. Confidence intervals for the LLLS and N–W estimators can then be obtained by using the asymptotic normality results. The key issues about the LLS estimators therefore involve the selection of kernel and window width. Regarding the choice of kernel we merely remind readers that for the large data sets it is now believed that the choice of smoothing kernel is not crucial, and that data should be transformed to a standardized from before entry into kernels. Also, in practice the product kernels are easy to use and perform well, that is $K(\psi_i) = \Pi_s K(\psi_{si})$ where $s = 1, \ldots, q$; and $K(\psi_{si})$ can be taken as the univariate normal with unbounded support or the Epanechnikov kernel with bounded support $K(\psi_{si}) = \frac{3}{4}(1 - \psi_{si}^2), |\psi_{si}| \leq 1$. These kernels are second-order kernels, implying their first moments are zero but the second are finite. Another class of kernels, known as higher order kernels with higher order moments as zero, are used in order to reduce the asymptotic bias problem in the LLS estimators. However, in practice the gains from these higher order kernels are not significant. For details on the choice of kernels see Silverman (1986).

The window width h controls the smoothness of the LLS estimate of $m(x)$ and in practice is crucial in obtaining a good estimate that controls the balance between the variance, which is high when h is too small, and the squared bias which is high when h is too large. With this in mind several window width selection procedures have tried to choose h to minimize a number of mean squared error (MSE) criteria, for example $\int (\hat{m}(x) - m(x))^2 dx$, $E\int ((\hat{m}(x) - m(x))^2 dx) = \int \mathrm{MSE}(\hat{m}(x)) dx$ = integrated MSE = IMSE and the average IMSE = AIMSE = $E\int (\hat{m}(x) - m(x))^2 f(x) dx$. The minimization of IMSE is known to provide the optimal h to be c $n^{-1/(q+4)}$ where c is a constant of proportionality which depends on unknown density and $m(x)$ and their derivatives. An initial estimate of c can be constructed giving "plug-in" estimators of h but this has not been a very popular procedure in practice. A recent proposal from Härdle and Bowman (1988) is to estimate AIMSE by bootstrapping and then minimizing the simulated AIMSE with respect to h. An advantage of this approach is that it also provides a confidence interval for $\hat{m}$.

Cross validation is a popular alternative procedure, which chooses h by minimizing the sum of squares of the estimated prediction error (EPE) or residual sum of squares (RSS), EPE = RSS = $\frac{1}{n}\sum_i^n (y_i - \hat{y}_{-i})^2 = \frac{1}{n}\sum_i^n \hat{u}_{-i}^2 = \frac{\hat{u}'\hat{u}}{n} = \frac{y'M'My}{n}$ where $\hat{y}_{-i} = \hat{m}_{-i}(x_i) = w_{-i}y$, $\hat{u}_{-i} = y_i - \hat{y}_{-i}$, $\hat{u} = y - W_{-i}y = My$ and $M = I - W_{-i}$; subscript $-i$ indicates the "leave-one-out" estimator, deleting ith observation in the sums is used. An alternative is to consider EPE* = $\frac{y'M^*y}{tr(M^*)}$ where $M^* = M'M$ and $tr(M^*)$ can be treated as the degrees of freedom in the nonparametric regression, as an analogue to the linear parametric regression case.

One drawback of the "goodness-of-fit function" EPE is that there is no penalty for large or small h. In view of this, many authors have recently considered the penalized goodness of fit function to choose h see Rice (1984) and Härdle, Hall, and Marron (1992). The principle is the same as in the case of penalty functions used in the parametric regression for the choice of number of parameters (variables), for example the Akaike criterion. The idea of a penalty function is, in general, an attractive one and it opens up the possibility of future research.

A related way to obtain h is to choose a value of h for which the square of correlation between y_i and $\hat{y}_i(\hat{\rho}_{y,\hat{y}}^2)$ is maximum, that is $0 \le R^2 = \hat{\rho}_{y,\hat{y}}^2 \le 1$ is maximum. One could also use the correlation between y and leave-one-out estimator $\hat{y}_{-i}$.

When $V(u_i | x_i) = \sigma^2(x_i)$, one can choose h such that an estimate of unconditional variance of u_i, $Eu_i^2 = E[E(u_i^2 | x_i)] = E[\sigma^2(x_i)] = \int \sigma^2(x) f(x) dx$ is minimum. That is, choose h such that $\mathrm{EPE}_1 = \hat{E}u_i^2 = \int \hat{\sigma}^2(x) d\hat{F}(x)$ where $\hat{\sigma}^2(x_i) = \hat{E}(\tilde{u}_i^2 | x_i)$ is obtained by the LPLS regression of $\tilde{u}_i^2$ on x_i; $\tilde{u}_i = y_i - \hat{m}(x_i)$ is the nonparametric residual, and $\hat{f}(x) = \sum_i^n w_i(x)$ is a nonparametric density estimator for some weight function $w_i(x)$ such that $\int w_i(x) dx = 1$. For the kernel density estimator $w_i(x) = K\left(\frac{x_i - x}{h}\right)/nh^q$, see Silverman (1986) and Pagan and Ullah (1999). It is better to use EPE_1 than EPE when there is a heteroskedasticity of unknown form. Also, since $\hat{E}(u_i^2)$ can be shown to be a consistent estimator of Eu_i^2 the nonparametric version of R^2,

$R_1^2 = 1 - \frac{EPE_1}{\frac{1}{n}\sum_i^n(y_i - \bar{y})^2}$ lies between 0 and 1, and it is an estimator of $\rho^2 = 1 - \frac{Eu_i^2}{V(y_i)} =$
$1 - \frac{E(y_i - m(x_i))^2}{V(y_i)}$.

Thus, an alternative is to choose h such that R_1^2 is maximum. One can also use EPE_1^* in R_1^2. This will correspond to $\bar{R}^2$ in the parametric regression. A simple way to calculate EPE_1 is to consider the empirical distribution function so that $EPE_1 = \frac{1}{n}\sum_i^n \hat{\sigma}^2(x_i)$.

In general the move from independent to dependent observations should not change the way window width selection is done. However, care has to be taken since, as indicated by Robinson (1986), a large window width might be needed for the dependent observations case due to the positive serial correlations (see Herrman, Gasser, and Kneip, 1992). Faraway (1990) considers the choice of varying window width. For details on the choices of h and their usefulness see Pagan and Ullah (1999).

3 COMBINED REGRESSION

Both the parametric and nonparametric regressions, when used individually, have certain drawbacks. For example, when the a priori specified parametric regression $m(x) = f(\beta, x)$ is misspecified even in the small regions of the data, the parametric fit may be poor (biased) though it may be smooth (low variance). On the other hand, the nonparametric regression techniques, which totally depend on the data and have no a priori specified functional form may trace the irregular pattern in the data well (less bias) but may be more variable (high variance). Thus, when the functional form of $m(x)$ is unknown, a parametric model may not adequately describe the data in its entire range, whereas a nonparametric analysis would ignore the important a priori information about the underlying model. A solution considered in the literature is to use a combination of parametric and nonparametric regressions which can improve upon the drawbacks of each when used individually, see Eubank and Spiegelman (1990), Fan and Ullah (1998), and Glad (1998). Essentially the combined regression estimator controls both the bias and variance and hence improves the MSE of the fit. To see the idea behind the combined estimation let us start with a parametric model $(m(x) = f(\beta, x))$ which can be written as

$$y_i = m(x_i) + u_i = f(\beta, x_i) + g(x_i) + \varepsilon_i,$$

where $g(x_i) = E(u_i \mid x_i) = m(x_i) - E(f(\beta, x_i) \mid x_i)$ and $\varepsilon_i = u_i - E(u_i \mid x_i)$ such that $E(\varepsilon_i \mid x_i) = 0$. Note that $f(\beta, x_i)$ may not be a correctly specified model so $g(x_i) \neq 0$. If it is indeed a correct specification $g(x_i) = 0$. The combined estimation of $m(x)$ can be written as

$$\hat{m}_c(x_i) = f(\hat{\beta}, x_i) + \hat{g}(x_i),$$

where $\hat{g}(x_i) = \hat{E}(\hat{u}_i \mid x_i)$ is obtained by the LLS estimation technique and $\hat{u}_i = y_i - f(\hat{\beta}, x_i)$ is the parametric residual.

An alternative way to combine the two models is to introduce a weight parameter λ and write $y_i = f(\beta, x_i) + \lambda g(x_i) + \varepsilon_i$. If the parametric model is correct, $\lambda = 0$. Thus, the parameter λ measures the degree of accuracy of the parametric model. A value of λ in the range 0 to 1 can be obtained by using the goodness of fit measures described in Section 2.1, especially R^2 and EPE. Alternatively, an LS estimator $\hat{\lambda}$ can be obtained by doing a density weighted regression of $y_i - f(\hat{\beta}, x_i) = \hat{u}_i$ on $\hat{g}(x_i)$, see Fan and Ullah (1998). The combined estimator of $m(x)$ can now be given by

$$\hat{m}_c^*(x_i) = f(\hat{\beta}, x_i) + \hat{\lambda}\hat{g}(x_i).$$

This estimation indicates that a parametric start model $f(\hat{\beta}, x)$ be adjusted by $\hat{\lambda}$ times $\hat{g}(x)$ to get a more accurate fit of the unknown $m(x)$.

Instead of additive adjustments to the parametric start in $\hat{m}_c(x)$ and $\hat{m}_{c*}(x)$, Glad (1998) proposed a multiplicative adjustment as given below. Write

$$m(x_i) = f(\beta, x_i)\frac{m(x_i)}{f(\beta, x_i)} = f(\beta, x_i)E(y_i^* \mid x_i),$$

where $y_i^* = y_i/f(\beta, x_i)$. Then $\hat{m}_g(x_i) = f(\hat{\beta}, x_i)\hat{E}(\hat{y}_i^* \mid x_i)$ is the estimator proposed by Glad (1998), where $\hat{y}_i^* = y_i/f(\beta, x_i)$, and $\hat{E}(\cdot)$ is obtained by the LLS estimator described above.

The asymptotic convergence rates of $\hat{m}_c(x)$ and its asymptotic normality are given in Fan and Ullah (1998). In small samples, the simulation results of Rahman and Ullah (1999) suggest that the combined estimators perform, in the MSE sense, as well as the parametric estimator if the parametric model is correct and perform better than both the parametric and nonparametric LLS estimators if the parametric model is incorrect.

4 ADDITIVE REGRESSIONS

In recent years several researchers have attempted to estimate $m(x_i)$ by imposing some structure upon the nature of the conditional mean $m(x_i)$. One popular solution is the generalized additive models of Hastie and Tibshirani (1990), which is

$$y_i = m(x_i) + u_i = m_1(x_{i1}) + m_2(x_{i1}) + \ldots + m_q(x_{iq}) + u_i,$$

where m_s, $s = 1, \ldots, q$, are functions of single variables with $Em_s(x_{is}) = 0$, $s = 2, \ldots, q$, for identification. Each of m_s and hence $m(x_i)$ is then estimated by one dimensional convergence rate of $(nh)^{1/2}$ which is faster than the convergence rate $(nh^q)^{1/2}$ achieved by direct nonparametric estimation of $m(x_i)$. The statistical properties of Hastie and Tibshirani (1990) estimation algorithm is complicated. For practical implementations, simpler estimation techniques are proposed in Linton and Nielson (1995) and Chen et al. (1996). The basic idea behind this is as follows. At the first stage estimate $\hat{m}(x_i) = \hat{m}(x_{i1}, \ldots, x_{iq}) = \hat{m}(x_{i1}, x_{\underline{i1}})$ by the nonparametric LLS procedure, where $x_{\underline{i1}}$ is a vector of $x_{i2} \ldots, x_{iq}$. Then, using $Em_s(x_{is}) = 0$, we note that

$$m_1(x_{i1}) = \int m(x_{i1}, x_{\underline{i1}}) dF(x_{\underline{i1}})$$

and hence $\hat{m}_1(x_{i1}) = \int \hat{m}(x_{i1}, x_{\underline{i1}}) d\hat{F}(x_{\underline{i1}})$. Using the empirical distribution one can calculate $\hat{m}_1(x_{i1}) = \frac{1}{n}\sum_{j=1}^{n} \hat{m}(x_{i1}, x_{\underline{i1}})$. $\hat{m}_s(x_{is})$ for any s can be similarly calculated. Under the assumptions that $[y_i, x_i]$ are iid, $nh^3 \to \infty$ and $nh^5 \to 0$ as $n \to \infty$, Linton and Nielson show the $(nh)^{1/2}$ convergence to normality for $\hat{m}_1$. For the test of additivity of $m(x_i)$ see Linton and Gozalo (1996), and for the application to estimating a production function see Chen *et al.* (1996).

Alternative useful approaches which impose structure on $m(x_i)$ are the projection pursuit regression and the neural networks procedures. For details on them, see Friedman and Tukey (1974), Breiman and Friedman (1985), Kuan and White (1994), Härdle (1990) and Pagan and Ullah (1999).

4.1 Semiparametric models

A partial solution to the dimensionality problem was also explored in Speckman (1988) and Robinson (1988). They considered the case where $x_i = (x_{i1}, x_{i2})$ and $m(x_i) = m(x_{i1}, x_{i2}) = m_1(x_{i1}) + m_2(x_{i2})$, but the researcher knows the functional form of $m_1(x_{i1})$ as $x_{i1}\beta$, where x_{i1} is a q_1 dimensional and x_{i2} is q_2 dimensional with no common elements. That is, they considered the partial linear models or semiparametric (SP) model of the following form

$$y_i = x_{i1}\beta + m(x_{i2}) + u_i,$$

where $E(u_i | x_i) = 0$. For example, in the earning functions log earning (y_i) may be an unknown function of age (x_{i2}) but a linear function of education (x_{i1}). The estimation of β can be carried out by first eliminating $m(x_{i2})$, and then using the following procedure of taking conditional expectations so that

$$E(y_i | x_{i2}) = E(x_{i1} | x_{i2})\beta + m(x_{i2})$$

and $y_i - E(y_i | x_{i2}) = (x_{i1} - E(x_{i1} | x_{i2}))\beta + u_i$ or $y_i^* = x_{i1}^*\beta + u_i$. This can then be estimated by the LS procedure as

$$\hat{\beta}_{SP} = \left(\sum_{i}^{n} x_{i1}^* x_{i1}^{*\prime}\right)^{-1} \sum_{i}^{n} x_{i1}^* y_i^*.$$

For the implementation we need to know y_i^* and x_{i1}^*, which can be obtained by estimating $E(y_i | x_{i2})$ and $E(x_{i1} | x_{i2})$ using the LLS procedures in Section 2. After obtaining $\hat{\beta}_{SP}$ one can proceed for the estimation of $m(x_{i2})$ by writing

$$y_i - x_{i1}\hat{\beta}_{SP} = y_i^{**} = m(x_{i2}) + u_i = E(y_i^{**} | x_{i2}) + u_i,$$

and then again doing the LLS regression of y_i^{**} on x_{i2}.

While the estimator of $m(x_{i2})$ achieves the nonparametric slow rate of convergence of $(nh^{q/2})^{1/2}$, the remarkable point is that the $\hat{\beta}_{SP}$ achieves the parametric rate of convergence of $n^{1/2}$. It is in this respect that this procedure is better than the univariate nonparametric convergence rates of generalized additive models above. However, in the partial linear model we need to be sure of the linearity of $x_{i1}\beta$. If $m(x_{i1}, \beta)$ is a nonlinear function of x_{i1} and β, then it is not clear how one proceeds with the above estimation technique, though it seems that a nonlinear semiparametric LS procedure might be helpful. For the empirical applications of the above models, see Engle *et al.* (1986) for an electricity expenditure estimation, Anglin and Gencay (1996) for a hedonic price estimation of Canadian housing.

There are various extensions of the idea of the partial linear models. Fan and Li (1997) combine the partial linearity with the generalized additive models to consider

$$y_i = x_{i1}\beta + m_2(x_{i2}) + m_3(x_{i3}) + \ldots + m_q(x_{iq}) + u_i$$

and suggest the $\sqrt{n}$ convergent estimate of β and $(nh)^{1/2}$ convergent estimates of $m_s(x_{is})$ for $s = 2, \ldots, q$. This improves upon the $(nh^q)^{1/2}$ state of convergence of $m(x_{i2})$ above.

The partially linear models have been extensively studied in the labor econometric literature on the selection models where $m(x_{i2}) = m(x_{i2}\delta)$ is an unknown function of single index $x_{i2}\delta$ and x_{i2} and x_{i1} may have some common variables. For details on this literature, see Pagan and Ullah (1999, chs. 7–9). For the maximum likelihood estimation of the purely parametric model, $y_i = x_i\beta + u_i$, partial linear, and selection models without the assumption about the form of the density of u_i, see the excellent work of Ai (1997). The estimation of panel data based partially linear models has been developed in Ullah and Roy (1998), Li and Ullah (1998) and Li and Stengos (1996), among others.

5 HYPOTHESIS TESTING

An obvious question is how to carry out various diagnostic tests done in the parametric econometrics within the nonparametric and semiparametric models. Several papers have appeared in the recent literature which deal with this issue. We present them here and show their links.

First consider the problem of testing a specified parametric model against a nonparametric alternative, $H_0 : f(\beta, x_i) = E(y_i | x_i)$ against $H_1 : m(x_i) = E(y_i | x_i)$. The idea behind the Ullah (1985) test statistic is to compare the parametric RSS (PRSS) $\sum \hat{u}_i^2$, $\hat{u}_i = y_i - f(\hat{\beta}, x_i)$ with the nonparametric RSS (NPRSS), $\sum \tilde{u}_i^2$, where $\tilde{u}_i = y_i - \hat{m}(x_i)$. His test statistic is

$$T_1 = \frac{(\text{PRSS} - \text{NPRSS})}{\text{NPRSS}} = \frac{\text{PRSS}}{\text{NPRSS}} - 1 = \frac{\sum \hat{u}_i^2 - \sum \tilde{u}_i^2}{\sum \tilde{u}_i^2},$$

or simply $T_1^* = (\text{PRSS} - \text{NPRSS})$, and reject the null hypothesis when T_1 is large. $\sqrt{n} T_1$ has a degenerage distribution under H_0. Lee (1994) uses density weighted residuals and compares $\sum w_i \hat{u}_i^2$ with $\sum \tilde{u}_i^2$ to avoid degeneracy, for other procedures see Pagan and Ullah (1999). Pagan and Ullah (1999) also indicate the normalizing factor needed for the asymptotic normality of T_1. An alternative suggested here is the following nonparametric bootstrap method:

1. Generate the bootstrap residuals u_i^* from the centered residuals $(\tilde{u}_i - \bar{\tilde{u}})$ where $\bar{\tilde{u}}$ is the average of $\tilde{u}_i$.
2. Generate $y_i^* = f(\hat{\beta}, x_i) + u_i^*$ from the null model.
3. Using the bootstrap sample $x_i, y_i^*, i = 1, \ldots, n$, estimate $m(x_i)$ nonparametrically, say and $\hat{m}^*(x_i)$, and obtain the bootstrap residual $\tilde{u}_i^* = y_i^* - \hat{m}^*(x_i)$.
4. Calculate the bootstrap test statistic $T_1^* = (\sum \hat{u}_i^2 - \sum \tilde{u}_i^{*})^2 / \sum \tilde{u}_i^{*2}$.
5. Repeat steps (1) to (4) B times and use the empirical distribution of T_1^* as the null distribution of T_1^*.

An alternative is to use wild bootstrap method or pivotal bootstrap which will preserve the conditional heteroskedasticity in the original residuals. Another alternative is to use the block bootstrap method (Bühlman and Künsch, 1995).

An alternative test statistic is based on comparing the parametric fit with the nonparametric fit. Defining $a(x)$ as a smooth weight function, this test statistic is

$$T_2 = \frac{1}{n} \sum_i^n (f(\hat{\beta}, x_i) - \hat{m}(x_i))^2 a(x_i) = \int (f(\hat{\beta}, x_i) - \hat{m}(x_i))^2 a(x_i) d\hat{F}(x),$$

where $\hat{F}$ is the empirical distribution function, see Ullah (1985) and Gozalo (1995), and Aït-Sahalia et al. (1998) who also indicate that $f(\hat{\beta}, x_i)$ and $\hat{m}(x_i)$ can also be replaced by $f(\hat{\beta}, x_i) - \int f(\hat{\beta}, x_i) \hat{f}(x_i) dx_i$ and $\hat{m}(x_i)$ by $\hat{m}(x_i) - \int \hat{m}(x_i) \hat{f}(x_i) dx_i$ without affecting the results in practice and provide the asymptotic normality of $nh^{q/2} T_2$.

Härdle and Mammen (1993) suggest a weighted integrated square difference between the nonparametric estimator and the kernel smoothed parametric estimator $\hat{f}(\beta, x_i) = \hat{E}(f(\hat{\beta}, x_i) | x_i)$ which can be calculated by the LLS procedures with y_i replaced by $f(\hat{\beta}, x_i)$. This is

$$T_3 = \int_x (\hat{f}(\hat{\beta}, x) - \hat{m}(x))^2 a(x) dx = \int_x [\hat{E}(\hat{u} | x)]^2 a(x) dx,$$

where $\hat{E}(\hat{u} | x) = \hat{E}(y | x) - \hat{E}(f(\hat{\beta}, x) | x) = \hat{m}(x) - \hat{f}(\hat{\beta}, x)$. It has been shown in Rahman and Ullah (1999) that the use of the kernel smoothed estimator $\hat{f}(\hat{\beta}, x)$ gives better size and power performances of the tests compared to the case of using $f(\hat{\beta}, x)$. T_3 is similar to T_2 if we write $a(x) = a(x)\hat{f}^{-1}(x)d\hat{F}(x)$ and use the empirical distribution. This test statistic is computationally involved. In view of this, Li and Wang (1998) and Zheng (1996) proposed a conditional moment test (CMT) which is easy to calculate, and has a better power performance. Its form is

$$T_4 = \frac{1}{n} \sum_i^n \hat{u}_i \hat{E}(\hat{u}_i | x_i) \hat{f}(x_i) = \frac{1}{n} \sum_i^n \hat{u}_i (\hat{m}(x_i) - \hat{f}(\hat{\beta}, x_i)) \hat{f}(x_i).$$

This statistic is based on the idea that under the null $E(u_i | x_i) = E[u_i E(u_i | x_i)] = E[(Eu_i | x_i)^2] = E[u_i E(u_i | x_i) a(x_i)] = 0$ for any positive $a(x_i)$. T_4 is an estimate of $E[u_i E(u_i | x_i) a(x_i)]$ for $a(x_i) = f(x_i)$. Eubank and Spiegelman (1990), however, tests for $E[(Eu_i | x_i)^2] = 0$ using a series type estimator of $E(u_i | x_i)$. The test statistic T_4 has $nh^{q/2}$ rate of convergence to normality.

An intuitive and simple test of the parametric specification follows from the combined regression $y_i = f(\beta, x_i) + \lambda g(x_i) + \varepsilon_i$ or $u_i = y_i - f(\beta, x_i) = \lambda E(u_i | x_i) + \varepsilon_i$ given in Section 3. The estimator of λ is then

$$\hat{\lambda} = \frac{\frac{1}{n} \sum_i^n \hat{u}_i \hat{E}(\hat{u}_i | x_i) a(x_i)}{\frac{1}{n} \sum_i^n (\hat{E}(\hat{u}_i | x_i))^2 a(x_i)} = \frac{\frac{1}{n} \sum_i^n \hat{u}_i (\hat{m}(x_i) - \hat{f}(\hat{\beta}, x_i)) a(x_i)}{\frac{1}{n} \sum_i^n (\hat{m}(x_i) - \hat{f}(\hat{\beta}, x_i))^2 a(x_i)} = \frac{\hat{\lambda}_N}{\hat{\lambda}_D},$$

which is the weighted LS of $\hat{u}_i$ on $\hat{E}(\hat{u}_i | x_i)$. Fan and Ullah (1998) considered the case where $a(x_i) = \hat{f}^2(x_i)$ and $\hat{f}(\hat{\beta}, x_i) = f(\hat{\beta}, x_i)$, and established the asymptotic normality of $h^{-q/2}\hat{\lambda}$ and $nh^{q/2}\hat{\lambda}_N$. Their test statistics for parametric specification, $H_0 : \lambda = 0$ are

$$T_5 = \frac{\hat{\lambda}}{\sqrt{V(\hat{\lambda})}} \text{ and } T_6 = \frac{\hat{\lambda}_N}{\sqrt{V(\hat{\lambda}_N)}},$$

and they indicate the better performances of size and power of T_6 compared to T_5. It is interesting to see the links between the test statistics T_1 to T_6. First, since $\hat{u}_i = y_i - f(\hat{\beta}, x_i)$ and $\tilde{u}_i = y_i - \hat{m}(x_i)$, it follows that

$$\frac{1}{n} \sum_i^n (\hat{u}_i^2 - \tilde{u}_i^2) a(x_i) = -\frac{1}{n} \sum_i^n (f(\hat{\beta}, x_i) - \hat{m}(x_i))^2 a(x_i) - \frac{2}{n} \sum \hat{u}_i (f(\hat{\beta}, x_i) - \hat{m}(x_i)) a(x_i)$$

or $T_1 = -T_2 + 2T_4$, except that T_4 has $\hat{f}(\hat{\beta}, x_i)$. Thus under the null hypothesis $T_4 \simeq 0$ and $T_2 \simeq 0$ may imply $T_1 \simeq 0$. We also note that T_6, with $a(x_i) = \hat{f}(x_i)$, is the Li–Wang and Zheng tests T_4.

All the above nonparametric tests are generally calculated with the leave-one-out estimators of $\hat{m}(x_i) = \hat{m}_{-i}(x_i)$ and the weight $a(x_i) = \hat{f}(x_i) = \hat{f}_{-i}(x_i)$. Theoretically, the use of leave-one-out estimators helps to get asymptotic normality centered at zero. The tests are consistent model specification tests in the sense that their power goes to one as $n \to \infty$ against all the alternatives. The usual parametric specification tests are however consistent against a specified alternative. An approach to developing consistent model specification test, without using any nonparametric estimator of $m(x)$, is the CMT due to Bierens–Newey–Tauchen, see Pagan and Ullah (1999) for details. An important difference between Bierens-type tests and the tests T_1 to T_6 is the treatment of h. While T_1 to T_6 tests consider $h \to 0$ as $n \to \infty$, Bierens (1982) type tests treat h to be fixed which makes the asymptotic distribution of their tests to be nonnormal but can detect the Pitman's local alternative that approach the null at the rate $O(n^{-1/2})$ compared to the slower rate of $O((nh^{q/2})^{-1/2})$ of T_1 to T_6. However, Fan and Li (1996) indicate that under high frequency type local alternatives the tests with vanishing h may be more powerful than tests based on fixed h. For asymptotic normality of the tests T_1 to T_6 for the dependent observations, see Li (1997).

The test statistics T_1 to T_6 can also be used for the problem of variable selections. For example, testing $H_0 : m(x_i) = m(x_{i1}, x_{i2}) = m(x_{i1})$ against $H_1 : m(x_i) \neq m(x_{i1})$ can be carried out by calculating the difference between the NPRSS due to $\hat{m}(x_{i1}, x_{i2})$ and the NPRSS due to $\hat{m}(x_{i1})$, or using $T_2 = n^{-1}\Sigma(\hat{m}(x_{i1}, x_{i2}) - \hat{m}(x_{i1}))^2 a(x_i)$ test, see Aït-Sahalia et al. (1998) for asymptotic normality. An alternative is suggested in Racine (1997). We can also do the diagnostics for variable selection by using the goodness of fit measures described in Section 2.1; in addition see Vien (1994) where the cross-validation method has been used.

The tests T_1 to T_6 can also be extended to do nonnested testing (Delgado and Mora, 1998), testing for parametric and semiparametric models $y_i = f(\beta, x_i) + \lambda m(x_i) + u_i$, (Li, 1997; Fan and Li, 1996) and single index models, Aït-Sahalia et al., 1998). Finally, for testing the restrictions on the parameters, testing heteroskedasticity, and testing serial correlation in the parametric model $y_i = f(\beta, x_i) + u_i$ with the unknown form of density, see Gonzalez-Rivera and Ullah (1999) where they develop the semiparametric Rao-score test (Lagrange multiplier) with the unknown density replaced by its kernel estimator. Also see Li and Hsiao (1998) for a semiparametric test of serial correlation.

Note

* The author is thankful to two referees for their constructive comments and suggestions. The research support from the Academic Senate, UCR, is gratefully acknowledged.

References

Ai, C. (1997). A semiparametric maximum likelihood estimator. *Econometrica* 65, 933–63.

Aït-Sahalia, Y., P.J. Bickel, and T.M. Stoker et al. (1998). Goodness-of-fit regression using kernel methods. Manuscript, University of Chicago.

Anglin, P., and R. Gencay (1996). Semiparametric estimation of a hedonic price function. *Journal of Applied Econometrics* 11, 633–48.

Bierens, H.J. (1982). Consistent model specification tests. *Journal of Econometrics* 20, 105–34.

Breiman, L., and J. Friedman (1985). Estimating optimal transformations for multiple regression and correlation. *Journal of the American Statistical Association* 80, 580–619.

Bühlman, P., and H.R. Künsch (1995). The blockwise bootstrap for general parameters of a stationary time series. *Scandinavian Journal of Statistics* 22, 35–54.

Chen, R., W. Härdle, O.B. Linton, and E. Sevarance-Lossin (1996). Nonparametric estimation of additive separable regression model. *Statistical Theory and Computational Aspect of Smoothing; Physica-Verlag* 247–65.

Cai, Z., J. Fan, and Q. Yao (1998). Functional-coefficient regression models for non-linear time series. Manuscript, University of North Carolina.

Delgado, M.A., and J. Mora (1998). Testing non-nested semiparametric models: An application to Engel curve specification. *Journal of Applied Econometrics* 13, 145–62.

Engel, R.F., C.W.J. Granger, J. Rice, and A. Weiss (1986). Semiparametric estimates of the relation between weather and electricity sales. *Journal of the American Statistical Association* 81, 310–20.

Eubank, R.L., and C.H. Spiegelman (1990). Testing the goodness-of-fit of the linear models via nonparametric regression techniques. *Journal of the American Statistical Association* 85, 387–92.

Fan, J., and I. Gijbels (1996). *Local Polynomial Modelling and Its Applications*. London: Chapman and Hall.

Fan, Y., and Q. Li (1996). Consistent model specification tests: Omitted variables and semiparametric functional forms. *Econometrica* 64, 865–90.

Fan, Y., and Q. Li (1997). On estimating additive partially linear models. Manuscript, University of Windsor.

Fan, Y., and A. Ullah (1998). Asymptotic normality of a combined regression estimator. *Journal of Multivariate Analysis* 71, 191–240.

Fan, Y., and A. Ullah (1999). On goodness-of-fit tests for weakly dependent processes using kernel method. *Journal of Nonparametric Statistics* 11, 337–60.

Faraway, J. (1990). Bootstrap selection for bandwidth and confidence bands for nonparametric regression. *Journal of Statistics Computational Simulations* 37, 37–44.

Friedman J.H., and J.W. Tukey (1974). A projection pursuit algorithm for exploratory data analysis. *IEEE. Transactions on Computers*, C-23, 881–90.

Glad, I.K. (1998). Parametrically guided nonparametric regression. *Scandinavian Journal of Statistics* 25, 649–68.

Gozalo, P.L. (1995). Nonparametric specification testing with $\sqrt{n}$–local power and bootstrap critical values. Working Paper no. 95–21R; Brown University.

Gonzalez-Rivera, G., and A. Ullah (1999). Rao's score test with nonparametric density estimators. *Journal of Statistical Planning and Inference*.

Härdle, W. (1990). *Applied Nonparametric Regression*. New York: Cambridge University Press.

Härdle, W., and A. Bowman (1988). Bootstrapping in nonparametric regression: Local adaptive smoothing and confidence bounds. *Journal of the American Statistical Association* 83, 102–10.

Härdle, W., P. Hall, and J.S. Marron (1992). Regression smoothing parameters that are not far from their optimum. *Journal of the American Statistical Association* 87, 277–33.

Härdle, W., and E. Mammen (1993). Comparing nonparametric versus parametric regression fits. *Annals of Statistics* 21, 1926–47.

Hastie, T., and R. Tibshirani (1990). *General Additive Models*. New York: Chapman and Hall.

Herrman, E., T. Gasser, and A. Kneip (1992). Choice of bandwidth for kernel regression when residuals are correlated. *Biometrika* 79, 783–95.

Kuan, C.M., and H. White (1994). Artificial neural networks: An econometric perspective. *Econometric Reviews* 13, 1–91.

Lee, B.J. (1994). Asymptotic distribution of the Ullah-type against the nonparametric alternative. *Journal of Quantitative Economics* 10, 73–92.

Lewbel, A., and O. Linton (1998). Nonparametric censored regression. Manuscript, no. 1186, Yale University.

Li, Q. (1997). Consistent model specification tests for time series models. Manuscript, University of Guelph.

Li, Q., and C. Hsiao (1998). Testing serial correlation in semiparametric panel data models. *Journal of Econometrics* 87, 207–37.

Li, Q., and T. Stengos (1996). Semiparametric estimation of partially linear panel data models. *Journal of Econometrics* 71, 389–97.

Li, Q., and A. Ullah (1998). Estimating partially linear panel data models with one way error components. *Econometric Reviews* 17, 145–66.

Li, Q., and S. Wang (1998). A simple consistent bootstrap test for a parametric regression function. *Journal of Econometrics* 87, 145–65.

Li, Q., C. Huang, and T.T. Fu (1998). Semiparametric smooth coefficient stochastic frontier models. Manuscript, Institute of Economics, Taiwan.

Linton, O., and D. Nielson (1995). Estimating structured nonparametric regression by the kernel method. *Biometrika* 82, 93–101.

Linton, O., and P.L. Gozalo (1996). Testing additivity in generalized nonparametric regression models. Working Paper, Yale University and Brown University.

Nadaraya, É.A. (1964). On estimating regression. *Theory of Probability and its Applications* 9, 141–2.

Newey, W.K. (1985). Maximum likelihood specification testing and conditional moment tests. *Econometrica* 53, 1047–70.

Newey, W.K. (1997). Convergence rates and asymptotic normality of series estimators. *Journal of Econometrics* 29, 147–68.

Pagan, A.R., and A. Ullah (1999). *Nonparametric Econometrics*. Cambridge: Cambridge University Press.

Phillips, P.C.B., and J.Y. Park (1998). Nonstationary density estimation and kernel autoregression. Manuscript, no. 1181, Yale University.

Powell, J.L., H. Stock, and T.M. Stoker (1989). Semiparametric estimation of index coefficients. *Econometrica* 57, 1403–30.

Prakasa Rao, B.L.S. (1983). *Nonparametric Functional Estimation*. New York: Academic Press.

Racine, J. (1997). Consistent significance testing for nonparametric regression. *Journal of Business and Economic Statistics* 15, 369–78.

Rahman, M., and A. Ullah (1999). Improved combined parametric and nonparametric regression: Estimation and hypothesis testing. Manuscript, University of California, Riverside.

Rice, J. (1984). Bandwidth choice for nonparametric regression. *Annals of Statistics* 12, 1215–30.

Robinson, P.M. (1988). Root-n-consistent semiparametric regression. *Econometrica* 56, 931–54.

Robinson, P.M. (1986). On the consistency and finite sample properties of nonparametric kernel time series regression, autoregression and density estimation. *Annals of the Institute of Statistical Mathematics* 38, 539–49.

Robinson, P.M. (1989). Nonparametric estimation of time varying parameters. In P. Hack (ed.) *Statistical Analysis and Forecasting of Economic Structional Change*. Springer-Verlag.

Silverman, B.W. (1986). *Density Estimation for Statistics and Data Analysis*. New York: Chapman and Hall.

Speckman, P. (1988). Kernel smoothing in a partial linear model. *Journal of Royal Statistical Society Series* B 50, 413–46.

Ullah, A. (1985). Specification analysis of econometric models. *Journal of Quantitative Economics* 1, 187–209.

Ullah, A., and N. Roy (1998). Nonparametric and semiparametric econometrics of panel data. In A. Ullah and D.E.A. Giles (eds.) *Handbook of Applied Economic Statistics*. ch. 17, pp. 579–604. Marcel Dekker.

Vien, P. (1994). Choice of regressors in nonparametric estimation. *Computational Statistics and Data Analysis* 17, 575–94.

Watson, G.S. (1964). Smooth regression analysis. *Sankhya Series* A 26, 359–72.

Zheng, J.X. (1996). Consistent test of functional form via nonparametric estimation techniques. *Journal of Econometrics* 75, 263–90.

Durations

Christian Gouriéroux and Joann Jasiak

1 INTRODUCTION

Duration data represent times elapsed between random arrivals of events. They play an important role in many areas of science such as engineering, management, physics, economics, and operational research. In economics, duration data frequently appear in labor and health studies, insurance analysis, and finance. For example, a commonly used duration-based statistic is the average individual lifetime, called the life expectancy, provided yearly by national surveys. It serves a variety of purposes. The macroeconomists quote it as an indicator of the level of development and welfare of the society, while applied microeconomists consider it implicitly in designing and pricing contracts such as life insurances. For specific projects, duration data are collected from a number of different sources. Various longitudinal studies are conducted on the national level to record durations of individual unemployment spells for job search studies. Data on durations of hospital treatments provide information on the anticipated expenses of the health care system. In academic research, the business cycle analysis and macroeconomic forecasting require studies of durations of recessions and expansions measuring times elapsed between subsequent turning points of the economy. Finally, in the private sector, businesses collect their own duration data. For example, insurance agencies record the times between reported car accidents to determine individual insurance premia or bonus–malus schemes, and learn about the attitude of their customers with respect to risk.

The probability theory often defines the distributional properties of durations with respect to the distribution of delimiting random events. In particular, the arrival frequency of these events has some major implications for research. For illustration, let us compare the durations of job searches to durations between consecutive transactions on a computerized stock market, like the New York Stock Exchange (NYSE). While a job search may last from a few days up to several months, a duration between trades may only amount to a fraction of a minute. We also expect that although the number of unemployment durations experienced by one person is theoretically unlimited, their total length cannot

exceed the maximum time during which the individual is able to actively participate in the labor force. In practice we do not observe more than a few unemployment spells per person, on average. For this reason researchers are mainly
interested in cross section studies of unemployment durations based on a large
number of individuals, rather than in investigating personal duration patterns.
This is not the case of intertrade durations where each stock generates a series of
durations consisting of thousands of observations per month. Such duration data
are primarily interesting from the point of view of their dynamics and fall into a
distinct category of duration time series. Therefore it is important to distinguish
between duration models applied to panel and time series data.

The dynamics of durations is often related to transitions of a stochastic process
between different admissible states. In this framework, a duration may be viewed
as the sojourn time spent in a given state (unemployment) before exiting this
state to enter into another state (employment). Besides the randomness related to
the exit time, its destination may also be stochastic. There exist durations which
may be terminated by events admitting several various states. An example of
such a duration is the length of a hospital stay, which may end up in a recovery
or a death of the patient. These durations data are called *transition data*.

An important issue in duration analysis concerns the measurement, or more
precisely the choice of the time scale of reference. Several economic applications
require time scales different from the conventional calendar time. The change
of the time scale is called time deformation. The *operational* time unit is often
selected with respect to some exogenous variables which may effect the speed
of the time flow. Intuitively, an individual has a different perception of the time
flow during busy working hours, and quiet periods of leisure. For objects like
machines and instruments a typical determinant of the time speed is the depre-
ciation rate. Accordingly, the time measuring the lifetime of a car flows at a
different speed for a new car which leaves the assembly line, from an old car
which has accumulated 100,000 km on the odometer. For this reason, a natural
time scale of reference seems to be in this example the calendar time discounted
by the mileage. As another example illustrating the economic sense of operational time, imagine an efficient stock trader who instead of measuring his time
spent on the market floor in minutes is using instead time units necessary to
trade, say, 1,000 shares or to make transactions worth 1,000 dollars. Obviously,
deformed time does not have equal, unitary increments, but it resembles the
calendar time in that it cannot stop or reverse its direction.

Finally, note that in everyday life we often encounter durations arising as
conditions specified by various contracts, such as lease agreements, rentals, or
credit terms. As such these predetermined durations are not of interest to analysts, who examine durations between events which are intrinsically random.
However the randomness reappears if a side of the contract is allowed to quit by
early termination, i.e. when, for example, borrowers have the option to prepay
the outstanding credit balances. Given that not all individuals display the same
behavior, this population is considered by a duration analyst as a heterogenous
one.

This chapter is organized as follows. In Section 2, we discuss the standard
characterizations of duration variables and present the main duration distribution

families. In Section 3, we introduce individual heterogeneity in parametric duration models. This heterogeneity is partly observed through individual explanatory
variables and partly unobserved. We discuss the effect of unobserved heterogeneity
in terms of negative duration dependence. Section 4 covers semiparametric models
with a parametric effect of observed explanatory variables, and an unspecified
baseline duration distribution. Finally, we introduce in Section 5 dynamic models
for the analysis of time series of durations which are especially useful for applications to financial transactions data.

2   Duration Variables

In this section we introduce basic concepts in duration analysis and present the
commonly used duration distributions.

2.1   Survivor and hazard functions

Let us consider a continuous duration variable Y measuring the time spent in a
given state, taking values in R^+. The probabilistic properties of Y can be defined
either by:

the probability density (pdf) function $f(y)$, assumed strictly positive,
or the cumulative distribution (cdf) function $F(y) = \int_0^y f(u)du$,
or the survivor function $S(y) = 1 - F(y) = \int_y^\infty f(u)du$.

The *survivor function* gives the probability of survival to y, or otherwise, the
chance of remaining in the present state for at least y time units. Essentially, the
survivor function concerns the future.

In many applications the exit time has an economic meaning and may signify
a transition into a desired or undesired state. Let us pursue the example of
individual life expectancy. A related important indicator is the instantaneous
mortality rate at age y. It is given by:

$$\lambda(y) = \lim_{dy \to 0} \frac{1}{dy} P[y \le Y < y + dy \mid Y \ge y]. \tag{21.1}$$

In this formula $\lambda(y)$ defines the probability per unit of time that a person dies
within a short interval of dy (seconds) given that he/she is still alive at age y.
It can easily be written in terms of the survivor function. Indeed we get:

$$\lambda(y) = \lim_{dy \to 0} \frac{1}{dy} \frac{P[y \le Y < y + dy]}{P[Y \ge y]}$$

$$= \lim_{dy \to 0} \frac{1}{dy} \frac{S(y) - S(y + dy)}{S(y)}$$

$$= -\frac{1}{S(y)} \frac{dS(y)}{dy},$$

$$\lambda(y) = \frac{f(y)}{S(y)}. \tag{21.2}$$

The *hazard function* is:

$$\lambda(y) = \frac{f(y)}{S(y)} = \lim_{dy \to 0} \frac{1}{dy} P[y < Y < y + dy \mid Y \geq y], \quad \forall y \in R^+. \tag{21.3}$$

It gives the instantaneous exit rate per unit of time evaluated at y. Among often encountered exit rates are, besides the aforementioned mortality rate, the bankruptcy rate, and the failure rate of instruments.

The duration variable can equivalently be defined by S, f or λ, in reason of the following relationship between the survivor function and the hazard function:

$$S(y) = \exp - \int_0^y \lambda(u)du. \tag{21.4}$$

This means that once we know the hazard function we can always find the survivor function.

2.2 Duration dependence

The duration dependence describes the relationship between the exit rate and the time already spent in the state. Technically it is determined by the hazard function, which may be a decreasing, increasing, or constant function of y. Accordingly, we distinguish (i) negative duration dependence; (ii) positive duration dependence; and (iii) absence of duration dependence.

NEGATIVE DURATION DEPENDENCE
The longer the time spent in a given state, the lower the probability of leaving it soon. This negative relationship is found for example in the job search analysis. The longer the job search lasts, the less chance an unemployed person has of finding a job.

POSITIVE DURATION DEPENDENCE
The longer the time spent in a given state, the higher the probability of leaving it soon. Positive duration dependence is observed in the failure rate of instruments which are getting used up in time, or depreciate gradually. For example, the longer a lightbulb works, the higher the probability that it fails within the next hour (say).

ABSENCE OF DURATION DEPENDENCE
The hazard function is constant. In this case there is no relationship between the duration spent in the state and the probability of exit.

The absence of duration dependence is often imposed as a simplifying although very restrictive assumption. It implies that items, such as instruments or machines, do not deteriorate: for example, an item, which has been in use for ten hours, is as good as a new item with regard to the amount of time remaining until the item fails. This effect is usually not supported by the data and durations observed in empirical research usually belong to the first or second category or else display a nonmonotone hazard function. For this reason empirical hazards often need to be studied case by case. Let us consider, for instance, a typical hazard function representing the rate of bankruptcies. A newly created firm has a low probability of failure; however six months to two years later the failure rate increases sharply. The bankruptcy rate usually shows a tendency to diminish for companies which operate for a fairly long time, acquire more experience, and become better known to their customers and suppliers.

2.3   Basic duration distributions

In this section we introduce some parametric families of duration distributions.

Exponential family

The exponentially distributed durations feature no duration dependence. In consequence of the time-independent durations, the hazard function is constant, $\lambda(y) = \lambda$. The cdf is given by the expression $F(y) = 1 - \exp(-\lambda y)$, and the survivor function is $S(y) = \exp(-\lambda y)$.

The density is given by:

$$f(y) = \lambda \exp(-\lambda y), \quad y > 0. \tag{21.5}$$

This family is parametrized by the parameter λ taking strictly positive values.

An important characteristic of the exponential distributions is that the mean and standard deviation are equal, as implied by $EY = \frac{1}{\lambda}$, $VY = \frac{1}{\lambda^2}$. In empirical research the data violating this condition are called over- or under-dispersed depending on whether the standard deviation exceeds the mean or is less than the mean.

Gamma family

This family of distributions depends on two positively valued parameters a and v. The density is given by:

$$f(y) = [a^v y^{v-1} \exp(-ay)]/\Gamma(v), \tag{21.6}$$

where $\Gamma(v) = \int_0^\infty \exp(-y) y^{v-1} dy$. When $v = n$ is integer valued, this distribution may be obtained by summing n independent exponentially distributed durations with parameter $\lambda = a$. In such a case $\Gamma(n) = (n - 1)!$.

The form of the hazard function depends on the parameter v.

1. If $v > 1$, the hazard function is decreasing and approaching asymptotically a.
2. If $v = 1$, the hazard function is a constant, and the model reduces to the exponential model.
3. If $v < 1$, the hazard function is decreasing from $+\infty$ and approaches an asymptote at a.

The gamma model is quite often employed in practice. The mean and variance of *gamma* distributed durations are $EY = \frac{v}{a}$, $VY = \frac{v}{a^2}$.

WEIBULL MODEL
This family of distributions also depends on two positive parameters a and b. The density is:

$$f(y) = aby^{b-1}\exp(-ay^b). \tag{21.7}$$

The formula of the survivor function is $S(y) = \exp(-ay^b)$. The behavior of the hazard function $\lambda(y) = aby^{b-1}$ is determined by b. It is increasing for $b > 1$ at either a growing or diminishing rate, and it is decreasing for values of $b < 1$.

LOGNORMAL FAMILY
These distributions, contrary to those discussed above, have a nonmonotone hazard function which is first increasing, and next decreasing in y. Therefore they can be used for the analysis of bankruptcy rates. The lognormal duration distribution is such that $\log Y$ follows a normal distribution with mean m and variance σ^2. The density is a function of the normal density denoted by ϕ:

$$f(y) = \frac{1}{\sigma y}\phi\left(\frac{\log y - m}{\sigma}\right). \tag{21.8}$$

The survivor function is $S(y) = 1 - \Phi(\frac{\log y - m}{\sigma})$, where Φ denotes the cdf of a standard normal. The hazard function can be written as the ratio:

$$\lambda(y) = \frac{1}{y}\frac{[1/\sigma\phi(x)]}{1 - \Phi(x)},$$

where $x = \frac{\log y - m}{\sigma}$.

3   PARAMETRIC MODELS

In empirical research we may wish to investigate the dependence of individual hazard functions on exogenous variables. These variables, called the control variates, depict in general various individual characteristics. Let us point out a few examples. In the job search analysis, a typical control variate is the amount of unemployment benefits, which influences the effort of unemployed individuals devoted to the job search and consequently the duration of unemployment. Empirical findings also suggest that family support provided by the state influences the birth rate, and that the expected increase of the insurance premium has an effect on the frequency of declared car accidents. As well, there is evidence indicating that the lengths of hospital stays depend on the cost incurred by patients, or else, the duration of an outstanding balance on a credit card is in part determined by the interest paid by the cardholder. Some explanatory variables differ accross individuals, and are invariant in time (e.g. gender), while others (e.g. age) are individual and time dependent. Such variables need to be doubly indexed by individual and time (see Hsiao, Chapter 16, in this volume). Other variables may have a common impact on all individuals in the sample and vary in time, like the rate of inflation or the global rate of unemployment.

Parametric duration models can accommodate the effect of observable or unobservable individual characteristics on durations. Let us denote by x_i the observable explanatory variables and by μ_i a latent heterogeneity factor. We proceed in two steps to define the extended duration model. First, we consider the conditional distribution of the duration variable Y_i given the observable covariates and heterogeneity. It is characterized by either the conditional pdf $f(y_i | x_i, \mu_i)$, or the conditional hazard function $\lambda(y_i | x_i, \mu_i)$. Next, we introduce a heterogeneity distribution $\pi(\mu_i)$ (say), which is used to derive the conditional distribution of the duration variable given the observable covariates only. This latter distribution is characterized by either the conditional pdf $f(y_i | x_i)$, or the conditional hazard function $\lambda(y_i | x_i)$.

In the first subsection we describe the exponential duration model without heterogeneity and its estimation by the maximum likelihood. In the following subsection we introduce a gamma distributed heterogeneity factor, which leads us to the Pareto regression model. The effect of unobservable heterogeneity and its relationship with the negative duration dependence are covered in the third part of this section. Finally, we discuss the problem of partial observability of duration variables due to truncation or censoring effects.

3.1 Exponential regression model

Recall that the exponential duration model depends on the parameter λ, which is the constant hazard rate. We now assume an exponential distribution for each individual duration, with a rate λ_i depending on the observable characteristics of this individual represented by explanatory variables. The positive sign of λ is ensured by assuming that:

$$\lambda_i = \exp(x_i\theta),$$

where θ is a vector of unknown parameters. The survivor function is given by:

$$S_i(y | x_i; \theta) = \exp[-(\exp x_i\theta)y],$$

whereas the conditional pdf of the duration variable given the covariates is:

$$f(y_i | x_i; \theta) = \lambda_i \exp(-\lambda_i y_i)$$
$$= \exp(x_i\theta)\exp[-y_i \exp(x_i\theta)]. \tag{21.9}$$

The parameter θ can be estimated by the maximum likelihood from a random sample of N observations on (x_i, y_i), $i = 1, \ldots, N$. The conditional loglikelihood function is:

$$\log l(y \mid x; \theta) = \sum_{i=1}^{N} \log f(y_i \mid x_i; \theta)$$

$$= \sum_{i=1}^{N} [x_i\theta - y_i \exp(x_i\theta)],$$

and the maximum likelihood estimator $\hat{\theta} = \text{Argmax}_\theta \log l(y \mid x; \theta)$ solves the optimization problem. The first order conditions are:

$$\frac{\partial \log l(y \mid x, \hat{\theta})}{\partial \theta} = 0$$

$$\Leftrightarrow \sum_{i=1}^{N} [1 - y_i \exp(x_i\hat{\theta})]x'_i = 0$$

$$\Leftrightarrow \sum_{i=1}^{N} \exp(x_i\hat{\theta})[y_i - \exp(-x_i\hat{\theta})]x'_i = 0. \tag{21.10}$$

Since the conditional expectation of the duration variable is $E[Y_i \mid x_i] = \exp(-x_i\hat{\theta})$, the first-order equations are equivalent to orthogonality conditions between the explanatory variables and the residuals: $\hat{u}_i = y_i - \exp(-x_i\hat{\theta})$, with weights $\exp(x_i\hat{\theta})$ due to the individual heteroskedasticity.

3.2 The exponential model with heterogeneity

The exponential regression model can easily be extended by introducing unobservable variables. We express the individual hazard rate as:

$$\lambda_i = \mu_i \exp(x_i\theta), \tag{21.11}$$

where μ_i is a latent variable representing the heterogeneity of individuals in the sample, called the heterogeneity factor. We assume that the heterogeneity factor is gamma distributed $\gamma(a, a)$, with two identical parameters to ensure $E\mu_i = 1$. The conditional duration distribution given the observable covariates is found by integrating out the unobservable heterogeneity.

$$f(y_i \mid x_i; \theta, a) = \int_0^\infty f(y_i \mid x_i, \mu; \theta)\pi(\mu; a)d\mu$$

$$= \int_0^\infty \mu \exp(x_i\theta) \exp[-y_i\mu \exp(x_i\theta)] \frac{a^a\mu^{a-1}\exp(-a\mu)}{\Gamma(a)}d\mu$$

$$= \frac{a^a \exp(x_i\theta)}{[a + y_i\exp(x_i\theta)]^{a+1}} \frac{\Gamma(a+1)}{\Gamma(a)}$$

$$f(y_i \mid x_i; \theta, a) = \frac{a^{a+1}\exp(x_i\theta)}{[a + y_i\exp(x_i\theta)]^{a+1}}. \tag{21.12}$$

We find that the conditional duration distribution is Pareto translated. The associated conditional survivor function is:

$$S(y_i \mid x_i; \theta, a) = \int_{y_i}^{\infty} \frac{a^{a+1} \exp(x_i\theta)}{[a + \mu \exp(x_i\theta)]^{a+1}} du$$

$$= \frac{a^a}{[a + y_i \exp(x_i\theta)]^a},$$

whereas the hazard function is:

$$\lambda(y_i \mid x_i; \theta, a) = \frac{a \exp(x_i\theta)}{a + y_i \exp(x_i\theta)}.$$

The hazard function of the Pareto distribution with drift is a decreasing function of y, and features negative duration dependence at the level of a representative individual. Hence, by aggregating exponentially distributed durations with constant hazards across infinitely many different individuals with a gamma distributed heterogeneity, we obtain a decreasing aggregate hazard function. The heterogeneity parameter a provides a natural measure of the negative duration dependence: the smaller a, the stronger the negative duration dependence. In the limiting case $a = +\infty$, we get $\mu_i = 1$, and $\lambda(y_i \mid x_i; \theta, a) = \exp(x_i\theta)$; there is no duration dependence and the Pareto regression model reduces to the exponential regression model.

For the Pareto regression model, the loglikelihood function is:

$$\log l(y \mid x; \theta, a) = \sum_{i=1}^{N} \log f(y_i \mid x_i; \theta, a)$$

$$= \sum_{i=1}^{N} \{(a+1)\log a + x_i\theta - (a+1)\log [a + y_i \exp(x_i\theta)]\}.$$

3.3   Heterogeneity and negative duration dependence

The effect of unobservable covariates can be measured by comparing models with and without heterogeneity. In this section we perform such a comparison using the exponential model. For simplicity we do not include observable covariates in the model. The conditional distribution of the duration variable given the heterogeneity factor μ_i is exponential with parameter $\lambda_i = \mu_i$ whereas the marginal distribution of the heterogeneity is π. Therefore, the conditional and marginal survivor functions are:

$$S(y_i \mid \mu_i) = \exp(-\mu_i y_i),$$

$$S(y_i) = \int_0^{\infty} \exp(-\mu y_i)\pi(\mu)d\mu.$$

The corresponding hazard functions are:

$$\lambda(y_i \mid \mu_i) = \mu_i,$$

$$\lambda(y_i) = -\frac{d \log S(y_i)}{dy} = -\frac{1}{S(y_i)} \frac{dS(y_i)}{dy}$$

$$= \frac{\int_0^\infty \exp(-\mu y_i) \mu \pi(\mu) d\mu}{\int_0^\infty \exp(-\mu y_i) \pi(\mu) d\mu}.$$

The marginal hazard rate is an average of the individual hazard rates μ_i with respect to a modified probability distribution with pdf:

$$\pi_{y_i}(\mu_i) = \exp(-\mu y_i) \pi(\mu) / \int_0^\infty \exp(-\mu y_i) \pi(\mu) d\mu. \tag{21.13}$$

We also get:

$$\lambda(y_i) = E_{\pi_{y_i}}[\lambda(y_i \mid \mu_i)] = E_{\pi_{y_i}}(\mu_i). \tag{21.14}$$

This marginal hazard function features negative duration dependence. Indeed, by taking the first-order derivative we find:

$$\frac{d\lambda(y_i)}{dy} = \frac{-\int_0^\infty \mu^2 \exp(-\mu y_i) \pi(\mu) d\mu}{\int_0^\infty \exp(-\mu y_i) \pi(\mu) d\mu} + \frac{[\int_0^\infty \exp(-\mu y_i) \mu \pi(\mu) d\mu]^2}{[\int_0^\infty \exp(-\mu y_i) \pi(\mu) d\mu]^2}$$

$$= -E_{\pi_{y_i}} \mu_i^2 + [E_{\pi_{y_i}}(\mu_i)]^2$$

$$= -\mathrm{var}_{\pi_{y_i}} \mu_i \leq 0.$$

We note that the negative duration dependence at level y_i is related to the magnitude of heterogeneity with respect to a modified probability.

To illustrate previous results let us consider a sample of individuals belonging to two categories with respective exit rates $\mu_1 > \mu_2$. The individuals in the first category with a high exit rate are called movers, whereas we call stayers the individuals belonging to the second category. The structure of the whole population at date 0 is $\pi_1 = \pi$, $\pi_2 = 1 - \pi$. The marginal hazard rate derived in the previous section becomes:

$$\lambda(y) = \frac{\pi_1 S_1(y) \mu_1 + \pi_2 S_2(y) \mu_2}{\pi_1 S_1(y) + \pi_2 S_2(y)}. \tag{21.15}$$

Between 0 and y some individuals exit from the population. The proportions of those who leave differ in the two subpopulations; they are given by $S_1(y) = \exp(-\mu_1 y) < S_2(y) = \exp(-\mu_2 y)$, which implies a modified structure of remaining individuals at date y. This modified structure is:

$$\pi_1(y) = \pi_1 S_1(y)/[\pi_1 S_1(y) + \pi_2 S_2(y)], \quad \pi_2(y) = 1 - \pi_1(y). \quad (21.16)$$

Since $S_1(y) < S_2(y)$, the proportion of movers is lower at date y than at date 0, which implies $\lambda(y) < \lambda(0) = \pi_1 \mu_1 + \pi_2 \mu_2$. Finally, we note that, for large y, $\pi_2(y)$ tends to one and the remaining population becomes homogenous including stayers only.

3.4   Truncation and censoring

Econometric data used in duration analysis are often panel data comprising a number of individuals observed over a fixed interval of time. Let us suppose that the survey concerns unemployment durations; the sampling period is January 2000–December 2000 and the individuals also provided information on their job history prior to January 2000. We can consider two different sampling schemes, which imply truncation and censoring.

CENSORING
Let us first consider a sample drawn from the population including both employed and unemployed people, and assume at most one unemployment spell per individual. Within this sample we find persons, who:

1.   are unemployed in January and remain unemployed in December too;
2.   are unemployed in January and find a job before December;
3.   are employed in January, lose their job before December and are still unemployed at this date;
4.   are employed in January, next lose their job and find new employment before December.

Due to the labor force dynamics, unemployment durations of some individuals are only partially observed. For groups (2) and (4) the unemployment spells are complete, whereas they are right censored for groups (1) and (3).

To identify the right censored durations we can introduce an indicator variable d_i. It takes value 1 if the observed duration spell for individual i is complete, and 0 if this observation is right censored. We also denote by T_i the date of the entry into the unemployment state, by ξ_i the total unemployment duration and by y_i the *observed* unemployment duration knowing that the sampling period ends at T.

The model involves two latent variables T_i and ξ_i. The observed variables d_i and y_i are related to the latent variables by:

$$\begin{cases} d_i = 1 \\ y_i = \xi_i \end{cases}, \qquad \text{if } T_i + \xi_i < T,$$

$$\begin{cases} d_i = 0 \\ y_i = T - T_i \end{cases}, \qquad \text{if } T_i + \xi_i > T,$$

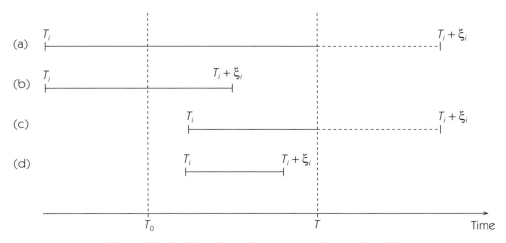

Figure 21.1   Censoring scheme: unemployment spells

Conditional on T_i the density of the observed pair (y_i, d_i) is:

$$l_i(y_i, d_i) = f_i(y_i)^{d_i} S_i(y_i)^{1-d_i}, \qquad (21.17)$$

or, otherwise:

$$l_i(y_i, d_i) = \lambda_i(y_i)^{d_i} S_i(y_i), \qquad (21.18)$$

by substituting the hazard expression into equation (21.17). The loglikelihood function for this model can be written by assuming that individual durations are independent conditional on explanatory variables:

$$\log L(y; d) = \sum_{i=1}^{N} \log l_i(y_i; d_i)$$

$$= \sum_{i=1}^{N} d_i \log \lambda_i(y_i) + \sum_{i=1}^{N} \log S_i(y_i).$$

Note that the duration distributions are conditioned on the date T_i. This information has generally to be introduced among the explanatory variables to correct for the so-called cohort effect.

TRUNCATION
We can also draw the sample in the subpopulation of people who are unemployed in January 2000 (date T_0, say). Within this sample we find persons, who:

1. are unemployed in January and remain unemployed in December too;
2. are unemployed in January and find a job before December.

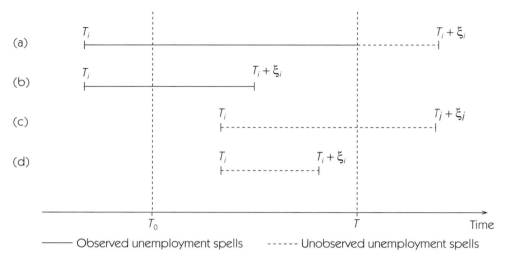

—— Observed unemployment spells   - - - - - - Unobserved unemployment spells

Figure 21.2 Truncation scheme

However, we now need to take into account the endogenous selection of the sample, which only contains unemployed people at T_0 (see Lung-Fei Lee, Chapter 16, in this volume). This sampling scheme is called left truncated, since compared to the previous scheme we have only retained the individuals with unemployment duration larger than $T_0 - T_i$. Conditional on T_i, the density of the pair (y_i, d_i) becomes:

$$l_i(y_i, d_i) = f_i(y_i)^{d_i} S_i(y_i)^{1-d_i} / S_i(T_0 - T_i).$$

4   Semiparametric Models

It is common to consider semiparametric specifications of duration models which distinguish a parametric scoring function and an unconstrained baseline distribution. We describe below the accelerated and proportional hazard models and introduce the estimation methods for the finite dimensional and functional parameters. For convenience we select an exponential specification of the score.

4.1   Accelerated hazard model

Accelerated hazard models rely on the assumption that individual durations follow the same distribution up to an individual change of the time scale (time deformation). For example, let us rescale the time by $\exp(x_i\theta)$, we get:

$$Y_i \exp(x_i\theta) \sim f_0, \tag{21.19}$$

where f_0 is the unconstrained baseline distribution and $\exp(x_i\theta)$ defines the change of the time unit. We deduce that the conditional hazard function given the observable covariates is:

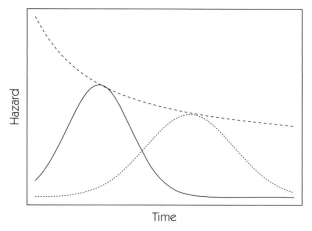

Figure 21.3 Hazard functions for accelerated hazard models

$$\lambda(y_i \,|\, x_i; \, \theta, f_0) = \lambda_0[y_i \exp(x_i\theta)]\exp(x_i\theta), \tag{21.20}$$

where the baseline hazard λ_0 corresponds to the f_0 distribution.

A consistent estimation method of the two types of parameters θ and f_0 is easily derived. Indeed from (21.20) we derive:

$$\log Y_i = -x_i\theta + u_i, \tag{21.21}$$

where the variables $\exp u_i$ are iid with the unknown distribution f_0. By introducing a constant term among the regressors, it is always possible to constrain the distribution f_0 so that $Eu_i = 0$. The finite dimensional parameter θ can be consistently estimated by ordinary least squares from a regression of the log-durations on the covariates x_i. Let us denote by $\hat{\theta}$ the OLS estimator. In the next step we can construct the corresponding residuals $\hat{u}_i = \log y_i + x_i\hat{\theta}$ and approximate the baseline distribution by the smoothed distribution of the exponential residuals $\exp\hat{u}_i = y_i \exp x_i\hat{\theta}$, $i = 1, \dots, N$.

4.2 Proportional hazard model

In this model the conditional hazard functions are assumed homothetic and the parametric term $\exp(x_i\theta)$ is introduced as the coefficient of proportionality:

$$\lambda(y_i \,|\, x_i; \, \theta, f_0) = \exp(x_i\theta)\lambda_0(y_i), \tag{21.22}$$

where λ_0 is an unconstrained baseline hazard function. It is defined up to a multiplicative scalar. The term proportional hazard indicates that the hazards for two individuals with regressor vectors x_1 and x_2 are in the same ratio. For

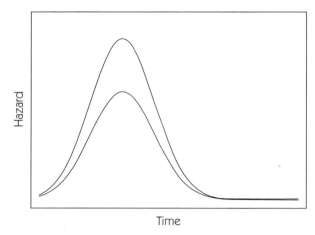

Figure 21.4 Hazard functions for proportional hazard models

example, the exponential model with $\lambda(y \mid x_i; \theta) = \exp(x_i\theta)$ is a proportional hazard model with $\lambda_0 = 1$.

The parameter θ can be consistently estimated by the partial maximum likelihood introduced by Cox (1975). The approach is the following. Let us first rank the duration data by increasing values $y_{(1)} < y_{(2)} < \ldots < y_{(N)}$, where we implicitly assume that all observed durations are different. Then we consider the subpopulation at risk just before the exit of the ith individual:

$$\mathcal{R}_{(i)} = \{j : y_{(j)} \geq y_{(i)}\}.$$

The probability that the first individual escaping from this subpopulation $\mathcal{R}_{(i)}$ is individual (i) is given by:

$$p_{(i)}(\theta, \lambda_0) = \frac{\lambda(y_{(i)} \mid x_{(i)}; \theta, \lambda_0)}{\sum_{j \in \mathcal{R}_{(i)}} \lambda[y_{(j)} \mid x_{(j)}; \theta, \lambda_0]}$$

$$= \frac{\exp(x_{(i)}\theta)}{\sum_{j \in \mathcal{R}_{(i)}} \exp(x_{(j)}\theta)}.$$

It no longer depends on the baseline distribution. The partial maximum likelihood estimation of θ is defined by:

$$\hat{\theta} = \operatorname*{argmax}_{\theta} \sum_{i=1}^{N} \log p_{(i)}(\theta, \lambda_0)$$

$$= \operatorname*{argmax}_{\theta} \sum_{i=1}^{N} \log \frac{\exp(x_{(i)}\theta)}{\sum_{j \in \mathcal{R}_{(i)}} \exp(x_{(j)}\theta)}. \tag{21.23}$$

5   DURATION TIME SERIES

In this section we focus our attention on duration time series, i.e. sequences of random durations, indexed by their successive numbers in the sequence and possibly featuring temporal dependence. In practice these data are generated, for example, by randomly occurring transactions on credit cards, by claims randomly submitted to insurance agencies at unequal intervals, or by assets traded at a time varying rate on stock markets. According to the traditional time series analysis the ultimate purpose of our study is to model and estimate the dynamics of these stochastic duration processes.

There are two major characteristics which account for the distinct character of duration time series. Unlike the familiar time series data, duration sequences are not indexed by time, but as mentioned earlier, by numbers indicating their position in the sequence. Such indices are necessarily integer valued, and in this respect dynamic durations belong to traditional discrete time series observed at a fixed frequency. Since the duration indices correspond to arrivals of some random events, researchers often employ the notion of an operational time scale with unitary increments set by the event arrivals.

Unlike the duration data discussed earlier in the text, duration time series do not represent patterns exhibited by a sample of individuals over a fixed span of calendar time. For example, in a sample of unemployed people, we may encounter individuals who, during the sampling period, experienced not one, but several unemployment spells. Yet, the study aims at finding the probabilistic structure of durations common to all individuals. At the individual level too few consecutive durations are available for inference on the dynamics, anyway. In contrast, the time series of durations represent times between many outcomes of the same repeated experiment (for example trading a stock), and always concern the same statistical individual (for example the IBM stock).

While the traditional duration analysis is essentially applied to cross section data, the analysis of stock trading dates, claim arrivals, or transactions on a bank account require a time series approach adapted to the specific features of durations. This field of research is quite recent. It originated from a growing interest in quote-by-quote data provided by electronic systems implemented on financial markets and has been developed in parallel to progressing computer capacities allowing for treatment of large data sets. The number of transactions on a particular stock in a stock market concluded during one day may be very large indeed and easily exceed several hundred thousands.

We begin this section with insights into the dynamics of durations in the simple case of the Poisson process. Next we cover some recent developments in this field including the Autoregressive Conditional Duration (ACD) model and the Stochastic Volatility Duration (SVD) model.

5.1   The Poisson process

There exist two alternative ways to study a sequence of event arrivals. First we can consider the sequence of arrival dates or equivalently the sequence of durations

$Y_1, \ldots, Y_n, \ldots$ between consecutive events. Secondly, we can introduce the counting process $[N(t), t$ varying$]$, which counts the number of events observed between 0 and t. The counting process is a jump process, whose jumps of unitary size occur at each arrival date. It is equivalent to know the sequence of durations or the path of the counting process.

The Poisson process is obtained by imposing the following two conditions:

1. The counting process has independent increments, i.e. $N(t_n) - N(t_{n-1})$, $N(t_{n-1}) - N(t_{n-2}), \ldots, N(t_1) - N(t_0)$ are independent for any $t_0 < t_1 < t_2 < \ldots < t_n$, and any n.
2. The rate of arrival of an event (a jump) is constant and two events cannot occur in a small time interval:

$$P[N(t + dt) - N(t) = 1] = \lambda dt + o(dt), \qquad (21.24)$$

$$P[N(t + dt) - N(t) = 0] = 1 - \lambda dt + o(dt), \qquad (21.25)$$

where the term $o(dt)$ is a function of dt such that $\lim_{dt \to 0} o(dt)/dt = 0$.

Under these assumptions it is possible to deduce the distributions of the counting process and of the sequence of durations.

1. For a Poisson process, the durations Y_i, $i = 1, \ldots, n$ are independent, identically exponentially distributed with parameter λ.
2. For a Poisson process, the increments $N(t_2) - N(t_1)$, with $t_2 > t_1$, follow Poisson distributions, with parameters $\lambda(t_2 - t_1)$.

This result explains why basic duration models are based on exponential distributions, whereas basic models for count data are based on Poisson distributions, and how these specifications are related (see Cameron and Trivedi, Chapter 15, in this volume).

Similarly, a more complex dynamics can be obtained by relaxing the assumption that either the successive durations, or the increments of the counting process are independent. In the following subsections we introduce the temporal dependence duration sequences.

5.2 The ACD model

This model was introduced by Engle and Russell (1998) to represent the dynamics of durations between trades on stock or exchange rate markets. Typically, intertrade durations are generated by a computerized order matching system which automatically selects trading partners who satisfy elementary matching criteria. Therefore, the timing of such automatically triggered transactions is a priori unknown and adds a significant element of randomness to the trading process. From the economic point of view, research on intertrade durations is motivated by the relevance of the time varying speed of trading for purposes such as strategic market interventions. Typically the market displays episodes of accelerated activity and slowdowns which reflect the varying *liquidity* of the asset. This concept is similar to the notion of velocity used in monetary macro-economics to describe the rate of money circulation (Gouriéroux, Jasiak, and Le Fol, 1999). In the context of stock markets, periods of intense trading are usually associated with short intertrade durations accompanied by high price volatilities and large traded volumes.

The intertrade durations plotted against time display dynamic patterns similar to stock price volatilities, termed in the literature the *clustering* effect. This means that long durations have a tendency to be followed by long durations, while short durations tend to be followed by short durations. To capture this behavior Engle and Russell (1998) proposed the ACD model. It accommodates the duration clustering in terms of temporal dependence of conditional means of durations. From the time series perspectives it is an analog of the GARCH model representing serial correlation in conditional variances of stock prices (see Engle, 1982) and from the duration analysis point of view it is an accelerated hazard model.

Let N be the number of events observed at random times. The N events are indexed by $i = 1, \ldots, N$ from the first observed event to the last. The ith duration is the time between the ith event and the $(i - 1)$th event. The distribution of the sequence of durations is characterized by the form of the conditional distribution of the duration Y_i given the lagged durations $\underline{Y_{i-1}} = \{Y_{i-1}, Y_{i-2}, \ldots\}$. The ACD(p, q) model is an accelerated hazard model, where the effect of the past is summarized by the conditional expectation $\psi_i = E(Y_i \mid \underline{Y_{i-1}})$:

$$f(y_i \mid \underline{y_{i-1}}) = \frac{1}{\psi_i} f_0\left(\frac{y_i}{\psi_i}\right), \qquad (21.26)$$

where f_0 is a baseline distribution with unitary mean, and the conditional mean ψ_i satisfies:

$$\psi_i = w + \alpha(L)Y_i + \beta(L)\psi_i, \qquad (21.27)$$

where L denotes the lag operator, $\alpha(L) = \alpha_1 L + \alpha_2 L^2 + \ldots + \alpha_q L^q$ and $\beta(L) = \beta_1 L + \beta_2 L^2 + \ldots + \beta_p L^p$ are lag polynomials of degrees p and q respectively. The coefficients $\alpha_j, j = 1, \ldots, q, \beta_j, j = 1, \ldots, p$ are assumed to be nonnegative to ensure the positivity of ψ_i. They are unknown and have to be estimated jointly with the baseline distribution. This specification implies that the effect of past durations on the current conditional expected value decays exponentially with the lag length. Indeed, the ACD(p, q) process may be rewritten as an ARMA(m, p) process in Y_i:

$$[1 - \alpha(L) - \beta(L)]Y_i = w + [1 - \beta(L)]v_i, \qquad (21.28)$$

where $m = \max(p, q)$, and $v_i = Y_i - \psi_i = Y_i - E(Y_i \mid \underline{Y_{i-1}})$ is the innovation of the duration process. The stationarity condition requires that the roots of $[1 - \alpha(L) - \beta(L)]$ and $[1 - \beta(L)]$ lie outside the unit circle, or equivalently since α_j, β_j are nonnegative $(\Sigma_j \alpha_j + \Sigma_j \beta_j) < 1$.

The baseline distribution can be left unspecified or constrained to belong to a parametric family, such as the Weibull family.

The ACD model was a pioneering specification in the domain of duration dynamics. Further research has focused on providing refinements of this model in order to improve the fit. Empirical results show for example that many duration data display autocorrelation functions decaying at a slow, hyperbolic rate. Indeed, the range of temporal dependence in durations may be extremely large suggesting that duration processes possess long memory. This empirical finding is at odds with the exponential decay rate assumed by construction in the ACD model. To accommodate the long persistence, a straightforward improvement consists in accounting for fractional integration in the ACD model (Jasiak, 1999). The corresponding fractionally integrated process is obtained by introducing a fractional differencing operator:

$$\phi(L)(1 - L)^d Y_i = w + [1 - \beta(L)]v_i, \tag{21.29}$$

where the fractional differencing operator $(1 - L)^d$ is defined by its expansion with respect to the lag operator:

$$(1 - L)^d = \sum_{k=0}^{\infty} \Gamma(k - d)\Gamma(k + 1)^{-1}\Gamma(-d)^{-1}L^k = \sum_{k=0}^{\infty} \pi_k L^k, \quad \text{say,} \tag{21.30}$$

where Γ denotes the gamma function and $0 < d < 1$.

Although this extension successfully captures serial correlation at long lags, it fails to solve the major drawback of the basic ACD model, which consists of tying together the movements of conditional mean and conditional variance by supposing that $E(Y_t | Y_{t-1}, Y_{t-2} \ldots) = \psi_t$ and $V(Y_t | Y_{t-1}, Y_{t-2} \ldots) = k_0\psi_t^2$, where the value k_0 depends on the baseline distribution. We see that even though overdispersion arises whenever $k_0 > 1$, its magnitude is supposed to be path independent. This is a stringent assumption which in practice is often violated by the data. Empirical results based on intertrade durations on stock markets suggest on the contrary, the presence of path dependent (under)overdispersion as well as the existence of distinct dynamic patterns of the conditional mean and dispersion. As an illustration we display in Figure 21.5 a scatterplot of squared means and variances of intertrade durations of the Alcatel stock traded on the Paris bourse. We observe that the cluster is relatively dispersed with a significant number of observations featuring (conditional) underdispersion. Therefore, the data provide evidence supporting the co-existence of (conditional) under- and overdispersion, generating marginal overdispersion.

5.3 The SVD model

This model represents dynamics of both the conditional mean and variance in duration data. In this way it allows for the presence of both conditional under- and overdispersion in the data. Technically, it shares some similarities with the stochastic volatility models used in finance. The main difference in SVD

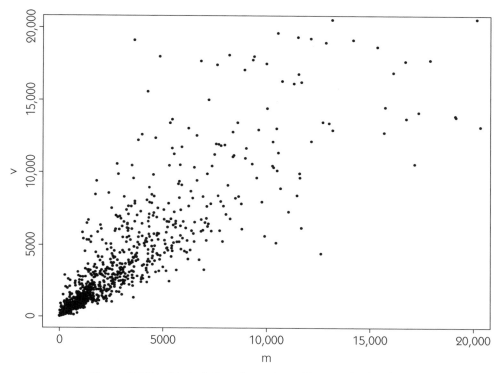

Figure 21.5 (Under) Overdispersion of intertrade durations

specification compared to ACD is that it relies on two latent factor variables which are assumed to follow autoregressive stochastic processes. Note that despite the fact that the conditional variance in the ACD model is stochastic it is entirely determined by past durations. The introduction of additional random terms enhances the structure of the model and improves significantly the fit. On the other hand it makes the model more complicated and requires more advanced estimation techniques.

The approach is based on an extension of the exponential duration model with gamma heterogeneity. In this model the duration variable Y is exponentially distributed with the pdf : $\lambda\exp(-\lambda y)$, conditional on the hazard rate λ. Therefore, the duration variable may be written as:

$$Y = U/\lambda, \tag{21.31}$$

where $U \sim \gamma(1, 1)$. The hazard rate depends on some heterogeneity component V:

$$\lambda = aV, \tag{21.32}$$

where $V \sim \gamma(b, b)$ is independent of U. The marginal distribution of this heterogeneity component is such that: $EV = 1$ and $\mathrm{Var}(V) = 1/b$, while the parameter a is a positive real number equal to the expected hazard rate.

Equations (21.31) and (21.32) yield the exponential model with gamma heterogeneity, namely:

$$Y = \frac{U}{aV},\tag{21.33}$$

where U, V are independent, $U \sim \gamma(1, 1)$ and $V \sim \gamma(b, b)$. This equation may be considered as a two factor model formula, where Y is a function of U and V. Some suitable nonlinear transformations can yield normally distributed factors. More explicitly, we get:

$$Y = \frac{G(1, \Phi(F_1))}{aG(b, \Phi(F_2))} = \frac{H(1, F_1)}{aH(b, F_2)},\tag{21.34}$$

where F_1, F_2 are iid standard normal variables, Φ is the cdf of the standard normal distribution and $G(b, .)$ the quantile function of the $\gamma(b, b)$ distribution. We have: $H(1, F_1) = -\log[1 - \Phi(F_1)]$. On the contrary, the function $H(b, F_2)$ has no simple analytical expression in the general case, but admits a simple approximation in the neighborhood of the homogeneity hypothesis; namely if $b \approx \infty$: $H(b, F_2) \approx 1 + (1/\sqrt{b})F_2 \approx \exp(F_2/\sqrt{b})$, where the latter follows by the Central Limit Theorem.

The dynamics is introduced into the model through the two underlying Gaussian factors which follow a bivariate VAR process $F_t = (F_{1t}, F_{2t})'$, where the marginal distribution of F_t is constrained to be $N(0, Id)$ to ensure that the marginal distribution of durations belongs to the class of exponential distributions with gamma heterogeneity.

This approach yields the class of Stochastic Volatility Duration (SVD) models (Ghysels, Gouriéroux, and Jasiak, 1997). They are defined by the following specification:

$$Y_t = \frac{1}{a}\frac{H(1, F_{1t})}{H(b, F_{2t})} = \frac{1}{a}\bar{H}(b, F_t), \quad \text{(say)}\tag{21.35}$$

where

$$F_t = \sum_{j=1}^{p} \Psi_j F_{t-j} + \varepsilon_t,\tag{21.36}$$

and ε_t is a Gaussian white noise random variable with variance–covariance matrix $\Sigma(\Psi)$ such that $\text{Var}(F_t) = Id$.

References

Cox, D.R. (1975). Partial likelihood. *Biometrika* 62, 269–76.
Cox, D.R., and D. Oakes (1984). Analysis of survival data. Chapman and Hall.
Engle, R.F. (1982). Autoregressive conditional heteroskedasticity with estimates of the variance of United Kingdom inflation. *Econometrica* 50, 987–1007.

Engle, R., and J.R. Russell (1998). The autoregressive conditional duration model. *Econometrica* 66, 1127–63.

Ghysels, E., C. Gouriéroux, and J. Jasiak (1997). The stochastic volatility duration model. D.P. CREST.

Gouriéroux, C. (1989). Econometrie des variables qualitatives. *Economica*.

Gouriéroux, C., J. Jasiak, and G. Le Fol (1999). Intra-day market activity. *Journal of Financial Markets* 2:3, 193–226.

Heckman, J. (1981). Heterogeneity and state dependence. In S. Rosen (ed.) *Studies in Labor Markets*. University of Chicago Press.

Heckman, J., and B. Singer (1974). Econometric duration analysis. *Journal of Econometrics* 24, 63–132.

Heckman, J., and B. Singer (1984). The identifiability of the proportional hazard model. *Review of Economic Studies* 231–45.

Jasiak, J. (1999). Persistence in intertrade durations. *Finance* 19, 166–95.

Kalbfleisch, J., and R. Prentice (1980). *The Statistical Analysis of Failure Time Data*. Wiley.

Lancaster, T. (1985). Generalized residuals and heterogenous duration models, with application to the Weibull model. *Journal of Econometrics* 28, 155–69.

Lancaster, T. (1990). *The Econometric Analysis of Transition Data*. Cambridge: Cambridge University Press.

Lee, L. (1981). Maximum likelihood estimation and specification test for normal distributional assumption for accelerated failure time models. *Journal of Econometrics* 24, 159–79.

Simulation Based Inference for Dynamic Multinomial Choice Models

John Geweke, Daniel Houser,
and Michael Keane

1 Introduction

Over the last decade econometric inference based on simulation techniques has become increasingly common, particularly for latent variable models. The reason is that such models often generate econometric objective functions that embed high-order integrals, and which, consequently, can be most easily evaluated using simulation techniques.[1] There are several well known classical techniques for inference by simulation. Perhaps most common are the Method of Simulated Moments (McFadden, 1989) and Simulated Maximum Likelihood or SML (Lerman and Manski, 1981). In practice, both methods require that reasonably accurate simulators be used to evaluate the integrals that enter the objective function (see Geweke, Keane, and Runkle, 1994). Bayesian techniques are also becoming quite popular. These techniques typically entail Markov Chain Monte Carlo (MCMC) simulation to evaluate the integrals that define the posterior densities of a model's parameters (see Geweke and Keane (1999b) for an overview of MCMC methods).

Our goal in this chapter is to explain concretely how to implement simulation methods in a very general class of models that are extremely useful in applied work: dynamic discrete choice models where one has available a panel of multinomial choice histories and partially observed payoffs. Many general surveys of simulation methods are now available (see Geweke, 1996; Monfort, Van Dijk, and Brown, 1995; and Gilks, Richardson, and Spiegelhalter, 1996), so in our view a detailed illustration of how to implement such methods in a specific case has greater marginal value than an additional broad survey. Moreover, the techniques we describe are directly applicable to a general class of models that includes static discrete choice models, the Heckman (1976) selection model, and all of the Heckman (1981) models (such as static and dynamic Bernoulli models, Markov models, and renewal processes). The particular procedure that we describe derives from a suggestion by Geweke and Keane (1999a), and has the advantages that it does not require the econometrician to solve the agents' dynamic optimization problem, or to make strong assumptions about the way individuals form expectations.

This chapter focuses on Bayesian inference for dynamic multinomial choice models via the MCMC method. Originally, we also hoped to discuss classical estimation of such models, so that readers could compare the two approaches. But, when we attempted to estimate the model developed below using SML it proved infeasible. The high dimension of the parameter vector caused an iterative search for the maximum of the simulated likelihood function via standard gradient based methods to fail rather dismally. In fact, unless the initial parameter values were set very close to the true values, the search algorithm would quickly stall. In contrast, the MCMC procedure was computationally feasible and robust to initial conditions. We concluded that Bayesian inference via MCMC has an important advantage over SML for high dimensional problems because it does not require a search for the optimum of the likelihood.

We consider dynamic, stochastic, parametric models with intertemporally additively separable preferences and a finite time horizon. Suppose that in each period $t = 1, \ldots, T$ $(T < \infty)$ each agent chooses among a finite set A_t of mutually exclusive alternatives. Let $\Re^{k_t}$ be the date-t state space, where k_t is a positive integer. Choosing alternative $a_t \in A_t$ in state $I_t \in \Re^{k_t}$ leads to period payoff $R(I_t, a_t; \theta)$, where θ is a finite-vector denoting the model's structural parameters.

The value to choosing alternative a_t in state I_t, denoted by $V_t(I_t, a_t)$, depends on the period payoff and on the way agents expect that choice to affect future payoffs. For instance, in the familiar case when agents have rational expectations, alternative specific values can be expressed:

$$V_t(I_t, a_t) = R(I_t, a_t; \theta) + \delta E_t \max_{a_{t+1} \in A_{t+1}} V_{t+1}(I_{t+1}, a_{t+1} \mid I_t, a_t) \ (t = 1, \ldots, T) \quad (22.1)$$

$$V_{T+1}(\cdot) \equiv 0 \quad (22.2)$$

$$I_{t+1} = H(I_t, a_t; \theta) \quad (22.3)$$

where δ is the constant rate of time preference, $H(I_t, a_t; \theta)$ is a stochastic law of motion that provides an intertemporal link between choices and states, and E_t is the date-t mathematical expectations operator so that expectations are taken with respect to the true distribution of the state variables $P_H(I_{t+1} \mid I_t, a_t; \theta)$ as generated by $H(\cdot)$. Individuals choose alternative a_t^* if and only if $V_t(I_t, a_t^*) > V_t(I_t, a_t)\ \forall a_t \in A_t,\ a_t,\ \neq a_t^*$. See Eckstein and Wolpin (1989) for a description of many alternative structural models that fit into this framework.

The econometrician is interested in drawing inferences about θ, the vector of structural parameters. One econometric procedure to accomplish this (see Rust, 1987 or Wolpin, 1984) requires using dynamic programming to solve system (22.1)–(22.3) at many trial parameter vectors. At each parameter vector, the solution to the system is used as input to evaluate a prespecified econometric objective function. The parameter space is systematically searched until a vector that "optimizes" the objective function is found. A potential drawback of this procedure is that, in general, solving system (22.1)–(22.3) with dynamic programming is extremely computationally burdensome. The reason is that the mathematical expectations that appear on the right-hand side of (22.1) are often impossible to compute analytically, and very time consuming to approximate well numerically. Hence, as a practical matter, this estimation procedure is useful only under very special circumstances (for instance, when there are a small number of state variables). Consequently, a literature has arisen that suggests alternative approaches to inference in dynamic multinomial choice models.

Some recently developed techniques for estimation of the system (22.1)–(22.3) focus on circumventing the need for dynamic programming. Several good surveys of this literature already exist, and we will not attempt one here (see Rust, 1994). Instead, we simply note that the idea underlying the more well known of these approaches, i.e., Hotz and Miller (1993) and Manski (1993), is to use choice and payoff data to draw inferences about the values of the expectations on the right-hand side of (22.1). A key limitation of these procedures is that, in order to learn about expectations, each requires the data to satisfy a strict form of stationarity in order to rule out cohort effects.

The technique proposed by Geweke and Keane (1999a) for structural inference in dynamic multinomial choice models also circumvents the need for dynamic programming. A unique advantage of their method is that it does not require the econometrician to make strong assumptions about the way people form expectations. Moreover, their procedure is not hampered by strong data requirements. It can be implemented when the data include only partially observed payoffs from a single cohort of agents observed over only part of their lifecycle.

To develop the Geweke–Keane approach, it is useful to express the value function (22.1) as:

$$V_t(I_t, a_t) = R(I_t, a_t; \theta) + F^H(I_t, a_t), \tag{22.4}$$

where $F^H(I_t, a_t) \equiv \delta E_t \max_{a_{t+1} \in A_{t+1}} V_{t+1}(a_{t+1}, H(I_t, a_t))$. Geweke and Keane (1999a) observed that the definition of $F^H(\cdot)$, henceforth referred to as the "future component", makes sense independent of the meaning of E_t. If, as assumed above, E_t is the mathematical expectations operator then $F^H(\cdot)$ is the rational expectations future component. On the other hand, if E_t is the zero operator, then future payoffs do not enter the individuals' decision rules, and $F^H(\cdot)$ is identically zero. In general, the functional form of the future component $F^H(\cdot)$ will vary with the way people form expectations. Unfortunately, in most circumstances the way people form expectations is unknown. Accordingly, the correct specification of the future component $F^H(\cdot)$ is also unknown.

There are, therefore, two important reasons why an econometrician may prefer not to impose strong assumptions about the way people form expectations, or, equivalently, on the admissible forms of the future component. First, such assumptions may lead to an intractable econometric model. Second, the econometrician may see some advantage to taking a less dogmatic stance with respect to behaviors about which very little, if any, a priori information is available.

When the econometrician is either unwilling or unable to make strong assumptions about the way people form expectations, Geweke and Keane (1999a) suggest that the future component $F^H(\cdot)$ be represented by a parameterized flexible functional form such as a high-order polynomial. The resulting value function can be written

$$V_t(I_t, a_t) = R(I_t, a_t; \theta) + F^H(I_t, a_t \mid \pi) \tag{22.5}$$

where π is a vector of polynomial coefficients that characterize expectation formation. Given functional forms for the contemporaneous payoff functions, and under the condition that θ and π are jointly identified, it is possible to draw inferences both about the parameters of the payoff functions and the structure of expectations.

This chapter focuses on an important case in which key structural and expectations parameters are jointly identified. We consider a model where an alternative's payoff is partially observed if and only if that alternative is chosen. In this case, after substitution of a flexible polynomial function for the future component as in (22.5), the model takes on a form similar to a static Roy (1951) model augmented to include influences on choice other than the current payoffs, as in Heckman and Sedlacek (1986). The key difference is that $F^H(\cdot)$ incorporates overidentifying restrictions on the non-payoff component of the value function that are implied by (22.1)–(22.3) and that are not typically invoked in the estimation of static selection models. Specifically, the parameters of the non-payoff component of the value function are constant across alternatives, and the arguments of the non-payoff component vary in a systematic way across alternatives that is determined by the law of motion $H(\cdot)$ for the state variables.

The structural model (22.1)–(22.3) also implies restrictions on the nature of the future component's arguments. For instance, if $H(\cdot)$ and $R(\cdot)$ jointly imply that the model's payoffs are path-independent, then the future component should be specified so that path-dependent expectation formation is ruled out.[2] Similarly, contemporaneous realizations of serially independent stochastic variables contain no information relevant for forecasting future outcomes, so they should not enter the arguments of the flexible functional form. Without such coherency conditions one might obtain results inconsistent with the logic of the model's specification.

A finite order polynomial will in general provide only an approximation to the true future component. Hence, it is important to investigate the extent to which misspecification of the future component may affect inference for the model's structural parameters. Below we report the outcome of some Monte Carlo experiments that shed light on this issue. The experiments are conducted under both correctly and incorrectly specified future components. We find that the Geweke–Keane approach performs extremely well when $F^H(\cdot)$ is correctly specified, and still very well under a misspecified future component. In particular, we find that assuming the future component is a polynomial when it is actually generated by rational expectations leads to only "second order" difficulties in two senses. First, it has a small effect on inferences with regard to the structural parameters of the payoff functions.[3] Second, the decision rules inferred from the data in the misspecified model are very close to the optimal rule in the sense that agents using the suboptimal rule incur "small" lifetime payoff losses.

The remainder of this chapter is organized as follows. Section 2 describes the application, and Section 3 details the Gibbs sampling algorithm. Section 4 reviews our experimental design and results, and Section 5 concludes.

2   The Dynamic Multinomial Choice Model

In this section we present an example of Bayesian inference for dynamic discrete choice models using the Geweke–Keane method of replacing the future component of the value function with a flexible polynomial function. The discussion is based on a model that is very similar to ones analyzed by Keane and Wolpin (1994, 1997).

In the model we consider, $i = 1, \ldots, N$ agents choose among $j = 1, \ldots, 4$ mutually exclusive alternatives in each of $t = 1, \ldots, 40$ periods. One can think of the first two alternatives as work in one of two occupations, the third as attending school and the fourth alternative as remaining at home. One component of the current period payoff in each of the two occupational alternatives is the associated wage, w_{ijt} ($j = 1, 2$). The log-wage equation is:

$$\ln w_{ijt} = \beta_{0j} + \beta_{1j} X_{i1t} + \beta_{2j} X_{i2t} + \beta_{3j} S_{it} + \beta_{4j} X_{ijt}^2 + \varepsilon_{ijt} \quad (j = 1, 2)$$

$$= Y'_{ijt} \beta_j + \varepsilon_{ijt} \quad (j = 1, 2), \tag{22.6}$$

where Y_{ijt} is the obvious vector, $\beta_j = (\beta_{0j}, \ldots, \beta_{4j})'$, S_{it} is the periods of school completed, $(X_{ijt})_{j=1,2}$ is the periods of experience in each occupation j, and the ε_{ijt} are serially independent productivity shocks, with $(\varepsilon_{i1t}, \varepsilon_{i2t})' \sim N(0, \Sigma_\varepsilon)$. Each occupational alternative also has a stochastic nonpecuniary payoff, v_{ijt}, so the complete current period payoffs are

$$u_{ijt} = w_{ijt} + v_{ijt} \quad (j = 1, 2). \tag{22.7}$$

The schooling payoffs include tuition costs. Agents begin with a tenth-grade education, and may complete two additional grades without cost. We assume there is a fixed undergraduate tuition rate α_1 for attending grades 13 through 16, and a fixed graduate tuition rate α_2 for each year of schooling beyond 16. We assume a "return to school" cost α_3 that agents face if they did not choose school the previous period. Finally, school has a nonstochastic, nonpecuniary benefit α_0 and a mean zero stochastic nonpecuniary payoff v_{i3t}. Thus we have

$$u_{i3t} = \alpha_0 + \alpha_1\chi(12 \leq S_{it} \leq 15) + \alpha_2\chi(S_{it} \geq 16) + \alpha_3\chi(d_{i,t-1} \neq 3) + v_{i3t} \equiv \Lambda_{it}\alpha + v_{i3t}, \tag{22.8}$$

where χ is an indicator function that takes value one if the stated condition is true and is zero otherwise, Λ_{it} is a vector of zeros and ones corresponding to the values of the indicator functions, $\alpha = (\alpha_0, \ldots, \alpha_3)'$, $d_{it} \in \{1, 2, 3, 4\}$ denotes the choice of i at t. Lastly, we assume that option four, home, has both a nonstochastic nonpecuniary payoff ϕ and a stochastic nonpecuniary payoff v_{ijt}, so

$$u_{i4t} = \phi + v_{i4t}. \tag{22.9}$$

We will set $u_{ijt} = \bar{u}_{ijt} + v_{ijt}$, $(j = 1, \ldots, 4)$. The nonpecuniary payoffs $(v_{ijt})_{j=1,4}$ are assumed serially independent.

The state of the agent at the time of each decision is

$$I_{it} = \{(X_{ijt})_{j=1,2}, S_{it}, t, d_{i,t-1}, (\varepsilon_{ijt})_{j=1,2}, (v_{ijt})_{j=1,\ldots4}\}. \tag{22.10}$$

We assume $d_{i0} = 3$. The laws of motion for experience in the occupational alternatives and school are: $X_{ij,t+1} = X_{ijt} + \chi(d_{it} = j)$, $j = 1, 2$, $S_{i,t+1} = S_{it} + \chi(d_{it} = 3)$. The number of "home" choices is excluded from the state-space as it is linearly dependent on the level of education, the period, and experience in the two occupations.

It is convenient to have notation for the elements of the state vector whose value in period $t + 1$ depends nontrivially on their value in period t or on the current choice. The reason, as we note below, is that these elements are the natural arguments of the future component. We define

$$I_{it}^* = \{(X_{ijt})_{j=1,2}, S_{it}, t, d_{i,t-1}\}.$$

The value of each alternative is the sum of its current period payoff, the stochastic nonpecuniary payoff and the future component:

$$V_{ijt}(I_{it}) = \bar{u}_{ijt}(I_{it}) + v_{ijt} + F(X_{i1t} + \chi(j = 1), X_{i2t} + \chi(j = 2),$$
$$S_{it} + \chi(j = 3), t + 1, \chi(j = 3)) \ (j = 1, \ldots 4) \ (t = 1, \ldots, 40)$$
$$\equiv \bar{u}_{ijt}(I_{it}) + v_{ijt} + F(I_{it}^*, j) \tag{22.11}$$

The function F represents agents' forecasts about the effects of their current state and choice on their future payoff stream. The function is fixed across alternatives, implying that forecasts vary across alternatives only because different choices lead to different future states, and it depends only on the choice and the state variables in I_{t+1}^*.[4]

Since choices depend only on relative alternative values, rather than their levels, we define for $j \in \{1, 2, 3\}$:

$$Z_{ijt} \equiv V_{ijt} - V_{i4t}$$

$$= \bar{u}_{ijt} + v_{ijt} + F(I^*_{it}, j) - \bar{u}_{i4t} - v_{i4t} - F(I^*_{it}, 4)$$

$$= \tilde{u}_{ijt} + f(I^*_{it}, j) + \eta_{ijt}, \tag{22.12}$$

where $\tilde{u}_{ijt} \equiv \bar{u}_{ijt} - \bar{u}_{i4t}$, $\{\eta_{ijt}\}_{j=1,2,3} \equiv (v_{ijt} - v_{i4t})_{j=1,2,3} \sim N(0, \Sigma_\eta)$ and $f(I^*_{it}, j) = F(I^*_{it}, j) - F(I^*_{it}, 4)$. Importantly, after differencing, the value ϕ of the home payoff is subsumed in f the relative future component. Clearly, if an alternative's future component has an intercept (as each of ours does) then it and the period return to home cannot be separately identified.

The value function differences Z_{it} are latent variables unobserved by the econometrician. The econometrician only observes the agents' choices $\{d_{it}\}$ for t = 1, ... , 40, and, in the periods when the agent works, the wage for the chosen alternative. Thus, payoffs are never completely observed, both because wages are censored and because the nonpecuniary components of the payoffs (v_{ijt}) are never observed. Nevertheless, given observed choices and partially observed wages, along with the functional form assumptions about the payoff functions, it is possible to learn both about the future component $F(\cdot)$ and the structural parameters of the payoff functions without making strong assumptions about how agents form expectations. Rather, we simply assume that the future component lies along a fourth-order polynomial in the state variables. After differencing to obtain $\{f(I^*_{it}, j)\}_{j=1,2,3}$, the polynomial contained 53 terms of order three and lower (see Appendix A). We express the future component as

$$f(I^*_{it}, j) = \psi'_{ijt}\pi \quad (j = 1, 2, 3), \tag{22.13}$$

where ψ_{ijt} is a vector of functions of state-variables that appear in the equation for $f(I^*_{it}, j)$ and π is a vector of coefficients common to each choice. Cross-equation restrictions of this type are a consequence of using the same future component function F for each alternative and reflect the consistency restrictions discussed earlier.

3 Implementing the Gibbs Sampling Algorithm

Bayesian analysis of this model entails deriving the joint posterior distribution of the model's parameters and unobserved variables. Recall that the value function differences $Z = \{(Z_{ijt})_{j=1,2,3;i=1,N;t=1,40}\}$ are never observed, and that wages $W = \{(w_{ijt})_{j=1,2,3;i=1,N;t=1,40}\}$ are only partially observed. Let W_1 and W_2 denote the set of observed and unobserved wages, respectively, and let $Y = \{Y_{ijt}\}_{i=1,N;j=1,2;t=1,40}$ denote the log-wage equation regressors. Then the joint posterior density is $p(W_2, Z, \beta_1, \beta_2, \alpha, \pi, \Sigma_\varepsilon^{-1}, \Sigma_\eta^{-1} \mid W_1, Y, \Lambda)$. By Bayes' law, this density is proportional to

$$p(W, Z \mid Y, \Lambda, \psi, \beta_1, \beta_2, \alpha, \pi, \Sigma_\varepsilon^{-1}, \Sigma_\eta^{-1}) \cdot p(\beta_1, \beta_2, \alpha, \pi, \Sigma_\varepsilon^{-1}, \Sigma_\eta^{-1}). \tag{22.14}$$

The first term in (22.14) is the so-called "complete data" likelihood function. It is the likelihood function that could be formed in the hypothetical case that we had data on N individuals observed over 40 periods each, and we observed all of the value function differences Z and the complete set of wages W for all alternatives. This is:

$$p(W, Z \mid Y, \Lambda, \psi, \beta_1, \beta_2, \alpha, \pi, \Sigma_\varepsilon^{-1}, \Sigma_\eta^{-1}) \propto$$

$$\prod_{i,t} |\Sigma_\varepsilon^{-1}|^{1/2} (w_{i1t} w_{i2t})^{-1} \exp\left\{ -\frac{1}{2} \begin{pmatrix} \ln w_{i1t} - Y'_{i1t}\beta_1 \\ \ln w_{i2t} - Y'_{i2t}\beta_2 \end{pmatrix} \Sigma_\varepsilon^{-1} \begin{pmatrix} \ln w_{i1t} - Y'_{i1t}\beta_1 \\ \ln w_{i2t} - Y'_{i2t}\beta_2 \end{pmatrix} \right\}$$

$$\cdot |\Sigma_\eta^{-1}|^{1/2} \exp\left\{ -\frac{1}{2} \begin{pmatrix} Z_{i1t} - w_{i1t} - \Psi'_{i1t}\pi \\ Z_{i2t} - w_{i2t} - \Psi'_{i2t}\pi \\ Z_{i3t} - \Lambda'_{it}\alpha - \Psi'_{i3t}\pi \end{pmatrix} \Sigma_\eta^{-1} \begin{pmatrix} Z_{i1t} - w_{i1t} - \Psi'_{i1t}\pi \\ Z_{i2t} - w_{i2t} - \Psi'_{i2t}\pi \\ Z_{i3t} - \Lambda'_{it}\alpha - \Psi'_{i3t}\pi \end{pmatrix} \right\}$$

$$\cdot \chi(Z_{ijt} > 0, Z_{ikt}(k \neq j) < 0 \text{ if } d_{it} = j \text{ and } j \in \{1, 2, 3\}, \{Z_{ijt}\}_{j=1,2,3} < 0 \text{ otherwise)}$$

$$(22.15)$$

The second term in (22.15) is the joint prior distribution. We assume flat priors on all parameters except the two precision matrices, for which we assume the standard noninformative priors (see Zellner, 1971, section 8.1):

$$p(\Sigma_\varepsilon^{-1}) \propto |\Sigma_\varepsilon^{-1}|^{-3/2}, \; p(\Sigma_\eta^{-1}) \propto |\Sigma_\varepsilon^{-1}|^{-2} \qquad (22.16)$$

The Gibbs sampler draws from a density that is proportional to the product of (22.15) and the two densities in (22.16).

The Gibbs sampling algorithm is used to form numerical approximations of the parameters' marginal posterior distributions. It is not feasible to construct these marginal posteriors analytically, since doing so requires high dimensional integrations over unobserved wages and value function differences. Implementing the Gibbs sampling algorithm requires us to factor the joint posterior defined by (22.14)–(22.16) into a set of conditional posterior densities, in such a way that each can be drawn from easily. Then, we cycle through these conditionals, drawing a block of parameters from each in turn. As the number of cycles grows large, the parameter draws so obtained converge in distribution to their respective marginal posteriors, given certain mild regularity conditions (see Tierney (1994) for a discussion of these conditions). An important condition is that the posterior distribution be finitely integrable, which we verify for this model in Appendix B. Given the posterior distribution of the parameters, conditional on the data, the investigator can draw exact finite sample inferences.

Our Gibbs sampling-data augmentation algorithm consists of six steps or "blocks." These steps, which we now briefly describe, are cycled through repeatedly until convergence is achieved.

Step 1. Draw value function differences $\{Z_{ijt}, i = 1, N; j = 1, 3; t = 1, 40\}$
Step 2. Draw unobserved wages $\{w_{ijt} \text{ when } d_{it} \neq j, (j = 1, 2)\}$

Step 3. Draw the log-wage equation coefficients β_j.
Step 4. Draw the log-wage equation error-covariance matrix Σ_ε.
Step 5. Draw the parameters of the future component π and school payoff parameters α.
Step 6. Draw the nonpecuniary payoff covariance matrix Σ_η.

Step 1

We chose to draw the $\{Z_{ijt}, i = 1, N; j = 1, 3; t = 1, 40\}$ one by one. Taking everything else in the model as given, it is evident from (22.14)–(22.16) that the conditional distribution of a single Z_{ijt} is truncated Gaussian. Dealing with the truncation is straightforward. There are three ways in which the Gaussian distribution might be truncated.

Case 1: Z_{ijt} is the value function difference for the chosen alternative. Thus, we draw $Z_{ijt} > \max\left\{0, (Z_{ikt})_{\substack{k\in\{1,2,3\} \\ k\neq j}}\right\}$.
Case 2: Z_{ijt} is not associated with the chosen alternative, and "home" was not chosen. Thus, we draw $Z_{ijt} < Z_{id_{it}t}$.
Case 3: "Home" was chosen. In this case, we draw $Z_{ijt} < 0$.

We draw from the appropriate univariate, truncated Gaussian distributions using standard inverse CDF methods.

Step 2

We chose to draw the unobserved wages $\{w_{ijt}$ when $d_{it} \neq j, (j = 1, 2, 3)\}$ one by one. Suppose w_{i1t} is unobserved. Its density, conditional on every other wage, future component difference and parameter being known, is from (22.14), (22.15) and (22.16) evidently given by:

$$g(w_{i1t}|\cdot) \propto \frac{1}{w_{i1t}}\exp\left\{-\frac{1}{2}\begin{pmatrix} \ln w_{i1t} - Y'_{i1t}\beta_1 \\ \ln w_{i2t} - Y'_{i2t}\beta_2 \end{pmatrix}\Sigma_\varepsilon^{-1}\begin{pmatrix} \ln w_{i1t} - Y'_{i1t}\beta_1 \\ \ln w_{i2t} - Y'_{i2t}\beta_2 \end{pmatrix}\right\}$$

$$\exp\left\{-\frac{1}{2}\begin{pmatrix} Z_{i1t} - w_{i1t} - \Psi'_{i1t}\pi \\ Z_{i2t} - w_{i2t} - \Psi'_{i2t}\pi \\ Z_{i3t} - \Lambda'_{it}\alpha - \Psi'_{i3t}\pi \end{pmatrix}'\Sigma_\eta^{-1}\begin{pmatrix} Z_{i1t} - w_{i1t} - \Psi'_{i1t}\pi \\ Z_{i2t} - w_{i2t} - \Psi'_{i2t}\pi \\ Z_{i3t} - \Lambda'_{it}\alpha - \Psi'_{i3t}\pi \end{pmatrix}\right\}. \qquad (22.17)$$

This distribution is nonstandard as wages enter in both logs and levels. Nevertheless, it is straightforward to sample from this distribution using rejection methods (see Geweke (1995) for a discussion of efficient rejection sampling). In brief, we first drew a candidate wage w^c from the distribution implied by the first exponential of (22.17), so that $\ln w^c \sim N(Y'_{i1t}\beta_1 + \lambda_{it}, \sigma_*^2)$, where $\lambda_{it} \equiv \Sigma_\varepsilon(1, 2)\varepsilon_{i2t}/\Sigma(2, 2)$ and $\sigma_*^2 \equiv \Sigma_\varepsilon(1, 1)(1 - (\Sigma_\varepsilon(1, 2)))^2/(\Sigma_\varepsilon(1, 1)\Sigma_\varepsilon(2, 2))$. This draw is easily accomplished, and w^c is found by exponentiating. The probability with which this draw is accepted is found by dividing the second exponential in

(22.17) by its conditional maximum over w_{i1t} and evaluating the resulting expression at $w_{i1t} = w^c$. If the draw is accepted then the unobserved w_{i1t} is set to w^c. Otherwise, the process is repeated until a draw is accepted.

STEP 3

Given all wages, value function differences, and other parameters, the density of (β_1, β_2) is:

$$g(\beta_1, \beta_2) \propto \exp\left\{-\frac{1}{2}\begin{pmatrix} \ln w_{i1t} - Y'_{i1t}\beta_1 \\ \ln w_{i2t} - Y'_{i2t}\beta_2 \end{pmatrix}' \Sigma_{\varepsilon}^{-1} \begin{pmatrix} \ln w_{i1t} - Y'_{i1t}\beta_1 \\ \ln w_{i2t} - Y'_{i2t}\beta_2 \end{pmatrix}\right\}. \qquad (22.18)$$

So that (β_1, β_2) is distributed according to a multivariate normal. In particular, it is easy to show that

$$\beta \sim N[(Y'\Sigma^{-1}Y)^{-1}Y'\Sigma^{-1} \ln W, (Y'\Sigma^{-1}Y)^{-1}],$$

where $\beta \equiv (\beta'_1, \beta'_2)'$, $\Sigma = \Sigma_{\varepsilon} \otimes I_{NT}$, $Y = \begin{bmatrix} Y_1 & 0 \\ 0 & Y_2 \end{bmatrix}$ and $\ln W = [\ln W'_1, \ln W'_2]'$, where Y_1 is the regressor matrix for the first log-wage equation naturally ordered through all individuals and periods, and similarly for Y_2, W_1 and W_2. It is straightforward to draw β from this multivariate normal density.

STEP 4

With everything else known $\Sigma_{\varepsilon}^{-1}$ has a Wishart distribution. Specifically, it is immediate from the joint posterior that $p(\Sigma_{\varepsilon}^{-1}) \propto |\Sigma_{\varepsilon}^{-1}|^{\frac{NT-3}{2}}\exp\{-\frac{1}{2}tr(S(\beta)\Sigma_{\varepsilon}^{-1})\}$, so that

$$\Sigma_{\varepsilon}^{-1} \sim W(S(\beta), NT),$$

where $S(\beta) = (\ln W_1 - Y_1\beta_1, \ln W_2 - Y_2\beta_2)'(\ln W_1 - Y_1\beta_1, \ln W_2 - Y_2\beta_2)$.
                                                                                    (22.19)

It is easy to draw from the Wishart and then invert the 2×2 matrix to obtain Σ_{ε}.

STEP 5

It is convenient to draw both the future component π parameters and the parameters α of the school payoff jointly. Since the future component for school contains an intercept, it and the constant in Λ cannot be separately identified. Hence, we omit α_0 as well as the first row from each Λ_{it}. Define the vector $\pi^* \equiv [\pi', \alpha']'$, where $\alpha = (\alpha_1, \alpha_2, \alpha_3)'$ and define $\Psi^*_{ijt} \equiv [\Psi'_{ijt}, 0'_3]'$ $(j = 1, 2)$, and $\Psi^*_{i3t} = [\Psi'_{i3t}, \Lambda'_{it}]'$. Note that π^* and the Ψ^*_{ijt} are 56-vectors. Then define $\Psi_k = [\Psi^*_{1k1} \ \Psi^*_{1k2} \ldots \Psi^*_{Nk,T-1}$ $\Psi^*_{NkT}]$, and set $\Psi = [\Psi_1 \ \Psi_2 \ \Psi_3]'$, so that Ψ is a $(3 \cdot NT \times 56)$ stacked-regressor matrix. Similarly, define the corresponding $3 \cdot NT$-vector Γ by $\Gamma = (\{Z_{i1t} - w_{i1t}\}'_{i,t},$ $\{Z_{i2t} - w_{i2t}\}'_{i,t}, \{Z_{i3t}\}'_{i,t})'$. It is immediate from (22.15), in which π^* enters only through the second exponential expressions that, conditional on everything else known, π^* has a multivariate normal density given by:

$$\pi^* \sim N[(\Psi'\Omega^{-1}\Psi)^{-1}\Psi'\Omega^{-1}\Gamma, (\Psi'\Omega^{-1}\Psi)^{-1}] \qquad (22.20)$$

where $\Omega = \Sigma_\eta \otimes I_{NT}$. We draw from this using a standard, multivariate normal random number generator.

STEP 6

With everything else known the distribution of Σ_η^{-1} is Wishart; $\Sigma_\eta^{-1} \sim W(SST_\eta, NT)$, where $SST_\eta = \Sigma_{i,t}(\eta_{i1t}\ \eta_{i2t}\ \eta_{i3t})'(\eta_{i1t}\ \eta_{i2t}\ \eta_{i3t})$, and with the η_{ijt} defined by (22.12). It is easy to draw from this distribution and then invert the 3×3 matrix to obtain Σ_η.

4   EXPERIMENTAL DESIGN AND RESULTS

This section details the design and results of a Monte Carlo experiment that we conducted to shed light on the performance of the Gibbs sampling algorithm discussed in Section 2. We generated data according to equations (22.6)–(22.12) using the true parameter values that are listed in column two of Table 22.3. The table does not list the discount rate and the intercepts in the school and home payoff functions, which were set to 0.95, 11,000, and 17,000 respectively, since these are not identified. In all of our experiments we set the number of people, N, to 2,000.

Data from this model were generated using two different assumptions about the way people formed expectations. First, we assumed that people had rational expectations. This required us to solve the resulting dynamic optimization problem once to generate the optimal decision rules. Since the choice set includes only four discrete alternatives it is feasible to do this. Then, to simulate choice and wage paths requires only that we generate realizations of the appropriate stochastic variables. It is important to note that the polynomial future component used in the estimation procedure does not provide a perfect fit to the rational expectations future component. Hence, analysis of this data sheds light on the effect that misspecification of the future component may have on inference.

Next, we assumed that agents used a future component that was actually a polynomial in the state variables to form decisions. Analysis of this data set sheds light on how the algorithm performs when the model is correctly specified. To ensure close comparability with the rational expectations case, we constructed this polynomial by regressing the rational expectations future components on a fourth-order polynomial in the state variables, constructed as described in the discussion preceding (22.13). We used the point estimates from this regression as the coefficients of our polynomial future component (see Appendix A for the specific form of the polynomial).

We found that a fourth-order polynomial provided a good approximation to the future component in the sense that if agents used the approximate instead of optimal decision rule they suffered rather small lifetime earnings losses. Evidence of this is given in Table 22.1, where we report the results of simulations

Table 22.1 Quality of the polynomial approximation to the true future component

Error set	1	2	3	4	5
Mean present value of payoffs with true future component*	356,796	356,327	355,797	355,803	355,661
Mean present value of payoffs with polynomial approximation*	356,306	355,978	355,337	355,515	355,263
Mean dollar equivalent loss*	491	349	460	287	398
Mean percent loss*	0.14%	0.10%	0.13%	0.08%	0.11%
Percent choice agreement Aggregate	91.81%	91.71%	91.66%	92.30%	91.80%
By period					
1	95.80%	95.55%	96.30%	96.10%	96.15%
2	95.35%	94.90%	95.85%	95.95%	95.30%
3	91.30%	90.45%	90.25%	91.15%	89.90%
4	88.00%	87.75%	89.00%	88.90%	88.45%
5	87.00%	88.30%	87.00%	89.20%	87.60%
10	92.70%	92.60%	92.70%	92.30%	92.30%
20	92.20%	93.00%	92.70%	93.05%	93.10%
30	91.55%	90.90%	90.55%	91.85%	90.85%
40	92.80%	92.15%	91.70%	92.75%	92.10%

* The mean present value of payoffs is the equally-weighted average discounted sum of ex-post lifetime payoffs over 2,000, 40 period lived agents. The values are dollar equivalents.

under optimal and suboptimal decision rules. The simulations were conducted as follows. First, for $N = 2,000$ people we drew five sets of lifetime ($T = 40$) realizations of the model's stochastic components $\{\varepsilon_{i1t}, \varepsilon_{i2t}, (\eta_{ijt})_{j=1,4}\}$. In Table 22.1 these are referred to as error sets one to five. For each of the five error sets we simulated lifetime choice histories for each of the 2,000 people under the optimal and approximate decision rules. We refer to the 10 data sets constructed in this way as 1-EMAX through 5-EMAX and 1-POLY through 5-POLY, respectively. We then calculated the mean of the present value of lifetime payoffs (pecuniary plus nonpecuniary) for each of the 2,000 people under the optimal and approximate decision rules, respectively, for each of the five error sets. These are reported in the second and third rows of Table 22.1. Holding the error set fixed, the source of any difference in the mean present value of lifetime payoffs lies in the use of different decision rules. The mean present values of dollar equivalent losses from using the suboptimal polynomial rules are small, ranging from 287 to 491. The percentage loss ranges from 8 hundredths of 1 percent to 14 hundredths of 1 percent. These findings are similar to those reported by Geweke and Keane (1999a) and Krusell and Smith (1995).

Table 22.2 reports the mean accepted wages and choice frequencies for the data generated from error-set two. The first set of columns report statistics for data generated according to the polynomial approximation (data set 2-POLY) while the second set of columns report results from the optimal decision rule (data set 2-EMAX). Under our parameterization, occupation one can be thought of as "unskilled" labor, while occupation two can be understood as "skilled" labor. The reason is the mean of the wage offer distribution is lower in occupation two early in life, but it rises more quickly with experience. The choice patterns and mean accepted wages are similar under the two decision rules. School is chosen somewhat more often under the optimal decision rule, which helps to generate slightly higher lifetime earnings. Finally, note that selection effects leave the mean accepted wage in occupation two higher than that in occupation one throughout the lifecycle under both decision rules.

Next, we ran the Gibbs algorithm described in section two for 40,000 cycles on each data set. We achieved about three cycles per minute on a Sun ultra-2 workstation.[5] Thus, while time requirements were substantial, they were minor compared to what estimation of such a model using a full solution of the dynamic programming problem would entail. Visual inspection of graphs of the draw sequences, as well as application of the split sequence diagnostic suggested by Gelman (1996) – which compares variability of the draws across subsequences – suggests that the algorithm converged for all 10 artificial data sets. In all cases, the final 15,000 draws from each run were used to simulate the parameters' marginal posterior distributions.

Table 22.3 reports the results of the Gibbs sampling algorithm when applied to the data generated with a polynomial future component. In this case, the econometric model is correctly specified. The first column of Table 22.3 is the parameter label, the second column is the true value, and the remaining columns report the structural parameters' posterior means and standard deviations for each of the five data sets.[6] The results are extremely encouraging. Across all runs, there was only one instance in which the posterior mean of a parameter for the first wage equation was more than two posterior standard deviations away from its true value: the intercept in data set one. In data sets four and five, all of the structural parameters' posterior means are within two posterior standard deviations of their true values. In the second data set, only the second wage equation's own experience term is slightly more than two posterior standard deviations from its true value. In the third data set the mean of the wage equation's error correlation is slightly more than two posterior standard deviations from the true value, as are a few of the second wage equation's parameters.

Careful examination of Table 22.3 reveals that the standard deviation of the nonpecuniary payoff was the most difficult parameter to pin down. In particular, the first two moments of the marginal posteriors of these parameters vary considerably across experiments, in relation to the variability of the other structural parameters' marginal posteriors. This result reflects earlier findings reported by Geweke and Keane (1999a). In the earlier work they found that relatively large changes in the value of the nonpecuniary component's standard deviation had only a small effect on choices. It appears that this is the case in the current experiment as well.

It is interesting to note that an OLS regression of accepted (observed) log-wages on the log-wage equation's regressors yields point estimates that differ sharply from the results of the Gibbs sampling algorithm. Table 22.4 contains point estimates and standard errors from such an accepted wage regression. Selection bias is apparent in the estimates of the log-wage equation's parameters in all data sets. This highlights the fact that the Bayesian simulation algorithm is doing an impressive job of implementing the appropriate dynamic selection correction.

Perhaps more interesting is the performance of the algorithm when taken to data that were generated using optimal decision rules. Table 22.5 reports the results of this analysis on data sets 1-EMAX to 5-EMAX. Again, the first column labels the parameter, and the second contains its data generating value. The performance of the algorithm is quite impressive. In almost all cases, the posterior means of the wage function parameters deviate only slightly from the true values in percentage terms. Also, the posterior standard deviations are in most cases quite small, suggesting that the data contain a great deal of information about these structural parameters – even without imposing the assumption that agents form the future component "optimally." Finally, despite the fact that the posterior standard deviations are quite small, the posterior means are rarely more than two posterior deviations away from the true values.[7] As with the polynomial data, the standard deviation of the nonpecuniary component seems difficult to pin down. Unlike the polynomial data, the school payoff parameters are not pinned down as well as the wage equation parameters. This is perhaps not surprising since school payoffs are never observed.

Figure 22.1 contains the simulated posterior densities for a subset of the structural parameters based on data set 3-EMAX. Each figure includes three triangles on its horizontal axis. The middle triangle defines the posterior mean, and the two flanking triangles mark the points two posterior standard deviations above and below the mean. A vertical line is positioned at the parameters' data generating (true) value. These distributions emphasize the quality of the algorithm's performance in that the true parameter values are typically close to the posterior means. The figures also make clear that not all the parameters have approximately normal distributions. For instance, the posterior density of the wage equations' error correlation is multi-modal.

The results of Table 22.5 indicate that in a case where agents form the future component optimally, we can still obtain reliable and precise inferences about structural parameters of the current payoff functions using a simplified and misspecified model that says the future component is a simple fourth-order polynomial in the state variables. But we are also interested in how well our method approximates the decision rule used by the agents. In Table 22.6 we consider an experiment in which we use the posterior means for the parameters π that

Table 22.2 Choice distributions and mean accepted wages in the data generated with true and OLS polynomial future components

Period	Data Set 2 – POLY				Mean accepted wage		Data Set 2 – EMAX				Mean accepted wage	
	Percent in occ. 1	Percent in occ. 2	Percent in school	Percent at home	Occ. 1	Occ. 2	Percent in occ. 1	Percent in occ. 2	Percent in school	Percent at home	Occ. 1	Occ. 2
1	0.10	0.00	0.75	0.15	13,762.19	17,971.88	0.09	0.00	0.79	0.12	13,837.93	19,955.02
2	0.23	0.01	0.58	0.17	11,822.16	19,032.16	0.23	0.01	0.60	0.15	11,941.31	18,502.51
3	0.41	0.04	0.34	0.21	11,249.67	16,521.61	0.39	0.03	0.39	0.18	11,275.37	16,786.46
4	0.52	0.06	0.20	0.22	11,167.03	16,209.88	0.50	0.04	0.27	0.19	11,208.15	17,778.61
5	0.60	0.06	0.14	0.20	11,417.94	16,141.39	0.57	0.05	0.20	0.18	11,598.75	16,965.70
6	0.63	0.08	0.10	0.19	11,802.61	16,427.58	0.63	0.06	0.14	0.16	11,897.28	17,100.50
7	0.65	0.09	0.07	0.18	12,257.30	16,987.46	0.68	0.08	0.08	0.16	12,286.26	17,634.68
8	0.69	0.10	0.05	0.16	12,701.01	17,067.03	0.72	0.09	0.05	0.13	12,751.92	17,300.99
9	0.69	0.10	0.05	0.16	13,167.06	18,442.74	0.72	0.10	0.05	0.13	13,159.23	19,498.18
10	0.70	0.11	0.05	0.14	13,709.21	18,274.23	0.74	0.09	0.05	0.12	13,790.83	19,125.16
11	0.72	0.12	0.05	0.11	14,409.81	19,391.23	0.75	0.11	0.04	0.10	14,546.63	19,867.95
12	0.71	0.14	0.04	0.12	14,511.54	19,730.21	0.74	0.12	0.04	0.10	14,650.45	20,320.53
13	0.72	0.14	0.05	0.10	15,216.89	21,641.41	0.75	0.14	0.03	0.08	15,439.04	21,723.49
14	0.74	0.13	0.03	0.09	15,943.12	21,866.44	0.76	0.14	0.02	0.08	16,150.59	22,096.07
15	0.73	0.16	0.03	0.07	16,507.05	22,177.61	0.75	0.16	0.03	0.06	16,773.15	22,764.69
16	0.74	0.16	0.03	0.07	17,129.96	22,624.51	0.75	0.16	0.03	0.06	17,437.26	22,786.18

17	0.75	0.17	0.02	0.06	17,886.20	24,194.23	0.75	0.18	0.02	0.05	18,276.74	24,804.59
18	0.73	0.17	0.02	0.07	18,408.75	24,318.34	0.74	0.18	0.01	0.06	18,786.43	24,476.18
19	0.72	0.19	0.02	0.06	19,590.88	25,385.99	0.73	0.20	0.01	0.05	19,961.17	25,719.67
20	0.74	0.19	0.02	0.05	20,186.07	25,161.39	0.75	0.20	0.01	0.04	20,571.89	25,422.50
21	0.71	0.23	0.01	0.05	21,113.74	26,409.20	0.71	0.24	0.01	0.04	21,613.91	26,613.20
22	0.70	0.25	0.01	0.04	22,002.82	26,935.39	0.70	0.25	0.00	0.04	22,488.94	27,566.90
23	0.67	0.29	0.01	0.03	23,259.72	28,191.41	0.67	0.29	0.01	0.03	23,655.61	28,952.46
24	0.66	0.30	0.00	0.03	23,119.46	28,634.21	0.66	0.31	0.00	0.03	23,706.23	29,491.67
25	0.66	0.30	0.00	0.04	24,085.78	30,826.10	0.66	0.31	0.00	0.03	24,535.54	31,403.33
26	0.62	0.34	0.01	0.04	25,399.34	30,707.99	0.63	0.34	0.00	0.03	26,003.31	31,157.72
27	0.62	0.34	0.00	0.04	26,971.71	32,251.61	0.62	0.35	0.00	0.03	27,482.83	33,112.86
28	0.60	0.37	0.00	0.03	27,074.62	32,024.07	0.60	0.37	0.00	0.02	27,805.46	32,743.79
29	0.57	0.40	0.00	0.03	29,049.11	32,411.14	0.58	0.39	0.00	0.03	29,596.82	33,872.97
30	0.55	0.42	0.00	0.04	30,492.25	34,513.76	0.56	0.41	0.00	0.03	31,216.48	35,462.35
31	0.52	0.45	0.00	0.03	30,745.54	35,672.21	0.52	0.45	0.00	0.03	31,744.63	36,763.93
32	0.50	0.48	0.00	0.03	32,078.16	36,076.17	0.51	0.47	0.00	0.03	33,016.52	37,028.17
33	0.46	0.50	0.00	0.04	34,202.82	37,460.57	0.47	0.51	0.00	0.03	34,905.34	38,435.23
34	0.43	0.54	0.00	0.02	34,578.60	38,293.38	0.44	0.54	0.00	0.02	35,656.54	39,212.14
35	0.42	0.55	0.00	0.04	37,084.91	39,690.50	0.43	0.54	0.00	0.03	38,195.57	40,767.33
36	0.39	0.58	0.00	0.03	37,580.47	40,970.75	0.40	0.57	0.00	0.03	39,119.51	41,740.41
37	0.36	0.60	0.00	0.04	40,129.34	41,885.28	0.37	0.60	0.00	0.03	41,228.89	42,901.62
38	0.33	0.64	0.00	0.03	40,101.57	43,929.61	0.34	0.63	0.00	0.03	41,477.02	45,076.14
39	0.28	0.67	0.00	0.05	43,282.44	44,724.22	0.30	0.66	0.00	0.04	44,266.27	46,039.50
40	0.26	0.70	0.00	0.03	44,462.69	45,703.45	0.28	0.69	0.00	0.03	45,668.36	46,847.68

Table 22.3 Descriptive statistics for posterior distributions of the model's structural parameters for several different data sets generated using polynomial future component

Parameter	True	Data Set 1 – POLY		Data Set 2 – POLY		Data Set 3 – POLY		Data Set 4 – POLY		Data Set 5 – POLY	
		Mean	SD	Mean	SD	Mean	SD	Mean	SD	Mean	SD
Occ. 1 intercept	9.00000	9.01300	0.00643	9.00125	0.00797	9.00845	0.00600	9.00256	0.00661	9.00309	0.00598
Occ. 1 own experience	0.05500	0.05440	0.00080	0.05540	0.00086	0.05429	0.00076	0.05462	0.00080	0.05496	0.00060
Occ. 2 experience	0.00000	0.00093	0.00095	-0.00121	0.00103	-0.00084	0.00092	0.00114	0.00112	-0.00129	0.00115
Education	0.05000	0.04806	0.00130	0.04881	0.00132	0.04850	0.00137	0.04938	0.00140	0.04924	0.00139
Occ. 1 exp. squared	-0.00025	-0.00024	0.00003	-0.00026	0.00003	-0.00025	0.00003	-0.00024	0.00003	-0.00026	0.00002
Occ. 1 error SD	0.40000	0.398	0.002	0.402	0.002	0.401	0.002	0.400	0.002	0.400	0.002
Occ. 2 intercept	8.95000	8.91712	0.01625	8.97693	0.01582	8.91699	0.01583	8.96316	0.01551	8.92501	0.01590
Occ. 2 own experience	0.04000	0.04049	0.00039	0.03918	0.00034	0.03946	0.00037	0.03968	0.00037	0.04055	0.00042
Occ. 1 experience	0.06000	0.06103	0.00175	0.06016	0.00178	0.06461	0.00173	0.05946	0.00180	0.06009	0.00178
Education	0.07500	0.07730	0.00187	0.07245	0.00161	0.07782	0.00178	0.07619	0.00167	0.07650	0.00171
Occ. 2 exp. squared	-0.00090	-0.00088	0.00008	-0.00093	0.00008	-0.00109	0.00008	-0.00092	0.00008	-0.00087	0.00008
Occ. 2 error SD	0.40000	0.409	0.003	0.399	0.003	0.407	0.003	0.397	0.003	0.399	0.003
Error correlation	0.50000	0.481	0.031	0.512	0.025	0.420	0.033	0.528	0.037	0.438	0.042
Undergraduate tuition	-5,000	-4,629	363	-5,212	464	-5,514	404	-4,908	464	-4,512	399
Graduate tuition	-15,000	-18,006	2,085	-16,711	1,829	-16,973	1,610	-16,817	1,692	-15,091	1,972
Return cost	-15,000	-14,063	531	-16,235	894	-15,809	554	-14,895	822	-15,448	679
Preference shock SD											
Occ. 1	9,082.95	10,121.05	255.49	9,397.38	577.26	10,578.31	537.01	9,253.22	615.27	9,494.74	354.07
Occ. 2	9,082.95	8,686.12	456.77	11,613.38	346.03	10,807.31	519.13	9,610.23	457.45	9,158.09	228.32
Occ. 3	11,821.59	11,569.93	281.18	12,683.67	803.09	13,418.79	358.98	12,019.38	417.75	12,247.80	401.15
Preference shock Corr.											
Occ. 1 with Occ. 2	0.89	0.90	0.01	0.96	0.01	0.93	0.01	0.91	0.01	0.90	0.02
Occ. 1 with Occ. 3	0.88	0.89	0.01	0.88	0.01	0.90	0.01	0.88	0.01	0.88	0.01
Occ. 2 with Occ. 3	0.88	0.89	0.01	0.89	0.01	0.89	0.01	0.89	0.01	0.89	0.01

Table 22.4 Log-wage equation estimates from OLS on observed wages generated under the polynomial future component*

Data Set	Occupation One					Occupation Two					Wage Error SDs	
	Intercept	Occ. 1 Experience	Occ. 2 Experience	Education	Occ. 1 Exp. Squared	Intercept	Occ. 1 Experience	Occ. 2 Experience	Education	Occ. 2 Exp. Squared	Occ. 1	Occ. 2
TRUE	9.00000	0.05500	0.00000	0.05000	-0.00025	8.95000	0.04000	0.06000	0.07500	-0.00090	0.40000	0.40000
1 – POLY	9.15261 *0.00520*	0.04236 *0.00076*	0.01708 *0.00074*	0.04247 *0.00133*	0.00012 *0.00003*	9.46735 *0.00906*	0.03516 *0.00037*	0.01953 *0.00146*	0.05589 *0.00179*	0.00038 *0.00008*	0.38845	0.36574
2 – POLY	9.14715 *0.00528*	0.04320 *0.00076*	0.01586 *0.00073*	0.04309 *0.00134*	0.00010 *0.00003*	9.47924 *0.00888*	0.03446 *0.00036*	0.02261 *0.00136*	0.05311 *0.00170*	0.00017 *0.00007*	0.38940	0.36300
3 – POLY	9.14895 *0.00528*	0.04230 *0.00076*	0.01732 *0.00072*	0.04420 *0.00135*	0.00011 *0.00003*	9.45851 *0.00914*	0.03482 *0.00036*	0.02335 *0.00140*	0.05665 *0.00177*	0.00016 *0.00007*	0.38935	0.36495
4 – POLY	9.15157 *0.00527*	0.04220 *0.00076*	0.01734 *0.00074*	0.04261 *0.00136*	0.00012 *0.00003*	9.46413 *0.00896*	0.03480 *0.00037*	0.02346 *0.00138*	0.05469 *0.00174*	0.00015 *0.00007*	0.38900	0.36217
5 – POLY	9.14838 *0.00521*	0.04274 *0.00076*	0.01695 *0.00073*	0.04408 *0.00135*	0.00011 *0.00003*	9.45131 *0.00880*	0.03570 *0.00036*	0.02021 *0.00139*	0.05671 *0.00173*	0.00035 *0.00007*	0.38772	0.35781

* Standard errors in italics.

Table 22.5 Descriptive statistics for posterior distributions of the model's structural parameters for several different data sets generated using true future component

Parameter	True	Data Set 1 – EMAX		Data Set 2 – EMAX		Data Set 3 – EMAX		Data Set 4 – EMAX		Data Set 5 – EMAX	
		Mean	SD	Mean	SD	Mean	SD	Mean	SD	Mean	SD
Occ. 1 intercept	9.00000	9.01342	0.00602	9.00471	0.00527	9.01436	0.00584	9.01028	0.00593	9.00929	0.00550
Occ. 1 own experience	0.05500	0.05427	0.00073	0.05489	0.00071	0.05384	0.00072	0.05394	0.00072	0.05410	0.00071
Occ. 2 experience	0.00000	0.00111	0.00093	0.00092	0.00114	0.00078	0.00126	0.00107	0.00100	0.00051	0.00093
Education	0.05000	0.04881	0.00118	0.05173	0.00126	0.04869	0.00129	0.04961	0.00123	0.05067	0.00124
Occ. 1 exp. squared	-0.00025	-0.00023	0.00002	-0.00025	0.00002	-0.00023	0.00002	-0.00022	0.00002	-0.00023	0.00002
Occ. 1 error SD	0.40000	0.397	0.002	0.399	0.002	0.399	0.002	0.397	0.002	0.397	0.002
Occ. 2 intercept	8.95000	8.90720	0.01704	8.98989	0.01970	8.93943	0.01850	8.93174	0.01649	8.94097	0.01410
Occ. 2 own experience	0.04000	0.04093	0.00037	0.03967	0.00037	0.03955	0.00038	0.04001	0.00037	0.04060	0.00039
Occ. 1 experience	0.06000	0.06087	0.00178	0.05716	0.00190	0.06200	0.00201	0.06211	0.00179	0.05880	0.00157
Education	0.07500	0.07822	0.00166	0.07338	0.00171	0.07579	0.00165	0.07743	0.00167	0.07613	0.00159
Occ. 2 exp. squared	-0.00090	-0.00087	0.00008	-0.00081	0.00008	-0.00098	0.00008	-0.00101	0.00008	-0.00084	0.00007
Occ. 2 error SD	0.40000	0.409	0.003	0.397	0.003	0.404	0.003	0.402	0.003	0.397	0.003
Error correlation	0.50000	0.517	0.023	0.607	0.029	0.484	0.044	0.521	0.035	0.488	0.028
Undergraduate tuition	-5,000	-2,261	313	-2,937	358	-3,407	371	-3,851	426	-3,286	448
Graduate tuition	-15,000	-10,092	1,046	-10,788	1,141	-11,983	1,188	-10,119	1,380	-11,958	1,823
Return cost	-15,000	-14,032	482	-16,014	431	-16,577	500	-16,168	662	-18,863	1,065
Preference shock SD											
Occ. 1	9,082.95	10,634.90	423.85	10,177.24	165.11	11,438.63	438.72	9,973.32	371.64	9,071.29	509.80
Occ. 2	9,082.95	9,436.10	372.86	12,741.02	405.25	11,432.19	287.69	9,310.37	718.15	7,770.66	555.39
Occ. 3	11,821.59	11,450.65	338.28	12,470.12	259.81	13,999.95	351.33	13,183.33	471.47	13,897.62	533.67
Preference shock corr.											
Occ. 1 with Occ. 2	0.89	0.93	0.01	0.98	0.00	0.94	0.01	0.91	0.02	0.86	0.03
Occ. 1 with Occ. 3	0.88	0.89	0.01	0.88	0.01	0.90	0.01	0.88	0.01	0.88	0.01
Occ. 2 with Occ. 3	0.88	0.87	0.01	0.90	0.01	0.90	0.01	0.89	0.02	0.89	0.02

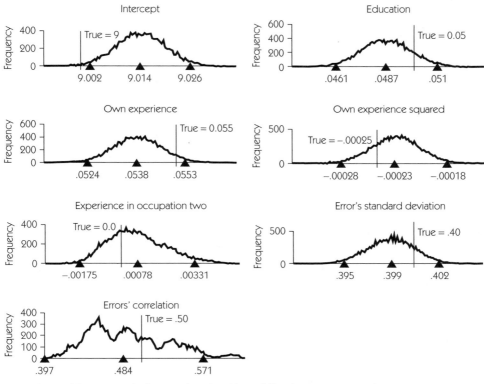

Figure 22.1 Marginal posterior densities of first log-wage equation's parameters from data set 3-EMAX*

* On each graph, the vertical line indicates the data generating parameter value. The middle triangle indicates the empirical mean, and the two flanking triangles are located two standard deviations from the mean

characterize how agents form expectations to form an estimate of agents' decision rules. We then simulate five new artificial data sets, using the exact same draws for the current period payoffs as were used to generate the original five artificial data sets. The only difference is that the estimated future component is substituted for the true future component in forming the decision rule. The results in Table 22.6 indicate that the mean wealth losses from using the estimated decision rule range from five-hundredths to three-tenths of 1 percent. The percentage of choices that agree between agents who use the optimal versus the approximate rules ranges from 89.8 to 93.5 percent. These results suggest that our estimated polynomial approximations to the optimal decision rules are reasonably accurate.

Figure 22.2 provides an alternative way to examine the quality of the polynomial approximation to the future component. This figure plots the value of the approximate and the true EMAX future components when evaluated at the mean

Table 22.6 Wealth loss when posterior polynomial approximation is used in place of true future component*

Data set	Using True EMAX**	Using Posterior EMAX**						
	Mean present value of payoffs***	Mean present value of payoffs***	Mean dollar equivalent loss	Mean percent loss (%)	Aggregate choice agreement (%)	Percent with 0–35 agreement (%)	Percent with 36–39 agreements (%)	Percent choosing same path (%)
1-EMAX	356,796	356,134	663	0.19	90.80	34.25	42.65	23.10
2-EMAX	356,327	355,836	491	0.14	91.34	33.00	44.00	23.00
3-EMAX	355,797	354,746	1,051	0.30	89.79	39.00	38.95	22.05
4-EMAX	355,803	355,450	353	0.10	93.48	24.60	38.45	36.95
5-EMAX	355,661	355,485	176	0.05	93.18	24.95	30.50	44.55

* Polynomial parameter values are set to the mean of their respective empirical posterior distributions.
** Each simulation includes 2,000 agents that live for exactly 40 periods.
*** The mean present value of payoffs is the equal-weight sample average of the discounted streams of ex-post lifetime payoffs.

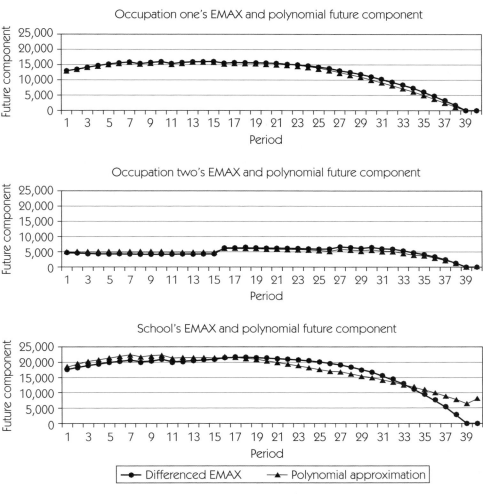

Figure 22.2 EMAX and polynomial future components evaluated at mean values of state variables at each period

of each period's state vector.[8] Each vertical axis corresponds to the value of the future component, and the horizontal axis is the period. Clearly, the approximation reflects the true EMAX future component's main features. The fit of the polynomial seems relatively strong for each occupational alternative throughout the lifecycle. The fit is good for school in early periods, but begins to deteriorate later. One reason is that school is chosen very infrequently after the first five periods, so there is increasingly less information about its future component. A second reason is that the contemporaneous return begins to dominate the future component in alternative valuations. Consequently, each data point in later periods contains relatively less information about the future component's value.

Overall, however, these figures furnish additional evidence that the polynomial approximation does a reasonable job of capturing the key characteristics of the true future component.

5   Conclusion

This chapter described how to implement a simulation based method for inference that is applicable to a wide class of dynamic multinomial choice models. The results of a Monte Carlo analysis demonstrated that the method works very well in relatively large state-space models with only partially observed payoffs where very high dimensional integrations are required. Although our discussion focused on models with discrete choices and independent and identically distributed stochastic terms, the method can also be applied to models with mixed continuous/discrete choice sets and serially correlated shocks (see Houser, 1999).

Appendix A   The Future Component

The future component we used was a fourth-order polynomial in the state variables. Below, in the interest of space and clarity, we will develop that polynomial only up to its third-order terms. The extension to the higher-order terms is obvious. From equation (22.12), the future component is the flexible functional form

$$F(X_{i1t} + \chi(j = 1), X_{i2t} + \chi(j = 2), S_{it} + \chi(j = 3), t + 1, \chi(j = 3))$$

Define $\iota_k \equiv \chi(j = k)$. Then, to third-order terms, we used the following polynomial to represent this function.

$$F(X_1 + \iota_1, X_2 + \iota_2, S + \iota_3, t + 1, \iota_3) = P_1 + P_2(X_1 + \iota_1) + P_3(X_2 + \iota_2) + P_4(S + \iota_3)$$
$$+ P_5(t + 1) + P_6(X_1 + \iota_1)^2 + P_7(X_2 + \iota_2)^2 + P_8(S + \iota_3)^2 + P_9(t + 1)^2 + P_{10}(X_1 + \iota_1)^3$$
$$+ P_{11}(X_2 + \iota_2)^3 + P_{12}(S + \iota_3)^3 + P_{13}(t + 1)^3 + P_{14}(X_1 + \iota_1)^2(X_2 + \iota_2) + P_{15}(X_1 + \iota_1)^2(S + \iota_3)$$
$$+ P_{16}(X_1 + \iota_1)^2(t + 1) + P_{17}(X_2 + \iota_2)^2(X_1 + \iota_1) + P_{18}(X_2 + \iota_2)^2(S + \iota_3) + P_{19}(X_2 + \iota_2)^2 (t + 1)$$
$$+ P_{20}(S + \iota_3)^2(X_1 + \iota_1) + P_{21}(S + \iota_3)^2 (X_2 + \iota_2) + P_{22}(S + \iota_3)^2 (t + 1) + P_{23}(t + 1)^2(X_1 + \iota_1)$$
$$+ P_{24}(t + 1)^2(X_2 + \iota_2) + P_{25}(t + 1)^2(S + \iota_3) + P_{26}\iota_3 + P_{27}\iota_3(X_1 + \iota_1) + P_{28}\iota_3(X_2 + \iota_2)$$
$$+ P_{29}\iota_3(S + \iota_3) + P_{30}\iota_3(t + 1) + P_{31}\iota_3(X_1 + \iota_1)^2 + P_{32}\iota_3(X_2 + \iota_2)^2 + P_{33}\iota_3(S + \iota_3)^2$$
$$+ P_{34}\iota_3(t + 1)^2$$

The differenced future components used above are defined by $f(I_{it}^*, j) = F(I_{it}^*, j) - F(I_{it}^*, 4)$. Several of the parameters of the level future component drop out due to differencing. For instance, the intercept P_1 and all coefficients of terms involving only $(t + 1)$ vanish. Simple algebra reveals the differenced future components have the following forms.

$$f(I_{it}^*, 1) = \pi_1 + \pi_2 g(X_1) + \pi_3 h(X_1) + \pi_4 X_2 g(X_1) + \pi_5 S g(X_1) + \pi_6 (t+1) g(X_1)$$
$$+ \pi_7 X_2^2 + \pi_8 S_2^2 + \pi_9 (t+1)^2.$$

$$f(I_{it}^*, 2) = \pi_4 X_1^2 + \pi_7 X_1 g(X_2) + \pi_{10} + \pi_{11} g(X_2) + \pi_{12} h(X_2) + \pi_{13} S g(X_2) + \pi_{14}(t+1) g(X_2)$$
$$+ \pi_{15} S^2 + \pi_{16}(t+1)^2.$$

$$f(I_{it}^*, 3) = \pi_5 X_1^2 + \pi_8 X_1 g(S) + \pi_{13} X_2^2 + \pi_{15} X_2 g(S) + \pi_{17} + \pi_{18} g(S) + \pi_{19} h(S) + \pi_{20} X_1^2$$
$$+ \pi_{21} X_2^2 + \pi_{22}(t+1) g(S) + \pi_{23}(t+1)^2 + \pi_{24} X_1 + \pi_{25} X_2 + \pi_{26}(t+1).$$

where $g(x) = 2x + 1$, and $h(x) = 3x^2 + 3x + 1$. Several of the parameters appear in multiple equations. Such cross equation restrictions reflect the specification's logical consistency. The future components' asymmetry arises since choosing school both augments school experience and removes the cost of returning to school that one would otherwise face. In contrast, choosing alternative one or two only augments experience within that alternative.

APPENDIX B   EXISTENCE OF JOINT POSTERIOR DISTRIBUTION

Let ω denote the number of missing wage observations, and let $\Omega \equiv [A_\Omega, B_\Omega]^\omega \in \mathfrak{R}_{++}^\omega$ be the domain of unobserved wages, where $0 < A_\Omega < B_\Omega < \infty$. Also, let $\Delta \equiv [A_\Delta, B_\Delta]^{3NT} \in \mathfrak{R}^{3NT}$ be the domain of latent relative utilities, where $-\infty < A_\Delta < B_\Delta < \infty$. We want to show that:

$$\int_{\Omega, \Delta, \beta, \pi, \Sigma_\varepsilon^{-1}, \Sigma_\eta^{-1}} \left(\prod_{i,t} (w_{i1t} w_{i2t})^{-1} \right) g(V, \beta, \Sigma_\varepsilon^{-1}) h(Z, W, \pi, \Sigma_\eta^{-1}) < \infty. \quad (22.\text{B}1)$$

Here, we have subsumed α and Λ into π and Ψ, respectively (as we did in Step 5 of Section 3) and defined

$$g(V, \beta, \Sigma_\varepsilon^{-1}) = |\Sigma_\varepsilon^{-1}|^{\frac{NT-3}{2}} \exp\{-\tfrac{1}{2}(V - Y\beta)'(\Sigma_\varepsilon^{-1} \otimes I_{NT})(V - Y\beta)\}, \quad (22.\text{B}2)$$

where

$$V = \begin{pmatrix} V_1 \\ V_2 \end{pmatrix}, \quad V_i = \begin{pmatrix} \ln w_{1it} \\ \vdots \\ \ln w_{NiT} \end{pmatrix}, \quad Y = \begin{bmatrix} Y_1 & 0 \\ 0 & Y_2 \end{bmatrix} \quad \text{and} \quad \beta = \begin{bmatrix} \beta_1 \\ \beta_2 \end{bmatrix}. \quad (22.\text{B}3)$$

We have also defined

$$h(Z, W, \pi, \Sigma_\eta^{-1}) = |\Sigma_\eta^{-1}|^{\frac{NT-4}{2}} \exp\{-\tfrac{1}{2}(Z - W - \Psi\pi)'(\Sigma_\eta^{-1} \otimes I_{NT})(Z - W - \Psi\pi)\}$$
$$\cdot I(Z_{ijt} > 0, Z_{ikt}(k \neq j) < 0 \text{ if } d_{it} = j \text{ and } j \in \{1, 2, 3\}, \{Z_{ijt}\}_{j=1,2,3} < 0 \text{ otherwise}),$$
$$(22.\text{B}4)$$

where

$$
Z = \begin{pmatrix} Z_1 \\ Z_2 \\ Z_3 \end{pmatrix}, \quad Z_i = \begin{pmatrix} Z_{i1} \\ \vdots \\ Z_{NiT} \end{pmatrix}, \quad W = \begin{pmatrix} W_1 \\ W_2 \\ W_3 \end{pmatrix}, \quad W_i = \begin{pmatrix} w_{i1} \\ \vdots \\ w_{NiT} \end{pmatrix} (i = 1, 2), \quad \text{and} \quad W_3 = (0).
$$

Since the only arguments common to both g and h are those that include functions of wages, we can express (22.B1) as

$$
\int_\Omega \left\{ \left(\prod_{i,t} (w_{i1t} w_{i2t})^{-1} \right) \int_{\beta, \Sigma_\varepsilon^{-1}} g(V, \beta, \Sigma_\varepsilon^{-1}) \int_{\Delta, \pi, \Sigma_\eta^{-1}} h(Z, W, \pi, \Sigma_\eta^{-1}) \right\}. \tag{22.B5}
$$

We first observe that for any configuration of unobserved wages in Ω,

$$
g(V) \equiv \int_{\beta, \Sigma_\varepsilon^{-1}} g(V, \beta, \Sigma_\varepsilon^{-1}) < \infty. \tag{22.B6}
$$

To see this, note that we can express $g(V, \beta, \Sigma_\varepsilon^{-1})$ as

$$
g(V, \beta, \Sigma_\varepsilon) = |\Sigma_\varepsilon^{-1}|^{\frac{NT-3}{2}} \exp\{-\tfrac{1}{2}\mathrm{tr}(S(\hat{\beta})\Sigma_\varepsilon^{-1}) - \tfrac{1}{2}(\beta - \hat{\beta})'Y'(\Sigma_\varepsilon^{-1} \otimes I_{NT})Y(\beta - \hat{\beta})\}, \tag{22.B7}
$$

where

$$
\hat{\beta} = (Y'(\Sigma_\varepsilon^{-1} \otimes I_{NT})Y)^{-1}Y'(\Sigma_\varepsilon^{-1} \otimes I_{NT})V
$$

$$
S(\hat{\beta}) = (V_1 - Y_1\hat{\beta}_1, V_2 - Y_2\hat{\beta}_2)'(V_1 - Y_1\hat{\beta}_1, V_2 - Y_2\hat{\beta}_2) \tag{22.B8}
$$

Hence, $g(V, \beta, \Sigma_\varepsilon)$ is proportional to a normal-Wishart density (Bernardo and Smith, 1994, p. 140), hence finitely integrable to a value $g(V)$ that, in general, will depend on the configuration of unobserved wages. Since $g(V)$ is finite over the compact set Ω, it follows that $g(V)$ is bounded over Ω.

Turn next to $h(Z, W, \pi, \Sigma_\eta^{-1})$. Since (22.B4) has the same form as (22.B2), just as (22.B7) we can write:

$$
h(Z, W, \pi, \Sigma_\eta^{-1}) = |\Sigma_\eta^{-1}|^{\frac{NT-4}{2}} \exp\{-\tfrac{1}{2}\mathrm{tr}(S(\hat{\pi})\Sigma_\eta^{-1}) - \tfrac{1}{2}(\pi - \hat{\pi})'\Psi'(\Sigma_\eta^{-1} \otimes I_{NT})\Psi(\pi - \hat{\pi})\}
$$
$$
\cdot I(Z_{ijt} > 0, Z_{iRt}(k \neq j) < 0 \text{ if } d_{it} = j \text{ and } j \in \{1, 2, 3\}, \{Z_{ijt}\}_{j=1,2,3} < 0 \text{ otherwise}) \tag{22.B9}
$$

where $\hat{\pi}$ and $S(\hat{\pi})$ are defined in a way that is exactly analogous to (22.B8).

Hence,

$$
h(Z, W) \equiv \int_{\Delta, \pi, \Sigma_\eta^{-1}} h(Z, W, \pi, \Sigma_\eta^{-1}) < \infty \tag{22.B10}
$$

for any configuration of unobserved wages in Ω and latent utilities in Δ. It follows that $h(Z, W)$ is bounded over $\Omega \times \Delta$. Thus, the integral (B1) reduces to

$$\int_{\Omega,\Delta} \left\{ \left(\prod_{i,t} (w_{i1t} w_{i2t})^{-1} \right) g(V) h(Z, W) \right\} \tag{22.B11}$$

which is finite since each element of the integrand is bounded over the compact domain of integration.

Notes

1 Currently, approaches to numerical integration such as quadrature and series expansion are not useful if the dimension of the integration is greater than three or four.

2 Restrictions of this type can be tested easily by estimating versions of the model with different but nested future components.

3 These findings are related to those of Lancaster (1997), who considered Bayesian inference in the stationary job search model. He found that if the future component is treated as a free parameter (rather than being set "optimally" as dictated by the offer wage function, offer arrival rate, unemployment benefit and discount rate) there is little loss of information about the structural parameters of the offer wage functions. (As in our example, however, identification of the discount factor is lost.) The stationary job search model considered by Lancaster (1997) has the feature that the future component is a constant (i.e. it is not a function of state variables). Our procedure of treating the future component as a polynomial in state variables can be viewed as extending Lancaster's approach to a much more general class of models.

4 As noted earlier, the future component's arguments reflect restrictions implied by the model. For instance, because the productivity and preference shocks are serially independent, they contain no information useful for forecasting future payoffs and do not appear in the future component's arguments. Also, given total experience in each occupation, the order in which occupations one and two were chosen in the past does not bear on current or future payoffs. Accordingly, only total experience in each occupation enters the future component.

5 To begin the Gibbs algorithm we needed an initial guess for the model's parameters (although the asymptotic behavior of the Gibbs sampler as the number of cycles grows large is independent of starting values). We chose to set the log-wage equation βs equal to the value from an OLS regression on observed wages. The diagonal elements of Σ_ε were set to the variance of observed log-wages, while the off-diagonal elements were set to zero. The school payoff parameters were all initialized at zero. All of the future component's π values were also started at zero, with the exception of the alternative-specific intercepts. The intercepts for alternatives one, two, and three were initialized at −5,000, 10,000, and 20,000, respectively. These values were chosen with an eye towards matching aggregate choice frequencies in each alternative. We initialized the Σ_η covariance matrix by setting all off-diagonal elements to zero, and each diagonal element to 5×10^8. We used large initial variances because doing so increases the size of the initial Gibbs steps, and seems to improve the rate of convergence of the algorithm.

6 Space considerations prevent us from reporting results for individual expectations parameters. Instead, below we will graphically compare the form of the estimated future component to that which was used to generate the data.

7   We also ran OLS accepted log-wage regressions for the 1-EMAX through 5-EMAX data sets. The results are very similar to those in Table 22.4, so we do not report them here. The estimates again show substantial biases for all the wage equation parameters. Thus, the Gibbs sampling algorithm continues to do an impressive job of implementing a dynamic selection correction despite the fact that the agents' decision rules are misspecified.

8   The mean state vectors were derived from the choices in data set 5-EMAX, and the coefficients of the polynomial were valued at the posterior means derived from the analysis of data set 5-EMAX.

References

Bernardo, J., and A.F.M. Smith (1994). *Bayesian Theory*. New York: John Wiley and Sons, Ltd.

Eckstein, Z., and K. Wolpin (1989). The specification and estimation of dynamic stochastic discrete choice models. *Journal of Human Resources* 24, 562–98.

Gelman, A. (1996). Inference and monitoring convergence. In W.R. Gilks, S. Richardson, and D.J. Spiegelhalter (eds.) *Markov Chain Monte Carlo in Practice*. pp. 131–43. London: Chapman & Hall.

Geweke, J. (1995). Priors for macroeconomic time series and their application. Working paper, Federal Reserve Bank of Minneapolis.

Geweke, J. (1996). Monte Carlo simulation and numerical integration. In H.M. Amman, D.A. Kendrick, and J. Rust (eds.) *Handbook of Computational Economics*, Volume 1, pp. 731–800.

Geweke, J., and M. Keane (1999a). Bayesian inference for dynamic discrete choice models without the need for dynamic programming. In Mariano, Schuermann, and Weeks (eds.) *Simulation Based Inference and Econometrics: Methods and Applications*. Cambridge: Cambridge University Press. (Also available as Federal Reserve Bank of Minneapolis working paper #564, January, 1996.)

Geweke, J., and M. Keane (1999b). Computationally intensive methods for integration in econometrics. In J. Heckman and E. Leamer (eds.) *Handbook of Econometrics*, Volume 5. Amsterdam: North-Holland.

Geweke, J., M. Keane, and D. Runkle (1994). Alternative computational approaches to inference in the multinomial probit model. *Review of Economics and Statistics* 76, 609–32.

Gilks, W.R., S. Richardson, and D.J. Spiegelhalter (1996). Introducing Markov Chain Monte Carlo. In W.R. Gilks, S. Richardson, and D.J. Spiegelhalter (eds.) *Markov Chain Monte Carlo in Practice*. pp. 1–20. London: Chapman & Hall.

Heckman, J. (1976). The common structure of statistical models of truncation, sample selection and limited dependent variables and a simple estimator for such models. *Annals of Economic and Social Measurement* 5, 475–92.

Heckman, J. (1981). Statistical models for discrete panel data. In C. Manski and D. McFadden (eds.) *Structural Analysis of Discrete Data with Econometric Applications*. pp. 115–78. Cambridge, MA: MIT Press.

Heckman, J., and G. Sedlacek (1985). Heterogeneity, aggregation and market wage functions: an empirical model of self-selection in the labor market. *Journal of Political Economy* 93, 1077–125.

Hotz, V.J., and R.A. Miller (1993). Conditional choice probabilities and the estimation of dynamic programming models. *Review of Economic Studies* 60, 497–530.

Houser, D. (1999). Bayesian analysis of a dynamic, stochastic model of labor supply and saving. Manuscript, University of Arizona.

Keane, M., and K. Wolpin (1994). Solution and estimation of discrete choice dynamic programming models by simulation and interpolation: Monte Carlo Evidence. *Review of Economics and Statistics* 76, 648–72.

Keane, M., and K. Wolpin (1997). The career decisions of young men. *Journal of Political Economy* 105, 473–522.

Krusell, P., and A.A. Smith (1995). Rules of thumb in macroeconomic equilibrium: a quantitative analysis. *Journal of Economic Dynamics and Control* 20, 527–58.

Lancaster, T. (1997). Exact structural inference in optimal job search models. *Journal of Business and Economic Statistics* 15, 165–79.

Lerman, S., and C. Manski (1981). On the use of simulated frequencies to approximate choice probabilities. In C. Manski and D. McFadden (eds.) *Structural Analysis of Discrete Data with Econometric Applications.* pp. 305–19. Cambridge, MA: MIT Press.

Manski, C. (1993). Dynamic choice in social settings. *Journal of Econometrics* 58, 121–36.

McFadden, D. (1989). A method of simulated moments for estimation of discrete response models without numerical integration. *Econometrica* 57, 995–1026.

Monfort, A., Van Dijk, H., and B. Brown (eds.) (1995). *Econometric Inference Using Simulation Techniques.* New York: John Wiley and Sons, Ltd.

Roy, A.D. (1951). Some thoughts on the distribution of earnings. *Oxford Economic Papers* 3, 135–46.

Rust, J. (1987). Optimal replacement of GMC bus engines: an empirical model of Harold Zurcher. *Econometrica* 55, 999–1033.

Rust, J. (1994). Estimation of dynamic structural models, problems and prospects: discrete decision processes. In C. Sims (ed.) *Advances in Econometrics, Sixth World Congress Vol. II.* pp. 119–70. Cambridge: Cambridge University Press.

Tierney, L. (1994). Markov chains for exploring posterior distributions. *Annals of Statistics* 22, 1701–32.

Wolpin, K. (1984). An estimable dynamic stochastic model of fertility and child mortality. *Journal of Political Economy* 92, 852–74.

Zellner, A. (1971). *An Introduction to Bayesian Inference in Econometrics.* New York: John Wiley and Sons.

Monte Carlo Test Methods in Econometrics

Jean-Marie Dufour and Lynda Khalaf*

1   INTRODUCTION

During the last 20 years, computer-based simulation methods have revolutionized the way we approach statistical analysis. This has been made possible by the rapid development of increasingly quick and inexpensive computers. Important innovations in this field include the bootstrap methods for improving standard asymptotic approximations (for reviews, see Efron, 1982; Efron and Tibshirani, 1993; Hall, 1992; Jeong and Maddala, 1993; Vinod, 1993; Shao and Tu, 1995; Davison and Hinkley, 1997; Horowitz, 1997) and techniques where estimators and forecasts are obtained from criteria evaluated by simulation (see Mariano and Brown, 1993; Hajivassiliou, 1993; Keane, 1993; Gouriéroux, Monfort, and Renault, 1993; Gallant and Tauchen, 1996). An area of statistical analysis where such techniques can make an important difference is hypothesis testing which often raises difficult distributional problems, especially in view of determining appropriate critical values.

This paper has two major objectives. First, we review some basic notions on hypothesis testing from a finite-sample perspective, emphasizing in particular the specific role of hypothesis testing in statistical analysis, the distinction between the level and the size of a test, the notions of exact and conservative tests, as well as randomized and non-randomized procedures. Second, we present a relatively informal overview of the possibilities of Monte Carlo test techniques, whose original idea originates in the early work of Dwass (1957), Barnard (1963) and Birnbaum (1974), in econometrics. This technique has the great attraction of providing provably *exact* (randomized) tests based on any statistic whose finite sample distribution may be intractable but can be simulated. Further, the validity of the tests so obtained does not depend on the number of replications employed (which can be small). These features may be contrasted with the bootstrap, which only provides asymptotically justified (although hopefully improved) large-sample approximations.

In our presentation, we will try to address the fundamental issues that will allow the practitioners to use Monte Carlo *test* techniques. The emphasis will be on concepts rather than technical detail, and the exposition aims at being intuitive. The ideas will be illustrated using practical econometric problems. Examples discussed include: specification tests in linear regressions contexts (normality, independence, heteroskedasticity and conditional heteroskedasticity), nonlinear hypotheses in univariate and SURE models, and tests on structural parameters in instrumental regressions. More precisely, we will discuss the following themes.

In Section 2, we identify the important statistical issues motivating this econometric methodology, as an alternative to standard procedures. The issues raised have their roots in practical test problems and include:

- an *exact* test strategy: what is it, and why should we care?;
- the *nuisance-parameter* problem: what does it mean to practitioners?;
- understanding the *size/level* control problem;
- pivotal and *boundedly-pivotal* test criteria: why is this property important?;
- identification and near non-identification: a challenging setting.

Further, the relevance and severity of the problem will be demonstrated using simulation studies and/or empirical examples.

Sections 3 and 4 describe the Monte Carlo (MC) test method along with various econometric applications of it. Among other things, the procedure is compared and contrasted with the bootstrap. Whereas bootstrap tests are asymptotically valid (as both the numbers of observations and simulated samples go to ∞), a formal demonstration is provided to emphasize the size control property of MC tests. Monte Carlo tests are typically discussed in parametric contexts. Extensions to nonparametric problems are also discussed. The theory is applied to a broad spectrum of examples that illustrate the usefulness of the procedure. We conclude with a word of caution on inference problems that cannot be solved by simulation. For convenience, the concepts and themes covered may be outlined as follows.

- MC tests based on pivotal statistics: an exact randomized test procedure;
- MC tests in the presence of nuisance parameters:
  (a) local MC p-value,
  (b) bounds MC p-value,
  (c) maximized MC p-value;
- MC tests versus the bootstrap:
  (a) fundamental differences/similarities,
  (b) the number of simulated samples: theory and guidelines;

- MC tests: breakthrough improvements and "success stories":
  - (a) The intractable null distributions problem (e.g. tests for normality, uniform linear hypothesis in multi-equation models, tests for ARCH),
  - (b) MC tests or Bartlett corrections?,
  - (c) The case of unidentified nuisance parameters (test for structural jumps, test for ARCH-M);
- MC tests may fail: where and why? a word of caution.

We conclude in Section 5.

2 Statistical Issues: A Practical Approach to Core Questions

The hypothesis testing problem is often presented as one of deciding between two hypotheses: the hypothesis of interest (the *null* H_0) and its complement (the *alternative* H_A). For the purpose of the exposition, consider a test problem pertaining to a *parametric* model $(\mathcal{Y}, P_\theta)$, i.e. the case where the data generating process (DGP) is determined up to a *finite* number of unknown real parameters $\theta \in \Theta$, where Θ refers to the parameter space (usually a vector space), $\mathcal{Y}$ is the sample space, P_θ is the family of probability distributions on $\mathcal{Y}$. Furthermore, let Y denote the observations, and Θ_0 the subspace of Θ compatible with H_0.

A statistical test partitions the sample space into two subsets: a set consistent with H_0 (the acceptance region), and its complements whose elements are viewed as inconsistent with H_0 (the rejection region, or the *critical region*). This may be translated into a decision rule based on a *test statistic* $S(Y)$: the rejection region is defined as the numerical values of the test statistic for which the null will be rejected.

Without loss of generality, we suppose the critical region has the form $S(Y) \geq c$. To obtain a test of level α, c must be chosen so that the probability of rejecting the null hypothesis $P_\theta[S(Y) \geq c]$ when H_0 is true (the probability of a *type I error*) is not greater than α, i.e. we must have:

$$\sup_{\theta \in \Theta_0} P_\theta[S(Y) \geq c] \leq \alpha. \tag{23.1}$$

Further, the test has *size* α if and only if

$$\sup_{\theta \in \Theta_0} P_\theta[S(Y) \geq c] = \alpha. \tag{23.2}$$

To solve for c in (23.1) or (23.2), it is necessary to extract the finite-sample distribution of $S(Y)$ when the null is true. Typically, $S(Y)$ is a complicated function of the observations and the statistical problem involved is often intractable. More importantly, it is evident from the definitions (23.1)–(23.2) that, in many cases of practical interest, the distribution of $S(Y)$ may be different for different parameter values. When the null hypothesis completely fixes the value of θ (i.e. Θ_0 is a point), the hypothesis is called a *simple hypothesis*. Most hypotheses encountered in practice are *composite*, i.e. the set Θ_0 contains more than one element. The null may uniquely define some parameters, but almost invariably some other parameters are not restricted to a point-set. In the context of composite hypotheses, some unknown parameters may appear in the distribution of $S(Y)$. Such parameters are called *nuisance parameters*.

When we talk about an *exact test*, it must be understood that attention is restricted to level-correct critical regions, where (23.1) must hold for a given finite sample size, for all values of the parameter θ compatible with the null. Consequently, in carrying out an exact test, one may encounter two problems. The first one is to extract the analytic form of the distribution of $S(Y)$. The second one is to maximize the rejection probability over the relevant nuisance parameter space, subject to the level constraint. We will see below that the first problem can easily be solved when Monte Carlo test techniques are applicable. The second one is usually more difficult to tackle, and its importance is not fully recognized in econometric practice.

A reasonable solution to both problems often exists when one is dealing with large samples. Whereas the null distribution of $S(Y)$ may be complicated and/or may involve unknown parameters, its asymptotic null distribution in many common cases has a known form and is nuisance-parameter-free (e.g., a normal or chi-square distribution). The critical point may conveniently be obtained using asymptotic arguments. The term *approximate critical point* is more appropriate here, since we are dealing with asymptotic levels: the critical values which yield the desired size α for a given sample size can be very different from these approximate values obtained through an asymptotic argument. For sufficiently large sample sizes, the standard asymptotic approximations are expected to work well. The question is, and will remain, *how large is large*? To illustrate this issue, we next consider several examples involving commonly used econometric methods. We will demonstrate, by simulation, that asymptotic procedures may yield highly unreliable decisions, with empirically relevant sample sizes. The problem, and our main point, is that *finite sample accuracy is not merely a small sample problem*.

2.1   Instrumental regressions

Consider the *limited information* (LI) structural regression model:

$$y = Y\beta + X_1\gamma_1 + u = Z\delta + u, \tag{23.3}$$

$$Y = X_1\Pi_1 + X_2\Pi_2 + V, \tag{23.4}$$

where Y and X_1 are $n \times m$ and $n \times k$ matrices which respectively contain the observations on the included endogenous and exogenous variables, $Z = [Y, X_1]$, $\delta = (\beta', \gamma_1')'$ and X_2 refers to the excluded exogenous variables. If more than m variables are excluded from the structural equation, the system is said to be *overidentified*. The associated LI reduced form is:

$$[y \quad Y] = X\Pi + [v \quad V], \quad \Pi = \begin{bmatrix} \pi_1 & \Pi_1 \\ \pi_2 & \Pi_2 \end{bmatrix}, \tag{23.5}$$

$$\pi_1 = \Pi_1\beta + \gamma_1, \quad \pi_2 = \Pi_2\beta. \tag{23.6}$$

The necessary and sufficient condition for identification follows from the relation $\pi_2 = \Pi_2\beta$. Indeed β is recoverable if and only if

$$\text{rank}(\Pi_2) = m. \tag{23.7}$$

To test the general linear hypothesis $R\delta = r$, where R is a full row rank $q \times (m + k)$ matrix, the well-known IV analog of the Wald test is frequently applied on grounds of computational ease. For instance, consider the two-stage least squares (2SLS) estimator

$$\hat{\delta} = [Z'P(P'P)^{-1}P'Z]^{-1}Z'P(P'P)^{-1}P'y, \tag{23.8}$$

where P is the following matrix of instruments $P = [X, X(X'X)^{-1}X'Y]$. Application of the Wald principle yields the following criterion

$$\tau_w = \frac{1}{s^2}(r - R\hat{\delta})'[R'(Z'P(P'P)^{-1}P'Z)^{-1}R](r - R\hat{\delta}), \tag{23.9}$$

where $s^2 = \frac{1}{n}(y - Z\hat{\delta})'(y - Z\hat{\delta})'$. Under usual regularity conditions and imposing identification, τ_w is distributed like a $\chi^2(q)$ variable, where $q = \text{rank}(R)$.

Bartlett (1948) and Anderson and Rubin (1949, henceforth AR) suggested an exact test that can be applied only if the null takes the form $\beta = \beta^0$. The idea behind the test is quite simple. Define $y^* = y - Y\beta^0$. Under the null, the model can be written as $y^* = X_1\gamma_1 + u$. On the other hand, if the hypothesis is not true, y^* will be a linear function of all the exogenous variables. Thus, the null may be assessed by the F-statistic for testing whether the coefficients of the regressors X_2 "excluded" from (23.3) are zero in the regression of y^* on all the exogenous variables, i.e. we simply test $\gamma_2 = 0$ in the extended linear regression $y^* = X_1\gamma_1 + X_2\gamma_2 + u$.

We first consider a simple experiment based on the work of Nelson and Startz (1990a, 1990b) and Staiger and Stock (1997). The model considered is a special case of (23.3) with two endogenous variables ($p = 2$) and $k = 1$ exogenous variables. The structural equation includes only the endogenous variable. The restrictions tested are of the form $H_{01} : \beta = \beta^0$. The sample sizes are set to $n = 25, 100, 250$. The exogenous regressors are independently drawn from the standard normal distribution. These are drawn only once. The errors are generated according to a multinormal distribution with mean zero and covariance matrix

$$\Sigma = \begin{bmatrix} 1 & .95 \\ .95 & 1 \end{bmatrix}. \tag{23.10}$$

Table 23.1   IV-based Wald/Anderson–Rubin tests: empirical type I errors

Π_2	$n = 25$		$n = 100$		$n = 250$	
	Wald	*AR*	*Wald*	*AR*	*Wald*	*AR*
1	0.061	0.059	0.046	0.046	0.049	0.057
0.9	0.063	0.059	0.045	0.046	0.049	0.057
0.7	0.071	0.059	0.046	0.046	0.052	0.057
0.5	0.081	0.059	0.060	0.046	0.049	0.057
0.2	0.160	0.059	0.106	0.046	0.076	0.057
0.1	0.260	0.059	0.168	0.046	0.121	0.057
0.05	0.332	0.059	0.284	0.046	0.203	0.057
0.01	0.359	0.059	0.389	0.046	0.419	0.057

The other coefficients are:

$$\beta = \beta^0 = 0; \quad \Pi_2 = 1, .9, .7, .5, .2, .1, .05, .01. \tag{23.11}$$

In this case, the 2SLS-based test corresponds to the standard t-test (see Nelson and Startz (1990b) for the relevant formulae). 1,000 replications are performed. Table 23.1 reports probabilities of type I error [$P(type\ I\ error)$] associated with the two-tailed 2SLS t-test for the significance of β and the corresponding Anderson–Rubin test. In this context, the identification condition reduces to $\Pi_2 \neq 0$; this condition can be tested using a standard F-test in the first stage regression.[1] It is evident that IV-based Wald tests perform very poorly in terms of size control. Identification problems severely distort test sizes. While the evidence of size distortions is notable even in identified models, the problem is far more severe in near-unidentified situations. More importantly, increasing the sample size does not correct the problem. In this regard, Bound, Jaeger, and Baker (1995) report severe bias problems associated with IV-based estimators, despite very large sample sizes. In contrast, the Anderson–Rubin test, when available, is immune to such problems: the test is exact, in the sense that the null distribution of the AR criterion does not depend on the parameters controlling identification. Indeed, the AR test statistic follows an $F(m, n - k)$ distribution, regardless of the identification status. The AR test has recently received renewed attention; see, for example, Dufour and Jasiak (1996) and Staiger and Stock (1997). Recall, however, that the test is not applicable unless the null sets the values of the coefficients of all the endogenous variables. On general linear structural restrictions, see Dufour and Khalaf (1998b).

Despite the recognition of the need for caution in the application of IV-based tests, standard econometric software packages typically implement IV-based Wald tests. In particular, the t-tests on individual parameters are routinely computed in the context of 2SLS or 3SLS procedures. Unfortunately, the Monte Carlo

experiments we have analyzed confirm that IV-based Wald tests realize computational savings at the risk of very poor reliability.

2.2   Normality tests

Let us now consider the fundamental problem of testing disturbance normality
in the context of the linear regression model:

$$Y = X\beta + u, \tag{23.12}$$

where $Y = (y_1, \ldots, y_n)'$ is a vector of observations on the dependent variable, X is
the matrix of n observations on k regressors, β is a vector of unknown coefficients
and $u = (u_1, \ldots, u_n)'$ is an n-dimensional vector of iid disturbances. The problem
consists in testing:

$$H_0 : f(u) = \varphi(u; 0, \sigma), \quad \sigma > 0, \tag{23.13}$$

where $f(u)$ is the probability density function (pdf) of u_i, and $\varphi(u; \mu, \sigma)$ is the
normal pdf with mean μ and standard deviation σ. In this context, normality
tests are typically based on the least squares residual vector

$$\hat{u} = y - X\hat{\beta} = M_X u, \tag{23.14}$$

where $\hat{\beta} = (X'X)^{-1} X'y$ and $M_X = I_n - X(X'X)^{-1}X'$. Let $\hat{u}_{1n} \leq \hat{u}_{2n} \leq \ldots \leq \hat{u}_{nn}$ denote the
order statistics of the residual, and

$$s^2 = (n - k)^{-1} \sum_{i=1}^{n} \hat{u}_{in}^2, \quad \hat{\sigma}^2 = n^{-1} \sum_{i=1}^{n} \hat{u}_{in}^2. \tag{23.15}$$

Here we focus on two tests: the Kolmogorov–Smirnov (KS) test (Kolmogorov,
1933; Smirnov, 1939), and the Jarque and Bera (1980, 1987; henceforth JB) test.

The KS test is based on a measure of discrepancy between the empirical and
hypothesized distributions:

$$KS = \max (D^+, D^-), \tag{23.16}$$

where $D^+ = \max_{1 \leq i \leq n}[(i/n) - \hat{z}_i]$ and $D^- = \max_{1 \leq i \leq n}[\hat{z}_i - (i - 1)/n]$, $\hat{z}_i = \Phi(\hat{u}_{in}/s)$,
$i = 1, \ldots, n$, and $\Phi(.)$ denotes the cumulative $N(0, 1)$ distribution function. The
exact and limiting distributions of the KS statistic are non-standard and even
asymptotic critical points must be estimated. We have used significance points
from D'Agostino and Stephens (1986, Table 4.7), although these were formally
derived for the location-scale model. The JB test combines the skewness (Sk) and
kurtosis (Ku) coefficients:

$$JB = n\left[\frac{1}{6}(Sk)^2 + \frac{1}{24}(Ku - 3)^2\right], \tag{23.17}$$

Table 23.2 Kolmogorov–Smirnov/Jarque–Bera residuals based tests: empirical type I errors

k_1		$n = 25$		$n = 50$		$n = 100$	
		KS	JB	KS	JB	KS	JB
0	STD	0.050	0.029	0.055	0.039	0.055	0.041
	MC	0.052	0.052	0.052	0.050	0.047	0.048
2, ($n = 25$)	STD	0.114	0.048	0.163	0.064	0.131	0.131
4, ($n > 25$)	MC	0.053	0.052	0.050	0.050	0.050	0.050
$k - 1$ ($n \leq 50$)	STD	0.282	0.067	0.301	0.084	0.322	0.322
8, ($n = 100$)	MC	0.052	0.048	0.050	0.047	0.047	0.047

STD refers to the standard normality test and MC denotes the (corresponding) Monte Carlo test.

where $Sk = n^{-1} \sum_{i=1}^{n} \hat{u}_{in}^3 / (\hat{\sigma}^2)^{3/2}$ and $Ku = n^{-1} \sum_{i=1}^{n} \hat{u}_{in}^4 / (\hat{\sigma}^2)^2$. Under the null and appropriate regularity conditions, the JB statistic is asymptotically distributed as $\chi^2(2)$; the statistic's exact distribution is intractable.

We next summarize relevant results from the simulation experiment reported in Dufour *et al.* (1998). The experiment based on (23.12) was performed as follows. For each disturbance distribution, the tests were applied to the residual vector, obtained as $\hat{u} = M_X u$. Hence, there was no need to specify the coefficients vector β. The matrix X included a constant term, k_1 dummy variables, and a set of independent standard normal variates. Table 23.2 reports rejection percentages (from 10,000 replications) at the nominal size of 5 percent under the null hypothesis, with $n = 25, 50, 100$, $k =$ the largest integer less than or equal to $\sqrt{n}$ and $k_1 = 0$, $2, 4, \ldots, k - 1$. Our conclusions may be summarized as follows. Although the tests appear adequate when the explanatory variables are generated as standard normal, the sizes of all tests vary substantially from the nominal 5 percent for all other designs, irrespective of the sample size. More specifically, (i) the KS test consistently overrejects, and (ii) the JB test based on $\hat{\sigma}$ underrejects when the number of dummy variables relative to normal regressors is small and overreject otherwise. We will discuss the MC tests results in Section 4.

2.3 Uniform linear hypothesis in multivariate regression models

Multivariate linear regression (MLR) models involve a set of p regression equations with cross-correlated errors. When regressors may differ across equations, the model is known as the seemingly unrelated regression model (SUR or SURE; Zellner, 1962). The MLR model can be expressed as follows:

$$\mathbf{Y} = XB + U, \tag{23.18}$$

where $Y = (Y_1, \dots, Y_p)$ is an $n \times p$ matrix of observation on p dependent variables, X is an $n \times k$ full-column rank matrix of fixed regressors, $B = [\beta_1, \dots, \beta_p]$ is a $k \times p$ matrix of unknown coefficients and $U = [U_1, \dots, U_p] = [\tilde{U}_1, \dots, \tilde{U}_n]'$ is an $n \times p$ matrix of random disturbances with covariance matrix Σ where det $(\Sigma) \neq 0$. To derive the distribution of the relevant test statistics, we also assume the following:

$$\tilde{U}_i = JW_i, \quad i = 1, \dots, n, \tag{23.19}$$

where the vector $w = \text{vec}(W_1, \dots, W_n)$ has a known distribution and J is an unknown, nonsingular matrix; for further reference, let $W = [W_1, \dots, W_n]' = UG'$, where $G = J^{-1}$. In particular, this condition will be satisfied when the normality assumption is imposed. An alternative representation of the model is

$$Y_{ij} = \alpha_j + \sum_{k=1}^{p} \beta_{jk} X_{ik}, \quad i = 1, \dots, n, \quad j = 1, \dots, p. \tag{23.20}$$

Uniform linear (UL) constraints take the special form

$$H_0 : RBC = D, \tag{23.21}$$

where R is a known $r \times k$ matrix of rank $r \leq k$, C is a known $p \times c$ matrix of rank $c \leq p$, and D is a known $r \times c$ matrix. An example is the case where the same hypothesis is tested for all equations

$$H_{01} : R\beta_i = \delta_i, \quad i = 1, \dots, p, \tag{23.22}$$

which corresponds to $C = I_p$. Here we shall focus on hypotheses of the form (23.22) for ease of exposition; see Dufour and Khalaf (1998c) for the general case.

Stewart (1997) discusses several econometric applications where the problem can be stated in terms of UL hypotheses. A prominent example includes the multivariate test of the capital asset pricing model (CAPM). Let $r_{jt}, j = 1, \dots, p$, be security returns for period t, $t = 1, \dots, T$. If it is assumed that a riskless asset r_F exists, then efficiency can be tested based on the following MLR-based CAPM model:

$$r_{jt} - r_{Ft} = \alpha_j + \beta_j (r_{Mt} - r_{Ft}) + \varepsilon_{jt}, \quad j = 1, \dots, p, \quad t = 1, \dots, T,$$

where r_{Mt} are the returns on the market benchmark. The hypothesis of efficiency implies that the intercepts α_j are jointly equal to zero. The latter hypothesis is a special case of (23.22) where R is the $1 \times p$ vector $(1, 0, \dots, 0)$. Another example concerns demand analysis. It can be shown (see, e.g., Berndt, 1991, ch. 9) that the translog demand specification yields a model of the form (23.20) where the hypothesis of linear homogeneity corresponds to

$$H_0 : \sum_{k=1}^{p} \beta_{jk} = 0, \quad j = 1, \dots, p. \tag{23.23}$$

Table 23.3 Empirical type I errors of multivariate tests: uniform linear hypotheses

Sample size	5 equations			7 equations			8 equations		
	LR	LR_c	LR_{MC}	LR	LR_c	LR_{MC}	LR	LR_c	LR_{MC}
20	0.295	0.100	0.051	0.599	0.250	0.047	0.760	0.404	0.046
25	0.174	0.075	0.049	0.384	0.145	0.036	0.492	0.190	0.042
40	0.130	0.066	0.056	0.191	0.068	0.051	0.230	0.087	0.051
50	0.097	0.058	0.055	0.138	0.066	0.050	0.191	0.073	0.053
100	0.070	0.052	0.042	0.078	0.051	0.041	0.096	0.052	0.049

LR, LR_c, LR_{MC} denote (respectively) the standard LR test, the Bartlett corrected test and the (corresponding) MC test.

In this context, the likelihood ratio (LR) criterion is:

$$\text{LR} = n \ln(\Lambda), \quad \Lambda = |\hat{U}_0'\hat{U}_0| / |\hat{U}'\hat{U}|, \tag{23.24}$$

where $\hat{U}_0'\hat{U}_0$ and $\hat{U}'\hat{U}$ are respectively the constrained and unconstrained SSE (sum of square error) matrices. On observing that, under the null hypothesis,

$$\hat{U}'\hat{U} = G^{-1}W'MW(G^{-1})', \tag{23.25}$$

$$\hat{U}_0'\hat{U}_0 = G^{-1}W'M_0W(G^{-1})', \tag{23.26}$$

where $M_0 = I - X(X'X)^{-1}(X'X - R'(R(X'X)^{-1}R')^{-1}R)(X'X)^{-1}X'$ and $M = I - X(X'X)^{-1}X'$, we can then rewrite Λ in the form

$$\Lambda = |W'M_0W| / |W'MW|, \tag{23.27}$$

where the matrix $W = UG'$ has a distribution which does not involve nuisance parameters. As shown in Dufour and Khalaf (1998c), decomposition (23.27) obtains only in the case of UL constraints. In Section 4 we will exploit the latter result to obtain exact MC tests based on the LR statistic.

To illustrate the performance of the various relevant tests, we consider a simulation experiment modeled after demand homogeneity tests, i.e. (23.20) and (23.23) with $p = 5, 7, 8, n = 20, 25, 40, 50, 100$. The regressors are independently drawn from the normal distribution; the errors are independently generated as iid $N(0, \Sigma)$ with $\Sigma = GG'$ and the elements of G drawn (once) from a normal distribution. The coefficients for all experiments are available from Dufour and Khalaf (1998c). The statistics examined are the relevant LR criteria defined by (23.24) and the Bartlett-corrected LR test (Attfield, 1995, section 3.3). The results are summarized in Table 23.3. We report the tests' empirical size, based on a nominal size of 5 percent and 1,000 replications. It is evident that the asymptotic LR test overrejects substantially. Second, the Bartlett correction, though providing some improvement, fails in larger systems. In this regard, it is worth noting that Attfield (1995, section 3.3) had conducted a similar Monte Carlo study to demonstrate the effectiveness of Bartlett adjustments in this framework, however the example analyzed was restricted to a two-equations model. We will discuss the MC test results in Section 4.

To conclude this section, it is worth noting that an exact test is available for hypotheses of the form $H_0 : RBC = D$, where $\min(r, c) \leq 2$. Indeed, Laitinen (1978) in the context of the tests of demand homogeneity and Gibbons, Ross, and Shanken (1989), for the problem of testing the CAPM efficiency hypothesis, independently show that a transformation of the relevant LR criterion has an exact F-distribution given normality of asset returns.[2]

2.4 Econometric applications: discussion

In many empirical problems, it is quite possible that the exact null distribution of the relevant test statistic $S(Y)$ will not be easy to compute analytically, even though it is nuisance-parameter-free. In this case, $S(Y)$ is called a pivotal statistic, i.e. the null distribution of $S(Y)$ is uniquely determined under the null hypothesis. In such cases, we will show that the MC test easily solves the size control problem, regardless of the distributional complexities involved. The above examples on normality tests and the UL hypotheses tests, all involve pivotal statistics. The problem is more complicated in the presence of nuisance parameters. We will first discuss a property related to nuisance-parameter-dependent test statistics which will prove to be fundamental in finite sample contexts.[3]

In the context of a right-tailed test problem, consider a statistic $S(Y)$ whose null distribution depends on nuisance parameters and suppose it is possible to find another statistic $S^*(Y)$ such that

$$S(Y) \leq S^*(Y), \quad \forall \theta \in \Theta_0, \tag{23.28}$$

and $S^*(Y)$ is pivotal under the null. Then $S(Y)$ is said to be *boundedly pivotal*. The implications of this property are as follows. From (23.28), we obtain

$$P_\theta[S(Y) \geq c] \leq P[S^*(Y) \geq c], \quad \forall \theta \in \Theta_0.$$

Then if we calculate c such that

$$P[S^*(Y) \geq c] = \alpha, \tag{23.29}$$

we solve the level constraint for the test based on $S(Y)$. It is clear that (23.28) and (23.29) imply

$$P_\theta[S(Y) \geq c] \leq \alpha, \quad \forall \theta \in \Theta_0.$$

As emphasized earlier, the size control constraint is easier to deal with in the case of $S^*(Y)$ because it is pivotal. Consequently, the maximization problem

$$\sup_{\theta \in \Theta_0} P_\theta[S(Y) \geq c]$$

has a non-trivial solution (less than 1) in the case of *boundedly pivotal statistics*. If this property fails to hold, the latter optimization problem may admit only the trivial solution, so that it becomes mathematically impossible to control the significance level of the test.

It is tempting to dismiss such considerations assuming they will occur only in "textbook" cases. Yet it can be shown (we will consider this issue in the next section) that similar considerations explain the poor performance of the Wald tests and confidence intervals discussed in Sections 2.1 and 2.3 above. *These are problems of empirical relevance in econometric practice.* In the next session, we will show that the bootstrap will also fail for such problems! For further discussion of the basic notions of statistical testing mentioned in this section, the reader may consult Lehmann (1986, ch. 3), Gouriéroux and Monfort (1995), and Dufour (1990, 1997).

3   THE MONTE CARLO TEST TECHNIQUE:
AN EXACT RANDOMIZED TEST PROCEDURE

If there were a machine that could check 10 permutations a second, the job would run something on the order of 1,000 years. The point is, then, that an impossible test can be made possible, if not always practical.

Dwass (1957)

The Monte Carlo (MC) test procedure was first proposed by Dwass (1957) in the following context. Consider two independent samples $X_1, \ldots, X_m$ and $Y_1, \ldots, Y_n$, where $X_1, \ldots, X_m \overset{iid}{\sim} F(x)$, $Y_1, \ldots, Y_n \overset{iid}{\sim} F(x - \delta)$ and the cdf $F(\cdot)$ is continuous. No further distributional assumptions are imposed. To test $H_0 : \delta = 0$, the following procedure may be applied.

- Let $z = (X_1, \ldots, X_m, Y_1, \ldots, Y_n)$ and $s = \frac{1}{m}\sum_{i=1}^{m} X_i - \frac{1}{n}\sum_{i=1}^{n} Y_i$.
- Obtain all possible $Q = (n + m)!$ permutations of z, $z^{(1)}, \ldots, z^{(Q)}$, and calculate the associated "permuted analogs" of s

$$s^{(j)} = \frac{1}{m}\sum_{i=1}^{m} z_i^{(j)} - \frac{1}{n}\sum_{i=m+1}^{m+n} z_i^{(j)}, \quad j = 1, \ldots, Q.$$

- Let r denote the number of $s^{(j)}$s for which $s \leq s^{(j)}$. Reject the null (e.g. against $H_A : \delta > 0$) if $r \leq k$, where k is a predetermined integer.

It is easy to see that $P(r \leq k) = k/Q$ under the null because the Xs and the Ys are exchangeable. In other words, the test just described is exactly of size k/Q.

The procedure is intuitively appealing, yet there are $(n + m)!$ permutations to examine. To circumvent this problem, Dwass (1957) proposed to apply the same principle to a sample of P permutations $\tilde{s}^{(1)}, \ldots, \tilde{s}^{(P)}$, *in a way that will preserve the size of the test.* The modified test may be applied as follows.

- Let $\tilde{r}$ denote the number of $\tilde{s}^{(j)}$s for which $s \leq \tilde{s}^{(j)}$. Reject the null (against $\delta > 0$) if $\tilde{r} \leq d$, where d is chosen such that

$$\frac{d+1}{P+1} = \frac{k}{Q}.$$

Dwass formally shows that with this choice for d, the size of the modified test is exactly k/Q = the size of the test based on all permutations. This means that, if we wish to get a 5 percent-level permutation test, and 99 random permutations can be generated, then $d + 1$ should be set to 5. The latter decision rule may be restated as follows: reject the null if the rank of s in the series $s, \tilde{s}^{(1)}, \ldots, \tilde{s}^{(P)}$ is less than or equal to 5. Since each $\tilde{s}^{(j)}$ is "weighted" by the probability that it is sampled from all possible permutations, the modification due to Dwass yields a randomized test procedure.

The principles underlying the MC test procedure are highly related to the randomized permutation test just described. Indeed, this technique is based on the above test strategy where the sample of permutations is replaced by *simulated samples*. Note that Barnard (1963) later proposed a similar idea.[4]

3.1   Monte Carlo tests based on pivotal statistics

In the following, we briefly outline the MC test methodology as it applies to the pivotal statistic context and a right-tailed test; for a more detailed discussion, see Dufour (1995) and Dufour and Kiviet (1998).

Let S_0 denote the observed test statistic S, where S is the test criterion. We assume S has a unique continuous distribution under the null hypothesis (S is a *continuous pivotal statistic*). Suppose we can generate N iid replications, S_j, $j = 1, \ldots, N$, of this test statistic under the null hypothesis. Compute

$$\hat{G}_N(S_0) = \frac{1}{N}\sum_{j=1}^{N} I_{[0,\infty]}(S_j - S_0), \quad I_A(z) = \begin{cases} 1, & \text{if } z \in A \\ 0, & \text{if } z \notin A \end{cases}.$$

In other words, $N\hat{G}_N(S_0)$ is the number of simulated statistics which are greater or equal to S_0, and provided none of the simulated values S_j, $j = 1, \ldots, N$, is equal to S_0, $\hat{R}_N(S_0) = N - N\hat{G}_N(S_0) + 1$ gives the rank of S_0 among the variables $S_0, S_1, \ldots, S_N$.[5] Then the critical region of a test with level α is:

$$\hat{p}_N(S_0) \leq \alpha, \tag{23.30}$$

where $0 < \alpha < 1$ and

$$\hat{p}_N(x) = \frac{N\hat{G}_N(x) + 1}{N + 1}. \tag{23.31}$$

The latter expression gives the *empirical probability* that a value as extreme or more extreme than S_0 is realized if the null is true. Hence $\hat{p}_N(S_0)$ may be viewed as a MC *p*-value.

Note that the MC decision rule may also be expressed in terms of $\hat{R}_N(S_0)$. Indeed the critical region

$$\frac{N\hat{G}_N(S_0) + 1}{N + 1} \le \alpha$$

is equivalent to

$$\hat{R}_N(S_0) \ge (N + 1)(1 - \alpha) + 1. \tag{23.32}$$

In other words, for 99 replications a 5 percent MC test is significant if the rank of S_0 in the series $S_0, S_1, \ldots, S_N$ is at least 96, or informally, if S_0 lies in the series top 5 percent percentile. We are now faced with the immediate question: does the MC test just defined achieve size control?

If the null distribution of S is nuisance-parameter-free and $\alpha(N + 1)$ is an integer, the critical region (23.30) is provably exact, in the sense that

$$P_{(H_0)}[\hat{p}_N(S_0) \le \alpha] = \alpha$$

or alternatively

$$P_{(H_0)}[\hat{R}_N(S_0) \ge (N + 1)(1 - \alpha) + 1] = \alpha.$$

The proof is based on the following theorem concerning the distribution of the ranks associated with a finite dimensional array of exchangeable variables; see Dufour (1995) for a more formal statement of the theorem and related references.

Theorem 23.1 Consider an $M \times 1$ vector of exchangeable real random variables $(Y_1, \ldots, Y_M)$ such that $P[Y_i = Y_j] = 0$ for $i \ne j$, and let R_j denote the rank of Y_j in the series $Y_1, \ldots, Y_M$. Then

$$P\left[\frac{R_j}{M} \ge z\right] = \frac{I[(1 - z)M] + 1}{M}, \quad 0 < z \le 1. \tag{23.33}$$

where $I(x)$ is the largest integer less than or equal to x.

If S is a continuous pivotal statistic, it follows from the latter result that

$$P_{(H_0)}[\hat{R}_N(S_0) \ge (N + 1)(1 - \alpha) + 1].$$

Indeed, in this case, the observed test statistic and the simulated statistic are exchangeable if the null is true. *Here it is worth recalling that the S_js must be simulated imposing the null.* Now using (23.33), it is easy to show that $P_{(H_0)}[\hat{R}_N(S_0) \ge (N + 1)(1 - \alpha) + 1] = \alpha$, provided N is chosen so that $\alpha(N + 1)$ is an integer.

We emphasize that the sample size and the number of replications are explicitly taken into consideration in the above arguments. No asymptotic theory has been used so far to justify the procedure just described.

It will be useful at this stage to focus on a simple illustrative example. Consider the Jarque and Bera normality test statistic,

$$\text{JB} = n\left[\frac{1}{6}(Sk)^2 + \frac{1}{24}(Ku - 3)^2\right],$$

in the context of the linear regression model $Y = X\beta + u$.[6] The MC test based on JB and N replications may be obtained as follows.

- Calculate the constrained OLS estimates $\hat{\beta}$, s and the associated residual $\hat{u}$.
- Obtain the Jarque–Bera statistic based on s and $\hat{u}$ and denote it $\text{JB}^{(0)}$.
- Treating s as fixed, repeat the following steps for $j = 1, \ldots, N$:
  (a) draw an $(n \times 1)$ vector $\tilde{u}^{(j)}$ as iid $N(0, s^2)$;
  (b) obtain the simulated independent variable $\tilde{Y}^{(j)} = X\hat{\beta} + \tilde{u}^{(j)}$;
  (c) regress $\tilde{Y}^{(j)}$ on X;
  (d) derive the Jarque–Bera statistic $\text{JB}^{(j)}$ associated with the regression of $\tilde{Y}^{(j)}$ on X.
- Obtain the rank $\hat{R}_N(\text{JB}^{(0)})$ in the series $\text{JB}^{(0)}, \text{JB}^{(1)}, \ldots, \text{JB}^{(N)}$.
- Reject the null if $\hat{R}_N(\text{JB}^{(0)}) \geq (N + 1)(1 - \alpha) + 1$.

Furthermore, an MC p-value may be obtained as $\hat{p}_N(S_0) = [N + 1 - \hat{R}_N(S_0)]/(N + 1)$. Dufour et al. (1998) show that the JB statistics can be computed from the standardized residual vector $\hat{u}/s$. Using (23.14), we see that

$$\hat{u}/s = \frac{\hat{u}}{(\hat{u}'\hat{u}/(n - k))^{1/2}} = (n - k)^{1/2}\frac{M_X u}{(u'M_X u)^{1/2}} = (n - k)^{1/2}\frac{M_X w}{(w'M_X w)^{1/2}}, \quad (23.34)$$

where $w = u/\sigma \overset{\text{iid}}{\sim} N(0, 1)$ when $u \sim N(0, \sigma^2 I_n)$. It follows that the simulated statistics $\text{JB}^{(j)}$ may be obtained using draws from a nuisance-parameter-free (standard normal) null distribution.

3.2 Monte Carlo tests in the presence of nuisance parameters

In Dufour (1995), we discuss extensions of MC tests when nuisance parameters are present. We now briefly outline the underlying methodology. In this section, n refers to the sample size and N the number of MC replications.

Consider a test statistic S for a null hypothesis H_0, and suppose the null distribution of S depends on an unknown parameter vector θ.

- From the observed data, compute:
  (a) the test statistic S_0, and
  (b) a restricted consistent estimator $\hat{\theta}_n^0$ of θ.

- Using $\hat{\theta}_n^0$, generate N simulated samples and, from them, N simulated values of the test statistic. Then compute $\hat{p}_N(S_0 \mid \hat{\theta}_n^0)$, where $\hat{p}_N(x \mid \bar{\theta})$ refers to $\hat{p}_N(x)$ based on realizations of S generated given $\theta = \bar{\theta}$ and $\hat{p}_N(x)$ is defined in (23.31).
- An MC test may be based on the critical region

$$\hat{p}_N(S_0 \mid \hat{\theta}_n^0) \leq \alpha, \quad \alpha \leq 0 \leq 1.$$

For further reference, we denote the latter procedure a *local Monte Carlo* (LMC) *test*. Under general conditions, this LMC test has the correct level asymptotically (as $n \to \infty$), i.e. under H_0,

$$\lim_{n \to \infty} \{P[\hat{p}_N(S_0 \mid \hat{\theta}_n^0) \leq \alpha] - P[\hat{p}_N(S_0 \mid \theta) \leq \alpha]\} = 0. \tag{23.35}$$

In particular, these conditions are usually met whenever the test criterion involved is asymptotically pivotal. We emphasize that no asymptotics on the number of replications is required to obtain (23.35).

- To obtain an exact critical region, the MC p-value ought to be maximized with respect to the intervening parameters. Specifically, in Dufour (1995), it is shown that the test (henceforth called a *maximized Monte Carlo* (MMC) *test*) based on the critical region

$$\sup_{\theta \in M_0} [\hat{p}_N(S_0 \mid \theta)] \leq \alpha \tag{23.36}$$

where M_0 is the subset of the parameter space compatible with the null hypothesis (i.e. the nuisance parameter space) is exact at level α.

The LMC test procedure is closely related to a parametric bootstrap, with however a fundamental difference. Whereas bootstrap tests are valid as $N \to \infty$, the number of simulated samples used in MC tests is explicitly taken into account. Further the LMC p-value may be viewed as exact in a *liberal* sense, i.e. if the LMC fails to reject, we can be sure that the exact test involving the maximum p-value is not significant at level α.

In practical applications of exact MMC tests, a global optimization procedure is needed to obtain the maximal randomized p-value in (23.36). We use the simulated annealing (SA) algorithm (Corana, Marchesi, Martini, and Ridella, 1987; Goffe, Ferrier, and Rogers, 1994). SA starts from an initial point (it is natural to use $\hat{\theta}_n^0$ here) and sweeps the parameter space (user defined) at random. An *uphill* step is always accepted while a downhill step may be accepted; the decision is made using the Metropolis criterion. The direction of all moves is determined by probabilistic criteria. As it progresses, SA constantly adjusts the step length so that *downhill* moves are less and less likely to be accepted. In this manner, the algorithm escapes local optima and gradually converges towards the most probable area for optimizing. SA is robust with respect to nonquadratic and even noncontinuous surfaces and typically escapes local optima. The procedure is known not to depend on starting values. Most importantly, SA readily handles problems involving a fairly large number of parameters.[7]

To conclude this section, we consider another application of MC tests which is useful in the context of boundedly pivotal statistics. Using the above notation, the statistic at hand S is boundedly pivotal if it is possible to find another statistic S^* such that

$$S \leq S^*, \quad \forall \theta \in \Theta_0, \tag{23.37}$$

and S^* is pivotal under the null. Let c and c^* refer to the α size-correct cut-off points associated with S and S^*. As emphasized earlier, inequality (23.37) entails that c^* may be used to define a critical region for S. The resulting test will have the correct level and may be viewed as *conservative* in the following sense: if the test based on c^* is significant, we can be sure that the exact test involving the (unknown!) c is significant at level α. The main point here is that it is easier to calculate c^*, because S^* is pivotal, whereas S is nuisance-parameter dependent. Of course, this presumes that the null exact distribution of S^* is known and tractable; see Dufour (1989, 1990) for the underlying theory and several illustrative examples. Here we argue that the MC test technique may be used to produce simulation-based conservative p-values based on S^* even if the analytic null distribution of S^* is unknown or complicated (but may be simulated). The procedure involved is the same as above, except that the S^* rather than S is evaluated from the simulated samples. We denote the latter procedure a bound MC (BMC) test.

A sound test strategy would be to perform the bounds tests first and, on failure to reject, to apply randomized tests. We recommend the following computationally attractive exact α test procedure:

1. compute the test statistic from the data;
2. if a bounding criterion is available, compute a BMC p-value; reject the null if: BMC p-value $\leq \alpha$;
3. if the observed value of the test statistic falls in the BMC acceptance region, obtain a LMC p-value; declare the test not significant if: LMC p-value $> \alpha$;
4. if the LMC p-value $\leq \alpha <$ BMC p-value, obtain the MMC p-value and reject the null if the latter is less than or equal to α.

4 MONTE CARLO TESTS: ECONOMETRIC APPLICATIONS

4.1 Pivotal statistics

In Dufour and Kiviet (1996, 1998), Kiviet and Dufour (1997), Dufour *et al.* (1998), Dufour and Khalaf (1998a, 1998c), Bernard, Dufour, Khalaf, and Genest (1998), Saphores, Khalaf, and Pelletier (1998), several applications of MC tests based on pivotal statistics are presented. The problems considered include: normality tests, heteroskedasticity tests including tests for (G)ARCH and tests for break in variance at unknown points, independence tests and tests based on autocorrelations.[8]

The reader will find in the above papers simulation results which show clearly that the technique of Monte Carlo tests completely corrects often important size distortions due to poor large sample approximations; power studies are also reported on a case by case basis to assess the performance of MC size corrected tests.

Relevant results pertaining to the examples considered above are included in Tables 23.2 and 23.3. It is evident from Table 23.2 that the size of the JB and KS tests is perfectly controlled for all designs considered.[9] Table 23.3 includes the empirical size of the MC LR test for linear restrictions. From (23.27), we see that under the distributional assumption (23.19), the simulated statistics may be obtained using draws from a nuisance-parameter free null distribution, namely the hypothesized distribution of the vector w. Consequently, application of the MC test procedure yields exact p-values. Indeed, it is shown in Table 23.3 that the MC LR test achieves perfect size control.[10]

Now to illustrate the feasibility of MMC tests and the usefulness of BMC tests, we will focus on examples involving nuisance parameters.

4.2   Monte Carlo tests in the presence of nuisance parameters: examples from the multivariate regression model

In this section, we provide examples from Dufour and Khalaf (1998a, 1998b) pertaining to LR test criteria in the MLR (reduced form) model. The model was introduced in Section 2.3. Consider the three equations system

$$Y_1 = \beta_{10} + \beta_{11}X_1 + U_1,$$

$$Y_2 = \beta_{20} + \beta_{22}X_2 + U_2,$$

$$Y_3 = \beta_{30} + \beta_{33}X_3 + U_3, \tag{23.38}$$

imposing normality, and the hypothesis $H_0 : \beta_{11} = \beta_{22} = \beta_{33}$. First restate H_0 in terms of the MLR model which includes the SURE system as a special case, so that it incorporates the SURE exclusion restrictions. Formally, in the framework of the MLR model

$$Y_1 = \beta_{10} + \beta_{11}X_1 + \beta_{12}X_2 + \beta_{13}X_3 + U_1,$$

$$Y_2 = \beta_{20} + \beta_{21}X_1 + \beta_{22}X_2 + \beta_{23}X_3 + U_2,$$

$$Y_3 = \beta_{30} + \beta_{31}X_1 + \beta_{32}X_2 + \beta_{33}X_3 + U_3, \tag{23.39}$$

H_0 is equivalent to the joint hypothesis

$$H_0^* : \beta_{11} = \beta_{22} = \beta_{33} \text{ and } \beta_{12} = \beta_{13} = \beta_{21} = \beta_{23} = \beta_{31} = \beta_{32} = 0. \tag{23.40}$$

The associated LR statistic is

$$LR = n \ln(\Lambda), \quad \Lambda = |\hat{\Sigma}_0| / |\hat{\Sigma}|, \qquad (23.41)$$

where $\hat{\Sigma}_0$ and $\hat{\Sigma}$ are the restricted and unrestricted SURE MLE. We also consider

$$LR^* = n \ln(\Lambda^*), \quad \Lambda^* = |\hat{\Sigma}_0| / |\hat{\Sigma}_u|, \qquad (23.42)$$

where $\hat{\Sigma}_u$ is the unconstrained estimate of Σ in the "nesting" MLR model. Since the restricted model is the same in both LR and LR*, while the unrestricted model used in LR* includes as a special case the one in LR, it is straightforward to see that LR ≤ LR*, so that the distribution function of LR* provides an upper bound on the distribution function of LR.

In order to apply a BMC test, we need to construct a set of UL restrictions that satisfy (23.40) so that the corresponding LRc criterion conforming with these UL restrictions yields a valid bound on the distribution of LR. Indeed, as emphasized above, the LR test statistic for UL restrictions is pivotal. Furthermore, by considering UL restrictions obtained as a special case of H_0^*, we can be sure that the associated statistic is always ≥ LR. Here, it is easy to see that the constraints setting the coefficients β_{ij}, $i, j = 1, \ldots, 3$, to specific values meet this criterion. Note that the statistic just derived serves to bound both LR and LR*.

Define $\theta \equiv C(\Sigma)$ as the vector of the parameters on or below the diagonal of the Cholesky factor $T(\Sigma)$ of the covariance matrix Σ (i.e. $T(\Sigma)$ is the lower triangular matrix such that $T(\Sigma)T(\Sigma)' = \Sigma$). The algorithm for performing MC tests based on LR*, at the 5 percent level with 99 replications, can be described as follows.

- Compute $\hat{\Sigma}_0$ and $\hat{\Sigma}$, the restricted and unrestricted SURE (iterative) MLE.
- Compute $\hat{\Sigma}_u$ as the unconstrained (OLS) estimate of Σ in the "nesting" MLR model.
- Compute $\Lambda^* = |\hat{\Sigma}_0| / |\hat{\Sigma}_u|$ and $LR^* = n \ln(\Lambda^*)$.
- Draw 99 realizations from a multivariate $(n, 3, I)$ normal distribution: $U^{(1)}$, $U^{(2)}, \ldots, U^{(p)}$ and store.
- Consider the linear constraints

$$H_{02} : \begin{bmatrix} 0 & 1 & 0 & 0 \\ 0 & 0 & 1 & 0 \\ 0 & 0 & 0 & 1 \end{bmatrix} \begin{bmatrix} \beta_{10} & \beta_{20} & \beta_{30} \\ \beta_{11} & \beta_{21} & \beta_{31} \\ \beta_{12} & \beta_{22} & \beta_{32} \\ \beta_{13} & \beta_{23} & \beta_{33} \end{bmatrix} = \begin{bmatrix} \hat{\beta}_{11} & 0 & 0 \\ 0 & \hat{\beta}_{22} & 0 \\ 0 & 0 & \hat{\beta}_{33} \end{bmatrix}$$

where $\hat{\beta}_{11} = \hat{\beta}_{22} = \hat{\beta}_{33}$ are the constrained SURE estimates calculated in the first step.

- Call the bound MC procedure BMC(θ), described below, for $\theta \equiv C(\hat{\Sigma}_0)$. The Cholesky decomposition is used to impose positive definiteness and avoid redundant parameters. The output is the BMC p-value. Reject the null if the latter is ≤ .05 and STOP.

- Otherwise, call the procedure MC(θ), also described below, for $\theta \equiv C(\hat{\Sigma}_0)$. It is important to note here that Σ is the only relevant nuisance parameter, for the example considered involves linear constraints (see Breusch, 1980). The output is the LMC p-value. Declare the test not significant if the latter *exceeds* .05 and STOP.
- Otherwise, call the maximization algorithm (for example, SA) for the function MC(θ) using $\theta \equiv C(\hat{\Sigma}_0)$ as a starting value. Obtain the MMC p-value and reject the null if the latter is $\leq$ .05. Note: if only a decision is required, the maximization algorithm may be instructed to exit as soon as a value larger than .05 is attained. This may save considerable computation time.

Description of the procedure MC(θ):

- Construct a triangular Ω from θ (this gives the Cholesky decomposition of the variance which will be used to generate the simulated model).
- Do for $j = 1, \ldots, N$ (independently)
  - (a) Generate the random vectors $Y_1^{(j)} Y_2^{(j)} Y_3^{(j)}$ conformably with the nesting MLR model, using the restricted SURE coefficient estimates, $U^{(j)}$, the observed regressors, and Ω.
  - (b) Estimate the MLR model with the observed regressors as dependent variable, and $Y_1^{(j)} Y_2^{(j)} Y_3^{(j)}$ as independent variables: obtain the unrestricted estimates and the estimates imposing H_0.
  - (c) From these estimates, form the statistics $\mathrm{LR}^{(j)}$ and store.
- Obtain the rank of LR^* in the series $\mathrm{LR}^*, \mathrm{LR}^{*(1)}, \ldots, \mathrm{LR}^{*(99)}$.
- This yields a MC p-value as described above which is the output of the procedure.
- The BMC(θ) procedure may be obtained as just described, replacing $\mathrm{LR}^{*(j)}$ by $\mathrm{LR}_c^{(j)}$. Alternatively, the BMC procedure may be rewritten following the methodology relating to MC tests of UL hypotheses so that no (unknown) parameters intervene in the generation of the simulated (bounding) statistics. Indeed, the bounding statistic satisfies (23.27) under (23.19). Thus $\mathrm{LR}_c^{(j)}$ may be obtained using draws from, e.g., the multivariate independent normal distribution.

In Dufour and Khalaf (1998c), we report the results of a simulation experiment designed according to this example. In particular, we examine the performance of LMC and BMC tests. We show that the MC test procedure achieves perfect size control and has good power. The same methodology may also be applied in simultaneous equations models such as (23.3). In Dufour and Khalaf (1998b), we present simulations which illustrate the performance of limited-information LR-based MC tests in this context. We have attempted to apply the MC test procedure to the IV-based Wald-type test for linear restrictions on structural parameters. In this case, the performance of the standard bootstrap was disappointing. The LMC Wald tests failed completely in near-unidentified conditions. Furthermore, in all cases examined, *the Wald tests maximal randomized p-values were always one.* This is a case (refer to Section 2.3) where the MC procedure does not (and cannot) correct the performance of the test.

In other words, Wald statistics do not constitute valid pivotal functions in such models and it is even impossible to bound their distributions over the parameter space (except by the trivial bound 0 and 1). (Dufour, 1997)

These results are also related to the non-invariance problems associated with Wald tests in nonlinear contexts (see, e.g. Dufour, 1997; Dagenais and Dufour, 1991). Indeed, it is evident from (23.3)–(23.5) that *seemingly linear* constraints on structural coefficients in instrumental regressions often involve nonlinear hypotheses implied by the structure. Of course, not all Wald tests will suffer from such problems. For instance, Wald tests for linear restrictions in linear regression models yield exact F-tests.

We conclude this section with a specific problem where the MC test strategy conveniently solves a difficult and non-standard distributional problem: the problem of unidentified nuisance parameters.

4.3 Non-identified nuisance parameters

The example we discuss here is the problem of testing for the significance of jumps in the context of a jump-diffusion model. For econometric applications and references, see Saphores *et al.* (1998). Formally, consider the following model written, for convenience, in discrete time:

$$S_t - S_{t-1} = \mu + \sigma\xi_t + \sum_{i=1}^{n_t} \ln(Y_t), \quad t = 1, \ldots, T,$$

where $\xi \overset{iid}{\sim} N(0, 1)$ and $\ln(Y) \overset{iid}{\sim} N(\theta, \delta^2)$ and n_t is the number of jumps which occur in the interval $[t-1, t]$; the arrival of jumps is assumed to follow a *Poisson* process with parameter λ. The associated likelihood function is as follows:

$$L_1 = -T\ln(\lambda) - \frac{T}{2}\ln(2\pi) + \sum_{t=1}^{T}\ln\left[\sum_{j=0}^{\infty}\frac{\lambda^j}{j!}\frac{1}{\sqrt{\sigma^2 + \delta^2 j}}\exp\left(\frac{-(x_t - \mu - \theta j)^2}{2(\sigma^2 + \delta^2 j)}\right)\right].$$

The hypothesis of no jumps corresponds to $\lambda = 0$. It is clear that in this case, the parameters θ, δ^2 are not identified under the null, and hence, following the results of Davies (1977, 1987), the distribution of the associated LR statistic is non-standard and quite complicated. Although this problem is well recognized by now, a $\chi^2(3)$ asymptotic distribution is often (inappropriately) used in empirical applications of the latter LR test. See Diebold and Chen (1996) for related arguments dealing with structural change tests.

Let $\hat{\mu}$, $\hat{\sigma}^2$ denote the MLE under the null, i.e. imposing a Geometric Brownian Motion. Here we argue that in this case, the MC p-value calculated as described above, drawing iid $N(\hat{\mu}, \hat{\sigma}^2)$ disturbances (with $\hat{\mu}$ and $\hat{\sigma}^2$ taken as given) will not depend on θ and δ^2. This follows immediately from the implications of non-identification. Furthermore, the invariance to location and scale (μ and σ) is straightforward to see. Consequently, the MC test described in the context of pivotal statistics will yield exact p-values.

The problem of unidentified nuisance parameters is prevalent in econometrics. Bernard *et al.* (1998) consider another illustrative example: testing for ARCH-in-mean effects, and show that the MC method works very well in terms of size and power.

5 Conclusion

In this chapter, we have demonstrated that finite sample concerns may arise in several empirically pertinent test problems. But, in many cases of interest, the MC test technique produces valid inference procedures no matter how small your sample is.

We have also emphasized that the problem of constructing a good test – although simplified – cannot be solved *just* using simulations. Yet in most examples we have reviewed, MC test techniques emerge as indispensable tools.

Beyond the cases covered above, it is worthwhile noting that the MC test technique may be applied to many other problems of interest. These include, for example, models where the estimators themselves are also simulation-based, e.g. estimators based on indirect inference or involving simulated maximum likelihood. Furthermore, the MC test technique is by no means restricted to nested hypotheses. It is therefore possible to compare nonnested models using MC LR-type tests; assessing the success of this strategy in practical problems is an interesting research avenue.

Of course, the first purpose of the MC test technique is to control the probability of type I errors (below a given *level*) so that rejections can properly be interpreted as showing that the null hypothesis is "incompatible" with the data. However, once level is controled, we can (and should) devote more attention to finding procedures with good *power* properties. Indeed, by helping to put the problem of level control out of the way, we think the technique of MC tests should help econometricians devote research to power issues as opposed to level. So an indirect consequence of the implementation of the technique may well be an increased emphasis on the design of more powerful tests.

Your data are valuable, and the statistical analysis you perform is often policy oriented. Why tolerate questionable *p*-values and confidence intervals, when exact or improved approximations are available?

Notes

*   The authors thank three anonymous referees and the Editor, Badi Baltagi, for several useful comments. This work was supported by the Bank of Canada and by grants from the Canadian Network of Centres of Excellence (program on *Mathematics of Information Technology and Complex Systems* (MITACS)), the Social Sciences and Humanities Research Council of Canada, the Natural Sciences and Engeneering Council of Canada, and the Government of Québec (Fonds FCAR).

1   The problem is more complicated when the structural equation includes more than one endogenous variable. See Dufour and Khalaf (1998b) for a detailed discussion of this case.

2   The underlying distributional result is due to Wilks (1932).

3 For a formal treatment see Dufour (1997).

4 Bera and Jarque (1982), Breusch and Pagan (1979, 1980) have also proposed related simulation-based techniques. However, these authors do not provide finite-sample theoretical justification for the proposed procedures. In particular, in contrast with Dwass (1957) and Barnard (1963) (and similarly to many other later authors who have proposed exploiting Monte Carlo techniques), they do not observe that appropriately randomized tests allow one to exactly control the level of a test in finite samples.

5 The subscript N in the notation adopted here may be misleading. We emphasize that $\hat{R}_N(T_0)$ gives the rank of S_0 in the $N + 1$ dimensional array $S_0, S_1, \ldots, S_N$. Throughout this section N refers to the number of MC replications.

6 See Section 2.2 for a formal presentation of the model and test statistics. Some equations are redefined here for convenience.

7 Global optimization is generally considered to be (relatively) computationally demanding. We have experimented (see Dufour and Khalaf, 1998c, 1998b) with several MMC tests where the number of nuisance parameters referred to the simulated annealing algorithm was up to 20. Our simulations show that the method works well. Convergence was slow in some cases (less than 5 per 1,000). Recall, however, that for the problem at hand, one just practically needs to check whether the maximized function exceeds α, which clearly reduces the computational burdens.

8 In connection, it is worth mentioning that the MC test procedure applied to the Durbin–Watson test for AR(1) disturbances solves the inconclusive region problem.

9 See Dufour *et al.* (1998) for the power study.

10 See Dufour and Khalaf (1998c) for the power study.

References

Anderson, T.W., and H. Rubin (1949). Estimation of the parameters of a single equation in a complete system of stochastic equations. *Annals of Mathematical Statistics* 20, 46–63.

Attfield, C.L.F. (1995). A Bartlett adjustment to the likelihood ratio test for a system of equations. *Journal of Econometrics* 66, 207–23.

Barnard, G.A. (1963). Comment on "The Spectral Analysis of Point Processes" by M.S. Bartlett. *Journal of the Royal Statistical Society, Series B* 25, 294.

Bartlett, M.S. (1948). A note on the statistical estimation of supply and demand relations from time series. *Econometrica* 16, 323–9.

Bera, A.K., and C.M. Jarque (1982). Model specification tests: A simultaneous approach. *Journal of Econometrics* 20, 59–82.

Bernard, J.-T., J.-M. Dufour, L. Khalaf, and I. Genest (1998). Monte Carlo tests for heteroskedasticity. Discussion paper, Département d'économique, Université Laval and CRDE, Université de Montréal.

Berndt, E.R. (1991). *The Practice of Econometrics: Classic and Contemporary*. Reading (MA): Addison-Wesley.

Birnbaum, Z.W. (1974). Computers and unconventional test-statistics. In F. Proschan, and R.J. Serfling (eds.) *Reliability and Biometry*, pp. 441–58. Philadelphia, PA: SIAM.

Bound, J., D.A. Jaeger, and R.M. Baker (1995). Problems with instrumental variables estimation when the correlation between the instruments and the endogenous explanatory variable is weak. *Journal of the American Statistical Association* 90, 443–50.

Breusch, T.S. (1980). Useful invariance results for generalized regression models. *Journal of Econometrics* 13, 327–40.

Breusch, T.S., and A.R. Pagan (1979). A simple test for heteroscedasticity and random coefficient variation. *Econometrica* 47, 1287–94.

Breusch, T.S., and A.R. Pagan (1980). The Lagrange multiplier test and its applications to model specification in econometrics. *Review of Economic Studies* 47, 239–54.

Corana, A., M. Marchesi, C. Martini, and S. Ridella (1987). Minimizing multimodal functions of continuous variables with the "Simulated Annealing" algorithm. *ACM Transactions on Mathematical Software* 13, 262–80.

Dagenais, M.G., and J.-M. Dufour (1991). Invariance, nonlinear models and asymptotic tests. *Econometrica* 59, 1601–15.

D'Agostino, R.B., and M.A. Stephens (eds.) (1986). *Goodness-of-Fit Techniques*. New York: Marcel Dekker.

Davies, R.B. (1977). Hypothesis testing when a nuisance parameter is present only under the alternative. *Biometrika* 64, 247–54.

Davies, R.B. (1987). Hypothesis testing when a nuisance parameter is present only under the alternative. *Biometrika* 74, 33–43.

Davison, A., and D. Hinkley (1997). *Bootstrap Methods and Their Application*. Cambridge: Cambridge University Press.

Diebold, F.X., and C. Chen (1996). Testing structural stability with endogenous breakpoint: A size comparison of analytic and bootstrap procedures. *Journal of Econometrics* 70, 221–41.

Dufour, J.-M. (1989). Nonlinear hypotheses, inequality restrictions, and nonnested hypotheses: Exact simultaneous tests in linear regressions. *Econometrica* 57, 335–55.

Dufour, J.-M. (1990). Exact tests and confidence sets in linear regressions with autocorrelated errors. *Econometrica* 58, 475–94.

Dufour, J.-M. (1995). Monte Carlo tests with nuisance parameters: A general approach to finite-sample inference and nonstandard asymptotics in econometrics. Discussion paper, C.R.D.E., Université de Montréal.

Dufour, J.-M. (1997). Some impossibility theorems in econometrics, with applications to structural and dynamic models. *Econometrica* 65, 1365–89.

Dufour, J.-M., A. Farhat, L. Gardiol, and L. Khalaf (1998). Simulation-based finite sample normality tests in linear regressions. *Econometrics Journal* 1, 154–73.

Dufour, J.M., and J. Jasiak (1996). Finite sample inference methods for simultaneous equations and models with unobserved and generated regressors. Discussion paper, C.R.D.E., Université de Montréal.

Dufour, J.-M., and L. Khalaf (1998a). Monte Carlo tests for contemporaneous correlation of disturbances in multiequation SURE models. Discussion paper, C.R.D.E., Université de Montréal.

Dufour, J.-M., and L. Khalaf (1998c). Simulation based finite and large sample inference methods in multivariate regressions and seemingly unrelated regressions. Discussion paper, C.R.D.E., Université de Montréal.

Dufour, J.-M., and L. Khalaf (1998b). Simulation-based finite and large sample inference methods in simultaneous equations. Discussion paper, C.R.D.E., Université de Montréal.

Dufour, J.-M., and J.F. Kiviet (1996). Exact tests for structural change in first-order dynamic models. *Journal of Econometrics* 70, 39–68.

Dufour, J.-M., and J.F. Kiviet (1998). Exact inference methods for first-order autoregressive distributed lag models. *Econometrica* 66, 79–104.

Dwass, M. (1957). Modified randomization tests for nonparametric hypotheses. *Annals of Mathematical Statistics* 28, 181–7.

Efron, B. (1982). *The Jackknife, the Bootstrap and Other Resampling Plans*, CBS-NSF Regional Conference Series in Applied Mathematics, Monograph No. 38. Society for Industrial and Applied Mathematics, Philadelphia, PA.

Efron, B., and R.J. Tibshirani (1993). *An Introduction to the Bootstrap*, vol. 57 of *Monographs on Statistics and Applied Probability*. New York: Chapman & Hall.

Gallant, A.R., and G. Tauchen (1996). Which moments to match? *Econometric Theory* 12, 657–81.

Gibbons, M.R., S.A. Ross, and J. Shanken (1989). A test of the efficiency of a given portfolio. *Econometrica* 57, 1121–52.

Goffe, W.L., G.D. Ferrier, and J. Rogers (1994). Global optimization of statistical functions with simulated annealing. *Journal of Econometrics* 60, 65–99.

Gouriéroux, C., and A. Monfort (1995). *Statistics and Econometric Models, Volumes One and Two*. Cambridge: Cambridge University Press.

Gouriéroux, C., A. Monfort, and E. Renault (1993). Indirect inference. *Journal of Applied Econometrics* 8S, 85–118.

Hajivassiliou, V.A. (1993). Simulation estimation methods for limited dependent variables. In G.S. Maddala, C.R. Rao, and H.D. Vinod (eds.) *Handbook of Statistics, Volume 11, Econometrics*. pp. 519–43. Amsterdam: North-Holland.

Hall, P. (1992). *The Bootstrap and Edgeworth Expansion*. New York: Springer-Verlag.

Horowitz, J.L. (1997). Bootstrap methods in econometrics: Theory and numerical performance. In D. Kreps, and K.W. Wallis (eds.) *Advances in Economics and Econometrics*, vol. 3, pp. 188–222. Cambridge: Cambridge University Press.

Jarque, C.M., and A.K. Bera (1980). Efficient tests for normality, heteroscedasticity and serial independence of regression residuals. *Economics Letters* 6, 255–9.

Jarque, C.M., and A.K. Bera (1987). A test for normality of observations and regression residuals. *International Statistical Review* 55, 163–72.

Jeong, J., and G.S. Maddala (1993). A perspective on application of bootstrap methods in econometrics. In G.S. Maddala, C.R. Rao, and H.D. Vinod (eds.) *Handbook of Statistics, Volume 11, Econometrics*, pp. 573–610. Amsterdam: North-Holland.

Keane, M.P. (1993). Simulation estimation for panel data models with limited dependent variables. In Maddala, Rao, and Vinod (1993), pp. 545–571.

Kiviet, J.F., and J.-M. Dufour (1997). Exact tests in single equation autoregressive distributed lag models. *Journal of Econometrics* 80, 325–53.

Kolmogorov, A.N. (1933). Sulla determinazione empiricadi una legge di distribtuzione. *Giorna. Ist. Attuari* 4, 83–91.

Laitinen, K. (1978). Why is demand homogeneity so often rejected? *Economics Letters* 1, 187–91.

Lehmann, E.L. (1986). *Testing Statistical Hypotheses*, 2nd edn. New York: John Wiley & Sons.

Maddala, G.S., C.R. Rao, and H.D. Vinod (eds.) (1993). *Handbook of Statistics, Volume 11, Econometrics*. Amsterdam: North-Holland.

Mariano, R.S., and B.W. Brown (1993). Stochastic simulation for inference in nonlinear errors-in-variables models. In Maddala, Rao, and Vinod (1993), pp. 611–27.

Nelson, C.R., and R. Startz (1990a). The distribution of the instrumental variable estimator and its *t*-ratio when the instrument is a poor one. *Journal of Business* 63, 125–40.

Nelson, C.R., and R. Startz (1990b). Some further results on the exact small properties of the instrumental variable estimator. *Econometrica* 58, 967–76.

Saphores, J.-D., L. Khalaf, and D. Pelletier (1998). Modelling unexpected changes in stumpage prices: an application to Pacific Northwest National Forests. Discussion paper, GREEN, Université Laval, Québec.

Shao, S., and D. Tu (1995). *The Jackknife and Bootstrap*. New York: Springer-Verlag.

Smirnov, N.V. (1939). Sur les écarts de la courbe de distribution empirique (Russian/French Summary). *Matematičeskiĭ Sbornik N.S.* 6, 3–26.

Staiger, D., and J.H. Stock (1997). Instrumental variables regression with weak instruments. *Econometrica* 65, 557–86.

Stewart, K.G. (1997). Exact testing in multivariate regression. *Econometric Reviews* 16, 321–52.

Vinod, H.D. (1993). Bootstrap methods: Applications in econometrics. in Maddala, Rao, and Vinod (1993), pp. 629–61.

Wilks, S.S. (1932). Certain generalizations in the analysis of variance. *Biometrika* 24, 471–94.

Zellner, A. (1962). An efficient method for estimating seemingly unrelated regressions and tests for aggregate bias. *Journal of the American Statistical Association* 57, 348–68.

Bayesian Analysis of Stochastic Frontier Models

Gary Koop and Mark F.J. Steel

1   INTRODUCTION

Stochastic frontier models are commonly used in the empirical study of firm[1] efficiency and productivity. The seminal papers in the field are Aigner, Lovell, and Schmidt (1977) and Meeusen and van den Broeck (1977), while a recent survey is provided in Bauer (1990). The ideas underlying this class of models can be demonstrated using a simple production model[2] where output of firm i, Y_i, is produced using a vector of inputs, X_i, $(i = 1 \ldots N)$. The best practice technology for turning inputs into output depends on a vector of unknown parameters, β, and is given by:

$$Y_i = f(X_i; \beta). \tag{24.1}$$

This so-called production frontier captures the maximum amount of output that can be obtained from a given level of inputs. In practice, actual output of a firm may fall below the maximum possible. The deviation of actual from maximum output is a measure of inefficiency and is the focus of interest in many applications. Formally, equation (24.1) can be extended to:

$$Y_i = f(X_i; \beta)\tau_i, \tag{24.2}$$

where $0 \leq \tau_i \leq 1$ is a measure of firm-specific efficiency and $\tau_i = 1$ indicates firm i is fully efficient.

In this chapter we will discuss Bayesian inference in such models. We will draw on our previous work in the area: van den Broeck, Koop, Osiewalski, and Steel (1994), Koop, Osiewalski, and Steel (1994, 1997, 1999, 2000) and Koop, Steel, and Osiewalski (1995), whereas theoretical foundations can be found in Fernández, Osiewalski, and Steel (1997). It is worthwhile to digress briefly as to why we think these models are worthy of serious study. Efficiency measurement is very important in many areas of economics[3] and, hence, worthy of study in and of itself. However, stochastic frontier models are also close to other classes of models and can be used to illustrate ideas relating to the linear and nonlinear regression models; models for panel data, variance components, random coefficients, and, generally, models with unobserved heterogeneity. Thus, stochastic frontier models can be used to illustrate Bayesian methods in many areas of econometrics. To justify our adoption of the Bayesian paradigm, the reader is referred to our work in the area. Suffice it to note here that the competitors to the Bayesian approach advocated here are the classical econometric stochastic frontier approach (see Bauer, 1990 for a survey) and the deterministic or nonparametric data envelopment analysis (DEA) approach (see, e.g., Färe, Grosskopf, and Lovell, 1994). Each of the three approaches has strengths and weaknesses, some of which will be noted in this chapter.

This chapter is intended to be reasonably self-contained. However, we do assume that the reader has a basic knowledge of Bayesian methods as applied to the linear regression model (e.g. Judge, Griffiths, Hill, Lütkepohl, and Lee, 1985, ch. 4 or Poirier, 1995, pp. 288–309 and 524–50). Furthermore, we assume some knowledge of simulation methods. Koop (1994, pp. 12–26) provides a simple survey of some of these methods. Osiewalski and Steel (1998) focuses on simulation methods in the context of stochastic frontier models. Casella and George (1992) and Chib and Greenberg (1995) are good expository sources for Gibbs sampling and Metropolis–Hastings algorithms, respectively. Geweke (1999) is a complete survey of both Bayesian methods and computation.

The remainder of the chapter is organized as follows. The second section considers the stochastic frontier model with cross-sectional data beginning with a simple loglinear model then considering a nonlinear extension and one where explanatory variables enter the efficiency distribution. The third section discusses the issues raised by the availability of panel data.

2   THE STOCHASTIC FRONTIER MODEL WITH CROSS-SECTIONAL DATA

2.1   Introduction and notation

The model given in equation (24.2) implicitly assumes that all deviations from the frontier are due to inefficiency. This assumption is also typically made in the DEA approach. However, following standard econometric practice, we add a random error to the model, ζ_i, to capture measurement (or specification) error,[4] resulting in:

$$Y_i = f(X_i; \beta)\tau_i\zeta_i. \tag{24.3}$$

The addition of measurement error makes the frontier stochastic, hence the term "stochastic frontier models". We assume that data for $i = 1 \ldots N$ firms is available and that the production frontier, $f(\cdot)$, is log-linear (e.g. Cobb–Douglas or translog). We define X_i as a $1 \times (k + 1)$ vector (e.g. $X_i = (1\ L_i\ K_i)$ in the case of a Cobb–Douglas frontier with two inputs, L and K) and, hence, (24.3) can be written as:

$$y_i = x_i \beta + v_i - z_i, \tag{24.4}$$

where $\beta = (\beta_0 \ldots \beta_k)'$, $y_i = \ln(Y_i)$, $v_i = \ln(\zeta_i)$, $z_i = -\ln(\tau_i)$ and x_i is the counterpart of X_i with the inputs transformed to logarithms. z_i is referred to as inefficiency and, since $0 \leq \tau_i \leq 1$, it is a nonnegative random variable. We assume that the model contains an intercept with coefficient β_0. Equation (24.4) looks like the standard linear regression model, except that the "error" is composed of two parts. This gives rise to another name for these models, viz. "composed error models".

For future reference, we define $y = (y_1 \ldots y_N)'$, $v = (v_1 \ldots v_N)'$, $z = (z_1 \ldots z_N)'$ and the $N \times (k + 1)$ matrix $x = (x_1' \ldots x_N')'$. Also, let $f_G(a \mid b, c)$ denote the density function of a Gamma distribution with shape parameter b and scale c so that a has mean b/c and variance b/c^2. $p(d) = f_N^r(d \mid g, F)$ indicates that d is r-variate normal with mean g and covariance matrix F. We will use $I(\cdot)$ to denote the indicator function; i.e. $I(G) = 1$ if event G occurs and is otherwise 0. Furthermore, I_N will indicate the $N \times N$ identity matrix and ι_N and $N \times 1$ vector of ones. Sample means will be indicated with a bar, e.g. $\bar{y} = \frac{1}{N} \iota_N' y$.

2.2 Bayesian inference

In order to define the sampling model,[5] we make the following assumptions about v_i and z_i for $i = 1 \ldots N$:

1. $p(v_i \mid h^{-1}) = f_N^1(v_i \mid 0, h^{-1})$ and the v_is are independent;
2. v_i and z_l are independent of one another for all i and l;
3. $p(z_i \mid \lambda^{-1}) = f_G(z_i \mid 1, \lambda^{-1})$ and the z_is are independent.

The first assumption is commonly made in cross-sectional analysis, but the last two require some justification. Assumption 2 says that measurement error and inefficiency are independent of one another. Assumption 3 is a common choice for the nonnegative random variable, z_i, although others (e.g. the half-normal) are possible. Ritter and Simar (1997) show that the use of very flexible one-sided distributions for z_i such as the unrestricted gamma may result in a problem of weak identification. Intuitively, if z_i is left too flexible, then the intercept minus z_i can come to look too much like v_i and it may become virtually impossible to distinguish between these two components with small data sets. The gamma with shape parameter 1 is the exponential distribution, which is sufficiently different from the normal to avoid this weak identification problem.[6] In addition, van den Broeck et al. (1994) found the exponential model the least sensitive to changes in prior assumptions in a study of the most commonly used models. Note that λ is the mean of the inefficiency distribution and let $\theta = (\beta', h, \lambda)'$ denote the parameters of the model.

The likelihood function is defined as:

$$L(y; \theta) = \prod_{i=1}^{N} p(y_i \mid x_i, \theta),$$

which requires the derivation of $p(y_i \mid x_i, \theta) = \int p(y_i \mid x_i, z_i, \theta) p(z_i \mid \theta) dz_i$. This is done in Jondrow, Lovell, Materov, and Schmidt (1982) for the exponential model and in van den Broeck *et al.* (1994) for a wider class of inefficiency distributions. However, we do not repeat the derivation here, since we do not need to know the explicit form of the likelihood function. To understand why isolating the likelihood function is not required, it is necessary to explain the computational methods that we recommend for Bayesian inference in stochastic frontier models.

Bayesian inference can be carried out using a posterior simulator which generates draws from the posterior, $p(\theta \mid y, x)$. In this case, Gibbs sampling with data augmentation is a natural choice for a posterior simulator. This algorithm relies on the fact that sequential draws, $\theta^{(s)}$ and $z^{(s)}$, from the conditional posteriors $p(\theta \mid y, x, z^{(s-1)})$ and $p(z \mid y, x, \theta^{(s)})$, respectively, will converge to draws from $p(\theta, z \mid y, x)$ from which inference on the marginal posteriors of θ or of functions of z (such as efficiencies) can immediately be derived. In other words, we do not need to have an analytical formula for $p(\theta \mid y, x)$ (and, hence, the likelihood function), but rather we can suffice with working out the full conditional distributions $p(\theta \mid y, x, z)$ and $p(z \mid y, x, \theta)$. Intuitively, the former is very easy to work with since, conditional on z, the stochastic frontier model reduces to the standard linear regression model.[7] If $p(\theta \mid y, x, z)$ as a whole is not analytically tractable, we can split up θ into, say, β and (h, λ) and draw sequentially from the full conditionals $p(\beta \mid h, \lambda, y, x, z)$, $p(h, \lambda \mid \beta, y, x, z)$, and $p(z \mid y, x, \beta, h, \lambda)$. However, before we can derive the Gibbs sampler, we must complete the Bayesian model by specifying a prior for the parameters.

The researcher can, of course, use any prior in an attempt to reflect his/her prior beliefs. However, a proper prior for h and λ^{-1} is advisable: Fernández *et al.* (1997) show that Bayesian inference is not feasible (in the sense that the posterior distribution is not well-defined) under the usual improper priors for h and λ^{-1}. Here, we will assume a prior of the product form: $p(\theta) = p(\beta)p(h)p(\lambda^{-1})$. In stochastic frontier models, prior information exists in the form of economic regularity conditions. It is extremely important to ensure that the production frontier satisfies these, since it is highly questionable to interpret deviations from a non-regular frontier as representing inefficiency. In an extreme case, if the researcher is using a highly flexible (or nonparametric) functional form for $f(\cdot)$ it might be possible for the frontier to fit the data nearly perfectly. It is only the imposition of economic regularity conditions that prevent this overfitting. The exact form of the economic regularity conditions depend on the specification of the frontier. For instance, in the Cobb–Douglas case, $\beta_i \geq 0$, $i = 1 \ldots k$ ensures global regularity of the production frontier. For the translog specification things are more complicated and we may wish only to impose local regularity. This requires checking certain conditions at each data point (see Koop *et al.*, 1999). In either case, we can choose a prior for β which imposes economic regularity. As emphasized by

Fernández *et al.* (1997), a proper or bounded prior is sufficient for β. Thus, it is acceptable to use a uniform (flat) prior:

$$p(\beta) \propto I(E), \qquad (24.5)$$

where $I(E)$ is the indicator function for the economic regularity conditions. Alternatively, a normal prior for β is proper and computationally convenient. In this chapter, we will use $p(\beta)$ as a general notation, but assume it is either truncated uniform or truncated normal. Both choices will easily combine with a normal distribution to produce a truncated normal posterior distribution.

For the other parameters, we assume gamma priors:

$$p(h) = f_G(h \mid a_h, b_h) \qquad (24.6)$$

and

$$p(\lambda^{-1}) = f_G(\lambda^{-1} \mid a_\lambda, b_\lambda). \qquad (24.7)$$

Note that, by setting $a_h = 0$ and $b_h = 0$ we obtain $p(h) \propto h^{-1}$, the usual noninformative prior for the error precision in the normal linear regression model. Here, the use of this improper prior is precluded (see Theorem 1 (ii) of Fernández *et al.*, 1997), but small values of these hyperparameters will allow for Bayesian inference (see Proposition 2 of Fernández *et al.*, 1997) while the prior is still dominated by the likelihood function. The hyperparameters a_λ and b_λ can often be elicited through consideration of the efficiency distribution. That is, researchers may often have prior information about the shape or location of the efficiency distribution. As discussed in van den Broeck *et al.* (1994), setting $a_\lambda = 1$ and $b_\lambda = -\ln(\tau^*)$ yields a relatively noninformative prior which implies the prior median of the efficiency distribution is τ^*. These are the values for a_λ and b_λ used in the following discussion.

The Gibbs sampler can be developed in a straightforward manner by noting that, if z were known, then we could write the model as $y + z = x\beta + v$ and standard results for the normal linear regression model can be used. In particular, we can obtain

$$p(\beta \mid y, x, z, h, \lambda^{-1}) = f_N^{k+1}(\beta \mid \hat{\beta}, h^{-1}(x'x)^{-1})p(\beta), \qquad (24.8)$$

where

$$\hat{\beta} = (x'x)^{-1}x'(y + z).$$

Furthermore,

$$p(h \mid y, x, z, \beta, \lambda^{-1}) = f_G\left(h \,\middle|\, a_h + \frac{N}{2}, b_h + \frac{(y - x\beta + z)'(y - x\beta + z)}{2}\right). \qquad (24.9)$$

Also, given z, the full conditional posterior for λ^{-1} can easily be derived:

$$p(\lambda^{-1} \mid y, x, z, \beta, h) = f_G(\lambda^{-1} \mid N + 1, z'\iota_N - \ln(\tau^*)). \qquad (24.10)$$

Equations (24.8), (24.9), and (24.10) are the full conditional posteriors necessary for setting up the Gibbs sampler *conditional on z*. To complete the posterior simulator, it is necessary to derive the posterior distribution of z conditional on θ. Noting that we can write $z = x\beta - y + v$, where v has pdf $f_N^N(v \mid 0, h^{-1}I_N)$ and z_i is a priori assumed to be iid $f_G(z_i \mid 1, \lambda^{-1})$,[8] we obtain:

$$p(z \mid y, x, \beta, h, \lambda^{-1}) \propto f_N^N(z \mid x\beta - y - h^{-1}\lambda^{-1}\iota_N, h^{-1}I_N) \prod_{i=1}^{N} I(z_i \geq 0). \qquad (24.11)$$

A Gibbs sampler with data augmentation on $(\beta, h, \lambda^{-1}, z)$ can be set up by sequentially drawing from (24.8), (24.9), (24.10), and (24.11), where (β, h) and λ^{-1} are independent given z, so that (24.10) can be combined with either (24.8) or (24.9) and there are only three steps in the Gibbs. Note that all that is required is random number generation from well known distributions, where drawing from the high-dimensional vector z is greatly simplified as (24.11) can be written as the product of N univariate truncated normals.

Given posterior simulator output, posterior properties of any of the parameters or of the individual τ_is can be obtained.[9] The latter can be calculated using simulated draws from (24.11) and transforming according to $\tau_i = \exp(-z_i)$. It is worth stressing that the Bayesian approach provides a finite sample distribution of the efficiency of each firm. This allows us to obtain both point and interval estimates, or even e.g. $P(\tau_i > \tau_j \mid y, x)$. The latter is potentially crucial since important policy consequences often hinge on one firm being labeled as more efficient in a statistically significant sense. Both DEA and classical econometric approaches typically only report point estimates. The DEA approach is nonparametric and, hence, confidence intervals for the efficiency measures obtained are very hard to derive.[10] Distributional theory for the classical econometric approach is discussed in Jondrow *et al.* (1982) and Horrace and Schmidt (1996). These papers point out that, although point estimates and confidence intervals for τ_i can be calculated, the theoretical justification is not that strong. For example, the maximum likelihood estimator for τ_i is inconsistent and the methods for constructing confidence intervals assume unknown parameters are equal to their point estimates. For this reason, it is common in classical econometric work to present some characteristics of the efficiency distribution as a whole (e.g. estimates of λ) rather than discuss firm specific efficiency. However, firm specific efficiencies are often of fundamental policy importance and, hence, we would argue that an important advantage of the Bayesian approach is its development of finite sample distributions for the τ_is.

2.3　Extensions

There are many ways of extending the previous model. For instance, we could allow for different distributions for z_i (see Koop *et al.*, 1995) or for many outputs to exist (see Fernández, Koop and Steel, 2000). Here we focus on two other extensions which are interesting in and of themselves, but also allow us to discuss some useful Bayesian techniques.

EXPLANATORY VARIABLES IN THE EFFICIENCY DISTRIBUTION

Consider, for instance, a case where data are available for many firms, but some are private companies and others are state owned. Interest centers on investigating whether private companies tend to be more efficient than state owned ones. This type of question can be formally handled by stochastic frontier models if we extend them to allow for explanatory variables in the efficiency distribution. Let us suppose that data exist on m variables which may affect the efficiency of firms (i.e. w_{ij}, for $i = 1 \ldots N$ and $j = 1 \ldots m$). We assume $w_{i1} = 1$ is an intercept and w_{ij} are 0–1 dummy variables for $j = 2 \ldots m$. The latter assumption could be relaxed at the cost of increasing the complexity of the computational methods. Since λ, the mean of the inefficiency distribution, is a positive random variable, a logical extension of the previous model is to allow it to vary over firms in the following manner:

$$\lambda_i^{-1} = \prod_{j=1}^{m} \phi_j^{w_{ij}}, \tag{24.12}$$

where the $\phi_j > 0$ are unknown parameters. Note that if $\phi_j = 1$ for $j = 2 \ldots m$ then this model reduces to the previous one. To aid in interpretation, observe how this specification allows, for instance, for private and state owned firms to have different inefficiency distributions. If $w_{i2} = 1$ indicates that firm i is private, then $\phi_2 > 1$ implies that the mean of the inefficiency distribution is lower for private firms and, hence, that private firms tend to be more efficient than state owned ones. We stress that such a finding would not imply that every private firm is more efficient than every state owned one, but rather that the former are drawing their efficiencies from a distribution with a higher mean. Such a specification seems very suitable for many sorts of policy issues and immediately allows for out-of-sample predictions.

For the new parameters, $\phi = (\phi_1 \ldots \phi_m)'$, we assume independent gamma priors: $p(\phi) = p(\phi_1) \ldots p(\phi_m)$ with $p(\phi_j) = f_G(\phi_j \mid a_j, b_j)$ for $j = 1 \ldots m$. If the explanatory variables have no role to play (i.e. $\phi_2 = \ldots = \phi_m = 1$), then ϕ_1 is equivalent to λ^{-1} in the previous model. This suggests one may want to follow the prior elicitation rule discussed above and set $a_1 = 1$ and $b_1 = -\ln(\tau^*)$. The other prior hyperparameters, a_j and b_j for $j = 2 \ldots m$, can be selected in the context of particular applications with moderate values for these parameters yielding a relatively noninformative prior. See Koop et al. (1997) for details.

A posterior simulator using Gibbs sampling with data augmentation can be set up as a straightforward extension of the one considered above. In fact, the posterior conditionals for β and h (i.e. equations (24.8) and (24.9)) are completely unaffected and the conditional for z in (24.11) is only affected in that $\lambda^{-1}\iota_N$ must be replaced by the vector $\eta = (\lambda_1^{-1} \ldots \lambda_N^{-1})'$, where λ_i^{-1} is given in equation (24.12). It can also be verified that for $j = 1 \ldots m$:[11]

$$p(\phi_j \mid y, x, z, \beta, h, w, \phi^{(-j)}) = f_G\left(\phi_j \left| a_j + \sum_{i=1}^{N} w_{ij}, b_j + \sum_{i=1}^{N} w_{ij} z_i \prod_{s \neq j} \phi_s^{w_{is}} \right.\right), \quad (24.13)$$

where $\phi^{(-j)} = (\phi_1 \ldots \phi_{j-1}, \phi_{j+1} \ldots \phi_m)'$. Hence, Bayesian inference in this model can again be conducted through sequential drawing from tractable distributions.

So far, we have focused on posterior inference. This stochastic frontier model with varying efficiency distribution can be used to illustrate Bayesian model comparison. Suppose $m = 2$ and we are interested in calculating the Bayes factor comparing model M_1 where $\phi_2 = 1$ (e.g. there is no tendency for state owned and private firms to differ in their efficiency distributions) against model M_2 with $\phi_2 \neq 1$. The prior for M_2 is given above. Define $\psi = (\beta, h, \phi^{(-2)})'$ as the parameters in the model M_1 and let $p_l(\cdot)$ indicate a density under M_l for $l = 1, 2$. If we make the reasonable assumption that $p_2(\psi \mid \phi_2 = 1) = p_1(\psi)$, then the Bayes factor in favor of M_1 can be written as the Savage–Dickey density ratio (see Verdinelli and Wasserman, 1995):

$$B_{12} = \frac{p_2(\phi_2 = 1 \mid y, x, w)}{p_2(\phi_2 = 1)}, \quad (24.14)$$

the ratio of posterior to prior density values at the point being tested. Note that the denominator of (24.14) is trivial to calculate since it is merely the gamma prior for ϕ_2 evaluated at a point. The numerator is also easy to calculate using (24.13). As Verdinelli and Wasserman (1995) stress, a good estimator of $p(\phi_2 = 1 \mid y, x, w)$ on the basis of R Gibbs replications is:

$$\frac{1}{R} \sum_{r=1}^{R} p(\phi_2 = 1 \mid y, x, z^{(r)}, \beta^{(r)}, h^{(r)}, w, \phi^{(-2)(r)}), \quad (24.15)$$

where superscript $^{(r)}$ denotes the rth draw in the Gibbs sampling algorithm. That is, we can just evaluate (24.13) at $\phi_2 = 1$ for each draw and average. Bayes factors for hypotheses such as this can be easily calculated without recourse to evaluating the likelihood function or adding steps to the simulation algorithm (as in the more general methods of Gelfand and Dey, 1994 and Chib, 1995, respectively).

NONLINEAR PRODUCTION FRONTIERS

The previous models both assumed that the production frontier was log-linear. However, many common production functions are inherently nonlinear in the parameters (e.g. the constant elasticity of substitution or CES or the asymptotically ideal model or AIM, see Koop et al., 1994). However, the techniques outlined above can be extended to allow for an arbitrary production function. Here we assume a model identical to the stochastic frontier model with common efficiency distribution (i.e. $m = 1$) except that the production frontier is of the form:[12]

$$y_i = f(x_i; \beta) + v_i - z_i. \quad (24.16)$$

The posterior simulator for everything except β is almost identical to the one given above. Equation (24.10) is completely unaffected, and (24.9) and (24.11) are slightly altered by replacing $x\beta$ by $f(x, \beta) = (f(x_1; \beta) \ldots f(x_N; \beta))'$.

However, the conditional posterior for β is more complicated, having the form:

$$p(\beta \mid y, x, z, h, \lambda^{-1}) \propto \exp\left(-\frac{h}{2}\sum_{i=1}^{N}(y_i - f(x_i; \beta) + z_i)^2\right)p(\beta). \qquad (24.17)$$

Equation (24.17) does not take the form of any well known density and the computational algorithm selected will depend on the exact form of $f(x; \beta)$. For the sake of brevity, here we will only point the reader in the direction of possible algorithms that may be used for drawing from (24.17). Two major cases are worth mentioning. First, in many cases, it might be possible to find a convenient density which approximates (24.17) well. For instance, in the case of the AIM model a multivariate-t density worked well (see Koop et al., 1994). In this case, importance sampling (Geweke, 1989) or an independence chain Metropolis–Hastings algorithm (Chib and Greenberg, 1995) should work well. On the other hand, if no convenient approximating density can be found, a random walk chain Metropolis–Hastings algorithm might prove a good choice (see Chib and Greenberg, 1995). The precise choice of algorithm will be case-specific and, hence, we do not discuss this issue in any more detail here.

3   THE STOCHASTIC FRONTIER MODEL WITH PANEL DATA

3.1   Time-invariant efficiency

It is increasingly common to use panel data[13] in the classical econometric analysis of the stochastic frontier model. Some of the statistical problems (e.g. inconsistency of point estimates of firm specific efficiency) of classical analysis are alleviated with panel data and the assumption of a particular distributional form for the inefficiency distribution can be dispensed with at the cost of assuming time-invariant efficiencies (i.e. treating them as "individual effects"). Schmidt and Sickles (1984) is an early influential paper which develops a relative efficiency measure based on a fixed effects specification and an absolute efficiency measure based on a random effects specification. In this paper, we describe a Bayesian alternative to this classical analysis and relate the random/fixed effects distinction to different prior structures for the efficiency distribution.

Accordingly, assume that data is available for $i = 1 \ldots N$ firms for $t = 1 \ldots T$ time periods. We will extend the notation of the previous section so that y_i and v_i are now $T \times 1$ vectors and x_i a $T \times k$ matrix containing the T observations for firm i. Note, however, that the assumption of constant efficiency over time implies that z_i is still a scalar and z an $N \times 1$ vector. For future reference, we now define $y = (y_1' \ldots y_N')'$ and $v = (v_1' \ldots v_N')'$ as $NT \times 1$ vectors and $x = (x_1' \ldots x_N')'$ as an $NT \times k$ matrix. In contrast to previous notation, x_i does not contain an intercept. We assume that the stochastic frontier model can be written as:

$$y_i = \beta_0 \iota_T + x_i \delta + v_i - z_i \iota_T, \tag{24.18}$$

where β_0 is the intercept coefficient and v_i is iid with pdf $f_N^T(v_i \,|\, 0, h^{-1} I_T)$. As discussed in Fernández et al. (1997), it is acceptable to use an improper noninformative prior for h when $T > 1$ and, hence, we assume $p(h) \propto h^{-1}$. We discuss different choices of priors for β_0 and z_i in the following material.

BAYESIAN FIXED EFFECTS MODEL

Equation (24.18) looks like a standard panel data model (see, e.g., Judge et al., 1985, ch. 13). The individual effect in the model can be written as:

$$\alpha_i = \beta_0 - z_i,$$

and the model rewritten as:

$$y_i = \alpha_i \iota_T + x_i \delta + v_i. \tag{24.19}$$

Classical fixed effects estimation of (24.19) proceeds by making no distributional assumption for α_i, but rather using firm-specific dummy variables. The Bayesian analog to this is to use flat, noninformative priors for the α_is.[14] Formally, defining $\alpha = (\alpha_1 \ldots \alpha_N)'$, we then adopt the prior:

$$p(\alpha, \delta, h) \propto h^{-1} p(\delta). \tag{24.20}$$

The trouble with this specification is that we cannot make direct inference about z_i (since β_0 is not separately identified) and, hence, the absolute efficiency of firm i: $\tau_i = \exp(-z_i)$. However, following Schmidt and Sickles (1984), we define relative inefficiency as:

$$z_i^{rel} = z_i - \min_j(z_j) = \max_j(\alpha_j) - \alpha_i. \tag{24.21}$$

In other words, we are measuring inefficiency relative to the most efficient firm (i.e. the firm with the highest α_i).[15] Relative efficiency is defined as $r_i^{rel} = \exp(-z_i^{rel})$ and we assume that the most efficient firm has $r_i^{rel} = 1$.

It is worth noting that this prior seems like an innocuous noninformative prior, but this initial impression is false since it implies a rather unusual prior for r_i^{rel}. In particular, as shown in Koop et al. (1997), $p(r_i^{rel})$ has a point mass of N^{-1} at full efficiency and is $p(r_i^{rel}) \propto 1/r_i^{rel}$ for $r_i^{rel} \in (0, 1)$. The latter is an L-shaped improper prior density which, for an arbitrary small $a \in (0, 1)$ puts an infinite mass in $(0, a)$ but only a finite mass in $(a, 1)$. In other words, this "noninformative" prior strongly favors low efficiency.

Bayesian inference in the fixed effects model can be carried out in a straightforward manner, by noting that for uniform $p(\delta)$, (24.19)–(24.20) is precisely a normal linear regression model with Jeffreys' prior. The vector of regression coefficients $(\alpha' \ \delta')'$ in such a model has a $(N + k)$-variate student-t posterior with $N(T - 1) - k$ degrees of freedom (where we have assumed that $N(T - 1) > k$, which implies $T > 1$). For typical values of N, T, and k the degrees of freedom are enormous and the student-t will be virtually identical to the normal distribution. Hence, throughout this subsection we present results in terms of this normal approximation.

Using standard Bayesian results for the normal linear regression model (e.g. Judge *et al.*, 1985, ch. 4), it follows that the marginal posterior for δ is given by (for general $p(\delta)$):

$$p(\delta \,|\, y, x) = f_N^k (\delta \,|\, \hat{\delta}, \hat{h}^{-1}S^{-1})p(\delta), \tag{24.22}$$

where

$$\hat{\delta} = S^{-1} \sum_{i=1}^N (x_i - \iota_T \overline{x}_i)'(y_i - \overline{y}_i \iota_T), \tag{24.23}$$

$$S = \sum_{i=1}^N S_i, \quad \overline{x}_i = \frac{1}{T}\iota_T' x_i$$

and

$$S_i = (x_i - \iota_T \overline{x}_i)'(x_i - \iota_T \overline{x}_i).$$

Note that (24.23) is the standard "within estimator" from the panel data literature. Finally,

$$\hat{h}^{-1} = \frac{1}{N(T-1)-k} \sum_{i=1}^N (y_i - \hat{\alpha}_i \iota_T - x_i \hat{\delta})'(y_i - \hat{\alpha}_i \iota_T - x_i \hat{\delta}),$$

where $\hat{\alpha}_i$ is the posterior mean of α_i defined below.

The marginal posterior of α is the N-variate normal with means

$$\hat{\alpha}_i = \overline{y}_i - \overline{x}_i \hat{\delta},$$

and covariances

$$\mathrm{cov}(\alpha_i, \alpha_j) = \hat{h}^{-1}\left(\frac{\Delta(i, j)}{T} + \overline{x}_i S^{-1}\overline{x}_j'\right),$$

where $\Delta(i, j) = 1$ if $i = j$ and 0 otherwise. Thus, analytical formulae for posterior means and standard deviations are available and, if interest centers on these, posterior simulation methods are not required. However, typically interest centers on the relative efficiencies which are a complicated nonlinear function of α, viz.,

$$r_i^{rel} = \exp(\alpha_i - \max_j (\alpha_j)), \tag{24.24}$$

and, hence, posterior simulation methods are required. However, direct Monte Carlo integration is possible since the posterior for α is multivariate normal and can easily be simulated. These simulated draws of α can be transformed using (24.24) to yield posterior draws of r_i^{rel}. However, this procedure is complicated by the fact that we do not know which firm is most efficient (i.e. which firm has largest α_j) and, hence, is worth describing in detail.

We begin by calculating the probability that a given firm, i, is the most efficient:

$$P(r_i^{rel} = 1 \,|\, y, x) = P(\alpha_i = \max_j (\alpha_j) \,|\, y, x), \tag{24.25}$$

which can be easily calculated using Monte Carlo integration. That is, (24.25) can simply be estimated by the proportion of the draws of α which have α_i being the largest.

Now consider the posterior for r_i^{rel} over the interval $(0, 1)$ (i.e. assuming it is *not* the most efficient):

$$p(r_i^{rel} \,|\, y, x) = \sum_{j=1, j \neq i}^{N} p(r_i^{rel} \,|\, y, x, r_j^{rel} = 1) P(r_j^{rel} = 1 \,|\, y, x). \tag{24.26}$$

Here $P(r_j^{rel} = 1 \,|\, y, x)$ can be calculated as discussed in the previous paragraph. In addition, $p(r_i^{rel} \,|\, y, x, r_j^{rel} = 1)$ can be calculated using the same posterior simulator output. That is, assuming firm j is most efficient, then $r_i^{rel} = \exp(\alpha_i - \alpha_j)$ which can be evaluated from those draws of α that correspond to $\alpha_j = \max_l(\alpha_l)$. Hence, posterior analysis of the relative efficiencies in a Bayesian fixed effects framework can be calculated in a straightforward manner.[16]

BAYESIAN RANDOM EFFECTS MODEL

The Bayesian fixed effects model described above might initially appeal to researchers who do not want to make distributional assumptions about the inefficiency distribution. However, as we have shown above, this model is implicitly making strong and possibly unreasonable prior assumptions. Furthermore, we can only calculate relative, as opposed to absolute, efficiencies. For these reasons, it is desirable to develop a model which makes an explicit distributional assumption for the inefficiencies. With such a model, absolute efficiencies can be calculated in the spirit of the cross-sectional stochastic frontier model of Section 2, since the distribution assumed for the z_is allows us to separately identify z_i and β_0. In addition, the resulting prior efficiency distributions will typically be more in line with our prior beliefs. Another important issue is the sensitivity of the posterior results on efficiency to the prior specification chosen. Since T is usually quite small, it makes sense to "borrow strength" from the observations for the other firms by linking the inefficiencies. Due to Assumption 3 in subsection 2.2, this is not done through the sampling model. Thus, Koop *et al.* (1997) define the difference between Bayesian fixed and random effects models through the prior for z_i. In particular, what matters are the prior links that are assumed between the z_is. Fixed effects models assume, a priori, that the z_is are fully separated.

Random effects models introduce links between the z_is, typically by assuming they are all drawn from distributions that share some common unknown parameter(s). In Bayesian language, the random effects model then implies a hierarchical prior for the individual effects.

Formally, we define a Bayesian random effects model by combining (24.18) with the prior:

$$p(\beta_0, \delta, h, z, \lambda^{-1}) \propto h^{-1}p(\delta)f_G(\lambda^{-1}\,|\,1, -\ln(\tau^*))\prod_{i=1}^{N} f_G(z_i\,|\,1, \lambda^{-1}). \qquad (24.27)$$

That is, we assume noninformative priors for h and β_0, whereas the inefficiencies are again assumed to be drawn from the exponential distribution with mean λ. Note that the z_is are now linked through this common parameter λ, for which we choose the same prior as in Section 2.

Bayesian analysis of this model proceeds along similar lines to the cross-sectional stochastic frontier model presented in Section 2. In particular, a Gibbs sampler with data augmentation can be set up. Defining $\beta = (\beta_0\ \delta')'$ and $X = (\iota_{NT} : x)$ the posterior conditional for the measurement error precision can be written as:

$$p(h\,|\,y, x, z, \beta, \lambda^{-1}) = f_G\left(h\,\bigg|\,\frac{NT}{2}, \frac{1}{2}[y - X\beta + (I_N \otimes \iota_T)z]'[y - X\beta + (I_N \otimes \iota_T)z]\right).$$
$$(24.28)$$

Next we obtain:

$$p(\beta\,|\,y, x, z, h, \lambda^{-1}) = f_N^{k+1}(\beta\,|\,\bar{\beta}, h^{-1}(X'X)^{-1})p(\delta), \qquad (24.29)$$

where

$$\bar{\beta} = (X'X)^{-1}\,[y + (I_N \otimes \iota_T)z].$$

The posterior conditional for the inefficiencies takes the form:

$$p(z\,|\,y, x, \beta, h, \lambda^{-1}) \propto f_N^N(z\,|\,(\iota_N : \tilde{x})\beta - \tilde{y} - (Th\lambda)^{-1}\iota_N, (Th)^{-1}I_N)\prod_{i=1}^{N} I(z_i \geq 0),$$
$$(24.30)$$

where $\tilde{y} = (\tilde{y}_1 \ldots \tilde{y}_N)'$ and $\tilde{x} = (\tilde{x}_1' \ldots \tilde{x}_N')'$.

Furthermore, the posterior conditional for λ^{-1}, $p(\lambda^{-1}\,|\,y, x, z, \beta, h)$, is the same as for the cross-sectional case (i.e. equation 24.10).

Using these results, Bayesian inference can be carried out using a Gibbs sampling algorithm based on (24.10), (24.28), (24.29), and (24.30). Although the formulas look somewhat complicated, it is worth stressing that all conditionals are either gamma or truncated normal.

3.2   Extensions

Extending the random effects stochastic frontier model to allow for a nonlinear production function or explanatory variables in the efficiency distribution can easily be done in a similar fashion as for the cross-sectional model (see subsection 2.3 and Koop *et al.*, 1997). Furthermore, different efficiency distributions can be allowed for in a straightforward manner and multiple outputs can be handled as in Fernández *et al.* (2000). Here we concentrate on extending the model in a different direction. In particular, we free up the assumption that each firm's efficiency, τ_i, is constant over time. Let us use the definitions of X and β introduced in the previous subsection and write the stochastic frontier model with panel data as:

$$y = X\beta - \gamma + v, \tag{24.31}$$

where γ is a $TN \times 1$ vector containing inefficiencies for each individual observation and y and v are defined as in subsection 3.1. In practice, we may want to put some structure on γ and, thus, Fernández *et al.* (1997) propose to rewrite it in terms of an M-dimensional vector u as:

$$\gamma = Du, \tag{24.32}$$

where $M \leq TN$ and D is a known $TN \times M$ matrix. Above, we implicitly assumed $D = I_N \otimes \iota_T$ which implies $M = N$ and $u_i = \gamma_{it} = z_i$. That is, firm-specific inefficiency was constant over time. However, a myriad of other possibilities exist. For instance, D can correspond to cases where clusters of firms or time periods share common efficiencies, or parametric time dependence exists in firm-specific efficiency. Also note the case $D = I_{TN}$, which allows each firm in each period to have a different inefficiency (i.e. $\gamma = u$). Thus, we are then effectively back in the cross section framework without exploiting the panel structure of the data. This case is considered in Koop *et al.* (1999, 2000), where interest is centered on the change in efficiency over time.[17] With all such specifications, it is possible to conduct Bayesian inference by slightly altering the posterior conditionals presented above in an obvious manner.

However, as discussed in Fernández *et al.* (1997), it is very important to be careful when using improper priors on any of the parameters. In some cases, improper priors imply that the posterior does not exist and, hence, valid Bayesian inference cannot be carried out. Intuitively, the inefficiencies can be interpreted as unknown parameters. If there are too many of these, prior information becomes necessary. As an example of the types of results proved in Fernández *et al.* (1997), we state one of their main theorems:

Theorem 24.1 (Fernández *et al.*, 1997, Theorem 1).   Consider the general model given in (24.31) and (24.32) and assume the standard noninformative prior for $h : p(h) \propto h^{-1}$. If rank$(X : D) < TN$ then the posterior distribution exists for any bounded or proper $p(\beta)$ and any proper $p(u)$. However, if rank$(X : D) = TN$, then the posterior does not exist.

The Bayesian random effects model discussed above has rank$(X : D) < TN$, so the posterior does exist even though we have used an improper prior for h. However, for the case where efficiency varies over time and across firms (i.e. $D = I_{TN}$), more informative priors are required in order to carry out valid Bayesian inference. Fernández *et al.* (1997, Proposition 2) show that a weakly informative (not necessarily proper) prior on h that penalizes large values of the precision is sufficient.

4   SUMMARY

In this chapter, we have described a Bayesian approach to efficiency analysis using stochastic frontier models. With cross-sectional data and a log-linear frontier, a simple Gibbs sampler can be used to carry out Bayesian inference. In the case of a nonlinear frontier, more complicated posterior simulation methods are necessary. Bayesian efficiency measurement with panel data is then discussed. We show how a Bayesian analog of the classical fixed effects panel data model can be used to calculate the efficiency of each firm relative to the most efficient firm. However, absolute efficiency calculations are precluded in this model and inference on efficiencies can be quite sensitive to prior assumptions. Accordingly, we describe a Bayesian analog of the classical random effects panel data model which can be used for robust inference on absolute efficiencies. Throughout we emphasize the computational methods necessary to carry out Bayesian inference. We show how random number generation from well known distributions is sufficient to develop posterior simulators for a wide variety of models.

Notes

1   Throughout this chapter, we will use the term "firm" to refer to the cross-sectional unit of analysis. In practice, it could also be the individual or country, etc.

2   In this chapter we focus on production frontiers. However, by suitably redefining Y and X, the methods can be applied to cost frontiers.

3   In addition to standard microeconomic studies of firm efficiencies, stochastic frontier models have been applied to e.g. environmental issues and macroeconomic growth studies.

4   This error reflects the stochastic nature of the frontier and we shall conveniently denote it by "measurement error". The treatment of measurement error is a crucial distinction between econometric and DEA methods. Most economic data sets are quite noisy and, hence, we feel including measurement error is important. DEA methods can be quite sensitive to outliers since they ignore measurement error. Furthermore, since the statistical framework for DEA methods is nonparametric, confidence intervals for parameter and efficiency estimates are very difficult to derive. However, econometric methods require the researcher to make more assumptions (e.g. about the error distribution) than do DEA methods. Recently, there has been some promising work on using the bootstrap with DEA methods which should lessen some of the

criticisms of DEA (see Simar and Wilson, 1998a, 1998b, and the references contained therein).

5   We use the terminology "sampling model" to denote the joint distribution of (y, z) given the parameters and shall base the likelihood function on the marginal distribution of y given the parameters.

6   In van den Broeck *et al.* (1994) and Koop *et al.* (1995), the Erlang distribution (i.e. the gamma distribution with fixed shape parameter, here chosen to be 1, 2, or 3) was used for inefficiency. The computational techniques necessary to work with Erlang distributions are simple extensions of those given in this section.

7   As shown in Fernández *et al.* (1997), the use of the full model with data augmentation also allows for the derivation of crucial theoretical results on the existence of the posterior distribution and moments.

8   The assumption that the inefficiencies are drawn from the exponential distribution with unknown common mean λ can be interpreted as a hierarchical prior for z_i. Alternatively, a classical econometrician would interpret this distributional assumption as part of the sampling model. This difference in interpretation highlights the fact that the division into prior and sampling model is to some extent arbitrary. See Fernández *et al.* (1997) for more discussion of this issue.

9   Note that we have not formally proven that the posterior mean and variance of θ exist (although numerical evidence suggests that they do). Hence, we recommend using the posterior median and interquartile range of θ to summarize properties of the posterior. Since $0 \leq \tau_i \leq 1$, we know that all posterior moments exist for the firm specific efficiencies.

10 Recent work on bootstrapping DEA frontiers is promising to surmount this problem and this procedure seems to be gaining some acceptance.

11 This is where the assumption that the w_{ij}s are 0–1 dummies is crucial.

12 The extension to a varying efficiency distribution as in (24.12) is trivial and proceeds along the lines of the previous model.

13 Of course, many of the issues which arise in the stochastic frontier model with panel data also arise in traditional panel data models. It is beyond the scope of the present chapter to attempt to summarize the huge literature on panel data. The reader is referred to Mátyás and Sevestre (1996) or Baltagi (1995) for an introduction to the broader panel data literature.

14 Note that this implies we now deviate from Assumption 3 in subsection 2.2.

15 It is worth noting that the classical econometric analysis assigns the status of most efficient firm to one particular firm and measures efficiency relative to this. The present Bayesian analysis also measures efficiency relative to the most efficient firm, but allows for uncertainty as to which that firm is.

16 This procedure can be computationally demanding since $P(r_j^{rel} = 1 \mid y, x)$ and $p(r_i^{rel} \mid y, x, r_j^{rel} = 1)$ must be calculated for every possible i and j. However, typically, $P(r_j^{rel} = 1 \mid y, x)$ is appreciable (e.g. > 0.001) for only a few firms and the rest can be ignored (see Koop *et al.*, 1997, p. 82).

17 Koop *et al.* (1999, 2000) also allow the frontier to shift over time and interpret such shifts as technical change. In such a framework, it is possible to decompose changes in output growth into components reflecting input change, technical change, and efficiency change. The ability of stochastic frontier models with panel data to calculate such decompositions is quite important in many practical applications. Also of interest are Baltagi and Griffin (1988) and Baltagi, Griffin, and Rich (1995), which develop a more general framework relating changes in the production function with technical change in a nonstochastic frontier panel data model.

References

Aigner, D., C.A.K. Lovell, and P. Schmidt (1977). Formulation and estimation of stochastic frontier production function models. *Journal of Econometrics* 6, 21–37.

Baltagi, B. (1995). *Econometric Analysis of Panel Data*. New York: John Wiley and Sons.

Baltagi, B., and J. Griffin (1988). A general index of technical change. *Journal of Political Economy* 90, 20–41.

Baltagi, B., J. Griffin, and D. Rich (1995). The measurement of firm-specific indexes of technical change. *Review of Economics and Statistics* 77, 654–63.

Bauer, P. (1990). Recent developments in the econometric estimation of frontiers. *Journal of Econometrics* 46, 39–56.

van den Broeck, J., G. Koop, J. Osiewalski, and M.F.J. Steel (1994). Stochastic frontier models: A Bayesian perspective. *Journal of Econometrics* 61, 273–303.

Casella, G., and E. George (1992). Explaining the Gibbs sampler. *The American Statistician* 46, 167–74.

Chib, S. (1995). Marginal likelihood from the Gibbs output. *Journal of the American Statistical Association* 90, 1313–21.

Chib, S., and E. Greenberg (1995). Understanding the Metropolis–Hastings algorithm. *The American Statistician* 49, 327–35.

Färe, R., S. Grosskopf, and C.A.K. Lovell (1994). *Production Frontiers*. Cambridge: Cambridge University Press.

Fernández, C., G. Koop, and M.F.J. Steel (2000). A Bayesian analysis of multiple output production frontiers. *Journal of Econometrics* 98, 47–9.

Fernández, C., J. Osiewalski, and M.F.J. Steel (1997). On the use of panel data in stochastic frontier models with improper priors. *Journal of Econometrics* 79, 169–93.

Gelfand, A., and D.K. Dey (1994). Bayesian model choice: Asymptotics and exact calculations. *Journal of the Royal Statistical Society, Series B* 56, 501–14.

Geweke, J. (1989). Bayesian inference in econometric models using Monte Carlo integration. *Econometrica* 57, 1317–40.

Geweke, J. (1999). Using simulation methods for Bayesian econometric models: Inference, development and communication (with discussion). *Econometric Reviews* 18, 1–126.

Horrace, W., and P. Schmidt (1996). Confidence statements for efficiency estimates from stochastic frontiers. *Journal of Productivity Analysis* 7, 257–82.

Jondrow, J., C.A.K. Lovell, I.S. Materov, and P. Schmidt (1982). On the estimation of technical inefficiency in the stochastic frontier production function model. *Journal of Econometrics* 19, 233–8.

Judge, G., W. Griffiths, R.C. Hill, H. Lütkepohl, and T.-C. Lee (1985). *The Theory and Practice of Econometrics*, 2nd edn. New York: John Wiley and Sons, Ltd.

Koop, G. (1994). Recent progress in applied Bayesian econometrics. *Journal of Economic Surveys* 8, 1–34.

Koop, G., J. Osiewalski, and M.F.J. Steel (1994). Bayesian efficiency analysis with a flexible form: The AIM cost function. *Journal of Business and Economic Statistics* 12, 93–106.

Koop, G., J. Osiewalski, and M.F.J. Steel (1997). Bayesian efficiency analysis through individual effects: Hospital cost frontiers. *Journal of Econometrics* 76, 77–105.

Koop, G., J. Osiewalski, and M.F.J. Steel (1999). The components of output growth: A stochastic frontier analysis. *Oxford Bulletin of Economics and Statistics* 61, 455–87.

Koop, G., J. Osiewalski, and M.F.J. Steel (2000). Modeling the sources of output growth in a panel of countries. *Journal of Business and Economic Statistics* 18, 284–99.

Koop, G., M.F.J. Steel, and J. Osiewalski (1995). Posterior analysis of stochastic frontier models using Gibbs sampling. *Computational Statistics* 10, 353–73.

Mátyás, L., and P. Sevestre (eds.) (1996). *The Econometrics of Panel Data*. Dordrecht: Kluwer Academic Publishers.

Meeusen, W., and J. van den Broeck (1977). Efficiency estimation from Cobb–Douglas production functions with composed errors. *International Economic Review* 8, 435–44.

Osiewalski, J., and M.F.J. Steel (1998). Numerical tools for the Bayesian analysis of stochastic frontier models. *Journal of Productivity Analysis* 10, 103–17.

Poirier, D. (1995). *Intermediate Statistics and Econometrics: A Comparative Approach*. Cambridge, MA: The MIT Press.

Ritter, C., and L. Simar (1997). Pitfalls of Normal–Gamma stochastic frontier models. *Journal of Productivity Analysis* 8, 167–82.

Schmidt, P., and R. Sickles (1984). Production frontiers and panel data. *Journal of Business and Economic Statistics* 2, 367–74.

Simar, L., and P.W. Wilson (1998a). A general methodology for bootstrapping in nonparametric frontier models. Manuscript.

Simar, L., and P.W. Wilson (1998b). Sensitivity analysis of efficiency scores: How to bootstrap in nonparametric frontier models. *Management Science* 44, 49–61.

Verdinelli, I., and L. Wasserman (1995). Computing Bayes factors using a generalization of the Savage–Dickey Density Ratio. *Journal of the American Statistical Association* 90, 614–18.

Parametric and Nonparametric Tests of Limited Domain and Ordered Hypotheses in Economics

Esfandiar Maasoumi*

1   INTRODUCTION

In this survey, technical and conceptual advances in testing multivariate linear and nonlinear inequality hypotheses in econometrics are summarized. This is discussed for economic applications in which either the null, or the alternative, or both hypotheses define more limited domains than the two-sided alternatives typically tested. The desired goal is increased power which is laudable given the endemic power problems of most of the classical asymptotic tests. The impediments are a lack of familiarity with implementation procedures, and characterization problems of distributions under some composite hypotheses.

Several empirically important cases are identified in which practical "one-sided" tests can be conducted by either the $\bar{\chi}^2$-*distribution*, or the union intersection mechanisms based on the Gaussian variate, or the increasingly feasible and popular resampling/simulation techniques. Point optimal testing and its derivatives find a natural medium here whenever unique characterization of the null distributions for the "least favorable" cases is not possible.

Most of the recent econometric literature in this area is parametric deriving from the multivariate extensions of the classical Gaussian means test with ordered alternatives. Tests for variance components, random coefficients, over-dispersion, heteroskedasticity, regime change, ARCH effects, curvature regularity conditions on flexible supply, demand, and other economic functions, are examples. But nonparametric tests for ordered relations between distributions, or their quantiles, or curvature regularity conditions on nonparametric economic relations, have witnessed rapid development and applications in economics and finance. We detail tests for Stochastic Dominance which indicate a major departure in the practice of empirical decision making in, so far, the areas of welfare and optimal financial strategy.

The additional information available when hypotheses can restrict attention to subspaces of the usual two-sided (unrestricted) hypotheses, can enhance the power of tests. Since good power is a rare commodity the interest in inequality restricted hypothesis tests has increased dramatically. In addition, the two-sided formulation is occasionally too vague to be of help when more sharply ordered alternatives are of interest. An example is the test of order relations (e.g. stochastic dominance) amongst investment strategies, or among income/welfare distributions. The two-sided formulation fails to distinguish between "equivalent" and "unrankable" cases.

In statistics, D.J. Bartholomew, H. Chernoff, V.J. Chacko, A. Kudo, and P.E. Nuesch are among the first to refine and extend the Neyman–Pearson testing procedure for one-sided alternatives, first in the one and then in the multivariate settings. For example, see Bartholomew (1959a, 1959b) and Kudô (1963). Later refinements and advances were obtained by Nuesch, Feder, Perlman, and others. At least in low dimensional cases, the power gains over the two-sided counterparts have been shown to be substantial, see Bartholomew (1959b), and Barlow *et al.* (1972). While Chernoff and Feder clarified the local nature of tests and gave some solutions when the true parameter value is "near" the boundaries of the hypotheses regions (see Wolak, 1989), Kudo, Nuesch, Perlman, and Shorack were among the first to develop the elements of the $\bar{\chi}^2$-*distribution* theory for the likelihood ratio and other classical tests. See Barlow *et al.* (1972) for references.

In econometrics, Gouriéroux, Holly, and Monfort (1980, 1982), heretofore GHM, are seminal contributions which introduced and extended this literature to linear and nonlinear econometric/regression models. The focus in GHM (1982) is on the following testing situation:

$$y = X\beta + u \tag{25.1}$$

$$R\beta \geq r, R : q \times K, q \leq K, \text{ the dimension of } \beta.$$

We wish to test

$$H_0 : R\beta = r, \ldots vs \ldots H_1 : R\beta \geq r. \tag{25.2}$$

u is assumed to be a Gaussian variate with zero-mean and finite variance Ω. Gouriéroux *et al.* (1982) derive the Lagrange multiplier (LM)/Kuhn–Tucker (KT) test, as well as the likelihood ratio (LR) and the Wald (W) tests with known and unknown covariance matrix, Ω, of the regression errors. With known covariance the three tests are equivalent and distributed exactly as a $\bar{\chi}^2$-*distribution*. They note that the problem considered here is essentially equivalent to the following in the earlier statistical literature: Let there be T independent observations from a p-dimensional $N(\mu, \Sigma)$. Test

$$H_0 : \mu = 0, \text{ against the alternative}$$

$$H_1 : \mu_i \geq 0, \text{ all } i, \text{ with at least one strict inequality} \qquad (25.3)$$

The LR test of this hypothesis has the $\bar{\chi}^2$-*distribution* which is a mixture of chi-squared distributions given by:

$$\sum_{j=0}^{p} w(p, j)\chi_{(j)}^2, \qquad (25.4)$$

with $\chi_{(0)}^2 = 1$ at the origin. The weights $w(\cdot)$ are probabilities to be computed in a multivariate setting over the space of alternatives. This is one of the practical impediments in this area, inviting a variety of solutions which we shall touch upon. These include obtaining bounds, exact tests for low dimension cases, and resampling/Monte Carlo techniques.

When Ω is unknown but depends on a finite set of parameters, GHM (1982) and others have shown that the same distribution theory applies asymptotically. GHM show that these tests are asymptotically equivalent and satisfy the usual inequality: $W \geq LR \geq LM(KT)$. We'll give the detailed form of these test statistics. In particular the LM version may be desirable as it can avoid the quadratic programming (QP) routine needed to obtain estimators under the inequality restrictions. We also point to routines that are readily available in Fortran and GAUSS (but alas not yet in the standard econometric software packages).

It should be noted that this simultaneous procedure competes with another approach based on the union intersection technique. In the latter, each univariate hypothesis is tested, with the decision being a rejection of the joint null if the least significant statistic is greater than the α-critical level of a standard Gaussian variate. Consistency of such tests has been established. We will discuss examples of these alternatives. Also, the nonexistence generally of an optimal test in the multivariable case has led to consideration of point optimal testing, and tests that attempt to maximize power in the least favorable case, or on suitable "averages". This is similar to recent attempts to deal with power computation when alternatives depend on nuisance parameters. For example see King and Wu (1997) and their references.

In the case of nonlinear models and/or nonlinear inequality restrictions, GHM (1980) and Wolak (1989, 1991) discuss the distribution of the same $\bar{\chi}^2$ tests, while Dufour considers modified classical tests. In this setting, however, there is another problem, as pointed out by Wolak (1989, 1991). When $q \leq K$ there is generally no unique solution for the "true β" from $R\beta = r$ (or its nonlinear counterpart). But convention dictates that in this-type case of composite hypotheses, power be computed for the "least favorable" case which arises at the boundary $R\beta = r$. It then follows that the asymptotic distribution (when Ω is consistently estimated in customary ways) cannot, in general, be uniquely characterized for the least favorable case. Sufficient conditions for a unique distribution are given in Wolak (1991) and will be discussed here. In the absence of these conditions, a "localized" version of the hypothesis is testable with the same $\overline{\chi}^2$-distribution.

All of the above developments are parametric. There is at least an old tradition for the nonparametric "two sample" testing of homogeneity between two distributions, often assumed to belong to the same family. Pearson type and Kolmogorov–Smirnov (KS) tests are prominent, as well as the Wilcoxan rank test. In the case of inequality or ordered hypotheses regarding relations between two unknown distributions, Anderson (1996) is an example of the modified Pearson tests based on relative cell frequencies, and Xu, Fisher, and Wilson (1995) is an example of quantile-based tests which incorporate the inequality information in the hypotheses and, hence lead to the use of $\overline{\chi}^2$-distribution theory. The multivariate versions of the KS test have been studied by McFadden (1989), Klecan, McFadden, and McFadden (1991), Kaur, Rao, and Singh (1994), and Maasoumi, Mills, and Zandvakili (1997). The union intersection alternative is also fully discussed in Davidson and Duclos (1998), representing a culmination of this line of development. The union intersection techniques do not exploit the inequality information and are expected to be less powerful. We discuss the main features of these alternatives.

In Section 2 we introduce the classical multivariate means problem and a general variant of it that makes it amenable to immediate application to very general econometric models in which an asymptotically normal estimator can be obtained. At this level of generality, one can treat very wide classes of processes, as well as linear and non-linear models, as described in Potscher and Prucha (1991a, 1991b). The linear model is given as an example, and the asymptotic distribution of the classical tests is described.

The next section describes the nonlinear models and the local nature of the hypothesis than can be tested. Section 4 is devoted to the nonparametric setting. Examples from economics and finance are cited throughout the chapter. Section 5 concludes.

2   The General Multivariate Parametric Problem

Consider the setting in (25.3) when $\hat{\mu} = \mu + v$, and $v \sim N(0, \Omega)$, is an available unrestricted estimator. Consider the restricted estimator $\tilde{\mu}$ as the solution to the following quadratic programming (QP) problem:

$$\min_{\mu} (\hat{\mu} - \mu)'\Omega^{-1}(\hat{\mu} - \mu), \quad \text{subject to } \mu \geq 0. \tag{25.5}$$

Then the likelihood ratio (LR) test of the hypothesis in (25.3) is:

$$LR = \tilde{\mu}'\Omega^{-1}\tilde{\mu}. \tag{25.6}$$

Several researchers, for instance Kudô (1963) and Perlman (1969), have established the distribution of the LR statistic under the null as:

$$\text{Sup}_{\mu \geq 0}.\ \text{pr}_{\mu,\Omega}(LR \geq c_\alpha) = \text{pr}_{0,\Omega}(LR \geq c_\alpha)$$

$$= \sum_{i=0}^{p} w(i, p, \Omega) \times \text{pr}(\chi^2_{(i)} \geq c_\alpha) \qquad (25.7)$$

a weighted sum of chi-squared variates for an exact test of size α. The weights $w(i, \cdot)$ sum to unity and each is the probability of $\tilde{\mu}$ having i positive elements.

If the *null* hypothesis is one of *inequality* restrictions, a similar distribution theory applies. To see this, consider:

$$H_0 : \mu \geq 0 \quad \text{vs.} \quad H_1 : \mu \in R^p, \qquad (25.8)$$

where $\hat{\mu} = \mu + v$, and $v \sim N(0, \Omega)$. Let $\tilde{\mu}$ be the restricted estimator from the following QP problem:

$$D = \min_{\mu} (\hat{\mu} - \mu)\Omega^{-1}(\hat{\mu} - \mu) \quad \text{subject to } \mu \geq 0. \qquad (25.9)$$

D is the LR statistic for (25.8). Perlman (1969) showed that the power function is monotonic in this case. In view of this result, taking C_α as the critical level of a test of size α, we may use the same distribution theory as in (25.7) above except that the weight $w(i.)$ will be the probability of $\tilde{\mu}$ having exactly $p - i$ positive elements.

There is a relatively extensive literature dealing with the computation of the weights $w(\cdot)$. Their computation requires evaluation of multivariate integrals which become tedious for $p \geq 8$. For example, Kudô (1963) provides exact expressions for $p \leq 4$, and Bohrer and Chow (1978) provide computational algorithms for $p \leq 10$. But these can be slow for large p. Kodde and Palm (1986) suggest an attractive bounds test solution which requires obtaining lower and upper bounds, c_l and c_u, to the critical value, as follows:

$$\alpha_l = \tfrac{1}{2}\text{pr}(\chi^2_{(1)} \geq c_l), \text{ and}$$

$$\alpha_u = \tfrac{1}{2}\text{pr}(\chi^2_{(p-1)} \geq c_u) + \tfrac{1}{2}\text{pr}(\chi^2_{(p)} \geq c_u) \qquad (25.10)$$

The null in (25.8) is rejected if $D \geq c_u$, but is inconclusive when $c_l \leq D \leq c_u$. Advances in Monte Carlo integration suggest resampling techniques may be used for large p, especially if the bounds test is inconclusive.

In the case of a single hypothesis ($\mu_1 = 0$), the above test is the one-sided UMP test. In this situation:

$$\text{pr}(LR \geq c_\alpha) = \text{pr}(\tfrac{1}{2}\chi^2_{(0)} + \tfrac{1}{2}\chi^2_{(1)} \geq c_\alpha) = \alpha \qquad (25.11)$$

The standard two-sided test would be based on the critical values c'_α from a $\chi^2_{(1)}$ distribution. But $pr(\chi^2_{(1)} \geq c'_\alpha) = \alpha$ makes clear that $c'_\alpha \geq c_\alpha$, indicating the substantial power loss which was demonstrated by Bartholomew (1959a, 1959b) and others.

In the two dimension ($p = 2$) case, under the null we have:

$$pr(LR \geq c_\alpha) = w(2, 0)\chi^2_{(0)} + w(2, 1)\chi^2_{(1)} + w(2, 2)\chi^2_{(2)} \tag{25.12}$$

where $w(2, 0) = pr[LR = 0] = pr[\hat{\mu}_1 \leq 0, \hat{\mu}_2 \leq 0]$, $w(2, 1) = \frac{1}{2}$, $w(2, 2) = \frac{1}{2} - w(2, 0)$. While difficult to establish analytically, the power gains over the standard case can be substantial in higher dimensions where UMP tests do not generally exist. See Kudô (1963) and GHM (1982).

2.1   LR, W, and LM tests

We give an account of the three classical tests in the context of the general linear regression model introduced in (25.1) above. We take R to be a $(p \times K)$ known matrix of rank $p \leq K$. Consider three estimators of β under the exact linear restrictions, under inequality restrictions, and when $\beta \in R^p$ (no restrictions). Denote these by $\bar{\beta}$, $\tilde{\beta}$, and $\hat{\beta}$, respectively. We note that $\hat{\beta} = (X'\Omega^{-1}X)^{-1}(X'\Omega^{-1}y)$ is the ML (GLS) estimator here. Let $(X'\Omega^{-1}X) = G$, and consider the following optimization programs:

$$\max - (y - X\beta)'\Omega^{-1}(y - X\beta), \quad \text{subject to } R\beta \geq r, \tag{25.13}$$

and the same objective function but with equality restrictions. Denote by $\tilde{\lambda}$ and $\bar{\lambda}$ the Lagrange multipliers, respectively, of these two programs (conventionally, $\lambda = 0$ for $\hat{\beta}$). Then:

$$\bar{\beta} = \hat{\beta} + G^{-1}R'\tilde{\lambda}/2, \quad \text{and} \quad \tilde{\beta} = \hat{\beta} + G^{-1}R'\bar{\lambda}/2. \tag{25.14}$$

See GHM (1982). Employing these relations it is straightforward to show that the following three classical tests are identical:

$$\xi_{LR} = -2 \log LR = 2(\tilde{L} - \bar{L}), \tag{25.15}$$

where $\bar{L}$ and $\tilde{L}$ are the logarithms of the maxima of the respective likelihood functions;

$$\xi_{LM} = \min (\lambda - \bar{\lambda})'RG^{-1}R'(\lambda - \bar{\lambda})/4, \quad \text{subject to } \lambda \leq 0 \tag{25.16}$$

is the Kuhn–Tucker/Lagrange multiplier (LM) test computed at $\tilde{\lambda}$, and,

$$\xi_W = (R\tilde{\beta} - r)'[RG^{-1}R']^{-1}(R\tilde{\beta} - r) \tag{25.17}$$

is the Wald test. In order to utilize the classical results stated above for problems in (25.3), or (25.8), it is customary to note that the LR test in (25.15) above is identical to the LR test of the following problem:

$$\hat{\beta} = \beta + v$$

$$R\beta \geq r$$

$$v \sim N(0, G^{-1}) \qquad\qquad (25.18)$$

For this problem ξ_{LR} is the optimum of the following QP problem:

$$\max - (\beta - \hat{\beta})'G(\beta - \hat{\beta}) + (\tilde{\beta} - \hat{\beta})'G(\tilde{\beta} - \hat{\beta})$$

subject to $R\beta \geq r.$ \qquad\qquad (25.19)

This is identical to the one-sided multivariate problem in (25.3). It also suggests that the context for applications can be very general indeed. All that is needed is normally distributed estimators, $\hat{\beta}$, which are then projected on to the cone defined by the inequality restrictions in order to obtain the restricted estimator $\tilde{\beta}$.

2.2   Asymtotically normal estimators

The assumption of normality can be relaxed for the situations that allow asymptotically normal estimators for β. This is because the inference theory developed for problems (25.3) or (25.8) is asymptotically valid for much broader classes of models and hypotheses. In fact, when consistent estimators of Ω are available and, in (25.18), v has the stated distribution *asymptotically*, an asymptotically exact test of size α is based on the same $\overline{\chi}^2$-*distribution* given above. To obtain this result one needs to replace Ω in the optimization problems with its corresponding consistent estimator. This is routinely possible when Ω is a continuous function of a finite set of parameters other than β.

The three tests are not identical in this situation, of course, but have the same asymptotic distribution. Furthermore, the usual inequality, viz. $\xi_W \geq \xi_{LR} \geq \xi_{LM}$ is still valid, see GHM (1982). Often the test which can avoid the QP problem is preferred, which means the LM test for the null of equality of the restrictions, and the Wald test when the null is one of inequality and the alternative is unrestricted. But much recent evidence, as well as invariance arguments, suggest that the LR test be used.

In the general linear regression models with linear and/or nonlinear inequality restrictions, other approaches are available. Kodde and Palm (1986, 1987), Dufour (1989), Dufour and Khalaf (1995), and Stewart (1997) are examples of theoretical and empirical applications in economics and finance. Dufour (1989) is an alternative "conservative" bounds test for the following type situation:

$$H_0 : R\beta \in \Gamma_0 \text{ against } H_1 : \beta \in \Gamma_1, \qquad\qquad (25.20)$$

where Γ_0 and Γ_1 are non-empty subsets, respectively of R^p and R^K. This also allows a consideration of such cases as $h(R\beta) = 0$, or $h(R\beta) \geq 0$. Dufour (1989) suggests a generalization of the well known, two-sided F-test in this situation as follows:

$$\text{pr}\left[\frac{SS_0 - SS_1}{SS_1} \geq \frac{p}{T-K} F_\alpha(p, T - K)\right] \leq \alpha, \tag{25.21}$$

where there are T observations from which SS_i, $i = 0, 1$, are calculated as residual sums of squares under the null and the alternative, respectively. Thus the traditional p-values will be upper-bounds for the true values and offer a conservative bounds testing strategy. Dufour (1989), Dufour and Khalaf (1993) and Stewart (1997), *inter alia*, consider "liberal bounds", and extensions to multivariate/simultaneous equations models and nonlinear inequality restrictions. Applications to demand functions and negativity constraints on the substitution matrix, as well as tests of nonlinear nulls in the CAPM models show size and power improvements over the traditional asymptotic tests. The latter are known for their tendency to overreject in any case. Stewart (1997) considers the performance of the standard LR, the Kodde and Palm (1986) bounds for the $\overline{\chi}^2$-*distribution*, and the Dufour-type bound test of negativity of the substitution matrix for the demand data for Germany and Holland. Stewart looks at, among other things, the hypothesis of negativity against an unrestricted alternative, and the null of negativity when symmetry and homogeneity are maintained. It appears that, while the Dufour test did well in most cases, certainly reversing the conclusions of the traditional LR test (which rejects everything!), the Kodde and Palm bounds test does consistently well when the conservative bounds test was not informative (with $\alpha = 1$). Both the lower and upper bounds for the $\overline{\chi}^2$-squared distribution are available, while the "liberal"/lower bounds for the Dufour adjustment are not in this case.

3   NONLINEAR MODELS AND NONLINEAR INEQUALITY RESTRICTIONS

Wolak (1989, 1991) gives a general account of this topic. He considers the general formulation in (25.18) with nonlinear restrictions. Specifically, consider the following problem:

$$\hat{\beta} = \beta + v$$

$$h(\beta) \geq 0$$

$$v \underset{a}{\sim} N(0, \Psi) \tag{25.22}$$

where $h(\cdot)$ is a smooth vector function of dimension p with a derivative matrix denoted by $H(\cdot)$. We wish to test

$$H_0 : h(\beta) \geq 0, \quad \text{vs.} \quad H_1 : \beta \in R^K. \tag{25.23}$$

This is very general since model classes that allow for estimation results given in (25.22) are very broad indeed. As the results in Potscher and Prucha (1991a, 1991b) indicate, many nonlinear dynamic processes in econometrics permit consistent and asymptotically normal estimators under regularity conditions.

In general an asymptotically exact size test of the null in (25.23) is not possible without a localization to some suitable neighborhood of the parameter space. To see this, let $h(\beta^0) = 0$ define β^0, and $H(\beta^0)$, *and* $I(\beta^0)$ the evaluations of $\partial h / \partial \beta = H(\beta)$, and the information matrix, respectively. Let

$$C = \{\beta \mid h(\beta) \geq 0, \beta \in \mathbb{R}^K\} \tag{25.24}$$

and $N_{\delta_T}(\beta^0)$ as a δ_T-neighborhood with $\delta_T = O(T^{-\frac{1}{2}})$. It is known that the global hypotheses of the type in (25.23)–(25.24) do not generally permit large sample approximations to the power function for fixed alternative hypotheses for nonlinear multivariate equality restrictions. See Wolak (1989). If we localize the null in (25.23) to only $\beta \in N_{\delta_T}(\beta^0)$, then *asymptotically* exact size tests are available and are as given by the appropriately defined chi-bar distribution. In fact, we would be testing whether $\beta \in \{$cone of tangents of C at $\beta^0\}$, where $\Psi = H(\beta^0)I(\beta^0)^{-1}H(\beta^0)$, in (25.22).

In order to appreciate the issues, we note that the asymptotic distribution of the test depends on Ψ, which in turn depends on $H(\cdot)$ and $I(\cdot)$. But the latter generally vary with β^0. Also, we note that $h(\beta^0) = 0$ does not have a unique solution unless it is linear and of rank $K = p$. Thus the case of $H_0 : \beta \geq 0$ does not have a problem. The case $R\beta \geq 0$, will present a problem in nonlinear models when rank $(R) < K$ since $I(\beta)$ will generally depend on the $K - p$ free parameters in β. It must be appreciated that this is specially serious since inequalities define composite hypotheses which force a consideration of power over regions. Optimal tests do not exist in multivariate situations. Thus other conventions must be developed for test selection. One method is to consider power in the least favorable case. Another is to maximize power at given points that are known to be "desirable", leading to point optimal testing. Closely related, and since such points may be difficult to select a priori, are tests that maximize mean power over sets of desirable points. See King and Wu (1997) for discussion. In the instant case, the "least favorable" cases are all those defined by $h(\beta^0) = 0$. Hence the indeterminacy of the asymptotic power function.

From this point on our discussion pertains to the "local" test whenever the estimates of Ψ cannot converge to a unique $H(\beta^0)I(\beta^0)^{-1}H(\beta^0) = \Psi$.

Let $x_t = (x_{t1}, x_{t2}, \ldots, x_{tn})'$, $t = 1, \ldots T$, be a realization of a random variable in $\mathbb{R}^n$, with a density function $f(x_t, \beta)$ which is continuous in β for all x_t. We assume a compact subspace of $\mathbb{R}^n$ contains β, $h(\cdot)$ is continuous with continuous partial derivatives $\partial h_i(\beta)/\partial \beta_j = H_{ij}$, defining the $p \times K$ matrix $H(\beta)$ that is assumed to have full rank $p \leq K$ at an interior point β^0 such that $h(\beta^0) = 0$. Finally, let β_T^0 denote the "true" value under the local hypothesis, then,

$$\beta_T^0 \in C_T = \{\beta \mid h(\beta) \geq 0, \beta \in N_{\delta_T}(\beta^0)\} \quad \textit{for all } T$$

and $(\beta_T^0 - \beta^0) = o(1)$ and $T^{\frac{1}{2}}(\beta_T^0 - \beta^0) = O(1)$. Let x represent T random observations from $f(x_t, \beta)$, and the loglikelihood function given below:

$$L(\beta) = L(x, \beta) = \sum_{t=1}^{T} \ln(f(x_t, \beta)). \tag{25.25}$$

Following GHM (1982), again we consider the three estimators of (β, λ), obtained under the inequality constraints, equality constraints, and no constraints as $(\tilde{\beta}, \tilde{\lambda})$, $(\bar{\beta}, \bar{\lambda})$, and $(\hat{\beta}, \hat{\lambda} = 0)$, respectively. It can be verified that (see Wolak, 1989) the three tests LR, Wald, and LM are asymptotically equivalent and have the distribution given earlier. They are computed as follows:

$$\xi_{LR} = 2[L(\hat{\beta}) - L(\tilde{\beta})] \tag{25.26}$$

$$\xi_W = T(h(\tilde{\beta}) - h(\hat{\beta}))'[H(\hat{\beta})I(\beta^0)^{-1}H(\hat{\beta})'](h(\tilde{\beta}) - h(\hat{\beta})) \tag{25.27}$$

$$\xi_W' = T(\tilde{\beta} - \hat{\beta})'I(\beta^0)(\tilde{\beta} - \hat{\beta}) \tag{25.28}$$

$$\xi_{LM} = T\tilde{\lambda}'H(\tilde{\beta})I(\beta^0)^{-1}H(\tilde{\beta})'\tilde{\lambda} \tag{25.29}$$

where $I(\beta^0)$ is the value of the information matrix, $\lim_{T \to \infty} T^{-1}E_{\beta^0}[-\partial^2 L/\partial\beta\partial\beta']$, at β^0, and (25.27)–(25.28) are two asymptotically equivalent ways of computing the Wald test. This testifies to its lack of invariance which has been widely appreciated in econometrics. The above results also benefit from the well known asymptotic approximations:

$$h(\beta^0) \simeq H(\beta^0)(\beta - \beta^0), \quad \text{and} \quad H(\beta^0) - H(\beta) \simeq 0,$$

which hold for all of the three estimators of β. As Wolak (1989) shows, these statistics are asymptotically equivalent to the generalized distance statistic D introduced in Kodde and Palm (1986):

$$D = \min_{\beta} T(\hat{\beta} - \beta)'I(\beta^0)(\hat{\beta} - \beta), \tag{25.30}$$

subject to $H(\beta^0)(\beta - \beta^0) \geq 0, \quad \text{and} \quad \beta \in N_{\delta_T}(\beta^0)$.

For local β defined above, all these statistics have the same $\bar{\chi}^2$-distribution given earlier. Kodde and Palm (1987) employ this statistic for an empirical test of the negativity of the substitution matrix of demand systems. They find that it outperforms the two-sided asymptotic LR test. Their bounds also appear to deal with the related problem of overrejection when nominal significance levels are used with other classical tests against the two-sided alternatives. Gouriéroux et al. (1982) give the popular artificial regression method of deriving the LM test. In the same general context, Wolak (1989) specializes the above tests to a test of joint nonlinear inequality and equality restrictions.

With the advent of cheap computing and Monte Carlo integration in high dimensions, the above tests are quite accessible. Certainly, the critical values from the bounds procedures deserve to be incorporated in standard econometric routines, as well as the exact bounds for low dimensional cases ($p \leq 8$). The power gains justify the extra effort.

4 NONPARAMETRIC TESTS OF INEQUALITY RESTRICTIONS

All of the above models and hypotheses were concerned with comparing means and/or variance parameters of either known or asymptotically normal distributions. We may not know the distributions and/or be interested in comparing more general characteristics than the first few moments, and the distributions being compared may not be from the same family. All of these situations require a nonparametric development that can also deal with ordered hypotheses.

Order relations between distributions present one of the most important and exciting areas of development in economics and finance. These include stochastic dominance relations which in turn include Lorenz dominance, and such others as likelihood and uniform orders. Below we focus on the example of stochastic dominance (SD) of various orders. An account of the definitions and tests is first given, followed by some applications.

4.1   Tests for stochastic dominance

In the area of income distributions and tax analysis, it is important to look at Lorenz curves and similar comparisons. In practice, a finite number of ordinates of the desired curves or functions are compared. These ordinates are typically represented by quantiles and/or conditional interval means. Thus, the distribution theory of the proposed tests are typically derived from the existing asymptotic theory for ordered statistics or conditional means and variances. A most up-to-date outline of the required asymptotic theory is Davidson and Duclos (1998). To control for the size of a sequence of tests at several points the union intersection (UI) and Studentized Maximum Modulus technique for multiple comparisons is generally favored in this area. In this line of inquiry the inequality nature of the order relations is not explicitly utilized in the manner described above for parametric tests. Therefore, procedures that do so may offer power gain. Some alternatives to these multiple comparison techniques have been suggested, which are typically based on Wald-type joint tests of *equality* of the same ordinates; e.g. see Anderson (1996). These alternatives are somewhat problematic since their implicit null and alternative hypotheses are typically not a satisfactory representation of the *inequality* (order) relations that need to be tested. For instance, Xu *et al.* (1995) take proper account of the inequality nature of such hypotheses and adapt econometric tests for inequality restrictions to testing for FSD and SSD, and to GL dominance, respectively. Their tests follow the $\bar{\chi}^2$ theory outlined earlier.

McFadden (1989) and Klecan *et al.* (1991) have proposed tests of first- and second-order "maximality" for stochastic dominance which are extensions of the

Kolmogorov–Smirnov statistic. McFadden (1989) assumes iid observations and independent variates, allowing him to derive the asymptotic distribution of his test, in general, and its exact distribution in some cases. He provides a Fortran and a GAUSS program for computing his tests. Klecan *et al.* generalize this earlier test by allowing for weak dependence in the processes and replace independence with exchangeability. They demonstrate with an application for ranking investment portfolios. The asymptotic distribution of these tests cannot be fully characterized, however, prompting Klecan *et al.* to propose Monte Carlo methods for evaluating critical levels. Similarly, Maasoumi *et al.* (1997) propose bootstrap-KS tests with several empirical applications. In the following subsections some definitions and results are summarized which help to describe these tests.

4.2   Definitions and tests

Let X and Y be two income variables at either two different points in time, before and after taxes, or for different regions or countries. Let $X_1, X_2, \ldots, X_n$ be n not necessarily iid observations on X, and $Y_1, Y_2, \ldots, Y_m$ be similar observations on Y. Let U_1 denote the class of all utility functions u such that $u' \geq 0$, (increasing). Also, let U_2 denote the subset of all utility functions in U_1 for which $u'' \leq 0$ (strict concavity), and U_3 denote a subset of U_2 for which $u''' \geq 0$. Let $X_{(i)}$ and $Y_{(i)}$ denote the ith order statistics, and assume $F(x)$ and $G(x)$ are continuous and monotonic cumulative distribution functions (cdfs) of X and Y, respectively. Let the quantile functions $X(p)$ and $Y(p)$ be defined by, for example, $Y(p) = \inf\{y : F(y) \geq p\}$.

Proposition 1.   X first-order stochastic dominates Y, denoted X FSD Y, if and only if any one of the following equivalent conditions holds:

1. $E[u(X)] \geq E[u(Y)]$ for all $u \in U_1$, with strict inequality for some u. This is the classical definition.
2. $F(x) \leq G(x)$ for all x in the support of X, with strict inequality for some x (e.g. see McFadden, 1989).
3. $X(p) \geq Y(p)$ for all $0 \leq p \leq 1$, with strict inequality for some p (e.g. see Xu *et al.*, 1995).

Proposition 2.   X second-order stochastic dominates Y, denoted X SSD Y, if and only if any of the following equivalent conditions holds:

1. $E[u(X)] \geq E[u(Y)]$ for all $u \in U_2$, with strict inequality for some u.
2. $\int_{-\infty}^{x} F(t)dt \leq \int_{-\infty}^{x} G(t)dt$ for all x in the support of X and Y, with strict inequality for some x.
3. $\Phi_X(p) = \int_0^p X(t)dt \geq \Phi_Y(p) = \int_0^p Y(t)dt$, for all $0 \leq p \leq 1$, with strict inequality for some value(s) p.

Weaker versions of these relations drop the requirement of strict inequality at some point. When either Lorenz or Generalized Lorenz Curves of two distributions cross, unambiguous ranking by FSD and SSD may not be possible. Shorrocks and Foster (1987) show that the addition of a "transfer sensitivity" requirement leads to third-order stochastic dominance (TSD) ranking of income distributions. This requirement is stronger than the Pigou–Dalton principle of transfers since it makes regressive transfers less desirable at lower income levels. TSD is defined as follows:

Proposition 3.   X third-order stochastic dominates Y, denoted X TSD Y, if any of the following equivalent conditions holds:

1. $E[u(X)] \geq E[u(Y)]$ for all $u \in U_3$, with strict inequality for some u.
2. $\int_{-\infty}^{x}\int_{-\infty}^{v}[F(t) - G(t)]dt\, dv \leq 0$, for all x in the support, with strict inequality for some x, with the end-point condition:

$$\int_{-\infty}^{+\infty} [F(t) - G(t)]dt \leq 0.$$

3.   When $E[X] = E[Y]$, X TSD Y iff $\bar{\sigma}_x^2(q_i) \leq \bar{\sigma}_y^2(q_i)$, for all Lorenz curve crossing points q_i, $i = 1, 2, \ldots, (n + 1)$; where $\bar{\sigma}_x^2(q_i)$ denotes the "cumulative variance" for incomes upto the ith crossing point. See Davies and Hoy (1995).

When $n = 1$, Shorrocks and Foster (1987) show that X TSD Y if (i) the Lorenz curve of X cuts that of Y from above, and (ii) var(X) ≤ var(Y). This situation seemingly revives the coefficient of variation as a useful statistical index for ranking distributions. But a distinction is needed between the well known (unconditional) coefficient of variation for a distribution, on the one hand, and the sequence of several conditional coefficients of variation involved in the TSD.
    The tests of FSD and SSD are based on empirical evaluations of conditions (2) or (3) in the above definitions. Mounting tests on conditions (3) typically relies on the fact that quantiles are consistently estimated by the corresponding order statistics at a finite number of sample points. Mounting tests on conditions (2) requires empirical cdfs and comparisons at a finite number of observed ordinates. Also, from Shorrocks (1983) it is clear that condition (3) of SSD is equivalent to the requirement of generalized Lorenz (GL) dominance. FSD implies SSD.
    The Lorenz and the generalized Lorenz curves are, respectively, defined by: $L(p) = (1/\mu) \int_0^p Y(u)du$, and $GL(p) = \mu L(p) = \int Y(u)du$, with $GL(0) = 0$, *and* $GL(1) = \mu$; see Shorrocks (1983).
    It is customary to consider K points on the L (or GL or the support) curves for empirical evaluation with $0 < p_1 < p_2 < \ldots < p_K = 1$, and $p_i = i/K$. Denote the corresponding quantiles by $Y(p_i)$, and the conditional moments $\gamma_i = E(Y | Y \leq Y(p_i))$, and $\bar{\sigma}_i^2 = E\{(Y - \gamma_i)^2 | Y \leq Y(p_i)\}$. The vector of GL ordinates is given by $\eta = (p_1\bar{\sigma}_1^2, p_2\bar{\sigma}_2^2, \ldots p_K\bar{\sigma}_K^2)'$. See Xu *et al.* (1995) who adopt the $\bar{\chi}^2$ approach described above to test quantile conditions (3) of FSD and SSD. A short description follows:
    Consider the random sequence $\{Z_t\} = \{X_t, Y_t\}'$, a stationary ϕ-*mixing* sequence of random vectors on a probability space $(\Omega, \Re, P)$. Similarly, denote the stacked

vector of GL ordinates for the two variables as $\eta^Z = (\eta^X, \eta^Y)'$, and the stacked vector of quantiles of the two variables by $q^Z = (q^X, q^Y)'$, where $q^X = (X(p_1),$ $X(p_2), \ldots X(p_K))'$, and similarly for Y. In order to utilize the general theory given for the $\overline{\chi}^2$-distribution, three ingredients are required. One is to show that the various hypotheses of interest in this context are representable as in (25.23) above. This is possible and simple. The second is to verify if and when the unrestricted estimators of the η and q functions satisfy the asymptotic representation given in (25.22). This is possible under conditions on the processes and their relationships, as we will summarize shortly. The third is to be able to empirically implement the $\overline{\chi}$ statistics that ensue. In this last step, resampling techniques are and will become even more prominent.

To see that hypotheses of interest are suitably representable, we note that for the case of conditions (3) of FSD and SSD, the testing problem is the following: $H_0 : h_K(q^Z) \geq 0$ against $H_1 : h_K(q^Z) \not\geq 0$, where $h_K(q^Z) = [I_K : -I_K]q^Z = I^*q^Z$, say, for FSD, and $h_K(q^Z) = BI^* \times q^Z$, for the test of SSD, where, $B = (B_{ij})$, $B_{ij} = 1, i \geq j$, $B_{ij} = 0$, otherwise, is the "summation" matrix which obtains the successive cumulated quantile (Φ) and other functions.

Tests for GL dominance (SSD) which are based on the ordinate vector η^Z are also of the "linear inequality" form and require $h(\eta^Z) = I^*\eta^Z$.

Sen (1972) gives a good account of the conditions under which sample quantiles are asymptotically normally distributed. Davidson and Duclos (1998) provide the most general treatment of the asymptotic normality of the nonparametric sample estimators of the ordinates in η. In both cases the asymptotic variance matrix, Ψ, noted in the general setup (25.22) is derived. What is needed is to appropriately replace R in the formulations of Kodde and Palm (1986), or Gouriéroux et al. (1982), and to implement the procedure with consistent estimates of Ω in $\Psi = R\Omega R'$.

For sample order statistics, $\hat{q}_T^Z$, it is well known that, if X and Y are independent,

$$\sqrt{T}(\hat{q}^Z - q^Z) \xrightarrow{d} N(0, \Omega)$$

$$\Omega = G^{-1}VG'^{-1}$$

$$G = \mathrm{diag}[f_x(X(p_i)), \ldots ; f_y(Y(p_i)), \ldots], i = 1, \ldots, K$$

$$V = \lim_{T \to \infty} E(gg'), g = T^{-1}(\mathfrak{F}_x \mathfrak{F}_y'),$$

$$\mathfrak{F}_x = [\{F(X(p_1)) - p_1\}, \ldots, \{F(X(p_K)) - p_K\}], \mathfrak{F}_y \text{ similarly defined.}$$

As is generally appreciated, these density components are notoriously difficult to estimate. Kernel density methods can be used, as can Newey–West type robust estimators. But it is desirable to obtain bootstrap estimates based on block bootstrap and/or iterated bootstrap techniques. These are equally accessible computationally, but may perform much better in smaller samples and for larger numbers of ordinates K. Xu et al. (1995) demonstrate with an application to the hypothesis of term premia based on one- and two-month US Treasury bills. This application was based on the Kodde and Palm (1986) critical bounds and encountered some realizations in the inconclusive region. Xu *et al.* (1995) employ Monte Carlo simulations to obtain the exact critical levels in those cases.

Sample analogs of η and similar functions for testing any stochastic order also have asymptotically normal distributions. Davidson and Duclos (1998) exploit the following interesting result which translates conditions (3) of the FSD and SSD into inequality restrictions among the members of the η functions defined above:

Let $D_X^1(x) = F_X(x)$, and $D_Y(y) = F_Y(y)$; then,

$$D_i^s(x) = \int_0^x D^{s-1}(u)du = \frac{1}{(s-1)!} \int_0^x (x-u)^{s-1} dF(u), \text{ for any } s \geq 2.$$

This last equality clearly shows that tests of any order stochastic dominance can be based on the conditional moments estimated at a suitable finite number of K ordinates as defined above. For instance, third order SD (s = 3) is seen to depend on the conditional/cumulative variance. Also, since poverty measures are often defined over lower subsets of the domain such that $x \leq$ poverty line, dominance relations over poverty measures can also be tested in the same fashion. Using empirical distribution functions, Davidson and Duclos (1998) demonstrate with an example from the panels for six countries in the Luxembourg study. It should be appreciated, however, that these tests do not exploit the inequality nature of the alternative hypotheses. The union intersection method determines the critical level of the inference process here. The cases of unrankable distributions include both "equivalence" and crossing (non-dominant) distributions. A usual asymptotic χ^2 test will have power in both directions. In order to improve upon this, therefore, one must employ the $\bar{\chi}^2$-distribution technique.

Similarly, Kaur *et al.* (1994) propose a test for condition (2) of SSD when iid observations are assumed for independent prospects X and Y. Their null hypothesis is condition (2) of SSD *for each x* against the alternative of strict violation of the same condition *for all x*. The test of SSD then requires an appeal to a union intersection technique which results in a test procedure with maximum asymptotic size of α if the test statistic at each x is compared with the critical value Z_α of the standard normal distribution. They showed their test is consistent. One rejects the null of dominance if any negative distances at the K ordinates is significant.

In contrast, McFadden (1989), and Klecan *et al.* (1991) test for dominance jointly *for all x*. McFadden's analysis of the multivariate Kolmogorov–Smirnov type test is developed for a set of variables and requires a definition of "maximal" sets, as follows:

Definition 1. Let $Æ = \{X_1, X_2, \ldots, X_K\}$ denote a set of K distinct random variables. Let F_k denote the cdf of the kth variable. The set Æ is first- (second-)order maximal if no variable in Æ is first- (second-)order weakly dominated by another.

Let $X_{.n} = (x_{1n}, x_{2n}, \ldots, x_{Kn})$, $n = 1, 2, \ldots, N$, be the observed data. We assume $X_{.n}$ is strictly stationary and α-*mixing*. As in Klecan *et al.*, we also assume $F_i(X_i)$, $i = 1$, $2, \ldots, K$ are *exchangeable* random variables, so that our resampling estimates of the test statistics converge appropriately. This is less demanding than the assumption of independence which is not realistic in many applications (as in before and after tax scenarios). We also assume F_k is unknown and estimated by the empirical distribution function $F_{kN}(X_k)$. Finally, we adopt Klecan *et al.*'s mathematical regularity conditions pertaining to von Neumann–Morgenstern (VNM) utility functions that generally underlie the expected utility maximization paradigm. The following theorem defines the tests and the hypotheses being tested:

Lemma Given the mathematical regularity conditions;

1. The variables in Æ are first-order stochastically maximal; i.e.

$$d = \min_{i \neq j} \max_x [F_i(x) - F_j(x)] > 0,$$

   if and only if for each i and j, there exists a continuous increasing function u such that $Eu(X_i) > Eu(X_j)$.
2. The variables in Æ are second-order stochastically maximal; i.e.

$$S = \min_{i \neq j} \max_x \int_{-\infty}^{x} [F_i(\mu) - F_j(\mu)]d\mu > 0,$$

   if and only if for each i and j, there exists a continuous increasing and strictly concave function u such that $Eu(X_i) > Eu(X_j)$.
3. Assuming, (i) the stochastic process $X_{.n}$, $n = 1, 2, \ldots$, to be strictly stationary and α-*mixing* with $\alpha(j) = O(j^{-\delta})$, for some $\delta > 1$, and (ii) the variables in the set are exchangeable (relaxing independence in McFadden, 1989): $d_{2N} \to d$, and $S_{2N} \to S$, where d_{2N} and S_{2N} are the empirical test statistics defined as:

$$d_{2N} = \min_{i \neq j} \max_x [F_{iN}(x) - F_{jN}(x)]$$

and

$$S_{2N} = \min_{i \neq j} \max_x \int_{0}^{x} [F_{iN}(\mu) - F_{jN}(\mu)]d\mu$$

Proof 1. See Theorems 1 and 5 of Klecan *et al.* (1991).

The null hypothesis tested by these two statistics is that, respectively, Æ is *not* first- (second-)order maximal – i.e. X_i FSD(SSD) X_j for some i and j. We reject the null when the statistics are positive and large. Since the null hypothesis in each case is composite, power is conventionally determined in the least favorable case of identical marginals $F_i = F_j$. As is shown in Kaur *et al.* (1994) and Klecan *et al.*

(1991), when X and Y are independent, tests based on d_{2N} and S_{2N} are consistent. Furthermore, the asymptotic distribution of these statistics are non-degenerate in the least favorable case, being Gaussian (see Klecan *et al.*, 1991, Theorems 6–7).

As is pointed out by Klecan *et al.* (1991), for non-independent variables, the statistic S_{2N} has, in general, neither a tractable distribution, nor an asymptotic distribution for which there are convenient computational approximations. The situation for d_{2N} is similar except for some special cases – see Durbin (1973, 1985), and McFadden (1989) who assume iid observations (not crucial), and indepen-dent variables in Æ (consequential). Unequal sample sizes may be handled as in Kaur *et al.* (1994).

Klecan *et al.* (1991) suggest Monte Carlo procedures for computing the signifi-cance levels of these tests. This forces a dependence on an assumed parametric distribution for generating MC iterations, but is otherwise quite appealing for very large iterations. Maasoumi *et al.* (1997) employ the bootstrap method to obtain the empirical distributions of the test statistics and of *p*-values. Pilot stud-ies show that their computations obtain similar results to the algorithm proposed in Klecan *et al.* (1991).

In the bootstrap procedure we compute d_{2N} and S_{2N} for a finite number K of the income ordinates. This requires a computation of sample frequencies, cdfs and sums of cdfs, as well as the differences of the last two quantities at all the K points. Bootstrap samples are generated from which empirical distributions of the differences, of the d_{2N} and S_{2N} statistics, and their bootstrap confidence intervals are determined. The bootstrap probability of these statistics being positive and/ or falling outside these intervals leads to rejection of the hypotheses. Maasoumi *et al.* (1997) demonstrate by several applications to the US income distributions based on the Current Population Survey (CPS) and the panel data from the Michigan study. In contrast to the sometimes confusing picture drawn by com-parisons based on inequality indices, they find frequent SSD relations, including between population subgroups, that suggest a "welfare" deterioration in the 1980s compared to the previous two decades.

5   CONCLUSION

Taking the one-sided nature of some linear and nonlinear hypotheses is both desirable and practical. It can improve power and lead to the improved computa-tion of the critical levels. A $\bar{\chi}^2$ and a multivariate KS testing strategy were described and contrasted with some alternatives, either the less powerful two-sided methods, or the union intersection procedures. The latter deserves to be studied further in comparison to the methods that are expected to have better power. Computa-tional issues involve having to solve QP problems to obtain inequality restricted estimators, and numerical techniques for computation of the weights in the $\bar{\chi}$ statistic. Bounds tests for the latter are available and may be sufficient in many cases.

Applications in the parametric/semiparametric, and the nonparametric testing area have been cited. They tend to occur in substantive attempts at empirical evaluation and incorporation of economic theories.

Note

* Comments from the editor and an anonymous referee helped improve this chapter. A more extensive bibliography and discussion is contained in the preliminary version of this chapter which is available upon request.

References

Anderson, G.J. (1996). Nonparametric tests of stochastic dominance in income distributions. *Econometrica* 64, 1183–93.

Barlow, R.E., D.J. Bartholomew, J.N. Bremner, and H.D. Brunk (1972). *Statistical Inference under Order Restrictions: The Theory and Applications of Isotonic Regression*. New York: John Wiley and Sons.

Bartholomew, D.J. (1959a). A test of homogeneity for ordered alternatives. *Biometrica* 46, 36–48.

Bartholomew, D.J. (1959b). A test of homogeneity for ordered alternatives. *Biometrica* 46, 328–35.

Bohrer, R., and W. Chow (1978). Weights of one-sided multivariate inference. *Applied Statistics* 27, 100–4.

Davidson, R., and J.-Y. Duclos (1998). Statistical inference for stochastic dominance and for the measurement of poverty and inequality. GREQAM, Doc. de Travail, no. 98A14.

Davies, J., and M. Hoy (1995). Making inequality comparisons when Lorenz curves intersect. *American Economic Review* 85, 980–6.

Dufour, J.-M. (1989). Nonlinear hypotheses, inequality restrictions and nonnested hypotheses: Exact simultaneous tests in linear regression. *Econometrica* 57, 335–55.

Dufour, J.-M., and L. Khalaf (1995). Finite sample inference methods in seemingly unrelated regressions and simultaneous equations. Technical report, University of Montreal.

Durbin, J. (1973). Distribution theory for tests based on the sample distribution function. Philadelphia, SIAM.

Durbin, J. (1985). The first passage density of a continuous Gaussian process to a general boundary. *Journal of Applied Probability* 22, 99–122.

Gouriéroux, C., A. Holly, and A. Monfort (1980). Kuhn–Tucker, likelihood ratio and Wald tests for nonlinear models with inequality constraints on the parameters. Harvard Institute of Economic Research, Mimeographed paper no. 770.

Gouriéroux, C., A. Holly, and A. Monfort (1982). Likelihood ratio test, Wald test and Kuhn–Tucker test in linear models with inequality constraints in the regression parameters. *Econometrica* 50, 63–80.

King, M.L., and Ping X. Wu (1997). Locally optimal one-sided tests for multiparameter hypotheses. *Econometric Reviews* 16, 131–56.

Kaur, A., B.L.S. Prakasa Rao, and H. Singh (1994). Testing for second-order stochastic dominance of two distributions. *Econometric Theory* 10, 849–66.

Klecan, L., R. McFadden, and D. McFadden (1991). A robust test for stochastic dominance. Working paper, Economics Dept., MIT.

Kodde, D.A., and F.C. Palm (1986). Wald criteria for jointly testing equality and inequality restrictions. *Econometrica* 50, 1243–8.

Kodde, D.A., and F. Palm (1987). A parametric test of the negativity of the substitution matrix. *Journal of Applied Econometrics* 2, 227–35.

Kudô, A. (1963). A multivariate analogue of the one-sided test. *Biometrica* 50, 403–18.

Maasoumi, E., J. Mills, and S. Zandvakili (1997). Consensus ranking of US income distributions: A bootstrap application of stochastic dominance tests. SMU, Economics.

McFadden, D. (1989). Testing for stochastic dominance. In Part II of T. Fomby and T.K. Seo (eds.) *Studies in the Economics of Uncertainty* (in honor of J. Hadar). Springer-Verlag.

Perlman, M.D. (1969). One-sided testing problems in multivariate analysis. *Annals of Mathematics and Statistics* 40, 549–62.

Potscher, B.M., and I.R. Prucha (1991a). Basic structure of the asymptotic theory in dynamic nonlinear econometric models: I. Consistency and approximation concepts. *Econometric Reviews* 10, 125–216.

Potscher, B.M., and I.R. Prucha (1991b). Basic structure of the asymptotic theory in dynamic nonlinear econometric models: II. Asymptotic Normality. *Econometric Reviews* 10, 253–326 (with comments).

Sen, P.K. (1972). On the Bahadur representation of sample quantiles for sequences of φ-mixing random variables. *Journal of Multivariate Analysis* 2, 77–95.

Shorrocks, A.F. (1983). Ranking income distributions. *Economica* 50, 3–17.

Shorrocks, A., and J. Foster (1987). Transfer sensitive inequality measures. *Review of Economic Studies* 54, 485–97.

Stewart, K.G. (1997). Exact testing in multivariate regression. *Econometric Reviews* 16, 321–52.

Wolak, F. (1989). Local and global testing of linear and nonlinear inequality constraints in nonlinear econometric models. *Econometric Theory* 5, 1–35.

Wolak, F. (1991). The local nature of hypothesis tests involving inequality constraints in nonlinear models. *Econometrica* 981–95.

Xu, K., G. Fisher, and D. Wilson (1995). New distribution-free tests for stochastic dominance. Working paper No. 95-02, February, Dept. of Economics, Dalhousie University, Halifax, Nova Scotia.

Spurious Regressions in Econometrics

Clive W.J. Granger

1 INTRODUCTION, HISTORY, AND DEFINITIONS

If X_t, Y_t are a pair of time series, independent of each other and one runs the simple ordinary least squares regression

$$Y_t = a + bX_t + e_t, \tag{26.1}$$

then one should expect to find no evidence of a relationship, so that the estimate of b is near zero and its associated t-statistics is insignificant. However, when the individual series have strong autocorrelations, it had been realized by the early 1970s by time series analysis that the situation may not be so simple; that apparent relationships may often be observed using standard interpretations of such regressions. Because a relationship appears to be found between independent series, they have been called "spurious". To appreciate part of the problem, note that if $b = 0$, then e_t must have the same time series properties as Y_t, that is will be strongly autocorrelated, and so the assumptions of the classical OLS regression will not be obeyed, as discussed in virtually any statistics or econometrics textbook. The possibility of getting incorrect results from regressions was originally pointed out by Yule (1926) in a much cited but insufficiently read paper that discussed "nonsense correlations." Kendall (1954) also pointed out if X_t, Y_t both obeyed the same autoregressive model of order one (AR (1))

$$\left. \begin{array}{l} X_t = a_1 X_{t-1} + \varepsilon_{xt} \\ Y_t = a_2 Y_{t-1} + \varepsilon_{yt} \end{array} \right\} \tag{26.2}$$

with $a_1 = a_2 = a$, where ε_{xt}, ε_{yt} are a pair of zero-mean, white noise (zero autocorrelated) series independent of each other at all pairs of times, then the sample correlation (R) between X_t, Y_t has

$$\text{var}(R) = n^{-1}(1 + a^2)/(1 - a^2),$$

where n is the sample size. Remember that R, being a correlation must be between -1 and 1, but if a is near one and n not very large, then var(R) will be quite big, which can only be achieved if the distribution of R values has large weights near the extreme values of -1 and 1, which will correspond to "significant" b values in (26.1).

2 SIMULATIONS

The obvious way to find evidence of spurious regressions is by using simulations. The first simulation on the topic was by Granger and Newbold (1974) who generated pairs of independent random walks, from (26.2) with $a_1 = a_2 = 1$. Each series had 50 terms and 100 repetitions were used. If the regression (26.1) is run, using series that are temporarily uncorrelated, one would expect that roughly 95 percent of values of $|t|$ on b would be less than 2. This original simulation using random walks found $|t| \leq 2$ on only 23 occasions, out of the 100, $|t|$ was between 2 and 4 on 24 times, between 4 and 7 on 34 times, and over 7 on the other 19 occasions.

The reaction to these results was to re-assess many of the previously obtained empirical results in applied time series econometrics, which undoubtedly involved highly autocorrelated series but had not previously been concerned by this fact. Just having a high R^2 value and an apparently significant value of b was no longer sufficient for a regression to be satisfactory or its interpretations relevant. The immediate questions were how one could easily detect a spurious regression and then correct for it. Granger and Newbold (1974) concentrated on the value of the Durbin–Watson statistic; if the value is too low, it suggests that the regressions results cannot be trusted. Quick fix methods such as using a Cochrane–Orcutt technique to correct autocorrelations in the residuals, or differencing the series used in a regression were inclined to introduce further difficulties and so cannot be recommended. The problem arises because equation (26.1) is misspecified, the proper reaction to having a possible spurious relationship is to add lagged dependent and independent variables, until the errors appear to be white noise, according to the Durbin–Watson statistic. A random walk is an example of an I(1) process, that is a process that needs to be differenced to become stationary. Such processes seem to be common in parts of econometrics, especially in macroeconomics and finance. One approach that is widely recommended is to test if X_t, Y_t are I(1) and, if yes, to difference before performing the regression (26.1). There are many tests available, a popular one is due to Dickey–Fuller (1979). However, as will be explained below, even this approach is not without its practical difficulties.

3 THEORY

A theoretical investigation of the basic unit root, ordinary least squares, spurious regression case was undertaken by Phillips (1986). He considered the asymptotic properties of the coefficients and statistics of equation (26.1), $\hat{a}$, $\hat{b}$, the t-statistic for b, R^2 and the Durbin–Watson statistics $\hat{\rho}$. To do this he introduced the link between normed sums of functions of unit root processes and integrals of Wiener processes. For example if a sample X_t of size T is generated from a driftless random walk then

$$T^{-3/2} \sum_1^T X_t \to \sigma_\varepsilon \int_0^1 W(t)dt$$

where σ_ε^2 is the variance of the shock,

$$T^{-2} \sum_1^T X_t^2 \to \sigma_\varepsilon^2 \int_0^1 W^2(t)dt$$

and if X_t, Y_t are an independent pair of such random walks, then

$$T^{-2} \sum_1^T X_t Y_t \to \sigma_\varepsilon \sigma_\eta \int_0^1 V(t)W(t)dt$$

where $V(t)$, $W(t)$ are independent Wiener processes. As a Wiener process is a continuous time random process on the real line [0, 1], the various sums are converging and can thus be replaced by integrals of a stochastic process. This transformation makes the mathematics of the investigation much easier, once one becomes familiar with the new tools. Phillips is able to show that

1. the distributions of the t-statistics for $\hat{a}$ and $\hat{b}$ from (26.1) diverge as t becomes large, so there is no asymptotically correct critical values for these conventional tests.
2. $\hat{b}$ converges to some random variable whose value changes from sample to sample.
3. Durbin–Watson statistics tend to zero.
4. R^2 does not tend to zero but to some random variable.

What is particularly interesting is that not only do these theoretical results completely explain the simulations but also that the theory deals with asymptotics, $T \to \infty$, whereas the original simulations had only $T = 50$. It seems that spurious regression occurs at all sample sizes.

Haldrup (1994) has extended Phillips' result to the case for two independent I(2) variables and obtained similar results. (An I(2) variable is one that needs differencing twice to get to stationarity, or here, difference once to get to random walk.) Marmol (1998) has further extended these results to fractionally integrated, I(d), processes. Unpublished simulation results also exist for various other long-memory processes, including explosive autoregressive processes, (26.2) with $a_1 = a_2 = a > 1$. Durlauf and Phillips (1988) regress an I(1) process on deterministic polynomials in time, thus polynomial trends, and found spurious relationships. Phillips (1998) has recently discussed how all such results can be interpreted by considering a decomposition of an I(1) series in terms of deterministic trends multiplied by stationary series.

4   Spurious Regressions with Stationary Processes

Spurious regressions in econometrics are usually associated with I(1) processes, which was explored in Phillips' well known theory and in the best known simulations. What is less appreciated is that the problem can just also occur, although less clearly, with stationary processes. Table 26.1, taken from Granger, Hyung, and Jeon (1998), shows simulation results from independent series generated by (26.2) with $0 < a_1 = a_2 = a \leq 1$ and e_{xt}, e_{yt} both Gaussian white noise series, using regression (26.1) estimated using OLS with sample sizes varying between 100 and 10,000.

It is seen that sample size has little impact on the percentage of spurious regressions found (apparent significance of the b coefficient in (26.1)). Fluctuations down columns do not change significantly with the number of iterations used. Thus, the spurious regression problem is not a small sample property. It is also seen to be a serious problem with pairs of autoregressive series which are not unit root processes. If $a = 0.75$ for example, then 30 percent of regressions will give spurious implications. Further results are available in the original paper but will not be reported in detail. The Gaussian error assumption can be replaced by other distributions with little or no change in the simulation results, except for an exceptional distribution such as the Cauchy. Spurious regressions also occur if $a_1 \neq a_2$, although less frequently, and particularly if the smaller of the two a values is at least 0.5 in magnitude.

The obvious implications of these results is that applied econometricians should not worry about spurious regressions only when dealing with I(1), unit root, processes. Thus, a strategy of first testing if a series contains a unit root before entering into a regression is not relevant. The results suggest that many more simple regressions need to be interpreted with care, when the series involved are strongly serially correlated. Again, the correct response is to move to a better specification, using lags of all variables.

Table 26.1   Regression between independent AR(1) series

Sample series	$a = 0$	$a = 0.25$	$a = 0.5$	$a = 0.75$	$a = 0.9$	$a = 1.0$
100	4.9	6.8	13.0	29.9	51.9	89.1
500	5.5	7.5	16.1	31.6	51.1	93.7
2,000	5.6	7.1	13.6	29.1	52.9	96.2
10,000	4.1	6.4	12.3	30.5	52.0	98.3

$a_1 = a_2 = a$ percentage of $|t| > 2$

5 RELATED PROCESSES

The final generalization would take variables generated by (26.2) but now allowing e_{xt}, e_{yt} to be correlated, say $\rho = \text{corr}(e_{xt}, e_{yt})$. Now the series are related and any relationship found in (26.2) will not be spurious, although the extent of the relationship is over-emphasized if the residual achieved is not white noise. The natural generalization is a bivariate vector autoregression or, if ρ is quite high, and if $a_1 = a_2 = 1$, the series will be cointegrated (as described in Chapter 30 on Cointegration), in which case an error-correction model is appropriate. In all these models, spurious regressions should not be a problem.

References

Dickey, D.A., and W.A. Fuller (1979). Distribution of the estimates for autoregressive time series with a unit root. *Journal of the American Statistical Association* 74, 427–31.

Durlauf, S.N., and P.C.B. Phillips (1988). Trends versus random walks in time series analysis. *Econometrica* 56, 1333–54.

Granger, C.W.J., N. Hyung, and Y. Jeon (1998). Spurious regression with stationary series. Working Paper, UCSD Department of Economics.

Granger, C.W.J., and P. Newbold (1974). Spurious regressions in econometrics. *Journal of Econometrics* 2, 111–20.

Haldrup, N. (1994). The asymptotics of single-equation cointegration regressions with I(1) and I(2) variables. *Journal of Econometrics* 63, 153–81.

Kendall, M.G. (1954). *Exercises in Theoretical Statistics*. London, Griffin.

Marmol, F. (1998). Spurious regression theory with non-stationary fractionally integrated processes. *Journal of Econometrics* 84, 233–50.

Phillips, P.C.B. (1986). Understanding spurious regressions in econometrics. *Journal of Econometrics* 33, 311–40.

Phillips, P.C.B. (1998). New tools for understanding spurious regressions. *Econometrica* 66, 1299–325.

Yule, G.U. (1926). Why do we sometimes get nonsense correlations between time series? *Journal of the Royal Statistical Society* 89, 1–64.

Forecasting Economic Time Series

*James H. Stock**

1 INTRODUCTION

The construction and interpretation of economic forecasts is one of the most publicly visible activities of professional economists. Over the past two decades, increased computer power has made increasingly sophisticated forecasting methods routinely available and the role of economic forecasting has expanded. Economic forecasts now enter into many aspects of economic life, including business planning, state and local budgeting, financial management, financial engineering, and monetary and fiscal policy. Yet, with this widening scope comes greater opportunities for the production of poor forecasts and the mis-interpretation of good forecasts. Responsible production and interpretation of economic forecasts requires a clear understanding of the associated econometric tools, their limits, and an awareness of common pitfalls in their application.

This chapter provides an introduction to the main methods used for forecast-ing economic time series. The field of economic forecasting is large, and, because of space limitations, this chapter covers only the most salient topics. The focus here will be on point forecasts, that is, forecasts of future values of the time series. It is assumed that the historical series is relatively "clean," in the sense of having no omitted observations, being observed at a consistent sampling fre-quency (e.g. monthly), and either having no seasonal component or having been seasonally adjusted. It is assumed that the forecaster has quadratic (i.e. mean squared error) loss. Finally, it is assumed that the time series is sufficiently long, relative to the forecast horizon, that the history of the time series will be informa-tive for making the forecast and for estimating parametric models.

This chapter has four substantive sections. Section 2 provides a theoretical framework for considering some of the tradeoffs in the construction of economic forecasts and for the comparison of forecasting methods. Section 3 provides a glimpse at some of the relevant empirical features of macroeconomic time series data. Section 4 discusses univariate forecasts, that is, forecasts of a series made using only past values of that series. Section 5 provides an overview of multivariate forecasting, in which forecasts are made using historical information on multiple time series.

There are many interesting and important aspects of economic forecasting that are not covered in this chapter. In some applications, it is of interest to estimate the entire distribution of future values of the variable of interest, conditional on current information, or certain functions of that conditional distribution. An example that arises in macroeconomics is predicting the probability of a recession, an event often modeled as two consecutive declines in real gross domestic product. Other functions of conditional distributions arise in finance; for examples, see Diebold, Gunther, and Tay (1998).

In some cases, time varying conditional densities might be adequately summarized by time varying conditional first and second moments, that is, by modeling conditional heteroskedasticity. For example, conditional estimates of future second moments of the returns on an asset can be used to price options written on that asset. Although there are various frameworks for estimating conditional heteroskedasticity, the premier tool for modeling conditional heteroskedasticity is Engle's (1982) so-called autoregressive conditional heteroskedasticity (ARCH) framework and variants, as discussed in Bollerslev, Engle, and Nelson (1994).

Another topic not explored in this chapter is nonquadratic loss. Quadratic loss is a natural starting point for many forecasting problems, both because of its tractability and because, in many applications, it is plausible that loss is symmetric and that the marginal cost of a forecast error increases linearly with its magnitude. However, in some circumstances other loss functions are appropriate. For example, loss might be asymmetric (would you rather be held responsible for a surprise government surplus or deficit?); see Granger and Newbold (1986, ch. 4.2) and West, Edison, and Cho (1993) for examples. Handling nonquadratic loss can be computationally challenging. The classic paper in this literature is Granger (1969), and a recent contribution is Christoffersen and Diebold (1997).

Another important set of problems encountered in practice but not addressed here involve data irregularities, such as missing or irregularly spaced observations. Methods for handling these irregularities tend to be model-dependent. Within univariate linear models and low-dimensional multivariate linear models, these are typically well handled using state space representations and the Kalman filter, as is detailed by Harvey (1989). A somewhat different set of issues arise with series that have large seasonal components. Issues of seasonal adjustment and handling seasonal data are discussed in Chapter 31 in this volume by Ghysels, Osborn, and Rodrigues.

Different issues also arise if the forecast horizon is long relative to the sample size (say, at least one-fifth the sample size) and the data exhibit strong serial correlation. Then the long-run forecast is dominated by estimates of the long-run correlation structure. Inference about the long-run correlation structure is typically nonstandard and, in some formulations, is related to the presence of large, possibly unit autoregressive roots and (in the multivariate setting) to possible cointegration among the series. Unit roots and cointegration are respectively discussed in this volume in Chapter 29 by Bierens and Chapter 30 by Dolado, Gonzalo, and Marmol. The construction of point forecasts and forecast intervals at long horizons entails considerable difficulties because of the sensitivity to the long-run dependence parameters, and methods for handling this are examined in Stock (1996).

A final area not addressed here is the combination of competing forecasts. When a variable is forecasted by two different methods that draw on different information sets and neither model is true, typically a combination of the two forecasts is theoretically preferred to either individual forecast (Bates and Granger, 1969). For an introduction to this literature, see Granger (1989), Diebold and Lopez (1995), and Chan, Stock, and Watson (1998).

This chapter makes use of concepts and methods associated with unit autoregressive roots, cointegration, vector autoregressions (VARs), and structural breaks. These are all topics of separate chapters in this volume, and the reader is referred to those chapters for background details.

2 ECONOMIC FORECASTING: A THEORETICAL FRAMEWORK

2.1 Optimal forecasts, feasible forecasts, and forecast errors

Let y_t denote the scalar time series variable that the forecaster wishes to forecast, let h denote the horizon of the forecast, and let F_t denote the set of data used at time t for making the forecast (F_t is sometimes referred to as the information set available to the forecaster). If the forecaster has squared error loss, the point forecast $\hat{y}_{t+h|t}$ is the function of F_t that minimizes the expected squared forecast error, that is, $E[(y_{t+h} - \hat{y}_{t+h|t})^2 \mid F_t]$. This expected loss is minimized when the forecast is the conditional expectation, $E(y_{t+h} \mid F_t)$. In general, this conditional expectation might be a time varying function of F_t. However, in this chapter we will assume that the data are drawn from a stationary distribution, that is, the distribution of $(y_s, \ldots, y_{s+T})$ does not depend on s (although some mention of structural breaks will be made later); then $E(y_{t+h} \mid F_t)$ is a time invariant function of F_t.

In practice, $E(y_{t+h} \mid F_t)$ is unknown and is in general nonlinear. Forecasts are constructed by approximating this unknown conditional expectation by a parametric function. This parametric function, or model, is denoted $\mu_h(F_t, \theta)$, where θ is a parameter vector which is assumed to lie in the parameter space Θ. The "best" value of this parameter, θ_0, is the value that minimizes the mean squared approximation error, $E[\mu_h(F_t, \theta) - E(y_{t+h} \mid F_t)]^2$.

Because θ_0 is unknown, it is typically estimated from historical data, and the estimate is denoted $\hat{\theta}$. To be concrete, suppose that F_t consists of observations on X_s, $1 \leq s \leq T$, where X_s is a vector time series (which typically includes y_s). Further suppose that only the first p lags of X_t are included in the forecast. Then θ could be estimated by least squares, that is, by solving,

$$\min_{\theta \in \Theta} \sum_{t=p+1}^{T-h} [y_{t+h} - \mu_h(F_t, \theta)]^2. \tag{27.1}$$

There are alternative methods for the estimation of θ. The minimization problem (27.1) uses an *h*-step ahead (nonlinear) least squares regression. Often an available alternative is to estimate a one-step ahead model (*h* = 1) by nonlinear least squares or maximum likelihood, and to iterate that model forward. The formulation (27.1) has the advantage of computational simplicity, especially for nonlinear models. Depending on the true model and the approximate model, approximation bias can be reduced by estimating the *h*-step ahead model (27.1). On the other hand, if the estimated model is correct, then iterating one-step ahead forecasts will be more efficient in the statistical sense. In general, the decision of whether to estimate parameters by *h*-step ahead or one-step ahead methods depends on the model being estimated and the type of misspecification that might be present. See Clements and Hendry (1996) for references to this literature and for simulation results comparing the two approaches.

It is useful to consider a decomposition of the forecast error, based on the various sources of that error. Let $\hat{e}_{t+h,t}$ denote the forecast error from the *h*-step ahead forecast of y_{t+h} using $\hat{y}_{t+h|t}$. Then,

$$\hat{e}_{t+h,t} = y_{t+h} - \hat{y}_{t+h|t}$$
$$= [y_{t+h} - E(y_{t+h}|F_t)] + [E(y_{t+h}|F_t) - \mu_h(F_t, \theta_0)] + [\mu_h(F_t, \theta_0) - \mu_h(F_t, \hat{\theta})].$$
$$(27.2)$$

The first term in brackets is the deviation of y_{t+h} from its conditional expectation, a source of forecast error that cannot be eliminated. The second term in brackets is the contribution of model misspecification, and is the error arising from using the best parameter value for the approximate conditional expectations function. The final term arises because this best parameter value is unknown, and instead θ is estimated from the data.

The decomposition (27.2) illustrates two facts. First, all forecasts, no matter how good, will have forecast error because of future, unknowable random events. Second, the quality of a forecasting method is therefore determined by its model approximation error and by its estimation error. These two sources of error generally entail a tradeoff. Using a flexible model with many parameters for μ_h can reduce model approximation error, but because there are many parameters estimation error increases.

2.2   Model selection using information criteria

Because the object of point forecasting is to minimize expected loss out-of-sample, it is not desirable to minimize approximation error (bias) when this entails adding considerable parameter estimation uncertainty. Thus, for example, model selection based on minimizing the sum of squared residuals, or maximizing the R^2, can lead to small bias and good in-sample fit, but very poor out-of-sample forecast performance.

A formal way to make this tradeoff between approximation error and estimation error is to use information criteria to select among a few competing models. When *h* = 1, information criteria (IC) have the form,

$$IC(p) = \ln \hat{\sigma}^2(p) + pg(T) \tag{27.3}$$

where p is the dimension of θ, T is the sample size used for estimation, $g(T)$ is a function of T with $g(T) > 0$ and $Tg(T) \to \infty$ and $g(T) \to 0$ as $T \to \infty$, and $\hat{\sigma}^2(p) =$ SSR$/T$, where SSR is the sum of squared residuals from the (in-sample) estimation. Comparing two models using the information criterion (27.3) is the same as comparing two models by their sum of squared residuals, except that the model with more parameters receives a penalty. Under suitable conditions on this penalty and on the class of models being considered, it can be shown that a model selected by the information criterion is the best in the sense of the trade-off between approximation error and sampling uncertainty about θ. A precise statement of such conditions in AR models, when only the maximum order is known, can be found in Geweke and Meese (1981), and extensions to infinite order autoregressive models are discussed in Brockwell and Davis (1987) and, in the context of unit root tests, Ng and Perron (1995). The two most common information criteria are the Akaike information criterion (AIC), for which $g(T) = 2/T$, and Schwarz's (1978) Bayes information criterion (BIC), for which $g(T) = \ln T/T$.

2.3   Prediction intervals

In some cases, the object of forecasting is not to produce a point forecast but rather to produce a range within which y_{t+h} has a prespecified probability of falling. Even if within the context of point forecasting, it is useful to provide users of forecasts with a measure of the uncertainty of the forecast. Both ends can be accomplished by reporting prediction intervals.

In general, the form of the prediction interval depends on the underlying distribution of the data. The simplest prediction interval is obtained by assuming that the data are conditionally homoskedastic and normal. Under these assumptions and regularity conditions, a prediction interval with asymptotic 67 percent coverage is given by $\hat{y}_{t+h|t} \pm \tilde{\sigma}_h$, where $\tilde{\sigma}_h = \text{SSR}_h/(T - p)$, where SSR$_h$ is the sum of squared residuals from the h-step ahead regression (27.1) and $T - p$ are the degrees of freedom of that regression.

If the series is conditionally normal but is conditionally heteroskedastic, this simple prediction error formula must be modified and the conditional variance can be computed using, for example, an ARCH model. If the series is conditionally nonnormally distributed, other methods, such as the bootstrap, can be used to construct asymptotically valid prediction intervals.

2.4   Forecast comparison and evaluation

The most reliable way to evaluate a forecast or to compare forecasting methods is by examining out of sample performance. To evaluate the forecasting performance of a single model or expert, one looks for signs of internal consistency. If the forecasts were made under squared error loss, the forecast errors should have mean zero and should be uncorrelated with any variable used to produce the forecast. For example, $\hat{e}_{t+h,t}$ should be uncorrelated with $\hat{e}_{t,t-h}$, although $\hat{e}_{t+h,t}$ will in general have an MA($h - 1$) correlation structure. Failure of out-of-sample forecasts to have mean zero and to be uncorrelated with F_t indicates a structural break, a deficiency of the forecasting model, or both.

Additional insights are obtained by comparing the out-of-sample forecasts of competing models or experts. Under mean squared error loss, the relative performance of two time series of point forecasts of the same variable can be compared by computing their mean squared forecast errors (MSFE). Of course, in a finite sample, a smaller MSFE might simply be an artifact of sampling error, so formal tests of whether the MSFEs are statistically significantly different are in order when comparing two forecasts. Such tests have been developed by Diebold and Mariano (1995) and further refined by West (1996), who built on earlier work by Nelson (1972), Fair (1980), and others.

Out of sample performance can be measured either by using true out-of-sample forecasts, or by a simulated out-of-sample forecasting exercise. While both approaches have similar objectives, the practical issues and interpretation of results is quite different. Because real time published forecasts usually involve expert opinion, a comparison of true out-of-sample forecasts typically entails an evaluation of both models and the expertise of those who use the models. Good examples of comparisons of real time forecasts, and of the lessons that can be drawn from such comparisons, are McNees (1990) and Zarnowitz and Braun (1993).

Simulated real time forecasting can be done in the course of model development and provides a useful check on the in-sample comparison measures discussed above. The essence of a simulated real time forecasting experiment is that all forecasts $\hat{y}_{t+h|t}$, $t = T_0, \ldots, T_1$, are functions only of data up through date t, so that all parameter estimation, model selection, etc., is done only using data through date t. This is often referred to as a recursive methodology (for linear models, the simulated out-of-sample forecasts can be computed using a recursion). In general this entails many re-estimations of the model, which for nonlinear models can be computationally demanding. For an example of simulated out-of-sample forecast comparisons, see Stock and Watson (1999a).

3 SALIENT FEATURES OF US MACROECONOMIC TIME SERIES DATA

The methods discussed in this chapter will be illustrated by application to five monthly economic time series for the US macroeconomy: inflation, as measured by the annual percentage change in the consumer price index (CPI); output growth, as measured by the growth rate of the index of industrial production; the unemployment rate; a short-term interest rate, as measured by the rate on 90-day US Treasury bills; and total real manufacturing and trade inventories, in logarithms.[1] Time series plots of these five series are presented as the heavy solid lines in Figures 27.1–27.5.

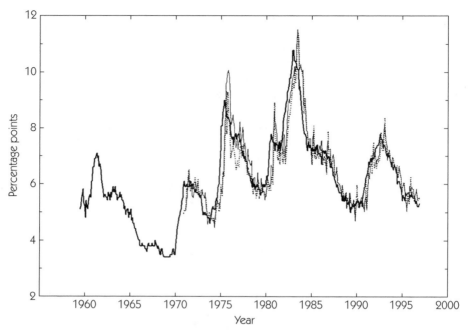

Figure 27.1   US unemployment rate (heavy solid line), recursive AR(BIC)/unit root pretest forecast (light solid line), and neural network forecast (dotted line)

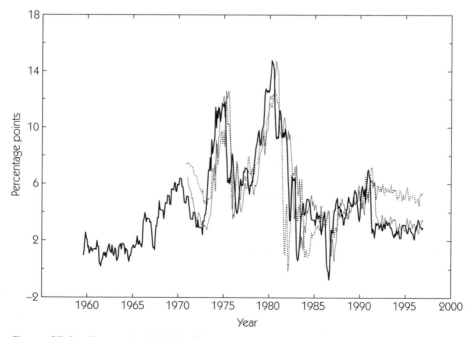

Figure 27.2   Six-month US CPI inflation at an annual rate (heavy solid line), recursive AR(BIC)/unit root pretest forecast (light solid line), and neural network forecast (dotted line)

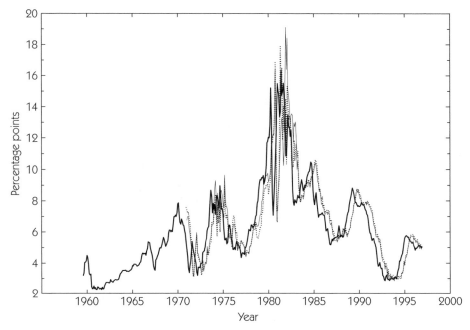

Figure 27.3 90-day Treasury bill at an annual rate (heavy solid line), recursive AR(BIC)/ unit root pretest forecast (light solid line), and neural network forecast (dotted line)

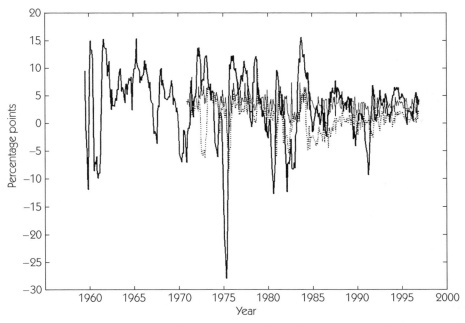

Figure 27.4 Six-month growth of US industrial production at an annual rate (heavy solid line), recursive AR(BIC)/unit root pretest forecast (light solid line), and neural network forecast (dotted line)

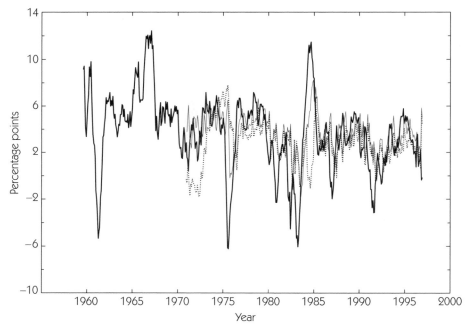

Figure 27.5 Six-month growth of total real US manufacturing and trade inventories at an annual rate (heavy solid line), recursive AR(BIC)/unit root pretest forecast (light solid line), and neural network forecast (dotted line)

In addition to being of interest in their own right, these series reflect some of the main statistical features present in many macroeconomic time series from developed economies. The 90-day Treasury bill rate, unemployment, inflation, and inventories all exhibit high persistence in the form of smooth long-run trends. These trends are clearly nonlinear, however, and follow no evident deterministic form, rather, the long-run component of these series can be thought of as a highly persistent stochastic trend. There has been much debate over whether this persistence is well modeled as arising from an autoregressive unit root in these series, and the issue of whether to impose a unit root (to first difference these data) is an important forecasting decision discussed below.

Two other features are evident in these series. All five series exhibit co-movements, especially over the two to four year horizons. The twin recessions of the early 1980s, the long expansions of the mid-1980s and the 1990s, and the recession in 1990 are reflected in each series (although the IP (industrial production) growth rate series might require some smoothing to see this). Such movements over the business cycle are typical for macroeconomic time series data; for further discussion of business cycle properties of economic time series data, see Stock and Watson (1999b). Finally, to varying degrees the series contain high frequency noise. This is most evident in inflation and IP growth. This high frequency noise arises from short-term, essentially random fluctuations in economic activity and from measurement error.

4   UNIVARIATE FORECASTS

Univariate forecasts are made solely using past observations on the series being forecast. Even if economic theory suggests additional variables that should be useful in forecasting a particular variable, univariate forecasts provide a simple and often reliable benchmark against which to assess the performance of those multivariate methods. In this section, some linear and nonlinear univariate forecasting methods are briefly presented. The performance of these methods is then illustrated for the macroeconomic time series in Figures 27.1–27.5.

4.1   Linear models

One of the simplest forecasting methods is the *exponential smoothing* or exponentially weighted moving average (EWMA) method. The EWMA forecast is,

$$\hat{y}_{t+h|t} = \alpha \hat{y}_{t+h-1|t-1} + (1 - \alpha)y_t, \tag{27.4}$$

where α is a parameter chosen by the forecaster or estimated by nonlinear least squares from historical data.

Autoregressive moving average (ARMA) models are a mainstay of univariate forecasting. The ARMA(p, q) model is,

$$a(L)y_t = \mu_t + b(L)\varepsilon_t, \tag{27.5}$$

where ε_t is a serially uncorrelated disturbance and $a(L)$ and $b(L)$ are lag polynomials of orders p and q, respectively. For y_t to be stationary, the roots of $a(L)$ lie outside the unit circle, and for $b(L)$ to be invertible, the roots of $b(L)$ also lie outside the unit circle. The term μ_t summarizes the deterministic component of the series. For example, if μ_t is a constant, the series is stationary around a constant mean. If $\mu_t = \mu_0 + \mu_1 t$, the series is stationary around a linear time trend. If $q > 0$, estimation of the unkown parameters of $a(L)$ and $b(L)$ entails nonlinear maximization. Asymptotic Gaussian maximum likelihood estimates of these parameters are a staple of time series forecasting computer packages. Multistep forecasts are computed by iterating forward the one-step forecasts. A deficiency of ARMA models is estimator bias introduced when the MA roots are large, the so-called unit MA root pileup problem (see Davis and Dunsmuir, 1996; and, for a general discussion and references, Stock, 1994).

An important special case of ARMA models are pure *autoregressive* models with lag order p (AR(p)). Meese and Geweke (1984) performed a large simulated out of sample forecasting comparison that examined a variety of linear forecasts, and found that long autoregressions and autoregressions with lags selected by information criteria performed well, and on average outperformed forecasts from ARMA models. The parameters can be estimated by ordinary least squares (OLS) and the order of the autoregression can be consistently estimated by, for example, the BIC.

Harvey (1989) has proposed a different framework for univariate forecasting, based on a decomposition of a series into various components: trend, cycle, seasonal, and irregular. Conceptually, this framework draws on an old concept in economic time series analysis in which the series is thought of as having different properties at different horizons, so that for example one might talk about the cyclical properties of a time series separately from its trend properties; he therefore calls these *structural time series models*. Harvey models these components as statistically uncorrelated at all leads and lags, and he parameterizes the components to reflect their role, for example, the trend can be modeled as a random walk with drift or a doubly integrated random walk, possibly with drift. Estimation is by asymptotic Gaussian maximum likelihood. The resulting forecasts are linear in historical data (although nonlinear in the parameters of the model) so these too are linear forecasts. Harvey (1989) argues that this formulation produces forecasts that avoid some of the undesirable properties of ARMA models. As with ARMA models, user judgment is required to select the models. One interesting application of these models is for trend estimation, see for example Stock and Watson (1998).

4.2   Nonlinear models

Outside of the normal distribution, conditional expectations are typically nonlinear, and in general one would imagine that these infeasible optimal forecasts would be nonlinear functions of past data. The main difficulty that arises with nonlinear forecasts is choosing a feasible forecasting method that performs well with the fairly short historical time series available for macroeconomic forecasting. With many parameters, approximation error in (27.2) is reduced, but estimation error can be increased. Many nonlinear forecasting methods also pose technical problems, such as having objective functions with many local minima, having parameters that are not globally identified, and difficulties with generating internally consistent h-step ahead forecasts from one-step ahead models.

Recognition of these issues has led to the development of a vast array of methods for nonlinear forecasting, and a comprehensive survey of these methods is beyond the limited scope of this chapter. Rather, here I provide a brief introduction to only two particular nonlinear models, smooth transition autoregressions (STAR) and artificial neural networks (NN). These models are interesting methodologically because they represent, respectively, parametric and nonparametric approaches to nonlinear forecasting, and they are interesting from a practical point of view because they have been fairly widely applied to economic data.

A third class of models that has received considerable attention in economics are the Markov switching models, in which an unobserved discrete state switches stochastically between regimes in which the process evolves in an otherwise linear fashion. Markov switching models were introduced in econometrics by Hamilton (1989) and are also known as hidden Markov models. However, space limitations preclude presenting these models here; for a textbook treatment, see Hamilton (1994). Kim and Nelson (1998, 1999) provide important extensions of this framework to multivariate models with unobserved components. The reader interested in further discussions of and additional references to other nonlinear time series forecasting methods should see the recent surveys and/or textbook treatments of nonlinear models by Granger and Teräsvirta (1993), Priestly (1989), and Samorodnitsky and Taqqu (1994).

An *artificial neural network* (NN) model relates inputs (lagged values) to outputs (future values) using an index model formulation with nonlinear transformations. There is considerable terminology and interpretation of these formulations which we will not go into here but which are addressed in a number of textbook treatments of these models; see in particular Swanson and White (1995, 1997) for discussions and applications of NN models to economic data. Here, we consider the simplest version, a feedforward NN with a single hidden layer and n hidden units. This has the form:

$$y_{t+h} = \beta_0(L)y_t + \sum_{i=1}^{n} \gamma_i g(\beta_i(L)y_t) + u_{t+h}, \qquad (27.6)$$

where $\beta_i(L)$, $i = 0, \ldots, n$ are lag polynomials, γ_i are unknown coefficients, and $g(z)$ is a function that maps $\Re \rightarrow [0, 1]$. Possible choices of $g(z)$ include the indicator function, sigmoids, and the logistic function. A variety of methods are available for the estimation of the unknown parameters of NNs, some specially designed for this problem; a natural estimation method is nonlinear least squares. NNs have a nonparametric interpretation when the number of hidden units (n) is increased as the sample size tends to infinity.

Smooth transition autoregressions are piecewise linear models and have the form:

$$y_{t+h} = \alpha(L)y_t + d_t\beta(L)y_t + u_{t+h}, \qquad (27.7)$$

where the mean is suppressed, $\alpha(L)$ and $\beta(L)$ are lag polynomials, and d_t is a nonlinear function of past data that switches between the "regimes" $\alpha(L)$ and $\beta(L)$. Various functions are available for d_t. For example, if d_t is the logistic function so $d_t = 1/(1 + \exp[\gamma_0 + \gamma_1'\zeta_t])$, then the model is referred to as the logistic smooth transition autoregression (LSTAR) model. The switching variable d_t determines the "threshold" at which the series switches, and depends on the data through ζ_t. For example, ζ_t might equal y_{t-k}, where k is some lag for the switch. The parameters of the model can be estimated by nonlinear least squares. Details about formulation, estimation and forecasting for TAR and STAR models can be found in Granger and Teräsvirta (1993) and in Granger, Teräsvirta, and Anderson (1993). For an application of TAR (and other models) to forecasting U.S. unemployment, see Montgomery, Zarnowitz, Tsay, and Tiao (1998).

4.3 Differencing the data

A question that arises in practice is whether to difference the data prior to construction of a forecasting model. This arises in all the models discussed above, but for simplicity it is discussed here in the context of a pure AR model. If one knows a priori that there is in fact a unit autoregressive root, then it is efficient to impose this information and to estimate the model in first differences. Of course, in practice this is not known. If there is a unit autoregressive root, then estimates of this root (or the coefficients associated with this root) are generally biased towards zero, and conditionally biased forecasts can obtain. However, the order of this bias is $1/T$, so for short horizon forecasts (h fixed) and T sufficiently large, this bias is negligible, so arguably the decision of whether to difference or not is unimportant to first-order asymptotically.

The issue of whether or not to difference the data, or more generally of how to treat the long-term dependence in the series, becomes important when the forecast horizon is long relative to the sample size. Computations in Stock (1996) suggest that these issues can arise even if the ratio, h/T, is small, .1 or greater. Conventional practice is to use a unit root pretest to make the decision about whether to difference or not, and the asymptotic results in Stock (1996) suggest that this approach has some merit when viewed from the perspective of minimizing either the maximum or integrated asymptotic risk, in a sense made precise in that paper. Although Dickey–Fuller (1979) unit root pretests are most common, other unit root tests have greater power, and tests with greater power produce lower risk for the pretest estimator. Unit root tests are surveyed in Stock (1994) and in Chapter 29 in this volume by Bierens.

4.4   Empirical examples

We now turn to applications of some of these forecasting methods to the five US macroeconomic time series in Figures 27.1–27.5.[2] In the previous notation, the series to be forecast, y_t, is the series plotted in those figures, for example, for industrial production $y_t = 200 \ln (\text{IP}_t/\text{IP}_{t-6})$, while for the interest rate y_t is the untransformed interest rate in levels (at an annual rate). The exercise reported here is a simulated out of sample comparison of six different forecasting models. All series are observed monthly with no missing observations. For each series, the initial observation date is 1959:1. Six-month ahead ($h = 6$) recursive forecasts of y_{t+6} are computed for $t = 1971:3, \ldots, 1996:6$; because a simulated out of sample methodology was used, all models were re-estimated at each such date t.

Eight different forecasts are computed: (a) EWMA, where the parameter is estimated by NLS; (b) AR(4) with a constant; (c) AR(4) with a constant and a time trend; (d) AR where the lag length is chosen by BIC ($0 \le p \le 12$) and the decision to difference or not is made using the Elliott–Rothenberg–Stock (1996) unit root pretest; (e) NN with a single hidden layer and two hidden units; (f) NN with two hidden layers, two hidden units in the first layer, and one hidden unit in the second layer; (g) LSTAR in levels with three lags and $\zeta_t = y_t - y_{t-6}$; and (h) LSTAR in differences with three lags and $\zeta_t = y_t - y_{t-6}$.

For each series, the simulated out of sample forecasts (b) and (e) are plotted in Figures 27.1–27.5. The root MSFEs for the different methods, relative to method (b), are presented in Table 27.1; thus method (b) has a relative root MSFE of 1.00 for all series. The final row of Table 27.1 presents the root mean squared forecast error in the native units of the series.

Several findings are evident. First, among the linear models, the AR(4) in levels with a constant performs well. This model dominates the AR(4) in levels with a

Table 27.1   Comparison of simulated out-of-sample linear and nonlinear forecasts for five US macroeconomic time series

Forecasting model	Relative root mean squared forecast errors				
	Unem.	Infl.	Int.	IP	Invent.
(a) EWMA	1.11	2.55	0.95	1.09	1.50
(b) AR(4), levels, constant	1.00	1.00	1.00	1.00	1.00
(c) AR(4), levels, constant and time trend	1.09	1.00	1.05	1.06	1.15
(d) AR(BIC), unit root pretest	1.05	0.84	1.07	0.99	1.01
(e) NN, levels, 1 hidden layer, 2 hidden units	1.07	1.76	9.72	1.05	1.54
(f) NN, levels, 2 hidden layers, 2(1) hidden units	1.07	0.99	0.99	1.07	1.25
(g) LSTAR, levels, 3 lags, $\zeta_t = y_t - y_{t-6}$	1.04	1.34	3.35	1.02	1.05
(h) LSTAR, differences, 3 lags, $\zeta_t = y_t - y_{t-6}$	1.04	0.89	1.17	1.01	1.03
Root mean squared forecast error for (b), AR(4), levels, constant	0.61	2.44	1.74	6.22	2.78

Sample period: monthly, 1959:1–1996:12; forecast period: 1971:3–1996:6; forecast horizon: six months.

Entries in the upper row are the root mean squared forecast error of the forecasting model in the indicated row, relative to that of model (b), so the relative root MSFE of model (b) is 1.00. Smaller relative root MSFEs indicate more accurate forecasts in this simulated out-of-sample experiment. The entries in the final row are the root mean squared forecast errors of model (b) in the native units of the series. The series are: the unemployment rate, the six-month rate of CPI inflation, the 90-day US Treasury bill annualized rate of interest, the six-month growth of IP, and the six-month growth of real manufacturing and trade inventories.

Table 27.2   Root mean squared forecast errors of VARs, relative to AR(4)

Forecasting model	Relative mean squared forecast errors				
	Unem.	Infl.	Int.	IP	Invent.
(i) VAR: $unemp_t$, $int.rate_t$, $\Delta lnIP_t$	0.98	—	1.05	0.93	—
(j) VAR: $unemp_t$, $\Delta lnCPI_t$, $int.rate_t$	1.03	0.95	1.03	—	—
(k) VAR: all five variables	1.03	1.10	1.04	0.94	0.96

Sample period: monthly, 1959:1–1996:12; forecast period: 1971:3–1996:6; forecast horizon: six months.

Entries are relative root MSFEs, relative to the root MSFE of model (b) in Table 27.1 (AR(4) with constant in levels). The VAR specifications have lag lengths selected by BIC; the six-month ahead forecasts were computed by iterating one-month ahead forecasts. All forecasts are simulated out of sample. See the notes to Table 27.1.

constant and time trend, in the sense that for all series the AR(4) with a constant and time trend has an RMSFE that is no less than the AR(4) with a constant. Evidently, fitting a linear time trend leads to poor out-of-sample performance, a result that would be expected if the trend is stochastic rather than deterministic. Using BIC lag length selection and a unit root pretest improves upon the AR(4) with a constant for inflation, has essentially the same performance for industrial production and inventories, and exhibits worse performance for the unemployment rate and the interest rate; averaged across series, the RMSFE is 0.99, indicating a slight edge over the AR(4) with a constant on average.

None of the nonlinear models uniformly improve upon the AR(4) with a constant. In fact, two of the nonlinear models ((e) and (g)) are dominated by the AR(4) with a constant. The greatest improvement is by model (h) for inflation; however, this relative RMSFE is still greater than the AR(BIC) forecast for inflation. Interestingly, the very simple EWMA forecast is the best of all forecasts, linear and nonlinear, for the interest rate. For the other series, however, it does not get the correct long-run trend, and the EWMA forecasts are worse than the AR(4).

The final row gives a sense of the performance of these forecasts in absolute terms. The RMSFE of the unemployment rate, six months hence, is only 0.6 percentage points, and the RMSFE for the 90-day Treasury bill rate is 1.7 percentage points. CPI inflation is harder to predict, with a six-month ahead RMSFE of 2.4 percentage points. Inspection of the graph of IP growth reveals that this series is highly volatile, and in absolute terms the forecast error is large, with a six-month ahead RMSFE of 6.2 percentage points.

Some of these points can be verified by inspection of the forecasts plotted in Figures 27.1–27.5. Clearly these forecasts track well the low frequency movements in the unemployment rate, the interest rate, and inflation (although the NN forecast does quite poorly in the 1990s for inflation). Industrial production and inventory growth has a larger high frequency component, which all these models have difficulty predicting (some of this high frequency component is just unpredictable forecast error).

These findings are consistent with the conclusions of the larger forecasting model comparison study in Stock and Watson (1999a). They found that, on average across 215 macroeconomic time series, autoregressive models with BIC lag length determination and a unit root pretest performed well, indeed, outperformed a range of NN and LSTAR models for six-month ahead forecasts. The autoregressive model typically improved significantly on no-change or EWMA models. Thus there is considerable ability to predict many U.S. macroeconomic time series, but much of this predictability is captured by relatively simple linear models with data-dependent determination of the specification.

5   MULTIVARIATE FORECASTS

The motivation for multivariate forecasting is that there is information in multiple economic time series that can be used to improve forecasts of the variable or variables of interest. Economic theory, formal and informal, suggests a large number of such relations. Multivariate forecasting methods in econometrics are usefully divided into four broad categories: structural econometric models; small linear time series models; small nonlinear time series models; and forecasts based on leading economic indicators.

Structural econometric models attempt to exploit parametric relationships suggested by economic theory to provide a priori restrictions. These models can be hundred-plus equation simultaneous systems, or very simple relations such as an empirical Phillips curve relating changes of inflation to the unemployment rate and supply shocks. Because simultaneous equations are the topic of Chapter 6 by Mariano in this volume, forecasts from simultaneous equations systems will be discussed no further here. Neither will we discuss further nonlinear multivariate models; although the intuitive motivation for these is sound, these typically have many parameters to be estimated and as such often exhibit poor out-of-sample performance (for a study of multivariate NNs, see Swanson and White (1995, 1997); for some positive results, see Montgomery *et al.*, 1998). This chapter therefore briefly reviews multivariate forecasting with small linear time series models, in particular, using VARs, and forecasting with leading indicators. For additional background on VARs, see the chapter in this volume by Lütkepohl.

5.1   Vector autoregressions

Vector autoregressions, which were introduced to econometrics by Sims (1980), have the form:

$$Y_t = \mu_t + A(L)Y_{t-1} + \varepsilon_t, \qquad (27.8)$$

where Y_t is a $n \times 1$ vector time series, ε_t is a $n \times 1$ serially uncorrelated disturbance, $A(L)$ is a pth order lag polynomial matrix, and μ_t is a $n \times 1$ vector of deterministic terms (for example, a constant or a constant plus linear time trend). If there are no restrictions on the parameters, the parameters can be estimated asymptotically efficiently (under Gaussianity) by OLS equation by equation. Multistep forecasts can be made either by replacing the left-hand side of (27.8) by Y_{t+h}, or by h-fold iteration of the one-step forecast.

Two important practical questions are the selection of the series to include in Y_t (the choice of n) and the choice of the lag order p in the VAR(p). Given the choice of series, the order p is typically unknown. As in the univariate case, it can be estimated by information criteria. This proceeds as discussed following (27.3), except that $\hat{\sigma}^2$ is replaced by the determinant of $\hat{\Sigma}$ (the MLE of the variance–covariance matrix of ε_t), and the relevant number of parameters is the total free parameters of the VAR; thus, if there are no deterministic terms, $IC(p) = \ln \det(\hat{\Sigma}) + n^2 p g(T)$. The choice of series is typically guided by economic theory, although the predictive least squares (PLS) criterion (which is similar to an information criterion) can be useful in guiding this choice, cf. Wei (1992).

The issue of whether to difference the series is further complicated in the multivariate context by the possible presence of cointegration among two or more of the n variables. The multiple time series Y_t is said to be cointegrated if each element of Y_t is integrated of order 1 (is I(1); that is, has an autoregressive unit root) but there are $k \geq 1$ linear combination, $\alpha'Y_t$, that are I(0) (that is, which do not have a unit AR root) (Engle and Granger, 1987). It has been conjectured that long-run forecasts are improved by imposing cointegration when it is present. However, even if cointegration is correctly imposed, it remains to estimate the parameters of the cointegrating vector, which are, to first-order, estimated consistently (and at the same rate) if cointegration is not imposed. If cointegration is imposed incorrectly, however, asymptotically biased forecasts with large risks can be produced. At short horizons, these issues are unimportant to first-order asymptotically. By extension of the univariate results that are known for long-horizon forecasting, one might suspect that pretesting for cointegration could improve forecast performance, at least as measured by the asymptotic risk. However, tests for cointegration have very poor finite sample performance (cf. Haug, 1996), so it is far from clear that in practice pretesting for cointegration will improve forecast performance. Although much of the theory in this area has been worked out, work remains on assessing the practical benefits of imposing cointegration for forecasting. For additional discussions of cointegration, see Watson (1994), Hatanaka (1996) and Chapter 30 in this volume by Dolado, Gonzalo, and Marmol.

It should be noted that there are numerous subtle issues involved in the interpretation of and statistical inference for VARs. Watson (1994) surveys these issues, and two excellent advanced references on VARs and related small linear time series models are Lütkepohl (1993) and Reinsel (1993). Also, VARs provide only one framework for multivariate forecasting; for a different perspective to the construction of small linear forecasting models, see Hendry (1995).

5.2   Forecasting with leading economic indicators

Forecasting with leading economic indicators entails drawing upon a large number of time series variables that, by various means, have been ascertained to lead the variable of interest, typically taken to be aggregate output (the business cycle). The first set of leading economic indicators was developed as part of the business cycle research program at the National Bureau of Economic Research, and was published by Mitchell and Burns (1938). More recent works using this general approach include Stock and Watson (1989) and the papers in Moore and Lahiri (1991).

The use of many variables and little theory has the exciting potential to exploit relations not captured in small multivariate time series models. It is, however, particularly susceptible to overfitting within sample. For example, Diebold and Rudebusch (1991) found that although historical values of the Index of Leading Economic Indicators (then maintained by the US Department of Commerce) fits the growth in economic activity well, the real time, unrevised index has limited predictive content for economic activity. This seeming contradiction arises primarily from periodic redefinitions of the index. Their sobering finding underscores the importance of properly understanding the statistical properties of each stage of a model selection exercise. The development of methods for exploiting large sets of leading indicators without overfitting is an exciting area of ongoing research.

5.3 Empirical examples

We now turn to an illustration of the performance of VARs as forecasting models. Like the experiment reported in Table 27.1, this experiment is simulated out of sample. Three families of VARs were specified. Using the numbering in Table 27.2, model (i) is a three-variable VAR with the unemployment rate, the interest rate, and the growth rate of industrial production. Model (j) is a three-variable VAR with the unemployment rate, CPI inflation, and the interest rate. Model (k) is a VAR with all five variables. The lags in all three models were kept the same in each equation of the VAR and were chosen recursively (at each forecast date, using only data through that date) by BIC, where $1 \leq p \leq 6$ for models (i) and (j), and $1 \leq p \leq 2$ for model (k). The VARs were estimated by OLS, equation by equation, with a one-step ahead specification, and six-month ahead forecasts were computed by iterating the one-month ahead forecasts.

The results are summarized in Table 27.2. In some cases, the VAR forecasts improve upon the AR forecasts. For example, for output growth, the VAR forecasts in (i) and (k) are respectively best and second-best of all the output growth forecasts in both tables. In contrast, for the interest rate, the VAR forecast is worse than the AR(4), and indeed the best forecast for the interest rate remains the EWMA forecast. However, the most notable feature of these forecasts is that eight of the eleven VAR forecasts in Table 27.2 have RMSFEs within 5 percent of the RMSFE of the AR(4), and all eleven have RMSFEs within 10 percent of the AR(4). For these specifications and these series, using additional information via a VAR results in forecasts that are essentially the same as those from an AR(4).

This finding, that forecasts from multivariate models often provide only modest improvements (or no improvement at all) over univariate forecasts, is not new.[3] One way to interpret this result is that additional macroeconomic series have little relationship to one another. This interpretation would, however, be incorrect, indeed, among the relationships in these VARs is the relation between the unemployment rate and inflation (the Phillips curve) and between interest rates and output (a channel of monetary policy), two links that have been studied in great detail and which are robust over the postwar period (cf. Stock and Watson, 1999b). An interpretation more in keeping with this latter evidence is that while these variables are related, there are sufficiently many parameters, which might not be stable over time, that these relations are not particularly useful for multivariate forecasting.

These negative results require some caveats. Supporters of VARs might suggest that the comparison in Table 27.2 is unfair because no attempt has been made to fine tune the VAR, to use additional variables, or to impose prior restrictions or prior information on the lag structure. This criticism has some merit, and methods which impose such structure, in particular Bayesian VARs, have a better track record than the unconstrained VARs reported here; see McNees (1990) and Sims (1993). Alternatively, others would argue that time series models developed specifically for some variables, such as an empirical Phillips curve (as in Gordon, 1998), would be expected to work better than unfocused application of a VAR. This too might be valid, but in evaluating such claims one must take great care to distinguish between in-sample fit and the much more difficult task of forecasting well out-of-sample, either in real time or in a simulated out-of-sample experiment. Finally, it should be emphasized that these conclusions are for macroeconomic time series. For example, in industry applications one can find series with more pronounced nonlinearities.

6   DISCUSSION AND CONCLUSION

One of the few truly safe predictions is that economic forecasters will remain the target of jokes in public discourse. In part this arises from a lack of understanding that all forecasts must in the end be wrong, and that forecast error is inevitable. Economic forecasters can, however, bolster their credibility by providing information about the possible range of forecast errors. Some consumers are uncomfortable with forecast uncertainty: when his advisors presented a forecast interval for economic growth, President Lyndon Johnson is said to have replied, "ranges are for cattle." Yet communication of forecast uncertainty to those who rely on forecasts helps them to create better, more flexible plans and supports the credibility of forecasters more generally.

A theme of this chapter has been the tradeoff between complex models, which either use more information to forecast or allow subtle nonlinear formulations of the conditional mean, and simple models, which require fitting a small number of parameters and which thereby reduce parameter estimation uncertainty. The empirical results in Tables 27.1 and 27.2 provide a clear illustration of this tradeoff. The short-term interest rate is influenced by expected inflation, monetary policy, and the general supply and demand for funds, and, because the nominal rate must be positive, the "true" model for the interest rate must be nonlinear. Yet, of the autoregressions, neural nets, LSTAR models, and VARs considered in Tables 27.1 and 27.2, the best forecast was generated by a simple exponentially weighted moving average of past values of the interest rate. No attempt has been made to uncover the source of the relatively poor performance of the more sophisticated forecasts of the interest rate, but presumably it arises from a combination of parameter estimation error and temporal instability in the more complicated models.

An important practical question is how to resolve this tradeoff in practice. Two methods have been discussed here. At a formal level, this tradeoff is captured by the use of information criteria. Information criteria can be misleading, however, when many models are being compared and/or when the forecasting environment changes over time. The other method is to perform a simulated out-of-sample forecast comparison of a small number of models. This is in fact closely related to information criteria (Wei, 1992) and shares some of their disadvantages. When applied to at most a few candidate models, however, this has the advantage of providing evidence on recent forecasting performance and how the forecasting performance of a model has evolved over the simulated forecast period. These observations, along with those above about reporting forecast uncertainty, suggest a simple rule: even if your main interest is in more complicated models, it pays to maintain benchmark forecasts using a simple model with honest forecast standard errors evaluated using a simulated real time experiment, and to convey the forecast uncertainty to the consumer of the forecast.

Finally, an important topic not addressed in this chapter is model instability. All forecasting models, no matter how sophisticated, are stylized and simplified ways to capture the complex and rich relations among economic time series variables. There is no particular reason to believe that these underlying relations are stable – technology, global trade, and macroeconomic policy have all evolved greatly over the past three decades – and even if they were, the implied parameters of the forecasting relations need not be stable. One therefore would expect estimated forecasting models to have parameters that vary over time, and in fact this appears to be the case empirically (Stock and Watson, 1996). Indeed, Clements and Hendry (1999) argue that most if not all major economic forecast failures arise because of unforeseen events that lead to a breakdown of the forecasting model; they survey existing methods and suggest some new techniques for detecting and adjusting to such structural shifts. The question of how best to forecast in a time-varying environment remains an important area of econometric research.

Notes

* The author thanks Lewis Chan for research assistance and four anonymous referees for useful suggestions.
1 All series were obtained from the Basic Economics Database maintained by DRI/ McGraw Hill. The series mnemonics are: PUNEW (the CPI); IP (industrial production); LHUR (the unemployment rate); FYGM3 (the 90 day U.S. Treasury bill rate); and IVMTQ (real manufacturing and trade inventories).
2 These results are drawn from the much larger model comparison exercise in Stock and Watson (1999a), to which the reader is referred for additional details on estimation method, model definitions, data sources, etc.
3 In influential work, Cooper (1972) and Nelson (1972) showed this in a particularly dramatic way. They found that simple ARMA models typically produced better forecasts of the major macroeconomic aggregates than did the main large structural macroeconomic models of the time. For a discussion of these papers and the ensuing literature, see Granger and Newbold (1986, ch. 9.4).

References

Bates, J.M., and C.W.J. Granger (1969). The combination of forecasts. *Operations Research Quarterly* 20, 451–68.
Bollerslev, T., R.F. Engle, and D.B. Nelson (1994). ARCH models. In R. Engle and D. McFadden (eds.), *Handbook of Econometrics*, Volume 4, pp. 2959–3038. Amsterdam: Elsevier.
Brockwell, P.J., and R.A. Davis (1987). *Time Series: Theory and Methods*. New York: Springer-Verlag.

Chan, Y.L., J.H. Stock, and M.W. Watson (1998). A dynamic factor model framework for forecast combination. *Spanish Economic Review* 1, 91–121.

Christoffersen, P.F., and F.X. Diebold (1997). Optimal prediction under asymmetric loss. *Econometric Theory* 13, 808–17.

Clements, M., and D.F. Hendry (1996). Multi-step estimation for forecasting. *Oxford Bulletin of Economics and Statistics* 58, 657–84.

Clements, M., and D.F. Hendry (1999). *Forecasting Non-Stationary Economic Time Series*. Cambridge: MIT Press.

Cooper, R.L. (1972). The predictive performance of quarterly econometric models of the United States. In B.G. Hickman (ed.) *Econometric Models of Cyclical Behavior*. New York: Columbia University Press.

Davis, R.A., and W.T.M. Dunsmuir (1996). Maximum likelihood estimation for MA(1) processes with a root on or near the unit circle. *Econometric Theory* 12, 1–29.

Diebold, F.X., T. Gunther, and A.S. Tay (1998). Evaluating density forecasts with applications to financial risk management. *International Economic Review* 39, 868–83.

Diebold, F.X., and J.A. Lopez (1995). Forecast evaluation and combination. In G.S. Maddala and C.R. Rao (eds.) *Handbook of Statistics* 14, 241–68.

Diebold, F.X., and R. Mariano (1995). Comparing predictive accuracy. *Journal of Business and Economic Statistics* 13, 253–63.

Diebold, F.X., and G. Rudebusch (1991). Forecasting output with the composite leading index: a real time analysis. *Journal of the American Statistical Association* 86, 603–10.

Elliott, G., T.J. Rothenberg, and J.H. Stock (1996). Efficient tests for an autoregressive unit root. *Econometrica* 64, 813–36.

Engle, R.F. (1982). Autoregressive conditional heteroskedasticity with estimates of the variance of U.K. inflation. *Econometrica* 50, 987–1008.

Engle, R.F., and C.W.J. Granger (1987). Co-integration and error correction: representation, estimation and testing. *Econometrica* 55, 251–76.

Fair, R.C. (1980). Evaluating the predictive accuracy of econometric models. *International Economic Review* 21, 355–78.

Geweke, J., and R. Meese (1981). Estimating regression models of finite but unknown order. *International Economic Review* 22, 55–70.

Gordon, R.J. (1998). Foundations of the Goldilocks economy: supply shocks and the time-varying NAIRU. *Brookings Papers on Economic Activity* 2, 297–333.

Granger, C.W.J. (1969). Prediction with a generalized cost of error function. *Operational Research Quarterly* 20, 199–207.

Granger, C.W.J. (1989). Combining forecasts – twenty years later. *Journal of Forecasting* 8, 167–73.

Granger, C.W.J., and P. Newbold (1986). *Forecasting Economic Time Series*, 2nd edn. Orlando: Academic Press.

Granger, C.W.J., and T. Teräsvirta (1993). *Modelling Non-linear Economic Relationships*. Oxford: Oxford University Press.

Granger, C.W.J., T. Teräsvirta, and H.M. Anderson (1993). Modeling nonlinearity over the business cycle. In J.H. Stock and M.W. Watson (eds.) *Business Cycles, Indicators, and Forecasting*, pp. 311–27. Chicago: University of Chicago Press for the NBER.

Hamilton, J.D. (1994). *Time Series Analysis*. Princeton: Princeton University Press.

Hamilton, J.D. (1989). A new approach to the economic analysis of nonstationary time series and the business cycle. *Econometrica* 57, 357–84.

Harvey, A.C. (1989). *Forecasting, Structural Time Series Models and the Kalman Filter*. Cambridge: Cambridge University Press.

Hatanaka, M. (1996). *Time-Series-Based Econometrics: Unit Roots and Cointegration*. Oxford: Oxford University Press.

Haug, A.A. (1996). Tests for cointegration: a Monte Carlo comparison. *Journal of Econometrics* 71, 89–115.

Hendry, D.F. (1995). *Dynamic Econometrics*. Oxford: Oxford University Press.

Kim, C.-J., and C.R. Nelson (1998). Business cycle turning points, a new coincident index, and tests of duration dependence based on a dynamic factor model with regime switching. *Review of Economics and Statistics* 80, 188–201.

Kim, C.-J., and C.R. Nelson (1999). *State-Space Models with Regime Switching: Classical and Gibbs Sampling Approaches with Applications*. Cambridge: MIT Press.

Lütkepohl, H. (1993). *Introduction to Multiple Time Series Analysis*, 2nd edn. New York: Springer-Verlag.

McNees, S.K. (1990). The role of judgment in macroeconomic forecasting accuracy. *International Journal of Forecasting* 6, 287–99.

Meese, R., and J. Geweke (1984). A comparison of autoregressive univariate forecasting procedures for macroeconomic time series. *Journal of Business and Economic Statistics* 2, 191–200.

Mitchell, W.C., and A.F. Burns (1938). *Statistical Indicators of Cyclical Revivals*. NBER Bulletin 69, New York. Reprinted in G.H. Moore (ed.) *Business Cycle Indicators*. Princeton: Princeton University Press, 1961.

Moore, G., and K. Lahiri (eds.) (1991). *The Leading Economic Indicators: New Approaches and Forecasting Records*. Cambridge: Cambridge University Press.

Montgomery, A.L., V. Zarnowitz, R.S. Tsay, and G.C. Tiao (1998). Forecasting the U.S. unemployment rate. *Journal of the American Statistical Association* 93, 478–93.

Nelson, C.R. (1972). The prediction performance of the FRB-MIT-PENN model of the U.S. economy. *American Economic Review* 62, 902–17.

Ng, S., and P. Perron (1995). Unit root tests in ARMA models with data dependent methods for the truncation lag. *Journal of the American Statistical Association* 90, 268–81.

Priestly, M.B. (1989). *Non-linear and Non-stationary Time Series Analysis*. London: Academic Press.

Reinsel, G.C. (1993). *Elements of Multivariate Time Series Analysis*. New York: Springer-Verlag.

Samorodnitsky, G., and M.S. Taqqu (1994). *Stable Non-Gaussian Random Processes*. New York: Chapman & Hall.

Schwarz, G. (1978). Estimating the dimension of a model. *Annals of Statistics* 6, 461–64.

Sims, C.A. (1980). Macroeconomics and reality. *Econometrica* 48, 1–48.

Sims, C.A. (1993). A nine-variable probabilistic macroeconomic forecasting model. In J.H. Stock and M.W. Watson (eds.) *Business Cycles, Indicators and Forecasting*. Chicago: University of Chicago Press for the NBER.

Stock, J.H. (1994). Unit roots, structural breaks, and trends. In R. Engle and D. McFadden (eds.) *Handbook of Econometrics*, Volume 4, pp. 2740–843. Amsterdam: Elsevier.

Stock, J.H. (1996). VAR, error correction and pretest forecasts at long horizons, *Oxford Bulletin of Economics and Statistics* 58, 685–701. Reprinted in A. Banerjee and D.F. Hendry (eds.) *The Econometrics of Economic Policy*, pp. 115–32. Oxford: Basil Blackwell, 1997.

Stock, J.H., and M.W. Watson (1989). New indexes of coincident and leading economic indicators. *NBER Macroeconomics Annual* 351–93.

Stock, J.H., and M.W. Watson (1996). Evidence on structural instability in macroeconomic time series relations. *Journal of Business and Economic Statistics*, 14, 11–30.

Stock, J.H., and M.W. Watson (1998). Median unbiased estimation of coefficient variance in a time varying parameter model. *Journal of the American Statistical Association* 93, 349–58.

Stock, J.H., and M.W. Watson (1999a). A comparison of linear and nonlinear univariate models for forecasting macroeconomic time series. Chapter 1 in R. Engle and H. White (eds.) *Cointegration, Causality and Forecasting: A Festschrift for C.W.J. Granger.* Oxford: Oxford University Press, 1–44.

Stock, J.H., and M.W. Watson (1999b). Business cycle fluctuations in U.S. macroeconomic time series. Chapter 1 in J. Taylor and M. Woodford (eds.) *Handbook of Macroeconomics.* Amsterdam: Elsevier, 3–64.

Swanson, N.R., and H. White (1995). A model selection approach to assessing the information in the term structure using linear models and artificial neural networks. *Journal of Business and Economic Statistics* 13, 265–75.

Swanson, N.R., and H. White (1997). A model selection approach to real-time macroeconomic forecasting using linear models and artificial neural networks. *Review of Economics and Statistics* 79, 540–50.

Watson, M.W. (1994). Vector autoregressions and cointegration. In R. Engle and D. McFadden (eds.) *Handbook of Econometrics,* Volume 4, pp. 2844–915. Amsterdam: Elsevier.

Wei, C.Z. (1992). On predictive least squares principles. *The Annals of Statistics* 20, 1–42.

West, K. (1996). Asymptotic inference about predictive ability. *Econometrica* 64, 1067–84.

West, K., H.J. Edison, and D. Cho (1993). A utility based evaluation of some models of exchange rate variability. *Journal of International Economics* 35, 23–46.

Zarnowitz, V., and Braun (1993). Twenty-two years of the NBER-ASA quarterly economic outlook surveys: aspects and comparisons of forecasting performance. In J.H. Stock and M.W. Watson (eds.) *Business Cycles, Indicators and Forecasting.* Chicago: University of Chicago Press for the NBER.

Time Series and Dynamic Models

Aris Spanos

1   INTRODUCTION

This chapter discusses certain dynamic statistical models of interest in modeling time series data. Particular emphasis is placed on the problem of *statistical adequacy*: the postulated model does not exhibit departures from the underlying assumptions. Statistical models are specified in terms of probabilistic assumptions on the observable stochastic processes involved, which can often be assessed a priori using graphical techniques. The primary objective is to render empirical modeling of time series an informed systematic procedure that gives rise to reliable empirical evidence.

1.1   Time series: a brief historical introduction

Time series data have been used since the dawn of empirical analysis in the mid-seventeenth century. In the "Bills of Mortality" John Graunt compared data on births and deaths over the period 1604–60 and across regions (parishes); see Stigler (1986). The time dimension of such data, however, was not properly understood during the early stages of empirical analysis. Indeed, it can be argued that the time dimension continued to bedevil statistical analysis for the next three centuries before it could be tamed in the context of proper statistical models for time series data.

THE DESCRIPTIVE STATISTICS PERIOD: 1665–1926
Up until the last quarter of the nineteenth century the time dimension of observed data and what that entails was not apparent to the descriptive statistics literature which concentrated almost exclusively in looking at histograms and

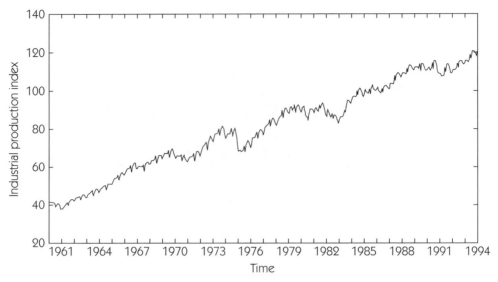

Figure 28.1 US industrial production index

certain associated numerical characteristics such as the mean and variance. By its very nature, histogram analysis and the associated descriptive statistics suppress the time dimension and concentrate on a single aspect of the data generating process, the *distribution*. Two other aspects raised by the time dimension, the *dependence* and *heterogeneity* with respect to the time index, were largely ignored, because implicit in this literature is the assumption that data exhibit independence and complete homogeneity. Questions concerning the *temporal independence/homogeneity* of time series data were first explicitly raised in the last quarter of the nineteenth century by Lexis and Bienayme (see Heyde and Seneta, 1977, ch. 3). By the mid-nineteenth century it became apparent that comparisons over time required a certain stability (temporal independence/homogeneity) of the measurements being compared; births, deaths, accidents, suicides, and murders. The proposed tests for stability took the form of comparing the sample variance of the time series in question with that of a stable (independent and homogeneous) binomially distributed process. The results on the basis of such a comparison were very discouraging, however, because, with the exception of the ratio of male to female births, it suggested that all other observed time series appeared to exhibit some form of instability.

This apparent instability was, at the time, associated with the cycles and trends exhibited by time series $\{y_1, y_2, \ldots, y_T\}$ when plotted over time (t-plot); in Figure 28.1 we can see a typical economic time series, the monthly US industrial production index for the period 1960–94. The two chance regularity patterns one can see in Figure 28.1 is the secular trend (increasing function of t) and the cycles around this trend. These cycles become more apparent when the data are de-trended as shown in Figure 28.2. By the end of the nineteenth century a time

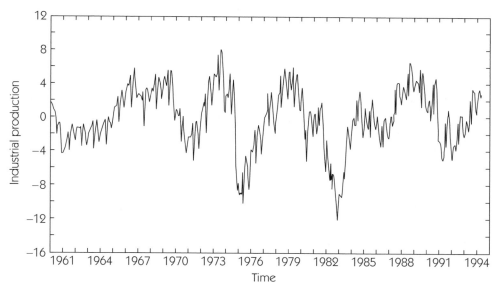

Figure 28.2 De-trended industrial production index

series was perceived as made up of three different components. As summarized by Davis:

> The problem of single time series, . . . , is concerned with three things: first, the determination of a trend; second, the discovery and interpretation of cyclical movements in the residuals; third, the determination of the magnitude of the erratic element in the data. (Davis, 1941, p. 59)

In view of this, it was only natural that time series focused on discovering the presence and capturing this instability (trends and cycles). In the early twentieth century the attempt to model observed cycles took two alternative (but related) forms. The first form attempted to capture the apparent cycles using sinusoidal functions (see Schuster, 1906). The objective was to discover any hidden periodicities using a technique appropriately called the *periodogram*. The second way to capture cycles came in the form of the temporal correlation, the *autocorrelation* coefficients, and their graph the *correlogram*; see Granger and Newbold (1977). This was a simple adaptation of Galton's (contemporaneous) correlation coefficient.

The early empirical studies indicated that the periodogram appeared to be somewhat unrealistic for economic time series because the harmonic scheme assumes strict periodicity. The correlogram was also partly unsuccessful because the sample correlogram gave rise to *spurious* correlations when it was applied to economic time series. Various techniques were suggested at the time in an attempt to deal with the spurious correlation problem, the most widely used being the differencing of the series and evaluating the correlogram using the differenced series (see Norton, 1902, Hooker, 1905). The first important use of these techniques with economic data was by Moore (1914) who attempted to discover the temporal interdependence among economic time series using both the periodogram and the temporal correlations. It was felt at the time that the problem of spurious correlation arises from the fact that time series are functions of time but there was no apparent functional form to be used in order to capture that effect; see Hendry and Morgan (1995). This literature culminated with the classic papers of Yule (1921, 1926) where the *spurious correlation* (and regression) problem was diagnosed as due to the apparent departures (exhibited by economic time series) from the assumptions required to render correlation analysis valid. Yule (1921) is a particularly important paper because it constitutes the first systematic attempt to relate misleading results of statistical analysis to the invalidity of the underlying probabilistic assumptions: *misspecification*. To this day, the problem of spurious correlation as due to the departures of probabilistic assumptions, necessary to render correlation analysis valid, is insufficiently understood. This is because the modeler is often unaware of the underlying probabilistic assumptions whose validity renders the analysis reliable. Such a situation arises when the statistical model is not explicitly specified and thus no assessment of the underlying assumptions can be conducted in order to ensure their validity. For instance, the sample (contemporaneous) correlation coefficient between two different series $\{(x_t, y_t),\ t = 1, 2, \ldots, T\}$ is a meaningful measure of first-order dependence only in cases where the means of both processes underlying the data are constant over $t : E(X_t) = \mu_x$, $E(Y_t) = \mu_y$, for all $t \in \mathbb{T}$; otherwise the measure is likely to be misleading.

THE STATISTICAL MODELING (PROPER) PERIOD: 1927–PRESENT

The formulation of explicit statistical models for time series began with the classic papers of Yule (1927) (Autoregressive (AR(p)) scheme):

$$y_t = \alpha_0 + \sum_{k=1}^{p} \alpha_k y_{t-k} + \varepsilon_t, \quad \varepsilon_t \sim \mathrm{NI}(0, \sigma^2), \quad t = 1, 2, \ldots,$$

where "NI" stands for "Normal, Independent" and Slutsky (1927) (Moving Average (MA(q)) scheme):

$$y_t = \gamma_0 + \sum_{k=1}^{q} \gamma_k \varepsilon_{t-k} + \varepsilon_t, \quad \varepsilon_t \sim \mathrm{NI}(0, \sigma^2), \quad t = 1, 2, \ldots.$$

Viewing these formulations from today's vantage point, it is clear that, at the time, they were proposed as nothing more than convenient descriptive models for time series data. Their justification was based exclusively on the fact that when simulated these schemes gave rise to data series which appear to exhibit cycles similar to those observed in actual time series data. It should be noted that, at the time, the difference between regular cycles due to seasonality and irregular cycles due to positive dependence was insufficiently understood.

The first attempt to provide a proper probabilistic foundation for these schemes is undoubtedly that of Wold (1938) who successfully fused these schemes with the appropriate probabilistic concepts necessary to model the chance regularity patterns exhibited by certain time series data. The appropriate probabilistic concepts were developed by Kolmogorov (1933) and Khinchine (1932). H. Cramer (1937) was instrumental in providing the missing link between the empirical literature on time series and the mathematical literature on *stochastic processes*; the probabilistic framework of modeling time series. Wold (1938), in his Ph.D. under Cramer, proposed the first proper statistical framework for modeling *stationary* time series. The lasting effect of Wold's work comes in the form of (i) his celebrated decomposition theorem (see Section 4), where under certain regularity restrictions a stationary process can be represented in the form of a MA(∞):

$$y_t = \gamma_0 + \sum_{k=1}^{\infty} \gamma_k \varepsilon_{t-k} + \varepsilon_t, \quad \sum_{k=1}^{\infty} |\gamma_k| < \infty, \quad \varepsilon_t \sim \text{NI}(0, \sigma^2), \quad t = 1, 2, \ldots,$$

and (ii) the ARMA(p, q) model:

$$y_t = \alpha_0 + \sum_{k=1}^{p} \alpha_k y_{t-k} + \sum_{k=1}^{q} \gamma_k \varepsilon_{t-k} + \varepsilon_t, \quad \varepsilon_t \sim \text{NI}(0, \sigma^2), \quad t = 1, 2, \ldots,$$

appropriate for time series exhibiting stationarity and weak dependence.

Wold's results provided the proper probabilistic foundations for the empirical analysis based on both the periodogram and the correlogram; the autocorrelations are directly related to the coefficients ($\alpha_0, \alpha_1, \ldots, \alpha_p, \gamma_1, \gamma_2, \ldots, \gamma_q$) and the periodogram can be directly related to the spectral representation of stationary stochastic processes; see Anderson (1971) for an excellent discussion.

The mathematical foundations of stationary stochastic processes were strengthened as well as delineated further by Kolmogorov (1941) but the ARMA(p, q) formulation did not become an empirical success for the next three decades because the overwhelming majority of times series appear to exhibit temporal heterogeneity (nonstationarity), rendering this model inappropriate. The state of the art, as it relates to the AR(p) family of models, was described at the time in the classic paper by Mann and Wald (1943).

The only indirect influence of the ARMA(p, q) family of models to econometric modeling came in the form of an extension of the linear regression model by adding an AR(1) model for the error term:

$$y_t = \beta^\top x_t + u_t, \quad u_t = \rho u_{t-1} + \varepsilon_t, \quad |\rho| < 1, \varepsilon_t \sim \text{NI}(0, \sigma^2), \quad t = 1, 2, \ldots, T. \tag{28.1}$$

This model provided the basis of the well known Durbin–Watson bounds test (see Durbin and Watson, 1950, 1951), which enabled econometricians to test for the presence of temporal dependence in the context of the linear regression model. This result, in conjunction with Cochrane and Orcutt (1949) who suggested a way to estimate the hybrid model (28.1), offered applied econometricians a way to use time series data in the context of the linear regression model without having to worry about *spurious regressions* (against which Yule (1926) cautioned time series analysts).

The important breakthrough in time series analysis came with Box and Jenkins (1970) who re-invented and popularized differencing as a way to deal with the apparent non-stationarity of time series:

$$\Delta^d y_t, \text{ where } \Delta := (1 - L), \quad d \text{ is a positive integer}, \quad t = 1, 2, \ldots,$$

in order to achieve (trend) stationarity and seasonal differencing of period s:

$$\Delta_s y_t := (1 - L^s) y_t = (y_t - y_{t-s}),$$

to achieve (seasonal) stationarity. They proposed the ARMA(p, q) model for the differenced series $\Delta_s^d y_t := y_t^*$, giving rise to the ARIMA(p, d, q) model:

$$y_t^* = \alpha_0 + \sum_{k=1}^{p} \alpha_k y_{t-k}^* + \sum_{k=1}^{q} \gamma_k \varepsilon_{t-k} + \varepsilon_t, \quad \varepsilon_t \sim \mathrm{NI}(0, \sigma^2), \quad t = 1, 2, \ldots$$

Box and Jenkins (1970) did not just propose a statistical model but a modeling strategy revolving around the ARIMA(p, d, q) model. This modeling procedure involved three stages. The first was *identification*: the choice of (p, d, q) using graphical techniques, the autocorrelations (correlogram) and the partial auto-correlations. The second stage was the *diagnostic checking* in order to assess the validity of the assumptions underlying the error term. The third stage was a for-mal *forecasting* procedure based on the estimated model. It must be noted that up until the 1970s the empirical forecasting schemes were based on *ad hoc* moving averages and exponential smoothing. The Box–Jenkins modeling strategy had a lasting effect on econometric modeling because it brought out an important weak-ness in econometric modeling: the insufficient attention paid to the temporal dependence/heterogeneity exhibited by economic time series; see Spanos (1986, 1987) for further discussion. This weakness was instrumental in giving rise to the LSE modeling methodology (see Hendry, 1993, for a collection of papers) and the popularization of the vector autoregressive (VAR(p)) model by Sims (1980).

The next important development in time series modeling came in the form of *unit root testing* in the context of the AR(p) model proposed by Dickey and Fuller (1979, 1981). The proposed tests provided the modeler with a way to decide whether the time series in question was stationary, trend nonstationary or unit root nonstationary. Since the 1930s it has been generally accepted that most eco-nomic time series can be viewed as stationary around a deterministic trend. Using the Dickey–Fuller testing procedures, Nelson and Plosser (1982) showed that, in contrast to conventional wisdom, most economic time series can be better described by the AR(p) model with a unit root. These results set off an explosion of time series research which is constantly revisiting and reconsidering the initial results by developing new testing procedures and techniques.

Phillips (1986, 1987) dealt effectively with the *spurious correlation* (regression) problem which was revisited in Granger and Newbold (1974), by utilizing and extending the Dickey and Fuller (1979, 1981) asymptotic distribution results. The same results were instrumental in formulating the notion of *cointegration* among time series with unit roots (see Granger, 1983; Engle and Granger, 1987; Johansen, 1991; Phillips, 1991) and explaining the empirical success of the error-correction models proposed by the LSE tradition (see Hendry, 1993).

2   A PROBABILISTIC FRAMEWORK FOR TIME SERIES

A time series is defined as a finite sequence of observed data $\{y_1, y_2, \ldots, y_T\}$ where the index $t = 1, 2, \ldots, T$, denotes time. The probabilistic concept which corresponds to this series is that of a real stochastic process: $\{Y_t, t \in \mathbb{T}\}$, defined on the probability space $(S, \mathfrak{F}, \mathbb{P}(\cdot)) : Y(\cdot, \cdot) : \{S \times \mathbb{T}\} \to \mathbb{R}_Y$, where S denotes the outcomes set, $\mathfrak{F}$ is the relevant σ–field, $\mathbb{P}(\cdot) : \mathfrak{F} \to [0, 1]$, $\mathbb{T}$ denotes the relevant index set (often $\mathbb{T} := \{1, 2, \ldots, T, \ldots\}$) and $\mathbb{R}_Y$ denotes a subset of the real line.

The probabilistic foundation of stochastic processes comes in the form of the finite joint distribution of the process $\{Y_t, t \in \mathbb{T}\}$ as formulated by Kolmogorov (1933) in the form of *Kolmogorov's extension theorem*. According to this result, the probabilistic structure of a stochastic process (under certain mild conditions) can be fully described by a finite dimensional joint distribution of the form:

$$f(y_1, y_2, \ldots, y_T; \psi), \quad \text{for all } (y_1, y_2, \ldots, y_T) \in \mathbb{R}_Y^T. \tag{28.2}$$

This joint distribution provides the starting point for the *probabilistic reduction (PR) approach* to modeling. The probabilistic structure of a stochastic process can be conveniently defined in the context of the joint distribution by imposing certain probabilistic assumptions from the following three categories:

Distribution: normal, student's t, gamma, beta, logistic, exponential, etc.
Dependence: Markov(p), ergodicity, m-dependence, martingale, mixing, etc.
Heterogeneity: identically distributed, stationarity (strict, kth order), etc.

Time series modeling can be viewed as choosing an appropriate statistical model which captures all the systematic information in the observed data series. Systematic statistical information comes to the modeler in the form of chance regularity patterns exhibited by the time series data. For example, the cycles exhibited by the time series data in Figures 28.1–28.2 constitute a chance regularity pattern associated with positive autocorrelation because they are not deterministic cycles that would indicate seasonality. For an extensive discussion on numerous chance regularity patterns and how they can be detected using a variety of graphical techniques including t-plots, scatter-plots, P-P and Q-Q plots, see Spanos (1999, chs 5–6).

The success for empirical modeling depends crucially on both recognizing these regularity patterns and then choosing the appropriate probabilistic concepts (in the form of assumptions) in order to model this information. The choice of these probabilistic assumptions amounts to specifying an appropriate statistical model. In the context of the PR approach all possible models ($\mathcal{P}$) are viewed as reductions from the joint distribution (28.2). That is, the chosen model $P_0 \in \mathcal{P}$, constitutes an element which arises by imposing certain reduction assumptions from the above three categories on the process $\{Y_t, t \in \mathbb{T}\}$. This methodological perspective, introduced by Spanos (1986), differs from the traditional view in so far as it does not view these models as just stochastic equations (linear, difference, differential, integral, etc.). In the next section we discuss the two alternative perspectives using the AR(1) model.

3 AUTOREGRESSIVE MODELS: UNIVARIATE

The objective of this section is to provide a brief overview of the most commonly used time series model, the AR(1), from both, the traditional and the probabilistic reduction (PR) perspectives.

3.1 AR(1): the traditional perspective

The traditional economic theory perspective for an AR(1) time series model was largely determined by the highly influential paper by Frisch (1933) as a linear (constant coefficient) stochastic difference equation:

$$y_t = \alpha_0 + \alpha_1 y_{t-1} + \varepsilon_t, \quad |\alpha_1| < 1, \quad \varepsilon_t \sim \text{NI}(0, \sigma^2), \quad t = 1, 2, \ldots, \quad (28.3)$$

with the probabilistic assumptions specified via the error process $\{\varepsilon_t, t \in \mathbb{T}\}$:

$$
\left.
\begin{array}{lll}
1^a & \text{zero mean:} & E(\varepsilon_t) = 0, \\
2^a & \text{constant variance:} & E(\varepsilon_t^2) = \sigma^2, \\
3^a & \text{no autocorrelation:} & E(\varepsilon_t \varepsilon_{t-\tau}) = 0, \tau \neq 0, \\
4^a & \text{Normality:} & \varepsilon_t \sim \text{N}(\cdot, \cdot),
\end{array}
\right\} t \in \mathbb{T}. \quad (28.4)
$$

These assumptions define the error $\{\varepsilon_t, t \in \mathbb{T}\}$ to be a Normal, white noise process. The formulation (28.3) is then viewed as a data generating mechanism (DGM) from right to left, the input being the error process (and the initial condition y_0) and the output the observable process $\{y_t, t \in \mathbb{T}\}$. The probabilistic structure of the latter process is generated from that of the error process via (28.3) by recursive substitution:

$$y_t = \alpha_0 + \alpha_1 y_{t-1} + \varepsilon_t = \alpha_1^t y_0 + \alpha_0 \left(\sum_{i=0}^{t-1} \alpha_1^i \right) + \left(\sum_{i=0}^{t-1} \alpha_1^i \varepsilon_{t-i} \right), \quad (28.5)$$

yielding the first two moments:

$$E(y_t) = \alpha_1^t E(y_0) + \alpha_0 \left(\sum_{i=0}^{t-1} \alpha_1^i \right), \quad \text{cov}(y_t, y_{t+\tau}) = \sigma^2 \alpha_1^\tau \left(\sum_{i=0}^{t-1} \alpha_1^{2i} \right), \quad \tau \geq 0.$$

Using the restriction $|\alpha_1| < 1$ we can simplify these to:

$$E(y_t) = \alpha_1^t E(y_0) + \alpha_0 \left(\frac{1 - \alpha_1^t}{1 - \alpha_1} \right), \quad \mathrm{cov}(y_t, y_{t+\tau}) = \sigma^2 \alpha_1^\tau \left(\frac{1 - \alpha_1^{2(t-1)}}{1 - \alpha_1^2} \right), \quad \tau \geq 0.$$

(28.6)

Viewed in terms of its first two moments, the stochastic process $\{y_t, t \in \mathbb{T}\}$ is both normal and Markov but second-order time heterogeneous. Traditionally, however, the time heterogeneity is sidestepped by focusing on the "steady-state":

$$\lim_{t \to \infty} E(y_t) = \frac{\alpha_0}{(1 - \alpha_1)}, \quad \lim_{t \to \infty} \mathrm{var}(y_t) = \frac{\sigma^2}{(1 - \alpha_1^2)}, \quad \lim_{t \to \infty} \mathrm{cov}(y_t, y_{t+\tau}) = \alpha_1^{|\tau|} \left(\frac{\sigma^2}{1 - \alpha_1^2} \right).$$

(28.7)

Hence, the (indirect) probabilistic assumptions underlying the observable process $\{y_t, t \in \mathbb{T}\}$, generated via the AR(1) (28.3), are:

1^b constant mean: $E(y_t) := \mu = \dfrac{\alpha_0}{(1 - \alpha_1)},$

2^b constant variance: $\mathrm{var}(y_t) := \sigma_0 = \dfrac{\sigma^2}{(1 - \alpha_1^2)},$

3^b Markov autocorrelation: $\mathrm{cov}(y_t, y_{t-\tau}) := \sigma_{|\tau|} = \alpha_1^{|\tau|} \left(\dfrac{\sigma^2}{1 - \alpha_1^2} \right), \tau \neq 0,$

4^b Normality: $y_t \sim \mathrm{N}(\cdot, \cdot),$

$$\left. \rule{0pt}{80pt} \right\} t \in \mathbb{T}.$$

(28.8)

As argued in the next subsection, the probabilistic reduction perspective reverses this viewpoint and contemplates (28.3) in terms of probabilistic assumptions regarding the process $\{y_t, t \in \mathbb{T}\}$ and not the error process $\{\varepsilon_t, t \in \mathbb{T}\}$. It must be emphasized that the probabilistic perspective provides an alternative viewpoint for statistical models which has certain advantages over the traditional theory viewpoint when the statistical aspects of modeling are of interest. In contrast, the traditional theory viewpoint has certain advantages when other aspects of modeling, such as the system properties, are of interest. Hence, the two viewpoints are considered as complimentary.

3.2   AR(1): the probabilistic reduction perspective

The probabilistic reduction perspective has been developed in Spanos (1986). This perspective begins with the observable process $\{y_t, t \in \mathbb{T}\}$ and specifies the statistical model exclusively in terms of this process. In particular, it contemplates the DGM (28.3) from left to right as an orthogonal decomposition of the form:

$$y_t = E(y_t \mid \sigma(Y_{t-1}^0)) + u_t, \ t \in \mathbb{T}, \tag{28.9}$$

where $Y_{t-1}^0 := (y_{t-1}, y_{t-2}, \ldots, y_0)$ and $u_t = y_t - E(y_t \mid \sigma(Y_{t-1}^0))$, with the underlying statistical model viewed as a reduction from the joint distribution of the underlying process $\{y_t, t \in \mathbb{T}\}$. The form of the autoregressive function depends on:

$$f(y_0, y_1, y_2, \ldots, y_T; \psi), \text{ for all } (y_0, y_1, y_2, \ldots, y_T) \in \mathbb{R}^{T+1},$$

in the sense of Kolmogorov (1933). In the present case, the *reduction assumptions* on the joint distribution of the process $\{y_t, t \in \mathbb{T}\}$, that would yield (28.3) are: (i) normal, (ii) Markov, and (iii) stationary.

Let us consider this in some detail. The assumption of Markovness for the underlying process enables one to concentrate on bivariate distributions since:

$$f(y_0, y_1, y_2, \ldots, y_T; \psi) = f(y_0; \phi_0) \prod_{t=1}^{T} f(y_t \mid y_{t-1}; \phi), \ (y_0, y_1, y_2, \ldots, y_T) \in \mathbb{R}^{T+1}. \tag{28.10}$$

The underlying bivariate distribution for model (28.3) is:

$$\begin{bmatrix} y_t \\ y_{t-1} \end{bmatrix} \sim N\left(\begin{bmatrix} \mu \\ \mu \end{bmatrix}, \begin{bmatrix} \sigma_0 & \sigma_1 \\ \sigma_1 & \sigma_0 \end{bmatrix} \right), \ t \in \mathbb{T}, \tag{28.11}$$

which, via the orthogonal decomposition (28.9) gives rise to:

$$y_t = \alpha_0 + \alpha_1 y_{t-1} + u_t, \ t \in \mathbb{T}. \tag{28.12}$$

The statistical parameters $\phi := (\alpha_0, \alpha_1, \sigma^2)$ are related to the primary parameters $\psi := (\mu, \sigma_0, \sigma_1)$ via:

$$\alpha_0 = (1 - \frac{\sigma_1}{\sigma_0})\mu \in \mathbb{R}, \quad \alpha_1 = \frac{\sigma_1}{\sigma_0} \in (-1, 1), \quad \sigma^2 = \sigma_0 - \frac{\sigma_1^2}{\sigma_0} \in \mathbb{R}_+, \tag{28.13}$$

and thus the two parameter spaces take the form:

$$\psi := (\mu, \sigma_1, \sigma_0) \in \mathbb{R}^2 \times \mathbb{R}_+, \quad \phi := (\alpha_0, \alpha_1, \sigma^2) \in \mathbb{R} \times (-1, 1) \times \mathbb{R}_+.$$

The inverse mapping from ϕ to ψ:

$$\mu = \frac{\alpha_0}{(1 - \alpha_1)}, \quad \sigma_0 = \frac{\sigma^2}{(1 - \alpha_1^2)}, \quad \sigma_1 = \frac{\alpha_1 \sigma^2}{(1 - \alpha_1^2)}, \tag{28.14}$$

reveals that the admissible range of values of α_1 is $(-1, 1)$, excluding unity. Note that the parameterization (28.13) can be derived directly from (28.12) by utilizing the assumptions $E(u_t \mid \sigma(y_{t-1})) = 0$, $E(u_t^2 \mid \sigma(y_{t-1})) = \sigma^2$; see Spanos (1995).

The probabilistic reduction approach views the AR(1) model specified in terms of (28.12) as comprising the following *model assumptions* concerning the conditional process $\{(y_t \mid Y_{t-1}^0), t \in \mathbb{T}\}$:

1ᶜ   normality: $f(y_t \mid Y^0_{t-1}; \psi)$ is normal
2ᶜ   linearity: $E(y_t \mid \sigma(Y^0_{t-1})) = \alpha_0 + \alpha_1 y_{t-1}$, linear in y_{t-1},
3ᶜ   homoskedasticity: $\text{var}(y_t \mid \sigma(Y^0_{t-1})) = \sigma^2$, free of Y^0_{t-1},
4ᶜ t-homogeneity: $(\alpha_0, \alpha_1, \sigma^2)$ are not functions of $t \in \mathbb{T}$,
5ᶜ   martingale difference: $\{(u_t \mid Y^0_{t-1}), t \in \mathbb{T}\}$ is a martingale difference process.

Note that the temporal dependence assumption underlying the observable process $\{y_t, t \in \mathbb{T}\}$ is Markov autocorrelation, whose general form (see (28.8)) is:

$$\text{cov}(y_t, y_{t-\tau}) := \sigma_{|\tau|} \le c\lambda^{|\tau|}, \quad c > 0, \quad 0 < \lambda < 1, \quad \tau \ne 0, \quad t = 1, 2, \ldots$$

The question that naturally arises at this stage is what kind of advantages the probabilistic reduction (PR) perspective offers (if any) when compared with the traditional DGM view. For a more systematic answer to this question we will consider the advantages at the different stages of empirical modeling: (i) specification, (ii) estimation, (iii) misspecification testing and (iv) respecification.

SPECIFICATION

This refers to the initial stage of choosing a statistical model in view of the observed data and the theoretical question(s) of interest. The postulated statistical model purports to provide an adequate description of the observable stochastic phenomenon of interest; model all the statistical systematic information exhibited by the observed data (see Spanos, 1999, ch. 1). The PR perspective of the AR(1) model (defined in terms of assumptions 1ᶜ–5ᶜ) has a distinct advantage over that of the traditional approach based on assumptions 1ᵃ–4ᵃ in so far as the latter assumptions are not a priori assessable because they are defined in terms of the unobservable error term process $\{\varepsilon_t, t \in \mathbb{T}\}$. In contrast, assumptions 1ᶜ–5ᶜ are specified directly in terms of the process $\{(y_t \mid Y^0_{t-1}), t \in \mathbb{T}\}$ and their validity can be assessed a priori via the reduction assumptions (i)–(iii) relating to $\{y_t, t \in \mathbb{T}\}$ using graphical techniques such as t-plots and scatter plots. The relationship between the model assumptions 1ᶜ–5ᶜ and the reduction assumptions is given by the following theorem.

Theorem 1.   Let $\{y_t, t \in \mathbb{T}\}$ by a stochastic process with bounded moments of order two. The process $\{y_t, t \in \mathbb{T}\}$ is normal, Markov and stationary *if and only if* the conditional process $\{(y_t \mid Y^0_{t-1}, t \in \mathbb{T}\}$ satisfies the model assumptions 1ᶜ–5ᶜ.

Proof.   The *if part*, (normality–Markovness–stationarity) $\Rightarrow$ 1ᶜ–5ᶜ, is trivial since:

$$f(y_0, y_1, y_2, \ldots, y_T; \psi) = f(y_0; \phi_0) \prod_{t=1}^{T} f(y_t \mid y_{t-1}, y_{t-2}, \ldots, y_0; \phi)$$

$$= f(y_0; \phi_0) \prod_{t=1}^{T} f_t(y_t \mid y_{t-1}; \phi_t) \qquad \text{– Markovness}$$

$$= f(y_0; \phi_0) \prod_{t=1}^{T} f(y_t \mid y_{t-1}; \phi) \qquad \text{– stationarity.}$$

These combined with normality implies assumptions 1^c–5^c. The *only if* part follows directly from Theorem 1 in Spanos (1995).   ■

Estimation

Given that the likelihood function is defined in terms of the joint distribution of the observable process $\{y_t, t \in \mathbb{T}\}$, the PR approach enjoys a minor advantage over the traditional approach because the need to transfer the probabilistic structure from the error process $\{\varepsilon_t, t \in \mathbb{T}\}$ onto the observable process does not arise. The primary advantage of the PR approach, however, arises from the implicit parameterization (28.13) which relates the model parameters $\phi := (\alpha_0, \alpha_1, \sigma^2)$ and primary parameters $\psi := (\mu, \sigma_0, \sigma_1)$. This parameterization plays an important role in bringing out the interrelationships among the model parameters as well as determining their admissible range. For instance, the PR statistical parameterization in (28.13) brings out two important points relating to the model parameters which are ignored by the traditional time series literature. The first point is that the admissible range of values of the model parameter α_1 is $(-1, 1)$ which excludes the values $|\alpha_1| = 1$. This has very important implications for the unit root testing literature. The second point is that the implicit restriction $\sigma^2 = \sigma_0(1 - \alpha_1^2)$ does not involve the initial condition (as traditionally assumed) but all observations. This has important implications for the MLEs of ϕ for α_1 near the unit root because the likelihood function based on (28.10); see Spanos and McGuirk (1999) for further details.

The PR approach can also help shed some light on the finite sample distribution of the OLS estimators of (α_0, α_1). In view of the similarity between the conditioning information set $\sigma(Y_{t-1}^0)$ of the AR(1) model and that of the stochastic normal/linear regression model $\sigma(X_t)$ (see Spanos, 1986, ch. 20), one can conjecture that the finite sampling distributions of $(\hat{\alpha}_0, \hat{\alpha}_1)$ are closer to the student's-t than the normal.

Misspecification testing

This refers to the testing of the model assumptions using misspecification tests which are probing beyond the boundaries of the postulated model; this should be contrasted with Neyman–Pearson testing which is viewed as testing within the boundaries (see Spanos, 1999, chs 14–15). The PR perspective has again certain distinct advantages over the traditional approach. First, the assumptions 1^c–5^c are specified explicitly in terms of the observable and not the error stochastic process (assumptions 1^a–4^a). This makes it easier to develop misspecification tests for these assumptions. In addition, the various misspecification tests developed in the context of the normal/linear regression model (see Spanos, 1986, chs 21–23) can be easily adapted to apply to the case of the AR(1) model with assumptions 1^c–5^c. Second, in the context of the PR approach, the connection between the reduction and model assumptions, utilized at the specification stage, can shed light on the likely directions of departures from 1^c–5^c, which can be useful in the choice of appropriate misspecification tests. Third, the same relationship can also be used to device joint misspecification tests (see Spanos, 1999, ch. 15).

RESPECIFICATION

This refers to the choice of an alternative statistical model when the original model is found to be statistically inadequate. In the context of the PR approach, respecification can be viewed as the choice of an alternative statistical model which can be devised by changing the reduction (not the model) assumptions in view of the misspecification testing results. For instance, if the misspecification testing has shown departures from assumptions 1^c and 3^c, the correspondence between reduction and model assumptions suggests changing the normality reduction assumption to another joint distribution with a linear autoregression and a heteroskedastic conditional variance; a member of the elliptically symmetric family of joint distributions, such as the Student's-t, suggests itself in this case. Changing the normal to the Student's-t distribution will give rise to a different AR(1) model with assumption 1^c replaced by the Student's-t and assumption 3^c to a particular dynamic heteroskedasticity formulation as suggested by the Student's-t distribution (see Spanos, 1994). In contrast, in the context of the traditional approach respecification takes the form of changing the model assumptions without worrying about the potential internal inconsistency among these assumptions. As shown in Spanos (1995), postulating some arbitrary dynamic heteroskedasticity formulation might give rise to internal inconsistencies.

3.3 Extending the autoregressive AR(1) model

The probabilistic reduction (PR) perspective, as it relates to respecification, provides a systematic way to extend AR(1) in several directions. It must be emphasized, however, the these extensions constitute alternative models. Let us consider a sample of such statistical models.

AR(P) MODEL

The extension of the AR(1) to the AR(p) model amounts to replacing the Markov (reduction) assumption with that of *Markov of order p*, yields:

$$y_t = \alpha_0 + \sum_{k=1}^{p} \alpha_k y_{t-k} + u_t, \quad t \in \mathbb{T},$$

with the model assumptions 1^c–5^c modified accordingly.

AR(1) MODEL WITH A TRENDING MEAN

Extending the AR(1) model in order to include a trend, amounts to replacing the reduction assumption of mean stationarity $E(y_t) = \mu$, for all $t \in \mathbb{T}$, with a particular form of mean-heterogeneity, say $E(y_t) = \mu t$, for all $t \in \mathbb{T}$. The implied changes in the bivariate distribution (28.11), via the orthogonal decomposition (28.9), give rise to:

$$y_t = \delta_0 + \delta_1 t + \alpha_1 y_{t-1} + u_t, \quad t \in \mathbb{T}, \tag{28.15}$$

where the statistical parameters $\phi := (\delta_0, \delta_1, \alpha_1, \sigma^2) \in \mathbb{R}^2 \times (-1, 1) \times \mathbb{R}_+$ and $\varphi := (\mu, \sigma_1, \sigma_0) \in \mathbb{R}^2 \times \mathbb{R}_+$, are interrelated via:

$$\delta_0 = \left(\frac{\sigma_1}{\sigma_0}\right)\mu \in \mathbb{R}, \quad \delta_1 = \left(1 - \left(\frac{\sigma_1}{\sigma_0}\right)\right)\mu, \quad \alpha_1 = \frac{\sigma_1}{\sigma_0} \in (-1, 1), \quad \sigma^2 = \sigma_0 - \frac{\sigma_1^2}{\sigma_0} \in \mathbb{R}_+,$$

$$(28.16)$$

$$\mu = \frac{\delta_0}{\alpha_1}, \quad \mu = \frac{\delta_1}{(1 - \alpha_1)}, \quad \sigma_0 = \frac{\sigma^2}{(1 - \alpha_1^2)}, \quad \sigma_1 = \frac{\alpha_1\sigma^2}{(1 - \alpha_1^2)}. \quad (28.17)$$

This is an important extension because it provides the backbone of Dickey–Fuller unit root testing (see Dickey and Fuller, 1979, 1981) based on $H_0 : \alpha_1 = 1$. A closer look at the above implicit parameterizations, however, suggests that when $\alpha_1 = 1$ $\Rightarrow (\delta_0 = \mu, \delta_1 = 0, \sigma^2 = 0)$; this raises important methodological issues concerning various aspects of these tests (see Spanos and McGuirk, 1999 for further details).

The extension of the AR(1) model to include higher-order trend terms and seasonal effects can be achieved by postulating mean-heterogeneity of the form

$$E(y_t) = \sum_{i=1}^{m} a_i D_{it} + \sum_{k=1}^{l} \mu_k t^k, \quad t \in \mathbb{T}, \text{ where } (D_{it}, i = 1, 2, \ldots, m)$$

can be either sinusoidal functions or/and dummy variables purporting to model the seasonal effects. We conclude this subsection by noting that following an analogous procedure one can specify AR(1) models with a trending variance; see Spanos (1990).

NON-NORMAL AUTOREGRESSIVE MODELS

By retaining the reduction assumptions of Markovness and stationarity and replacing normality with an alternative joint distribution one can specify numerous nonnormal autoregressive models; see Spanos (1999, ch. 8). The normal autoregressive model can also be extended in the direction of nonlinear models; see Granger and Teräsvirta (1993) for several important nonlinear time series models.

4   MOVING AVERAGE MODELS

4.1   The traditional approach

A *moving average model* of order q, denoted by MA(q):

$$y_t = a_0 + \sum_{k=1}^{q} a_k \varepsilon_{t-k} + \varepsilon_t, \quad \varepsilon_t \sim \text{NI}(0, \sigma^2), \quad t \in \mathbb{T}, \quad (28.18)$$

is traditionally viewed as a DGM with a normal white noise process $\{\varepsilon_t, t \in \mathbb{T}\}$ (see (28.4)) as the input and $\{y_t, t \in \mathbb{T}\}$, as the output process.

The question which naturally arises at this stage is "how does the DGM (28.18) fit into the orthogonal decomposition given in (28.9)?" A naïve answer will be $y_t = E(y_t \mid \sigma(\varepsilon_{t-1}, \varepsilon_{t-2}, \ldots, \varepsilon_{t-q})) + \varepsilon_t, \ t \in \mathbb{T}$. However, such an answer is misleading because operational conditioning cannot be defined in terms of an unobserved stochastic process $\{\varepsilon_t, \ t \in \mathbb{T}\}$. In view of this, the next question is "how is the formulation (28.18) justified as a statistical Generating Mechanism?" The answer lies with the following theorem.

Wold decomposition theorem. Let $\{y_t, \ t \in \mathbb{T}\}$, be a normal stationary process and define the unobservable derived process $\{\varepsilon_t, \ t \in \mathbb{T}\}$, by:

$$\varepsilon_t = y_t - E(y_t \mid \sigma(Y_{t-1}^0)), \text{ with } E(\varepsilon_t) = 0, \quad E(\varepsilon_t^2) = \sigma^2 > 0. \tag{28.19}$$

Then, the process $\{y_t, \ t \in \mathbb{T}\}$, can be expressed in the form:

$$y_t - \mu = w_t + \sum_{k=0}^{\infty} a_k \varepsilon_{t-k}, \quad t \in \mathbb{T}. \tag{28.20}$$

(i) $\varepsilon_t \sim \text{NI}(0, \sigma^2), \ t = 1, 2, \ldots,$

(ii) $\displaystyle\sum_{k=0}^{\infty} a_k^2 < \infty$, for $a_k = \dfrac{\text{cov}(y_t, \varepsilon_{t-k})}{\text{var}(\varepsilon_{t-k})}, \ k = 0, 1, 2, \ldots,$

(iii)   for $w_t = \displaystyle\sum_{k=1}^{\infty} \gamma_k w_{t-k}, \ E(w_t \varepsilon_s) = 0$, for all $t, s = 1, 2, \ldots$

It is important to note that the process $\{w_t, \ t \in \mathbb{T}\}$, is *deterministic* in the sense that it's perfectly predictable from its own past; since $\sigma(w_{t-1}, w_{t-2}, \ldots) = \cap_{t=-\infty}^{\infty} \sigma(Y_{t-1}^0)$, the right-hand side being the remote past of the process $\{y_t, \ t \in \mathbb{T}\}$ (see Wold, 1938). In view of this, the MA(∞) decomposition often excludes the remote past:

$$y_t - \mu = \sum_{k=1}^{\infty} a_k \varepsilon_{t-k} + \varepsilon_t, \quad t \in \mathbb{T}. \tag{28.21}$$

As it stands, the MA(∞) formulation is non-operational because it involves an infinite number of unknown parameters. The question arises whether one can truncate the MA(∞) at some finite value $q < T$, in order to get an operational model. As the Wold decomposition theorem stands, no such truncation is justifiable. For such a truncation to be formally justifiable we need to impose certain temporal dependence restrictions on the covariances $\sigma_{|\tau|} = \text{cov}(y_t, y_{t-\tau})$. The most natural dependence restriction in the case of stationary processes is that of ergodicity; see Hamilton (1994) and Phillips (1987).

4.2   MA(q): the probabilistic reduction perspective

At this point it is important to emphasize that the above discussion relating to the convergence of certain partial sums of the MA(∞) coefficients is not helpful from the empirical modeling viewpoint because the restrictions cannot be assessed a priori. Alternatively, one can consider restrictions on the temporal covariances of the observable process $\{y_t, t \in \mathbb{T}\}$ which we can assess a priori:

1^d constant mean: $E(y_t) := \mu, t \in \mathbb{T},$
2^d constant variance: $\text{var}(y_t) := \sigma_0, t \in \mathbb{T},$

3^d m-autocorrelation: $\text{cov}(y_t, y_{t-\tau}) := \begin{cases} \sigma_{|\tau|}, & \tau = 1, 2, \ldots, q, \\ 0, & \tau > q, \end{cases}$

4^d normality: $y_t \sim N(\cdot, \cdot), t \in \mathbb{T}.$ (28.22)

where the first two moments in terms of the statistical parameterization $\phi := (a_0, a_1, \ldots, a_q, \sigma^2)$ take the form:

$$\mu = a_0, \quad \sigma_0 = \sigma^2\left(1 + \sum_{k=1}^{q} a_k^2\right), \quad \sigma_{|\tau|} = \sigma^2(a_\tau + a_1 a_{\tau+1} + \ldots + a_{q-\tau}a_q). \quad (28.23)$$

In view of the fact that the likelihood function is defined in terms of the joint distribution of the observable process $\{y_t, t \in \mathbb{T}\}$, it is apparent that:

$$L(\phi) \propto (2\pi)^{-\frac{T}{2}}(\det \Omega(\phi))^{-\frac{1}{2}}\exp\{-\tfrac{1}{2}(y - 1a_0)^\top \Omega(\phi)^{-1}(y - 1a_0)\},$$

where the $T \times T$ temporal variance–covariance $\Omega(\phi)$ takes the banded Toeplitz form with all elements along the diagonal and off-diagonals up to q coincide and are nonzero but after the qth off-diagonal the covariances are zero. This gives rise to a loglikelihood function whose first-order conditions with respect to ϕ are nonlinear and the estimation requires numerical optimization; see Anderson (1971).

Returning to the Wold decomposition theorem we note that the probabilistic structure of the observable process $\{y_t, t \in \mathbb{T}\}$ involves only normality and stationarity which imply that the variance–covariance matrix is Toeplitz, which, when compared with $\Omega(\phi)$ the result becomes apparent; the banded Toeplitz covariance matrix in $\Omega(\phi)$ as $T \to \infty$ gives rise to a MA(q) formulation and the unrestricted Toeplitz covariance matrix as $T \to \infty$ gives rise to a MA(∞) formulation. Does this mean that to get an operational model we need to truncate the temporal covariance matrix, i.e. assume that $\sigma_\tau = 0$ for all $\tau > q$, for some $q > 1$? This assumption will give rise to the MA(q) model but there are more general models we can contemplate that do not impose such a strong restriction. Instead, we need some restrictions which ensure that $\sigma_\tau \to 0$ as $\tau \to \infty$ at a "reasonable" rate such as:

$$|\sigma_\tau| \leq c\lambda^\tau, \quad c > 0, \quad 0 < \lambda < 1, \quad \tau = 1, 2, 3, \ldots \quad (28.24)$$

This enables us to approximate the non-operational MA(∞) representation with operational models from the broader ARMA(p, q) family. This should be contrasted with stochastic processes with long memory (see Granger, 1980) where:

$$|\sigma_\tau| \leq c\tau^{(2d-1)}, \quad c > 0, \quad 0 < d < .5, \quad \tau = 1, 2, 3, \ldots \quad (28.25)$$

In cases where, in addition to the normality and stationarity, we assume that the process $\{y_t, t \in \mathbb{T}\}$ satisfies the dependence restriction (28.24), we can proceed to approximate the infinite polynomial in the lag operator L, $a_\infty(L) = 1 + a_1 L + \ldots + a_k L^k + \ldots$, of the MA($\infty$) representation:

$$y_t = \mu + \sum_{k=1}^{\infty} a_k \varepsilon_{t-k} + \varepsilon_t = \mu + a_\infty(L) \cdot \varepsilon_t, \ t \in \mathbb{T}, \quad (28.26)$$

by a ratio of two finite order polynomials $a_\infty(L) = \frac{\gamma_q(L)}{\delta_p(L)} := \frac{(1 + \gamma_1 L + \gamma_2 L^2 + \ldots + \gamma_q L^q)}{(1 + \delta_1 L + \delta_2 L^2 + \ldots + \delta_p L^p)}$, $p \geq q \geq 0$; (see Dhrymes, 1971). After re-arranging the two polynomials:

$$y_t = \mu + \frac{\gamma_q(L)}{\alpha_p(L)} \varepsilon_t \Rightarrow \alpha_p(L) y_t = \mu + \gamma_q(L) \varepsilon_t, \quad t \in \mathbb{T},$$

yields the autoregressive-moving average model ARMA(p, q) popularized by Box and Jenkins (1970):

$$y_t + \sum_{k=1}^{p} \alpha_k y_{t-k} = \mu + \sum_{k=1}^{q} \gamma_k \varepsilon_{t-k} + \varepsilon_t, \quad t \in \mathbb{T}.$$

Such models proved very efficient in capturing the temporal dependence in time series data in a parsimonious way but failed to capture the imagination of economic modelers because it's very difficult to relate such models to economic theory.

The question that arises in justifying this representation is why define the statistical GM in terms of the errors? The only effective justification is when the modeler has a priori evidence that the dependence exhibited by the time series data is of the q-autocorrelation form and q is reasonably small. On the other hand, if the dependence is better described by (28.24), the AR(p) representation provides a much more effective description. The relationship between the MA(q) representation (28.18) and the autoregressive AR(∞) representation takes the form:

$$y_t = \sum_{k=1}^{\infty} b_k y_{t-k} + \varepsilon_t, \quad t \in \mathbb{T},$$

where the coefficients are related (by equating the coefficients) via:

$$b_1 = a_1, \ b_2 = a_2 + a_1 b_1, \ b_3 = a_3 + a_1 b_2 + a_2 b_1, \ldots, \ldots,$$

$$b_q = a_q + a_1 b_{q-1} + a_2 b_{q-2} + \ldots + a_{q-1} b_1, \ b_\tau = \sum_{k=1}^{q} a_k b_{\tau-k}, \ \tau > q.$$

Given that $b_\tau \xrightarrow{\tau \to \infty} 0$, the modeler can assume that the latter representation can be approximated by a finite AR(p) model; which is often preferred for forecasting.

5   ARMA TYPE MODELS: MULTIVARIATE

The above discussion of the AR(p) and MA(q) models can be extended to the case where the observable process is a vector $\{Z_t, t \in \mathbb{T}\}$, $Z_t : (m \times 1)$. This stochastic vector process is said to be second-order stationary if:

$$E(Z_t) = \mu, \quad \text{cov}(Z_t, Z_{t-\tau}) = E((Z_t - \mu)(Z_{t-\tau} - \mu)^\top) = \Sigma(\tau).$$

Note that $\Sigma(\tau)$ is not symmetric since $\sigma_{ij}(\tau) = \sigma_{ji}(-\tau)$; see Hamilton (1994).

The ARMA representations for the vector process $\{Z_t, t \in \mathbb{T}\}$ take the form:

$$VAR(p): \qquad Z_t = \alpha_0 + A_1 Z_{t-1} + A_2 Z_{t-2} + \ldots + A_p Z_{t-p} + \varepsilon_t,$$

$$VMA(q): \qquad Z_t = \mu + \Phi_1 \varepsilon_{t-1} + \Phi_2 \varepsilon_{t-2} + \ldots + \Phi_q \varepsilon_{t-q} + \varepsilon_t,$$

$$VARMA(p, q): \quad Z_t = \gamma_0 + A_1 Z_{t-1} + \ldots + A_p Z_{t-p} + \Theta_1 \varepsilon_{t-1} + \ldots + \Theta_q \varepsilon_{t-q} + \varepsilon_t,$$

where the vector error process is of the form: $\varepsilon_t \sim NI(0, \Omega)$.

In direct analogy to the univariate case, the probabilistic assumptions are:

$$
\left.
\begin{array}{llll}
1^e & \text{zero mean:} & E(\varepsilon_t) = 0, \\
2^e & \text{constant variance:} & E(\varepsilon_t \varepsilon_t^\top) = \Omega, \\
3^e & \text{no autocorrelation:} & E(\varepsilon_t \varepsilon_{t-\tau}^\top) = 0, \ \tau \neq 0, \\
4^e & \text{normality:} & \varepsilon_t \sim N(\cdot, \cdot),
\end{array}
\right\} t \in \mathbb{T}. \qquad (28.27)
$$

Looking at the above representations from the PR perspective we need to translate 1^e–4^e into assumptions in terms of the observable vector $\{Z_t, t \in \mathbb{T}\}$.

5.1   The probabilistic reduction perspective

The probabilistic reduction perspective contemplates the DGM of the Vector Autoregressive representation from left to right as an orthogonal decomposition:

$$Z_t = E(Z_t \,|\, \sigma(Z_{t-1}^0)) + u_t, \quad t \in \mathbb{T}, \qquad (28.28)$$

where $Z_{t-1}^0 := (Z_{t-1}, Z_{t-2}, \ldots, Z_0)$ and $u_t = Z_t - E(Z_t \,|\, \sigma(Z_{t-1}^0))$, with the underlying statistical model viewed as reduction from the joint distribution of the underlying process $\{Z_t, t \in \mathbb{T}\}$. In direct analogy to the univariate case the *reduction assumptions* on the joint distribution of the process $\{Z_t, t \in \mathbb{T}\}$, that would yield VAR(1) model are: (i) normal, (ii) Markov, and (iii) stationary.

Let us consider the question of probabilistic reduction in some detail by imposing the reduction assumptions in a certain sequence in order to reduce the joint distribution to an operational model:

$$D(Z_0, Z_1, \ldots, Z_T; \psi) = D(Z_0; \phi_0) \prod_{t=1}^{T} D_t(Z_t \mid Z_{t-1}^0; \phi_t),$$

$$\stackrel{M}{=} D(Z_0; \phi_0) \prod_{t=1}^{T} D(Z_t \mid Z_{t-1}; \phi),$$

$$\stackrel{M\&S}{=} D(Z_0; \phi_0) \prod_{t=1}^{T} D(Z_t \mid Z_{t-1}; \phi), \quad (Z_0, \ldots, Z_T) \in \mathbb{R}^{m(T+1)}.$$

(28.29)

The first equality does not entail any assumptions, but the second follows from the Markovness (M) and the third from the stationarity (S) assumption. In order to see what happens to $D(Z_t \mid Z_{t-1}; \phi)$ when the normality assumption:

$$\begin{bmatrix} Z_t \\ Z_{t-1} \end{bmatrix} \sim N\left(\begin{bmatrix} \mu \\ \mu \end{bmatrix}, \begin{bmatrix} \Sigma(0) & \Sigma(1) \\ \Sigma(1)^\top & \Sigma(0) \end{bmatrix} \right), \quad t \in \mathbb{T}, \quad (28.30)$$

is imposed, the orthogonal decomposition (28.28) gives rise to:

$$Z_t = \alpha_0 + A_1 Z_{t-1} + u_t, \quad t \in \mathbb{T}. \quad (28.31)$$

The statistical parameters $\phi := (\alpha_0, A_1, \Omega)$ are related to the primary parameters $\psi = (\mu, \Sigma(0), \Sigma(1))$ via:

$$\alpha_0 = (I - A_1)\mu, \quad A_1 = \Sigma(1)^\top \Sigma(0)^{-1}, \quad \Omega = \Sigma(0) - \Sigma(1)^\top \Sigma(0)^{-1} \Sigma(0), \quad (28.32)$$

and the discussion concerning the interrelationships between two parameter spaces is analogous to the univariate case discussed in the previous section and will not be pursued any further; see Spanos (1986, chs 22–23).

The probabilistic reduction approach views the VAR(1) model specified in terms of (28.12) as comprising the following *model assumptions* concerning the conditional process $\{(Z_t \mid Z_{t-1}^0), t \in \mathbb{T}\}$:

1^f normality: $D(Z_t \mid Z_{t-1}^0; \psi)$ is normal,
2^f linearity: $E(Z_t \mid \sigma(Z_{t-1}^0)) = \alpha_0 + A_1 Z_{t-1}$, linear in Z_{t-1},
3^f homoskedasticity: $\text{cov}(Z_t \mid \sigma(Z_{t-1}^0)) = \Omega$, free of Z_{t-1}^0,
4^f t-homogeneity: (α_0, A_1, Ω) are not functions of $t \in \mathbb{T}$,
5^f martingale difference: $\{(u_t \mid Z_{t-1}^0), t \in \mathbb{T}\}$ is a vector martingale difference process.

Continuing with the analogies between the vector and univariate cases, the temporal dependence assumption for the process $\{Z_t, t \in \mathbb{T}\}$ is Markov autocorrelation:

$$\text{cov}(Z_{it}, Z_{j(t-\tau)}) = \sigma_{ij\tau} \leq c\lambda^{|\tau|}, \ c > 0, \ 0 < \lambda < 1, \ \tau \neq 0, \ i, j = 1, 2, \ldots, \ t = 1, 2, \ldots$$

For the VAR(1) model as specified by (28.31) and assumptions 1^f–5^f above to be statistically adequate, the modeler should test the underlying assumptions, with the misspecification tests being modifications of the ones for the univariate case (see Spanos, 1986, ch. 24).

The VAR(1) is much richer than the univariate ARMA(p, q) specification because, in addition to the self-temporal structure, it enables the modeler to consider the cross-temporal structure, fulfilling Moore's basic objective in the classic (1914) study. This can be seen in the simplest case of a VAR(1) model with $m = 2$:

$$\begin{pmatrix} Z_{1t} \\ Z_{2t} \end{pmatrix} = \begin{pmatrix} a_{10} \\ a_{20} \end{pmatrix} + \begin{pmatrix} a_{11} & a_{12} \\ a_{21} & a_{22} \end{pmatrix}\begin{pmatrix} Z_{1(t-1)} \\ Z_{2(t-1)} \end{pmatrix} + \begin{pmatrix} u_{1t} \\ u_{2t} \end{pmatrix}, \quad \Omega = \begin{pmatrix} \omega_{11} & \omega_{12} \\ \omega_{21} & \omega_{22} \end{pmatrix}.$$

The coefficients (a_{12}, a_{21}) measure the cross-temporal dependence between the two processes. In the case where $a_{12} = 0$, Z_{2t} does not *Granger cause* Z_{1t}, and vice versa in the case where $a_{21} = 0$. This is an important concept in the context of forecasting. The covariance ω_{12} constitutes a measure of the contemporaneous ($\text{cov}(Z_{1t}, Z_{2t} \mid Z_{t-1}^0)$) dependence. As argued in the next subsection, the dynamic linear regression model can be viewed as a further reduction of the VAR model which purports to model this contemporaneous dependence. For further discussion of the VAR model see Hamilton (1994).

6 Time Series and Linear Regression Models

6.1 Error autocorrelation vs. temporal dependence

The classic paper of Yule (1926) had a lasting effect on econometric modeling in so far as his cautionary note that using time series data in the context of linear regression can often lead to spurious results, resulted in reducing the number of empirical studies using such data. As mentioned above, the results of Cochrane and Orcutt (1949) and Durbin and Watson (1950, 1951) were interpreted by the econometric literature as a way to sidestep the spurious regression problem raised by Yule, and legitimize the use of time series data in the context of the linear regression model. *Stage 1*: estimate the linear regression model:

$$y_t = \beta^\top x_t + u_t, \quad u_t \sim \text{NI}(0, \sigma^2), \quad t \in \mathbb{T}, \tag{28.33}$$

and test for error autocorrelation using the Durbin–Watson test based on:

$$DW(y) = \frac{\sum_{t=2}^{T}(\hat{u}_t - \hat{u}_{t-1})^2}{\sum_{t=1}^{T}\hat{u}_t^2}, \quad \hat{u}_t = y_t - \hat{\beta}^\top x_t, \quad \hat{\beta} = (X^\top X)^{-1}X^\top y.$$

The alternative model that gives rise to this test is the modified model:

$$y_t = \beta^\top x_t + u_t, \quad u_t = \rho u_{t-1} + \varepsilon_t, \quad \varepsilon_t \sim \text{NI}(0, \sigma_\varepsilon^2), \quad |\rho| < 1, \quad t \in \mathbb{T}, \tag{28.34}$$

and the test is based on the hypothesis $H_0 : \rho = 0$, $H_1 : \rho \neq 0$. *Stage 2*: if the null hypothesis is not rejected, the modeler assumes that the original model (28.33) does not indicate the presence of error autocorrelation, otherwise the modeler can "cure" the problem by adopting the alternative model (28.34), which can be estimated using the Cochrane–Orcutt procedure. In the context of the traditional Gauss–Markov specification in matrix notation:

$$y = X\beta + u, \quad y : T \times 1, \quad X : T \times k,$$

$$1^g \ E(u) = 0, \quad 2^g\text{–}3^g \ E(uu') = \sigma^2 I_T \quad 4^g \ x_t \text{ is fixed}, \quad 5^g \ \text{Rank}(X) = k, \ (T > k),$$

the presence of error autocorrelation takes the form $3^g \ E(uu^\top) = V_T \neq \sigma^2 I_T$. Under $E(uu^\top) = V_T$, (i.e. $E(u_t u_s) \neq 0$, $t \neq s$, $t, s = 1, 2, \ldots, T$) the OLS estimator $\hat{\beta} = (X^\top X)^{-1} X^\top y$ is no longer best, linear unbiased estimator (BLUE); it is said to retain its *unbiasedness* and *consistency* but forfeit its *relative efficiency* since:

$$\text{cov}(\hat{\beta}) = (X^\top X)^{-1}(X^\top V_T X)(X^\top X)^{-1} \geq (X^\top V_T^{-1} X) = \text{cov}(\tilde{\beta}),$$

where $\tilde{\beta} = (X^\top V_T^{-1} X)^{-1} X^\top V_T^{-1} y$ is the generalized least squares (GLS) estimator. This traditional discussion has often encouraged applied econometricians to argue that the use of time series data in the context of the linear regression model with assumptions 1^g–5^g would forfeit only the relative efficiency of the OLS estimators. As argued in Spanos (1986, chs 22–23), the above suggestion is very misleading because the traditional textbook scenario is highly unlikely in empirical modeling. In order to see this we need to consider the above discussion from the probabilistic reduction (PR) perspective. Viewing (28.33) from this perspective reveals that the implicit parameterization of $\theta := (\beta, \sigma^2)$ is:

$$\beta = \text{cov}(X_t)^{-1}\text{cov}(X_t, y_t), \quad \sigma^2 = \text{var}(y_t) - \text{cov}(y_t, X_t)\text{cov}(X_t)^{-1}\text{cov}(X_t, y_t).$$

In the context of the PR specification, assumption 3^g corresponds to $(y_1, y_2, \ldots, y_T)$ being "temporally" independent (see Spanos, 1986, p. 373). In the context of the PR approach, respecification amounts to replacing the original reduction assumptions on the vector process $\{Z_t, \ t \in \mathbb{T}\}$ where $Z_t := (y_t \ X_t^\top)^\top$, i.e. (i) normality; (ii) (temporal) independence; and (iii) identically distributed, with assumptions such as (i)′ normality; (ii)′ Markov; and (iii)′ stationarity. The PR approach replaces the original conditioning information set $\mathcal{D}_t = \{X_t = x_t\}$ with $\mathcal{D}_t^* = \{X_t = x_t, Z_{t-1}^0\}$, $Z_{t-1}^0 = \{Z_{t-1}, \ldots, Z_0\}$, which (under (i)′–(iii)′) gives rise to the *dynamic linear regression*:

$$y_t = \beta_0^\top x_t + \alpha_1^\top Z_{t-1} + \varepsilon_t, \quad t \in \mathbb{T}. \tag{28.35}$$

where the implicit statistical parameterization is:

$$\beta_0 = \text{cov}(X_t \mid Z_{t-1})^{-1} \left[\text{cov}(X_t, y_t) - \text{cov}(X_t, Z_{t-1}) \left[\text{cov}(Z_{t-1}) \right]^{-1} \text{cov}(Z_{t-1}, y_t) \right],$$

$$\alpha_1 = \text{cov}(Z_{t-1} \mid X_t)^{-1} \left[\text{cov}(Z_{t-1}, y_t) - \text{cov}(Z_{t-1}, X_t) \left[\text{cov}(X_t) \right]^{-1} \text{cov}(X_t, y_t) \right],$$

$$\sigma_\varepsilon^2 = \text{var}(y_t) - (\text{cov}(y_t, X_t^*)) (\text{cov}(X_t^*))^{-1} (\text{cov}(X_t^*, y_t)), \ X_t^* = (X_t^\top, Z_{t-1}^\top)^\top.$$

The important point to emphasize is that the statistical parameterization of β_0 is very different from that of β in the context of the linear regression model since:

$$\beta_0 \neq \mathrm{cov}(X_t)^{-1}\mathrm{cov}(X_t, y_t),$$

unless $\mathrm{cov}(X_t, Z_{t-1}) = 0$; there is no temporal correlation between X_t and Z_{t-1}. Given that the latter case is excluded by assumption, the only other case when the two parameterizations coincide arises in the case where the appropriate model is (28.34). In order to understand what the latter model entails let us consider how it can be nested within the dynamic linear regression model (28.35). Substituting out the error autocorrelation in the context of (28.34) yields:

$$y_t = \beta^\top x_t - \rho\beta^\top x_{t-1} + \rho y_{t-1} + \varepsilon_t, \quad |\rho| < 1, \quad t \in \mathbb{T},$$

which is a special case of the dynamic linear regression model (28.35):

$$y_t = \beta_0^\top x_t + \beta_1^\top x_{t-1} + \alpha_1 y_{t-1} + u_t, \quad t \in \mathbb{T},$$

when one imposes the so-called *common factor restrictions* (see Hendry and Mizon, 1978) $\beta_0\alpha_1 + \beta_1 = 0$. As shown in Spanos (1987), these restrictions are highly unlikely in empirical modeling because their validity presupposes that all the individual components of the vector process $\{Z_t, t \in \mathbb{T}\}$ are Granger noncausal and their temporal structure is "almost identical". Under this PR scenario the OLS estimator $\hat{\beta} = (X^\top X)^{-1}X^\top y$ under the assumption that the vector process $\{Z_t, t \in \mathbb{T}\}$ is "temporally" dependent is both *biased* and *inconsistent*!

6.2   Dynamic linear regression models

The dynamic linear regression model (28.35) discussed above, constitutes a reduction of the VAR(1) model (28.31), given that we can decompose $D(Z_t | Z_{t-1}; \phi)$ further, based on the separation $Z_t = (y_t^\top, X_t^\top)^\top$, $y_t : m_1 \times 1$, to yield:

$$D(Z_0, Z_1, \ldots, Z_T; \psi) \overset{\text{M\&s}}{=} D(Z_0; \phi_0) \prod_{t=1}^{T} D(Z_t | Z_{t-1}; \phi)$$

$$= D(Z_0; \phi_0) \prod_{t=1}^{T} D(y_t | X_t, Z_{t-1}; \varphi)D(X_t | Z_{t-1}; \phi).$$

$$(28.36)$$

Under the normality reduction assumption this gives rise to the multivariate dynamic linear regression model (MDLR):

$$y_t = B_0^\top x_t + B_1^\top x_{t-1} + A_1^\top y_{t-1} + u_t, \quad t \in \mathbb{T}, \qquad (28.37)$$

where $A = \begin{pmatrix} A_{11} & A_{12} \\ A_{21} & A_{22} \end{pmatrix}$, $\Omega := \begin{pmatrix} \Omega_{11} & \Omega_{12} \\ \Omega_{21} & \Omega_{22} \end{pmatrix}$, are reparameterized into:

$$B_0^\top = \Omega_{22}^{-1}\Omega_{21}, \quad B_1^\top = A_{12} - \Omega_{12}\Omega_{22}^{-1}A_{22}, \quad A_1^\top = A_{11} - \Omega_{12}\Omega_{22}^{-1}A_{21},$$

$$\mathrm{cov}(y_t \mid X_t, Z_{t-1}) = \Omega_{11} - \Omega_{12}\Omega_{22}^{-1}\Omega_{21}.$$

As we can see, the statistical parameters of the MDLR(1) (28.37) differ from those of the VAR(1) model (28.31) in so far as the former goes one step further purporting to model (in terms of the extra conditioning) the "contemporaneous dependence" captured in Ω in the context of the former model. This model is particularly interesting in econometrics because it provides a direct link to the simultaneous equations model; see Spanos (1986), p. 645.

7 CONCLUSION

Statistical models, such as AR(p), MA(q), ARMA(p, q) and the linear regression model with error autocorrelation, often used for modeling time series data, have been considered from a particular viewing angle we called the probabilistic reduction (PR) approach. The emphasis of this approach is placed on specifying statistical models in terms of a consistent set of probabilistic assumptions regarding the observable stochastic process underlying the data, as opposed to the error term. Although the discussion did not cover the more recent developments in time series econometrics, it is important to conclude with certain remarks regarding these developments. The recent literature on unit roots and cointegration, when viewed from the PR viewpoint, can be criticized on two grounds. The *first* criticism is that the literature has largely ignored the statistical adequacy issue. When the estimated AR(p) models are misspecified, however, the unit root test inference results will often be misleading. The *second* criticism concerns the inadequate attention paid by the recent literature on the implicit parameterizations (discussed above) and what they entail (see Spanos and McGuirk, 1999).

References

Anderson, T.W. (1971). *The Statistical Analysis of Time Series*. Wiley, New York.

Box, G.E.P., and G.M. Jenkins (1970). *Time Series Analysis: Forecasting and Control*, revised edn 1976. Holden-Day, San Francisco.

Cochrane, D., and G.H. Orcutt (1949). Application of least-squares regression to relationships containing autocorrelated error terms. *Journal of the American Statistical Association* 44, 32–61.

Cramer, H. (1937). *Random Variables and Probability Distributions*. Cambridge: Cambridge University Press.

Davis, T.H. (1941). *The Analysis of Economic Time Series*. Cowles Commission Monograph No. 6, The Principia Press, Indiana.

Dhrymes, P.J. (1971). *Distributed Lags: Problems of Estimation and Formulation*. Edinburgh: Oliver and Boyd.

Dickey, D.A., and W.A. Fuller (1979). Distribution of the estimators for autoregressive time series with a unit root. *Journal of the American Statistical Association* 74, 427–31.

Dickey, D.A., and W.A. Fuller (1981). Likelihood ratio statistics for autoregressive time series with a unit root. *Econometrica* 49, 1057–72.

Durbin, J., and G.S. Watson (1950). Testing for serial correlation in least squares regression I. *Biometrika* 37, 409–28.

Durbin, J., and G.S. Watson (1951). Testing for serial correlation in least squares regression II. *Biometrika* 38, 159–78.

Engle, R.F., and C.W.J. Granger (1987). Cointegration and error-correction representation: estimation and testing. *Econometrica* 55, 251–76.

Frisch, R. (1933). Propagation problems and impulse problems in dynamic economics. In *Economic Essays in Honor of Gustav Cassel*. London: Macmillan.

Granger, C.W.J. (1980). Long memory relationships and the aggregation of dynamic models. *Journal of Econometrics* 14, 227–38.

Granger, C.W.J. (1983). Cointegrated variables and error-correcting models. UCSD discussion paper 83–13.

Granger, C.W.J. (ed.) (1990). *Modelling Economic Series: Readings on the Methodology of Econometric Modeling*. Oxford: Oxford University Press.

Granger, C.W.J., and P. Newbold (1974). Spurious regressions in econometrics. *Journal of Econometrics* 2, 111–20.

Granger, C.W.J., and P. Newbold (1977). *Forecasting Economic Time Series*. London: Academic Press.

Granger, C.W.J., and T. Teräsvirta (1993). *Modelling Nonlinear Economic relationships*. Oxford: Oxford University Press.

Hamilton, J.D. (1994). *Time Series Analysis*. New Jersey: Princeton University Press.

Hendry, D.F. (1993). *Econometrics: Alchemy or Science?*. Oxford: Blackwell.

Hendry, D.F., and G.E. Mizon (1978). Serial correlation as a convenient simplification not a nuisance: a comment on a study of the demand for money by the Bank of England. *Economic Journal* 88, 549–63.

Hendry, D.F., and M.S. Morgan (1995). *The Foundations of Economic Analysis: An Introduction*. New York: Cambridge University Press.

Heyde, C.C., and E. Seneta (1977). *I.J. Bieyname: Statistical Theory Anticipated*. New York: Springer-Verlag.

Hooker, R. (1901). Correlation of the marriage rate with trade. *Journal of the Royal Statistical Society* 64, 485–603.

Hooker, R. (1905). On the correlation of successive observations: illustrated by corn prices. *Journal of the Royal Statistical Society* 68, 696–703.

Johansen, S. (1991). Estimation and hypothesis testing of cointegrating vectors in Gaussian vector autoregressive models. *Econometrica* 59, 1551–81.

Khinchine, A.Y. (1932). Selle successioni stazioarie di eventi. *Giorn. Ist. Ital. Attuari* 3, 267–74.

Kolmogorov, A.N. (1933). *Grundbegriffe der Wahrscheinlichkeitrechnung*, Berlin. *Foundations of the Theory of Probability*, 2nd English edn. New York: Chelsea Publishing Co.

Kolmogorov, A.N. (1941). Stationary sequences in Hilbert space. *Byull. Moskov. Gos. Univ. Mat.* 2, 1–40. English translation reprinted in Shiryayev (1992), pp. 228–71.

Mann, H.B. and A. Wald (1943). On the statistical treatment of linear stochastic difference equations. *Econometrica* 11, 173–220.

Moore, H.L. (1914). *Economic Cycles: Their Law and Cause*. New York: Macmillan.

Nelson, C.R., and C.I. Plosser (1982). Trends and random walks in macro-economic time series: some evidence and implications. *Journal of Monetary Economics* 10, 139–62.

Norton, J. (1902). *Statistical Studies in the New York Money Market*. New York: Macmillan.

Phillips, P.C.B. (1986). Understanding spurious regression in econometrics. *Journal of Econometrics* 33, 311–40.

Phillips, P.C.B. (1987). Time series regressions with a unit root. *Econometrica* 55, 227–301.

Phillips, P.C.B. (1991). Optimal inference in cointegrating systems. *Econometrica* 59, 283–306.

Schuster, A. (1906). On the periodicities of sunspots. *Philosophical Transactions of Royal Society of London* A, 206, 69–100.

Shiryayev, A.N. (ed.) (1992). *Selected Works of A.N. Kolmogorov, vol. II: Probability Theory and Mathematical Statistics*. Dordrecht: Kluwer.

Sims, C.A. (1980). Macroeconomics and reality. *Econometrica* 48, 1–48.

Slutsky, E. (1927). The summation of random causes as the source of cyclic processes (in Russian); English translation in *Econometrica* 5, (1937).

Spanos, A. (1986). *Statistical Foundations of Econometric Modelling*. Cambridge: Cambridge University Press.

Spanos, A. (1987). Error autocorrelation revisited: the AR(1) case. *Econometric Reviews* 6, 285–94.

Spanos, A. (1990). Unit roots and their dependence of the conditioning information set. *Advances in Econometrics* 8, 271–92.

Spanos, A. (1995). On normality and the linear regression model. *Econometric Reviews* 14, 195–203.

Spanos, A. (1999). *Probability Theory and Statistical Inference: Econometric Modeling with Observational Data*. Cambridge: Cambridge University Press.

Spanos, A., and A. McGuirk (1999). The power of unit root tests revisited. Mimeo, Virginia Polytechnic Institute and State University.

Stigler, S.M. (1986). *The History of Statistics: the Measurement of Uncertainty before 1900*, Cambridge, MA: Harvard University Press.

Wold, H.O. (1938). *A Study in the Analysis of Stationary Time Series* (revised 1954) Uppsala: Almquist and Wicksell.

Yule, G.U. (1921). On the time-correlation problem. *Journal of the Royal Statistical Society* 84, 497–526.

Yule, G.U. (1926). Why do we sometimes get nonsense correlations between time series – a study in sampling and the nature of time series. *Journal of the Royal Statistical Society* 89, 1–64.

Yule, G.U. (1927). On a method of investigating periodicities in disturbed series, with special reference to Wolfer's sunspot numbers. *Philosophical Transactions of the Royal Society* series A, 226, 267–98.

Unit Roots

Herman J. Bierens*

1 INTRODUCTION

In this chapter I will explain the two most frequently applied types of unit root tests, namely the Augmented Dickey–Fuller tests (see Fuller, 1996; Dickey and Fuller, 1979, 1981), and the Phillips–Perron tests (see Phillips, 1987; Phillips and Perron, 1988). The statistics and econometrics levels required for understanding the material below are Hogg and Craig (1978) or a similar level for statistics, and Green (1997) or a similar level for econometrics. The functional central limit theorem (see Billingsley, 1968), which plays a key role in the derivations involved, will be explained in this chapter by showing its analogy with the concept of convergence in distribution of random variables, and by confining the discussion to Gaussian unit root processes.

This chapter is not a review of the vast literature on unit roots. Such a review would entail a long list of descriptions of the many different recipes for unit root testing proposed in the literature, and would leave no space for motivation, let alone proofs. I have chosen for depth rather than breadth, by focusing on the most influential papers on unit root testing, and discussing them in detail, without assuming that the reader has any previous knowledge about this topic.

As an introduction to the concept of a unit root and its consequences, consider the Gaussian AR(1) process $y_t = \beta_0 + \beta_1 y_{t-1} + u_t$, or equivalently $(1 - \beta_1 L)y_t = \beta_0 + u_t$, where L is the lag operator: $Ly_t = y_{t-1}$, and the u_ts are iid $N(0, \sigma^2)$. The lag polynomial $1 - \beta_1 L$ has root equal to $1/\beta_1$. If $|\beta_1| < 1$, then by backwards substitution we can write $y_t = \beta_0/(1 - \beta_1) + \sum_{j=0}^{\infty} \beta_1^j u_{t-j}$, so that y_t is strictly stationary, i.e. for arbitrary natural numbers $m_1 < m_2 < \ldots < m_{k-1}$ the joint distribution of y_t, y_{t-m_1}, y_{t-m_2}, $\ldots$, $y_{t-m_{k-1}}$ does not depend on t, but only on the lags or leads $m_1, m_2, \ldots$, m_{k-1}. Moreover, the distribution of y_t, $t > 0$, conditional on $y_0, y_{-1}, y_{-2}, \ldots$, then converges to the marginal distribution of y_t if $t \to \infty$. In other words, y_t has a vanishing memory: y_t becomes independent of its past, $y_0, y_{-1}, y_{-2}, \ldots$, if $t \to \infty$.

If $\beta_1 = 1$, so that the lag polynomial $1 - \beta_1 L$ has a unit root, then y_t is called a unit root process. In this case the AR(1) process under review becomes $y_t = y_{t-1} +$

$\beta_0 + u_t$, which by backwards substitution yields for $t > 0$, $y_t = y_0 + \beta_0 t + \sum_{j=1}^{t} u_j$. Thus now the distribution of y_t, $t > 0$, conditional on $y_0, y_{-1}, y_{-2}, \ldots$, is $N(y_0 + \beta_0 t, \sigma^2 t)$, so that y_t has no longer a vanishing memory: a shock in y_0 will have a persistent effect on y_t. The former intercept β_0 now becomes the *drift* parameter of the unit root process involved.

It is important to distinguish stationary processes from unit root processes, for the following reasons.

1. Regressions involving unit root processes may give spurious results. If y_t and x_t are mutually independent unit root processes, i.e. y_t is independent of x_{t-j} for all t and j, then the OLS regression of y_t on x_t for $t = 1, \ldots, n$, with or without an intercept, will yield a significant estimate of the slope parameter if n is large: the absolute value of the t-value of the slope converges in probability to ∞ if $n \to \infty$. We then might conclude that y_t depends on x_t, while in reality the y_ts are independent of the x_ts. This phenomenon is called *spurious regression*.[1] One should therefore be very cautious when conducting standard econometric analysis using time series. If the time series involved are unit root processes, naive application of regression analysis may yield nonsense results.

2. For two or more unit root processes there may exist linear combinations which are stationary, and these linear combinations may be interpreted as long-run relationships. This phenomenon is called *cointegration*,[2] and plays a dominant role in modern empirical macroeconomic research.

3. Tests of parameter restrictions in (auto)regressions involving unit root processes have in general different null distributions than in the case of stationary processes. In particular, if one would test the null hypothesis $\beta_1 = 1$ in the above AR(1) model using the usual t-test, the null distribution involved is nonnormal. Therefore, naive application of classical inference may give incorrect results. We will demonstrate the latter first, and in the process derive the Dickey–Fuller test (see Fuller, 1996; Dickey and Fuller, 1979, 1981), by rewriting the AR(1) model as

$$\Delta y_t = y_t - y_{t-1} = \beta_0 + (\beta_1 - 1)y_{t-1} + u_t = \alpha_0 + \alpha_1 y_{t-1} + u_t, \quad (29.1)$$

say, estimating the parameter α_1 by OLS on the basis of observations $y_0, y_1, \ldots, y_n$, and then testing the unit root hypothesis $\alpha_1 = 0$ against the stationarity hypothesis $-2 < \alpha_1 < 0$, using the t-value of α_1. In Section 2 we consider the case where $\alpha_0 = 0$ under both the unit root hypothesis and the stationarity hypothesis. In Section 3 we consider the case where $\alpha_0 = 0$ under the unit root hypothesis but not under the stationarity hypothesis.

The assumption that the error process u_t is independent is quite unrealistic for macroeconomic time series. Therefore, in Sections 4 and 5 this assumption will be relaxed, and two types of appropriate unit root tests will be discussed: the augmented Dickey–Fuller (ADF) tests, and the Phillips–Perron (PP) tests.

In Section 6 we consider the unit root *with* drift case, and we discuss the ADF and PP tests of the unit root with drift hypothesis, against the alternative of trend stationarity.

Finally, Section 7 contains some concluding remarks.

2   THE GAUSSIAN AR(1) CASE WITHOUT INTERCEPT: PART 1

2.1   Introduction

Consider the AR(1) model without intercept, rewritten as[3]

$$\Delta y_t = \alpha_0 y_{t-1} + u_t, \text{ where } u_t \text{ is iid } N(0, \sigma^2), \tag{29.2}$$

and y_t is observed for $t = 1, 2, \ldots, n$. For convenience I will assume that

$$y_t = 0 \text{ for } t \le 0. \tag{29.3}$$

This assumption is, of course, quite unrealistic, but is made for the sake of transparency of the argument, and will appear to be innocent.

The OLS estimator of α_0 is:

$$\hat{\alpha}_0 = \frac{\sum\limits_{t=1}^{n} y_{t-1}\Delta y_t}{\sum\limits_{t=1}^{n} y_{t-1}^2} = \alpha_0 + \frac{\sum\limits_{t=1}^{n} y_{t-1} u_t}{\sum\limits_{t=1}^{n} y_{t-1}^2}. \tag{29.4}$$

If $-2 < \alpha_0 < 0$, so that y_t is stationary, then it is a standard exercise to verify that $\sqrt{n}\,(\hat{\alpha}_0 - \alpha_0) \to N(0, 1 - (1 + \alpha_0)^2)$ in distribution. On the other hand, if $\alpha_0 = 0$, so that y_t is a unit root process, this result reads: $\sqrt{n}\,\hat{\alpha}_0 \to N(0, 0)$ in distribution, hence $\text{plim}_{n\to\infty}\sqrt{n}\,\hat{\alpha}_0 = 0$. However, we show now that a much stronger result holds, namely that $\hat{\rho}_0 \equiv n\hat{\alpha}_0$ converges in distribution, but the limiting distribution involved is nonnormal. Thus, the presence of a unit root is actually advantageous for the efficiency of the OLS estimator $\hat{\alpha}_0$. The main problem is that the t-test of the null hypothesis that $\alpha_0 = 0$ has no longer a standard normal asymptotic null distribution, so that we cannot test for a unit root using standard methods. The same applies to more general unit root processes.

In the unit root case under review we have $y_t = y_{t-1} + u_t = y_0 + \sum_{j=1}^{t} u_j = \sum_{j=1}^{t} u_j$ for $t > 0$, where the last equality involved is due to assumption (29.3). Denoting

$$S_t = 0 \text{ for } t \le 0, \; S_t = \sum_{j=1}^{t} u_j \text{ for } t \ge 1. \tag{29.5}$$

and $\hat{\sigma}^2 = (1/n)\sum_{t=1}^{n} u_t^2$, it follows that

$$\frac{1}{n}\sum_{t=1}^{n} u_t y_{t-1} = \frac{1}{2n}\sum_{t=1}^{n}((u_t + y_{t-1})^2 - y_{t-1}^2 - u_t^2) = \frac{1}{2}\left(\frac{1}{n}\sum_{t=1}^{n} y_t^2 - \frac{1}{n}\sum_{t=1}^{n} y_{t-1}^2 - \frac{1}{n}\sum_{t=1}^{n} u_t^2\right)$$

$$= \frac{1}{2}(y_n^2/n - y_0^2/n - \hat{\sigma}^2) = \frac{1}{2}(S_n^2/n - \hat{\sigma}^2), \tag{29.6}$$

and similarly,

$$\frac{1}{n^2} \sum_{t=1}^{n} y_{t-1}^2 = \frac{1}{n} \sum_{t=1}^{n} (S_{t-1}/\sqrt{n})^2. \tag{29.7}$$

Next, let

$$W_n(x) = S_{[nx]}/(\sigma\sqrt{n}) \quad \text{for } x \in [0, 1], \tag{29.8}$$

where $[z]$ means truncation to the nearest integer $\leq z$. Then we have:[4]

$$\frac{1}{n} \sum_{t=1}^{n} u_t y_{t-1} = \frac{1}{2}(\sigma^2 W_n(1)^2 - \hat{\sigma}^2)$$

$$= \frac{1}{2}(\sigma^2 W_n(1)^2 - \sigma^2 - O_p(1/\sqrt{n})) = \sigma^2 \frac{1}{2}(W_n(1)^2 - 1) + o_p(1), \tag{29.9}$$

and

$$\frac{1}{n^2} \sum_{t=1}^{n} y_{t-1}^2 = \frac{1}{n} \sum_{t=1}^{n} \sigma^2 W_n((t-1)/n)^2 = \int W_n(x)^2 dx, \tag{29.10}$$

where the integral in (29.10) *and below, unless otherwise indicated,* is taken over the unit interval [0, 1]. The last equality in (29.9) follows from the law of large numbers, by which $\hat{\sigma}^2 = \sigma^2 + O_p(1/\sqrt{n})$. The last equality in (29.10) follows from the fact that for any power m,

$$\int W_n(x)^m dx = \int_0^1 W_n(x)^m dx = \frac{1}{n} \int_0^n W_n(z/n)^m dz = \frac{1}{n} \sum_{t=1}^{n} \int_{t-1}^{t} W_n(z/n)^m dz$$

$$= \frac{1}{n^{1+m/2}} \sum_{t=1}^{n} \int_{t-1}^{t} (S_{[z]}/\sigma)^m dz = \frac{1}{n^{1+m/2}} \sum_{t=1}^{n} (S_{t-1}/\sigma)^m. \tag{29.11}$$

Moreover, observe from (29.11), with $m = 1$, that $\int W_n(x)dx$ is a linear combination of iid standard normal random variables, and therefore normal itself, with zero mean and variance

$$E\left(\int W_n(x)dx\right)^2 = \iint E(W_n(x)W_n(y))dxdy$$

$$= \iint \frac{\min([nx], [ny])}{n} dxdy \rightarrow \iint \min(x, y)dxdy = \frac{1}{3}. \tag{29.12}$$

Thus, $\int W_n(x)dx \rightarrow N(0, 1/3)$ in distribution. Since $\int W_n(x)^2dx \geq (\int W_n(x)dx)^2$, it follows therefore that $\int W_n(x)^2dx$ is bounded away from zero:

$$\left(\int W_n(x)^2\,dx\right)^{-1} = O_p(1). \tag{29.13}$$

Combining (29.9), (29.10), and (29.13), we now have:

$$\hat{\rho}_0 \equiv n\hat{\alpha}_0 = \frac{(1/n)\sum_{t=1}^{n} u_t y_{t-1}}{(1/n^2)\sum_{t=1}^{n} y_{t-1}^2} = \frac{(1/2)(W_n(1)^2 - 1) + o_p(1)}{\int W_n(x)^2\,dx} = \frac{1}{2}\left(\frac{W_n(1)^2 - 1}{\int W_n(x)^2\,dx}\right) + o_p(1).$$

$$\tag{29.14}$$

This result does not depend on assumption (29.3).

2.2   Weak convergence of random functions

In order to establish the limiting distribution of (29.14), and other asymptotic results, we need to extend the well known concept of convergence in distribution of random variables to convergence in distribution of a sequence of random functions. Recall that for random variables X_n, X, $X_n \rightarrow X$ in distribution if the distribution function $F_n(x)$ of X_n converges pointwise to the distribution function $F(x)$ of X in the continuity points of $F(x)$. Moreover, recall that distribution functions are uniquely associated to probability measures on the Borel sets,[5] i.e. there exists one and only one probability measure $\mu_n(B)$ on the Borel sets B such that $F_n(x) = \mu_n((-\infty, x])$, and similarly, $F(x)$ is uniquely associated to a probability measure μ on the Borel sets, such that $F(x) = \mu((-\infty, x])$. The statement $X_n \rightarrow X$ in distribution can now be expressed in terms of the probability measures μ_n and $\mu : \mu_n(B) \rightarrow \mu(B)$ for all Borel sets B with boundary δB satisfying $\mu(\delta B) = 0$.

In order to extend the latter to random functions, we need to define Borel sets of functions. For our purpose it suffices to define Borel sets of continuous functions on $[0, 1]$. Let $C[0, 1]$ be the set of all continuous functions on the unit interval $[0, 1]$. Define the distance between two functions f and g in $C[0, 1]$ by the sup-norm: $\rho(f, g) = \sup_{0\leq x\leq 1}|f(x) - g(x)|$. Endowed with this norm, the set $C[0, 1]$ becomes a metric space, for which we can define open subsets, similarly to the concept of an open subset of $\mathbb{R}$: A set B in $C[0, 1]$ is open if for each function f in B we can find an $\varepsilon > 0$ such that $\{g \in C[0, 1] : \rho(g, f) < \varepsilon\} \subset B$. Now the smallest σ-algebra of subsets of $C[0, 1]$ containing the collection of all open subsets of $C[0, 1]$ is just the collection of Borel sets of functions in $C[0, 1]$.

A random element of $C[0, 1]$ is a random function $W(x)$, say, on $[0, 1]$, which is continuous with probability 1. For such a random element W, say, we can define a probability measure μ on the Borel sets B in $C[0, 1]$ by $\mu(B) = P(W \in B)$. Now a sequence W_n^* of random elements of $C[0, 1]$, with corresponding probability measures μ_n, is said to converge weakly to a random element W of $C[0, 1]$, with corresponding probability measure μ, if for each Borel set B in $C[0, 1]$ with boundary δB satisfying $\mu(\delta B) = 0$, we have $\mu_n(B) \to \mu(B)$. This is usually denoted by: $W_n^* \Rightarrow W$(on $[0, 1]$). Thus, weak convergence is the extension to random functions of the concept of convergence in distribution.

In order to verify that $W_n^* \Rightarrow W$ on $[0, 1]$, we have to verify two conditions. See Billingsley (1963). First, we have to verify that the finite distributions of W_n^* converge to the corresponding finite distributions of W, i.e. for arbitrary points $x_1, \ldots, x_m$ in $[0, 1]$, $(W_n^*(x_1), \ldots, W_n^*(x_m)) \Rightarrow (W(x_1), \ldots, W(x_m))$ in distribution. Second, we have to verify that W_n^* is tight. Tightness is the extension of the concept of stochastic boundedness to random functions: for each ε in $[0, 1]$ there exists a compact (Borel) set K in $C[0, 1]$ such that $\mu_n(K) > 1 - \varepsilon$ for $n = 1, 2, \ldots$ Since convergence in distribution implies stochastic boundedness, we cannot have convergence in distribution without stochastic boundedness, and the same applies to weak convergence: tightness is a necessary condition for weak convergence.

As is well known, if $X_n \to X$ in distribution, and Φ is a continuous mapping from the support of X into a Euclidean space, then by Slutsky's theorem, $\Phi(X_n) \to \Phi(X)$ in distribution. A similar result holds for weak convergence, which is known as the continuous mapping theorem: if Φ is a continuous mapping from $C[0, 1]$ into a Euclidean space, then $W_n^* \Rightarrow W$ implies $\Phi(W_n^*) \to \Phi(W)$ in distribution. For example, the integral $\Phi(f) = \int f(x)^2 dx$ with $f \in C[0, 1]$ is a continuous mapping from $C[0, 1]$ into the real line, hence $W_n^* \Rightarrow W$ implies that $\int W_n^*(x)^2 dx \to \int W(x)^2 dx$ in distribution.

The random function W_n defined by (29.8) is a step function on $[0, 1]$, and therefore not a random element of $C[0, 1]$. However, the steps involved can be smoothed by piecewise linear interpolation, yielding a random element W_n^* of $C[0, 1]$ such that $\sup_{0 \le x \le 1} | W_n^*(x) - W_n(x) | = o_p(1)$. The finite distributions of W_n^* are therefore asymptotically the same as the finite distributions of W_n. In order to analyze the latter, redefine W_n as

$$W_n(x) = \frac{1}{\sqrt{n}} \sum_{t=1}^{[nx]} e_t \text{ for } x \in [n^{-1}, 1], \quad W_n(x) = 0 \text{ for } x \in [0, n^{-1}), \quad e_t \text{ is iid } N(0, 1).$$

$$(29.15)$$

(Thus, $e_t = u_t / \sigma$), and let

$$W_n^*(x) = W_n\left(\frac{t-1}{n}\right) + (nx - (t - 1))\left(W_n\left(\frac{t}{n}\right) - W_n\left(\frac{t-1}{n}\right)\right)$$

$$= W_n(x) + (nx - (t - 1))\frac{e_t}{\sqrt{n}} \text{ for } x \in \left(\frac{t-1}{n}, \frac{t}{n}\right], t = 1, \ldots, n, W_n^*(0) = 0.$$

$$(29.16)$$

Then

$$\sup_{0 \leq x \leq 1} | W_n^*(x) - W_n(x) | \leq \frac{\max\limits_{1 \leq t \leq n} |e_t|}{\sqrt{n}} = o_p(1). \tag{29.17}$$

The latter conclusion is not too hard an exercise.[6]

It is easy to verify that for *fixed* $0 \leq x < y \leq 1$ we have

$$\begin{pmatrix} W_n(x) \\ W_n(y) - W_n(x) \end{pmatrix} = \frac{1}{\sqrt{n}} \begin{pmatrix} \sum\limits_{t=1}^{[nx]} e_t \\ \sum\limits_{t=[nx]+1}^{[ny]} e_t \end{pmatrix} \sim N_2 \left(\begin{pmatrix} 0 \\ 0 \end{pmatrix}, \begin{pmatrix} \dfrac{[nx]}{n} & 0 \\ 0 & \dfrac{[ny] - [nx]}{n} \end{pmatrix} \right)$$

$$\rightarrow \begin{pmatrix} W(x) \\ W(y) - W(x) \end{pmatrix} \text{ in distribution,} \tag{29.18}$$

where $W(x)$ is a random function on $[0, 1]$ such that for $0 \leq x < y \leq 1$,

$$\begin{pmatrix} W(x) \\ W(y) - W(x) \end{pmatrix} \sim N_2 \left(\begin{pmatrix} 0 \\ 0 \end{pmatrix}, \begin{pmatrix} x & 0 \\ 0 & y - x \end{pmatrix} \right). \tag{29.19}$$

This random function $W(x)$ is called a standard Wiener process, or Brownian motion. Similarly, for arbitrary fixed x, y in $[0, 1]$,

$$\begin{pmatrix} W_n(x) \\ W_n(y) \end{pmatrix} \rightarrow \begin{pmatrix} W(x) \\ W(y) \end{pmatrix} \sim N_2 \left(\begin{pmatrix} 0 \\ 0 \end{pmatrix}, \begin{pmatrix} x & \min(x, y) \\ \min(x, y) & y \end{pmatrix} \right) \text{ in distribution} \tag{29.20}$$

and it follows from (29.17) that the same applies to W_n^*. Therefore, the finite distributions of W_n^* converge to the corresponding finite distributions of W. Also, it can be shown that W_n^* is tight (see Billingsley, 1963). Hence, $W_n^* \Rightarrow W$, and by the continuous mapping theorem,

$$\left(W_n^*(1), \int W_n^*(x)dx, \int W_n^*(x)^2 dx, \int x W_n^*(x)dx \right)^T \rightarrow$$

$$\left(W(1), \int W(x)dx, \int W(x)^2 dx, \int x W(x)dx \right)^T \tag{29.21}$$

in distribution. This result, together with (29.17), implies that:

Lemma 1.   For W_n defined by (29.15), $(W_n(1), \int W_n(x)dx, \int W_n(x)^2 dx, \int x W_n(x)dx)^T$ converges jointly in distribution to $(W(1), \int W(x)dx, \int W(x)^2 dx, \int x W(x)dx)^T$.

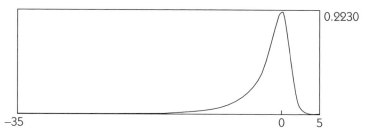

Figure 29.1 Density of ρ_0

2.3 Asymptotic null distributions

Using Lemma 1, it follows now straightforwardly from (29.14) that:

$$\hat{\rho}_0 \equiv n\hat{\alpha}_0 \rightarrow \rho_0 \equiv \frac{1}{2}\left(\frac{W(1)^2 - 1}{\int W(x)^2 dx}\right) \text{ in distribution.} \tag{29.22}$$

The density[7] of the distribution of ρ_0 is displayed in Figure 29.1, which clearly shows that the distribution involved is nonnormal and asymmetric, with a fat left tail.

Also the limiting distribution of the usual t-test statistic of the null hypothesis $\alpha_0 = 0$ is nonnormal. First, observe that due to (29.10), (29.22), and Lemma 1, the residual sum of squares (RSS) of the regression (29.2) under the unit root hypothesis is:

$$\text{RSS} = \sum_{t=1}^{n}(\Delta y_t - \hat{\alpha}_0 y_{t-1})^2 = \sum_{t=1}^{n} u_t^2 - (n\hat{\alpha}_0)^2(1/n^2)\sum_{t=1}^{n} y_{t-1}^2 = \sum_{t=1}^{n} u_t^2 + O_p(1).$$

$$\tag{29.23}$$

Hence $\text{RSS}/(n-1) = \sigma^2 + O_p(1/n)$. Therefore, similarly to (29.14) and (29.22), the Dickey–Fuller t-statistic $\hat{\tau}_0$ involved satisfies:

$$\hat{\tau}_0 \equiv n\hat{\alpha}_0 \frac{\sqrt{(1/n^2)\sum_{t=1}^{n} y_{t-1}^2}}{\sqrt{\text{RSS}/(n-1)}} = \frac{(W_n(1)^2 - 1)/2}{\sqrt{\int W_n(x)^2 dx}} + o_p(1) \rightarrow$$

$$\tau_0 \equiv \frac{(W(1)^2 - 1)/2}{\sqrt{\int W(x)^2 dx}} \text{ in distribution.} \tag{29.24}$$

Note that the unit root tests based on the statistics $\hat{\rho}_0 \equiv n\hat{\alpha}_0$ and $\hat{\tau}_0$ are left-sided: under the alternative of stationarity, $-2 < \alpha_0 < 0$, we have $\text{plim}_{n\rightarrow\infty}\hat{\alpha}_0 = \alpha_0 \leq 0$, hence $\hat{\rho}_0 \rightarrow -\infty$ in probability at rate n, and $\hat{\tau}_0 \rightarrow -\infty$ in probability at rate $\sqrt{n}$.

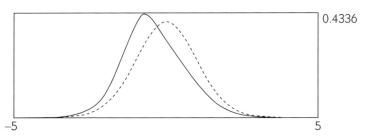

Figure 29.2   Density of τ_0 compared with the standard normal density (dashed curve)

The nonnormality of the limiting distributions ρ_0 and τ_0 is no problem, though, as long one is aware of it. The distributions involved are free of nuisance parameters, and asymptotic critical values of the unit root tests $\hat{\rho}_0$ and $\hat{\tau}_0$ can easily be tabulated, using Monte Carlo simulation. In particular,

$$P(\tau_0 \leq -1.95) = 0.05, \quad P(\tau_0 \leq -1.62) = 0.10, \tag{29.25}$$

(see Fuller, 1996, p. 642), whereas for a standard normal random variable e,

$$P(e \leq -1.64) = 0.05, \ P(e \leq -1.28) = 0.10. \tag{29.26}$$

In Figure 29.2 the density of τ_0 is compared with the standard normal density. We see that the density of τ_0 is shifted to left of the standard normal density, which causes the difference between (29.25) and (29.26). Using the left-sided standard normal test would result in a type 1 error of about twice the size: compare (29.26) with

$$P(\tau_0 \leq -1.64) \approx 0.09, \quad P(\tau_0 \leq -1.28) \approx 0.18 \tag{29.27}$$

3   The Gaussian AR(1) Case with Intercept under the Alternative of Stationarity

If under the stationarity hypothesis the AR(1) process has an intercept, but not under the unit root hypothesis, the AR(1) model that covers both the null and the alternative is:

$$\Delta y_t = \alpha_0 + \alpha_1 y_{t-1} + u_t, \quad \text{where } \alpha_0 = -c\alpha_1. \tag{29.28}$$

If $-2 < \alpha_1 < 0$, then the process y_t is stationary around the constant c:

$$y_t = -c\alpha_1 + (1 + \alpha_1)y_{t-1} + u_t = \sum_{j=0}^{\infty} (1 + \alpha_1)^j(-c\alpha_1 + u_{t-j}) = c + \sum_{j=0}^{\infty} (1 + \alpha_1)^j u_{t-j}, \tag{29.29}$$

hence $E(y_t^2) = c^2 + (1 - (1 + \alpha_1)^2)^{-1}\sigma^2$, $E(y_t y_{t-1}) = c^2 + (1 + \alpha_1)(1 - (1 + \alpha_1)^2)^{-1}\sigma^2$, and

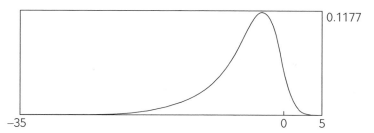

Figure 29.3 Density of ρ_1

$$\operatorname*{plim}_{n\to\infty} \hat{\alpha}_0 = \frac{E(y_t y_{t-1})}{E(y_{t-1}^2)} - 1 = \frac{\alpha_1}{1 + (c/\sigma)^2(1 - (1 + \alpha_1)^2)}, \tag{29.30}$$

which approaches zero if $c^2/\sigma^2 \to \infty$. Therefore, the power of the test $\hat{\rho}_0$ will be low if the variance of u_t is small relative to $[E(y_t)]^2$. The same applies to the t-test $\hat{\tau}_0$. We should therefore use the OLS estimator of α_1 and the corresponding t-value in the regression of Δy_t on y_{t-1} *with* intercept.

Denoting $\bar{y}_{-1} = (1/n)\sum_{t=1}^{n} y_{t-1}$, $\bar{u} = (1/n)\sum_{t=1}^{n} u_t$, the OLS estimator of α_1 is:

$$\hat{\alpha}_1 = \alpha_1 + \frac{\displaystyle\sum_{t=1}^{n} u_t y_{t-1} - n\bar{u}\bar{y}_{-1}}{\displaystyle\sum_{t=1}^{n} y_{t-1}^2 - n\bar{y}_{-1}^2}. \tag{29.31}$$

Since by (29.8), $\sqrt{n}\bar{u} = \sigma W_n(1)$, and under the null hypothesis $\alpha_1 = 0$ and the maintained hypothesis (29.3),

$$\bar{y}_{-1}/\sqrt{n} = \frac{1}{n\sqrt{n}}\sum_{t=1}^{n} S_{t-1} = \sigma \int W_n(x)dx, \tag{29.32}$$

where the last equality follows from (29.11) with $m = 1$, it follows from Lemma 1, similarly to (29.14) and (29.22) that

$$\hat{\rho}_1 \equiv n\hat{\alpha}_1 = \frac{(1/2)(W_n(1)^2 - 1) - W_n(1)\int W_n(x)dx}{\int W_n(x)^2 dx - (\int W_n(x)dx)^2} + o_p(1)$$

$$\to \rho_1 \equiv \frac{(1/2)(W(1)^2 - 1) - W(1)\int W(x)dx}{\int W(x)^2 dx - (\int W(x)dx)^2} \quad \text{in distribution.} \tag{29.33}$$

The density of ρ_1 is displayed in Figure 29.3. Comparing Figures 29.1 and 29.3, we see that the density of ρ_1 is farther left of zero than the density of ρ_0, and has a fatter left tail.

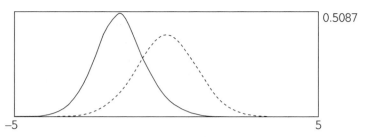

0.5087

−5   5

Figure 29.4   Density of τ_1 compared with the standard normal density (dashed curve)

As to the *t*-value $\hat{\tau}_1$ of α_1 in this case, it follows similarly to (29.24) and (29.33) that under the unit root hypothesis,

$$\hat{\tau}_1 \to \tau_1 \equiv \frac{(1/2)(W(1)^2 - 1) - W(1)\int W(x)dx}{\sqrt{\int W(x)^2 dx - (\int W(x)dx)^2}} \quad \text{in distribution.} \qquad (29.34)$$

Again, the results (29.33) and (29.34) do not hinge on assumption (29.3).

The distribution of τ_1 is even farther away from the normal distribution than the distribution of τ_0, as follows from comparison of (29.26) with

$$P(\tau_1 \le -2.86) = 0.05, \quad P(\tau_1 \le -2.57) = 0.1 \qquad (29.35)$$

See again Fuller (1996, p. 642). This is corroborated by Figure 29.4, where the density of τ_1 is compared with the standard normal density.

We see that the density of τ_1 is shifted even more to the left of the standard normal density than in Figure 29.2, hence the left-sided standard normal test would result in a dramatically higher type 1 error than in the case without an intercept: compare

$$P(\tau_1 \le -1.64) \approx 0.46, \quad P(\tau_1 \le -1.28) \approx 0.64 \qquad (29.36)$$

with (29.26) and (29.27).

4   GENERAL AR PROCESSES WITH A UNIT ROOT, AND THE AUGMENTED DICKEY–FULLER TEST

The assumption made in Sections 2 and 3 that the data-generating process is an AR(1) process, is not very realistic for macroeconomic time series, because even after differencing most of these time series will still display a fair amount of dependence. Therefore we now consider an AR(p) process:

$$y_t = \beta_0 + \sum_{j=1}^{p} \beta_j y_{t-j} + u_t, \quad u_t \sim \text{iid } N(0, \sigma^2). \qquad (29.37)$$

By recursively replacing y_{t-j} by $\Delta y_{t-j} + y_{t-1-j}$ for $j = 0, 1, \ldots, p - 1$, this model can be written as

$$\Delta y_t = \alpha_0 + \sum_{j=1}^{p-1} \alpha_j \Delta y_{t-j} + \alpha_p y_{t-p} + u_t, \quad u_t \sim \text{iid } N(0, \sigma^2), \tag{29.38}$$

where $\alpha_0 = \beta_0$, $\alpha_j = \sum_{i=1}^{j} \beta_i - 1$, $j = 1, \ldots, p$. Alternatively and equivalently, by recursively replacing y_{t-p+j} by $y_{t-p+j+1} - \Delta y_{t-p+j+1}$ for $j = 0, 1, \ldots, p - 1$, model (29.37) can also be written as

$$\Delta y_t = \alpha_0 + \sum_{j=1}^{p-1} \alpha_j \Delta y_{t-j} + \alpha_p y_{t-1} + u_t, \quad u_t \sim \text{iid } N(0, \sigma^2), \tag{29.39}$$

where now $\alpha_j = -\sum_{i=1}^{j} \beta_i$, $j = 1, \ldots, p - 1$, $\alpha_p = \sum_{i=1}^{p} \beta_i - 1$.

If the AP(p) process (29.37) has a unit root, then clearly $\alpha_p = 0$ in (29.38) and (29.39). If the process (29.37) is stationary, i.e. all the roots of the lag polynomial $1 - \sum_{i=1}^{p} \beta_j L^j$ lie outside the complex unit circle, then $\alpha_p = \sum_{i=1}^{p} \beta_j - 1 < 0$ in (29.38) and (29.39).[8] The unit root hypothesis can therefore be tested by testing the null hypothesis $\alpha_p = 0$ against the alternative hypothesis $\alpha_p < 0$, using the t-value $\hat{\tau}_p$ of α_p in model (29.38) or model (29.39). This test is known as the augmented Dickey–Fuller (ADF) test.

We will show now for the case $p = 2$, with intercept under the alternative, i.e.

$$\Delta y_t = \alpha_0 + \alpha_1 \Delta y_{t-1} + \alpha_2 y_{t-1} + u_t, \quad u_t \sim \text{iid } N(0, \sigma^2), t = 1, \ldots, n. \tag{29.40}$$

that under the unit root (without drift[9]) hypothesis the limiting distribution of $n\hat{\alpha}_p$ is proportional to the limiting distribution in (29.33), and the limiting distribution of $\hat{\tau}_p$ is the same as in (29.34).

Under the unit root hypothesis, i.e. $\alpha_0 = \alpha_2 = 0$, $|\alpha_1| < 1$, we have

$$\Delta y_t = \alpha_1 \Delta y_{t-1} + u_t = (1 - \alpha_1 L)^{-1} u_t = (1 - \alpha_1)^{-1} u_t + [(1 - \alpha_1 L)^{-1} - (1 - \alpha_1)^{-1}] u_t$$

$$= (1 - \alpha_1)^{-1} u_t - \alpha_1 (1 - \alpha_1)^{-1} (1 - \alpha_1 L)^{-1} (1 - L) u_t = (1 - \alpha_1)^{-1} u_t + v_t - v_{t-1}, \tag{29.41}$$

say, where $v_t = -\alpha_1 (1 - \alpha_1)^{-1} (1 - \alpha_1 L)^{-1} u_t = -\alpha_1 (1 - \alpha_1)^{-1} \sum_{j=0}^{\infty} \alpha_1^j u_{t-j}$ is a stationary process. Hence:

$$y_t / \sqrt{n} = y_0 / \sqrt{n} + v_t / \sqrt{n} - v_0 / \sqrt{n} + (1 - \alpha_1)^{-1} (1/\sqrt{n}) \sum_{j=1}^{t} u_j$$

$$= y_0 / \sqrt{n} + v_t / \sqrt{n} - v_0 / \sqrt{n} + \sigma (1 - \alpha_1)^{-1} W_n(t/n) \tag{29.42}$$

and therefore, similarly to (29.6), (29.7), and (29.32), it follows that

$$(1/n) \sum_{t-1}^{n} y_{t-1} / \sqrt{n} = \sigma (1 - \alpha_1)^{-1} \int W_n(x) dx + o_p(1), \tag{29.43}$$

$$(1/n^2) \sum_{t-1}^{n} y_{t-1}^2 = \sigma^2(1 - \alpha_1)^{-2} \int W_n(x)^2 dx + o_p(1), \tag{29.44}$$

$$(1/n) \sum_{t=1}^{n} u_t y_{t-1} = (1/n) \sum_{t=1}^{n} u_t \left((1 - \alpha_1)^{-1} \sum_{j=1}^{t-1} u_j + y_0 + v_{t-1} - v_0 \right)$$

$$= (1 - \alpha_1)^{-1}(1/n) \sum_{t=1}^{n} u_t \sum_{j=1}^{t-1} u_j + (y_0 - v_0)(1/n) \sum_{t=1}^{n} u_t + (1/n) \sum_{t=1}^{n} u_t v_{t-1}$$

$$= \frac{(1 - \alpha_1)^{-1}\sigma^2}{2} (W_n(1)^2 - 1) + o_p(1). \tag{29.45}$$

Moreover,

$$\plim_{n \to \infty} (1/n) \sum_{t=1}^{n} \Delta y_{t-1} = E(\Delta y_t) = 0, \quad \plim_{n \to \infty} (1/n) \sum_{t=1}^{n} (\Delta y_{t-1})^2 = E(\Delta y_t)^2 = \sigma^2/(1 - \alpha_1^2) \tag{29.46}$$

and

$$(1/n) \sum_{t=1}^{n} y_{t-1} \Delta y_{t-1} = (1/n) \sum_{t=1}^{n} (\Delta y_{t-1})^2 + (1/n) \sum_{t=1}^{n} y_{t-2} \Delta y_{t-1}$$

$$= (1/n) \sum_{t=1}^{n} (\Delta y_{t-1})^2 + \frac{1}{2} \left((1/n) \sum_{t=1}^{n} y_{t-1}^2 - (1/n) \sum_{t=1}^{n} y_{t-2}^2 - (1/n) \sum_{t=1}^{n} (\Delta y_{t-1})^2 \right)$$

$$= \frac{1}{2} \left((1/n) \sum_{t=1}^{n} (\Delta y_{t-1})^2 + y_{n-1}^2/n - y_{-1}^2/n \right)$$

$$= \frac{1}{2} (\sigma^2/(1 - \alpha_1^2) + \sigma^2(1 - \alpha_1)^{-2} W_n(1)^2) + o_p(1) \tag{29.47}$$

hence

$$(1/n) \sum_{t=1}^{n} y_{t-1} \Delta y_{t-1}/\sqrt{n} = O_p(1/\sqrt{n}). \tag{29.48}$$

Next, let $\hat{\alpha} = (\hat{\alpha}_0, \hat{\alpha}_1, \hat{\alpha}_2)^T$ be the OLS estimator of $\alpha = (\alpha_0, \alpha_1, \alpha_2)^T$. Under the unit root hypothesis we have

$$\begin{pmatrix} \sqrt{n}\hat{\alpha}_0 \\ \sqrt{n}(\hat{\alpha}_1 - \alpha_1) \\ n\hat{\alpha}_2 \end{pmatrix} = \sqrt{n} D_n \hat{\Sigma}_{xx}^{-1} \hat{\Sigma}_{xu} = (D_n^{-1} \hat{\Sigma}_{xx} D_n^{-1})^{-1} \sqrt{n} D_n^{-1} \hat{\Sigma}_{xu}, \tag{29.49}$$

where

$$D_n = \begin{pmatrix} 1 & 0 & 0 \\ 0 & 1 & 0 \\ 0 & 0 & \sqrt{n} \end{pmatrix}, \tag{29.50}$$

$$\hat{\Sigma}_{xx} = \begin{pmatrix} 1 & (1/n)\sum_{t=1}^{n}\Delta y_{t-1} & (1/n)\sum_{t=1}^{n}y_{t-1} \\ (1/n)\sum_{t=1}^{n}\Delta y_{t-1} & (1/n)\sum_{t=1}^{n}(\Delta y_{t-1})^2 & (1/n)\sum_{t=1}^{n}y_{t-1}\Delta y_{t-1} \\ (1/n)\sum_{t=1}^{n}y_{t-1} & (1/n)\sum_{t=1}^{n}y_{t-1}\Delta y_{t-1} & (1/n)\sum_{t=1}^{n}y_{t-1}^2 \end{pmatrix}, \tag{29.51}$$

and

$$\hat{\Sigma}_{xu} = \begin{pmatrix} (1/n)\sum_{t=1}^{n}u_t \\ (1/n)\sum_{t=1}^{n}u_t\Delta y_{t-1} \\ (1/n)\sum_{t=1}^{n}u_t y_{t-1} \end{pmatrix}. \tag{29.52}$$

It follows from (29.43) through (29.48) that

$$D_n^{-1}\hat{\Sigma}_{xx}D_n^{-1} = \begin{pmatrix} 1 & 0 & \sigma(1-\alpha_1)^{-1}\int W_n(x)dx \\ 0 & \sigma^2/(1-\alpha_1^2) & 0 \\ \sigma(1-\alpha_1)^{-1}\int W_n(x)dx & 0 & \sigma^2(1-\alpha_1)^{-2}\int W_n(x)^2 dx \end{pmatrix} + o_p(1), \tag{29.53}$$

hence, using the easy equality

$$\begin{pmatrix} 1 & 0 & a \\ 0 & b & 0 \\ a & 0 & c \end{pmatrix}^{-1} = \frac{1}{c-a^2}\begin{pmatrix} c & 0 & -a \\ 0 & b^{-1}(c-a^2) & 0 \\ -a & 0 & 1 \end{pmatrix},$$

it follows that

$$(D_n^{-1}\hat{\Sigma}_{xx}D_n^{-1})^{-1} = \frac{\sigma^{-2}(1-\alpha_1)^2}{\int W_n(x)^2 dx - (\int W_n(x)dx)^2}$$

$$\times \begin{pmatrix} \sigma^2(1-\alpha_1)^{-2}\int W_n(x)^2 dx & 0 & -\sigma(1-\alpha_1)^{-1}\int W_n(x)dx \\ 0 & \dfrac{\int W_n(x)^2 dx - (\int W_n(x)dx)}{(1-\alpha_1^2)(1-\alpha_1)^2} & 0 \\ -\sigma(1-\alpha_1)^{-1}\int W_n(x)dx & 0 & 1 \end{pmatrix}$$

$$+ o_p(1). \tag{29.54}$$

Moreover, it follows from (29.8) and (29.45) that

$$
\sqrt{n}D_n^{-1}\hat{\Sigma}_{xu} = \begin{pmatrix} \sigma W_n(1) \\ (1/\sqrt{n})\sum_{t=1}^{n} u_t \Delta y_{t-1} \\ \sigma^2(1 - \alpha_1)^{-2}(W_n(1)^2 - 1)/2 \end{pmatrix} + o_p(1). \tag{29.55}
$$

Combining (29.49), (29.54) and (29.55), and using Lemma 1, it follows now easily that

$$
\frac{n\hat{\alpha}_2}{1 - \alpha_1} = \frac{\frac{1}{2}(W_n(1)^2 - 1) - W_n(1)\int W_n(x)dx}{\int W_n(x)^2 dx - (\int W_n(x)dx)^2} + o_p(1) \to \rho_1 \text{ in distribution}, \tag{29.56}
$$

where ρ_1 is defined in (29.33). Along the same lines it can be shown:

Theorem 1. Let y_t be generated by (29.39), and let $\hat{\alpha}_p$ be the OLS estimator of α_p. Under the unit root hypothesis, i.e. $\alpha_p = 0$ and $\alpha_0 = 0$, the following hold: If model (29.39) is estimated without intercept, then $n\hat{\alpha}_p \to (1 - \sum_{j=1}^{p-1}\alpha_j)\rho_0$ in distribution, where ρ_0 is defined in (29.22). If model (29.39) is estimated with intercept, then $n\hat{\alpha}_p \to (1 - \sum_{j=1}^{p-1}\alpha_j)\rho_1$ in distribution, where ρ_1 is defined in (29.33). Moreover, under the stationarity hypothesis, $\text{plim}_{n\to\infty}\hat{\alpha}_p = \alpha_p < 0$, hence $\text{plim}_{n\to\infty}\hat{\alpha}_p = -\infty$, provided that in the case where the model is estimated without intercept this intercept, α_0, is indeed zero.

Due to the factor $1 - \sum_{j=1}^{p-1}\alpha_j$ in the limiting distribution of $n\hat{\alpha}_p$ under the unit root hypothesis, we cannot use $n\hat{\alpha}_p$ directly as a unit root test. However, it can be shown that under the unit root hypothesis this factor can be consistently estimated by $1 - \sum_{j=1}^{p-1}\hat{\alpha}_j$, hence we can use $n\hat{\alpha}_p/|1 - \sum_{j=1}^{p-1}\hat{\alpha}_j|$ as a unit root test statistic, with limiting distribution given by (29.22) or (29.33). The reason for the absolute value is that under the alternative of stationarity the probability limit of $1 - \sum_{j=1}^{p-1}\hat{\alpha}_j$ may be negative.[10]

The actual ADF test is based on the t-value of α_p, because the factor $1 - \sum_{j=1}^{p-1}\alpha_j$ will cancel out in the limiting distribution involved. We will show this for the AR(2) case.

First, it is not too hard to verify from (29.43) through (29.48), and (29.54), that the residual sum of squares RSS of the regression (29.40) satisfies:

$$
\text{RSS} = \sum_{t=1}^{n} u_t^2 + O_p(1). \tag{29.57}
$$

This result carries over to the general AR(p) case, and also holds under the stationarity hypothesis. Moreover, under the unit root hypothesis it follows easily from (29.54) and (29.57) that the OLS standard error, s_2, say, of $\hat{\alpha}_2$ in model (29.40) satisfies:

$$ns_2 = \sqrt{\frac{(\text{RSS}/(n-3))\sigma^{-2}(1-\alpha_1)^2}{\int W_n(x)^2 \, dx - (\int W_n(x) dx)^2}} + o_p(1)$$

$$= \frac{1-\alpha_1}{\sqrt{\int W_n(x)^2 \, dx - (\int W_n(x) dx)^2}} + o_p(1), \tag{29.58}$$

hence it follows from (29.56) that the t-value $\hat{t}_2$ of $\hat{\alpha}_2$ in model (29.40) satisfies (29.34). Again, this result carries over to the general AR(p) case:

Theorem 2. Let y_t be generated by (29.39), and let $\hat{t}_p$ be t-value of the OLS estimator of α_p. Under the unit root hypothesis, i.e. $\alpha_p = 0$ and $\alpha_0 = 0$, the following hold: If model (29.39) is estimated without intercept, then $\hat{t}_p \to \tau_0$ in distribution, where τ_0 is defined in (29.24). If model (29.39) is estimated with intercept, then $\hat{t}_p \to \tau_1$ in distribution, where τ_1 is defined in (29.34). Moreover, under the stationarity hypothesis, $\text{plim}_{n\to\infty} \hat{t}_p/\sqrt{n} < 0$, hence $\text{plim}_{n\to\infty} \hat{t}_p = -\infty$, provided that in the case where the model is estimated without intercept this intercept, α_0, is indeed zero.

5 ARIMA PROCESSES, AND THE PHILLIPS–PERRON TEST

The ADF test requires that the order p of the AR model involved is finite, and correctly specified, i.e. the specified order should not be smaller than the actual order. In order to analyze what happens if p is misspecified, suppose that the actual data generating process is given by (29.39) with $\alpha_0 = \alpha_2 = 0$ and $p > 1$, and that the unit root hypothesis is tested on the basis of the assumption that $p = 1$. Denoting $e_t = u_t/\sigma$, model (29.39) with $\alpha_0 = \alpha_2 = 0$ can be rewritten as

$$\Delta y_t = \left(\sum_{j=0}^{\infty} \gamma_j L^j \right) e_t = \gamma(L)e_t, \quad e_t \sim \text{iid } N(0, 1), \tag{29.59}$$

where $\gamma(L) = \alpha(L)^{-1}$, with $\alpha(L) = 1 - \sum_{j=1}^{p-1} \alpha_j L^j$. This data generating process can be nested in the auxiliary model

$$\Delta y_t = \alpha_0 + \alpha_1 y_{t-1} + u_t, \quad u_t = \gamma(L)e_t, \quad e_t \sim \text{iid } N(0, 1). \tag{29.60}$$

We will now determine the limiting distribution of the OLS estimate $\hat{\alpha}_1$ and corresponding t-value $\hat{t}_1$ of the parameter α_1 in the regression (29.60), derived under the assumption that the u_ts are independent, while in reality (29.59) holds.

Similarly to (29.41) we can write $\Delta y_t = \gamma(1)e_t + v_t - v_{t-1}$, where $v_t = [(\gamma(L) - \gamma(1))/(1 - L)]e_t$ is a stationary process. The latter follows from the fact that by construction the lag polynomial $\gamma(L) - \gamma(1)$ has a unit root, and therefore contains a factor $1 - L$. Next, redefining $W_n(x)$ as

$$W_n(x) = (1/\sqrt{n}) \sum_{t=1}^{[nx]} e_t \quad \text{if } x \in [n^{-1}, 1], \quad W_n(x) = 0 \quad \text{if } x \in [0, n^{-1}), \tag{29.61}$$

it follows similarly to (29.42) that

$$y_t/\sqrt{n} = y_0/\sqrt{n} + v_t/\sqrt{n} - v_0/\sqrt{n} + \gamma(1)W_n(t/n),\qquad(29.62)$$

hence

$$y_n/\sqrt{n} = \gamma(1)W_n(1) + O_p(1/\sqrt{n}),\qquad(29.63)$$

and similarly to (29.43) and (29.44) that

$$\bar{y}_{-1}/\sqrt{n} = \frac{1}{n}\sum_{t=1}^{n} y_{t-1}/\sqrt{n} = \gamma(1)\int W_n(x)dx + o_p(1),\qquad(29.64)$$

and

$$\frac{1}{n^2}\sum_{t=1}^{n} y_{t-1}^2 = \gamma(1)^2\int W_n(x)^2 dx + o_p(1).\qquad(29.65)$$

Moreover, similarly to (29.6) we have

$$\frac{1}{n}\sum_{t=1}^{n}(\Delta y_t)y_{t-1} = \frac{1}{2}\left(y_n^2/n - y_0^2/n - \frac{1}{n}\sum_{t=1}^{n}(\Delta y_t)^2\right)$$

$$= \frac{1}{2}\left(\gamma(1)^2 W_n(1)^2 - \frac{1}{n}\sum_{t=1}^{n}(\gamma(L)e_t)^2\right) + o_p(1)$$

$$= \gamma(1)^2\frac{1}{2}(W_n(1) - \lambda) + o_p(1),\qquad(29.66)$$

where

$$\lambda = \frac{E(\gamma(L)e_t)^2}{\gamma(1)^2} = \frac{\displaystyle\sum_{j=0}^{\infty}\gamma_j^2}{\left(\displaystyle\sum_{j=0}^{\infty}\gamma_j\right)^2}.\qquad(29.67)$$

Therefore, (29.33) now becomes:

$$n\hat{\alpha}_1 = \frac{(1/2)(W_n(1)^2 - \lambda) - W_n(1)\int W_n(x)dx}{\int W_n(x)^2 dx - (\int W_n(x)dx)^2} + o_p(1) \rightarrow$$

$$\rho_1 + \frac{0.5(1-\lambda)}{\int W(x)^2 dx - (\int W(x)dx)^2}\qquad(29.68)$$

in distribution, and (29.34) becomes:

$$\hat{t}_1 = \frac{(1/2)(W_n(1)^2 - \lambda) - W_n(1)\int W_n(x)dx}{\sqrt{\int W_n(x)^2\,dx - (\int W_n(x)dx)^2}} + o_p(1) \to$$

$$\tau_1 + \frac{0.5(1 - \lambda)}{\sqrt{\int W(x)^2\,dx - (\int W(x)dxt)^2}} \tag{29.69}$$

in distribution. These results carry straightforwardly over to the case where the actual data generating process is an ARIMA process $\alpha(L)\Delta y_t = \beta(L)e_t$, simply by redefining $\gamma(L) = \beta(L)/\alpha(L)$.

The parameter $\gamma(1)^2$ is known as the long-run variance of $u_t = \gamma(L)e_t$:

$$\sigma_L^2 = \lim_{n\to\infty} \text{var}\left[(1/\sqrt{n})\sum_{t=1}^n u_t\right] = \gamma(1)^2 \tag{29.70}$$

which in general is different from the variance of u_t itself:

$$\therefore \sigma_u^2 = \text{var}(u_t) = E(u_t^2) = E\left(\sum_{j=0}^\infty \gamma_j e_{t-j}\right)^2 = \sum_{j=0}^\infty \gamma_j^2. \tag{29.71}$$

If we would know σ_L^2 and σ_u^2, and thus $\lambda = \sigma_u^2/\sigma_L^2$, then it follows from (29.64), (29.65), and Lemma 1, that

$$\frac{\sigma_L^2 - \sigma_u^2}{(1/n^2)\sum_{t=1}^n(y_{t-1} - \bar{y}_{-1})^2} \to \frac{1 - \lambda}{\int W(x)^2\,dx - (\int W(x)dx)^2} \quad \text{in distribution.} \tag{29.72}$$

It is an easy exercise to verify that this result also holds if we replace y_{t-1} by y_t and $\bar{y}_{-1}$ by $\bar{y} = (1/n)\sum_{t=1}^n y_t$. Therefore, it follows from (29.68) and (29.72) that:

Theorem 3. (Phillips–Perron test 1) Under the unit root hypothesis, and given consistent estimators $\hat{\sigma}_L^2$ and $\hat{\sigma}_u^2$ of σ_L^2 and σ_u^2, respectively, we have

$$\hat{Z}_1 = n\left(\hat{\alpha}_1 - \frac{(\hat{\sigma}_L^2 - \hat{\sigma}_u^2)/2}{(1/n)\sum_{t=1}^n(y_t - \bar{y})^2}\right) \to \rho_1 \quad \text{in distribution.} \tag{29.73}$$

This correction of (29.68) has been proposed by Phillips and Perron (1988) for particular estimators $\hat{\sigma}_L^2$ and $\hat{\sigma}_u^2$, following the approach of Phillips (1987) for the case where the intercept α_0 in (29.60) is assumed to be zero.

It is desirable to choose the estimators $\hat{\sigma}_L^2$ and $\hat{\sigma}_u^2$ such that under the stationarity alternative, $\text{plim}_{n\to\infty}\hat{Z}_1 = -\infty$. We show now that this is the case if we choose

$$\hat{\sigma}_u^2 = \frac{1}{n}\sum_{t=1}^n \hat{u}_t^2, \quad \text{where } \hat{u}_t = \Delta y_t - \hat{\alpha}_0 - \hat{\alpha}_1 y_{t-1}, \tag{29.74}$$

and $\hat{\sigma}_L^2$ such that $\bar{\sigma}_L^2 = \text{plim}_{n\to\infty}\hat{\sigma}_L^2 \geq 0$ under the alternative of stationarity.

First, it is easy to verify that $\hat{\sigma}_u^2$ is consistent under the null hypothesis, by verifying that (29.57) still holds. Under stationarity we have $\mathrm{plim}_{n\to\infty}\hat{\alpha}_1 = \mathrm{cov}(y_t, y_{t-1})/\mathrm{var}(y_t) - 1 = \alpha_1^*$, say, $\mathrm{plim}_{n\to\infty}\hat{\alpha}_0 = -\alpha_1^* E(y_t) = \alpha_0^*$, say, and $\mathrm{plim}_{n\to\infty}\hat{\sigma}_u^2 = (1 - (\alpha_1^* + 1)^2)\mathrm{var}(y_t) = \sigma_*^2$, say. Therefore,

$$\mathrm{plim}_{n\to\infty} \hat{Z}_1/n = -0.5(\alpha_1^{*2} + \bar{\sigma}_L^2/\mathrm{var}(y_t)) < 0. \tag{29.75}$$

Phillips and Perron (1988) propose to estimate the long-run variance by the Newey–West (1987) estimator

$$\hat{\sigma}_L^2 = \hat{\sigma}_u^2 + 2\sum_{i=1}^{m}[1 - i/(m+1)](1/n)\sum_{t=i+1}^{n}\hat{u}_t\hat{u}_{t-i}, \tag{29.76}$$

where $\hat{u}_t$ is defined in (29.74), and m converges to infinity with n at rate $o(n^{1/4})$. Andrews (1991) has shown (and we will show it again along the lines in Bierens, 1994) that the rate $o(n^{1/4})$ can be relaxed to $o(n^{1/2})$. The weights $1 - j/(m+1)$ guarantee that this estimator is always positive. The reason for the latter is the following. Let $u_t^* = u_t$ for $t = 1, \ldots, n$, and $u_t^* = 0$ for $t < 1$ and $t > n$. Then,

$$\hat{\sigma}_L^{*2} \equiv \frac{1}{n}\sum_{t=1}^{n+m}\left(\frac{1}{\sqrt{m+1}}\sum_{j=0}^{m}u_{t-j}^*\right)^2 = \frac{1}{m+1}\sum_{j=0}^{m}\frac{1}{n}\sum_{t=1}^{n+m}u_{t-j}^{*2} + 2\frac{1}{m+1}\sum_{j=0}^{m-1}\sum_{i=1}^{m-j}\frac{1}{n}\sum_{t=1}^{n+m}u_{t-j}^*u_{t-j-i}^*$$

$$= \frac{1}{m+1}\sum_{j=0}^{m}\frac{1}{n}\sum_{t=1-j}^{n+m-j}u_t^{*2} + 2\frac{1}{m+1}\sum_{j=0}^{m-1}\sum_{i=1}^{m-j}\frac{1}{n}\sum_{t=1-j}^{n+m-j}u_t^*u_{t-i}^*$$

$$= \frac{1}{n}\sum_{t=1}^{n}u_t^2 + 2\frac{1}{m+1}\sum_{j=0}^{m-1}\sum_{i=1}^{m-j}\frac{1}{n}\sum_{t=i+1}^{n}u_t u_{t-i}$$

$$= \frac{1}{n}\sum_{t=1}^{n}u_t^2 + 2\frac{1}{m+1}\sum_{i=1}^{m}(m+1-i)\frac{1}{n}\sum_{t=i+1}^{n}u_t u_{t-i} \tag{29.77}$$

is positive, and so is $\hat{\sigma}_L^2$. Next, observe from (29.62) and (29.74) that

$$\hat{u}_t = u_t - \sqrt{n}\hat{\alpha}_1\gamma(1)W_n(t/n) - \hat{\alpha}_1 v_t + \hat{\alpha}_1(v_0 - y_0) - \hat{\alpha}_0. \tag{29.78}$$

Since

$$E\left|(1/n)\sum_{t=1+i}^{n}u_t W_n((t-i)/n)\right| \le \sqrt{(1/n)\sum_{t=1+i}^{n}E(u_t^2)}\sqrt{(1/n)\sum_{t=1+i}^{n}E(W_n((t-i)/n)^2)} = O(1),$$

it follows that $(1/n)\sum_{t=1+i}^{n}u_t W_n((t-i)/n) = O_p(1)$. Similarly, $(1/n)\sum_{t=1+i}^{n}u_{t-i}W_n(t/n) = O_p(1)$. Moreover, $\hat{\alpha}_1 = O_p(1/n)$, and similarly, it can be shown that $\hat{\alpha}_0 = O_p(1/\sqrt{n})$. Therefore, it follows from (29.77) and (29.78) that

$$\hat{\sigma}_L^2 - \hat{\sigma}_L^{*2} = O_p(1/n) + O_p\left(\sum_{i=1}^{m}[1 - i/(m+1)]/\sqrt{n}\right) = O_p(1/n) + O_p(m/\sqrt{n}). \tag{29.79}$$

A similar result holds under the stationarity hypothesis. Moreover, substituting $u_t = \sigma_L^2 e_t + v_t - v_{t-1}$, and denoting $e_t^* = e_t$, $v_t^* = v_t$ for $t = 1, \ldots, n$, $v_t^* = e_t^* = 0$ for $t < 1$ and $t > n$, it is easy to verify that under the unit root hypothesis,

$$\hat{\sigma}_L^{*2} = \frac{1}{n} \sum_{t=1}^{n+m} \left(\sigma_L \frac{1}{\sqrt{m+1}} \sum_{j=0}^{m} e_{t-j}^* + \frac{v_t^* - v_{t-m}^*}{\sqrt{m+1}} \right)^2$$

$$= \sigma_L^2 \frac{1}{n} \sum_{t=1}^{n+m} \left(\frac{1}{\sqrt{m+1}} \sum_{j=0}^{m} e_{t-j}^* \right)^2 + 2\sigma_L \frac{1}{n} \sum_{t=1}^{n+m} \left(\frac{1}{\sqrt{m+1}} \sum_{j=0}^{m} e_{t-j}^* \right) \left(\frac{v_t^* - v_{t-m}^*}{\sqrt{m+1}} \right)$$

$$+ \frac{1}{n} \sum_{t=1}^{n+m} \left(\frac{v_t^* - v_{t-m}^*}{\sqrt{m+1}} \right)^2 = \sigma_L^2 + O_p(\sqrt{m/n}) + O_p(1/\sqrt{m}) + O_p(1/m). \quad (29.80)$$

A similar result holds under the stationarity hypothesis. Thus:

Theorem 4. Let m increase with n to infinity at rate $o(n^{1/2})$. Then under both the unit root and stationarity hypothesis, $\text{plim}_{n\to\infty}(\hat{\sigma}_L^2 - \hat{\sigma}_L^{*2}) = 0$. Moreover, under the unit root hypothesis, $\text{plim}_{n\to\infty}\hat{\sigma}_L^{*2} = \sigma_L^2$, and under the stationarity hypothesis, $\text{plim}_{n\to\infty}\hat{\sigma}_L^{*2} > 0$. Consequently, under stationarity, the Phillips–Perron test satisfies $\text{plim}_{n\to\infty}\hat{Z}_1/n < 0$.

Finally, note that the advantage of the PP test is that there is no need to specify the ARIMA process under the null hypothesis. It is in essence a nonparametric test. Of course, we still have to specify the Newey–West truncation lag m as a function of n, but as long as $m = o(\sqrt{n})$, this specification is asymptotically not critical.

6   UNIT ROOT WITH DRIFT VS. TREND STATIONARITY

Most macroeconomic time series in (log) levels have an upwards sloping pattern. Therefore, if they are (covariance) stationary, then they are stationary around a deterministic trend. If we would conduct the ADF and PP tests in Sections 4 and 5 to a linear trend stationary process, we will likely accept the unit root hypothesis, due to the following. Suppose we conduct the ADF test under the hypothesis $p = 1$ to the trend stationary process $y_t = \beta_0 + \beta_1 t + u_t$, where the u_ts are iid $N(0, \sigma^2)$. It is a standard exercise to verify that then $\text{plim}_{n\to\infty}n\hat{\alpha}_1 = 0$, hence the ADF and PP tests in sections 4 and 5 have no power against linear trend stationarity!

Therefore, if one wishes to test the unit root hypothesis against linear trend stationarity, then a trend term should be included in the auxiliary regressions (29.39) in the ADF case, and in (29.60) in the PP case: Thus the ADF regression (29.39) now becomes

$$\Delta y_t = \alpha_0 + \sum_{j=1}^{p-1} \alpha_j \Delta y_{t-j} + \alpha_p y_{t-1} + \alpha_{p+1} t + u_t, \quad u_t \sim \text{iid } N(0, \sigma_2) \quad (29.81)$$

where the null hypothesis of a unit root with drift corresponds to the hypothesis $\alpha_p = \alpha_{p+1} = 0$, and the PP regression becomes:

$$\Delta y_t = \alpha_0 + \alpha_1 y_{t-1} + \alpha_2 t + u_t, \quad u_t = \gamma(L)e_t, \quad e_t \sim \text{iid } N(0, 1). \tag{29.82}$$

The asymptotic null distributions of the ADF and PP tests for the case with drift are quite similar to the ADF test without an intercept. The difference is that the Wiener process $W(x)$ is replaced by the de-trended Wiener process:

$$W^{**}(x) = W(x) - 4\int W(z)dz + 6\int zW(z)dz + 6\left(\int W(z)dz - 2\int zW(z)dz\right)x$$

After some tedious but not too difficult calculations it can be shown that effectively the statistics $n\hat{\alpha}_p/(1 - \sum_{j=1}^{p}\alpha_j)$ and $\hat{t}_p$ are asymptotically equivalent to the Dickey–Fuller tests statistics $\hat{\rho}_0$ and $\hat{\tau}_0$, respectively, applied to de-trended time series.

Theorem 5. Let y_t be generated by (29.81), and let $\hat{\alpha}_p$ and $\hat{t}_p$ be the OLS estimator and corresponding t-value of α_p. Under the unit root with drift hypothesis, i.e. $\alpha_p = \alpha_{p+1} = 0$, we have $n\hat{\alpha}_p \to (1 - \sum_{j=1}^{p-1}\alpha_j)\rho_2$ and $\hat{t}_p \to \tau_2$ in distribution, where

$$\rho_2 = \frac{1}{2}\left(\frac{W^{**}(1) - 1}{\int W^{**}(x)^2 dx}\right), \quad \tau_2 = \frac{1}{2}\left(\frac{W^{**}(1) - 1}{\sqrt{\int W^{**}(x)^2 dx}}\right).$$

Under the trend stationarity hypothesis, $\text{plim}_{n\to\infty}\hat{\alpha}_p = \alpha_p < 0$, hence $\text{plim}_{n\to\infty}\hat{t}_p/\sqrt{n} < 0$.

The densities of ρ_2 and τ_2 (the latter compared with the standard normal density), are displayed in Figures 29.5 and 29.6, respectively. Again, these densities are farther to the left, and heavier left-tailed, than the corresponding densities displayed in Figures 29.1–29.4. The asymptotic 5 percent and 10 percent critical values of the Dickey–Fuller t-test are:

$$P(\tau_2 < -3.41) = 0.05, \quad P(\tau_2 < -3.13) = 0.10$$

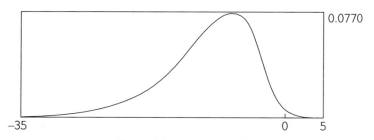

Figure 29.5 Density of ρ_2

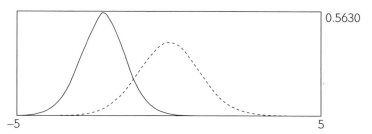

Figure 29.6 Density of τ_2 compared with the standard normal density (dashed curve)

Moreover, comparing (29.26) with

$$P(\tau_2 \leq -1.64) \approx 0.77, \quad P(\tau_2 \leq -1.28) \approx 0.89,$$

we see that the standard normal tests at the 5 percent and 10 percent significance level would reject the correct unit root with drift hypothesis with probabilities of about 0.77 and 0.89, respectively!

A similar result as in Theorem 5 can be derived for the PP test, on the basis of the OLS estimator of α_1 in, and the residuals $\hat{u}_t$ of, the auxiliary regression (29.82):

Theorem 6. (Phillips–Perron test 2) Let $\hat{r}_t$ be the residuals of the OLS regression of y_t on t and a constant, and let $\hat{\sigma}_u^2$ and $\hat{\sigma}_L^2$ be as before, with the $\hat{u}_t$s the OLS residuals of the auxiliary regression (29.82). Under the unit root with drift hypothesis,

$$\hat{Z}_2 = n\left(\hat{\alpha}_1 - \frac{(\hat{\sigma}_L^2 - \hat{\sigma}_u^2)/2}{(1/n)\sum_{t=1}^{n}\hat{r}_t^2} \right) \to \rho_2 \text{ in distribution,} \tag{29.83}$$

whereas under trend stationarity $\operatorname{plim}_{n\to\infty}\hat{Z}_2/n < 0$.

7 CONCLUDING REMARKS

In the discussion of the ADF test we have assumed that the lag length p of the auxiliary regression (29.81) is fixed. It should be noted that we may choose p as a function of the length n of the time series involved, similarly to the truncation width of the Newey–West estimator of the long-run variance in the Phillips–Perron test. See Said and Dickey (1984).

We have seen that the ADF and Phillips–Perron tests for a unit root against stationarity around a constant have almost no power if the correct alternative is linear trend stationarity. However, the same may apply to the tests discussed in Section 6 if the alternative is trend stationarity with a broken trend. See Perron (1988, 1989, 1990), Perron and Vogelsang (1992), and Zivot and Andrews (1992), among others.

All the tests discussed so far have the unit root as the null hypothesis, and (trend) stationarity as the alternative. However, it is also possible to test the other way around. See Bierens and Guo (1993), and Kwiatkowski *et al.* (1992). The latter test is known as the KPSS test.

Finally, note that the ADF and Phillips–Perron tests can easily be conducted by various econometric software packages, for example TSP, EViews, RATS, and *EasyReg*.[11]

Notes

*   The useful comments of three referees are gratefully acknowledged.

1   See Chapter 26 on spurious regression in this volume. This phenomenon can easily be demonstrated by using my free software package *EasyReg*, which is downloadable from website http://econ.la.psu.edu/~hbierens/EASYREG.HTM (Click on "Tools", and then on "Teaching tools").

2   See Chapter 30 on cointegration in this volume.

3   The reason for changing the subscript of α from 1 in (29.1) to 0 is to indicate the number of other parameters at the right-hand side of the equation. See also (29.39).

4   Recall that the notation $o_p(a_n)$, with a_n a deterministic sequence, stands for a sequence of random variables or vectors x_n, say, such that $\text{plim}_{n\to\infty} x_n/a_n = 0$, and that the notation $O_p(a_n)$ stands for a sequence of random variables or vectors x_n such that x_n/a_n is stochastically bounded: $\forall \varepsilon \in (0, 1) \, \exists \, M \in (0, \infty)$: $\sup_{n\geq 1} P(|x_n/a_n| > M) < \varepsilon$. Also, recall that convergence in distribution implies stochastic boundedness.

5   The Borel sets in $\mathbb{R}$ are the members of the smallest σ-algebra containing the collection $\mathfrak{C}$, say, of all half-open intervals $(-\infty, x]$, $x \in \mathbb{R}$. Equivalently, we may also define the Borel sets as the members of the smallest σ-algebra containing the collection of open subsets of $\mathbb{R}$. A collection $\mathcal{F}$ of subsets of a set Ω is called a σ-algebra if the following three conditions hold: $\Omega \in \mathcal{F}$; $A \in \mathcal{F}$ implies that its complement also belongs to $\mathcal{F}$: $\Omega \backslash A \in \mathcal{F}$ (hence, the empty set ϕ belongs to $\mathcal{F}$); $A_n \in \mathcal{F}$, $n = 1, 2, 3, \ldots$, implies $\bigcup_{n=1}^{\infty} A_n \in \mathcal{F}$. The smallest σ-algebra containing a collection $\mathfrak{C}$ of sets is the intersection of all σ-algebras containing the collection $\mathfrak{C}$.

6   Under the assumption that e_t is iid $N(0, 1)$,

$$P(\max_{1\leq t\leq n} |e_t| \leq \varepsilon \sqrt{n}) = \left(1 - 2\int_{\varepsilon\sqrt{n}}^{\infty} \frac{\exp(-x^2/2)}{\sqrt{2\pi}} dx\right)^n \to 1$$

   for arbitrary $\varepsilon > 0$.

7   This density is actually a kernel estimate of the density of $\hat{\rho}_0$ on the basis of 10,000 replications of a Gaussian random walk $y_t = y_{t-1} + e_t$, $t = 0, 1, \ldots, 1,000$, $y_t = 0$ for $t < 0$. The kernel involved is the standard normal density, and the bandwidth $h = c.s10,000^{-1/5}$, where s is the sample standard error, and $c = 1$. The scale factor c has been chosen by experimenting with various values. The value $c = 1$ is about the smallest one for which the kernel estimate remains a smooth curve; for smaller values of c the kernel estimate becomes wobbly. The densities of ρ_1, τ_1, ρ_2, and τ_2 in Figures 29.2–29.6 have been constructed in the same way, with $c = 1$.

8   To see this, write $1 - \sum_{j=1}^{p} \beta_j L^j = \prod_{j=1}^{p}(1 - \rho_j L)$, so that $1 - \sum_{j=1}^{p} \beta_j = \prod_{j=1}^{p}(1 - \rho_j)$, where the $1/\rho_j$s are the roots of the lag polynomial involved. If root $1/\rho_j$ is real valued, then the stationarity condition implies $-1 < \rho_j < 1$, so that $1 - \rho_j > 0$. If some roots are complex-valued, then these roots come in complex-conjugate pairs, say $1/\rho_1 = a + i.b$ and $1/\rho_2 = a - i.b$, hence $(1 - \rho_1)(1 - \rho_2) = (1/\rho_1 - 1)(1/\rho_2 - 1)\rho_1\rho_2 = ((a - 1)^2 + b^2)/(a^2 + b^2) > 0$.

9   In the sequel we shall suppress the statement "without drift." A unit root process is from now on by default a unit root without drift process, except if otherwise indicated.

10 For example, let $p = 2$ in (29.37) and (29.39). Then $\alpha_1 = -\beta_1$, hence if $\beta_1 < -1$ then $1 - \alpha_1 < 0$. In order to show that $\beta_1 < -1$ can be compatible with stationarity, assume that $\beta_1^2 = 4\beta_2$, so that the lag polynomial $1 - \beta_1 L - \beta_2 L^2$ has two common roots $-2/|\beta_1|$. Then the AR(2) process involved is stationary for $-2 < \beta_1 < -1$.

11 The most important difference with other econometric software packages is that *EasyReg* is free. See footnote 1. *EasyReg* also contains my own unit root tests, Bierens (1993, 1997), Bierens and Guo (1993), and the KPSS test.

References

Andrews, D.W.K. (1991). Heteroskedasticity and autocorrelation consistent covariance matrix estimators. *Econometrica* 59, 817–58.

Bierens, H.J. (1993). Higher order sample autocorrelations and the unit root hypothesis. *Journal of Econometrics* 57, 137–60.

Bierens, H.J. (1997). Testing the unit root hypothesis against nonlinear trend stationarity, with an application to the price level and interest rate in the U.S. *Journal of Econometrics* 81, 29–64.

Bierens, H.J. (1994). *Topics in Advanced Econometrics: Estimation, Testing and Specification of Cross-Section and Time Series Models*. Cambridge: Cambridge University Press.

Bierens, H.J., and S. Guo (1993). Testing stationarity and trend stationarity against the unit root hypothesis. *Econometric Reviews* 12, 1–32.

Billingsley, P. (1968). *Convergence of Probability Measures*. New York: John Wiley.

Dickey, D.A., and W.A. Fuller (1979). Distribution of the estimators for autoregressive times series with a unit root. *Journal of the American Statistical Association* 74, 427–31.

Dickey, D.A., and W.A. Fuller (1981). Likelihood ratio statistics for autoregressive time series with a unit root. *Econometrica* 49, 1057–72.

Fuller, W.A. (1996). *Introduction to Statistical Time Series*. New York: John Wiley.

Green, W. (1997). *Econometric Analysis*. Upper Saddle River, NJ: Prentice Hall.

Hogg, R.V., and A.T. Craig (1978). *Introduction to Mathematical Statistics*. London: Macmillan.

Kwiatkowski, D., P.C.B. Phillips, P. Schmidt, and Y. Shin (1992). Testing the null of stationarity against the alternative of a unit root. *Journal of Econometrics* 54, 159–78.

Newey, W.K., and K.D. West (1987). A simple positive definite heteroskedasticity and autocorrelation consistent covariance matrix. *Econometrica* 55, 703–8.

Perron, P. (1988). Trends and random walks in macroeconomic time series: further evidence from a new approach. *Journal of Economic Dynamics and Control* 12, 297–332.

Perron, P. (1989). The great crash, the oil price shock and the unit root hypothesis. *Econometrica* 57, 1361–402.

Perron, P. (1990). Testing the unit root in a time series with a changing mean. *Journal of Business and Economic Statistics* 8, 153–62.

Perron, P., and T.J. Vogelsang (1992). Nonstationarity and level shifts with an application to purchasing power parity. *Journal of Business and Economic Statistics* 10, 301–20.

Phillips, P.C.B. (1987). Time series regression with a unit root. *Econometrica* 55, 277–301.

Phillips, P.C.B., and P. Perron (1988). Testing for a unit root in time series regression. *Biometrika* 75, 335–46.

Said, S.E., and D.A. Dickey (1984). Testing for unit roots in autoregressive-moving average of unknown order. *Biometrika* 71, 599–607.

Zivot, E., and D.W.K. Andrews (1992). Further evidence on the great crash, the oil price shock, and the unit root hypothesis. *Journal of Business and Economic Statistics* 10, 251–70.

Cointegration

Juan J. Dolado, Jesús Gonzalo, and Francesc Marmol

1   INTRODUCTION

A substantial part of economic theory generally deals with long-run equilibrium relationships generated by market forces and behavioral rules. Correspondingly, most empirical econometric studies entailing time series can be interpreted as attempts to evaluate such relationships in a dynamic framework.

At one time, conventional wisdom was that in order to apply standard inference procedures in such studies, the variables in the system needed to be stationary since the vast majority of econometric theory is built upon the assumption of stationarity. Consequently, for many years econometricians proceeded as if stationarity could be achieved by simply removing deterministic components (e.g. drifts and trends) from the data. However, stationary series should at least have constant unconditional mean and variance over time, a condition which hardly appears to be satisfied in economics, even after removing those deterministic terms.

Those problems were somehow ignored in applied work until important papers by Granger and Newbold (1974) and Nelson and Plosser (1982) alerted many to the econometric implications of nonstationarity and the dangers of running *nonsense* or *spurious* regressions; see, e.g. Chapter 26 by Granger in this volume for further details. In particular, most of the attention focused on the implications of dealing with integrated variables which are a specific class of nonstationary variables with important economic and statistical properties. These are derived from the presence of unit roots which give rise to stochastic trends, as opposed to pure deterministic trends, with innovations to an integrated process being permanent rather than transitory.

The presence of, at least, a unit root in economic time series is implied in many economic models. Among them, there are those based on the rational use of available information or the existence of very high adjustment costs in some markets. Interesting examples include future contracts, stock prices, yield curves, exchange rates, money velocity, hysteresis theories of unemployment, and, perhaps the most popular, the implications of the permanent income hypothesis for real consumption under rational expectations.

Statisticians, in turn, following the influential approach by Box and Jenkins (1970), had advocated transforming integrated time series into stationary ones by successive differencing of the series before modelization. Therefore, from their viewpoint, removing unit roots through differencing ought to be a prerequisite for regression analysis. However, some authors, notably Sargan (1964), Hendry and Mizon (1978) and Davidson *et al.* (1978), *inter alia*, started to criticize on a number of grounds the specification of dynamic models in terms of differenced variables only, especially because of the difficulties in inferring the long-run equilibrium from the estimated model. After all, if deviations from that equilibrium relationship affect future changes in a set of variables, omitting the former, i.e. estimating a differenced model, should entail a misspecification error. However, for some time it remained to be well understood how both variables in differences and levels could coexist in regression models.

Granger (1981), resting upon the previous ideas, solved the puzzle by pointing out that a vector of variables, all of which achieve stationarity after differencing, could have linear combinations which are stationary in levels. Later, Granger (1986) and Engle and Granger (1987) were the first to formalize the idea of integrated variables sharing an equilibrium relation which turned out to be either stationary or have a lower degree of integration than the original series. They denoted this property by *cointegration*, signifying comovements among trending variables which could be exploited to test for the existence of equilibrium relationships within a fully dynamic specification framework. Notice that the notion of "equilibrium" used here is that of a state to which a dynamic system tends to converge over time after any of the variables in the system is perturbed by a shock. In economics, the strength of attraction to such a state depends on the actions of a market or on government intervention. In this sense, the basic concept of cointegration applies in a variety of economic models including the relationships between capital and output, real wages and labor productivity, nominal exchange rates and relative prices, consumption and disposable income, long- and short-term interest rates, money velocity and interest rates, price of shares and dividends, production and sales, etc. In particular, Campbell and Shiller (1987) have pointed out that a pair of integrated variables that are related through a present value model, as it is often the case in macroeconomics and finance, must be cointegrated.

In view of the strength of these ideas, a burgeoning literature on cointegration has developed over the last decade. In this chapter we will explore the basic conceptual issues and discuss related econometric techniques, with the aim of offering an introductory coverage of the main developments in this new field of research. Section 2 provides some preliminaries on the implications of cointegration and the basic estimation and testing procedures in a single equation framework, when variables have a single unit root. In Section 3, we extend the previous techniques to more general multivariate setups, introducing those system-based approaches to cointegration which are now in common use. Section 4, in turn, presents some interesting developments on which the recent research on cointegration has been focusing. Finally, Section 5 draws some concluding remarks.

Nowadays, the interested reader, who wants to deepen beyond the introductory level offered here, could find a number of textbooks (e.g. Banerjee *et al.*, 1993; Johansen, 1995; Hatanaka, 1996; Maddala and Kim, 1998) and surveys (e.g. Engle and Granger, 1991; Watson, 1994) on cointegration where more general treatments of the relevant issues covered in this chapter are presented. Likewise, there are now many software packages that support the techniques discussed here (e.g. Gauss-COINT, E-VIEWS and PC-FIML).

2 Preliminaries: Unit Roots and Cointegration

2.1 Some basic concepts

A well known result in time series analysis is Wold's (1938) decomposition theorem which states that a stationary time series process, after removal of any deterministic components, has an infinite moving average (MA) representation which, under some technical conditions (absolute summability of the MA coefficients), can be represented by a finite autoregressive moving average (ARMA) process.

However, as mentioned in the introduction, many time series need to be appropriately differenced in order to achieve stationarity. From this comes the definition of integration: a time series is said to be integrated of order d, in short I(d), if it has a stationary, invertible, non-deterministic ARMA representation after differencing d times. A white noise series and a stable first-order autoregressive AR(1) process are well known examples of I(0) series, a random walk process is an example of an I(1) series, while accumulating a random walk gives rise to an I(2) series, etc.

Consider now two time series y_{1t} and y_{2t} which are both I(d) (i.e. they have compatible long-run properties). In general, any linear combination of y_{1t} and y_{2t} will be also I(d). However, if there exists a vector $(1, -\beta)'$, such that the linear combination

$$z_t = y_{1t} - \alpha - \beta y_{2t} \tag{30.1}$$

is I($d - b$), $d \geq b > 0$, then, following Engle and Granger (1987), y_{1t} and y_{2t} are defined as cointegrated of order (d, b), denoted $y_t = (y_{1t}, y_{2t})' \sim \text{CI}(d, b)$, with $(1, -\beta)'$ called the cointegrating vector.

Several features in (30.1) are noteworthy. First, as defined above, cointegration refers to a linear combination of nonstationary variables. Although theoretically it is possible that nonlinear relationships may exist among a set of integrated variables, the econometric practice about this more general type of cointegration is less developed (see more on this in Section 4). Second, note that the cointegrating vector is not uniquely defined, since for any nonzero value of λ, $(\lambda, -\lambda\beta)'$ is also a cointegrating vector. Thus, a normalization rule needs to be used; for example,

$\lambda = 1$ has been chosen in (30.1). Third, all variables must be integrated of the same order to be candidates to form a cointegrating relationship. Notwithstanding, there are extensions of the concept of cointegration, called *multicointegration*, when the number of variables considered is larger than two and where the possibility of having variables with different order of integration can be addressed (see, e.g. Granger and Lee, 1989). For example, in a trivariate system, we may have that y_{1t} and y_{2t} are I(2) and y_{3t} is I(1); if y_{1t} and y_{2t} are CI(2, 1), it is possible that the corresponding combination of y_{1t} and y_{2t} which achieves that property be itself cointegrated with y_{3t} giving rise to an I(0) linear combination among the three variables. Fourth, and most important, most of the cointegration literature focuses on the case where variables contain a single unit root, since few economic variables prove in practice to be integrated of higher order. If variables have a strong seasonal component, however, there may be unit roots at the seasonal frequencies, a case that we will briefly consider in Section 4; see Chapter 30 by Ghysels, Osborn, and Rodrigues in this volume for further details. Hence, the remainder of this chapter will mainly focus on the case of CI(1, 1) variables, so that z_t in (30.1) is I(0) and the concept of cointegration mimics the existence of a long-run equilibrium to which the system converges over time. If, e.g., economic theory suggests the following long-run relationship between y_{1t} and y_{2t},

$$y_{1t} = \alpha + \beta y_{2t}, \tag{30.2}$$

then z_t can be interpreted as the equilibrium error (i.e. the distance that the system is away from the equilibrium at any point in time). Note that a constant term has been included in (30.1) in order to allow for the possibility that z_t may have nonzero mean. For example, a standard theory of spatial competition argues that arbitrage will prevent prices of similar products in different locations from moving too far apart even if the prices are nonstationary. However, if there are fixed transportation costs from one location to another, a constant term needs to be included in (30.1).

At this stage, it is important to point out that a useful way to understand cointegrating relationships is through the observation that CI(1, 1) variables must share a set of stochastic trends. Using the example in (30.1), since y_{1t} and y_{2t} are I(1) variables, they can be decomposed into an I(1) component (say, a random walk) plus an irregular I(0) component (not necessarily white noise). Denoting the first components by μ_{it} and the second components by u_{it}, $i = 1, 2$, we can write

$$y_{1t} = \mu_{1t} + u_{1t} \tag{30.3}$$

$$y_{2t} = \mu_{2t} + u_{2t}. \tag{30.3'}$$

Since the sum of an I(1) process and an I(0) process is always I(1), the previous representation must characterize the individual stochastic properties of y_{1t} and y_{2t}. However, if $y_{1t} - \beta y_{2t}$ is I(0), it must be that $\mu_{1t} = \beta \mu_{2t}$, annihilating the I(1) component in the cointegrating relationship. In other words, if y_{1t} and y_{2t} are

CI(1, 1) variables, they must share (up to a scalar) the same stochastic trend, say μ_t, denoted as *common trend*, so that $\mu_{1t} = \mu_t$ and $\mu_{2t} = \beta\mu_t$. As before, notice that if μ_t is a common trend for y_{1t} and y_{2t}, $\lambda\mu_t$ will also be a common trend implying that a normalization rule is needed for identification. Generalizing the previous argument to a vector of cointegration and common trends, then it can be proved that if there are $n - r$ common trends among the n variables, there must be r cointegrating relationships. Note that $0 < r < n$, since $r = 0$ implies that each series in the system is governed by a different stochastic trend and that $r = n$ implies that the series are I(0) instead of I(1). These properties constitute the core of two important dual approaches toward testing for cointegration, namely, one that tests directly for the number of cointegrating vectors (r) and another which tests for the number of common trends ($n - r$). However, before explaining those approaches in more detail (see Section 3), we now turn to another useful representation of CI(1, 1) systems which has proved very popular in practice.

Engle and Granger (1987) have shown that if y_{1t} and y_{2t} are cointegrated CI(1, 1), then there must exist a so-called *vector error correction model* (VECM) representation of the dynamic system governing the joint behavior of y_{1t} and y_{2t} over time, of the following form

$$\Delta y_{1t} = \theta_{10} + \theta_{11}z_{t-1} + \sum_{i=1}^{p_1} \theta_{12,i}\Delta y_{1,t-i} + \sum_{i=1}^{p_2} \theta_{13,i}\Delta y_{2,t-i} + \varepsilon_{1t}, \tag{30.4}$$

$$\Delta y_{2t} = \theta_{20} + \theta_{21}z_{t-1} + \sum_{i=1}^{p_3} \theta_{22,i}\Delta y_{1,t-i} + \sum_{i=1}^{p_4} \theta_{23,i}\Delta y_{2,t-i} + \varepsilon_{2t}, \tag{30.4'}$$

where Δ denotes the first-order time difference (i.e. $\Delta y_t = y_t - y_{t-1}$) and where the lag lengths p_i, $i = 1, \ldots, 4$ are such that the innovations $\varepsilon_t = (\varepsilon_{1t}, \varepsilon_{2t})'$ are iid $(0, \Sigma)$. Furthermore, they proved the converse result that a VECM generates cointegrated CI(1, 1) series as long as the coefficients on z_{t-1} (the so-called *loading or speed of adjustment parameters*) are not simultaneously equal to zero.

Note that the term z_{t-1} in equations (30.4) and (30.4') represents the extent of the disequilibrium levels of y_1 and y_2 in the previous period. Thus, the VECM representation states that changes in one variable not only depends on changes of the other variables and its own past changes, but also on the extent of the disequilibrium between the levels of y_1 and y_2. For example, if $\beta = 1$ in (30.1), as many theories predict when y_{1t} and y_{2t} are taken in logarithmic form, then if y_1 is larger than y_2 in the past ($z_{t-1} > 0$), then $\theta_{11} < 0$ and $\theta_{21} > 0$ will imply that, everything else equal, y_1 would fall and y_2 would rise in the current period, implying that both series adjust toward its long-run equilibrium. Notice that both θ_{11} and θ_{21} cannot be equal to zero. However, if $\theta_{11} < 0$ and $\theta_{21} = 0$, then all of the adjustment falls on y_1, or vice versa if $\theta_{11} = 0$ and $\theta_{21} > 0$. Note also that the larger are the speed of adjustment parameters (with the right signs), the greater is the convergence rate toward equilibrium. Of course, at least one of those terms must be nonzero, implying the existence of Granger causality in cointegrated systems in at least one direction; see Chapter 32 by Lütkepohl in this volume for the formal definition of causality. Hence, the appeal of the VECM formulation is that it combines flexibility in dynamic specification with desirable long-run properties: it could be seen as capturing the transitional dynamics of the system to the long-run equilibrium suggested by economic theory (see, e.g. Hendry and Richard, 1983). Further, if cointegration exists, the VECM representation will generate better forecasts than the corresponding representation in first-differenced form (i.e. with $\theta_{11} = \theta_{21} = 0$), particularly over medium- and long-run horizons, since under cointegration z_t will have a finite forecast error variance whereas any other linear combination of the forecasts of the individual series in y_t will have infinite variance; see Engle and Yoo (1987) for further details.

2.2 Estimation and testing for cointegration in a single equation framework

Based upon the VECM representation, Engle and Granger (1987) suggest a two-step estimation procedure for single equation dynamic modeling which has become very popular in applied research. Assuming that $y_t \sim I(1)$, then the procedure goes as follows:

1. First, in order to test whether the series are cointegrated, the *cointegration regression*

$$y_{1t} = \alpha + \beta y_{2t} + z_t \qquad (30.5)$$

is estimated by ordinary least squares (OLS) and it is tested whether the *cointegrating residuals* $\hat{z}_t = y_{1t} - \hat{\alpha} - \hat{\beta} y_{2t}$ are I(1). To do this, for example, we can perform a Dickey–Fuller test on the residual sequence $\{\hat{z}_t\}$ to determine whether it has a unit root. For this, consider the autoregression of the residuals

$$\Delta \hat{z}_t = \rho_1 \hat{z}_{t-1} + \varepsilon_t, \qquad (30.6)$$

where no intercept term has been included since the $\{\hat{z}_t\}$, being residuals from a regression equation with a constant term, have zero mean. If we can reject the null hypothesis that $\rho_1 = 0$ against the alternative $\rho_1 < 0$ at a given significance level, we can conclude that the residual sequence is I(0) and, therefore, that y_{1t} and y_{2t} are CI(1, 1). It is noteworthy that for carrying out this test it is not possible to use the Dickey–Fuller tables themselves since $\{\hat{z}_t\}$ are a generated series of residuals from fitting regression (30.5). The problem is that the OLS estimates of α and β are such that they minimize the residual variance in (30.5) and thus prejudice the testing procedure toward finding stationarity. Hence, larger (in absolute value) critical levels than the standard Dickey–Fuller ones are needed. In this respect, MacKinnon (1991) provides appropriate tables to test the null hypothesis $\rho_1 = 0$ for any sample size and also when the number of regressors in (30.5) is expanded from one to several variables. In general, if the $\{\hat{\varepsilon}_t\}$ sequence exhibits serial correlation, then an augmented Dickey–Fuller (ADF) test should be used, based this time on the extended autoregression

$$\Delta \hat{z}_t = \rho_1 \hat{z}_{t-1} + \sum_{i=1}^{p} \zeta_i \Delta \hat{z}_{t-i} + \varepsilon_t, \tag{30.6'}$$

where again, if $\rho_1 < 0$, we can conclude that y_{1t} and y_{2t} are CI(1, 1). Alternative versions of the test on $\{\hat{z}_t\}$ being I(1) versus I(0) can be found in Phillips and Ouliaris (1990). Banerjee *et al.* (1998), in turn, suggest another class of tests based this time on the direct significance of the loading parameters in (30.4) and (30.4') where the β coefficient is estimated alongside the remaining parameters in a single step using nonlinear least squares (NLS).

If we reject that $\hat{z}_t$ are I(1), Stock (1987) has shown that the OLS estimate of β in equation (30.5) is *super-consistent*, in the sense that the OLS estimator $\hat{\beta}$ converges in probability to its true value β at a rate proportional to the inverse of the sample size, T^{-1}, rather than at $T^{-1/2}$ as is the standard result in the ordinary case where y_{1t} and y_{2t} are I(0). Thus, when T grows, convergence is much quicker in the CI(1, 1) case. The intuition behind this remarkable result can be seen by analyzing the behavior of $\hat{\beta}$ in (30.5) (where the constant is omitted for simplicity) in the particular case where $z_t \sim$ iid $(0, \sigma_z^2)$, and that $\theta_{20} = \theta_{21} = 0$ and $p_3 = p_4 = 0$, so that y_{2t} is assumed to follow a simple random walk

$$\Delta y_{2t} = \varepsilon_{2t}, \tag{30.7}$$

or, integrating (30.7) backwards with $y_{20} = 0$,

$$y_{2t} = \sum_{i=1}^{t} \varepsilon_{2i}, \tag{30.7'}$$

with ε_{2t} possibly correlated with z_t. In this case, we get $\text{var}(y_{2t}) = t \, \text{var}(\varepsilon_{21}) = t\sigma_2^2$, exploding as $T \uparrow \infty$. Nevertheless, it is not difficult to show that $T^{-2}\sum_{t=1}^{T} y_{2t}^2$ converges to a random variable. Similarly, the cross-product $T^{-1/2}\sum_{t=1}^{T} y_{2t} z_t$ will explode, in contrast to the stationary case where a simple application of the central limit theorem implies that it is asymptotically normally distributed. In the I(1) case, $T^{-1}\sum_{t=1}^{T} y_{2t} z_t$ converges also to a random variable. Both random variables are functionals of Brownian motions which will be denoted henceforth, in general, as $f(B)$. A Brownian motion is a zero-mean normally distributed continuous (a.s.) process with independent increments, i.e. loosely speaking, the continuous version of the discrete random walk; see Phillips (1987), and Chapter 29 by Bierens in this volume for further details.

Now, from the expression for the OLS estimator of β, we obtain

$$\hat{\beta} - \beta = \frac{\sum_{t=1}^{T} y_{2t} z_t}{\sum_{t=1}^{T} y_{2t}^2}, \tag{30.8}$$

and, from the previous discussion, it follows that

$$T(\hat{\beta} - \beta) = \frac{T^{-1} \sum\limits_{t=1}^{T} y_{2t} z_t}{T^{-2} \sum\limits_{t=1}^{T} y_{2t}^2} \tag{30.9}$$

is asymptotically (as $T \uparrow \infty$) the ratio of two non-degenerate random variables that in general, is not normally distributed. Thus, in spite of the super-consistency, standard inference cannot be applied to $\hat{\beta}$ except in some restrictive cases which are discussed below.

2. After rejecting the null hypothesis that the cointegrating residuals in equation (30.5) are I(1), the $\hat{z}_{t-1}$ term is included in the VECM system and the remaining parameters are estimated by OLS. Indeed, given the super-consistency of $\hat{\beta}$, Engle and Granger (1987) show that their asymptotic distributions will be identical to using the true value of β. Now, all the variables in (30.4) and (30.4′) are I(0) and conventional modeling strategies (e.g. testing the maximum lag length, residual autocorrelation or whether either θ_{11} or θ_{21} is zero, etc.) can be applied to assess model adequacy; see Chapter 32 by Lütkepohl in this volume for further details.

In spite of the beauty and simplicity of the previous procedure, however, several problems remain. In particular, although $\hat{\beta}$ is super-consistent, this is an asymptotic result and thus biases could be important in finite samples. For instance, assume that the rates of convergence of two estimators are $T^{-1/2}$ and $10^{10}T^{-1}$. Then, we will need huge sample sizes to have the second estimator dominating the first one. In this sense, Monte Carlo experiments by Banerjee *et al.* (1993) showed that the biases could be important particularly when z_t and Δy_{2t} are highly serially correlated and they are not independent. Phillips (1991), in turn, has shown analytically that in the case where y_{2t} and z_t are independent at all leads and lags, the distribution in (30.9) as T grows behaves like a Gaussian distribution (technically is a *mixture of normals*) and, hence, the distribution of the *t*-statistic of β is also asymptotically normal. For this reason, Phillips and Hansen (1990) have developed an estimation procedure which corrects for the previous bias while achieving-asymptotic normality. The procedure, denoted as a *fully modified ordinary least squares estimator* (FM-OLS), is based upon a correction to the OLS estimator given in (30.8) by which the error term z_t is conditioned on the whole process $\{\Delta y_{2t}, t = 0, \pm 1, \ldots\}$ and, hence, orthogonality between regressors and disturbance is achieved by construction. For example, if z_t and ε_{2t} in (30.5) and (30.7) are correlated white noises with $\gamma = E(z_t \varepsilon_{2t})/\text{var}(\varepsilon_{2t})$, the FM-OLS estimator of β, denoted $\hat{\beta}_{FM}$, is given by

$$\hat{\beta}_{FM} = \frac{\sum\limits_{t=1}^{T} y_{2t}(y_{1t} - \hat{\gamma} \Delta y_{2t})}{\sum\limits_{t=1}^{T} y_{2t}^2}, \tag{30.10}$$

where $\hat{\gamma}$ is the empirical counterpart of γ obtained from regressing the OLS residuals $\hat{z}_t$ on Δy_{2t}. When z_t and Δy_{2t} follow more general processes, the FM-OLS estimator of β is similar to (30.10) except that further corrections are needed in its numerator. Alternatively, Saikkonen (1991) and Stock and Watson (1993) have shown that, since $E(z_t | \{\Delta y_{2t}\}) = h(L)\Delta y_{2t}$, where $h(L)$ is a two-sided filter in the lag operator L, regression of y_{1t} on y_{2t} and leads and lags of Δy_{2t} (suitably truncated), using either OLS or GLS, will yield an estimator of β which is asymptotically equivalent to the FM-OLS estimator. The resulting estimation approach is known as *dynamic* OLS (respectively GLS) or DOLS (respectively, DGLS).

3   System-Based Approaches to Cointegration

Whereas in the previous section we confined the analysis to the case where there is at most a single cointegrating vector in a bivariate system, this setup is usually quite restrictive when analyzing the cointegrating properties of an n-dimensional vector of I(1) variables where several cointegration relationships may arise. For example, when dealing with a trivariate system formed by the logarithms of nominal wages, prices, and labor productivity, there may exist two relationships, one determining an employment equation and another determining a wage equation. In this section we survey some of the popular estimation and testing procedures for cointegration in this more general multivariate context, which will be denoted as system-based approaches.

In general, if y_t now represents a vector of n I(1) variables its Wold representation (assuming again no deterministic terms) is given by

$$\Delta y_t = C(L)\varepsilon_t, \qquad (30.11)$$

where now $\varepsilon_t \sim \text{nid}(0, \Sigma)$, Σ being the covariance matrix of ε_t and $C(L)$ an $(n \times n)$ invertible matrix of polynomial lags, where the term "invertible" means that $|C(L)=0|$ has all its roots strictly larger than unity in absolute value. If there is a cointegrating $(n \times 1)$ vector, $\beta' = (\beta_{11}, \dots, \beta_{nn})$, then, premultiplying (30.11) by β' yields

$$\beta'\Delta y_t = \beta'[C(1) + \tilde{C}(L)\Delta]\varepsilon_t, \qquad (30.12)$$

where $C(L)$ has been expanded around $L = 1$ using a first-order Taylor expansion and $\tilde{C}(L)$ can be shown to be an invertible lag matrix. Since the cointegration property implies that $\beta'y_t$ is I(0), then it must be that $\beta'C(1) = 0$ and hence $\Delta(= 1 - L)$ will cancel out on both sides of (30.12). Moreover, given that $C(L)$ is invertible, then y_t has a vector autoregressive representation such that

$$A(L)y_t = \varepsilon_t, \qquad (30.13)$$

where $A(L)C(L) = (1 - L)I_n$, I_n being the $(n \times n)$ identity matrix. Hence, we must have that $A(1)C(1) = 0$, implying that $A(1)$ can be written as a linear combination of the elements β, namely, $A(1) = \alpha\beta'$, with α being another $(n \times 1)$ vector. In the same manner, if there were r cointegrating vectors $(0 < r < n)$, then $A(1) = B\Gamma'$, where B and Γ are this time $(n \times r)$ matrices which collect the r different α and β vectors. Matrix B is known as the *loading matrix* since its rows determine how many cointegrating relationships enter each of the individual dynamic equations in (30.13). Testing the rank of $A(1)$ or $C(1)$, which happen to be r and $n - r$, respectively, constitutes the basis of the following two procedures.

3.1   The Johansen's method

Johansen (1995) develops a maximum likelihood estimation procedure based on the so-called *reduced rank regression method* that, as the other methods to be later discussed, presents some advantages over the two-step regression procedure described in the previous section. First, it relaxes the assumption that the cointegrating vector is unique, and, second, it takes into account the short-run dynamics of the system when estimating the cointegrating vectors. The under-lying intuition behind Johansen's testing procedure can be easily explained by means of the following example. Assume that y_t has a VAR(1) representation, that is, $A(L)$ in (30.13) is such that $A(L) = I_n - A_1L$. Hence, the VAR(1) process can be reparameterized in the VECM representation as

$$\Delta y_t = (A_1 - I_n)y_{t-1} + \varepsilon_t. \tag{30.14}$$

If $A_1 - I_n = -A(1) = 0$, then y_t is I(1) and there are no cointegrating relationships $(r = 0)$, whereas if rank$(A_1 - I_n) = n$, there are n cointegrating relationships among the n series and hence $y_t \sim$ I(0). Thus, testing the null hypothesis that the number of cointegrating vectors (r) is equivalent to testing whether rank$(A_1 - I_n) = r$. Likewise, alternative hypotheses could be designed in different ways, e.g. that the rank is $(r + 1)$ or that it is n.

Under the previous considerations, Johansen (1995) deals with the more general case where y_t follows a VAR(p) process of the form

$$y_t = A_1y_{t-1} + A_2y_{t-2} + \ldots + A_py_{t-p} + \varepsilon_t, \tag{30.15}$$

which, as in (30.4) and (30.4'), can be rewritten in the ECM representation

$$\Delta y_t = D_1\Delta y_{t-1} + D_2\Delta y_{t-2} + \ldots + D_{p-1}\Delta y_{t-p+1} + Dy_{t-1} + \varepsilon_t. \tag{30.16}$$

Where $D_i = -(A_{i+1} + \ldots + A_p)$, $i = 1, 2, \ldots, p - 1$, and $D = (A_1 + \ldots + A_p - I_n) = -A(1)$ $= -B\Gamma'$. To estimate B and Γ, we need to estimate D subject to some identification restriction since otherwise B and Γ could not be separately identified. Maximum likelihood estimation of D goes along the same principles of the basic partitioned regression model, namely, the regressand and the regressor of interest (Δy_t and y_{t-1}) are regressed by OLS on the remaining set of regressors ($\Delta y_{t-1}, \ldots, \Delta y_{t-p+1}$) giving rise to two matrices of residuals denoted as $\hat{e}_0$ and $\hat{e}_1$ and the regression model $\hat{e}_{ot} = \hat{D}\hat{e}_{1t} +$ residuals. Following the preceding discussion, Johansen (1995) shows that testing for the rank of $\hat{D}$ is equivalent to test for the number of canonical correlations between $\hat{e}_0$ and $\hat{e}_1$ that are different from zero. This can be conducted using either of the following two test statistics

$$\lambda_{tr}(r) = -T \sum_{i=r+1}^{n} \ln(1 - \hat{\lambda}_i) \tag{30.17}$$

$$\lambda_{max}(r, r+1) = -T \ln(1 - \hat{\lambda}_{r+1}), \tag{30.18}$$

where the $\hat{\lambda}_i$s are the eigenvalues of the matrix $S_{10}S_{00}^{-1}S_{01}$ with respect to the matrix S_{11}, ordered in decreasing order $(1 > \hat{\lambda}_1 > \ldots > \hat{\lambda}_n > 0)$, where $S_{ij} = T^{-1}\sum_{t=1}^{T}\hat{e}_{it}\hat{e}_{jt}'$, $i, j = 0, 1$. These eigenvalues can be obtained as the solution of the determinantal equation

$$|\lambda S_{11} - S_{10}S_{00}^{-1}S_{01}| = 0. \tag{30.19}$$

The statistic in (30.17), known as the *trace statistic*, tests the null hypothesis that the number of cointegrating vectors is less than or equal to r against a general alternative. Note that, since $\ln(1) = 0$ and $\ln(0)$ tends to $-\infty$, it is clear that the trace statistic equals zero when all the $\hat{\lambda}_i$s are zero, whereas the further the eigenvalues are from zero the more negative is $\ln(1 - \hat{\lambda}_i)$ and the larger is the statistic. Likewise, the statistic in (30.18), known as the *maximum eigenvalue statistic*, tests a null of r cointegrating vectors against the specific alternative of $r + 1$. As above, if $\hat{\lambda}_{r+1}$ is close to zero, the statistic will be small. Further, if the null hypothesis is not rejected, the r cointegrating vectors contained in matrix Γ can be estimated as the first r columns of matrix $\hat{V} = (\hat{v}_1, \ldots, \hat{v}_n)$ which contains the eigenvectors associated to the eigenvalues in (30.19) computed as

$$(\lambda_i S_{11} - S_{10}S_{00}^{-1}S_{01})\hat{v}_i = 0, \quad i = 1, 2, \ldots, n$$

subject to the length normalization rule $\hat{V}'S_{11}\hat{V} = I_n$. Once Γ has been estimated, estimates of the B, D_i, and Σ matrices in (30.16) can be obtained by inserting $\hat{\Gamma}$ in their corresponding OLS formulae which will be functions of Γ.

Osterwald-Lenum (1992) has tabulated the critical values for both tests using Monte Carlo simulations, since their asymptotic distributions are multivariate $f(B)$ which depend upon: (i) the number of nonstationary components under the null hypothesis $(n - r)$ and (ii) the form of the vector of deterministic components, μ (e.g. a vector of drift terms), which needs to be included in the estimation of the ECM representation where the variables have nonzero means. Since, in order to simplify matters, the inclusion of deterministic components in (30.16) has not been considered so far, it is worth using a simple example to illustrate the type of interesting statistical problems that may arise when taking them into account. Suppose that $r = 1$ and that the unique cointegrating vector in Γ is normalized to be $\beta' = (1, \beta_{22}, \ldots, \beta_{nn})$, while the vector of speed of adjustment parameters, with which the cointegrating vector appears in each of the equations for the n variables, is $\alpha' = (\alpha_{11}, \ldots \alpha_{nn})$. If there is a vector of drift terms $\mu' = (\mu_1, \ldots \mu_n)$ such that they satisfy the restrictions $\mu_i = \alpha_{11}\mu_1$ (with $\alpha_{11} = 1$), it then follows that all Δy_{it} in (30.16) are expected to be zero when $y_{1,t-1} + \beta_{22}y_{2,t-1} + \cdots + \beta_{nn}y_{n,t-1} + \mu_1 = 0$ and, hence, the general solution for each of the $\{y_{it}\}$ processes, when integrated, will not contain a time trend. Many other possibilities, like, for example, allowing for a linear trend in each variable but not in the cointegrating relations, may be considered. In each case, the asymptotic distribution of the cointegration tests given in (30.17) and (30.18) will differ, and the corresponding sets of simulated critical values can be found in the reference quoted above. Sometimes, theory will guide the choice of restrictions; for example, if one is considering the relation between short-term and long-term interest rates, it may be wise to impose the restriction that the processes for both interest rates do not have linear trends and that the drift terms are restricted to appear in the cointegrating relationship interpreted as the "term structure." However, in other instances one may be interested in testing alternative sets of restrictions on the way μ enters the system; see, e.g. Chapter 32 by Lütkepohl in this volume for further details.

In that respect, the Johansen's approach allows to test restrictions on μ, B, and Γ subject to a given number of cointegrating relationships. The insight to all these tests, which turn out to have asymptotic chi-square distributions, is to compare the number of cointegrating vectors (i.e. the number of eigenvalues which are significantly different from zero) both when the restrictions are imposed and when they are not. Since if the true cointegration rank is r, only r linear combinations of the variables are stationary, one should find that the number of cointegrating vectors does not diminish if the restrictions are not binding and vice versa. Thus, denoting by $\hat{\lambda}_i$ and λ_i^* the set of r eigenvalues for the unrestricted and restricted cases, both sets of eigenvalues should be equivalent if the restrictions are valid. For example, a modification of the trace test in the form

$$T \sum_{i=1}^{r} [\ln (1 - \lambda_i^*) - \ln (1 - \hat{\lambda}_i)] \tag{30.20}$$

will be small if the λ_i^*s are similar to the $\hat{\lambda}_i$s, whereas it will be large if the λ_i^*s are smaller than the $\hat{\lambda}_i$s. If we impose s restrictions, then the above test will reject the null hypothesis if the calculated value of (30.20) exceeds that in a chi-square table with $r(n - s)$ degrees of freedom.

Most of the existing Monte Carlo studies on the Johansen methodology point out that dimension of the data series for a given sample size may pose particular problems since the number of parameters of the underlying VAR models grows very large as the dimension increases. Likewise, difficulties often arise when, for a given n, the lag length of the system, p, is either over- or under-parameterized. In particular, Ho and Sorensen (1996) and Gonzalo and Pitarakis (1999) show, by numerical methods, that the cointegrating order will tend to be overestimated as the dimension of the system increases relative to the time dimension, while serious size and power distortions arise when choosing too short and too long a lag length, respectively. Although several degrees of freedom adjustments to improve the performance of the test statistics have been advocated (see, e.g. Reinsel and Ahn, 1992), researchers ought to have considerable care when using the Johansen estimator to determine cointegration order in high dimensional systems with small sample sizes. Nonetheless, it is worth noticing that a useful approach to reduce the dimension of the VAR system is to rely upon exogeneity arguments to construct smaller conditional systems as suggested by Ericsson (1992) and Johansen (1992a). Equally, if the VAR specification is not appropriate, Phillips (1991) and Saikkonen (1992) provide efficient estimation of cointegrating vectors in more general time series settings, including vector ARMA processes.

3.2   Common trends representation

As mentioned above, there is a dual relationship between the number of cointegrating vectors (r) and the number of common trends ($n - r$) in an n-dimensional system. Hence, testing for the dimension of the set of "common trends" provides an alternative approach to testing for the cointegration order in a VAR//VECM representation. Stock and Watson (1988) provide a detailed study of this type of methodology based on the use of the so-called Beveridge–Nelson (1981) decomposition. This works from the Wold representation of an I(1) system, which we can write as in expression (30.11) with $C(L) = \sum_{j=0}^{\infty} C_j L^j$, $C_0 = I_n$. As shown in expression (30.12), $C(L)$ can be expanded as $C(L) = C(1) + \tilde{C}(L)(1 - L)$, so that, by integrating (30.11), we get

$$y_t = C(1)Y_t + \tilde{w}_t, \tag{30.21}$$

where $\tilde{w}_t = \tilde{C}(L)\varepsilon_t$ can be shown to be covariance stationary, and $Y_t = \sum_{i=1}^{t} \varepsilon_i$ is a latent or unobservable set of random walks which capture the I(1) nature of the data. However, as above mentioned, if the cointegration order is r, there must be an $(r \times n)$ Γ matrix such that $\Gamma'C(1) = 0$ since, otherwise, $\Gamma'y_t$ would be I(1) instead of I(0). This means that the $(n \times n)$ $C(1)$ matrix cannot have full rank. Indeed, from standard linear algebra arguments, it is easy to prove that the rank of $C(1)$ is $(n - r)$, implying that there are only $(n - r)$ independent common trends in the system. Hence, there exists the so-called *common trends representation* of a cointegrated system, such that

$$y_t = \Phi y_t^c + \tilde{w}_t, \tag{30.22}$$

where Φ is an $n \times (n - r)$ matrix of loading coefficients such that $\Gamma'\Phi = 0$ and y_t^c is an $(n - r)$ vector random walk. In other words, y_t can be written as the sum of $(n - r)$ common trends and an I(0) component. Thus, testing for $(n - r)$ common trends in the system is equivalent to testing for r cointegrating vectors. In this sense, Stock and Watson's (1988) testing approach relies upon the observation that, under the null hypothesis, the first-order autoregressive matrix of y_t^c should have $(n - r)$ eigenvalues equal to unity, whereas, under the alternative hypothesis of higher cointegration order, some of those eigenvalues will be less than unity. It is worth noticing that there are other alternative strategies to identify the set of common trends, y_t^c, which do not impose a vector random walk structure. In particular, Gonzalo and Granger (1995), using arguments embedded in the Johansen's approach, suggest identifying y_t^c as linear combinations of y_t which are not caused in the long-run by the cointegration relationships $\Gamma'y_{t-1}$. These linear combinations are the orthogonal complement of matrix B in (30.16), $y_t^c = B_\perp y_t$, where $B_\perp$ is an $(n \times (n - r))$ full ranked matrix, such that $B'B_\perp = 0$, that can be estimated as the last $(n - r)$ eigenvectors of the second moments matrix $S_{01}S_{11}^{-1}S_{10}$ with respect to S_{00}. For instance, when some of the rows of matrix B are zero, the common trends will be linear combinations of those I(1) variables in the system where the cointegrating vectors do not enter into their respective adjustment equations. Since common trends are expressed in terms of observable variables, instead of a latent set of random walks, economic theory can again be quite useful in helping to provide useful interpretation of their role. For example, the rational expectations version of the permanent income hypothesis of consumption states that consumption follows a random walk whilst saving (disposable income minus consumption) is I(0). Thus, if the theory is a valid one, the cointegrating vector in the system formed by consumption and disposable income should be $\beta' = (1, -1)$ and it would only appear in the second equation (i.e. $\alpha' = (0, \alpha_{22})$), implying that consumption should be the common trend behind the nonstationary behavior of both variables.

To give a simple illustration of the conceptual issues discussed in the previous two sections, let us consider the following Wold (MA) representation of the bivariate I(1) process $y_t = (y_{1t}, y_{2t})'$,

$$(1 - L)\begin{pmatrix} y_{1t} \\ y_{2t} \end{pmatrix} = (1 - 0.2L)^{-1}\begin{pmatrix} 1 - 0.6L & 0.8L \\ 0.2L & 1 - 0.6L \end{pmatrix}\begin{pmatrix} \varepsilon_{1t} \\ \varepsilon_{2t} \end{pmatrix}.$$

Evaluating $C(L)$ at $L = 1$ yields

$$C(1) = \begin{pmatrix} 0.5 & 1 \\ 0.25 & 0.5 \end{pmatrix},$$

so that rank $C(1) = 1$. Hence, $y_t \sim CI(1, 1)$. Next, inverting $C(L)$, yields the VAR representation

$$\begin{pmatrix} 1 - 0.6L & -0.8L \\ -0.2L & 1 - 0.6L \end{pmatrix}\begin{pmatrix} y_{1t} \\ y_{2t} \end{pmatrix} = \begin{pmatrix} \varepsilon_{1t} \\ \varepsilon_{2t} \end{pmatrix},$$

where

$$A(1) = \begin{pmatrix} 0.4 & -0.8 \\ -0.2 & 0.4 \end{pmatrix},$$

so that rank $A(1) = 1$ and

$$A(1) = \begin{pmatrix} 0.4 \\ -0.2 \end{pmatrix}(1, -2) = \alpha\beta'.$$

Hence, having normalized on the first element, the cointegrating vector is $\beta' = (1, -2)$, leading to the following VECM representation of the system

$$(1 - L)\begin{pmatrix} y_{1t} \\ y_{2t} \end{pmatrix} = \begin{pmatrix} -0.4 \\ 0.2 \end{pmatrix}(1, -2)\begin{pmatrix} y_{1,t-1} \\ y_{2,t-1} \end{pmatrix} + \begin{pmatrix} \varepsilon_{1t} \\ \varepsilon_{2t} \end{pmatrix}.$$

Next, given $C(1)$ and normalizing again on the first element, it is clear that the common factor is $y_t^c = \sum_{i=1}^t \varepsilon_{1i} + 2\sum_{i=1}^t \varepsilon_{2i}$, whereas the loading vector Φ and the common trend representation would be as follows

$$\begin{pmatrix} y_{1t} \\ y_{2t} \end{pmatrix} = \begin{pmatrix} 0.5 \\ 0.25 \end{pmatrix}y_t^c + \tilde{w}_t.$$

Notice that $\beta' y_t$ eliminates y_t^c from the linear combination which achieves cointegration. In other words, Φ is the orthogonal complement of β once the normalization criteria has been chosen.

Finally, to examine the effects of drift terms, let us add a vector $\mu = (\mu_1, \mu_2)'$ of drift coefficients to the VAR representation. Then, it is easy to prove that y_{1t} and y_{2t} will have a linear trends with slopes equal to $\mu_1/2 + \mu_2$ and $\mu_1/4 + \mu_2/2$, respectively. When $2\mu_1 + \mu_2 \neq 0$ the data will have linear trends, whereas the cointegrating relationship will not have them, since the linear combination in β annihilates the individual trends for any μ_1 and μ_2.

The interesting case arises when the restriction $2\mu_1 + \mu_2 = 0$ holds, since now the linear trend is purged from the system, leading to the restricted ECM representation

$$(1 - L)\begin{pmatrix} y_{1t} \\ y_{2t} \end{pmatrix} = \begin{pmatrix} -0.4 \\ 0.2 \end{pmatrix}(1, -2, -\mu_1^*)\begin{pmatrix} y_{1,t-1} \\ y_{2,t-1} \\ 1 \end{pmatrix} + \begin{pmatrix} \varepsilon_{1t} \\ \varepsilon_{2t} \end{pmatrix},$$

where $\mu_1^* = \mu_1/0.4$.

4   Further Research on Cointegration

Although the discussion in the previous sections has been confined to the possibility of cointegration arising from linear combinations of I(1) variables, the literature is currently proceeding in several interesting extensions of this standard setup. In the sequel we will briefly outline some of those extensions which have drawn a substantial amount of research in the recent past.

4.1   Higher order cointegrated systems

The statistical theory of I(d) systems with $d = 2, 3, \ldots$, is much less developed than the theory for the I(1) model, partly because it is uncommon to find time series, at least in economics, whose degree of integration higher than two, partly because the theory is quite involved as it must deal with possibly multicointegrated cases where, for instance, linear combinations of levels and first differences can achieve stationarity. We refer the reader to Haldrup (1999) for a survey of the statistical treatment of I(2) models, restricting the discussion in this chapter to the basics of the CI(2, 2) case.

Assuming, thus, that $y_t \sim$ CI(2, 2), with Wold representation given by

$$(1 - L)^2 y_t = C(L)\varepsilon_t, \tag{30.23}$$

then, by means of a Taylor expansion, we can write $C(L)$ as

$$C(L) = C(1) - C^*(1)(1 - L) + \tilde{C}(L)(1 - L)^2,$$

with $C^*(1)$ being the first derivative of $C(L)$ with respect to L, evaluated at $L = 1$. Following the arguments in the previous section, $y_t \sim$ CI(2, 2) implies that there exists a set of cointegrating vectors such that $\Gamma'C(1) = \Gamma'C^*(1) = 0$, from which the following VECM representation can be derived

$$A^*(L)(1 - L)^2 y_t = -B_1\Gamma' y_{t-1} - B_2\Gamma'\Delta y_{t-1} + \varepsilon_t \tag{30.24}$$

with $A^*(0) = I_n$. Johansen (1992b) has developed the maximum likelihood estimation of this class of models, which, albeit more complicated than in the CI(1, 1) case, proceeds along similar lines to those discussed in Section 3.

Likewise, there are systems where the variables have unit roots at the seasonal frequencies. For example, if a seasonally integrated variable is measured every half-a-year, then it will have the following Wold representation

$$(1 - L^2)y_t = C(L)\varepsilon_t. \tag{30.25}$$

Since $(1 - L^2) = (1 - L)(1 + L)$, the $\{y_t\}$ process could be cointegrated by obtaining linear combinations which eliminate the unit root at the zero frequency, $(1 - L)$, and/or at the seasonal frequency, $(1 + L)$. Assuming that Γ_1 and Γ_2 are sets of cointegrating relationships at each of the two above mentioned frequencies, Hylleberg et al. (1990) have shown that the VECM representation of the system this time will be

$$A^*(L)(1 - L^2)y_t = -B_1\Gamma_1'\Delta y_{t-1} - B_2\Gamma_2'(y_{t-1} + y_{t-2}) + \varepsilon_t, \tag{30.26}$$

with $A^*(0) = I_n$. Notice that if there is no cointegration in $(1 + L)$, $\Gamma_2 = 0$ and the second term in the right-hand side of (30.26) will vanish, whereas lack of cointegration in $(1 - L)$ implies $\Gamma_1 = 0$ and the first term will disappear. Similar arguments can be used to obtain VECM representations for quarterly or monthly data with seasonal difference operators of the form $(1 - L^4)$ and $(1 - L^{12})$, respectively.

4.2 Fractionally cointegrated systems

As discussed earlier in this chapter, one of the main characteristics of the existence of unit roots in the Wold representation of a time series is that they have "long memory," in the sense that shocks have permanent effects on the levels of the series so that the variance of the levels of the series explodes. In general, it is known that if the differencing filter $(1 - L)^d$, d being now a real number, is needed to achieve stationarity, then the coefficient of ε_{i-j} in the Wold representation of the I(d) process has a leading term j^{d-1} (e.g. the coefficient in an I(1) process is unity, since $d = 1$) and the process is said to be *fractionally integrated of order d*. In this case, the variance of the series in levels will explode at the rate T^{2d-1} (e.g. at the rate T when $d = 1$) and then all that is needed to have this kind of long memory is a degree of differencing $d > 1/2$.

Consequently, it is clear that a wide range of dynamic behavior is ruled out a priori if d is restricted to integer values and that a much broader range of cointegration possibilities are entailed when fractional cases are considered. For example, we could have a pair of series which are I(d_1), $d_1 > 1/2$, which cointegrate to obtain an I(d_0) linear combination such that $0 < d_0 < 1/2$. A further complication arises in this case if the various integration orders are not assumed to be known and need to be estimated for which frequency domain regression methods are normally used. Extensions of least squares and maximum likelihood methods of estimation and testing for cointegration within this more general framework can be found in Jeganathan (1996), Marmol (1998) and Robinson and Marinucci (1998).

4.3 Nearly cointegrated systems

Even when a vector of time series is I(1), the size of the unit root in each of the series could be very different. For example, in terms of the common trend representation of a bivariate system discussed above, it could well be the case that $y_{1t} = \phi_1 y_t^c + \tilde{w}_{1t}$ and $y_{2t} = \phi_2 y_t^c + \tilde{w}_{2t}$ are such that ϕ_1 is close to zero and that ϕ_2 is large. Then y_{1t} will not be different from $\tilde{w}_{1t}$ which is an I(0) series while y_{2t} will be clearly I(1). The two series are cointegrated, since they share a common trend. However, if we regress y_{1t} on y_{2t}, i.e. we normalize the cointegrating vector on the coefficient of y_{1t}, the regression will be nearly unbalanced, namely, the regressand is almost I(0) whilst the regressor is I(1). In this case, the estimated coefficient on y_{2t} will converge quickly to zero and the residuals will resemble the properties of y_{1t}, i.e. they will look stationary. Thus, according to the Engle and Granger testing approach, we will often reject the null of no cointegration. By contrast, if we regress y_{2t} on y_{1t}, now the residuals will resemble the I(1) properties of the regressand and we will often reject cointegration. Therefore, normalization plays a crucial role in least squares estimation of cointegrating vectors in nearly cointegrated systems. Consequently, if one uses the static regression approach to estimate the cointegrating vector, it follows from the previous discussion that it is better to use the "less integrated" variable as the regressand. Ng and Perron (1997) have shown that these problems remain when the equations are estimated using more efficient methods like FM-OLS and DOLS, while the Johansen's methodology provides a better estimation approach, since normalization is only imposed on the length of the eigenvectors.

4.4 Nonlinear error correction models

When discussing the role of the cointegrating relationship z_t in (30.3) and (30.3'), we motivated the EC model as the disequilibrium mechanism that leads to the particular equilibrium. However, as a function of an I(0) process is generally also I(0), an alternative more general VECM model has z_{t-1} in (30.3) and (30.3') replaced by $g(z_{t-1})$ where $g(z)$ is a function such that $g(0) = 0$ and $E[g(z)]$ exists. The function $g(z)$ is such that it can be estimated nonparametrically or by assuming a particular parametric form. For example, one can include $z^+ = \max\{0, z_t\}$ and $z^- = \min\{0, z_t\}$ separately into the model or large and small values of z according to some prespecified threshold in order to deal with possible sign or size asymmetries in the dynamic adjustment. Further examples can be found in Granger and Teräsvirta (1993). The theory of nonlinear cointegration models is still fairly incomplete, but nice applications can be found in Gonzalez and Gonzalo (1998) and Balke and Fomby (1997).

4.5 Structural breaks in cointegrated systems

The parameters in the cointegrating regression model (30.5) may not be constant through time. Gregory and Hansen (1995) developed a test for cointegration allowing for a structural break in the intercept as well as in the slope of model (30.5). The new regression model now looks like

$$y_{1t} = \alpha_1 + \alpha_2 D(t_0) + \beta_1 y_{2t} + \beta_2 y_{2t} D(t_0) + z_t, \qquad (30.27)$$

where $D(t_0)$ is a dummy variable such that $D(t_0) = 0$ if $0 < t \le t_0$ and $D(t_0) = 1$ if $t_0 < t \le T$. The test for cointegration is conducted by testing for unit roots (for instance, with an ADF test) on the residuals $\hat{z}_t$ for each t_0. Gregory and Hansen propose and tabulate the critical values of the test statistic

$$ADF^* = \inf_{1 < t_0 < T} \{ADF(t_0)\}.$$

The null hypothesis of no cointegration and no structural break is rejected if the statistic ADF^* is smaller than the corresponding critical value. In this case the structural break will be located at time t^* where the inf of the ADF test is obtained. The work of Gregory and Hansen is opening an extensive research on analyzing the stability of the parameters of multivariate possibly cointegrated systems models like the VECM in (30.16). Further work in this direction can be found in Hansen and Johansen (1993), Quintos (1994), Juhl (1997), and Arranz and Escribano (2000).

5   CONCLUDING REMARKS

The considerable gap in the past between the economic theorist, who had much to say about equilibrium but relatively less to say about dynamics and the econometrician whose models concentrated on the short-run dynamics disregarding the long-run equilibrium, has been bridged by the concept of cointegration. In addition to allowing the data to determine the short-run dynamics, cointegration suggest that models can be significantly improved by including long-run equilibrium conditions as suggested by economic theory. The generic existence of such long-run relationships, in turn, should be tested using the techniques discussed in this chapter to reduce the risk of finding spurious conclusions.

The literature on cointegration has greatly enhanced the existing methods of dynamic econometric modeling of economic time series and should be considered nowadays as a very valuable part of the practitioner's toolkit.

References

Arranz, M.A., and A. Escribano (2000). Cointegration testing under structural breaks: A robust extended error correction model. *Oxford Bulletin of Economics and Statistics* 62, 23–52.

Balke, N., and T. Fomby (1997). Threshold cointegration. *International Economic Review* 38, 627–45.

Banerjee, A., J.J. Dolado, J.W. Galbraith, and D.F. Hendry (1993). *Co-integration, Erroe Correction and the Econometric Analysis of Non-stationary Data*, Oxford: Oxford University Press.

Banerjee, A., J.J. Dolado, and R. Mestre (1998). Error-correction mechanism tests for cointegration in a single-equation framework. *Journal of Time Series Analysis* 19, 267–84.

Beveridge, S., and C.R. Nelson (1981). A new approach to decomposition of economic time series into permanent and transitory components with particular attention to measurement of the "Business Cycle". *Journal of Monetary Economics* 7, 151–74.

Box, G.E.P., and G.M. Jenkins (1970). *Time Series Analysis: Forecasting and Control*, San Francisco: Holden Day.

Campbell, J.Y., and R.J. Shiller (1987). Cointegration and tests of present value models. *Journal of Political Economy* 95, 1062–88.

Davidson, J.E.H., D.F. Hendry, F. Srba, and S. Yeo (1978). Econometric modelling of the aggregate time series relationships between consumer's expenditure and income in the United Kingdom. *Economic Journal* 88, 661–92.

Engle, R.F., and C.W.J. Granger (1987). Co-integration and error correction: Representation, estimation and testing. *Econometrica* 55, 251–76.

Engle, R.F. and C.W.J. Granger (eds.) (1991). *Long-run Economic Relationships: Readings in Cointegration*. Oxford: Oxford University Press.

Engle, R.F., and B.S. Yoo (1987). Forecasting and testing in cointegrated systems. *Journal of Econometrics* 35, 143–59.

Ericsson, N.R. (1992). Cointegration, exogeneity and policy analysis: An overview. *Journal of Policy Modeling* 14, 424–38.

Gonzalez, M., and J. Gonzalo (1998). Inference in threshold error correction model. *Discussion Paper*, Universidad Carlos III de Madrid.

Gonzalo, J., and C.W.J. Granger (1995). Estimation of common long memory components in cointegrated systems. *Journal of Business and Economic Statistics* 13, 27–36.

Gonzalo, J., and J.-Y. Pitarakis (1999). Dimensionality effect in cointegrated systems. In Granger Festschrift edited by R. Engle and H. White (eds.). Oxford: Oxford, University Press.

Granger, C.W.J. (1981). Some properties of time series data and their use in econometric model specification. *Journal of Econometrics* 23, 121–30.

Granger, C.W.J. (1986). Developments in the study of cointegrated economic variables. *Oxford Bulletin of Economics and Statistics* 48, 213–28.

Granger, C.W.J., and T.H. Lee (1989). Multicointegration. *Advances in Econometrics* 8, 71–84.

Granger, C.W.J., and P. Newbold (1974). Spurious regressions in econometrics. *Journal of Econometrics* 2, 111–20.

Granger, C.W.J., and T. Teräsvirta (1993). *Modelling Nonlinear Economic Relationships*. Oxford: Oxford University Press.

Gregory, A.W., and B.E. Hansen (1995). Residual-based tests for cointegration in models with regime shifts. *Journal of Econometrics* 70, 99–126.

Haldrup, N. (1999). A review of the econometric analysis of I(2) variables. In L. Oxley and M. McAleer (eds.) *Practical Issues in Cointegration Analysis*. Oxford: Blackwell.

Hansen, H., and S. Johansen (1993). Recursive estimation in cointegrated VAR models. *Preprint* 1, Institute of Mathematical Statistics, University of Copenhagen.

Hatanaka, M. (1996). *Time Series-Based Econometrics*. Oxford: Oxford University Press.

Hendry, D.F., and G.E. Mizon (1978). Serial correlation as a convenient simplification not a nuisance: A comment on a study of the demand for money by the Bank of England. *Economic Journal* 88, 549–63.

Hendry, D.F., and J.-F. Richard (1983). The econometric analysis of economic time series (with discussant). *International Statistical Review* 51, 111–63.

Hylleberg, S., R.F. Engle, C.W.J. Granger, and B.S. Yoo (1990). Seasonal integration and cointegration. *Journal of Econometrics* 44, 215–28.

Ho, M. and B. Sorensen (1996). Finding cointegration rank in high dimensional systems using the Johansen test: An illustration using data based on Monte Carlo simulations. *Review of Economics and Statistics* 78, 726–32.

Jeganathan, P. (1996). On asymptotic inference in cointegrated time series with fractionally integrated errors. *Discussion Paper*, University of Michigan.

Johansen, S. (1992a). A representation of vector autoregressive processes integrated of order 2. *Econometric Theory* 8, 188–202.

Johansen, S. (1992b). Cointegration in partial systems and the efficiency of single-equation analysis. *Journal of Econometrics* 52, 389–402.

Johansen, S. (1995). *Likelihood-Based Inference in Cointegrated Vector Auto-regressive Models*, Oxford: Oxford University Press.

Juhl, T., (1997), Likelihood ratio tests for cointegration in the presence of multiple breaks. Discussion Paper, University of Pennsylvania.

MacKinnon, J.G. (1991). Critical values for cointegration tests. In R.F. Engle and C.W.J. Granger (eds.) *Long-run Economic Relationships: Readings in Cointegration*. Oxford: Oxford University Press.

Maddala, G.S., and I.M. Kim (1998) *Unit Roots, Cointegration and Structural Change*. Cambridge: Cambridge University Press.

Marmol, F. (1998). Spurious regression theory with nonstationary fractionally integrated processes. *Journal of Econometrics* 84, 232–50.

Nelson, C.R., and C.I. Plosser (1982). Trends and random walks in macroeconomic time series: Some evidence and implications. *Journal of Monetary Economics* 10, 139–62.

Ng, S., and P. Perron (1997). Estimation and inference in nearly unbalanced nearly cointegrated systems. *Journal of Econometrics* 79, 53–81.

Osterwald-Lenum, M. (1992). A note with quantiles of the asymptotic distribution of the maximum likelihood cointegration rank test statistics. *Oxford Bulletin of Economics and Statistics* 54, 461–72.

Phillips, P.C.B. (1987). Time series regression with a unit root. *Econometrica* 55, 277–301.

Phillips, P.C.B. (1991). Optimal inference in cointegrated systems. *Econometrica* 59, 283–306.

Phillips, P.C.B., and B.E. Hansen (1990). Statistical inference in instrumental variables regression with I(1) processes. *Review of Economic Studies* 57, 99–125.

Phillips, P.C.B., and S. Ouliaris (1990). Asymptotic properties of residual based tests for cointegration. *Econometrica* 58, 165–94.

Quintos, C. (1994). Rank constancy tests in cointegrating regressions. Discussion Paper, Yale University.

Reinsel, G.C., and S.K. Ahn (1992). Vector autoregressive models with unit roots and reduced rank structure: Estimation, likelihood ratio test, and forecasting. *Journal of Time Series Analysis* 13, 353–75.

Robinson, P., and D. Marinucci (1998). Semiparametric frequency domain analysis of fractional cointegration. Discussion Paper, London School of Economics.

Saikkonen, P. (1991). Asymptotically efficient estimation of cointegrated regressions. *Econometric Theory* 7, 1–21.

Saikkonen, P. (1992). Estimation and testing of cointegrated systems by an autoregressive approximation. *Econometric Theory* 8, 1–27.

Sargan, J.D. (1964). Wages and prices in the United Kingdom: A study in econometric methodology. In D.F. Hendry and K.F. Wallis (eds.) *Econometrics and Quantitative Economics*. Oxford: Blackwell.

Stock, J.H. (1987). Asymptotic properties of least squares estimators of cointegrating vectors. *Econometrica* 55, 277–302.

Stock, J.H., and M.W. Watson (1988). Testing for common trends. *Journal of the American Statistical Association* 83, 1097–107.

Stock, J.H., and M.W. Watson (1993). A simple estimator of cointegrating vectors in higher order integrated systems. *Econometrica* 61, 783–820.

Watson, M.W. (1994). Vector autoregressions and cointegration. In Engle, R.F. and D.L. McFadden (eds.) *Handbook of Econometrics IV*, New York: Elsevier.

Wold, H. (1938). *A Study in the Analysis of Stationary Time Series*, Stockholm: Almqvist and Wiksell.

Seasonal Nonstationarity and Near-Nonstationarity*

*Eric Ghysels, Denise R. Osborn,
and Paulo M.M. Rodrigues**

1 INTRODUCTION

Over the last three decades there has been an increasing interest in modeling seasonality. Progressing from the traditional view that the seasonal pattern is a nuisance which needed to be removed, it is now considered to be an informative feature of economic time series which should be modeled explicitly (see for instance Ghysels (1994) for a review).

Since the seminal work by Box and Jenkins (1970), the stochastic properties of seasonality have been a major focus of research. In particular, the recognition that the seasonal behavior of economic time series may be varying and changing over time due to the presence of seasonal unit roots (see for example Canova and Ghysels (1994), Hylleberg (1994), Hylleberg, Jørgensen, and Sørensen (1993) and Osborn (1990)), has led to the development of a considerable number of testing procedures (*inter alia*, Canova and Hansen (1995), Dickey, Hasza, and Fuller (1984), Franses (1994), Hylleberg, Engle, Granger, and Yoo (1990) and Osborn, Chui, Smith, and Birchenhall (1988)).

In this chapter, we review the properties of stochastic seasonal nonstationary processes, as well as the properties of several seasonal unit root tests. More specifically, in Section 2 we analyze the characteristics of the seasonal random walk and generalize our discussion for seasonally integrated ARMA (autoregressive moving average) processes. Furthermore, we also illustrate the implications that can emerge when nonstationary stochastic seasonality is posited as deterministic.

In Section 3 we consider the asymptotic properties of the seasonal unit root test procedures proposed by Dickey *et al.* (1984) and Hylleberg *et al.* (1990). Section 4 generalizes most of the results of Section 3 by considering the behavior of the test procedures in a near seasonally integrated framework. Finally, Section 5 concludes the chapter.

To devote a chapter on the narrow subject of seasonal nonstationarity deserves some explanation. Seasonal time series appear nonstationary, a feature shared by many economic data recorded at fixed time intervals. Whether we study so-called seasonal adjusted data or raw series, the question of seasonal unit roots looms behind the univariate models being used. The standard seasonal adjustment programs like X-11 and X-12/ARIMA involve removal of seasonal unit roots (for details of seasonal adjustment programs see for instance Findley *et al.* (1998) or Ghysels and Osborn (2000)). Removing such roots may be unwarranted if they are not present and may cause statistical problems such as non-invertible MA roots (see Maravall, 1993, for further discussion). When unadjusted series are considered, then the question of seasonal unit roots is a basic issue of univariate time series model specification. Since we are particularly interested in how the asymptotic results for conventional unit root processes generalize to the seasonal context we will use the large sample distribution theory involving Brownian motion representations.

2   PROPERTIES OF SEASONAL UNIT ROOT PROCESSES

The case of primary interest in the context of seasonal unit roots occurs when the process y_t is nonstationary and annual differencing is required to induce stationarity. This is often referred to as *seasonal integration*. More formally:

Definition 1.   The nonstationary stochastic process y_t, observed at $\mathbb{S}$ equally spaced time intervals per year, is said to be seasonally integrated of order d, denoted $y_t \sim \mathrm{SI}(d)$, if $\Delta_{\mathbb{S}}^d y_t = (1 - L^{\mathbb{S}})^d y_t$ is a stationary, invertible ARMA process.

Therefore, if first order annual differencing renders y_t a stationary and invertible process, then $y_t \sim \mathrm{SI}(1)$. The simplest case of such a process is the seasonal random walk, which will be the focus of analysis throughout most of this chapter. We refer to $\mathbb{S}$ as the number of seasons per year for y_t.

2.1   The seasonal random walk

The seasonal random walk is a seasonal autoregressive process of order 1, or SAR(1), such that

$$y_t = y_{t-\mathbb{S}} + \varepsilon_t, \quad t = 1, 2, \ldots, T \tag{31.1}$$

with $\varepsilon_t \sim \mathrm{iid}(0, \sigma^2)$. Denoting the season in which observation t falls as s_t, with $s_t = 1 + (t - 1) \bmod \mathbb{S}$, backward substitution for lagged y_t in this process implies that

$$y_t = y_{s_t-\mathbb{S}} + \sum_{j=0}^{n_t-1} \varepsilon_{t-\mathbb{S}j}, \tag{31.2}$$

where $n_t = 1 + [(t-1)/\mathbb{S}]$ and $[\cdot]$ represents the greatest integer less or equal to $(t-1)/\mathbb{S}$. As noted by Dickey et al. (1984) and emphasized by Osborn (1993), the random walk in this case is defined in terms of the disturbances for the specific season s_t only, with the summation over the current disturbance ε_t and the disturbance for this season in the $n_t - 1$ previous years of the observation period. The term $y_{s_t-\mathbb{S}} = y_{t-n_t\mathbb{S}}$, refers to the appropriate starting value for the process. Equation (31.1) is, of course, a generalization of the conventional nonseasonal random walk. Note that the unconditional mean of y_t from (31.2) is

$$E(y_t) = E(y_{s_t-\mathbb{S}}). \tag{31.3}$$

Thus, although the process (31.1) does not explicitly contain deterministic seasonal effects, these are implicitly included when $E(y_{s_t-\mathbb{S}})$ is nonzero and varies over $s_t = 1, \ldots, \mathbb{S}$. In their analysis of seasonal unit roots, Dickey et al. (1984) separate the y_t corresponding to each of the $\mathbb{S}$ seasons into distinct series. Notationally, this is conveniently achieved using two subscripts, the first referring to the season and the second to the year. Then

$$y_t = y_{s+\mathbb{S}(n-1)} = y_{sn}, \tag{31.4}$$

where s_t and n_t are here written as s and n for simplicity of notation. Correspondingly $\mathbb{S}$ disturbance series can be defined as

$$\varepsilon_t = \varepsilon_{s_t+\mathbb{S}(n_t-1)} = \varepsilon_{sn}. \tag{31.5}$$

Using these definitions, and assuming that observations are available for precisely N ($N = T/\mathbb{S}$) complete years, then (31.1) can be written as

$$y_{sn} = y_{s,0} + \sum_{j=1}^{n} \varepsilon_{sj} \quad s = 1, \ldots, \mathbb{S} \quad \text{and} \quad n = 1, \ldots, N \tag{31.6}$$

which simply defines a random walk for each season $s = 1, \ldots, \mathbb{S}$. Because the disturbances ε_t of (31.1) are uncorrelated, the random walks defined by (31.6) for the $\mathbb{S}$ seasons of the year are also uncorrelated. Thus, any linear combination of these processes can itself be represented as a random walk. The accumulation of disturbances allows the differences to wander far from the mean over time, giving rise to the phenomenon that "summer may become winter."

2.2   More general processes

To generalize the above discussion, weakly stationary autocorrelations can be permitted in the SI(1) process. That is, (31.1) can be generalized to the seasonally integrated ARMA process:

$$\phi(L)\Delta_{\mathbb{S}} y_t = \theta(L)\varepsilon_t, \quad t = 1, 2, \ldots, T, \tag{31.7}$$

where, as before, $\varepsilon_t \sim \text{iid}(0, \sigma^2)$, while the polynomials $\phi(L)$ and $\theta(L)$ in the lag operator L have all roots outside the unit circle. It is, of course, permissible that these polynomials take the multiplicative form of the seasonal ARMA model of Box and Jenkins (1970). Inverting the stationary autoregressive polynomial and defining $z_t = \phi(L)^{-1}\theta(L)\varepsilon_t$, we can write (31.7) as:

$$\Delta_{\mathbb{S}} y_t = z_t, \quad t = 1, \ldots, T. \tag{31.8}$$

The process superficially looks like the seasonal random walk, namely (31.1). There is, however, a crucial difference in that z_t here is a stationary, invertible ARMA process. Nevertheless, performing the same substitution for lagged y_t as above leads to the corresponding result, which can be written as

$$y_{sn} = y_{s,0} + \sum_{j=1}^{n} z_{sj} \quad s = 1, \ldots, \mathbb{S} \quad \text{and} \quad n = 1, \ldots, N. \tag{31.9}$$

As in (31.6), (31.9) implies that there are $\mathbb{S}$ distinct unit root processes, one corresponding to each of the seasons. The important distinction is that these processes in (31.9) may be autocorrelated and cross-correlated. Nevertheless, it is only the stationary components which are correlated.

Defining the observation and (weakly stationary) disturbance vectors for year n as $Y_n = (y_{1n}, \ldots, y_{\mathbb{S}n})'$ and $Z_n = (z_{1n}, \ldots, z_{\mathbb{S}n})'$ respectively, the vector representation of (31.9) is:

$$\Delta Y_n = Z_n, \quad n = 1, \ldots, N. \tag{31.10}$$

The disturbances here follow a stationary vector ARMA process

$$\Phi(L)Z_n = \Theta(L)E_n. \tag{31.11}$$

It is sufficient to note that $\Phi(L)$ and $\Theta(L)$ are appropriately defined $\mathbb{S} \times \mathbb{S}$ polynomial matrices in L with all roots outside the unit circle and $E_n = (\varepsilon_{1n}, \ldots, \varepsilon_{\mathbb{S}n})'$. The seasonal difference of (31.7) is converted to a first difference in (31.10) because $\Delta Y_n = Y_n - Y_{n-1}$ defines an annual (that is, seasonal) difference of the vector Y_t. Now, in (31.10) we have a vector ARMA process in ΔY_n, which is a vector ARIMA process in Y_n. In the terminology of Engle and Granger (1987), the $\mathbb{S}$ processes in the vector Y_t cannot be cointegrated if this is the data generating process (DGP). Expressed in a slightly different way, if the process is written in terms of the level Y_n, the vector process will contain $\mathbb{S}$ unit roots due to the presence of the factor $\Delta = 1 - L$ in each of the equations. Therefore, the implication drawn from the seasonal random walk of (31.1) that any linear combination of the separate seasonal series is itself an I(1) process carries over to this case too.

For the purpose of this chapter, only the simple seasonal random walk case will be considered in the subsequent analysis. It should, however, be recognized that the key results extend to more general seasonally integrated processes.

2.3 Asymptotic properties

Consider the DGP of the seasonal random walk with initial values $y_{-S+s} = \ldots = y_0 = 0$. Using the notation of (31.6), the following S independent partial sum processes (PSPs) can be obtained:

$$S_{sn} = \sum_{j=1}^{n} \varepsilon_{sj} \quad s = 1, \ldots, S, \quad n = 1, \ldots, N \tag{31.12}$$

where n represents the number of years of observations to time t. From the functional central limit theorem (FCLT) and the continuous mapping theorem (CMT) the appropriately scaled PSPs in (31.12) converge as $N \to \infty$ to

$$\frac{1}{\sqrt{N}} S_{sn} \Rightarrow \sigma W_s(r), \tag{31.13}$$

where $\Rightarrow$ indicates convergence in distribution, while $W_s(r)$, $s = 1, \ldots, S$ are independent standard Brownian motions. Furthermore, the following Lemma collecting the relevant convergence results for seasonal unit root processes of periodicity S can be stated:

Lemma 1. Assuming that the DGP is the seasonal random walk in (31.1) with initial values equal to zero, $\varepsilon_t \sim \text{iid}(0, \sigma^2)$ and $T = SN$, then from the CMT, as $T \to \infty$,

(a) $\quad T^{-1/2} y_{t-k} \Rightarrow S^{-1/2} \sigma L^k W_s$

(b) $\quad T^{-3/2} \sum_{t=1}^{T} y_{t-k} \Rightarrow S^{-3/2} \sigma \sum_{s=1}^{S} \int_0^1 W_s dr$

(c) $\quad T^{-2} \sum_{t=1}^{T} y_{t-i} y_{t-k} \Rightarrow S^{-2} \sigma^2 \sum_{s=1}^{S} \int_0^1 W_s (L^{k-i} W_s) dr \quad k \geq i$

(d) $\quad T^{-1} \sum_{t=1}^{T} y_{t-k} \varepsilon_t \Rightarrow S^{-1} \sigma^2 \sum_{s=1}^{S} \int_0^1 (L^k W_s) dW_s$

where $k = 1, \ldots, S$, $W_s(r)$ ($s = 1 + (t - 1) \bmod S$) are independent standard Brownian motions, L is the lag operator which shifts the Brownian motions between seasons ($L^k W_s = W_{s-k}$ with $W_{s-k} = W_{S+s-k}$ for $s - k \leq 0$) and $W_s = W_s(r)$ for simplicity of notation.

It is important to note the circular property regarding the rotation of the W_k, so that after S lags of y_t the same sum of S integrals emerges. The Lemma is established in Osborn and Rodrigues (1998).

2.4   Deterministic seasonality

A common practice is to attempt the removal of seasonal patterns via seasonal dummy variables (see, for example, Barsky and Miron, 1989; Beaulieu and Miron, 1991; Osborn, 1990). The interpretation of the seasonal dummy approach is that seasonality is essentially deterministic so that the series is stationary around seasonally varying means. The simplest deterministic seasonal model is

$$y_t = \sum_{s=1}^{\mathbb{S}} \delta_{st} m_s + \varepsilon_t \tag{31.14}$$

where δ_{st} is the seasonal dummy variable which takes the value 1 when t falls in season s and $\varepsilon_t \sim$ iid$(0, \sigma^2)$. Typically, y_t is a first difference series in order to account for the zero frequency unit root commonly found in economic time series. When a model like (31.14) is used, the coefficient of determination (R^2) is often computed as a measure of the strength of the seasonal pattern. However, as Abeysinghe (1991, 1994) and Franses, Hylleberg, and Lee (1995) indicate, the presence of seasonal unit roots in the DGP will have important consequences for R^2.

To illustrate this issue, take the seasonal random walk of (31.1) as the DGP and assume that (31.14) is used to model the seasonal pattern. As is well known, the OLS estimates of m_s, $s = 1, \ldots, \mathbb{S}$ are simply the mean values of y_t in each season. Thus, using the notation of (31.4),

$$\hat{m}_s = \frac{1}{N} \sum_{t=1}^{T} \delta_{st} y_t = \frac{1}{N} \sum_{t=1}^{N} y_{sn} \tag{31.15}$$

where (as before) T and N are the total number of observations and the total number of complete years of observations available, respectively, and it is again assumed for simplicity that $T = \mathbb{S}N$. As noted by Franses et al. (1995), the estimated seasonal intercepts diverge under the seasonal random walk DGP. In particular, the appropriately scaled $\hat{m}_s$ converges to a normal random variable

$$N^{-1/2} \hat{m}_s = N^{-3/2} \sum_{t=1}^{T} \delta_{st} y_t \Rightarrow \sigma \int_0^1 W_s(r)\, dr = N(0, \sigma^2/3), \quad s = 1, \ldots, \mathbb{S} \tag{31.16}$$

where the latter follows from Banerjee et al. (1993, pp. 43–5) who show that $\int_0^1 W(r)dr = N(0, 1/3)$. For this DGP, the R^2 from (31.14) has the non-degenerate asymptotic distribution,[1]

$$R^2 = \frac{\sum_{t=1}^{T} (\hat{y}_t - \bar{y})^2}{\sum_{t=1}^{T} (y_t - \bar{y})^2} \Rightarrow \frac{\sum_{s=1}^{\mathbb{S}} \left(\int_0^1 W_s(r)dr \right)^2 - \frac{1}{\mathbb{S}} \left[\int_0^1 \left(\sum_{s=1}^{\mathbb{S}} W_s(r) \right) dr \right]^2}{\sum_{s=1}^{\mathbb{S}} \int_0^1 W_s^2(r)dr - \frac{1}{\mathbb{S}} \left[\int_0^1 \left(\sum_{s=1}^{\mathbb{S}} W_s(r) \right) dr \right]^2}. \tag{31.17}$$

Consequently, high values for this statistic are to be anticipated, as concluded by Franses *et al.* These are spurious in the sense that the DGP contains no deterministic seasonality since $E(y_t) = 0$ when the starting values for (31.1) are zero. Hence a high value of R^2 when (31.14) is estimated does not constitute evidence in favor of deterministic seasonality.

3   Testing the Seasonal Unit Root Null Hypothesis

In this section we discuss the test procedures proposed by Dickey *et al.* (1984) and Hylleberg, Engle, Granger, and Yoo (HEGY) (1990) to test the null hypothesis of seasonal integration. It should be noted that while there are a large number of seasonal unit root tests available (see, for example, Rodrigues (1998) for an extensive survey), casual observation of the literature shows that the HEGY test is the most frequently used procedure in empirical work. For simplicity of presentation, throughout this section we assume that augmentation of the test regression to account for autocorrelation is unnecessary and that presample starting values for the DGP are equal to zero.

3.1   The Dickey–Hasza–Fuller test

The first test of the null hypothesis $y_t \sim SI(1)$ was proposed by Dickey, Hasza, and Fuller (DHF) (1984), as a direct generalization of the test proposed by Dickey and Fuller (1979) for a nonseasonal AR(1) process. Assuming that the process is known to be a SAR(1), then the DHF test can be parameterized as

$$\Delta_S y_t = \alpha_S y_{t-S} + \varepsilon_t. \tag{31.18}$$

The null hypothesis of seasonal integration corresponds to $\alpha_S = 0$, while the alternative of a stationary stochastic seasonal process implies $\alpha_S < 0$. The appropriately scaled least squares bias obtained from the estimation of α_S under the null hypothesis is

$$T\hat{\alpha}_S = \frac{\dfrac{1}{T}\sum_{t=1}^{T} y_{t-S}\varepsilon_t}{\dfrac{1}{T^2}\sum_{t=1}^{T} y_{t-S}^2} \tag{31.19}$$

and the associated *t*-statistic is

$$t_{\hat{\alpha}_S} = \frac{\dfrac{1}{T}\sum_{t=1}^{T} y_{t-S}\varepsilon_t}{\tilde{\sigma}\left[\dfrac{1}{T^2}\sum_{t=1}^{T} y_{t-S}^2\right]^{\frac{1}{2}}}, \tag{31.20}$$

where $\tilde{\sigma}$ is the usual degrees of freedom corrected estimator of σ. Similarly to the usual Dickey–Fuller approach, the test is typically implemented using (31.20). Using the results in (c) and (d) of Lemma 1, it is straightforward to establish that (31.19) and (31.20) converge to

$$\frac{T}{\mathbb{S}}\hat{\alpha}_{\mathbb{S}} \Rightarrow \frac{\sum_{s=1}^{\mathbb{S}}\int_0^1 W_s(r)dW_s(r)}{\sum_{s=1}^{\mathbb{S}}\int_0^1 W_s^2(r)dr} \tag{31.21}$$

and

$$t_{\hat{\alpha}_{\mathbb{S}}} \Rightarrow \frac{\sum_{s=1}^{\mathbb{S}}\int_0^1 W_s(r)dW_s(r)}{\left[\sum_{s=1}^{\mathbb{S}}\int_0^1 W_s^2(r)dr\right]^{\frac{1}{2}}}, \tag{31.22}$$

respectively. Note that $\tilde{\sigma}^2 \xrightarrow{P} \sigma^2$.

The asymptotic distribution of the DHF statistic given by (31.22) is non-standard, but is of similar type to the Dickey–Fuller t-distribution. Indeed, it is precisely the Dickey–Fuller t-distribution in the special case $\mathbb{S} = 1$, when the test regression (31.18) is the usual Dickey–Fuller test regression for a conventional random walk. It can also be seen from (31.22) that the distribution for the DHF t-statistic depends on $\mathbb{S}$, that is on the frequency with which observations are made within each year. On the basis of Monte Carlo simulations, DHF tabulated critical values of $\frac{T}{\mathbb{S}}\hat{\alpha}_{\mathbb{S}}$ and $t_{\hat{\alpha}_{\mathbb{S}}}$ for various T and $\mathbb{S}$. Note that the limit distributions presented as functions of Brownian motions can also be found in Chan (1989), Boswijk and Franses (1996) and more recently in Osborn and Rodrigues (1998). To explore the dependence on $\mathbb{S}$ a little further, note first that

$$\int_0^1 W_s(r)dW_s(r) = \frac{1}{2}\{[W_s(1)]^2 - 1\}, \tag{31.23}$$

where $[W_s(1)]^2$ is $\chi^2(1)$ (see, for example, Banerjee et al., 1993, p. 91). The numerator of (31.22) involves the sum of $\mathbb{S}$ such terms which are mutually independent and hence

$$\sum_{s=1}^{\mathbb{S}}\int_0^1 W_s(r)dW_s(r) = \frac{1}{2}\sum_{s=1}^{\mathbb{S}}\{[W_s(1)]^2 - 1\}$$

$$= \frac{1}{2}\{\chi^2(\mathbb{S}) - \mathbb{S}\}, \tag{31.24}$$

which is half the difference between a $\chi^2(\mathbb{S})$ statistic and its mean of $\mathbb{S}$. It is well known that the Dickey–Fuller t-statistic is not symmetric about zero. Indeed,

Fuller (1996, p. 549) comments that asymptotically the probability of (in our nota-tion) $\hat{\alpha}_1 < 0$ is 0.68 for the nonseasonal random walk because $\Pr[\chi^2(1) < 1] = 0.68$. In terms of (31.22), the denominator is always positive and hence $\Pr[\chi^2(\mathbb{S}) < \mathbb{S}]$ dictates the probability that $t_{\hat{\alpha}_s}$ is negative. With a seasonal random walk and quarterly data, $\Pr[\chi^2(4) < 4] = 0.59$, while in the monthly case $\Pr[\chi^2(12) < 12] = 0.55$. Therefore, the preponderance of negative test statistics is expected to de-crease as $\mathbb{S}$ increases. As seen from the percentiles tabulated by DHF, the disper-sion of $t_{\hat{\alpha}_s}$ is effectively invariant to $\mathbb{S}$, so that the principal effect of an increasing frequency of observation is a reduction in the asymmetry of this test statistic around zero.

3.2 Testing complex unit roots

Before proceeding to the examination of the procedure proposed by Hylleberg et al. (1990) it will be useful to consider some of the issues related to testing complex unit roots, because these are an intrinsic part of any SI(1) process.

The simplest process which contains a pair of complex unit roots is

$$y_t = -y_{t-2} + u_t, \tag{31.25}$$

with $u_t \sim \text{iid}(0, \sigma^2)$. This process has $\mathbb{S} = 2$ and, using the notation identifying the season s and year n, it can be equivalently written as

$$y_{sn} = -y_{s,n-1} + u_{sn} \quad s = 1, 2. \tag{31.26}$$

Notice that the seasonal patterns reverse each year. Due to this alternating pat-tern, and assuming $y_0 = y_{-1} = 0$, it can be seen that

$$y_t = S^*_{sn} = \sum_{i=0}^{n-1} (-1)^i u_{s,n-i} = -S^*_{s,n-1} + u_{sn}, \tag{31.27}$$

where, in this case, $n = \left[\frac{t+1}{2}\right]$. Note that S^*_{sn} ($s = 1, 2$) are independent processes, one corresponding to each of the two seasons of the year. Nevertheless, the nature of the seasonality implied by (31.25) is not of the conventional type in that S^*_{sj} (for given s) tends to oscillate as j increases. Moreover, it can be observed from (31.27) that aggregation of the process over full cycles of two years annihilates the nonstationarity as $S^*_{s,n-1} + S^*_{sn} = u_{sn}$. To relate these S^*_{sn} to the $\mathbb{S}$ independent random walks of (31.6), let $\varepsilon_{sj} = (-1)^j u_{sj}$ which (providing the distribution of u_t is symmetric) has identical properties. Then

$$S^*_{sn} = \begin{cases} \displaystyle\sum_{j=1}^{n} (-1)^{j+1} u_{sj} = -\sum_{j=1}^{n} \varepsilon_{sj} = -S_{jn}, & n \text{ odd} \\[2em] \displaystyle\sum_{j=1}^{n} (-1)^j u_{sj} = \sum_{j=1}^{n} \varepsilon_{sj} = S_{jn}, & n \text{ even} \end{cases} \tag{31.28}$$

where S_{jn} is defined in (31.12). Analogously to the DHF test, the unit root process (31.25) may be tested through the t-ratio for $\hat{\alpha}_2^*$ in

$$(1 + L^2)y_t = \alpha_2^* y_{t-2} + u_t. \tag{31.29}$$

The null hypothesis is $\alpha_2^* = 0$ with the alternative of stationarity implying $\alpha_2^* > 0$. Then, assuming $T = 2N$, under the null hypothesis

$$T\hat{\alpha}_2^* = \frac{T^{-1}\sum_{t=1}^{T} y_{t-2} u_t}{T^{-2}\sum_{t=1}^{T} y_{t-2}^2} = \frac{(2N)^{-1}\sum_{s=1}^{2}\sum_{j=1}^{N} S_{s,j-1}^*(S_{s,j}^* + S_{s,j-1}^*)}{(2N)^{-2}\sum_{s=1}^{2}\sum_{j=1}^{N} (S_{s,j-1}^*)^2}. \tag{31.30}$$

and

$$t(\hat{\alpha}_2^*) = \frac{\sum_{t=1}^{T} y_{t-2} u_t}{\tilde{\sigma}\left[\sum_{t=1}^{T} y_{t-2}^2\right]^{\frac{1}{2}}} = \frac{(2N)^{-1}\sum_{s=1}^{2}\sum_{j=1}^{N} S_{s,j-1}^*(S_{s,j}^* + S_{s,j-1}^*)}{\tilde{\sigma}\left[(2N)^{-2}\sum_{s=1}^{2}\sum_{j=1}^{N} (S_{s,j-1}^*)^2\right]^{\frac{1}{2}}}. \tag{31.31}$$

If, for further expositional clarity, we assume that N is even, then using (31.28), we have

$$\sum_{j=1}^{N} S_{s,j-1}^*(S_{s,j}^* + S_{s,j-1}^*) = \sum_{i=1}^{N/2} [S_{s,2i-2}^*(S_{s,2i-1}^* + S_{s,2i-2}^*) + S_{s,2i-1}^*(S_{s,2i}^* + S_{s,2i-1}^*)]$$

$$= \sum_{i=1}^{N/2} [S_{s,2i-2}(-S_{s,2i-1} + S_{s,2i-2}) - S_{s,2i-1}(S_{s,2i} - S_{s,2i-1})]$$

$$= -\sum_{j=1}^{N} S_{s,j-1}(S_{s,j} - S_{s,j-1}).$$

Thus, there is a "mirror image" relationship between the numerator of (31.30) and (31.31) compared with that of (31.19) and (31.20) with $\mathbb{S} = 2$. The corresponding denominators are identical as $(S_{sj}^*)^2 = S_{sj}^2$. Thus, by applying similar arguments as in the proof of Lemma 1:

$$\frac{T}{2}\hat{\alpha}_2^* \Rightarrow -\frac{\sum_{s=1}^{2}\int_0^1 W_s(r)dW_s(r)}{\sum_{s=1}^{2}\int_0^1 [W_s(r)]^2 dr} \tag{31.32}$$

and

$$t_{\hat{\alpha}_2^*} \Rightarrow -\frac{\displaystyle\sum_{s=1}^{2}\int_0^1 W_s(r)dW_s(r)}{\left\{\displaystyle\sum_{s=1}^{2}\int_0^1 [W_s(r)]^2 dr\right\}^{\frac{1}{2}}}, \tag{31.33}$$

which can be compared with (31.21) and (31.22) respectively. This mirror image property of these test statistics has also been shown by Chan and Wei (1988) and Fuller (1996, pp. 553–4). One important practical consequence of (31.33) is that with a simple change of sign, the DHF tables with $\mathbb{S} = 2$ apply to the case of testing $\alpha_2^* = 0$ in (31.29). Under the assumed DGP (31.25), we may also consider testing the null hypothesis $\alpha_1^* = 0$ against the alternative $\alpha_1^* \neq 0$ in

$$(1 + L^2)y_t = \alpha_1^* y_{t-1} + u_t. \tag{31.34}$$

The test here is not, strictly speaking, a unit root test, since the unit coefficient on L^2 in (31.34) implies that the process contains two roots of modulus one, irrespective of the value of α_1^*. Rather, the test of $\alpha_1^* = 0$ is a test of the null hypothesis that the process contains a half-cycle every $\mathbb{S} = 2$ periods, and hence a full cycle every four periods. The appropriate alternative hypothesis is, therefore, two-sided. For this test regression,

$$T\hat{\alpha}_1^* = \frac{T^{-1}\displaystyle\sum_{t=1}^{T} y_{t-1}u_t}{T^{-2}\displaystyle\sum_{t=1}^{T} y_{t-1}^2}.$$

Again referring to (31.27) and (31.28), we can see that

$$T\hat{\alpha}_1^* = \frac{(2N)^{-1}\displaystyle\sum_{j=1}^{N}[-S_{2,j-1}(S_{1,j} - S_{1,j-1}) + S_{1,j}(S_{2,j} - S_{2,j-1})]}{(2N)^{-2}\displaystyle\sum_{j=1}^{N}(S_{1,j-1}^2 + S_{2,j}^2)}. \tag{31.35}$$

Thus, (31.35) converges to,

$$\frac{T}{2}\hat{\alpha}_1^* \Rightarrow \frac{\displaystyle\int_0^1 W_1(r)dW_2(r) - \int_0^1 W_2(r)dW_1(r)}{\displaystyle\sum_{s=1}^{2}\int_0^1 [W_s(r)]^2 dr}, \tag{31.36}$$

and consequently,

$$
t_{\hat{\alpha}_1^*} \Rightarrow \frac{\displaystyle\int_0^1 W_1(r)dW_2(r) - \int_0^1 W_2(r)dW_1(r)}{\left\{\displaystyle\sum_{s=1}^2 \int_0^1 [W_s(r)]^2 dr\right\}^{\frac{1}{2}}}. \tag{31.37}
$$

Indeed, the results for the distributions associated with the test statistics in (31.29) and (31.34) continue to apply for the test regression

$$
(1 + L^2)y_t = \alpha_1^* y_{t-1} + \alpha_2^* y_{t-2} + \varepsilon_t \tag{31.38}
$$

because the regressors y_{t-1} and y_{t-2} can be shown to be asymptotically orthogonal (see, for instance, Ahtola and Tiao (1987) or Chan and Wei (1988) for more details).

3.3   The Hylleberg–Engle–Granger–Yoo test

It is well known that the seasonal difference operator $\Delta_\mathbb{S} = 1 - L^\mathbb{S}$ can always be factorized as

$$
1 - L^\mathbb{S} = (1 - L)(1 + L + L^2 + \ldots + L^{\mathbb{S}-1}). \tag{31.39}
$$

Hence, (31.39) indicates that an SI(1) process always contains a conventional unit root and a set of $\mathbb{S} - 1$ seasonal unit roots. The approach suggested by Hylleberg *et al.* (1990), commonly known as HEGY, examines the validity of $\Delta_\mathbb{S}$ through exploiting (31.39) by testing the unit root of 1 and the $\mathbb{S} - 1$ separate nonstationary roots on the unit circle implied by $1 + L + \ldots + L^{\mathbb{S}-1}$. To see the implications of this factorization, consider the case of quarterly data ($\mathbb{S} = 4$) where

$$
\begin{aligned}
1 - L^4 &= (1 - L)(1 + L + L^2 + L^3) \\
&= (1 - L)(1 + L)(1 + L^2).
\end{aligned} \tag{31.40}
$$

Thus, $\Delta_4 = 1 - L^4$ has four roots on the unit circle,[2] namely 1 and -1 which occur at the 0 and π frequencies respectively, and the complex pair $\pm i$ at the frequencies $\frac{\pi}{2}$ and $\frac{3\pi}{2}$. Hence, in addition to the conventional unit root, the quarterly case implies three seasonal unit roots, which are -1 and the complex pair $\pm i$.

Corresponding to each of the three factors of (31.40), using a Lagrange approximation, HEGY suggest the following linear transformations:

$$
y_{(1),t} = (1 + L)(1 + L^2)y_t = y_t + y_{t-1} + y_{t-2} + y_{t-3} \tag{31.41}
$$

$$
y_{(2),t} = -(1 - L)(1 + L^2)y_t = -y_t + y_{t-1} - y_{t-2} + y_{t-3} \tag{31.42}
$$

$$
y_{(3),t} = -(1 - L)(1 + L)y_t = -y_t + y_{t-2}. \tag{31.43}
$$

By construction, each of the variables in (31.41) to (31.43) accepts all the factors of Δ_4 except one. That is, $y_{(1),t}$ assumes the factors $(1 + L)$ and $(1 + L^2)$, $y_{(2),t}$ assumes $(1 - L)$ and $(1 + L^2)$, while $y_{(3),t}$ assumes $(1 - L)$ and $(1 + L)$. The test regression for quarterly data suggested by HEGY has the form:

$$\Delta_4 y_t = \pi_1 y_{(1),t-1} + \pi_2 y_{(2),t-1} + \pi_3 y_{(3),t-2} + \pi_4 y_{(3),t-1} + \varepsilon_t, \quad t = 1, 2, \ldots, T \quad (31.44)$$

where $y_{(1),t}$, $y_{(2),t}$, and $y_{(3),t}$ are defined in (31.41), (31.42), and (31.43), respectively. Note that these regressors are asymptotically orthogonal by construction. The two lags of $y_{(3),t}$ arise because the pair of complex roots $\pm i$ imply two restrictions on a second order polynomial $1 + \phi_1 L + \phi_2 L^2$, namely $\phi_1 = 0$ and $\phi_2 = 1$ (see Section 3.2). The overall null hypothesis $y_t \sim \text{SI}(1)$ implies $\pi_1 = \pi_2 = \pi_3 = \pi_4 = 0$ and hence $\Delta_4 y_t = \varepsilon_t$ as for the DHF test. The HEGY regression (31.44) and the associated asymptotic distributions can be motivated by considering the three factors of $\Delta_4 = (1 - L)(1 + L)(1 + L^2)$ one by one. Through the variable $y_{(1),t}$, we may consider the DGP

$$y_{(1),t} = y_{(1),t-1} + \varepsilon_t. \quad (31.45)$$

Therefore, when y_t is generated from a seasonal random walk, $y_{(1),t}$ has the properties of a conventional random walk process and hence, with initial values equal to zero,

$$y_{(1),t} = \sum_{j=0}^{t-1} \varepsilon_{t-j}. \quad (31.46)$$

Since $\Delta_1 y_{(1),t} = \Delta_4 y_t$, the Dickey–Fuller test regression for the DGP (31.45) is

$$\Delta_4 y_t = \pi_1 y_{(1),t-1} + \varepsilon_t, \quad (31.47)$$

where we test $\pi_1 = 0$ against $\pi_1 < 0$. Considering

$$T\hat{\pi}_1 = \frac{T^{-1} \sum_{t=1}^{T} y_{(1),t-1}\varepsilon_t}{T^{-2} \sum_{t=1}^{T} y_{(1),t-1}^2} = \frac{T^{-1} \sum_{t=1}^{T} (y_{t-1} + y_{t-2} + y_{t-3} + y_{t-4})\varepsilon_t}{T^{-2} \sum_{t=1}^{T} (y_{t-1} + y_{t-2} + y_{t-3} + y_{t-4})^2}, \quad (31.48)$$

then from Lemma 1 and (31.13) it can be observed that under the seasonal random walk null hypothesis

$$T^{-1} \sum_{t=1}^{T} (y_{t-1} + y_{t-2} + y_{t-3} + y_{t-4})\varepsilon_t \Rightarrow \frac{\sigma^2}{4} \left\{ \int_0^1 W_{(1)}(r)dW_{(1)}(r) \right\} \quad (31.49)$$

and

$$T^{-2} \sum_{t=1}^{T} (y_{t-1} + y_{t-2} + y_{t-3} + y_{t-4})^2 \Rightarrow \frac{\sigma^2}{16} \int_0^1 4W_{(1)}^2(r)dr, \qquad (31.50)$$

where $W_{(1)}(r) = \sum_{s=1}^{4} W_s(r)$. Substituting (31.49) and (31.50) into (31.48) gives:

$$T\hat{\pi}_1 \Rightarrow \frac{\int_0^1 W_{(1)}(r)dW_{(1)}(r)}{\int_0^1 [W_{(1)}(r)]^2 dr}. \qquad (31.51)$$

The associated t-statistic, which is commonly used to test for the zero frequency unit root, can be expressed as

$$t_{\hat{\pi}_1} \Rightarrow \frac{\int_0^1 W_1^*(r)dW_1^*(r)}{\left\{\int_0^1 [W_1^*(r)]^2 dr\right\}^{\frac{1}{2}}} \qquad (31.52)$$

where $W_1^*(r) = W_{(1)}(r)/2$. Division by 2 is undertaken here so that $W_1^*(r)$ is standard Brownian motion, whereas $W_{(1)}(r)$ is not. Therefore, (31.52) is the conventional Dickey–Fuller t-distribution, tabulated by Fuller (1996).

Similarly, based on (31.42), the seasonal random walk (31.1) implies

$$-(1 + L)y_{(2),t} = \varepsilon_t. \qquad (31.53)$$

Notice the "bounce back" effect in (31.53) which implies a half cycle for $y_{(2),t}$ every period and hence a full cycle every two periods. Also note that (31.53) effectively has the same form as (31.26). Testing the root of -1 implied by (31.53) leads to a test of $\phi_2 = 1$ against $\phi_2 < 1$ in

$$-(1 + \phi_2 L)y_{(2),t} = \varepsilon_t.$$

Equivalently, defining $\pi_2 = \phi_2 - 1$ and again using (31.42) yields:

$$\Delta_4 y_t = \pi_2 y_{(2),t-1} + \varepsilon_t, \qquad (31.54)$$

with null and alternative hypotheses $\pi_2 = 0$ and $\pi_2 < 0$, respectively. Under the null hypothesis, and using analogous reasoning to Section 3.2 combined with Lemma 1, we obtain

$$T\hat{\pi}_2 \Rightarrow \frac{\displaystyle\int_0^1 W_{(2)}(r)dW_{(2)}(r)}{\displaystyle\int_0^1 [W_{(2)}(r)]^2 dr} \tag{31.55}$$

and

$$t_{\hat{\pi}_2} \Rightarrow \frac{\displaystyle\int_0^1 W_2^*(r)dW_2^*(r)}{\left\{\displaystyle\int_0^1 [W_2^*(r)]^2 dr\right\}^{\frac{1}{2}}}, \tag{31.56}$$

where the Brownian motion $W_{(2)}(r) = W_1(r) - W_2(r) + W_3(r) - W_4(r)$ is standardized as $W_2^*(r) = W_{(2)}(r)/2$. Like (31.52), (31.56) is the conventional Dickey–Fuller distribution tabulated by Fuller (1996). It is important to note that, as indicated by Chan and Wei (1988) and Fuller (1996), the distributions of the least squares bias and corresponding t-statistic when the DGP is an AR(1) with a -1 root are the "mirror image" of those obtained when testing the conventional random walk. However, in (31.55) and (31.56), this mirror image is incorporated through the design of the HEGY test regression in that the linear transformation of $y_{(2),t}$ is defined with a minus sign as $-(1 - L)(1 + L^2)$.

Finally, from (31.43) it follows that $y_t \sim \text{SI}(1)$ as in (31.1) with S = 4 implies

$$-(1 + L^2)y_{(3),t} = \varepsilon_t. \tag{31.57}$$

This process implies a "bounce back" after two periods and a full cycle after four. This process has the complex root form identical to (31.25). Hence, the results presented for that process carry over directly for this case. Noting again that $-(1 + L^2)y_{(3),t} = \Delta_4 y_t$, we can test $\phi_3 = 1$ and $\phi_4 = 0$ in

$$-(1 + \phi_4 L + \phi_3 L^2)y_{(3),t} = \varepsilon_t$$

through the regression

$$\Delta_4 y_t = \pi_3 y_{(3),t-2} + \pi_4 y_{(3),t-1} + \varepsilon_t \tag{31.58}$$

with $\pi_3 = \phi_3 - 1$ and $\pi_4 = -\phi_4$. Testing against stationarity implies null and alternative hypotheses of $\pi_3 = 0$ and $\pi_3 < 0$. However, while $\pi_4 = 0$ is also indicated under the null hypothesis, the alternative here is $\pi_4 \neq 0$. The reasoning for this two-sided alternative is precisely that for the test regression (31.34) and (31.58) has the same form as (31.38). Therefore, using similar arguments to Section 3.2, and noting that the "mirror image" property discussed there is incorporated through the minus sign in the definition of $y_{(3),t}$, it can be seen that

$$t_{\hat{\pi}_3} \Rightarrow \frac{\int_0^1 W_3^*(r)dW_3^*(r) + \int_0^1 W_4^*(r)dW_4^*(r)}{\left\{ \int_0^1 [W_3^*(r)]^2 dr + \int_0^1 [W_4^*(r)]^2 dr \right\}^{\frac{1}{2}}} \tag{31.59}$$

and

$$t_{\hat{\pi}_4} \Rightarrow \frac{\int_0^1 W_4^*(r)dW_3^*(r) - \int_0^1 W_3^*(r)dW_4^*(r)}{\left\{ \int_0^1 [W_3^*(r)]^2 dr + \int_0^1 [W_4^*(r)]^2 dr \right\}^{\frac{1}{2}}}, \tag{31.60}$$

where $W_3^*(r) = [W_1(r) - W_3(r)]/\sqrt{2}$ and $W_4^*(r) = [W_2(r) - W_4(r)]/\sqrt{2}$ are independent standard Brownian motions. Note that the least squares bias $T\hat{\pi}_3$ and $T\hat{\pi}_4$ can also be obtained from (31.32) and (31.36).

HEGY suggest that π_3 and π_4 might be jointly tested, since they are both associated with the pair of nonstationary complex roots $\pm i$. Such joint testing might be accomplished by computing $F(\hat{\pi}_3 \cap \hat{\pi}_4)$ as for a standard F-test, although the distribution will not, of course, be the standard F-distribution. Engle, Granger, Hylleberg, and Lee (1993) show that the limiting distribution of $F(\hat{\pi}_3 \cap \hat{\pi}_4)$ is identical to that of $\frac{1}{2}[t_{\hat{\pi}_3}^2 + t_{\hat{\pi}_4}^2]$, where the two individual components are given in (31.59) and (31.60). More details can be found in Smith and Taylor (1998) or Osborn and Rodrigues (1998).

Due to the asymptotic orthogonality of the regressors in (31.47), (31.54) and (31.58), these can be combined into the single test regression (31.44) without any effect on the asymptotic properties of the coefficient estimators.

3.4   Extensions to the HEGY approach

Ghysels, Lee, and Noh (1994), or GLN, consider further the asymptotic distribution of the HEGY test statistics for quarterly data and present some extensions. In particular, they propose the joint test statistics $F(\hat{\pi}_1 \cap \hat{\pi}_2 \cap \hat{\pi}_3 \cap \hat{\pi}_4)$ and $F(\hat{\pi}_2 \cap \hat{\pi}_3 \cap \hat{\pi}_4)$, the former being an overall test of the null hypothesis $y_t \sim SI(1)$ and the latter a joint test of the seasonal unit roots implied by the summation operator $1 + L + L^2 + L^3$. Due to the two-sided nature of all F-tests, the alternative hypothesis in each case is that one or more of the unit root restrictions is not valid. Thus, in particular, these tests should not be interpreted as testing seasonal integration against stationarity for the process. From the asymptotic independence of $t_{\hat{\pi}_i}$, $i = 1, \ldots, 4$, it follows that $F(\hat{\pi}_1 \cap \hat{\pi}_2 \cap \hat{\pi}_3 \cap \hat{\pi}_4)$ has the same asymptotic distribution as $\frac{1}{4}\sum_{i=1}^4 (t_{\hat{\pi}_i})^2$, where the individual asymptotic distributions are given by (31.52), (31.56), (31.59) and (31.60). Hence, $F(\hat{\pi}_1 \cap \hat{\pi}_2 \cap \hat{\pi}_3 \cap \hat{\pi}_4)$ is asymptotically distributed as the simple average of the squares of each of two Dickey–Fuller distributions, a DHF distribution with $\mathbb{S} = 2$ and (31.60). It is straightforward to see that a similar expression results for $F(\hat{\pi}_2 \cap \hat{\pi}_3 \cap \hat{\pi}_4)$, which is a simple average of the squares of a Dickey–Fuller distribution, a DHF distribution with $\mathbb{S} = 2$ and (31.60).

GLN also observe that the usual test procedure of Dickey and Fuller (DF) (1979) can validly be applied in the presence of seasonal unit roots. However, this validity only applies if the regression contains sufficient augmentation. The essential reason derives from (31.39), so that the SI(1) process $\Delta_{\mathbb{S}} y_y = \varepsilon_t$ can be written as

$$\Delta_1 y_t = \alpha_1 y_{t-1} + \phi_1 \Delta_1 y_{t-1} + \ldots + \phi_{\mathbb{S}-1} \Delta_1 y_{t-\mathbb{S}+1} + \varepsilon_t \qquad (31.61)$$

with $\alpha_1 = 0$ and $\phi_1 = \ldots = \phi_{\mathbb{S}-1} = -1$. With (31.61) applied as a unit root test regression, $t_{\hat{\alpha}_1}$ asymptotically follows the usual DF distribution, as given in (31.52). See Ghysels, Lee, and Siklos (1993), Ghysels et al. (1994) and Rodrigues (2000a) for a more detailed discussion.

Beaulieu and Miron (1993) and Franses (1991) develop the HEGY approach for the case of monthly data.[3] This requires the construction of at least seven transformed variables, analogous to $y_{(1),t}$, $y_{(2),t}$, and $y_{(3),t}$ used in (31.41) to (31.43), and the estimation of twelve coefficients π_i ($i = 1, \ldots, 12$). Beaulieu and Miron present the asymptotic distributions, noting that the t-type statistics corresponding to the two real roots of $+1$ and -1 each have the usual Dickey–Fuller form, while the remaining coefficients correspond to pairs of complex roots. In the Beaulieu and Miron parameterization, each of the five pairs of complex roots leads to a $t_{\hat{\pi}_i}$ with a DHF distribution (again with $\mathbb{S} = 2$) and a $t_{\hat{\pi}_i}$ with the distribution (31.60).

Although both Beaulieu and Miron (1993) and Franses (1991) discuss the use of joint F-type statistics for the two coefficients corresponding to a pair of complex roots, neither considers the use of the F-tests as in Ghysels et al. (1994) to test the overall Δ_{12} filter or the eleven seasonal unit roots. Taylor (1998) supplies critical values for these overall joint tests in the monthly case.

Kunst (1997) takes an apparently different approach to testing seasonal integration from that of HEGY, but his approach is easily seen to be related to that of DHF. Kunst is primarily concerned with the distribution of a joint test statistic. Although apparently overlooked by Kunst, it is easy to see that his joint test is identical to the joint test of all coefficients which arises in the HEGY framework. Ghysels and Osborn (2000) and Osborn and Rodrigues (1998) discuss in detail the equivalence between the tests proposed by Kunst and prior existing tests. Also, comparison of the percentiles tabulated by Ghysels et al. (1994) and Kunst with $\mathbb{S} = 4$ are effectively identical.[4] Naturally, these results carry over to the monthly case, with the HEGY F-statistic of Taylor (1998) being equivalent to that of Kunst with $\mathbb{S} = 12$. Kunst does, however, provide critical values for other cases, including $\mathbb{S} = 7$, which is relevant for testing the null hypothesis that a daily series is seasonally integrated at a period of one week.

3.5 Multiple tests and levels of significance

It is notable that many tests of the seasonal unit root null hypothesis involve tests on multiple coefficients. In particular, for the application of the HEGY test (31.44),

Hylleberg *et al.* (1990) recommend that one-sided tests of π_1 and π_2 should be applied, with (π_3, π_4) either tested sequentially or jointly. The rationale for applying one-sided tests for π_1, π_2, and π_3 is that it permits a test against stationarity, which is not the case when a joint F-type test is applied. Thus, the null hypothesis is rejected against stationarity only if the null hypothesis is rejected for each of these three tests. Many applied researchers have followed HEGY's advice, apparently failing to recognize the implications of this strategy for the overall level of significance for the implied joint test of $\pi_1 = \pi_2 = \pi_3 = \pi_4 = 0$.

Let us assume that separate tests are applied to π_1 and π_2, with a joint test applied to (π_3, π_4), with each of these three tests applied at the same level of significance, α. Conveniently, these tests are mutually independent, due to the asymptotic orthogonality of the regressors, as discussed in Section 3.3. Therefore, the overall probability of not rejecting the SI(1) null hypothesis when it is true is $(1 - \alpha)^3 \approx 1 - 3\alpha$ for α small. Thus, with $\alpha = .05$, the implied level of significance for the overall test is $1 - .95^3 = .14$, or approximately three times that of each individual test. With monthly data the issue is even more important of course.

In conclusion, the impact of multiple tests must be borne in mind when applying seasonal unit root tests. To date, however, these issues have received relatively little attention in this literature.

4   Near Seasonal Integration

As noted in Section 3.1 for the DHF test, $\Pr[t_{\hat{\alpha}_s} < 0] = \Pr[\chi^2(\mathbb{S}) < \mathbb{S}]$ seems to be converging to $1/2$ as $\mathbb{S}$ increases. However, for the periodicities typically considered this probability always exceeds $1/2$. This phenomenon indicates that a standard normal distribution may not be a satisfactory approximation when the characteristic root is close to 1 and the sample size is moderate, as Chan and Wei (1987) point out. It is also a well established fact that the power of unit root tests is quite poor when the parameter of interest is in the neighborhood of unity (see, for example, Evans and Savin (1981, 1984) and Perron (1989)). This suggests a distributional gap between the standard distribution typically assumed under stationarity and the function of Brownian motions obtained when the DGP is a random walk. To close this gap, a new class of models have been proposed, which allow the characteristic root of a process to be in the neighborhood of unity. This type of process is often called near integrated. Important work concerning near integration in a conventional AR(1) process includes Bobkoski (1983), Cavanagh (1986), Phillips (1987, 1988), Chan and Wei (1987), Chan (1988, 1989), and Nabeya and Perron (1994). In the exposition of the preceding sections, it has been assumed that the DGP is a special case of

$$y_t = \phi_{\mathbb{S}} y_{t-\mathbb{S}} + \varepsilon_t \tag{31.62}$$

with $\phi_{\mathbb{S}} = 1$ and $y_{-\mathbb{S}+1} = \ldots = y_0 = 0$. In this section we generalize the results by considering a class of processes characterized by an autoregressive parameter $\phi_{\mathbb{S}}$ close to 1.

Analogously to the conventional near integrated AR(1), a noncentrality parameter c can be considered such that

$$\phi_\mathbb{S} = e^{c/N} \simeq 1 + \frac{c}{N} = 1 + \frac{\mathbb{S}c}{T}. \tag{31.63}$$

This characterizes a near seasonally integrated process, which can be locally stationary $(c < 0)$, locally explosive $(c > 0)$, or a conventional seasonal random walk $(c = 0)$. This type of near seasonally integrated process has been considered by Chan (1988, 1989), Perron (1992), Rodrigues (2000b), and Tanaka (1996). Similarly to the seasonal random walk, when the DGP is given by (31.62) and (31.63), and assuming that the observations are available for exactly N $(N = T/\mathbb{S})$ complete years, then

$$S_{sn} = \sum_{j=0}^{n-1} e^{\frac{jc}{N}} \varepsilon_{s,n-j} = \sum_{j=1}^{n} e^{(n-j)\frac{c}{N}} \varepsilon_{s,j} \quad s = 1, \dots, \mathbb{S}. \tag{31.64}$$

This indicates that each season represents a near integrated process with a common noncentrality parameter c across seasons. One of the main features of a process like (31.62) with $\phi_\mathbb{S} = e^{c/N}$, is that

$$\frac{1}{N^{1/2}} y_{sn} = \frac{1}{N^{1/2}} S_{sn} \Rightarrow \sigma^2 J_{sc}(r), \quad s = 1, \dots, \mathbb{S}, \tag{31.65}$$

where S_{sn} is the PSP corresponding to season s and $J_{sc}(r)$ is a Ornstein–Uhlenbeck process and not a Brownian motion as in the seasonal random walk case. Note that, as indicated by, for example, Phillips (1987) or Perron (1992), this diffusion process is generated by the stochastic differential equation

$$dJ_{sc}(r) = cJ_{sc}(r)dr + dW_s(r), \tag{31.66}$$

so that

$$J_{sc}(r) = W_s(r) + c \int_0^1 e^{(r-v)c} W_s(v)dv \tag{31.67}$$

and $J_{sc}(0) = 0$.

Applying results given by Phillips (1987), and following analogous steps to those underlying Section 3.1, yields:

$$\frac{T}{\mathbb{S}}(\hat{\phi}_\mathbb{S} - \phi_\mathbb{S}) = \frac{\displaystyle\sum_{s=1}^{\mathbb{S}} \int_0^1 J_{sc}(r)dW_s(r)}{\displaystyle\sum_{s=1}^{\mathbb{S}} \int_0^1 J_{sc}^2(r)dr}, \tag{31.68}$$

where $J_{sc}(r)$ and $W_s(r)$, $s = 1, \ldots, \mathbb{S}$, are independent Ornstein–Uhlenbeck processes and standard Brownian motions, respectively. Similarly, the t-statistic converges to

$$t_{(\hat{\phi}_s - \phi_s)} = \frac{\sum_{s=1}^{\mathbb{S}} \int_0^1 J_{sc}(r) dW_s(r)}{\left[\sum_{s=1}^{\mathbb{S}} \int_0^1 J_{sc}^2(r) dr \right]^{\frac{1}{2}}}. \tag{31.69}$$

A more detailed analysis appears in Chan (1988, 1989), Perron (1992), Rodrigues (2000b) and Tanaka (1996). The result in (31.69) is the asymptotic power function for the DHF t-test. It is straightforward to observe that the distributions in (31.21) and (31.22) are particular cases of (31.68) and (31.69) respectively with $c = 0$.

The examination of the HEGY procedure in a near seasonally integrated framework is slightly more involved. As indicated by Rodrigues (2000b), $(1 - (1 + \frac{c}{N})L^4)$ can be approximated by,

$$\left[1 - \left(1 + \frac{c}{4N} + O(N^{-2}) \right) L \right] \left[1 + \left(1 + \frac{c}{4N} + O(N^{-2}) \right) L \right] \times \left[1 + \left(1 + \frac{c}{2N} + O(N^{-2}) \right) L^2 \right]. \tag{31.70}$$

The results provided by Jeganathan (1991), together with the orthogonality of the regressors in the HEGY test regression, yield the distributions of the HEGY statistics in the context of a near seasonally integrated process. Rodrigues (2000b) establishes the limit results for the HEGY test regression. One important result also put forward by Rodrigues (2000b) is that the distributions are still valid when we allow different noncentrality parameters for each factor in (31.70).

5 Conclusion

We have considered only the simple seasonal random walk case, which was used to present the general properties of seasonally integrated processes. It should be noted, however, that the effect of nonzero initial values and drifts on the distributions of the seasonal unit root test statistics can easily be handled substituting the standard Brownian motions by demeaned or detrended independent Brownian motions.

Among other issues not considered are the implications of autocorrelation and mean shifts for unit root tests. The first is discussed in detail in Ghysels et $al.$ (1994), Hylleberg (1995), and Rodrigues and Osborn (1999). It is known that strong MA components can distort the power of these procedures. To a certain extent, however, these distortions can be corrected by augmenting the test regression with lags of the dependent variable.

The negative impact of mean shifts on the unit root test procedures, was noted by Ghysels (1991). Recently, Smith and Otero (1997) and Franses and Vogelsang

(1998) have shown, using artificial data, that the HEGY test is strongly affected by seasonal mean shifts. This led Franses and Vogelsang to adapt the HEGY test so as to allow for deterministic mean shifts (Smith and Otero also present relevant critical values for the HEGY procedure in this context).

Notes

* We would like to thank three referees for their valuable comments.
1 The proof of the result appears in the Appendix to the companion working paper Ghysels, Osborn, and Rodrigues (1999).
2 Notice that the unit roots of a monthly seasonal random walk are:

$$1, -1, \pm i, -\tfrac{1}{2}(1 \pm \sqrt{3}\,i), \tfrac{1}{2}(1 \pm \sqrt{3}\,i), -\tfrac{1}{2}(\sqrt{3} \pm i), \tfrac{1}{2}(\sqrt{3} \pm i).$$

The first is, once again, the conventional nonseasonal, or zero frequency, unit root. The remaining 11 seasonal unit roots arise from the seasonal summation operator $1 + L + L^2 + \ldots + L^{11}$ and result in nonstationary cycles with a maximum duration of one year. As can be observed, this monthly case implies five pairs of complex roots on the unit circle.
3 The reparameterization of the regressors proposed for monthly data by Beaulieu and Miron (1993) is typically preferred because, in contrast to that of Franses (1991), the constructed variables are asymptotically orthogonal.
4 Once again, due to the definition of his F-type statistic, the Kunst (1997) percentiles have to be divided by 4 to be comparable with those of Ghysels *et al.* (1994). In the monthly case, the Kunst values have to be divided by 12 for comparison with Taylor (1998). Since these percentiles are obtained from Monte Carlo simulations, they will not be identical across different studies.

References

Abeysinghe, T. (1991). Inappropriate use of seasonal dummies in regression. *Economic Letters* 36, 175–9.

Abeysinghe, T. (1994). Deterministic seasonal models and spurious regressions. *Journal of Econometrics* 61, 259–72.

Ahtola, J., and G.C. Tiao (1987). Distributions of least squares estimators of autoregressive parameters for a process with complex roots on the unit circle. *Journal of Time Series Analysis* 8, 1–14.

Banerjee, A., J. Dolado, J.W. Galbraith, and D. Hendry (1993). *Cointegration, Error-Correction and the Econometric Analysis of Nonstationary Data.* Oxford: Oxford University Press.

Barsky, R.B., and J.A. Miron (1989). The seasonal cycle and the business cycle. *Journal of Political Economy* 97, 503–35.

Beaulieu, J.J., and J.A. Miron (1991). The seasonal cycle in U.S. manufacturing. *Economics Letters* 37, 115–18.

Beaulieu, J.J., and J.A. Miron (1993). Seasonal unit roots in aggregate U.S. data. *Journal of Econometrics* 55, 305–28.

Bobkoski, M.J. (1983). Hypothesis testing in nonstationary time series. Ph.D. thesis, University of Wisconsin, Madison.

Boswijk, H.P., and P.H. Franses (1996). Unit roots in periodic autoregressions. *Journal of Time Series Analysis* 17, 221–45.

Box, G.E.P., and G.M. Jenkins (1970). *Time Series Analysis: Forecasting and Control*. San Francisco: Holden-Day.

Cavanagh, C. (1986). Roots local to unity. Manuscript, Department of Economics, Harvard University, Cambridge, MA.

Canova, F., and E. Ghysels (1994). Changes in seasonal patterns: are they cyclical? *Journal of Economic Dynamics and Control* 18, 1143–71.

Canova, F., and B.E. Hansen (1995). Are seasonal patterns constant over time? a test for seasonal stability. *Journal of Business and Economic Statistics* 13, 237–52.

Chan, N.H. (1988). The parameter inference for nearly nonstationary time series. *Journal of the American Statistical Association* 83, 857–62.

Chan, N.H. (1989). On the nearly nonstationary seasonal time series. *Canadian Journal of Statistics* 17, 279–84.

Chan, N.H., and C.Z. Wei (1987). Asymptotic inference for nearly nonstationary AR(1) processes. *Annals of Statistics* 15, 1050–63.

Chan, N.H., and C.Z. Wei (1988). Limiting distributions of least squares estimates of unstable autoregressive processes. *Annals of Statistics* 16, 367–401.

Dickey, D.A., D.P. Hasza, and W.A. Fuller (1984). Testing for unit roots in seasonal time series. *Journal of the American Statistical Association* 79, 355–67.

Dickey, D.A., and W.A. Fuller (1979). Distribution of the estimators for autoregressive time series with a unit root. *Journal of the American Statistical Association* 74, 427–31.

Engle, R.F., and C.W.J. Granger (1987). Cointegration and error correction: representation, estimation and testing. *Econometrica* 55, 251–76.

Engle, R.F., C.W.J. Granger, S. Hylleberg, and H.S. Lee (1993). Seasonal cointegration: the Japanese consumption function. *Journal of Econometrics* 55, 275–98.

Evans, G.B.A., and N.E. Savin (1981). Testing for unit roots: 1. *Econometrica* 49, 753–79.

Evans, G.B.A., and N.E. Savin (1984). Testing for unit roots: 2. *Econometrica* 52, 1241–69.

Findley, D.F., B.C. Monsell, W.R. Bell, M.C. Otto, and B.-C. Chen (1998). New capabilities and methods of the X-12-ARIMA seasonal-adjustment program. *Journal of Business and Economic Statistics* 16, 127–52.

Franses, P.H. (1991). Seasonality, nonstationarity and forecasting monthly time series. *Journal of Forecasting* 7, 199–208.

Franses, P.H. (1994). A multivariate approach to modelling univariate seasonal time series. *Journal of Econometrics* 63, 133–51.

Franses, H.P., S. Hylleberg, and H.S. Lee (1995). Spurious deterministic seasonality. *Economics Letters* 48, 249–56.

Franses, P.H., and T.J. Vogelsang (1998). Testing for seasonal unit roots in the presence of changing seasonal means. *Review of Economics and Statistics* 80, 231–40.

Fuller, W.A. (1996). *Introduction to Statistical Time Series*, 2nd edn. New York: John Wiley.

Ghysels, E. (1991). On seasonal asymmetries and their implications on deterministic and stochastic models of seasonality. Mimeo, C.R.D.E., Université de Montréal.

Ghysels, E. (1994). On the economics and econometrics of seasonality. In C.A. Sims (ed.) *Advances in Econometrics*, pp. 257–316. Cambridge: Cambridge University Press.

Ghysels, E., H.S. Lee, and P.L. Siklos (1993). On the (mis)specification of seasonality andits consequences: an empirical investigation with US data. *Empirical Economics* 18, 747–60.

Ghysels, E., H.S. Lee, and J. Noh (1994). Testing for unit roots in seasonal time series: some theoretical extensions and a Monte Carlo investigation. *Journal of Econometrics* 62, 415–42.

Ghysels, E., and D.R. Osborn (2000). *The Econometric Analysis of Seasonal Time Series*. Cambridge: Cambridge University Press.

Ghysels, E., D.R. Osborn, and P.M.M. Rodrigues (1999). Seasonal nonstationarity and near-nonstationarity. Discussion paper 99s-05, CIRANO, available at http://ftp.cirano.umontreal.ca/pub/publication/99s-05.pdf.zip.

Hylleberg, S. (1994). Modelling seasonal variation in nonstationary time series analysis and cointegration. In C. Hargreaves (ed.) *Non-Stationary Time Series Analysis and Cointegration*, pp. 153–178. Oxford: Oxford University Press.

Hylleberg, S. (1995). Tests for seasonal unit roots: general to specific or specific to general?. *Journal of Econometrics* 69, 5–25.

Hylleberg, S., C. Jørgensen, and N.K. Sørensen (1993). Seasonality in macroeconomic time series. *Empirical Economics* 18, 321–35.

Hylleberg, S., R.F. Engle, C.W.J. Granger, and B.S. Yoo (1990). Seasonal integration and cointegration. *Journal of Econometrics* 44, 215–38.

Kunst, R.M. (1997). Testing for cyclical non-stationarity in autoregressive processes. *Journal of Time Series Analysis* 18, 325–30.

Jeganathan, P. (1991). On the asymptotic behavior of least-squares estimators in AR time series with roots near the unit circle. *Econometric Theory* 7, 269–306.

Maravall, A. (1993). Stochastic linear trends: models and estimators. *Journal of Econometrics* 56, 5–38.

Nabeya, S., and P. Perron (1994). Local asymptotic distribution related to the AR(1) model with dependent errors. *Journal of Econometrics* 62, 229–64.

Osborn, D.R. (1990). A survey of seasonality in UK macroeconomic variables. *International Journal of Forecasting* 6, 327–36.

Osborn, D.R. (1993). Discussion on "Seasonal Cointegration: The Japanese Consumption Function". *Journal of Econometrics* 55, 299–303.

Osborn, D.R., A.P.L. Chui, J.P. Smith, and C.R. Birchenhall (1988). Seasonality and the order of integration for consumption. *Oxford Bulletin of Economics and Statistics* 50, 361–77.

Osborn, D.R., and P.M.M. Rodrigues (1998). The asymptotic distributions of seasonal unit root tests: a unifying approach. University of Manchester, School of Economic Studies Discussion Paper Series No. 9811.

Perron, P. (1989). The calculation of the limiting distribution of the least-squares estimator in a near-integrated model. *Econometric Theory* 5, 241–55.

Perron, P. (1992). The limiting distribution of the least-squares estimator in nearly integrated seasonal models. *Canadian Journal of Statistics* 20, 121–34.

Phillips, P.C.B. (1987). Towards a unified asymptotic theory for autoregression. *Biometrika* 74, 535–47.

Phillips, P.C.B. (1988). Regression theory for near-integrated time series. *Econometrica* 56, 1021–43.

Rodrigues, P.M.M. (1998). Inference in seasonal nonstationary processes. Unpublished Ph.D. thesis, School of Economic Studies, University of Manchester.

Rodrigues, P.M.M. (2000a). A note on the application of the DF test to seasonal data. *Statistics and Probability Letters* 47, 171–5.

Rodrigues, P.M.M. (2000b). Near seasonal integration. *Econometric Theory*, forthcoming.

Rodrigues, P.M.M., and D.R. Osborn (1999). Performance of seasonal unit root tests for monthly data. *Journal of Applied Statistics* 26, 985–1004.

Smith, J., and J. Otero (1997). Structural breaks and seasonal integration. *Economics Letters* 56, 13–19.

Smith, R.J., and A.M.R. Taylor (1998). Additional critical values and asymptotic representations for seasonal unit root tests. *Journal of Econometrics* 85, 269–88.

Tanaka, K. (1996). *Time Series Analysis: Nonstationarity and Noninvertible Distribution Theory*. New York: John Wiley.

Taylor, A.M.R. (1998). Testing for unit roots in monthly time series. *Journal of Time Series Analysis* 19, 349–68.

Vector Autoregressions

Helmut Lütkepohl*

1 INTRODUCTION

The last 60 years have witnessed a rapid development in the field of econometrics. In the 1940s and 1950s the foundations were laid by the Cowles Commission researchers for analyzing econometric simultaneous equations models. Once the basic statistical theory was available many such models were constructed for empirical analysis. The parallel development of computer technology in the 1950s and 1960s has resulted in simultaneous equations models of increasing size with the accompanying hope that more detailed models would result in better approximations to the underlying data generation mechanisms. It turned out, however, that increasing the number of variables and equations of the models did not generally lead to improvements in performance in terms of forecasting, for instance. In fact, in some forecast comparisons univariate time series models were found to be superior to large scale econometric models. One explanation of this failure of the latter models is their insufficient representation of the dynamic interactions in a system of variables.

The poor performance of standard macroeconometric models in some respects resulted in a critical assessment of econometric simultaneous equations modeling as summarized by Sims (1980) who advocated using vector autoregressive (VAR) models as alternatives. In these models all variables are often treated as a priori endogenous and allowance is made for rich dynamics. Restrictions are imposed to a large extent by statistical tools rather than by prior beliefs based on uncertain theoretical considerations. Although VAR models are, now, standard instruments in econometric analyses, it has become apparent that certain types of interpretations and economic investigations are not possible without incorporating nonstatistical a priori information. Therefore, so-called *structural* VAR models are now often used in practice. Moreover, the invention of cointegration by Granger

(1981) and Engle and Granger (1987) has resulted in specific parameterizations which support the analysis of the cointegration structure. The cointegrating relations are often interpreted as the connecting link to the relations derived from economic theory. Therefore they are of particular interest in an analysis of a set of time series variables.

In the following I will first discuss some of the related models which are now in common use. I will then consider estimation and specification issues in Sections 3 and 4, respectively. Possible uses of VAR models are presented in Section 5. Conclusions and extensions are considered in Section 6. Nowadays a number of books are available which treat modern developments in VAR modeling and dynamic econometric analysis more generally in some detail. Surveys of vector autoregressive modeling include Watson (1994) and Lütkepohl and Breitung (1997).

2   VAR Models

2.1   Characteristics of variables

The characteristics of the variables involved determine to some extent which model is a suitable representation of the data generation process (DGP). For instance, the trending properties of the variables and their seasonal fluctuations are of importance in setting up a suitable model. In the following a variable is called *integrated* of order d ($I(d)$) if stochastic trends or unit roots can be removed by differencing the variable d times (see also Chapter 29 by Bierens in this volume). In the present chapter it is assumed that all variables are at most $I(1)$ if not otherwise stated so that, for any time series variable y_{kt} it is assumed that $\Delta y_{kt} \equiv y_{kt} - y_{k,t-1}$ has no stochastic trend. Note, however, that Δy_{kt} may still have deterministic components such as a polynomial trend and a seasonal component whereas seasonal unit roots are excluded. Note also that a variable without a stochastic trend or unit root is sometimes called $I(0)$. In other words, a variable is $I(0)$ if its stochastic part is stationary. A set of $I(1)$ variables is called *cointegrated* if a linear combination exists which is $I(0)$. Occasionally it is convenient to consider systems with both $I(1)$ and $I(0)$ variables. In this case the concept of cointegration is extended by calling any linear combination which is $I(0)$ a cointegration relation although this terminology is not in the spirit of the original definition because it can result in a linear combination of $I(0)$ variables being called a cointegration relation. Further discussion of cointegration may also be found in Chapter 30 by Dolado, Gonzalo, and Marmol in this volume.

As mentioned earlier, we allow for deterministic polynomial trends. For these terms we assume for convenience that they are at most linear. In other words, we exclude higher order polynomial trend terms. For practical purposes this assumption is not a severe limitation.

2.2   Alternative models and model representations

Given a set of K time series variables $y_t = (y_{1t}, \ldots, y_{Kt})'$, the basic VAR model is of the form

$$y_t = A_1 y_{t-1} + \ldots + A_p y_{t-p} + u_t, \tag{32.1}$$

where $u_t = (u_{1t}, \ldots, u_{Kt})'$ is an unobservable zero-mean independent white noise process with time invariant positive definite covariance matrix $E(u_t u_t') = \Sigma_u$ and the A_i are $(K \times K)$ coefficient matrices. This model is often briefly referred to as a VAR(p) process because the number of lags is p.

The process is *stable* if

$$\det(I_K - A_1 z - \ldots - A_p z^p) \neq 0 \text{ for } |z| \leq 1. \tag{32.2}$$

Assuming that it has been initiated in the infinite past, it generates stationary time series which have time invariant means, variances, and covariance structure. If the determinantal polynomial in (32.2) has roots for $z = 1$ (i.e. unit roots), then some or all of the variables are I(1) and they may also be cointegrated. Thus, the present model is general enough to accommodate variables with stochastic trends. On the other hand, it is not the most suitable type of model if interest centers on the cointegration relations because they do not appear explicitly in the VAR version (32.1). They are more easily analyzed by reparameterizing (32.1) to obtain the so-called *vector error correction model* (VECM):

$$\Delta y_t = \Pi y_{t-1} + \Gamma_1 \Delta y_{t-1} + \ldots + \Gamma_{p-1} \Delta y_{t-p+1} + u_t, \tag{32.3}$$

where $\Pi = -(I_K - A_1 - \ldots - A_p)$ and $\Gamma_i = -(A_{i+1} + \ldots + A_p)$ for $i = 1, \ldots, p - 1$. This representation of the process is obtained from (32.1) by subtracting y_{t-1} from both sides and rearranging terms. Because Δy_t does not contain stochastic trends by our assumption that all variables can be at most I(1), the term Πy_{t-1} is the only one which includes I(1) variables. Hence, Πy_{t-1} must also be I(0). Thus, it contains the cointegrating relations. The Γ_j ($j = 1, \ldots, p - 1$) are often referred to as the short-term or short-run parameters while Πy_{t-1} is sometimes called long-run or long-term part. The model in (32.3) will be abbreviated as VECM(p) because p is the largest lag of the levels y_t that appears in the model. To distinguish the VECM from the VAR model the latter is sometimes called the levels version. Of course, it is also possible to determine the A_j levels parameter matrices from the coefficients of the VECM as $A_1 = \Gamma_1 + \Pi + I_K$, $A_i = \Gamma_i - \Gamma_{i-1}$ for $i = 2, \ldots, p - 1$, and $A_p = -\Gamma_{p-1}$.

If the VAR(p) process has unit roots, that is, $\det(I_K - A_1 z - \ldots - A_p z^p) = 0$ for $z = 1$, the matrix Π is singular. Suppose it has rank r, that is, rank(Π) = r. Then it is well known that Π can be written as a product $\Pi = \alpha \beta'$, where α and β are $(K \times r)$ matrices with rank(α) = rank(β) = r. Premultiplying an I(0) vector by some matrix results again in an I(0) process. Hence, premultiplying $\Pi y_{t-1} = \alpha \beta' y_{t-1}$ by $(\alpha' \alpha)^{-1} \alpha'$ shows that $\beta' y_{t-1}$ is I(0) and, therefore, contains the cointegrating relations. Hence, there are $r = $ rank(Π) linearly independent cointegrating relations among the components of y_t. The matrices α and β are not unique so that there are many possible β matrices which contain the cointegrating relations or linear transformations of them. Consequently, cointegrating relations with economic content cannot be extracted purely from the observed time series. Some nonsample information is required to identify them uniquely.

Special cases included in (32.3) are I(0) processes for which $r = K$ and systems that have a stable VAR representation in first differences. In the latter case, $r = 0$ and the term Πy_{t-1} disappears in (32.3). These boundary cases do not represent cointegrated systems in the usual sense. There are also other cases where no cointegration in the original sense is present although the model (32.3) has a cointegrating rank strictly between 0 and K. Still it is convenient to include these cases in the present framework because they can be accommodated easily as far as estimation and inference are concerned.

In practice the basic models (32.1) and (32.3) are usually too restrictive to represent the main characteristics of the data. In particular, deterministic terms such as an intercept, a linear trend term or seasonal dummy variables may be required for a proper representation of the data. There are two ways to include deterministic terms. The first possibility is to represent the observed variables y_t as a sum of a deterministic term and a stochastic part,

$$y_t = \mu_t + x_t, \tag{32.4}$$

where μ_t is the deterministic part and x_t is a stochastic process which may have a VAR or VECM representation as in (32.1) or (32.3), that is, $x_t = A_1 x_{t-1} + \ldots + A_p x_{t-p} + u_t$ or $\Delta x_t = \Pi x_{t-1} + \Gamma_1 \Delta x_{t-1} + \ldots + \Gamma_{p-1} \Delta x_{t-p+1} + u_t$. In that case, if μ_t is a linear trend term, that is, $\mu_t = \mu_0 + \mu_1 t$, then y_t has a VAR(p) representation of the form

$$y_t = \nu_0 + \nu_1 t + A_1 y_{t-1} + \ldots + A_p y_{t-p} + u_t, \tag{32.5}$$

where $\nu_0 = -\Pi\mu_0 + (\sum_{j=1}^{p} j A_j)\mu_1$ and $\nu_1 = -\Pi\mu_1$. In other words, ν_0 and ν_1 satisfy a set of restrictions. Note, however, that if (32.5) is regarded as the basic model without restrictions for ν_i, $i = 0, 1$, the model can in principle generate quadratic trends if I(1) variables are included, whereas in (32.4) with a deterministic term $\mu_t = \mu_0 + \mu_1 t$ a linear trend term is permitted only. The fact that in (32.4) a clear partitioning of the process in a deterministic and a stochastic component is available is sometimes advantageous in theoretical derivations. Also, in practice, it may be possible to subtract the deterministic term first and then focus the analysis on the stochastic part which usually contains the behavioral relations. Therefore this part is often of primary interest in econometric analyses. Of course, a VECM(p) representation equivalent to (32.5) also exists.

In practice, these representations with possibly additional deterministic terms may still not be general enough. At times one may wish to include stochastic exogenous variables on top of the deterministic part. A fairly general VECM form which includes all these terms is

$$\Delta y_t = \Pi y_{t-1} + \Gamma_1 \Delta y_{t-1} + \ldots + \Gamma_{p-1} \Delta y_{t-p+1} + CD_t + Bz_t + u_t, \tag{32.6}$$

where the z_t are exogenous variables, D_t contains all regressors associated with deterministic terms, and C and B are parameter matrices.

All the models we have presented so far are reduced form models in that they do not include instantaneous relations between the endogenous variables y_t. In practice it is often desirable to model the contemporaneous relations as well and therefore it is useful to consider a structural form

$$\Gamma_0^* \Delta y_t = \Pi^* y_{t-1} + \Gamma_1^* \Delta y_{t-1} + \ldots + \Gamma_{p-1}^* \Delta y_{t-p+1} + C^* D_t + B^* z_t + v_t, \qquad (32.7)$$

where v_t is a $(K \times 1)$ zero mean white noise process with covariance matrix Σ_v and the Π^*, Γ_j^* $(j = 0, \ldots, p - 1)$, C^* and B^* are structural form parameter matrices. The reduced form corresponding to the structural model (32.7) is given in (32.6) with $\Gamma_j = (\Gamma_0^*)^{-1} \Gamma_j^*$ $(j = 1, \ldots, p - 1)$, $C = (\Gamma_0^*)^{-1} C^*$, $\Pi = (\Gamma_0^*)^{-1} \Pi^*$, $B = (\Gamma_0^*)^{-1} B^*$ and $u_t = (\Gamma_0^*)^{-1} v_t$. Of course, a number of restrictions are usually imposed on the general forms of our models. These restrictions are important at the estimation stage which will be discussed next.

3   ESTIMATION

Because estimation of some of the special case models is particularly easy these cases will be considered in more detail in the following. We begin with the levels VAR representation (32.1) under the condition that no restrictions are imposed. Then estimation of the VECM (32.3) is treated and finally more general model variants are discussed.

3.1   Estimation of unrestricted VARs and VECMs

Given a sample $y_1, \ldots, y_T$ and presample values $y_{-p+1}, \ldots, y_0$, the K equations of the VAR (32.1) may be estimated separately by least squares (LS) without losing efficiency relative to generalized LS (GLS) approaches. In fact, in this case LS is identical to GLS. Under standard assumptions, the LS estimator $\hat{A}$ of $A = [A_1 : \ldots : A_p]$ is consistent and asymptotically normally distributed (see, e.g., Lütkepohl, 1991),

$$\sqrt{T} \, \text{vec}(\hat{A} - A) \xrightarrow{d} N(0, \Sigma_{\hat{A}}) \quad \text{or, more intuitively,} \quad \text{vec}(\hat{A}) \overset{a}{\sim} N(\text{vec}(A), \Sigma_{\hat{A}}/T). \tag{32.8}$$

Here vec denotes the column stacking operator which stacks the columns of a matrix in a column vector, $\xrightarrow{d}$ signifies convergence in distribution and $\overset{a}{\sim}$ indicates "asymptotically distributed as".

Although this result also holds for I(1) cointegrated systems (see Sims, Stock, and Watson, 1990; Lütkepohl, 1991, ch. 11) it is important to note that in this case the covariance matrix $\Sigma_{\hat{A}}$ is singular whereas it is nonsingular in the usual I(0) case. In other words, if there are integrated or cointegrated variables, some estimated coefficients or linear combinations of coefficients converge with a faster rate than $\sqrt{T}$. Therefore, the usual t-, χ^2-, and F-tests for inference regarding the VAR parameters may not be valid in this case (see, e.g. Toda and Phillips, 1993). Although inference problems may arise in VAR models with I(1) variables, there are also many unproblematic cases. Dolado and Lütkepohl (1996) show that if all variables are I(1) or I(0) and if a null hypothesis is considered which does not restrict elements of each of the A_i $(i = 1, \ldots, p)$ the usual tests have their standard asymptotic properties. For example, if the VAR order $p \geq 2$, the t-ratios have their usual asymptotic standard normal distributions (see also Toda and Yamamoto (1995) for a related result).

If the white noise process u_t is normally distributed (Gaussian) and the process y_t is I(0), then the LS estimator is identical to the maximum likelihood (ML) estimator conditional on the initial values. It is also straightforward to include deterministic terms such as polynomial trends in the model (32.1). In this case the asymptotic properties of the VAR coefficients remain essentially the same as in the case without deterministic terms (Sims *et al.*, 1990).

If the cointegrating rank of the system under consideration is known and one wishes to impose a corresponding restriction, working with the VECM form (32.3) is convenient. If the VAR order is $p = 1$ the estimators may be obtained by applying reduced rank regression (RRR) to $\Delta y_t = \Pi y_{t-1} + u_t$ subject to rank(Π) = r. The approach is easily extended to higher order VAR processes as well (see Johansen, 1995). Under Gaussian assumptions the ML estimators conditional on the presample values may, in fact, be obtained in this way. However, in order to estimate the matrices α and β in $\Pi = \alpha\beta'$ consistently, it is necessary to impose identifying restrictions. Without such restrictions only the product $\alpha\beta' = \Pi$ can be estimated consistently. If uniqueness restrictions are imposed it can be shown that $T(\hat{\beta} - \beta)$ and $\sqrt{T}(\hat{\alpha} - \alpha)$ converge in distribution (Johansen, 1995). Hence, the estimator of β converges with the fast rate T and is therefore sometimes called *super-consistent*. In contrast, the estimator of α converges with the usual rate $\sqrt{T}$. The estimators of $\Gamma = [\Gamma_1 : \ldots : \Gamma_{p-1}]$ and Π are consistent and asymptotically normal under general assumptions. The asymptotic distribution of $\hat{\Gamma}$ is nonsingular so that standard inference may be used for the short-term parameters Γ_j. On the other hand, the asymptotic distribution of $\hat{\Pi}$ is singular if $r < K$. This result is due to two forces. On the one hand, imposing the rank constraint in estimating Π restricts the parameter space and, on the other hand, Π involves the cointegrating relations which are estimated super-consistently.

It is perhaps interesting to note that an estimator of A can be computed via the estimates of Π and Γ. That estimator has the advantage of imposing the cointegrating restrictions on the levels version of the VAR process. However, its asymptotic distribution is the same as in (32.8) where no restrictions have been imposed in estimating A.

3.2   Estimation of restricted models and structural forms

Efficient estimation of a general structural form model such as (32.7) with restrictions on the parameter matrices is more complicated. Of course, identifying restrictions are necessary for consistent estimation. In practice, various over-identifying restrictions are usually available, typically in the form of zero restrictions on Γ_j^* $(j = 0, \ldots, p - 1)$, C^* and B^*. In addition, there may be a rank restriction for Π^* given by the number of cointegrating relations. Alternatively,

Π^* may be replaced by the product $\alpha^*\beta^{*\prime}$, if identifying restrictions are available for the cointegrating relations and/or the loading matrix α^*. Restrictions for α^* are typically zero constraints, meaning that some cointegrating relations are excluded from some of the equations of the system. In some cases it is possible to estimate β^* in a first stage, for example, using a reduced form procedure which ignores some or all of the structural restrictions on the short-term parameters. Let the estimator be $\hat{\beta}^*$. Because the estimators of the cointegrating parameters converge at a better rate than the estimators of the short-term parameters they may be treated as fixed in a second-stage procedure for the structural form. In other words, a systems estimation procedure may be applied to

$$\Gamma_0^* \Delta y_t = \alpha^* \hat{\beta}^{*\prime} y_{t-1} + \Gamma_1^* \Delta y_{t-1} + \ldots + \Gamma_{p-1}^* \Delta y_{t-p+1} + C^* D_t + B^* z_t + \hat{v}_t. \qquad (32.9)$$

If only exclusion restrictions are imposed on the parameter matrices in this form, standard three-stage LS or similar methods may be applied which result in estimators of the short-term parameters with the usual asymptotic properties. Important results on estimating models with integrated variables are due to Phillips and his co-workers (e.g. Phillips, 1987, 1991).

If deterministic variables are to be included in the cointegration relations this requires a suitable reparameterization of the model. Such reparameterizations for intercepts and linear trend terms are presented in Section 4.2, where tests for the cointegrating rank are discussed. In that context a proper treatment of deterministic terms is of particular importance. Therefore, a more detailed discussion is deferred to Section 4.2. In a subsequent analysis of the model the parameters of the deterministic terms are often of minor interest and therefore the properties of the corresponding estimators are not treated in detail here (see, however, Sims et al., 1990).

4 MODEL SPECIFICATION AND MODEL CHECKING

4.1 Choosing the model order

Unrestricted VAR models usually involve a substantial number of parameters which in turn results in rather imprecise estimators. Therefore, it is desirable to impose restrictions that reduce the dimensionality of the parameter space. Such restrictions may be based on economic theory or other nonsample information and on statistical procedures. Of course, for structural models nonsample information is required for imposing identifying constraints. On top of that there may be further overidentifying constraints on the basis of a priori knowledge.

Tests are common statistical procedures for detecting possible restrictions. For example, t-ratios and F-tests are available for this purpose. These tests retain their usual asymptotic properties if they are applied to the short-run parameters in a VECM whereas problems may arise in the levels VAR representation as explained in the previous section. A particular set of restrictions where such problems occur is discussed in more detail in Section 5.2. In case of doubt it may be preferable to work on the VECM form. This form also makes it easy to test restrictions on the cointegration vectors (see Chapter 30 by Dolado, Gonzalo, and Marmol in this volume).

Because the cointegrating rank r is usually unknown when the choice of p is made, it is useful to focus on the VAR form (32.1) at this stage. Various model selection criteria are available that can be used in this context. In practice, it is not uncommon to start from a model with some prespecified maximum lag length, say $p_{\max}$, and apply tests sequentially, eliminating one or more variables in each step until a relatively parsimonious representation with significant parameter estimates has been found. Instead of sequential tests one may alternatively choose the lag length or determine exclusion restrictions by model selection procedures. For example, for determining the VAR order, the general approach is to fit VAR(m) models with orders $m = 0, \ldots, p_{\max}$ and choose an estimator of the order p which minimizes a criterion such as

$$\text{AIC}(m) = \log \det(\tilde{\Sigma}_u(m)) + \frac{2}{T} m K^2,$$

(see Akaike, 1974);

$$\text{HQ}(m) = \log \det(\tilde{\Sigma}_u(m)) + \frac{2 \log \log T}{T} m K^2$$

proposed by Hannan and Quinn (1979); or

$$\text{SC}(m) = \log \det(\tilde{\Sigma}_u(m)) + \frac{\log T}{T} m K^2$$

due to Schwarz (1978). Here det($\cdot$) denotes the determinant, log is the natural logarithm and $\tilde{\Sigma}_u(m) = T^{-1}\sum_{t=1}^{T}\hat{u}_t\hat{u}_t'$ is the residual covariance matrix estimator for a model of order m. The term $\log \det(\tilde{\Sigma}_u(m))$ measures the fit of a model with order m. Since there is no correction for degrees of freedom in the covariance matrix estimator the log determinant decreases (or at least does not increase) when m increases. Note that the sample size is assumed to be held constant and, hence, the number of presample values set aside for estimation is determined by the maximum order $p_{\max}$. The last terms in the criteria penalize large VAR orders. In each case the estimator $\hat{p}$ of p is chosen to be the order which minimizes the desired criterion so that the two terms in the sum on the right-hand sides are balanced optimally.

The AIC criterion asymptotically overestimates the order with positive probability whereas the last two criteria estimate the order consistently (plim $\hat{p} = p$ or $\hat{p} \to p$ a.s.) under quite general conditions, if the actual DGP has a finite VAR order and the maximum order $p_{\max}$ is larger than the true order. These results not only hold for I(0) processes but also for I(1) processes with cointegrated variables (Paulsen, 1984). Denoting the orders selected by the three criteria by $\hat{p}(\text{AIC})$, $\hat{p}(\text{HQ})$, and $\hat{p}(\text{SC})$, respectively, the following relations hold even in small samples of fixed size $T \geq 16$ (see Lütkepohl, 1991, chs 4 and 11): $\hat{p}(\text{SC}) \leq \hat{p}(\text{HQ}) \leq \hat{p}(\text{AIC})$.

Model selection criteria may also be used for identifying single coefficients that may be replaced by zero or other exclusion restrictions. After a model has been set up, a series of checks may be employed to confirm the model's adequacy. Some such checks will be mentioned briefly in a subsequent section. Before that issue is taken up, procedures for specifying the cointegrating rank will be reviewed.

4.2 Specifying the cointegrating rank

In practice, the cointegrating rank r is also usually unknown. It is commonly determined by a sequential testing procedure based on likelihood ratio (LR) type tests. Because for a given cointegrating rank Gaussian ML estimates for the reduced form VECM are easy to compute, as mentioned in Section 3.1, LR test statistics are also easily available. The following sequence of hypotheses may be considered:

$$H_0(r_0) : \text{rank}(\Pi) = r_0 \quad \text{versus} \quad H_1(r_0) : \text{rank}(\Pi) > r_0, \quad r_0 = 0, \dots, K - 1.$$

(32.10)

The testing sequence terminates if the null hypothesis cannot be rejected for the first time. If the first null hypothesis, $H_0(0)$, cannot be rejected, a VAR process in first differences is considered. At the other end, if all the null hypotheses can be rejected, the process is assumed to be I(0) in levels.

In principle, it is also possible to investigate the cointegrating rank by testing hypotheses $H_0 : \text{rank}(\Pi) \leq r_0$ versus $H_1 : \text{rank}(\Pi) > r_0$, $r_0 = K - 1, \dots, 1, 0$, that is, by testing in reverse order from the largest to the smallest rank. The cointegrating rank is then chosen as the last r_0 for which H_0 is not rejected. From a theoretical viewpoint such a procedure has a drawback, however. Strictly speaking the critical values for the tests to be discussed in the following apply for the situation that rank(Π) is equal to r_0 and not smaller than r_0. Moreover, starting with the smallest rank as in (32.10) means to test the most restricted model first. Thus, a less restricted model is considered only if the data are strongly in favor of removing the restrictions.

Although, under Gaussian assumptions, LR tests can be used here, it turns out that the limiting distribution of the LR statistic under $H_0(r_0)$ is non-standard. It depends on the difference $K - r_0$ and on the deterministic terms included in the DGP. In particular, the deterministic trend terms in the DGP have an impact on the null distribution of the LR tests. Therefore, LR type tests have been derived under different assumptions regarding the deterministic trend parameters. Fortunately, the limiting null distributions do not depend on the short-term dynamics if the latter are properly specified and, hence, critical values for LR type tests have been tabulated for different values of $K - r_0$ under alternative assumptions for deterministic trend terms.

In this context it turns out that the model (32.4), where the deterministic and stochastic parts are separated, is a convenient point of departure. Therefore we consider the model

$$y_t = \mu_0 + \mu_1 t + x_t$$

(32.11)

Table 32.1 Models and LR type tests

Assumption for deterministic term	Model	Reference
μ_0 arbitrary $\mu_1 = 0$	$\Delta y_t = \nu_0 + \Pi y_{t-1} + \sum_{j=1}^{p-1} \Gamma_j \Delta y_{t-j} + u_t$	Johansen (1995)
	$\Delta y_t = [\Pi : \nu_0] \begin{bmatrix} y_{t-1} \\ 1 \end{bmatrix} + \sum_{j=1}^{p-1} \Gamma_j \Delta y_{t-j} + u_t$	Johansen and Juselius (1990)
	$\Delta y_t = \Pi(y_{t-1} - \tilde{\mu}_0) + \sum_{j=1}^{p-1} \Gamma_j \Delta y_{t-j} + u_t$	Saikkonen and Luukkonen (1997)
μ_0 arbitrary $\mu_1 \neq 0$, $\beta'\mu_1 = 0$	$\Delta y_t = \nu_0 + \Pi y_{t-1} + \sum_{j=1}^{p-1} \Gamma_j \Delta y_{t-j} + u_t$	Johansen (1995)
	$\Delta y_t - \hat{\mu}_1 = \Pi(y_{t-1} - \hat{\mu}_0) + \sum_{j=1}^{p-1} \Gamma_j (\Delta y_{t-j} - \hat{\mu}_1) + u_t$	Saikkonen and Lütkepohl (2000b)
μ_0, μ_1 arbitrary	$\Delta y_t = \nu + [\Pi : \nu_1] \begin{bmatrix} y_{t-1} \\ t-1 \end{bmatrix} + \sum_{j=1}^{p-1} \Gamma_j \Delta y_{t-j} + u_t$	Johansen (1995)
	$\Delta y_t = \nu_0 + \nu_1 t + \Pi y_{t-1} + \sum_{j=1}^{p-1} \Gamma_j \Delta y_{t-j} + u_t$	Perron and Campbell (1993)
	$\Delta y_t - \hat{\mu}_1 = \Pi(y_{t-1} - \hat{\mu}_0 - \hat{\mu}_1(t-1))$ $+ \sum_{j=1}^{p-1} \Gamma_j (\Delta y_{t-j} - \hat{\mu}_1) + u_t$	Saikkonen and Lütkepohl (2000a) Lütkepohl and Saikkonen (2000)

with

$$\Delta x_t = \Pi x_{t-1} + \Gamma_1 \Delta x_{t-1} + \ldots + \Gamma_{p-1} \Delta x_{t-p+1} + u_t. \tag{32.12}$$

It is easy to see that the process y_t has a VECM representation

$$\Delta y_t = \nu_0 + \nu_1 t + \Pi y_{t-1} + \sum_{j=1}^{p-1} \Gamma_j \Delta y_{t-j} + u_t$$

$$= \nu + [\Pi : \nu_1] \begin{bmatrix} y_{t-1} \\ t-1 \end{bmatrix} + \sum_{j=1}^{p-1} \Gamma_j \Delta y_{t-j} + u_t$$

$$= \nu + \Pi^+ y_{t-1}^+ + \sum_{j=1}^{p-1} \Gamma_j \Delta y_{t-j} + u_t, \tag{32.13}$$

where ν_0 and ν_1 are as defined below (32.5), $\nu = \nu_0 + \nu_1$, $\Pi^+ = [\Pi : \nu_1]$ and $y_{t-1}^+ = [y_{t-1}' : t-1]'$. Depending on the assumptions for μ_0 and μ_1, different LR type tests can be obtained in this framework by appropriately restricting the parameters of the deterministic part and using RR regression techniques. An overview is given in Table 32.1 which is adopted from Table 1 of Hubrich, Lütkepohl and Saikkonen (2001) where more details on the tests may be found.

For instance, if $\mu_1 = 0$ and μ_0 is unrestricted, a nonzero mean term is accommodated whereas a deterministic linear trend term is excluded by assumption. Three variants of LR type tests have been considered in the literature for this situation plus a number of asymptotically equivalent modifications. As can be seen from Table 32.1, the three statistics can be obtained easily from VECMs. The first test is obtained by dropping the $\nu_1 t$ term in (32.13) and estimating the intercept term in the VECM in unrestricted form and hence, the estimated model may generate linear trends. The second test enforces the restriction that there is no linear deterministic trend in computing the test statistic by absorbing the intercept into the cointegration relations. Finally, in the third test the mean term μ_0 is estimated in a first step and is subtracted from y_t. Then the estimation procedure with rank restriction for Π is applied to (32.12) with x_t replaced by $\tilde{x}_t = y_t - \tilde{\mu}_0$. A suitable estimator $\tilde{\mu}_0$ is proposed by Saikkonen and Luukkonen (1997) who also give the asymptotic distribution of the resulting test statistic under the null hypothesis. It is shown in Saikkonen and Lütkepohl (1999) that the latter test can have considerably more local power than the other two LR tests. Thus, based on local power it is the first choice if $\mu_1 = 0$.

If μ_0 is arbitrary, $\mu_1 \neq 0$ and $\beta' \mu_1 = 0$, at least one of the variables has a deterministic linear trend because $\mu_1 \neq 0$, whereas the cointegration relations do not have a linear trend due to the constraint $\beta' \mu_1 = 0$. The resulting tests are perhaps the most frequently used ones for determining the cointegrating rank in applied work. It may be worth emphasizing, however, that for the $(K \times r)$ matrix β to satisfy $\beta' \mu_1 = 0$, $\mu_1 \neq 0$ implies that $r < K$. Hence, if a trend is known to be present then it should also be allowed for under the alternative and consequently even under the alternative the rank must be smaller than K. In other words, in the present setting only tests of null hypotheses rank$(\Pi) = r_0 < K - 1$ make sense. This result is a consequence of the fact that a linear trend is assumed in at least one of the variables ($\mu_1 \neq 0$) whereas a stable model with an intercept cannot generate a linear trend. Two different LR type tests are available for this case.

In the third case, both μ_0 and μ_1 are unrestricted so that the variables and the cointegrating relations may have a deterministic linear trend. Three different LR type tests and some asymptotically equivalent relatives have been proposed for this situation. Again, these test statistics can be obtained conveniently via the VECMs using the techniques mentioned in Section 3. The first model is set up in such a way so as to impose the linearity of the trend term. The second model includes the trend term in unrestricted form. As mentioned earlier, in principle such a model can generate quadratic trends. Finally, the last test in Table 32.1 is again based on prior trend adjustment and estimation of the resulting VECM for the trend adjusted variables. The trend parameters are again estimated in a first step by a generalized LS procedure. Critical values for all these tests may be found in the references given in Table 32.1.

Instead of the pair of hypotheses in (32.10) one may alternatively test $H_0(r_0)$: rank$(\Pi) = r_0$ versus $H_1^*(r_0)$: rank$(\Pi) = r_0 + 1$. LR tests for this pair of hypotheses were also pioneered by Johansen and are known as *maximum eigenvalue tests*. They can be applied for all the different cases listed in Table 32.1. They also have non-standard limiting distributions. Critical values can be found in the literature cited in the foregoing.

A comprehensive survey of the properties of LR type tests for the cointegrating rank as well as a substantial number of other tests that have been proposed in the literature is given by Hubrich *et al.* (2001). We refer the interested reader to that article for further details.

4.3 Model checking

Once a model has been specified and estimated its adequacy is usually checked with a range of tests and other statistical procedures. Many of these model checking tools are based on the residuals of the final model. Some of them are applied to the residuals of individual equations and others are based on the full residual vectors. Examples of specification checking tools are visual inspection of the plots of the residuals and their autocorrelations. In addition, autocorrelations of squared residuals may be considered to check for possible autoregressive conditional heteroskedasticity (ARCH). Although it may be quite insightful to inspect the autocorrelations visually, formal statistical tests for remaining residual autocorrelation should also be applied. Such tests are often based on LM (Lagrange multiplier) or Portmanteau statistics. Moreover, normality tests of the Lomnicki–Jarque–Bera type may be applied to the residuals (see, e.g. Lütkepohl, 1991; Doornik and Hendry, 1997).

If model defects are detected at the checking stage this is usually regarded as an indication of the model being a poor representation of the DGP and efforts are made to find a better representation by adding other variables or lags to the model, by including nonlinear terms or changing the functional form, by modifying the sampling period or getting other data.

5 Uses of Vector Autoregressive Models

When an adequate model for the DGP of a system of variables has been found it may be used for forecasting and economic analysis. Different tools have been proposed for the latter purpose. For instance, there has been an extensive discussion of how to analyze causal relations between the variables of a system of interest. In this section forecasting VAR processes will be discussed first. Forecasting in more general terms is discussed in Chapter 27 by Stock in this volume. In subsection 5.2 the concept of Granger-causality will be introduced which is based on forecast performance. It has received considerable attention in the theoretical and empirical literature. In subsection 5.3 impulse responses are considered. They may also be regarded as instruments for analyzing causal relations between variables. Finally, forecast error variance decompositions and policy analysis are discussed in subsections 5.4 and 5.5, respectively.

5.1 Forecasting VAR processes

Neglecting deterministic terms and exogenous variables the levels VAR form (32.1) is particularly convenient to use in forecasting the variables y_t. Suppose the

u_t are generated by an independent rather than just uncorrelated white noise process. Then the optimal (minimum MSE) one-step forecast in period T is the conditional expectation,

$$y_{T+1|T} = E(y_{T+1} \,|\, y_T, y_{T-1}, \dots) = A_1 y_T + \dots + A_p y_{T+1-p}. \tag{32.14}$$

Forecasts for larger horizons $h > 1$ may be obtained recursively as

$$y_{T+h|T} = A_1 y_{T+h-1|T} + \dots + A_p y_{T+h-p|T}, \tag{32.15}$$

where $y_{T+j|T} = y_{T+j}$ for $j \leq 0$. The corresponding forecast errors are

$$y_{T+h} - y_{T+h|T} = u_{T+h} + \Phi_1 u_{T+h-1} + \dots + \Phi_{h-1} u_{T+1}, \tag{32.16}$$

where it is easy to see by successive substitution that $\Phi_s = \sum_{j=1}^s \Phi_{s-j} A_j$ ($s = 1, 2, \dots$) with $\Phi_0 = I_K$ and $A_j = 0$ for $j > p$ (see Lütkepohl, 1991, sec. 11.3). Hence, the forecasts are unbiased, that is, the forecast errors have expectation 0 and their MSE matrix is

$$\Sigma_y(h) = E\{(y_{T+h} - y_{T+h|T})(y_{T+h} - y_{T+h|T})'\} = \sum_{j=0}^{h-1} \Phi_j \Sigma_u \Phi_j'. \tag{32.17}$$

For any other h-step forecast with MSE matrix $\Sigma_y^*(h)$, say, the difference $\Sigma_y^*(h) - \Sigma_y(h)$ is a positive semidefinite matrix. This result relies on the assumption that u_t is independent white noise, i.e. u_t and u_s are independent for $s \neq t$. If u_t is uncorrelated white noise and not necessarily independent over time, these forecasts are just best linear forecasts in general (see Lütkepohl, 1991, sec. 2.2.2).

The forecast MSEs for integrated processes are generally unbounded as the horizon h goes to infinity. Thus the forecast uncertainty increases without bounds for forecasts of the distant future. This contrasts with the case of I(0) variables for which the forecast MSEs are bounded by the unconditional covariance Σ_y of y_t. This means, in particular, that forecasts of cointegration relations have bounded MSEs even for horizons approaching infinity. The corresponding forecast intervals reflect this property as well. Assuming that the process y_t is Gaussian, that is, $u_t \sim \text{iid } N(0, \Sigma_u)$, the forecast errors are also multivariate normal. This result may be used to set up forecast intervals in the usual way.

In practice the parameters of a VAR process are usually estimated. Denoting by $\hat{y}_{T+h|T}$ the forecast based on estimated coefficients corresponding to $y_{T+h|T}$ the associated forecast error is

$$y_{T+h} - \hat{y}_{T+h|T} = [y_{T+h} - y_{T+h|T}] + [y_{T+h|T} - \hat{y}_{T+h|T}].$$

At the forecast origin T the first term on the right-hand side involves future residuals only whereas the second term involves present and past variables only, provided only past variables have been used for estimation. Consequently, if u_t is independent white noise, the two terms are independent. Moreover, under standard assumptions, the difference $y_{T+h|T} - \hat{y}_{T+h|T}$ is small in probability as the sample size used for estimation gets large. Hence, the forecast error covariance matrix in this case is

$$\Sigma_{\hat{y}}(h) = E\{[y_{T+h} - \hat{y}_{T+h|T}][y_{T+h} - \hat{y}_{T+h|T}]'\}$$
$$= \Sigma_y(h) + o(1),$$

where $o(1)$ denotes a term which approaches zero as the sample size tends to infinity. Thus, for large samples the estimation uncertainty may be ignored in evaluating the forecast precision and setting up forecast intervals. In small samples, including a correction term is preferable, however. In this case the precision of the forecasts will depend on the precision of the estimators. Hence, if precise forecasts are desired, it is a good strategy to look for precise parameter estimators.

5.2   Granger-causality analysis

THE CONCEPT

The causality concept introduced by Granger (1969) is perhaps the most widely discussed form of causality in the econometrics literature. Granger defines a variable y_{1t} to be causal for another time series variable y_{2t} if the former helps predicting the latter. Formally, denoting by $y_{2,t+h|\Omega_t}$ the optimal h-step predictor of y_{2t} at origin t based on the set of all the relevant information in the universe Ω_t, y_{1t} may be defined to be Granger-noncausal for y_{2t} if and only if

$$y_{2,t+h|\Omega_t} = y_{2,t+h|\Omega_t\setminus\{y_{1,s}|s\le t\}}, \quad h = 1, 2, \ldots. \tag{32.18}$$

Here $\Omega_t\setminus\mathcal{A}$ denotes the set containing all elements of Ω_t which are not in the set $\mathcal{A}$. In other words, y_{1t} is not causal for y_{2t} if removing the past of y_{1t} from the information set does not change the optimal forecast for y_{2t} at any forecast horizon. In turn, y_{1t} is Granger-causal for y_{2t} if the equality in (32.18) is violated for at least one h and, thus, a better forecast of y_{2t} is obtained for some forecast horizon by including the past of y_{1t} in the information set. If $\Omega_t = \{(y_{1,s}, y_{2,s})'\,|\,s \le t\}$ and $(y_{1t}, y_{2t})'$ is generated by a bivariate VAR(p) process,

$$\begin{bmatrix} y_{1t} \\ y_{2t} \end{bmatrix} = \sum_{i=1}^p \begin{bmatrix} \alpha_{11,i} & \alpha_{12,i} \\ \alpha_{21,i} & \alpha_{22,i} \end{bmatrix} \begin{bmatrix} y_{1,t-i} \\ y_{2,t-i} \end{bmatrix} + u_t, \tag{32.19}$$

then (32.18) is easily seen to be equivalent to

$$\alpha_{21,i} = 0, \quad i = 1, 2, \ldots, p. \tag{32.20}$$

Of course, Granger-causality can also be investigated in the framework of the VECM (see, e.g. Mosconi and Giannini, 1992).

Economic systems usually consist of more than two relevant variables. Hence, it is desirable to extend the concept of Granger-causality to higher dimensional systems. Different possible extensions have been considered (see, e.g. Lütkepohl, 1993; Dufour and Renault, 1998). One possible generalization assumes that the vector of all variables, y_t, is partitioned into two subvectors so that $y_t = (y'_{1t}, y'_{2t})'$. Then the definition in (32.18) may be used for the two subvectors, y_{1t}, y_{2t}, rather than two individual variables. If $\Omega_t = \{y_s \mid s \leq t\}$ and y_t is a VAR process of the form (32.19), where the $\alpha_{kh,i}$ are now matrices of appropriate dimensions, the restrictions for noncausality are the same as in the bivariate case so that y_{1t} is Granger-noncausal for y_{2t} if $\alpha_{21,i} = 0$ for $i = 1, \ldots, p$ (Lütkepohl, 1991, sec. 2.3.1).

This approach is not satisfactory if interest centers on a causal relation between two variables within a higher dimensional system because a set of variables being causal for another set of variables does not necessarily imply that each member of the former set is causal for each member of the latter set. Therefore it is of interest to consider causality of y_{1t} to y_{2t} if there are further variables in the system. In this context, different causality concepts have been proposed which are most easily explained in terms of the three-dimensional VAR process

$$
y_t = \begin{bmatrix} y_{1t} \\ y_{2t} \\ y_{3t} \end{bmatrix} = \sum_{i=1}^{p} \begin{bmatrix} \alpha_{11,i} & \alpha_{12,i} & \alpha_{13,i} \\ \alpha_{21,i} & \alpha_{22,i} & \alpha_{23,i} \\ \alpha_{31,i} & \alpha_{32,i} & \alpha_{33,i} \end{bmatrix} \begin{bmatrix} y_{1,t-i} \\ y_{2,t-i} \\ y_{3,t-i} \end{bmatrix} + u_t.
\tag{32.21}
$$

Within this system causality of y_{1t} for y_{2t} is sometimes checked by testing

$$
H_0 : \alpha_{21,i} = 0, \quad i = 1, \ldots, p.
\tag{32.22}
$$

These restrictions are not equivalent to (32.18), however. They are equivalent to equality of the one-step forecasts, $y_{2,t+1|\Omega_t} = y_{2,t+1|\Omega_t \setminus \{y_{1,s}|s \leq t\}}$. The information in past y_{1t} may still help improving the forecasts of y_{2t} more than one period ahead if (32.22) holds (Lütkepohl, 1993). Intuitively, this happens because there may be indirect causal links, e.g. y_{1t} may have an impact on y_{3t} which in turn may affect y_{2t}. Thus, the definition of noncausality corresponding to the restrictions in (32.22) is not in line with an intuitive notion of the term. For higher dimensional processes the definition based on (32.18) results in more complicated nonlinear restrictions for the VAR coefficients. Details are given in Dufour and Renault (1998).

TESTING FOR GRANGER-CAUSALITY

Wald tests are standard tools for testing restrictions on the coefficients of VAR processes because the test statistics are easy to compute in this context. Unfortunately, they may have non-standard asymptotic properties if the VAR contains I(1) variables. In particular, Wald tests for Granger-causality are known to result in nonstandard limiting distributions depending on the cointegration properties of the system and possibly on nuisance parameters (see Toda and Phillips, 1993).

Dolado and Lütkepohl (1996) and Toda and Yamamoto (1995) point out a simple way to overcome the problems with these tests in the present context. As mentioned in Section 3.1, the non-standard asymptotic properties of the standard tests on the coefficients of cointegrated VAR processes are due to the singularity of the asymptotic distribution of the LS estimators. Hence, the idea is to get rid of the singularity by fitting a VAR process whose order exceeds the true order. It can be shown that this device leads to a nonsingular asymptotic distribution of the relevant coefficients, overcoming the problems associated with standard tests and their complicated non-standard limiting properties.

More generally, as mentioned in Section 3.1, Dolado and Lütkepohl (1996) show that whenever the elements in at least one of the complete coefficient matrices A_i are not restricted at all under the null hypothesis, the Wald statistic has its usual limiting χ^2-distribution. Thus, if elements from all A_i, $i = 1, \ldots, p$, are involved in the restrictions as, for instance, in the noncausality restrictions in (32.20) or (32.22), simply adding an extra (redundant) lag in estimating the parameters of the process, ensures standard asymptotics for the Wald test. Of course, if the true DGP is a VAR(p) process, then a VAR($p + 1$) with $A_{p+1} = 0$ is also an appropriate model. The test is then performed on the A_i, $i = 1, \ldots, p$, only.

For this procedure to work it is not necessary to know the cointegration properties of the system. Thus, if there is uncertainty with respect to the integration properties of the variables an extra lag may simply be added and the test may be performed on the lag augmented model to be on the safe side. Unfortunately, the procedure is not fully efficient due to the redundant parameters. A generalization of these ideas to Wald tests for nonlinear restrictions representing, for instance, other causality definitions, is discussed by Lütkepohl and Burda (1997).

5.3 Impulse response analysis

Tracing out the effects of shocks in the variables of a given system may also be regarded as a type of causality analysis. If the process y_t is I(0), it has a Wold moving average (MA) representation

$$y_t = \Phi_0 u_t + \Phi_1 u_{t-1} + \Phi_2 u_{t-2} + \ldots, \tag{32.23}$$

where $\Phi_0 = I_K$ and the Φ_s may be computed recursively as in (32.16). The coefficients of this representation may be interpreted as reflecting the responses to impulses hitting the system. The (i, j)th elements of the matrices Φ_s, regarded as a function of s, trace out the expected response of $y_{i,t+s}$ to a unit change in y_{jt} holding constant all past values of y_t. Since the change in y_{it} given $\{y_{t-1}, y_{t-2}, \ldots\}$ is measured by the innovation u_{it}, the elements of Φ_s represent the impulse responses of the components of y_t with respect to the u_t innovations. In the presently considered I(0) case, $\Phi_s \to 0$ as $s \to \infty$. Hence, the effect of an impulse is transitory as it vanishes over time. These impulse responses are sometimes called *forecast error impulse responses* because the u_t are the one-step ahead forecast errors.

Although the Wold representation does not exist for nonstationary cointegrated processes it is easy to see that the Φ_s impulse response matrices can be computed in the same way as in (32.16) (Lütkepohl, 1991, ch. 11; Lütkepohl and Reimers, 1992). In this case the Φ_s may not converge to zero as $s \to \infty$ and, consequently, some shocks may have permanent effects. Assuming that all variables are I(1), it is also reasonable to consider the Wold representation of the stationary process Δy_t,

$$\Delta y_t = \Xi_0 u_t + \Xi_1 u_{t-1} + \Xi_2 u_{t-2} + \dots, \tag{32.24}$$

where $\Xi_0 = I_K$ and $\Xi_j = \Phi_j - \Phi_{j-1}$ ($j = 1, 2, \dots$). Again, the coefficients of this representation may be interpreted as impulse responses. Because $\Phi_s = \sum_{j=0}^{s} \Xi_j$, $s = 1, 2, \dots$, the Φ_s may be regarded as accumulated impulse responses of the representation in first differences.

A critique that has been raised against forecast error impulse responses is that the underlying shocks are not likely to occur in isolation if the components of u_t are not instantaneously uncorrelated, that is, if Σ_u is not diagonal. Therefore, in many applications the innovations of the VAR are orthogonalized using a Cholesky decomposition of the covariance matrix Σ_u. Denoting by P a lower triangular matrix such that $\Sigma_u = PP'$, the orthogonalized shocks are given by $\varepsilon_t = P^{-1} u_t$. Hence, in the stationary case we get from (32.23),

$$y_t = \Psi_0 \varepsilon_t + \Psi_1 \varepsilon_{t-1} + \dots, \tag{32.25}$$

where $\Psi_i = \Phi_i P$ ($i = 0, 1, 2, \dots$). Here $\Psi_0 = P$ is lower triangular so that an ε shock in the first variable may have an instantaneous effect on all the other variables as well, whereas a shock in the second variable cannot have an instantaneous impact on y_{1t} but only on the remaining variables and so on.

Since many matrices P exist which satisfy $PP' = \Sigma_u$, using this approach is to some extent arbitrary. Even if P is found by a lower triangular Choleski decomposition, choosing a different ordering of the variables in the vector y_t may produce different shocks. Hence, the effects of a shock may depend on the way the variables are arranged in the vector y_t. In view of this difficulty, Sims (1981) recommends trying various triangular orthogonalizations and checking the robustness of the results with respect to the ordering of the variables. He also recommends using a priori hypotheses about the structure if possible. The resulting models are known as *structural* VARs. They are of the general form (32.7). In addition, the residuals may be represented as $v_t = R\varepsilon_t$, where R is a fixed $(K \times K)$ matrix and ε_t is a $(K \times 1)$ vector of structural shocks with covariance matrix $E(\varepsilon_t \varepsilon_t') = \Sigma_\varepsilon$. Usually it is assumed that Σ_ε is a diagonal matrix so that the structural shocks are instantaneously uncorrelated. The relation to the reduced form residuals is given by $\Gamma_0^* u_t = R\varepsilon_t$.

In recent years, different types of identifying restrictions were considered (see, e.g. Watson (1994) and Lütkepohl and Breitung (1997) for discussions). The aforementioned triangular system is a special case of such a class of structural models with $P = \Gamma_0^{*-1} R$. Obviously, identifying restrictions are required to obtain a unique structural representation. In the early literature, linear restrictions on Γ_0^* or R were used to identify the system (e.g. Pagan, 1995). Later Blanchard and Quah

(1989), King, Plosser, Stock, and Watson (1991), Gali (1992) and others introduced nonlinear restrictions. To motivate the nonlinear constraints it is useful to consider the moving average representation (32.24) and write it in terms of the structural residuals:

$$\Delta y_t = \Theta_0 \varepsilon_t + \Theta_1 \varepsilon_{t-1} + \Theta_2 \varepsilon_{t-2} + \ldots, \qquad (32.26)$$

where $\Theta_s = \Xi_s \Gamma_0^{*-1} R$ $(s = 0, 1, \ldots)$. The long run impact of the structural shocks on y_t is given by $\lim_{n \to \infty} \partial y_{t+n} / \partial \varepsilon_t' = \lim_{n \to \infty} \Phi_n \Gamma_0^{*-1} R = \sum_{s=0}^{\infty} \Theta_s \equiv \bar{\Theta}$. If the shock ε_{jt} has a transitory effect on y_{it}, then the (i, j)th element of $\bar{\Theta}$ is zero. Hence, the restriction that ε_{jt} does not affect y_{it} in the long run may be written as the nonlinear constraint

$$e_i' \bar{\Theta} e_j = e_i'(I_K + \Xi_1 + \Xi_2 + \ldots) \Gamma_0^{*-1} R e_j = 0.$$

Here e_i (e_j) is the ith $(j$th) column of the identity matrix. It can be shown that for a cointegrated system with cointegrating rank r, the matrix $\bar{\Theta}$ has rank $n - r$ so that there exist $n - r$ shocks with permanent effects (e.g. Engle and Granger, 1987).

Imposing this kind of nonlinear restrictions in the estimation procedure requires that nonlinear procedures are used. For instance, generalized methods of moments (GMM) estimation may be applied (see Watson, 1994). If an estimator $\hat{\alpha}$, say, of the VAR coefficients summarized in the vector α is available, estimators of the impulse responses may be obtained as $\hat{\phi}_{ij,h} = \phi_{ij,h}(\hat{\alpha})$. Assuming that $\hat{\alpha}$ has a normal limiting distribution, the $\hat{\phi}_{ij,h}$ are also asymptotically normally distributed. However, due to the nonlinearity of the functional relationship, the latter limiting distribution may be singular. Moreover, the asymptotic covariance matrix of $\hat{\alpha}$ may also be singular if there are constraints on the coefficients or, as mentioned earlier, if there are I(1) variables. Therefore, standard asymptotic inference for the impulse response coefficients may fail.

In practice, bootstrap methods are often used to construct confidence intervals (CIs) for impulse responses because these methods occasionally lead to more reliable small sample inference than asymptotic theory (e.g. Kilian, 1998). Moreover, the analytical expressions of the asymptotic variances of the impulse response coefficients are rather complicated. Using the bootstrap for setting up CIs, the precise expressions of the variances are not needed and, hence, deriving the analytical expressions explicitly can be avoided. Unfortunately, the bootstrap does not necessarily overcome the problems due to the aforementioned singularity in the asymptotic distribution. In other words, in these cases bootstrap CIs may not have the desired coverage. For a critical discussion see Benkwitz, Lütkepohl, and Neumann (2000).

5.4   Forecast error variance decomposition

In practice forecast error variance decompositions are also popular tools for interpreting VAR models. Expressing the h-step forecast error from (32.16) in terms of the orthogonalized impulse responses $\varepsilon_t = (\varepsilon_{1t}, \ldots, \varepsilon_{Kt})' = P^{-1}u_t$ from (32.25), where P is a lower triangular matrix such that $PP' = \Sigma_u$, gives

$$y_{T+h} - y_{T+h|T} = \Psi_0\varepsilon_{T+h} + \Psi_1\varepsilon_{T+h-1} + \ldots + \Psi_{h-1}\varepsilon_{T+1}.$$

Denoting the (i, j)th element of Ψ_n by $\psi_{ij,n}$, the kth element of the forecast error vector becomes

$$y_{k,T+h} - y_{k,T+h|T} = \sum_{n=0}^{h-1} (\psi_{k1,n}\varepsilon_{1,T+h-n} + \cdots + \psi_{kK,n}\varepsilon_{K,T+h-n}).$$

Using the fact that the ε_{kt} are contemporaneously and serially uncorrelated and have unit variances by construction, it follows that the corresponding forecast error variance is

$$\sigma_k^2(h) = \sum_{n=0}^{h-1} (\psi_{k1,n}^2 + \cdots + \psi_{kK,n}^2) = \sum_{j=1}^{K} (\psi_{kj,0}^2 + \cdots + \psi_{kj,h-1}^2).$$

The term $(\psi_{kj,0}^2 + \ldots + \psi_{kj,h-1}^2)$ is interpreted as the contribution of variable j to the h-step forecast error variance of variable k. This interpretation makes sense if the ε_{it} can be interpreted as shocks in variable i. Dividing the above terms by $\sigma_k^2(h)$ gives the percentage contribution of variable j to the h-step forecast error variance of variable k,

$$w_{kj}(h) = (\psi_{kj,0}^2 + \ldots + \psi_{kj,h-1}^2)/\sigma_k^2(h).$$

These quantities, computed from estimated parameters, are often reported for various forecast horizons. Clearly, their interpretation as forecast error variance components may be criticized on the same grounds as orthogonalized impulse responses because they are based on the latter quantities.

5.5 Policy analysis

If there are exogenous variables in the system (32.7), the model may also be used directly for policy analysis. In other words, if a policy maker affects the values or properties of z_t the effect on the endogenous variables may be investigated within the conditional model (32.7). If the policy maker sets the values of z_t the effect of such an action can be analyzed by considering the resulting dynamic effects on the endogenous variables similar to an impulse response analysis. In general, if z_t represents stochastic variables, it is more natural to think of policy actions as changes in the distribution of z_t. For instance, a policy maker may shift the mean of z_t. Again, such changes can be analyzed in the context of our extended VAR models. For details see, for example, Hendry and Mizon (1998).

6   CONCLUSIONS AND EXTENSIONS

Since the publication of Sims' (1980) critique of classical econometric modeling, VAR processes have become standard tools for macroeconometric analyses. A brief introduction to these models, their estimation, specification, and analysis has been provided. Special attention has been given to cointegrated systems. Forecasting, causality, impulse response, and policy analysis are discussed as possible uses of VAR models. In some of the discussion exogenous variables and deterministic terms are explicitly allowed for and, hence, the model class is generalized slightly relative to standard pure VAR processes.

There are now different software packages that support VAR analyses. For example, PcFiml (see Doornik and Hendry, 1997) and EVIEWS may be used. Furthermore, packages programmed in GAUSS exist which simplify a VAR analysis (see, e.g. Haase *et al.*, 1992).

In practice, further model generalizations are often useful. For instance, to obtain a more parsimonious parameterization allowing for MA terms as well and, hence, considering the class of vector autoregressive moving average processes may be desirable (see Hannan and Deistler, 1988; Lütkepohl and Poskitt, 1996). Generalizations of the concept of cointegration may be found in Chapter 30 by Dolado, Gonzalo, and Marmol in this volume. Especially for financial time series modeling the conditional second moments is sometimes of primary interest. Multivariate ARCH type models that can be used for this purpose are, for instance, discussed by Engle and Kroner (1995). Generally, nonlinearities of unknown functional form may be treated nonparametrically, semiparametrically, or semi-nonparametrically. A large body of literature is currently developing on these issues.

Note

*   I thank Jörg Breitung and Moses Salau for helpful comments on an earlier draft of this chapter and the Deutsche Forschungsgemeinschaft, SFB 373, as well as the European Commission under the Training and Mobility of Researchers Programme (contract No. ERBFMRXCT980213) for financial support. An extended version of this chapter with more explanations, examples and references is available from the internet at http://sfb.wiwi.hu-berlin.de in subdirectory bub/papers/sfb373.

References

Akaike, H. (1974). A new look at the statistical model identification. *IEEE Transactions on Automatic Control* AC-19, 716–23.

Benkwitz, A., H. Lütkepohl, and M.H. Neumann (2000). Problems related to confidence intervals for impulse responses of autoregressive processes. *Econometric Reviews* 19, 69–103.

Blanchard, O., and D. Quah (1989). The dynamic effects of aggregate demand and supply disturbances. *American Economic Review* 79, 655–73.

Dolado, J.J., and H. Lütkepohl (1996). Making Wald tests work for cointegrated systems. *Econometric Reviews* 15, 369–86.

Doornik, J.A., and D.F. Hendry (1997). *Modelling Dynamic Systems Using PcFiml 9.0 for Windows*. London: International Thomson Business Press.

Dufour, J.-M., and E. Renault (1998). Short run and long run causality in time series: Theory, *Econometrica* 66, 1099–125.

Engle, R.F., and C.W.J. Granger (1987). Cointegration and error correction: Representation, estimation and testing. *Econometrica* 55, 251–76.

Engle, R.F., and K.F. Kroner (1995). Multivariate simultaneous generalized GARCH. *Econometric Theory* 11, 122–50.

Gali, J. (1992). How well does the IS-LM model fit postwar U.S. data. *Quarterly Journal of Economics* 107, 709–38.

Granger, C.W.J. (1969). Investigating causal relations by econometric models and cross-spectral methods. *Econometrica* 37, 424–38.

Granger, C.W.J. (1981). Some properties of time series data and their use in econometric model specification. *Journal of Econometrics* 16, 121–30.

Haase, K., H. Lütkepohl, H. Claessen, M. Moryson, and W. Schneider (1992). *MulTi: A Menu-Driven GAUSS Program for Multiple Time Series Analysis*. Kiel, Germany: Universität Kiel.

Hannan, E.J., and M. Deistler (1988). *The Statistical Theory of Linear Systems*. New York: John Wiley.

Hannan, E.J., and B.G. Quinn (1979). The determination of the order of an autoregression. *Journal of the Royal Statistical Society* B41, 190–5.

Hendry, D.F., and G.E. Mizon (1998). Exogeneity, causality, and co-breaking in economic policy analysis of a small econometric model of money in the UK. *Empirical Economics* 23, 267–94.

Hubrich, K., H. Lütkepohl, and P. Saikkonen (2001). A review of systems cointe-gration tests. *Econometric Reviews*, 20, 247–318.

Johansen, S. (1995). *Likelihood Based Inference in Cointegrated Vector Autoregressive Models*. Oxford: Oxford University Press.

Johansen, S., and K. Juselius (1990). Maximum likelihood estimation and inference on cointegration – with applications to the demand for money. *Oxford Bulletin of Economics and Statistics* 52, 169–210.

Kilian, L. (1998). Small-sample confidence intervals for impulse response functions. *Review of Economics and Statistics* 80, 218–30.

King, R.G., C.I. Plosser, J.H. Stock, and M.W. Watson (1991). Stochastic trends and economic fluctuations. *American Economic Review* 81, 819–40.

Lütkepohl, H. (1991). *Introduction to Multiple Time Series Analysis*. Berlin: Springer-Verlag.

Lütkepohl, H. (1993). Testing for causation between two variables in higher dimensional VAR models. In H. Schneeweiss and K.F. Zimmermann (eds.) *Studies in Applied Econometrics*, pp. 75–91. Heidelberg: Physica-Verlag.

Lütkepohl, H., and J. Breitung (1997). Impulse response analysis of vector autoregressive processes. In C. Heij, H. Schumacher, B. Hanzon, and C. Praagman (eds.) *System Dynamics in Economic and Financial Models*. Chichester: John Wiley.

Lütkepohl, H., and M.M. Burda (1997). Modified Wald tests under nonregular conditions. *Journal of Econometrics* 78, 315–32.

Lütkepohl, H., and D.S. Poskitt (1996). Specification of echelon form VARMA models. *Journal of Business and Economic Statistics* 14, 69–79.

Lütkepohl, H., and H.-E. Reimers (1992). Impulse response analysis of cointegrated systems. *Journal of Economic Dynamics and Control* 16, 53–78.

Lütkepohl, H., and P. Saikkonen (2000). Testing for the cointegrating rank of a VAR process with a time trend. *Journal of Econometrics* 95, 177–98.

Mosconi, R., and C. Giannini (1992). Non-causality in cointegrated systems: Representation, estimation and testing. *Oxford Bulletin of Economics and Statistics* 54, 399–417.

Pagan, A. (1995). Three econometric methodologies: An update. In L. Oxley, D.A.R. George, C.J. Roberts, and S. Sayer (eds.) *Surveys in Econometrics* Oxford: Basil Blackwell.

Paulsen, J. (1984). Order determination of multivariate autoregressive time series with unit roots. *Journal of Time Series Analysis* 5, 115–27.

Perron, P., and J.Y. Campbell (1993). A note on Johansen's cointegration procedure when trends are present. *Empirical Economics* 18, 777–89.

Phillips, P.C.B. (1987). Time series regression with a unit root. *Econometrica* 55, 277–301.

Phillips, P.C.B. (1991). Optimal inference in cointegrated systems. *Econometrica* 59, 283–306.

Saikkonen, P., and H. Lütkepohl (1999). Local power of likelihood ratio tests for the cointegrating rank of a VAR process. *Econometric Theory* 15, 50–78.

Saikkonen, P., and H. Lütkepohl (2000a). Trend adjustment prior to testing for the cointegrating rank of a VAR process. *Journal of Time Series Analysis*, 21, 435–56.

Saikkonen, P., and H. Lütkepohl (2000b). Testing for the cointegrating rank of a VAR process with an intercept. *Econometric Theory* 16, 373–406.

Saikkonen, P., and R. Luukkonen (1997). Testing cointegration in infinite order vector autoregressive processes. *Journal of Econometrics* 81, 93–126.

Schwarz, G. (1978). Estimating the dimension of a model. *Annals of Statistics* 6, 461–4.

Sims, C.A. (1980). Macroeconomics and reality. *Econometrica* 48, 1–48.

Sims, C.A. (1981). An autoregressive index model for the U.S. 1948–1975. In J. Kmenta and J.B. Ramsey (eds.) *Large-Scale Macro-Econometric Models*. pp. 283–327. Amsterdam: North-Holland.

Sims, C.A., J.H. Stock, and M.W. Watson (1990). Inference in linear time series models with some unit roots. *Econometrica* 58, 113–44.

Toda, H.Y., and P.C.B. Phillips (1993). Vector autoregressions and causality. *Econometrica* 61, 1367–93.

Toda, H.Y., and T. Yamamoto (1995). Statistical inference in vector autoregressions with possibly integrated processes. *Journal of Econometrics* 66, 225–50.

Watson, M.W. (1994). Vector autoregressions and cointegration. In: R.F. Engle and D.L. McFadden (eds.) *Handbook of Econometrics*, Volume 4. New York: Elsevier.

Index